COMPREHENSIVE HANDBOOK
OF
PERSONALITY AND PSYCHOPATHOLOGY

COMPREHENSIVE HANDBOOK OF PERSONALITY AND PSYCHOPATHOLOGY

VOLUME 3
CHILD PSYCHOPATHOLOGY

Robert T. Ammerman
Volume Editor

Michel Hersen
Jay C. Thomas
Editors-in-Chief

John Wiley & Sons, Inc.

This book is printed on acid-free paper. ∞

Copyright © 2006 by John Wiley & Sons, Inc. All rights reserved.

Published by John Wiley & Sons, Inc., Hoboken, New Jersey.
Published simultaneously in Canada.

No part of this publication may be reproduced, stored in a retrieval system, or transmitted in any form or by any means, electronic, mechanical, photocopying, recording, scanning, or otherwise, except as permitted under Section 107 or 108 of the 1976 United States Copyright Act, without either the prior written permission of the Publisher, or authorization through payment of the appropriate per-copy fee to the Copyright Clearance Center, Inc., 222 Rosewood Drive, Danvers, MA 01923, (978) 750-8400, fax (978) 750-4470, or on the web at www.copyright.com. Requests to the Publisher for permission should be addressed to the Permissions Department, John Wiley & Sons, Inc., 111 River Street, Hoboken, NJ 07030, (201) 748-6011, fax (201) 748-6008, or online at http://www.wiley.com/go/permissions.

Limit of Liability/Disclaimer of Warranty: While the publisher and author have used their best efforts in preparing this book, they make no representations or warranties with respect to the accuracy or completeness of the contents of this book and specifically disclaim any implied warranties or merchantability or fitness for a particular purpose. No warranty may be created or extended by sales representatives or written sales materials. The advice and strategies contained herein may not be suitable for your situation. You should consult with a professional where appropriate. Neither the publisher nor author shall be liable for any loss of profit or any other commercial damages, including but not limited to special, incidental, consequential, or other damages.

For general information on our other products and services or for technical support, please contact our Customer Care Department within the United States at (800) 762-2974, outside the United States at (317) 572-3993 or fax (317) 572-4002.

Wiley also publishes its books in a variety of electronic formats. Some content that appears in print may not be available in electronic books. For more information about Wiley products, visit our web site at www.wiley.com.

Library of Congress Cataloging-in-Publication Data:

Comprehensive handbook of personality and psychopathology / Michel Hersen & Jay C. Thomas, editors-in-chief.
    p. ; cm.
    Includes bibliographical references.
    ISBN-13 978-0-471-47945-1 (cloth : alk. paper : set)
    ISBN-10 0-471-47945-4 (cloth : alk. paper : set) —
    ISBN-13 978-0-471-48837-8 (cloth : alk. paper : v. 1)
    ISBN-10 0-471-48837-2 (cloth : alk. paper : v. 1) —
    ISBN-13 978-0-471-48838-5 (cloth : alk. paper : v. 2)
    ISBN-10 0-471-48838-0 (cloth : alk. paper : v. 2) —
    ISBN-13 978-0-471-48839-2 (cloth : alk. paper : v. 3)
    ISBN-10 0-471-48839-9 (cloth : alk. paper : v. 3)
      1. Psychology, Pathological—Handbooks, manuals, etc. 2. Child psychopathology— Handbooks, manuals, etc. 3. Personality—Handbooks, manuals, etc. 4. Psychology— Handbooks, manuals, etc. I. Hersen, Michel. II. Thomas, Jay C., 1951–
      [DNLM: 1. Mental Disorders—therapy. 2. Personality. 3. Psychological Theory. WM 400 C737 2006] 1951–
  RC456.C66 2006
  618.92′89—dc22
                                                                  2005043981

Printed in the United States of America.

10 9 8 7 6 5 4 3 2 1

To the memory of Dr. Samuel M. Turner

Contents

Handbook Preface xi

Preface to Volume 3 xiii

Contributors xv

PART ONE
GENERAL ISSUES

1   DIAGNOSIS AND CLASSIFICATION 3
      Leigh Anne Faul and Alan M. Gross

2   GENETIC CONTRIBUTIONS 16
      Danielle M. Dick and Richard D. Todd

3   NEUROPSYCHIATRIC CONTRIBUTIONS 29
      Roger A. Brumback and C. Edward Coffey

4   COGNITIVE AND BEHAVIORAL CONTRIBUTIONS 38
      Brad Donohue, Valerie Romero, and Gregory Devore

5   SOCIOLOGICAL CONTRIBUTIONS 47
      Terrance J. Wade and John Cairney

6   TEMPERAMENT IN EARLY DEVELOPMENT 64
      Susan D. Calkins and Kathryn A. Degnan

7   INFANT MENTAL HEALTH 85
      Mary Margaret Gleason and Charles H. Zeanah

8   DEVELOPMENTAL PSYCHOPATHOLOGY 100
      Gabriel P. Kuperminc and Kathryn A. Brookmeyer

PART TWO
MAJOR DISORDERS AND PROBLEMS

9   GENERALIZED ANXIETY DISORDER 117
      Joanna A. Robin, Anthony C. Puliafico, Torrey A. Creed, Jonathan S. Comer, Stacey A. Hofflich, Andrea J. Barmish, Cynthia Suveg, and Philip C. Kendall

10   SOCIAL ANXIETY DISORDER 135
      Robert T. Ammerman, Kelly L. McGraw, Lori E. Crosby, Deborah C. Beidel, and Samuel M. Turner

11 POST-TRAUMATIC STRESS DISORDER   148
    Melissa K. Runyon, Esther Deblinger, Leah Behl, and Beth Cooper

12 MAJOR DEPRESSION   165
    Judy Garber and Jocelyn Smith Carter

13 BIPOLAR DISORDERS   217
    Robert A. Kowatch and Mary A. Fristad

14 MENTAL RETARDATION   233
    James M. Bebko and Jonathan A. Weiss

15 PERVASIVE DEVELOPMENTAL DISORDERS   254
    Bryna Siegel and Michelle Ficcaglia

16 LEARNING DISABILITIES   272
    James W. Loomis

17 OPPOSITIONAL DEFIANT DISORDER   285
    Ross W. Greene

18 CONDUCT DISORDER   299
    Eva R. Kimonis and Paul J. Frick

19 ATTENTION-DEFICIT/HYPERACTIVITY DISORDER   316
    Jack Stevens and Jeanne Ward-Estes

20 EATING DISORDERS   330
    Eric Stice, Stephen Wonderlich, and Emily Wade

21 SUBSTANCE USE DISORDERS   348
    Eric F. Wagner and Ashley M. Austin

22 CHILD PHYSICAL ABUSE AND NEGLECT   367
    David DiLillo, Andrea R. Perry, and Michelle Fortier

23 CHILD SEXUAL ABUSE   388
    Anthony P. Mannarino and Judith A. Cohen

24 SOMATIZATION DISORDERS   403
    Brenda Bursch

PART THREE
TREATMENT APPROACHES

25 PSYCHODYNAMIC TREATMENTS   425
    Sandra W. Russ

26	**COGNITIVE-BEHAVIORAL TREATMENTS** 438
	Joseph A. Durlak

27	**PHARMACOLOGICAL TREATMENTS** 448
	Sanjeev Pathak

Author Index   467

Subject Index   483

Handbook Preface

Remarkably, the linkage between personality and psychopathology, although extensive, has not been underscored in the larger tomes on these subjects. In the last decade there have been many books on personality, adult psychopathology, and child psychopathology, but none seems to have related the three in an integrated fashion. In part, this three-volume *Comprehensive Handbook of Personality and Psychopathology* (CHOPP), with the first volume on *Personality and Everyday Functioning,* the second on *Adult Psychopathology,* and the third on *Child Psychopathology,* is devoted to remedying this gap in the literature. Another unique feature of CHOPP appears in the volumes on *Adult Psychopathology* and *Child Psychopathology,* where impact of adult and child psychopathology on family, work, school, and peers is highlighted, in addition to the relation of specific psychopathology to normal development. Given the marked importance of such impact, contributors were asked to delineate the negative impact of psychopathology on the individual's daily environments.

In light of the aforementioned features, we trust that CHOPP is timely and that it will be well received in many quarters in psychology. The work should stand as an entity as a three-volume endeavor. However, given the structure of each volume, we believe that it is possible to break up the set into individual volumes for relevant courses on personality, normal development, adult psychopathology, and child psychopathology.

Volume 1 (*Personality and Everyday Functioning*) contains 23 chapters divided into four parts (Foundations, Broad-Range Theories and Systems, Mid-Range Theories, and Special Applications). This volume is unique in that it encompasses both the broad theories of personality and those theories with a more limited range, known as mid-range theories. Broad-range theories were originally developed to explain the behavior of normal people in everyday situations. But it also is important to have a reference point for those individuals suffering from various sorts of psychopathology. Chapters in this section follow a general format where possible:

A. Statement of the Theory
B. Developmental Considerations
C. Biological/Physiological Relationships
D. Boundaries of the Theory
E. Evidence in Support of and against the Theory
F. Predictions for Everyday Functioning
  1. Family Life
  2. Work or School
  3. Retirement
  4. Recreation

Thus, Volume 1 sets the stage for Volumes 2 and 3 while at the same time standing on its own for understanding everyday life from the personality perspective.

Volume 2 (*Adult Psychopathology*) contains 30 chapters divided into three parts (General Issues, Major Disorders and Problems, Treatment Approaches). Volume 3 (*Child Psychopathology*) contains 27 chapters divided into three parts (General Issues, Major Disorders and Problems, Treatment Approaches). As previously noted, a unique feature in these volumes is mention of the impact of psychopathology on the family, work, school, and peers, often neglected in standard works. In both Volumes 2 and 3, most of the contributors have adhered to a relatively standard format for Part Two. In some instances, some of the authors have opted to combine sections.

A. Description of the Disorder
B. Epidemiology
C. Clinical Picture
D. Etiology
E. Course, Complications, and Prognosis
F. Assessment and Diagnosis
G. Impact on the Environment
  1. Family
  2. Work or School
  3. Peer Interactions
H. Treatment Implications

In addition, authors in Volume 3 include the sections Personality Development and Psychopathology and Implications for Future Personality Development. We trust that the relatively uniform format in Part Two of Volumes 2 and 3 will make for ease of reading and some interchapter comparisons within and across volumes.

Many individuals have worked very hard to bring this series of volumes to fruition. First, we thank our editor at John

Wiley, Tracey Belmont, for once again understanding the import and scope of the project and having confidence in our ability to execute in spite of interfering hurricanes, other natural events, and varied life events. Second, we thank our editors of the specific volumes for planning, recruiting, and editing. Third, we thank our eminent contributors for taking time out from their busy schedules to add yet one more writing task in sharing their expertise. Claire Huismann, our project manager at Apex Publishing, deserves special recognition for her extraordinary efforts, competence, and patience throughout the creation of this series. And finally, but hardly least of all, we thank all at John Wiley and Pacific University, including Carole Londeree, Linda James, Alison Brodhagen, Greg May, and Cynthia Polance, for their excellent technical assistance.

Michel Hersen and Jay C. Thomas
Forest Grove and Portland, Oregon

Preface to Volume 3

In the past decade, our understanding of the origins, manifestations, and course of child psychopathology has dramatically increased. It is clear that most adult psychopathology emerges in childhood. Delineation of the processes by which psychological and psychiatric disturbance develop and change over time has important implications for treatment and prevention. There are several unique issues in examining childhood psychopathology. First, psychopathology must be considered against the backdrop of unfolding developmental processes. Indeed, the field of developmental psychopathology explicitly acknowledges and emphasizes the juxtaposition of maturation and development and the emergence of psychological and psychiatric disturbance and has greatly contributed to advances in our understanding of child disorders. Second, changes in development over time require methodological procedures that include longitudinal designs, measurement that is developmentally appropriate and psychometrically sound, and assessments that use multiple methods and informants. And third, contextual factors have enormous influence over the etiology, course, and presentation of psychopathology. Poverty, trauma, exposure to violence, and parental mental illness are but a few of the most important ecological determinants of long-term outcomes in children.

The overarching purpose of this book is to examine the relationship between personality and child psychopathology. Traditionally, these domains have been viewed as separate and distinct. Yet, recent research and new theoretical conceptualizations have documented the synergistic and integrated ways in which they influence each other. In fact, early personality traits (such as temperament and behavioral inhibition) are now believed to be precursors to the development of childhood disorders. The stable nature of personality also impacts the course of disorders, vulnerability to comorbidity, and response to treatment. Thus, a book devoted to the consideration of both personality and psychopathology in childhood is timely as well as practical. The 27 chapters of this book are divided into three parts. Part One, General Issues, examines areas important to understanding child development in general and the emergence of psychopathology in particular. These include chapters on diagnosis and classification, genetics, pediatric neuropsychiatry, cognitive and behavioral considerations, sociological contributions, temperament and early personality development, infant mental health, and developmental psychopathology. Part Two, Major Disorders and Problems, includes chapters on generalized anxiety disorder, social anxiety disorder, post-traumatic stress disorder, major depression, bipolar disorder, mental retardation, pervasive developmental disorders, learning disorders, oppositional defiant disorder, conduct disorder, attention-deficit/hyperactivity disorder, eating disorders, substance use disorders, child physical abuse and neglect, child sexual abuse, and somatization disorders. Part Three, Treatment Approaches, contains chapters covering psychodynamic, cognitive-behavioral, and pharmacological treatments.

Authors have drawn on their respective literatures to construct chapters that reflect recent scientific advances and state-of-the-art clinical approaches. Moreover, authors in Chapters 9–24 have used a predetermined format that includes the following headings: Description of the Disorder/Problem and Clinical Picture; Personality Development and Psychopathology; Epidemiology; Etiology; Course, Complications, and Prognosis; Assessment and Diagnosis; Impact on Environment (Family, School, Peer Interactions); Implications for Future Personality Development; and Treatment Implications.

A number of individuals have assisted in bringing this book to fruition, and we acknowledge their help and support. We are especially grateful to the contributors to this book for sharing their expertise and insights. Our editor at John Wiley & Sons, Tracey Belmont, was instrumental in shaping the scope and breadth of this book. Her patience and guidance in bringing the book to fruition is appreciated. We also extend our thanks to Pam Malone, who assisted in the various stages of compiling the book. Finally, we wish to express our sadness at the untimely death of Dr. Samuel M. Turner, a contributor to this book. Dr. Turner was a consummate scholar and a major figure in child and adult psychopathology. He will be sorely missed, and we extend our condolences to his family, friends, and colleagues.

Robert T. Ammerman
Cincinnati, Ohio

Contributors

Robert T. Ammerman, PhD
University of Cincinnati College of Medicine—Cincinnati Children's Hospital Medical Center
Cincinnati, OH

Ashley M. Austin, MSW
Florida International University
Miami, FL

Andrea J. Barmish, BA
Temple University
Philadelphia, PA

James M. Bebko, PhD
York University
Toronto, Ontario, Canada

Leah Behl, PhD
University of Medicine and Dentistry of New Jersey—School of Osteopathic Medicine
Stratford, NJ

Deborah C. Beidel, PhD
University of Maryland
College Park, MD

Kathryn A. Brookmeyer, MA
Georgia State University
Atlanta, GA

Roger A. Brumback, MD
Creighton University School of Medicine
Omaha, NE

Brenda Bursch, PhD
David Geffen School of Medicine at UCLA
Los Angeles, CA

John Cairney, PhD
Centre for Addiction and Mental Health, University of Toronto
Toronto, Ontario, Canada

Susan D. Calkins, PhD
University of North Carolina at Greensboro
Greensboro, NC

Jocelyn Smith Carter, MS
Vanderbilt University
Nashville, TN

C. Edward Coffey, MD
Henry Ford Health System
Detroit, MI

Judith A. Cohen, MD
Allegheny General Hospital & Drexel University College of Medicine
Pittsburgh, PA

Jonathan S. Comer, MA
Temple University
Philadelphia, PA

Beth Cooper, MS
University of Medicine and Dentistry of New Jersey—School of Osteopathic Medicine
Stratford, NJ

Torrey A. Creed, MA
Temple University
Philadelphia, PA

Lori E. Crosby, PsyD
University of Cincinnati College of Medicine—Cincinnati Children's Hospital Medical Center
Cincinnati, OH

Esther Deblinger, PhD
New Jersey Child Abuse, Research, and Education Services Institute (NJ CARES)
Stratford, NJ

Kathryn A. Degnan, MA
University of North Carolina at Greensboro
Greensboro, NC

Gregory Devore, BA
University of Nevada, Las Vegas
Las Vegas, NV

Danielle M. Dick, PhD
Washington University School of Medicine
St. Louis, MO

David DiLillo, PhD
University of Nebraska–Lincoln
Lincoln, NE

Brad Donohue, PhD
University of Nevada, Las Vegas
Las Vegas, NV

Joseph A. Durlak, PhD
Loyola University Chicago
Chicago, IL

Leigh Anne Faul, MA
University of Mississippi
University, MS

Michelle Ficcaglia, PhD
University of California, San Francisco
San Francisco, CA

Michelle Fortier, MA
University of Nebraska–Lincoln
Lincoln, NE

Paul J. Frick, PhD
University of New Orleans
New Orleans, LA

Mary A. Fristad, PhD
The Ohio State University
Columbus, OH

Judy Garber, PhD
Vanderbilt University
Nashville, TN

Mary M. Gleason, MD
Tulane University Health Sciences Center
New Orleans, LA

Ross W. Greene, PhD
Massachusetts General Hospital
Newton Corner, MA

Alan M. Gross, PhD
University of Mississippi
University, MS

Stacey A. Hofflich, BA
Temple University
Philadelphia, PA

Philip C. Kendall, PhD
Temple University
Philadelphia, PA

Eva R. Kimonis, MS
University of New Orleans
New Orleans, LA

Robert A. Kowatch, MD
University of Cincinnati College of Medicine—University of Cincinnati Medical Center
Cincinnati, OH

Gabriel P. Kuperminc, PhD
Georgia State University
Atlanta, GA

James W. Loomis, PhD
Center for Children with Special Needs
Glastonbury, CT

Anthony P. Mannarino, PhD
Allegheny General Hospital & Drexel University College of Medicine
Pittsburgh, PA

Kelly L. McGraw, PsyD
University of Cincinnati College of Medicine—Cincinnati Children's Hospital Medical Center
Cincinnati, OH

Sanjeev Pathak, MD
University of Cincinnati College of Medicine—Cincinnati Children's Hospital Medical Center
Cincinnati, OH

Andrea R. Perry, MA
University of Nebraska–Lincoln
Lincoln, NE

Anthony C. Puliafico, MA
Temple University
Philadelphia, PA

Joanna A. Robin, MA
Temple University
Philadelphia, PA

Valerie Romero, BS
University of Nevada, Las Vegas
Las Vegas, NV

Melissa K. Runyon, PhD
University of Medicine and Dentistry of New Jersey—School of Osteopathic Medicine
Stratford, NJ

Sandra W. Russ, PhD
Case Western University
Cleveland, OH

Bryna Siegel, PhD
University of California, San Francisco
San Francisco, CA

Jack Stevens, PhD
Columbus Children's Hospital
Columbus, OH

Eric Stice, PhD
University of Texas
Austin, TX

Cynthia Suveg, PhD
Temple University
Philadelphia, PA

Richard D. Todd, PhD, MD
Washington University School of Medicine
St. Louis, MO

Samuel M. Turner, PhD
University of Maryland
College Park, MD

Emily Wade, BS
University of North Dakota School of Medicine
Fargo, North Dakota

Terrance J. Wade, PhD
Brock University
St. Catharines, Ontario, Canada

Eric F. Wagner, PhD
Florida International University
Miami, FL

Jeanne Ward-Estes, BS
Ohio State University
Columbus, OH

Jonathan A. Weiss, MA
York University
Toronto, Ontario, Canada

Stephen Wonderlich, PhD
University of North Dakota School of Medicine
Fargo, ND

Charles H. Zeanah, MD
Tulane University Health Sciences Center
New Orleans, LA

PART ONE
GENERAL ISSUES

CHAPTER 1

Diagnosis and Classification

LEIGH ANNE FAUL AND ALAN M. GROSS

INTRODUCTION

Classification is among the first steps in scientific methodology, accompanying observation and description of the phenomena of interest. In psychology, classification is the process by which behavior is categorized along a spectrum of abnormality. Classification organizes and conveys information to aid in clinical decision making and interpretation of data (e.g., base rates or prevalence rates of disorders in the general population). Classification allows for comparison of differences in functioning among individuals by providing a uniform taxonomy. Acting also as an heuristic to empirical investigation, classification facilitates understanding of the nature and causes of psychological disorders. A widely recognized and utilized classification system of behavior is very important to enhance communication and understanding among professionals in the research as well as the clinical and applied fields of psychology. Thus, classification is critical so that psychology can move from scientific identification of similarities and differences in human behavior to span subsidiary objectives such as understanding of symptom array, etiology, epidemiology, prognosis, and treatment of specific disorders.

Within applied psychology, classification takes the specific form of diagnosis. To diagnose means "to distinguish or to know apart" (from the Greek *dia,* "apart," and *gignoskein,* "to know"). Diagnosis permits the assignment of cases to categories of a classification system of disorders or diseases. Diagnostic criteria are used to rule cases into or out of diagnostic categories. Diagnosis comprises the formulation of suppositions about a problem or disorder, serving as the foundation upon which a functional assessment is conducted and a treatment plan is devised (Hayes & Follette, 1992).

Diagnostic classification begins with one of two primary processes: inductive methodology or deductive methodology. In clinical psychology, these two processes reflect differences between the idiographic approach and the nomothetic approach (congruent with inductive and deductive reasoning, respectively; Cone, 1988). In the inductive, also called bottom-up, approach, one accrues multiple observations of behavior, spanning the range of normality and abnormality, and aligns these along dimensions of congruency, creating a taxonomy that serves as the basis for additional observations and the inception and formulation of a theory. Within the deductive, or top-down, approach, developing theories of psychopathology (based on clinical observations) are used to formulate categories, criteria, and future data collection that either substantiate or refute the theory. Classification and diagnosis of pathological behavior lie within a nomothetic framework. Definitions of adaptive and maladaptive behavior are formed via deductive methodology. The purpose of this chapter is to review basic principles, historical and current systems, special concerns and issues, and methodology within diagnosis and classification of childhood psychopathology.

PRINCIPLES OF PSYCHOPATHOLOGY

Defining Normal Behavior

In psychology, no consensus exists as to what constitutes normal behavior. The operational definition of adaptive behavior is a default; functionally, it is the absence of abnormal behavior. Defining psychopathology as aberration while normality and its boundaries (from which maladaptive behavior is said to deviate) are left unspecified is inherently problematic. Given that psychology did not begin with a conceptualization (either theoretical or empirical) of normal behavior, there is no standard taxonomy with which to define, identify, and investigate deviations. Though broad parameters have been posited, no single classification system of adaptive behavior has been widely adopted (Adams & Cassidy, 1993; Buss, 1966; Jahoda, 1958). There are numerous definitions of adaptive behavior. *Normal behavior* generally is viewed as what people do and wish to do weighed against what is required by the environment (Wicks-Nelson & Israel, 1991). *Mental health,* an outcome of consistent patterns of adaptive behavior, is in part made up of the ability to think logically and rationally, to cope effectively with life events, and to display emotional stability and growth. These conceptualizations form loose guidelines that help to delineate maladaptive behavior (Wicks-Nelson & Israel, 1991).

Defining Psychopathology

Terms such as *abnormal behavior* and *psychopathology* span a wide variety of difficulties, from reduced competence in the completion of daily tasks to reality-defying delusions. Describing behavior as maladaptive generally implies that a problem behavior is being exhibited, with resultant difficulties in daily living and distress on the part of the individual or others (i.e., inability to cope, exceptional stress or distress, or feelings of vulnerability). Different approaches from statistical to theoretical have been used in the endeavor to produce a coherent classification system for psychopathology.

A conventional way to define deviant behavior is assessment of its occurrence (frequency, duration, and intensity) within the general population. This can be accomplished via a categorical or dimensional approach. Psychopathology has been defined by two basic methodologies: the class model and the multivariate model. The class or qualitative difference model operates under the tenet that some disorders or behaviors do not occur in the general population. This categorical-type model assumes that, within a given subset of the population, symptomatologies of disorders covary in distinct patterns and are functionally related (Adams, Luscher, & Bernat, 2001).

Conversely, the multivariate model of psychopathology places all behavior on a continuum. Deviant behavior is posited as dimensional, present in every individual to some degree. The multivariate model uses two criteria to define psychopathology: (1) establishing that a behavior pattern is deviant or rare; and (2) demonstrating that behavior patterns are clinically significant, causing objective or subjective distress to the person or others. The first criterion, labeled deviance, is relative, varying by culture, time, and location. The second criterion, adjustment, is a measure of how well individuals cope with environmental milieus. Wakefield's supposition of "harmful dysfunction" has replaced the criterion of adjustment (1992). Thus, psychopathology is conceptualized as behavior that in some way violates social norms and causes dysfunction in a subset of the population who exhibit behavior at problematic and clinical levels.

Attempts to define maladaptive, deviant, or disordered behavior historically have been as abundant as they have been controversial, resulting in added confusion rather than much-coveted clarification. From stigmatization, labeling effects, and reification to the imperfection of diagnostic categories (i.e., overlap of symptoms across disorders, indistinct boundaries between disorders), numerous criticisms have been leveled at the classification of abnormal behavior. Despite criticism and controversy, tremendous progress has been made in the last 25 years in classifying abnormal behavior. With increasingly defined goals and a history of refinement, diagnosis and classification of childhood abnormal behavior have shown marked improvement.

DIAGNOSIS AND CLASSIFICATION: THEN AND NOW

Historical Antecedents

The need to classify types of human behavior predates written records. From the bodily humors of Hippocrates and Galen (i.e., melancholic, phlegmatic, choleric, and sanguine) to Gall's phrenology and Sheldon's phenotypes (i.e., mesomorph, ectomorph, endomorph), many cultures ascribed individual behavioral tendencies to physical characteristics. This was the dominant trend in diagnosis and classification until the late 1890s. In 1899, Emil Kraepelin made a pivotal contribution to psychological classification, publishing the sixth edition of *Textbook of Psychiatry,* which listed 16 major categories of psychopathology. Kraepelin's diagnostic model serves as the framework for current diagnostic systems. Based on Kraepelin's model of classification, the first diagnostic system of the American Psychiatric Association (*Standard Classified Nomenclature of Diseases,* 1933) included 24 categories of adult psychopathology.

Current Systems

The Diagnostic and Statistical Manual of Mental Disorders

The Diagnostic and Statistical Manual of Mental Disorders (*DSM*) is the most widely adopted classification system of mental disorders. It contains standard terms and definitions that mental health professionals use in research and treatment. First published in 1952 by the American Psychiatric Association, the *DSM* has undergone a series of revisions as current knowledge has been incorporated. In the first edition, 108 diagnoses were outlined within three major classes of psychopathology: organic brain syndromes, functional disorders, and mental deficiency. Disorders of childhood and adolescence were largely excluded. Only one diagnosis specific to children was detailed, adjustment reaction of childhood and adolescence (APA, 1952).

The second edition of the *DSM* (APA, 1968) expanded the number of categories from 8 to 11 and the number of diagnoses from 108 to 182. More importantly, this edition included a diagnostic section devoted to children, "Behavior Disorders of Childhood-Adolescence." Diagnoses listed in this section included unsocialized reaction, withdrawing reaction, overanxious reaction, group delinquent reaction, aggressive reaction, runaway reaction, and hyperkinetic reaction.

The first two versions of the *DSM* were characterized by vague and unreliable diagnostic criteria. *DSM-III* (APA, 1980) represented a major improvement over previous editions with the inclusion of specific criteria (using a categorical scheme), a multiaxial system of classification, and the removal of unsupported theoretical inferences. Five axes—clinical syndromes, personality disorders and developmental disorders, physical disorders and conditions, psychosocial stressors, and global assessment of functioning—and 265 diagnoses were included. The multiaxial system allows for diagnosis and assessment of functioning in a broader and more meaningful sense in that it encompasses a basic description and diagnosis of the presenting difficulty as well as its effects within and across individual, family, and community contexts.

The trend of increasing diagnostic specificity was evident in the revision of the *DSM-III* (*DSM-III-R,* APA, 1987). Empirical findings were emphasized as operational criteria for disorders were developed. Moreover, disorders related specifically to children and adolescents were placed in a section titled "Disorders First Evident in Childhood or Adolescence." The *DSM-III-R* specified five major diagnostic categories of childhood problems.

Similar to the *DSM-III-R,* the most recent editions of the *DSM* (*DSM-IV,* APA, 1994; *DSM-IV-TR,* APA, 2000) use operationally defined criteria and empirical findings in delineating diagnostic entities. A number of major changes are also found in these editions. These include the assimilation of several child categories within corresponding diagnoses formerly only for adults (e.g., avoidant disorder of childhood has been incorporated within social phobia) as well as the addition of new categories. Interestingly, despite emphasis on empirical literature, a focus on situational and contextual factors is noticeably absent in these editions (Scotti, Morris, McNeil, & Hawkins, 1996).

Despite its widespread acceptance in both research and practice, the *DSM* has been criticized for a number of issues. Criticisms of the *DSM* classification system include its exclusion of a definition of normality, lack of emphasis on situational and contextual factors that precede and maintain behavioral difficulties, overlap of symptom criteria across diagnostic categories, and high comorbidity rates among disorders. Additionally, the tendency toward reification of disorders (i.e., when a psychological disorder is viewed as a causal agent rather than a convenient, descriptive label for exhibited symptomatology) is also criticized, although this is an artifact of usage rather than an inherent design flaw.

International Statistical Classification of Diseases *and Related Health Problems*

The first *International Classification of Diseases* (*ICD*), formalized in 1893 as the *Bertillon Classification* (later titled *International List of Causes of Death*), was intended to provide physicians and researchers a standard format for presentation of epidemiological statistics on physical conditions (specifically, mortality and morbidity rates). In 1948, a classification system for mental disorders, complete with diagnostic categories and symptom criteria, was included in the sixth edition of the *ICD* (World Health Organization, 1948). The newly included section for mental disorders comprised 10 categories of psychoses; 9 categories of psychoneuroses; and 7 categories of disorders of character, intelligence, and behavior. This addition allowed the *ICD* to function as an inclusive diagnostic classification system, spanning both mental and physical problems. Since its inception, the *ICD* has undergone revision roughly once every decade. The *ICD-10,* the most recent edition, is compatible with the most widely used classification system of mental disorders, *DSM-IV.*

Ancillary Classification Systems

Supplemental classification schemes have been suggested to augment the scope of diagnostic classification. Some of these supplemental systems address oversights in the *DSM*. Independent classification systems for young children (specifically, ages 0–3) have been devised to supplement the *DSM,* addressing the paucity of diagnostic criteria and consideration of this age group in the current edition of the *DSM*. For example, the National Center for Clinical Infant Programs developed the *Diagnostic Classification: 0–3* (*DC: 0–3;* Zero to Three/National Center for Clinical Infant Programs, 1994), a multiaxial system for classifying problems occurring in early childhood and spanning multiple domains of functioning. The *DC: 0–3* has five axes spanning functional emotional developmental level, relationship disorder, primary diagnosis, psychosocial stressors, and medical and developmental problems. The *DC: 0–3* is similar to the *DSM-IV* in the inclusion of similarly named disorders, such as traumatic stress disorder, disorders of affect (subtypes of anxiety and depression), adjustment disorder, sleep behavior disorder, and eating behavior disorder (Dunitz-Scheer, Scheer, Kvas, & Macari, 1996; Thomas & Clark, 1998). However, not all of the ancillary systems employ a categorical approach to classification, nor do they correspond to the *DSM-IV* (1994).

Based on the tenet that human behavior can be examined along a number of independent dimensions, dimensional classification systems have been developed. One of the most widely recognized systems is the Child Behavior Checklist (CBCL), an empirically based dimensional system developed by Thomas Achenbach (Achenbach & Edelbrock, 1981; Achenbach, 1991). The Child Behavior Checklist-4–18 and 1991 Profile (CBCL-4–18) combines a 113-item behavior-problems checklist with a seven-part social competency checklist. Parental responses to both checklists result in comprehensive descriptions of child behavior that clinicians can use to distinguish between typical children and those having significant behavioral disturbances. The scoring profile for the CBCL-4–18 includes (a) three competence scales (activities, social, and school); (b) a total competence scale score; (c) eight syndrome scales (aggressive behavior, attention problems, delinquent behavior, social problems, somatic complaints, thought problems, anxious-depressed, and withdrawn); (d) an internalizing problem scale score; (e) an externalizing problem scale score; and (f) a total problem scale score. Unlike the *DSM* diagnoses, the CBCL syndromes are entirely empirical in their derivation, based upon repeated and comprehensive analyses of parent ratings of children's behaviors. The checklists are part of a larger effort by Achenbach (1993) to create an empirical taxonomy of behavioral disturbance in which syndromes describe features of behavior that co-occur in children, and profiles represent combinations of syndromes that occur at greater than chance levels. The CBCL checklists and syndromes have become a standard against which many other clinical decision-making tools are compared (Edelbrock & Costello, 1988).

Using a dimensional approach, Reynolds and Kamphaus (1992) developed the Behavioral Assessment Scale for Children (BASC). Responses to questionnaires from multiple informants result in the identification of symptom clusters organized across broad dimensional syndromes (internalizing problems, externalizing problems, behavioral symptoms index, emotional symptoms index, clinical maladjustment, school problems, clinical adjustment, and others). Additionally, narrower problematic behavior clusters, within the broad dimensional syndromes, are also delineated (e.g., aggression, hyperactivity, and conduct problems within externalizing problems) (Reynolds & Kamphaus, 1992). These and other ancillary classification systems are useful as supplementary sources of diagnostic information.

Reliability, Validity, and Clinical Utility

Reliability, validity, and clinical utility are benchmark indicators of the efficacy and accuracy of any diagnostic system.

(These three standards [reliability, validity, and clinical utility] can also be applied to the specific assessment tools or methods used in the diagnostic process.) Reliability refers to the consistency with which clinicians apply the same categories or diagnoses to describe a child's behavior. Reliability also relates to the consistency of a diagnostic category over time. In the past, diagnostic reliability has been problematic. Interrater agreement (i.e., interrater reliability) is acceptable for a majority of the major *DSM-IV* childhood categories; lower levels of reliability are found when examining diagnostic agreement within *DSM-IV* childhood subcategories (Frick et al., 1994; Lahey et al., 1998; Werry, 1992). The specific assessment instruments used in an evaluation often determine the level of diagnostic reliability (Scotti & Morris, 2000). Diagnostic reliability has markedly improved with increased specificity of diagnostic criteria (within the *DSM-IV*) and the use of standardized assessment instruments.

Validity generally refers to issues of correctness, meaningfulness, and relevancy (Werry, 1992). It relates to the ability of a diagnostic system to measure what it has been designed to measure. Although there is general acceptance of the validity of *DSM* diagnostic categories, questions of validity remain as the result of the frequently reported observation of comorbidity of disorders. Comorbidity exists when individuals simultaneously meet criteria for more than one diagnosis or disorder (e.g., anxiety and depression). The rate of comorbidity in childhood disorders is relatively high (Angold, Costello, & Erkanli, 1999; Costello, Mustillo, Erkanli, Keeler, & Angold, 2003; Ford, Goodman, & Meltzer, 2003; Jensen et al., 2002; Lillienfeld, 2003; van Dulmen et al., 2002; Volkmar & Woolston, 1997; Werry, 1992) and may be due in part to symptom overlap (overlapping definitional criteria). A number of *DSM* disorders share common features and criteria. Other explanations for this problem include distinct disorders sharing a common vulnerability factor, or that comorbidity is an artifact of a classification system that allows two diagnoses to be assigned to what may be one disorder.

In addition to content validity, external validity is also important to classification systems. Diagnoses should provide information regarding prognosis, etiology, and treatment (i.e., predictive validity). Evidence for this comes from the development of empirically supported treatments (Chambless et al., 1996), such as those for phobic and anxiety disorders in childhood (American Psychological Association Division 12 Task Force, 1995; King, Hamilton, & Ollendick, 1994; Lonigan, Elbert, & Johnson, 1998; Ollendick & King, 1998). Recent advances in diagnostic conceptualization (Barlow, Allen, & Choate, 2004) have posited a common mechanism underlying the emotional disorders (as evidenced by comorbidity rates and commonalities in etiology and structure).

Specifically, an underlying syndrome of negative affect has been posited in anxiety and depressive disorders and within all anxiety disorders (Barlow, Allen, & Choate, 2004). With a reconceptualization of concomitant disorders (e.g., anxiety and depression) comes the possibility of attenuated comorbidity rates and improved external validity as well as more efficacious treatments. Diagnostic validity and comorbidity are being addressed by continuing theoretical and empirical work (Brestan & Eyberg, 1998; Kazdin, 1997; Pelham, Wheeler, & Chronis, 1998). It is important that clinicians cultivate an accurate understanding of validity and comorbidity, especially as these factors relate to the quality of current diagnostic systems.

A classification system is also judged by its clinical utility. Clinical utility refers to the degree of completeness and usefulness of a diagnostic system. Kendell (1989) stated that "diagnostic terms are no more than convenient labels for arbitrary groupings of clinical phenomena" and that these are "concepts justified only by their usefulness" (p. 51). Clinical utility is implied through modifications made to the existing classification system (measure of flexibility and responsiveness to change) and the development of alternative forms of classification. Critics have argued that diagnostic classification provides no explanation of the child's difficulties or necessary steps for remediation. However, by providing a method of systematically grouping behavioral disorders, the *DSM* has facilitated efforts to systematically examine the etiology of complex behavior problems. Moreover, the clinical utility of the *DSM* is also reflected in the recent emphasis on the development and use of empirically supported treatments corresponding to specific diagnoses.

ISSUES AND CHALLENGES

Pragmatic Considerations

Working with a clinical child population raises specific issues. It is important that professionals have knowledge of both the diagnostic tools being utilized as well as issues and guidelines unique to conducting evaluations with children. Unlike adults who seek treatment for problems, children participate in assessment and treatment as a result of the concerns of parents, teachers, or both. Children are often incapable of understanding the assessment process. It is important that clinicians make every effort to ensure that the child and parents understand the purpose and the process of the diagnostic evaluation. The primary goal is to improve daily functioning at home, at school, and in the community. It is important to express this clearly to children given that they might mistake the evaluation's purpose (e.g., they might believe they are in trouble), potentially causing them distress and possibly affecting their cooperativeness. Clarifying the purpose of the assessment and the process by which it will be achieved should be one of the initial steps in the evaluation.

Establishing good rapport between the child and the clinician is essential to successful child evaluation. A child who is uncomfortable with or mistrustful of the clinician might not respond openly to questions, resulting in an inaccurate picture of functioning. The clinician should display qualities such as warmth, openness, and empathy toward the child to help alleviate anxiety. Asking simple, direct questions also will aid the clinician in improving the assessment experience for the youngster (as well as increasing the quality of information he or she provides). Spending time talking with the child about his or her interests, or playing a game the child enjoys, can be used to promote rapport. Regardless of the method chosen, the clinician should make concerted efforts to ensure that rapport is established early and maintained throughout the diagnostic process.

It is important that the child's interest and motivation be maintained across the assessment. Results might also be compromised if the assessment is overly tiring or taxing. The child's age and developmental level should be taken into account when deciding the administration format of the evaluation. It may be necessary to schedule the assessment across several days to avoid the effects of fatigue and waning enthusiasm or cooperation.

Ethical Issues

In addition to pragmatic and practical issues, clinicians must also bear in mind numerous ethical issues in childhood diagnostic classification. Maintaining confidentiality of information is an important matter. As will be addressed later, multiple informants are often used in the assessment of children. In addition to family members (parents, siblings) serving as informants, assessment data may also be requested of the child's teachers, day care staff, or other relevant adults. When requesting these data, clinicians must take care not to reveal sensitive information. This can be particularly challenging as these individuals may request some explanation concerning why they are being asked to provide this information. Additionally, ensuring that the family and child understand the limits to confidentiality as well as how their private information is to be managed is key. It is beneficial to clarify the boundaries of confidentiality when reviewing the format of the evaluation.

Another ethical dilemma involves balancing the need to maintain good rapport with a child against the need to notify parents of risky behavior. Although this issue may not interfere with data collection during the diagnostic evaluation, it may have a significant impact on a youngster's responsiveness to working with the clinician in therapy. Suicidal ideation, abuse, and victimization are clear-cut examples of events to report to parents. The decision is more ambiguous in situations where a child endorses engagement in risky behavior such as unprotected sex, drug or alcohol experimentation, truancy, or violations of curfew. As such, it is important at the outset of the diagnostic process to outline confidentiality and its terms to both the child and his or her parents. To help preserve rapport and engender trust, it may be useful to consider explaining to both the child and the parents that if confidentiality is to be broken (e.g., if the clinician decides to notify parents of certain behavior a child is displaying), the clinician will discuss it with the child before informing the parents.

Cultural Considerations

It is increasingly important that psychologists possess the knowledge and skills necessary to work effectively with ethnically diverse populations. This is especially true in diagnostic classification of ethnic minority children and adolescents. Cultures vary in their definition of acceptable and deviant behavior. Strong cultural values may influence children and parents in what symptoms they develop, how they understand the symptoms, coping methods, and use and satisfaction with diagnostic and clinical services (Canino & Spurlock, 2000). Parents of one ethnicity may be more likely to view and report certain behaviors as more problematic relative to other ethnicities. Failure to understand cultural practices and beliefs can result in incorrect diagnoses. As such, it is important to consider cultural differences when interpreting parent reports used in formulating diagnostic and treatment recommendations.

Great diversity exists within any cultural group, especially in terms of level of assimilation into mainstream culture. This is problematic in that clinicians are left to decide what factors and norms are most relevant in evaluating and understanding the child's problematic behavior. As such, clinicians should be aware of within-group ethnic and cultural diversity as well as between-group cultural differences when making a diagnosis. In addition, ethnically diverse children might also experience poverty, discrimination, and conflicts with assimilation into the larger culture. For example, poverty and history of discrimination could evoke wariness in the child or parents, causing some hesitancy to cooperate fully with the clinician and thus affecting the accuracy of the diagnosis. In some cases, parents might seek an evaluation not because of what the clinician would consider to be symptoms of psychopathology, but because their child is exhibiting behavior congruent with majority cultural norms and incongruent with their native cultural practices.

Ethnic minorities are underrepresented in mental health research, thus hampering the development of culturally inclusive diagnostic methods (Rogler, 1996). Behavioral and developmental differences due to culture, ethnicity, and socioeconomic status remain largely unexamined in diverse populations. The absence of culturally relevant data concerning behavior problems has resulted in default, and perhaps inappropriate, comparisons to Euro American (white) children as the normative sample (Sue & Sue, 1999). Clinicians who work with ethnically diverse children are at a disadvantage as there are limited data to shape diagnostic formulations in a culturally informed manner (Sue & Sue, 1999). Until an adequate culturally diverse empirical diagnostic research base exists, clinicians must make every effort to recognize the potential impact of cultural variables on the diagnostic process. Moreover, this must be done without making broad generalizations about cultural variables or losing sight of the role of regional, generational, and socioeconomic factors on these variables.

Language poses an additional challenge in the diagnostic classification of ethnically diverse children. When the clinician is not fluent in the primary language of the child and parents, the potential for communication problems is great. Language differences may lead to miscommunication concerning the delineation of symptoms, difficulties identifying the contingencies supporting problem behaviors, and a failure to recognize the significance of symptoms for the individual and his or her family. Obviously, communication problems set the stage for misdiagnosis. Having an examiner present who is familiar with both the clients' native language and with diagnostic terminology may minimize these potential hazards.

Developmental Considerations

In the early stages of the field of child clinical psychology, theories of adult psychopathology were unsuccessfully applied to childhood problems. Theory and taxonomy were primarily devised by an extension of adult models downward while developmental contexts were disregarded. Within the last 15 years, professionals have begun to integrate a developmental perspective in the study of child psychopathology.

To accurately judge the significance of problem behaviors, it is necessary to have a solid understanding of normal child development. Behaviors considered typical at one age are deemed problematic at another age or developmental level. For example, oppositional behavior and enuresis are not regarded as significant problems for 2-year-olds, whereas they are considered significant difficulties in 11-year-olds. Similarly, determining the meaning of various child behaviors also requires consideration of the youngster's intellectual capabilities. Children with attenuated or impaired cognitive abilities cannot be expected to function at the same levels as children of normal intelligence across all areas of development. Moreover, children are often referred because they exhibit problems in academic settings. Though it may be that behavioral difficulties are interfering with learning, cognitive problems (e.g., a reading disorder or developmental delay) might prompt a child to display behaviors designed to promote avoidance of or removal from challenging tasks or environments. Failure to consider cognitive and developmental variables could compound problems the child is experiencing. Familiarity with norms concerning cognitive, physical, and social development facilitates interpretation of their impact on presenting behavior, thus affecting diagnostic conceptualization (Coie & Jacobs, 1993; Sroufe, 1979.)

Problematic behavior also varies by gender. Prevalence rates reveal higher ratios of males to females for a number of childhood disorders (e.g., autism is three times more likely in males than in females; Cohen et al., 1993). Sex differences can be attributed to several factors. Boys appear to be more biologically vulnerable than girls (as evidenced by higher death rates and heightened effects of malnutrition, disease, and poverty relative to girls; Birns, 1976; Eme, 1979). Alternatively, broad gender norms regarding controversial child behaviors may result in differential attention from adults. For example, adults may show less tolerance for the display of high activity levels and disruptiveness when exhibited by girls compared to boys (Chess & Thomas, 1972; Huston, 1983; Jensen et al., 1996; Lyons & Serbin, 1986). These biases may influence referrals as well as adult reporting during diagnostic data gathering. This suggests that in some cases so-called gender differences in diagnosis may be artifacts of sociocultural factors (Butcher, Narikiyo, & Bemis Vitousek, 1993; Dana, 1993; Lytton & Romeny, 1993). An understanding of gender norms and stereotypes is necessary to guard against these variables having an adverse impact on the diagnostic process.

Children within Contexts

In addition to the developmental contexts outlined previously, it is imperative that maladaptive behavior be defined and understood within the social context in which it occurs (Maccoby & Martin, 1983). Behavior in the absence of context is meaningless. Current family dynamics can exacerbate or influence problematic behavior. For example, recent changes such as the birth of a sibling, family relocation, changing schools, death of a family member or pet, or an imminent divorce can affect the child's functioning. Similarly, parental psychopathology and marital distress also have been shown to be related to child behavior problems (Campbell & Cohn, 1997; Conger, McCarty, Yang, Lahey, & Kropp, 1984; Emery, 1982; Forehand, McCombs, & Brody, 1987; Jouriles et al., 1991; Katz & Gottman, 1993; Lyons-Ruth, 1992). Although parents may not recognize the relevance of these types of events, these factors may color how the behavior of the child, specifically degree of intensity, frequency, and severity, is presented to the clinician. A child referral can be more indicative of the parents' level of functioning, ability to manage their child's behavior, or both than it is of actual child dysfunction. As such, it is important to establish early rapport with the parents and to assess the impact of current family functioning on presenting problem behavior.

Recognition of contextual factors may help determine the function of the problem behavior, increasing diagnostic accuracy. For example, inattention and oppositional behavior at home and school are symptoms seen in several childhood disorders. Defiance and inattention may be the result of poor child-management practices on the part of the parent, a consequence of excessive motor activity and deficits in attentional abilities (making it difficult for the youngster to follow instructions), a response to environmental contingencies that reward defiance over compliance (to increase peer status), or the child's tendency to avoid tasks in which they fear they might fail. Careful scrutiny of environmental contingencies may reveal different functions for these behaviors, offering important diagnostic information.

Differential diagnosis refers to the determination of which diagnosis best captures the problem behaviors the child is exhibiting. Because one purpose of diagnosis is to inform treatment, determining accurately the function of problem behavior is essential to selecting the appropriate diagnosis and intervention. Inaccuracy, especially if it goes unnoticed, ends in failure to diagnose and treat the presenting problem in an effective manner. Beyond identification of the symptom cluster of the problematic behavior, careful examination of contextual factors surrounding and maintaining problematic behavior aids the process of differential diagnosis (cf. Last & Strauss, 1990; Scotti & Morris, 2000).

DIAGNOSTIC ASSESSMENT TOOLS AND METHODS

In any evaluation, it is important that the question guide the process. There are numerous reasons children are referred for diagnostic evaluation. The presenting problem and reason for referral form the initial evaluative framework, indicating what information is necessary, what sources are important, and what tools are appropriate to use in the collection and organization of information.

Core Components of Child Diagnostic Evaluation

The foundation of diagnostic assessment is the initial interview. During the interview, the clinician learns the difficulties the child is experiencing while establishing rapport necessary to work with the child and parents. The initial interview provides the basis for the initial case conceptualization. As information is added, the diagnostic picture takes shape. Via delineation of the problem, the clinician develops ideas regarding the nature of the dysfunction as well as preliminary diagnoses to be ruled in or out. The clinical interview also guides the selection of assessment instruments to be included.

Although unstructured clinical interviews frequently provide the basis for diagnostic decision making, the use of structured and semistructured interviews provides systematic methods that may enhance diagnostic reliability and accuracy. These devices ensure that clinicians ask the necessary questions to determine whether the child's behavior meets specific diagnostic criteria. Some examples of structured assessment instruments include the Diagnostic Interview Schedule for Children (DISC-IV) and the Child and Adolescent Psychiatric Assessment (CAPA). Semistructured interview formats include the Interview Schedule for Children and Adolescents (ISCA), the Schedule for Affective Disorders and Schizophrenia for School-Aged Children (K-SADS), and the Diagnostic Interview for Children and Adolescents (DICA). Though a thorough review of these instruments is beyond the scope of this chapter, brief descriptions of them follow.

Structured Interview Formats

The National Institute of Mental Health's (NIMH) Diagnostic Interview Schedule for Children (DISC-IV; Shaffer, Fisher, Lucas, Dulcan, & Schwab-Stone, 2000) is a reliable, highly structured diagnostic interview designed to assess more than 30 psychiatric disorders occurring in children and adolescents aged 6–17 years. The DISC-IV, widely used in clinical settings, is designed to assess for syndromes corresponding to *DSM-IV* criteria (Bravo, Ribera, & Rubio-Stipec, 2001; Garland et al., 2001; Jensen et al., 1996; Shaffer, 1994; Shaffer et al., 2000). It has undergone several revisions paralleling the revisions to both the *DSM* (i.e., *DSM-IV;* American Psychiatric Association, 1994) and the *International Classification of Diseases* (*ICD-10;* World Health Organization, 1992). It includes youth and parent forms, each using a stem-contingent question format. Informants answer all 358 stem questions; if a stem is endorsed, the informant is asked a series of contingent queries, providing additional specific information on symptomatology (frequency, severity, and duration) to be compared to *DSM-IV* criteria (Reitman, Hummel, Franz, & Gross, 1998; Shaffer et al., 2000).

The Child and Adolescent Psychiatric Assessment (CAPA; Angold et al., 1995) is a structured interview for use with children aged 9–17 years. Questions assess for symptomatology (severity, onset, and duration) in order to assign diagnoses based on *DSM-IV* and *ICD-10* criteria. The CAPA has a modular format with both parent and child forms. The CAPA may be administered in whole or in part at the interviewer's discretion. For example, if it is suspected that a youngster's problem involves a mood disorder, the clinician can administer that specific module while omitting modules associated with diagnostic categories viewed as irrelevant to the individuals (Boggs, Griffin, & Gross, 2003). The CAPA Glossary, a unique feature, provides operational definitions of terms to reduce subjectivity and confusion on the part of the clinician in administration and scoring (Angold & Costello, 2000).

Semistructured Interview Formats

The Interview Schedule for Children and Adolescents (ISCA; Kovacs, 1997) is a semistructured interview for use with children aged 8–17 years. Two versions of the schedule exist, the ISCA and the Follow-up Interview Schedule for Adults (FISA). The FISA is used in the collection of longitudinal data from adults and young adults formerly diagnosed using the ISCA (Boggs et al., 2003; Sherrill & Kovacs, 2000). The ISCA, consisting of five sections and one global assessment of functioning, queries and provides diagnoses in several *DSM-IV* categories including mood disorders, anxiety disorders, externalizing disorders, and elimination disorders. Ancillary questionnaires can be administered to assess for presence of other disorders of childhood, substance disorders, eating disorders, other anxiety disorders not addressed by the core instrument, and personality disorders (Sherrill & Kovacs, 2000). Though it offers uniform queries, there are no stem-contingent questions on the ISCA as provided by the DISC-IV (Kovacs, 1997; Sherrill & Kovacs, 2000).

The Schedule for Affective Disorders and Schizophrenia for School-Aged Children (K-SADS; Puig-Antich & Chambers, 1978), also referred to as the "Kiddie-SADS," is a semistructured interview for children aged 6–18 years. There are three modular format versions with varying foci (providing information on epidemiology in K-SADS-E, providing present and lifetime diagnoses in K-SADS-PL, and assessing present state in K-SADS-P IVR; Ambrosini, 2000; Kaufman et al., 1997). Each form provides a psychiatric diagnosis using *DSM-IV* diagnostic criteria. The most commonly used form is the K-SADS-PL (Kaufman, Birmaher, Brent, Rao, & Ryan, 1996). Following a section to obtain information on child and family background and the presenting problem, the screen interview section is administered, which has a stem-branch format. This section is designed to obtain information on broad presenting symptomatology, thus determining which of five modules (behavioral, affective, anxiety, psychotic, and substance abuse) are to be subsequently administered. Per protocol instructions, probe questions are not required to be administered verbatim.

The Diagnostic Interview for Children and Adolescents (DICA-R; Reich & Welner, 1998) is a semistructured interview for children aged 6–17 years. Its aim is to arrive at a lifetime diagnosis within *DSM-IV* or *ICD-10* criteria (Reich, 2000) while also addressing perinatal and early development and assessing for psychosocial stressors. The format of the DICA-R requires exact wording and presentation of questions limited to specific sections of the protocol while allowing for certain deviations and specific probes for further inquiry. There are separate interview sections for parents, children, and adolescents. In addition to providing a diagnosis, the DICA-R also contains sections to assess stressors in psychosocial areas as well as perinatal and early development (Boggs et al., 2003; Reich, 2000).

Whether structured or semistructured, diagnostic interview schedules that have been subjected to empirical scrutiny offer improved evaluative reliability and validity to clinicians, enhancing diagnostic accuracy. As such, thorough knowledge of tools designed for assessment of child behavior problems allows for increased diagnostic accuracy.

Multiple Informants and Auxiliary Measures

As the diagnostic formulation gains clarity, it may be necessary to include additional sources of information or use supplementary methods. Reliance on a single source of information may lead to misdiagnosis. A comprehensive evaluation of problematic behavior (encompassing behavioral and emotional functioning) incorporates information from relevant sources, such as parents, teachers, peers, siblings, involved family members, other relevant adults, and the children themselves. Rich with contextual details, this multi-informant strategy facilitates comparisons of the child's functioning across settings.

Clinicians may choose from a multitude of assessment tools, too numerous to mention, to obtain additional information from the child and relevant other sources. Direct behavioral observation (Dadds & Sanders, 1992) and behavioral monitoring forms (Beidel, Neal, & Lederer, 1991) may provide details regarding the function of the behavior as well as help to identify relevant contextual variables. Child report measures might be used to assess broad-based functioning (YRF: Youth Report Form; Achenbach, 1991). Auxiliary measures also might be used to assess specific symptomatology such as aggression, anxiety, and inattention. Examples of these instruments include the Continuous Performance Task for impulsivity (CPT-3: Conners, 1995), Barkley's ADHD Behavior Rating Scale for attention and hyperactivity problems (Barkley, 1990), peer sociometric report for aggression (Coie, Dodge, & Copotelli, 1982), and the Childhood Anxiety Sensitivity Index (CASI: Silverman, Fleisig, Rabian, & Peterson, 1991) for anxiety. The availability of reliable and valid assessment tools that target specific problem areas provides a variety of avenues for symptom-specific data collection. Moreover, the diversity of instruments available makes easy the task of selecting an instrument that is relevant to the informant.

Diagnostic Labeling

It is also important to consider the potential impact a diagnosis can have on children and their families (Corrigan, 1998; Dickerson, 1998; Holmes & River, 1998; Lundin, 1998; Mayville & Penn, 1998). Though clinicians recognize that a diagnosis simply summarizes a symptom cluster and suggests a course of intervention, parents, teachers, and children may interpret diagnostic labels quite differently. Failure to understand the meaning of a diagnosis may have implications for how children with such problems are perceived and treated. Adults influenced by labels may assume that all children with a particular diagnosis are more alike than they actually are, leading to oversight of the child's individual needs. People, reacting to the child's diagnostic label, may notice or focus only on behavior or information that is consistent with the label. Moreover, individuals may lower their expectations for the child, believing alternative behavior to be beyond his or her capabilities. Such a response from the environment may encourage maladaptive child behavior (e.g., it may create a self-fulfilling prophecy; Rutter & Gould, 1985).

The preceding discussion highlights the importance of carefully presenting and interpreting results of a child's diagnostic evaluation to the parents. If a diagnosis is offered, care should be taken to emphasize that it is a descriptive label that summarizes the cluster of problematic behaviors rather than the cause of the problem. Etiology and prognosis, as well as typical treatments for specific dysfunction, should be conveyed clearly. With younger children, rather than present a diagnosis, it may be most appropriate to explain the results in terms of the impact these challenging behaviors may have on the child's daily life. Potential treatment ideas also might be conveyed.

SUMMARY

The effort to define and classify abnormal behavior has an extensive history. In this chapter a brief discussion concerning the issues surrounding attempts to define normal and abnormal behavior was presented. This was followed by a brief review of the evolution of diagnostic classification of childhood psychopathology. From preliminary forms to current systems, the progression of diagnostic classification was outlined. Included was a discussion of the *DSM*, the most widely used system of psychiatric diagnostic classification. Additionally, criteria by which diagnostic systems are critiqued were discussed.

Diagnosis and classification of behavior problems is a complex process designed to delineate dysfunction or difficulties that individuals display. Myriad issues exist in diagnostic classification, some of which are unique to children. Special ethical concerns were highlighted, as were the potential negative effects of labeling. Challenges associated with diagnosing child behavior problems were also examined, such as the paucity of data on cultural and ethnic differences, the presence of diagnostic comorbidity, and the complex process of differential diagnosis. The importance of recognizing the impact of developmental, cognitive, and family variables on child functioning was also discussed. Additionally, contextual factors were also emphasized as important parts of a thorough child evaluation.

The core components of diagnostic assessment were outlined. Central to the discussion of methodology was the clinical interview. Use of clinical interview formats was recommended, and several structured and semistructured instruments were briefly reviewed. As a follow-up to the clinical interview, the use of multiple informants and supplemental assessment tools was suggested to garner information regarding specific problem areas. The importance of identifying contextual factors contributing to the problem behavior was emphasized throughout the chapter. Finally, negative implications resulting from diagnostic classification were mentioned.

Recent emphasis on developmental psychopathology (the pathways approach) has expanded understanding of how problem behavior develops and changes in children and adolescents. With this knowledge comes increased precision in diagnostic classification of maladaptive behavior via refinements and alterations to theory and practice.

REFERENCES

Achenbach, T. M. (1991). *Manual for the Child Behavior Checklist/ 4–18 and 1991 Profile*. Burlington: University of Vermont, Department of Psychiatry.

Achenbach, T. M. (1993). Implications of multiaxial empirically based assessment for behavior therapy with children. *Behavior Therapy, 24,* 91–116.

Achenbach, T. M., & Edelbrock, C. S. (1981). Behavioral problems and competencies reported by parents of normal and disturbed children ages four through sixteen. *Monographs of the Society for Research in Child Development, 46*(1, Serial No. 188).

Adams, H. E., & Cassidy, J. F. (1993). The classification of abnormal behavior: An overview. In P. B. Sutker & H. E. Adams (Eds.), *Comprehensive handbook of psychopathology* (2nd ed., pp. 3–25). New York: Plenum Press.

Adams, H. E., Luscher, K. A., & Bernat, J. A. (2001). Classification of abnormal behavior: An overview. In P. B. Sutker & H. E. Adams (Eds.), *Comprehensive handbook of psychopathology* (pp. 3–28). New York: Kluwer/Plenum Press.

Ambrosini, P. (2000). Historical development and present status of the Schedule for Affective Disorders and Schizophrenia for School-Age Children (K-SADS). *Journal of the American Academy of Child and Adolescent Psychiatry, 39,* 49–58.

American Psychiatric Association. (1933). *Standard classified nomenclature of diseases.* Washington, DC: Author.

American Psychiatric Association. (1952). *Diagnostic and statistical manual of mental disorders.* Washington, DC: Author.

American Psychiatric Association. (1968). *Diagnostic and statistical manual of mental disorders* (2nd ed.). Washington, DC: Author.

American Psychiatric Association. (1980). *Diagnostic and statistical manual of mental disorders* (3rd ed.). Washington, DC: Author.

American Psychiatric Association. (1987). *Diagnostic and statistical manual of mental disorders* (3rd ed., rev.). Washington, DC: Author.

American Psychiatric Association. (1994). *Diagnostic and statistical manual of mental disorders* (4th ed.). Washington, DC: Author.

American Psychiatric Association. (2000). *Diagnostic and statistical manual of mental disorders* (4th ed., text rev.). Washington, DC: Author.

American Psychological Association Division 12 Task Force on Promotion and Dissemination of Psychological Procedures. (1995). Training in and dissemination of empirically-validated psychological treatments: Report and recommendations. *Clinical Psychologist, 48,* 3–23.

Angold, A., & Costello, E. (2000). The child and adolescent psychiatric assessment (CAPA). *Journal of the American Academy of Child and Adolescent Psychiatry, 39,* 39–48.

Angold, A., Costello, E., & Erkanli, A. (1999). Comorbidity. *Journal of Child Psychology and Psychiatry, 40,* 57–87.

Angold, A., Prendergast, M., Cox, A., Harrington, R., Simonoff, E., & Rutter, M. (1995). The Child and Adolescent Assessment (CAPA). *Psychological Medicine, 25,* 739–753.

Barkley, R. A. (1990). *Attention deficit hyperactivity disorder: A handbook for diagnosis and treatment.* New York: Guilford Press.

Barlow, D., Allen, L., & Choate, M. (2004). Toward a unified treatment for emotional disorders. *Behavior Therapy, 35,* 205–230.

Beidel, D., Neal, A., & Lederer, A. (1991). The feasibility and validity of a daily diary for the assessment of anxiety in children. *Behavior Therapy, 22,* 505–517.

Birns, B. (1976). The emergence and socialization of sex differences in the earliest years. *Merrill-Palmer Quarterly, 22,* 229–254.

Boggs, K., Griffin, R., & Gross, A. M. (2003). Children. In M. Hersen (Ed.), *Diagnostic interviewing* (pp. 393–413). New York: Kluwer-Plenum Press.

Bravo, M., Ribera, J., & Rubio-Stipec, M. (2001). Test-retest reliability of the Spanish version of the Diagnostic Interview Schedule for Children (DISC-IV). *Journal of Abnormal Child Psychology, 29,* 433–444.

Brestan, E., & Eyberg, S. (1998). Effective psychosocial treatments for conduct-disordered children and adolescents: 29 years, 82 studies, and 5,272 kids. *Journal of Clinical Child Psychology, 27,* 180–189.

Buss, A. H. (1966). *Psychopathology.* New York: Wiley.

Butcher, J., Narikiyo, T., & Bemis Vitousek, K. (1993). Understanding abnormal behavior in cultural context. In P. Sutker & H. Adams (Eds.), *Comprehensive handbook of psychopathology* (2nd ed., pp. 83–105). New York: Plenum Press.

Campbell, S., & Cohn, S. (1997). The timing and chronicity of postpartum depression: Implications for infant development. In L. Murray & P. Cooper (Eds.), *Postpartum depression and child development* (pp. 165–197). Berlin: Springer-Verlag.

Canino, I., & Spurlock, J. (2000). *Culturally diverse children and adolescents.* New York: Guilford Press.

Chambless, D., Sanderson, W., Shoham, V., Johnson, S., Pope, K., Crits-Christoph, P., et al. (1996). An update on empirically validated therapies. *Clinical Psychologist, 49,* 5–18.

Chess, S., & Thomas, A. (1972). Differences in outcome with early intervention in children with behavior disorders. In M. Roff, L. Robins, & M. Pollack (Eds.), *Life history research in psychopathology* (Vol. 2). Minneapolis: University Press.

Cohen, P., Cohen, J., Kasen, S., Velez, C., Hartmark, C., Rojas, M., et al. (1993). An epidemiological study of disorders in late childhood and adolescence: I. Age- and gender-specific prevalence. *Journal of Child Psychology and Psychiatry, 34,* 851–867.

Coie, J. D., Dodge, K. A., & Copotelli, H. (1982). Dimensions and types of social status: A cross-age perspective. *Developmental Psychology, 18,* 557–570.

Coie, J. D., & Jacobs, M. R. (1993). The role of social context in the prevention of conduct disorder. *Development and Psychopathology, 5,* 263–275.

Cone, J. D. (1988). Psychometric considerations and the multiple models of behavioral assessment. In A. S. Bellack & M. Hersen (Eds.), *Conceptual foundations of behavioral assessment* (pp. 111–128). New York: Guilford Press.

Conger, R., McCarty, J., Yang, R., Lahey, B., & Kropp, J. (1984). Perception of child, child-rearing values, and emotional distress as mediating links between environmental stressors and observed maternal behavior. *Child Development, 55,* 2234–2247.

Conners, C. (1995). *Conners' Continuous Performance Test computer program 3.0: User's manual.* Toronto: MultiHealth Systems.

Corrigan, P. (1998). The impact of stigma on severe mental illness. *Cognitive and Behavioral Practice, 5,* 201–222.

Costello, J., Mustillo, S., Erkanli, A., Keeler, G., & Angold, A. (2003). Prevalence and development of psychiatric disorders in childhood and adolescence. *Archives of General Psychiatry, 60,* 837–844.

Dadds, M., & Sanders, M. (1992). Family interaction and child psychopathology: A comparison of two observation strategies. *Journal of Child and Family Studies, 1,* 371–391.

Dana, R. (1993). *Multicultural assessment perspectives for professional psychology.* Boston: Allyn & Bacon.

Dickerson, F. (1998). Strategies that foster empowerment. *Cognitive and Behavioral Practice, 5,* 255–275.

Dunitz-Scheer, M., Scheer, P., Kvas, E., & Macari, S. (1996). Psychiatric diagnosis in infancy: A comparison. *Infant Mental Health Journal, 17,* 12–24.

Edelbrock, C., & Costello, A. J. (1988). Convergence between statistically derived behavior problem syndromes and child psychiatric diagnoses. *Journal of Abnormal Child Psychology, 16,* 219–231.

Eme, R. (1979). Sex differences in childhood psychopathology: A review. *Psychological Bulletin, 86,* 574–595.

Emery, R. (1982). Interparental conflict and the children of discord and divorce. *Psychological Bulletin, 92,* 310–330.

Ford, T., Goodman, R., & Meltzer, H. (2003). The British Child and Adolescent Mental Health Survey 1999: The prevalence of *DSM-IV* disorders. *Journal of the American Academy of Child and Adolescent Psychiatry, 42,* 1203–1211.

Forehand, R., McCombs, A., & Brody, G. (1987). The relationship between parental depressive mood state and child functioning. *Advances in Behavior Research and Therapy, 9,* 1–20.

Frick, P. J., Lahey, B. B., Applegate, B., Kerdyck, L., Ollendick, T., Hynd, G. W., et al. (1994). DSM-IV field trials for the disruptive behavior disorders: Symptom utility estimates. *Journal of the*

American Academy of Child and Adolescent Psychiatry, 33, 529–539.

Hayes, S. C., & Follette, W. C. (1992). Can functional analysis provide a substitute for syndromal classification? *Behavioral Assessment, 14,* 345–355.

Holmes, E., & River, L. (1998). Individual strategies for coping with the stigma of mental illness. *Cognitive and Behavioral Practice, 5,* 231–239.

Huston, A. (1983). Sex-typing. In P. Mussen (Ed.), *Handbook of child psychology* (Vol. 4). New York: Wiley.

Jahoda, M. (1958). *Current concepts of positive mental health.* New York: Basic Books.

Jensen, P., & members of the MTA cooperative group. (2002). ADHD comorbidity findings from the MTA study: New diagnostic subtypes and their optimal treatments. In J. Helzer & J. Hudziak (Eds.), *Defining psychopathology in the 21st century: DSM-IV and beyond.* Washington, DC: American Psychiatric Association.

Jensen, P., Watanabe, H., Richters, J., Roper, M., Hibbs, E., Salzberg, A., et al. (1996). Scales, diagnoses, and child psychopathology: II. Comparing the CBCL and the DISC against external validators. *Journal of Abnormal Child Psychology, 24,* 151–168.

Jouriles, E., Murphy, C., Farris, A., Smith, D., Richters, J., & Waters, E. (1991). Marital adjustment, parental disagreements about child rearing, and behavior problems in boys: Increasing the specificity of marital assessment. *Child Development, 62,* 1424–1433.

Katz, L., & Gottman, J. (1993). Patterns of marital conflict predict children's externalizing and internalizing behaviors. *Developmental Psychology, 29,* 940–950.

Kaufman, J., Birmaher, B., Brent, D., Rao, U., Flynn, C., Moreci, P., et al. (1997). Schedule for Affective Disorders and Schizophrenia for School-Age Children—Present and Lifetime Version (K-SADS-PL): Initial reliability and validity data. *Journal of the American Academy of Child and Adolescent Psychiatry, 36,* 980–988.

Kaufman, J., Birmaher, B., Brent, D., Rao, U., & Ryan, N. (1996). *Kiddie-SADS—Present and Lifetime Version (K-SADS-PL).* Retrieved April 3, 2004, from http://www.wpic.pitt.edu/ksads

Kazdin, A. (1997). A model for developing effective treatments: Progression and interplay of theory, research, and practice. *Journal of Clinical Child Psychology, 26,* 114–129.

Kendell, R. E. (1989). Clinical validity. In L. N. Robins & J. E. Barret (Eds.), *The validity of psychiatric diagnosis* (pp. 305–322). New York: Raven Press.

King, H., Hamilton, D., and Ollendick, T. (1994). *Children's phobias: A behavioral perspective.* Oxford, England: Wiley.

Kovacs, M. (1997). *The Interview Schedule for Children and Adolescents (ISCA): Current and Lifetime (ISCA-C & L) and Current and Interim (ISCA-C & I) versions.* Pittsburgh: Western Psychiatric Institute and Clinic.

Lahey, B. B., Loeber, R., Quay, H. C., Applegate, B., Shaffer, D., Waldman, I., et al. (1998). Validity of *DSM-IV* subtypes of conduct disorder based on age of onset. *Journal of the American Academy of Child and Adolescent Psychiatry, 37,* 435–442.

Last, C., & Strauss, C. (1990). School refusal in anxiety disordered children and adolescents. *Journal of the American Academy of Child and Adolescent Psychiatry, 29,* 31–35.

Lillienfeld, S. (2003). Comorbidity between and within childhood externalizing and internalizing disorders: Reflections and directions. *Journal of Abnormal Child Psychology, 31,* 285–291.

Lonigan, C., Elbert, J., & Johnson, S. (1998). Empirically supported psychosocial interventions for children: An overview. *Journal of Clinical Child Psychology, 27,* 138–145.

Lundin, R. (1998). Living with mental illness: A personal experience. *Cognitive and Behavioral Practice, 5,* 223–230.

Lyons, J., & Serbin, L. (1986). Observer bias in scoring boys' and girls' aggression. *Sex Roles, 14,* 301–313.

Lyons-Ruth, K. (1992). Maternal depressive symptoms, disorganized infant-mother attachment relationships, and hostile-aggressive behavior in the preschool classroom: A prospective longitudinal view from infancy to age five. In D. Cichetti & S. Toth (Eds.), *Developmental perspectives on depression. Rochester symposium on developmental psychology* (pp. 131–172). Rochester, NY: University Press.

Lytton, H., & Romeny, D. (1993). Parents' differential socialization of boys and girls: A meta-analysis. *Psychological Bulletin, 109,* 267–296.

Maccoby, E. E., & Martin, J. A. (1983). Socialization in the context of the family: Parent-child interaction. In E. M. Hetherington (Ed.), *Handbook of child psychology* (Vol. 4, 4th ed., pp. 1–101). New York: Wiley.

Mayville, E., & Penn, D. (1998). Changing societal attitudes toward persons with severe mental retardation. *Cognitive and Behavioral Practice, 5,* 241–253.

Ollendick, T., & King, N. (1998). Empirically supported treatments for children with phobic and anxiety disorders: Current status. *Journal of Clinical Child Psychology, 27,* 156–167.

Pelham, W., Wheeler, T., & Chronis, A. (1998). Empirically supported psychosocial treatments for attention deficit hyperactivity disorder. *Journal of Clinical Child Psychology, 27,* 190–205.

Puig-Antich, J., & Chambers, W. (1978). *The Schedule for Affective Disorders and Schizophrenia for School-Age Children (K-SADS).* New York: New York State Psychiatric Institute.

Reich, W. (2000). Diagnostic Interview Schedule for Children and Adolescents (DICA). *Journal of the American Academy of Child and Adolescent Psychiatry, 39,* 58–66.

Reich, W., & Welner, A. (1998). *Revised version of the Diagnostic Interview Schedule for Children and Adolescents (DICA-R).* St. Louis: Washington University School of Medicine, Department of Psychiatry.

Reitman, D., Hummel, R., Franz, D., & Gross, A. M. (1998). A review of methods and instruments for assessing externalizing disorders: Theoretical and practical considerations in rendering a diagnosis. *Clinical Psychology Review, 18,* 555–584.

Reynolds, C. R., & Kamphaus, R. W. (1992). *Behavioral Assessment Scale for Children.* Circle Pines, MN: American Guidance Service.

Rogler, L. (1996). Framing research on culture in psychiatric diagnosis: The case of the *DSM-IV. Psychiatry, 59,* 145–155.

Rutter, M., & Gould, M. (1985). Classification. In M. Rutter & L. Hersov (Eds.), *Child and adolescent psychiatry: Modern approaches.* Oxford: Blackwell.

Scotti, J. R., & Morris, T. L. (2000). Diagnosis and classification. In M. Hersen & R. T. Ammerman (Eds.), *Advanced abnormal child psychology* (pp. 15–32). Mahwah, NJ: Erlbaum.

Scotti, J. R., Morris, T. L., McNeil, C. B., & Hawkins, R. P. (1996). DSM-IV and disorders of childhood and adolescence: Can structural criteria be functional? *Journal of Consulting and Clinical Psychology, 64,* 1177–1191.

Shaffer, D. (1994). Structured interviews for assessing children. *Journal of Child Psychology and Psychiatry and Allied Disciplines, 35,* 783–784.

Shaffer, D., Fisher, P., Lucas, C., Dulcan, M., & Schwab-Stone, M. (2000). NIMH Diagnostic Interview for Children Version IV (NIMH DISC-IV): Description, differences from previous versions, and reliability of some common diagnoses. *Journal of the American Academy of Child and Adolescent Psychiatry, 39,* 28–38.

Sherrill, J., & Kovacs, M. (2000). Interview Schedule for Children and Adolescents (ISCA). *Journal of the American Academy of Child and Adolescent Psychiatry, 39,* 67–75.

Silverman, W., Fleisig, W., Rabian, B., & Peterson, R. (1991). Childhood anxiety sensitivity index. *Journal of Clinical Child Psychology, 20,* 162–168.

Sroufe, L. A. (1979). The coherence of individual development. *American Psychologist, 34,* 834–841.

Sue, D., & Sue, D. (1999). *Counseling the culturally different.* New York: Wiley.

Thomas, J., & Clark, R. (1998). Disruptive behaviors in the very young child: Diagnostic classification: 0–3 guides identification of risk factors and relational intervention. *Infant Mental Health Journal, 19,* 229–244.

Van Dulmen, M., Grotevant, H., Dunbar, N., Miller, B., Bayley, B., Christensen, M., et al. (2002). Connecting national survey data with *DSM-IV* criteria. *Journal of Adolescent Health, 31,* 475–481.

Volkmar, F., & Woolston, J. (1997). Comorbidity of psychiatric disorders in children and adolescents. In S. Wetzler & W. Anderson (Eds.), *Treatment strategies for patients with psychiatric comorbidity* (pp. 307–322). New York: Wiley.

Wakefield, J. (1992). Disorder as harmful dysfunction: A conceptual critique of *DSM*'s definition of mental disorder. *Psychological Review, 99,* 232–247.

Werry, J. S. (1992). Child psychiatric disorders: Are they classifial600ble? *British Journal of Psychiatry, 161,* 472–480.

Wicks-Nelson, R., & Israel, A. C. (1991). *Behavior disorders of children.* Englewood Cliffs, NJ: Prentice Hall.

World Health Organization. (1948). *International classification of diseases* (6th rev.). Geneva, Switzerland: Author.

World Health Organization. (1992). *International classification of diseases* (10th rev.). Geneva, Switzerland: Author.

Zero to Three/National Center for Clinical Infant Programs. (1994). *Diagnostic classification of mental health and developmental disorders of infancy and early childhood (Diagnostic classification: 0–3).* Washington, DC: Author.

CHAPTER 2

Genetic Contributions

DANIELLE M. DICK AND RICHARD D. TODD

INTRODUCTION

Historically, childhood disorders were thought to be the result of poor or inconsistent parenting. More recently it has been recognized that there are significant genetic contributions to many childhood disorders. It is now widely accepted that most childhood psychopathology results from complex interactions of genetic predispositions and environmental circumstances. This chapter will review the methodologies used to determine whether genetic influences impact a behavior, new developments in the kinds of questions being addressed by researchers interested in the genetics of psychopathology, and advances in our ability to detect specific genes involved in psychopathology. For illustrative purposes, many of the examples provided focus on adolescent substance use and related behavioral disorders, but the issues raised are broadly applicable to the study of other forms of behavioral and psychiatric phenotypes.

TRADITIONAL METHODS TO DETECT GENETIC INFLUENCE

Family Studies

Family studies are traditionally used as the first step in establishing whether a disorder is under a degree of genetic influence. If a certain disorder runs in families, then it is possible that the disorder is under genetic influence. If a disorder is influenced by genes, individuals who are more closely related genetically should be more likely to be affected. For example, the data shown in Figure 2.1 (Gottesman, 1991) clearly indicate that individuals who are more closely related genetically have a greater risk of schizophrenia.

However, the problem with family studies is that it is not possible to tease apart genetic and environmental influences. Individuals who are more closely related genetically (e.g., siblings as compared to cousins) are also more likely to spend more time together and share more environmental influences. Thus, genetic and environmental influences are confounded in the traditional family study. In the literature, it is not uncommon to see parent-child correlations for a particular behavior interpreted as support for the importance of environmental influences such as parenting practices. Although probably correct for some behaviors, in general, this is a faulty experimental design, in that parent-child correlations (among biological, nonadopted family members) can result from shared genes, environmental influences, gene-environment interactions, and so forth.

Adoption Studies

Another study design that has been employed to evaluate the degree to which genetic influences impact a particular behavior or disorder is the study of adopted children. When a child is adopted by individuals who are not biological relatives, it provides, in theory, a clear separation of genetic and environmental influences. These adopted children share their rearing environment with individuals with whom they share no genes, and they share genes, but not their environment, with their biological parents. Accordingly, the degree of resemblance between adopted-apart biological relatives indicates the importance of genetic influences, whereas the degree of resemblance among nonbiological adoptive relatives indicates the degree of influence of the shared environment.

A classic adoption study was conducted by Heston in the mid-1900s and had a significant impact on the way the field views the etiology of schizophrenia. A sample of nearly 50 children who were born to schizophrenic mothers between 1915 and 1945 in Oregon's state psychiatric hospitals were separated from their mothers within the first few days of life and adopted by nonschizophrenic parents. These children were followed up through age 36 and were compared to a control group of foster children whose mothers had no record of psychiatric problems, and who were matched on sex and type of placement. Of the foster-reared children of schizophrenics, 17 percent developed schizophrenia, whereas none

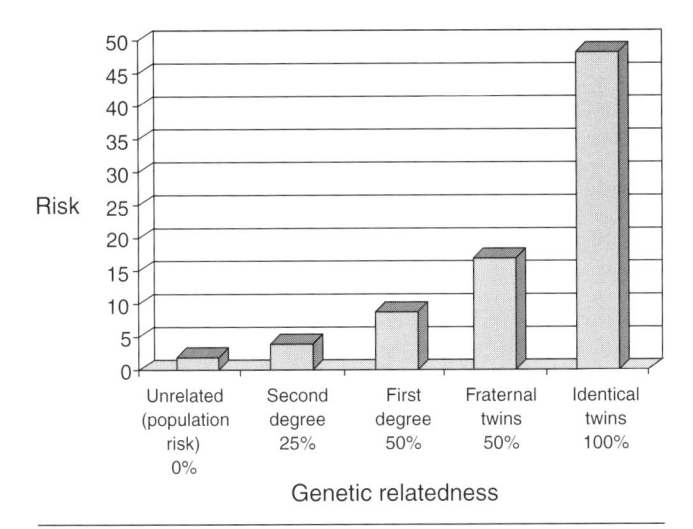

Figure 2.1 Risk of developing schizophrenia among individuals of different genetic relatedness to a schizophrenic proband (adapted from Gottesman, 1991).

of the control children did (Heston & Denney, 1967). These findings suggest that biological predispositions are involved in the development of schizophrenia, and this study helped dispel the myth of schizophrenia being caused by so-called schizophrenogenic mothers.

Another influential adoption study was Cloninger's study of alcoholism among Swedish men adopted by nonrelatives at an early age (Cloninger, Bohman, & Sigvardsson, 1981). He distinguished between two forms of alcoholism: Type 1, characterized by a later age of onset and loss of control when drinking, and Type 2, characterized by an early age of onset and high novelty seeking and antisocial behavior. Alcoholism in adoptive parents was not associated with alcoholism in their adoptive children, suggesting little role of the familial environment in causing either type of alcoholism. However, when both a genetic predisposition *and* environmental provocation were present, the risk of Type 1 alcoholism increased. In contrast, a genetic predisposition alone was sufficient to increase the risk of Type 2 alcoholism in adopted-away offspring of Type 2 alcoholics (Cloninger, 1987).

Limitations

Despite their utility in teasing apart the relative influence of genetic and environmental factors on outcome, adoption studies suffer from a number of limitations. Adoptive parents are often a biased sample of the population by virtue of adoptive agencies' screening processes. They are often higher in socioeconomic status and they have lower rates of mental illness compared to the general population. Systematic investigation of this bias has demonstrated that the restricted range of family environments observed in adoption studies can lead to substantial underestimates of the importance of the environment and upwardly biased estimates of genetic effects (Stoolmiller, 1998). Biological parents of children who are adopted away are often biased in the opposite direction, having higher rates of mental illness and a lower social standing. There are higher rates of poor prenatal care and in utero exposure to drugs, alcohol, and nicotine in adopted-away children. Another limitation of adoption studies is selective placement. If the adoptive parents are matched to the biological parents on a particular variable that influences the outcome under study, this will create an artificial inflation in the correlation between biological parents and their adopted children. For example, if the adopted family is matched to the biological parents on socioeconomic status (SES), and SES influences the behavioral trait of interest, then the estimate of heritability based on biological parent–adopted child traits will be inflated due to the selective placement. Another problem with adoption studies is that so-called open adoptions are increasingly common, in which the biological parents maintain some contact with their adopted child. This confounds the traditional separation of genetic and environmental influences that exists with the traditional adoption study. Finally, the number of children given up for adoption is decreasing, given that the stigma attached to abortion and single mothers has decreased.

Twin Studies

Twin studies are one of the most widely used methodologies to establish genetic influence on a trait of interest. Twins account for 3 percent of live births in the United States, and the rate of twinning has risen in recent years (Arias, MacDorman, Strobino, & Guyer, 2003). Monozygotic (MZ) twins (also called identical twins) result when a single fertilized egg splits during the process of cell division. It is not clear what causes this split that leads to the development of MZ twins (Hall, 2003). Because they arose from a single fertilized egg, MZ twins are identical genetically. Dizygotic (DZ) twins, also called fraternal twins, result when two separate eggs are fertilized by two sperm cells. The release of two eggs is related to increased concentration of follicle-stimulating hormone (FSH) in the mother (Hall, 2003). Dizygotic twinning is found to run in some families, likely due to genetic influence on FSH levels. In addition, FSH levels increase with age; accordingly, the chance of conceiving DZ twins increases with maternal age. Because DZ twins result from the fertilization of two eggs, they share, on average, 50 percent of their segregating genes, just as do ordinary siblings. However, unlike ordinary siblings, DZs are the same age and also share an intrauterine environment.

Comparisons of MZ and DZ twins yield estimates of the degree to which a particular behavior or disorder is influenced by genetics, the environment, or both. Traditional twin studies divide observed behavioral variance into three unobserved (latent) sources: variance attributable to genetic effects, that due to environmental influences shared by siblings (called common or shared environmental influences), and that arising in unshared environmental experience that makes siblings differ from one another (called unique environmental influence). Variance attributed to genetic effects can be further divided into additive genetic influences and dominant genetic influences. Except for the sex chromosomes, individuals have two copies (called alleles) at any given genetic locus, one inherited from each parent. Under an additive system, each copy contributes additively to the outcome, so individuals with one copy of the genetic variant have a phenotype intermediate to individuals with zero copies and individuals with two copies. When there is dominance, only one copy is necessary for the effect on the outcome; individuals with one or two copies look equivalent to each other and different from individuals with no copies. It is not possible to estimate both dominant genetic influences and common environment at the same time when only twin data are available.

Because MZs share more of their segregating genes than do DZs, but both types of twins, when raised together, share their home environment, increased similarity among MZs is interpreted as evidence for genetic effects. As an example, consider a behavior on which MZ twins correlate at 0.8 and DZ twins correlate at 0.5. The fact that MZs are more alike than DZs are would suggest genetic influence on this behavior. More specifically, we can get a rough estimate of the degree to which genes influence the behavior by doubling the difference between MZs and DZs [$2 \times (0.8 - 0.5) = 0.6$]. Accordingly, the amount of variance that would be attributed to additive genetic effects (A) for this behavior would be 60 percent. This estimate is called a heritability estimate. It indicates the proportion of variance that can be attributed to genetic variance out of the total variance in the behavior. One can imagine that if the correlation between MZs and DZs is identical, the heritability would be 0, and there would be no evidence that genes influence this behavior. Heritability estimates are specific to a particular population at the particular point in time at which it was studied. (More details about this are included later in the chapter.) Common environmental influences (C) are those that make siblings more similar to one another. These could include a shared home environment and parental rearing practices; shared peers; and shared societal factors, such as religion or a shared school. Common environmental influences are suggested when the DZ correlation is greater than half the MZ correlation, because half the MZ correlation is the degree of similarity expected based on genetic influences alone. When DZ twins are more alike than what is expected based on their degree of genetic similarity, it suggests that common environmental influences are acting on the trait. When the correlation for DZ twins is less than half that of MZ twins, it suggests dominant genetic effects (D). As previously mentioned, C and D effects cannot be estimated simultaneously; however, the ratio of the DZ correlation to the MZ correlation can be used to determine whether a model testing C effects or D effects is more appropriate. Finally, unique environmental effects (E) are influences that make siblings dissimilar to one another. These can include influences such as different peers or differential parental treatment of the twins. E effects also include the so-called slings and arrows of outrageous fortune, that is, unexpected environmental effects that impact a single individual. E effects are suggested when the MZ correlation is less than 1. In the case of our hypothetical behavioral example, an MZ correlation of 0.8 would suggest that (1.0–0.8) 20 percent of the variance is due to unique environmental effects. Error is also included in the E term. If a behavior is under only genetic influence, MZ twins should be identical for the behavior. The fact that MZ twins are not perfectly correlated for most behaviors of interest suggests that unique environmental effects play a role, there is error in our measurement of the phenotype, or both. Monozygotic twins cannot be any more correlated than the same individual assessed at two time points. Some genetically informative models have attempted to take into account reliability of the measurement (Kendler, Neale, Kessler, Heath, & Eaves, 1993).

Limitations

Twin studies make certain assumptions in order to draw conclusions about the relative importance of genetic and environmental effects. The primary assumption of the twin design is the equal environments assumption. In the classic twin design, any excess similarity in MZ twins, relative to DZ twins, is attributed to genetic influence. If identical twins are treated more similarly than fraternal twins, they may be more alike for reasons other than their additional shared genes. For example, if physical similarity influences social treatment, which subsequently influences psychiatric outcome, then MZ twins would be more similar than DZs, in part for nongenetic reasons. Twin researchers have used a number of methods to test the equal environments assumption. In one study, researchers made home visits to evaluate similarities in the ways parents treated MZ and DZ twins. Any excess similarity in the treatment of MZs was found to be caused by parental responses to the children's behavior (which was presumably more similar in MZs to the extent that genetic influences impact behavior) (Lytton, 1977). There is no question that MZ twins have increased shared experience; MZ twins report more frequently sharing the same room and being dressed alike as children, and parents report treating their MZ twins more similarly. The issue is whether this type of shared experience influences the trait or disorder of interest. Most studies have found no correlation between the report of these types of environmental experiences and similarity for personality, intelligence, and most psychiatric disorders. Finally, a number of twins and parents are misinformed about the twins' zygosity. If expectations about MZ twins lead to greater similarity in parental treatment and outcome, we would expect DZ twins misclassified as MZs to be more similar than DZ twins correctly classified. For a variety of traits, there has been no evidence that perceived zygosity influences outcome. Thus, the majority of studies that have tested the equal environment assumption have found that it is correct for most behavioral outcomes of interest, such as personality and psychopathology. Minimally, it appears that the equal environment assumption does not contribute any substantial bias to the conclusions of twin studies (Cronk et al., 2002).

In addition, twin studies have been criticized because twins differ from singletons with respect to their prenatal and perinatal development. Twins are more likely to have a lower birth weight, and they are more likely to experience congenital abnormalities. To the extent that birth weight and prenatal development may influence the outcome under study, twins may not be representative of the risk factors that most individuals experience. However, no excess in rates of psychopathology has been found in twins (Kendler, 1993).

THE EVOLVING FIELD OF BEHAVIOR GENETICS

Historically, the field of behavior genetics had a single and simple goal: to demonstrate that some of the variation in behavior is attributable to genetic variance. This may seem to be a simple idea, but it was met with much resistance at the time it was put forth, as the predominant view was that psychopathology was the result of abnormal childhood development. Now, less than 50 years after the first text on behavior genetics was published (Fuller & Thompson, 1960), a diverse array of behaviors has been investigated with twin and adoption designs, yielding evidence that genetic variation contributes to individual differences in virtually all behavioral domains (McGuffin, Riley, & Plomin, 2001). The questions addressed by researchers interested in the genetics of both normal and abnormal behavior are now increasingly complex. Several factors have contributed to this advance. One of these developments has been the establishment of population-based twin registries. Early studies often used small sample sizes and clinically ascertained twins. This limited the conclusions one could draw, in that individuals who seek treatment for their disorder may not be representative of the majority of affected individuals. Additionally, the presence of multiple psychiatric problems also influences treatment seeking. Population-based twin registries allow one to make population estimates, to study both normal and abnormal phenotypes, and to study large numbers of twins. Several population-based twin registries have been established in the United States, such as one in Virginia using driver's license records (Kendler, Neale, Kessler, Heath, & Eaves, 1992) and one in Missouri using birth records (Kendler et al., 1992; Todd et al., 2001). In addition, some of the most famous population-based twin registries have been established in European countries, in which central population registries have allowed investigators access to birth records and current addresses for the country's residents (Boomsma, 1998; Kaprio, Pulkkinen, & Rose, 2002). Population-based twin registries have also made it possible to ascertain and prospectively study large samples of twins, necessary for the complex models now being applied to twin data.

The application of biometrical modeling to twin data is a second advance that has drastically expanded the type and complexity of questions that can be addressed regarding the genetics of behavior. Model fitting allows one to statistically specify a hypothesis and then test the fit of the data to that hypothesis. Competing hypotheses can also be specified and statistically tested. In addition, model fitting allows for more accurate parameter estimates and for confidence intervals to be obtained for those estimates. Detailed in the following sections are several of the more complex kinds of questions, regarding *how* genetic influences impact a particular trait, that can now be addressed through biometrical modeling of twin data.

Developmental Changes

We know that the impact of genes is not static, but rather that the importance of genetic factors can vary across development. Such changes can be dramatic and rapid, particularly across childhood and adolescence. For example, in a sample of adolescent Finnish twins assessed on three occasions from ages 16 to 18.5, genetic contributions to individual differences in drinking frequency increased over time, accounting for only a third of the variation at age 16 but half of it just 30 months later (Rose, Dick, Viken, & Kaprio, 2001). Concurrently, the effects of sharing a common environment decreased in importance. Analyses of another sample of Finnish twins, assessed for the initiation of alcohol use by age 14, found that even earlier in adolescence the effect of genes on drinking patterns was negligible, accounting for only 18 percent of the variation among drinking initiation in girls and having no significant effect yet at this age in boys (Rose, Dick, Viken, Pulkkinen, & Kaprio, 2001).

Dramatic changes in the heritability of IQ across development have also been documented. Developmental comparisons have demonstrated that, for general cognitive ability, heritability increases from infancy (about 20 percent) to childhood (40 percent) to adolescence (50 percent) to adulthood (60 percent; McGue, Bouchard, Iacono, & Lykken, 1993), a finding that has been extended into twins aged 80 years or older (McClearn et al., 1997). Interestingly, analyses of smoking frequency in the same population of Finnish twins described previously found little change in the importance of genetic and environmental effects across ages 16–18.5, illustrating the trait specificity of gene-environment dynamics: some effects are stable across a developmental period, whereas others change.

Gene-Environment Interaction

Standard twin models yield estimates of the amount of variance attributable to genetic and environmental effects for a given population. These models average across any group differences that may exist in the population. As an overly simplistic example, a heritability of 50 percent could mean that for half of the population studied the trait is completely determined by genetic influences, and for the other half, the trait is completely determined by environmental influences. Additionally, if not explicitly modeled, gene-environment interaction effects could be subsumed under estimates of genetic influence (Heath, 2003). Therefore, a more sophisticated understanding of the etiology of any particular trait should provide insight into how genetic influences act within the context of particular environments (McClearn, 2004).

Early documentation of the potential importance of gene-environment interaction on behavioral outcome was found in data from the Australian twin registry: marital status moderated the relative importance of genetic effects on alcohol consumption (Heath, Jardine, & Martin, 1989) and on depression symptoms (Heath, Eaves, & Martin, 1998) in females. Having a marriagelike relationship reduced the impact of genetic influences on drinking. A marriagelike relationship also reduced the influence of genetic liability to depression symptoms: genetic factors accounted for far less of the variance in depression scores among married women, as compared to unmarried females (Heath et al., 1998). This study illustrated that environments can moderate the impact of genetic and environmental influences on behavior and suggested that a protective environment, characterized by a marriagelike relationship, may reduce the impact of genetic predispositions to various clinical problems.

Interestingly, there is reason to believe that genetic influences on adolescent behavior may be particularly susceptible to moderation by environmental effects. Adolescent substance use provides an illustrative example. Because substance use is illegal for most adolescents, exposure to particular environments allowing access to the substance are necessary before individuals have the opportunity to express genetic predispositions for patterns of use and abuse. Thus, genetic influences on adolescent substance use may be particularly dependent on the environmental context. As an illustration, in results from the Minnesota Twin Family Study, boys who had inherited a high genetic risk (based on their parents' alcohol use) were at increased risk of developing substance use by age 14 if they were exposed to a high-risk environment, such as deviant peers. However, genetic risk was largely irrelevant among boys whose environment was characterized as low risk (positive peer influences, a positive relationship with the mother, and participation in religious and school activities; Legrand, McGue, & Iacono, 1999).

In data from the Finnish Twin Studies, we have also found evidence of a strong moderating effect of the community environment on adolescent alcohol use. At age 16, we found that genetic influences accounted for nearly two times as much variance in drinking frequency in urban environments as compared to rural environments. Conversely, common environmental effects played a larger role in rural settings (Rose, Dick, Viken, & Kaprio, 2001). Further exploration of this effect illustrated that this moderation was dramatically enhanced when we incorporated more detailed information about specific aspects of the adolescent's community. For example, in neighborhoods with low stability (high rates of migration in and out), genetic influences accounted for more than 60 percent of the variation in drinking patterns, and common environmental effects played no detectable role. However, in neighborhoods with the most stability, common environmental factors played the largest role, accounting for nearly 50 percent of the variance, while genetic factors accounted for only 20 percent. These results suggest that communities characterized by greater social mobility allow for increased expression of genetic dispositions that contribute to individual differences in adolescent drinking. Conversely, communities with more social structure create opportunities in which common environmental effects assume greater importance, presumably by engendering more accountability for one's actions and more shared pressure to engage, or not engage, in certain behaviors (Dick, Rose, Viken, Kaprio, & Koskenvuo, 2001).

Subtyping Disorders

Two questions central to conceptions of disease for complex phenotypes are whether the disorder represents a continuum of severity (such as, for example, hypertension) or whether the disorder represents one or more discrete illnesses (for example, pneumonia, which represents hundreds of different discrete pathogens and mechanisms resulting in somewhat overlapping clinical presentations). Twin studies, especially when carried out on a population- or community-based sample, are well suited to address both of these issues. First, clustering of specific symptoms across the population can help determine whether there is a discrete grouping of symptoms, which occurs more frequently than expected by chance. If so, this would imply that a categorical form of illness may be the appropriate phenotype. If not, then this would give weight to the conception of severity of disorder being a continuously distributed trait in the population. If evidence is found for the discrete clustering of symptoms into two or more classes, whether these are genetically discrete or overlapping syndromes can be tested by looking at monozygotic and dizygotic twin concordance rates (as also described in the next section for comorbidity).

An example of this approach is provided by recent studies of attention-deficit/hyperactivity disorder (ADHD; Rasmussen et al., 2002, 2004; Todd et al., 2001). In this case, complete symptom information for *DSM-IV*-defined ADHD was collected on two population-based samples of twins. Clustering of symptoms within individuals was tested for (in this case by latent class analysis) and evidence found for multiple categories of ADHD symptoms. When monozygotic and dizygotic twin concordance rates were compared for these population-based definitions of ADHD subtypes, each subtype was found to be highly heritable, but there was no evidence for cross-heritability between the subtypes. In this case, ADHD symptoms identify a number of genetically discrete illness subtypes, which only partially overlap with *DSM-IV* ADHD subtypes. Using the same approaches, the opposite conclusion has been reached for autistic symptoms (Constantino, Przybeck, Friesen, & Todd, 2000; Constantino & Todd, 2003).

Comorbidity between Disorders

Twin studies also allow us to examine interesting questions about the causes of comorbidity between disorders. Comorbidity is the presence of two or more disorders in an individual. Many disorders seen in adolescence show substantial overlap. For example, comorbidity among ADHD, oppositional defiant disorder (ODD), and conduct disorder (CD) has been reported in both epidemiological and clinical samples (Biederman, Newcorn, & Sprich, 1991; Jensen, Martin, & Cantwell, 1997; Simonoff et al., 1997). However, the causes for the interrelationships between ADHD, ODD, and CD are not well understood. Do these disorders frequently co-occur because common environmental factors contribute to all of them? Or do shared genetic factors contribute to the observed overlap? A number of twin studies have now investigated this question (Dick, Viken, Kaprio, Pulkkinen, & Rose, 2004; Nadder, Rutter, Silberg, Maes, & Eaves, 2002; Silberg et al., 1996; Thapar, Harrington, & McGuffin, 2001; Waldman, Rhee, Levy, & Hay, 2001; Young, Stallings, Corley, Krauter, & Hewitt, 2000), studying twins varying in age and assessed with a variety of methods, including self-report and maternal questionnaire and interview. The results from these studies have been remarkably consistent in demonstrating that shared genetic factors largely contribute to the overlap observed among the disorders, with shared environmental factors making only modest (if any) contributions to comorbidity. However, the extent to which genetic influences are shared among these disorders remains controversial. For example, one twin study found that CD and ODD had completely overlapping genetic influences, such that analyses of these data have considered these behaviors as a joint construct (Nadder et al., 2002; Silberg et al., 1996), whereas others have not found this to be the case (Dick et al., 2004; Waldman et al., 2001). Similarly, at least one study has concluded that ADHD symptoms and CD symptoms are explained by a single genetic liability (Thapar, Hervas, & McGuffin, 1995), whereas other studies have found that constraining these disorders to share the exact same genetic factors, disallowing any unique genetic variance, did not fit the data well (Dick et al., 2004). The majority of the evidence at this point seems to support the assertion that genetic factors are primarily responsible for the overlap among ADHD, ODD, and CD. A single genetic liability, however, does not fully explain the heritability of these disorders, suggesting that these three externalizing disorders are not simply alternative manifestations of the same underlying genetic predisposition. Thus, some genes likely predispose to factors such as temperament, personality, or behavioral disinhibition that increase the risk for all externalizing disorders, whereas other genetic factors contribute to symptoms specific to the individual disorders.

It is also possible that genetic contributions to comorbidity between disorders can change across time. For example, CD is a robust predictor of both concurrent and future alcohol problems. This predictive association has been demonstrated in both school-based and clinically ascertained samples (Crowley, Milkulich, MacDonald, Young, & Zerbe, 1998; White, Zie, Thompson, Loeber, & Stouthamer-Loeber, 2001). Data from an Australian adult twin study found that the overlap between childhood CD (reported retrospectively) and the later development of adult alcohol dependence was due largely to shared genetic factors that contributed to the two disorders (Slutske et al., 1997). This suggests that some of the same genes that contribute to CD in childhood may also contribute to alcohol dependence in adulthood. However, a study of CD and alcohol problems measured prospectively in Finnish twin adolescents at age 14 found that the overlap between CD and concurrent alcohol dependence symptoms was due entirely to shared environmental factors (Rose et al., 2004). Alcohol problems showed no evidence of genetic effects at this age. Thus, analyses of CD and alcohol dependence symptoms *in adolescence* suggest that comorbidity between conduct and alcohol problems during this developmental period is largely due to environmental factors, such as deviant peers or a lack of parental supervision. However, CD already showed evidence of genetic effects at age 14. These findings suggest that CD (rather than alcohol problems, which appear to be an environmental phenomenon in early adolescence) may be a childhood manifestation of the genetic predisposition that later contributes to alcohol dependence in adulthood.

IDENTIFYING SPECIFIC GENES INVOLVED IN DISORDERS

Advances in genetics have now made it possible to move beyond the identification of latent sources of genetic influence, such as are indicated in classic twin studies, and to begin to identify the specific genes involved in disorders. To explain these methods, some background on the human genome is helpful. In most cells of the human body, genetic information is contained in 46 microscopic structures in the nucleus, called the chromosomes. The first 22 chromosomes are present in pairs, and the 23rd pair consists of either two X chromosomes (female) or an X and a Y chromosome (male). The chromosomes are inherited from the parents, with each parent providing one set of 23 chromosomes. These chromosomes contain a large molecule called deoxyribonucleic acid (DNA), which consists of four building blocks called nucleotides that are arranged in a specific order. This sequence of nucleotides encodes the genetic information necessary for the organism to develop and function. The DNA segments that determine those characteristics of an individual that are inherited from one generation to the next are called genes.

In contrast to the relatively simple gene structures present in prokaryotes, eukaryotic genes are characterized by interruptions in the DNA sequences that will eventually be transcribed and translated into protein. As shown in Figure 2.2, regions of protein coding genes that are eventually translated into protein (termed exons) are interrupted by regions of nucleic acid sequence that are translated into RNA but subsequently spliced out (termed introns). This process of transcription and splicing of RNA to yield the mature messenger RNA that is translated into protein appears to be the rule in eukaryotic genes. Also, indicated in the figure are two structural regions frequently found in genes that regulate their transcription. First is the promoter, which is always at the 5' end of genes (although it may be some distance away). Specific proteins can enhance the binding of RNA polymerase to this region and increase transcription of the gene. Also shown are possible enhancer regions that can increase transcription of genes when regulating proteins bind to them. These enhancers have the unusual characteristics of having the same effect on gene transcription no matter in which direction they appear in the DNA sequence and of being located anywhere in the gene (5', 3', or in introns). Either through direct messenger RNA or protein sequencing efforts or through new statistical programs, the identity of exons is known with high precision. The locations of promoters and enhancer regions is much more difficult to define at present.

Many variations in the DNA exist among the genes and noncoding DNA regions of different individuals. Such variants of a DNA sequence are called alleles. A DNA region for which several alleles exist is said to be polymorphic—that is, it exists in many forms. The identification of these var-

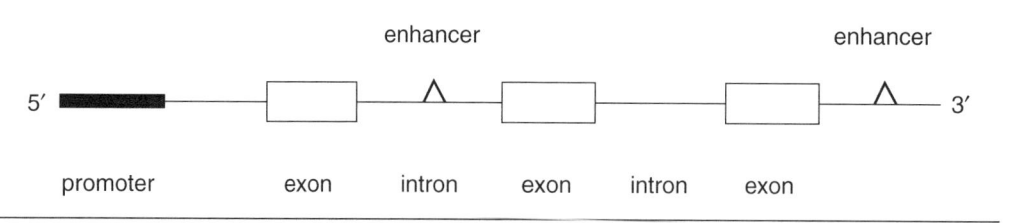

Figure 2.2 Example of a gene structure, illustrating different parts of the gene.

Comparative DNA sequence: ATGCCG**TA**GGGAGTT

Microsatellite marker: ATGCCG**TATATA**GGGAGTT

Comparative DNA sequence: ATGCCG**T**AGGGAGTT

SNP marker: ATGCCG**C**AGGGAGTT

Figure 2.3 Different types of genetic polymorphisms. Differences in the DNA sequence are bold and underlined.

iants has revolutionized the study of genetics because they allow researchers to study the inheritance of the alleles and to associate specific alleles with the presence of certain diseases. Several types of polymorphisms are commonly used for genetic analyses, including microsatellite markers and single-nucleotide polymorphisms (SNPs; see Figure 2.3). Microsatellite markers are DNA sequences in which short motifs of 2, 3, or 4 nucleotides are repeated several times, with the number of repetitions varying from person to person. Microsatellite markers are typically found in noncoding DNA regions. Single-nucleotide polymorphisms consist of the exchange of single nucleotides in the DNA and can be found in both coding and noncoding DNA regions. If SNPs occur within a gene or within a DNA region controlling the activity of a gene (such as a promoter or enhancer region), they can result in disease. However, many subtle changes in gene sequence—as well as many other DNA markers used in genetic analyses—have no apparent consequence.

Methods Used to Identify Genes

Linkage Approaches

To identify as-yet unknown genes involved in complex psychopathological phenotypes, investigators can search the entire genome by testing for linkage between polymorphic markers and the expression of the disorder or a related behavior. This means that they analyze whether specific alleles of those markers are more commonly found in people with the disorder or behavior than in people without it, by studying families with multiple affected individuals. Using markers that are evenly spaced across all chromosomes, one can analyze the entire genome using this approach and thereby identify susceptibility genes with no, or only limited, prior knowledge about the mechanisms underlying the disease process.

Studies using this approach initially focused on understanding the genetic mechanisms underlying disorders that are caused by defects in a single gene and for which the inheritance pattern could be clearly specified. These studies

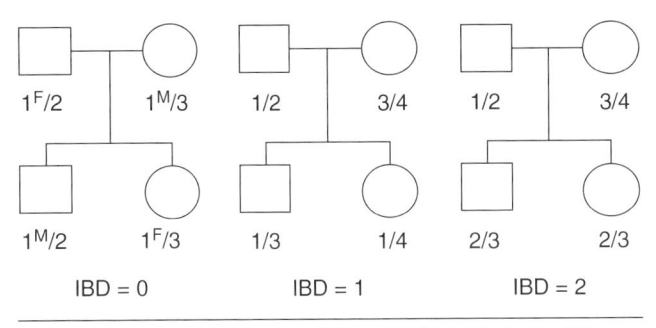

1^F/2 1^M/3	1/2 3/4	1/2 3/4
1^M/2 1^F/3	1/3 1/4	2/3 2/3
IBD = 0	IBD = 1	IBD = 2

Figure 2.4 Pedigrees illustrating siblings who have inherited a different number of alleles identical by descent (IBD).

involved statistical tests called parametric linkage analyses, which use DNA markers to locate, or map, a disease gene to a particular chromosomal region. Such analyses led to the identification of the genes causing Huntington's disease, cystic fibrosis, Duchenne muscular dystrophy and hundreds of other genetic disorders (Online Mendelian Inheritance in Man; http://www3.ncbi.nlm.nih.gov/Omim/).

However, psychopathology has a complex inheritance, with multiple genetic and environmental factors contributing to each disorder. As a result, it may be impossible to specify a particular inheritance pattern for any given complex disease. In this instance, researchers can use another type of statistical test called nonparametric linkage analysis as a powerful tool to identify genes involved in the disorder. This statistical approach does not require a specific model of how a disease is inherited. Such nonparametric linkage analyses typically involve identifying families with multiple affected family members who are thought to have inherited genes that increase the risk for disease susceptibility.

All nonparametric linkage analyses are based on a concept called identity by descent (IBD) marker allele sharing. If siblings inherit the same marker allele from the same parent, the allele is called IBD (Figure 2.4). In the figure, three nuclear families, each consisting of the parents and two offspring, are shown. In each nuclear family, the genotype for a marker with four alleles is listed. In the left panel, the two siblings have both inherited allele 1. However, the brother inherited this allele 1 from his mother whereas his sister inherited this allele 1 from her father. Therefore, they have no alleles IBD (IBD = 0). In the middle panel, both siblings inherited allele 1 from the father (IBD = 1). In the right panel, both siblings inherited allele 2 from their father and allele 3 from their mother (IBD = 2).

If the marker being tested is in close physical proximity to a gene influencing the disease or trait under study, then siblings who are similar for the trait would be expected to share more IBD marker alleles. Conversely, siblings who are dissimilar would be expected to exhibit fewer IBD marker alleles near the gene influencing the trait. More recently, nonparametric linkage methods allow the inclusion of more extended families beyond sibling pairs in the genetic analysis. Thus, more genetic information can be gained by studying additional affected family members. Nonparametric linkage analyses can be used to study both traits that exist in an either-or fashion (i.e., qualitative or categorical traits, such as having or not having a disorder) and traits that vary in severity along a continuum (i.e., quantitative traits, such as quantity or frequency of alcohol use).

Association Studies and Candidate Genes

Whereas linkage analyses can identify a broad chromosomal region that likely contains a gene contributing to a disorder or behavior, association analyses are able to more accurately pinpoint the gene or genes that influence the outcome. One of the most commonly employed experimental designs to identify genes contributing to a disease is that of candidate gene analysis, which seeks to test the association between a particular allele of the candidate gene and a specific outcome. A candidate gene typically is chosen because it is suspected to play a role in the disorder, either because researchers have some information about the gene's function that might be related to the disease or because the gene lies in a DNA region that has already been linked to the disorder through linkage methods (described previously). In the future, researchers hope to be able to conduct genome-wide association studies in which SNPs spaced across the entire genome are tested to identify potential associations with a disease, rather than having to focus on candidate regions or genes. Two primary methods are currently available to test for association with a particular gene.

Case-Control Association Studies. Many candidate gene studies use methods that compare the genes of groups of people that differ on the disorder or behavior of interest. For example, in alcoholism research such analyses would involve two samples: a group of alcoholic patients and a control group of nonalcoholic individuals. Ideally, the two groups would be matched with respect to numerous factors (e.g., age and ethnicity) so that they differ only in disease status. The investigators would then compare the frequencies of various alleles of a marker (e.g., a SNP) within or near the candidate gene. Evidence of differences in allele frequencies between the two groups is typically interpreted as evidence that the candidate gene contributes to the disease. For example, in Figure 2.5 illustrating the case-control design, 8/10 of the cases carry the "1" allele, whereas only 2/10 of the controls do. Because this allele is more prevalent among the cases

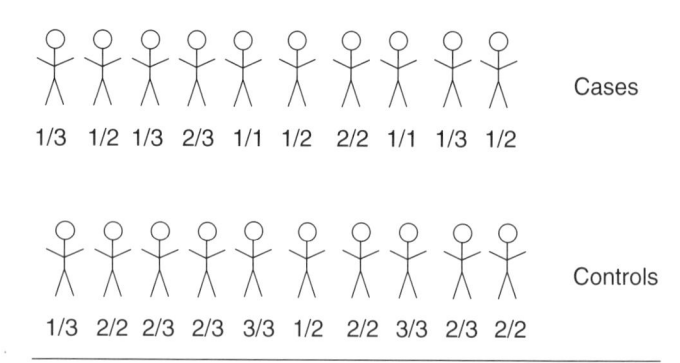

Figure 2.5 Example of a case-control association design showing genotypes for two groups of individuals. Allele 1 is found more often in the cases, suggesting that it may be involved in disease susceptibility.

than among the controls, it suggests that this genetic variant may be involved in the disorder on which the individuals were selected.

As discussed earlier, a gene can be a candidate gene based on the known biology of the disorder or its treatment or by the gene residing under a linkage peak. In the case of ADHD, a good rationale exists for the selection of candidate genes based on the known pathophysiology of dopamine in ADHD as well as the mechanism of action of stimulant medications. This has led to a number of candidate gene studies involving dopamine pathway genes such as the dopamine transporter (DAT) and the dopamine DRD4 and DRD5 receptor genes. One drawback of many candidate gene studies is the use of relatively small sample sizes for case-control or within-family comparison studies and difficulties with phenotype definition. In the case of combined subtype ADHD, however, meta-analyses have demonstrated the involvement across multiple studies of a coding region expansion repeat polymorphism in the DRD4 receptor gene (Faraone, Doyle, Mick, & Biederman, 2001) and a 3′ flanking repeat polymorphism near the DRD5 receptor gene (Lowe et al., 2004). In both these cases the effect size for each gene was relatively small (odds ratios approximately equal to 1.3) but established over multiple independent samples.

Because of their simplicity, case-control association studies of candidate genes have been widely used, and perhaps abused. Although this approach appears to have been successful in identifying genes involved in ADHD, there are several major problems with this approach in studying complex disorders (such as alcoholism). The first problem is the choice of candidate gene. Numerous biochemical pathways are likely involved in addictive behavior, including pathways related to alcohol metabolism. These pathways involve numerous enzymes and other molecules, and the genes encoding all of these molecules are therefore potential candidate genes. Thus, the number of candidate genes is large and increases daily with the application of new technologies to alcohol research. The second problem is that with a disorder that involves multiple genes, as in alcoholism, the effects of each gene are probably small. Therefore, large sample sizes in multiple populations are often required to detect such genes. Finally, spurious associations between certain alleles and the disorder are likely to show up if the two samples (i.e., alcoholics and nonalcoholics) are not well matched with respect to important characteristics, such as ethnicity.

Family-Based Association Studies. To avoid the pitfalls of population-based association studies, Spielman and Ewens (1996) developed a family-based association test—the transmission disequilibrium test (TDT). The primary advantage of the TDT is that it avoids the necessity of including a matched control sample. As originally proposed, the TDT analyzes a nuclear trio consisting of an affected individual and his or her parents, as shown in Figure 2.6.

For these three individuals, one determines the genotype of a marker in or near the candidate gene. If each parent carries two different alleles of the marker gene, then one allele from each parent will be transmitted to the affected offspring and one allele will not be transmitted. Those alleles that have been transmitted from the parents to the affected offspring are considered the case sample, and the remaining alleles are used as the control sample. The TDT tests the hypothesis that a particular marker allele is more frequently transmitted to affected offspring from heterozygous parents. In the example in Figure 2.6, the father is heterozygous at the marker and transmits allele 2 but not allele 1 to his affected son. The mother is homozygous and can transmit to her affected son only allele 1 and, therefore, does not provide information toward the TDT. Using the information on the transmission of various alleles from many families, one can conduct statistical analyses to determine if a particular allele of the marker being tested is associated with disease development. Through the use of such a within-family design, the control sample of alleles is perfectly matched to the case sample of alleles because both samples are transmitted from the same two parents. To expand the use of the TDT, researchers recently have begun to apply it to other designs, such as family-based association tests that include data from both affected and unaffected siblings or from even more extended pedigrees. In addition, the test has been extended to the analysis of quantitative traits in addition to qualitative traits.

Use of Twins to Identify Specific Genes

A relatively new use of twins has emerged that can lead directly to the demonstration of specific genes or specific bio-

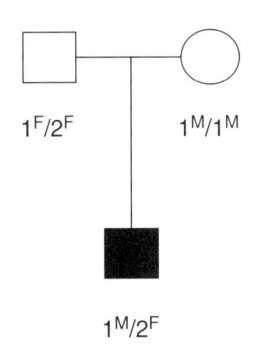

Figure 2.6 Example of the transmission disequilibrium test (TDT). In the pedigree shown, the child has inherited allele 1 from the mother and allele 2 from the heterozygous father.

logical pathways involved in the genesis of disorder. This approach takes advantage of the presence of discordant monozygotic twins. We will briefly describe two examples of this approach.

Recently, Kondo et al. (2002) identified two monozygotic twins who were discordant for Van der Woude syndrome, which is an autosomal dominant disorder that is the most common syndromic form of cleft lip or palate. Previous linkage studies identified a critical region for development of the syndrome located on chromosome 1q32–q41. Kondo et al. identified a nonsense mutation in the affected twin in the IRF6 gene in this region. They subsequently were able to demonstrate mutations in the same gene in a number of other Van der Woude syndrome pedigrees. In this case, a mutation in the IRF6 gene occurred following division of the fertilized ovum into two identical embryos, resulting in illness in one twin.

In an example from a more complex disorder, Kakiuchi et al. (2003) used DNA micro array analysis of messenger RNA from lymphoblastoid cells from two pairs of twins discordant for bipolar disorder. They found down-regulated expression of genes related to the endoplasmic reticulum (ER) stress response in both affected twins from the discordant pairs. They were then able to identify a polymorphism in the promoter region of the ER stress response gene XBP1, which was significantly more common in both Japanese and U.S. bipolar disorder patients. Further biological studies based on this observation suggest that this particular polymorphism in the XBP1 gene causes an impairment in a positive feedback system, increasing the risk for bipolar disorder.

CONCLUSIONS

In conclusion, psychiatry and psychology have undergone a revolution in the past century regarding how childhood disorders are viewed. It is now widely recognized that genetic influences play some role in most behaviors of interest, and that childhood behavior, both normal and abnormal, likely results from an interaction of both environmental and genetic factors. Family studies, adoption studies, and twin studies have been pivotal in demonstrating genetic influence on behavioral outcome. The methods and limitations of each of these designs have been discussed. A number of new extensions of the twin design are now allowing genetic researchers to address more complex questions regarding how genetic influences impact behavior. These include studying developmental trajectories of the importance of genetic and environmental risk factors across time, elucidating how genetic and environmental risk factors interact, and studying how genetic and environmental factors contribute to the comorbidity observed among many disorders. More recently, efforts have begun to identify specific genes involved in disorders. Linkage analyses, based on allele-sharing methods, have allowed researchers to identify chromosomal regions that are likely to contain genes predisposing to certain behaviors. Association analyses are then employed to test whether specific genetic variants are likely to be involved. Better characterization of specific genes and environmental influences, and how these risk and protective factors act and interact, promises to dramatically enhance our understanding of the etiology of childhood disorders.

REFERENCES

Arias, E., MacDorman, M. F., Strobino, D. M., & Guyer, B. (2003). Annual summary of vital statistics—2002. *Pediatrics, 112,* 1215–1230.

Biederman, J., Newcorn, J., & Sprich, S. (1991). Comorbidity of attention deficit hyperactivity disorder with conduct, depressive, anxiety, and other disorders. *American Journal of Psychiatry, 148,* 564–577.

Boomsma, D. I. (1998). Twin registers in Europe: An overview. *Twin Research, 1,* 34–51.

Cloninger, C. R. (1987). Neurogenetic adaptive mechanisms in alcoholism. *Science, 236,* 410–416.

Cloninger, C. R., Bohman, M., & Sigvardsson, S. (1981). Inheritance of alcohol abuse: Cross-fostering analysis of adopted men. *Archives of General Psychiatry, 38,* 861–868.

Constantino, J. N., Przybeck, T., Friesen, D., & Todd, R. D. (2000). Reciprocal social behavior in children with and without pervasive developmental disorders. *Journal of Developmental and Behavioral Pediatrics, 21,* 2–11.

Constantino, J. N., & Todd, R. D. (2003). Autistic traits in the general population: A twin study. *Archives of General Psychiatry, 60,* 524–530.

Cronk, N. J., Slutske, W. S., Madden, P. A., Bucholz, K. K., Reich, W., & Heath, A. C. (2002). Emotional and behavioral problems among female twins: An evaluation of the equal environments assumption. *Journal of the American Academy of Child and Adolescent Psychiatry, 41,* 829–837.

Crowley, T. J., Milkulich, S. K., MacDonald, M., Young, S. E., & Zerbe, G. O. (1998). Substance-dependent, conduct-disordered adolescent males: Severity of diagnosis predicts 2-year outcome. *Drug & Alcohol Dependence, 49,* 225–237.

Dick, D. M., Rose, R. J., Viken, R. J., Kaprio, J., & Koskenvuo, M. (2001). Exploring gene-environment interactions: Socioregional moderation of alcohol use. *Journal of Abnormal Psychology, 110,* 625–632.

Dick, D. M., Viken, R. J., Kaprio, J., Pulkkinen, L., & Rose, R. J. (2005). Understanding the covariation between childhood externalizing symptoms: Genetic and environmental influences on conduct disorder, attention deficit hyperactivity disorder, and oppositional defiant disorder symptoms. *Journal of Abnormal Child Psychology, 33,* 219–229.

Faraone, S. V., Doyle, A. E., Mick, E., & Biederman, J. (2001). Meta-analysis of the association between the 7-repeat allele of the dopamine D(4) receptor gene and attention deficit hyperactivity disorder. *American Journal of Psychiatry, 158,* 1052–1057.

Fuller, J. L., & Thompson, W. R. (1960). *Behavior genetics.* New York: Wiley.

Gottesman, I. I. (1991). *Schizophrenia genesis: The origins of madness.* New York: Freeman.

Hall, J. G. (2003). Twinning. *Lancet, 362,* 735–743.

Heath, A. C. (2003, June). *Annual Distinguished Researcher Award address.* Paper presented at the 26th Annual Meeting of the Research Society on Alcoholism, Miami, FL.

Heath, A. C., Eaves, L. J., & Martin, N. G. (1998). Interaction of marital status and genetic risk for symptoms of depression. *Twin Research, 1,* 119–122.

Heath, A. C., Jardine, R., & Martin, N. G. (1989). Interactive effects of genotype and social environment on alcohol consumption in female twins. *Journal of Studies on Alcohol, 50,* 38–48.

Heston, L. L., & Denney, D. (1967). Interactions between early life experience and biological factors in schizophrenia. In D. Rosenthal & S. S. Kety (Eds.), *The transmission of schizophrenia* (pp. 363–376). Oxford: Pergamon Press.

Jensen, P. S., Martin, D., & Cantwell, D. P. (1997). Comorbidity in ADHD: Implications for research, practice of *DSM-IV. Journal of the American Academy of Child and Adolescent Psychiatry, 36,* 1065–1079.

Kakiuchi, C., Iwamoto, K., Ishiwata, M., Bundo, M., Kasahara, T., Kusumi, I., et al. (2003). Impaired feedback regulation of XBP1 as a genetic risk factor for bipolar disorder. *Nature Genetics, 35,* 171–175.

Kaprio, J., Pulkkinen, L., & Rose, R. J. (2002). Genetic and environmental factors in health-related behaviors: Studies on Finnish twins and twin families. *Twin Research, 5,* 358–365.

Kendler, K. S. (1993). Twin studies of psychiatric illness: Current status and future directions. *Archives of General Psychiatry, 50,* 905–915.

Kendler, K. S., Neale, M. C., Kessler, R. C., Heath, A. C., & Eaves, L. J. (1992). A population-based twin study of major depression in women. *Archives of General Psychiatry, 49,* 257–266.

Kendler, K. S., Neale, M. C., Kessler, R. C., Heath, A. C., & Eaves, L. J. (1993). The lifetime history of major depression in women: Reliability of diagnosis and heritability. *Archives of General Psychiatry, 50,* 863–870.

Kondo, S., Schutte, B. C., Richardson, R. J., Bjork, B. C., Knight, A. S., Watanabe, Y., et al. (2002). Mutations in IRF6 cause Van der Woude and popliteal pterygium syndromes. *Nature Genetics, 32,* 285–289.

Legrand, L., McGue, M., & Iacono, W. G. (1999). Search for interactive effects in the etiology of early-onset substance use. *Behavior Genetics, 29,* 433–444.

Lowe, N., Kirley, A., Hawi, Z., Sham, P. C., Wickham, H., Kratochvil, C. J., et al. (2004). Joint analyses of the DRD5 marker concludes association with attention deficit/hyperactivity disorder confined to the predominantly inattentive and combined subtypes. *American Journal of Human Genetics, 74,* 348–356.

Lytton, H. (1977). Do parents create, or respond to, differences in twins? *Developmental Psychology, 13,* 456–459.

McClearn, G. E. (2004). Nature and nurture: Interaction and coaction. *American Journal of Medical Genetics (Neuropsychiatric Genetics), 124B,* 124–130.

McClearn, G. E., Johansson, B., Berg, S., Pedersen, N., Ahern, F., Petrill, S. A., et al. (1997). Substantial genetic influence on cognitive abilities in twins 80 or more years old. *Science, 276,* 1560–1563.

McGue, M., Bouchard, T. J. Jr., Iacono, W. G., & Lykken, D. T. (1993). Behavioral genetics of cognitive ability: A life-span perspective. In R. Plomin & G. E. McClearn (Eds.), *Nature, nurture, and psychology* (pp. 59–76). Washington, DC: American Psychological Association.

McGuffin, P., Riley, B., & Plomin, R. (2001). Toward behavioral genomics. *Science, 291,* 1232–1249.

Nadder, T. S., Rutter, M., Silberg, J. L., Maes, H. H., & Eaves, L. J. (2002). Genetic effects on the variation and covariation of attention deficit-hyperactivity disorder (ADHD) and oppositional-defiant disorder/conduct disorder (ODD/CD) symptomatologies across informant and occasion of measurement. *Psychological Medicine, 32,* 39–53.

Rasmussen, E. R., Neuman, R. J., Heath, A. C., Levy, F., Hay, D. A., & Todd, R. D. (2002). Replication of the latent class structure of attention-deficit/hyperactivity disorder (ADHD) subtypes in a sample of Australian twins. *Journal of Child Psychology and Psychiatry and Allied Disciplines, 43,* 1018–1028.

Rasmussen, E. R., Neuman, R. J., Heath, A. C., Levy, F., Hay, D. A., & Todd, R. D. (2004). Familial clustering of latent class and DSM-IV defined attention-deficit/hyperactivity disorder subtypes. *Journal of Child Psychology and Psychiatry and Allied Disciplines, 45,* 589–598.

Rose, R. J., Dick, D. M., Viken, R. J., & Kaprio, J. (2001). Gene-environment interaction in patterns of adolescent drinking: Regional residency moderates longitudinal influences on alcohol use. *Alcoholism: Clinical and Experimental Research, 25,* 637–643.

Rose, R. J., Dick, D. M., Viken, R. J., Pulkkinen, L., & Kaprio, J. (2001). Drinking or abstaining at age 14: A genetic epidemiological study. *Alcoholism: Clinical and Experimental Research, 25,* 1594–1604.

Rose, R. J., Dick, D. M., Viken, R. J., Pulkkinen, L., Nurnberger, J. I., Jr., & Kaprio, J. (2004). Genetic and environmental effects on conduct disorder, alcohol symptoms, and their covariation at age 14. *Alcoholism: Clinical and Experimental Research, 28,* 1541–1548.

Silberg, J. L., Rutter, M., Meyer, J. M., Maes, H. H., Hewitt, J. K., Simonoff, E., et al. (1996). Genetic and environmental influences on the covariation between hyperactivity and conduct disturbance in juvenile twins. *Journal of Child Psychology and Psychiatry, 37,* 803–816.

Simonoff, E., Pickles, A., Meyer, J. M., Silberg, J. L., Maes, H. H., Loeber, R., et al. (1997). The Virginia Twin Study of Adolescent Behavioral Development. *Archives of General Psychiatry, 54,* 800–808.

Slutske, W. S., Heath, A. C., Dinwiddie, S. H., Madden, P. A. F., Bucholz, K. K., Dunne, M. P., et al. (1997). Modeling genetic and environmental influences in the etiology of conduct disorder: A study of 2,682 adult twin pairs. *Journal of Abnormal Psychology, 106,* 266–279.

Spielman, R. S., & Ewens, W. J. (1996). the TDT and other family-based tests for linkage disequilibrium and association. *American Journal of Human Genetics, 59,* 983–989.

Stoolmiller, M. (1998). Correcting estimates of shared environmental variance for range restriction in adoption studies using a truncated multivariate normal model. *Behavior Genetics, 28,* 429–441.

Stoolmiller, M. (1999). Implications of the restricted range of family environments for estimates of heritability and nonshared environment in behavior-genetic adoption studies. *Psychological Bulletin, 125,* 392–409.

Thapar, A., Harrington, R., & McGuffin, P. (2001). Examining the comorbidity of ADHD-related behaviours and conduct problems using a twin study design. *British Journal of Psychiatry, 179,* 224–229.

Thapar, A., Hervas, A., & McGuffin, P. (1995). Childhood hyperactivity scores are highly heritable and show sibling competition effects: Twin study evidence. *Behavior Genetics, 25,* 537–544.

Todd, R. D., Rasmussen, E. R., Neuman, R. J., Reich, W., Hudziak, J. J., Bucholz, K. K., et al. (2001). Familiality and heritability of subtypes of attention deficit hyperactivity disorder in a population sample of adolescent female twins. *American Journal of Psychiatry, 158,* 1891–1898.

Waldman, I., Rhee, S. H., Levy, F., & Hay, D. A. (2001). Causes of the overlap among symptoms of ADHD, oppositional defiant disorder, and conduct disorder. In F. Levy & D. A. Hay (Eds.), *Attention, genes, and ADHD* (pp. 115–138). New York: Brunner-Routledge.

White, H. R., Zie, M., Thompson, W., Loeber, R., & Stouthamer-Loeber, M. (2001). Psychopathology as a predictor of adolescent drug use trajectories. *Psychology of Addictive Behaviors, 15,* 210–218.

Young, S. E., Stallings, M. C., Corley, R. P., Krauter, K. S., & Hewitt, J. K. (2000). Genetic and environmental influences on behavioral disinhibition. *American Journal of Medical Genetics, 96,* 684–695.

CHAPTER 3

Neuropsychiatric Contributions

ROGER A. BRUMBACK AND C. EDWARD COFFEY

HISTORICAL PERSPECTIVE

For centuries, the problem of behavioral abnormalities in the young was clouded in mysticism, religion, and philosophical discussions about the nature of humankind. Infanticide was one solution for any child considered defective. Because normal speech was a prerequisite for Roman citizenship, the Latin term *infans* (meaning unable to speak) was applied to children as well as to individuals with deafness, mutism, insanity, or mental retardation (Accardo, 1996; Gilson, 1955; Gordon, 1959). From biblical times, individuals with epilepsy were regarded as possessed by demons:

> A man in the crowd answered, "Teacher, I brought you my son, who is possessed by a sprit that has robbed him of speech. Whenever it seizes him, it throws him to the ground. He foams at the mouth, gnashes his teeth and becomes rigid." "Bring the boy to me." So they brought him. When the spirit saw Jesus, it immediately threw the boy into a convulsion. He fell to the ground and rolled around, foaming at the mouth. Jesus asked the boy's father, "How long has he been like this?" "From childhood," he answered. "It has often thrown him into fire or water to kill him. But if you can do anything, take pity on us and help us." When Jesus saw that a crowd was running to the scene, he rebuked the evil spirit. "You deaf and mute spirit," he said, "I command you, come out of him and never enter him again." The spirit shrieked, convulsed him violently and came out. The boy looked so much like a corpse that many said, "He's dead." But Jesus took him by the hand and lifted him to his feet, and he stood up. (Mark 9:17–27, *New International Version*)

During the Middle Ages, an abnormal child was often considered to be a "changeling" substituted at birth for a normal child by fairies. By the late thirteenth century, the preferred method of dealing with those who were disabled, epileptic, mentally retarded, or mentally ill was confinement in *lazars,* which had originally been built to house individuals afflicted with leprosy but became relatively empty as the leprosy population declined. These institutions became known as asylums for individuals considered defective or unable to fit into so-called normal society. By the seventeenth century, it was estimated that 1 percent of the Paris population was housed in asylums, which were little better than prisons and kept these individuals off the streets by providing meager food and shelter (Benson, 1996; Foucault, 1965). In the early seventeenth century, Burton (1621/1924) suggested that melancholy in children was transmitted to them either in utero by pregnant mothers or in infancy by wet nurses. The term cripple was used to describe anyone with physical deformities, whether congenital, acquired, or secondary to central or peripheral abnormalities.

The scientific investigation of nervous system abnormalities had its advent in the nineteenth century, and the beginning of neuropsychiatry can probably be dated to the meticulous anatomical observations of Franz-Josef Gall (1809), who (with his pupil Johann Christoph Spurzheim) showed that the brain was the organ of the mind and had localizable functions. Although Gall's reputation is clouded by his advocacy of the discredited theories of phrenology, Pierre Paul Broca (1888) acknowledged Gall as the inspiration for subsequent studies defining cerebral localization (including his own 1861 description of a patient with aphasia as a result of a lesion of the inferior frontal gyrus of the left cerebral hemisphere).

The second half of the nineteenth century was an era of increasing interest in the study of the nervous system and its relationship not only to obvious neurological diseases but also to behavior. Despite priority battles fought between individual scientists and laboratories or hospitals, significant advances were made by a variety of specialists, including internists and orthopedists as well as neuropsychiatrists. In England, the orthopedic surgeon William John Little (Little, 1853) delineated a disorder with motor, behavioral, and cognitive abnormalities and hypothesized that it was a "third outcome" for neonatal asphyxia, which contradicted the accepted dogma that children with asphyxia neonatorum either died or developed normally (Accardo, 1989). Childhood spastic diplegia was then known as Little's disease, until Sir William Osler used the term cerebral palsy for this condition in his neurological monograph documenting the clinical features of 151 patients from the Infirmary for Nervous Diseases in Philadelphia (McHenry, 1993; Osler, 1889). In Austria, the young neurologist Sigmund Freud published a monograph in which he devised a classification system for subtypes of cerebral palsy (which is still the basis for modern classification schemes) and documented a relationship among epilepsy, mental retardation, and cerebral palsy (Accardo, 1982; Freud, 1897/1968). Two English physicians, John Langdon Haydon Down and William Witherspoon Ireland, tried to characterize "idiocy" or "imbecility" (mental retardation). Down defined subtypes of mental retardation on the basis of associated physical abnormalities (Down, 1866, 1887) using the concept of recapitulation (ontogeny recapitulates phylogeny) and theorizing that abnormalities in children and adults were the result of arrested development at stages of lower animals or lower human races (he considered Malay, Aztec, and Mongolian as lower races, and thus he used the term "Mongolian idiot" for the mental retardation disorder now know as Down syndrome). Ireland (1877) classified mental retardation based on etiology and provided specific definitions (for example, microcephaly was defined as a head circumference of less than 17 inches). Meanwhile, controversy raged about whether children could show evidence of insanity. Sir James Crichton-Browne (1860) argued that melancholia was "incompatible with early life," while Henry Maudsley (1867) included melancholia among his seven subtypes of childhood insanity. Previously, in Germany, one of the most popular children's books was produced by the physician Heinrich Hoffmann (1845), who had been both a general practitioner and the director of the state mental hospital in Frankfurt am Main. The book *Der Struwwelpeter* (which Hoffmann published and illustrated himself) described a variety of children with behavioral problems (Zipes, 2000), including "Fidget Philipp," who was a hyperactive boy modeled after Hoffmann's own son. Also in Germany, the ophthalmologist R. Berlin (1884, 1887) coined the term dyslexia to describe the condition of disturbed reading in adults with normal visual function and postulated an abnormality in the left cerebral hemisphere in right-handed individuals. Inspired by the ophthalmologist James Hinshelwood (1900, 1907), the English general practitioner W. Pringle Morgan (1896) published the first description of congenital word blindness in a normally intelligent 14-year-old boy who could not learn to read.

With the dawn of the twentieth century, clear territorial distinctions in medicine and psychology appeared. Freud fueled a movement that changed thoughts about behavior from categorical (medical model) to dimensional. Instead of the categorical approach of defining clear distinctions between abnormal behaviors (indicating disease) and normal functioning, Freud advanced a dimensional approach in which abnormal behavior was viewed as a deviation along a continuum from the normal behaviors that was experienced by everyone at different stages of development. The ultimate result was a splintering of the medical field of neuropsychiatry into neurology (for those clinicians interested in the signs and symptoms of clearly defined nervous system lesions [the categorical or medical model approach of delineating specific disease processes]) and psychiatry (for those interested in behavior and cognitive processes [the dimensional approach of describing variations related to development]). As the professional gulf between the medical disciplines of neurology and psychiatry grew, interest in the child's nervous system related only to how it was molded to produce the adult brain. Thus, the study of brain-behavior relations in children was virtually abandoned to the ever-enlarging medical specialty of pediatrics, which rapidly grew (along with the proliferation of specialty pediatric hospitals) to subsume all care of children and adolescents. The dogma instilled into pediatric trainees was that only a pediatrician could provide the comprehensive care necessary to treat all medical problems in children—not only disorders with definite nervous system lesions but also those manifesting as behavioral or cognitive difficulties. For example, pediatricians such as George Frederick Still (1902) described the syndrome of childhood hyperactivity, Charles Bradley (1937) identified the benefits of amphetamine treatment for hyperactive children, and Samuel Livingston (1954) produced early protocols for the treatment of childhood epilepsy. Pediatric dysmorphologists began to define developmental brain malformations, and pediatric geneticists identified the chromosomal, biochemical, and molecular biological bases of many nervous system disorders (Jones, 1997; Warkany, 1971).

It was rare for neuroscience to impinge on developmental psychiatry, in that nearly all pediatric patients with behavioral disorders were cared for in community child guidance clinics, which embraced the psychoanalytic model of psychopathology, looking for the ways in which behavior deviated from normal development. Treatment for the large number of patients with severe cognitive or communication deficits was provided mostly by behavioral psychologists with variable knowledge of developmental neuroscience. This demedicalization of care for the developmentally disabled was furthered by the insistence of advocates (parents and government) that the care of such youth not be mixed in with that of the severely and persistently mentally ill individuals (adults) who occupied state mental institutions.

By the 1960s, it became apparent that brain and behavior were inextricably linked, as medical scientists began to identify the neurochemical, neurophysiological, and neuropathological etiologies underlying many neurological and psychiatric syndromes, and as they began to develop specific neuropsychopharmacological treatments (Cummings, 1985). Thus, the field of neuropsychiatry was reborn, but at first only in the areas of adult disorders. Following the advances in basic neurobiology, it became imperative that clinicians adopt a scientific approach. Propelled by the intellectual ferment stimulated by Eli Robins and Samuel B. Guze in the Department of Psychiatry at the Washington University (St. Louis) School of Medicine, a categorical approach to behavioral illnesses in adults was developed (Feighner et al., 1972; Spitzer, Endicott, & Robins, 1975), returning clinical psychiatry to a neurobiologic medical model and to a closer association with clinical neurology. In that same feverish academic environment, Warren A. Weinberg (a pediatrician with training in both child neurology and psychiatry) examined behavior problems in children from a similar neurobiologic viewpoint. Weinberg defined affective illness (both depression and mania) as disorders afflicting children that could be treated with the newer neuropsychopharmacological agents (Brumback, Dietz-Schmidt & Weinberg, 1977; Brumback & Weinberg, 1977; Weinberg & Brumback, 1976; Weinberg, Rutman, Sullivan, Penick, & Dietz, 1973). Thus came the rebirth of pediatric neuropsychiatry, and over the past 30 years there has been an explosion of information concerning the developing nervous system and the consequences of perturbation of that development (Coffey & Brumback, 1998; Fletcher & Butler, 1992; Gualtieri, 1991).

ADVANCES OF MODERN PEDIATRIC NEUROPSYCHIATRY

The modern field of pediatric neuropsychiatry brings together specialists with different viewpoints, encompassing a broad range of disciplines including child neurology, child psychiatry, pediatric psychology, pediatric neuropsychology, behavioral pediatrics, developmental pediatrics, pediatric neurosurgery, pediatric orthopedics, pediatric genetics, dysmorphology, neuroembryology, pediatric neuroradiology, and adolescent medicine (Brumback & Coffey, 1998). The relative absence of territorial divisions among clinical disciplines studying disorders such as those discussed previously has fostered many different outlooks, leading to the rush of new understanding about pediatric nervous system disorders. Clinicians and researchers in the field of pediatric neuropsychiatry employ a broad range of tools including molecular biology; neurophysiology; and a variety of imaging techniques such as computerized electroencephalography (EEG), magnetic resonance imaging (MRI) and spectroscopy (MRS), positron emission tomography (PET), and single-photon emission computed tomography (SPECT), which together have begun to unravel the brain mechanisms underlying normal and abnormal development of behavioral and cognitive skills in infants, children, and adolescents. In addition, investigators are increasingly able to elucidate the effects of a wide variety of insults on the dynamic processes of brain growth and development, and the most exciting part is that it may soon be possible to understand not only anatomic and physiological bases of normal cognitive development but also the ways in which these normal maturational processes can be altered by nervous system disease. The advances in pediatric neuropsychiatry have also provided an unprecedented increase in the availability of behavioral and pharmacological treatments that provide practitioners with a varied and powerful armamentarium with which to combat neuropsychiatric illness in the infant, child, or adolescent. This improved understanding of the interrelationships of brain and behavior is leading to enhanced care for large numbers of infants, children, and adolescents—an important investment in the future of our society. In the following sections we describe a sampling of some of these advances.

Autism

Autism was first defined by Leo Kanner (1943), a psychiatrist working with children in the Harriet Lane Home of the Johns Hopkins Hospital, as a disorder in which the children had an "inability to form the usual, biologically provided affective contact with people." Autism was at first thought to be a disorder resulting from poor parenting or parental psychopathology. Initially considered a rare disorder, subsequent epidemiologic studies showed prevalence rates of greater than 2 per 1,000 live births (Lingham et al., 2003). Further investigations revealed frequent mental retardation, dysmorphic features, and neurologic signs in autistic individuals, and family studies suggested increased incidence among siblings and high concordance among monozygotic twins (Ritvo et al., 1985). Further investigations involving the use of diagnostic criteria developed in the various versions of the American Psychiatric Association's *Diagnostic and Statistical Manual of Mental Disorders* have demonstrated that autism is a heterogeneous symptom complex found associated with many genetic and nongenetic disorders. Careful neuropsychiatric studies of patients with some of these disorders has produced significant contributions to the understanding of genetic factors underlying brain development. For example, studies of the fragile X syndrome have permitted a greater understanding of the role of early synaptic activity (in part from environmental stimulation) in shaping neuronal structure (Greenough et al., 2001). Similarly, neuropsychiatric investigations of another autistic disorder, Rett syndrome, has led to additional insights into neuronal plasticity in the developing nervous system as well as the potential for environmental modification to affect this plasticity (Johnston, 2004). Investigations of autism have also led to new understanding of the role of the cerebellum in behavior (a function previously considered to be reserved for the cerebrum alone; Allen, Müller, & Courchesne, 2004). Additionally, a number of individuals demonstrating abnormal interpersonal interactions suggestive of autism but with normal or superior intelligence have been identified as having Asperger's syndrome (Frith, 1991; Wing, 1981). Collaborative imaging investigations by neuropsychiatrists and neuroradiologists have provided insights into the functions of the frontal lobes and right cerebral hemisphere in mediating social and emotional behavior (Brumback, Harper, & Weinberg, 1996; Herbert, 2004; McKelvey, Lambert, Mottron, & Shevell, 1995; Volkmar et al., 1996).

Hyperactivity, Attention, and Attention-Deficit/Hyperactivity Disorder

Despite the popularity of the descriptions by Heinrich Hoffmann of the hyperactive "Fidget Philipp" and the inattentive "Johnny Look-in-the-Air" (Hoffmann, 1845), not until Bradley (1937) identified the benefit of amphetamines in the behavior of hyperactive children did this problem evoke the interest of neuropsychiatrists. Still, it took many decades before an understanding developed of the relationship between motor restlessness and attentional functions of the brain (Voeller & Heilman, 1988). Research has focused on defining associations with attention-deficit/hyperactivity disorder (ADHD), clearly indicating that it is a symptom complex found in a wide variety of conditions with a prevalence in the school-age population possibly as high as 10 percent, with nearly two thirds of these being boys (McCracken, 1998; Voeller, 2004; Weinberg & Brumback, 1992) and with persistence of the symptoms into adulthood in about 70 percent of cases (Kaplan & Stevens, 2002). A large number of clinical, electrophysiologic, and imaging studies have identified a variety of abnormalities that could potentially underlie ADHD symptoms. Some of these findings have included smaller total cerebral volume, reduced frontal lobe volume, smaller basal ganglia, and reduced thickness of the right prefrontal and left occipital cerebral gray matter. Functional imaging studies have also suggested lower activity in the right frontal premotor cortex, right temporal cortex, and bilaterally in the posterior putamen and middle cingulate cortex (Voeller, 2004). Nonetheless, no consistent hypothesis to explain the sometimes contradictory findings has so far been forthcoming. The pharmacotherapeutic effects of a variety of agents that alter amine neurotransmission have led to hypotheses implicating dopaminergic and noradrenergic systems involving the brainstem, striatum, and cerebral cortex, while neuropsychological testing has suggested disturbances in frontal lobe or other cerebral cortical circuits (Braun, Archambault, Daigneault, & Larocque, 2000; Voeller, 1999). Prefrontal executive dysfunction has also been hypothesized as an explanation for some aspects of ADHD (Powell & Voeller, 2004). The Weinberg syndrome is a novel explanation for some families with multiple generations affected by mixed patterns of inattentive and hyperactive forms of ADHD, in which the underlying problem appears to be a disturbance of systems mediating vigilance (wakefulness or arousal; Brumback, 2000; Clarke, Barry, McCarthy, & Selikowitz, 2001; Clarke, Barry, McCarthy, Selikowitz, & Brown, 2002; Weinberg & Brumback, 1990; Weinberg, Harper, & Brumback, 1999a, 1999b). Genetic and molecular studies have suggested that polymorphisms in the dopamine D_4 receptor (DRD4) and the dopamine transporter (DAT1) genes could predispose to the symptoms of ADHD and affect the response to pharmacologic treatment (Qian, Wang, Zhou, Yang, & Faraone, 2004; Rohde et al., 2003; Roman, Rohde, & Hutz, 2004).

Obsessive-Compulsive Disorder, Tics and Tourette's Syndrome, and Sydenham Chorea and PANDAS

Tourette's syndrome has been known since the description by George Gilles de la Tourette in 1885 of patients with motor and phonic tics. There was relatively little interest in the problem of tics and Tourette's syndrome until the finding that antipsychotic medications (particularly haloperidol) could control the symptoms (Shapiro, Shapiro, & Wayne, 1973) that include simple and complex motor tics and vocal tics involving palilalia (repetition of one's own words), echolalia (repetition of the words of others), and copralalia (compulsive use of obscene language). The discovery of therapeutic options led to more investigative interest. Studies that identified overlap of clinical symptoms between Tourette's syndrome and obsessive-compulsive disorder were followed by functional imaging studies that showed involvement of the striatum in both conditions (Lucey et al., 1997; Singer & Minzer, 2003). Other investigators identified children who developed obsessive-compulsive symptoms (and occasionally tics) after a streptococcal infection, designating this condition *pediatric autoimmune neuropsychiatric disorder associated with streptococcus* (PANDAS; Garvey, Giedd, & Swedo, 1998). Patients with PANDAS have a clinical course similar to that of Sydenham chorea (in which children develop choreiform movements and behavioral symptoms several weeks to months after a group A beta-hemolytic streptococcal infection;

Snider & Swedo, 2003). In both PANDAS and Sydenham chorea, imaging studies have shown abnormalities in the basal ganglia (Citak et al., 2004). Tic symptoms have also been reported in relation to the mood disturbances associated with affective disorder (Brumback & Staton, 1981). The familial clustering of obsessive-compulsive disorder and of Tourette's syndrome has also led investigators to a variety of potential gene loci, but no definite responsible gene has been identified (Tourette Syndrome Association International Consortium for Genetics, 1999).

Affective Illness

Depression and mania (grouped under the category of affective illness) have been recognized in adults, but not until the 1970s was there acceptance that affective illness could afflict children (Emslie, Weinberg, & Kowatch, 1999; Weinberg et al., 1973). Subsequently, the emphasis in most investigations was developing criteria for the psychological characteristics that could be used to define this mood disturbance in children (Kashani et al., 1983; Kashani & Simonds, 1979; Poznanski, Mokros, Grossman, & Freeman, 1985). Taking a cue from the research in adults with affective illness, investigators began to identify similar endocrine problems (dysfunction in the hypothalamic-pituitary-adrenal, hypothalamic-pituitary-thyroid, and hypothalamic-pituitary-growth hormone regulatory systems) in children with affective illness (Emslie et al., 1999). Although the possibility that neurological signs of cerebral dysfunction could be associated with affective illness was first described in 1895 in a case report of a 47-year-old Welsh sailor with recurrent manic-depressive illness, not until the 1980s did studies describe the common occurrence of such signs in children with affective illness (Brumback, 1985a, 1985b, 1988; Emslie et al., 1999; Staton, Wilson, & Brumback, 1981). It was also apparent that the first symptoms of an affective illness could be neurological problems (mimicking cerebral palsy; Brumback & Staton, 1983; Brumback, Staton, & Wilson, 1984) or learning disability (Weintraub & Mesulam, 1983). The presence of these signs also seemed to be useful in predicting the response to pharmacologic treatment of the affective illness (Brumback, 1988). Brain imaging studies are just now being performed in children with affective illness, but few consistent results have been found (Emslie et al., 1999; Farchione, Moore, & Rosenberg, 2002; MacMillan et al., 2003; Smith et al., 2003).

Verbal and Nonverbal Learning Disabilities

Estimates suggest that specific developmental learning disabilities are evident in as many as 30 percent of school-age children (according to the 2000 U.S. Census, there are approximately 60 million children between the ages of 5 and 18 years), for a total of about 18 million affected children and adolescents (Brumback & Weinberg, 1990; Cantwell & Forness, 1982; Dworkin, 1985; Feagans, 1983). It has also been estimated that up to 2 percent of the same age group shows evidence of school failure secondary to depression (Brumback, 1988; Kashani & Simonds, 1979; Kashani et al., 1983; Staton & Brumback, 1981), which adds another 1 million individuals to the population of youth with school problems. These estimates explain the reports from epidemiologic studies that 5 percent of all office visits to pediatricians are for behavior or learning problems at home or at school (Anders, 1977). The problems of educating children have been at the forefront of national political concerns for the past several decades, and verbal learning disabilities (particularly reading disability or dyslexia) have been blamed on both poor parental attitudes toward education and teacher incompetence. Considerable efforts have been made to develop curricula that will assist children in their attempts to read. At the same time investigators have been attempting to develop a medical-scientific explanation for reading disability (Lyon, Gray, Kavanaugh, & Krasnegor, 1993). A wide variety of neuropathological and neuroimaging changes have been identified in the brains of children with dyslexia (Backes et al., 2002; Galaburda, 1988, 1993; Galaburda, Sherman, Rosen, Aboitiz, & Geschwind, 1985; Lyon & Rumsey, 1996; Papanicolaou et al., 2003), probably reflecting the diverse underlying conditions that can all materialize as reading problems. Some of the imaging findings could prove useful in prognosis and in delineating the appropriate curricular approach for a given individual (Shaywitz et al., 2003, 2004).

A wide variety of forms of learning disability in which reading is relatively normal also exist (Weinberg, Harper, & Brumback, 1999a). Recently, a great deal of attention has been paid to a group of conditions that have been variously termed clumsy child syndrome, visual-motor disability, developmental dyspraxia, developmental dysgraphia, developmental Gerstmann syndrome, developmental dyscalculia, right hemisphere learning disabilities, or nonverbal learning disabilities (Brumback, 1988; Brumback, Harper, & Weinberg, 1996; Brumback & Staton, 1982; Brumback & Weinberg, 1990; Geschwind, 1984; Rourke, 1989, 1995; Shalev, 2004; Voeller, 1986, 1995). These children have a variety of clinical signs and symptoms, including impaired coordination, clumsy and messy pencil-and-paper tasks and eye-hand activities (such as difficulties catching and hitting a ball or improperly gripping and using a knife and fork or a pen), impaired recognition of visual images (such as faces, leading to improper matching of names and faces), difficulties with directions (getting lost), problems with body orientation (leading to dressing difficulties), problems conceptualizing the whole as a series of interconnected parts (leading to difficulty performing multistep tasks), and impaired humor. Many of these children are socially incapacitated due to their difficulties understanding the social cues in speech (prosody or melody of speech) and in body language (particularly facial expression). As more investigators have studied these children, it has become apparent that there is considerable overlap with autism and Asperger's syndrome (Fast, 2004; Klin, Volkmar, & Sparrow, 2000).

THE FUTURE

The emerging field of pediatric neuropsychiatry seeks to establish a link between the neurobiology of major psychiatric illness and the neurobiology of brain disorders that cause behavioral disturbances in youth, and in so doing to stimulate consideration of fundamental brain-behavior relationships as they evolve against the backdrop of the developing nervous system. The neurobiology of brain development is at the frontier of scientific discovery, and we now have extremely powerful tools to elucidate the impact of development (both normal and abnormal) upon behavior. Pediatric neuropsychiatrists are developing an array of safe and effective treatments for pediatric neuropsychiatric disorders, giving new hope to and improving the lives of children with many of the most challenging disorders in all of medicine.

REFERENCES

Accardo, P. J. (1982). Freud on diplegia: Commentary and translation. *American Journal of Diseases of Children, 136,* 452–456.

Accardo, P. J. (1989). William John Little (1810–1894) and cerebral palsy in the nineteenth century. *Journal of the History of Medicine and Allied Sciences, 44,* 56–71.

Accardo, P. J. (1996). A medical history of developmental disabilities. In A. J. Capute & P. J. Accardo, (Eds.), *The spectrum of developmental disabilities* (Vol. 2, 2nd ed., pp. 1–13). Baltimore: Paul H. Brookes.

Allen, G., Müller, R. A, & Courchesne, E. (2004). Cerebellar function in autism: Functional magnetic resonance image activation during a simple motor task. *Biological Psychiatry 56,* 269–278.

Anders, T. F. (1977). Child psychiatry and pediatrics: The state of the relationship. *Pediatrics, 60,* 616–620.

Backes, W., Vuurman, E., Wennekes, R., Spronk, P., Wuisman, M., van Engelshoven, J., et al. (2002). Atypical brain activation of reading processes in children with developmental dyslexia. *Journal of Child Neurology, 17,* 867–871.

Benson, D. F. (1996). Neuropsychiatry and behavioral neurology: Past, present, and future. *Journal of Neuropsychiatry and Clinical Neuroscience, 8,* 351–357.

Berlin, R. (1884). Uber dyslexie. *Archiv fur Psychiatrie, 15,* 276–278.

Berlin, R. (1887). *Eine besondere art der wortblindheit (dyslexie).* Wiesbaden, Germany: Bergmann.

Bradley, C. (1937). The behavior of children receiving Benzedrine. *American Journal of Psychiatry, 94,* 577–585.

Braun, C. M., Archambault, M. A., Daigneault, S., & Larocque, C. (2000). Right body side performance decrement in congenitally dyslexic children and left body side performance decrement in congenitally hyperactive children. *Neuropsychiatry, Neuropsychology, and Behavioral Neurology, 13,* 89–100.

Broca, P. (1888). *Memoires d'anthropologie.* Paris: Reinwald.

Brumback, R. A. (1985a). Wechsler performance IQ deficit in depression in children. *Perceptual and Motor Skills, 61,* 331–335.

Brumback, R. A. (1985b). Neurology of depression. *Neurology and Neurosurgery Update Series, 7,* 1–8.

Brumback, R. A. (1988). Childhood depression and medically treatable learning disability. In D. L. Molfese & S. J. Segalowitz (Eds.), *Developmental implications of brain lateralization* (pp. 463–505). New York: Guilford Press.

Brumback, R. A. (2000). Weinberg's syndrome: A disorder of attention and behavior problems needing further research. *Journal of Child Neurology, 15,* 478–480.

Brumback, R. A., & Coffey, C. E. (1998). Pediatric neuropsychiatry. In C. E. Coffey & R. A. Brumback (Eds.), *Textbook of pediatric neuropsychiatry* (pp. 3–8). Washington, DC: American Psychiatric Press.

Brumback, R. A., Dietz-Schmidt, S. G., & Weinberg, W. A. (1977). Depression in children referred to an educational diagnostic center: Diagnosis and treatment. II. Analysis of criteria and literature review. *Diseases of the Nervous System, 38,* 529–535.

Brumback, R. A., Harper, C. R., & Weinberg, W. A. (1996). Nonverbal learning disabilities, Asperger's syndrome, pervasive developmental disorder—should we care? *Journal of Child Neurology, 11,* 427–429.

Brumback, R. A., & Staton, R. D. (1981). Depression-induced neurologic dysfunction. *New England Journal of Medicine, 305,* 642.

Brumback, R. A., & Staton, R. D. (1982). An hypothesis regarding the commonality of right hemisphere involvement in learning disability, attentional disorder, and childhood major depressive disorder. *Perceptual and Motor Skills, 55,* 1091–1097.

Brumback, R. A., & Staton, R. D. (1983). Learning disability and childhood depression. *American Journal of Orthopsychiatry, 53,* 269–281.

Brumback, R. A., Staton, R. D., & Wilson, H. (1984). Right cerebral hemisphere dysfunction. *Archives of Neurology, 41,* 248–250.

Brumback, R. A., & Weinberg, W. A. (1977). Mania in childhood. II. Therapeutic trial of lithium carbonate and further description of manic-depressive illness in children. *American Journal of Diseases of Children, 131,* 1122–1126.

Brumback, R. A., & Weinberg, W. A. (1990). Pediatric behavioral neurology: An update on the neurologic aspects of depression, hyperactivity, and learning disabilities. *Neurologic Clinics, 8,* 677–703.

Burton, R. (1924/1621). *The anatomy of melancholy.* New York: Empire State.

Cantwell, D., & Forness, S. R. (1982). Learning disorders. *Journal of the American Academy of Child Psychiatry, 21,* 417–419.

Citak, E. C., Gucuyener, K., Karabacak, N. I., Serdaroglu, A., Okuyaz, C., & Aydin, K. (2004). Functional brain imaging in Sydenham's chorea and streptococcal tic disorders. *Journal of Child Neurology, 19,* 387–390.

Clarke, A. R., Barry, R. J., McCarthy, R., & Selikowitz, M. (2001). EEG-defined subtypes of children with attention-deficit/hyperactivity disorder. *Clinical Neurophysiology, 112,* 2098–2105.

Clarke, A. R., Barry, R. J., McCarthy, R., Selikowitz, M., & Brown, C. R. (2002). EEG evidence for a new conceptualisation of attention deficit hyperactivity disorder. *Clinical Neurophysiology, 113,* 1036–1044.

Coffey, C. E., & Brumback, R. A. (Eds.). (1998). *Textbook of pediatric neuropsychiatry.* Washington, DC: American Psychiatric Press.

Crichton-Browne, J. (1860). Psychical diseases of early life. *Journal of Mental Science, 6,* 284–320.

Cummings, J. L. (1985). *Clinical neuropsychiatry.* Orlando, FL: Grune & Stratton.

Down, J. L. H. (1866). Observations on an ethnic classification of idiots. *London Hospital Reports, 3,* 259–262.

Down, J. L. H. (1887). *Mental affections of children and youth.* London: Churchill.

Dworkin, P. H. (1985). *Learning and behavior problems of school children.* Philadelphia: Saunders.

Emslie, G. J., Weinberg, W. A., & Kowatch, R. A. (1999). Mood disorders. In C. E. Coffey & R. A. Brumback (Eds.), *Textbook of pediatric neuropsychiatry* (pp. 359–392). Washington, DC: American Psychiatric Press.

Farchione, T. R., Moore, G. J., & Rosenberg, D. R. (2002). Proton magnetic resonance spectroscopic imaging in pediatric major depression. *Biological Psychiatry, 52,* 86–92.

Fast, Y. (2004). *Employment for individuals with Asperger syndrome or non-verbal learning disability.* London: Jessica Kingsley.

Feagans, L. (1983). A current view of learning disabilities. *Journal of Pediatrics, 102,* 487–493.

Feighner, J. P., Robins, E., Guze, S. B., Woodruff, R. A., Winokur, G., & Munoz, R. (1972). Diagnostic criteria for use in psychiatric research. *Archives of General Psychiatry, 26,* 57–63.

Fletcher, J. M., & Butler, I. J. (1992). The behavioral sciences and issues in child neurology and developmental pediatrics. *Journal of Child Neurology, 7,* 131–134.

Foucault, M. (1965). *Madness and civilization: A history of insanity in the age of reason* (R. Howard, Trans.). New York: Pantheon.

Freud, S. (1968). *Infantile cerebral paralysis* (L. A. Russin, Trans.). Coral Gables, FL: University of Miami Press. (Original work published 1897)

Frith, U. (Ed.). (1991). *Autism and Asperger syndrome.* Cambridge: Cambridge University Press.

Galaburda, A. M. (1988). The pathogenesis of childhood dyslexia. *Research Publications—Association for Research in Nervous and Mental Disorders, 66,* 127–137.

Galaburda, A. M. (1993). Neuroanatomic basis of developmental dyslexia. *Neurologic Clinics, 11,* 161–173.

Galaburda, A. M., Sherman, F. G., Rosen, G. D., Aboitiz, F., & Geschwind, N. (1985). Developmental dyslexia: Four consecutive patients with cortical anomalies. *Annals of Neurology, 18,* 222–233.

Gall, F. J., & Spurzheimer, J. C. (1809). *Untersuchungen fiber die anatomie des nervensystems uberhaupt und des gehirns insbesondere.* Paris: Treuttel & Wurtz.

Garvey, M. A., Giedd, J., & Swedo, S. E. (1998). PANDAS: The search for environmental triggers of pediatric neuropsychiatric disorders. Lessons from rheumatic fever. *Journal of Child Neurology, 13,* 413–423.

Geschwind, N. (1984). The brain of a learning-disabled individual. *Annals of Dyslexia, 34,* 319–327.

Gille de la Tourette, G. (1885). Étude sur une affection nerveuse caractérisée par l'incoordination motrice accompagnée d'écholalie et de coprolalie. *Archives de Neurologie, 9,* 19–42, 158–200.

Gilson, E. (1955). *History of Christian philosophy in the middle ages.* New York: Random House.

Gordon, B. L. (1959). *Medieval and renaissance medicine.* New York: Philosophical Library.

Greenough, W. T., Klintsova, A. Y., Irwin, S. A., Galvez, R., Bates, K. E., & Weiler, I. J. (2001). Synaptic regulation of protein synthesis and the fragile X protein. *Proceedings of the National Academy of Science, 98,* 7101–7106.

Gualtieri, C. T. (1991). *Neuropsychiatry and behavioral pharmacology.* New York: Springer-Verlag.

Herbert, M. R. (2004). Neuroimaging in disorders of social and emotional functioning: What is the question? *Journal of Child Neurology, 19,* 772–784.

Hinshelwood, J. (1900). Congenital wordblindness. *Lancet, 1,* 1506–1508.

Hinshelwood, J. (1907). Four cases of congenital word-blindness occurring in the same family. *British Medical Journal, 2,* 1229–1232.

Hoffmann, H. (1845). *Der Struwwelpeter.* Self-published by author.

Ireland, W. W. (1877). *Idiocy and imbecility.* London: J & A Churchill.

Johnston, M. V. (2004). Clinical disorders of brain plasticity. *Brain and Development, 26,* 73–80.

Jones, K. L. (1997). *Smith's recognizable patterns of human malformation* (5th ed.). Philadelphia: Saunders.

Kanner, L. (1943). Autistic disturbances of affective contact. *Nervous Child, 2,* 217–250.

Kaplan, R. F., & Stevens, M. A (2002). Review of adult ADHD: A neuropsychological and neuroimaging perspective. *CNS Spectrums, 7,* 355–362.

Kashani, J., McGee, R. O., Clarkson, S. E., Anderson, J. C., Walton, L. A., Williams, S., et al. (1983). Depression in a sample of 9-year old children: Prevalence and associated characteristics. *Archives of General Psychiatry, 40,* 1217–1223.

Kashani, J., & Simonds, J. F. (1979). The incidence of depression in children. *American Journal of Psychiatry, 136,* 1203–1205.

Klin, A., Volkmar, F. R., & Sparrow, S. S. (2000). *Asperger syndrome.* New York: Guilford Press.

Lingam, R., Simmons, A., Andrews, E., Miller, E., Stowe, J., & Taylor, B. (2003). Prevalence of autism and parentally reported triggers in a north east London population. *Archives of Disease in Childhood, 88,* 666–670.

Little, W. J. (1853). *On the nature and treatment of the deformities of the human frame.* London: Longman Brown.

Livingston, S. (1954). *The diagnosis and treatment of convulsive disorders in children.* Springfield, IL: Charles C Thomas.

Lucey, J. V., Costa, D. C., Busatto, G., Pilowsky, L. S., Marks, I. M., Ell, P. J., et al. (1997). Caudate regional cerebral blood flow in obsessive-compulsive disorder, panic disorder and healthy controls on single photon emission computerised tomography. *Psychiatry Research, 74,* 25–33.

Lyon, G. R., Gray, D. B., Kavanagh, J. F., & Krasnegor, N. (Eds.). (1993). *Better understanding learning disabilities: New views from research and their implications for education and public policies.* Baltimore: Paul H. Brookes.

Lyon, G. R., & Rumsey, J. M. (Eds.). (1996). *Neuroimaging: A window to the neurological foundations of learning and behavior in children.* Baltimore: Paul H. Brookes.

MacMillan, S., Szeszko, P. R., Moore, G. J., Madden, R., Lorch, E., Ivey, J., et al. (2003). Increased amygdala: Hippocampal volume ratios associated with severity of anxiety in pediatric major depression. *Journal of Child and Adolescent Psychopharmacology, 13,* 65–73.

Maudsley, H. (1867). *The physiology and pathology of the mind.* London: Macmillan.

McCracken, J. T. (1999). Attention-deficit hyperactivity disorder II: Neuropsychiatric aspects. In C. E. Coffey & R. A. Brumback (Eds.), *Textbook of pediatric neuropsychiatry* (pp. 483–501). Washington, DC: American Psychiatric Press.

McHenry, L. C., Jr. (1993). William Osler: A Philadelphia neurologist. *Journal of Child Neurology, 8,* 416–422.

McKelvey, J. R., Lambert, R., Mottron, L., & Shevell, M. I. (1995). Right-hemisphere dysfunction in Asperger's syndrome. *Journal of Child Neurology, 10,* 310–314.

Morgan, W. P. (1896). A case of congenital word-blindness. *British Medical Journal, 2,* 1378–1379.

Osler, W. (1889). *The cerebral palsies of children: A clinical study from the Infirmary for Nervous Diseases.* Philadelphia: Blakiston.

Papanicolaou, A. C., Simos, P. G., Breier, J. I., Fletcher, J. M., Foorman, B. R., Francis, D., et al. (2003). Brain mechanisms for reading in children with and without dyslexia: A review of studies of normal development and plasticity. *Developmental Neuropsychology, 24,* 593–612.

Powell, K. B., & Voeller, K. K. S. (2004). Prefrontal executive function syndromes in children. *Journal of Child Neurology, 19,* 785–797.

Poznanski, E., Mokros, H. B., Grossman, J., & Freeman, L. N. (1985). Diagnostic criteria in childhood depression. *American Journal of Psychiatry, 142,* 1168–1173.

Qian, Q., Wang, Y., Zhou, R., Yang, L., & Faraone, S. V. (2004). Family-based and case-control association studies of DRD4 and DAT1 polymorphisms in Chinese attention deficit hyperactivity disorder patients suggest long repeats contribute to genetic risk for the disorder. *American Journal of Medical Genetics, 128B,* 84–89.

Ritvo, E. R., Spence, M. A., Freeman, B. J., Mason-Brother, A., Mo, A., & Marazita, M. I. (1985). Evidence for autosomal recessive inheritance in 46 families with multiple incidences of autism. *American Journal of Psychiatry, 142,* 187–192.

Rohde, L. A., Roman, T., Szobot, C., Cunha, R. D., Hutz, M. H., & Biederman, J. (2003). Dopamine transporter gene, response to methylphenidate and cerebral blood flow in attention-deficit/hyperactivity disorder: A pilot study. *Synapse, 48,* 87–89.

Roman, T., Rohde, L. A., & Hutz, M. H. (2004). Polymorphisms of the dopamine transporter gene: Influence on response to methylphenidate in attention deficit-hyperactivity disorder. *American Journal of Pharmacogenomics, 4,* 83–92.

Rourke, B. P. (1989). *Nonverbal learning disabilities: The syndrome and the model.* New York: Guilford Press.

Rourke, B. P. (Ed.). (1995). *Syndrome of nonverbal learning disabilities: Neurodevelopmental manifestations.* New York: Guilford Press.

Shalev, R. S. (2004). Developmental dyscalculia. *Journal of Child Neurology, 19,* 765–771.

Shapiro, A. K., Shapiro, E., & Wayne, H. (1973). Treatment of Tourette's syndrome with haloperidol, review of 34 cases. *Archives of General Psychiatry, 28,* 92–97.

Shaywitz, B. A., Shaywitz, S. E., Blachman, B. A., Pugh, K. R., Fulbright, R. K., Skudlarski, P., et al. (2004). Development of left occipitotemporal systems for skilled reading in children after a phonologically-based intervention. *Biological Psychiatry, 55,* 926–933.

Shaywitz, S. E., Shaywitz, B. A., Fulbright, R. K., Skudlarski, P., Mencl, W. E., Constable, R. T., et al. (2003). Neural systems for compensation and persistence: Young adult outcome of childhood reading disability. *Biological Psychiatry, 54,* 25–33.

Singer, H. S., & Minzer, K. (2003). Neurobiology of Tourette's syndrome: Concepts of neuroanatomic localization and neurochemical abnormalities. *Brain Development, 25*(Suppl. 1), S70–S84.

Smith, E. A., Russell, A., Lorch, E., Banerjee, S. P., Rose, M., Ivey, J., et al. (2003). Increased medial thalamic choline found in pediatric patients with obsessive-compulsive disorder versus major depression or healthy control subjects: A magnetic resonance spectroscopy study. *Biological Psychiatry, 54,* 1399–1405.

Snider, L. A., & Swedo, S. E. (2003). Post-streptococcal autoimmune disorders of the central nervous system. *Current Opinion in Neurology, 16,* 359–365.

Spitzer, R. L., Endicott, J., & Robins, E. (1975). *Research diagnostic criteria (RDC).* New York: Biometrics Research, New York State Psychiatric Institute.

Staton, R. D., & Brumback, R. A. (1981). Non-specificity of motor hyperactivity as a diagnostic criterion. *Perception of Motor Skills, 52,* 219–234.

Staton, R. D., Wilson, H., & Brumback, R. A. (1981). Cognitive improvement associated with tricyclic antidepressant treatment of childhood major depressive illness. *Perception of Motor Skills, 53,* 219–234.

Still, G. F. (1902). The Coulstonian lectures on some abnormal psychical conditions in children. *Lancet, i,* 1008–1012, 1077–1082, 1163–1168.

Sundheim, S. T. P. V., & Voeller, K. K. S. (2004). Psychiatric implications of language disorders and learning disabilities: Risks and management. *Journal of Child Neurology, 19,* 814–826.

Tourette Syndrome Association International Consortium for Genetics. (1999). A complete genome screen in sib pairs affected by Gilles de la Tourette syndrome. *American Journal of Human Genetics, 65,* 1428–1436.

Tuke, D. H. (Ed.). (1892). *A dictionary of psychological medicine* (Vol. 2). London: J & A Churchill.

Voeller, K. K. S. (1986). Right-hemisphere deficit syndrome in children. *American Journal of Psychiatry, 143,* 1004–1009.

Voeller, K. K. S. (1995). Clinical neurologic aspects of right-hemisphere deficit syndrome. *Journal of Child Neurology, 10*(Suppl. 1), S16–S22.

Voeller, K. K. S. (1999). Attention-deficit hyperactivity disorder I: Neurobiological and clinical aspects of attention and disorders of attention. In C. E. Coffey & R. A. Brumback (Eds.), *Textbook of pediatric neuropsychiatry* (pp. 449–482). Washington, DC: American Psychiatric Press.

Voeller, K. K. S. (2004). Attention-deficit hyperactivity disorder (ADHD). *Journal of Child Neurology, 19,* 798–814.

Voeller, K. K. S., & Heilman, K. M. (1988). Attention deficit disorder in children: A neglect syndrome? *Neurology, 38,* 806–808.

Volkmar, F. R., Klin, A., Schultz, R. B., Bronen, R., Marans, W. D., Sparrow, S., et al. (1996). Grand rounds in child psychiatry: Asperger syndrome. *Journal of the American Academy of Child and Adolescent Psychiatry, 35,* 118–123.

Warkany, J. (1971). *Congenital malformations: Notes and comments.* Chicago: Year Book Medical.

Weinberg, W. A., & Brumback, R. A. (1976). Mania in childhood: Case studies and literature review. *American Journal Disturbed Children, 130,* 380–385.

Weinberg, W. A., & Brumback, R. A. (1990). Primary disorder of vigilance: A novel explanation of inattentiveness, daydreaming, boredom, restlessness, and sleepiness. *Journal of Pediatrics, 116,* 720–725.

Weinberg, W. A., & Brumback, R. A. (1992). The myth of attention deficit-hyperactivity disorder: Symptoms resulting from multiple causes. *Journal of Child Neurology 7,* 431–445.

Weinberg, W. A., Harper, C. R., & Brumback, R. A. (1999a). Examination II: Clinical evaluation of cognitive/behavioral function. In C. E. Coffey & R. A. Brumback (Eds.), *Textbook of pediatric neuropsychiatry* (pp. 171–219). Washington, DC: American Psychiatric Press.

Weinberg, W. A., Harper, C. R., & Brumback, R. A. (1999b). Attention-deficit hyperactivity disorder III: Disturbances of vigilance (wakefulness). In C. E. Coffey & R. A. Brumback (Eds.), *Textbook of pediatric neuropsychiatry* (pp. 503–525). Washington, DC: American Psychiatric Press.

Weinberg, W. A., Rutman, J., Sullivan, L., Penick, E. C., & Dietz, S. G. (1973). Depression in children referred to an educational diagnostic center: Diagnosis and treatment. *Journal of Pediatrics 83,* 1065–1072.

Weintraub, S., & Mesulam, M. M. (1983). Developmental learning disabilities of the right hemisphere: Emotional, interpersonal, and cognitive components. *Archives of Neurology, 40,* 463–468.

Wing, L. (1981). Asperger's syndrome: A clinical account. *Psychological Medicine, 11,* 115–129.

Zipes, J. D. (2000). *Sticks and stones: The troublesome success of children's literature from Slovenly Peter to Harry Potter.* New York: Routledge.

CHAPTER 4

Cognitive and Behavioral Contributions

BRAD DONOHUE, VALERIE ROMERO, AND GREGORY DEVORE

INTRODUCTION

Understanding the development of psychopathology is complicated, because it is influenced by many factors that are reciprocally interactive and ever changing. Empirically validated interventions for psychopathology have increasingly focused on the modification of thoughts and behaviors. However, the predominant theoretical underpinnings supporting the need to address thoughts and behaviors in child psychopathology are seldom conceptualized broadly in a clinical context. Therefore, this chapter delineates behavioral and cognitive contributions to the development of psychopathology, with a focus on associative learning, operant conditioning, modeling, and various cognitive theories. Throughout the text, clinical examples help illustrate how cognitions and behaviors act to shape personality development and psychopathology.

Behavior, cognitions, and feelings are each significantly influenced by the environment (Hergenhan, 2001). Indeed, environmental experiences assist in determining patterns of behavioral responding (Barker, 2001), including those that are relevant to the development and maintenance of psychopathology. Behavioral repertoires have traditionally been recognized as observable actions that are influenced by (a) antecedent stimuli that occur prior to behavior (e.g., hunger, lack of companionship, anger, battering), (b) concomitant stimuli that occur during behavior (e.g., intoxication, lecturing, fatigue), and (c) consequent stimuli that occur after behavior (e.g., praise and rewards, punishment, high blood pressure; see Pierce & Cheney, 2004). In general, it is adaptive to develop new behavioral repertoires as cognitive functioning improves. Children, however, sometimes acquire behavioral patterns that may be adaptive in circumscribed situations but counterproductive outside these situations. For instance, assertive behavior is necessary to maintain independent living, whereas nonassertive behavior might be more appropriate during an aggressive father's tirade. Expressions of feelings and thoughts follow similar principles. Indeed, fearful thoughts of sailing boats in storms may protect an individual from drowning, but if this fear generalizes to sailing boats in calm weather the individual will likely lose reinforcement opportunities, such as affection from a boat-loving spouse or other joys associated with sailing boats (Albano, Chorpita, & Barlow, 2003). Thus, in understanding abnormal behavior, it is imperative to examine the environmental context in which the behavior occurs (Todd & Bohart, 1999), as well as thought processes, which in turn influence feelings (McHugh & Wierzbicki, 1998).

ASSOCIATIVE LEARNING

Associative learning was first empirically examined in dozens of controlled trials involving animals (Pavlov, 1960). While examining digestion processes involving dogs, Ivan Pavlov realized the dogs made associations between various stimuli. Specifically, when feeding the dogs he noticed that if the presentation of food (labeled an unconditioned stimulus because it elicited the unconditioned response of salivation) was accompanied by various stimuli that did not elicit salivation (labeled neutral stimuli because these stimuli did not elicit the response of salivation), these stimuli would eventually elicit salivation without the accompanying food and would thus be labeled conditioned stimuli. Salivation occurring consequent to the conditioned stimulus was labeled a conditioned response because the dogs learned to salivate in response to the conditioned stimulus (i.e., the sound of a bell). This basic associative process exemplifies classical conditioning. However, Pavlov and others have demonstrated more sophisticated models to explain behavior (see Sarafino, 2001).

An interesting extension of classical conditioning is higher order conditioning. The first phase of this process is identical to classical conditioning. In the second phase, however, the conditioned stimulus is paired with a second neutral stimulus. This neutral stimulus later becomes the second conditioned stimulus, in that it elicits the conditioned response by itself. The implications of higher order conditioning are extraordinary because the second conditioned stimulus is paired with a conditioned stimulus, not an unconditioned stimulus (as is the case in classical conditioning). This process is perhaps best exemplified in a clinical scenario. A boy enjoys listening to his father talk about the boy's baseball talent and potential to play professional baseball (neutral stimulus 1). Later, the boy's father begins to drink alcohol excessively while he lectures his son for extended periods about things the boy is not doing properly to become a great athlete. These aversively perceived lectures include many unconditioned stimuli (e.g., bad breath, screaming, shaking) that bring about the unconditioned response of anger in the child. Alternating throughout these aversive lectures are compliments from the father about the boy's baseball talents and potential (neutral stimulus 1). After a few of the aforementioned lectures, whenever the father, whether sober or intoxicated, compliments the boy on his talent, the boy evidences the unconditioned response of anger. Thus, the first neutral stimulus (discussing the boy's baseball talent and potential) becomes a conditioned stimulus because it elicits, by itself, the conditioned response of anger.

In the second phase of higher order conditioning, the boy's mother compliments her son while the father compliments him. She does this because the father usually explodes with anger when people do not support his position. The mother's compliments previously brought about good feelings in the boy that were relevant to pride and a sense of accomplishment, but certainly not anger (i.e., neutral stimulus 2). After several pairings with the first conditioned stimulus (i.e., the father's compliments), however, the mother's compliments also bring about the conditioned response of anger in the boy. Thus, the mother's compliments become a conditioned stimulus, even though this stimulus is never paired with unconditioned stimuli. Interestingly, this example helps explain why some children respond to praise whereas others do not. Indeed, in this scenario, the boy may go on to resent people who compliment him, caused in part by stimulus generalization.

Another model of associative learning that is relevant to children is sensory preconditioning. In sensory preconditioning, if two or more neutral stimuli are paired, and one of these neutral stimuli is subsequently paired with an unconditioned stimulus, both of these neutral stimuli may become conditioned stimuli. Neutral stimuli do not have to be associated with unconditioned stimuli to elicit conditioned responses. For instance, an adolescent repeatedly listens to the Beatles at a friend's house and never feels anxious. If this youth experiences anxiety (unconditioned response) consequent to an incident of extreme marijuana use while listening to the Beatles, listening to the Beatles in the future may elicit the conditioned response of anxiety. Hence, listening to the Beatles would be considered a conditioned stimulus. However, visiting the friend's house may also elicit anxiety because this experience was previously associated with listening to the Beatles. This is interesting because visiting the friend's house was never associated with anxiety that occurred during the drug use situation (i.e., the unconditioned stimulus).

Thus, associative learning is a complicated process that obviously makes clinical assessment difficult because interviewees may be unable to determine how their personality characteristics and behavioral repertoires developed. This is unfortunate in that insight pertaining to the conditioning process may be beneficial. For instance, if an adolescent girl was raped, it would be important to conceptualize to a boyfriend that the victim might perceive hugging, kissing, or other signs of affection typically considered to be supportive as aversive due to their associations with unconditioned stimuli associated with the rape.

Understanding the development of problem behavior is further complicated because many neutral stimuli may be associated with many unconditioned stimuli. Moreover, if unconditioned stimuli are traumatic, the conditioning may be rapid and nonsensible. For instance, a child who was wearing a seat belt during a car accident may develop a fear of wearing seat belts, even though the seat belt may have saved the child's life. Irrational thoughts and attributions that occur during traumatic experiences may also become conditioned stimuli that elicit conditioned responses. A young child, for example, may think he caused a hurricane to destroy his home because God was upset that he did not perform his chores that day, or an adolescent may think she caused a young man to rape her because she dressed seductively. Obviously, these faulty attributions may contribute to the development of anxiety-based disorders if allowed to occur without intervention. Along a similar vein, it is common for individuals to avoid conditioned stimuli (e.g., small insects, storms, large men with tattoos) that elicit aversive conditioned responses (e.g., fear, anxiety, anger, upset). Avoidance behavior reinforces the respective aversive response through negative reinforcement; that is, confronting the conditioned stimulus temporarily increases the intensity of the aversive response. Subsequent avoidance of the conditioned stimulus, however, reduces the intensity of the aversive response, thus reinforcing future avoidance behavior and maintaining aversive responding (see Frick & Silverthorn, 2001).

OPERANT CONDITIONING

Reinforcement

Behavioral repertoires are also acquired through operant conditioning. As exemplified by B. F. Skinner in his studies of animals, operant conditioning involves a contingency between a stimulus and a response (Mynatt & Doherty, 1999). Reinforcement involves an increase in the frequency of behavior after a stimulus is provided or removed (Barlow, 1968). Therefore, stimuli that result in an increase in behavior are considered reinforcers, and reinforcers may be delivered naturally or through planning (Shull & Lawrence, 1998). A stimulus that occurs after the individual performs the behavior is labeled a positive reinforcer (e.g., food, toys, tokens, smiles, nodding, praise, pats on the back, money). Negative reinforcement occurs when a stimulus that is usually perceived to be aversive is present (e.g., yelling, lecturing, loud noise, intense heat), and a behavior is performed (e.g., yelling louder, punching, pulling hand away) that results in the withdrawal of this stimulus. If the frequency of the behavior increases in the future, negative reinforcement has occurred (Crosbie, 1998). A good example of negative reinforcement is Gerald Patterson's negative coercion theory, which assists in explaining the escalation of aversive communication patterns (Patterson, Reid, & Dishion, 1992). For instance, a girl is lectured to by her mother. The girl raises her voice, and the mother terminates the aversively perceived lecture. The termination of this aversive stimulus influences the girl to raise her voice in response to future lectures (negative reinforcement). Several days later, the mother initiates a lecture, and the girl expectedly raises her voice. However, this day the mother does not terminate her lecture but instead raises her voice. The surprised girl closes her mouth and listens to the remaining lecture. Thus, both have been reinforced to raise their voices, resulting in future screaming matches and poor communication skills that have been indicated in various psychological disorders (e.g., conduct disorders, mood and anxiety disorders, personality disorders, substance use disorders).

Reinforcers are usually most effective when they are provided, or removed, immediately and consistently after the respective behavior occurs (Barker, 2001), although the strength of a reinforcer will vary across time, individuals, situations, and behaviors. For instance, a candy bar might be enough to motivate a boy to wash the dishes when he is 8 years old, but not when he is a teenager. Twenty dollars may motivate an adolescent raised in poverty to dig a hole, but an adolescent raised in affluence may refuse to do so for that amount. Parental attention may motivate a child to read a comic book but do little to motivate the child to read a science book in studying for an exam. Other factors must also be considered, including noncontingent accessibility of the reinforcer, and satiation. Indeed, for a child who has unlimited access to ice cream, ice cream will probably be an ineffective reinforcer. Using potato chips as reinforcers may motivate an autistic child to attempt to speak words during discrete trials, but not on a full stomach.

Ample amounts of reinforcement for prosocial behaviors are likely to assist in building behavioral repertoires that act to facilitate coping skills that buffer against psychopathology and personality deficits. Contrarily, aversively perceived stimulation is associated with behavioral deficits, poor assertiveness, and greater risk of developing psychopathology (Skinner, 1953). Moreover, insufficient, inadequate, or maladaptive reinforcement contributes to the development and maintenance of psychopathology (Mash & Dozois, 2003). Overindulgence or spoiling is a good example. If a child is freely provided various reinforcers without having to earn them through contingent reinforcement, the child may experience upset when the provider of reinforcement (e.g., the parent) is unavailable. Indeed, a child who is accustomed to getting reinforcers with few performance demands may throw a tantrum or engage in other undesired behaviors when denied these reinforcers. These inappropriate behaviors may then lead to aversive experiences with others (e.g., being teased or isolated from peers or significant others). Of course, this may result in less opportunity to learn social skills that have been indicated to buffer against various pathologies in youth (see Bourke & Donohue, 1996; Donohue, Acierno, & Kogan, 1996; Donohue, Van Hasselt, Hersen, & Perrin, 1999). Reinforcement for problem behaviors may also lead to dysfunctional behavioral repertoires. Indeed, among gang members, social recognition and praise for shooting rival gang members will increase the risk of performing behaviors that are consistent with conduct disorders.

The role of negative reinforcement is clearly evidenced by youth who suffer from anxiety-based disorders. In the development of obsessive-compulsive disorder, an obsessive thought (e.g., concern as to whether an alarm clock was set) results in anxiety. If the child checks the clock and determines that the alarm was indeed set, this will immediately relieve anxiety and thus reinforce the child to continue engaging in compulsive checking behaviors in the future (Barrett & Healy, 2003). Similar processes occur in fears; avoiding the feared stimulus results in an immediate reduction in fear, thus reinforcing the fear response and leading to future avoidance behavior.

When used correctly, reinforcement can serve as a protective barrier against the development of psychopathology, in that treatment for these disorders usually involves consistent increases in reinforcement for prosocial or functional behavior. To illustrate this point, reinforcing a child for nonaggressive behavioral repertoires significantly reduces the likelihood that this child will develop tendencies to be aggressive or physically violent. Similarly, a child who is reinforced for remaining calm in social situations is unlikely to develop social anxieties.

Punishment

Punishment involves a decrease in the frequency of behavior after a stimulus is provided or removed (Mynatt & Doherty, 1999). In positive punishment, a stimulus is added consequent to the respective behavior, and a decrease in the future frequency of that behavior is evidenced (Pierce & Cheney, 2004). For instance, if a boy who regularly engages in throwing spitballs is later required to perform extra chores as a consequence, positive punishment would occur if the child significantly decreases the frequency of throwing spitballs.

It is important to realize that although the punisher is typically perceived to be aversive, the stimulus may be nonaversive. Nathan Azrin's positive practice procedure (see Donohue, Van Hasselt, Miller, & Hersen, 1997, for full description) is an example of a relatively nonaversive discipline that follows the tenets of positive punishment. In this procedure the consequent stimulus is an instruction to practice the desired behavior several times. If a child slams a door, for example, the child would be instructed to shut the door softly several times after being told the slam was probably caused by some circumstance outside the child's control (e.g., a strong wind). This intervention has been shown to be effective in the amelioration of problem behaviors in children (e.g., Azrin, Donohue, Besalel, Kogan, & Acierno, 1994; Donohue & Van Hasselt, 1999). It is important to emphasize that punishment involves a reduction in the frequency of behavior, not whether the stimulus is perceived to be aversive. It is certainly aversive to receive a slap in the face after coming home late for curfew. However, if the frequency of behavior does not change, the slap is not a punisher. Indeed, a parent may find that the frequency of the child's coming home late *increases* consequent to the slap, indicating that the slap is either inconsequential or potentially a reinforcer.

Negative punishment involves a decrease in behavior consequent to a stimulus being removed (Pierce & Cheney, 2004). The stimulus is typically something desired, and examples include a time-out from positive reinforcement and response cost (Miltenberger, 1997). Time-out involves removing the child from a reinforcing situation, such as restricting a child from a play area or placing the child in a quiet corner for a specified time. Response cost involves the removal of a desired stimulus from the existing situation after the behavior occurs, such as taking a toy away for a specified time after a child is observed hitting another child.

Punishment can have the desired effect of decreasing unwanted behaviors rapidly, which may explain its widespread use. However, unexpected side effects often result when using aversive punishments, including aggression, fear, and emotional problems (Miltenberger, 1997). The recipient of punishment often focuses on avoiding or escaping from the punisher and, therefore, may be unable to focus on learning to perform the desired behavior. Indeed, avoidance of the punisher will lead to less opportunity to supervise and to reinforce desired behavior. Interestingly, continued use of punishment is usually caused by the punisher's being negatively reinforced, not a decrease in the child's behavior. From the parent's perspective, a spanking results in removal of an aversive stimulus and, therefore, increases the parent's likelihood to spank in the future, although no positive long-term behavior change may have resulted. Punishment is typically short-lived, as it usually only suppresses undesired behavior—that is, when the contingency maintaining punishment is removed, the unwanted response often recurs (Skinner, 1953). Another problem with punishment arises when punishment is intermittently administered. In these cases, a lack of consistency in punishment contributes to the child's uncertainty as to what behaviors are truly punishable, a situation that may result in anxiety.

When a response is followed by an aversive stimulus, other stimuli that are associated with the response are also punished (Skinner, 1953). To exemplify this point, imagine a child being spanked because he did not look both ways before crossing a street. Any thoughts or behaviors the child was having at the time the punishment was administered (e.g., excitement about seeing his father) may also be punished. Similarly, nontargeted prosocial behaviors may be repressed or not encouraged to develop when punishment is used routinely. For example, if a child learns to be quiet when reprimanded due to fear of exacerbating the punishment, a maladaptive behavior (i.e., lack of negative assertion) has now developed, whereas the targeted problem behavior is merely suppressed. Another problem in the application of punishment is that the punishing caregiver often feels guilty for having used the aversive discipline, which causes the punisher to subsequently overindulge the child (e.g., take the child out for ice cream, provide reassurance that the child is loved).

Sometimes anticipation of attention may act to motivate the child to perform undesired behavior, particularly if the child is neglected. For instance, a baby pulls pots and pans from a kitchen cabinet despite being repeatedly reprimanded by the mother in a stern voice and with a firm tap on the child's bottom. After each incident of corporal punishment, the mother feels sorry for the child, discontinues her other activity, and begins to play with the child. In this scenario, the baby is willing to tolerate the reprimand and relatively nonpainful pat on the bottom to receive attention from the mother. Unfortunately, the baby is learning at a very young age that attention can be achieved consequent to performing undesired behavior or upsetting the mother. The mother is also being reinforced to use aversive methods because there is an immediate suppression of the baby's undesired behavior and subsequent playtime with the baby.

The moderately high probability of physical and emotional harm to the individual being punished has led to ethical concerns regarding instruction in corporal punishment (Crosbie, 1998). Indeed, if corporal punishment is to be effective in suppressing undesired behavior, at least in the immediate situation, its severity needs to increase continuously (see Skinner, 1953). A gentle pat on a toddler's bottom may result in the toddler stopping all activities to observe the face of the punisher. If the punisher demonstrates a stern and disapproving face, the toddler will usually cry and terminate the initiated behavior. However, if the caregiver regularly pats the toddler on the bottom when undesired behaviors occur, the toddler will likely become desensitized to strikes on the bottom (i.e., demonstrate no upset). In part this is because the initial novelty of the stern face wears off. When this inevitably occurs, the caregiver will usually increase the severity of the spanking, and the toddler will again show upset and terminate the initiated undesired behavior. If the caregiver relies on this method of discipline, the spankings may escalate until the caregiver uses objects (e.g., wooden spoons, paddles) to deliver sufficiently intense spankings. Thus, the intensity of aversiveness may increase to the extent that fear, anger, frustration, and even child abuse can occur (see Donohue, Ammerman, & Zelis, 1998). To avoid this liability, many nursery schools and day care centers no longer use aversive disciplines (e.g., corporal punishment, time-out) and instead have increased their training in reinforcement-based strategies to influence the children in their care to comply with program rules. In summary, although punishment may be effective in the short term, it rarely terminates problem behavior, and overreliance on punishment often leads to undesired consequences.

SOCIAL LEARNING

Modeling, or learning from the observation of others, is a major contributor to the development of behavioral repertoires (e.g., moral development, expression of emotions, empathy, assertiveness, anxiety and fear, problem solving, kindness, child care; Sigelman & Rider, 2003). As Petri (1996) reported, several circumstances must be present for the modeled behavior to occur, including attention to the model, retention of the information observed, and perceived ability and motivation to perform the modeled behavior. Motivation to perform the modeled behavior is more likely to occur if the model is similar to the observer, physically attractive, popular (but not overly so), well liked, and reinforced for the modeled behavior (Chance, 1999). Indeed, a child who sees an adolescent steal a candy bar without getting punished is more likely to steal in the future, particularly if the model is esteemed and the same age, gender, and ethnicity.

Modeling can lead to the development of both normal and deviant behavioral repertoires. Bandura, Ross, and Ross (1961) clearly demonstrated the influence of modeling on aggression. In a classic study, children were exposed to adults who were instructed to act violently (i.e., hitting, kicking, verbal aggression) toward a Bobo doll (an inflatable, self-righting "punching bag"–type toy). When subsequently exposed to Bobo dolls, these children were observed to imitate the aggressive acts that were modeled. The results of this study are consistent with findings from other studies reporting that children who are exposed to domestic violence are likely to display aggressive tendencies with others. Evidence also suggests that aggression to oneself is influenced by imitation, in that suicide rates increase by as much as 7 percent after a highly publicized case (Holmes, 2001).

Just as imitation can increase rates of maladaptive behavior, it can also increase rates of adaptive behavior. For example, children can learn through imitation how to cope with negative emotional states by observing calm models getting reinforced for prosocial behaviors. Indeed, good morals are influenced by observation of people performing good deeds (Sigelman & Rider, 2003), and the modeling of positive moral behavior (e.g., sharing, telling the truth, altruistic behavior) can act to buffer against the development of maladaptive behavioral patterns. This is particularly true if the child who imitates the modeled behavior is told that performance of the moralistic behavior is a result of the child's character (e.g., "You're a very kind and considerate boy").

COGNITION

Cognition involves mental processes associated with problem solving, creativity, decision making, and language. Aaron Beck, one of the founders of modern cognitive therapy, described cognitions as (a) *automatic,* in that they occur without prior reflection or reasoning; (b) *involuntary,* in that they occur even when the individual does not want them to occur or is actively trying to avoid them; and (c) *plausible,* meaning they are relevant and uncritical in origin (Beck, 1963). Beck (1967) found that children and adults arrive at self-defeating conclusions based on consistent and illogical cognitions. His work with depression identified a number of illogical thought processes, such as overgeneralization. In overgeneralization, wide-ranging negative conclusions are derived based on a single inconsequential event. For example, an adolescent might think she is a poor athlete because she loses a 100-meter sprint. That thought might lead to a depressed mood if this girl believes it is important to be a good athlete. This suggests that children with psychological disorders and problems can both develop and overcome their problems by restructuring their thoughts. Therefore, many theorists have focused on the influence of cognitions in the development and maintenance of psychopathology.

Irrational beliefs are a recurrent theme in most applied cognitive theories, and they have been classified into distinct categories (David, Schnur, & Belloiu, 2002). For instance, demandingness occurs when a child thinks in absolutist terms expressed as musts or shoulds (e.g., "I must win the race"). Such statements are pathologically oriented because perfectionism is extremely unlikely, and if the child expects it to occur, this often leads to upset. Awfulizing occurs when a child believes situations are worse than they actually are or grossly devalues situations. For example, failing a test causes the child to believe he has no hope of being admitted to an esteemed university despite his having high marks on all other tests. Self-loathing occurs when an individual is highly self-critical and consistently makes general negative self-evaluations. Certainly, these perspectives are associated with negativistic thinking patterns that often result in upset, lack of assertiveness, and greater likelihood of evidencing various psychopathologies. Indeed, children with depression exhibit greater encoding biases of negative material and less recall of positive feedback than nondepressed children.

Cognitive theorists believe that thoughts and feelings are inextricably intertwined. In the two-factor theory of emotion proposed by Schachter and Singer (1962), the authors hypothesized that children are relatively unfamiliar with their feelings and attitudes. Because internal reactions are ambiguous, however, children look to their own behavior and aspects of the external world for clues about the nature of their feelings. Obviously, chaotic and inconsistent aversive environments make it difficult for children to make sense of their emotions. For instance, aggressive children often misinterpret their emotional arousal as hostile when the intentions of their peers are unclear, when harm is accidental, and even when a peer is trying to be helpful (Dodge, 1985; Dodge & Somberg, 1987). Indeed, these children appear to misinterpret their internal feelings because they misread cues from their environment, which leads them to act aggressively and thus lose opportunities to gain reinforcement from their peers.

Another way in which cognition can affect emotions is through the activation of cognitive schemas containing strong affect. Suppose an adolescent is introduced to others as "extremely smart." Based on this label, others may activate cognitive schema that are relevant to their understanding of smart children. This bias will likely influence the way individuals think about, and treat, this adolescent. Indeed, some symptoms of schizophrenia may erroneously result from being labeled schizophrenic (Holmes, 2001). For instance, if an adolescent who has been diagnosed with schizophrenia is asked multiple times if schizophrenic symptoms are present, this youth may falsely identify, confuse, and exacerbate normal feelings with unnatural extremes associated with this disorder. In this way, the perceived expectations of others are fulfilled. In the case of delusions, the youth may confuse normal feelings of being special to the family with delusions of grandiosity. As such, cognitions that denote labels can activate emotional contexts that not only affect how others feel about the individual but also change the individual's self-perceptions and perpetuate self-fulfilling prophecies relevant to inducement of psychopathological symptoms that do not exist, or exacerbate existing psychopathology (Lee, Uhlemann, & Barak, 1999).

In everyday life, individuals perceive ambiguous stimuli more favorably when they are in a pleasant mood than when they are in an unpleasant mood (Isen, 1993). Children who evidence depressed mood states are biased to develop unfavorable evaluations of themselves and others, and they are also primed to recollect negative events (Bower, 1987). Therefore, depressed mood states cause children to view their life experiences negatively, which in turn influences them to engage in negativistic thought patterns that often lead to insufficient motivation and behavioral repertoires (David et al., 2002).

Similar to the self-fulfilling prophesy, the expectations of others act to guide children's decision making (Madon, Guyll, Spoth, Cross, & Hilberg, 2003). Along a slightly different vein, negative appraisals and low expectations of children by teachers can seriously undermine students' chances for success (Eckenrode, Laird, & Doris, 1993). For instance, in a landmark study (Rosenthal & Jacobson, 1968), teachers were provided false information that some students were likely to show large gains in their IQ scores during the coming year. Consistent with a self-fulfilling prophecy, the IQ scores of these students increased more than those of a control group of students. Negative outcome expectations of youth are also indicated in clinical populations (e.g., child maltreatment, substance abuse, delinquency, depression). When positive expectations are lacking, children from these backgrounds are likely to conclude that traditional routes of occupational success will be closed to them. In turn, these children may seek rewards from antisocial peer groups and criminal behavior (Patterson et al., 1992). Therefore, therapists should emphasize the positive aspects of youth to parents, particularly youth with whom parents and others are biased to have low expectations (Coie & Dodge, 1998). Indeed, positive expectations of children by parents, teachers, and peer groups can greatly influence children to enhance their self-evaluations and can buffer against psychopathology.

Interestingly, many studies have shown that positive cognitions are associated with greater health. A longitudinal study of Harvard graduates demonstrated that participants who were judged to be relatively optimistic at the beginning of the study were healthiest when reexamined more than 30 years later (Peterson, Seligman, & Vaillant, 1988). Furthermore, optimists appear to cope well with physical adversity (Aspinwall & Taylor, 1997). In studies of cancer patients it has been found that openness to fighting illness is positively associated with greater immune function, decreased recurrence rates, and longer life spans, even among patients who are in advanced stages of cancer (Levy, Herberman, Maluish, Achlien, & Lippman, 1985). Alternatively, worrisome thoughts have been found to exacerbate medical and psychiatric conditions. For instance, children who suffer from post-traumatic stress disorder experience high levels of cognitively based anxiety problems and report greater incidences of nightmares and nocturnal awakenings (Germain & Nielsen, 2003). Nocturnal awakenings, often a result of stress brought about by worrisome thoughts, have been found to reduce quality of sleep and exacerbate mental health conditions (Pilcher & Walters, 1997).

In general, individuals who have irrational beliefs, particularly regarding receipt of criticism, tend to experience maladaptive negative emotions (David et al., 2002). Therefore, it is important to teach children to think optimistically and not let criticism negatively affect their self-esteem. Children also need to be taught to interpret information accurately, however. Of course, irrational beliefs may be prevented by teaching youth to use positive, albeit accurate, self-efficacious thoughts (see Frick & Silverthorn, 2001). Indeed, if a parent consistently tells a child to avoid dogs because they may bite, a fear of dogs may develop. It would obviously be more beneficial to let the child know that most dogs do not bite, although some do on occasion.

Interpretation of interpersonal responses and social judgment has also been indicated in child psychopathology. For example, youth who evidence conduct disorders appear to make errors in their interpretation of social cues and clarification of social goals as well as decision-making processes (Hinshaw & Lee, 2003). Thus, cognition plays a critical role in determining behavior in that the interpretation of environmental stimuli acts to motivate children to action.

CONCLUSION

Leading cognitive and behavioral theories were examined in this chapter to demonstrate some of the ways in which behaviors and thoughts contribute to the initial development of personality constructs and child psychopathology. Although the review of theories in this paper was not comprehensive, ample support was provided to indicate that cognitive and behavioral repertoires each have prominent roles in the prevention of problem behaviors and emotions in children. Given experiential complexities, however, it is clearly apparent that behaviors and cognitions affect the development of each child's personality uniquely.

REFERENCES

Albano, A. M., Chorpita, B. F., & Barlow, D. H. (2003). Childhood anxiety disorders. In E. J. Mash & R. A. Barkley (Eds.), *Child psychopathology* (pp. 279–329). New York: Guilford Press.

Aspinwall, L. G., & Taylor, S. E. (1997). A stitch in time: Self-regulation and proactive coping. *Psychological Bulletin, 121,* 417–436.

Azrin, N. H., Donohue, B., Besalel, V., Kogan, E., & Acierno, R. (1994). Youth drug abuse treatment: A controlled outcome study. *Journal of Child and Adolescent Substance Abuse, 3,* 1–16.

Bandura, A., Ross, D., & Ross, S. A. (1961). Transmission of aggression through imitation of aggressive models. *Journal of Abnormal and Social Psychology, 63,* 575–582.

Barker, L. M. (2001). *Learning and behavior.* Saddle River, NJ: Prentice Hall.

Barlow, J. A. (1968). *Stimulus and response.* New York: Harper and Row.

Barrett, P. M., & Healy, L. J. (2003). An examination of the cognitive processes involved in childhood obsessive-compulsive disorders. *Behaviour Research and Therapy, 41,* 285–299.

Beck, A. T. (1963). Thinking and depression. *Archives of General Psychiatry, 9,* 324–333.

Beck, A. T. (1967). *Depression: Clinical, experimental, and theoretical aspects.* New York: Harper and Row.

Bourke, M., & Donohue, B. (1996). Assessment and treatment of juvenile sexual offenders: An empirical review. *Journal of Child Sexual Abuse, 5,* 47–70.

Bower, G. H. (1987). Commentary on mood and memory. *Behavioral Research and Therapy, 25,* 443–455.

Chance, P. (1999). *Learning and behaviour.* Pacific Grove, CA: Brooks/Cole.

Coie, J. D., & Dodge, K. A. (1998). Aggression and antisocial behavior. In N. Eisenberg (Ed.), *Handbook of child psychology: Vol. 3. Social, emotional, and personality development* (5th ed., pp. 779–862). New York: Wiley.

Crosbie, J. (1998). Negative reinforcement and punishment. In K. A. Lattal & M. Perone (Eds.), *Handbook of research methods in human operant behavior* (pp. 163–189). New York: Plenum Press.

David, D., Schnur, J., & Belloiu, A. (2002). Another search for the hot cognitions: Appraisal, irrational beliefs, attributions, and their relation to emotion. *Journal of Emotion and Cognitive-Behavior Therapy, 20,* 93–131.

Dodge, K. A. (1985). Attributional bias in aggressive children. In P. C. Kendal (Ed.), *Advances in cognitive-behavioral research and therapy* (pp. 73–110). San Diego: Academic Press.

Dodge, K. A., & Somberg, (1987). Hostile attributional biases among aggressive boys are exacerbated under conditions of threats to the self. *Child Development, 58,* 213–224.

Donohue, B., Acierno, R., & Kogan, E. (1996). Relationship of depression with measures of social functioning in adult drug abusers. *Addictive Behaviors, 21,* 211–216.

Donohue, B., Ammerman, R. T., & Zelis, K. (1998). Child physical abuse and neglect. In S. T. Watson & F. M. Gresham (Eds.), *Handbook of child behavior therapy* (pp. 183–202). New York: Plenum Press.

Donohue, B., Miller, E., Van Hasselt, V. B., & Hersen, M. (1998). An ecobehavioral approach to child maltreatment. In V. B. Van Hasselt & M. Hersen (Eds.), *Handbook of psychological treatment protocols for children and adolescents* (pp. 279–358). Mahwah, NJ: Erlbaum.

Donohue, B., & Van Hasselt, V. B. (1999). Development of an ecobehavioral treatment program for child maltreatment. *Behavioral Interventions, 14,* 55–82.

Donohue, B., Van Hasselt, V. B., Hersen, M., & Perrin, S. (1999). Role-play assessment of social skills in conduct-disordered and substance abusing adolescents: An empirical review. *Journal of Child and Adolescent Substance Abuse, 9,* 1–29.

Donohue, B., Van Hasselt, V. B., Miller, E., & Hersen, M. (1997). An ecobehavioral approach to child maltreatment. In V. B. Van Hasselt & M. Hersen (Eds.), *Handbook of psychological treatment manuals with children and adolescents.* Hillsdale, NJ: Erlbaum.

Eckenrode, J., Laird, M., & Doris, J. (1993). School performance and disciplinary problems among abused and neglected children. *Developmental Psychology, 29,* 53–62.

Frick, P. J., & Silverthorn, P. (2001). Psychopathology in children. In H. E. Adams & P. B. Sutker (Eds.), *Comprehensive handbook of psychopathology* (pp. 881–920). New York: Plenum Press.

Germain, A., & Nielsen, T. A. (2003). Sleep pathophysiology in posttraumatic stress disorder and idiopathic nightmare sufferers. *Biological Psychiatry, 54,* 1092–1098.

Hergenhan, B. R. (2001). *An introduction to the history of psychology.* Belmont, CA: Thomson.

Hinshaw, S. P., & Lee, S. S. (2003). Conduct and oppositional defiant disorders. In E. J. Mash & R. A. Barkley (Eds.), *Child psychopathology* (pp. 144–189). New York: Guilford Press.

Holmes, D. S. (2001). *Abnormal psychology.* Needham Heights, MA: Allyn & Bacon.

Isen, A. M. (1993). Positive affect and decision making. In M. Lewis & J. M. Haviland (Eds.), *Handbook of emotion* (pp. 216–277). New York: Guilford Press.

Lee, D. Y., Uhlemann, M. R., & Barak, A. (1999). Effects of diagnostic suggestion on the clinical judgments and recall memories of autobiography. *Journal of Social Clinical Psychology, 18,* 35–46.

Levy, S. M., Herberman, R., Maluish, A., Achlien, B., & Lippman, M. (1985). Prognostic risk assessment in primary breast cancer by behavioral and immunological parameters. *Health Psychology, 4,* 99–113.

Madon, S., Guyll, M., Spoth, R. L., Cross, S. E., & Hilbert, S. J. (2003). The self-fulfilling influence of mother expectations on children's underage drinking. *Journal of Personality and Social Psychology, 84,* 1188–1205.

Mash, E. J., & Dozois, D. J. A. (2003). Child psychopathology: A developmental systems perspective. In E. J. Mash & R. A. Barkley (Eds.), *Child psychopathology* (pp. 3–71). New York: Guilford Press.

McHugh, K. M., & Wierzbicki, M. (1998). Prediction of responses to cognitive and behavioral mood inductions. *Journal of Psychology, 132,* 33–41.

Miltenberger, R. G. (1997). *Behavior modification: Principles and procedures.* Pacific Grove, CA: Brooks/Cole.

Mynatt, C. R., & Doherty, M. E. (1999). *Understanding human behavior.* Needham Heights, MA: Allyn & Bacon.

Patterson, G. R., Reid, J. B., & Dishion, T. J. (1992). *Antisocial boys.* Eugene, OR: Castalia.

Pavlov, I. P. (1960). *Conditioned reflexes.* London: Oxford University Press.

Peterson, C., Seligman, M. E. P., & Vaillant, G. E. (1988). Pessimistic explanatory style is a risk factor for physical illness. A thirty-five-year longitudinal study. *Journal of Personality and Social Psychology, 55,* 23–27.

Petri, H. L. (1996). *Motivation.* Pacific Grove, CA: Brooks/Cole.

Pierce, W. D., & Cheney, C. D. (2004). *Behavior analysis and learning.* Mahwah, NJ: Erlbaum.

Pilcher, J. J., & Walters, A. S. (1997). How sleep deprivation affects psychological variables related to college students' cognitive performance. *Journal of American College Health, 46,* 121–126.

Rosenthal, R., & Jacobson, L. (1968). *Pygmalion in the classroom: Teacher expectation and pupils' intellectual development.* New York: Rinehart and Winston.

Sarafino, E. P. (2001). *Behavior modification.* Mountain View, CA: Mayfield.

Schachter, S., & Singer, J. (1962). Cognitive, social, and physiological determinants of emotional state. *Psychological Review, 69,* 379–399.

Shull, R. L., & Lawrence, P. S. (1998). Reinforcement. In K. A. Lattal & M. Perone (Eds.), *Handbook of research methods in human operant behavior* (pp. 95–129). New York: Plenum Press.

Sigelman, C. K., & Rider, E. A. (2003). Life span human development. Belmont, CA: Thomson.

Skinner, B. F. (1953). *Science and human behavior.* New York: Macmillan.

Todd, J., & Bohart, A. C. (1999). *Foundations of clinical and counseling psychology.* New York: Longman.

CHAPTER 5

Sociological Contributions

TERRANCE J. WADE AND JOHN CAIRNEY

INTRODUCTION

On the many occasions that Dr. Dan Offord, one of Canada's most distinguished child psychiatrists and a world-renowned expert in child psychiatric epidemiology, spoke to groups of scientists, community leaders, and policy makers on child health and development, he would often evoke the metaphor that growing up in Canada (and North America more generally) was like being part of a running race. The issue to him was not that some children would finish first and others last; that is a given in any competition. The issue is one of social justice—is the race fair for all children? To Dr. Offord, the answer was, and continues to be, no. Not all children start at the same line. Some have hurdles along the way. And for other children, the path is relatively unobstructed. Of course, he was speaking about children from socially and economically deprived families and how the disadvantages they face early in life can lead to a negative developmental trajectory across their lives. Our job, he believed, is to make sure the race is fair, to eliminate roadblocks, and to level the playing field for all children.

The power in this metaphor lies not only in the call to action to alleviate the suffering of children; it also reminds us as researchers to pay attention to how the race is structured, because this will be a powerful determinant of whether all children will have an equitable chance of winning. This equity in opportunity is the basis of various national initiatives that have been designed to structure the start of this race more fairly (e.g., Head Start and No Child Left Behind). The chapter presented here is rooted in this perspective. In it, we examine the process of how background disadvantage shapes the proximal contexts in which children live and the health consequences that result from these daily lived experiences.

In the first section of the chapter, we focus our discussion within a sociological framework to emphasize the importance of social and structural determinants on health and health behaviors. This perspective is contrasted to current individual-based approaches, most notably epidemiology. Second, we differentiate between distal and proximal risk factors for child psychopathology and healthy development. We present and describe a model linking constructs (and literatures) together to show the influence of socioenvironmental factors on both the developmental contexts in which children grow and on child health directly. Third, we present a review of some of the literature that has focused on specific components of our model in an attempt to demonstrate how they can potentially be integrated into a more unifying framework. In the final section, we discuss the need to examine not only how various social and economic factors may operate independently but also how they may work in tangent with one another as a constellation of social-structural disadvantage.

EPIDEMIOLOGIC VERSUS SOCIOLOGIC APPROACHES: SOCIAL CONDITIONS AS FUNDAMENTAL CAUSES OF DISEASE

Greater attention to the social and environmental determinants of disease has enjoyed a resurgence in the medical sciences over the past couple of decades. Under the banner of population health, clinicians and researchers have restored the prominent role that both the physical environment and social environment play in disease etiology. In epidemiology in particular, this renaissance of sorts is linked to the increasing influence of other disciplines, including sociology, psychology, and geography. A product or consequence of the infiltration of these disciplines into epidemiology has been to broaden the unit of analysis from the individual to the social environment. Most epidemiologic research, however, continues to focus on individuals as the principal level of analysis to understand the etiology of disease processes (see Diez-Roux, 1998; Rose, 1985; and Schwartz & Carpenter, 1999, for discussions). The designs most commonly em-

---

Acknowledgment: In memory of Dr. David (Dan) R. Offord (1933–2004). Dr. Wade is funded by the Canada Research Chairs program.

ployed in epidemiologic research—case control and cohort designs—detect individual-level differences between those who are diagnosed or identified with a particular disease or disorder (cases) and those who are not (controls; Rose, 1985). Because method is undeniably related to results, the role that the social environment plays in disease etiology in these studies is often neglected or disregarded altogether in favor of the individual as the most appropriate unit. Yet, sociology informs us that where we live and the resources we possess (e.g., knowledge, income) are important determinants of well-being across the life course. These things are firmly entrenched in early work by Gough (1948), Robins (1966), and the Gluecks (1950) and population health literature more recently by Evans, Barer, and Marmor (1994). Both researchers and clinicians are becoming increasingly aware that the context in which people live is not just a backdrop but also an important component of development that cannot be ignored. When the focus is on child health and development, a sociological framework directs attention toward the familial (not just family) environmental factors in which children develop, forcing researchers to consider the ways in which these contexts can be modified, enhanced, or restructured altogether to improve child outcomes.

Link and Phelan (1995, 2000) provide a useful heuristic for restoring the primacy of context into the research enterprise in population health and epidemiology. They make an important distinction between different kinds of risk factors in terms of the spatial-temporal referents of distal and proximal. Essentially, distal risk factors refer to conditions such as poverty and neighborhood disorganization that we might think of as upstream risk factors for disease—they are contextual effects. Proximal risk factors, in turn, are those downstream factors, often behavioral, that are directly linked to poor health outcomes (e.g., smoking, sedentary lifestyle, stress). If we think in terms of a causal model, proximal factors may be thought of as mediating or intervening components between distal risk factors and health outcomes. However, investigation of this process is more an exception than a rule. Overattention to proximal risk factors has hindered both the scientific understanding of the role that social-structural and economic factors play in the etiology of illness and the development of public health interventions that move beyond individual behavioral modification and change to address contextual risk factors for illness and disease (Shy, 1997). Using smoking as an example, it would be difficult to find anyone who does not know that smoking is hazardous to one's health. Yet, smoking rates continue to be high and are also differentially distributed across subpopulations, principally by age and social class. To better understand why people smoke requires one to examine more closely the social conditions associated with smoking.

Link and Phelan's (1995) argument is trenchant and persuasive: If we focus only on those risk factors most proximate to health outcomes (e.g., smoking), we fail to consider the enduring social structures that condition exposure to those risk factors in the first place (e.g., poverty, life circumstances). Stated another way, Link and Phalen challenge us to consider what puts individuals at risk for the very factors that epidemiologists currently treat as risk factors for disease; that is, what places individuals at risk for risk factors. Social conditions are fundamental determinants because although proximal risk factors change (e.g., smoking rates in the population over time have changed), distal factors remain invariant (i.e., poverty has always been a risk factor for disease). Therefore, if we want to improve the health of a population, we need to modify the fundamental factors that produce disease. From a sociological perspective, this is simply a call to attend to the structural and economic context in which individual behaviors are situated.

What are these enduring or fundamental conditions? Link and Phelan (1995) define them in terms of access to resources that allow individuals to protect themselves from potentially damaging elements in the social environment—particularly those resources associated with social and economic deprivation. Fundamental conditions could also be thought of as both the power and the means to control one's own environment, making it more favorable and less harmful. It is the knowledge to make informed decisions and the ability to successfully implement and act on those decisions. This could include the knowledge and ability to be able to afford to live in a more desirable neighborhood and send one's children to a more desirable school, and access better health care resources. It also includes behavioral decisions that flow from both knowledge and means, such as buying food that is more nutritious and seeking appropriate health care resources.

Fundamentally, these resources are connected to the unequal distribution of power within societies (economic and social). When power is differentially distributed, sociologists refer to the stratification of the population in terms of a social hierarchy. Regardless of the characteristics (ascribed or achieved) or combinations of characteristics form the basis of this social hierarchy, people will be differentially sorted with regard to access to power and resources, which in turn results in differential health outcomes (e.g., House et al., 1994). In the sociological literature, the determinants of social status or social position include gender; socioeconomic status (education and income); social class (occupational status); race and ethnicity; and, to a lesser extent, age (see Turner & Lloyd, 1999). To this list we would also add family structure (two-headed versus single-headed households), which may be thought of as the intersection between gender, socioeconomic status, and social class. Single-parent households are becoming increasingly more prevalent in most Western societies. For example, in the United States, the percentage of single-parent families has more than doubled, from 12 percent in 1970 to 27 percent in 1998 (U.S. Department of Health and Human Services, 2001). Rates in Canada, though much lower than those in the United States, have increased from 9.4 percent in 1970 to 12 percent in 1999. Of these, more than 80 percent are female-headed single-parent families. While many single-parent families are the result of marital dissolution, never-married women with children are becoming increasingly more common. For example, only 5 percent of all U.S. births in 1960 were to unmarried women compared to 37 percent in 1997, and the majority of this increase is attributable to increases among teenage mothers (U.S. Department of Health and Human Services, 2001). As a social condition, single-parent families are more likely to be disadvantaged economically for a variety of reasons, including inability to continue with education due to parenting obligations and limited job opportunities resulting from educational deficits, child-care obligations, and gender inequality in the workplace. And given that the majority of single-parent families are headed by single mothers, they are both a socially and an economically deprived group (Cairney, Boyle, Lipman, & Racine, 2004; Cairney, Boyle, Offord, & Racine, 2003).

Together, these markers of social position reflect real differences in material and psychosocial resources that are also associated with health and illness. Not surprisingly, the relationships between these characteristics and morbidity and mortality have been extensively studied (Kaplan & Keil, 1993; Lynch, Kaplan, Cohen, Tuomilehto, & Salonen, 1996; Mackenbach & Kunst, 1997) and are typically thought of as the pillars of social epidemiology (Berkman & Kawachi, 2000). In the child epidemiological literature, social position usually refers to the family, since children themselves are not directly part of a social hierarchy but are connected to social structure through their parents or primary caregivers. How, then, is position in the social structure at the family level connected to child health and psychopathology? To use the language of Link and Phelan (1995), what is the relationship between distal and proximal factors in shaping children's well-being? In the next section, we explore this question and present a unifying conceptualization to illustrate the process that connects these factors with child health.

A CONCEPTUAL MODEL OF PROCESS LINKING CHILD PSYCHOPATHOLOGY WITH PROXIMAL AND DISTAL RISK FACTORS

Similar to the epidemiological literature on adults, research on the role that social conditions, particularly social structural factors (e.g., socioeconomic status, family structure), play in shaping child health outcomes is problematic. We are not claiming, however, that social structure is neglected or absent from current research on child psychopathology. In fact, we argue quite the opposite. Social structure and socioeconomic status (SES) are so ubiquitous that their role and importance as fundamental conditions are often almost unrecognized or taken for granted. But the pursuit of trying to identify what places people (or families) at risk for risk requires us to attend to how social conditions influence proximal risk factors in this process.

The majority of research on child health takes one of two approaches to examining the effect of background social-structural forces. First, it attends to the *independent* associations of both proximal factors and distal factors on child health and development. Here, social-structural factors are examined as acting independently of proximal factors while the emphasis is most often placed on the proximal effects. It is common to read statements such as "controlling for race [or controlling for income], . . . maternal depression [or hostile parenting, or another proximal risk factor] is related to child mental illness." Although the effect of the background factors may be statistically significant and independent of the proximal family factors, little consideration is given to how they may have a direct bearing on exposure to proximal factors. Alternatively, other studies of proximal effects on child health indicate that the researchers have adjusted for social conditions as though these were simply noises that need to be filtered out. In both of these cases, the conceptual and statistical significance of social structure is lost. We believe this may be connected to the search for that programmatic so-called magic bullet that can be affected at the individual level. Factors such as SES are perceived as confounding elements that interfere with the variables of interest. But we cannot discount these background characteristics as independent or statistically extraneous.

This is indicative of most child development models focusing on the immediate context and interrelationships (interpersonal or interactional factors) that influence child health. For example, Bronfenbrenner's (1979) ecological model is composed of a set of interactional systems expanding from the family, or the microsystem at the center, to the larger society through the mesosystem, exosystem, and macrosystem. The microsystem stresses the importance of interpersonal interactions within the family domain and other domains such as school as the child ages. The mesosystem captures the interactions between developmental domains that the child participates within, such as family and school. These two systems directly impact the child. While Bronfenbrenner (1979) also accounts for larger societal forces within the exosystem and macrosystem, the focus is on interactions between institutions and individuals and between the institutions themselves. Similarly, Belsky (1984) focuses on interpersonal relations between parents and children. According to Belsky (1994), these interactions are dictated principally by parent personality and well-being, which have direct bearing on parenting behaviors.

We do not disregard the utility of these proximal-level factors and the importance of interpersonal relationships. Both Bronfenbrenner (1979) and Belsky (1984) and others provide compelling evidence for their importance in this process. But little attention is given to the material resources of parents and the structural factors in which these material resources are generally derived. Proximal risks based on parent-child interaction are present in the daily lives of children, providing the context in which children develop. However, these risks do not occur in a social vacuum; that is, they are not randomly distributed within the population. Albeit with some exceptions (discussed in the next section), it is our contention that much of the research has attended to them as though they are randomly distributed. We argue that greater attention to the contextualization of the classic developmental contexts (home, school, and community) of child health and development is required. This means more than simply attending to different facets of the developmental context. A comprehensive conceptual framework that connects social conditions at the family level to child health outcomes through the mediating influences of home, school, and community environments or subsystems is required (see Figure 5.1).

We do not take credit for the creation of this model given that many of the specific pathways have been proposed and tested in the extant literature. Indeed, in the sections that follow we provide brief reviews of current literature connecting various components of the model. We offer the model as a challenge to researchers to think about synthesizing the literature already produced into a coherent framework that can account for variation in child outcomes and the variations in findings across studies. We argue in particular that insufficient attention has been paid to understanding the process of how a family's position in the social structure shapes exposure to other, well-established risk factors (e.g., parenting practices, crowding in the home) across different developmental contexts (e.g., home, neighborhood, school) that are proximal and predictive of child psychopathology. Moreover, we argue that greater attention to understanding this process will ultimately assist in the development of more effective, targeted interventions.

The model presents four key pathways. Path 1 shows the direct link between proximal contexts and child psychopathology. It is the relationship that has garnered the overwhelming majority of attention in both the research literature

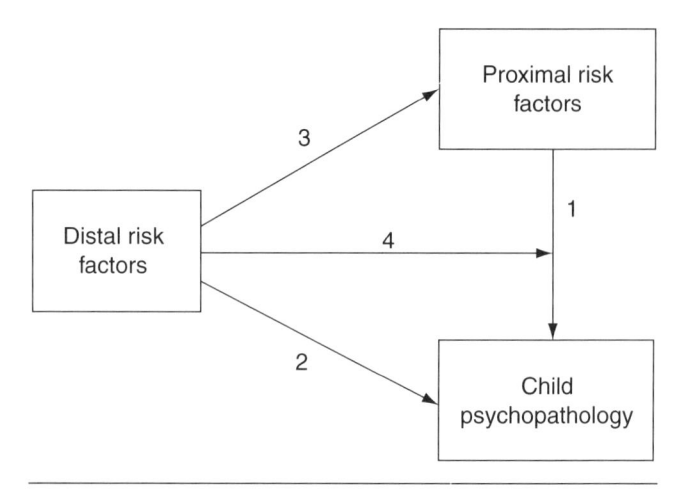

Figure 5.1 The relationship between distal and proximal risk factors on child psychopathology: A unifying framework.

and programmatic and policy development. Path 2 illustrates the direct effect of background social-structural disadvantage on child psychopathology, independent of the effect of more proximal factors. This is equivalent to controlling for background factors as discussed previously. The final two relationships move beyond direct, independent effects, identifying the links across various factors. We can think of these pathways as process models in the sense that Pearlin (1989) and others have conceptualized models linking stress to mental health outcomes. The process here begins with structural disadvantage and flows through proximal contexts to child psychopathology. It is a process because earlier or distal effects condition exposure to more proximal factors, which in turn produces differential health outcomes.

The first process is based on the social exposure hypothesis (see Turner & Lloyd, 1999; Turner, Wheaton, & Lloyd, 1995); background factors such as class, family structure, age, and gender exert their influence on child psychopathology, but they do so by undermining the social processes of the key normative proximal environments that directly impact the child. Consequently, poverty and other facets of social structure are causes of child psychopathology. But not all children who come from disadvantaged environments manifest mental health problems. Nor do all children who manifest mental health problems come from disadvantaged environments. The key is exposure to the intervening variables—the effectiveness of proximal environments that are largely, but not exclusively, determined by the background factors. Socioeconomic disadvantage creates a fertile environment for the development of child psychopathology because it *exposes* these children to increased levels of noxious stimuli within their proximal environments; the greater the level of exposure, the greater the risk.

The final process is based on the social vulnerability hypothesis (see Kessler, 1979; Kessler & McLeod, 1984; Kessler, Turner, & House, 1988): Children in disadvantaged families may not have the resources available to permit them to adequately prepare for or compensate for exposure. This hypothesis involves a somewhat different explanation for the impact of social factors on child health in that it is not exposure per se that leads to poor health outcomes, but rather reactivity to exposure to the noxious conditions. For example, maternal depression is a well-established risk factor (proximal) for child psychopathology (e.g., Orvaschel, Walsh-Allis, & Ye, 1988; Pevalin, Wade, & Brannigan, 2003; Wade, Pevalin, & Brannigan, 1999; Williams & Carmichael, 1991). Yet, the impact of this risk factor on child health is not likely to be the same for all families. The economic resources of the household may buffer the negative impact of maternal depression by providing greater opportunities and resources to cope with the illness (e.g., access to mental health care, opportunity to provide paid supportive care for both mother and child). Conversely, families who are poor will not be able to bring the same kind of resources to bear on the problem. At the extreme end of the distribution, female-headed single-parent families who are poor not only lack economic resources, but they are also disadvantaged in terms of the number of immediate caregivers. When a single parent becomes sick, there is often little or no support for the child. Therefore, the vulnerability hypothesis/pathway is somewhat different from the exposure pathway in the sense that not only do disadvantaged families suffer disproportionately more exposure to stress and strains, but also their resources and ability to cope with problems are seriously compromised as a result of their relative deprivation. We could add even greater complexity to the issue by including the intersection of additional structural factors such as race, age of mother, and so forth. Differential vulnerability challenges us to consider not only how proximal risk factors are distributed across social status characteristics, but also how social status may alter the effect of risk factors on child psychopathology.

This proposed pathway has been the most neglected in research on child psychopathology to date. But it is likely the most important from a programmatic and policy perspective. Framed against the literature on best practices, it suggests that not all groups will benefit equally from the same intervention. A targeted intervention based on established best practices may be more or less successful for some groups under certain conditions compared to other groups or under different conditions (McCracken, 2001). In the context of the example presented earlier, the kind of interventions enacted to deal with the problem of maternal depression may have differential efficacy when other characteristics (e.g., family structure) are taken into account. Simply controlling for these characteristics statistically is not sufficient to identify who may benefit and under what conditions.

In the next section, we provide a review of the proximal and distal risk factors across several disciplines including developmental and social psychology, criminology, sociology, and epidemiology. We also present research that has attempted to move beyond the independent, direct effects of various factors on child psychopathology to examine the links between factors through both social exposure and social vulnerability frameworks.

TOWARD A UNIFYING FRAMEWORK: A REVIEW OF CURRENT LITERATURE

Proximal Risk Factors of Child Psychopathology

With regard to the path between proximal factors and child psychopathology, an exhaustive review of the various risk factors at this level is beyond the scope of this chapter. In fact, just within the family itself, there is a dizzying amount of research on child psychopathology and behavior from both social psychology and human developmental perspectives (i.e., more than 5,000 published articles before 1995; see Zeitlin et al., 1995). We can classify as proximal risk factors those central environments in which the child lives, including family, school, neighborhood, and peer groups.

Risk factors within the family environment may include family dysfunction, maternal and paternal well-being and substance use, parental-child bonding and attachment, parenting skills such as supervision as well as hostile and punitive versus positive and consistent parenting, and child abuse and neglect. Poor parenting practices, especially harsh and inconsistent punishment and low levels of monitoring, have been correlated with, and predictive of, higher levels of antisocial behavior in children (Patterson, Reid, & Dishon, 1992; Shaw, Owens, Giovannelli, & Winslow, 2001; Tremblay et al., 1992; West, 1982; West & Farrington, 1973). In studies of early childhood and preadolescence, Fagot and Leve (1998) found that coercive parenting when the child was 18 months old was predictive of teacher-rated externalizing behaviors at age 5. Campbell and colleagues (Campbell, 1994; Campbell, Pierce, Moore, Marakovitz, & Newby, 1996) identified harsh parenting during preschool years as predictive of child behavior problems in elementary school. Children of families marked with high levels of conflict and negative family interaction are also prone to manifest elevated levels of mental health problems. Marital conflict and poor parent-child interactions are strongly associated with health problems among children (Hetherington, Cox, & Cox, 1982; Peterson & Zill, 1986; Wierson, Forehand, & McCombs, 1988). Others have identified a range of risk factors within the family environment that are associated with various manifestations of child psychopathology including both externalizing and internalizing behaviors such as ineffective family functioning (Henry, Moffitt, Robins, Earls, & Silva, 1993; Leblanc et al., 1991; Ruchkin, Eisemann, & Hägglöf, 1998; Tolan, 1987); marital problems, conflict, aggression, and distress (Depner, Leino, & Chun, 1992; Emery, 1982; Jouriles, Murphy, & O'Leary, 1989; Katz & Gottman 1993; Lahey et al., 1988; Shaw, Keenan, & Vondra, 1994); child neglect (Erickson & Egeland, 1996); physical, sexual, and verbal child abuse (Johnson et al., 2001; Kendler et al., 2000; Nelson, Heath, & Madden, 2002); parental alcoholism and substance use (Carbonneau et al., 1998; Martin, Romig, & Kirisci, 2000; Vitaro, Tremblay, & Zoccolillo, 1999); domestic violence (Acierno & Resnick, 1997; Maker & Kemmelmeier, 1998); family stress, negative life events, and family adversity (Barocas, Seifer, & Sameroff, 1985; Campbell et al., 1996; Heller, Baker, Henker, & Hinshaw, 1996); social support (Guidubaldi, Perry, & Nastasi, 1987); and maternal mental health (Beardslee, Gladstone, Wright, & Cooper, 2003; Canino, Bird, Rubio-Stipec, Bravo, & Alegria, 1990; Shaw et al., 1994; Wade et al., 1999). Whether some of these family factors are causal in the onset of the child's antisocial behavior or merely aggravating or prolonging the behavior in a reciprocal relationship is open to some debate (Anderson, Lytton, & Romney, 1986; Lytton, 2000), but the overwhelming evidence, both cross-sectional and longitudinal, point to family factors preceding the onset of behavioral problems.

The physical environment of the family and neighborhood, such as the play environment and physical safety, is also related to internalizing and externalizing behaviors (Attar, Guerra, & Tolan, 1994; Cohen & Brook, 1987; Elardo & Bradley, 1981). These proximal contextual factors, including such things as neighborhood safety and cohesion, residential stability, and the neighborhood environment (e.g., litter, absence of playgrounds, prevalence of crime), are linked to the development of child psychopathology (Eckenrode, Rowe, Laird, & Braithwaite, 1995; Lindgren, Harper, & Blackman, 1986; Melton, 1992; Wade et al., 1999). Community violence is also a consistent predictor of child psychosocial outcomes (Barbarin, Richter, & deWet, 2001).

What is salient for the role of proximal factors, specifically parenting and its relationship with antisocial behavior and psychopathology, is that it is generally seen as modifiable and thus represents a key area for intervention (see Barlow & Stewart-Brown, 2000; Yoshikawa, 1995). Intervention studies based on this premise include a mix of home-based (e.g., Olds & Eckenrode, 1997), center-based (e.g., Chicago Child Parent Center; see Reynolds, 1999, 2000), and integrated home and center-based models (e.g., Carolina Abecedarian Project, see Ramey & Campbell, 1984; Houston Parent-Child Development Center, see Johnson & Walker, 1987; Syracuse University Family Development Research Program, see Lally, Mangione, & Honig, 1988). Even the federally sponsored Head Start preschool program for low-income children contains intervention components directed toward several aspects of the family identified as strong predictors of development and child psychopathology, such as parenting practices and hostile parenting, parent-child bonding, and social and behavioral child development. Most of these child interventions were approximately two years in duration, but positive results have been observed long after the intervention (e.g., see Barlow & Stewart-Brown, 2000; Eckenrode et al., 2001; Olds & Eckenrode, 1997; Olds et al., 1998; Olds, Henderson, Kitzman, Cole, & Tatelbaum, 1999). One of the most common underlying themes of the interventions listed previously as well as most others (e.g., Montreal Longitudinal Experiment, see Tremblay et al., 1992; Tremblay, Pagni-Kurtz, Masse, Vitaro, & Pihl, 1995; High Scope Perry Study, see Weikart, Berrueta-Clement, Schweinhart, Barnett, & Epstein, 1984; Weikart, Schweinhart, & Barnes, 1993) is the overwhelming targeting of children living in disadvantaged social conditions. Clearly, these proximal risk factors that are targets of intervention do not occur randomly or haphazardly across the general population. Families experiencing socioeconomic disadvantage are more likely to be the recipients of these interventions because these proximal risk factors tend to cluster disproportionately among this population.

Distal Risk Factors of Child Psychopathology

If we explore some of the seminal work in psychiatric epidemiology across various countries, we see strong evidence for the direct effect of social structure on child psychopathology (Figure 5.1, Path 2). For example, in the Isle of Wight Study in Great Britain of a cohort of 10- to 11-year-olds, Rutter (1973) found that children experiencing economic hardship had significantly higher levels of mental health problems. The Midtown Manhattan Survey of Psychiatric Impairment in Urban Children in New York City focused on children ages 6–18 from 1,034 randomly selected families and 1,000 mothers on welfare (Langner et al., 1974; Langner, McCarthy, Gersten, Simca-Fagan, & Eisenberg, 1979; Srole, Langner, Micheal, Opler & Rennie, 1962). They found strong evidence that children of families on welfare were almost twice as likely to manifest impaired health and behavior ratings. In Canada, the Ontario Child Health Study examined a random sample of 3,294 children aged 4–16 from 1,869 families and identified children from families with very low incomes, receiving welfare, or both as significantly more likely to have at least one of four disorders—hyperactivity, conduct disorder, emotional disorder, and somatization—compared to other children; however, the finding for income was weaker when each disorder was examined separately (Offord, Boyle, & Jones, 1987; Offord, Boyle, & Racine, 1989). The link between a disadvantaged social structural environment and an increased prevalence of psychiatric disorder is even more alarming in light of their finding that 68.2 percent of children with one of the four disorders manifested at least one additional disorder (Offord, Boyle, Fleming, Blum, & Grant, 1989). As such, not only do they manifest significantly more disorders, but also the resulting impairment from psychiatric problems is increased with increased comorbidity. In one of the most ambitious research studies to test the direct effect of poverty on child health, Leventhal and Brooks-Gunn (2003) reported on the experimental randomized controlled trial intervention Moving to Opportunity. This project took families from public housing in poor neighborhoods and randomly placed them in near-poverty and nonpoor neighborhoods. The authors reported significant three-year differences in child mental health improvements, but only for boys compared to girls and only for those in the younger age cohort compared to older children.

Given the connection between social and economic deprivation and child health, the increasing poverty rates in the United States as well as in Canada point toward increasing prevalence rates among children (Corcoran & Chaudry, 1997; Rank & Hirschl, 1999). In fact, Corcoran and Chaudry (1997) found that one third of all children in the United States will experience at least one year of poverty during childhood, and 26 percent of Black adults and 10 percent of White adults experience poverty for more than 50 percent of their childhood. As a serious risk factor for the development of child psychopathology, the effect of poverty seems to persist well into early adulthood and further. But is there a specific threshold that defines when poverty becomes a risk factor? Exploring this question, some have examined the effect of relative income levels on health status, indicating an incremental effect of socioeconomic and income gradients on health (e.g., Goodman, 1999; Goodman, Huang, Wade, & Kahn, 2003; Wilkinson, 1996; Willms, 2002). For example, among adolescents, Goodman (1999) found that moving down five income categories, depressive symptomatology increased concomitantly. Moreover, relative individual-level income and relative school-level income were both related to depression (Goodman et al., 2003).

Race and ethnicity, though often difficult to disentangle from poverty, are also predictive of child psychopathology. For example, Ezpeleta, Keeler, Erkanli, Costello, and Angold (2001) found that ethnic minorities manifested higher levels of disruptive behaviors compared to Whites. Nyborg and Curry (2003) argued that among African American boys the higher prevalence of externalizing problems may be a result of perceived racism. Wagner, Lloyd, and Gil (2002) also found significant variation across race and ethnicity for both incidence and age of onset for teenage alcohol use disorders.

Among other components of social structure, family structure and changes in family structure have also been identified as important. Prevalence of child disorder is higher among children in single-parent families (e.g., Lipman, Boyle, Dooley, & Offord, 2002; Liu & Guo, 2000; O'Connor, Dunn, Jenkins, Pickering, & Rashbash, 2001; Pevalin et al., 2003; Rousseau, Drapeau, & Platt, 2000; Weitoft, Hjern, Haglund, & Rosen, 2003). Investigation on the effect of changes in family composition has found that family disruption is associated with deficits in children's behavior during the initial adjustment phase (Hetherington, 1979; Hetherington, Cox, & Cox, 1982; Shaw & Emery, 1987; Wallerstein & Kelly, 1975, 1980). Others have also found that the negative effects of marital separation on mental and physical health among children persist for years after the event (e.g., Avison & McAlpine, 1992; Guidubaldi, Cleminshaw, Perry, Nastasi & Lightel, 1986; Peterson & Zill, 1986; Rutter, 1971). Similar to those children of marital disruption, children of unwed mothers also manifest higher levels of behavioral disorders and lower levels of social competence, and this difference appears to be greatest among adolescents (Avison & McAlpine, 1992; Furstenberg, Brooks-Gunn, & Morgan, 1987).

Not all research, however, finds negative outcomes for children of divorced parents. In a meta-analysis of more than 90 different studies of psychopathology among children of divorced families, Amato and Keith (1991) argued that although some evidence was present for economic disadvantage as a determinant, the presence of family conflict tended to best predict mental health problems among children. In fact, they concluded that children from intact families with high levels of family conflict had lower psychological well-being compared to children of divorced families. But treating family conflict and family structure as independent of each other and arguing for the importance of family conflict over family structure neglects the potential of process. Family conflict may be a key variable, but we would argue that it is also an intervening variable. Family conflict certainly exists in intact families as well as divorced families, but it is more likely to occur in divorced families, as either a precipitating factor or a consequence of the event itself.

The Social Exposure Hypothesis: Social Conditions, Developmental Contexts, and Child Psychopathology

A history of parallel theoretical work across several disciplines has proposed an exposure-based model, presented in Figure 5.1 (Path 3 to Path 1), as a process to explain a variety of outcomes, including child IQ, health, health behavior, and delinquent behaviors. Although these literatures focus on different discipline-specific outcomes (e.g., criminogenic vs. health outcomes), they provide insight into the consequences of exposure to distal risk factors for child psychopathology (see Wade, 2001). For example, in criminology, Hirschi (1969) and Gottfredson and Hirschi (1990) argued that deviant behavior is largely the result of a deficit in self-control, which is itself a result of early negative interaction between parent and child. According to this theory, parental nurturance and proper discipline and training in the early childhood years are essential to the development of strong internal self-control among children. Ineffective child rearing, nurturance, and parental discipline inhibit the development of high levels of self-control, which leads to deviant or criminal behaviors. But ineffective parenting on all levels is largely a consequence of structural disadvantage in that these behaviors cluster disproportionately across social classes. Work by Jessor and colleagues (Donovan & Jessor, 1985; Jessor & Jessor, 1977) on problem behavior theory identified a connection between structural disadvantage, proximal family processes, and adolescent risk- and health-behavior problems. They argued that the development of a syndrome, not unlike the trait of self-control proposed by Gottfredson and Hirschi (1990), predisposes some children to be more prone to a diverse array of problem behaviors such as substance use, delinquency, risky sexual behavior, and risky driving behavior. Based on the Rochester Longitudinal Study, developmental psychologist Arnold Sameroff (1995, 1998) and colleagues (Sameroff, Seifer, Baldwin, & Baldwin, 1993; Sameroff, Seiver, & Zax, 1982; Sameroff, Seifer, Zax, & Greenspan, 1987) identified that exposure to 10 key family risk factors was cumulatively related to lower IQ among children. Five of these risks are social-structural (i.e., mother not attending high school, head of household employed in a semiskilled occupation, father not living in the home, minority group status, and four or more children living in the household) and five were proximal within the family (i.e., maternal mental illness, severe maternal anxiety, little positive mother-child interaction, high exposure to stressful events, rigid maternal values on child development). Whereas Sameroff (1998) stressed the importance of what he defines as intermediate variables (maternal mental illness) and proximal variables (mother-child interaction), he also acknowledged the importance of distal factors in this development as a process by creating a trajectory that renders youths more likely to suffer lower competence and increased mental health problems from birth to 18 years of age.

Within criminology, Loeber and Stouthamer-Loeber (1986), in a review of more than 30 studies, found strong support for both socioeconomic disadvantage and poor parent-child relations leading to children's behavior problems and delinquency, suggesting a cascading of risk factors where the familial environment, specifically parenting practices, mediates the effect of a disadvantaged social-structural background. In a thorough review across various disciplines (e.g., sociology, criminology, social and developmental psychology) of the social-structural and proximal determinants of child psychopathology, Gotlib and Avison (1993) also suggested an intervening process whereby structural disadvantage causes child psychopathology through exposure to marital discord and poor child-parent bonds. There is also some empirical evidence connecting social and structural disadvantage (poverty, parental education and occupation, race and ethnic minority, single-parent status, teenager at birth of child) to child psychopathology through increased exposure to various dimensions of poor family interaction (i.e., family functioning, parent-child interaction and parenting, and maternal and paternal mental illness and substance use; Brody et al., 2003; Dodge, Bates, & Pettit, 1990; Haapsalano & Tremblay, 1994; Henry et al., 1993; Jackson, 2003; Jackson, Brooks-Gunn, Huang, & Glassman, 2000; Kilgore, Snyder, & Lentz, 2000; Marchand & Hock, 1998; McLoyd, 1990, 1998; O'Connor et al., 2001; Olson, Ceballo, & Park, 2002; Patterson et al., 1992; Ruchkin et al., 1998; Snyder & Patterson, 1995; Spieker, Larson, Lewis, Keller, & Gilchrist, 1999; Tolan, 1987; Wakschlag & Hans, 1999; West, 1982; Widom, 1991). For example, Conger, Ge, Elder, Lorenz, & Simons (1994) investigated the role of economic pressure on parenting and found that coercive disagreements between spouses over financial matters were associated with increased hostility in their parenting, which in turn led to increased behavioral problems in their adolescent children. Jackson (2003) and Jackson et al. (2000) found that maternal education and financial strain were linked to both maternal depression and quality of parenting, which were linked to child behavior problems. Finally, the interventions discussed previously targeting proximal risk factors also reflect this process. Though they focus on proximal context for the actual intervention, they target children who are most at risk for exposure—children from impoverished backgrounds including poverty, racial and ethnic minority groups, and teenage single parents.

The Social Vulnerability Hypothesis: Social Conditions Moderating the Effect of Proximal Risk Factors on Child Psychopathology

It appears clear from this review that social-structural disadvantage provides increased exposure to these proximal factors, leading ultimately to an increased likelihood of child psychopathology. This framework implies that the process will be equivalent for all children, across all levels of a specific social-structural status. But children and families possess differential resources that may enable them to more adequately prepare for or compensate for exposure. In the preceding section, we discussed that the link between maternal depression and child outcomes may be different depending on family structure. Although the likelihood of maternal depression among recently separated and divorced single mothers is higher than among mothers in two-parent families (Cairney, Thorpe, Rietschlin, & Avison, 1999; Wade & Pevalin, 2004), maternal depression still exists in many two-parent families. And where it exists, regardless of family structure, the exposure to this risk factor is similar. Yet, the consequences of maternal depression on the child may be different based in part on the resources that different family units have available to effectively compensate for this exposure—that is, instead of maternal depression being just merely a product of the cumulative or total exposure to risk factors, families and children may be differentially susceptible based on their social conditions. Proximal risk factors will have a differential impact on child outcomes depending on the characteristics of various subpopulations.

To explore this avenue, it is necessary to move beyond the simple additive research models that are commonly employed and begin to attend to the conditional relationships between distal and proximal risk factors. For example, Grzywacz, Almeida, Neupert, and Ettner (2004) found that although both education status and daily stressors predicted daily physical health symptoms and daily reported negative affect, there was also a significant interaction between them— that is, the stressor-health relationship was not merely a matter of differential exposure based on education. Education appears to buffer (protect) persons from the negative consequences of exposure.

This process can also be illustrated by a comparison of recent analyses on child behavioral outcomes. In a recent analysis by Nagin and Tremblay (2000) of their longitudinal study of boys identified at kindergarten as displaying high levels of opposition and hyperactivity, they found that low levels of maternal education and teenage onset of childbearing are important predictors of persistent high levels of aggression. In this analysis, structural circumstances such as age of the mother, number of children in the household, and having a single parent raised the likelihood of boys' increasing levels of antisocial behavior over time or being less likely to reduce levels in those already at a high level. In an analysis of the National Longitudinal Survey of Children and Youth (Pevalin et al., 2003), however, we found that the predictors of antisocial behavior varied across gender. Similar to the results of Nagin and Trembley (2000), our results for boys centered around structural factors and included age of mother, number of children in the household, and single-parent status. Among girls, however, these structural factors had little effect. Investigation of the proximal family context showed that although maternal depression was predictive of antisocial behavior for both boys and girls, positive parenting was significant for girls only. Hostile parenting was significant for both girls and boys in predicting an increase in antisocial behavior among those originally categorized in the lowest-risk group, but reductions in hostile parenting behavior significantly reduced antisocial behavior only among girls. Findings by Becker and McCloskey (2002) support the differential effect of structural factors and parenting factors across boys and girls. They found that family violence predicted conduct problems and delinquency among girls but failed to predict conduct problems or delinquency in boys.

From a population perspective, these results suggest that structural factors may have relatively greater importance in the development and stability of antisocial behavior for boys than for girls. Perhaps girls may be more affected by family processes than boys; factors that have traditionally been the target of intervention programs. Attention to potential differences across groups, whether based on gender, poverty, family structure, age, or another factor, will provide more clarity as to whether social and structural factors condition the relationship between proximal risks and child psychopathology and provide insight as to why some interventions may work for some groups but not others.

THE CONSTELLATION OF SOCIAL STRUCTURE AND SOCIOECONOMIC STATUS: THE MULTIPLEXITY OF DISTAL RISK FACTORS

Up to this point, we have identified an array of various social-structural determinants including gender, family structure, education, income, occupational status, race and ethnicity, and age. We have presented these determinants as factors that condition more proximal risk factors leading to child psychopathology through exposure. We have argued that it is also important to assess whether background factors may moderate the relationship between proximal risk factors and child health—that is, to explore whether exposure to various proximal risk factors may be more deleterious for some children compared to others.

Throughout this discussion, we have presented these distal factors as additive in their effect on these various processes. However, this is unlikely to be the case. Quite simply, neither individuals nor families occupy single sociodemographic categories (e.g., families can be poor, non-White, and headed by a teenage single mother). Because our concern is with social-structural determinants of illness and disease, we must attend to how families are organized within the structure of modern society. This necessitates recognition that this structure is multiplex, and therefore we must consider the health consequences of occupying multiple-status positions simultaneously. Dimensions of social position cannot be conceptualized individually but need to be considered as a constellation. Yet, most social and child epidemiologic research focuses on the additive relationships between distal risk factors and health outcomes.

As presented previously, an impressive body of research has documented relationships between sociodemographic risk factors and health. Indeed, documenting the effect of these variables on health has become the mainstay of population health research. Virtually all of this work uses a similar analytic and conceptual approach to the study of social differences in health. First, the population is categorized into social groups usually based on income, education, occupation, gender, age, or marital status. Next, differences in the prevalence of disease are documented across one or more of these categories; this, in fact, is considered evidence of social differentials in illness and disease. Sometimes, multivariate statistical models are used to document, for example, income differences in disease while controlling for other factors simultaneously (e.g., age, gender, marital status, or any combination of these). The implicit assumption in this approach is that the variable of interest (in this example, income) is a *master status*. In other words, income differences for a particular outcome, net of other factors, suggest that economic factors rather than gender or age or marital status are the most important structural determinants of illness (i.e., to be poor, regardless of age and sex, increases the likelihood of ill health).

Although it is important to better understand how specific aspects of social structure influence health and well-being, we must also recognize that this approach tends to obscure the fact that master statuses are problematic in societies stratified hierarchically across a number of different factors. In other words, inequality is linked not to a single status but to multiple, intersecting positions. In North American society, for example, people are stratified not only by income, education, or occupation but by gender, family structure, age, and race as well. People do not occupy single social positions; they occupy multiple positions. Social structure, then, cannot be defined by just socioeconomic status; it is composed of many bases of inequality.

This is not a new idea in sociology even though relatively little work explicitly makes reference to the multiplexity of social status. For example, sociologists interested in examining the mental and physical health consequences of occupying two or more disadvantaged social positions have proposed the double or multiple-jeopardy hypothesis (e.g., Clark, Maddox, & Steinhauser, 1993; Dowd & Bengtson, 1978; Ferraro & Farmer, 1996; Markides, Timbers, & Osberg, 1984). Most of this work has focused on age and race and the interactive effect that these two measures of social position have on mortality and morbidity. From a conceptual point of view, the importance of this work lies in the explicit recognition that the experience of old age is not uniform across other social categories. Rather, an important intersection between variables like age and race/ethnicity leads to unique, compounded structural disadvantages. Quite simply, to be old is to be generally disadvantaged in Western society. But to be old and Black is to occupy a more precarious position compared to someone who is old and White. Multiple jeopardy is used in this context to recognize that the systems of inequality (e.g., gender, socioeconomic status, race) operate simultaneously to sift and sort individuals into hierarchies, leading to the differential distribution of health and well-being that is characteristic of modern societies.

In the literature of the sociology of aging, McMullin (1995, 2000) also discussed the theoretical importance of considering intersecting systems of social inequality. She used the relationship between gender and social class as the starting point for her argument. Many feminist scholars argue that sociology's traditional concern with the study of the impact of social class on personal circumstances disregards the fact that modern Western societies are patriarchal. Therefore, the influence of social class on determining access to resources such as wealth is different for men than for women. Women in lower socioeconomic positions, unlike men in similar socioeconomic positions, suffer the double disadvantage of living in both a capitalist and a patriarchal system where social advantages are distributed on the basis of socioeconomic status and gender. McMullin (1995) argued that we must theorize about how all of these social structures influence personal circumstances simultaneously rather than simply focus on one aspect of social stratification.

These bodies of work suggest a new direction for sociologists and others interested in understanding the social determinants of child psychopathology. To gain a more complete grasp of how various social and economic factors may operate to influence both proximal risk factors and child health necessitates an understanding as to how they may work in tangent with each other as a constellation of social-structural disadvantage. This creates both conceptual and methodological challenges. From a conceptual standpoint, more attention must be paid to how various dimensions may interact with each other. Similar to our discussion on social vulnerability and the conditional nature of relationships, we can also frame this argument as the interaction between multiple occupancies in the various roles. For example, in the United States, being Black is generally considered a structural risk factor for children. Moreover, poverty is another risk factor and a strong determinant of child health. But does being Black *and* poor increase a child's risk for psychopathology beyond being Black *or* poor? We can further increase the complexity of status by including gender. It is well established that gender differences in depression emerge at age 14, with females being about twice as likely to manifest depression starting at this age compared to males (Wade, Cairney, & Pevalin, 2002). Though all three factors are predictive of mental health problems separately, does occupying additional statuses increase a child's risk? In this example, is the gap in depression between male and female adolescents consistent across race *or* poverty? Is the gap consistent across race *and* poverty?

From a methodological perspective, researchers must pay greater attention to sampling and sample sizes to ensure that specific subgroups of interest are included in any sampling frame and that the samples of each subgroup are large enough to facilitate analysis. For example, the National Longitudinal Survey of Adolescent Health (AddHealth; see Udry, 1997) was attentive to this very question in its design. The survey deliberately oversampled from the population of Black high-income students to provide a large enough sample to examine the multiplexity of these two social-structural positions. In one analysis using the AddHealth data examining risk behavior, specifically weapon-related violence, cigarette and alcohol use, suicidal thoughts or attempts, and sexual intercourse, Blum et al. (2000) looked at the multiplexity of gender, race and ethnicity, income, and family structure independently and with two-way and three-way interactions. They reported only the results of the main effects, arguing that the models that included the interaction terms did not significantly improve the model fit. However, whether the interactions improve the model fit is only one issue. Significant interactions between any of these factors implies that the factors are not independent of one another—that is, the effect of one status on any of these outcomes may be conditional upon the level of another status. Coming back to our earlier example, the effect of being Black on these outcomes may or may not be contingent upon their poverty status, their gender, or both.

SUMMARY

In this chapter, we presented a sociological perspective that emphasizes the need to attend more to the primacy of social-structural disadvantage as a distal risk factor for child psychopathology and other negative health outcomes. We presented a model to move beyond merely controlling for the independent effects of social structure by describing two distinct but overlapping processes—social exposure and social vulnerability—and how they may expose children to differential levels of proximal risks and how they may condition the effect of proximal risk factors on child psychopathology. This model unifies existing literature across several disciplines including sociology, epidemiology, psychology, and criminology within a common, mutually inclusive causal framework to better inform research and interventions. We also argued that even acknowledging the primacy of social structure in this process may still not be sufficient. To simply include social-structural factors in any statistical model in an additive fashion or test statistical interactions between social structural factors and proximal risk factors neglects the multiplexity of social status. Children occupy several social positions simultaneously, creating uniquely disadvantaged subpopulations. As a discipline, sociology is as guilty as others for not attending to the constellation of social-structural disadvantage. However, given sociology's disciplinary focus on social structure, social stratification, and social problems, sociologists are in a unique position to correct this current deficit. Assessing how these constellations may influence proximal risk factors and child psychopathology offers enhanced opportunities for better understanding through research. And it offers the potential for more efficacious interventions that better target resources to those who may benefit while providing further insight for the development of new interventions that may address children with different socioeconomic constellations.

To conclude, we return to the metaphor of a running race among children as a way to examine the hierarchical ranking of members of society. As is true in all other races, this race will certainly result in both winners and losers. People will be stratified within society, occupying higher or lower social positions. This is not to imply that the resulting social hierarchy is necessarily unjust. Within any democratic meritocracy, it is assumed, rightly or wrongly, that people have opportunities to move up in the social hierarchy if they work hard enough. The social injustice occurs when the opportunity for upward mobility for some children, regardless of personal ability, is blocked or severely limited through no fault of their own. As scientists, clinicians, policy makers, and community leaders, it is our collective responsibility to attend to social-structural disadvantages because, as we argue, they are central determinants in the development of child psychopathology.

REFERENCES

Acierno, R., & Resnick, H. S. (1997). Health impact of interpersonal violence 1: Prevalence rates, case identification, and risk factors for sexual assault, physical assault, and domestic violence in men and women. *Behavioral Medicine, 23,* 53–64.

Amato, P. R., & Keith, B. (1991). Parental divorce and the well-being of children: A meta-analysis. *Psychological Bulletin, 110,* 26–46.

Anderson, K. E., Lytton, H., & Romney, D. M. (1986). Mothers' interactions with normal and conduct-disordered boys—who affects whom? *Developmental Psychology, 22,* 604–609.

Attar, B. K., Guerra, N. G., & Tolan, P. H. (1994). Neighborhood disadvantage, stressful life events, and adjustment in urban elementary school children. *Journal of Clinical Child Psychology, 23,* 391–400.

Avison, W. R., & McAlpine, D. D. (1992). Gender differences in symptoms of depression among adolescents. *Journal of Health and Social Behavior, 33,* 77–96.

Barbarin, O. A., Richter, L., & deWet, T. (2001). Exposure to violence, coping resources, and psychological adjustment of South African children. *American Journal of Orthopsychiatry, 71,* 16–25.

Barlow, J., & Stewart-Brown, S. (2000). Behavior problems and group-based parent education programs. *Journal of Developmental and Behavioral Pediatrics 21,* 356–370.

Barocas, R., Seifer, R., & Sameroff, A. J. (1985). Defining environmental risk: Multiple dimensions of psychological vulnerability. *American Journal of Community Psychology, 13,* 433–447.

Beardslee, W. R., Gladstone, T. R., Wright, E. J., & Cooper, A. B. (2003). A family-based approach to the prevention of depressive symptoms in children at risk: Evidence of parental and child change. *Pediatrics, 112,* 119–131.

Becker, K. B., & McCloskey, L. A. (2002). Attention and conduct problems in children exposed to family violence. *American Journal of Orthopsychiatry, 72,* 83–91.

Belsky, J. (1984). The determinants of parenting: A process model. *Child Development, 55,* 83–96.

Berkman, L. F., & Kawachi, I. (2000). *Social epidemiology.* New York: Oxford University Press.

Blum, R. W., Beuhring, T., Shew, M. L., Bearinger, L. H., Sieving, R. E., & Resnick, M. D. (2000). The effects of race/ethnicity, income, and family structure on adolescent risk behaviors. *American Journal of Public Health, 90,* 1879–1884.

Brody, G. H., Ge, X., Kim, S. Y., Murry, V. M., Simons, R. L., Gibbons, F. X., et al. (2003). Neighborhood disadvantage moderates associations of parenting and older sibling problems, attitudes and behaviour with conduct disorders in African American children. *Journal of Consulting and Clinical Psychology, 71,* 211–222.

Bronfenbrenner, U. (1979). *The ecology of human development: Experiments by nature and design.* Cambridge, MA: Harvard University Press.

Cairney, J., Boyle, M. H., Lipman, E. L., & Racine, Y. (2004). Single mothers and the use of professionals for mental health care reasons. *Social Science and Medicine, 59*(12), 2535–2546.

Cairney, J., Boyle, M., Offord, D. R., & Racine, Y. (2003). Stress, social support and depression in single and married mothers. *Social Psychiatry and Psychiatric Epidemiology, 38,* 442–449.

Cairney, J., Thorpe, C., Rietschlin, J., & Avison, W. R. (1999). 12-month prevalence of depression among single and married mothers in 1994. National Population Health Survey. *Canadian Journal of Public Health, 90,* 320–324.

Campbell, S. B. (1994). Hard-to-manage preschool boys—externalizing behaviour, social competence, and family context at 2-year follow-up. *Journal of Abnormal Child Psychology, 22,* 147–166.

Campbell, S. B., Pierce, E. W., Moore, G., Marakovitz, S., & Newby, K. (1996). Boys' externalizing problems at elementary school age: Pathways from early behavior problems, maternal control, and family stress. *Development and Psychopathology, 8,* 701–719.

Canino, G. J., Bird, H. R., Rubio-Stipec, M., Bravo, M., & Alegria, M. (1990). Children of parents with psychiatric disorder in the community. *Journal of the American Academy of Child and Adolescent Psychiatry, 29,* 398–406.

Carbonneau, R., Tremblay, R. E., Vitaro, F., Dobkin, P. L., Saucier, J. F., & Pihl, R. O. (1998). Paternal alcoholism, paternal absence and the development of problem behaviors in boys from age six to twelve years. *Journal of Studies of Alcohol, 59,* 387–398.

Clark, D. O., Maddox, G. L., & Steinhauser, K. (1993). Race, aging and functional health. *Journal of Aging and Health, 5,* 537–554.

Cohen, P., & Brook, J. (1987). Family factors related to the persistence of psychopathology in childhood and adolescence. *Psychiatry, 50,* 332–345.

Conger, R. D., Ge, X. J., Elder, G. H., Lorenz, F. O., & Simons R. L. (1994). Economic stress, coercive family process, and developmental problems of adolescents. *Child Development, 65,* 541–561.

Corcoran, M. E., & Chaudry, A. (1997). The dynamics of childhood poverty. *Future of Children, 7,* 40–54.

Depner, C. E., Leino, E. V., & Chun, A. (1992). Interparental conflict and child adjustment: A decade review and meta-analysis. *Family and Conciliation Courts Review, 30,* 323–341.

Diez-Roux, A. V. (1998). Bringing context back into epidemiology: Variables and fallacies in multilevel analysis. *American Journal of Public Health, 88,* 216–222.

Dodge, K. A., Bates, J. E., & Pettit, G. S. (1990). Mechanisms in the cycle of violence. *Science, 250,* 1678–1683.

Donovan, J. E., & Jessor, R. (1985). Structure of problem behavior in adolescence and young adulthood. *Journal of Consulting and Clinical Psychology, 53,* 890–904.

Dowd, J. J., & Bengtson, V. L. (1978). Aging in minority populations: An examination of the double jeopardy hypothesis. *Journal of Gerontology, 33,* 427–436.

Eckenrode, J., Rowe, E., Laird, M., & Braithwaite, J. (1995). Mobility as a mediator of the effects of child maltreatment on academic performance. *Child Development, 66,* 1130–1142.

Eckenrode, J., Zielinski, D., Smith. E., Marcynyszyn, L. A., Henderson, C. R., Kitzman, H., et al. (2001). Child maltreatment and the early onset of problem behaviors: Can a program of nurse home visitation break the link? *Development and Psychopathology, 13,* 873–890.

Elardo, R., & Bradley, R. H. (1981). The Home Observation of Measurement of the Environment (HOME) scale: A review of research. *Developmental Review, 1,* 113–145.

Emery, R. E. (1982). Interparental conflict and the children of discord and divorce. *Psychological Bulletin, 92,* 310–330.

Erickson, M., & Egeland, B. (1996). Child neglect. In J. Briere & L. Berliner (Eds.), *The APSAC handbook of child maltreatment* (pp. 4–20). Thousand Oaks, CA: Sage.

Evans, R. G., Barer, M. L., & Marmor, T. R. (Eds.). (1994). *Why are some people healthy and others not?* Hawthorne, NY: Aldine de Gryter.

Ezpeleta, L., Keeler, G., Erkanli, A., Costello, E. J., & Angold, A. (2001). Epidemiology of psychiatric disability in childhood and adolescence. *Journal of Child Psychology and Psychiatry and Allied Disciplines, 42,* 901–914.

Fagot, B. I., & Leve, L. D. (1998). Teacher ratings of externalizing behavior at school entry for boys and girls. Similar early predictors and different correlates. *Journal of Child Psychology and Psychiatry and Allied Disciplines, 39,* 555–566.

Ferraro, K. F., & Farmer, M. M. (1996). Double jeopardy to health hypothesis for African Americans: Analysis and critique. *Journal of Health and Social Behavior, 37,* 27–43.

Furstenberg, F. F., Brooks-Gunn, J., & Morgan, S. P. (1987). *Adolescent mothers in later life.* New York: Cambridge University Press.

Glueck, S., & Glueck, E. (1950). *Unraveling juvenile delinquency.* Cambridge, MA: Harvard University Press.

Goodman, E. (1999). The role of socioeconomic status gradients in explaining differences in U.S. adolescents' health. *American Journal of Public Health, 89,* 1522–1528.

Goodman, E., Huang, B., Wade, T. J., & Kahn, R. S. (2003). A multilevel analysis of the relation of socioeconomic status to adolescent depressive symptoms: Does school context matter? *Journal of Pediatrics, 143,* 451–546.

Gotlib, I. H., & Avison, W. R. (1993). Children at risk for psychopathology. In C. G. Costello (Ed.), *Basic issues in psychopathology* (pp. 271–319). Stanford, CA: Stanford University Press.

Gottfredson, M., & Hirschi, T. (1990). *A general theory of crime.* Stanford, CA: Stanford University Press.

Gough, H. G. (1948). A sociological theory of psychopathy. *American Journal of Sociology, 53,* 359–366.

Grzywacz, J. G., Almeida, D. M., Neupert, S. D., & Ettner, S. L. (2004). Socioeconomic status and health: A micro-level analysis of exposure and vulnerability to daily stressors. *Journal of Health and Social Behavior, 45,* 1–16.

Guidubaldi, J., Cleminshaw, H. K., Perry, J. D., Nastasi, B. K., & Lightel, J. (1986). The role of selected family environmental factors in children's post-divorce adjustment. *Family Relations, 35,* 141–151.

Guidubaldi, J., Perry, J., & Nastasi, B. K. (1987). Growing up in a divorced family: Initial and long-term perspectives on children's adjustment. *Applied Social Psychology Annual, 7,* 202–237.

Haapsalano, J., & Tremblay, R. E. (1994). Physically aggressive boys from ages 6 to 12—family background, parenting behavior, and prediction of delinquency. *Journal of Consulting and Clinical Psychology, 62,* 1044–1052.

Heller, T. L., Baker, B. L., Henker, B., & Hinshaw, S. P. (1996). Externalizing behavior and cognitive functioning from preschool to first grade: Stability and predictors. *Journal of Clinical Child Psychology, 25,* 376–387.

Henry, B., Moffitt, T. E., Robins, L. N., Earls, F., & Silva, P. A. (1993). Early family predictors of child and adolescent antisocial behaviour: Who are the mothers of delinquents? *Criminal Behavior and Mental Health, 3,* 97–118.

Hetherington, E. M. (1979). Divorce: A child's perspective. *American Psychologist, 34,* 851–858.

Hetherington, M. E., Cox, M. E., & Cox, R. (1982). Effects of divorce of parents and children. In M. Lamb (Ed.), *Non-traditional families* (pp. 233–288). Hillsdale, NJ: Erlbaum.

Hirschi, T. (1969). *Causes of delinquency.* Berkeley: University of California Press.

House, J. S., Lepkowski, J. M., Kinney, A. M., Mero, R. P., Kessler, R. C., & Herzog, A. R. (1994). The social stratification of aging and health. *Journal of Health and Social Behavior, 35,* 213–234.

Jackson, A. P. (2003). The effects of family and neighborhood characteristics on the behavioral and cognitive development of poor Black children: A longitudinal study. *American Journal of Community Psychology, 32,* 175–186.

Jackson, A. P., Brooks-Gunn, J., Huang, C. C., & Glassman, M. (2000). Single mothers in low-wage jobs: Financial strain, parenting, and preschoolers' outcomes. *Child Development, 71,* 1409–1423.

Jessor, R., & Jessor, S. L. (1977). *Problem behavior and psychosocial development: A longitudinal study of youth*. New York: Academic Press.

Johnson, D. L., & Walker, T. (1987). Primary prevention of behavior problems in Mexican-American children. *American Journal of Community Psychology, 15*, 375–385.

Johnson, J. G., Cohen, P., Smailes, E. M., Skodol, A. E., Brown, J., & Oldham, J. M. (2001). Childhood verbal abuse and risk for personality disorders during adolescence and early adulthood. *Comprehensive Psychiatry, 24*, 16–23.

Jouriles, E. N., Murphy, C. M., & O'Leary, K. E. (1989). Interpersonal aggression, marital discord and child problems. *Journal of Consulting and Clinical Psychology, 57*, 453–455.

Kaplan, G. A., & Keil, J. E. (1993). Socioeconomic factors and cardiovascular disease: A review of the literature. *Circulation, 88*, 1973–1994.

Katz, L. F., & Gottman, J. M. (1993). Patterns of marital conflict predict children's internalizing and externalizing behaviors. *Developmental Psychology, 29*, 940–950.

Kendler, K. S., Bulik, C. M., Silberg, J., Hettema, J. M., Myers, J., & Prescott, C. A. (2000). Childhood sexual abuse and adult psychiatric and substance use disorders in women: An epidemiological and co-twin control analysis. *Archives of General Psychiatry, 57*, 953–959.

Kessler, R. C. (1979). A strategy for studying differential vulnerability to the psychological consequences of stress. *Journal of Health and Social Behavior, 20*, 100–108.

Kessler, R., & McLeod, J. (1984). Sex differences in vulnerability to undesirable life events. *American Sociological Review, 49*, 620–631.

Kessler, R. C., Turner, J. B., & House, J. S. (1988). Effects of unemployment on health in a community survey: Main, modifying, and mediating effects. *Journal of Health and Social Behavior, 44*, 69–85.

Kilgore, K., Snyder, J., & Lentz, C. (2000). The contribution of parental discipline, parental monitoring, and school risk to early-onset conduct problems in African American boys and girls. *Developmental Psychology, 36*, 835–845.

Lahey, B. B., Hartdagen, S. E., Frick, P. J., McBurnett, K., Conner, R., & Hynd, G. W. (1988). Conduct disorder: Parsing the confounded relation to parental divorce and antisocial personality. *Journal of Abnormal Psychology, 97*, 334–337.

Lally, J. R., Mangione, P. L., & Honig, A. S. (1988). The Syracuse University Family Development Research Program: Long-range impact on an early intervention with low-income children and their families. In D. Powell (Ed.), *Parent education as early childhood intervention* (pp. 79–104). Norwood, NJ: Ablex.

Langner, T. S., Gersten, J. C., Green, E. L., Eisenberg, J. G., Herson, J. H., & McCarthy, E. D. (1974). Treatment of psychological disorders among urban children. *Journal of Consulting and Clinical Psychology, 42*, 170–179.

Langner, T. S., McCarthy, E. D., Gersten, J. C., Simcha-Fagan, O., & Eisenberg, J. G. (1979). Factors in children's behavior and mental health over time: The family research project. In R. G. Simmons (Ed.), *Research in community and mental health* (Vol. 1, pp. 127–181). Greenwich, CT: JAI Press.

LeBlanc, M., McDuff, P., Charlebois, P., Gagnon, C., Larrivee, S., & Tremblay, R. E. (1991). Social and psychological consequences, at 10 years old, of an earlier onset of self-reported delinquency. *Psychiatry, 54*, 133–147.

Leventhal, T., & Brooks-Gunn, J. (2003). Moving to opportunity: An experimental study of neighbourhood effects on mental health. *American Journal of Public Health, 93*, 1576–1582.

Lindgren, S. D., Harper, D. C., & Blackman, J. A. (1986). Environmental influences and perinatal risk factors in high-risk children. *Journal of Pediatric Psychology, 11*, 531–547.

Link, B. G., & Phelan, J. (1995). Social conditions as fundamental causes of disease. *Journal of Health and Social Behavior, Extra Issue*, 80–94.

Link, B., & Phelan, J. (2000). Evaluating the fundamental cause explanation for social disparities in health. In C. Bird, P. Conrad, & A Fremont (Eds.), *The handbook of medical sociology* (pp. 33–46). Upper Saddle River, NJ: Prentice Hall.

Lipman, E. L., Boyle, M. H., Dooley, M. D., & Offord, D. R. (2002). Child well-being in single-mother families. *Journal of the American Academy of Child and Adolescent Psychiatry, 41*, 75–82.

Liu, X., & Guo, C. (2000). Behavioral and emotional problems in Chinese children of divorced parents. *Journal of the American Academy of Child and Adolescent Psychiatry, 39*, 896–903.

Loeber, R., & Stouthamer-Loeber, M. (1986). Family factors as correlates and predictors of delinquency. In M. Tonry & N. Morris (Eds.), *Crime and justice: An annual review of research* (Vol. 7, pp. 29–149). Chicago: University of Chicago Press.

Lynch, J. W., Kaplan, G. A., Cohen, R. D., Tuomilehto, J., & Salonen, J. T. (1996). Do cardiovascular risk factors explain the relation between socioeconomic status, risk of all-cause mortality, cardiovascular mortality, and acute myocardial infarction? *American Journal of Epidemiology, 144*, 934–942.

Lytton, H. (2000). Toward a model of family-environmental and child-biological influence on development. *Developmental Review, 20*, 150–179.

Mackenbach, J. P., & Kunst, A. E. (1997). Measuring the magnitude of socio-economic inequalities in health: An overview of available measures illustrated with two examples from Europe. *Social Science and Medicine, 44*, 757–771.

Maker, A. H., & Kemmelmeier, M. (1998). Long term psychological consequences in women witnessing parental physical conflict and experiencing abuse in childhood. *Journal of Interpersonal Violence, 13*, 574–590.

Marchand, J. F., & Hock, E. (1998). The relation of problem behaviors in preschool children to depressive symptoms in mothers and fathers. *Journal of Genetic Psychology, 159*, 353–356.

Markides, K. S., Timbers, D. M., & Osberg, J. S. (1984). Aging and health: A longitudinal study. *Archives of Gerontology and Geriatrics, 3,* 33–49.

Martin, C. S., Romig, C. J., & Kirisci, L. (2000). *DSM-IV* learning disorders in 10- to 12-year-old boys with and without a parental history of substance use disorders. *Prevention Science, 1,* 107–113.

McCracken, A. (2001). The dangers of best practices. *Foundation News and Commentary, 3,* 30–32.

McLoyd, V. C. (1998). Socio-economic disadvantage and child development. *American Psychologist, 53,* 185–204.

McLoyd, V. C. (1990). The impact of economic hardship on Black families and children: Psychological distress, parenting, and socioemotional development. *Child Development, 61,* 311–346.

McMullin, J. A. (2000). Diversity and the state of sociological aging theory. *Gerontologist, 40,* 517–530.

McMullin, J. A. (1995). Theorizing age and gender relations. In S. Arber and J. Ginn (Eds.), *Conceptualizing gender and ageing: A sociological approach* (pp. 30–41). Buckingham, England: Open University Press.

Melton, G. B. (1992). It's time for neighborhood research and action. *Child Abuse and Neglect, 16,* 909–913.

Nagin, D. S., & Tremblay, R. E. (2000). Parental and early childhood predictors of persistent physical aggression in boys from kindergarten to high school. *Archives of General Psychiatry, 58,* 389–394.

Nelson, E., Heath, A., & Madden, P. (2002). Association between self-reported childhood sexual abuse and adverse psychosocial outcomes: Results from a twin study. *Archives of General Psychiatry, 59,* 139–146.

Nyborg, V. M., & Curry, J. F. (2003). The impact of perceived racism: Psychological symptoms among African American boys. *Journal of Clinical Child and Adolescent Psychology, 32,* 258–266.

O'Connor, T. G., Dunn, J., Jenkins, J. M., Pickering, K., & Rasbash, J. (2001). Family settings and children's adjustment: Differential adjustment within and across families. *British Journal of Psychiatry, 179,* 110–115.

Offord, D. R., Boyle, M. H., Fleming, J. E., Blum, H. M., & Grant, N. I. (1989). Ontario child health study: Summary of selected results. *Canadian Journal of Psychiatry, 34,* 483–491.

Offord, D. R., Boyle, M. H., & Jones, B. R. (1987). Psychiatric disorder and poor school performance among welfare children in Ontario. *Canadian Journal of Psychiatry, 32,* 518–525.

Offord, D. R., Boyle, M. D., Racine, Y. (1989). Ontario Child Health Study: Correlates of disorder. *Journal of the American Academy of Child and Adolescent Psychiatry, 28,* 856–860.

Olds, D., & Eckenrode, J. (1997). Long-term effects of home visitation on maternal life course and child abuse and neglect: 15-year follow-up of a randomized trial. *Journal of the American Medical Association, 278,* 637–643.

Olds, D. J., Eckenrode, J., Henderson, C. R., Kitzman, H., Jr., Powers, J., Cole, R., et al. (1997). Long-term effects of nurse home visitation on children's criminal and antisocial behavior: 15-year follow-up of a randomized trial. *Journal of the American Medical Association, 278*(8), 637–643.

Olds, D. L., Henderson, C. R., Kitzman, H. J., Cole, R. E., & Tatelbaum, R. C. (1999). Prenatal and infancy home visitation by nurses: Recent findings. *The Future of Children, 9,* 44–65.

Olson, S. L., Ceballo, R., & Park, C. (2002). Early problem behavior among children from low-income, mother-headed families: A multiple risk perspective. *Journal of Clinical Child and Adolescent Psychology, 31,* 419–430.

Orvaschel, H., Walsh-Allis, G., & Ye, W. J. (1988). Psychopathology in children of parents with recurrent depression. *Journal of Abnormal Child Psychology, 16,* 17–28.

Patterson, G. R., Reid, J. B., & Dishon, T. J. (1992). *Antisocial boys.* Eugene, OR: Castalia.

Pearlin, L. I. (1989). The sociological study of stress. *Journal of Health and Social Behavior, 30,* 241–256.

Peterson, J., & Zill, N. (1986). Marital disruption, parent-child relationship and behavior problems in children. *Journal of Marriage and the Family, 48,* 295–307.

Pevalin, D. J., Wade, T. J., & Brannigan, A. (2003). Precursors, consequences and implications for stability and change in preadolescent antisocial behaviors. *Prevention Science, 4,* 123–136.

Ramey, C. T., & Campbell, F. A. (1984). Preventive education for high-risk children: Cognitive consequences of the Carolina Abecedarian Project. *American Journal of Mental Deficiency, 88,* 515–523.

Rank, M. R., & Hirschl, T. A. (1999). The economic risk of childhood in America: Estimating the probability of poverty across the formative years. *Journal of Marriage and the Family, 61,* 1058–1067.

Reynolds, A. J. (1999). Educational success in high-risk settings: Contributions of the Chicago Longitudinal Study. *Journal of School Psychology, 31,* 345–354.

Reynolds, A. J. (2000). *Success in early intervention: The Chicago child-parent centers.* Lincoln: University of Nebraska Press.

Robins, L. (1966). *Deviant children grow up.* Baltimore: Williams and Wilkins.

Rose, G. (1985). Sick individuals and sick populations. *International Journal of Epidemiology, 14,* 23–38.

Rousseau, C., Drapeau, A., & Platt, R. (2000). Living conditions and emotional profiles of Cambodian, Central American, and Quebecois youth. *Canadian Journal of Psychiatry, 45,* 905–911.

Ruchkin, V. V., Eisemann, M., & Hägglöf, B. (1998). Parental rearing and problem behaviors in male delinquent adolescents versus controls in Northern Russia. *Social Psychiatry and Psychiatric Epidemiology, 33,* 477–482.

Rutter, M. (1971). Parent-child separation: Psychological effects on the children. *Journal of Child Psychology and Psychiatry, 12,* 233–260.

Rutter, M. (1973). Why are London children so disturbed? *Proceedings of the Royal Society of Medicine, 66,* 1221–1225.

Sameroff, A. J. (1995). General systems theories and developmental psychopathology. In D. Cicchetti & D. Cohen (Vol. eds.), *Developmental and Psychopathology* (Vol. 4, pp. 659–695). New York: Wiley.

Sameroff, A. J. (1998). Management of clinical problems and emotional care: Environmental risk factors in infancy. *Pediatrics, 102,* 1287–1292.

Sameroff, A. J., Seifer, R., Baldwin, A. L., & Baldwin, C. A. (1993). Stability of intelligence from preschool to adolescence: The influence of social and family risk factors. *Child Development, 64,* 80–97.

Sameroff, A. J., Seifer, R., Barocas, R., Zax, M., & Greenspan, S. (1987). Intelligence quotient scores of 4-year-old children: Social environmental risk factors. *Pediatrics, 79,* 343–350.

Sameroff, A. J., Seifer, R., & Zax, M. (1982). Early development of children at risk for emotional disorder. *Monographs of the Society for Research in Child Development, 47,* 1–82.

Schwartz, S., & Carpenter, K. M. (1999). The right answer for the wrong question: Consequences of type III error for public health research. *American Journal of Public Health, 89,* 1175–1180.

Shaw, D. S., & Emery, R. E. (1987). Parental conflict and other correlates of the adjustment of school-age children whose parents have separated. *Journal of Abnormal Child Psychology, 15,* 269–281.

Shaw, D. S., Keenan, K., & Vondra, J. (1994). Developmental precursors of externalizing behavior: Ages 1 to 3. *Developmental Psychology, 30,* 355–364.

Shaw, D. S., Owens, E. B., Giovannelli, J., & Winslow, E. B. (2001). Infant and toddler pathways leading to early externalizing disorders. *Journal of the American Academy of Child and Adolescent Psychiatry, 40,* 36–43.

Shy, C. M. (1997). The failure of academic epidemiology: Witness for the prosecution. *American Journal of Epidemiology, 145,* 479–484.

Snyder, J. J., & Patterson, G. R. (1995). Individual differences in social aggression: A test of a reinforcement model of socialization in the natural environment. *Behavior Therapy, 26,* 371–391.

Spieker, S. J., Larson, N. C., Lewis, M. S., Keller, T. E., & Gilchrist, L. (1999). Developmental trajectories of disruptive behavior problems in preschool children of adolescent mothers. *Child Development, 70,* 443–458.

Srole, L., Langer, T. S., Micheal, S. T., Opler, M. K., & Rennie, T. A. C. (1962). *The Midtown Manhattan Study.* New York: McGraw Hill.

Tolan, P. H. (1987). Implications of age of onset for delinquency risk. *Journal of Abnormal Child Psychology, 15,* 47–65.

Tremblay, R. E., Vitaro, F., Bertrand, L., Le Blanc, M., Beauchesne, H., Boileau, H., et al. (1992). Parent and child training to prevent early onset of delinquency: The Montreal longitudinal-experimental study. In J. McCord & R. E. Tremblay (Eds.), *Preventing antisocial behavior: Interventions from birth through adolescence* (pp. 117–138). New York: Guilford Press.

Tremblay, R. E., Pagni-Kurtz, L., Masse, L. C., Vitaro, R., & Pihl, R. O. (1995). A bimodal preventive intervention for disruptive kindergarten boys: Its impact through mid-adolescence. *Journal of Consulting and Clinical Psychology, 63,* 560–568.

Turner, R. J., & Lloyd, D. A. (1999). The stress process and the social distribution of depression. *Journal of Health and Social Behavior, 40,* 374–404.

Turner, R. J., Wheaton, B., & Lloyd, D. A. (1995). The epidemiology of social stress. *American Sociological Review, 60,* 104–125.

Udry, J. R. (1997). *The National Longitudinal Study of Adolescent Health (Add Health), wave 1,* 1994–1996 (Data Set 48–50, Kelley, M. S., Peterson, E. C., & Peterson, J. L.; machine-readable data file and documentation). Chapel Hill, NC: Carolina Population Center, University of North Carolina at Chapel Hill (Producer). Los Altos, CA: Sociometrics Corporation, American Family Data Archive (Producer & Distributor).

U.S. Department of Health and Human Services. (2001). *Trends in the well-being of America's children and youth.* Washington, DC: Westat.

Vitaro, F., Tremblay, R. E., & Zoccolillo, M. (1999). The alcoholic father, psychotropic drug abuse during adolescence and protective influences. *Canadian Journal of Psychiatry, 44,* 901–908.

Wade, T. J. (2001). Delinquency and health among adolescents: Multiple outcomes of a similar social and structural process. *International Journal of Law and Psychiatry, 24,* 447–467.

Wade, T. J., Cairney, J., & Pevalin, D. J. (2002). Emergence of gender differences in depression during adolescence: National panel results from three countries. *Journal of the American Academy of Child and Adolescent Psychiatry, 41,* 190–198.

Wade, T. J., & Pevalin, D. J. (2004). Marital transitions and mental health. *Journal of Health and Social Behavior, 45,* 155–170.

Wade, T. J., Pevalin, D. J., & Brannigan, A. (1999). The clustering of severe behavioural, health and educational deficits in Canadian children: Preliminary evidence from the National Longitudinal Survey of Children and Youth. *Canadian Journal of Public Health, 90,* 253–259.

Wagner, E. F., Lloyd, D. A., & Gil, A. G. (2002). Racial/ethnic and gender differences in the incidence and onset age of *DSM-IV* alcohol use disorder symptoms among adolescents. *Journals of Studies on Alcohol, 63,* 609–619.

Wakschlag, L. S., Hans, S. L. (1999). Relation of maternal responsiveness during infancy to the development of behavior problems in high-risk youths. *Developmental Psychology, 35,* 569–579.

Wallerstein, J. S., & Kelly, J. B. (1975). The effects of parental divorce: Experiences of the preschool child. *Journal of the American Academy of Child Psychiatry, 14,* 600–616.

Wallerstein, J. S., & Kelly, J. B. (1980). *Surviving the breakup: How children and parents cope with divorce.* New York: Basic Books.

Weikart, D. P., Berrueta-Clement, J. R., Schweinhart, L., Barnett, W. S., & Epstein, A. S. (1984). *Changed lives: The effects of the Perry Preschool Program on youths through age 19.* Ypsilanti, MI: High Scope Press.

Weikart, D. P., Schweinhart, L., & Barnes, H. V. (1993). *Significant benefits: The high scope Perry Preschool Study through age 27.* Ypsilanti, MI: High Scope Press.

Weitoft, G. R., Hjern, A., Haglund, B., & Rosen, M. (2003). Mortality, severe morbidity, and injury in children living with single parents in Sweden: A population-based study. *Lancet, 361,* 289–295.

Werner, E. E. (1982). High-risk children in young adulthood: A longitudinal study from birth to 32 years. *American Journal of Orthopsychiatry, 59,* 72–81.

West, D. J. (1982). *Delinquency: Its roots, careers, and prospects.* London: Heinemann.

West, D. J., & Farrington, D. P. (1973). *Who becomes delinquent?* London: Heinemann.

Widom, C. S. (1991). Avoidance of criminality in abused and neglected children. *Psychiatry, 54,* 162–174.

Wierson, M., Forehand, R., & McCombs, A. (1988). The relationship of early adolescent functioning to parent-reported and adolescent-perceived interparental conflict. *Journal of Abnormal Child Psychology, 16,* 707–718.

Wilkinson, R. G. (1996). *Unhealthy societies: The afflictions of inequalities.* London: Routledge.

Williams, H., & Carmichael, A. (1991). Depression in mothers and behaviour problems with their preschool children. *Journal of Paediatrics and Child Health, 27,* 76–82.

Willms, D. J. (2002). Socioeconomic gradients for childhood vulnerability. In D. J. Willms (Ed.), *Vulnerable children* (pp. 71–102). Edmonton, AB: University of Alberta Press.

Yoshikawa, H. (1995). Long-term effects of early childhood programs on social outcomes and delinquency. *Future of Children, 5,* 51–75.

Zeitlin, M. F., Megawangi, R., Kramer, E. M., Colletta, N. D., Babatunde, E. D., & Garman, D. (1995). *Strengthening the family—implications for international development.* New York: United Nations University Press.

CHAPTER 6

Temperament in Early Development

SUSAN D. CALKINS AND KATHRYN A. DEGNAN

INTRODUCTION

The construct of temperament has been the focus of considerable developmental and clinical psychology research because it has the potential to capture the contribution of the child to early developmental processes. Temperament refers to individual characteristics that are assumed to have a biological or genetic basis; that determine the individual's affective, attentional, and motoric responding cross-situationally; and that play a role in subsequent social interactions and social functioning. Early temperament research focused on establishing taxonomies of temperament dimensions, addressing measurement issues, and examining stability of temperament across time. More recent longitudinal research has focused on the extent to which temperament affects adjustment and the development of psychopathology. In this chapter, we provide a brief and selective review of the domain of infant temperament, with an emphasis on different conceptual and empirical perspectives. Then we examine recent research documenting the effects of early temperament on child adjustment, with a specific focus on externalizing and internalizing disorders, broadly considered. This body of work has been conducted in several different countries, with both boys and girls, using different measurement tools. These studies are consistent in finding modest direct effects of early temperament dimensions, most notably temperamental distress, on the display of externalizing and internalizing behavior problems at later ages (Calkins & Dedmon, 2000; Caspi, Henry, McGee, Moffitt, & Silva, 1995; Prior, Smart, Sanson, & Oberklaid, 1993; Shaw, Owens, Giovanelli, & Winslow, 2001).

Finally, and by way of an alternative perspective on the development of early psychopathology, we present a framework for integrating the construct of temperament with processes and mechanisms that may be implicated in the development of childhood psychopathologies, and that provide an explication of the possible indirect effects of temperament on the development of childhood adjustment. This framework focuses on the self-regulatory component of temperament that develops over the course of infancy and childhood; that influences, and is influenced by, relationships with caregivers; and that provides a more proximal mechanism for understanding the relation between temperament and childhood psychopathology. Self-regulatory processes, particularly those involved in the regulation of affect, have been described as core features of many disorders of childhood (Barkley, 1997; Keenan, 2000; Posner & Rothbart, 2000). A coherent account of the developmental processes and pathways involved in childhood psychopathology must account for the development of these core deficits.

Temperament and Early Emotional Development

Theories of Temperament

The construct of temperament is commonly viewed as the basic organization of personality that is observable as early as infancy and that becomes elaborated over the course of development as the individual's skills, abilities, cognitions, and motivations become more sophisticated (Rothbart & Bates, 1998; Shiner & Caspi, 2003). Temperament thus refers primarily to early differences in emotional and behavioral characteristics that are relatively stable traits with genetic and biological components (DiLalla & Jones, 2000; Goldsmith, Lemery, Aksan, & Buss, 2000).

Current theorizing about infant and child temperament and its role in emotional functioning and behavioral adjustment has its roots in the work of Thomas and Chess (Thomas, Birch, Chess, Hertzig, & Korn, 1964; Thomas & Chess, 1977; Thomas, Chess, & Birch, 1970). Thomas and Chess conducted a longitudinal study of children's behavioral styles, later termed temperament, in an effort to understand how children's personality emerged and interacted with their environments. On the basis of interviews with parents about

---

Acknowledgment: This chapter was supported by National Institute of Health grants to the author first (MH 55584 and MH 58144).

children's reactions to a variety of stimuli and situations, they described nine different behavioral dimensions that clustered into three types, labeled easy, difficult, and slow-to-warm-up temperaments. Children displaying these different profiles exhibited characteristic patterns of responding across a variety of situations. Importantly, though, Thomas and Chess viewed the critical predictor of this adaptation to be the goodness of fit between a child's temperament and his environment. With their work, Thomas and Chess introduced the idea that children bring with them to their development, and to their interactions with others, their own style that plays a role in subsequent behavioral adaptation.

Thomas and Chess's work stimulated a number of researchers interested in early socioemotional development to explore the notion that inborn characteristics of the child contributed substantively to later behavior, and to try to develop measurement strategies to capture these characteristics. Subsequent theories of temperament have varied in the numbers of temperament dimensions proposed, the emphasis on emotion versus behavior, and the extent to which the environment influences these initial tendencies (Fox, Henderson, & Marshall, 2002; Goldsmith et al., 1987; Rothbart & Bates, 1998). For example, Seifer (Seifer & Sameroff, 1986; Seifer, Schiller, Sameroff, Resnick, & Riordan, 1996) has extended Thomas and Chess's theory to incorporate the notion that the goodness of fit between parent and child is influenced by a number of factors, including infant behavior, parent expectations and parenting practices, and the context in which the interactions occur. Alternatively, Goldsmith and Campos focused on the expression of specific emotions in specific contexts (Goldsmith & Campos, 1990), with less attention to the potential interactional nature of temperament. Kagan (1994; Kagan & Snidman, 1991) focused his temperament theory on two extreme types of children—inhibited and uninhibited—that he argued represented distinct biobehavioral profiles leading to patterns of approach versus withdrawal tendencies across childhood. Rothbart and colleagues (Derryberry & Rothbart, 1997; Rothbart, 1981; Rothbart & Bates, 1998; Rothbart & Derryberry, 1981) have articulated one of the most influential theories of early temperament and one that has generated a great deal of research on infant development over the last 10 years (Buss & Goldsmith, 1998; Calkins & Fox, 1992; Calkins, Dedmon, Gill, Lomax, & Johnson, 2002; Stifter & Braungart, 1995). This theory defines temperament along two broad dimensions of reactivity and self-regulation, which then subsume six subscales that place a greater emphasis on basic emotion, attention, and motor processes.

With respect to the reactive dimension of temperament, Rothbart notes that the initial responses of an infant may be characterized by their physiological and behavioral reactions to sensory stimuli of different qualities and intensities. This reactivity is believed to be present and observable at birth and reflects a relatively stable characteristic of the infant (Rothbart, Derryberry, & Hershey, 2000). Moreover, infants will differ initially in their threshold to respond to visual or auditory stimuli as well as in their level of reactivity to stimuli designed to elicit negative affect (e.g., Calkins, Fox, & Marshall, 1996). These initial affective responses that are characterized by vocal and facial indices of negativity are presumed to reflect generalized distress. Thus, this initial negative reactivity has neither the complexity nor the range of later emotional responses. Rather, it is a rudimentary form of the more sophisticated and differentiated emotions that will in later infancy be labeled as fear, anger, or sadness. These emotions undergo further differentiation with cognitive development and the emergence of self-awareness during early childhood (Bronson, 2000).

The second dimension proposed by Rothbart, that of self-regulation, has been described largely in terms of attentional and motoric control mechanisms that emerge across early development. For example, the development of attention and its use in the control of emotional reactivity begins to emerge in the first year of life and continues throughout the preschool and school years (Posner & Rothbart, 2000; Rothbart, 1989; Rothbart & Bates, 1998). Individual differences in the ability to voluntarily sustain focus or shift attention are critical components of self-control of attention. Attentional orienting skills, in particular, have been identified as a critical component of the regulatory process, as orienting has the direct effect of amplifying, at a neural level, the stimuli toward which attention is directed, thus changing the affective experience of the individual (Rothbart, Posner, & Rosicky, 1994). Thus, orienting skills assist in the management of both negative and positive emotions, and consequently to the development of adaptive control of emotion and behavior. Qualitative shifts in attention skills across the first 12 months of life may be integral to the qualitative shifts in emotional regulation that are observed during this period. However, there are clear individual differences in the ability to use attention to successfully control emotion. For example, Rothbart (1981, 1986) found increases in positive affect and decreases in distress from 3 to 6 months during episodes of focused attention, suggesting that control of attention is tied to affective experience. Moreover, negative affectivity is believed to interfere with the child's ability to deploy attention to explore and learn about the environment (Rothbart, Posner, & Rosicky, 1994; Ruff & Rothbart, 1996). Clearly, attention must be considered a central process that links temperamental reactivity to later adjustment very early in development.

Another key construct in Rothbart's theory of temperament that would be classified under the broad rubric of self-regulation is effortful control, defined as the ability to inhibit responses to stimuli in the immediate environment while pursuing a cognitively represented goal (Rothbart & Posner, 1985). As a temperamental dimension, effortful control refers to a special class of self-regulatory processes that develop with the maturation of attentional mechanisms, particularly the anterior attention system (Posner & Rothbart, 1992). Although it is believed that effortful control begins to emerge at the end of the first year of life, its development continues at least through the preschool years and again is a likely factor in the development of childhood psychopathology due to its role in the control of behavioral systems, particularly those involved in the control of impulsivity and compliance to external demands.

In sum, although a number of different approaches to conceptualizing and studying infant temperament have been proposed, Rothbart's theory of temperament has the potential to elucidate processes related to adjustment because it takes into account the emotional and reactive elements of temperament, as well as the regulatory dimensions. The incorporation of both makes the theory unique in the field of infant temperament. Rothbart views the very young infant as a highly reactive organism whose behavior becomes, with development, increasingly controlled by regulatory processes. And, although research and theory on the relations between temperament and adjustment, which will be reviewed in the next section, have largely focused on the negative and reactive dimensions of temperament (e.g., anger and fear), it is the regulatory processes that may ultimately determine the young child's degree of success at mastering developmental achievements (Calkins, 1994; Cicchetti, Ganiban, & Barnett, 1991; Kopp, 1982).

Behavioral Assessments of Temperament

Efforts to assess endogenous infant traits described in temperament theory that may influence subsequent personality development and childhood adjustment have generated a variety of methodologies involving both laboratory and questionnaire techniques. The work of Thomas and Chess and their colleagues (Thomas, Birch, Chess, Hertzig, & Korn, 1968) on the New York Longitudinal Study began the discussion of how to measure individual differences among infants using temperament constructs and specific temperament dimensions. This approach construed temperament in terms of behavioral style, which is thought to be stable over time and reflected in the similarity of responses across different emotional elicitors and situations that the infant commonly confronts during the course of early development. Various theorists have proposed particular dimensions of temperament that reflect, in general, the child's emotionality, activity level, and attention (Buss & Plomin, 1984; Rothbart, 1981; Thomas & Chess, 1977). In addition, these approaches assume a biological component of individual differences. Finally, most of these approaches are similar in that the measurement of these traits is achieved through the completion of a questionnaire that requires mothers to rate the frequency of particular infant behaviors observed during the previous week.

The measurement of specific temperament dimensions using questionnaire techniques has led to a great deal of research concerning the stability of temperament, its convergent validity with observations of behavior, and its role in developing social relationships (c.f. Isabella, Ward, & Belsky, 1985; Worobey, 1986). Two of these issues, stability and convergence, are at the core of the challenge of developing accurate temperament assessment instruments. For if, as the major theoretical positions maintain, temperament is stable, measuring temperament should produce cross-age correlations on the different dimensions, and these assessments should also correlate with observed behavior. Critics of these instruments maintain that maternal report of temperament is biased and ought to be validated by other sorts of information (Isabella, Ward, & Belsky, 1985; Vaughn, 1986; Worobey, 1986). However, recent reconciliation of these issues has been achieved through the acknowledgment of contextual effects on children's behavior that may undermine cross-informer consistency rather than attributing the lack of consistency to biased caregiver reports (see Mangelsdorf, Schoppe, & Buur, 2000). Finally, studies utilizing maternal report of temperament are often focused on the reactive component of temperament, with less emphasis on the attentional and motoric self-regulatory dimensions of temperament.

Direct observations of temperament in the home or laboratory have been proposed as one means of validating maternal assessments via questionnaire. The Laboratory Temperament Assessment Battery (LAB-TAB; Goldsmith & Rothbart, 1993), developed in the tradition of Rothbart's model of temperament, employs a standard set of tasks that may be used to assess temperament in the laboratory and that are scored along a number of dimensions, yielding measurements of such temperament dimensions as fear, positive affectivity, and frustration. A number of recent studies have used such batteries to assess temperament and its relation to social development and adjustment (Buss & Goldsmith, 1998; Calkins & Dedmon, 2000). However, it is important to note that the primary emphasis in many studies is on the emotional reactivity component of the child's response to a particular task or situation, including the latency, intensity, and duration of distress, with less-explicit emphasis on the potential regulatory component of the child's response. In addition, observational methods are vulnerable to distortion as well, because the period of observation is short and the range of behaviors observed may be constricted. Matheny and others (Calkins et al., 2002; Matheny, Riese, & Wilson, 1985; Rothbart & Bates, 1998) have argued in favor of multimethod assessments that include both laboratory and maternal assessments. Such multimethod approaches validate maternal assessment and provide a measure of temperament that takes into account behaviors that are observed over the course of several days or weeks.

Psychobiological Assessments of Temperament

In addition to finding reliable and valid measurement instruments to assess the behavioral component of temperament, it is useful for temperament theorists to try to account for the biological or physiological component of the construct as well. That is, if, as temperament theorists propose, temperamental types or characteristics reflect the behavioral manifestation of some underlying biological process, it would be helpful to observe convergent validity of behavior and biology. Indeed, some researchers, notably Kagan (1991), Fox (1989, 1991; Fox & Card, 1999), and Gunnar (1990), place a greater emphasis on exploring the underlying physiological base of temperament that is often referenced only hypothetically in other theories. Three primary types of measures have been used to study relations between physiology and emotional responsivity to a variety of elicitors: measures of heart rate, brain electrical activity, and adrenocortical activity. Excellent reviews of the use of these three measures in both the adult and child literature have been conducted (Fox, Schmidt, & Henderson, 2000; Porges, 1991; Stansbury & Gunnar, 1994). Briefly, we describe these measures and representative findings from the temperament literature.

Heart Rate. The use of heart rate measures of emotion has a long and varied history (see Porges, 1991, for a review). Assessment of heart rate among infant populations is a nonintrusive, painless procedure. Numerous studies have examined individual differences in heart rate and heart rate variability among different groups of infants and children (Calkins et al., 2002; Fox & Gelles, 1984; Kagan, Reznick, & Snidman, 1987). Fox and Gelles (1984) found that infants differing on level of heart rate variability also differed in the degree of facial expressivity. Infants with greater heart rate variability were also more expressive. Kagan et al. (1987) found that behaviorally inhibited children display faster and less-variable heart rates compared to behaviorally extroverted children. They interpreted these differences as reflecting differences in the degree of sympathetic activation between the two groups.

Other studies have examined individual differences in vagal tone, or heart rate variability that occurs at the frequency of breathing (respiratory sinus arrhythmia, or RSA), which is thought to reflect parasympathetic activity, and its relation to emotional reactivity in infancy (Calkins et al., 2002; Fox, 1989; Porges, Doussard-Roosevelt, Portales, & Greenspan, 1996; Stifter, Fox, & Porges, 1989; Stifter & Fox, 1990). In a series of studies Porges and his colleagues have demonstrated that vagal tone is related to both emotional reactivity and regulation (Porter, Porges, & Marshall, 1988; Stifter, Fox, & Porges, 1989). Infants with high vagal tone tend to be more reactive emotionally; Porges speculates that this responsivity may be predictive of better regulatory ability. Further, developmental changes in vagal tone may be a contributor to normative changes in emotion expression observed during infancy (Porges, 1991).

Recent work has examined a measure of cardiac activity that may be more directly related to the kinds of self-regulatory behaviors children begin to display in toddlerhood and early childhood. This measure is vagal regulation of the heart as indexed by a decrease (suppression) in RSA during situations where coping or emotional and behavioral regulation is required. Vagal regulation in the form of suppression of RSA during demanding tasks may reflect physiological processes that allow the child to shift focus from internal homeostatic demands to demands that require internal processing or the generation of coping strategies to control affective or behavioral arousal. Thus, suppression of RSA is thought to be a physiological strategy that permits sustained attention and behaviors indicative of active coping that are mediated by the parasympathetic nervous system (Porges, 1991, 1996; Wilson & Gottman, 1996). Recent research indicates that suppression of RSA during challenging situations is related to better state regulation, greater self-soothing, and more attentional control in infancy (DeGangi, DiPietro, Greenspan, & Porges, 1991; Huffman et al., 1998).

Brain Electrical Activity. A second physiological measure that has recently been used in the study of infant temperament is the electroencephalogram (EEG), low-level electrical activity recorded off the scalp. Researchers interested in the pattern of activation between the right and left hemispheres have computed ratio scores of the difference in power or energy between the two hemispheres. These ratio or difference scores present relative differences in power and a score that reflects the degree to which one hemisphere or region in a hemisphere exhibits greater activation than a homologous region. An extensive literature exists on EEG asymmetry patterns during verbal versus spatial tasks (Davidson, Chapman, Chapman, & Henriques, 1990) and during the expression and perception of different emotions (Davidson, 1984; Fox & Davidson, 1986).

In applying these methods to the study of infant emotion, Fox and Davidson (Davidson & Fox, 1982, 1989; Fox & Davidson, 1986, 1987, 1988) examined whether differences in hemispheric asymmetry are markers for individual differences in emotionality or temperament in infancy (Davidson & Fox, 1989; Fox & Davidson, 1991). In their study of infants' reactions to maternal separation, they found that infants who displayed less left-sided activation in the frontal region during a baseline condition were more likely to cry to brief separation (Fox & Davidson, 1987). Fox and Davidson (1991) argued that infants who show a characteristic right-sided frontal activation may have a lower threshold for experiencing negative emotion. More recently this work has been extended to examine differences among behaviorally inhibited and uninhibited children. Data from several longitudinal cohorts of infants and children suggest that infants selected for temperamental characteristics predictive of inhibition are more likely to exhibit greater relative right frontal activation (Calkins, Fox, & Marshall, 1996) and that children who continue to show inhibited and shy behavior in childhood also display a similar frontal asymmetry (Fox, Schmidt, Calkins, Rubin, & Coplan, 1996).

Adrenocortical Functioning. A third physiological measure that has recently been applied to the study of temperament is that of adrenocortical activity as measured in plasma and salivary cortisol. Cortisol is the primary hormone of the adrenocortical system, whose production varies fairly rhythmically during the course of the 24-hour cycle of day and night. In addition, however, cortisol levels change in response to both physiological and psychological elicitors. In using cortisol as a measure of emotional reactivity, then, the aim is to compare changes in cortisol levels from basal to stressor conditions, with consideration to the activity of the system relative to its daily cycle (Gunnar & Davis, 2003; Stansbury & Gunnar, 1994). Measurement of adrenocortical activity in infants is further complicated by the developmental changes occurring in the pattern of daily cortisol activity during the first year of life. Nevertheless, recent improvements in the radioimmune assays used to analyze salivary cortisol make this method of obtaining psychophysiological data from very young infants quite feasible.

In examining the relations between measures of cortisol and emotion, debate exists as to whether observed increases in cortisol reflect reactivity to stress or whether changes in cortisol level reflect reactivity to novelty and uncertainty. The first hypothesis implies that elevations in cortisol levels will be observed consistently in response to stressors producing negative affect, whereas the second hypothesis predicts habituation of the adrenocortical response once the novelty of the event or stimulus has dissipated (Gunnar, 1990). A third hypothesis recently proposed suggests that control or regulation of the affective response may be the critical factor related to observed changes in cortisol (Stansbury & Gunnar, 1994).

A growing number of temperament and emotion researchers are examining the psychobiological correlates of these processes. One challenge to psychobiological temperament research, however has been the integration of various physiological systems at both a conceptual and an empirical level. This challenge is partially a function of the difficulty in collecting different physiological measures simultaneously, though little in the way of theoretical integration has been attempted. Recent developmental neuroscience work suggests that one way of integrating this work is around the constructs of attention and emotion processes (Bell & Wolfe, 2004; Blair, 2002) that may be integral to the development of self-regulation (Calkins, 2004). Such an approach may explain how the individual might recruit different physiological systems at various points during the processing of emotional stimuli.

Temperament and the Development of Psychopathology

The emphasis on infant and child temperament as a predictor of childhood psychopathology grew largely out of basic research in developmental psychology demonstrating that considerable variability existed in children's behavioral style and that this variability could influence a range of possible experiences the child would have in the course of development (Rothbart & Bates, 1998). Though a number of studies demonstrating concurrent relations between early temperament and adjustment have been conducted, the power of such studies to demonstrate causality is weak. In addition, potential overlap of the measurement of temperament and behavior problems is sometimes discussed as a possible explanation for modest effects between the two domains. However, two recent studies eliminated such confounds in their data and found significant relations between negative temperament in toddlerhood and childhood adjustment (Lemery, Essex, & Smider, 2002; Lengua, West, & Sandler, 1998). Reviews of both concurrent and longitudinal studies are presented by Bates (Bates & McFadyen-Ketchum, 2000; Rothbart & Bates, 1998). Here, we focus primarily on representative longitudinal studies examining direct and indirect effects of temperament on the two broad dimensions of childhood psychopathology, internalizing and externalizing (Achenbach, 1982).

Temperament and Internalizing Problems

Internalizing spectrum behavior includes social withdrawal, inhibition, shyness, anxiety, and depression (Achenbach & Edelbrock, 1978, 1981; Hinshaw, 1987; Rubin & Asendorpf, 1993; Zahn-Waxler, Klimes-Dougan, & Slattery, 2000). Much of the early research linking temperament to behaviors characteristic of internalizing problems focused on the phenomena of behavioral inhibition to the unfamiliar. Behavioral inhibition captures a child's initial response to novel events or unfamiliar people. First described by Kagan and colleagues (Garcia-Coll, Kagan & Reznick, 1984; Kagan & Snidman, 1991), this research indicated that infants and young children who are behaviorally inhibited display low approach tendencies, become and remain vigilant for the duration of exposure to the novel object, and often seek the proximity of a caregiver when exposed to novel events or situations. This behavioral pattern appears to have a distinct physiological profile. Kagan, Snidman, and Arcus (1993) reported that inhibited and uninhibited infants differ in the magnitude of cardiac acceleration and pupillary dilation to mild stress. The origins of behavioral inhibition are negative reactivity and high motor activity in infancy.

Complementing Kagan's research is more recent work demonstrating other physiological correlates of early negative reactivity and inhibition, as well as increased risk for internalizing problems. For example, Calkins, Fox, and Marshall (1996) found that infants with greater relative right frontal EEG activation displayed more negative affect and motor activity at 9 months of age than infants with greater relative left frontal activation, and that these infants were more likely to exhibit inhibited behavior in toddlerhood. In addition, this work revealed that the consequence of an early inhibited temperament appears to be social withdrawal, one index of internalizing difficulties (Fox et al., 1995). Children who exhibit social withdrawal when confronted with unfamiliar peers do not engage in social interaction, nor do they initiate or respond with social behaviors to social bids from unfamiliar peers. In examining the pattern of brain electrical activity that characterizes inhibition and social withdrawal (Calkins et al., 1996; Fox et al., 1995, 1996), Fox has repeatedly found an asymmetrical pattern of activation biased toward the right hemisphere. Moreover, Suomi (1987) found that a small group of rhesus monkeys that were fearful and timid to the unfamiliar also displayed physiological characteristics such as high heart rate and resembled the profile of inhibited children identified in human research. Kagan has argued that limbic system differences underlie the pattern of emotional and behavioral responding seen in inhibited children and animals (Kagan, 1989). However, Calkins (1994) suggested that these emotional and behavioral differences are at the core of a regulatory style that limits inhibited children's exposure to novel events and stimuli that are beyond the regulatory abilities of these children. The consequence of this regulatory style is low social competence and withdrawal from the peer group.

Negative emotionality is another dimension of temperament that has been linked to internalizing spectrum problems (Rothbart & Bates, 1998), although it has been measured in different ways by different investigators. Researchers have found that negative temperamental reactivity early in development is related to internalizing behavior in children age 7–17 years (Merikangas, Swendsen, Preisig, & Chazan, 1998). Other research has found that withdrawal behavior (Mun, Fitzgerald, Von Eye, Puttler, & Zucker, 2001) and irritable distress (Morris et al., 2002) were predictive of internalizing behavior problems in children.

Other studies have measured negative temperament more broadly in studying the relations between temperament and adjustment. For example, using a more global measure of negative temperament, Mathijssen and colleagues found that children with an easy temperament had fewer internalizing behavior problems (Mathijssen, Koot, & Verhulst, 1999), and Keenan and colleagues found that infants and toddlers with a difficult temperament were more likely to have higher internalizing problems in preschool and early childhood, regardless of gender (Keenan, Shaw, Delliquadri, Giovannelli, & Walsh, 1998). Another study that formed composites based on temperament dimensions found that children's level of negative affect and avoidance tendencies predicted greater self-reported anxiety and depression, and children's level of positive affect or sociability predicted less self-reported anxiety and depression (Phillips, Lonigan, Driscoll, & Hooe, 2002). In addition, Anthony and colleagues found that a child composite of negative temperamental traits was related to more child depression and anxiety, whereas a child composite of positive temperamental traits was related to less child depression (Anthony, Lonigan, Hooe, & Phillips, 2002). Thus, global measures of positive versus negative affectivity seem to be associated with the experiences of anxiety and depression as reported by both parents and children.

Other temperament dimensions such as persistence and adaptability have also been found to relate to internalizing behavior problems (Keiley, Lofthouse, Bates, Dodge, & Pettit, 2003; St. John Seed & Weiss, 2002). Research has also found that child reports on multiple domains of temperament, including activity level, flexibility, approach/withdrawal, mood, rhythmicity, and task orientation, are associated with self-report of depression. In addition, self-report of anxiety is mostly related to the temperament domains of activity level and flexibility (Bussing, Gary, & Mason, 2003).

Thus, several dimensions of temperament, reflecting fear, withdrawal, distress, and unadaptability, have been linked to internalizing spectrum behavior problems characterized by anxiety, depression, and social withdrawal in childhood. It is important to note, however, that in most studies, the direct effects of these temperament dimensions are modest (Rothbart & Bates, 1998). Moreover, the mechanism through which these temperament dimensions affect the development of internalizing problems is largely left unspecified.

Temperament and Externalizing Problems

Externalizing behavior refers to problems characterized by acting out, including aggressive and destructive behaviors. Approximately 8 percent of toddlers exhibit a level of externalizing behavior requiring clinical intervention (Achenbach, 1991). The emphasis on understanding these types of problems is largely due to the observation that such problems are moderately stable and are predictive of other, more serious kinds of disorders in middle childhood (Olson, Bates, Sandy, & Schilling, 2002) and adolescence (Moffit, Caspi, Dickson, Silva, & Stanton, 1996). A number of large-scale longitudinal studies have been conducted to examine the role of temperament in externalizing spectrum disorders and behavior, with a particular emphasis on aggression and disruptive behavior. These studies have been conducted in Australia by Prior and colleagues, in the United States by Shaw and Bates and their colleagues, and in New Zealand by Caspi and colleagues. Despite the differences across these studies in terms of the country of origin, the gender and age of the participants, and the specific temperament scales and tools used, these studies are consistent in finding modest direct effects of early temperament dimensions such as negativity, resistance to control, and activity level on the display of externalizing, or acting out behavior problems, at later ages (Bates, Bayles, Bennett, Ridge, & Brown, 1991; Caspi, Henry, McGee, Moffitt, & Silva, 1995; Prior, Smart, Sanson, Pedlow, & Oberklaid, 1992; Shaw et al., 2001). In addition, a number of smaller studies, many of them cross-sectional, conducted across the period of infancy, childhood, and adolescence largely confirm these findings, although, again, the dimensions of temperament vary across studies.

The New Zealand study provided some of the earliest findings regarding the implications of temperament for subsequent development. The earliest temperament measure was collected when the participant children were 3 years old.

Across a number of different reports, the investigative team found that the temperament dimension referred to as undercontrol was predictive of personality, functioning, and psychopathology over the period of childhood, adolescence, and adulthood (Caspi, Moffitt, Newman, & Silva, 1996; Caspi & Silva, 1995; Moffitt et al., 1996). The limitations of this work are that the measure of temperament was assessed well beyond the period when it could be considered purely a characteristic of the child. Nevertheless, these data provide evidence for both continuity in personality and the role of personality in the development of psychopathology.

A second set of reports from a longitudinal study of children also found continuity and relations to psychopathology. This study examined the correlates of the stability of aggression in childhood and used a composite of parent- and teacher-reported temperamental difficulty along with many other measures (Kingston & Prior, 1995). Maternal report of child difficult temperament at 2–3, 3–4, 5–6, and 7–8 years of age was a significant discriminator between stable aggressive and nonaggressive groups of children at the later ages (Kingston & Prior, 1995). In addition, teacher reports of child temperamental difficultness (reactivity in particular) was a significant discriminator between the late-onset and nonaggressive groups (Kingston & Prior, 1995).

Work by Bates and colleagues and Shaw and colleagues in the United States has used a more comprehensive approach to assessing temperament, caregiving, and child outcomes by using a multimeasure longitudinal approach. Shaw's work has focused exclusively on high-risk low-income boys, who display a higher incidence of externalizing problems than do girls. Both sets of studies examined dimensions of child behavior that are considered challenging to caregivers, difficultness and resistance. Difficultness reflects temperamental reactivity and thus may be a more pure measure of temperament, whereas resistance might reflect the dynamic between parent and child. Nevertheless, both sets of studies report modest main effects of early temperament and, importantly, interactions between temperament and caregiving in the prediction of externalizing behavior problems (Bates et al., 1991; Bates & McFadyen-Ketchum, 2000; Bates, Pettit, Dodge, & Ridge, 1998; Shaw, Keenan, & Vondra, 1994; Shaw, Owens, Vondra, Keenan, & Winslow, 1996). The significant finding from these studies is that children in less-than-optimal caregiving environments and relationships that exacerbate children's tendencies to be emotionally reactive, difficult, or resistant were at greatest risk for the development of aggression and disruptive behavior problems. Again, though the mechanisms are specified as temperament and caregiving, the specific behaviors and processes that are implicated in the display of problematic behaviors are left unspecified.

A number of other studies have examined the direct and indirect effects of temperament on early problem behavior in children. A smaller cross-sectional study of a low-risk sample by Rubin and colleagues (Rubin, Hastings, Chen, Stewart, & McNichol, 1998) examined temperament using observed measures of toddlers' anger/frustration tolerance and self-control/approach motivation, which were combined to form an index of observed undercontrol. This measure was positively related to concurrent observed levels of aggression with peers for boys and girls (Rubin et al., 1998). Calkins (2002) examined observed toddler distress (vocal affective responses of the children), aggression (venting behavior), and defiance (to maternal commands) in a sample of low-risk girls and boys at 18 and 24 months of age. At 18 months of age, all three aversive behaviors were correlated with each other, but at 24 months, distress was related to only aggressive behavior, not defiance (Calkins, 2002). In addition, an 18-month composite variable of the aversive behaviors was found to be significantly related to aggression at 24 months, but only when maternal positive guidance was low at 18 months (Calkins, 2002).

Another study, using the same construct of difficultness at both 6 and 13 months of age, examined relations between temperament in infancy and problem behavior at 5 years of age (Andersson & Sommerfelt, 1999). Temperamental difficultness at both ages was correlated with the problem behavior measure, but difficultness predicted problem behavior only when it interacted with social risk at 6 months of age (Andersson & Sommerfelt, 1999). Infants' level of difficultness at 6 months was positively related to problem behavior at 5 years of age, but only for those children of low socio-economic status (Andersson & Sommerfelt, 1999).

Studies have also examined precursors of the combination of aggression and hyperactivity across childhood (Sanson, Smart, Prior, & Oberklaid, 1993). Sanson and colleagues (Sanson et al., 1993) used parent report of activity-reactivity and irritability from an Australian adaptation of the Revised Infant Temperament Questionnaire (ITC) at 4–8 months of age and 32–36 months of age in relation to parent and teacher ratings of aggression at 32–36 months, 44–48 months, 5–6 years, and 7–8 years of age. The hyperactive-aggressive and aggressive-only groups showed more evidence of difficult temperament in infancy, and difficult behaviors in infancy were more strongly related to aggression at school age than hyperactivity (Sanson et al., 1993). In a study by Schmitz and colleagues (Schmitz et al., 1999) parent report of temperamental emotionality and activity (Colorado Child Temperament Inventory, CCTI) at 14, 20, 24, and 36 months of age was examined in relation to problem behavior at 4 years of age. The emotionality scale from all ages was significantly correlated with the measure of problem behavior at age 4 (Schmitz et al., 1999).

A study using another temperament questionnaire, the Dimensions of Temperament Survey (DOTS), examined the subscales of activity level and reactivity during preschool in relation to externalizing problems during early childhood (Mun et al., 2001). Across the entire sample, the parent report of reactivity was related to the level of externalizing problems in early childhood, whereas the report of activity level was related to the externalizing problems only for children with parents high on psychopathology (Mun et al., 2001). Another study used the DOTS parent report of temperament at 6 years of age in relation to aggression at 10, 11, and 12 years of age (Vitaro, Brendgen, & Tremblay, 2002). In addition, the researchers separated the measure of aggression into that of reactive and proactive aggression. They found that the reactive-only and reactive-proactive aggression groups were more active and negatively reactive than the nonaggressive group. In addition, the reactive-only group was rated as more negatively reactive than the reactive-proactive group (Vitaro et al., 2002).

Other studies have examined multiple dimensions of temperament in relation to both internalizing and externalizing problems. Eisenberg and colleagues (Eisenberg et al., 2001) examined parent and teacher reports of anger, frustration, sadness, fear, impulsivity, and inhibitory control between children grouped on the basis of parent and teacher report of externalizing problems. Children high on externalizing were found to be higher on sadness and impulsivity than the control and internalizing children and higher on anger than the control children (Eisenberg et al., 2001). This work suggests that specificity between type of negative temperament observed and type of psychopathology is an important consideration of this research, though problems of comorbidity of internalizing and externalizing complicate the search for such specificity (Zahn-Waxler et al., 2000).

Other studies have examined the interactions between child temperament and dimensions of family functioning other than parenting behavior in relation to externalizing behavior. One study examined parent report of temperament at 12, 18, and 30 months of age, using the Dutch Temperament Questionnaire, in relation to externalizing problems, rated by both the teacher and the parent at 7 years of age (Stams, Juffer, & Ijzendoorn, 2002). A composite measure of difficult temperament across infancy and toddlerhood was predictive of externalizing behavior in middle childhood above and beyond many other variables, including maternal sensitivity, the parent-child relationship composite, and attachment (Stams et al., 2002). A study by Tschann and colleagues (Tschann, Kaiser, Chesney, Alkon, & Boyce, 1996) also examined the possible interaction of temperament and family functioning in relation to externalizing behavior and observed aggression. They found that temperament interacted with family functioning to predict outcome. Preschool children with difficult temperaments were found to have the most teacher-rated externalizing problems when they were living in high-conflict families and were found to show more observed aggression if their families were more expressive (Tschann et al., 1996). Interestingly, preschool children with less-difficult temperament were less aggressive when their families were more expressive. Finally, Russell and colleagues (Russell, Hart, Robinson, & Olsen, 2003) examined mother ratings of temperament using the Emotionality, Activity, and Sociability temperament survey and found that temperamental activity scores related significantly to teacher ratings of physical and relational aggression in preschool children. In addition, the study examined parenting and temperament interactions but found none to be significantly related to aggressive behavior (Russell et al., 2003).

A Self-Regulatory Framework for Examining Temperament-Psychopathology Relations

The important question of how temperament might affect subsequent adjustment and the development of behavior problems in childhood is receiving increasing attention (Rothbart & Bates, 1998; Shiner & Caspi, 2003). Studies that have reported modest direct effects of temperament have motivated theorists and researchers to search for causal mechanisms in the development of childhood psychopathology (Hinshaw, 2002). Multiple models of such mechanisms have been proposed, including, most frequently, those that focus on the moderational role of the caregiving environment (see Bates & McFadyen-Ketchum, 2000, for a complete review of these studies). However, less work has focused on the processes that might mediate the relation between such temperament dimensions as distress or negativity, caregiving contexts, and behavioral patterns characterized by withdrawal or aggression. One hypothesis that follows directly from Rothbart's theory is that temperament exerts its effects on child behavior via the developing self-regulatory system. Indeed, the development of deficits of emotional self-regulation in particular is viewed by many to be one of the key symptoms in behavior problems of childhood (Barkley, 1997; Calkins, 2004; Keenan & Shaw, 2003; Nigg & Huang-Pollock, 2003). For example, in characterizing the behavior of children with early externalizing behavior problems, there is often reference to a lack of control, undercontrol, or poor regulation (Campbell, 1995; Lewis & Miller, 1990). In characterizing the behavior of children with internalizing disorders, there is often a discussion of overcontrol (Calkins & Fox, 2002; Zahn-Waxler et al., 2000). Examination of the possible mediational effects of self-regulation and emotion regulation may provide a more proximal mechanism for the development of different forms of behavioral adjustment difficulties characteristic of childhood.

One hypothesis generated as a result of an examination of the temperament literature is that the temperamental characteristic of negative reactivity in particular plays a role in at least the display, if not the development, of emotion-regulation skills that are integral to appropriate functioning (Calkins, 1994; Keenan & Shaw, 2003). In turn, the absence of these skills is seen as contributing to both internalizing and externalizing behavior problems (Calkins, 1994; Gilliom, Shaw, Beck, Schonberg, & Lukon, 2002; Keenan, 2000; Mangelsdorf, Shapiro, & Marzolf, 1995; Stifter & Braungart, 1995; Zahn-Waxler et al., 2000). From this perspective, it is assumed that the inborn personality characteristic of temperamental distress that differentiates infants and children from one another influences, either directly or indirectly, the kinds of emotion-regulatory skills and strategies that children develop as a function of attentional and inhibitory control mechanisms on the one hand and parenting behavior on the other (Calkins, 1994; Keenan & Shaw, 2003), and the patterns of emotional control that lead to problematic adjustment.

Our rationale for examining the differentiation, development, and integration of these regulatory processes as a function of temperamental reactivity emanates from recent work in the area of developmental neuroscience that has identified specific brain regions that may play a functional role in the deployment of attention and in the processing and regulation of emotion, cognition, and behavior (Posner & Rothbart, 1994, 1998). This work has identified areas of the prefrontal cortex as central to the effortful regulation of behavior via the anterior attention system. This system is guided by the anterior cingulate cortex (ACC), which includes two major subdivisions. One subdivision governs cognitive and attentional processes and has connections to the prefrontal cortex. A second subdivision governs emotional processes and has connections with the limbic system and peripheral autonomic, visceromotor, and endocrine systems (Lane & McRae, 2004; Luu & Tucker, 2004).

Recent research suggests that these subdivisions of the ACC have a reciprocal relation (Davidson, Putnam & Larson, 2000; Davis, Bruce, & Gunnar, 2002). Moreover, the functional relation between these two areas of the cortex provides a biological mechanism for the developmental integration of reactive and self-regulatory processes in childhood. Recent developmental neuroscience work suggests that because of their dependence on the maturation of prefrontal-limbic connections, the development of self-regulatory processes are relatively protracted (Beauregard, Levesque, & Paquette, 2004), from the development of basic and automatic regulation of physiology in infancy and toddlerhood to the more self-conscious and intentional regulation of cognition emerging in middle childhood (Ochsner & Gross, 2004). From a developmental psychopathology perspective, then, opportunities for success and failure of self-regulation are numerous over the course of childhood, particularly given the potential of environmental factors such as parenting to facilitate or disrupt development in these domains (Calkins, Smith, Gill, & Johnson, 1998). In the next section, we describe normative developments in these domains, with a particular focus on emotion regulation, as well as the consequences of failures for individual behavioral functioning.

Normative Developments in Self-Regulation

Self-regulatory processes refer to mechanisms that allow an organism to exert control over processes that occur at the level of biology, attention, emotion, behavior, and cognition (Vohs & Baumeister, 2004). Moreover, this system of regulation emerges and becomes integrated over time. Much of the research on the development of emotion-regulation skills and abilities has focused on infancy and toddlerhood, primarily because dramatic developments may be observed during this period of development. The developmental process itself may be described broadly as one in which the relatively passive and reactive neonate becomes a child capable of self-initiated behaviors that serve a regulatory function (Calkins, 1994; Kopp, 1982; Sroufe, 1996). In addition, this process has also been described as one in which the infant progresses from near complete reliance on caregivers for regulation to independent self-regulation. As the infant makes this transition, the use of specific strategies and behaviors becomes organized into the infant's repertoire of emotional self-regulation that may be used in a variety of contexts and that leads to independent functioning across a variety of skill domains.

Kopp (1982) provides an excellent overview of the early developments in emotional self-regulation. This description has been verified by studies of both normative development (Buss & Goldsmith, 1998; Mangelsdorf, Shapiro, & Marzolf, 1995; Rothbart, Ziaie, & O'Boyle, 1992) and studies of individual differences (Stifter & Braungart, 1995; Mangelsdorf et al., 1995). These descriptions provide an explanation of how infants develop and utilize a rich behavioral repertoire of strategies in the service of reducing, inhibiting, amplifying, and balancing different affective responses. Moreover, it is also clear from these descriptions that functioning in a variety of nonemotional domains, including motor, language and cognition, and social development, is implicated in these changes as well (Kopp, 1989, 1992). So though emotion regulation is critical to positive adjustment, it is often difficult to isolate it from basic developments in other domains.

Early efforts at emotional self-regulation, specifically those occurring before about 3 months of age, are thought to be controlled largely by physiological mechanisms that are innate (Kopp, 1982). By 3 months of age, primitive mechanisms of self-soothing, such as sucking; simple motor movements such as turning away; and reflexive signaling in response to discomfort, often in the form of crying, are the primary processes operating, independent of caregiver intervention (Kopp, 1982; Rothbart et al., 1992).

The period between 3 and 6 months of age marks a major transition in infant development. First, biological functioning, specifically sleep-wake cycles and eating and elimination processes, have become more predictable, signaling an important biological transition that is implicated in self-regulation. Second, the ability of the infant to voluntarily control arousal levels begins to emerge. This control depends largely on attentional control mechanisms and simple motor skills (Rothbart et al., 1992; Ruff & Rothbart, 1996) and leads to coordinated use of attention engagement and disengagement, particularly in contexts that evoke negative affect. Infants are now capable of engaging in self-initiated distraction, moving attention away from the source of negative arousal to more neutral nonsocial stimuli. For example, the ability to shift attention away from a negative event (such as something frightening) to a positive distracter may lead to decreases in the experience of negative affect. Importantly, though, clear individual differences exist in the ability to use attention to successfully control emotion and behavior. Rothbart (1981, 1986) found increases in positive affect and decreases in distress from 3 to 6 months during episodes of focused attention, suggesting that attentional control is tied to affective experience. Mangelsdorf and colleagues also found that younger infants tended to rely on simple attentional means such as gaze avoidance to control negative affect (Mangelsdorf et al., 1995). These empirical findings are important to an understanding of the long-term implications of early emotional regulation because the experience of negative affect is believed to interfere with the child's ability to explore and learn about the environment (Ruff & Rothbart, 1996). Consequently, there are clear implications of early emotional self-regulation for development in a range of domains.

By the end of the first year of life, infants become much more active and purposeful in their attempts to control affective arousal (Kopp, 1982; Mangelsdorf et al., 1995). First, they begin to employ organized sequences of motor behavior that enable them to reach, retreat, redirect, and self-soothe in a flexible manner that suggests they are responsive to environmental cues. Second, their signaling and redirection become explicitly social as they recognize that caregivers and others may behave in a way that will assist them in the regulation of affective states (Rothbart et al., 1992).

During the second year of life, the transition from passive to active methods of emotional regulation is complete (Rothbart et al., 1992). Although infants are not entirely capable of controlling their own affective states by this age, they are capable of using specific strategies to attempt to manage different affective states, albeit sometimes unsuccessfully (Calkins & Dedmon, 2000; Calkins, Smith, Gill, & Johnson, 1998). Moreover, during this period, infants begin to respond to caregiver directives, and as a consequence of this responsivity, compliance and behavioral self-control begin to emerge (Kopp, 1989). This shift is supported by developments in the motor domain as well as changes in representational ability and the development of language skills. Brain maturation contributes as well, and by the end of toddlerhood, children have executive control abilities that allow control of arousal, regulation of affective expression, and inhibition and activation of behavior (Bronson, 2000), skills that will support adaptive behavior across a range of contexts.

The description of the developmental process of emerging self-regulation, including emotional self-regulation, has been subject to inquiry regarding the role of factors that contribute to these developments. Empirical evidence supports the theoretical notion that multiple dimensions of the caregiving environment play a role in the development of emotion-regulation skills (Braungart & Stifter, 1991; Nachmias, Gunnar, Mangelsdorf, Parritz, & Buss, 1996). Clearly, though, emotional regulatory processes begin to develop as a function of very early behavioral and biological reactive tendencies, or temperament. In the next section, the relation between temperamental reactivity, most notably negative emotionality, and the development of emotional self-regulation is examined.

Temperament and the Development of Self-Regulation

There are several possible ways that temperamental distress may affect the display and development of emotion regulation and, consequently, the development of behavior problems (Calkins, 1994, 2004). One hypothesis is that temperament directly constrains the development of specific regulatory behaviors that are integral to behavioral control and social functioning (Calkins & Johnson, 1998). A second hypothesis is that temperament is moderated by specific kinds of caregiving behaviors or environments that then alter the trajectories of self-regulation. A third hypothesis is that temperamental distress might be mediated by other basic regulatory processes, such as attention or physiology (Calkins & Dedmon, 2000; Harmon, Rothbart, & Posner, 1997; Shipman, Schneider, & Brown, 2004), that then affect the development of emotional regulation in context. Failures of these basic regulatory processes have cascading consequences. First, they contribute directly to behaviors that are disruptive to the child's functioning in the situations in which they occur (Calkins & Dedmon, 2000). Second, because the child is unable to control negative affect, these failures limit opportunities to learn adaptive skills in social-interactional contexts with parents and peers (Keane & Calkins, 2004).

Direct Effects of Temperament. Characteristics of the infant that are most often explored in the study of emotional self-regulation are temperamental dimensions such as proneness to distress (Calkins & Fox, 1992; Mangelsdorf, Gunnar, Kestenbaum, Lang, & Andreas, 1990; Seifer, Schiller, Sameroff, Resnick, & Riordan, 1996). Hypothetically, one might imagine an infant who is highly negatively reactive to novel stimuli. Such an infant might cry easily, intensely, and for a long duration when exposed to new people, objects, or environments. Given the level of behavioral disorganization that might accompany such a response, such a child might be unable to display, and therefore practice, the skills of gaze aversion, social referencing, distraction, or self-soothing that typically lead to a reduction in the experience and expression of negative affect. Under repeated exposures to novelty, the opportunities for the acquisition of early regulatory behaviors become limited. As the child develops, the likelihood of having a rich behavioral repertoire of strategies to draw upon also becomes limited. In this way, temperamental reactivity to novelty may function to limit concurrent strategy use as well as the practice and development of more sophisticated skills that build on early primitive strategies such as gaze aversion or self-soothing, and that are critical to adaptive functioning across a range of more challenging contexts.

Such a scenario has found support in a small number of studies that have investigated the role of temperament in displays of emotional regulation. For example, in a recent series of studies, several researchers have suggested that frustration reactivity, elicited in response to physical restraint or denial, may constrain both the use and the development of appropriate regulatory behaviors (Calkins, 1994; Calkins & Fox, 1992; Fox & Calkins, 1993; Stifter & Fox, 1990). In one study, Stifter and Braungart (1995) examined the types of regulatory behaviors infants use to manage emotional reactivity and observed that relations existed between these behaviors and changes in negative affect. In another study of the efficacy of regulatory behaviors, Rothbart and colleagues (Rothbart, Posner, & Boylan, 1990) observed that at least one specific emotion-regulation behavior, that of attentional control, is related to decreases in negative emotionality in infancy. And Buss and Goldsmith (1998) observed that a number of different behaviors that infants display when observed in frustrating or constraining situations appear to reduce negative affect.

In our work, we have demonstrated that relations exist between level of reactivity to frustration, both behaviorally and physiologically, and emotional and physiological regulation. For example, the magnitude of baseline resting heart rate variability, or vagal tone, which is often used as a marker of temperament, predicted the magnitude of physiological regulation in response to frustration during infancy, toddlerhood, and preschool age (Calkins, 1997; Calkins et al., 2002; Calkins, Smith, Gill, & Johnson, 1998). We have also demonstrated that relations exist between regulatory behaviors and the tendency to be distressed to frustrating situations during toddlerhood (Calkins and Johnson, 1998). And we found that a group of infants characterized by low frustration tolerance differed from less-frustrated infants in terms of physiological regulation, emotion-regulation strategies, attention, and activity level (Calkins et al., 2002). Similarly, a group of toddlers characterized by disruptive behavior displayed fewer emotion-regulation behaviors and poorer physiological regulation (Calkins & Dedmon, 2000). The implications of these behavioral and physiological profiles for longer-term emotional regulation are unclear. However, the notion that certain behaviors serve to minimize frustration reactivity has gained clear support, as has the notion that greater levels of frustration are linked to both less regulation and the use of less-adaptive types of regulation.

A second issue with respect to frustration reactivity is its effect over time on developing regulatory ability. Braungart-Rieker and Stifter (1996) demonstrated that frustration reactivity at 5 months of age was related to the use of fewer emotion-regulation behaviors at 10 months of age. What is unclear, though, is whether some types of emotion-regulation behaviors are more likely to be associated with heightened frustration over time than others. A small number of studies conducted with children of various ages suggest that it might be possible to identify profiles of infants at higher risk for regulatory difficulties. For example, Aksan and colleagues (Aksan et al., 1999) reported that a preschool temperament type characterized by noncontrolled-expressive behavior was predicted by infant distress to limitations. Thus, there seems to be evidence that the dimension of frustration, as it is displayed in infancy, at least, is linked both concurrently and predictively to the use of less-adaptive emotion-regulation skills.

Moderated Effects of Temperament. A second way that temperament might affect emotional regulation is that it is moderated by some environmental influence such as parenting behavior (Calkins, 1994). Such a hypothesis implies that temperament affects emotional regulation when it is displayed in the context of specific type of parenting. So, for example, an infant who has a tendency to be easily frustrated might have difficulties developing appropriate emotion-regulation skills only when the infant's caregiver does not provide sensitive and responsive care. Such an infant might be forced to rely on immature or ineffective self-regulation skills because the caregiver is not providing the appropriate, indeed necessary, emotional support that will allow the child to become a skilled practitioner of emotion regulation even in the absence of the caregiver.

There is considerable evidence that caregiving behavior is directly related to both proximal and distal measures of emotion regulation, as well as to both behavioral and biological measures of such behavior (Braungart & Stifter, 1991; Calkins et al., 1998; Diener, Mangelsdorf, McHale, & Frosch, 2002; Donovan & Leavitt, 1985; Nachmias et al., 1996). The question of indirect effects is one that has been examined in studies of both specific emotion-regulation strategies (proximal effects) and behavior problems (distal effects).

Empirical investigations of the moderational hypothesis of temperament by caregiving interactions with respect to proximal measures of emotion regulation are quite uncommon. Gilliom and colleagues (Gilliom et al., 2002) conducted a study that examined specific emotion-regulation strategy use beyond the infancy period. The focus of this investigation was on preschoolers' use of specific anger-control strategies during a waiting paradigm. Specific strategies involving the control of attention were found to predict the anger reaction of the children in this situation. In addition, though, maternal negative control was found to moderate this temperament effect. Children who displayed a difficult temperament and whose mothers used more negative control developed different, potentially less effective strategies for regulating anger when they were of school age (Gilliom et al., 2002).

Mediational Effects of Temperament. A third way that temperament may affect the development of emotional regulation is through processes or mechanisms that mediate this relation. As defined by Baron and Kenny (1986), a mediator is a variable that serves as the mechanism through which a predictor affects an outcome. Because mediational analyses allow one to specify possible mechanisms or processes that explain how one variable affects another, they are thus quite useful in developing an understanding of developmental process. Although few studies have specified the goal of defining the mechanism through which temperament affects regulation, it is possible to extrapolate, at least on a theoretical level, some of these processes given the existing literature.

For example, one hypothesized central process in the emergence of emotion regulation is the control of attention (Kopp, 2002). A number of investigators have reported that specific attention-regulating behaviors have a direct influence on the experience and expression of both positive and negative affective states (Calkins et al., 2002; Rothbart, Posner, & Rosicky, 1994; Stifter & Moyer, 1991). Clearly, attention must be considered a central process that links temperamental reactivity to emotional regulation very early in development.

A second process that may link temperament to emotional regulation in early development may be physiological in nature. Descriptions of processes underlying the maturation and differentiation of the frontal lobes have been provided by Fox (1989, 1994), who noted that the frontal lobes of the brain are differentially specialized for approach versus avoidance and that these tendencies influence the behaviors that children engage in when emotionally and behaviorally aroused. He further noted that maturation of the frontal cortex provides a mechanism for the more sophisticated and planful regulatory behaviors of older children versus infants. Porges (Porges, Doussard-Roosevelt, & Maita, 1994; Porges, 1996) also described an important role for biological maturation, specifically maturation of the parasympathetic nervous system, which plays a key role in regulation of state, motor activity, and emotion. Moreover, Porges noted that individual differences in nervous system functioning might mediate the expression and regulation of emotion (Porges et al., 1994). Physiological measures of autonomic nervous system (ANS) activity such as heart rate variability have been linked to both temperamental reactivity and emotion regulation. Regulation or suppression of vagal tone during emotional challenge is thought to be a physiological strategy that permits sustained attention and behaviors indicative of active coping that are mediated by the parasympathetic nervous system (Porges, 1991, 1996; Wilson & Gottman, 1996). The degree to which the organism experiences ANS arousal, as reflected in heart rate variability, may affect the successful generation of emotional coping skills because of the organism's capacity to regulate physiological arousal. Thus, childhood psychological problems that have been linked to temperamental reactivity may, in fact, be caused by the failure of these children to acquire adaptive regulatory skills to cope with their physiological reactivity to novelty and uncertainty (Calkins, 1994; Rothbart & Bates, 1998).

Although physiological and attentional control mechanisms have been hypothesized to mediate the relation between reactivity and emotional regulation (Calkins, 1994; Kopp, 2002; Porges, 1996), there has been only indirect empirical evidence to support this relation (Calkins et al., 2002). Explicit tests of such a model are needed to verify these relations. Greater emphasis on physiological processes in studies of early emotional development will significantly enhance our ability to understand these relations and their potential contribution to the development of psychopathology.

Self-Regulation and Childhood Psychopathology

Within the framework outlined, temperamental distress is hypothesized to affect the development of psychopathology via its influence on developing self-regulation and emotional regulation. Relations between specific dimensions of self-regulation and emotional regulation and childhood psychopathology are now the focus of much developmental and clinical psychology research, though with greater emphasis on the emotion-psychopathology associations. However, evidence is growing that physiological measures of regulation are related to behavior problems in young children. Specifically, several measures of cardiac functioning show consistent relations to self-regulation and externalizing behavior. Children with low RSA may be at risk because they may have difficulty attending and reacting to environmental stimulation (Porges, 1991; Wilson & Gottman, 1996). Heart rate variability has been found to be reduced in children with conduct disorder (Pine et al., 1998). Eisenberg et al. (1995) found that greater heart rate variability was also related to better social competence. Pine and colleagues (Pine et al., 1998) recently reported that 11-year-old boys with externalizing symptoms had lower heart rate variability. Mezzacappa and colleagues (Mezzacappa et al., 1997) reported similar findings among adolescent males. These researchers concluded that such relations may occur because of parasympathetic links to regulatory abilities involving attentional and behavioral control.

While growing evidence suggests that physiological regulatory processes may underlie young children's behavioral difficulties, considerable research has established that emotion regulation very early in life is also predictive of later behavior and behavior problems (Cole, Michel, & Teti, 1994). Stifter, Spinrad, and Braungart-Rieker (1999) found that emotional regulation in response to frustration in infancy was related to compliance to adult requests in toddlerhood. Eisenberg and her colleagues (Eisenberg et al., 1994, 1996; Eisenberg, Murphy, Maszk, Smith, & Karbon, 1995) have consistently found relations among emotion regulation and behavior problems and peer competence.

One example of how problematic emotion regulation may lead to deficiencies in social competence is in the relation between anger management and aggression that Eisenberg has observed across a number of studies (Eisenberg et al., 1993, 1994; Fabes & Eisenberg, 1992). Eisenberg found that individuals who are highly emotional in response to anger-inducing events and low in regulation are likely to display aggression. Eisenberg hypothesizes that the intensity of anger is related to a loss of behavioral control. Strategies such as attentional control, avoidance, and instrumental coping may be useful in dealing with anger (Eisenberg et al., 1993, 1994).

Although most of the research examining deficits in children with externalizing behavior problems has focused on the role of emotion regulation, more sophisticated types of regulation are also implicated in these disorders. For example, evidence exists for a negative relation between the child's success at behavioral regulation (compliance, control of impulsivity, and delay of gratification ability) and externalizing problem behavior. Eisenberg and colleagues have examined the relation between behavioral regulation and externalizing behaviors among older children. In one study, Eisenberg found that teacher and parent ratings of children's problem behavior were related to children's persistence on a behavioral regulation task. In addition, parent ratings of impulsivity, inhibition control, and global self-control predicted parent ratings of later problem behavior and teacher ratings of children's social competence (Eisenberg et al., 1997). In a separate sample of 214 children (ages 4.5–8), Eisenberg et al. (2001) found a negative correlation between child persistence and mother report of externalizing behavior. There was also a negative correlation between both teacher and parent ratings of regulation and the other reporters' rating of externalizing behavior. Though clearly a direct link exists between behavioral regulation and externalizing behavior in young children, Eisenberg et al. (2001) have explored behavioral regulation as a mediator of these relations. They found that regulation mediated the relation between maternal positive and negative expressivity and children's internalizing and externalizing behaviors. These findings suggest that behavioral regulation plays an important role in how parenting behaviors affect child outcomes, both directly and indirectly.

Given evidence that self-regulation is related to externalizing behavior, it is not surprising that regulatory processes have also been investigated in relation to internalizing disorders in young children (Cicchetti & Toth, 1991; Fox & Calkins, 1993; Schultz, Izard, Ackerman, & Youngstrom, 2001). These disorders may appear to be less common in younger children, but this may be due to the fact that such disorders may be less obvious and less disruptive to parents and teachers. Again, much research in this area involving infants and very young children has focused on the phenomenon of behavioral inhibition and its relation to social withdrawal. However, an examination of the studies with a focus on regulatory behavior such as attention and inhibition suggest that temperamental reactivity likely interacts with emotion regulation to predict internalizing problems (Rubin, Coplan, Fox, & Calkins, 1995). Fox (1994) speculates that a stable resting pattern of frontal EEG asymmetry found among negatively reactive and socially withdrawn children may reflect an underlying trait disposition for the motivational states of approach or withdrawal and that such motivational states may facilitate adaptive regulatory behavior under conditions of emotional challenge (Fox, 1994; Fox et al., 1996, 2001). Superimposed on this foundation of lateralized brain function are processes such as attention that function to provide competencies to the child for adaptive emotion regulation. It is the interaction of lateralization, which predisposes the child to engage in approach versus withdrawal behaviors (depending on whether the left or right frontal region is more activated), and attention skills that enables the child to use specific strategies. A child with well-developed attention-control skills who is predisposed to withdraw from a threatening stimulus may be better able to engage in self-distraction than a child with a similar predisposition, but without such skills (Calkins & Fox, 2002).

Behavioral regulation may also predict internalizing in children from a very young age. Behaviorally inhibited toddlers have been found to be more socially wary and reticent than their uninhibited counterparts when interacting with peers at 4 years of age (Calkins & Fox, 1995). Vondra, Shaw, Swearingen, Cohen, and Owens (2001) found that 2-year-old children who displayed greater behavioral regulation had fewer internalizing behavior problems at age 3.5. Brody and Flor (1998) found a strong correlation between behavioral regulation and teacher ratings of withdrawal, anxiety, and depression in a sample of African American 6- to 9-year-olds living in single-parent households. Moreover, behavioral regulation mediated the connection between maternal measures (maternal parenting style, mother-child relationship, and maternal school involvement) and internalizing problems. This is consistent with findings by Eisenberg et al. (2001) that children's behavioral regulation mediated the relation between maternal emotional expressivity and children's internalizing problems. These findings suggest that behavioral regulation may not simply be a direct predictor of internalizing behavior but may also play a role in the link between parenting and internalizing for young children.

SUMMARY AND FUTURE DIRECTIONS

The theoretical and empirical work reviewed to this point suggests that there are clear implications of temperamental reactivity, particularly distress, for the development of childhood psychopathology. However, this effect may not be direct; the mechanism that allows temperament to exert its effects may be self-regulation, a set of processes that are considered under the rubric of temperament but that develop over the course of infancy and childhood. For example, the level of distress an infant experiences, which is thought to be reflective of a stable, biologically based trait, influences the tendency to use specific emotion-regulation strategies, the subsequent level of distress, the likelihood of the future use of particular strategies, and the development of problematic profiles of emotion regulation that are core features of internalizing (overcontrol) and externalizing (undercontrol) problems. In addition, there is evidence from the psychophysiological literature that predictable biological responses can be expected from infants in contexts that activate the emotion systems during the course of early development, but that these physiological response systems may interact with attention and cognition processes to influence subsequent behavior. Multimethod, multilevel assessments of these physiological and behavioral control systems are clearly needed for us to understand the processes and pathways involved in the development of psychopathology.

Beyond direct effects and mediational models of temperament, it is clear that the moderational role of parenting, with respect to reactivity, self-regulation, and psychopathology, must also be explored. However, because these effects have not been systematically assessed with respect to the specific types of moderators and mediators, the age at which such processes are observable, and the proximal versus distal outcomes involved, clear explication of the role of temperament, self-regulation, and environment is not yet possible. Moreover, it is clear that the direction of effects in development is not always from child to outcome. Transactional influences from the environment to the child and back again are responsible for some pathways in development (Cummings, Davies, & Campbell, 2000). The child plays an important role in the dyadic interactions with caregivers that lead to the development of relationships that are themselves critical to the development of emotion regulation (Calkins, 1994, 2004; Thompson, 1994). Consequently, these transactional influences may obscure the identification of longer-term effects of temperament on emotional processes, but they are clearly important to an understanding of the developmental pathways to childhood psychopathology (Cicchetti, 1984, 1993).

REFERENCES

Achenbach, T. M. (1982). *Developmental psychopathology* (2nd ed.). New York: Wiley.

Achenbach, T. M. (1991). *Manual for the Child Behavior Checklist/ 4–18 and 1991 Profile*. Burlington: University of Vermont Department of Psychology.

Achenbach, T. M., & Edelbrock, C. S. (1978). The classification of child psychopathology: A review and analysis of empirical efforts. *Psychological Bulletin, 85,* 1275–1301.

Achenbach, T. M., & Edelbrock, C. S. (1981). Behavioral problems and competencies reported by parents of normal and disturbed children aged four through sixteen. *Monographs of the Society for Research in Child Development, 46*(1, Serial No. 188).

Aksan, N., Goldsmith, H. H., Smider, N., Essex, M., Clark, R., Klein, M., & Vandell, D. (1999). Derivation and prediction of temperamental types among preschoolers. *Developmental Psychology, 35,* 958–971.

Andersson, H. W., & Sommerfelt, K. (1999). Infant temperamental factors as predictors of problem behavior and IQ at age 5 years: Interactional effects of biological and social risk factors. *Child Study Journal, 29,* 207–226.

Anthony, J. L, Lonigan, C. J., Hooe, E. S., & Phillips, B. M. (2002). An affect-based, hierarchical model of temperament and its relations with internalizing symptomatology. *Journal of Clinical Child and Adolescent Psychology, 31,* 480–490.

Barkley, R. A. (1997). *ADHD and the nature of self-control.* New York: Guilford Press.

Baron, R. M., & Kenny, D. A. (1986). The moderator-mediator variable distinction in social psychological research: Conceptual, strategic, and statistical considerations. *Journal of Personality and Social Psychology, 51,* 1173–1182.

Bates, J. E., Bayles, K., Bennett, D. S., Ridge, B., & Brown, M. M. (1991). Origins of externalizing behavior problems at eight years of age. In D. Pepler & K. Rubin (Eds.), *Development and treatment of childhood aggression* (pp. 93–120). Hillsdale, NJ: Erlbaum.

Bates, J. E., & McFadyen-Ketchum, S. (2000). Temperament and parent-child relations as interacting factors in children's behavioral adjustment. In V. J. Molfese & D. L. Molfese (Eds.), *Temperament and personality development across the lifespan* (pp. 141–176). Mahwah, NJ: Erlbaum.

Bates, J. E., Pettit, G., Dodge, K., & Ridge, B. (1998). Interaction of temperamental resistance to control and restrictive parenting in the development of externalizing behavior. *Developmental Psychology, 34,* 982–995.

Beauregard, M., Levesque J., & Paquette, V. (2004). Neural basis of conscious and voluntary self-regulation of emotion. In M. Beauregard (Ed.), *Consciousness, emotional self-regulation and the brain* (pp. 163–194). Amsterdam: John Benjamins.

Bell, M. A., & Wolf, C. (2004). Emotion and cognition: An intricately bound developmental process. *Child Development, 75,* 366–370.

Blair, C. (2002). School readiness: Integrating cognition and emotion in a neurobiological conceptualization of children's functioning at school entry. *American Psychologist, 57,* 111–127.

Braungart, J. M., & Stifter, C. A. (1991). Regulation of negative reactivity during the Strange Situation: Temperament and attachment in 12-month-old infants. *Infant Behavior and Development, 14,* 349–367.

Braungart-Rieker, J., & Stifter, C. (1996). Infants' responses to frustrating situations: Continuity and change in reactivity and regulation. *Child Development, 67,* 1767–1769.

Brody, G. H., & Flor, D. L. (1998). Maternal resources, parenting practices, and child competence in rural, single-parent African American families. *Child Development, 69,* 803–816.

Bronson, M. B. (2000). *Self-regulation in early childhood: Nature and nurture.* New York: Guilford Press.

Buss, A. H., & Goldsmith (1998). Fear and anger regulation in infancy: Effects on the temporal dynamics of affective expression. *Child Development, 69,* 359–374.

Buss, A. H., & Plomin, R. (1984). *Temperament: Early developing personality traits.* Hillsdale, NJ: Erlbaum.

Bussing, R., Gary, F. A., & Mason, D. M. (2003). Child temperament, ADHD and caregiver strain: Exploring relationships in an epidemiological sample. *Journal of the American Academy of Child and Adolescent Psychiatry, 42,* 184–192.

Calkins, S. D. (1994). Origins and outcomes of individual differences in emotional regulation. In N. A. Fox (Ed.), *Emotion regulation: Behavioral and biological considerations. Monographs of the Society for Research in Child Development, 59*(2–3, Serial No. 240), pp. 53–72.

Calkins, S. D. (1997). Cardiac vagal tone indices of temperamental reactivity and behavioral regulation in young children. *Developmental Psychobiology, 31,* 125–135.

Calkins, S. D. (2002). Does aversive behavior during toddlerhood matter? The effects of difficult temperament on maternal perceptions and behavior. *Infant Mental Health Journal, 23,* 381–402.

Calkins, S. D. (2004). Early attachment processes and the development of emotional self-regulation. In R. F. Baumeister & K. D. Vohs (Eds.), *Handbook of self regulation* (pp. 324–339). New York: Guilford Press.

Calkins, S. D., & Dedmon, S. A. (2000). Physiological and behavioral regulation in two-year-old children with aggressive/destructive behavior problems. *Journal of Abnormal Child Psychology, 2,* 103–118.

Calkins, S. D., Dedmon, S., Gill, K., Lomax, L., & Johnson, L. (2002). Frustration in infancy: Implications for emotion regulation, physiological processes, and temperament. *Infancy, 3,* 175–198.

Calkins, S. D., & Fox, N. A. (1992). The relations among infant temperament, security of attachment, and behavioral inhibition at 24 months. *Child Development, 63,* 1456–1472.

Calkins, S. D., & Fox, N. A. (1995). *Longitudinal correlates of toddler inhibition.* Paper presented at the Biennial Meeting of the Society for Research in Child Development, Indianapolis, IN.

Calkins, S. D., & Fox, N. A. (2002). Self-regulatory processes in early personality development: A multilevel approach to the study of childhood social withdrawal and aggression. *Development and Psychopathology, 14,* 477–498.

Calkins, S. D., Fox, N. A., & Marshall, T. R. (1996). Behavioral and physiological antecedents of inhibition in infancy. *Child Development, 67,* 523–540.

Calkins, S. D., & Johnson, M. C. (1998). Toddler regulation of distress to frustrating events: Temperamental and maternal correlates. *Infant Behavior and Development, 21,* 379–395.

Calkins, S. D., Smith, C. L., Gill, K. L., & Johnson, M. C. (1998). Maternal interactive style across contexts: Relations to emotional, behavioral and physiological regulation during toddlerhood. *Social Development, 7,* 350–369.

Campbell, S. B. (1995). Behavior problems in preschool children: A review of recent research. *Journal of Child Psychology and Psychiatry, 36,* 113–149.

Caspi, A., Henry, B., McGee, R., Moffitt, T., & Silva, P. (1995). Temperamental origins of child and adolescent behavior problems: From age three to fifteen. *Child Development, 66,* 55–68.

Caspi, A., Moffit, T. E., Newman, D. L., & Silva, P.A. (1996). Behavioral observations at age 3 predict adult psychiatric disorders: Longitudinal evidence from a birth cohort. *Archives of General Psychiatry, 53,* 1033–1039.

Caspi, A., & Silva, P. A. (1995). Temperamental qualities at age three predict personality traits in young adulthood: Longitudinal evidence from a birth cohort. *Child Development, 66,* 486–498.

Cicchetti, D. (1984). The emergence of developmental psychopathology. *Child Development, 55,* 1–7.

Cicchetti, D. (1993). Developmental psychopathology: Reactions, reflections, projections. *Developmental Review, 13,* 471–502.

Cicchetti, D., Ganiban, J., & Barnett, D. (1991). Contributions from the study of high-risk populations to understanding the development of emotional regulation. In J. Garber & K. A. Dodge (Eds.), *The development of emotion regulation and dysregulation* (pp. 69–88). New York: Cambridge University Press.

Cicchetti, D., & Toth, S. L. (Eds.). (1991). *Internalizing and externalizing expressions of dysfunction.* Hillsdale, NJ: Erlbaum.

Cole, P. M., Michel, M. K., & Teti, L. O. (1994). The development of emotion regulation and dysregulation: A clinical perspective. *Monographs of the Society for Research in Child Development, 59,* 73–100, 250–283.

Cummings, E. M., Davies, P. T., & Campbell, S. B. (2000). *Developmental psychopathology and family process: Theory, research, and clinical implications.* New York: Guilford Press.

Davidson, R. J. (1984). Affect, cognition, and hemispheric specialization. In C. E. Izard, J. Kagan, & R. Zajonc (Eds.), *Emotion, cognition, and behavior.* New York: Cambridge University Press.

Davidson, R. J., Chapman, J. P., Chapman, L. J., & Henriques, J. B. (1990). Asymmetrical brain electrical activity discriminates between psychometrically-matched verbal and spatial cognitive tasks. *Psychophysiology, 27,* 528–543.

Davidson, R. J., & Fox, N. A. (1982). Asymmetrical brain activity discriminates between positive versus negative affective stimuli in human infants. *Science, 218,* 1235–1237.

Davidson, R. J., & Fox, N. A. (1989). Frontal brain asymmetry predicts infants' response to maternal separation. *Journal of Abnormal Psychology, 98,* 127–131.

Davidson, R. J., Putnam, K. M., & Larson, C. L. (2000). Dysfunction in the neural circuitry of emotion regulation—a possible prelude to violence. *Science, 289,* 591–594.

Davis, E. P., Bruce, J., & Gunnar, M. R. (2002). The anterior attention network: Associations with temperament and neuroendocrine activity in 6-year-old children. *Developmental Psychobiology, 40,* 43–65.

DeGangi, G. A., DiPietro, J. A., Greenspan, S. I., & Porges, S. W. (1991). Psychophysiological characteristics of the regulatory disordered infant. *Infant Behavior and Development, 14,* 37–50.

Derryberry, D., & Rothbart, M. K. (1997). Reactive and effortful processes in the organization of temperament. *Development and Psychopathology, 9,* 633–652.

Diener, M., Mangelsdorf, S., McHale, J., & Frosch, C. (2002). Infants' behavioral strategies for emotion regulation with fathers and mothers: Associations with emotional expressions and attachment quality. *Infancy, 3,* 153–174.

DiLalla, L. F., & Jones, S. (2000). Genetic and environmental influences on temperament in preschoolers. In V. J. Molfese & J. A. Card (Eds.), *Temperament and personality development across the life span* (pp. 33–55). Mahwah, NJ: Erlbaum.

Donovan, W. L., & Leavitt, L. A. (1985). Physiologic assessment of mother-infant attachment. *Journal of the American Academy of Child Psychiatry, 24,* 65–70.

Eisenberg, N., Cumberland, A., Spinrad, T. L., Fabes, R. A., Shepard, S. A., Reiser, M., et al. (2001). The relations of regulation and emotionality to children's externalizing and internalizing problem behavior. *Child Development, 72,* 1112–1134.

Eisenberg, N., Fabes, R. A., Bernzweig, J., Karbon, M., Poulin, R., & Hanish, L. (1993). The relations of emotionality and regulation to preschoolers' social skills and sociometric status. *Child Development, 64,* 1418–1438.

Eisenberg, N., Fabes, R., Guthrie, I., Murphy, B., Maszk, P., Holmgren, R., et al. (1996). The relations of regulation and emotionality to problem behavior in elementary school. *Development and Psychopathology, 8,* 141–162.

Eisenberg, N., Fabes, R. A., Nyman, M., Bernzweig, J., Bernzweig, J., & Pinuelas, A. (1994). The relations of emotionality and regulation to children's anger-related reactions. *Child Development, 65,* 109–128.

Eisenberg, N., Fabes, R. A., Shephard, S. A., Murphy, B. C., Guthrie, I. K., Jones, S., et al. (1997). Contemporaneous and longitudinal prediction of children's social functioning from regulation and emotionality. *Child Development, 68,* 642–664.

Eisenberg, N., Murphy, B. C., Maszk, P., Smith, M., & Karbon, M. (1995). The role of emotionality and regulation in children's social functioning: A longitudinal study. *Child Development, 66,* 1360–1384.

Fabes, R. A., & Eisenberg, N. (1992). Young children's coping with interpersonal anger. *Child Development, 63,* 116–128.

Fox, N. A. (1989). Psychophysiological correlates of emotional reactivity during the first year of life. *Developmental Psychology, 25,* 364–372.

Fox, N. A. (1991). If it's not left, it's right: Electroencephalogram asymmetry and the development of emotion. *American Psychologist, 46,* 863–872.

Fox, N. A. (1994). Dynamic cerebral process underlying emotion regulation. In N. A. Fox (Ed.), *Emotion regulation: Behavioral and biological considerations. Monographs of the Society for Research in Child Development, 59*(2–3, Serial No. 240), pp. 152–166.

Fox, N. A., & Calkins, S. D. (1993). Pathways to aggression and social withdrawal: Interactions among temperament, attachment and regulation. In K. Rubin & J. Asendorpf (Eds.), *Social withdrawal, shyness and inhibition in childhood* (pp. 81–100). Hillsdale, NJ: Erlbaum.

Fox, N. A., Calkins, S. D., Porges, S. W., Rubin, K., Coplan, R. J., Stewart, S., et al. (1995). Frontal activation asymmetry and social competence at four years of age. *Child Development, 66,* 1770–1784.

Fox, N. A., & Card, J. A. (1999). Psychophysiological measures in the study of attachment. In J. Cassidy & P. Shaver (Eds.), *Handbook of attachment: Theory, research, and clinical applications* (pp. 226–245). New York: Guilford Press.

Fox, N. A., & Davidson, R. J. (1986). Taste-elicited changes in facial signs of emotion and the asymmetry of brain electrical activity in human newborns. *Neuropsychologia, 24,* 417–422.

Fox, N. A., & Davidson, R. J. (1987). Electroencephalogram asymmetry in response to the approach of a stranger and maternal separation. *Developmental Psychology, 23,* 233–240.

Fox, N. A., & Davidson, R. J. (1988). Patterns of brain electrical activity during the expression of discrete emotions in ten-month-old infants. *Developmental Psychology, 24,* 230–236.

Fox, N. A., & Davidson, R. J. (1991). Hemispheric asymmetry and attachment behaviors: Developmental processes and individual differences in separation protest. In J. L. Gewirtz & W. M. Kurtines (Eds.), *Intersections with attachment* (pp. 147–164). Hillsdale, NJ: Erlbaum.

Fox, N. A., & Gelles, M. (1984). Face to face interactions with term and preterm infants. *Infant Mental Health Journal, 5,* 192–208.

Fox, N. A., Henderson, H. A., & Marshall, P. J. (2002). The biology of temperament: An integrative approach. In C. A. Nelson & M. Luciana (Eds.), *The Handbook of developmental cognitive neuroscience.* Cambridge, MA: MIT Press.

Fox, N. A., Henderson, H. A., Rubin, K. H., Calkins, S. D., & Schmidt, L. A. (2001). Continuity and discontinuity of behavioral inhibition and exuberance: Psychophysiological and behavioral influences across the first four years of life. *Child Development, 72,* 1–21.

Fox, N. A., Schmidt, L. A., Calkins, S. D., Rubin, K. H., & Coplan, R. J. (1996). The role of frontal activation in the regulation and dysregulation of social behavior during the preschool years. *Developmental and Psychopathology, 8,* 89–102.

Fox, N. A., Schmidt, L. A., & Henderson, H. A. (2000). Developmental psychophysiology: Conceptual and methodological perspectives. In J. Cacioppo, L. Tassinary, & G. Berntson (Eds.), *Handbook of psychophysiology* (pp. 665–686). New York: Cambridge University Press.

Garcia Coll, C., Kagan, J., & Reznick, J. S. (1984). Behavioral inhibition to the unfamiliar. *Child Development, 55,* 1005–1019.

Gilliom, M., Shaw, D., Beck, J., Schonberg, M., & Lukon, J. (2002). Anger regulation in disadvantaged preschool boys: Strategies, antecedents, and the development of self-control. *Developmental Psychology, 38,* 222–235.

Goldsmith, H. H., Buss, A., Plomin, R., Rothbart, M., Thomas, A., Chess, S., et al. (1987). Roundtable: What is temperament? Four approaches. *Child Development, 58,* 505–529.

Goldsmith, H. H., & Campos, J. J. (1990). The structure of temperamental fear and pleasure in infants: A psychometric perspective. *Child Development, 61,* 1944–1964.

Goldsmith, H. H., Lemery, K. S., Aksan, N., & Buss, K. A. (2000). Temperamental substrates of personality. In V. J. Molfese & D. L. Molfese (Eds.), *Temperament and personality development across the life span* (pp. 1–32). Mahwah, NJ: Erlbaum.

Goldsmith, H. H., & Rothbart, M. K. (1993). *The laboratory temperament assessment battery (LAB-TAB).* Madison: University of Wisconsin.

Gunnar, M. R. (1990). The psychobiology of infant temperament. In J. F. Colombo & J. Fagan (Eds.), *Individual differences in infancy: Reliability, stability, prediction* (pp. 387–409). Hillsdale, NJ: Erlbaum.

Gunnar, M. R., & Davis, E. P. (2003). Stress and emotion in early childhood. In R. M. Lerner, M. A. Easterbrooks, & J. Mistry (Eds.), *Handbook of psychology: Vol. 6. Developmental psychology* (pp. 113–134). Hoboken, NJ: Wiley.

Harman, C., Rothbart, M. K., & Posner, M. I. (1997). Distress and attention interactions in early infancy. *Motivation and Emotion, 21,* 27–43.

Hinshaw, S. P. (1987). Hyperactivity, attention deficit disorders, and learning disabilities. In V. B. Van Hasselt & M. Hersen (Eds.), *Psychological evaluation of the developmentally and physically disabled.* New York: Erlbaum.

Hinshaw, S. P. (2002). Process, mechanism, and explanation related to externalizing behavior in developmental psychopathology. *Journal of Abnormal Child Psychology, 30,* 431–446.

Huffman, L. C., Bryan, Y. E., del Carmen, R., Pederson, F. A., Doussard-Roosevelt, J. A., & Porges, S. W. (1998). Infant temperament and cardiac vagal tone: Assessments at twelve weeks of age. *Child Development, 69,* 624–635.

Isabella, R. A., Ward, M. J., & Belsky, J. (1985). Convergence of multiple sources of information on infant individuality: Neonatal behavior, infant behavior, and temperament reports. *Infant Behavior and Development, 8,* 283–291.

Kagan, J. (1989). The concept of behavioral inhibition to the unfamiliar. In J. S. Reznick (Ed.), *Perspectives on behavioral inhibition. The John D. and Catherine T. MacArthur Foundation series on mental health and development* (pp. 1–23). Chicago: University Chicago Press.

Kagan, J. (1991). Etiologies of adolescents at risk. *Journal of Adolescent Health, 12,* 591–596.

Kagan, J. (1994). On the nature of emotion. In N. A. Fox (Ed.), *Emotion regulation: Behavioral and biological considerations. Monographs of the Society for Research in Child Development,* 59(2–3, Serial No. 240), pp. 7–24.

Kagan, J., Reznick, J. S., & Snidman, N. (1987). The physiology and psychology of behavioral inhibition in children. *Child Development, 58,* 1459–1473.

Kagan, J., & Snidman, N. (1991). Temperamental factors in human development. *American Psychologist, 46,* 856–862.

Kagan, J., Snidman, N., & Arcus, D. (1993). On the temperamental categories of inhibited and uninhibited children. In K. H. Rubin & J. B. Asendorpf (Eds.), *Social withdrawal, inhibition, and shyness in childhood* (pp. 19–28). Hillsdale, NJ: Erlbaum.

Keane, S. P., & Calkins, S. D. (2004). Predicting kindergarten peer social status from toddler and preschool problem behavior. *Journal of Abnormal Child Psychology, 32,* 409–423.

Keenan, K. (2000). Emotion dysregulation as a risk factor for child psychopathology. *Clinical Psychology: Science and Practice, 7,* 418–434.

Keenan, K., & Shaw, D. S. (2003). Exploring the etiology of antisocial behavior in the first years of life. In B. B. Lahey, T. E. Moffitt, & A. Caspi (Eds.), *Causes of conduct disorder and juvenile delinquency* (pp. 153–181). New York: Guilford Press.

Keenan, K., Shaw, D. S., Delliquadri, E., Giovannelli, J., & Walsh, B. (1998). Evidence for the continuity of early problem behaviors: Application of a developmental model. *Journal of Abnormal Psychology, 26,* 441–452.

Keiley, M. K., Lofthouse, N., Bates, J. E., Dodge, K. A., & Pettit, G. S. (2003). Differential risks of covarying and pure components in mother and teacher reports of externalizing and internalizing behavior across ages 5 to 14. *Journal of Abnormal Child Psychology, 31,* 267–283.

Kingston, L., & Prior, M. (1995). The development of patterns of stable, transient, and school age onset aggressive behavior in young children. *Journal of the American Academy of Child and Adolescent Psychiatry, 34,* 348–358.

Kopp, C. (1982). Antecedents of self-regulation: A developmental perspective. *Developmental Psychology, 18,* 199–214.

Kopp, C. (1989). Regulation of distress and negative emotions: A developmental view. *Developmental Psychology, 25,* 243–254.

Kopp, C. (1992). Emotional distress and control in young children. In N. Eisenberg & R. Fabes (Eds.), *Emotion and its regulation in early development. New directions for child development* (pp. 7–23). San Francisco: Jossey-Bass/Pfeiffer.

Kopp, C. (2002). The codevelopment of attention and emotion regulation. *Infancy, 3,* 199–208.

Lane, R. D., & McRae, K. (2004). Neural substrates of conscious emotional experience. In M. Beauregard (Ed.), *Consciousness, emotional self-regulation and the brain* (pp. 87–122). Amsterdam: John Benjamins.

Lemery, K. S., Essex, M. J., & Smider, N. A. (2002). Revealing the relation between temperament and behavior problem symptoms by eliminating measurement confounding: Expert ratings and factor analyses. *Child Development, 73,* 867–882.

Lengua, L. J., West, S. G., & Sandler, I. N. (1998). Temperament as a predictor of symptomatology in children: Addressing contamination of measures. *Child Development, 69,* 164–181.

Lewis, M., & Miller, S. (1990). *Handbook of developmental psychopathology.* New York: Plenum Press.

Luu, P., & Tucker, D. M. (2004). Self-regulation by the medial frontal cortex: Limbic representation of motive set-points. In M. Beauregard (Ed.), *Consciousness, emotional self-regulation and the brain* (pp. 123–162). Amsterdam: John Benjamins.

Mangelsdorf, S., Gunnar, M., Kestenbaum, R., Lang, S., & Andreas, D. (1990). Infant proneness-to-distress temperament, maternal personality, and mother-infant attachment: Associations and goodness of fit. *Child Development, 61,* 820–831.

Mangelsdorf, S. C., Schoppe, S. J., & Buur, H. (2000). The meaning of parental reports: A contextual approach to the study of temperament and behavior problems in childhood. In V. J. Molfese & D. L. Molfese (Eds.), *Temperament and personality development across the lifespan* (pp. 121–140). Mahwah, NJ: Erlbaum.

Mangelsdorf, S., Shapiro, J., & Marzolf, D. (1995). Developmental and temperamental differences in emotional regulation in infancy. *Child Development, 66,* 1817–1828.

Matheny, A. P., Riese, M. L., & Wilson, R. S. (1985). Rudiments of infant temperament: Newborn to 9 months. *Developmental Psychology, 21,* 486–494.

Mathijssen, J. P., Koot, H. M., & Verhulst, F. C. (1999). Predicting change in problem behavior from child and family characteristics and stress in referred children and adolescents. *Development and Psychopathology, 11,* 305–320.

Merikangas, K. R., Swendsen, J. D., Preisig, M. A., & Chazan, R. Z. (1998). Psychopathology and temperament in parents and offspring: Results of a family study. *Journal of Affective Disorders, 51,* 63–74.

Mezzacappa, E., Tremblay, R., Kindlon, D., Saul, J., Arsenault, L., Seguin, J., et al. (1997). Anxiety, antisocial behavior, and heart rate regulation in adolescent males. *Journal of Child Psychology and Psychiatry and Allied Disciplines, 38,* 457–469.

Moffit, T. E., Caspi, A., Dickson, N., Silva, P. A., & Stanton, W. (1996). Childhood-onset versus adolescent-onset antisocial conduct in males: Natural history from ages 3 to 18. *Development and Psychopathology, 8,* 399–424.

Morris, A. S., Silk, J. S., Steinberg, L., Sessa, F. M., Avenevoli, S., & Essex, M. J. (2002). Temperamental vulnerability and negative parenting as interacting of child adjustment. *Journal of Marriage and Family, 64,* 461–471.

Mun, E., Fitzgerald, H., Von Eye, A., Puttler, L. I., & Zucker, R. (2001). Temperamental characteristics as predictors of externalizing and internalizing child behavior problems in the context of high and low parental psychopathology. *Infant Mental Health Journal, 22,* 393–415.

Nachmias, M., Gunnar, M., Mangelsdorf, S., Parritz, R., & Buss, K. (1996). Behavioral inhibition and stress reactivity: The moderating role of attachment security. *Child Development, 67,* 508–522.

Nigg, J. T., & Huang-Pollock, C. L. (2003). An early-onset model of the role of executive functions and intelligence in conduct disorder/delinquency. In B. B. Lahey, T. E. Moffit, & A. Caspi (Eds.), *Causes of conduct disorder and juvenile delinquency* (pp. 227–253). New York: Guilford Press.

Ochsner, K. N., & Gross, J. J. (2004). Thinking makes it so: A social cognitive neuroscience approach to emotion regulation. In R. F. Baumeister & K. D. Vohs (Eds.), *Handbook of self-regulation: Research, theory and applications* (pp. 229–258). New York: Guilford Press.

Olson, S. L., Bates, J. E., Sandy, J. M., & Schilling, E. M. (2002). Early developmental precursors of impulsive and inattentive behavior: From infancy to middle childhood. *Journal of Child Psychology and Psychiatry and Allied Disciplines, 43,* 435–448.

Phillips, B. M., Lonigan, C. J., Driscoll, K., & Hooe, E. S. (2002). Positive and negative affectivity in children: A multitrait-multimethod investigation. *Journal of Clinical Child and Adolescent Psychology, 31,* 465–479.

Pine, D. S., Wasserman, G. A., Miller, L., Coplan, J. D., Bagiella, E., Kovelenku, P., et al. (1998). Heart period variability and psychopathology in urban boys at risk for delinquency. *Psychophysiology, 35,* 521–529.

Porges, S. W. (1991). Vagal tone: An autonomic mediatory of affect. In J. A. Garber & K. A. Dodge (Eds.), *The development of affect regulation and dysregulation* (pp. 11–128). New York: Cambridge University Press.

Porges, S. W. (1996). Physiological regulation in high-risk infants: A model for assessment and potential intervention. *Development and Psychopathology, 8,* 43–58.

Porges, S. W., Doussard-Roosevelt, J. A., & Maita, A. K. (1994). Vagal tone and the physiological regulation of emotion. In N. A. Fox (Ed.), *Emotion regulation: Behavioral and biological con-*

siderations. *Monographs of the Society for Research in Child Development, 59,* 167–186.

Porges, S. W., Doussard-Roosevelt, J. A., Portales, A. L., & Greenspan, S. I. (1996). Infant regulation of the vagal "brake" predicts child behavior problems: A psychobiological model of social behavior. *Developmental Psychobiology, 29,* 697–712.

Porter, F. L., Porges, S. W., & Marshall, R. E. (1988). Newborn pain cries and vagal tone: Parallel changes in response to circumcision. *Child Development, 59,* 495–505.

Posner, M. I., & Rothbart, M. K. (1992). Attentional mechanisms and conscious experience. In D. Milner & M. Ruggs (Eds.), *The neuropsychology of consciousness* (pp. 91–111). San Diego: Academic Press.

Posner, M. I., & Rothbart, M. K. (1994). Attentional regulation: From mechanism to culture. In P. Bertelson & P. Eelen (Eds.), *International perspectives on psychological science. Vol. 1. Leading themes* (pp. 41–55). Hillsdale, NJ: Erlbaum.

Posner, M. I., & Rothbart, M. K. (1998). Summary and commentary: Developing attentional skills. In J. Richards (Ed.), *Cognitive neuroscience of attention: A developmental perspective* (pp. 317–323). Mahwah, NJ: Erlbaum.

Posner, M. I., & Rothbart, M. K. (2000). Developing mechanisms of self-regulation. *Development and Psychopathology, 12,* 427–441.

Prior, M., Smart, D., Sanson, A., & Oberklaid, F. (1993). Sex differences in psychological differences in psychological adjustment from infancy to 8 years. *Journal of the American Academy of Child and Adolescent Psychiatry, 32,* 291–304.

Prior, M., Smart, D., Sanson, A., Pedlow, R., & Oberklaid, F. (1992). Transient versus stable behavior problems in a normative sample: Infancy to school age. *Journal of Pediatric Psychology, 17,* 423–443.

Rothbart, M. K. (1981). Measurement of temperament in infancy. *Child Development, 52,* 569–578.

Rothbart, M. K. (1986). Longitudinal observation of infant temperament. *Developmental Psychology, 22,* 356–365.

Rothbart, M. K. (1989). Temperament and development. In G. Kohnstamm, J. Bates, & M. K. Rothbart (Eds.), *Temperament in childhood* (pp. 187–248). Chichester, England: Wiley.

Rothbart, M. K., & Bates, J. E. (1998). Temperament. In W. Damon (Series ed.) & N. Eisenberg (Vol. ed.), *Handbook of child psychology: Vol. 4. Social, emotional, and personality development* (5th ed., pp. 105–176). New York: Wiley.

Rothbart, M. K., & Derryberry, D. (1981). Development of individual differences in temperament. In M. E. Lamb & A. L. Brown (Eds.), *The neuropsychology of individual differences: A developmental perspective* (pp. 93–123). New York: Plenum Press.

Rothbart, M. K., Derryberry, D., & Hershey, K. (2000). Stability of temperament in childhood: laboratory infant assessment to parent report at seven years. In V. Molfese & D. Molfese (Eds.), *Temperament and personality development across the lifespan* (pp. 85–119). Mahwah, NJ: Erlbaum.

Rothbart, M. K., & Posner, M. I. (1985). Temperament and the development of self-regulation. In L. C. Hartlage & C. F. Telzrow (Eds.), *The neuropsychology of individual differences: A developmental perspective* (pp. 93–123). New York: Plenum Press.

Rothbart, M. K., Posner, M. I., & Boylan, A. (1990). Regulatory mechanisms in infant development. In J. Enns (Ed.), *The development of attention: Research and theory* (pp. 139–160). Amsterdam: Elsevier.

Rothbart, M. K., Posner, M. I., & Rosicky, J. (1994). Orienting in normal and pathological development. *Development and Psychopathology, 6,* 635–652.

Rothbart, M., Ziaie, H., & O'Boyle, C. (1992). Self-regulation and emotion in infancy. In N. Eisenberg & R. Fabes, (Eds.), *Emotion and its regulation in early development. New directions for child development* (pp. 7–23). San Francisco: Jossey-Bass/Pfeiffer.

Rubin, K. H., & Asendorpf, J. B. (1993). *Social withdrawal, inhibition, and shyness in childhood.* Hillsdale, NJ: Erlbaum.

Rubin, K. H., Coplan, R. J., Fox, N. A., & Calkins, S. D. (1995). Emotionality, emotion regulation and preschoolers' social adaptation. *Development and Psychopathology 7,* 49–62.

Rubin, K. H., Hastings, P., Chen, X., Stewart, S., & McNichol, K. (1998). Interpersonal and maternal correlates of aggression, conflict, and externalizing problems in toddlers. *Child Development, 69,* 1614–1629.

Ruff, H., & Rothbart, M. K. (1996). *Attention in early development.* New York: Oxford University Press.

Russell, A., Hart, C. H., Robinson, C. C., & Olsen, S. F. (2003). Children's sociable and aggressive behaviour with peers: A comparison of the US and Australia, and contributions of temperament and parenting styles. *International Journal of Behavioural Development, 27,* 74–86.

Sanson, A., Smart, D., Prior, M., & Oberklaid, F. (1993). Precursors of hyperactivity and aggression. *Journal of the American Academy of Child and Adolescent Psychiatry, 32,* 1207–1216.

Schmitz, S., Fulker, D. W., Plomin, R., Zahn-Waxler, C., Emde, R. N., & DeFries, J. C. (1999). Temperament and problem behavior during early childhood. *International Journal of Behavioral Development, 23,* 333–355.

Schultz, D., Izard, C. E., Ackerman, B. P., & Youngstrom, E. A. (2001). Emotion knowledge in economically disadvantaged children: Self-regulatory antecedents and relations to social difficulties and withdrawal. *Development and Psychopathology, 13,* 53–67.

Seifer, R., & Sameroff, A. J. (1986). The concept, measurement, and interpretation of temperament in young children: A survey of research issues. *Advances in Developmental and Behavioral Pediatrics, 7,* 1–43.

Seifer, R., Schiller, M., Sameroff, A., Resnick, S., & Riordan, K. (1996). Attachment, maternal sensitivity, and infant temperament during the first year of life. *Developmental Psychology, 32,* 12–25.

Shaw, D. S., Keenan, K., & Vondra, J. I. (1994). Developmental precursors of externalizing behavior: Ages 1 to 3. *Developmental Psychology, 30,* 355–364.

Shaw, D., Owens, E., Giovanelli, J., & Winslow, E. (2001). Infant and toddler pathways leading to early externalizing disorders. *Journal of the American Academy of Child and Adolescent Psychiatry, 40,* 36–43.

Shaw, D., Owens, E., Vondra, J., Keenan, K., & Winslow, E. (1996). Early risk factors and pathways in the development of early disruptive behavior problems. *Development and Psychopathology, 4,* 679–700.

Shiner, R., & Caspi, A. (2003). Personality differences in childhood and adolescence: Measurement, development, and consequences. *Journal of Child Psychology and Psychiatry and Allied Disciplines, 44,* 2–32.

Shipman, K., Schneider, R., & Brown, A. (2004). Emotion dysregulation and psychopathology. In M. Beauregard (Ed.), *Consciousness, emotional self-regulation and the brain* (pp. 61–85). Amsterdam: John Benjamins.

Sroufe, A. L. (1996). *Emotional development: The organization of emotional life in the early years.* New York: Cambridge University Press.

Stams, G. J., Juffer, F., & Ijzendoorn, M. H. (2002). Maternal sensitivity, infant attachment, and temperament in early childhood predict adjustment in middle childhood: The case of adopted children and their biologically unrelated parents. *Developmental Psychology, 38,* 806–821.

Stansbury, K., & Gunnar, M. R. (1994). Adrenocortical activity and emotion regulation. In N. A. Fox (Ed.), *The development of emotion regulation: Biological and behavioral considerations* (pp. 108–134). *Monographs of the Society for Research in Child Development, 59*(2–3, Serial No. 240).

Stifter, C. A., & Braungart, J. M. (1995). The regulation of negative reactivity in infancy: Function and development. *Developmental Psychology, 31,* 448–455.

Stifter, C. A., & Fox, N. A. (1990). Infant reactivity: Physiological correlates of newborn and 5-month temperament. *Developmental Psychology, 26,* 582–588.

Stifter, C. A., Fox, N. A., & Porges, S. W. (1989). Facial expressivity and vagal tone in 5- and 10-month-old infants. *Infant Behavior and Development, 12,* 127–137.

Stifter, C. A., & Moyer, D. (1991). The regulation of positive affect: Gaze aversion activity during mother-infant interaction. *Infant Behavior and Development, 14,* 111–123.

Stifter, C. A., Spinrad, T. L., & Braungart-Rieker, J. M. (1999). Toward a developmental model of child compliance: The role of emotion regulation in infancy. *Child Development, 70,* 21–32.

St. Jonn Seed, M., & Weiss, S. (2002). Maternal expressed emotion as a predictor of emotional and behavioral problems in low birth weight children. *Issues in Mental Health Nursing, 23,* 649–672.

Suomi, S. J. (1987). Genetic and maternal contributions to individual differences in rhesus monkey biobehavioral development. In W. P. Smotherman, M. A. Hofer, & N. A. Krasnegor (Eds.), *Perinatal development: A psychobiological perspective. Behavioral biology* (pp. 397–419). San Diego: Academic Press.

Thomas, A., Birch, H., Chess, S., Hertzig, M., & Korn, S. (1964). *Behavioral individuality in early childhood.* New York: New York University Press.

Thomas, A., & Chess, S. (1977). *Temperament and development.* New York: Brunner/Mazel.

Thomas, A., Chess, S., & Birch, H. G. (1970). The origins of personality. *Scientific American, 223,* 102–109.

Thompson, R. A. (1994). Emotion regulation: A theme in search of definition. In N. A. Fox (Ed.), *The development of emotion regulation: Biological and behavioral considerations. Monographs of the Society for Research in Child Development, 59*(2–3 Serial No. 240), pp. 25–52.

Tschann, J. M., Kaiser, P., Chesney, M. A., Alkon, A., & Boyce, W. T. (1996). Resilience and vulnerability among preschool children: Family functioning, temperament, and behavior problems. *Journal of the American Academy of Child and Adolescent Psychiatry, 35,* 184–192.

Vaughn, B. (1986). The doubtful validity of infant temperament assessments by means of questionnaires like the ITQ. In G. A. Kohnstamm (Ed.), *Temperament discussed: Temperament and development in infancy and childhood.* (pp. 35–42). Bristol, PA: Swets & Zeitlinger.

Vitaro, F., Brendgen, M., & Tremblay, R. E. (2002). Reactively and proactively aggressive children: Antecedent and subsequent characteristics. *Journal of Child Psychology and Psychiatry, 43,* 495–505.

Vohs, K. D., & Baumeister, R. F. (2004). Understanding self-regulation: An introduction. In R. F. Baumeister & K. D. Vohs (Eds.), *Handbook of self-regulation: Research, theory and applications* (pp. 1–13). New York: Guilford Press.

Vondra, J. I., Shaw, D. S., Swearingen, L., Cohen, M., & Owens, E. B. (2001). Attachment stability and emotional and behavioral regulation from infancy to preschool age. *Development and Psychopathology, 13,* 13–33.

Wilson, B., & Gottman, J. (1996). Attention—the shuttle between emotion and cognition: Risk, resiliency, and physiological bases. In E. Hetherington & E. Blechman (Eds.), *Stress, coping and resiliency in children and families.* Mahwah, NJ: Erlbaum.

Worobey, J. (1986). Convergence among assessments of temperament in the first month. *Child Development, 57,* 47–55.

Zahn-Waxler, C., Klimes-Dougan, B., & Slattery, M. J. (2000). Internalizing problems of childhood and adolescence: Prospects, pitfalls, and progress in understanding the development of anxiety and depression. *Development and Psychopathology, 12,* 443–466.

CHAPTER 7

Infant Mental Health

MARY MARGARET GLEASON AND CHARLES H. ZEANAH

INTRODUCTION

Infant mental health is a clinical discipline that focuses on psychological disturbances in children in the first several years of life as well as in their families. Infant mental health also encompasses multidisciplinary approaches to enhancing the social and emotional competence of infants through their biological, relationship, and cultural contexts. Infant mental health has been defined as "the young child's capacity to experience, regulate, and express emotions, form close and secure relationships, and explore the environment and learn. All of these capacities will be best accomplished within the context of the caregiving environment that includes family, community, and cultural expectations for young children" (Zero to Three, 2002).

Infant mental health is multidisciplinary because navigating the complex, interrelated nature of human development and its deviations requires expertise and conceptualizations beyond the capabilities of any particular discipline. The complexity of the clinical problems of infants and toddlers invites multidisciplinary collaboration to minimize suffering, enhance development, and promote competence. Therefore, it is likely that the field of infant mental health will remain pluralistic, a subspecialty within a number of different disciplines rather than an integrated and distinct discipline in itself.

Two distinctive themes of infant mental health are especially relevant for clinicians. The first theme is development. Young children develop and change in the early years at a pace that is unique in the life cycle. Clinicians require a thorough knowledge of infant development to appreciate both developmental delays and developmental deviance. Furthermore, clinicians must be focused on developmental trajectories. This means thinking about not only where the infant is now, but also where the infant has been and where the infant is going. A second major distinctive feature of infancy is the importance of multiple interrelated *contexts* (parent-infant relationship, family, cultural, and so forth) within which infants develop. Of these, we propose that the relationship context is the most important, and this is the most distinctive focus of infant mental health efforts. Understanding the contexts in which infants develop requires understanding risk and protective factors as they impact developmental trajectories. Both development and the child's relationship and cultural contexts must be considered in the core activities of assessment and intervention with infants and their families.

In this chapter, we begin by describing the development and the contexts of infant mental health within which risk and protective factors exert their effects. Next, we turn to an overview of psychopathology in the early years. We then describe the assessment of young children experiencing or at risk for psychopathology. Finally, we review principles of intervention, both prevention and treatment of established conditions, and provide illustrative examples of approaches.

DEVELOPMENT

A useful way of conceptualizing development in the first few years of life is to consider periods in which rapid qualitative changes occur in an infant's capacity for social interactions and relationships. Three of these times occur in the first 2 years. As shown in Table 7.1, these shifts occur around 2 months, 7 months, and 18 months. These biobehavioral shifts are believed to be tied to underlying neurobiological developmental changes, although little is known at this point about the specifics of what those changes entail.

With these three periods of rapid developmental change identified, it is possible to consider the four developmental epochs created by these periods (see Table 7.1). The first 2 months of life constitute a period often described as a phase of homeostasis. This is a time in which extrauterine adaptation by the infant predominates, and social interaction is less apparent.

From 2 to 7 months, however, the infant blossoms socially and engages in frequent, socially reciprocal interchanges with

TABLE 7.1 Biobehavior Shifts in Infant Development

	0–2 months	Shift 1 2–3 months	2–7 months	Shift 2 7–9 months	7–18 months	Shift 3 18–20 months	18–36 months
Cognitive	Recognition of maternal face Emergence of perceptual recognition (especially olfactory and auditory)		Emergence of classical and operant conditioning Development of habituation		Object permanence Exploration of objects' properties		Symbolic representation Pretend play Emergence of personal pronouns
Language	Crying, cooing predominate		Responsive cooing, polysyllabic babbling		Intentional communication (mostly gestural at first), then developing vocabulary up to 10 words		Rapid expansion of vocabulary Use of 2–3 word combinations Decreased need for context cues in receptive language skills
Emotional	Ability to express distress, contentment, and interest		Able to display differentiated expressions of sadness, disgust, anger, joy and contentment, interest and surprise		Instrumental use of affect develops Begins to use social referencing		18 months—demonstrates embarrassment, empathy, and envy 24 months—pride and shame appear as distinct emotional displays
Social	Physical and social attributes attract adults for social interactions		Social smile develops Eye contact emerges Able to engage adults in reciprocal social interactions		Focused attachment to primary caregiver Separation protest and stranger reactions develop Intersubjectivity evident		Able to express needs Develops negotiating abilities with caregivers Increased interest in peers—moves toward interactive play
Motor	Tracks past midline Begins to be able to lift head while prone		Increased mobility and perspective taking from rolling over and sitting		Increased physical independence with walking (12 months) and the emergency of self-feeding abilities		Ability for fine-motor skills allows for self-care skills including helping with dressing

Adapted from Zeanah, Boris, & Larrieu, 1997.

caregivers. From 7 to 18 months, the infant is in a phase of focused attachment and intersubjectivity. Attachment is heralded by the onset of stranger wariness and separation protest as infants begin to seek comfort, support, nurturance, and protection from a small number of caregiving adults. Qualitative differences in attachment relationships are predictive of subsequent psychosocial adaptation. Intersubjectivity refers to the infant's discovery of the ability to share thoughts, feelings, and intentions with others. This ability provides the foundation for a number of important achievements, including social referencing, intentional communication, and affect attunement. Finally, following the shift occurring around 18 to 20 months, the infant is in the phase of symbolic representation as the ability to communicate verbally and the ability to imagine something other than immediate reality become apparent. These capacities enormously enhance the complexity of the young child's social repertoire at a time when the child is beginning to move out into the wider social world.

BIOLOGICAL, RELATIONSHIP, AND CULTURAL CONTEXTS

The importance of the contexts, or environments, in which infants grow and develop is well established. In fact, the inclusion of context in studies of development has been asserted to be the most important research advance in developmental psychology in the latter part of the twentieth century (Sameroff, 1992). Appreciating the complexities and importance of context has enhanced our understanding of infant development and our ability to predict developmental trajectories (Sameroff & Fiese, 2000). Contexts exert their effects from within and from without, determining the experiences an infant has as well as how that infant affects those experiences.

Intrinsic (within the individual) characteristics that contribute to context may derive from individual differences in genetic endowment (specific genetic defects or genetic susceptibility for affective or behavioral disorders) as well as from noninherited neurobiological differences. Although individual differences in infant characteristics may be identified readily, there is surprisingly little predictive power about subsequent outcomes when infant characteristics are considered alone. For example, studies of preterm infants, many of whom experienced significant perinatal insults, have shown repeatedly that the best predictors of social, emotional, and cognitive outcomes are family rather than infant biological or health-related characteristics. In fact, social class of the infant's family is the single best predictor of outcome in these children (Sameroff & Fiese, 2000). When considered within the context of their caregiving relationships, however, infant characteristics are much more predictive of later-emerging behavior problems (Mangelsdorf, Gunnar, Kestenbaum, Lang, & Andreas, 1990; Sanson, Oberklaid, Pedlow, & Prior, 1991).

Infant-caregiver relationships are the most important *experience-near* context for infant development. A considerable body of research has documented the importance of the quality of the infant-caregiver relationship and its impact on infant development. Positive qualities in infant-parent relationships, such as warmth, reciprocity, and successful resolution of distress, have been linked to more optimal social, emotional, and cognitive development (see Crockenberg & Leerkes, 2000; Lyons-Ruth & Zeanah, 1993; Zeanah, Boris, & Larrieu, 1997).

Infant-parent relationships moderate intrinsic risk factors in infants (McCarton et al., 1997; Ramey et al., 1992). In other words, infants with biological difficulties such as the complications of prematurity have better outcomes when their caregiving environments are supportive and more problematic outcomes when their caregiving environments are less supportive.

Infant-parent relationships also are the conduit through which infants experience environmental risk factors. Infants experience risk factors such as poverty, maternal mental illness, and partner violence primarily through their effects on infant-parent relationships. Through their specific relationship experiences, infants are affected by the risk factors that characterize their caregiving environments.

Finally, increasingly we are learning that the way psychopathology is expressed in young children depends on the types of relationships they have with their caregivers (Zeanah, Boris, & Scheeringa, 1997). Research has shown that infants construct different types of relationships with different caregivers (Steele, Steele, & Fonagy, 1996; Suess, Grossman, & Sroufe, 1992); they also may express symptoms in the presence of one caregiver but not with another (Zeanah & Boris, 2000).

For all of the preceding reasons, the focus of infant mental health has been dominated by a relational approach. This means that infants are best understood, assessed, and treated in the context of their primary caregiving relationships. Or,
as Sroufe (1989) put it, "Almost all problems in the early years, while often manifest poignantly in child behavior, are best conceptualized as relationship problems" (p. 70).

Beyond the caregiver-infant dyad, we must consider infant development in the context of the entire family. Considerable evidence, for example, indicates that the marital relationship is one of the most important influences on child development (Cummings, 1998). An infant's relationships with various family members are influenced by various other relationships within the family (Emde, 1991). Beyond the immediate family of the infant, other family influences are important. From its early clinical roots, infant mental health has recognized the importance of intergenerational influences on infant development. These have been demonstrated empirically in various studies of infant-parent attachment. Using a structured interview, the Adult Attachment Interview (George, Kaplan, & Main, 1984), to assess classifications of attachment in parents, and a laboratory procedure, the Strange Situation Procedure (Ainsworth, Blehar, Waters, & Wall, 1978), to assess classifications of attachment in infants, investigators have examined predicted associations between secure and insecure attachments between caregivers and their infants, and caregivers and their parents. In a recent meta-analysis, van Ijzendoorn (1995) reported a 75 percent concordance between secure attachment in parents and infants, with a substantial effect size of 1.06 for 854 infant-parent dyads. One of the clearest demonstrations of intergenerational influences was provided by Benoit and Parker (1994). They demonstrated significant associations between mothers' and infants' attachment classifications, between mothers and their own mothers' attachment classifications, and between grandmothers' and their grandchildren's attachment classifications.

Infants also grow and develop within cultural contexts. Cultural beliefs and value systems define the assumptions of the group about what is important as well as the rules about raising children a certain way. Parenting beliefs and parents' explanations and interpretations of infant behavior are among the most important aspects of the cultural context of infant development (Garcia-Coll & Meyer, 1993; Lewis, 2000). These beliefs include shared cultural assumptions about what facilitates infant development; the roles and relevance of parenting; and the causes and amelioration of psychopathology, the topic we consider next.

PSYCHOPATHOLOGY IN EARLY CHILDHOOD

The idea of psychiatric disorders in infants and young children makes many uncomfortable. Nevertheless, in clinical practice, examples of patterns of serious psychopathology are impossible to avoid. Young children present consistent patterns of impairing symptoms that compromise their functioning and development. The debate is about whether these patterns of symptoms comprise disorders or whether they are best conceptualized as risk factors for subsequent disorders. A growing body of research supports the reliability and validity of diagnoses in early childhood (American Academy of Child and Adolescent Psychiatry [AACAP], 2003; Frankel, Boyum, & Harmon, 2004; Luby, Heffelfinger, et al., 2003; Luby, Mrakotsky, et al., 2003; Scheeringa, Zeanah, Myers, & Putnam, 2003). In addition, children with early mental health disorders are at risk for continued psychiatric problems later (Lavigne et al., 1998).

Nevertheless, very real challenges exist in the diagnosis of young children. In particular, measurement problems, rapidity of development, distinguishing normal variation from true psychopathology, and the relationship context all have been cited (Zeanah, Boris, & Scheeringa, 1997). Further, the primary tool for psychiatric diagnosis, the *DSM-IV*, was developed primarily for adults, with limited empirical attention for diagnoses in childhood and adolescence (American Psychiatric Association [APA], 2000; Stafford, Zeanah, & Scheeringa, 2003). Alternative diagnostic systems have been proposed, and the field continues to fine-tune the definition of disorders in young children. Diagnostic classifications allow effective communication with parents and colleagues about our understanding of the problem and provide a common foundation for research to understand the validity, prognosis, and intervention effects of the identified symptom constellations.

Diagnostic Systems

Many researchers and clinicians have been concerned about the usefulness of the *DSM-IV* diagnostic criteria in evaluating the symptoms of infants and toddlers because the diagnoses were primarily written for adults and used limited empirical data related to preschoolers. In 1994, Zero to Three published the *Diagnostic Classification of Mental Health and Developmental Disorders of Infancy and Early Childhood* (*DC: 0–3*; Zero to Three, 1994). This diagnostic framework provides a supplemental system to the *DSM* criteria, using a clinically driven set of developmentally derived criteria for disorders of early childhood (Zero to Three, 1994). A primary difference between the *DSM-IV* and the *DC: 0–3* is the transformation of Axis II to focus on the primary caregiving relationship and disorders within that relationship. The *DC: 0–3* also sharpens the diagnostic focus on a child's developmental level, by both changing Axis III to include developmental conditions and specifically characterizing Axis V (functioning) in the context of the child's developmental achievement. Although the system may be clinically useful and provides new diagnostic entities that clinicians will use, research on the validity of the criteria has been slow (Emde & Wise, 2003; Stafford et al., 2003). In addition, *DC: 0–3* often is not accepted by third-party insurers and must be translated back into a *DSM-IV* or *ICD-10* code. The AACAP has responded to the need for increased reliability in diagnostic criteria for the preschool age group by developing the Research Diagnostic Criteria for Infants and Preschool Children (AACAP, 2003). The task force reviewed the available literature on reliability and validity of preschool diagnoses and revised diagnostic criteria for disorders affecting young children, with the goal that the criteria may stimulate further research focused on validity and reliability of the *DSM* criteria in young children.

Disorders in Clinical Settings

Rates of *DSM-IV* diagnoses in young children appear to be similar to those in older children. Using consensus diagnosis based on questionnaires and structured interviews, Lavigne demonstrated that 21 percent of preschoolers in a pediatric office met *DSM-IV* criteria for at least one diagnosis and 9 percent of preschoolers had a severe disorder (Lavigne et al., 1996). Disorders with prominent externalizing symptoms (attention-deficit/hyperactivity disorder [ADHD], oppositional defiant disorder [ODD], and conduct disorder [CD] in the *DSM-IV* classification system; regulatory disorders of *DC: 0–3* classification system) are common diagnoses in most referred and nonreferred populations, and trauma-related disorders also are prominent (Frankel et al., 2004; Lavigne et al., 1996; Thomas & Clark, 1998). The rates of other disorders, particularly those characterized as internalizing disorders, vary in different reports, perhaps as a reflection of difficulties with detection.

Externalizing Disorders

Externalizing symptoms, including impulsivity, oppositional behaviors, attentional difficulties, hyperactivity, and temper tantrums, are commonly described in the preschool age group and are the most common reason children are referred for infant mental health evaluations (e.g., Thomas & Clark, 1998). To some degree, these so-called symptoms can represent a part of normal development. The clinical dilemma in diagnosing these disorders in preschool children revolves around the developmental appropriateness of some of the symptoms. As children develop an enhanced sense of autonomy and they test the limits of their emotional and physical dependence, parental report of oppositional behaviors often increases (Achenbach, 1992). Parental reports of aggression and externalizing behaviors peak at age 2 and then begin to decrease to some extent (Achenbach, 1992; Shaw, Gilliom, & Giovannelli, 2000). However, there are clearly cases in which a child's behaviors reflect an impulsivity and dysregulation out of proportion to the normal developmental phase.

The triumvirate of externalizing diagnoses in the *DSM* nosology includes ADHD; ODD; and, less commonly, CD. These diagnoses are among the best-validated disorders in the preschool age group (AACAP, 2003) and they show stability over time, with 70 percent of children diagnosed at ages 2–3 continuing to have a disruptive behavior disorder diagnosis 4 years later (Lavigne et al., 1998).

Inattention/Hyperactivity

ADHD is defined as a maladaptive and developmentally inappropriate level of either inattention or hyperactivity and impulsivity (APA, 2000) and has a general prevalence in children 2–5 years old of 2 percent in the primary care setting (Lavigne et al., 1996). Children with ADHD may also present with a combined type in which they meet criteria for both inattentive and hyperactive-impulsive types of ADHD. Like older children with ADHD, preschoolers with ADHD present with either hyperactive, hypermotoric, impulsive symptoms or with notable inattention and disorganization. Because of the diagnostic challenges of assessing young children with these symptoms, it is especially important to obtain information about the child's behavior in multiple settings and from various caregivers, especially day care providers, to rule out differential diagnoses such as anxiety disorders, learning disorders, or relationship-based disorders.

Oppositional Defiant Disorder

In a general primary care setting, the most common psychiatric disorder identified by a number of standardized checklists and observations was ODD in children ages 2–5 years, with a prevalence of 16.8 percent with a peak at age 3, and with boys displaying a higher prevalence than girls (Lavigne et al., 1996). Oppositional defiant disorder is characterized by a pattern of "negativistic, hostile, and defiant behaviors" (p. 243) including arguing with adults; losing temper; refusing to follow directions; and seeming angry, resentful, or spiteful (APA, 2000). Children with ODD often have co-morbid ADHD (Lavigne et al., 1996), which is associated with a worse outcome 2 years later (Speltz, McClellan, DeKlyen, & Jones, 1999). Also associated with a worse outcome are specific ODD symptoms, including being "touchy and easily annoyed" and "spiteful and vindictive" (Speltz et al., 1999).

Conduct Disorder

CD, a more extreme disorder of disruptive, aggressive, and destructive behaviors, is less common in the preschool population, with fewer than 0.5 percent of children meeting the diagnostic criteria (Lavigne et al., 1996). Nevertheless, with developmentally sensitive criteria, it does appear that CD can be diagnosed in preschool children (AACAP, 2003; Keenan and Wakschlag, 2002, 2004). Keenan and Wakschlag (2002) described the utility of identifying the "pervasiveness, intensity, and intransigence" (p. 352) of disruptive behaviors in distinguishing between disordered behaviors and developmentally normal autonomy and demonstrations of frustration.

Some have suggested that not all children who present with disruptive behaviors as their chief complaints have a disruptive behavior disorder. In a study of 64 children who were referred to one infant mental health clinic for disruptive behaviors, for example, only 27 percent were diagnosed with ADHD or ODD using *DSM-IV* criteria. Using the *DC: 0–3* criteria, 41 percent had a disorder of affect, 30 percent a regulatory disorder, and 23 percent a traumatic stress disorder (Thomas & Clark, 1998). Thomas and Clark emphasized that these disruptive behaviors may represent a final common pathway for the expression of inner turmoil or distress.

Internalizing Disorders

Internalizing disorders in early childhood include disorders of mood and anxiety as well as somatic complaints. These are less well studied than externalizing disorders, and they may be more difficult to recognize because they can be associated with social withdrawal rather than intrusive disruptive symptoms.

Depressive Disorders

Depression in young children looks similar to depression in older children and adults, although with more variability in mood states and with fewer vegetative symptoms. In young children, irritability or sadness can be the core symptom of depression. In addition, children can have notable sleep, appetite, or concentration disturbances as well as preoccupation with death or excessive guilty feelings. Unlike adults, preschoolers with depression may not demonstrate the consistent daily symptoms for 2 weeks (Luby, Mrakotsky, et al., 2003). Recent data indicate that somatic symptoms do occur within the context of preschool depression, but depressive symptoms predominate the clinical picture (Luby, Heffelfinger, et al., 2003).

Anxiety Disorders

Anxiety symptoms are prominent in early childhood, with the fears peaking in the toddler years and then usually decreasing over time before entering school. It is during this time that young children can develop fears of the dark and of monsters. However, it is also possible for children to present with impairing anxiety symptoms. Young children present with specific phobias during this period. It is not clear whether young children experience social phobia, panic disorders, or acute stress disorders (AACAP, 2003).

Researchers interested in anxiety tendencies in children have described a group of children who are behaviorally inhibited, that is, they tend to demonstrate fear and withdrawal in new situations. Behavioral inhibition appears to be physiologically mediated, in that these children have significantly different cardiac responses to new situations than noninhibited children. Behavioral inhibition shows stability across the preschool years, with moderate correlations between measurements at 21 and 48 months of age (Kagan, Reznick, Clarke, Snidman, & Garcia-Coll, 1984). Behavioral inhibition is also related to the development of anxiety disorders, particularly social anxiety symptoms (Biederman et al., 2001).

It is clear that young children experience post-traumatic stress disorder (PTSD) after traumatic events including motor vehicle accidents, abuse, and witnessing violence. In the preschool age group, the most commonly described symptoms include *reexperiencing symptoms,* such as distress in response to a reminder of the trauma or repetitive play related to the traumatic event; *avoidance of reminders* of the trauma, such as not wanting to go in the car; and increased *arousal,* evidenced by increased irritability and temper tantrums as well as hypervigilance and hyperstartle responses (Scheeringa, Peebles, & Cook, 2001; Scheeringa et al., 2003). The context of the traumatic event is an important mediator in the development of PTSD. Children who experience a single major traumatic event are more likely to develop reexperiencing signs of PTSD than those who experience chronic traumas, who are more likely to experience signs of numbing (Scheeringa & Zeanah, 1995). The parent-child relationship can protect children from symptoms related to a traumatic event (Scheeringa & Zeanah, 2001).

Regulatory Disorders

The category of regulatory disorders of the *DC: 0–3* system provides a particular focus on early dysregulation of affect, motor, sensory, and attentional processes. These disorders are categorized as hypersensitive, underreactive, and motorically disorganized, and they are believed to reflect constitutional differences in young children. Though these disorders do not have equivalents in *DSM-IV,* they provide descriptive categories related to early childhood dysregulation and have demonstrated some predictive validity, with disordered infants having more emotional, behavioral, and developmental problems at 4 years of age (DeGangi, Porges, Sickel, & Greenspan, 1993).

Feeding Disorders

Soon after birth, and throughout the early years, feeding is one of the major activities of a parent and child. Feeding disorders are only briefly identified in the *DSM-IV,* but they are extensively described in the research diagnostic criteria, with eight subcategories of disorders. Most feeding disorders involve an inability to eat or food refusal associated with an inability to maintain appropriate weight gain. Feeding disorders can present with extreme disengagement in the feeding process or with intense conflict. Though some feeding disorders can be related to specific events (e.g., nasogastric feeding or traumatic intubations), most appear to have multifactorial etiologies. Sensory processing, attachment relationship, state regulation, and medical conditions all may play a role in the development or perpetuation of feeding disorders (AACAP, 2003; Benoit, 2000; Coolbear & Benoit, 1999). Regardless of the etiology, symptoms related to feeding are also common, in that up to 25 percent of children may experience feeding problems in the early years (Benoit, 2000). The more severe of these constitute disorders and can be quite stressful for parents and for the parent-child relationship.

Sleep Disorders

Sleep is a central factor in early childhood state regulation. Newborns spend up to 18 hours of every 24 sleeping. As infants develop, they begin to exhibit a diurnal sleep pattern, sleeping more in the evening and being awake more during the daytime. Variations in these developmental processes may manifest themselves as so-called sleep problems. Classifying these problems by frequency and duration helps to distinguish between normal variants and true disorders (Anders, Goodlin-Jones, & Sadeh, 2000). Disorders of sleep in young children can occur around sleep onset (primary insomnia or sleep refusal), or during sleep, in the form of night wakenings or parasomnias. In the preschool age group, the normal developmental process of tonsillar and adenoidal hypertrophy can produce snoring and, when excessive, sleep apnea symptoms. Sleep disturbances affect children's attention and behavior (Chervin, Dillon, Archbokd, & Ruzicka, 2003), as well as impact family sleep practices and relationships (Anders & Eiben, 1997).

Relationship Disorders

In young children, a relationship with a nurturing, sensitive, responsive caregiver is one of the most important protective factors for healthy development. Individual differences in qualitative features of the relationship, such as quality of attachment, have been associated with increased or decreased risk of problematic outcomes subsequently (van Ijzendoorn, Schuengel, & Bakersmans-Krankenburg, 1999). In fact, many aspects of the parent-child relationship may be associated with positive or negative child outcomes (Belsky & Fearson, 2002). To highlight the power of the relationship, *DC: 0–3* uses a separate axis from the clinical disorder axis to diagnose relationship disturbances. In some dyads, the pattern of relationship and distortion of perceptions in the relationship can impair at the level of a disorder. A disturbed parent-infant relationship may arise from problems within the infant, problems within the parent, or from problems between the parent and infant. Regardless of etiology, impairments in the relationship are associated with behavior problems in the child subsequently (Aoki, Zeanah, Heller, & Bakshi, 2002). The literature continues to reflect controversy and lack of consensus about the best means of conceptualizing and diagnosing these disorders (AACAP, 2003; APA, 2000; Sameroff & Emde, 1989; Stafford et al., 2003; Zeanah & Boris, 2000).

Attachment Disorders

A particular type of relationship disorder, attachment disorders have been defined reliably and also have growing evidence of validity (Zeanah & Boris, 2000; Zeanah et al., in press). Whatever the specific diagnostic criteria used, it is clear that clinically relevant disturbances in children's attachment behaviors exist. Young children with healthy attachments to a caregiver or parent are able to balance safe exploration of their environment with use of the attachment figure as a source of comfort, support, and nurturance.

Children with attachment disorders can generally demonstrate two major patterns of behaviors: inhibited and disinhibited behaviors. Children with the inhibited form of reactive attachment disorder (RAD) tend to be affectively restricted and overly cautious and do not seek out comfort from a discriminated caregiver in an effective manner (AACAP, 2003; APA, 2000). In the disinhibited type, children are excessively and indiscriminately friendly with unfamiliar adults and rarely check back with their parent, even in new environments where they may not know anyone. The *ICD-10* classification system (World Health Organization, 1992) also includes disturbance of emotional dysregulation as representing a central part of this form of RAD. These two patterns of RAD are not mutually exclusive; children can also present with features of both patterns. Although these disorders occur in the context of a disordered relationship, indiscriminate behavior patterns have been shown to persist in children from institutions, even after a child has developed an attachment relationship with a stable caregiver (Chisolm, 1998). Though it is clear that disturbances of attachment may continue to put children at risk for disorders, RAD has not been studied in children older than 5 years, and the current descriptions of these disorders may not be helpful in the older age group (AACAP, 2003).

ASSESSMENT

Infant mental health assessments are multimodal evaluations that usually involve a number of appointments in different settings. A thorough history, careful observations, and collateral information are critical components of the evaluation. Formal assessments, including structured questionnaires, developmental assessments, and relationship assessments, can add additional understanding to the child and the relationships that define his or her world.

Content of the Assessment

Direct assessments of infant behavior without major consideration of the environmental and relationship contexts are of limited value in infant mental health. Instead, infant assessments are most commonly conducted as infant-caregiver relationship assessments (Clark, Paulson, & Conlin, 1993; Zeanah, Larrieu, Heller, & Valliere, 2000), and this relationship is understood within a broader social and cultural context. Major components of the relationship assessed include the overt patterns of interaction that characterize a particular dyad as well as the subjective experience of each member of the dyad (Stern-Bruschweiler & Stern, 1989). Assessment should include evaluations of both behavior and the meaning of behavior for the members of the dyad.

Domains of the parent-child relationship have been proposed by Emde (1989) and modified for use in relationship assessment by Zeanah et al. (2000). In this model, certain parent behaviors are conceptually linked with emerging infant behaviors and qualities. Thus, parents' emotional availability is associated with infants' emerging capacities for emotion regulation. Parents' nurturance and warmth are associated with infants' sense of trust and security. Parents' response to distress is related to infants' learning to seek comfort for distress. Further, parents' protection of their infants is related to the infants' feelings of safety and the later development of the capacity for self-protection. Parents are important play partners for their infants, and play is an important domain of the infant-parent relationship. Parents also are teachers of their infants, and these efforts relate to infants' curiosity, sense of mastery, and interest in learning. Parents' ability to provide structure, routines, and instrumental care affects the infants' development of a sense of predictability and the capacity for self-regulation. Finally, parents set limits and discipline as needed to help young children develop self-control and a reasonable degree of compliance and cooperation. Although the importance of the parent's role in these domains is clear, it is important to note that the infant also plays an active role in these dyadic developmental achievements.

These domains can be assessed through a combination of parent report and observation of infant-parent interaction in naturalistic and clinic settings. Naturalistic settings like the family's home offer the advantages of observing interaction in real-world contexts, without the limits imposed by more structured settings on behavior of the dyad. Clinic settings, on the other hand, afford clinicians opportunities to structure situations to examine specific behaviors of interest and to make standardized comparisons across many caregiver-infant dyads. Caregiver-infant interactional assessments, usually conducted in clinic settings, generally include both less- and more-structured activities for parent and child to determine how the dyad negotiate each of these (Clark et al., 1993; Zeanah et al., 2000).

The meaning of the child's behavior for the parent may be assessed by careful attention to how the parent perceives and experiences the child. In some settings, this is formally assessed using structured interviews (Zeanah & Benoit, 1995), although most often, this may be noted less formally. A major advance in understanding parent perceptions of their infants has been the recognition that, in addition to the content of the parent's narrative about the child, qualitative features, such as coherence, emotional tone, and flexibility of the parent's internal working model of the child, provide valuable information about how the parent conceptualizes the infant. In other words, to understand how the parent understands and thinks about the child, it is essential to pay attention to not only what the parent reports, but also how the parent talks about the child.

Standardized assessments, including structured questionnaires, developmental assessments, and clinical interviews, can add additional understanding to the child and the relationships that define his or her world. As shown in Table 7.2, many methods are available to clinicians conducting comprehensive assessments.

Process of the Assessment

Infant mental health assessments require careful attention to process. Infant mental health can be a novel or frightening idea for many parents, and they often bring with them unspoken fears, guilt, or attributions about their role in their child's difficulties. Because of these potential concerns, one of the first steps in an evaluation is to address the parents' concerns about the evaluation itself and provide a clear explanation of the goals and process of the evaluation. Furthermore, the assessment process should be just as oriented to the identification of strengths as to problems.

A primary goal of the assessment is to develop an understanding of the problem from the parents' perspective, including the meaning of the problem behaviors in the context of the family and within the relationships of the family. In addition, the evaluation should clarify the parents' major concerns in the context of the child's developmental level, his or her genetic and medical predispositions, and social factors. Developmental delays and disorders, particularly speech and language delays, as well as medical problems are more common in children with behavioral or emotional problems. These conditions can exacerbate mental health problems and sometimes have not been diagnosed before a mental health referral has been made. Identification and treatment of these disorders is an essential part of understanding and addressing infant mental health concerns. Because clinical work with infants and toddlers is, by its very nature, a preventive endeavor, strengths of the child as an individual and of the family should be identified as well as risk factors. With the family's collaboration, the evaluator will develop a treatment plan designed to meet the parents' explicit goals and address the problems identified during the evaluation.

Infant behavior is important to assess, but most important is observing the infant's behavior with one or more caregivers. Infants may behave quite differently with different caregivers, so the only way to distinguish within-the-child characteristic behaviors rather than relationship-specific behaviors is to observe the infant interacting with all important caregivers (Zeanah et al., 2000). Videotaping such observations may be useful for clinical review as well as for review with the family.

Merely being in a clinic setting with a stranger (the clinician) is a mild stressor for an older infant or toddler. Thus, the beginning of the evaluation provides an opportunity to observe how the child and the parent interact under mild dis-

TABLE 7.2 Approaches to Assessments in Infant Mental Health

Target	Methods	Sample instruments	Ages	Areas measured	Number of items or time
General development	Parent report questionnaire	Ages and Stages Questionnaire (Squires, Bricker, & Potter, 1997)	3–60 months	Communication, gross motor, fine motor, problem solving, and personal-social	20 min
	Parent report questionnaire	Parent Evaluation of Development Scales (Glascoe, 2000)	0–8 years	Parental concern of child's speech and language, fine motor, gross motor, behavior, and social skills	2 min
	Structured infant evaluation	Bayley Scales (Bayley, 1993)	1–42 months	Mental scale, motor scale, behavior rating scale	45 min
	Structured infant evaluation	Vineland Scales of Adaptive Behavior (Sparrow, Ball, & Cicchetti, 1984)	0–18 years	Adaptive behavior composite and 4 domain scores: communication, daily living, socialization, motor skills	20–60 min
Behavioral or emotional problems	Parent report questionnaire	Ages and Stages Questionnaire: Social Emotional (Squires, Bricker, & Twombly 2002)	6–60 months	Self-regulation, compliance, communication, adaptive functioning, autonomy, affect, and interaction with people	10–15 min
	Parent report questionnaire	CBCL 1½–5 (Achenbach, 1992)	18–60 months	Internalizing, externalizing, and total problem scores	15 min
	Clinical observation	Disruptive Behavior Diagnostic Observation (Keenan & Wakschlag, 2002)	30–66 months	Disruptive Behavior Scale	
	Semistructured parent interview	Disturbance of Attachment Interview (Smyke, Dumitrescu, & Zeanah, 2002)	10–60 months	Presence of focused attachment, inhibited and indiscriminate attachment behaviors	10 min
	Parent interview	Preschool Age Psychiatric Assessment (PAPA) (Egger, Ascher, & Angold, 2003)	24–72 months	Psychiatric diagnoses and impairment based on *DSM-IV*, DC: 0–3 and RDC: Preschool age	2 hours
Parent–child interactions	Naturalistic observations		All	Qualitative observations	
	Interview and observation	Clinical Observation of Attachment (Boris et al., 2004)	18–48 months	Symptoms of *DSM-IV* reactive attachment disorder, symptoms of nonattachment and secure base distortions	30 min
	Structured evaluation	Crowell Procedure (Zeanah et al., 2000)	10–60 months	Tone, responsive, reciprocal, contingent parent-child behaviors	Approximately 45 min
Parent perceptions of infant	Semistructured interview	Working Model of the Child Interview (Zeanah & Benoit, 1995)	All, including prenatal	Narrative features, affective tone, engagement, and balanced perceptions	45–60 min

tress and how the child uses the parent for comfort. Some children will initially cling to the parent, whereas others may explore the room freely but check back visually or physically with the parent. As the interview progresses or in subsequent appointments, a child usually becomes more comfortable in the setting, and the observations become more representative of the dyad's usual interactions.

Table 7.3 outlines one approach (The Crowell Procedure, Crowell & Feldman, 1988; Zeanah et al., 2000) to interactional assessment. Observing free play is often a way to see how the dyad functions in a low-demand situation. While observing dyadic play, the evaluator can note the level of mutual engagement; shared attention; reciprocity; and, with verbal children, shared representational play themes (AACAP, 1997). Clean-up and teaching tasks are more demanding situations in which the dyad is supposed to accomplish a goal. Clinicians may observe the degree to which the dyad is able to make a demanding situation into a fun or enjoyable experience.

Across all episodes, the tone of the interaction and the dyad's comfort together also reflect the nature of the relationship. Observing the nature of the child's affective interchanges, particularly whether the child is excessively inhibited or indiscriminate with strangers, can provide information about the child's quality of attachment with his or her primary caregiver (Boris, Fueyo, & Zeanah, 1997).

TABLE 7.3 One Approach to Assessment of Child-Parent Interaction: The Crowell Procedure (12–60 months)

Episode	Time	Behaviors of interest
Free play	6–10 min	Warmth, reciprocity, joint attention, imaginative play, exploration, task-oriented vs. fun-oriented togetherness and comfort, familiarity of "play"
Cleanup	3–5 min	Compliance, cooperations, transitions
Bubbles	3–5 min	Positive affect sharing, joint attention, sponteneity, turn taking, pacing
Tasks #1–4	3–6 min	Independence vs. dependence, attempt to master, reliance for help, accomplishment vs. experience, emotional tone, transitions
Separation	3 min	Stress, self-soothing behavior, activates attachment
Reunion	3 min	Reconnection following brief separation, resolution of distress

Depending on the child's age and the nature of the parent's concerns, it can be informative to negotiate a separation and reunion during the evaluation to provide an informal window into the attachment relationship. This will include observing how the parent prepares the child for the separation, but especially the dyad's ability to acknowledge distress related to the separation and to demonstrate an ability to resolve this distress together during the reunion (Boris et al., 1997; Zeanah et al., 2000).

With infants in the early months of life, observing face-to-face interaction or feedings may afford opportunities to observe interactive behaviors. Developmentally appropriate eye contact and tracking, vocalizations and communication, state and emotion regulation, display and reading of cues, and other regulatory behaviors all can be noted (AACAP, 1997).

INTERVENTION

In early childhood, intervention includes efforts to identify young children at high risk for adverse outcomes and to prevent those outcomes, as well as to treat those already suffering from established psychopathology. The evidence base of intervention in early childhood is limited but growing. In this section, we illustrate different types of prevention and treatment efforts and highlight their distinctive features.

Prevention

Prevention of future problems generally focuses on infants at high risk for the emergence of these problems even before they become apparent. The emphasis of preventive interventions is on altering infant and parent behaviors and family functioning in order to preserve or restore infants to more normative developmental trajectories. Sometimes intrinsic infant risk factors, such as difficult temperament, cannot be prevented, but the adverse consequences of difficult temperament, such as the emergence of behavior problems, may be the focus of prevention efforts. Other environmental risk factors known to be associated with infant developmental compromise, such as maternal depression, also may focus on preventing sequelae. Abuse and neglect constitute a risk factor for infant development that has been targeted for prevention efforts, with efforts aimed at groups believed to be at risk.

One particularly powerful example of primary prevention directed at the reduction of abuse and neglect in a high-risk, impoverished sample is the work of David Olds and his colleagues. They pioneered a public health nurse home visitation intervention with first-time, impoverished mothers. The Nurse Family Partnership, as it has come to be known, begins in pregnancy and continues through the child's second birthday and focuses comprehensively on personal health, environmental health, quality of caregiving for the infant, maternal life course development, and social support. Essentially, the model involves having a nurse establish a therapeutic relationship with the mother and the mother using this relationship to enhance her relationship with her child and her own competence. Among other findings, this program demonstrated an 80 percent reduction in child maltreatment among families from birth through the child's second birthday, 56 percent reduction in health care encounters for accidental injuries in children, a 43 percent reduction in subsequent pregnancies, and a reduction in children's antisocial behaviors at age 15 years (Kitzman et al., 1997; Olds et al., 1997, 1998). Importantly, although the program was relatively expensive to implement, program costs were recovered with benefits by the time the target children were 4 years of age (Olds, Henderson, Phelps, Kitzman, & Hanks, 1993), and by the time children reached the age of 15 years, the program had yielded savings of four times its cost (Olds et al., 1997).

Other preventive efforts target children already affected by adverse experience. Young children who have been abused and neglected, for example, are at dramatically increased risk for poor outcomes across a variety of domains (Cicchetti & Toth, 1995). Our group recently demonstrated that a comprehensive, individualized, relationship-focused preventive intervention dramatically reduced recidivism for young maltreated children in foster care (Zeanah et al., 2001). Not only were the maltreated children less likely to return to foster placement a second time, but maltreating mothers also were less likely to have another child removed from them and placed in foster care subsequently. Thus, a systems-directed preventive intervention for maltreated infants and toddlers also yielded primary prevention effects for siblings born subsequently.

Another promising prevention approach currently being evaluated is the Circle of Security (Marvin, Cooper, Hoffman, & Powell, 2002). Drawn from attachment theory and research, this is a video-based group therapy approach that involves helping parents identify their own defensive styles and how those impact their relationships with their toddlers. It is currently being evaluated with various high-risk mothers and their infants.

Treatment

Treatment of already identified problems may be focused primarily on changing the infant (Benoit, Wang, & Zlotkin, 2000), the parent and her experience (Cramer et al., 1990), or the infant-parent relationship (Lieberman, Silverman, & Pawl, 2000; McDonough, 2000). Stern (1995) has argued that these different forms of intervention actually use different points of entry into the parent-infant relationship and use different therapeutic strategies, but that all are concerned with altering the infant-parent relationship as a way of changing infant behavior and ensuring that the changes are enduring.

For this reason, most often there is an explicit effort to work with parent and infant together on changing their relationship in order to change the infant. An important therapeutic aim is to develop a good working alliance between parents and therapist, that is, a shared commitment in working together in the best interest of the child (Zeanah & McDonough, 1989). The relationship between the therapist and the parent becomes an important component of treatment, although most therapeutic effort is concerned with appreciating the parent's emotional experience of the young child, and the young child's experience of the parent.

Most commonly, these approaches take the form of dyadic therapy, in which parent and child are seen together. Two of the most common dyadic approaches are infant-parent psychotherapy (Lieberman et al., 2000) and interaction guidance (McDonough, 2000). In each of these approaches, the presence of the child is considered vital for several reasons. First, the therapist is able to witness and to intervene directly in conflicted or problematic interactions that occur during the session. Second, the presence of the child focuses the treatment on the relationship between parent and child rather than on a myriad of other possible concerns. Finally, the child's presence communicates hope about the possibility of change through his or her developmental progress during treatment.

Infant-parent psychotherapy, or child-parent psychotherapy with older toddlers and preschoolers, involves identifying patterns of relationship disturbances as enacted in interactions and emotional miscommunication between members of a young child and parent dyad. The therapist's focus is on enhancing communication through clarification and reinterpretation of the needs and wishes of both parent and child. The therapist is vigilant about identifying and making explicit relationship reenactments from a parent's previous relationships as they occur in the parent-child relationship. Some preliminary evidence supports the efficacy of this treatment approach with 1- to 2-year-olds (Lieberman, Weston, & Pawl, 1991), and at present it is being actively evaluated with older children.

Interaction guidance involves liberal use of videotape of parent-child interactions and a focus on here-and-now interactions. After some initial rapport-building sessions, each session begins by videotaping a few minutes of interaction between parent and child, and the remainder of the session is spent reviewing the tape. The therapist takes care to focus exclusively on what the parent is doing well. Other concerns are brought into treatment only as they relate to the here-and-now interaction focus of the treatment. This approach also has some preliminary support for its efficacy (Cramer et al., 1990), and it is being actively evaluated in young children with relationship disturbances.

A cognitive behavioral approach (cognitive-behavioral therapy, or CBT) for sexually abused preschool girls has been demonstrated to be effective in reducing post-traumatic symptoms immediately after treatment and 1 year later (Cohen & Mannarino, 1996, 1997). In keeping with the importance of the caregiving relationship in early childhood, this approach also involves parallel work with mothers that is likely to be crucial to the success of the approach. Other efforts to apply CBT to young children are being actively evaluated at present.

SUMMARY

Infant mental health is an emerging field, but already research has established basic tenets of infant mental health assessment and intervention. The foundations of infant mental health are the understanding of the infant in the context of his or her developmental stage and within the primary caregiving relationship through which the child experiences the world. The assessment of infants in clinical settings, the conceptualizations of diagnostic categories, and the development of prevention and treatment interventions are built upon these foundations. Assessments must focus on the child's current developmental abilities and delays, and interventions must use the infant's strengths and provide support in areas of weakness or delays. Similarly, the role of the parent-child relationship should always be on the mind of the clinician. The parent's perceptions impact the way in which parents present their concerns as well as affect all of their interactions with their child. The quality of the parent-child relationship and the contributions of both the parent and the infant to this relationship are sometimes the primary focus of clinical intervention and always have the potential to modify other areas of clinical concern. Clinicians have an opportunity to intervene within this relationship that provides the most important way in which infants experience the world around them. Research in early intervention for young children with diagnosable conditions and high-risk infants can have a long-lasting impact on the development, mental health, and safety of children and their families.

REFERENCES

Achenbach, T. M. (1992). *Manual for the Child Behavior Checklist 2/3 and 1992 profile.* Burlington: University of Vermont Department of Psychiatry.

Ainsworth, M. D. S., Blehar, M., Waters, E., & Wall, S. (1978). *Patterns of attachment: A psychological study of the strange situation.* Hillsdale, NJ: Erlbaum.

American Academy of Child and Adolescent Psychiatry. (1997). Practice parameters for the psychiatric assessment of infants and toddlers (0–36 Months). *Journal of the American Academy of Child and Adolescent Psychiatry, 36,* 21S–36S.

American Academy of Child and Adolescent Psychiatry Task Force on Research Diagnostic Criteria. (2003). Research diagnostic criteria—preschool age: The process and empirical support. *Journal of the American Academy of Child and Adolescent Psychiatry, 42,* 1502–1512.

American Psychiatric Association. (2000). *Diagnostic and statistical manual of mental disorders* (4th ed., text rev.). Washington, DC: Author.

Anders, T. F., & Eiben, L. A. (1997). Pediatric sleep disorders: A review of the past 10 years. *Journal of the American Academy of Child and Adolescent Psychiatry, 36,* 9–20.

Anders, T., Goodlin-Jones, B., & Sadeh, A. (2000). Sleep disorders. In C. H. Zeanah (Ed.), *Handbook of infant mental health* (pp. 326–338). New York: Guilford Press.

Aoki, Y., Zeanah, C. H., Heller, S. S., & Bakshi, S. (2002). The parent-infant relationship global assessment scale: A study of predictive validity. *Psychiatry and Clinical Neurosciences, 56,* 493–497.

Bayley, N. (1993). *Bayley Scales of Infant Development* (2nd ed.). San Antonio, TX: Harcourt Press.

Belsky, J., & Fearon, R. M. P. (2002). Infant-mother attachment: Security, contextual risk and early development: A moderational analysis. *Developmental Psychology, 14,* 293–301.

Benoit, D. (2000). Feeding disorders, failure to thrive and obesity. In C. H. Zeanah (Ed.), *Handbook of infant mental health* (pp. 339–352). New York: Guilford Press.

Benoit, D., & Parker, K. (1994). Stability and transmission of attachment across three generations. *Child Development, 65,* 1444–1457.

Benoit, D., Wang, E. E., & Zlotkin, S. H. (2000). Discontinuation of enterostomy tube feeding by behavioral treatment in early childhood: A randomized controlled trial. *Journal of Pediatrics, 137,* 498–503.

Biederman, J., Hirshfeld-Becker, D. R., Rosenbaum, J. F., Herot, C., Friedman, D., Snidman, N., et al. (2001). Further evidence of association between behavioral inhibition and social anxiety in children. *American Journal of Psychiatry, 158,* 1673–1679.

Boris, N. W., Fueyo, M., & Zeanah, C. H. (1997). The clinical assessment of attachment in children under five. *Journal of the American Academy of Child and Adolescent Psychiatry, 36,* 291–293.

Boris, N. W., Hinshaw-Fuselier, S. S., Smyke, A. T., Scheeringa, M. S., Heller, S. S., & Zeanah, C. H. (2004). Comparing criteria for attachment disorders: Establishing reliability and validity in high-risk samples. *Journal of the American Academy of Child and Adolescent Psychiatry, 43,* 568–577.

Chervin, R. D., Dillon, J. E., Archbokd, K. H., & Ruzicka, D. L. (2003). Conduct problems and symptoms of sleep disorders in children. *Journal of the American Academy of Child and Adolescent Psychiatry, 42,* 201–208.

Chisolm, K. (1998). A three year follow-up of attachment and indiscriminate friendliness in children adopted from Romanian orphanages. *Child Development, 69,* 1092–1106.

Cicchetti, D., & Toth, S. L. (1995). A developmental psychopathology perspective on child abuse and neglect. *Journal of the American Academy of Child and Adolescent Psychiatry, 34,* 541–565.

Clark, R., Paulson, A., & Conlin, S. (1993). Assessment of developmental status and parent-infant relationships: The therapeutic process of evaluation. In C. H. Zeanah (Ed.), *Handbook of infant mental health* (pp. 191–209). New York: Guilford Press.

Cohen, J. A., & Mannarino, A. P. (1996). A treatment outcome study for sexually abused preschool children: Initial findings. *Journal of the American Academy of Child and Adolescent Psychiatry, 35,* 42–50.

Cohen, J. A., & Mannarino, A. P. (1997). A treatment study for sexually abused preschool children: Outcome during a one-year follow-up. *Journal of the American Academy of Child and Adolescent Psychiatry, 36,* 1228–1235.

Coolbear, J., & Benoit, D. (1999). Failure to thrive: Risk for clinical attachment disturbance. *Infant Mental Health Journal, 20,* 84–107.

Cramer, B., Robert-Tissot, C., Stern, D. N., Serpa-Rusconi, S., DeMuralt, M., Besson, G., et al. (1990). Outcome evaluation in brief mother-infant psychotherapy: A brief report. *Infant Mental Health Journal, 11,* 278–300.

Crockenberg, S., & Leerkes, E. (2000). Infant social and emotional development. In C. H. Zeanah (Ed.), *Handbook of infant mental health* (pp. 60–90). New York: Guilford Press.

Crowell, J. A., & Feldman, S. S. (1988) Mothers' internal models of relationships and children's behavioral and developmental status: A study of mother-child interaction. *Child Development, 59,* 1273–1285.

Cummings, E. M. (1998). Children exposed to marital conflict and violence: Conceptual and theoretical directions. In W. Holden & R. Geffner (Eds.), *Children exposed to marital violence: Theory, research, and applied issues* (pp. 55–93). Washington, DC: American Psychological Association.

DeGangi, G., Porges, S., Sickel, R., & Greenspan, S. (1993). Four year follow-up of a sample of regulatory disordered infants. *Infant Mental Health Journal, 14,* 330–343.

Egger, H. L., Ascher, B. H., & Angold, A. (2003). *Preschool Age Psychiatric Assessment Parent Interview Version 1.3.* Durham, NC: Duke University.

Emde, R. N. (1989). The infant's relationship experience: Developmental and affective aspects. In A. J. Sameroff & R. N. Emde (Eds.), *Relationship disturbances in early childhood: A developmental approach* (pp. 33–51). New York: Basic Books.

Emde, R. N. (1991). The wonder of our complex enterprise: Steps enabled by attachment and the effects of relationships on relationships. *Infant Mental Health Journal, 12,* 164–173.

Emde, R. N., & Wise, B. K. (2003). The cup is half-full: Initial clinical trials of *DC: 0–3* and recommendations for revision. *Infant Mental Health Journal, 24,* 437–446.

Frankel, K. A., Boyum, L. A., & Harmon, R. J. (2004). Diagnoses and presenting symptoms in an infant psychiatry clinic: Comparison of two diagnostic systems. *Journal of the American Academy of Child and Adolescent Psychiatry, 43,* 578–587.

Garcia-Coll, C. T., & Meyer, E. C. (1993). The sociocultural context of infant development. In C. H. Zeanah (Ed.), *Handbook of infant mental health* (pp. 56–69). New York: Guilford Press.

George, C., Kaplan, N., & Main, M. (1984). *Adult Attachment Interview.* Unpublished manuscript, University of California at Berkeley.

Glascoe, F. P. (2000). Early detection of developmental and behavioral problems. *Pediatrics in Review, 21,* 272–279.

Kagan, J., Reznick, S., Clarke, C., Snidman, N., & Garcia-Coll, C. (1984). Behavioral inhibition to the unfamiliar. *Child Development, 55,* 2212–2225.

Keenan, K., & Wakschlag, L. S. (2002). Can a valid diagnosis of disruptive behavior disorder be made in preschool children? *American Journal of Psychiatry, 159,* 351–358.

Keenan, K., & Wakschlag, L. S. (2004). Are oppositional defiant and conduct disorder symptoms normative behaviors in preschoolers? A comparison of referred and nonreferred children. *American Journal of Psychiatry, 161,* 356–358.

Kitzman, H., Olds, D. L., Henderson, C. R. Jr., Hanks, C., Cole, R., Tatelbaum, R., et al. (1997). Effect of prenatal and infancy home visitation by nurses on pregnancy outcomes, childhood injuries, and repeated childbearing. A randomized controlled trial. *Journal of the American Medical Association, 278,* 644–652.

Lavigne, J. V., Gibbons, R. D., Christoffel, K. K., Arend, R., Rosenbaum, D., Binns, H., et al. (1996). Prevalence rates and correlates of psychiatric disorders among preschool children. *Journal of the American Academy of Child and Adolescent Psychiatry, 35,* 204–214.

Lavigne, J., Arend, R., Rosenbaum, D., Binns, H., Christoffel, K. K., & Gibbons, R. (1998). Psychiatric disorders with onset in the preschool years: II. Correlates and predictors of stable case status. *Journal of the American Academy of Child and Adolescent Psychiatry, 37,* 1255–1261.

Lewis, M. L. (2000). The cultural context of infant mental health: The developmental niche of infant-caregiver relationships. In C. H. Zeanah (Ed.), *Handbook of infant mental health* (pp. 91–108). New York: Guilford Press.

Lieberman, A. F., Silverman, R., & Pawl, F. H. (2000). Infant-parent psychotherapy: Core concepts and current approaches. In C. Zeanah (Ed.), *Handbook of infant mental health* (pp. 472–484). New York: Guilford Press.

Lieberman, A. F., Weston, D. R., & Pawl, J. H. (1991). Preventive intervention and outcome with anxiously attached dyads. *Child Development, 62,* 199–209.

Luby, J. L., Heffelfinger, A. K., Mrakotsky, C., Brown, K., Hessler, M., & Wallis, J. S. (2003). Clinical picture of depression in preschool children. *Journal of the American Academy of Child and Adolescent Psychiatry, 42,* 340–348.

Luby, J. L., Mrakotsky, C., Heffelfinger, A., Brown, K., Hessler, M., & Spitznagel, E. (2003). Modification of *DSM-IV* criteria for depressed preschool children. *Journal of American Psychiatry, 160,* 1169–1172.

Lyons-Ruth, K., & Zeanah, C. H. (1993). The family context of infant mental health: Affective development in the primary caregiving relationship. In C. H. Zeanah (Ed.), *Handbook of infant mental health* (pp. 14–37). New York: Guilford Press.

Mangelsdorf, S., Gunnar, M., Kestenbaum, R., Lang, S., & Andreas, D. (1990). Infant proneness-to-distress temperament, maternal personality, and mother-infant attachment: Associations and goodness of fit. *Child Development, 61,* 820–831.

Marvin, R., Cooper, G., Hoffman, K., & Powell, B. (2002). The Circle of Security project: Attachment-based intervention with caregiver-pre-school child dyads. *Attachment and Human Development, 4,* 107–124.

McCarton, C. M., Brooks-Gunn, J., Wallace, I. F., Bauer, C. R., Bennett, F. C., Bernbaum, J. C., et al. (1997). Results at age 8 years of early intervention for low-birth-weight premature infants. The Infant Health and Development Program. *Journal of the American Medical Association, 277,* 126–132.

McDonough, S. C. (2000). Interaction guidance: An approach for difficult-to-engage families. In C. H. Zeanah (Ed.), *Handbook of infant mental health* (pp. 485–493). New York: Guilford Press.

Olds, D. L., Eckenrode, J., Henderson, C. R. Jr., Kitzman, H., Powers, J., Cole, R., et al. (1997). Long-term effects of home visitation on maternal life course and child abuse and neglect. Fifteen-year follow-up of a randomized trial. *Journal of the American Medical Association, 278,* 637–643.

Olds, D. L., Henderson, C. R., Cole, R., Eckenrode, J., Kitzman, H., Luckey, D., et al. (1998). Long-term effects of nurse home visitation on children's criminal and antisocial behavior. Fifteen-year follow-up of a randomized controlled trial. *Journal of the American Medical Association, 280,* 1238–1244.

Olds, D. L., Henderson, C. R., Phelps, C., Kitzman, H., & Hanks, C. (1993). Effect of prenatal infancy nurse home visitation on government spending. *Medical Care, 31,* 155–174.

Ramey, C. T., Bryant, D. M., Wasik, B. H., Sparling, J. J., Fendt, K. H., & LaVange, L. M. (1992). Infant health and development program for low birth weight, premature infants: Program elements, family participation, and child intelligence. *Pediatrics, 89,* 454–465.

Sameroff, A. J. (1992). Systems, development, and early intervention. *Monographs of the Society for Research in Child Development, 57,* 154–163.

Sameroff, A. J., & Emde, R. N. (1989). *Relationship disturbances in early childhood: A developmental approach.* New York: Basic Books.

Sameroff, A. J., & Fiese, B. J. (2000). Models of development and developmental risk. In C. H. Zeanah (Ed.), *Handbook of infant mental health* (pp. 3–19). New York: Guilford Press.

Sanson, A., Oberklaid, F., Pedlow, R., & Prior, M. (1991). Risk indicators: Assessment of infancy predictors of pre-school behavioural maladjustment. *Journal of Child Psychology and Psychiatry 32,* 609–626.

Scheeringa, M. S., Peebles, C. D., & Cook, C. A. (2001). Toward establishing procedural, criterion, and discriminant validity for PTSD in early childhood. *Journal of the American Academy of Child and Adolescent Psychiatry, 40,* 52–60.

Scheeringa, M. S., & Zeanah, C. H. (1995). Symptom expression and trauma variables in children under 48 months of age. *Infant Mental Health Journal, 16,* 259–270.

Scheeringa, M. S., & Zeanah, C. H. (2001) A relationship perspective on PTSD in infancy. *Journal of Traumatic Stress, 14,* 799–815.

Scheeringa, M. S., Zeanah, C. H., Myers, L., & Putnam, F. W. (2003). New findings of alternative criteria for PTSD. *Journal of the American Academy of Child and Adolescent Psychiatry, 42,* 561–570.

Shaw, D. S., Gilliom, M., & Giovannelli, J. (2000). Aggressive behavior disorders. In C. H. Zeanah (Ed.), *Handbook of infant mental health* (pp. 397–411). New York: Guilford Press.

Smyke, A. T., Dumitrescu, A., & Zeanah, C. H. (2002). Attachment disturbances in young children I: The continuum of caretaking casualty. *Journal of the American Academy of Child and Adolescent Psychiatry, 41,* 972–982.

Sparrow, S., Ball, D., & Cicchetti, D. V. (1984). *Vineland Adaptive Behavior Scales.* Circle Pines, MN: American Guidance Service.

Speltz, M. L., McClellan, J., DeKlyen, M., & Jones, K. (1999). Preschool boys with oppositional defiant disorder: Clinical presentation and diagnostic change. *Journal of the American Academy of Child and Adolescent Psychiatry, 38,* 833–845.

Squires, J., Bricker, D., & Potter, L. (1997). Revision of a parent-completed development screening tool: Ages and Stages Questionnaires. *Pediatric Psychology, 22,* 313–328.

Squires, J., Bricker, D., & Twombly, E. (2002). *Ages & Stages Questionnaires: Social-Emotional.* Baltimore: Paul H. Brookes.

Sroufe, L. A. (1989). Relationships and relationship disturbances. In A. Sameroff & R. Emde (Eds.), *Relationship disturbances in early childhood* (pp. 97–124). New York: Basic Books.

Stafford, B., Zeanah, C. H., & Scheeringa, M. S. (2003). Exploring psychopathology in early childhood: PTSD and attachment disorders in *DC: 0–3* and *DSM-IV. Infant Mental Health Journal, 24,* 398–409.

Steele, H., Steele, M., & Fonagy, P. (1996). Associations among attachment classifications of mothers, fathers, and their infants. *Child Development, 67,* 541–555.

Stern, D. N. (1995). *The motherhood constellation: A unified view of parent-infant psychotherapy.* New York: Basic Books.

Stern-Bruschweiler, N., & Stern, D. N. (1989). A model for conceptualizing the role of the mother's representational world in various mother infant therapies. *Infant Mental Health Journal, 10,* 142–156.

Suess, G. J., Grossman, K. E., & Sroufe, L. A. (1992). Effects of infant attachment to mother and father on quality of adaptation in preschool: From dyadic to individual organization of self. *International Journal of Behavioral Development, 15,* 43–65.

Thomas, J. R., & Clark, R. (1998). Disruptive behavior in the very young child: Diagnostic criteria: 0–3 guides identification of risk factors and intervention. *Infant Mental Health Journal, 19,* 222–244.

van Ijzendoorn, M. (1995). Adult attachment representations, parental responsiveness, and infant attachment: A meta-analysis on the predictive validity of the adult attachment interview. *Psychological Bulletin, 117,* 387–403.

van Ijzendoorn, M. G., Schuengel, C., & Bakersmans-Krankenburg, M. K. (1999). Disorganized attachment in early childhood: Meta-analysis of precursors, concomitants and sequelae. *Development and Psychopathology, 11,* 225–249.

World Health Organization.(1992). *ICD 10 classification of behavioural and mental disorders: Clinical descriptions and diagnostic guidelines.* Geneva: Author.

Zeanah, C. H., & Benoit, D. (1995). Clinical applications of a parent perception interview in infant mental health. *Child and Adolescent Psychiatric Clinics of North America, 4,* 539–554.

Zeanah, C. H., & Boris, N. W. (2000). Disturbances and disorders of attachment in early childhood. In C. H. Zeanah (Ed.), *Handbook of infant mental health* (pp. 326–338). New York: Guilford Press.

Zeanah, C. H., Boris, N. W., & Larrieu, J. A. (1997). Infant development and developmental risk: A review of the past 10 years. *Journal of the American Academy of Child and Adolescent Psychiatry, 36,* 165–178.

Zeanah, C. H., Boris, N. W., & Scheeringa, M. S. (1997). Psychopathology in infancy. *Journal of Child Psychology and Psychiatry, 38,* 81–99.

Zeanah, C. H., Larrieu, J. A., Heller, S. S., & Valliere, J. (2000). Infant-parent relationship assessment. In C. H. Zeanah (Ed.), *Handbook of infant mental health* (pp. 222–235). New York: Guilford Press.

Zeanah, C. H., Larrieu, J. A., Heller, S. S., Valliere, J., Hinshaw-Fuselier, S., Aoki, Y., et al. (2001). Evaluation of a preventive intervention for maltreated infants and toddlers in foster care. *Journal of the American Academy of Child and Adolescent Psychiatry, 40,* 214–221.

Zeanah, C. H., & McDonough, S. (1989). Clinical approaches to families in early intervention. *Seminars in Perinatology, 13,* 513–522.

Zeanah, C. H., Scheeringa, M. S., Boris, N. W., Heller, S. S., Smyke, A. T., & Trapani, J. (in press). Reactive attachment disorder in maltreated toddlers. *Child Abuse & Neglect.*

Zero to Three. (2002). *About infant mental health.* Retrieved August 23, 2004, from http://www.zerotothree.org/Search/index2.cfm

Zero to Three National Center for Clinical Infant Programs. (1994). *Diagnostic Classification: 0–3.* Arlington, VA: Author.

CHAPTER 8

Developmental Psychopathology

GABRIEL P. KUPERMINC AND KATHRYN A. BROOKMEYER

INTRODUCTION

The basic working principle of the field of developmental psychopathology is that "we can learn about the normal functioning of an organism by studying its pathology, and likewise, more about its pathology by studying its normal condition" (Cicchetti, 1984, p. 1). Developmental psychopathology is an interdisciplinary field, drawing from developmental psychology, academic psychology, clinical psychology, and psychiatry (Cicchetti, 1984; Sroufe, 1990; Sroufe & Rutter, 1984).

Interest in the developmental roots of psychopathology can be found in the work of Freud and the early psychoanalytic theorists, whose *organismic* models of development tended to view abnormal functioning as a distortion of normative development, and in the work of behaviorists, such as Skinner, whose *mechanistic* perspective viewed individuals as passive recipients of information, stimulus, and reinforcement from the outside world (cf. Cicchetti, 1984; Ollendick, Grills, & King, 2001). With its emphasis on development as primarily a maturational process occurring within individuals, the organismic perspective failed to account adequately for environmental inputs. In contrast, the mechanistic model was limited primarily in its failure to recognize the effects individuals can have on their environments (Bell, 1968). More recently, the *transactional* perspective (Sameroff, 1975) addressed limitations of mechanistic and organismic models by proposing that developmental changes come about as products of continuous and reciprocal interactions between individuals and their environments.

Drawing from this transactional model, the developmental psychopathology orientation challenges simple cause-and-effect explanations of behavior and emphasizes the importance of understanding the mechanisms and processes of development that contribute to either maladaptive or adaptive behavioral outcomes. Indeed, such a perspective highlights the need to approach developmental processes with a complexity that matches the diversity of developmental outcomes. For example, Cicchetti and Toth (1997) note that childhood maltreatment is associated with a wide range of psychiatric symptoms and diagnoses during childhood, including higher incidence of attention deficit and hyperactivity, oppositional, and post-traumatic stress disorders. Childhood maltreatment has also been implicated in adulthood psychiatric problems, including (among others) panic and anxiety disorders, depression, eating disorders, dissociation, and hysterical symptoms. Cicchetti and Toth's review illustrates the effects of maltreatment on how individuals negotiate developmental tasks from infancy to adolescence, including affect regulation, formation of attachments, peer relations, and adaptation to school. Early manifestations of disorder (e.g., deficits in affect regulation) may lead in cyclical fashion to conditions in the environment that foster the further development of disorder (e.g., social incompetence leading to peer rejection; Sroufe, 1990).

Challenges for the Field

The example of childhood maltreatment illustrates several fundamental challenges for the study of psychopathology and development. First, the field must be able to account for *multifinality,* in which a single vulnerability factor can eventuate in diverse outcomes (e.g., the broad array of childhood and adult diagnoses associated with a history of maltreatment), and *equifinality,* in which varied developmental pathways can lead to a similar outcome (e.g., not all cases of anxiety disorder can be traced to a history of maltreatment; Cicchetti & Toth, 1997). Such diversity in both precursors and expressions of disorder requires recognition that childhood exposure to conditions of risk cannot be seen as causative, but rather as indicating greater likelihood of the emergence of disorder. Further, this recognition of risk as probabilistic

---

Acknowledgment: This work was made possible by funding from the W. T. Grant Foundation (W. T. Grant Scholars Program) and by a Research Program Enhancement Award from Georgia State University to the first author.

rather than causative requires special consideration of the factors associated with resilient outcomes, cases in which exposure to conditions of risk does not lead to disorder.

A second challenge involves accounting for so-called disordered behavior in the context of rapid physical, cognitive, and social developmental growth. This "moving target" problem can take several forms. Consider, for example, that childhood disorders share both similarities and differences with corresponding adulthood disorders. Also, disordered behavior in childhood can resolve itself by adulthood with little or no intervention, such as when many juvenile delinquents appear to grow out of their deviant behavior by early adulthood (Allen, Moore, & Kuperminc, 1997). Moreover, behavior falling within the normal range at one developmental phase (e.g., dependency on adults) can be considered deviant if it persists through a subsequent phase (Kazdin, 2003). The converse may also be true, in that behaviors may change from one developmental phase to another but reflect the same underlying risk for disorder (Bell, 1986). Considering developmental context complicates the task of determining whether a given behavior is problematic, and whether to intervene (Kazdin, 2003; Ollendick et al., 2001).

A third challenge involves achieving greater clarity in accounting for the interplay between child characteristics and the environment. Despite research documenting a wealth of information about the many risk factors associated with youth violence, ranging from genetic and biological predispositions to parenting and familial interaction patterns and sociocultural variables, some observers have cautioned that research on the role of context in development has offered little more than the conclusion that " 'bad' things have 'bad' effects among some—but not all—people, some—but not all—of the time" (Steinberg & Avenevoli, 2000, p. 66).

Addressing the Challenges—Key Concepts

The preceding discussion illustrates the complexity inherent in applying a developmental psychopathology approach to understanding adaptation and disorder during childhood and adolescence. In this section we define several key concepts underlying developmental psychopathology. These include the concepts of risk and protection, person-environment transactions, and the ecological orientation.

Risk and Protection

Risk and protective processes include characteristics of individuals (e.g., intelligence, temperament), families, communities, and the interconnections among them. Risk processes are related to increased likelihood of onset, greater severity, and longer duration of mental health problems (Coie et al., 1993). Risk factors include enduring conditions that persist over time and transient events, whose influence is likely to vary with the developmental period in which they occur (Cicchetti & Toth, 1997). Protective factors mitigate the effects of risk exposure through direct (counteracting) effects, interactive (buffering) effects, or effects that disrupt the causal link between risk and dysfunction (Coie et al., 1993). In many cases, risk and protective factors are continuous variables (e.g., poor to adequate parenting) that can be conceptualized as two sides of a coin (Masten, 2001). Whereas the need to consider both risk and protective processes has now gained wide acceptance, greater conceptual clarity and specificity are needed regarding risk and protective processes (Luthar, Cicchetti, & Becker, 2000).

Resilience

Masten (2001) has described resilience as an ordinary developmental process, such that individuals who appear to succeed despite growing up under adverse circumstances are viewed not as invulnerable, but as benefiting from protective processes that offset the effects of exposure to risk. Resilient youth participate actively in that they appear to generate health-promoting opportunities for themselves, for example, by forging connections to competent and caring adults in their families and communities. Masten (2001) notes that resilience involves an inference based on two fundamental judgments—first, that the person is functioning adequately, and second, that the individual has been exposed to significant adversity. Although there is some debate about what constitutes adequate functioning (e.g., absence of psychopathology, better than average academic performance, etc.), consensus is growing that the concept of resilience has utility for increasing understanding of both adaptive and maladaptive functioning (Luthar et al., 2000).

Person-Environment Transactions

Sameroff (1975) has argued that risk does not exist in the child but rather should be considered a transaction between the child and his or her environment. Transactional processes involve bidirectional and reciprocal influences extending over time between individuals and their environments. These processes are nicely illustrated by the classic studies of Thomas, Chess, and Birch (1968; cf. Sameroff & MacKenzie, 2003), which found that temperamentally difficult infants often elicit maladaptive parenting, which in turn can lead to maladaptive behavior later in life.

Ecological-Transactional Model

The ecological perspective provides an overarching framework, taking processes of risk and resilience and person-environment transactions into account and increasing understanding of how multiple factors play a role in development. This perspective identifies multiple levels of influence on the developing child, ranging from characteristics of individuals to broad cultural beliefs and values (Bronfenbrenner, 1979). The ecological-transactional model organizes environmental characteristics hierarchically, from proximal features (e.g., family interactions) that exert direct influences on children's psychological development and behavioral adaptation to distal features that exert more indirect influences. For example, cultural beliefs and values about child rearing and the instrumental competencies needed for successful development set the stage for variations in parenting practices (Cauce, 2002). Cicchetti and Toth (1997) incorporate a transactional perspective into the ecological model, proposing that the environment influences the developing child's organization of environmental inputs; the child's task, in turn, is to coordinate and integrate information from the environment to negotiate the tasks of each developmental phase.

Ontogenetic development lies at the center of the ecological-transactional model and refers to factors within the person that contribute to development and adaptation (Cicchetti & Toth, 1997). Foci of ontogenetic development include aspects of personality that contribute to vulnerability for maladjustment (e.g., Blatt's notion of self-critical and dependent depressive vulnerabilities; see Leadbeater, Kuperminc, Blatt, & Hertzog, 1999) or neurobiological processes (e.g., brain structures involved in emotion regulation; see Cicchetti, 2002; Steinberg & Avenevoli, 2000). The *microsystem* refers to the immediate settings in which the individual lives, usually including the family, school, and peer group. More distal levels include the *exosystem,* which includes aspects of the communities in which children and their families live, and the *macrosystem,* which includes underlying cultural values and beliefs (Cicchetti & Toth, 1997).

Summary and Organization of the Chapter

The developmental psychopathology approach takes account of normative changes that occur over the life span and attends to the role of risk and protective processes occurring within the individual and the environment that can modify the individual's developmental trajectory toward either adaptive or maladaptive functioning. In the remainder of this chapter, we use an ecological-transactional model as a framework for discussing the utility of developmental psychopathology for conceptualization, assessment, prevention, and treatment of a range of childhood psychological disorders. These include externalizing and internalizing disorders, substance abuse related disorders, learning and mental disabilities, and severe or pervasive psychopathology (Kazdin, 2003). Also considered are problem or risk behaviors that increase the likelihood in the future of adverse psychological, social, and health outcomes (e.g., truancy, unprotected sexual activity).

In the sections that follow, we review illustrative studies focused on developmental processes at the ontogenetic, microsystemic, exosystemic, and macrosystemic levels. We describe processes at each ecological level in greater detail and use these studies as exemplars of research that informs understanding of both normative and problematic development. The studies address a broad array of processes and outcomes, ranging from personality factors that contribute to risk for depression to effects of community violence exposure on aggressive or oppositional behavior (see Table 8.1). We expand on the studies' findings to illustrate linkages between and across ecological levels, with a particular focus on the interplay of risk and protective factors.

ONTOGENETIC PROCESSES IN DEVELOPMENT

The study of ontogenetic development allows a focus on both the universality of developmental processes and the mechanisms involved in deviating from a typical developmental trajectory. Studying typical and atypical development together allows lessons from one population to increase understanding of the other (Burack, 1997). However, it is not enough to simply study typical populations and then to define deviations from the norm (Sroufe, 1990). Although individual development is always veiled within a more complex environment of family, peers, school, neighborhoods, race, and income, this section considers factors within the individual that affect development. Subsequent sections discussing microsystemic, exosystemic, and macrosystemic processes will illuminate how factors within the individual are involved within a grander interplay of factors across multiple levels of the environment.

Lessons from Cognitive Universals

Universals, as defined by early development theorists, provide a rich background for learning about typical and atypical pathways in development. Indeed, traditional understandings or theories of development can serve to highlight continuities and discontinuities in developmental organization. The continuum of typical and atypical development was underscored

TABLE 8.1 Elements and Illustrations of a Transactional Ecological Model in Developmental Psychopathology

Ecological level	Definition	Illustrative findings
Ontogenetic	Factors within the child that contribute to development and adaptation	Children with and without mental retardation (MR) experience a "similar sequence" of milestones in cognitive development (Weisz & Zigler, 1979). Children with MR seek more adult support in solving simple cognitive tasks than comparison children without MR matched on mental age, illustrating the importance of taking individual histories into account (Bybee & Zigler, 1992).
Microsystem	Transactions with the immediate settings in which the child lives, usually including the family, school, peers, and neighborhood	Secure attachment facilitates growth in autonomy during adolescence; both processes linked to adaptive psychosocial functioning (Allen et al., 1997). Positive perceptions of school climate buffer the effects of young adolescents' self-critical vulnerability on the emergence of internalizing and externalizing problems (Kuperminc, Leadbeater, & Blatt, 2001). Peer influences on prosocial and antisocial behavior operate through selection (friends with similar characteristics) and socialization (friends encourage each other's behavior) (Berndt & Keefe, 1995).
Exosystem	Linkages across two or more settings in which children and/or families live	Family support moderates the effects of violence exposure on adolescents (Gorman-Smith & Tolan, 1998). The genetic contribution to IQ is stronger than environmental contributions for children in affluent families; the reverse is true for children in socioeconomically disadvantaged families (Turkheimer, Haley, Waldron, D'Onofrio, & Gottesman, 2003).
Macrosystem	Overarching patterns of ideology, values, and beliefs as well as the organization of social systems that are common to a particular culture or subculture.	Reflecting differences in gender roles, greater stability in interpersonal vulnerability, and sensitivity to changes in peer and parent relationships underlies increases in internalizing problems for girls, whereas greater stability in self-critical vulnerability partly accounts for increases in externalizing problems for boys (Leadbeater et al., 1999). Perhaps reflecting a collectivistic orientation, ethnic minority youth (Black and Latino) are more vulnerable to changes in peer and parent relationships than White youth, whereas White youth are more vulnerable to experiences that threaten sense of self (Kuperminc, Blatt, Shahar, Henrich, & Leadbeater, 2004). Extensive filial responsibilities in immigrant Latino youth may mark both culturally prescribed socialization practices that support positive development or stress-related overreliance on children, depending on the extent of fairness/reciprocity in the family system (Jurkovic et al., 2004).

by Weisz and Zigler (1979) in their testing of mentally retarded and typical cognitive developing children, using Piaget's cognitive stages as a model of universals. Those authors questioned whether these generalities in cognitive development truly exist, and if the sequence of cognitive achievement can be considered without exception across populations, specifically for those with mental retardation. The researchers tested Piaget's theory of cognitive universals against the similar sequence hypothesis, or the idea that both mentally retarded and typically developing children traverse the same stages of cognitive development in the same order, distinct only in the speed in which cognitive milestones are reached and the eventual developmental ceiling attained. Results of cross-sectional and longitudinal assessments of mentally retarded and non–mentally retarded individuals on a variety of Piagetian tasks revealed strong support for the similar sequence hypothesis.

Support for the similar sequence hypothesis illustrates how we can learn about continuities in development from studying atypical cognitive development. However, the idea of continuities in development can be expanded through the examination of discrepancies of cognitive performance of individuals with similar levels of cognitive ability. Specifically, it is crucial to take into account the life experiences and specific characteristics of an individual, such as personality or motivation, when attempting to understand the developmental outcome of cognitive ability (Zigler & Hodapp, 1986). For example, children both with and without mental retardation who were matched on mental age (MA) looked to the adult researcher for information cues in resolving a novel and ambiguous cognitive task. However, on a relatively simplistic and straightforward cognitive task, only those children with mental retardation looked to the adult for cues on how to respond, a strategy characteristic of children with lower MA than those in the study (Bybee & Zigler, 1992). It may be that children with mental retardation relied on adults even when it may not have been necessary because of a consistent history of failure in cognitive tasks. This finding reveals the complexity involved in attaining a particular developmental outcome. Specifically, Bybee and Zigler illustrate the necessity of considering the mechanism by which a developmental outcome was achieved rather than simply considering the outcome itself.

Conceptualizing individuals as agents of change within their environments and having the power to affect their own development (Sameroff, 1975) has important consequences for children with and without developmental disabilities. For example, mastery motivation—a concept related to intrinsic motivation, or the desire to learn (Hauser-Cram, Warfield, Shonkoff, & Krauss, 2001)—is said to stimulate independent, focused, and persistent efforts to solve a problem or master skills or tasks that are perceived as being at least moderately difficult. Research indicates that higher levels of mastery motivation observed during infancy and toddlerhood are related to the level of performance achieved on problem-solving tasks and cognitive ability 1 to 2 years later for children both with and without disabilities (Jennings, Yarrow, & Martin, 1984). Motivation to succeed in skill or task mastery, then, affects typically developing and developmentally delayed children alike. Indeed, the degree of persistence by children illustrates the child's own role in impacting his or her own cognitive development and cognitive achievements over time.

Lessons from Language Development

The study of language development is another aspect of cognitive development fraught with conceptual milestones, here involving language production and language comprehension. By the end of the first year of life, the rudiments of communication and language skills are already present in typical developmental pathways. However, for some children, especially those with severe mental retardation, those milestones do not emerge in such timely fashion. Romski and Sevcik (2002) have focused much of their research on developing instructional approaches, which compensate for the lack of language production in these populations. Such efforts have led to the refinement of augmentative communication devices, computer-based speech production devices that either augment or replace children's existing expressive skills. Use of these devices is expected to reduce the impact that lack of speech production wields on overall development, including social-emotional skills and abilities.

Findings from research on children with severe mental retardation who are given augmentative communication devices have served to advance understanding of language development in typically developing populations. For example, Sevcik and Romski's (1997) work with such children found that speech comprehension not only precedes language production, but also serves as a foundation for speech production to occur. It appears that speech comprehension may well be developing even when children do not have the capacity to produce speech themselves. Indeed, because previous research had been unable to pinpoint the order in which speech comprehension and production develop, the work of Romski and Sevcik on atypical populations has allowed researchers to virtually slow down the process of language development, revealing insights relevant to understanding development in children both with and without developmental disabilities.

In sum, understanding how individual factors affect development can inform knowledge of both typical and atypical developmental pathways. Studies of children with mental retardation illustrate that not only are developmental outcomes key to an understanding of the overall trajectory of development, but characteristics of the individual also impact the nature of the outcome. Although providing only one piece of a complex story of development, the study of ontogenetic development affords insights into the more elusive aspects of developmental processes for both typically and nontypically developing children alike.

MICROSYSTEMIC PROCESSES IN DEVELOPMENT

Beyond the study of ontogenetic development, a recognition of the many interacting environments in which the individual is embedded is also critical for gaining insight into the continuities and discontinuities observed in development (Cicchetti & Toth, 1997). Emerging as a theme in this chapter, environmental levels operate both proximately and distally to impact the developmental process and adjustment outcomes of the individual.

Research has shown that the more immediate the influence, the more directly the environmental factor will impact the individual (Cicchetti & Toth, 1997). Thus, the *microsystem*, defined as any immediate environmental setting that includes the individual, is a key level of influence (Bronfenbrenner, 1979). The microsystem encompasses individuals' transactions with the school, family, and peer group.

Further complicating the dynamics of the interacting microsystems are the risk and protective factors operating within each environmental setting. For instance, risk factors may not only be markers of the development and progression of disorder and maladaptation, but may also serve to reveal the mechanisms through which poor functioning within the microsystem has occurred (Kazdin, 1997). Multiple risk factors can interact with one another between and within microsystems to create more adverse circumstances for the individual and can have both independent and cumulative effects, such that having one risk factor may make the individual more prone to the development of another. For example, poor academic achievement in middle and high school may lead to truancy, which may in turn lead to dropping out of school, leading to an elevated risk for conduct disorder (Kazdin, 1997). Yet even under severe circumstances of risk, individuals may adapt and even thrive, experiencing no disordered outcomes (Luthar, 1991; Luthar et al., 2000; Masten, 2001).

Understanding how protective factors interact with risk factors across and within multiple layers of the microsystem can lead to a more comprehensive understanding of developmental outcomes (Masten, 2001). The studies highlighted here, which include investigations of the quality of parent-child relationships, the impact of peers, and the role of school climate, illustrate the complex nature of risk and protection and the diversity in developmental processes.

Quality of Parent-Child Relationships

The family represents the most central microsystem in the lives of most children, and not surprisingly, it has been the focus of the greatest amount of research at the nexus of child development and psychopathology. Attachment theory, through its focus on how early experiences influence individuals' representations of themselves and others, has gained wide acceptance within developmental psychopathology as providing useful conceptualizations for understanding normative and disordered behavior and for formulating therapeutic intervention strategies (Thompson & Raikes, 2003).

Of particular relevance to developmental psychopathology is the concept of internal working models, which Bowlby (1982) put forward as the internalized representations about self and experiences in relationships that provide individuals with a sort of working theory about how to interact with others. In theory, individuals continually revise their representations as they gain greater sophistication in cognitive abilities and incorporate ongoing experience with the social world, but the representations remain resistant to easy change because they are formulated from experience and maintained by ongoing relationships. Yet, considerable gaps remain in empirical knowledge about stability and change in attachment processes, how early attachments contribute to behavior later in life, and how contextual risk (and protection) experienced across the life span affect individuals' models of attachment and transact with those models to affect behavior (Thompson & Raikes, 2003).

One pertinent question is whether attachment representations remain as central organizing guidelines for individuals throughout their development. The period of adolescence, for example, raises the potential for conflict between the attachment system and young people's emergent strivings for behavioral and emotional autonomy from parents. However, recent research has revealed some of the mechanisms underlying intergenerational continuities in attachment organization from mothers to adolescents (Allen et al., 2003) and show that adolescents are best able to establish autonomy in the context of secure relationships with parents (Allen & Land, 1999; Allen et al., 1997). Indeed, attachment security is associated broadly with positive indexes of psychosocial functioning, including competence with peers and low levels of internalizing and externalizing difficulties (Allen, Moore, Kuperminc, & Bell, 1998).

The work of Patterson and colleagues on the role of coercive family interactions in the etiology of antisocial behavior (Patterson, 1993; Patterson, DeBaryshe, & Ramsey, 1989) provides another example of transactional processes involving the individual and the family microsystem. In this model, a cycle of coercive interactions escalates over time within the family system and then is carried over by the child to other settings. The combination of unskilled parenting, difficult child temperament, and exposure to ecological stress appears to contribute particularly high risk for these coercive cycles, which have been found to lead to antisocial behavior, peer rejection, school failure, and low self-esteem (Sameroff & MacKenzie, 2003).

Impact of Peers

The peer group, another proximal system within the microsystem, has been found to wield a great deal of influence on decision making during adolescence (Buhrmester, 1996; Perrino, González-Soldevilla, Pantin, & Szapocznik, 2000). By adolescence, peers become important behavioral referents for both positive and negative behaviors, and much research has documented similarities in levels of risk behavior within peer groups (e.g., Boyer, Tschann, & Shafer, 1999; Henrich, Kuperminc, Sack, Blatt, & Leadbeater, 2000; Romer et al., 1994). Specifically, deviant peer networks have been implicated in the incidence not only of adolescent problem behavior (e.g., Dishion, Bullock & Granic, 2002; Prinstein,

Boergers, & Spirito, 2001), but also of growth in problem behaviors over time (Patterson, 1993).

The association of affiliation with risk-taking or deviant peers and subsequent adolescent risk-taking behavior appears to be a product of both selection and socialization processes (Berndt & Keefe, 1995). Selection effects occur when youth choose to become friends with peers who evidence similar behavior patterns (Dishion et al., 2002). Socialization effects occur when youth either overtly or passively encourage one another to engage in either prosocial or risky behaviors (e.g., Bandura, 1986). Studies attempting to disentangle this link have found that in the case of risk behavior, peer influences appear to exceed selection effects (Dishion et al., 2002).

Research investigating peers across multiple risk behaviors shows that although peers are influential, their effects need not necessarily be negative (Berndt & Keefe, 1995). In addition, peer influences on adolescent risk-taking behaviors may not be direct but may depend on the specific risk under consideration. For example, whereas adolescents' perceived connectedness to friends has been associated with having fewer sexual partners (Rotheram-Borus, Reid, & Rosario, 1994), supportive friendships may also predict elevated levels of substance use, especially when peers exhibit high levels of substance use (Wills, Mariani, & Filer, 1996; Wills & Vaughan, 1989).

This brief review of peer effects and adolescent risk taking shows that, though peers are often implicated as causing adolescent risk behavior, the links may not be so straightforward. Indeed, the role of the individual in peer relationships must be considered, as does the specific risk behavior under investigation.

Role of School Climate

Understanding how children and adolescents adapt within the proximal setting of the school serves to further illustrate the ways in which an individual's characteristics interact with microsystem settings to predict adaptive or maladaptive outcomes (Kuperminc, Leadbeater, Emmons, & Blatt, 1997). Kuperminc et al. (2001) examined how school climate perceptions interacted with individual vulnerabilities to explain changes in behavioral and emotional problems during the middle school years. Using a person-environment fit framework, the researchers posited that a mismatch between student and school attributes would place the students at increased risk for internalizing and externalizing problems over time. Findings revealed that highly self-critical students were buffered from both internalizing problems and externalizing problems when they perceived their school climate as positive. Additionally, perceiving a positive school climate protected against increases in internalizing problems for adolescents who were low in perceived self-efficacy. Importantly, school climate perceptions could not be predicted prospectively from earlier adjustment difficulties, indicating that school climate perceptions are not mere reflections of maladjustment.

Results from investigations of school settings illustrate that psychosocial problems do not result only from an individual's characteristics or from the perceived characteristics of a school setting, but rather the dynamic interaction between the two levels of context acts to predict either adaptive or maladaptive outcomes. The fit or match between these two levels of context is key to understanding the process by which developmental outcomes evolve (Kuperminc et al., 2001). These studies suggest that it is not enough to try to understand a student's social adjustment through examining one environment without taking into account the individual's role in creating and perceiving that context.

EXOSYSTEMIC AND MACROSYSTEMIC PROCESSES

Exosystemic and macrosystemic processes represent the most distal levels of influences on development. The *exosystem* can be described as consisting of the linkages across two or more settings in which children and families live. Cicchetti and Toth (1997) include linkages across settings that contain the child within the exosystem (which Bronfenbrenner, 1979, 1988, identified as the mesosystem) as well as settings that do not necessarily contain the child (e.g., the parent's workplace). The *macrosystem* refers to the overarching patterns of ideology, values, and beliefs, as well as the organization of social systems, that are common to a particular culture or subculture. These processes are perhaps the least researched, owing in part to the complexity inherent in conceptualization and measurement of processes so distal to the child and yet so intimately interwoven into children's, families', and communities' lives as to be almost taken for granted.

Bronfenbrenner (1988) distinguishes two broad approaches that have been used in research examining ecological processes in human development. In research using *class theoretical paradigms*, exosystemic and macrosystemic processes are typically reduced to a social address—simple markers of status that differentiate members of different ethnic or cultural groups, families at high as compared to low socioeconomic status, and so forth. Class theoretical studies range from simple comparisons among children growing up in different social addresses (e.g., differences in academic achievement among Black/African American as compared to White children) to more complex models that take into account characteristics of individuals, families, or other microsystems. Such studies are limited, however. For example, growing up in persistent poverty involves far more than a lack of financial resources; among other things, poverty often means limited access to health care alongside increased exposure to unhealthy environments, chronic stress that negatively affects parents' ability to supervise and discipline children effectively, and living in dangerous neighborhoods (McLoyd, 1998). In a similar vein, racial or ethnic categories are poor proxies for culture in that they tell us little about the distinct social and cultural experiences of diverse groups or about the diversity that exists within them (Betancourt & López, 1993).

Process paradigms comprise the second approach described by Bronfenbrenner. The simplest of process models examine characteristics of individuals (ontogenetic), or microsystemic processes, or both to identify unique and combined effects of two or more processes on development. Studies of infant temperament and individual differences in parenting (Thomas et al., 1968) referred to previously provide an example of such a model.

The Moderating Role of Gender and Ethnicity

Studies that compare developmental processes across gender, race or ethnicity, and social class serve to highlight both the similarities and differences in developmental pathways encountered by members of different groups (Rowe, Vazsonyi, & Flannery, 1994). Such studies may consider group membership as a moderator of the links between and across processes at the ontogenetic and microsystemic levels as they relate to adjustment outcomes.

It is virtually a given that by adolescence the rates of internalizing problems in girls exceed those of boys and, conversely, the rates of externalizing problems in boys outpace those of girls. Leadbeater et al. (1999) examined a multivariate model of gender differences in these processes and found that the overall developmental pathways leading to internalizing and externalizing problems among young adolescent girls and boys were quite similar. However, increases in internalizing problems among girls were explained by greater stability in interpersonal vulnerabilities and greater sensitivity to changes in the quality of relationships with parents and peers. In contrast, increases in externalizing problems observed in boys were partly explained by greater stability in boys' vulnerability to self-criticism.

Clarifying the nature of ethnic or cultural group differences in emotional and behavioral problems is no simple task, because observed differences might reflect variations in the true prevalence of depression and internalizing disorders, differences in how researchers conceptualize and measure the disorders, culturally anchored variations in symptom expression and reporting, differences in the effects of risk or protective processes contributing to development (Allen & Mitchell, 1998), or any combination of these. To address some of these issues, Kuperminc et al. (2004) examined a large sample of Black, White, and Latino young adolescents (ages 11–14) for ethnic group differences in self-definition (self-worth and efficacy), interpersonal relatedness (quality of relationships with parents and peers), and academic and psychological adjustment over a 1-year period. Consistent with past research, Black and Latino youth reported more overall adjustment difficulties than White youth; however, patterns of change were similar across ethnic groups, suggesting cultural equivalence in developmental processes across most domains. In further analyses, ethnicity moderated the associations of relatedness and self-definition with psychological and school adjustment such that Black and Latino youth appeared particularly vulnerable to experiences that threaten closeness and trust in relationships. In contrast, White youth appeared particularly vulnerable to experiences that threaten their sense of self-worth. One might speculate that a collectivistic orientation underlies the specific vulnerability of the ethnic minority youth to relational risk factors, whereas an individualistic orientation underlies the specific vulnerability of White youth to risk factors within the self system.

Social Class Differences in the Heritability of Intelligence

Failure to take broad aspects of context into account can lead to unwarranted conclusions with potentially far-reaching implications. Recent research on the role of socioeconomic status in the heritability of cognitive ability illustrates this point. Based on findings from numerous twin and adoption studies, many researchers have concluded that genetic effects on intelligence (measured by IQ) outweigh the effects of family environment (Turkheimer et al., 2003). Studies of children rescued from poverty, in contrast, find large environmental effects on IQ. Turkheimer and colleagues point out that few twin or adoption studies include children from impoverished backgrounds, and this failure to consider socioeconomic status might help account for inconsistencies in the findings of studies using diverse methodologies. Drawing on data from a nationally representative sample of twins, those researchers found a negligible genetic contribution to IQ among children in impoverished families but a strong genetic contribution to IQ among children in affluent families. These findings illustrate how unaccommodating environments can constrain normative development and suggest the possibility that in some cases, interventions directed at ameliorating environments may be as effective as person-centered interventions.

Community Violence: Direct and Distal Processes

By going beyond simple markers of group membership, process-oriented research attempts to bring the exosystemic and macrosystemic contexts of development into sharper relief. Variables describing community and cultural context, for instance, can be examined in transaction with characteristics of individuals and their proximal contexts.

Numerous studies have reported that urban adolescents are witnessing disturbingly large amounts of violence in their neighborhoods and communities (Fitzpatrick & Boldizar, 1993; Osofsky, Wewers, Hann, & Fick, 1993; Richters & Martinez, 1993; Schwab-Stone et al., 1995). In a recent survey of adolescents in New Haven, Connecticut, more than 40 percent had witnessed a shooting or stabbing in the past year, and 74 percent reported feeling unsafe in one or more familiar contexts (Schwab-Stone et al., 1999).

Not only do violent neighborhoods have direct links to children's rates of witnessing and being victimized by violence, but there are also links between witnessing community violence and committing acts of violence. Witnessing violence has been shown to be positively related to subsequent increases in the frequency of violent behavior and has also been found to be among the most consistent predictors of the use of violence (Brookmeyer, Henrich, & Schwab-Stone, in press; Farrell & Bruce, 1997; Gorman-Smith & Tolan, 1998; Miller, Wasserman, Neugebauer, Gorman-Smith, & Kamboukos, 1999). For example, Gorman-Smith and Tolan (1998) found that witnessing violence was related to increases in aggressive behavior over a 1-year period, even after controlling for previous levels of aggression.

However, not all links between living in violent neighborhoods and maladaptive outcomes are so direct. In fact, aspects of the family microsystem have been shown to moderate some of the effects of living in violent communities, albeit in complicated and sometimes counterintuitive ways. Miller et al. (1999), for example, found that boys who witnessed high levels of violence were actually more vulnerable to engaging in antisocial behavior when the levels of conflict in their families were low. In contrast, Gorman-Smith and Tolan (1998) showed that family structure (i.e., dependability, support, and intolerance for deviance) moderated the effects of rates of violence exposure on aggressive behavior, such that in the context of high levels of family structure, violence exposure was correlated with increases in aggressive behavior over time. Such studies suggest the ability of parent support to either temper or exacerbate the potential adverse effects of community violence. More broadly, this research exemplifies how microsystems can act to alter the effects of macrosystemic stress (Cicchetti & Toth, 1997).

Immigration and Acculturation

The United States is currently undergoing a dramatic demographic shift, driven in large part by immigration. Children of immigrants now make up 20 percent of all youth in the United States (Suárez-Orozco & Suárez-Orozco, 2001). The dynamics of immigration and resettlement, including acculturation of family members to a new host setting and changes occurring in communities to accommodate the influx of culturally diverse new residents, provide an extraordinary opportunity to investigate the role of macrosystemic processes in normative and pathological development. Numerous investigators have observed that children of immigrants often learn English more rapidly than their parents and subsequently take on responsibilities as language and culture brokers; they also have been observed to take on added responsibility for sibling caregiving, cooking and cleaning, and mediating household conflict (Jurkovic et al., 2004). These responsibilities raise the concerns of clinicians sensitive to issues of parentification and role reversal that can have deleterious consequences for the children. Among researchers of culture, however, children's assumption of instrumental and emotional caregiving roles within the family may be seen as the extension of culturally based attitudes that place obligation and loyalty to the family at the center of normative development.

To reconcile these contrasting viewpoints, Jurkovic and colleagues (2004) have proposed the term filial responsibility to refer to children's instrumental and emotional contributions to family welfare, and they have argued that the ethical context (e.g., the extent of fairness, reciprocity, and acknowledgment by parents) in which children take on caregiving roles plays a pivotal role in whether such responsibilities will have positive or negative consequences. Initial studies have supported this hypothesis. For example, Kuperminc, Jurkovic, and Lapidus (2003) found that perceptions of fairness moderated the relations of adolescents' caregiving with both competence and adjustment problems as reported by teachers. Instrumental caregiving in the family was associated with teacher perceptions of better adjustment and greater competence for high school students, suggesting positive effects of caregiving for mid- to late adolescents. Emotional caregiving was associated with better adjustment and greater competence, but only in the context of a high degree of fairness. Overall, findings are consistent with the notion that young people's contributions to family well-being can promote positive developmental outcomes. However, more work is needed to identify sex and age differences in levels and effects of family responsibilities for immigrant and U.S.-born Latino youth.

IMPLICATIONS FOR ASSESSMENT

In this section, we outline some implications for the clinical assessment of children and adolescents based on the transactional-ecological perspective espoused in this chapter. Attention to developmental change requires the use of assessment tools that are reliable and valid within specific age groups and techniques that maximize the likelihood of obtaining accurate and useful information. Ollendick et al. (2001) recommended a normative-developmental approach to assessment that attends to qualitative and quantitative changes that occur with development, judged with respect to normative behavior within appropriate reference groups. Normative data from children of the same age offer the most common point of reference, and the usefulness of such normative data can be enhanced with the availability of information related to gender, socioeconomic status, and ethnic or cultural variations. Ollendick et al. urged particular caution in the use of downward extensions of instruments that were developed and validated with adults and may not capture developmental differences in symptomatology. In a similar vein, upward extensions of instruments validated for very young children may also fail to capture developmental changes.

Change is the hallmark of development, and it follows that developmentally sensitive assessment should adopt a longitudinal perspective. Such assessment draws attention beyond presenting symptoms at a given point in time to consideration of stability and change in overt behaviors as well as exposure to risk and protective processes involved in the etiology or maintenance of behavior. Hinshaw (2002) differentiates the notion of *developmental pathways,* the predictable sequences of psychosocial and psychobiological processes that characterize normative development, from the notion of *developmental trajectories,* the specific sequences traversed by particular subgroups. Comparing information about the developmental trajectories of target individuals against normative pathways can provide critical information useful in diagnosis and treatment.

Furthermore, attention to transactional-ecological processes requires that clinicians account for the extent of consistency in behavior across settings and the social contexts in which behavior occurs. Algozzine, Serna, and Patton (2001) outline a practical approach to ecological assessment that elicits information about the expectations and tolerances of key individuals within the major settings affecting the target child.

For very young children it may be sufficient to focus such assessment on the family, but for school-age children and adolescents assessment strategies may need to be expanded to additional settings, including the school, neighborhood, and peer group (Hinshaw, 2002). It has been noted that children are typically referred for treatment by parents or teachers and often do not believe they have a problem (Algozzine et al., 2001; Ollendick et al., 2001). A possibility that cannot be overlooked is that a child's presenting problems may reveal more about the expectations and tolerances of adults in key settings than about the child per se. In such cases, the primary target of intervention involves processes external to the child (e.g., parent training). However, when troubling behavior appears consistently across diverse settings and is perceived as problematic by multiple observers, intervention targets are more likely to center on the child.

IMPLICATIONS FOR INTERVENTION

The transactional-ecological perspective also has implications for intervention. Mindful of the potential for resilient outcomes, we advocate an approach to intervention that spans a continuum from prevention to treatment. Key contributions from prevention research include its attention to epidemiology, risk and protective processes, and developmental trajectories (Tolan & Gorman-Smith, 2002). Preventive interventions typically proceed from the assumption that changes in the environment can alter developmental trajectories, usually via strategies to reduce exposure to risk (e.g., training parents in effective discipline practices) or increasing exposure to protective processes (e.g., increasing available supports through provision of adult mentors or establishment of after-school programs). Such strategies are likely to have universal benefits for children and youth. When widely implemented in schools or community settings, a preventive orientation can also be useful in identifying children at particularly high risk who might benefit from additional, targeted intervention (Tolan & Gorman-Smith, 2002).

A developmental orientation also reminds us that different strategies may be useful at different ages. For example, cognitive-behavioral techniques may need to be modified for very young children, who are unlikely to possess the experience and cognitive information-processing capacities necessary to reflect on negative cognitions and weigh potential benefits of alternative solutions to problems. Treatment outcome studies typically have not examined effectiveness for children and youth of differing ages; however, there is some evidence that family-based intervention for childhood anxiety (e.g., helping parents deal with their own anxieties and providing strategies for managing children's anxiety and avoidance) may be more effective with young children, ages 7–10, than individually focused treatment alone. For older children, ages 11–14, family-based treatment adds little value to individual therapies focused on cognitive processing and exposure to feared stimuli (cf. Ollendick et al., 2001).

The context of intervention also requires concerted attention. Changing the conditions that elicit or serve to reinforce disordered behavior in one setting may or may not have consequences for the child's behavior in another setting. At a minimum, this suggests the need for ongoing attention to the child's transactions with multiple settings throughout the course of intervention. In many instances, effective treatment may require intervening at multiple levels, including not only person-centered strategies (e.g., skills training), but also strategies directed at environmental change (e.g., efforts to improve school climate). The utility of comprehensive approaches is illustrated by the superiority of multisystemic treatment for juvenile offenders relative to traditional services (Henggeler, 2003).

FUTURE DIRECTIONS

In this chapter we have highlighted processes at multiple ecological levels that contribute to both normative and disordered behavior in children and adolescents. Drawing from illustrative studies and reviews of research on specific classes of disorder, including Ollendick et al.'s (2001) focus on anxiety disorders and Hinshaw's (2002) focus on impulsivity and disruptive behavior, we have described implications of the transactional-ecological model for assessment and intervention across a broad spectrum of behavior. Revisiting progress from 1975 to the beginning of the twenty-first century, Sameroff and MacKenzie (2003) highlighted advances in longitudinal research design and analytic tools that have enabled increasingly sophisticated examination of transactional processes across time and across levels of the ecology. Yet several challenges remain, including the need for stronger linkages between basic and applied research to build stronger theory and at the same time yield practical guidance for clinical practice. In addition, gaps exist in current knowledge of processes at the macrosocial and the intraindividual levels, and in our understanding of the dynamics of influence across levels.

The joining of basic and applied perspectives is needed for greater understanding of lawful processes of development and for yielding practical insights useful in designing effective interventions. Facilitated by the development of sophisticated analytic tools that enable multilevel modeling of bidirectional effects across ecological levels and estimation of growth curves across multiple observations, research has made significant strides in the ability to examine transactional-ecological models of development. But even the most sophisticated longitudinal investigations are limited in two ways from the perspective of clinical intervention (Sameroff & MacKenzie, 2003). First, longitudinal research can hint at, but not establish, causal links underlying normative and pathological development. The design of effective intervention strategies requires information that goes beyond description of which risk factors predict which problematic behaviors toward providing information about the processes and mechanisms through which those factors are linked to onset or maintenance (Hinshaw, 2002; Steinberg & Avenevoli, 2000). Only through systematic experimentation to reduce hypothesized risk factors or increase protective processes can we begin to untangle causal mechanisms—information that is critical for both advancing theory and refining intervention strategies. Although some progress has been made in documenting effective intervention approaches spanning prevention (Weissberg, Kumpfer, & Seligman, 2003) and treatment (Kazdin, 2003), the majority of treatments for children and adolescents have not been evaluated empirically (Kazdin, 2003). Kazdin (2003) describes a cycle of basic and applied research to inform effective treatments, encompassing (a) theory and research on the nature of clinical dysfunction; (b) theory and research on the change processes or mechanisms of treatment; (c) specification of treatment; (d) tests of treatment outcome; (e) tests of moderators; and (f) tests of generalization and applicability.

A second limitation of much current research is the assumption of linear, variable-centered data analytic approaches that are useful in documenting associations across a wide array of processes but may not describe the experiences of any one person in particular. Understanding variations in developmental processes for specific groups of individuals is needed to help guide the refinement of prevention and treatment efforts. A move toward mixed approaches that include both variable-centered and person-centered data analyses is a step in the right direction (Masten, 2001). For example, Seidman and his colleagues (Seidman & Pedersen, 2003) employ a pattern-centered strategy to identify homogeneous subgroups of individuals with similar risk profiles (e.g., similar patterns of functional to dysfunctional family transactions) and then examine trajectories of development within and across those profiles.

The transactional-ecological perspective that has formed the framework for this chapter focuses attention away from static markers of normative versus disordered behavior toward the dynamic processes of development, but gaps in knowledge of processes remain. Looking inward to ontogenetic processes, some observers have noted that developmental psychopathologists have lent insufficient attention to biological processes, including transactions involving neurobiological systems (Cicchetti, 2002; Steinberg & Avenevoli, 2000). Looking outward toward sociocultural processes, we continue to have only an elementary understanding of the role of exosystemic and macrosystemic processes. Pinquart and Silbereisen (2004), for example, note the lack of specific theories regarding the consequences of social change. Social change is ubiquitous, ranging from demographic transformations toward greater cultural diversity and an older populace, to managing the threats of terrorism. Drawing from their research on East and West Germans following the reunification of Germany, Pinquart and Silbereisen offer a comprehensive model to examine the developmental consequences of coping with social change. Finally, looking across ecological levels, a need remains for studies that include person, process, and context to provide synthesis of effects across different levels of the ecology (Hinshaw, 2002). One of the greatest strengths of the developmental psychopathology perspective remains its ability to draw from multiple scientific traditions to look inward, outward, and across individual and environmental influences on behavior to critically examine questions of typical and atypical development.

REFERENCES

Algozzine, R., Serna, L., & Patton, J. R. (2001). *Childhood behavior disorders: Applied research and educational practices* (2nd ed.). Austin, TX: Pro-ed.

Allen, J. P., & Land, D. (1999). Attachment in adolescence. In J. Cassidy and P. R. Shaver (Eds.), *Handbook of attachment* (pp. 319–335). New York: Guilford Press.

Allen, J. P., McElhaney, K. B., Land, D. J., Kuperminc, G. P., Moore, C. W., O'Beirne-Kelly, H., et al. (2003). A secure base in adolescence: Markers of attachment security in the mother-adolescent relationship. *Child Development, 74,* 292–307.

Allen, J. P., Moore, C., & Kuperminc, G. P. (1997). Developmental approaches to understanding adolescent deviance. In S. S. Luthar, J. A. Burack, D. Cicchetti, & J. R. Weisz (Eds.), *Developmental psychopathology: Perspectives on adjustment, risk, and disorder* (pp. 548–567). New York: Cambridge University Press.

Allen, J. P., Moore, C., Kuperminc, G., & Bell, K. (1998). Attachment and adolescent psychosocial functioning. *Child Development, 69,* 1406–1419.

Allen, L., & Mitchell, C. (1998). Racial and ethnic differences in patterns of problematic and adaptive development: An epidemiological review. In V. C. McLoyd & L. Steinberg (Eds.), *Studying minority adolescents: Conceptual, methodological, and theoretical issues* (pp. 29–54). Mahwah, NJ: Erlbaum.

Bandura, A. (1986). *Social foundations of thought and action: A social-cognitive theory.* Upper Saddle River, NJ: Prentice Hall.

Bell, R. Q. (1968). A reinterpretation of the direction of effects in studies of socialization. *Psychological Review, 75,* 81–95.

Bell, R. Q. (1986). Age-specific manifestations in changing psychosocial risk. In D. Farran & J. D. McKinney (Eds.), *The concept of risk in intellectual and psychosocial development* (pp. 169–185). New York: Academic Press.

Berndt, T. J., & Keefe, K. (1995). Friends' influence on adolescents' adjustment to school. *Child Development, 66,* 1312–1329.

Betancourt, H., & López, S. R. (1993). The study of culture, ethnicity, and race in American psychology. *American Psychologist, 48,* 629–637.

Bowlby, J. (1982). *Attachment and loss: Vol. 1. Attachment* (2nd ed.). New York: Basic Books.

Boyer, C. B., Tschann, J. M., & Shafer, M. (1999). Predictors of risk for sexually transmitted diseases in ninth-grade urban high-school students. *Journal of Adolescent Research, 14,* 448–465.

Bronfenbrenner, U. (1979). *The ecology of human development.* Cambridge, MA: Harvard University Press.

Bronfenbrenner, U. (1988). Interacting systems in human development. Research paradigms: Present and future. In N. Bolger, A. Caspi, G. Downey, & M. Moorehouse (Eds.), *Persons in context: Developmental perspectives* (pp. 25–49). New York: Cambridge University Press.

Brookmeyer, K. A., Henrich, C. C., & Schwab-Stone, M. (in press). Adolescents who witness community violence: Can prenatal support and prosocial cognitions protect them from committing violence? *Child Development.*

Buhrmester, D. (1996). Need fulfillment, interpersonal competence, and the developmental contexts of early adolescent friendship. In W. M. Bukowski, A. F. Newcomb, & W. W. Hartup (Eds.), *The company they keep: Friendship in childhood and adolescence* (pp. 158–185). New York: Cambridge University Press.

Burack, J. A. (1997). The study of atypical and typical populations in developmental psychology: The quest for a common science. In S. S. Luthar, J. A. Burack, D. Cicchetti, & J. R. Weisz (Eds.), *Developmental psychopathology: Perspectives on adjustment, risk, and disorder* (pp. 139–165). New York: Cambridge University Press.

Bybee, J., & Zigler, E. (1992). Is outerdirectedness employed in a harmful or beneficial manner by normal and mentally retarded children? *American Journal on Mental Retardation, 96,* 512–521.

Cauce, A. M. (2002). Examining culture within a quantitative empirical framework. *Human Development, 45,* 294–298.

Cicchetti, D. (1984). The emergence of developmental psychopathology. *Child Development, 55,* 1–7.

Cicchetti, D. (2002). The impact of social experience on neurobiological systems: Illustration from a constructivist view of child maltreatment. *Cognitive Development, 17,* 1407–1428.

Cicchetti, D., & Toth, S. L. (1997). Transactional ecological systems in developmental psychopathology. In S. S. Luthar, J. A. Burack, D. Cicchetti, & J. R. Weisz (Eds.), *Developmental psychopathology: Perspectives on adjustment, risk, and disorder* (pp. 317–349). New York: Cambridge University Press.

Coie, J. D., Watt, N. F., West, S. G., Hawkins, J. D., Asarnow, J. R., Markman, H. J., et al. (1993). The science of prevention: A conceptual framework and some directions for a national research program. *American Psychologist, 48,* 1013–1022.

Dishion, T. J., Bullock, B. M., & Granic, I. (2002). Pragmatism in modeling peer influence: Dynamics, outcomes and change processes. *Development and Psychopathology, 14,* 969–981.

Farrell, A. D., & Bruce, S. E. (1997). Impact of exposure to community violence on violent behavior and emotional distress among urban adolescents. *American Journal of Preventive Medicine, 12,* 13–21.

Fitzpatrick, K. M., & Boldizar, J. P. (1993). The prevalence and consequences of exposure to violence among African-American youth. *Journal of the American Academy of Child and Adolescent Psychiatry, 32,* 424–430.

Gorman-Smith, D., & Tolan, P. (1998). The role of exposure to community violence and developmental problems among inner-city youth. *Development and Psychopathology, 10,* 101–116.

Hauser-Cram, P., Warfield, M. E., Shonkoff, J. P., & Krauss, M. W. (2001). Children with disabilities. *Monographs of the Society for Research in Child Development, 66*(3, Serial No. 266).

Henggeler, S. W. (2003). Advantages and disadvantages of multisystemic therapy and other evidence-based practices for treating juvenile offenders. *Journal of Forensic Psychology Practice, 3,* 53–59.

Henrich, C. C., Kuperminc, G. P., Sack, A., Blatt, S. J., & Leadbeater, B. J. (2000). Characteristics and homogeneity of early friendship groups: A comparison of male and female clique and nonclique members. *Applied Developmental Science, 4,* 15–26.

Hinshaw, S. P. (2002). Process, mechanism, and explanation related to externalizing behavior in developmental psychopathology. *Journal of Abnormal Child Psychology, 30,* 431–446.

Jennings, K. D., Yarrow, L. J., & Martin, P. P. (1984). Mastery motivation and cognitive development: A longitudinal study from infancy to 3 1/2 years of age. *International Journal of Behavioral Development, 7,* 441–461.

Jurkovic, G. J., Kuperminc, G., Perilla, J., Murphy, A., Ibañez, G., & Casey, S. (2004). Ecological and ethical perspectives on filial responsibility: Implications for primary prevention with immigrant Latino adolescents. *Journal of Primary Prevention, 25,* 81–104.

Kazdin, A. E. (1997). Conduct disorder across the lifespan. In S. S. Luthar, J. A. Burack, D. Cicchetti, & J. R. Weisz (Eds.), *Developmental psychopathology: Perspectives on adjustment, risk, and disorder* (pp. 248–273). New York: Cambridge University Press.

Kazdin, A. E. (2003). Psychotherapy for children and adolescents. *Annual Review of Psychology, 54,* 253–276.

Kuperminc, G. P., Blatt, S. J., Shahar, G., Henrich, C., & Leadbeater, B. J. (2004). Cultural equivalence and cultural variance in longitudinal associations of young adolescent self-definition and interpersonal relatedness to psychological and school adjustment. *Journal of Youth and Adolescence, 33,* 13–30.

Kuperminc, G. P., Jurkovic, G. J., & Lapidus, R. B. (2003, April). *The role of filial responsibility in the school-based adjustment of immigrant Latino adolescents.* Presented at the biennial meeting of the Society for Research in Child Development, Tampa, FL.

Kuperminc, G. P., Leadbeater, B. J., & Blatt, S. J. (2001). School social climate and individual differences to psychopathology among middle school students. *Journal of School Psychology, 39,* 141–159.

Kuperminc, G. P., Leadbeater, B. J., Emmons, C., & Blatt, S. (1997). Perceived school climate and difficulties in the social adjustment of middle school students. *Applied Developmental Science, 1,* 76–88.

Leadbeater, B. J., Kuperminc, G. P., Blatt, S. J., & Hertzog, C. (1999). A multivariate model of gender differences in adolescents' internalizing and externalizing problems. *Developmental Psychology, 35,* 1268–1282.

Luthar, S. S. (1991). Vulnerability and resilience: A study of high-risk adolescents. *Child Development, 62,* 600–616.

Luthar, S. S., Cicchetti, D., & Becker, B. (2000). The construct of resilience: A critical evaluation and guidelines for future work. *Child Development, 71,* 543–562.

Masten, A. S. (2001). Ordinary magic: Resilience processes in development. *American Psychologist, 56,* 227–238.

McLoyd, V. (1998). Socioeconomic disadvantage and child development. *American Psychologist, 53,* 185–204.

Miller, L. S., Wasserman, G. A., Neugebauer, R., Gorman-Smith, D., & Kamboukos, D. (1999). *Journal of Clinical Child Psychology, 28,* 2–11.

Ollendick, T. H., Grills, A. E., & King, N. J. (2001). Applying developmental theory to the assessment and treatment of childhood disorders: Does it make a difference? *Clinical Psychology and Psychotherapy, 8,* 304–314.

Osofsky, J. D., Wewers, S., Hann, D. M., & Fick, A. C. (1993). Chronic community violence: What is happening to our children? *Psychiatry, 56,* 36–45.

Patterson, G. R. (1993). Orderly change in a stable world: The antisocial trait as a chimera. *Journal of Consulting and Consulting Psychology, 61,* 911–919.

Patterson, G. R., DeBaryshe, B. D., & Ramsey, E. (1989). A developmental perspective on antisocial behavior. *American Psychologist, 44,* 329–335.

Perrino, T., Gonzalez-Soldevilla, A., Pantin, H., & Szapocznik, J. (2000). The role of families in adolescent HIV prevention: A review. *Clinical Child and Family Psychiatry, 3,* 81–96.

Pinquart, M., & Silbereisen, R. K. (2004). Human development in times of social change: Theoretical considerations and research needs. *International Journal of Behavioral Development, 28,* 289–298.

Prinstein, M. J., Boegers, J., & Spirito, A. (2001). Adolescents' and their friends' health risk behavior: Factors that alter or add to peer influence. *Journal of Pediatric Psychology, 26,* 287–298.

Richters, J. E., & Martinez, P. (1993). The NIMH community violence project: I. Children as victims of and witnesses to violence. *Psychiatry, 56,* 7–21.

Romer, D., Black, M., Ricardo, I., Feigelman, S., Kaljee, L., Galbraith, J., et al. (1994). Social influences on the sexual behavior of youth at risk for HIV exposure. *American Journal of Public Health, 84,* 977–985.

Romski, M., & Sevcik, R. A. (2002). Patterns of language development through augmentative means in youth with mental retardation. In D. L. Molfese & V. J. Molfese (Eds.), *Developmental variations in learning: Applications to social, executive function, language, and reading skills* (pp. 257–274). Mahwah, NJ: Erlbaum.

Rotheram-Borus, M., Reid, H., & Rosario, M. (1994). Factors mediating changes in sexual HIV risk behaviors among gay and bisexual male adolescents. *American Journal of Public Health, 84,* 1938–1946.

Rowe, D. C., Vazsonyi, A. T., & Flannery, D. J. (1994). No more than skin deep: Racial and ethnic similarity in developmental process. *Psychological Review, 101,* 396–413.

Sameroff, A. (1975). Transactional models in early social relations. *Human Development, 18,* 65–79.

Sameroff, A. J., & MacKenzie, M. J. (2003). Research strategies for capturing transactional models of development: The limits of the possible. *Development and Psychopathology, 15,* 613–640.

Schwab-Stone, M. E., Ayers, T., Kasprow, W., Voyce, C., Barone, C., Shriver, T., et al. (1995). No safe haven: A study of violence exposure in an urban community. *Journal of the American Academy of Child and Adolescent Development, 34,* 1343–1352.

Schwab-Stone, M., Chen, C., Greenberger, E., Silver, D., Lichtman, J., & Voyce, C. (1999). No safe haven II: The effects of violence exposure on urban youth. *Journal of the American Academy of Child and Adolescent Psychiatry, 38,* 359–367.

Seidman, E., & Pedersen, S. (2003). Holistic contextual perspectives on risk, protection, and competence among low-income urban adolescents. In S. S. Luthar (Ed.), *Resilience and vulnerability: Adaptation in the context of childhood adversities.* New York: Cambridge University Press.

Sevcik, R. A., & Romski, M. (1997). Comprehension and language acquisition: Evidence from youth with severe cognitive disabilities. In L. B. Adamson & M. Romski (Eds.), *Communication and language acquisition: Discoveries from atypical development.* Baltimore: Brookes.

Sroufe, L. A. (1990). Considering normal and abnormal together: The essence of developmental psychopathology. *Development and Psychopathology, 2,* 335–347.

Sroufe, L. A., & Rutter, M. (1984). The domain of developmental psychopathology. *Child Development, 55,* 17–29.

Steinberg, L., & Avenevoli, S. (2000). The role of context in the development of psychopathology: A conceptual framework and some speculative propositions. *Child Development, 71,* 66–74.

Suárez-Orozco, C., & Suárez-Orozco, M. M. (2001). *Children of immigration.* Cambridge, MA: Harvard University Press.

Thomas, A., Chess, S., & Birch, H. G. (1968). *Temperament and behavior disorders in children.* New York: New York University Press.

Thompson, R. A., & Raikes, H. A. (2003). Toward the next quarter century: Conceptual and methodological challenges for attachment theory. *Development and Psychopathology, 15,* 691–718.

Tolan, P. H., & Gorman-Smith, D. (2002). What violence prevention research can tell us about developmental psychopathology. *Development and Psychopathology, 14,* 713–729.

Turkheimer, E., Haley, A., Waldron, M., D'Onofrio, B., & Gottesman, I. I. (2003). Socioeconomic status modifies heritability of IQ in young children. *Psychological Science, 14,* 623–628.

Weissberg, R. P., Kumpfer, K. L., & Seligman, M. E. P. (2003). Prevention that works for children and youth: An introduction. *American Psychologist, 58,* 425–432.

Weisz, J. R., & Zigler, E. (1979). Cognitive development in retarded and nonretarded persons: Paigetian tests of the similar sequence hypothesis. *Psychological Bulletin, 86,* 831–851.

Wills, T. A., & Vaughan, R. (1989). Supportive relationships and substance use in early adolescence. *Journal of Behavioral Medicine, 12,* 321–339.

Wills, T. A., Mariani, J., & Filer, M. (1996). The role of family and peer relationships in adolescent substance use. In G. P. Pierce, B. R. Sarason, & I. G. Sarason (Eds.), *Handbook of social support and the family* (pp. 251–549). New York: Plenum Press.

Zigler, E., & Hodapp, R. M. (1986). *Understanding mental retardation.* New York: Cambridge University Press.

PART TWO
MAJOR DISORDERS AND PROBLEMS

CHAPTER 9

Generalized Anxiety Disorder

JOANNA A. ROBIN, ANTHONY C. PULIAFICO, TORREY A. CREED, JONATHAN S. COMER, STACEY A. HOFFLICH, ANDREA J. BARMISH, CYNTHIA SUVEG, AND PHILIP C. KENDALL

DESCRIPTION OF THE DISORDER AND CLINICAL PICTURE

The syndrome of excessive, impairing childhood worry has changed over time (see also Silk, Nath, Siegel, & Kendall, 2000). In *DSM-II* (American Psychiatric Association [APA], 1968), excessive worry in childhood was introduced as a diagnostic category, characterized as "overanxious reaction of childhood." Modifications occurred in *DSM-III* (APA, 1980) and *DSM-III-R* (APA, 1987), where the pattern of excessive worry was labeled overanxious disorder (OAD). The OAD designation was often considered a residual, catchall diagnostic category and was criticized as a vague categorization of symptoms that had too much overlap with other disorders (e.g., Beidel, 1991; Werry, 1991). Further, a large number of nondisordered children exhibited OAD symptoms, suggesting that it was not a clear diagnostic category for pathology (Bell-Dolan, Last, & Strauss, 1990). *DSM-IV* (APA, 1994) removed the OAD diagnosis, instead subsuming many of the symptoms under generalized anxiety disorder (GAD), which had previously been an adult diagnosis. The more specific criteria for GAD were conducive to empirical study (Tracey, Chorpita, Douban, & Barlow, 1997) and facilitated the establishment of GAD in childhood as a disorder. Some data suggest that there are no meaningful differences among the youth who received the different diagnoses (OAD [*DSM-III-R*] to GAD [*DSM-IV*]; Kendall & Warman, 1996).

Children with GAD have been described by their caretakers as "little adults" or "worrywarts" due to their pseudomaturity and their common worries about adhering to rules, being on time, and other details (Kendall, Krain, & Treadwell, 1999). Although worry about daily events and activities are not unique to youth with GAD, children with this disorder self-report much more intense worry than nonclinical children (Weems, Silverman, & LaGreca, 2000). Children with GAD often experience their worries as uncontrollable, which leads to both distress and interference in the child's life.

Children with GAD may suffer from increased levels of tension and distress caused by their recurrent dwelling on numerous subjects. They may worry about issues such as school performance (e.g., homework, tests, class work), athletic or musical performance (e.g., gym class, choir), interpersonal issues (e.g., physical appearance, friendships), perfectionism (e.g., keeping schedules, never making mistakes), health (e.g., death or becoming seriously ill), family (e.g., divorce, family finances), or community issues or world events (e.g., poverty, crime, war). Worries about health of self and others, school, natural or human-made disasters, and personal harm are the most commonly reported domains of worry for children with GAD (Weems, Silverman, & La Greca, 2000).

In addition to recurrent and intrusive worries, children with GAD often present with uncomfortable physical symptoms, including restlessness or edginess, fatigue, impaired concentration, irritability, sleep disturbance, and muscle tension (APA, 2000). Although not included in the *DSM-IV-TR* criteria, headaches, stomachaches, trembling, sweating, and enuresis are also common (Eisen & Engler, 1995). Children with GAD commonly experience excessive physiological arousal. This may be manifested in many ways, including disruption of sleep (e.g., difficulty falling asleep, waking during the night, waking earlier than intended) or fidgetiness such as nail biting or skin picking (Albano, Chorpita, & Barlow, 2003). These worries and associated physical symptoms may adversely affect a child's life by causing problems ranging from missed school days and social events to an inability to function in carrying out daily responsibilities. Due to the general nature of the worry, several types of events can trigger anxiety, making it difficult for the child to concentrate, pay attention to schoolwork, or fall asleep at night.

Distorted cognitive processes can be common. For example, children with GAD may overestimate the likelihood of the negative consequences of their actions, expect much more negative outcomes than are likely, and underestimate their ability to cope with problems (Albano, Chorpita, &

Barlow, 1996). Poor problem-solving skills (Leger, Ladouceur, & Dugas, 2003) may compound the children's difficulties in dealing with potential outcomes to situations. Intolerance of uncertainty, or the inability to tolerate not knowing what will happen in the future (Laugesen, Dugas, & Bukowski, 2003), is also commonly seen in children with GAD.

Perfectionism is a common feature of GAD. Children with perfectionistic tendencies will evaluate their own behavior in an all-or-nothing manner and suffer from unrealistic expectations or severe self-criticism (Kendall et al., 1999). For example, a child may despair over a small mistake during a basketball game, despite winning the game. Children may perceive small errors as equivalent to complete failure, leading them to sometimes avoid any activity with a chance of less-than-perfect performance (Flannery-Schroeder, 2004). As close adherence to rules and social norms are often seen as desirable, children with GAD may be overlooked for treatment or even praised for their perfectionistic tendencies.

Children with GAD often seek excessive reassurance from caregivers, teachers, and others about daily activities and may be overly self-critical and self-conscious (Flannery-Schroeder, 2004). They may ask numerous times for reassurance that they are doing things well, while doubting this fact for themselves. These children may then avoid situations in which they fear they may be less than perfect.

PERSONALITY DEVELOPMENT AND PSYCHOPATHOLOGY

Children suffering from GAD share similar personality traits or temperaments. Although little is known about the relationship between these characteristics and the development of GAD, some research has suggested that certain personality factors may contribute to the onset or maintenance of anxiety disorders in general. Personality characteristics that have received significant attention in this context include behavioral inhibition, negative affect, and effortful control.

Behavioral Inhibition

Behavioral inhibition (BI) has been described as the tendency for young children to become withdrawn, nervous, and avoidant when faced with new or unfamiliar stimuli (Garcia-Coll, Kagan, & Reznick, 1984; Kagan, Reznick, Clarke, Snidman, & Garcia-Coll, 1984). These stimuli may include unfamiliar people or environments, or even new toys. Infants as young as 4 months have displayed aspects of BI behavior, and it has been suggested that as many as 10 percent to 20 percent of young children can be classified as BI (Kagan, 1989). Although BI is often linked to infancy or young childhood, evidence suggests that BI behavior often persists through middle childhood (Kagan, Reznick, Snidman, Gibbons, & Johnson, 1988).

Considering the behavioral similarities between BI and anxious behavior, it has been hypothesized that BI may act as a diathesis for the development of anxiety disorders in children. Longitudinal research suggests that BI is associated with the subsequent development of anxiety disorders (e.g., Biederman et al., 1993). Recently, much attention has been given to a specific connection between BI and one anxiety disorder, social phobia (SP). Several studies found that children with BI tendencies at an early age later develop SP, but not other anxiety disorders (Biederman et al., 2001; Hayward, Killen, Kraemer, & Taylor, 1998). Nevertheless, other studies have suggested that BI may be associated with symptoms of later GAD. For example, Biederman and colleagues (1990) reported that BI children were more likely to meet criteria for OAD when they were between the ages of 5 and 8, and Muris, Merckelbach, Wessel, and van de Ven (1999) noted that self-reported, behaviorally inhibited children were more likely to worry more frequently than children without self-reported BI.

Currently, the degree of specificity in the association between BI and GAD is unclear. Whereas BI may be most strongly linked to SP, it may still act as a diathesis for other anxiety disorders, including GAD. It is the role of future research to more clearly determine the connection between BI and GAD.

Negative Affect

Clark and Watson (1991) described a tripartite model as a way to understand the relationship between anxiety and depression. Three affective factors comprise the model—positive affect (PA), negative affect (NA), and physiological hyperarousal (PH). Whereas PA can be described as feelings of pleasure, satisfaction, and positive engagement with one's environment, NA represents feelings of distress, displeasure, and negative engagement with one's environment. Finally, PH can be described as changes in autonomic functioning in the presence of potentially anxiety-provoking stimuli. However, the role of PH in the tripartite model has been questioned (Chorpita, 2002; Chorpita, Plummer, & Moffitt, 2000; Clark, Watson, & Mineka, 1994) and is not often considered in studies of the model.

Clark and Watson's theory suggests that both individuals with anxiety and those with depression experience high NA. Individuals with depression, however, experience low PA whereas anxious individuals generally do not. Numerous studies have suggested that the tripartite model effectively distinguishes anxiety and depression in adults (Brown, Chorpita, & Barlow, 1998; Watson, Clark, & Carey, 1988). Although the utility of the tripartite model in youth populations has not been examined to the same extent, several studies have found the model to be useful in children and adolescents as well. For example, Lonigan, Carey, and Finch (1994) found that children and adolescents hospitalized for anxiety were similar to children hospitalized for depression on the NA factor, but the two groups differed on the PA factor. Joiner, Catanzaro, and Laurent (1996) and Joiner and Lonigan (2000) later replicated these findings. Studies of anxiety-disordered children (Chorpita, Albano, & Barlow, 1998) and community members (Anthony, Lonigan, Hooe, & Phillips, 2002; Lonigan, Phillips, & Hooe, 2003) have also found that high NA, but not low PA, is associated with anxiety in children.

Unfortunately, the utility of the tripartite model with regard to GAD specifically has not been investigated in youth populations. In a study of adults with anxiety and depressive disorders, Brown et al. (1998) found that individuals with GAD experience high NA but not low PA. Furthermore, the correlation between NA and GAD was higher than the correlation between NA and other anxiety disorders, including panic disorder, obsessive-compulsive disorder (OCD), and SP. A relatively strong relationship between NA and GAD has been found in other studies as well (e.g., Brown, Chorpita, Korotitsch, & Barlow, 1997). Empirical work assessing the association between NA and GAD in children and adolescents has yet to be conducted.

Effortful Control

Another personality factor that has been discussed within the context of child anxiety is effortful control (EC), which is the ability to conduct executive self-regulatory processes. Thus, EC is a measure of an individual's ability to regulate his or her emotional responses to external stimuli and to attend to appropriate aspects of the environment. Some researchers have hypothesized that low EC is associated with anxiety in children. Lonigan and Phillips (2001) hypothesized that high NA was most likely not a sufficient diathesis for an anxiety disorder, but that high NA combined with low EC places children and adolescents at high risk for anxiety. They reasoned that high NA youth with moderate to high EC would be able to control reactivity to anxiety-provoking stimuli. The inability of high NA/low EC youth to exert such control makes these children more likely to develop an anxiety disorder.

Several studies provide support for the presence of low EC and high NA in children with internalizing disorders (Eisenberg et al., 2001; John, Caspi, Robins, Moffitt, & Stouthamer-Loeber, 1994; Lengua, 2002). In a 12-year longitudinal study, Caspi, Henry, McGee, Moffitt, and Silva (1995) found that high NA/low EC children at ages 3–5 were more likely to display internalizing symptoms between the ages of 9 and 15. Most recently, Lonigan and colleagues (Lonigan, Vasey, Phillips, & Hazen, 2004) proposed a model suggesting that NA directly increases risk for an anxiety disorder but also predisposes individuals to an attentional bias toward threat cues, which also acts as a risk factor. This attentional bias is moderated by the individual's EC capacity. This model provides an interactive understanding of the interplay between personality factors, namely NA and EC, and anxiety psychopathology in children.

EPIDEMIOLOGY

Anxiety disorders are said to be the most prevalent mental health disorders in children and adolescents (Kashani & Orvaschel, 1988, 1990; McGee et al., 1990). A recent community study assessing the prevalence of *DSM-IV* psychiatric disorders found that approximately 2.4 percent of children ages 9–16 met criteria for at least one anxiety disorder (Costello, Mustillo, Erkanli, Keeler, & Angold, 2003). A large amount of variability exists in the reported prevalence rates of OAD/GAD, most likely caused by the use of different interviewing procedures and reporters, and the degree of severity required for diagnoses (Clark, Smith, Neighbors, Skerlec, & Randall, 1994).

Community prevalence rates of OAD/GAD range from 2.9 percent to 17 percent (e.g., Bowen, Offord, & Boyle, 1990; Cohen et al., 1993; Costello, 1989; Kashani & Orvaschel, 1990). Anderson, Williams, McGee, and Silva (1987) found an estimated 2.9 percent of 11-year-old children in the general population meeting criteria for OAD. Rates of GAD may increase with age. For example, OAD/GAD was the most prevalent psychiatric disorder (5.9 percent) in adolescents aged 15 from a general population (McGee et al., 1990), and 17 percent of 17-year-olds in a community sample met criteria for OAD/GAD (Kashani & Orvaschel, 1990). Prevalence rates for OAD/GAD of approximately 10 percent have been observed in child psychiatry clinics (e.g., Beitchman, Wekerle, & Hood, 1987), and referrals to specialized anxiety clinics report rates of OAD/GAD as high as 85 percent (Keller et al., 1992; Kendall & Brady, 1995).

Data regarding gender differences in individuals with OAD/GAD are inconsistent. A greater self-reported prevalence and intensity of nonclinical fear and anxiety among girls has been observed (e.g., Bell-Dolan et al., 1990). In clinical samples of children, however, OAD/GAD does not seem to be differentially diagnosed by gender (Last, Perrin, Hersen, & Kazdin, 1992; Silverman & Nelles, 1988; Treadwell, Flannery-Schroeder, & Kendall, 1995). Gender differences have been observed in adolescence, with more females meeting criteria for GAD than males (Bowen et al., 1990; McGee et al., 1990). Similarly, a drop in the rates of OAD/GAD has been observed for boys between the ages of 10 and 20 but not for girls (Cohen et al., 1993). Cohen et al. (1993) reported the OAD/GAD prevalence rate for girls aged 14–16 and 17–20 at 14 percent, but a prevalence of only 5 percent for boys in the same age range. The gender differences observed in adolescents are consistent with those found in adults (e.g., APA, 2000; Rapee, 1991).

Data on differential diagnosis of OAD/GAD across ethnicities is less available. Treatment studies conducted in specialized anxiety clinics demonstrate higher rates of Caucasians than minority children in their samples (Last et al., 1992; Treadwell et al., 1995). Despite the lower rates of treatment-seeking ethnic minorities, studies suggest that no differences exist in the manifestation and severity of anxiety disorders across ethnicities (e.g., Last & Perrin, 1993; Treadwell et al., 1995).

ETIOLOGY

Researchers investigating the etiology of GAD have faced significant challenges. First, studies of GAD have likely suffered from shifting definitions of the disorder, in that across the multiple editions of the *DSM,* the symptoms that actually constitute GAD have not always been consistent or clear. Second, the disorder is not characterized by a clear onset of disturbance; rather, individuals with GAD typically report a slow and insidious development of pervasive worry (see Rapee, 2001). With the temporal boundaries of the disorder unclear, in a given case it is not always apparent whether a particular phenomenon is a risk factor for, or a manifestation of, GAD. Moreover, high comorbidity among the anxiety disorders (e.g., Kendall, Brady, & Verduin, 2001) makes it difficult to discern the origins of GAD specifically rather than of anxiety disorders more broadly. Consequently, what follows is a discussion of risk factors identified in the development of *any* anxiety disorder, with reference to research addressing specific relationships to the development of GAD where available.

Genetics

Behavioral genetics research suggests that at least some of the risk for the development of an anxiety disorder is inherited (see Eley, 2001). Although consistent with genetic and familial explanations, top-down research examining the offspring of individuals with anxiety disorders has consistently found that children of anxiety-disordered adults report more anxious symptomatology (e.g., Turner, Beidel, & Costello, 1987) and are more likely themselves to meet criteria for an anxiety disorder (e.g., Biederman, Rosenbaum, Bolduc, Faraone, & Hirshfeld, 1991). Bottom-up research examining adult relatives of children with anxiety disorders has also indicated the high familial prevalence of anxiety (e.g., Last, Hersen, Kazdin, Orvaschel, & Perrin, 1991). More compelling evidence for genetic influence can be found in twin and adoption studies, and these studies suggest that genetic influences account for as much as one third of the variance in anxiety (Andrews, Stewart, Allen, & Henderson, 1990; Kendler, Neale, Kessler, Heath, & Eaves, 1992; Kendler et al., 1995).

The majority of work in this area has failed to identify genetic vulnerabilities for specific anxiety disorders (Hudson & Rapee, 2004). Rather, research suggests the heritability of a disposition toward anxiety or mood disorder, or both, more broadly. Regarding the specific case of GAD, a large twin study conducted by Kendler and colleagues (1995) identified a shared genetic risk for GAD and major depressive disorder. Interestingly, results from this study also indicated that risk for panic disorder and phobias may be linked to a separate genetic factor.

Although more research is needed, it appears that the development of GAD is at least in part genetically influenced, and that such genetic vulnerability may be specific not to GAD but rather to disorders characterized by negative affectivity more broadly. With genetic influences accounting for only a portion of the variance in an anxiety disorder, what, then, accounts for the remaining variance? Growing evidence points to the impact of environmental factors, such as parenting behavior and parent-child attachment quality. We now turn our attention to these factors.

Environmental Contributions

The family environment constitutes the most salient and immediate context within which children develop. Investigations of parenting behavior have consistently identified controlling and overprotective parenting as associated with anxiety disorders (see Hudson & Rapee, 2004; Rapee, 1997). For instance, Kagan, Snidman, Archus, and Reznick (1994) reported that the degree to which mothers held their infants when they did not need help prospectively predicted fear among infants 1 year later.

Research suggests that mothers of anxious youth are more intrusive and overinvolved when helping their children complete a stressful task than mothers of nonanxious youth (Hudson & Rapee, 2002). Further, empirical work suggests that parents of anxious children exhibit similar levels of overinvolvement when interacting with their anxious child's sibling (Hudson & Rapee, 2002), suggesting that anxious children may not simply evoke such parenting behavior. Siqueland, Kendall, and Steinberg (1996) found parents of anxious children to be less granting of autonomy than parents of nonclinical children (as determined by observational ratings). This study also reported that children with anxiety disorders rated their parents as less accepting than nonclinical children rated their parents.

Parents of anxious youth support, even if unwittingly, more avoidant coping behavior in their children than do parents of nonanxious youth (Dadds, Barrett, Rapee, & Ryan, 1996). Whereas nonclinical youth and youth suffering from externalizing pathologies report less avoidant responses to a hypothetical threat situation after discussing the situation with their parents, anxious youth have been found to report more avoidant responses after discussing the situation with their parents (Barrett, Rapee, Dadds, & Ryan, 1996). Further, research suggests that levels of parental anxiety may influence the extent to which parents support avoidant coping in their children, with maternal distress found to correlate with anxious children's increased avoidance following family discussion (Shortt, Barrett, Dadds, & Fox, 2001). Parents may also model fearful responding in their children via nonverbal behavior. Recently, Gerull and Rapee (2002) reported that infants are more likely to avoid novel stimuli after mothers reacted to such stimuli with a fearful expression.

Attachment, referring to the enduring emotional connection between the child and caregiver, provides another familial context within which children's behavior develops. Although related to parenting behavior, the construct of attachment is a relationship construct and is consequently measured via assessment of the relationship between parents and child, rather than a parent's caregiving behavior. Children exhibiting insecure attachments with their caregivers are said to experience uncertainty regarding the availability of their caregivers and demonstrate heightened vigilance for threat cues and less exploration in their play. Research suggests that an insecure attachment may place the child at risk for anxiety (see Thompson, 2001). Warren, Huston, Egeland, and Sroufe (1997) found that 28 percent of a sample of children assessed during infancy as insecurely attached developed an anxiety disorder by age 17. Research has not shown a specific relationship between attachment quality and the development of GAD.

In addition to the family environment, other environments play a role in the development of anxiety disorders. Research has yet to explore the potential roles of several such powerful socialization agents (e.g., peers, teachers, and the media). Further, although research broadly indicates that nonspecific stressful events are related to the development of anxiety disorders (see Craske, 1999; Rapee, 2001), the relationship between stressful life events and the development of GAD is less clear.

Current etiological models of GAD (e.g., Rapee, 2001) highlight the role of cumulative vulnerability. For example, a child with a genetic predisposition for anxiety may develop GAD but only in the context of parenting behavior that supports his or her avoidance behavior. Another child in the context of parenting behavior supporting autonomy and independence may not develop an anxiety disorder, whether or not that child is at risk.

COURSE, COMPLICATIONS, AND PROGNOSIS

Developmental Course and Associated Complications

Too little is known about the exact course of childhood GAD. Findings suggest that young children (2.5–6 years) do not experience specific anxiety disorders, including GAD, but suffer nonspecific anxiety (Spence, Rapee, McDonald, & Ingram, 2001). However, GAD (or OAD) has been identified in children as young as 8 years old (e.g., Kendall et al., 1997).

Findings about the stability of GAD in childhood are mixed. Several studies reported that childhood internalizing disorders are often persistent and unremitting without treatment (see Ollendick & King, 1994), and these findings are in accord with evidence that adult GAD is a chronic disorder with low rates of remission (Keller, 2002). However, some earlier reports suggested that childhood OAD/GAD is not generally chronic (Cantwell & Baker, 1989). Last, Hansen, and Franco (1997) found that children with anxiety and depression are more likely as adults to have psychological problems and difficulties in school and work. Given that children with anxiety disorders are at risk for developing other difficulties, including depression and alcohol abuse, childhood GAD should not be viewed as a fleeting problem that will remit in time.

In children, GAD is often associated with other behavior that negatively impacts functioning. Children with GAD can display school refusal behavior (Kearney, 2001) that may interfere with academic functioning. For example, Ialongo and colleagues (Ialongo, Edelsohn, Werthamer-Larsson, Crockett, & Kellam, 1995) reported that children who experienced symptoms of anxiety in first grade were more likely to be in the academic lower third of their class in fifth grade. Additionally, GAD in childhood is often associated with negative social expectations and lower self-competence (Chansky & Kendall, 1997). Such negatively biased social cognition is consistent with anxious children's increased attention toward threat cues in general (Bogels & Zigterman, 2000; Taghavi, Neshat-Doost, Moradi, Yule, & Dalgleish, 1999).

Childhood GAD can lead to difficulties later in life. Presence of GAD in childhood is associated with increased risk for alcohol use (Kaplow, Curran, Angold, & Costello, 2001) and abuse (Lewinsohn, Zinbarg, Seeley, Lewinsohn, & Sack, 1997) in adolescence. For example, Kaplow and colleagues (2001) reported that after controlling for symptoms of depression, early symptoms of GAD were associated with increased risk for initiation of alcohol use in youth. Kaplow and colleagues suggested that youth with GAD are more likely to worry about peer acceptance, which may increase their likelihood to engage in alcohol use to fit in with a peer group. The authors also suggested that after initial use, these youth may continue to use alcohol to decrease physiological arousal and worries associated with GAD.

Youth with GAD may also have a greater risk of suicidal behavior later in life. Strauss and colleagues (Strauss et al., 2000) found that in older youth (age >15 years), GAD was more prevalent in suicidal ideators than nonideators. More research on the associations between GAD and both alcohol use and suicidal behavior are crucial to a better understanding of the long-term impacts of childhood GAD.

Comorbidity

Comorbidity rates for childhood anxiety disorders, including GAD, are generally high (Kendall, 1994; Newman et al., 1996), which is consistent with research findings in adult GAD (e.g., Bruce, Machan, Dyck, & Keller, 2001). Several studies indicate GAD to be frequently comorbid with other anxiety disorders. For instance, in a study of comorbidity using *DSM-III* criteria, Last, Strauss, and Francis (1987) found that children diagnosed with OAD most frequently also suffered from social anxiety. In a more recent study, Verduin and Kendall (2003) reported that GAD was most often comorbid with specific phobias, followed by SP and separation anxiety disorder (SAD) (the comorbidity rates for those three disorders and GAD were all above 20 percent).

Childhood GAD is also frequently comorbid with depressive disorders. Masi and colleagues (Masi, Mucci, Favilla, Romano, & Poli, 1999) reported that approximately half of all children with GAD assessed at a specific time were suffering from a concurrent depressive episode. Consistent with adult literature, childhood anxiety may be a risk factor for the onset of depression (Brady & Kendall, 1992). High comorbidity rates between GAD and depression is concerning in that youth with both anxiety and depression suffer from more severe anxiety symptoms (Masi et al., 1999) and are much more likely to attempt suicide than youth with only an anxiety disorder (Lewinsohn, Rohde, & Seeley, 1995).

ASSESSMENT AND DIAGNOSIS

Diagnostic Criteria

The *DSM-IV-TR* (APA, 2000) defines GAD as unrealistic or excessive worry about a number of things (e.g., academic performance; health of oneself or significant others, or both; the future). The worry must be difficult to control and must be interfering and distressing for more days than not for at least 6 months. The worry cannot be better accounted for by another disorder, cannot result from a medical condition or the effects of a substance, or cannot occur only during a psychotic episode or mood disorder. The diagnostic criteria for GAD are the same for adults as for children, except that children are required to have only one of six somatic complaints, which include restlessness, fatigue, poor concentration, irritability, muscle tension, and sleep disturbance.

Differential Diagnosis

Because the worries of GAD youth will be in multiple domains, it is possible that the content of a child's worries resembles fears or concerns often seen in other childhood anxiety disorders (e.g., SAD or SP). If a child's fears are about safety, accidents, or other events that could lead to separation, but are not specifically about the fear of separation, then GAD may be the more appropriate diagnosis. However, if a child reports a fear of situations that revolve around separation from loved ones (e.g., getting lost or being kidnapped, parents getting into a car accident), then SAD seems more appropriate. In addition, if a child's worries are (a) limited to social situations and not about multiple domains, or (b) about how others will evaluate them as opposed to how they are evaluating themselves, then SP may be more appropriate.

Differentiating GAD from obsessive-compulsive disorder in anxious children can be difficult given the phenomenological overlap between worries and obsessions (see Comer, Kendall, Franklin, Hudson, & Pimentel, in press). In short, both processes involve recurrent and persistent anticipatory cognitive activity that the individual experiences as uncontrollable and intrusive. Comer and colleagues suggested that, despite overlap in the two processes, worry and obsessions may be differentiated by content (i.e., worries tend to regard realistic and mundane concerns; obsessions can be bizarre), form (i.e., worries are predominantly abstract and verbal; obsessions are often imaginal), and the presence or absence of an identifiable trigger (i.e., GAD children more apt to report a specific trigger; OCD children are less so).

The physical symptoms associated with GAD may appear similar to symptoms of attention-deficit/hyperactivity disorder (ADHD) or to those of major depression. Children with GAD often have difficulty paying attention, relaxing, and sitting still—but this behavior occurs in the context of worrying and may vary in severity across time. Children with ADHD display similar behavior, but the behavior must be present before age 7, must occur across settings, and must occur in more than one domain. Worrying (as in GAD) can affect children's sleep patterns, energy, and mood—similar to depression. Interestingly, children with depression are usually sad, irritable, or both versus apprehensive, and they withdraw due to their mood as opposed to actively seeking help and reassurance.

Differential diagnosis is important—the outcome is linked to variations in treatment, and there are several empirically supported treatments for each of these mental health problems. Optimally, diagnoses are based on a thorough multimethod and multi-informant assessment, and when the symptom criteria are met, it is appropriate for multiple diagnoses to be assigned.

Assessment

A comprehensive assessment of childhood GAD involves a multi-informant and multimethod evaluation that considers developmental level, cultural context, family factors, and normative comparisons (Albano et al., 2003; Barrios & Hartmann, 1997; Kendall et al., 1999). Various methods are used to assess the presence and severity of GAD, such as diagnostic interviews, self-report questionnaires, and parent and teacher reports.

Diagnostic Interviews

Diagnostic structured and semistructured interviews assess a broad range of psychopathology. These interviews provide information on the severity, duration, and interference of disorder. Examples of such clinical interviews are the Diagnostic Interview for Children and Adolescents—Revised (DICA-R; Reich, Shayka, & Taibleson, 1991), the National Institute of Mental Health Diagnostic Interview Schedule for Children Version IV (DISC-IV; Shaffer, Fisher, Lucas, Dulan, & Schwab-Stone, 2000), and the Schedule for Affective Disorders and Schizophrenia for School-Aged Children—Present and Lifetime Version (K-SADS-PL; Kaufman, Birmaher, & Brent, 1997). The Anxiety Disorders Interview Schedule—Child/Parent (ADIS-C/P; Silverman & Albano, 1996) focuses primarily on anxiety disorders (Stallings & March, 1995) and provides a clinician severity rating (CSR), ranging from 0 (not at all) to 8 (very, very much), that is based on the combined child and parent ratings of the severity of symptoms and degree of interference the symptoms cause for the child in school, at home, and with friends. The ADIS-C/P has strong psychometric properties. For example, Silverman, Saavedra, and Pina (2001) used a 7- to 14-day retest interval and reported that diagnoses derived from the ADIS-C/P had high temporal stability. Kappa coefficients for uncontrollable worry ranged from .31 to .63 on the child interview and .43 to .78 on the parent interview. Kappa coefficients for physiological symptoms ranged from .54 to .81 on the child interview and .23 to .67 on the parent interview. These clinical interviews involve individual child and parent assessments, yet parent-child agreement has often been found to be low (Kendall & Pimentel, 2003). Self-reports offer additional information and provide a time-efficient, dimensional way to assess symptoms of GAD in youth.

Self-Report Questionnaires

Although self-report questionnaires alone are not sufficient to assess diagnostic criteria, they do provide valuable data regarding symptomatology, severity, and distress of worrying. Historically the Revised Children's Manifest Anxiety Scale (RCMAS; Reynolds & Richmond, 1978) and the State-Trait Anxiety Interview for Children (STAIC; Spielberger, 1973) have been used. The RCMAS is a 37-item questionnaire assessing the presence of worry, fear, and physiological symptoms. The STAIC has two 20-item scales that assess state and trait anxiety. However, these measures may be limited by high correlations with NA and depression (March & Albano, 2002). Two newer measures, the Screen for Childhood Anxiety Related Emotional Disorders (SCARED-R; Birmaher et al., 1999) and the Multidimensional Anxiety Scale for Children (MASC; March, Parker, Sullivan, Stallings, & Conners, 1997), both assess *DSM-IV* symptomatology and are sensitive to anxiety disorders. The SCARED is a 41-item questionnaire assessing the frequency of panic, generalized anxiety, separation anxiety, SP, and school phobia symptoms. The MASC is a 39-item scale of the frequency of physical symptoms, social anxiety, harm avoidance, and separation anxiety. Christophersen (2001) reports that these measures have adequate internal and test-retest reliability and adequate convergent validity. The Penn State Worry Questionnaire—Child (PSWQ-C; Chorpita, Tracey, Brown, Colica, & Barlow, 1997), an adaptation of the PSWQ (Meyer, Miller, Metzger, & Borkovec, 1990), assesses frequency and severity of worry. The PSWQ-C was found to have excellent test-retest reliability, good internal consistency, and favorable convergent and discriminant validity in initial studies (Chorpita et al., 1997). Clinicians must consider developmental level and cognitive ability when using self-report measures.

Parent and Teacher Reports

Most parent and teacher report measures assess for psychopathology in general and not GAD specifically. However, the SCARED, for example, assesses GAD symptoms and has a parent version. The Child Behavior Checklist (CBCL; Achenbach, 1991a) and the Teacher's Report Form (TRF; Achenbach, 1991b) are checklists of behavioral problems and social competencies and allow for comparison between behavior at home and at school. Although the CBCL has adequate psychometric properties, it has not been found to distinguish among the anxiety disorders. The Behavior Assessment System for Children (BASC; Reynolds & Kamphaus, 1992) assesses for broadband internalizing disorders as well as specific disorders and has been reported as psychometrically sound (Christophersen, 2001). The Revised Behavior Problem Checklist (RBPC; Quay & Peterson, 1987) has adequate reliability and validity (Daugherty & Shapiro, 1994) and is similar to the CBCL and TRF in that it measures a more general anxiety or withdrawal factor that has been associated with worrying, nervousness, and fearfulness (Strauss, 1994).

IMPACT ON ENVIRONMENT

Mental health professionals working with anxious youth are typically aware of the impact that child anxiety has on the family, school, and peers. However, empirical research on the impact of childhood GAD in these settings is sparse. Researchers have suggested that children with GAD worry excessively about events that have a low probability of occurring and have difficulty recognizing that perception of the probability of the event occurring is distorted (e.g., Butler & Matthews, 1983; Muris et al., 2000). In addition, children with GAD have a low perception of the controllability of events (Rapee, 1991). This cognitive style impacts not only the child's quality of life but also interactions with family, school, and peers.

Family

By the time parents seek treatment for their child with GAD, they may be frustrated and overwhelmed by the intensity of their child's worries and excessive need for reassurance. At first, the child's concerns or worries may be valued, admired, and rewarded with attention and praise, but when these worries become excessive and uncontrollable, parents may become unsure about how to best respond to their child. Parents are often troubled by their child's consistent need for reassurance about safety, health, and performance. They tend to be confused about how these worries developed and why the worries persist when there is no present threat. Parents often respond to children's worries by offering reassurance, but this does not seem to alleviate the worries (Kearney & Albano, 2000; Kendall et al., 1999) and may actually maintain the child's anxiety. For example, parents may try to reason with their child by telling them, "Don't worry, because I won't let something bad happen to you." This type of response may help children with GAD maintain the belief that they are unable to cope with world on their own and that, therefore, it is necessary to be vigilant in cases when they feel their parents are not alert.

As mentioned in a previous section, children with GAD often present with perfectionism. Their desire for perfection can manifest in several ways and impact the people in their lives. Although many parents would be very pleased if their children demonstrated dedication to their schoolwork or extracurricular activities, children with GAD often exhibit such high expectations and self-criticism when completing homework assignments and projects that it may begin to interfere with family relationships and increase parent-child conflict. One child with GAD doubted her ability to provide correct answers on her homework assignment, so she kept erasing her answers so many times that she ripped her papers. Her parents were unable to console her or convince her that if she completed the assignment incorrectly, it would be okay. The fear was so intense that she would throw temper tantrums and beg her parents to let her skip school the next day.

These types of interactions often lead parents to become frustrated with their children's rigidity and need for reassurance. The intensity of children's worrying and the associated irritability may make it difficult for parents to respond in a sensitive manner. Instead of offering reassurance, they may act punitively in hopes of decreasing the unwanted behavior. An intermittent reinforcement schedule is established, whereby parents sometimes respond by offering reassurance in a sensitive manner and at other times respond with harshness and criticism. This pattern may help to maintain reassurance seeking, while increasing tension and hostility between parent and child.

School

Children with GAD typically like to please their teachers, are conscientious about completing assignments, and adhere to school rules. Often, these children are considered the "good" students and can be overlooked by teachers because they require less redirection. In other cases, the symptoms associated with GAD may negatively impact the classroom environment and the teacher-child relationship. Children who seek reassurance from parents may also seek reassurance from teachers at school. They may have difficulty completing assignments autonomously because they will repeatedly ask their teachers for reassurance about whether they are completing assignments correctly (Flannery-Schroeder, 2004).

Children with perfectionism concerns are often satisfied only with perfect scores on exams, have difficulty tolerating making mistakes, and are afraid of breaking rules and getting into trouble at school. Ironically, children with GAD rarely do get into trouble at school and are often praised by teachers for being very well behaved. Yet, the fear of getting into trouble with a teacher can become so intense that the child may have difficulty completing assignments for fear of making a mistake. For example, one child with GAD refused to participate in any group activities that required the child to provide opinions. This activity was too difficult for him because he feared his opinions would be *wrong*.

In extreme situations, severe perfectionism can lead to school refusal problems. This may occur when a child encounters a new teacher who has higher expectations of the child or is stricter than previous teachers. For example, one child with GAD told his mother that he did not want to go to school because he was getting yelled at by the teacher almost every day. When the mother questioned the teacher about this, she replied that she had yelled at the class several times during the week, but her displeasure was never directed individually at the child.

As mentioned previously, children often suffer from several physical symptoms associated with excessive worrying, such as headaches and stomachaches, muscle tension, and perspiration (Eisen & Engler, 1995). Because children with GAD may not understand or connect physical symptoms to feared events, they will seek treatment from the nurse or convince their parents that they cannot go to school due to these somatic complaints. School nurses often cannot find the cause of the physical symptoms and are unsure how to help the child. Many times they allow the child to go home or spend the rest of the day in the nurses' office.

Peer Interactions

Research examining peer relationships of youth with GAD is relatively scarce, and little is known about how the symptoms of GAD impact children's social relationships and social status. Several studies on peer relationships and peer status of anxious youth show that anxious youth do make an impact on their peers. For example, Strauss and colleagues (Strauss, Frame, & Forehand, 1987) found that teacher-rated anxious youth were most likely to be nominated by their peers as shy or socially withdrawn. Another study by Strauss and colleagues demonstrated that anxious children are often socially neglected by peers and less likely to be nominated as "most liked" by their peers (Strauss, Lahey, Frick, Frame, & Hynd, 1988). Although there were significant differences in peer social status between anxious and nonanxious youth, a majority of the anxious youth in the sample did not show peer social status deficits. Thus, the authors suggested that not all anxious children are at risk for peer-related difficulties. Anxious children are typically thought to be more neglected than rejected by peers, but a recent study by Waas and Graczyk (1999) found that school-age children were more likely to reject peers who were described to them as anxious and socially withdrawn.

Given the variety of worries and concerns that children with GAD will present with, the impact on peers may also vary. Albano and Hack (2004) suggested that an increasing pattern of avoidance can occur for children with worries regarding performance and social evaluation. These children may begin to avoid peer-related activities because of lower levels of confidence in interpersonal and performance situations (Chansky & Kendall, 1997). Unfortunately, withdrawal from peer-related activities may lead the child to be less well known and liked by peers (Strauss et al., 1988). Thus, it becomes unlikely that the child will be included in future peer-related activities. Ultimately, the lack of peer contact may reinforce the child's belief that he or she will be unaccepted by his peers.

Children who display perfectionism, rigidity, or excessive need to adhere to rules may also have difficulty with peer relationships. Their need to behave correctly and difficulty tolerating uncertainty may make it difficult for these children to regulate anxiety in peer interactions. This inability to regulate anxiety may lead to difficulties in interpersonal interactions because children may be more likely to ignore or reject children who display anxiety (Rubin, Bukowski, & Parker, 1998).

The inability of children with GAD to perceive threat accurately and their lack of confidence in their ability to cope with situations independently may increase the likelihood that they seek adult interaction for peer-related conflict, which may lead to peer rejection. For example, a child with GAD was so afraid that she would get in trouble for another child's inappropriate behavior that she repeatedly "told on him" whenever he violated any rules. Soon after, the other children labeled her as a "teacher's pet" and a "tattletale."

Childhood GAD impacts not only the child's life, but also the lives of those around the child. Interactions that cause conflict and rejection can prevent the child with GAD from developing self-confidence and self-esteem. It is essential that clinicians working with GAD youth promote positive interactions with the adults and children in the child's life and work to prevent maladaptive patterns from continuing.

IMPLICATIONS FOR FUTURE PERSONALITY DEVELOPMENT

Impairment associated with childhood anxiety has long-term implications for adult functioning (Kendall, 1992), yet little research has examined childhood GAD and adult personality traits. Given this lack of empirical work, this section will focus on (1) studies that use retrospective reports of adults with childhood-onset GAD, and (2) studies on the relationship between comorbid personality functioning and GAD in adults.

Personality Problems of Adults with Childhood Onset GAD

Although there are no prospective studies that examine personality functioning in adults with childhood GAD, retrospective studies of adults with childhood-onset GAD suggest that childhood-onset GAD may be associated with increased comorbidity of Axis I disorders, impaired personality functioning, or both. When GAD develops in childhood, children have more time to approach situations with avoidance or uncertainty without having opportunities to learn that both this style and worrying itself are unproductive (Campbell, Brown, & Grisham, 2003). If GAD is left untreated or is treated unsuccessfully, children continue maladaptive patterns of worrying, and being a worrier may eventually become part of their identity (Campbell et al., 2003). As this style of interacting with the world becomes ingrained, it may begin to affect different areas of adult functioning. Empirical evidence of retrospective studies supports this hypothesis. For example, Hoehn-Saric, Hazlett, and McLeod (1993) reported that adults with childhood-onset GAD have higher scores on measures of neuroticism, trait anxiety, depression, and obsessional features than adults with adult-onset GAD. Interestingly, the two groups did not differ on current symptom severity. Campbell et al. (2003) reported childhood-onset GAD was associated with higher symptom severity and higher scores on a measure of temperamental vulnerability, which was made up of measures of NA, neuroticism, and behavioral inhibition. Given that earlier onset of GAD is associated with increased impairment in adulthood, it is likely that children who suffer from GAD that is not successfully treated may have subsequent personality difficulties in adulthood.

Personality Disorders in Adults with GAD

Literature on adult personality traits in patients with GAD is also scarce. Some work suggests that adults with GAD often present with comorbid personality disorders (Reich et al., 1994; Sanderson, Wetzler, Beck, & Bertz., 1994). For example, Sanderson and colleagues (1994) reported that almost half (49 percent) of the sample of outpatients with GAD met criteria for a personality disorder. Individuals with GAD are more likely to present with personality pathology compared to individuals with agoraphobia or panic disorder (Reich et al., 1994). Findings are mixed on the types of personality disorders that are associated with GAD, although a key feature among adults with GAD is a concern about interpersonal relationships (Roemer, Mollina, & Borkevec, 1997). For example, adults with GAD have more interpersonal difficulties (e.g., distress and rigidity) than nonanxious controls (Pincus & Borkevec, 1994).

Sanderson and Wetzler (1991) found that avoidant personality disorder and dependent personality disorder were the most common personality disorders in patients with GAD. Both of these personality disorders are "characterized by feelings of inadequacy, hypersensitivity to criticism, and a need for reassurance . . ." (*DSM-IV,* APA, 2000, p. 720). However, individuals with these personality disorders cope with their feelings differently. According to the *DSM* (*DSM-IV,* APA, 1994), adults with avoidant personality disorder withdraw until they are assured of acceptance, and those with dependent personality disorder are more likely to actively attempt to maintain close relationships to feel safe. A study on comorbid personality traits and GAD by Blashfield and colleagues (1994) reported results that contrasted those of Sanderson and Wetzler (1991). They found that patients with GAD reported more antisocial personality traits than patients with panic disorder (controlling for age and gender).

The literature suggests that individuals with childhood-onset GAD that does not remit in adulthood may be at increased risk for a variety of adjustment difficulties in adulthood, including personality disorders. Unfortunately, full or partial remission of GAD is less likely in adult patients with a comorbid personality disorder (Yonkers, Dyck, Warshaw, & Keller, 2000). Furthermore, individuals with GAD and a comorbid personality disorder are more likely to drop out of treatment than individuals with only GAD (Sanderson, Beck,

& McGinn, 2002). These findings are discouraging for adults coping with GAD and support the effort to provide effective treatment to youth with GAD. We now turn our attention to treatment implications for children with GAD.

TREATMENT IMPLICATIONS

Only a handful of studies (e.g., Eisen & Silverman, 1993, 1998; Kane & Kendall, 1989) have specifically examined the psychosocial treatment of GAD, and these studies had very small sample sizes. However, the majority of youth in the samples studied in the randomized clinical trials that are reviewed herein had a principal diagnosis of GAD. In general, research has identified cognitive-behavioral therapy (CBT) approaches as probably efficacious in the treatment of anxiety disorders in youth (Ollendick & King, 2000). The pharmacological treatment of GAD in youth is less researched, and thus it is not yet possible to draw solid conclusions. Preliminary research suggests that the use of selective serotonin reuptake inhibitors (SSRIs) might be helpful, at least in the short term, in treating GAD in youth (Research Units on Pediatric Psychopharmacology Anxiety Study Group, 2001).

Cognitive-Behavioral Therapy

Kendall and colleagues manualized CBT for use with anxiety-disordered youth (Kendall, 1994), although many adaptations of this model now exist (e.g., child-focused CBT, family CBT, group CBT). Despite the particular variant of CBT, the program (e.g., Kendall, 1990, 2000) consists of approximately 16 sessions during which time the anxious youth first learns skills to manage anxiety and then practices the skills in actual anxiety-provoking situations. The main principles of the CBT program are presented using the FEAR acronym to facilitate learning and include (1) recognizing bodily symptoms of anxiety (i.e., **F**eeling frightened?), (2) identifying maladaptive cognition in anxiety-provoking situations (i.e., **E**xpecting bad things to happen?), (3) developing a repertoire of coping strategies (i.e., **A**ttitudes and actions that can help), and (4) behavioral reinforcement (i.e., **R**esults and rewards). Various behavioral strategies are implemented during the therapy process and include modeling, role-playing, imaginal and in vivo exposure, and relaxation training (for a practical discussion regarding the design and implementation of exposures, see Kendall et al., 2005). Lastly, STIC (**S**how **T**hat **I** **C**an) tasks are assigned as weekly homework to provide the child an opportunity to practice the skills learned in the session. In carrying out CBT, it is crucial that the therapist focus attention on the child's individual needs and development level (i.e., social, emotional, and cognitive) (e.g., Silverman & Ollendick, 1999). In this way, the therapist is encouraged to apply the manual flexibly within the CBT model (Kendall, Chu, Gifford, Hayes, & Nauta, 1998).

The use of CBT for treating anxiety in youth has undergone empirical scrutiny. Multiple baseline evaluations and several randomized clinical trials have reported efficacy for individual (Eisen & Silverman, 1993, 1998; Kendall, 1994, 1997), group (Barrett, 1998; Flannery-Schroeder & Kendall, 2000; Silverman et al., 1999), and family-focused (e.g., Barrett, Dadds, & Rapee, 1996; Cobham, Dadds, & Spence, 1998; Shortt, Barrett, & Fox, 2001) applications. In the first clinical trial (Kendall, 1994), 47 children with anxiety disorder (ages 9–13) participated. Thirty of the 47 children were diagnosed with overanxious disorder (now GAD); the remaining participants had a diagnosis of either SAD or SP. Results revealed both statistically significant and clinically meaningful gains at posttreatment: 64 percent no longer exhibited their primary diagnosis, and comparable percentages were within the normative range on self-, parent-, and teacher-report measures. Overall, gains were comparable for children with GAD (relative to other principal anxiety disorders) and were maintained at 1-year and 3.5-year follow-up (Kendall & Southam-Gerow, 1996).

A second randomized clinical trial found similar support for an individual CBT (Kendall et al., 1997). Perhaps more interesting, however, is the 7.4-year follow-up of that treated sample (see Kendall, Safford, Flannery-Schroeder, & Webb, 2004), which examined not only the maintenance of treatment effects, but also the effects of treatment on potential sequelae of childhood anxiety. The follow-up included 86 of the 94 children in the original sample (ages 9–13 at intake) with a principal diagnosis of GAD ($n = 55$), SAD ($n = 22$), or SP ($n = 17$), and the results indicated that for the majority of participants, treatment gains were maintained. Results also indicated that those who responded positively to CBT used alcohol and other substances less and had fewer difficulties related to substance use than less positive CBT responders. No relation between CBT response and the development of a mood disorder was found.

As noted previously in the Etiology section, family factors contribute to both the etiology and maintenance of childhood anxiety. Although the literature examining the role of the family in treatment is relatively scant, the research that is available has suggested that younger children may benefit more from including parents and families than older children (e.g., Barrett et al., 1996; Cobham et al., 1998). For example, Barrett et al. (1996) randomly assigned children to individual CBT, CBT plus a family anxiety management (FAM), or a wait-list control condition. Results indicated that younger children (≤10 years) responded best in the CBT + FAM condition, whereas older children (≥11 years) responded equally in both CBT conditions. Cobham et al. (1998) examined the role of parental anxiety in a group of 67 children with a primary anxiety disorder, 40 of whom had GAD as a principal diagnosis. Children were randomly assigned to individual CBT or CBT plus parental anxiety management (PAM). Results indicated that children who had at least one anxious parent responded better to the CBT + PAM condition. Children who did not have an anxious parent responded equally well to the CBT as to the CBT + PAM conditions. However, a more detailed review of the role of parents in treating anxious youth revealed variability across the nature, type, format, and duration of parental involvement in treatment, with few solid conclusions (Barmish & Kendall, in press).

Adaptations to the general CBT are appropriate for children with different primary disorders. First, given the major worry component of GAD, it is helpful for the clinician to spend increased time addressing the cognitive aspects of CBT. This may be especially helpful for younger or cognitively delayed youth, who may have difficulty with the cognitive components of treatment (e.g., identification of anxious cognition, use of coping thoughts). Given that youth with GAD worry about a number of domains, ongoing assessment of both previous and newly developed worry areas is important.

Pharmacological Treatment

The literature on the pharmacological treatment of GAD in youth (for a review see Walkup, Labellarte, & Ginsburg, 2002; Stein & Seedat, 2004) is at present less developed than the psychosocial approaches (see also Kendall, Pimentel, Rynn, Angelosante, & Webb, 2004). In short, the literature suggests lack of support for the use of tricyclic antidepressants (TCAs) in youth with GAD, and neither of the controlled trials examining the efficacy of benzodiazepine use in childhood anxiety disorders that included GAD in the diagnostic profile yielded positive results (Graee, Milner, Rizzotoo, & Klein, 1994; Simeon et al., 1992). However, preliminary findings for SSRI use in children with GAD are promising. A double-blind multisite study examined Fluvoxamine in 134 children with GAD, SAD, SP, or a combination of these, and the results indicated improvement on self- and other report measures (RUPP Anxiety Study Group, 2001). Other smaller trials also reported short-term efficacy of SSRIs in treating childhood anxiety disorders, including GAD (e.g., Birmaher et al., 1994, 2003; Rynn, Siqueland, & Rickels, 2001).

Future Directions for Treatment of Youth with GAD

Although advances in the treatment of anxiety in youth have been made, challenges remain (Kendall & Ollendick, 2004). First, there are no published studies examining the relative efficacy of a monotherapeutic approach as compared to a combined psychological and pharmacologic approach. Yet, at least for some children (e.g., those with severe GAD), a combined approach may be needed and appropriate (see Compton, McKnight, & March, 2004). Second, given that a considerable percentage of treated youth continue to experience symptomatology following treatment, more studies examining treatment nonresponse and ways to enhance current treatments are very much needed.

REFERENCES

Achenbach, T. M. (1991a). *Manual for the Child Behavior Checklist/4–18 and 1991 profile:* Burlington: University of Vermont, Department of Psychiatry.

Achenbach, T. M. (1991b). *Manual for the Teacher's Report Form and 1991 profile.* Burlington: University of Vermont, Department of Psychiatry.

Albano, A. M., Chorpita, B. F., & Barlow, D. H. (1996). Anxiety disorders. In E. J. Mash & R. A. Barkley (Eds.), *Child psychopathology* (pp. 196–241). New York: Guilford Press.

Albano, A. M., Chorpita, B. F. & Barlow, D. H. (2003).Childhood anxiety disorders. In E. J. Mash & R. A. Barkley (Eds.), *Child psychopathology* (2nd ed., pp. 279–329). New York: Guilford Press.

Albano, A. M., & Hack, S. (2004). Children and adolescents. In R. Heimberg, C. L. Turk, & D. S. Mennin (Eds.), *Generalized anxiety disorder: Advances in research and practice* (pp. 383–408). New York: Guilford Press.

American Psychiatric Association. (1968). *Diagnostic and statistical manual of mental disorders* (2nd ed.). Washington, DC: Author.

American Psychiatric Association. (1980). *Diagnostic and statistical manual of mental disorders* (3rd ed.). Washington, DC: Author.

American Psychiatric Association. (1987). *Diagnostic and statistical manual of mental disorders* (3rd ed., rev.). Washington, DC: Author.

American Psychiatric Association. (1994). *Diagnostic and statistical manual of mental disorders* (4th ed.). Washington, DC: Author.

American Psychiatric Association. (2000). *Diagnostic and statistical manual of mental disorders* (4th ed., text rev.). Washington, DC: Author.

Anderson, J. C., Williams, S., McGee, R., & Silva, P. A. (1987). *DSM-II* disorders in preadolescent children. *Archives of General Psychiatry, 44,* 69–76.

Andrews, G., Stewart, G. W., Allen, R., & Henderson, A. S. (1990). The genetics of six neurotic disorders: A twin study. *Journal of Affective Disorders, 19,* 23–29.

Anthony, J. L., Lonigan, C. J., Hooe, E. S., & Phillips, B. M. (2002). An affect-based, hierarchical model of temperament and its relations with internalizing symptomatology. *Journal of Clinical Child and Adolescent Psychology, 31,* 480–490.

Barmish, A., & Kendall, P. C. (in press). Should parents be co-clients in treating anxious youth with CBT? *Journal of Clinical Child and Adolescent Psychology.*

Barrett, P. M. (1998). Evaluation of cognitive-behavioral group treatments for childhood anxiety disorders. *Journal of Clinical Child Psychology, 27,* 459–468.

Barrett, P. M, Dadds, M. R., & Rapee, R. M. (1996). Family treatment for childhood anxiety: A controlled trial. *Journal of Consulting and Clinical Psychology, 64,* 333–342.

Barrett, P. M., Rapee, R. M., Dadds, M. R., & Ryan, S. (1996). Family enhancement of cognitive style in anxious and aggressive children. *Journal of Abnormal Child Psychology, 24,* 187–203.

Barrios, B. A., & Hartmann, D. P. (1997). Fears and anxieties. In E. J. Mash & L. G. Terdal (Eds.), *Assessment of childhood disorders* (3rd ed., pp. 230–327). New York: Guilford Press.

Beidel, D. C. (1991). Social phobia and overanxious disorder in school-age children. *Journal of the American Academy of Child and Adolescent Psychiatry, 30,* 545–552.

Beitchman, J. H., Wekerle, C., & Hood, J. (1987). Diagnostic continuity from preschool to middle childhood. *Journal of the American Academy of Child and Adolescent Psychiatry, 26,* 694–699.

Bell-Dolan, D. J., Last, C. G., & Strauss, C. C. (1990). Symptoms of anxiety disorders in normal children. *Journal of the American Academy of Child and Adolescent Psychiatry, 29,* 759–765.

Biederman, J., Hirshfeld-Becker, D. R., Rosenbaum, J. F., Friedman, D., Snidman, N., Kagan, J., et al. (2001). Further evidence of an association between behavioral inhibition and social anxiety in children. *American Journal of Psychiatry, 158,* 1673–1679.

Biederman, J., Rosenbaum, J. F., Bolduc, E. A., Faraone, S. V., & Hirshfeld, D. R. (1991). A high risk study of young children of parents with panic disorder and agoraphobia with and without comorbid major depression. *Psychiatry Research, 37,* 333–348.

Biederman, J., Rosenbaum, J. F., Bolduc-Murphy, E. A., Faraone, S. V., Charloff, J., Hirshfeld, D. R., et al. (1993). A 3-year follow-up of children with and without behavioral inhibition. *Journal of the American Academy of Child and Adolescent Psychiatry, 32,* 814–821.

Biederman, J., Rosenbaum, J. F., Hirshfeld, D. R., Faraone, S. V., Bolduc, E. A., Gersten, M., et al. (1990). Psychiatric correlates of behavioral inhibition in young children of parents with and without psychiatric disorders. *Archives of General Psychiatry, 47,* 21–26.

Birmaher, B., Axelson, M. D., Monk, K., Kalas, C., Clark, D., Ehmann, M., Bridge, J., et al. (2003). Fluoxetine for the treatment of childhood anxiety disorders. *Journal of the American Academy of Child and Adolescent Psychiatry, 42*(4), 415–423.

Birmaher, B., Brent, D. A., Chiappetta, L., Bridge, J., Monga, S., & Baugher, M. (1999). Psychometric properties of the Screen for Child Anxiety Related Emotional Disorders (SCARED): A replication study. *Journal of the American Academy of Child and Adolescent Psychiatry, 38,* 1230–1236.

Birmaher, B., Waterman, G. S., Ryan, N., Cully, M., Balach, L., Ingram, J., et al. (1994). Fluoxetine for childhood anxiety disorders. *Journal of the American Academy of Child and Adolescent Psychiatry, 33,* 993–999.

Blashfield, R., Noyes, R., Reich, J., Woodman, C., Cook, B. L., & Garvey, M. J. (1994). Personality disorder traits in generalized anxiety and panic disorder patients. *Comprehensive Psychiatry, 35,* 329–334.

Bogels, S. M., & Zigterman, D. (2000). Dysfunctional cognitions in children with social phobia, separation anxiety disorder, and generalized anxiety disorder. *Journal of Abnormal Child Psychology, 28,* 205–211.

Bowen, R. C., Offord, D. R., & Boyle, M. H. (1990). The prevalence of overanxious disorder and separation disorder in the community: Results from the Ontario Mental Health Study. *Journal of the American Academy of Child and Adolescent Psychiatry, 29,* 753–758.

Brady, E. U., & Kendall, P. C. (1992). Comorbidity of anxiety and depression in children and adolescents. *Psychological Bulletin, 111,* 244–255.

Brown, T. A., Chorpita, B. F., & Barlow, D. H. (1998). Structural relations among dimensions of the *DSM-IV* anxiety and mood disorders and dimensions of negative affect, positive affect, and autonomic arousal. *Journal of Abnormal Psychology, 107,* 179–192.

Brown, T. A., Chorpita, B. E, Korotitsch, W., & Barlow, D. H. (1997). Psychometric properties of the Depression Anxiety Stress Scales (DASS) in clinical samples. *Behaviour Research and Therapy, 35,* 79–89.

Bruce, S. E., Machan, J. T., Dyck, I., & Keller, M. B. (2001). Infrequency of "pure" GAD: Impact of psychiatric comorbidity on clinical course. *Depression and Anxiety, 14,* 219–225.

Butler, G., & Matthews, A. (1983). Cognitive process in anxiety. *Advances in Behavior Research and Therapy, 5,* 51–62.

Campbell, L. A., Brown, T. A., & Grisham, J. R. (2003). Relevance of age of onset to the psychopathology of generalized anxiety disorder. *Behavior Therapy, 34,* 31–48.

Cantwell, D. P., & Baker, L. (1989). Stability and natural history of *DSM-III* childhood diagnoses. *Journal of the American Academy of Child and Adolescent Psychiatry, 29,* 691–700.

Caspi, A., Henry, B., McGee, O. R., Moffitt, T. E., & Silva, P. A. (1995). Temperamental origins of child and adolescent behavior problems: From age three to age fifteen. *Child Development, 66,* 55–68.

Chansky, T. E., & Kendall, P. C. (1997). Social expectancies and self-perceptions in anxiety disordered children. *Journal of Anxiety Disorders, 11,* 347–364.

Chorpita, B. F. (2002).The tripartite model and dimensions of anxiety and depression: An examination of structure in a large school sample. *Journal of Abnormal Child Psychology, 30,* 177–190.

Chorpita, B. F., Albano, A. M., & Barlow, D. H. (1998). The structure of negative emotions in a clinical sample of children and adolescents. *Journal of Abnormal Psychology, 107,* 74–85.

Chorpita, B. F., Plummer, C. M., & Moffitt, C. E. (2000). Relations of tripartite dimensions of emotion to childhood anxiety and mood disorders. *Journal of Abnormal Child Psychology, 28,* 299–310.

Chorpita, B. F., Tracey, S. A., Brown, T. A., Collica, T. J., & Barlow, D. H. (1997). Assessment of worry in children and adolescents: An adaptation of the Penn State Worry Questionnaire. *Behaviour Research and Therapy, 35,* 569–581.

Christophersen, E. R. (2001). Diagnosis and management of anxiety disorders. In E. R. Christophersen & S. Mortweet (Eds.), *Treatments that work with children: Empirically supported strategies for managing childhood problems* (pp. 49–78). Washington, DC: American Psychological Association.

Clark, D. B., Smith, M. G., Neighbors, B. D., Skerlec, L. M., & Randall, J. (1994). Anxiety disorders in adolescents: Characteristics, prevalence, and comorbidities. *Clinical Psychology Review, 14,* 113–137.

Clark, L. A., & Watson, D. (1991). Tripartite model of anxiety and depression: Psychometric evidence and taxonomic implications. *Journal of Abnormal Psychology, 100,* 316–336.

Clark, L. A., Watson, D., & Mineka, S. (1994). Temperament, personality, and the mood and anxiety disorders. *Journal of Abnormal Psychology, 103,* 103–116.

Cobham, V. E., Dadds, M. R., & Spence, S. H. (1998). The role of parental anxiety in the treatment of child anxiety. *Journal of Consulting and Clinical Psychology, 66,* 893–905.

Cohen, P., Cohen, J., Kasen, S., Velez, C. N., Hartmark, C., Johnson, J., et al. (1993). An epidemiological study of disorders in late childhood and adolescence: Age and gender specific prevalence. *Journal of Child Psychology and Psychiatry, 34,* 851–867.

Comer, J. S., Kendall, P. C., Franklin, M. E., Hudson, J., & Pimentel, S. (in press). Obsessing/worrying about the overlap between obsessive-compulsive disorder and generalized and anxiety disorder in youth. *Clinical Psychology Review.*

Compton, S. N., McKnight, C. D., & March, J. S. (2004). Combining medication and psychosocial treatments. In T. L. Morris & J. S. March (Eds.), *Anxiety disorders in children and adolescents* (2nd ed., pp. 355–370). New York: Guilford Press.

Costello, E. J. (1989). Developments in child psychiatric epidemiology. *Journal of the American Academy of Child and Adolescent Psychiatry, 28,* 836–841.

Costello, E. J., Mustillo, S., Erkanli, A., Keeler, G., & Angold, A. (2003). Prevalence and development of psychiatric disorders in childhood and adolescence. *Archives of General Psychiatry, 60,* 837–844.

Craske, M. G. (1999). *Anxiety disorders: Psychological to theory and treatment.* Boulder, CO: Westview.

Dadds, M. R., Barrett, P. M., Rapee, R. M., & Ryan, S. (1996). Family process and child anxiety and aggression: An observational analysis. *Journal of Abnormal Child Psychology, 24,* 715–734.

Daugherty, T. K., & Shapiro, S. E. (1994). Behavior checklists and rating forms. In T. H. Ollendick & N. J. King (Eds.), *International handbook of phobic and anxiety disorders in children and adolescents* (pp. 331–347). New York: Plenum Press.

Eisen, A. R., & Engler, L. B. (1995). Chronic anxiety. In A. R. Eisen, C. A. Kearney, & C. A. Schaefer (Eds.), *Clinical handbook of anxiety disorders in children and adolescents.* Northvale, NJ: Aronson.

Eisen, A. R., & Silverman, W. K. (1993). Should I relax or change my thoughts? A preliminary examination of cognitive therapy, relaxation training, and their combination with overanxious children. *Journal of Cognitive Psychotherapy, 7,* 265–279.

Eisen, A. R., & Silverman, W. K. (1998). Prescriptive treatment for generalized anxiety disorder in children. *Behavior Therapy, 29,* 105–121.

Eisenberg, N., Cumberland, A., Spinrad, T. L., Fabes, R. A., Shepard, S. A., Reiser, M., et al. (2001). The relations of regulation and emotionality to children's externalizing and internalizing problem behavior. *Child Development, 72,* 1112–1134.

Eley, T. C. (2001). Contributions of behavioral genetics research: Quantifying genetic, shared environmental and nonshared environmental influences. In M. W. Vasey & M. R. Dadds (Eds.), *The developmental psychopathology of anxiety* (pp. 45–59). New York: Oxford University Press.

Flannery-Schroder, E. (2004). Generalized anxiety disorder. In T. L. Morris & J. S. March, *anxiety disorders in children and adolescents* (2nd ed., pp. 125–140). New York: Guilford Press.

Flannery-Schroeder, E., & Kendall, P. C. (2000). Group and individual cognitive-behavioral treatments for youth with anxiety disorders: A randomized clinical trial. *Cognitive Therapy and Research, 24,* 251–278.

Garcia-Coll, C., Kagan, J., & Reznick, J. S. (1984). Behavioral inhibition in young children. *Child Development, 55,* 1005–1019.

Gerull, F. C., & Rapee, R. M. (2002). Mother knows best: Effects of maternal modeling on the acquisition of fear and avoidance behaviour in toddlers. *Behaviour Research and Therapy, 40,* 279–287.

Graae, F., Milner, J., Rizzotto, L., & Klein, R. G. (1994). Clonazepam in childhood anxiety disorders. *Journal of the American Academy of Child and Adolescent Psychiatry, 33,* 372–376.

Hayward, C., Killen, J., Kraemer, H. C., & Taylor, C. B. (1998). Linking self-reported childhood behavioral inhibition to adolescent social phobia. *Journal of the American Academy of Child and Adolescent Psychiatry, 37,* 1308–1316.

Hoehn-Saric, R., Hazlett, R. L., & McLeod, D. R. (1993). Generalized anxiety disorder with early and late onset of anxiety symptoms. *Comprehensive Psychiatry, 34,* 291–298.

Hudson, J. L., & Rapee, R. M. (2002). Parent-child interactions in clinically anxious children and their siblings. *Journal of Clinical Child and Adolescent Psychology, 31,* 548–555.

Hudson, J. L., & Rapee, R. M. (2004). From anxious temperament to disorder. In R. G. Heimberg, C. L. Turk, & D. S. Mennin (Eds.), *Generalized anxiety disorder: Advances in research and practice* (pp. 51–74). New York: Guilford Press.

Ialongo, N., Edelsohn, G., Werthamer-Larsson, L., Crockett, L., & Kellam, S. (1995). The significance of self-reported anxious symptoms in first grade children: Prediction to anxious symptoms and adaptive functioning in fifth grade. *Journal of Child Psychology and Psychiatry, 36,* 427–437.

John, O. P., Caspi, A., Robbins, R. W., Moffitt, T. E., & Stouthamer-Loeber, M. (1994). The "little five": Exploring the nomological network of the five-factor model of personality in adolescent boys. *Child Development, 65,* 160–178.

Joiner, T. E., Jr., Catanzaro, S., & Laurent, J. (1996). The tripartite structure of positive and negative affect, depression, and anxiety in child and adolescent psychiatric inpatients. *Journal of Abnormal Psychology, 105,* 401–409.

Joiner, T. E., Jr., & Lonigan, C. J. (2000). Tripartite model of depression and anxiety in youth psychiatric inpatients: Relations with diagnostic status and future symptoms. *Journal of Clinical Child Psychology, 29,* 372–382.

Kagan, J. (1989). Temperamental contributions to social behavior. *American Psychologist, 44,* 668–674.

Kagan, J., Reznick, J. S., Clarke, C., Snidman, N., & Garcia-Coll, C. (1984). Behavioral inhibition to the unfamiliar. *Child Development, 55,* 2212–2225.

Kagan, J., Reznick, J. S., Snidman, N., Gibbons, J., & Johnson, M. O. (1988). Childhood derivatives of inhibition and lack of inhibition to the unfamiliar. *Child Development, 59,* 1580–1589.

Kagan, J., Snidman, N., Archus, D., & Reznick, J. S. (1994). *Galen's prophecy: Temperament in human nature.* New York: Basic Books.

Kane, M. T., & Kendall, P. C. (1989). Anxiety disorders in children: A multiple baseline evaluation of a cognitive-behavioral treatment. *Behavior Therapy, 20,* 499–508.

Kaplow, J. B., Curran, P. J., Angold, A., & Costello, E. J. (2001). The prospective relation between dimensions of anxiety and the initiation of adolescent alcohol abuse. *Journal of Clinical Child Psychology, 30,* 316–326.

Kashani, J. H., & Orvaschel, H. (1988). Anxiety disorders in mid-adolescence: A community sample. *American Journal of Psychiatry, 145,* 960–964.

Kashani, J. H., & Orvaschel, H. (1990). A community study of anxiety in children and adolescents. *American Journal of Psychiatry, 147,* 313–318.

Kaufman, J., Birmaher, B., & Brent, D. (1997). Schedule for Affective Disorders and Schizophrenia for School-Age Children—Present and Lifetime Version (K-SADS-PL): Initial reliability and validity data. *Journal of the American Academy of Child and Adolescent Psychiatry, 36,* 980–988.

Kearney, C. A. (2001). *School refusal behavior in youth: A functional approach to assessment and treatment.* Washington, DC: American Psychological Association.

Kearney, C. A. & Albano, A. M. (2000). *When children refuse school: A cognitive behavioral therapy approach: Therapist's manual.* San Antonio, TX: Psychological Corporation.

Keller, M. B. (2002). The long-term clinical course of generalized anxiety disorder. *Journal of Clinical Psychiatry, 63,* 11–16.

Keller, M. B., Lavori, P. W., Wunder, J., Beardslee, W. R., Schwartz, C. E., & Roth, J. (1992). Chronic course of anxiety disorders in children and adolescents. *Journal of the American Academy of Child and Adolescent Psychiatry, 31,* 595–599.

Kendall, P. C. (1990). *Coping cat workbook.* Ardmore, PA: Workbook.

Kendall, P. C. (2000). *Cognitive-behavioral therapy for anxious children: Therapist manual* (2nd ed.). Ardmore, PA: Workbook.

Kendall, P. C. (1992). Childhood coping: Avoiding a lifetime of anxiety. *Behavioral Change, 9,* 1–8.

Kendall, P. C. (1994). Treating anxiety disorders in children: Results of a randomized clinical trial. *Journal of Consulting and Clinical Psychology, 62,* 100–110.

Kendall, P. C., & Brady, E. U. (1995). Comorbidity in the anxiety disorders of childhood. In K. D. Craig & K. S. Dobson (Eds.), *Anxiety and depression in adults and children.* Newbury Park, CA: Sage.

Kendall, P. C., Brady, E. U., & Verduin, T. L. (2001). Comorbidity in childhood anxiety disorders and treatment outcome. *Journal of the American Academy of Child and Adolescent Psychiatry, 40,* 787–794.

Kendall, P. C., Chu, B., Gifford, A., Hayes, C., & Nauta, M. (1998). Breathing life into a manual: Flexibility and creativity with manual-based treatments. *Cognitive and Behavioral Practice, 5,* 177–198.

Kendall, P. C., Flannery-Schroeder, E., Panichelli-Mindel, S. M, Southam-Gerow, M. A., Henin, A., & Warman, M. (1997). Therapy for youths with anxiety disorders: A second randomized clinical trial. *Journal of Consulting and Clinical Psychology, 65,* 366–380.

Kendall, P. C., Krain, A., & Treadwell, K. R. (1999). Generalized anxiety disorders. In R. T. Ammerman, M. Hersen, & C. G. Last (Eds.), *Handbook of prescriptive treatments for children and ad-*

olescents (2nd ed., pp. 155–171). Needham Heights, MA: Allyn & Bacon.

Kendall, P. C., & Ollendick, T. H. (2004). Setting the research and practice agenda for anxiety in children and adolescence: A topic comes of age. *Cognitive and Behavioral Practice, 11,* 65–74.

Kendall, P. C., & Pimentel, S. S. (2003). On the physiological symptom constellation in youth with generalized anxiety disorder (GAD). *Journal of Anxiety Disorders, 17,* 211–221.

Kendall, P. C., Pimentel, S., Rynn, M., Angelosante, A., & Webb, A. (2004). Generalized anxiety disorder. In T. Ollendick & J. March (Eds.), *Phobic and anxiety disorders in children and adolescents* (pp. 534–580). New York: Oxford University Press.

Kendall, P. C., Robin, J., Hedtke, K., Suveg, C., Flannery-Schroeder, E., & Gosch, E. (2005). Conducting CBT with anxious youth? Think exposures. *Journal of Cognitive-Behavior Practice, 12,* 136–148.

Kendall, P. C., Safford, S., Flannery-Schroeder, E., & Webb, A. (2004). Child anxiety treatment: Outcome in adolescence and impact on substance use and depression at 7.4-year follow-up. *Journal of Consulting and Clinical Psychology, 72,* 276–287.

Kendall, P. C., & Southam-Gerow, M. A. (1996). Long-term follow-up of a cognitive-behavioral therapy for anxiety-disordered youth. *Journal of Consulting and Clinical Psychology, 64,* 724–730.

Kendall, P. C., & Warman, M. J. (1996). Anxiety disorders in youth: Diagnostic consistency across *DSM-III-R* and *DSM-IV*. *Journal of Anxiety Disorders, 10,* 453–463.

Kendler, K. S., Neale, M. C., Kessler, R. C., Heath, A. C., & Eaves, L. J. (1992). Major depression and generalized anxiety disorder: Same genes, (partly) different environments? *Archives of General Psychiatry, 49,* 716–722.

Kendler, K. S., Walters, E. E., Neale, M. C., Kessler, R. C., Heath, A. C., & Eaves, L. J. (1995). The structure of the genetic and environmental risk factors for six major psychiatric disorders in women: Phobia, generalized anxiety disorder, panic disorder, bulimia, major depression, and alcoholism. *Archives of General Psychiatry, 52,* 374–383.

Last, C. G., Hansen, C., & Franco, N. (1997). Anxious children in adulthood: A prospective study of adjustment. *Journal of the American Academy of Child and Adolescent Psychiatry, 36,* 645–652.

Last, C. L., Hersen, M., Kazdin, A. E., Orvaschel, H., & Perrin, S. (1991). Anxiety disorders in children and their families. *Archives of General Psychiatry, 48,* 928–934.

Last, C. G., & Perrin, S. (1993). Anxiety disorders in African-American and White children. *Journal of Abnormal Child Psychology, 21,* 153–164.

Last, C. G., Perrin, S., Hersen, M., & Kazdin, A. E. (1992). *DSM-III-R* anxiety disorders in children: Sociodemographic and clinical characteristics. *Journal of the American Academy of Child and Adolescent Psychiatry, 31,* 1070–1076.

Last, C. G., Strauss, C. C., & Francis, G. (1987). Comorbidity among childhood anxiety disorders. *Journal of Nervous and Mental Disease, 175,* 726–730.

Laugesen, N., Dugas, M. J., & Bukowski, W. M. (2003). Understanding adolescent worry: The application of a cognitive model. *Journal of Abnormal Child Psychology, 31,* 55–64.

Leger, E., Ladouceur, R., & Dugas, M. J. (2003). Cognitive-behavioral treatment of generalized anxiety disorder among adolescents: A case series. *Journal of the American Academy of Child and Adolescent Psychiatry, 42,* 327–330.

Lengua, L. J. (2002). The contribution of emotionality and self-regulation to the understanding of children's response to multiple risk. *Child Development, 73,* 144–161.

Lewinsohn, P. M., Rohde, P., & Seeley, J. R. (1995). Adolescent psychopathology: III. The clinical consequences of comorbidity. *Journal of the American Academy of Child and Adolescent Psychiatry, 34,* 510–519.

Lewinsohn, P. M., Zinbarg, R., Seeley, J. R., Lewinsohn, M., & Sack, W. H. (1997). Lifetime comorbidity among anxiety disorders and between anxiety disorders and other mental disorders in adolescents. *Journal of Anxiety Disorders, 11,* 377–394.

Lonigan, C. J., Carey, M. P., & Finch, A. J., Jr. (1994). Anxiety and depression in children and adolescents: Negative affectivity and the utility of self-reports. *Journal of Consulting and Clinical Psychology, 62,* 1000–1008.

Lonigan, C. J., & Phillips, B. M. (2001). Temperamental basis of anxiety disorders in children. In M. W. Vasey and M. R. Dadds (Eds.), *The developmental psychopathology of anxiety* (pp. 60–91). New York: Oxford University Press.

Lonigan, C. J., Phillips, B. M., & Hooe, E. S. (2003). Relations of positive and negative affectivity to anxiety and depression in children: Evidence from a latent variable longitudinal study. *Journal of Consulting and Clinical Psychology, 71,* 465–481.

Lonigan, C. J., Vasey, M. W., Phillips, B. M., & Hazen, R. A. (2004). Temperament, anxiety, and the processing of threat-relevant stimuli. *Journal of Clinical Child and Adolescent Psychology, 33,* 8–20.

March, J. S., & Albano, A. M. (2002). Anxiety disorders in children and adolescents. In D. J. Stein & E. Hollander (Eds.), *Textbook of anxiety disorders* (pp. 415–427). Washington, DC: American Psychiatric Press.

March, J. S., Parker, J., Sullivan, K., Stallings, P., & Conners, C. (1997). The Multidimensional Anxiety Scale for Children (MASC): Factor structure, reliability and validity. *Journal of the American Academy of Child and Adolescent Psychiatry, 36*(4), 554–565.

Masi, G., Mucci, M., Favilla, L., Romano, R., & Poli, P. (1999). Symptomatology and comorbidity of generalized anxiety disorder in children and adolescents. *Comprehensive Psychiatry, 40,* 210–215.

McGee, R., Feehan, M., Williams, S., Partridge, F., Silva, P., & Kelly, J. (1990). *DSM-III* disorders in large sample of adolescents. *Journal of the American Academy of Child and Adolescent Psychiatry, 26,* 611–619.

Meyer, T. J., Miller, M. L., Metzger, R. L., & Borkovec, T. D. (1990) Development and validation of the Penn State Worry Questionnaire. *Behaviour Research and Therapy, 28,* 487–495.

Muris, P., Kindt, M., Bogels, S., Merckelbach, H., Gadet, B., & Moulaert, V. (2000). Anxiety and threat perceptions abnormalities in normal children. *Journal of Psychopathology and Behavioral Assessment, 22,* 183–199.

Muris, P., Merckelbach, H., Wessel, I., & van de Ven, M. (1999). Psychopathological correlates of self-reported behavioural inhibition in normal children. *Behavior Research and Therapy, 51,* 44–58.

Newman, D. I., Moffitt, T. E., Caspi, A., Magdol, L., Silva, P. A., & Stanton, W. R. (1996). Psychiatric disorder in a birth cohort of young adults: Prevalence, comorbidity, clinical significance, and new case incidence from ages 11 to 21. *Journal of Consulting and Clinical Psychology, 64,* 552–562.

Ollendick, T. H., & King, N. J. (1994). Diagnosis, assessment, and treatment of internalizing problems in children: The role of longitudinal data. *Journal of Consulting and Clinical Psychology, 62,* 918–927.

Ollendick, T. H., & King, N. J. (2000). Empirically supported treatments for children and adolescents. In P. C. Kendall (Ed.), *Child and adolescent therapy: Cognitive-behavioral procedures* (2nd ed., pp. 386–425). New York: Guilford Press.

Pincus, A. L., & Borkovec, T. D. (1994, June). *Interpersonal problems in generalized anxiety disorder: Preliminary clustering of patients' interpersonal dysfunction.* Paper presented at the annual meeting of the American Psychological Society, New York.

Quay, H. C., & Peterson, D. R. (1987). *Manual for the revised behavior problem checklist.* Unpublished manuscript, University of Miami, Coral Gables, FL.

Rapee, R. M. (1991). Generalized anxiety disorder: A review of clinical features and theoretical concepts. *Clinical Psychology Review, 11,* 419–440.

Rapee, R. M. (1997). The potential role of childrearing practices in the development of anxiety and depression. *Clinical Psychology Review, 17,* 47–67.

Rapee, R. M. (2001). The development of generalized anxiety disorder. In M. W. Vasey & M. R. Dadds (Eds.), *The Developmental Psychopathology of Anxiety* (pp. 481–504). New York: Oxford University Press.

Reich, J. H., Perry, J. C., Shera, D., Dyck, I., Vasile, R., Goisman, R. M., et al. (1994). Comparison of personality disorders in different anxiety disorder diagnoses: Panic, agoraphobia, generalized anxiety disorder, and social phobia. *Annals of Clinical Psychiatry, 6,* 125–134.

Reich, W., Shayka, J. J., & Taibleson, C. (1991). *Diagnostic Interview for Children and Adolescents—DICA-R.* Unpublished manuscript, Division of Child Psychiatry, Washington University, St. Louis.

Research Units on Pediatric Psychopharmacology Anxiety Study Group. (2001). Fluvoxamine for the treatment of anxiety disorders in children and adolescents. *New England Journal of Medicine, 344,* 1679–1685.

Reynolds, C. R., & Kamphaus, R. W. (1992). *Behavior Assessment System for Children.* Circle Pines, MN: American Guidance Service.

Reynolds, C. R., & Richmond, B. O. (1978). What I think and feel: A revised measure of children's manifest anxiety. *Journal of Abnormal Child Psychology, 6,* 271–280.

Roemer, L., Mollina, S., & Borkevec, T. D. (1997). An investigation of worry content among generally anxious individuals. *Journal of Nervous and Mental Disease, 185,* 314–319.

Rosenbaum, J. F., Biederman, J., Hirshfeld-Becker, D. R., Kagan, J., Snidman, N., Friedman, D., et al. (2000). A controlled study of behavioral inhibition in children of parents with panic disorder and depression. *American Journal of Psychiatry, 157,* 2002–2010.

Rubin, K. H., Bukowski, W., & Parker, J. G. (1998). Peer interactions, relationships, and groups. In W. Damon (Ed.) & N. Eisenberg (Vol. ed.), *Handbook of child psychology: Vol. 3. Social, emotional, and personality development* (5th ed., pp. 619–700). New York: Wiley.

Rynn, M. A., Siqueland, L., & Rickels, K. (2001). Placebo-controlled trial of sertraline in the treatment of children with generalized anxiety disorder. *American Journal of Psychiatry, 158,* 2008–2014.

Sanderson, W. C., Beck, A. T., & McGinn, L. K. (2002). Cognitive therapy for generalized anxiety disorder: Significance of comorbid personality disorders. In R. L. Leahy & E. T. Dowd (Eds.), *Clinical advances in cognitive psychotherapy: Theory and application* (pp. 287–293). New York: Springer.

Sanderson, W. C., & Wetzler, S. (1991). Chronic anxiety and generalized anxiety disorder: issues in comorbidity. In R. M. Rapee & D. H. Barlow (Eds.), *Chronic anxiety: Generalized anxiety disorder and mixed anxiety-depression* (pp. 119–135). New York: Guilford Press.

Sanderson, W. C., Wetzler, S., Beck, A. T., & Bertz, F.(1994). Prevalence of personality disorders among patients with anxiety disorder. *Psychiatry Research, 51,* 167–174.

Shaffer, D., Fisher, P., Lucas, C. P., Dulcan, M., & Schwab-Stone, M. E. (2000). NIMH Diagnostic Interview Schedule for Children, Version IV (NIMH DISC-IV): Description, differences from previous versions and reliability of some common diagnoses. *Journal of the American Academy of Child and Adolescent Psychiatry, 39,* 28–38.

Shortt, A. L., Barrett, P. M., Dadds, M. R., & Fox, T. L. (2001). The influence of family and experimental context on cognition in anxious children. *Journal of Abnormal Child Psychology, 6,* 585–596.

Shortt, A. L., Barrett, P. M., & Fox, T. L. (2001). Evaluating the FRIENDS program: A cognitive-behavioral group treatment for anxious children. *Journal of Clinical Child Psychology, 30,* 525–535.

Silk, J., Nath, S., Siegel, L., & Kendall, P. C. (2000). Conceptualizing mental disorders in children: Where have we been and where are we going? *Development and Psychopathology, 12,* 713–735.

Silverman, W. K., & Albano, A. M. (1996). *The Anxiety Disorders Interview Schedule for DSM-IV Child and Parent Versions.* San Antonio, TX: Graywind/Psychological.

Silverman, W. K., Kurtines, W. M., Ginsburg, G. S., Weems, C. F., Lumpkin, P. W., & Carmichale, D. H. (1999). Treating anxiety disorders in children with group cognitive-behavioral therapy: A randomized clinical trial. *Journal of Consulting and Clinical Psychology, 67,* 995–1003.

Silverman, W. K., & Nelles, W. B. (1998). The Anxiety Disorders Interview Schedule for Children. *Journal of the American Academy of Child and Adolescent Psychiatry, 27,* 772–778.

Silverman, W. K., & Ollendick, T. H. (1999). *Developmental issues in the clinical treatment of children.* Boston: Allyn & Bacon.

Silverman, W. K., Saavedra, L. M., & Pina, A. A. (2001). Test-retest reliability of anxiety symptoms and diagnoses with the Anxiety Disorders Interview Schedule for *DSM-IV*: Child and Parent Versions. *Journal of the American Academy of Child and Adolescent Psychiatry, 40,* 937–944.

Simeon, J. G., Ferguson, H. B., Knott, V., Roberts, N., Gauthier, B., Dubois, C., et al. (1992). Clinical, cognitive, and neurophysiological effects of alprazolam in children and adolescents with overanxious and avoidant disorders. *Journal of the American Academy of Child and Adolescent Psychiatry, 31,* 29–33.

Siqueland, L., Kendall, P. C., & Steinberg, L. (1996). Anxiety in children: Perceived family environments and observed family interactions. *Journal of Clinical Child Psychology, 25,* 225–237.

Spence, S. H., Rapee, R., McDonald, C., & Ingram, M. (2001). The structure of anxiety symptoms among preschoolers. *Behaviour Research and Therapy, 39,* 1293–1316.

Spielberger, C. D. (1973). *Manual for the State-Trait Anxiety Inventory for Children.* Palo Alto, CA: Consulting Psychologists Press.

Stallings, P., & March, J. (1995). Assessment. In J. S. March (Ed.), *Anxiety disorders in children and adolescents* (pp. 125–147). New York: Guilford Press.

Stein, M. B., & Seedat, S. (2004). Pharmacotherapy. In T. L. Morris & J. S. March (Eds.), *Anxiety disorders in children and adolescents* (2nd ed., pp. 329–354). New York: Guilford Press.

Strauss, C. C. (1994) Overanxious disorder. In: T. H. Ollendick & N. J. King (Eds.), *International handbook of phobic and anxiety disorders in children and adolescents* (pp. 187–206). New York: Plenum Press.

Strauss, C. C., Frame, C. L., & Forehand, R. (1987). Psychosocial impairment associated with anxiety in children. *Journal of Clinical Child Psychology, 16,* 235–239.

Strauss, C. C., Lahey, B. B., Frick, P., Frame, C. L., & Hynd, G. W. (1988). Peer social status of children with anxiety disorders. *Journal of Consulting and Clinical Psychology, 56,* 137–141.

Strauss, G., Birmaher, B., Bridge, J., Axelson, D., Chiappetta, L., Brent, D., et al. (2000). Anxiety disorders in suicidal youth. *Canadian Journal of Psychiatry, 45,* 739–745.

Taghavi, M. R., Neshat-Doost, H. T., Moradi, A. R., Yule, W., & Dalgleish, T. (1999). Biases in visual attention in children and adolescents with clinical anxiety and mixed anxiety-depression. *Journal of Abnormal Child Psychology, 27,* 215–223.

Thompson, R. L. (2001). Childhood anxiety disorders from the perspective of emotion regulation and attachment. In M. W. Vasey & M. R. Dadds (Eds.), *The developmental psychopathology of anxiety* (pp. 160–182). New York: Oxford University Press.

Tracey, S. A., Chorpita, B. F., Douban, J., & Barlow, D. F. (1997). Empirical validation of *DSM-IV* generalized anxiety disorder criteria in children and adolescents. *Journal of Clinical Child Psychology, 26,* 404–414.

Treadwell, K. H., Flannery-Schroeder, E. C., & Kendall, P. C. (1995). Ethnicity and gender in relation to adaptive functioning, diagnostic status, and treatment outcome in children from an anxiety clinic. *Journal of Anxiety Disorders, 9,* 373–384.

Turner, S. M., Beidel, D. C., & Costello, A. (1987). Psychopathology in the offspring of anxiety disordered patients. *Journal of Consulting and Clinical Psychology, 55,* 229–235.

Verduin, T. L., & Kendall, P. C. (2003). Differential occurrence of comorbidity within childhood anxiety disorders. *Journal of Clinical Child and Adolescent Psychology, 32,* 290–295.

Waas, G. A., & Graczyk, P. A. (1999). Child behaviors leading to peer rejection: A view from the peer group. *Child Study Journal, 29,* 291–305.

Walkup, J. T., Labellarte, M. J., & Ginsburg, G. S. (2002). The pharmacological treatment of childhood anxiety disorders. *International Review of Psychiatry, 14,* 135–142.

Warren, S. L., Huston, L., Egeland, B., & Sroufe, L. A. (1997). Child and adolescent anxiety disorders and early attachment. *Journal of the American Academy of Child and Adolescent Psychiatry, 36,* 637–641.

Watson, D., Clark, L. A., & Carey, G. (1988). Positive and negative affectivity and their relation to anxiety and depressive disorders. *Journal of Abnormal Psychology, 97,* 346–353.

Weems, C. F., Silverman, W. K., & La Greca, A. M. (2000). What do youth referred for anxiety problems worry about? Worry and its relation to anxiety and anxiety disorders in children and adolescents. *Journal of Abnormal Child Psychology, 28,* 63–72.

Werry, J. S. (1991). Overanxious disorder: A review of its taxonomic properties. *Journal of the American Academy of Child and Adolescent Psychiatry, 30,* 533–544.

Yonkers, K., Dyck, I. R., Warshaw, M., & Keller, M. B. (2000). Factors predicting the clinical course of generalized anxiety disorder. *British Journal of Psychiatry, 176,* 544–549.

CHAPTER 10

Social Anxiety Disorder

ROBERT T. AMMERMAN, KELLY L. MCGRAW, LORI E. CROSBY, DEBORAH C. BEIDEL, AND SAMUEL M. TURNER

DESCRIPTION OF THE DISORDER AND CLINICAL PICTURE

Social anxiety disorder (SAD; also known as social phobia) is characterized by a marked and persistent fear of social and performance situations in which negative scrutiny by others and embarrassment may occur. Individuals with SAD experience such intense distress or avoid anxiety-producing situations to such an extent that significant problems in social or occupational/academic functioning occur. For example, children may miss a significant amount of school due to social and performance fears. Two subtypes of SAD are currently recognized: generalized and specific. Individuals with the generalized subtype experience significant distress across a range of situations, whereas those with a specific presentation may experience anxiety in only one or a few social or performance situations. The generalized subtype is more common, with 70 percent of individuals with SAD falling within this category (Turner, Beidel, & Cooley, 1994).

SAD was first recognized as a clinical disorder in the third edition of the *Diagnostic and Statistical Manual of Mental Disorders* (*DSM-III;* American Psychiatric Association, 1980). At that time, SAD was thought to develop only in midadolescence. However, findings in the last decade suggest that SAD can be diagnosed in children as early as age 8 (Beidel & Turner, 1988; Strauss & Last, 1993). In the more recent psychiatric nosology (*DSM-IV;* American Psychiatric Association, 1994), two important factors in making a diagnosis of SAD in children are noted. First, for a clinician to diagnose SAD in childhood, the child must have the capacity to develop age-appropriate social relationships. Thus, children with pervasive developmental disorders, such as autism, would not qualify for the diagnosis. Parents of children with SAD are likely to report that their children are socially engaged with siblings, cousins, or close family friends. However, once outside this circle, the child invariably becomes anxious around adults and peers. And second, the child's anxiety must occur in the context of interacting with peers, and not solely with adults.

An additional consideration when making a diagnosis of SAD in childhood is that some children are unable to recognize or articulate that they are experiencing anxiety or the social fears that accompany it. Young children in particular have yet to acquire the advanced cognitive and perceptual skills to consistently identify anxiety and the excessive or irrational nature of their fear. When asked about social situations, children with SAD underreport the extent of their social difficulties. Parents may provide conflicting information on the qualitative aspects of peer interactions (e.g., refusing to attend parties or invite friends to do things), and given this discrepancy, parental report of symptoms is critical to making an accurate diagnosis (Beidel & Turner, 1998).

In addition to core symptoms of SAD, children may present with other psychosocial difficulties including school refusal or avoidance, separation anxiety, somatic complaints, and oppositional behavior. Social fears can often be misinterpreted by others, primarily due to a lack of understanding of the disorder. For example, children who refuse to attend school may be perceived as having conduct problems, when in fact social anxiety is the primary cause. Indeed, a study examining children with school refusal found that 30 percent did not attend school due to social fears (Last, Perrin, Hersen, & Kazdin, 1992).

As with other anxiety disorders, individuals with SAD typically experience an array of physiological symptoms. The most common symptoms include rapid heart rate, blushing, sweating, and shaking (Gorman & Gorman, 1987). Beidel, Christ, and Long (1991) found the most common physical symptoms in 8- to 12-year-old children with social evaluative fears included choking, flushing or chills, heart palpitations, fainting, shaking, feeling like dying, and headaches. The *DSM-IV* criteria for SAD describe a possible "situationally

---

Acknowledgment: This chapter was written with the support of Grant No. RO1 MH53703–05 from the National Institute on Mental Health to the fourth and fifth authors.

bound" panic attack in response to a feared social situation. Though this may occur in adults or adolescents, panic attacks are considered a relatively rare experience for children. Children are more likely to express anxiety by crying, freezing, or having a temper tantrum in response to an anxiety-provoking situation (American Psychiatric Association, 1994).

Children with SAD experience distress in a number of social and performance situations. In a sample of children with SAD, Beidel (1991) found that 89 percent feared public speaking (e.g., giving an oral report or reading aloud), 39 percent feared eating in front of others (e.g., in the school cafeteria, in a restaurant, or at home), 28 percent feared writing on the blackboard, 28 percent feared going to parties, 24 percent feared using public restrooms, and 21 percent feared speaking to authority figures. Additional feared situations included taking tests, making phone calls, and asking questions.

Albano, DiBartolo, Heimburg, and Barlow (1995) examined behavioral and cognitive manifestations of social anxiety among children. Common behavioral problems included stuttering, making poor eye contact, mumbling, nail biting, and speaking in a trembling voice. In addition, the authors found that children described feeling as if they would be negatively evaluated by others and would experience failure, humiliation, embarrassment, inadequacy, and self-criticism. Many children reported frequently having thoughts about how to escape the feared situations in order to decrease anxiety.

In many cases, the play activities of children with SAD look different from those without the disorder. In a study of recreational interests in children with SAD, Albano et al. (1995) found unusual hobbies, including collecting facts about particular events, programming computers, or tracking weather reports. These researchers felt that the lack of more common interests (e.g., playing sports, going to the mall) was likely caused by a decreased opportunity to participate in everyday activities rather than a lack of desire.

Several researchers have examined the frequency of distressful events among children with SAD using a daily self-monitoring diary (Beidel, Neal, & Lederer, 1991). Results show that socially phobic children encounter distressful events about every other day. In some cases children experience distress throughout the day. Not surprisingly, children reported that distressful events most often occur at school during unstructured social situations. For example, children reported anxiety when talking or playing with another child during recess or lunch or while working in a group.

PERSONALITY DEVELOPMENT AND PSYCHOPATHOLOGY

Of all the psychiatric disorders, SAD has the most extensive overlap with personality constructs. Personality theorists have sought to identify core personality traits that emerge early in life, are stable and durable across the life span, are believed to be strongly heritable, and are readily measured. Of particular relevance to SAD, empirically based personality systems have consistently identified social inhibition and general anxiety in factor analyses of the general population. For example, Eysenk (1994) identified the bipolar personality "super traits" of introversion-extraversion and neuroticism-stability. Elements of SAD are evident in the characteristics of both introversion (avoidance, timidity, low activity, fear of novelty) and neuroticism (anxiety, tension, shyness). More recently, the Five Factor Model (McCrae & Costa, 1997) proposed five personality dimensions, two of which conceptually map onto SAD (extraversion [and its polar opposite, introversion] and neuroticism). With regard to examining competing theories, it is noteworthy that these two traits are integral to virtually all theoretical conceptualizations of personality.

In childhood, temperament describes the earliest manifestation of personality traits. Temperament refers to the behavioral and physiological characteristics of infants that reflect adaptations to internal and external events. Temperament emerges early, is stable, and is considered to be primarily genetically determined. Once again, organizational models of temperament include features that mirror characteristics of SAD. These include emotional reactivity, adaptability, approach/withdrawal, and mood (Thomas & Chess, 1977).

Behavioral inhibition (BI) has been identified as trait emergent in infancy and toddlerhood that is strongly related to subsequent development of SAD. BI reflects fear, avoidance, and reticence upon encountering unfamiliar people and situations. It is detectable through behavioral observations and is evident in physiological measurement. Measurement of BI changes across development. In infancy, BI is manifested as distress, withdrawal, and restricted exploratory behavior. For toddlers, BI is expressed as fear, comfort seeking, emotional upset, and inhibition. Later in childhood BI is characterized by timidity, anxiousness, reticence, and avoidance. BI is stable over time. Moderate levels of stability have been documented from infancy/toddlerhood into middle childhood (Fordham & Stevenson-Hinde, 1999) and into young adulthood (Caspi & Silva, 1995).

There is considerable evidence of heritability of BI. BI has been attributed to several biological mechanisms, including hyperarousal of the sympathetic nervous system and lower thresholds of reactivity to novelty in the limbic-hypothalamic alert system (Kagan, 2003). Taken together, it is evident that BI is an emotional and behavioral construct linked to a biological substrate that is durable across development. It has been suggested that BI reflects a diathesis that increases vulnerability to the development of anxiety disorders in general, and SAD in particular. Researchers have explored the contribution of BI to the development of SAD and other anxiety disorders by prospectively following children with BI into later childhood and adulthood, retrospective measurement of BI characteristics in adolescents and adults with SAD and other forms of psychopathology, and linking BI to parental psychiatric disorders.

Although the literature linking BI to the subsequent development of SAD is impressive, several caveats limit the strength of this relationship. First, methodological shortcomings in studies on BI temper interpretation of findings. Sampling strategies have resulted in primarily Caucasian samples, restricting generalizability. Second, differences in measurement and definitions of BI and SAD (and related diagnostic categories) complicate synthesis of results across studies. And third, it is noteworthy that most children rated as high on BI do not subsequently develop SAD (Biederman et al., 2001). BI is neither a necessary nor a sufficient precondition for the development of SAD (Beidel & Turner, 1998). As a result, BI must be viewed as one of several potential pathways to the acquisition of SAD.

EPIDEMIOLOGY

SAD is one of the most common psychiatric disorders in the general population and exists across age groups, gender, and ethnicity. Kessler et al. (1994) found that SAD was the third most common psychiatric disorder behind depression and alcohol abuse. Epidemiological data suggest a 12-month prevalence rate of 8 percent across age groups (Kessler et al., 1994). Given the high prevalence of the disorder, SAD is recognized as a considerable public health concern (Furmark, 2002).

Furmark (2002) reviewed 43 published articles in which SAD was clearly defined and found lifetime prevalence rates of 2 percent to 3 percent in the United States. When using diagnostic criteria from the *DSM-III-R*, higher prevalence rates of SAD were found. In the National Comorbidity Survey (Magee, Eaton, Wittchen, McGonagle, & Kessler, 1996) a lifetime prevalence rate of 13 percent was found.

Several researchers have examined the prevalence of SAD among children and adolescents. Last et al. (1992) reported that 15 percent of children presenting to an anxiety clinic had a primary diagnosis of SAD. Albano et al. (1995) found that 18 percent of children seen at an anxiety clinic met criteria for SAD.

Among children, girls are generally more likely than boys to report social fears. In one study, 70 percent of the children referred from a local school district who were diagnosed with SAD were female (Beidel & Turner, 1992). However, using information gathered from clinic data, the gender distribution is more equal. For example, Last et al. (1992) found that 44 percent of children seeking treatment were female.

ETIOLOGY

Both Biedel and Turner (1998) and Ollendick and Hirshfeld-Becker (2002) underscore the developmental psychopathology of SAD. Specifically, within this framework, SAD emerges from the synergistic interplay of multiple etiologic factors. The transactional relationships between risk and protective factors, interacting with the unfolding developmental staging of cognitive, emotional, and social capabilities, contribute to the manifestation of SAD. As a result, no single etiologic pathway for SAD has been identified, although multiple contributing factors have been implicated in the onset and maintenance of the disorder.

Familial Aggregation and Genetics

It has long been observed that anxiety disorders cluster in families, and research has confirmed this finding in SAD. A number of studies have found an aggregation of anxiety disorders in general, and SAD in particular, in the first-degree relatives of persons diagnosed with SAD. Relatives of persons with SAD exhibit increased prevalence of phobias, panic disorder, and depression (Ollendick & Hirshfeld-Becker, 2002). Yet there is also a high degree of specificity to SAD (Merikangas, Lieb, Wittchen, & Avenevoli, 2003). For example, Reich and Yeates (1988) reported a threefold increase in risk for SAD in relatives of persons with SAD in contrast to those who do not have relatives with the disorder. Risk is particularly elevated for the generalized subtype. Stein et al. (1998) found that relatives of probands with generalized SAD were almost 10 times as likely to manifest the disorder relative to controls (lifetime prevalence 26.4 percent vs. 2.7 percent). After controlling for panic disorder, Merikangas et al. (2003) found an adjusted odds ratio of 2.0 for SAD in relatives of probands with SAD.

Familial aggregation of SAD suggests a genetic transmission of the disorder or of broader vulnerabilities to developing SAD. Twin studies provide partial support for the genetic transmission of SAD. Kendler, Neale, Kessler, Heath, and Eaves (1992) found a 30 percent heritability of SAD in female twins, a finding consistent with a genetic contribution but also suggesting considerable environmental influence. As noted earlier, behavioral inhibition is a potential biobehavioral precursor to SAD, and it has been found to have a moderate degree of heritability (Kagan & Snidman, 1999). More recently, Gelernter, Page, Stein, and Woods (2004) identified a possible genomic location for SAD. Results indicated a suggestive linkage involving a gene implicated in a norepinephrine transporter protein. Taken together, family aggregation and genetic studies strongly suggest some form of genetic transmission. It is unclear if this pathway is specific to SAD, is common to several disorders, involves broad predisposing vulnerabilities, or any combination of these.

Observational Learning and Conditioning

Observational learning is a powerful means of behavior acquisition, and some have argued that familial aggregation of SAD is at least partly explained by children's modeling of fearful and anxious behavior in affected adults (Ost, 1985). In such scenarios, it is believed that children are exposed to verbal and nonverbal features of parental anxiety, including avoidance of feared situations. Through vicarious learning, children model such behavior in their own social interactions. Yet, although some adults with SAD report that observing social anxiety in others was an important determinant of their own disorders, no prospective studies have documented the causal role of observational learning in the onset of SAD.

It has long been recognized that conditioning is an important mechanism in the development of phobias. Evidence exists that persons with SAD have traumatic experiences that condition subsequent fear responses. Specifically, according to this view, SAD emerges following experiences in which the person is shamed, humiliated, or ridiculed in social situations. Indeed, Ost (1985) found that 58 percent of adults with SAD attributed their disorder to a specific traumatic incident. In another study, Stemberger, Turner, Beidel, and Calhoun (1995) reported that 44 percent of adults with SAD recounted a traumatic social incident; in turn, recounting such an incident was found to be more prevalent in those with the specific subtype in contrast to the generalized subtype. Twenty percent of control participants (without a psychiatric disorder) also reported a traumatic social experience, underscoring that traumatic experiences are neither necessary nor sufficient for development of SAD. Rather, they may be most likely to contribute to onset of SAD in those persons already vulnerable due to temperament (BI), trait anxiety, or some other factor. Beidel and Turner (1998) suggested that the accumulation of less-intense social rejections, rather than a single incident, may contribute to conditioned fear and subsequent avoidance. As in observational learning, the literature on traumatic condition relies on retrospective methodologies and is thus prone to biased recall. The etiologic role of traumatic conditioning remains unclear in the absence of prospective research.

Parenting Practices

It has been proposed that SAD can develop because of specific parenting practices that engender anxiety and avoidance. Some adults with SAD retrospectively report experiencing high levels of parental overprotectiveness, criticism, and rejection in childhood (Bruch & Heimberg, 1994). Research on children with SAD and their parents has not found significant aberrations in reports and perceptions of parenting practices (Bogels, van Oosten, Muris, & Smulders, 2001). An observational study of a laboratory play interaction also failed to find overt overprotectiveness and excessive criticism in anxious parents, only a few of whom had SAD (Turner, Beidel, Roberson-Nay, & Tervo, 2003). Although the contribution of authoritarian parenting practices to the etiology of SAD has not been conclusively established, there is evidence that families of children with SAD are more likely to have dysfunctional family systems. Bogels et al. (2001) found that children with SAD and their mothers reported decreased sociability, and Turner et al. (2003) documented decreased family expressiveness and lower cohesion.

Collectively, the literature on parenting practices in SAD is characterized by retrospective or cross-sectional methodologies, and it is unclear if parenting practices precede the onset of SAD, co-occur with the disorder, or develop as an adaptation to clinically significant social anxiety. A more definitive picture of the etiologic importance of parenting practices can emerge only in the context of prospective longitudinal research.

COURSE, COMPLICATIONS, AND PROGNOSIS

The age of onset for SAD is typically reported to be middle to late adolescence. From a developmental perspective, this is an age in which individuals develop an increasing awareness and concern of evaluation by others (Westenberg, Drewes, Goedhart, Siebelink, & Treffers, 2004). However, age of onset findings are largely drawn from retrospective studies conducted in adulthood, and considerable support exists for an earlier onset in many cases (Beidel & Turner, 1998). As previously noted, premorbid personality features (e.g., inhibition) appear at earlier developmental stages, including infancy (Woodward, Lenzenweger, Kagan, Snidman, & Arcus, 2000). Identification of SAD in younger children is complicated by their limited cognitive abilities to detect and report concerns about negative scrutiny and evaluations by others. As a result, it is possible that a sizable proportion of children with SAD experience an earlier age of onset than that reported in the adult literature. In one study, earlier age of onset was associated with poorer treatment outcomes in adults with SAD (Van Ameringen, Oakman, Mancini, Pipe, & Chung, 2004).

The course of SAD in childhood has not been fully elucidated. Several lines of research point toward a chronic course with progressive worsening over time. Unlike other fears in childhood, social fears are relatively stable and unremitting. The same pattern is evident in the temperament and personality precursors to SAD, such as social anxiety and introversion (Goodwin, Fergusson, & Horwood, 2004). In one study, Davidson (1993) reported that onset of SAD before age 11 was predictive of subsequent nonrecovery. In a retrospective study, Otto et al. (2001) found that 79 percent of adults with SAD also reported meeting diagnostic criteria for the disorder in childhood. On the other hand, some children resolve social fears over time. At this point, it is not known what proportion of children with SAD will remit or continue to exhibit clinically significant symptoms into adolescence and adulthood, or what variables might differentially predict these outcomes. Longitudinal studies of newly diagnosed children with SAD have not been conducted, and such research is needed to more definitively delineate the course of the disorder through childhood.

Beidel et al. (2005) contrasted adolescents with SAD and those without a diagnosis on a variety of indices of social, emotional, and behavioral functioning. Results indicated that adolescents with SAD experienced greater functional impairment, increased distress, increased internalizing symptoms, more comorbidities, greater avoidance, and pervasive social skills deficits. The authors noted that although there is an overlap in clinical presentation between preadolescents and adolescents with SAD, adolescents appear to exhibit greater severity and distress than their younger counterparts. These findings are consistent with a course that is deteriorating over time.

The course of SAD in adulthood is clearer and consists of a predominately unremitting presentation. Longitudinal studies in adulthood have consistently documented a largely unchanged clinical picture and stability in functional impairment over time. The Harvard/Brown Research Program (HARP; findings reviewed by Keller, 2003) has reported on the 11- to 13-year following of a cohort of adults with SAD. Results from this study reveal little improvement over time, in contrast to the relatively more optimistic prognoses of panic disorder and other anxiety disorders. For example, 6 months after the index diagnosis of SAD, 8 percent of study participants experienced full remission, increasing to 20 percent at 2 years, 27 percent at 5 years, and only 36 percent at 8 years. Of those who fully remitted, 29 percent experienced a relapse within 5 years.

The functional impairment associated with SAD is substantial. In children with SAD, loneliness and social isolation are common consequences. Poor school performance may result from failure to participate in class or seek needed help from teachers, and poor test performance secondary to anxiety. Social skills deficits have been documented in children with SAD (Beidel, Turner, & Morris, 1999), and these contribute to social incompetence and isolation. Studies of children identified as shy during childhood document functional impairments into adulthood and maladaptation to developmental roles. For example, Caspi, Elder, and Bem (1988) tracked shy children over a 30-year period into adulthood. Shy boys delayed entry into parenthood, marriage, and stable occupations. Shy girls were found to be more likely to pursue more conventional roles (marriage, child rearing, homemaking) than their nonshy counterparts. Role restrictions were also identified in shy male and female children in Sweden who were assessed in adulthood (Kerr, Lambert, & Bem, 1996). Adults with SAD receive less education, are less likely to be employed, and are less likely to marry (Lepine & Pelissolo, 2000). In the HARP study of adults with SAD, Keller (2003) noted that SAD was associated with moderate difficulty in social and occupational functioning and that about 20 percent had attempted suicide. Indeed, SAD leads to more severe psychiatric disability than most other mental health problems. The European Study of the Epidemiology of Mental Disorders (ESEMeD/MHEDEA 2000; Investigators, 2004) measured quality of life and social and occupational disability in 21,425 adults. Of nine mental disorders, SAD (in addition to dysthymia, major depression, PTSD, and panic disorder) had the highest impact on quality of life and daily functioning. SAD had the greatest negative impact on workdays lost because of illness when contrasted with other disorders.

A notable complicating feature of SAD is psychiatric comorbidity. In fact, concurrent psychiatric disorders appear to be the rule rather than the exception in this population. Beidel et al. (1999) found that 60 percent of a sample of children with SAD had an additional psychiatric disorder. Other anxiety disorders were observed in 36 percent of participants, followed by ADHD (10 percent) and major depression (6 percent). It was also observed that the majority (87 percent) of patients exhibited clinically significant anxiety symptoms, even if some did not meet full diagnostic criteria for other anxiety disorders. Compared to normative scale scores, children with SAD had elevated levels of depressive symptoms and internalizing problems (as reported by parents and teachers). Otto et al. (2001) found that 56 percent of adults with SAD retrospectively reported having an additional psychiatric disorder in childhood. Overanxious disorder was most prevalent (49 percent), followed by avoidant disorder (26 percent) and separation anxiety disorder (13 percent).

Comorbidity has also been documented in adults with SAD. Weiller, Bisserbe, Boyer, Lepine, and Lecrubier (1996) found that 33 percent of adults with SAD had major depression, followed by 27 percent with generalized anxiety disorder and 19 percent with agoraphobia. Keller (2003) reported that, in the HARP study, 76 percent of adults with SAD had a concurrent psychiatric disorder, and 32 percent had two or more comorbid disorders. Depression was found in 56 percent of participants, followed by panic disorder with agoraphobia, generalized anxiety disorder, simple phobia, and obsessive-compulsive disorder. In general, research suggests that SAD typically precedes the development of comorbid depression (Keller, 2003) and alcohol abuse (Schuckit et al., 1997). Furthermore, concurrent depression is associated with earlier onset of SAD, greater symptom severity, and increased functional impairment.

A final point addresses the importance of treatment on the course of SAD. It is noteworthy that effective treatments for SAD have been developed for both children and adults. Yet, although many children and adults with psychiatric disorders fail to seek treatment, SAD is remarkable in terms of the extent to which treatment is not sought or obtained. A partial explanation for this phenomenon is the pervasiveness of normative social anxiety in the general population and the corresponding diminishment of clinically significant social anxiety. For children with SAD, parents and other adults often view the disorder as a manifestation of so-called normal shyness, or view symptoms as immutable personality traits for which treatment is likely to be inappropriate or ineffective. The nature of the disorder is also a barrier to obtaining effective treatment. Both children and adults with SAD avoid social interactions that elicit anxiety, and the process of seeking and receiving treatment may be aversive and restrict participation. For parents, concerns about medication side effects (Chavira, Stein, Bailey, & Stein, 2004) and safety may discourage seeking treatment (Young et al., 2005). Although psychological treatments may be more acceptable to parents (Chavira et al.), the frequency and intensity of treatment required for optimal response may pose a barrier for some families. Identifying ways to improve access to and acceptability of effective treatments for SAD is a priority for future research.

ASSESSMENT AND DIAGNOSIS

Assessment and diagnosis of SAD in children can be a difficult task given the complexity of the disorder and high rate of comorbidity. Thus, it is imperative that clinicians conduct a comprehensive evaluation to facilitate accurate diagnosis and treatment planning. Because some children with SAD underreport the severity of their symptoms, multiple informants should be utilized (Schniering, Hudson, & Rapee, 2000).

Several structured and semistructured interviews based on diagnostic classification systems have been developed to gather information and assist clinicians in making a diagnosis of SAD. Although the use of structured interviews can be time-consuming, information gained can provide a wealth of information for use in planning treatment. Structured and semistructured interviews for children include the Diagnostic Interview Schedule for Children—Revised (Shaffer et al., 1993), the Diagnostic Interview for Children and Adolescents (Herjanic & Reich, 1982), the Kiddie Schedule for Affective Disorders and Schizophrenia—Present and Lifetime Version (K-SADS-PL; Kaufman, Birmaher, Brent, Rao, & Ryan, 1997), the Children's Assessment Schedule (Hodges, Kline, Stern, Cytryn, & McKnew, 1982), the Child and Adolescent Psychiatric Assessment (Angold et al., 1995) and the Anxiety Disorders Interview Schedule for Children (ADIS-IV-C; Silverman & Albano, 1995).

The ADIS-IV-C (Silverman & Albano, 1995) is one of the most comprehensive and widely used semistructured interviews specifically designed for the diagnosis of anxiety disorders in children. The ADIS-IV-C can be used to diagnose a range of anxiety disorders, mood disorders, and other comorbidities. The ADIS-IV-C also compiles information regarding severity of impairment; family history; and cognitive, physiological, and behavioral manifestations of the disorders. In addition, situational parameters or triggers of anxiety can be explored. The ADIS-IV-C includes a specific SAD module that includes child and parent reports of fear ratings for 13 different social and performance situations (e.g., giving an oral report or reading aloud, talking to unfamiliar individuals, attending a party or activity). Parents and children provide an overall rating of functional impairment resulting from the disorder. Information regarding the child's current and previous social relationships, frequency of participation in social activities, and problems in family functioning can be obtained.

Although structured and semistructured interviews are highly recommended for a comprehensive assessment of SAD, self-report measures can also be used for diagnostic purposes. A number of self-report instruments are used to examine symptoms of anxiety in children, and many provide separate anxiety subscales. These measures include the Child Behavior Checklist (Achenbach, 1991), the Behavior Assessment Scale for Children (Reynolds & Kamphaus, 1992), and the

Revised Children's Manifest Anxiety Scale for Children (Reynolds & Richmond, 1978).

Several questionnaires have been designed to look specifically at symptoms of SAD. The Social Anxiety Scale for Children—Revised (La Greca & Stone, 1993) assesses social fears in children and yields three subscales: social avoidance and distress in general, social avoidance and distress in new situations, and fear of negative evaluation. La Greca and Stone (1993) reported adequate internal consistency for each of the three subscales ($r \geq 0.65$) and concurrent validity in a sample of preadolescent children. Beidel, Turner, and Morris (1995) developed the Social Phobia and Anxiety Inventory for Children, a self-report measure of SAD in children. This measure consists of three factors: assertiveness/general conversation, traditional social encounters, and a public performance factor. Beidel, Turner, and Fink (1996) reported excellent internal consistency and high test-retest reliability. Moreover, this measure is sensitive to changes as a result of treatment (Beidel, Turner, & Morris, 2000).

Physiological measures have also been used to measure anxiety in children with SAD. However, there have been few empirical investigations of such measures as diagnostic tools. Beidel (1988) examined heart rate among children reading aloud as part of an assessment for SAD. Children who were socially anxious displayed increased heart rate throughout the task compared to nonclinical controls, who showed a reduction in heart rate as they progressed through the task. Physiological measures may be difficult to use in clinical practice, and not every individual with anxiety experiences physiological arousal.

IMPACT ON ENVIRONMENT

Family

In the Etiology section, the causal role of family factors was considered. In this section, we consider the impact of SAD on families. Although it is readily acknowledged that children with SAD and other family members influence each other in a bidirectional manner, such interrelationships have not been adequately disaggregated. As a result, it is often difficult to differentiate family variables that precede or result from children's SAD symptoms and their associated features. As with any psychiatric disorder, however, families often struggle to adapt to the challenges arising from SAD. For example, parents may experience great frustration in urging their children with SAD to interact with other children. Daily struggles often accompany SAD, including the child's refusal to go to school, vague somatic complaints, refusal to talk on the phone, and reticence with strangers or more familiar peers and adults. Children with SAD may be excessively clingy and reluctant to separate from parents, refusing to participate in developmentally appropriate activities such as organized sports, boys' and girls' clubs, or sleepovers at friends' houses. In some cases, children with SAD will use avoidant strategies while participating in activities, such as sitting in the back of a group so as not to be noticed or rushing through a task so that it ends quickly. Academic underachievement secondary to social anxiety (not participating in class, test anxiety), social isolation and minimal peer networks, and loneliness further increase parental frustration and disappointment.

Social anxiety in general, and SAD in particular, result in daily hassles for families that compound stress and may have deleterious effects on family relationships. In a survey of mothers of young children identified as shy, Warnke and Evans (1996) documented such commonly encountered difficulties. Sleep problems (difficulty falling and staying asleep, having to sleep with parents) and difficulty separating emerged as the two most commonly reported concerns. Additional issues included wariness of strangers, oversensitivity to noises, poor adaptation to changes in routine, and resistance to novel experiences (new foods, new activities). Although it is unclear whether these concerns extend to children with identified SAD or to older populations, they are consistent with clinical reports and other research on core features of the disorder (Beidel & Turner, 1998).

To effectively parent a child with SAD, it is necessary to (1) have a high frustration tolerance, (2) have a good understanding of the nature of the disorder, (3) be highly structured and authoritative in parenting style, and (4) advocate effectively in settings in which other adults (teachers, coaches, physicians) may underappreciate the potential severity of the disorder. As previously noted, parents of children with SAD are often anxious themselves and report increased levels of family conflict. As a result, incorporation of families into treatment may be an important component of achieving successful outcomes.

School

School is a setting in which SAD is often most pronounced. In school, children encounter numerous and varied social interactions. These can involve exposure to unfamiliar people, situations, and demands, all of which are especially challenging to children with SAD. Moreover, in the classroom, children are called upon to show initiative (e.g., asking questions if they do not understand the material), answer questions in front of others, and participate in explicitly evaluative activities (e.g., tests, oral reports, writing on the blackboard).

In analyzing daily diaries of distressing events, Beidel et al. (1999) found that most of the difficult situations children with SAD encountered occurred in school. In terms of assessment, most measures of SAD query respondents about anxiety and avoidance in situations occurring in school.

Children with SAD sometimes avoid going to or staying in school in order to minimize exposure to distressing situations. Such children may defiantly refuse to attend school or may avoid attendance by convincing caregivers to allow them to stay home secondary to somatic complaints (e.g., stomachaches) or obtaining early release from school because of anxiety-related physical ailments. For the majority of children with SAD who regularly attend school, avoidance can manifest itself in other ways. These include low levels of class participation, not asking questions and minimizing overall verbal expression, and restricting encounters with anxiety-eliciting situations (Evans, 2001).

Teacher and parent reports of social anxiety in children are only modestly correlated. Achenbach, McConaughy, and Howell (1987) found a correlation of only .21 between parent and teacher reports of inhibition and social withdrawal, a statistic considerably lower than that obtained for externalizing problems. This is in part attributable to differences in child behavior in home and at school. Evans (2001) noted that teachers tend to emphasize quality of peer relationships in determining shy and withdrawn behavior, whereas parents are more likely to place greater emphasis on timidity when meeting strangers and aversion to being the center of attention in social situations. Teachers are often more concerned about excessive time spent with children who have disruptive behavior disorders, such as attention-deficit/hyperactivity disorder and oppositional defiant disorder. Because children with SAD are typically shy and withdrawn, they rarely cause problems of such magnitude that require frequent redirection or intervention. However, teachers may experience considerable frustration resulting from unsuccessful efforts to engage children with SAD and encourage them to be more interactive in the classroom.

There is evidence that academic performance is impacted by SAD. Test anxiety is relatively common in SAD, with about 60 percent of children with SAD or overanxious disorder affected, in contrast with 40 percent of school-aged children in general (Beidel & Turner, 1988). Indeed, the prevalence of test anxiety in these populations suggests that it might be a useful screening indicator for more significant anxiety problems. Research on shy and withdrawn children (a broader category but one that likely subsumes children with SAD) indicates that they may be less academically competent than their more outgoing peers, particularly in verbal expression and comprehension (e.g., Masten, Morison, & Pellegrini, 1985: Rubin, 1982). The nature of the relationship between social withdrawal/inhibition and academic performance has not been elucidated. It is possible that less competence in academic abilities leads to reluctance to engage in activities in which poor performance will be evident, or perhaps inhibition restricts opportunities to fully learn and practice academic skills (especially of a verbal nature), resulting in insufficient mastery. A body of research also suggests that teachers have a general negative impression of academic abilities in shy and withdrawn children (e.g., Rubin, Hymel, & Chen, 1994). Such children are viewed as less competent in a variety of academic areas, raising the possibility that negative and biased expectations of inhibited children by teachers may also contribute to lowered academic performance.

Peer Interactions

Children with SAD have great difficulty initiating and maintaining interactions with peers, and they typically avoid social interactions that may elicit anxiety (Rubin, LeMare, & Lollis, 1990). Therefore, it is not surprising that a body of research has emerged that documents extensive difficulties with peers. Beidel et al. (1999) reported that, in a sample of 50 children with SAD, 75 percent reported having no or few friends, and 50 percent were not involved in any structured peer activities. This study also found a high level of self-reported loneliness. Sociometric investigations have supported a link between social anxiety and neglected peer group status. For example, Strauss, Lahey, Frick, Frame, and Hynd (1988) reported that socially anxious children were more likely to be rated by peers as neglected (in contrast to rejected or popular) than their conduct-disordered and non–psychiatrically impaired counterparts. In another study, La Greca, Dandes, Wick, Shaw, and Stone (1988) found that neglected children were more likely to be socially anxious than rejected and popular children.

Socially anxious children often report negative interactions and social ineptness with their peers. Social skills deficits in children with SAD have been implicated as possible contributors to peer relationship difficulties. Given their limited interactions with peers (resulting from avoidance and neglect by others), children with SAD have few opportunities to acquire and practice developmentally appropriate social skills. In the only study to directly assess social skills in children with SAD, Beidel et al. (1999) found that blind raters viewed children with SAD as less socially skilled and more anxious in a structured role-play test. In another study, Simonian, Beidel, Turner, Berkes, and Long (2001) found that children with SAD exhibited deficits in recognizing social affect, a critical element of social skills and social competence. It is unclear if social skills deficits in children with SAD reflect a failure to acquire necessary skills, or if anxiety interferes with the expression of adequately learned behaviors and abilities (Kashdan & Herbert, 2001). It seems likely that both factors are involved in social interaction problems in SAD, and successful treatment is dependent on addressing each of them.

IMPLICATIONS FOR FUTURE PERSONALITY DEVELOPMENT

One of the most striking features of SAD is its unremitting course in adulthood (Keller, 2003). Not surprisingly, the core personality features of SAD that have been identified in childhood (e.g., BI, introversion, neuroticism) are also evident throughout the life span. BI, the earliest temperamental indicator of social anxiety and avoidance, is moderately stable into adulthood. Schwartz, Wright, Shin, Kagan, and Rauch (2003) examined the long-term expression of BI in 13 young adults categorized as behaviorally inhibited at age 2, and contrasted them with 9 counterparts categorized as noninhibited. Individuals were exposed to familiar and unfamiliar stimuli, and amygdalar response was measured using functional MRI. Results indicated greater arousal in response to novel stimuli in the behaviorally inhibited subjects, providing support for both the stability of behavioral inhibition into young adulthood and the importance of the amygdala as the biological mechanism undergirding inhibition and wariness of novel stimuli. Interestingly, only 2 of the 13 behaviorally inhibited participants were diagnosed with SAD, further underscoring the fact that BI may increase vulnerability to developing the disorder, but it is neither a sufficient nor a specific etiologic pathway.

Several studies have investigated personality profiles in adults with SAD. These efforts have sought to describe personality structures in those with SAD and to relate variability in personality structure to expression, severity, and course. Not surprisingly, introversion and neurotic anxiety have emerged as strong correlates of SAD. Marteinsdottir, Furmark, Tillfors, Frederikson, and Ekselius (2001) contrasted adults with and without SAD using the Karolinska Scales of Personality. Findings revealed that those with SAD had elevated scores on trait anxiety scales (somatic anxiety, muscular tension) than controls. Moreover, they also reported maladaptive levels of irritability, indirect aggression, socialization, and detachment. Pélissolo et al. (2002) compared 178 adults with SAD to 602 community controls using the Temperament and Character Inventory. SAD was associated with high levels of harm avoidance, a trait that was correlated with symptom severity, social avoidance, and the generalized SAD subtype. Individuals with SAD also had lower scores on the character scales of this measure, including self-directedness, cooperativeness, and self-transcendence. In another study, Alnaes and Torgerson (1999) found that low emotional expressiveness and avoidant personality features were most predictive of chronicity of SAD at six-year follow up.

Taken together, the aforementioned studies describe a SAD personality profile characterized by inhibition, neurotic anxiety, avoidance, social wariness, and emotional inexpressiveness. However, it does not appear that these personality features are highly specific to SAD. On the contrary, each of these personality traits has been found in other anxiety disorders as well (Alnaes & Torgersen, 1999). As such, these personality traits are viewed as stable manifestations of core features of anxiety disorders (and SAD in particular) throughout the life span.

A sizable body of research has accrued that examines the relationship between SAD and Axis II personality disorders, particularly avoidant personality disorder (APD). Prevalence rates of APD in persons diagnosed with SAD vary across studies depending on criteria used and methodological differences, although they are consistently on the high end, ranging from 21 percent to 90 percent (Johnson, Turner, Beidel, & Lydiard, 1995). It is unclear if SAD and APD represent distinct disorders, the same disorders, or a continuum of severity in which APD is a more severe manifestation of SAD. Disaggregating these two disorders is complicated by two issues. First, symptoms overlap considerably. APD is characterized by a pervasive pattern of social inhibition, hypersensitivity to negative evaluation, and persistent avoidance of social situations, all of which are primary elements of SAD. And second, the chronic and unremitting course of SAD in adulthood blurs the distinction between Axis I and Axis II diagnoses (Axis I conditions typically have acute manifestations separated by intervals of partial or full remission, in contrast to Axis II conditions in which the clinical presentation is largely unchanged over time). Yet evidence exists that APD may be an important moderating variable. It is generally believed that the co-occurrence of SAD and APD (or other personality disorders) may mitigate treatment response (Johnson et al., 1995). Also, concurrent APD is associated with lower probability of remission in adults with generalized SAD (Keller, 2003).

TREATMENT IMPLICATIONS

Treatment of SAD in childhood and adolescence is in the early stages of development. Treatments have largely been derived from those used in adults with SAD, incorporating to varying degrees such strategies as exposure, social skills training, cognitive restructuring, and pharmacotherapy. Psychological treatments typically differ in their emphases on cognitive features of the disorder, fear and avoidance behavior, involvement of family members, and tailoring to developmental level (Kashdan & Herbert, 2001). Moreover, research on psychological treatments is limited by infrequent use of attention control groups, small sample sizes, and minimal replication. That having been said, several approaches have emerged as particularly promising and efficacious. Research on pharmacotherapy has been less extensive, although preliminary work supports the use of selective seratonin reuptake inhibitors (a mainstay of pharmacological treatment for adults with SAD) with children and adolescents.

Social Effectiveness Therapy for Children (SET-C; Beidel, Turner, & Morris, 1998) is a comprehensive behavioral treatment program for children with SAD designed to enhance social skills and decrease social anxiety. In addition, it is one of the few programs to be rigorously evaluated through comparison to an attention control (Beidel et al., 2000). The program consists of parent and child education, 12 weekly individual in vivo exposure sessions, and 12 weekly group sessions. Children are also given individualized exposure-based homework assignments. A unique feature of the program is Peer Generalization Programming, in which children are paired with outgoing peer volunteers while participating in a developmentally normal activity. This component allows the children to practice newly learned social skills in a naturalistic setting. Results from a controlled trial (Beidel et al., 2004) revealed that participation in SET-C resulted in decreased social fears, general anxiety, and distress as well as increased social skills and improvements in daily social functioning relative to a control condition (Testbusters, a program to improve study skills and test taking). At posttreatment, 67 percent of children in SET-C no longer met diagnostic criteria for SAD, in contrast to 5 percent in the Testbusters condition. Of the 73 percent of children in SET-C who participated in a six-month follow up, 85 percent did not meet diagnostic criteria for SAD. Beidel, Turner, Young, and Paulson (in press) reported findings from a three-year follow-up of this sample of children with SAD. Findings revealed maintenance of gains over this time interval, with 72.4 percent of children remaining free of a SAD diagnosis.

Hayward et al. (2000) examined a group cognitive-behavioral treatment (CBT) in 35 females with SAD who were randomly assigned to the treatment condition or wait list control. The 16-week intervention focused on education about the disorder, exposure, and family communication (which was facilitated by parent involvement in selected sessions). Posttreatment analyses revealed a significant reduction in SAD diagnosis and severity in the treatment group, although group differences were not found at the subsequent one-year follow up. The CBT "coping cat" program (Kendall, 1990) is a 16-session intervention for children with anxiety disorders that has been delivered in both individual and group formats. In a series of studies of children with anxiety disorders (some of whom had SAD), the treatment has been superior to wait list controls (Kashdan & Herbert, 2001). Another study compared a CBT-based treatment to an attention placebo and found no differences between treated children and controls (Silverman et al., 1999).

There are few controlled trials of pharmacological treatments for children and adolescents with SAD. Birmaher et al. (2003) found fluoxetine to be superior to placebo in the treatment of childhood anxiety disorders, including SAD. More recently, a large-scale, multisite trial of paroxetine (Wagner et al., 2004) found similar positive results. Long-term effects of these medications on SAD are unknown and in need of further research.

REFERENCES

Achenbach, T. M. (1991). *Manual for the Child Behavior Checklist/4–18 and 1991 profile.* Burlington, VT: Department of Psychiatry, University of Vermont.

Achenbach, T. M., McConaughy, S. H., & Howell, C. T. (1987). Implication of cross-informant correlations. *Psychological Bulletin, 101,* 213–232.

Albano, A. M., DiBartolo, P. M., Heimberg, R. G., & Barlow, D. H. (1995). Children and adolescents: Assessment and treatment. In R. G. Heimberg, M. R. Liebowitz, D. A. Hope, & F. R. Schneider (Eds.), *Social phobia: Diagnosis, assessment and treatment* (pp. 387–425). New York: Guilford Press.

Alnaes, R., & Torgersen, S. (1999). A 6-year follow-up study of anxiety disorders in psychiatric outpatients: Development and continuity with personality disorders and personality traits as predictors. *Nordic Journal of Psychiatry, 53,* 409–416.

American Psychiatric Association. (1980). *Diagnostic and statistical manual of mental disorders* (3rd ed.). Washington, DC: Author.

American Psychiatric Association. (1987). *Diagnostic and statistical manual of mental disorders* (3rd ed., rev.). Washington, DC: Author.

American Psychiatric Association. (1994). *Diagnostic and statistical manual of mental disorders* (4th ed.) Washington, DC: Author.

Angold, A., Prendergast, M., Cox, A., Harrington, R., Simonoff, E., & Rutter, M. (1995). The Child and Adolescent Psychiatric Assessment (CAPA). *Psychological Medicine, 25,* 739–753.

Beidel, D. C. (1988). Psychophysiological assessment of anxious emotional states in children. *Journal of Abnormal Psychology, 97,* 80–82.

Beidel, D. C. (1991). Social phobia and overanxious disorder in school-age children. *Journal of the American Academy of Child and Adolescent Psychiatry, 30,* 545–552.

Beidel, D. C., Christ, M. A. G., & Long, P. J. (1991). Somatic complaints in anxious children. *Journal of Abnormal Child Psychology, 19,* 659–670.

Beidel, D. C, Neal, A. M., & Lederer, A. S. (1991). The feasibility and validity of a daily diary for the assessment of anxiety in children. *Behavior Therapy, 22,* 505–517.

Beidel, D. C., & Turner, S. M. (1988). Comorbidity of test anxiety and other anxiety disorders in children. *Journal of Abnormal Child Psychology, 16,* 275–287.

Beider, D. C., & Turner, S. M. (1992, October). *Are social phobic children the same as social phobic adults?* Paper presented at the American Academy of Child and Adolescent Psychiatry Annual Meeting, Washington, DC.

Beidel, D. C., & Turner, S. M. (1998). *Shy children, phobic adults. Nature and treatment of social phobia.* Washington, DC: American Psychological Association.

Beidel, D. C., Turner, S. M., & Fink, C. M. (1996). The assessment of childhood social phobia: Construct, convergent, and discriminative validity of the SAD and Anxiety Inventory for Children (SPAI-C). *Psychological Assessment, 8,* 235–240.

Beidel, D. C., Turner, S. M., & Morris, T. L. (1995). A new inventory to assess childhood social anxiety and phobia: The Social Phobia and Anxiety Inventory for Children. *Psychological Assessment, 7,* 73–79.

Beidel, D. C., Turner, S. M., & Morris, T. L. (1998). *Social Effectiveness Therapy for Children: A treatment manual.* Unpublished manuscript, Medical University of South Carolina.

Beidel, D. C., Turner, S. M., & Morris, T. L. (1999). Psychopathology of childhood social phobia. *Journal of the American Academy of Child and Adolescent Psychiatry, 38,* 643–650.

Beidel, D. C., Turner, S. M., & Morris, T. L. (2000). Behavioral treatment of childhood social phobia. *Journal of Consulting and Clinical Psychology, 68,* 1072–1080.

Beidel, D. C., Turner, S. M., Young, B. J., Ammerman, R. T., Sallee, F. R., & Crosby, L. A. (2005). *Psychopathology of adolescent social phobia.* Unpublished manuscript, University of Maryland, College Park.

Beidel, D. C., Turner, S. M., Young, B., & Paulson, A. (in press). Social Effectiveness Therapy for Children: Three-year follow-up. *Journal of Consulting and Clinical Psychology.*

Biederman, J., Hirshfeld-Becker, D. R., Rosenbaum, J. F., Herot, C., Friedman, D., Snidman, N., et al. (2001). Further evidence of association between behavioral inhibition and social anxiety in children. *American Journal of Psychiatry, 158,* 1673–1679.

Birmaher, B., Axelson, D. A., Mond, K., Kalas, C., Clark, D. B., Ehmann, M., et al. (2003). Fluoxetine for the treatment of childhood anxiety disorders. *Journal of the American Academy of Child and Adolescent Psychiatry, 42,* 415–423.

Bogels, S. M., van Oosten, A., Muris, P., & Smulders, D. (2001). Familial correlates of social anxiety in children and adolescents. *Behaviour Research and Therapy, 39,* 273–287.

Bruch, B., & Heimberg, R. (1994). Differences in perceptions of parental and personal characteristics between generalized and nongeneralized social phobics. *Journal of Anxiety Disorders, 8,* 155–168.

Caspi, A., Elder, G. H., Jr., & Bem, D. J. (1988). Moving away from the world: Life course patters of shy children. *Developmental Psychology, 24,* 824–831.

Caspi, A., & Silva, P. A. (1995). Temperamental qualities at age 3 predict personality traits in young adulthood: Longitudinal evidence from a birth cohort. *Child Development, 66,* 486–498.

Chavira, D. A., Stein, M. B., Bailey, K., & Stein, M. T. (2004). Comorbidity of generalized social anxiety disorder and depression in a pediatric primary care sample. *Journal of Affective Disorders, 80,* 163–171.

Davidson, J. (1993). *Childhood histories of adult social phobics.* Paper presented at the Anxiety Disorders Association Annual Convention, Charleston, SC.

The European Study of the Epidemiology of Mental Disorders: A European Assessment in Year 2000 (ESEMeD/MHEDEA 2000) Investigators. (2004). Disability and quality of life impact of mental disorders in Europe: Results from the European Study of the Epidemiology of Mental Disorders (ESEMeD) project. *Acta Psychiatrica Scandinavica, 420,* 38–46.

Evans, M. A. (2001). Shyness in the classroom and home. In W. R. Crozier & L. E. Alden (Eds.), *International handbook of social anxiety: Concepts, research and interventions relating to the self and shyness* (pp. 159–183). New York: Wiley.

Eysenck, H. J. (1994). The Big Five or giant three: Criteria for a paradigm. In C. F. Halverson, G. A. Kohnstamm, & R. P. Martin, *Developing structure of temperament and personality from infancy to adulthood* (pp. 37–51). Hillsdale, NJ: Erlbaum.

Fordham, K., & Stevenson-Hinde, J. (1999). Shyness, friendship quality, and adjustment during middle childhood. *Journal of Child Psychology and Psychiatry, 40,* 757–768.

Furmark, T. (2002). Social phobia: Overview of community surveys. *Acta Psychiatrica Scandinavica, 105,* 84–93.

Gelernter, J., Page, G. P., Stein, M. B., & Woods, S. W. (2004). Genome-wide linkage scan for loci predisposing to social phobia: Evidence for a chromosome 16 risk locus. *American Journal of Psychiatry, 161,* 59–66.

Goodwin, R. D., Fergusson, D. M., & Horwood, L. J. (2004). Early anxious/withdrawn behaviours predict later internalising disorders. *Journal of Child Psychology and Psychiatry, 45,* 874–883.

Gorman, J. M., & Gorman, L. F. (1987). Drug treatment of social phobia. *Journal of Affective Disorders, 13,* 183–192.

Hayward, C. Varady, S., Albano, A. M., Thienemann, M., Henderson, L., & Schatzberg, A. F. (2000). Cognitive behavioral group therapy for social phobia in female adolescents: Results of a pilot study. *Journal of the American Academy of Child and Adolescent Psychiatry, 39,* 1–6.

Herjanic, B., & Reich, W. (1982). Development of a structured psychiatric interview for children: Agreement between child and parent on individual symptoms. *Journal of Abnormal Child Psychology, 10,* 307–324.

Hodges, K. H., Kline, J., Stern, L., Cytryn, L., & McKnew, D. (1982). The development of a Child Assessment Schedule for research and clinical use. *Journal of Abnormal Child Psychology, 10,* 173–189.

Johnson, M. R., Turner, S. M., Beidel, D. C., & Lydiard, R. B. (1995). Personality function and social phobia. In M. D. Stein (Ed.), *Social phobia: Clinical perspectives and research* (pp. 77–117). Washington, DC: American Psychiatric Press.

Kagan, J. (2003). Biology, context, and developmental inquiry. *Annual Review of Psychology, 54,* 1–23.

Kagan, J., & Snidman, N. (1999). Early childhood predictors of adult anxiety disorders. *Society of Biological Psychiatry, 46,* 1536–1541.

Kashdan, T. B., & Herbert, J. D. (2001). Social anxiety disorder in childhood and adolescence: Current status and future directions. *Clinical Child and Family Psychology, 4,* 37–61.

Kaufman, J., Birmaher, B., Brent, D., Rao, U., & Ryan, N. (1997). Schedule for Affective Disorders and Schizophrenia for School-Age Children—Present and lifetime version (K-SADS-PL): Initial reliability and validity data. *Journal of the American Academy of Child and Adolescent Psychiatry, 36,* 980–988.

Keller, M. B. (2003). The lifelong course of social anxiety disorder: A clinical perspective. *Acta Psychiatrica Scandinavica, 108* (Suppl. 417), 85–94.

Kendall, P. C. (1990). *Coping cat workbook.* Ardmore, PA: Workbook.

Kendler, K., Neale, M., Kessler, R., Heath, A., & Eaves, L. (1992). The genetic epidemiology of phobias in women: The interrelationship of agoraphobia, social phobia, situational phobia, and simple phobia. *Archives of General Psychiatry, 49,* 273–281.

Kerr, M., Lambert, W. W., & Bem, D. J. (1996). Life course sequelae of childhood shyness in Sweden: Comparison with the United States. *Developmental Psychology, 32,* 1100–1105.

Kessler, R. C., McGonagle, K. A., Zhao, S., Nelson, C. B., Hughes, M., Eshelman, S., et al. (1994). Lifetime and 12-month prevalence of *DSM-III-R* psychiatric disorders in the United States. *Archives of General Psychiatry, 51,* 8–19.

La Greca, A. M., Dandes, S. K., Wick, P., Shaw, K., & Stone, W. L. (1988). Development of the social anxiety scale for children: Reliability and concurrent validity. *Journal of Clinical Child Psychology, 17,* 84–91.

La Greca, A. M., & Stone, W. L. (1993). Social Anxiety Scale for Children—Revised: Factor structure and concurrent validity. *Journal of Clinical Child Psychology, 22,* 17–27.

Last, C. G., Perrin, S., Hersen, M., & Kazdin, A. E. (1992). *DSM-III-R* anxiety disorders in children: Sociodemographic and clinical characteristics. *Journal of the American Academy of Child and Adolescent Psychiatry, 31,* 928–934.

Lepine, J.-P., & Pelissolo, A. (2000). Why take social anxiety disorder seriously? *Depression and Anxiety, 11,* 87–92.

Magee, W. J., Eaton, W. W., Wittchen, H. U., McGonagle, K. A., & Kessler, R. C. (1996). Agoraphobia, simple phobia and SAD in the National Comorbidity Survey. *Archives of General Psychiatry, 53,* 159–168.

Marteinsdottir, I., Furmark, T., Tillfors, M., Fredrikson, M., & Ekselius, L. (2001). Personality traits in social phobia. *European Psychiatry, 16,* 143–150.

Masten, A., Morison, P., & Pellegrini, D. (1985). A revised class play method of peer assessment. *Developmental Psychology, 21,* 523–533.

McCrae, R. R., & Costa, P. T., Jr. (1997). Personality trait structure as a human universal. *American Psychologist, 52,* 509–516.

Merikangas, K. R., Lieb, R., Wittchen, H.-U., & Avenevoli, S. (2003). Family and high-risk studies of social anxiety disorder. *Acta Psychiatrica Scandinavica, 108*(Suppl. 417), 28–37.

Ollendick, T. H., & Hirshfeld-Becker, D. R. (2002). The developmental psychopathology of social anxiety disorder. *Biological Psychiatry, 51,* 44–58.

Ost, L. (1985). Ways of acquiring phobias and outcome of behavioral treatments. *Behaviour Research and Therapy, 23,* 683–689.

Otto, M. S., Pollack, M. H., Maki, K. M., Gould, R. A., Worthington, J. J., III, Smoller, J. W., et al. (2001). Childhood history of anxiety disorders among adults with social phobia: Rates, correlates, and comparisons with patients with panic disorder. *Depression and Anxiety, 14,* 209–213.

Pélissolo, A., Andre, C., Pujol, H., Yao, S. N., Servant, D., Braconnier, A., et al. (2002). Personality dimensions in social phobics with or without depression. *Acta Psychiatrica Scandinavica 105,* 94–103.

Reich, J., & Yates, W. (1988). Family history of psychiatric disorders in social phobia. *Comprehensive Psychiatry, 29,* 72–75.

Reynolds, C. R., & Kamphaus, R. W. (1992). Behavior Assessment System for Children. Circle Pines, MN: AGS.

Reynolds, C. R., & Richmond, B. O. (1978). A revised measure of Children's Manifest Anxiety Scale. *Journal of Abnormal Child Psychology, 6,* 271–280.

Rubin, K. H. (1982). Social and social-cognitive characteristics of young isolate, normal, and social children. In K. H. Rubin &

S. H. Ross (Eds.), *Peer relationships and social skills in childhood* (pp. 353–374). New York: Springer-Verlag.

Rubin, K. H., & Asendorpf, J. B. (1993). Social withdrawal, inhibition, and shyness in childhood: Conceptual and definitional issues. In K. H. Rubin & J. B. Asendorpf (Eds.), *Social withdrawal, inhibition, and shyness in childhood* (pp. 3–17). Hillsdale, NJ: Erlbaum.

Rubin, K. H., Hymel, S., & Chen, X. (1994). The social-emotional characteristics of extremely aggressive and extremely withdrawn children. *Merrill-Palmer Quarterly, 39,* 518–534.

Rubin, K. H., LeMare, L. J., & Lollis, S. (1990). Social withdrawal in childhood: Developmental pathways to peer rejection. In S. R. Asher & J. D. Coie (Eds.), *Peer rejection in childhood* (pp. 217–249). Cambridge, England: Cambridge University Press.

Schneier, F. R., Johnson, J., Hornig, C. D., Liebowitz, M. R., & Weissman, M. M. (1992). Social phobia, comorbidity and morbidity in an epidemiological sample. *Archives of General Psychiatry, 49,* 282–288.

Schniering, C. A., Hudson, J. L., & Rapee, R. M. (2000). Issues in the diagnosis and assessment of anxiety disorders in children and adolescents. *Clinical Psychology Review, 20,* 453–478.

Schuckit, M. A., Tipp, J. E., Bucholz, K. K., Nurnberger, J. I., Jr., Hesselbrock, V. M., Crowe, R. R., et al. (1997). The life-time rates of three major mood disorders and four major anxiety disorders in alcoholics and controls. *Addiction, 92,* 1289–1304.

Schwartz, C. E., Wright, C. I., Shin, L. M., Kagan, J., & Rauch, S. L. (2003). Inhibited and uninhibited infants "grown up": Adult amygdalar response to novelty. *Science, 300,* 1952–1954.

Shaffer, D., Schwab-Stone, M., Fisher, P., Cohen, P., Piacentini, J., Davies, M., et al. (1993). The Diagnostic Interview Schedule for Children—Revised Version (DISC-R): I. Preparation, field testing, interrater reliability, and acceptability. *Journal of the American Academy of Child and Adolescent Psychiatry, 32,* 643–650.

Silverman, W. K., & Albano, A. M. (1995). *Anxiety Disorders Interview Schedule for Children.* San Antonio, TX: Psychological Corp.

Silverman, W. K., Jurtines, W. M., Ginsburg, G. S., Weems, C. F., Lumpkin, P. W., & Carmichael, D. H. (1999). Treating anxiety disorders in children with group cognitive-behavioral therapy: A randomized clinical trial. *Journal of Consulting and Clinical Psychology, 67,* 995–1003.

Simonian, S. J., Beidel, D. C., Turner, S. M., Berkes, J. L., & Long, J. H. (2001). Recognition of facial affect by children and adolescents diagnosed with social phobia. *Child Psychiatry and Human Development, 32,* 137–145.

Stein, M. B., Chartier, M. J., Hazen, A. L., Kozac, M. V., Tancer, M. E., Lander, S., et al. (1998). A direct-interview family study of generalized social phobia. *American Journal of Psychiatry, 155,* 90–97.

Stemberger, R. T., Turner, S. M., Beidel, D. C., & Calhoun, K. S. (1995). Social phobia: An analysis of possible developmental factors. *Journal of Abnormal Psychology, 104,* 526–531.

Strauss, C. C., Lahey, B. B., Frick, P., Frame, C. L., & Hynd, G. W. (1988). Peer social status of children with anxiety disorders. *Journal of Consulting and Clinical Psychology, 56,* 137–141.

Strauss, C. C., & Last, C. G. (1993). Social and simple phobia in children. *Journal of Anxiety Disorders, 1,* 141–152.

Thomas, A., & Chess, S. (1977). *Temperament and development.* New York: Brunner/Mazel.

Turner, S. M., Beidel, D. C., Borden, J. W., Stanley, M. R., & Jacob, R. G. (1991). Social phobia: Axis I and Axis II correlates. *Journal of Abnormal Psychology, 100,* 102–106.

Turner, S. M, Beidel, D. C., & Cooley, M. R. (1994). *Social Effectiveness Therapy: A program for overcoming social anxiety and SAD.* Mount Pleasant, SC: Turndel.

Turner, S. M., Beidel, D. C., Roberson-Nay, R., & Tervo, K. (2003). Parenting behaviors in parents with anxiety disorders. *Behaviour Research and Therapy, 41,* 541–554.

Van Ameringen, M., Oakman, J., Mancini, C., Pipe, B., & Chung, H. (2004). Predictors of response in generalized social phobia: Effect of age of onset. *Journal of Clinical Psychopharmacology, 24,* 42–48.

Wagner, A. D., Berard, R., Stein, M. B., Wetherhold, E., Carpenter, D. J., Perera, P., et al. (2004). A multicenter, randomized, double-blind, placebo-controlled trial of paroxetine in children and adolescents with social anxiety disorder. *Archives of General Psychiatry, 61,* 1153–1162.

Warnke, S., & Evans, M. A. (1996, July). *Don't blame mother: Parenting styles associated with childhood shyness.* Paper presented at the International Society for the Study of Behavioural Development, Quebec City.

Weiller, E., Bisserbe, J. C., Boyer, P., Lepine, J. P., & Lecrubier, Y. (1996). Social phobia in general health care: An unrecognized undertreated disabling disorder. *British Journal of Psychiatry, 168,* 169–174.

Westenberg, P. M., Drewes, M. J., Goedhart, A. W., Siebelink, B. M., & Treffers, P. D. (2004). A developmental analysis of self-reported fears in late childhood through mid-adolescence: Social-evaluative fears on the rise? *Journal of Child Psychology and Psychiatry, 45,* 481–495.

Woodward, S. A., Lenzenweger, M. F., Kagan, J., Snidman, N., & Arcus, D. (2000). Taxonic structure of infant reactivity: Evidence from a taxometric perspective. *Psychological Science, 11,* 296–301.

Young, B., Beidel, D. C., Turner, S. M., McGraw, K., Ammerman, R. T., & Coaston, S. C. (2005, March). *Study refusal due to medication in a randomized clinical trial for child and adolescent social phobia.* Paper presented at the Anxiety Disorders Association of America Annual Conference, Seattle.

CHAPTER 11

Post-Traumatic Stress Disorder

MELISSA K. RUNYON, ESTHER DEBLINGER, LEAH BEHL, AND BETH COOPER

DESCRIPTION OF THE DISORDER AND CLINICAL PICTURE

It is imperative that mental health professionals have an understanding of post-traumatic stress disorder (PTSD) given that an estimated 25 percent of all children will experience some type of trauma prior to their 16th birthday (Costello, Erkanli, Fairbank, & Angold, 2002). Indeed, PTSD has been documented in children who have experienced various types of trauma, including but not limited to child sexual abuse, child physical abuse, exposure to domestic violence, war, natural disasters, and community violence (see Cohen, Berliner, & Mannarino, 2000). However, a majority of children who experience traumatic events do not develop full-blown PTSD as defined by *DSM-IV.* For example, McLeer, Deblinger, Atkins, Foa, and Ralphe (1988) documented the frequency of PTSD and associated symptoms in a group of sexually abused children who were referred for psychiatric treatment and reported that 48.4 percent of children met full criteria, and 80.6 percent of those who did not meet full criteria met partial criteria for PTSD. Others indicate that PTSD symptoms may not be identified in young children due to a child's inability to provide verbal accounts of some symptoms (Scheeringa, Zenah, Drel, & Larrieu, 1995). This factor has resulted in researchers and clinicians alike questioning the applicability of adult-focused diagnostic criteria for identifying PTSD in children (Cohen et al., 2000). Despite this debate, professionals have focused on refining the assessment of PTSD symptoms in children (Scheeringa et al., 1995) and have developed effective treatment strategies (see Cohen et al., 2000) within the conceptual framework of PTSD that incorporate those children who meet full-blown criteria for PTSD as well as those who have partial PTSD symptoms.

Initially, PTSD criteria provided no distinction in the manifestation of symptoms between adults and children. However, diagnostic criteria for posttrauma response have evolved over the past four decades to provide some guidance to those professionals who are attempting to assess trauma symptoms in children. Symptoms characteristic of the syndrome currently known as PTSD were historically documented as "soldier's heart" in soldiers during the American Civil War (Kaplan & Sadock, 1991). According to Kaplan and Sadock, these symptoms reappeared in the soldiers of the first and second world wars, as well as in survivors of Nazi concentration camps and atomic bombings.

The *Diagnostic and Statistical Manual-I (DSM-I),* published by the American Psychiatric Association (APA) in 1952, labeled the cluster of symptoms as *gross stress reaction,* a syndrome that was believed to abate rather quickly unless maintained by preexisting personality pathology. Following an analogous principle, the *Diagnostic and Statistical Manual-II (DSM-II;* APA, 1968) coined the diagnosis *transient situational disturbance* or *anxiety neurosis.*

When PTSD was initially presented in the diagnostic nomenclature of the *Diagnostic and Statistical Manual-III (DSM-III;* APA, 1980), diagnostic criteria were not explicitly applied to children and adolescents. Although *DSM-III* diagnostic criteria did not address this particular issue, professionals reportedly began to recognize that severe traumatic experiences could produce long-term psychological consequences in adults with no premorbid character problems (Green, Lindy, & Grace, 1985).

Finally, the revised version of the *DSM (DSM-III-R;* APA, 1987) addressed some of the concerns of professionals in the field by including in the criteria the statement that the stressor producing the syndrome would be markedly distressing to almost anyone and is most commonly experienced with intense terror and helplessness. The diagnosis also became applicable to children in that it was deemed to occur at any age, but it was offered with the qualifying statement that the disorder was most likely to occur in older children. At that time, the utility of the PTSD diagnostic category with children continued to be questioned despite these modifications in the *DSM-III-R* criteria. The *DSM-III-R* cautioned that children who suffered some form of maltreatment (i.e., physical, sexual, or psychological) may present with a variety of emotional and behavioral reactions and recommended that additional diagnoses, such as reactive attachment disorder of infancy or early childhood and adjustment disorder, be considered.

Further refinement of PTSD criteria occurred with the publication of the fourth edition of the diagnostic manual (*DSM-IV;* APA, 1994), which delineated the potential for differences in the symptom presentation of children as compared to adults with PTSD. This version of the *DSM* also noted greater overlap among the symptoms of major depressive disorder (MDD) and those of PTSD than did the previous versions. These refinements addressed criteria issues that had been a source of much criticism of earlier versions of the *DSM*. According to Amaya-Jackson and March (1995), overlap among criteria groups can result in PTSD symptoms being confounded by spurious comorbidity. For example, these authors reported that affective constriction in PTSD may be misinterpreted as anhedonia in MDD. Another example these authors provided is a child who appears depressed and inattentive as a result of lack of sleep caused by trauma-related nightmares. Indeed, similarity between symptoms may increase the difficulty of differential diagnosis.

With regard to PTSD diagnostic criteria, children of all ages may experience repetitive intrusive thoughts during inactive times and before falling asleep. Reminders or cues in the child's environment may also provoke strong negative emotional responses related to the trauma. According to *DSM-IV* diagnostic criteria, young children are more likely to engage in repetitive trauma-related play, reenact the trauma, and experience nightmares (Scheeringa et al., 1995), whereas adolescents and adults are more likely to report flashbacks, body memories, and dissociation. Children's play may incorporate rescue fantasies and happy endings in an attempt to master the traumatic situation. On the other hand, counterphobic "acting out" as a method for gaining mastery is common in adolescents, as evidenced by their propensity for risk-taking behaviors such as self-injury, substance abuse, and angry outbursts. One-month posttrauma nightmares of children with PTSD, according to *DSM-IV,* typically generalize from reexperiencing the traumatic event to nightmares of monsters and other scary things. Children generally do not have the sense that they are reliving the past experience; hence it is extremely important to obtain adult reports concerning the child's behavior. This absence of certain symptoms in young children could be an artifact of the difficulty involved in assessing these symptoms with this population given that 8 of 18 *DSM-IV* symptoms require children to have sufficiently expressive language skills to describe their internal experiences (Scheeringa et al., 1995).

Other symptoms include avoidance of trauma-related stimuli and numbing of general responsiveness, which are less common in children, as well as hyperarousal (e.g., sleep disturbance, irritability, difficulty concentrating, hypervigilance, exaggerated startle response). Angry outbursts, somatic complaints, and sleep difficulties are symptoms common in children under this criterion cluster. These problems can impair concentration and result in decreased school performance.

Because the child's developmental level impacts the way symptoms are expressed (American Academy of Child and Adolescent Psychiatry, 1998; Scheeringa et al., 1995), age-specific features of PTSD were included in the 2000 text revision of the *DSM-IV* (*DSM-IV-TR;* APA, 2000). For example, children can express recurrent and distressing recollections of the event through repetitive play with traumatic themes; recurrent or distressing dreams about the event may be replaced by frightening dreams or nightmares without recognizable content (e.g., the content of the dream may have no direct link to the traumatic event); and instead of flashbacks, children may experience trauma-specific reenactment such as reenacting sexual activities that were experienced during sexual abuse. Scheeringa and colleagues (1995) developed alternate criteria for diagnosing PTSD in very young children. These criteria are based on observable behaviors instead of subjective experiences that may be difficult for the child to express or for the assessor to interpret. For example, reexperiencing symptoms has been reworded to more accurately reflect how PTSD may be manifested in children, including posttraumatic play, play reenactment, recurrent recollections of the traumatic event, nightmares with or without an obvious link to the trauma, and episodes with dissociative features (Scheeringa et al., 1995). A new criterion was also introduced that includes aggression, separation anxiety, fear of going to the bathroom alone, being afraid of the dark, and other fears that may not be obviously related to the trauma (Scheeringa et al., 1995). As children mature, however, they begin to exhibit more adultlike PTSD symptoms (American Academy of Child and Adolescent Psychiatry, 1998).

Similar to the recommendations made in *DSM-IV,* Lipovsky (1992) highlights the importance of obtaining information from multiple sources concerning the child's emotional and behavioral functioning. This is important because of the difficulty of diagnosing PTSD in children. For example, a child who experiences intrusive and repetitive symptoms may report that he thinks about abuse all the time. Parental reports of the child waking from nightmares provide further evidence for this symptom. Behaviorally, reexperiencing the traumatic event may be demonstrated by the child's play with traumatic themes. Symptoms of avoidance are even more difficult to recognize in children. If a clinician is informed that the child has experienced a potentially traumatic event, the professional may look for a child who denies the event or refuses to discuss it, a child who moves away from the interviewer or changes activity when the subject of abuse is broached, and parental reports of the child isolating from peers. Hyperarousal in children is often demonstrated by self- and parent-reported sleep difficulties and observable changes in rate of breathing when questioned about abuse.

PERSONALITY DEVELOPMENT AND PSYCHOPATHOLOGY

Factors Moderating the Development of PTSD in Children

Though experiencing a traumatic event is necessary for a diagnosis of PTSD, not all children who are exposed to trauma develop PTSD. A meta-analysis by Fletcher (1996b) indicated that only approximately 36 percent of children exposed to traumatic events in the studies evaluated met full criteria for PTSD. A number of variables may moderate symptom presentation and treatment response for children who have been exposed to trauma, which explains the variability in the development of PTSD in children. A review of 25 studies in the practice parameters of the American Academy of Child and Adolescent Psychiatry (1998) identified three factors that may moderate the development of PTSD symptomatology: severity of the trauma, parental distress associated with the trauma, and temporal proximity to the traumatic event. High level of parental support and a positive emotional response to the trauma by the parent have been associated with positive posttrauma outcomes for children (see American Academy of Child and Adolescent Psychiatry, 1998). Though this holds true for children who have experienced a variety of traumatic events, it has probably been best documented for children who have suffered sexual abuse (Everson, Hunter, Runyan, Edelson, & Coulter, 1989).

The variability in PTSD symptoms reported by traumatized children may also be related to individual traits such as personality traits, attributions, coping styles, and preexisting psychopathology as well. Personality factors have been suggested as both potential protective and risk factors for the development of PTSD (Paris, 2000). Personality can be defined as "a constellation of attributes, or traits, that describe, explain, and predict an individual's behavior" (Schnurr & Vielhauer, 1999, p. 195). Research suggests that five general personality factors exist: conscientiousness, agreeableness, extroversion, openness to experience, and neuroticism for both adults (e.g., McCrae & Costa, 1987) and children (e.g., Ahadi, Rothbart, & Ye, 1993). There are many paths in which an individual's personality may influence the development of PTSD.

An individual's personality may increase or decrease the likelihood of being exposed to a trauma (Breslau, Davis, & Andreski, 1995). Individuals who are more impulsive may place themselves in higher risk situations and consequently may be more likely to experience a traumatic event. For example, an impulsive girl may be more likely to get drunk at a party where she does not know many people and to accept a ride home from someone she just met. This behavior may place her at a higher risk for experiencing a sexual assault. It is important to note that this in no way means the girl is responsible for the sexual assault. Someone who is less impulsive may be less likely to attend a party where she does not know many people, would be less likely to get drunk if there, and probably would not accept a ride from someone she did not know. All of these choices may decrease the likelihood of her experiencing a traumatic sexual assault.

Frequently, traumatic events occur regardless of an individual's behavior. Therefore, a conscientious individual who thinks through every action may also experience a traumatic event. Once a person experiences a trauma, their personality may impact how they actually experience the event. An individual's personality can influence the level of emotions surrounding the event. For example, people who are anxious or behaviorally inhibited may have an increased physiological response to events due to an increased baseline activity for catecholamine and cortisol responses (DeBellis et al., 1999). Both catecholamine and cortisol responses have been seen to play a prominent role in the development and maintenance of PTSD. Consequently, the neurotic individual may develop a typical sympathetic nervous system response to a stressor, whereas another individual may experience minimal physiological reaction.

A child's perception of the traumatic event(s) has also been identified as a variable that moderates PTSD development in children following exposure to child abuse (Brown & Kolko, 1999; Feiring, Taska, & Lewis, 1998; Runyon & Kenny, 2002). Cognitive behavioral theory suggests that how an individual thinks about an event will change how they feel about it (Beck, 1995). For example, one person may experience a hurricane as something that they are very afraid of because it can seriously injure them and therefore may view the hurricane as a traumatic event, whereas another individual may experience the same hurricane as an awesome display of nature's power and may experience the event with wonder and amazement at the world around them. In this scenario both individuals may have the same physiological reaction, but they interpret it in two different ways; the first individual may interpret their physiological reaction as being afraid for their lives, whereas the second individual may interpret their physiological reaction as excitement and fascination. Consequently, what the individual focuses on during the trauma and how they interpret their reactions have a large impact on whether they develop a negative stress reaction. Given this association, it seems imperative that treatment approaches address children's general and abuse-related attributions and cognitions and coping strategies.

Research has suggested that preexisting anxiety may place a child at a higher risk for the development of PTSD (e.g., Asarnow et al., 1999; La Greca, Silverman, & Wasserstein, 1998; Lonigan, Shannon, Taylor, Finch, & Sallee, 1994). Lonigan and colleagues (1994) even found that children's levels of both trait anxiety and reported negative emotional reactivity during Hurricane Hugo predicted more PTSD symptoms 3 months after the hurricane than exposure factors (e.g., subjective severity of the hurricane, degree of damage to the child's home). Lonigan et al. (1994) suggested that the higher predictive power of negative emotional reactivity of the children reflected an interaction between the severity of the trauma and the children's personal disposition. Pynoos, Steinberg, and Piacentini (1999) suggested that preexisting anxiety may contribute to traumatic stress reactions, like those of PTSD, due to the anxious child's higher physiological reactivity, fewer attributions of controllability, catastrophizing bodily sensations, cognitive discrimination, inability to calm down, and inability to be comforted by efforts at safety improvement or parental reassurances, all of which may be influenced by a child's personality.

Yet another way that personality may influence the development of PTSD is by influencing how the individual copes with the traumatic event. For example, after a traumatic event an extrovert may choose to be around their friends and family to help them, whereas an introvert may pull away from people. In this scenario the extroverted individual will receive the benefit of social support, which according to research may protect them and may make it less likely that they will develop PTSD.

Studies have also suggested that survivors whose coping responses are characterized by avoidance, denial, self-blame, or a combination of these tend to exhibit more negative psychological outcomes (Leitenberg, Greenwald, & Cado, 1992). An individual's personality may also determine how they cope with the traumatic event, which may also affect others' responses to them, potentially affecting their exposure to secondary trauma. For example, people with high levels of neuroticism may be more negative in response to traumatic events. Their negativism may make it more difficult for others to be comfortable around them, which may result in the unwillingness of others to help or even more severe negative reactions to the traumatized individuals. Others' unwillingness to help may prolong the recovery from the initial trauma, and other, more severe reactions may create a second experience of trauma for the individual.

PTSD's Influence on Personality Development

It is also important to understand what impact the development of PTSD has on both general (or so-called normal) and pathological personality development. Though literature exists on the relationship between a diagnosis of PTSD and the development of personality disorders (e.g., Fauerbach, Lawrence, Schmidt, Munster, & Costa, 2000; Holeva & Tarrier, 2001; Nightingale & Williams, 2000), the literature on the relationship between PTSD and long-term general personality development is sparse.

There are four diagnostic features of PTSD: the trauma experience, avoidance, hyperarousal, and reexperiencing (APA, 1994), which are further described in the Assessment and Diagnosis section of this chapter (see "Diagnostic Criteria for PTSD"). Although little research has been carried out on the impact of these diagnostic features on personality development, the relationships are theoretically possible. Each of the diagnostic features of PTSD may potentially determine if and how traumatic experiences have a long-lasting impact on the lives of children who experience them.

Trauma and Personality Development

Many aspects of a child's traumatic experience may impact that child's future personality development. The type of trauma is one such aspect. Was the traumatic event a single, isolated incident or a chronic stressor? Was it a natural disaster or an accident? Was the trauma brought about by a stranger or by someone the child trusted? Additionally, how the child interprets the trauma may also impact how he or she interacts with the world (e.g., a child's ability to view the world as a safe place may impact his or her level of comfort in that world). Indeed, in an adult sample, Bramsen, van der Ploeg, van der Kamp, and Ader (2002) found support for the idea that traumatic events may force individuals to change their worldviews, which consequently may make them more likely to develop higher levels of neuroticism (i.e., emotional instability).

The child's developmental level at the time of the trauma—for example, the type and number of coping skills that the child has available to him or her—can also impact a child's personality development (Rutter, 1989). Limited or dysfunctional coping skills may significantly decrease the likelihood of the child successfully coping with the event (Fletcher, 1996b) and its aftermath, which in turn can affect the child's future personality development. The inability to regulate emotions may lead to problems with peers, which may decrease the child's level of extroversion. The child's developmental level at the time of the trauma may also play a role in determining what meaning the child gives to the event. Children who believe that their actions led to the trauma or caused it to occur may become overcontrolled or highly conscientious in all areas of their lives.

Finally, the presence of a secondary trauma brought on by the original traumatic experience can impact personality development. For example, a child who witnesses the murder of her mother has to cope with the trauma of the event and has to grow up without the support and love of her mother. This secondary loss may negatively impact her self-confidence (among other things) and consequently decrease her level of overall extroversion.

It is important to note that consequences of traumatic experiences are not all negative; positive outcomes may occur after an individual experiences a traumatic event. There may be some truth to the adage "that which does not kill you makes you stronger." For example, successfully overcoming traumatic experiences may lead to increases in the individual's self-efficacy. Feeling that he or she can be effective in handling extreme situations may also increase a person's self-esteem and feelings of pride. In addition to potentially feeling better about their abilities, people who use different coping mechanisms to deal with traumatic events may also gain more confidence and the ability to use coping skills in the future, such as cognitive coping, processing thoughts, frustration management, or anxiety tolerance. Treatment can help individuals reduce the negative impact of experiencing traumatic events and highlight the strengths gained from overcoming adversity.

Avoidance and Personality Development

Although little research exists on the relationship between avoidance and personality development, avoidance symptoms associated with PTSD have the potential to influence personality development in many ways. Avoidance of trauma-related cues tends to result in the continuation of fear related to the traumatic experience (Mowrer, 1960). The negative reinforcement that a child receives by avoiding reminders of the traumatic event may reinforce avoidance coping and, therefore, impede more functional problem-solving coping. An extreme avoidance of traumatic cues may also lead to a failure to maintain responsibilities and may cause the child to be less conscientious. In some instances, the avoidance symptoms associated with PTSD may lead to increasing social isolation, thereby restricting the child's opportunities to develop effective relationship skills.

Reexperiencing and Personality Development

The biological changes associated with PTSD may also impact a child's personality development. The development and maintenance of PTSD is associated with an increase in baseline activity for catecholamine and cortisol responses (DeBellis et al., 1999). This increased baseline activity may create a higher level of general anxiety in children who have experienced a traumatic event, potentially impacting their level of neuroticism. The dysregulation and experience of painful emotions combined with trauma-related negative self-attributions may also create an increased fear of negative social evaluation (Pynoos et al., 1999), which in turn may lead to a decrease in the child's level of extroversion.

Hyperarousal and Personality Development

Hyperarousal symptoms may contribute to personality development in children in a number of ways. First, the increased attention given to being watchful for danger creates an attentional bias in the child. A child who is looking for things that could be dangerous is more likely to find danger in the surrounding world. This increased attention on the unsafe aspects of the world may create increased anxiety in the child. Second, the increased arousal may manifest itself as increased irritability, which in turn can create negative interaction patterns with the people in the child's life. These negative interaction patterns may impact how the child is perceived by others, including the feedback about himself that he receives from others, and ultimately can impact how the child sees himself. Difficulty concentrating may be another way in which hyperarousal symptoms impact the self-esteem of the child. A child who has difficulty concentrating is likely to do poorly in school and other aspects of achievement. This decreased ability to achieve may lead the child to think that she is dumb or that she cannot do anything right, resulting in decreased levels of confidence and self-esteem.

PTSD and Personality Disorders

Research suggests that individuals who are high or low on certain personality dimensions are more likely to have particular personality disorders. The two personality dimensions that appear to be associated with PTSD are neuroticism (e.g., Fauerbach et al., 2000; Holeva & Tarrier, 2001; Schnurr & Vielhauer, 1999) and extroversion (e.g., Davidson, Kudler, & Smith, 1987; Fauerbach et al., 2000; Nightingale & Williams, 2000; Schnurr & Vielhauer, 1999). For example, Blais, Hilsenroth, and Castlebury (1997) found that people who are high in neuroticism are more likely to develop PTSD and borderline, antisocial, histrionic, and avoidant personality disorders. People who are low in extroversion are also more likely to develop PTSD and schizoid personality disorder. Although a correlation exists between certain personality dimensions and PTSD, and research on the relationship between personality dimensions and personality disorders suggests that these factors are related, causality and even correlation between PTSD and personality disorders cannot be inferred.

Research has also suggested that there may be a connection between childhood trauma and personality disorders (Johnson, Cohen, Brown, Smailes, & Bernstein, 1999; Paris, 1998). For example, Johnson and colleagues (1999) found that after controlling for age, parental education, parental psychopathology, and other abuse, individuals with documented childhood abuse were more than four times likely to be diagnosed with a personality disorder than those who did not have a history of abuse or neglect. In this study, sexual abuse was associated with higher symptom levels of histrionic, depressive, and borderline personality disorders, and physical abuse was associated with higher symptom levels of antisocial, passive-aggressive, schizotypal, and borderline personality disorders.

Indeed, a number of researchers have suggested a strong relationship between PTSD and borderline personality disorder (Gunderson & Sabo, 1993). Research has suggested that borderline personality disorder often has trauma involved with its etiology. Perhaps both PTSD and borderline personality disorder are caused in part by traumatic events.

Johnson and colleagues (1999) also found that neglect, which by definition is considered the absence of an action and is not considered a traumatic event, was also associated with higher symptom levels of avoidant, dependent, narcissistic, passive-aggressive, schizotypal, antisocial, and borderline personality disorders. These findings suggest that PTSD may contribute to the development of certain personality disorders, but it may not be the cause. Indeed, not all people who are diagnosed with borderline personality disorder have a trauma history (Gunderson & Sabo, 1993; Paris, 1998). It is likely that traumatic experiences are not a sole cause of borderline personality disorder and that other, perhaps more important factors also contribute to the development of any personality disorder. Further research is needed to elucidate these factors.

EPIDEMIOLOGY

According to *DSM-IV* (American Psychiatric Association, 1994), lifetime prevalence rates of PTSD range from 1 percent to 14 percent for adults in the general population. Less is known about the occurrence of PTSD in children who have been traumatized. One study examining adolescents from the general population reported that 1 percent of boys and 3 percent of girls met full *DSM-IV* criteria for PTSD (Cuffe et al., 1998). Prevalence rates of PTSD are much higher for children who have experienced trauma as compared to the general population. Conservative estimates indicate that 30 percent of children exposed to traumatic events will develop PTSD (Perry, 1999). These rates vary depending on the methodology used to assess PTSD and the type of trauma experienced. Though little epidemiological data is available regarding the prevalence rates of PTSD in children and adolescents, the occurrence of PTSD is clearly more likely in youth exposed to life-threatening trauma than in those whose lives are not threatened. For example, researchers reported the following rates of PTSD for specific trauma populations in their samples: 35 percent of adolescents diagnosed with cancer (Pelcovitz et al., 1998), 93 percent of children witnessing domestic violence (Kilpatrick & Williams, 1998), 50 percent of Cambodian adolescents exposed to severe trauma during war (Kinzie, Sack, Angell, & Manson, 1986), and 48 percent of children experiencing sexual abuse (McLeer, Deblinger, Atkins, Foa, & Ralphe, 1988). Studies have also provided support for the association between PTSD and child physical abuse (Ackerman, Newton, McPherson, Jones, & Dykman, 1998), with rates of PTSD ranging from 6.9 percent to 36 percent (Ackerman et al., 1998; Deblinger, McLeer, Atkins, Ralphe, & Foa, 1989). These statistics may even be an underestimate given the difficulty of diagnosing PTSD in young children, as well as the fact that children in the samples who met partial criteria for PTSD were not included in the calculation of PTSD rates.

Demographic variables, such as gender and ethnicity, may also be associated with PTSD. In adult samples, research has indicated that women are 2.42 times more likely than men to develop PTSD, even after those experiencing sexual trauma were excluded from the sample (Stein, Walker, & Forde, 2000). Research findings are variable as to whether gender has a differential effect on PTSD rates in children. Some studies have suggested that more females than males develop PTSD, but other investigations have not replicated these findings (American Academy of Child and Adolescent Psychiatry, 1998).

ETIOLOGY

Several theoretical models have been proposed to conceptualize the development and maintenance of PTSD in children. Early psychoanalytic theories postulated that unresolved conflicts from early childhood or infancy are reactivated when a traumatic event is experienced (Kaplan & Sadock, 1991). From this viewpoint, children who experience psychogenic amnesia may be defending against painful experiences by blocking them out and may be less aware of the distress related to the trauma they are experiencing (cf. Freud, 1959; Terr, 1991; van der Kolk, 1984). Freud (1948) describes the behavioral manifestation of this unresolved unconscious conflict as the repetition compulsion, when victims repeatedly play out traumatic themes in an effort to master the trauma.

The two-factor learning theory (Mowrer, 1960), based on behavioral principles, is one of the most widely used conceptual models of PTSD and emphasizes the role of classical and operant conditioning in explaining PTSD-related behaviors and symptoms. Through classical conditioning, a child learns a fearful response (or conditioned response), such as avoidance, to previously neutral stimuli (e.g., the basement) when the neutral stimuli are repeatedly paired with an anxiety-provoking or traumatic event (e.g., the child's brother fondling the child). The basement, a conditioned stimulus, elicits the fear. The fearful response is maintained through operant conditioning when a child's avoidant behavior is reinforced by a reduction in the child's fear, which in turn increases the likelihood of the child avoiding the conditioned stimulus (the basement) in the future. The PTSD-related fearful response may also generalize to other neutral stimuli (e.g., males, males with black hair, basements in all houses).

Though classical and operant conditioning explains the development of PTSD, contemporary learning theorists, such as Hayes, Follette, and Follette (1996), discuss the role of environmental contingencies in the maintenance of abuse-related and general behavior problems. For example, parents may inadvertently reinforce fears and PTSD-related behaviors, such as avoidance, in their children. The findings of a recent investigation (Deblinger, Steer, & Lippmann, 1999), in fact, demonstrated that sexually abused children exhibited higher levels of PTSD symptoms and acting-out behaviors when they perceived their parents as using psychologically controlling or anxiety- or guilt-provoking appeals to influence the children's behavior (e.g., "Someday you'll be sorry you didn't behave better").

Given the association of PTSD symptoms with self-blame and negative beliefs in traumatized children (Brown & Kolko, 1999; Feiring et al., 1998; Runyon & Kenny, 2002), many researchers have gone beyond a pure behavioral model and have highlighted the need to include cognitions as an important element of PTSD conceptual models (Deblinger & Heflin, 1996; Kolko & Swenson, 2002; Runyon, Deblinger, Ryan, & Thakkar-Kolar, 2004). Some of these models include emotional processing theory (see Foa & Rothbaum, 1998) and overaccommodation (Resick & Schnicke, 1992). Detailed reviews of these conceptual models are available (see Foa & Rothbaum, 1998; Rothbaum, Meadows, Resick, & Foy, 2000).

Cognitive theory (Beck, 1970) operates from the underlying tenet that faulty cognitions and beliefs about the self, world, and future can contribute to the development of symptoms. More recent theorists such as Janoff-Bulman and Frieze (1983) attribute trauma reactions and feelings of helplessness and hopelessness to changes in cognitive schemata associated with a sense of loss of personal safety, meaning, and available options. When a child experiences a traumatic event, his or her schemas and basic assumptions about personal safety, self-worth, and the environment can be altered. These negative beliefs about self, world, and future may trigger underlying dysfunctional schemata that have been ingrained throughout childhood and predispose the child to PTSD. For example, a child's negative assumptions about herself, the world, and her future may have been shaped by her inconsistent and nonsupportive family environment. She was physically abused and emotionally berated by her father, which further reinforced her negative self-statements and feelings of worthlessness and self-blame. She also experienced significant losses (i.e., separation from her father, perceived betrayal by her siblings) that she seemed to misinterpret as more evidence of her being a worthless person, which in turn contributed to her posttrauma symptoms. Her schema of the world as a predictable and safe place may further be altered by her experiences of physical abuse, inconsistent parenting, and neglect. Her schemas and basic assumptions about personal safety, self-worth, and self-blame predisposed her to PTSD. She believes that she had done something wrong and deserved to be abused by her father. Her feelings of guilt and worthlessness were reinforced as she began to blame herself for the abuse (trauma) she had endured. In addition, she learned that she is unable to control events in her life. Symptoms of PTSD in response to this loss of control associated with trauma is not uncommon in children. This conceptualization highlights the important need to address children's faulty cognitions, in conjunction with the behavioral manifestations of the disorder, in treatment.

COURSE, COMPLICATIONS, AND PROGNOSIS

The course of PTSD is variable. In some childhood cases, PTSD symptoms may be present in a few days or weeks following exposure to a traumatic event and persist for years or months. For many children, PTSD symptoms dissipate over time, whereas others experience chronic trauma-related symptoms. For instance, a sample of children who were kidnapped and buried alive continued to suffer posttrauma symptoms at the four-year follow-up (Terr, 1984). Not only can symptoms be experienced for years, but the child's proximity to the traumatic event can impact the length of time that symptoms persist. Of 159 children ages 5–13, assessed one month after witnessing a fatal sniper attack on a school playground, 77 percent who were on the playground and 67 percent who watched from the school building met criteria for PTSD (Pynoos et al., 1987). At follow-up 14 months after exposure to trauma, almost all of the children (74 percent) who were on the playground continued to exhibit PTSD, whereas only 19 percent who were in the school continued to be symptomatic (Nader, Pynoos, Fairbanks, & Frederick, 1990). Other longitudinal studies examining the course of PTSD symptoms have produced varying results. (For a thorough review, see the American Academy of Child and Adolescent Psychiatry, 1998.)

ASSESSMENT AND DIAGNOSIS

Diagnostic Criteria for PTSD

Post-traumatic stress disorder is the only diagnostic category that requires an etiological agent to be present for diagnosis—an identified traumatic event. According to *DSM-IV* diagnostic specifications (American Psychiatric Association, 1994), the individual must have been exposed to a traumatic event that involved experiencing, witnessing, or confronting actual or threatened death, serious injury, or threat to the physical integrity of self or others that resulted in the individual responding with intense fear, helplessness, or horror. In children, these feelings may be depicted by disorganized or agitated behavior. This anxiety disorder is classified by symptom clusters of reexperiencing, avoidance, and hyperarousal following exposure to a traumatic event. One reexperiencing symptom, three avoidance or numbing symptoms, and two symptoms of hyperarousal must be present for the affected person to meet the diagnostic criteria for PTSD.

Specifically, the trauma is reexperienced in at least one of the following ways: (1) having recurrent, intrusive memories of the trauma; (2) having recurrent nightmares about the event; (3) reliving the experience through dissociation or flashbacks; and (4) experiencing intense distress or physiological reactivity provoked by exposure to situations symbolic of or similar to the event. In addition to these symptoms, children may engage in repetitive trauma-related play, reenact the trauma, and experience nightmares that may not be about the traumatic event.

Other symptoms include avoidance of trauma-related stimuli and numbing of general responsiveness as well as hyperarousal (e.g., sleep disturbance, irritability, difficulty concentrating, hypervigilance, exaggerated startle response). Duration of symptom presentation must be greater than one month and must impair daily functioning. Recent diagnostic criteria for PTSD has placed greater emphasis on duration of symptoms by specifying acute or chronic. Acute is specified when the symptoms have persisted for a duration of less than three months, whereas chronic is specified when symptoms have persisted for three months or longer. In *DSM-IV* a second diagnosis, acute stress disorder, is incorporated to illustrate the brief symptom picture once thought to be the predominant posttrauma course.

Assessing PTSD Symptoms in Children and Adolescents

The assessment of PTSD symptoms to determine whether a child meets the aforementioned criteria is a complex, multifaceted process that begins with establishing that the child or adolescent was exposed to a traumatic event. It is good practice for the assessor to conduct extensive interviews about the history of traumatic events with both the child and the caregiver, as well as to gather all documented information, including medical records, police reports, and reports from eyewitnesses (Perrin, Smith, & Yule, 2000) to aid in the verification of the traumatic event.

The next step in the assessment process is to ascertain whether the child is experiencing the requisite number of reexperiencing, avoidant, and hyperarousal symptoms. Unfortunately, there is no specific instrument for determining PTSD (Cohen et al., 2000). As such, it is necessary to use a multimethod approach that includes parent-report instruments, self-report instruments, semistructured interviews, psychophysiological assessments, or a combination of these in conjunction with observations of the child and any other documented information that may aid in the diagnosis. For children younger than five years of age, it is critical to obtain parent reports of symptoms (LaGreca, 2001). School-age children and adolescents are likely the best reporters of their own symptomatology, given that research has documented that caregivers may underestimate PTSD symptoms in children (LaGreca, 2001). To make the best possible diagnostic assessment, it is preferable to use a multimodal assessment to gather information from multiple sources (e.g., child, parent, teacher) when assessing trauma-related symptoms. Some of the standardized measures are described in the next section; however, it is beyond the scope of this chapter to list all the measures that are currently available to assess PTSD in children and adolescents. See Ohan, Myers, and Collett

(2002) for a more comprehensive review of available instruments for the assessment of PTSD.

Self-Administered Instruments

Parent Report

Several parent-report measures are available to elicit the parent or caregiver's observations regarding the child's PTSD symptoms. These include the Parent Report of Post-Traumatic Symptoms (PROPS; Greenwald & Rubin, 1999), the Parent Report of Children's Reaction to Stress (Fletcher, 1996a), and the PTSD Checklist Parent Report on Child (PCL-PR; Ford & Thomas, 2000). These measures assess *DSM-IV* diagnostic criteria for PTSD.

Child Report

Numerous self-report instruments have been developed to assess PTSD-related symptoms, but a majority of these are not diagnostic. For example, the Trauma Symptom Checklist for Children (TSCC; Briere, 1996) is a 54-item self-report measure designed to assess symptoms related to traumatic experiences, such as avoidance, numbing, nightmares, and intrusive thinking, in children ages 8–16 years. The child chooses from a Likert rating scale to indicate how often he or she experiences each of the symptoms.

The Children's Impact of Traumatic Events Scale—Revised (CITES-R; Wolfe, Gentile, Michienzi, Sas, & Wolfe, 1991) is a 78-item self-report measure that assesses PTSD features (i.e., intrusive thoughts, avoidance, hyperarousal, and sexual anxiety), social reactions (i.e., social support), and attributions about abuse (e.g., self-blame, personal vulnerability) associated with child sexual abuse. Though the CITES-R is potentially a useful tool for assessing PTSD-related symptomatology, it is limited in that it assesses only PTSD related to sexual abuse in children who have previously been identified as experiencing sexual abuse. Questions are specific to the previously identified perpetrator of the abuse. For example, the child is asked to respond to the statement "(*Perpetrator's name*) was to blame for what happened" with one of three replies: very true, somewhat true, or not true.

The Child Report of Post-Traumatic Symptoms (CROPS; Greenwald & Rubin, 1999) is another self-report measure that assesses trauma-related symptoms but does not yield a diagnosis.

A number of self-report measures do assist in the diagnosis of PTSD in children. One example of such an instrument is the When Bad Things Happen Scale (WBTH; Fletcher, 1997b), a measure that assesses *DSM-IV* and *DSM-III-R* PTSD criteria in children age eight and older.

Another self-report measure of PTSD in children is the Child PTSD Symptom Scale (CPSS; Foa, Johnson, Feeny, & Treadwell, 2001). This relatively new measure provides a PTSD symptom severity score by assessing all of the PTSD symptoms in the three symptom clusters as well as providing an assessment of functional impairment. A preliminary examination of this instrument's psychometric properties suggests that the CPSS is a useful instrument for the assessment of PTSD in children ages 8–18 (Foa et al., 2001). However, further research is needed to determine the reliability and validity of the measure.

Clinician-Administered Scales

To improve diagnostic accuracy, a semistructured interview that elicits *DSM* PTSD symptoms for the child from both the parent and the child is recommended (Perrin et al., 2000). One such semistructured interview is the Schedule for Affective Disorders and Schizophrenia for School-Aged Children—Present and Lifetime Version—PTSD Section (K-SADS-PL PTSD; Kaufman et al., 1997). The K-SADS can be used with children ages 6–18 years and provides data on the presence but not the severity of symptoms. The child and the caregiver are interviewed separately by a single interviewer, who records their responses on a common answer sheet. During the interview, the interviewer obtains information regarding the child's experiences of the three symptom clusters. A summary of symptoms is generated from this information. This instrument has demonstrated good reliability (Kaufman et al., 1997).

Both the Diagnostic Interview Schedule for Children (DISC; Costello, Edelbrock, Dulcan, Kalis, & Klaric, 1984) and the Diagnostic Interview for Children and Adolescents (DICA; Welner, Reich, Herjanic, Jung, & Amado, 1987) include supplemental questions for assessing PTSD (PTSD Supplemental Module for the DISC-2.1; Fisher & Kranzler, 1990). However, Lipovsky (1992) suggests that questions regarding identification of occurrence of a traumatic event are weak and specific to physical or sexual abuse.

The Post-Traumatic Stress Disorder Reaction Index (PTSD-RI; Frederick, 1985, 1986; Pynoos et al., 1987) is administered by the clinician and consists of 20-items that assess the child's reactions to a traumatic event. The original version was not diagnostic in nature, but scores in the moderate to severe distress range did correlate highly with PTSD diagnoses in children. More recently, the UCLA PTSD-RI (Pynoos, Rodriguez, Steinberg, Stuber, & Frederick, 1998) revised the semistructured interview, which currently includes a section to elicit history of traumatic events and questions to assess all *DSM-IV* diagnostic criteria. Child, adolescent, and parent versions are available (Pynoos et al., 1998).

The Diagnostic Interview Schedule—PTSD (Garrison et al., 1995) and the Childhood PTSD Interview—Child Form (Fletcher, 1997a) are other examples of semistructured interviews that clinicians can use to assess PTSD symptomatology in children who have experienced trauma.

The Children's PTSD Inventory (CPTSDI) (Saigh et al., 2000) is a clinician-administered scale for children between the ages of 7 and 18 years. This relatively new scale was developed based on the *DSM-IV* PTSD diagnostic criteria and has demonstrated moderate to good reliability (Saigh et al., 2000). The instrument provides data on the presence as well as the severity of symptoms. One study conducted with a previous version of the CPTSDI (Saigh, 1989) as a screening device for PTSD in children demonstrated an 84 percent true positive hit rate (Saigh, 1989).

Psychophysiological Assessments

Psychophysiological assessment of the presence of PTSD symptoms is less dependent on the child's or the parent's report (Orr & Roth, 2000). Physiological measures include increased galvanic skin response, heart rate, and respiration. These measures can help validate self-reports and provide useful information with nonverbal children (Perrin & Yule, 2000). Other symptoms of PTSD that lend themselves to psychophysiological assessment include exaggerated startle and difficulty concentrating, two of the hallmarks of PTSD (Orr & Roth, 2000).

IMPACT ON ENVIRONMENT

Family

In addition to their emotional and behavioral impact on the child, PTSD symptoms can affect others involved in the child's life. Many of the symptoms of PTSD, particularly internalizing symptoms (e.g., intrusive thoughts, avoidance, restricted affect), are not highly disruptive to the environment. Thus, the family may be unaware of the difficulties a child may be experiencing. In fact, children and adolescents may suffer silently for months, sometimes years, before others become aware of their PTSD-related difficulties. Although PTSD symptoms can develop in the immediate aftermath of a traumatic experience (e.g., within the first 3 months), it is not unusual for symptoms to be delayed or episodic in their occurrence. Unfortunately, a delayed or episodic presentation also increases the likelihood that the difficulties will not be linked to the original trauma(s), thereby reducing the likelihood that a PTSD diagnosis will be made. Difficulties in sleeping and concentration, for example, are common symptoms of PTSD, but if they are not recognized as such, they may lead to deteriorating grades that family members, particularly parents, may attribute to laziness or attention problems. Clearly, such conclusions might lead parents to take actions that would be unlikely to result in improved grades if PTSD was actually the underlying cause.

On the other hand, some PTSD symptoms are highly disruptive and can create immediate difficulties in terms of a youngster's functioning at home. Distress related to PTSD may be triggered by trauma reminders (e.g., individuals who look like abusive perpetrators, weather reminiscent of the day of the disaster) that may lead to fear or avoidance responses, somatic symptoms, unexplained angry outbursts, or any combination of these. For example, Steiner, Garcia, and Matthews (1997) documented a high rate of externalizing disorders among victimized juvenile delinquents that they attributed to the loss of impulse control and diminished anger control that may be associated with PTSD. Specific to ongoing stressors such as physical abuse, Pelcovitz et al. (1994) hypothesized that externalizing symptoms in youth may initially emerge, followed by PTSD symptoms. Thus, those children who do not receive treatment that addresses their anger and PTSD may exhibit an ongoing and escalating pattern of aggressive behavior that impacts their relationships with family members and may place them at greater risk for revictimization (i.e., in cases of child physical abuse).

When a child exhibits ongoing PTSD-related emotional and behavioral problems (e.g., PTSD-related hyperarousal, fearfulness, aggressive behavior, or a combination of these), the parent may be likely to interpret these symptoms as noncompliance. This in turn may contribute to a negative cycle of parent-child interactions.

Fear of the dark or of being alone can lead to sleeping difficulties that can be highly disruptive to family relationships, particularly when children suffering PTSD refuse to sleep in their own beds. Though these difficulties often can be overcome with effective intervention within several weeks, untreated children can go on sleeping in their parents' beds for years at a time. Not only can this pattern lead to parental sleeping difficulties, but it can inadvertently create marital problems as well.

School

Symptoms of PTSD may also impact the child's functioning at school regardless of whether the traumatic event occurred on school property or outside the school. Following an assaultive experience in a school, PTSD-related avoidance symptoms can take the form of repeated visits to the school nurse or numerous unexplained school absences, despite the suspension of the perpetrator. Not only are such difficulties likely to impair school performance, but also they often strain the child's relationship with school personnel as struggles ensue around efforts to encourage school attendance. Children experiencing PTSD as a result of abusive experiences may also be particularly prone to overreact to seemingly threatening but innocuous interpersonal cues. Even when these difficulties are recognized as traumatic responses, a child's ability to interact effectively with school personnel may be greatly impaired. Interestingly, these difficulties often increase when parents' or teachers' responses are on either end of the spectrum from overly punishing to highly lenient.

Symptoms related to PTSD such as flashbacks and intrusive thoughts can contribute to concentration difficulties that impair a child's school performance. These difficulties frequently result in a child being misdiagnosed with attention-deficit/hyperactivity disorder. Unfortunately, the treatment offered does not address PTSD and the traumatic event frequently remains unidentified, leaving the child to suffer silently.

Peer Interactions

Children who experience trauma are at increased risk of victimizing others or being revictimized themselves. Those children who are exposed to violence frequently display aggressive behavior, poor social problem-solving skills and communication skills, and lower levels of empathy and sensitivity toward others (e.g., Dodge, Pettit, & Bates, 1994; Salzinger, Feldman, Hammer, & Rosario, 1993). Research has suggested that these externalizing difficulties are associated with PTSD (Pelcovitz et al., 1994; Steiner et al., 1997). Children exposed to violence may also be more likely than nonabused children to interpret interactions with peers as hostile (Dodge, Pettit, & Bates, 1990) and as such may be more likely to retaliate against their peers. This pattern of aggressive behavior exhibited by school-aged children tends to alienate them from social groups (Salinger et al., 1993). Without appropriate intervention, these behaviors may also escalate, as evidenced by studies demonstrating that exposure to violence has been associated with violent, criminal behavior in adolescents (Herrenkohl, Egolf, & Herrenkohl, 1997) and adults (Widom, 1989), abusive or coercive behaviors in dating relationships (Wolfe, Wekerle, Reitzel-Jaffe, & Lefebvre, 1998), and an increased risk for victimization during adulthood (Root & Fallon, 1988). Unfortunately, aggressive behavior associated with PTSD may impact a child's interpersonal relationships across all developmental stages.

As trauma-related cues become increasingly generalized (e.g., from men who look like the perpetrator to all men), it becomes difficult for youngsters to avoid all of the reminders that exist in their environment. Thus, they may resort to social isolation, substances use, or both to help them avoid the reminders and to dampen their emotional responses. Clearly, the longer that chronic PTSD goes unrecognized and untreated, the more likely it is for difficulties, like those described previously, to multiply. Ultimately, these difficulties tend to negatively impact all the environments in which children function. Sadly, as children's difficulties become more disruptive to their environments, the children may be more likely to be referred for psychotherapeutic interventions. However, too often, these services may target disruptive symptoms and behaviors as opposed to assessing and therapeutically addressing the underlying traumatic experience(s).

IMPLICATIONS FOR FUTURE PERSONALITY DEVELOPMENT

Exposure to a traumatic event can have an immediate emotional and behavioral impact on the child that is expressed by PTSD symptoms. These symptoms in turn can be associated with long-term personality traits in adulthood. The adult literature suggests that a relationship exists between PTSD and both neuroticism and extroversion. It suggests that there is a positive correlation with neuroticism (e.g., Fauerbach et al., 2000; Holeva & Tarrier, 2001; Schnurr & Vielhaur, 1999) and a negative correlation with extroversion (e.g., Davidson et al., 1987; Fauerbach et al., 2000; Nightingale & Williams, 2000; Schnurr & Vielhaur, 1999) and PTSD. Drawing conclusions about the development of PTSD and personality in children from research on adults is problematic (e.g., other factors may modify the relationship, such as developmental stages, coping mechanisms, and so forth).

Unfortunately, the literature on the relationship between general personality dimensions and PTSD in children is sparse. Because the key feature of neuroticism is highly emotional reactions to negative events and the criteria for being diagnosed with PTSD includes an experience of a traumatic event (definitely negative) combined with symptoms that include high distress at the reminder of the event, the correlation between neuroticism and development of PTSD could be expected in children as well. Individuals who have a high level of neuroticism may have a higher physiological reaction and are more likely to interpret a traumatic event in a more negative manner than those who have fewer neurotic characteristics (Paris, 2000).

Exploring the child literature for the relationship between PTSD and facets of neuroticism provides more empirical support for a relationship. Facets of the neuroticism construct include anxiety, depression, hostility, impulsiveness, self-consciousness, and vulnerability (Fauerbach et al., 2000).

Extroversion is the second personality factor that has been suggested to play a role in the development of PTSD. The adult literature suggests a strong negative correlation between extroversion and PTSD (Davidson et al., 1987; Fauerbach et al., 2000; Schnurr & Vielhaur, 1999). Although the children's PTSD literature has not examined the direct relationship between extroversion and PTSD, there is minimal support for the relationship when examining the social support in relation to extroversion and PTSD (Vernberg, LaGreca, Silverman, & Prinstein, 1996). It is possible given the correlations that children who are higher in extroversion are more likely to have social supports and, therefore, are less likely to develop PTSD symptoms.

There is little research that has implicated conscientiousness, agreeableness, or openness to experience in the development PTSD. However, given the paucity of PTSD and personality literature available with children, few conclusions regarding the presence or absence of their protective or risk status can be drawn. More research is needed to further illuminate the relationship between all personality factors and the development of PTSD.

TREATMENT IMPLICATIONS

Given the prevalence and potentially significant impact that PTSD can have on children's cognitive, emotional, behavioral, social, and personality development, the importance of early, effective intervention cannot be overstated. However, in the aftermath of traumatic experiences, some children and adults will not suffer PTSD or will experience PTSD-like symptoms that may spontaneously remit with the passage of time alone. Our ability to identify and understand the factors that lead to this type of natural resilience is only in its infancy. Still, this type of research may be critical to enhancing our success in reaching those more likely to suffer chronic PTSD. Unfortunately, children who continue to experience PTSD symptoms episodically or chronically in the aftermath of trauma may suffer a lifetime of difficulties that may impact many areas of their development and functioning.

The clinical literature examining the treatment of trauma-related difficulties in childhood and adolescence is quite rich with descriptions of interventions based on crisis intervention, psychodynamic, family systems, interpersonal, cognitive behavioral, and eclectic models of treatment (Deblinger & Heflin, 1996; Friedrich, 1995; Gil, 1991; Kolko, 1996; Pynoos & Nader, 1988; Runyon et al., 2004). Similarly, clinical reports have described the use of various medications for children suffering PTSD symptomatology (Famularo, Kadushin, & Fenton, 1988; Harmon & Riggs, 1996). However, with the exception of cognitive behavioral interventions, the psychosocial and psychopharmacological approaches described in the literature have not been extensively evaluated in terms of their efficacy from a scientific standpoint. In fact, to date there have been no rigorously controlled randomized trials evaluating the impact of psychiatric medications on the treatment of PTSD in children and adolescents. Thus, physicians must rely heavily on their clinical judgment in determining the appropriate use of psychotropic medications when treating children and adolescents exhibiting PTSD. It has been recommended, for example, that clinicians be well advised to prescribe psychiatric medications for youth experiencing PTSD (e.g., SSRIs, imipramine) based on the presence of comorbid conditions such as depression, anxiety, ADHD symptoms, or a combination of these (American Academy Child and Adolescent Psychiatry, 1998).

Several recent reviews of the empirical literature, particularly in terms of the psychological treatment of children who have endured abuse, have identified trauma-focused cognitive behavioral therapy (TF-CBT) as the treatment of choice for children experiencing PTSD and related difficulties (Saunders, Berliner, & Hanson, 2003; http://modelprograms.samhsa.gov). To date, over a dozen studies have examined cognitive behavioral interventions for children who have experienced a wide array of traumas including sexual abuse, physical abuse, natural disasters, and community violence. These studies have examined CBT interventions delivered via individual as well as group therapy and have taken place in clinics as well as school settings (Berliner & Saunders, 1996; Deblinger, McLeer, & Henry, 1990; Goenjian et al., 1997; March, Amaya-Jackson, Murray, & Schulte, 1998; Stauffer & Deblinger, 1999). The findings of a subset of these investigations that have used the most scientifically rigorous randomized controlled designs have been remarkably consistent (Cohen & Mannarino, 1996, 1998; Cohen, Deblinger, Mannarino, & Steer, 2004; Deblinger, Lippmann, & Steer, 1996; Deblinger, Stauffer, & Steer, 2001; King et al., 2000; Kolko, 1996). In sum, the results have not only documented the superior benefits of trauma-focused CBT as compared to alternative conditions including wait list, supportive counseling, client-centered and community treatment conditions, but the results have also revealed the beneficial impact of encouraging the involvement of parents whenever possible.

Trauma-focused CBT integrates trauma-sensitive interventions with cognitive behavioral strategies designed to assist parents and children in their efforts to cope with the traumas experienced. The initial stages of therapy are generally conducted with children and parents participating in individual sessions, with the goal of bringing them together for joint sessions that provide opportunities for parents and children to practice skills and communicate openly and more effectively about the trauma(s). These joint parent-child sessions generally occur during the second half of treatment, once parents are prepared to serve as more effective coping role models for their children. Trauma-focused CBT generally involves four overlapping phases of treatment, including the initial phase in which rapport is developed, treatment plans and rationales are explained, and collaborative therapy relationships are established. Next is the skill-building phase, in which the clinician encourages children and parents to develop and practice coping skills that will help them manage distress and also prepare them for the subsequent phases of therapy when they will be encouraged to focus on and explore thoughts and feelings related to the trauma(s) experienced. More specifically, during the skill-building phase modeling, behavioral rehearsal, praise, and corrective feedback are used to teach relaxation, emotional expression, and cognitive coping skills.

During the third phase, children and parents engage in trauma-focused work during which they are encouraged to participate in gradual exposure and processing exercises that help children work through the traumatic experience(s) suffered. This CBT component, designed to target PTSD symptoms, involves gradual imaginal or in vivo exposure, or both, to anxiety-provoking stimuli (e.g., memories, thoughts, innocuous reminders) in the context of a supportive, therapeutic environment (Cohen, Deblinger, & Mannarino, 2004; Deblinger & Heflin, 1996; Kolko & Swenson, 2002; Runyon et al., 2004). With children, exposure exercises most frequently take the form of sharing trauma memories through the development of narratives, drawings, or doll play, or any combination of these, that describe or depict the details of the traumatic experiences as well as associated thoughts and feelings. In addition, parents may assist with in vivo exposure homework assignments, for example, by encouraging positive play activities in the otherwise safe place (e.g., the basement) where the trauma may have occurred. With repeated exposure to trauma-related memories, thoughts, and other reminders, the intensity of children's conditioned emotional responses are expected to diminish, thus allowing children to more comfortably reveal and process dysfunctional trauma/abuse-related thoughts and worries. The identification and correction of developing dysfunctional beliefs about one's self, one's relationships, and the world in general may have the most significant implications for children's long-term emotional well-being. The final phase of therapy incorporates psychoeducation, personal safety skill and relapse-prevention activities designed to prepare clients for termination while ensuring that they will use the skills and knowledge they have gained beyond the termination of treatment. Studies of CBT that have incorporated follow-up assessments have documented the maintenance of symptom improvements over one- and two-year follow-up periods, respectively (Cohen & Mannarino, 1997; Deblinger et al., 1999).

Interestingly, regardless of their theoretical underpinnings, many of the treatment models described in the clinical literature and widely used in community settings incorporate some of the same basic components that are included in the more rigorously tested CBT approaches. It is particularly noteworthy that authors representing a wide array of theoretical orientations have suggested that some type of trauma-focused discussion or working-through activity is central to effective treatment with this population (Benedek, 1985; Friedrich, 1996; Pynoos & Nader, 1988; Terr, 1991). Some researchers have suggested that trauma-focused CBT provides the structure, skills, and guidelines for engaging children and parents in trauma-focused work in a time-limited, cost-effective manner.

REFERENCES

Ackerman, P. T., Newton, J. E. O., McPherson, W. B., Jones, J. G., & Dykman, R. A. (1998). Prevalence of posttraumatic stress disorder and other psychiatric diagnoses in three groups of abused children (sexual, physical, and both). *Child Abuse & Neglect, 22,* 759–774.

Ahadi, S. A., Rothbart, M. K., & Ye, R. (1993). Children's temperament in the US and China: Similarities and differences. *European Journal of Personality, 7,* 359–377.

Amaya-Jackson, L., & March, J. S. (1995). Post-traumatic stress disorder. In J. March (Ed.), *Anxiety disorders in children and adolescents* (pp. 276–300). New York: Guilford Press.

American Academy of Child and Adolescent Psychiatry. (1998). Practice parameters for the assessment and treatment of children and adolescents with posttraumatic stress disorder. *Journal of the American Academy of Child and Adolescent Psychiatry, 37,* 4–26.

American Psychiatric Association. (1952). *Diagnostic and statistical manual of mental disorders.* Washington, DC: Author.

American Psychiatric Association. (1968). *Diagnostic and statistical manual of mental disorders* (2nd ed.). Washington, DC: Author.

American Psychiatric Association. (1980). *Diagnostic and statistical manual of mental disorders* (3rd ed.). Washington, DC: Author.

American Psychiatric Association. (1987). *Diagnostic and statistical manual of mental disorders—Revised* (3rd ed., rev.). Washington, DC: Author.

American Psychiatric Association. (1994). *Diagnostic and statistical manual of mental disorders* (4th ed.). Washington, DC: Author

American Psychiatric Association. (2000). *Diagnostic and statistical manual of mental disorders* (4th ed., text rev.). Washington, DC: Author

Asarnow, J., Glynn, S., Pynoos, R. S., Guthrie, D., Cantwell, D. P., & Franklin, B. (1999). When the earth stops shaking: Earthquake sequelae among children diagnosed for pre-earthquake psychopathology. *Journal of the American Academy of Child and Adolescent Psychiatry, 38,* 1016–1023.

Beck, A. T. (1970). Cognitive therapy: Nature and relation to behavior therapy. *Behavior Therapy, 1,* 184–200.

Beck, J. S. (1995). *Cognitive therapy.* New York: Guilford Press.

Benedek, E. P. (1985). Children and psychic trauma: A brief review of contemporary thinking. In S. Eth & R. S. Pynoos (Eds.), *Posttraumatic stress disorder in children* (pp. 1–16). Washington, DC: American Psychiatric Press.

Berliner, L., & Saunders, B. (1996). Treating fear and anxiety in sexually abused children: Results of a controlled 2-year follow-up study. *Child Maltreatment, 1,* 294–309.

Blais, M. A., Hilsenroth, M. J., & Castlebury, F. D. (1997). Content validity of the *DSM-IV* borderline and narcissistic personality disorder criteria sets. *Comprehensive Psychiatry, 38,* 31–37.

Bramsen, I., van der Ploeg, H. M., van der Kamp, L. J., & Ader, H. J. (2002). Exposure to traumatic war events and neuroticism: The mediating role of attributing meaning. *Personality and Individual Differences, 32,* 747–760.

Breslau, N., Davis, G. C., & Andreski, P. (1995). Risk factors for PTSD-related traumatic events: A prospective analysis. *American Journal of Psychiatry, 152,* 529–535.

Briere, J. (1996). *The Trauma Symptom Checklist for Children (TSCC), professional manual.* Odessa, FL: Psychological Assessment Resources.

Brown, E. J., & Kolko, D. J. (1999). Child victims' attributions about being physically abused: An examination of factors associated with symptom severity. *Journal of Abnormal Child Psychology, 27,* 311–322.

Cohen, J. A., Berliner, L., & Mannarino, A. (2000). Treating traumatized children: A research review and synthesis. *Trauma, Violence, and Abuse, 1,* 29–46.

Cohen, J. A., Deblinger, E., & Mannarino, A. P. (2004). Trauma-focused cognitive behavioral therapy for sexually abused children. *Psychiatric Times, 21,* 52–53.

Cohen, J. A., Deblinger, E., Mannarino, A. P., & Steer, R. (2004). A multi-site, randomized controlled trial for children with sexabuse-related PTSD symptoms. *Journal of the American Academy of Child and Adolescent Psychiatry, 43,* 393–402.

Cohen, J. A., & Mannarino A. P. (1996). A treatment outcome study for sexually abused preschooler children: Initial findings. *Journal of the American Academy of Child and Adolescent Psychiatry, 35,* 42–50.

Cohen, J. A., & Mannarino A. P. (1997). A treatment study of sexually abused preschool children: Outcome during one year follow-up. *Journal of the American Academy of Child and Adolescent Psychiatry, 36,* 1228–1235.

Cohen, J. A., & Mannarino A. P. (1998). Interventions for sexually abused children: Initial treatment findings. *Child Maltreatment, 3,* 17–26.

Costello, A. J., Edelbrock, C. S., Dulcan, M. K., Kalis, R., & Klaric, S. H. (1984). *Report on the NIMH Diagnostic Interview Schedule for Children (DISC).* Washington, DC: National Institute of Mental Health.

Costello, E. J., Erkanli, A., Fairbank, J. A., & Angold, A. (2002). The prevalence of potentially traumatic events in childhood and adolescents. *Journal of Traumatic Stress, 15,* 99–112.

Davidson, J., Kudler, H., & Smith, R. (1987). Personality in chronic post-traumatic stress disorder: A study of the Eysenck Inventory. *Journal of Anxiety Disorders, 1,* 295–300.

De Bellis, M. D., Baum, A. S., Birmaher, B., Keshavan, M. S., Eccard, C. H., Boring, A. M., et al. (1999). Developmental traumatology. Part I: Biological stress systems. *Biological Psychiatry, 45,* 1259–1270.

Deblinger, E., & Heflin, A. (1996). *Treating sexually abused children and their non-offending parents: A cognitive-behavioral approach.* Thousand Oaks, CA: Sage.

Deblinger, E., Lippmann, J., & Steer, R. (1996). Sexually abused children suffering posttraumatic stress symptoms: Initial treatment outcome findings. *Child Maltreatment, 1,* 310–321.

Deblinger, E., McLeer, S., Atkins, M. S., Ralphe, D., & Foa, E. (1989). Post-traumatic stress in sexually abused, physically abused, and non-abused children. *Child Abuse & Neglect, 13,* 403–408.

Deblinger, E., McLeer, S. V., & Henry, D. E. (1990). Cognitive/behavioral treatment for sexually abused children suffering posttraumatic stress: Preliminary findings. *Journal of the American Academy of Child and Adolescent Psychiatry, 29,* 747–752.

Deblinger, E., Stauffer, L. B., & Steer, R. (2001). Comparative efficacies of supportive and cognitive-behavioral group therapies for young children who have been sexually abused and their non-offending mothers. *Child Maltreatment, 6,* 332–343.

Deblinger, E., Steer, B., & Lippmann, J. (1999). Maternal factors associated with sexually abused children's psychosocial adjustment. *Child Maltreatment, 4,* 13–20.

Dodge, K. A., Pettit, G. S., & Bates, J. E. (1990). Mechanisms in the cycle of violence. *Science, 250,* 1678–1683.

Dodge, K. A., Pettit, G. S., & Bates, J. E. (1994). Effects of physical maltreatment on the development of peer relations. *Development and Psychopathology, 6,* 43–55.

Everson, M. D., Hunter, W. M., Runyan, D. K., Edelson, G. A., & Coulter, M. L. (1989). Maternal support following disclosure of incest. *American Journal of Orthopsychiatry, 59,* 197–207.

Famularo, R., Kadushin, C., & Fenton, T. (1988). Propranolol treatment for childhood posttraumatic stress after two years. *American Journal Diseases of Children, 142,* 1244–1247.

Fauerbach, J. A., Lawrence, J. W., Schmidt, C. W., Munster, A. M., & Costa, P. T. (2000). Personality predictors of injury-related posttraumatic stress disorder. *Journal of Nervous and Mental Disease, 188,* 510–517.

Feiring, C., Taska, L. S., & Lewis, M. (1998). The role of shame and attributional style in children's and adolescents' adaptation to sexual abuse. *Child Maltreatment, 3,* 129–142.

Fisher, P., & Kranzler, E. (1990). *Post-traumatic stress disorder: Supplemental module for the DISC-2.1.* New York: New York State Psychiatric Institute.

Fletcher, K. (1996a). Psychometric review of the Parent Report of Child's Reaction to Stress. In B. H. Stamm (Ed.), *Measurement of stress, trauma, and adaptation* (pp. 225–227). Lutherville, MD: Sidran Press.

Fletcher, K. E. (1996b). Childhood posttraumatic stress disorder. In E. J. Mash & R. A. Barkley (Eds.), *Child psychopathology.* (pp. 242–276). New York: Guilford Press.

Fletcher, K. (1997a). Childhood PTSD Interview—Child Form. In E. B. Carlson (Ed.), *Trauma assessments: A clinician's guide* (pp. 248–250). New York: Guilford Press.

Fletcher, K. (1997b). When Bad Things Happen Scale. In E. B. Carlson (Ed.), *Trauma assessments: A clinician's guide* (pp. 257–259). New York: Guilford Press.

Foa, E. B., Johnson, K. M., Feeny, N. C., & Treadwell, K. R. H. (2001). The child PTSD symptom scale: A preliminary examination of its psychometric properties. *Journal of Clinical Child Psychology, 3,* 376–384.

Foa, E. B., & Rothbaum, B. O. (1998). *Treating the trauma of rape: Cognitive-behavioral therapy for PTSD.* New York: Guilford Press.

Ford, J. D., & Thomas, J. (2000). Child maltreatment, other trauma exposure, and posttraumatic symptomatology among children with oppositional defiant and attention deficit hyperactivity disorders. *Child Maltreatment, 5,* 205–217.

Frederick, C. (1985). Selected foci in the spectrum of posttraumatic stress disorders. In J. Laube & S. A. Murray (Eds.), *Perspectives on disaster recovery* (pp. 110–130). East Norwalk, CT: Appleton.

Freud, S. (1948). Inhibitions, symptoms, and anxiety. In J. Strachey (Ed.), *The standard edition of the complete psychological works of Sigmund Freud* (pp. 87–174). London: Hogarth.

Freud, S. (1959). Beyond the pleasure principle. In J. Strachey (Ed.), *The standard edition of the complete psychological works of Sigmund Freud* (Vol. 18, pp. 7–64). London: Hogarth.

Friedrich, W. N. (1995). *Psychotherapy with sexually abused boys: An integrated approach.* Thousand Oaks, CA: Sage.

Friedrich, W. N. (1996). An integrated model of psychotherapy for abused children. In J. Briere, L. Berliner, J. A. Bulkley, C. Jenny, & T. Reid (Eds.), *The APSAC handbook on child maltreatment* (pp. 104–118). Thousand Oaks, CA: Sage.

Garrison, C. Z., Bryant, E. S., Addy, C. L., Spurrier, P. G., Freedy, J. R., & Kilpatrick, D. G. (1995). Posttraumatic stress disorder in adolescents after Hurricane Andrew. *Journal of the American Academy of Child and Adolescent Psychiatry, 34,* 1193–1201.

Gil, E. (1991). *The healing power of play: Working with abused children.* New York: Guilford Press.

Goenjian, A. K., Karayan, I., Pynoos, R. S., Minassian, D., Najarian, L. M., Steinberg, A. M., et al. (1997). Outcome of psychotherapy among early adolescents after trauma. *American Journal of Psychiatry, 154,* 536–542.

Green, B. L., Lindy, J. D., & Grace, M. C. (1985). Post-traumatic stress disorder toward *DSM-IV. Journal of Nervous and Mental Disease, 7,* 406–411.

Greenwald, R., & Rubin, A. (1999). Assessment of posttraumatic symptoms in children: Development and preliminary validation of parent and child scales. *Research on Social Work Practice, 9,* 61–75.

Gunderson, J. G., & Sabo, A. N. (1993). The phenomenological and conceptual interface between borderline personality disorder and PTSD. *American Journal of Psychiatry, 150,* 19–27.

Harmon, R. J., & Riggs, P. D. (1996). Clonidine for posttraumatic stress disorder in preschool children. *Journal of the American Academy of Child and Adolescent Psychiatry, 35,* 1247–1249.

Hayes, S. C., Follette, W. C., & Follette, V. M. (1996). Behavior therapy: A contextual approach. In A. S. Gurman & S. B. Messer (Eds.), *Essential psychotherapies: Theory and practice* (pp. 128–181). New York: Guilford Press.

Herrenkohl, R. C., Egolf, B. P., & Herrenkohl, E. C. (1997). Preschool antecedents of adolescent assaultive behavior: A longitudinal study. *American Journal of Orthopsychiatry, 67,* 422–432.

Holeva, V., & Tarrier, N. (2001). Personality and peritraumatic dissociation in the prediction of PTSD in victims of road traffic accidents. *Journal of Psychosomatic Research, 51,* 687–692.

Janoff-Bulman, R., & Frieze, I. H. (1983). A theoretical perspective for understanding reactions to victimization. *Journal of Social Issues, 39,* 1–17.

Johnson, J. G., Cohen, P., Brown, J., Smailes, E., & Bernstein, D. P. (1999). Childhood maltreatment increases risk for personality disorders during early adulthood. *Archives of General Psychiatry, 56,* 600–606.

Kaplan, H. I., & Sadock, B. J. (1991). *Synopsis of psychiatry* (6th ed.). Baltimore: Williams & Wilkins.

Kaufman, J., Birmaher, B., Brent, D., Rao, U., Flynn, C, Moreci, P., et al. (1997). Schedule for Affective Disorders and Schizophrenia for School-Age Children—Present and Lifetime Version (K-SADS-PL): Initial reliability and validity data. *Journal of the American Academy of Child and Adolescent Psychiatry, 36,* 980–988.

Kilpatrick, K. L., & Williams, L. M. (1998). Potential mediators of posttraumatic stress disorder in child witnesses to domestic violence. *Child Abuse & Neglect, 22,* 319–330.

King, N., Tonge, B. J., Mullen, P., Myerson, N., Heyne, D., Rollings, S., et al. (2000). Treating sexually abused children with posttraumatic stress symptoms: A randomized clinical trial. *Journal of the American Academy of Child and Adolescent Psychiatry, 59,* 1347–1355.

Kinzie, J. D., Sack, W., Angell, R., & Manson, S. (1986). The psychiatric effects of massive trauma on Cambodian children. Part I. The children. *Journal of the American Academy of Child and Adolescent Psychiatry, 25,* 370–376.

Kolko, D. J. (1996). Individual cognitive-behavioral treatment and family therapy for physically abused children and their offending parents: A comparison of clinical outcomes. *Child Maltreatment, 1,* 322–342.

Kolko, D. J., & Swenson, C. C. (2002). *Assessing and treating physically abused children and their families: A cognitive-behavioral approach.* Thousand Oaks, CA: Sage.

LaGreca, A. M. (2001). Children experiencing disasters: Prevention and intervention. In J. N. Hughes (Ed.), *Handbook of psychological services for children and adolescents* (pp. 195–222). New York: Oxford University Press.

LaGreca, A. M., Silverman, W. K., & Wasserstein, S. B. (1998). Children's predisaster functioning as a predictor of posttraumatic stress following Hurricane Andrew. *Journal of Consulting and Clinical Psychology, 66,* 883–892.

Leitenberg, H., Greenwald, E., & Cado, S. (1992). A retrospective study of long-term methods of coping with having been sexually abused during childhood. *Child Abuse & Neglect, 16,* 399–407.

Lipovsky, J. A. (1992). Assessment and treatment of post-traumatic stress disorder in child survivors of sexual assault. In D. W. Foy (Ed.), *Treating PTSD: Cognitive-behavioral strategies* (pp. 127–164). New York: Guilford Press.

Lonigan, C. J., Shannon, M. P., Taylor, C. M., Finch, A. J., & Sallee, F. R. (1994). Children exposed to disaster: II. Risk factors for the development of post-traumatic symptomatology. *Journal of the American Academy of Child and Adolescent Psychiatry, 33,* 94–105.

March, J. S., Amaya-Jackson, L., Murray, M. C., & Schulte, A. (1998). Cognitive-behavioral psychotherapy for children and adolescents with posttraumatic stress disorder after a single-incident stressor. *Journal of the American Academy of Child and Adolescent Psychiatry, 37,* 585–593.

McCrae, R. R., & Costa, P. T. (1987). Validation of the five-factor model across instruments and observers. *Journal of Personality and Social Psychology, 49,* 710–727.

McLeer, S. V., Deblinger, E., Atkins, M. S., Foa, E. B., & Ralphe, D. L. (1988). Post-traumatic stress disorder in sexually abused children. *Journal of the American Academy of Child and Adolescent Psychiatry, 27,* 650–654.

Mowrer, O. A. (1960). *Learning theory and behavior.* New York: Wiley.

Nader, K., Pynoos, R. S., Fairbanks, L., & Frederick, C. (1990). Children's post-traumatic stress disorder reactions one year after a sniper attack at their school. *American Journal of Psychiatry, 147,* 1526–1530.

Nightingale, J., & Williams, R. M. (2000). Attitudes to emotional expression and personality in predicting post-traumatic stress disorder. *British Journal of Clinical Psychology, 39,* 243–254.

Ohan, J. L., Myers, K., & Collett, B. R. (2002). Ten-year review of rating scales. IV: Scales assessing trauma and its effects. *Journal of the American Academy of Child and Adolescent Psychiatry, 41,* 1401–1422.

Orr, S. P., & Roth, W. T. (2000). Psychophysiological assessment: Clinical applications for PTSD. *Journal of Affective Disorders, 61,* 225–240.

Paris, J. (1998). Does childhood trauma cause personality disorders in adults? *Canadian Journal of Psychiatry, 43,* 148–153.

Paris, J. (2000). Predispositions, personality traits and posttraumatic stress disorder. *Harvard Review of Psychiatry, 8,* 175–183.

Pelcovitz, D., Kaplan, S., Goldenberg, B., Mandel, F., Lehane, J., & Guarrera, J. (1994). Post-traumatic stress disorder in physically abused children. *Journal of the American Academy of Child and Adolescent Psychiatry, 33,* 305–312.

Perrin, S., Smith, P., & Yule, W. (2000). Practitioner review: The assessment and treatment of post-traumatic stress disorder in children and adolescents. *Journal of Child Psychology and Psychiatry, 41,* 277–289.

Perry, B. D. (1999). Post-traumatic stress disorders in children and adolescents. *Current Options in Pediatrics, 11,* 15.

Pynoos, R. S., Frederick, C., Nader, K., Arroyo, W., Steinberg, A., Eth, S., et al. (1987). Life threat and post-traumatic stress in school-age children. *Archives of General Psychiatry, 44,* 1057–1063.

Pynoos, R. S., & Nader, K. (1988). Psychological first aid and treatment approach to children exposed to community violence: Research implications. *Journal of Traumatic Stress, 1,* 445–473.

Pynoos, R., Rodriguez, N., Steinberg, A. M., Stuber, M., & Frederick, C. (1998). *UCLA Post-Traumatic Stress Reaction Index.* Copyrighted instrument. Los Angeles: UCLA Trauma Psychiatry Service.

Pynoos, R. S., Steinberg, A. M., & Piacentini, J. C. (1999). A developmental psychopathology model of childhood traumatic stress and intersection with anxiety disorders. *Biological Psychiatry, 46,* 1542–1554.

Resick, P. A., & Schnicke, M. K. (1992). Cognitive processing therapy for sexual assault victims. *Journal of Consulting and Clinical Psychology, 60,* 748–756.

Root, M. P., & Fallon, P. (1988). The incidences of victimization experiences in a bulimic sample. *Journal of Interpersonal Violence, 3,* 161–173.

Rothbaum, B. O., Meadows, E. A., Resick, P., & Foy, D. (2000). Cognitive behavioral therapy. In E. B. Foa, T. M. Keane, & M. J. Friedman (Eds.), *Effective treatments for PTSD* (pp. 60–83). New York: Guilford Press.

Runyon, M. K., Deblinger, E., Ryan, E., & Thakkar-Kolar, R. (2004). An overview of child physical abuse: Developing an integrated parent-child cognitive-behavioral treatment approach. *Trauma, Violence, and Abuse: A Review Journal, 5,* 65–85.

Runyon, M. K., & Kenny, M. (2002). Relationship of attributional style, depression, and post-trauma distress among children who suffered physical or sexual abuse. *Child Maltreatment, 7,* 254–264.

Rutter, M. (1989). Pathways from childhood to adult life. *Journal of Child Psychology and Psychiatry and Allied Disciplines, 30,* 23–51.

Saigh, P. A. (1989). The development and validation of the children's post-traumatic stress disorder inventory. *International Journal of Special Education, 4,* 75–84.

Saigh, P. A., Yasik, A. E., Oberfield, R. A., Green, B. L., Halamandaris, P. V., Rybenstein, H., et al. (2000). The Children's PTSD Inventory: Development and reliability. *Journal of Traumatic Stress, 13,* 369–380.

Salzinger, S., Feldman, R. S., Hammer, M., & Rosario, M. (1993). The effects of physical abuse on children's social relationships. *Child Development, 64,* 169–187.

Saunders, B. E., Berliner, L., & Hanson, R. F. (Eds.) (2003). *Child physical and sexual abuse: Guidelines for treatment* (Revised Report: April 26, 2004). Charleston, SC: National Crime Victims Research and Treatment Center. Available from www.musc.edu/cvc.

Scheeringa, M. S., Zenah, C. H., Drel, M. J., & Larrieu, J. A. (1995). Two approaches to the diagnosis of posttraumatic stress disorder in infancy and early childhood. *Journal of the American Academy of Child and Adolescent Psychiatry, 34,* 191–200.

Schnurr, P. P., & Vielhauer, M. J. (1999). Personality as a risk factor for PTSD. In R. Yehuda (Ed.), *Risk factors for posttraumatic stress disorder* (pp. 191–222). Washington, DC: American Psychiatric Press.

Stauffer, L., & Deblinger, E (1999). Cognitive behavioral groups for nonoffending mothers and their young sexually abused children: A preliminary treatment outcome study. *Child Maltreatment 1,* 65–76.

Stein, M. B., Walker, J. R., & Forde, D. R. (2000). Gender differences in susceptibility to posttraumatic stress disorder. *Behaviour Research and Therapy, 38,* 619–628.

Steiner, H., Garcia, I. G., & Matthews, Z. (1997). Posttraumatic stress disorder in incarcerated juvenile delinquents. *Journal of the American Academy of Child and Adolescent Psychiatry, 36,* 357–365.

Terr, L. C. (1984). Chowchilla revisited: The effects of psychic trauma four years after a school-bus kidnapping. *Annual Progress in Child Psychiatry and Child Development, 71,* 300–317.

Terr, L. C. (1991). Childhood trauma: An outline and overview. *American Journal of Psychiatry, 148,* 10–19.

van der Kolk, B. (1984). *Psychological trauma.* Washington, DC: American Psychiatric Press.

Vernberg, E. M., LaGreca, A.M., Silverman, W. K., & Prinstein, M. J. (1996). Prediction of posttraumatic stress symptoms in children after Hurricane Andrew. *Journal of Abnormal Psychology, 105,* 237–248.

Welner, Z., Reich, W., Herjanic, B., Jung, K. G., & Amado, H. (1987). Reliability, validity, and parent-child agreement studies of the Diagnostic Interview for Children and Adolescents (DICA). *Journal of the American Academy of Child and Adolescent Psychiatry, 26,* 649–653.

Widom, C. S. (1989). Child abuse, neglect, and adult behavior. *Criminology, 27,* 251–271.

Wolfe, D. A., Wekerle, C., Reitzel-Jaffe, D., & Lefebvre, L. (1998). Factors associated with abusive relationships among maltreated and nonmaltreated youth. *Development and Psychopathology, 10,* 61–85.

Wolfe, V. V., Gentile, C., Michienzi, T., Sas, L., & Wolfe, D. A. (1991). The children's impact of traumatic events scale: A measure of post-sexual-abuse PTSD symptoms. *Behavioral Assessment, 13,* 359–383.

CHAPTER 12

Major Depression

JUDY GARBER AND JOCELYN SMITH CARTER

DESCRIPTION OF THE DISORDERS AND CLINICAL PICTURE

Major depressive disorder (MDD) is categorized as a mood disorder in the fourth edition of the *Diagnostic and Statistical Manual*—Text Revision (*DSM-IV-TR;* American Psychiatric Association [APA], 2000) and is characterized by one or more major depressive episodes (MDEs). To be diagnosed with an MDE, individuals must have at least five of the nine symptoms listed in Table 12.1, for most of the day nearly every day, for at least 2 weeks, and clinically significant distress or impairment. Dysthymic disorder (DD) is a more chronic but less severe condition than MDD. The depressed mood (or irritability in children and adolescents) generally is present most of the day for more days than not, with at least two additional symptoms as listed in Table 12.2. The required duration is at least 2 years (at least 1 year in children and adolescents), and the individual cannot be without these symptoms for more than 2 months at a time. Thus, the two minor developmental variations in *DSM-IV-TR* are that for children and adolescents, irritability is considered a manifestation of dysphoric mood, and the duration of dysthymia is 1 rather than 2 years.

Depressive disorders that do not meet criteria for MDD, dysthymia, or an adjustment disorder with depressed mood may be classified as depressive disorder not otherwise specified (D-NOS). Some examples of D-NOS include (a) premenstrual dysphoric disorder, with symptoms that last longer than a week and are severe enough to interfere with functioning; (b) minor depressive disorder, with depressive symptoms of at least 2 weeks but fewer symptoms than the five required for a diagnosis of MDE; or (c) recurrent brief depressive disorder, with depressive episodes from 2 days up to 2 weeks that occur at least once a month for at least a year (APA, 2000). D-NOS may be a subsyndromal level of depression that can be a risk for subsequent episodes of MDD (Hays, Wells, Sherbourne, Rogers, & Spritzer, 1995; Judd et al., 1998).

Although current psychiatric nomenclature (i.e., *DSM-IV-TR*) categorizes depression into qualitatively distinct diagnoses, some also consider depression to fall on a quantitative continuum of severity from normal sadness to a depressive disorder (e.g., Compas, Ey, & Grant, 1993; Flett, Vredenburg, & Krames, 1997; Ruscio & Ruscio, 2000). The single symptom of sadness is a subjective state that most individuals experience at various points in their lives and by itself is not necessarily pathological. The syndrome of depression is made up of more than an isolated dysphoric mood and occurs in combination with other symptoms (e.g., as listed in Table 12.1) to form a symptom complex or syndrome. When this clinical syndrome has a specifiable course, outcome, etiology, and treatment response, then it is considered a distinct nosologic disorder.

An important question is whether the specific symptoms that comprise the syndrome of depression differ with development. Although certain core symptoms invariantly may be a part of depression at any age, other symptoms may vary with developmental level, and different combinations of symptoms may characterize depression at different ages. In other words, some cognitive or physiological symptoms might not be present in children until they have reached a certain level of abstract thinking or biological maturity, respectively, and therefore may not be part of the depressive syndrome at a young age. For example, with development come the increasing capacities to maintain a negative self-view and negative expectation about the future, which then can sustain negative emotions beyond the immediate situation (Harris, 1989). Thus, although young children might be able to experience

---

Acknowledgments: Judy Garber was supported in part by grants (R01MH57822; R01MH64735) and a Research Scientist Development Award (K02 MH66249) from the National Institute of Mental Health and a grant from the William T. Grant Foundation (173096) during completion of this work. Jocelyn Smith Carter was supported in part from a Ford Foundation Fellowship and a Dean's Graduate Fellowship and Peabody Fellowship from Vanderbilt University.

TABLE 12.1 Symptoms of Major Depression

Depressed mood or irritability.
Anhedonia.
Decrease or increase in appetite, non-intentional weight loss or gain, or failure to make expected weight gains.
Sleep problems.
Fatigue or loss of energy.
Psychomotor agitation or retardation.
Feelings of worthlessness or excessive or inappropriate guilt.
Difficulty concentrating or making decisions.
Thoughts of death, suicidal ideation, suicide attempt.

TABLE 12.2 Symptoms of Dysthymic Disorder

Decreased or increased appetite.
Sleep problems.
Fatigue or low energy.
Low self-esteem.
Difficulty concentrating or making decisions.
Sense of hopelessness.

transient sadness, particularly in response to acute stressors, they might be less able to experience some depressive symptoms such as guilt, worthlessness, and hopelessness that require a higher level of cognitive development (Weiner, 1985).

Although the overall syndrome of depression seems to be fairly stable over time (e.g., Holsen, Kraft, & Vitterso, 2000; Nolen-Hoeksema, Girgus, & Seligman, 1992), there is less continuity with regard to particular symptoms across episodes. The few longitudinal studies of depressive disorders that have followed the same children across time have found evidence of both stability and change in specific depressive symptoms as children developed. In a sample of 87 depressed patients first identified at ages 8–13 years old and followed through young adulthood (age 21), Kovacs, Obrosky, and Sherrill (2003) found that as the children got older, they were increasingly likely to report pessimism, social withdrawal, sleep disturbances (both hyposomnia and insomnia), and neurovegetative complaints, whereas more stable patterns were found for guilt, worthlessness, and feeling unloved. Lewinsohn, Pettit, Joiner, and Seeley (2003) examined the stability of symptoms across multiple depressive episodes in a sample of high school students followed until age 24 and found that the most stable symptom was anhedonia, whereas the remaining symptoms had low symptom concordance (kappas < .30) from one episode to the next.

Weiss and Garber (2003) conducted a meta-analysis to examine whether there are developmental differences in the phenomenology of depression at both the individual symptom and syndrome levels. At the symptom level, 19 of the 29 depressive symptoms evaluated showed significant variability across studies, indicating that some as-yet unknown, between-study factors influenced the magnitude of these effects. Moreover, 6 of the 10 symptoms that did not have significant variability showed significant developmental effects, indicating higher levels of these symptoms (anhedonia, hopelessness, hypersomnia, weight gain, social withdrawal) among more developmentally advanced individuals. Thus, there were developmental differences in the rates at which some depressive symptoms were endorsed.

At the syndrome level, two studies supported developmental isomorphism, two studies supported developmental differences in depression, and one provided some support for each position. Based on this review of the empirical data available at that point, Weiss and Garber (2003) asserted that it may be premature to conclude that depression is developmentally isomorphic, at either the symptom or syndrome level. This does not mean that clinicians cannot identify children who meet the adult diagnostic criteria for depression (e.g., Ryan et al., 1987). However, the presence of children who fit these criteria does not preclude the possibility that other symptoms (e.g., somatic complaints, social withdrawal) are part of childhood depression, or that some of the adult symptoms are not part of the child syndrome. Thus, the extent to which there are meaningful developmental changes in the phenomenology of depressive symptoms and syndrome from early childhood through adulthood remains an unresolved issue in need of further investigation.

PERSONALITY DEVELOPMENT AND PSYCHOPATHOLOGY

Temperament generally is defined as a behavioral, emotional, or cognitive style that is relatively stable across time and consistent across situations (Rothbart & Bates, 1998; Rothbart, Posner, & Hershey, 1995; Shiner, 1998). Although temperament is thought to have a genetic or biological basis (e.g., Goldsmith, 1986; Gray, 1987), experience, particularly within the social context, can affect its development and expression (Caspi, Henry, McGee, Moffitt, & Silva, 1995; Hartup & van Lieshout, 1995). Moreover, some personality characteristics can be learned. Temperament and character are considered to be two components of personality, with the former being largely genetic and the latter being primarily learned (Cloninger, Svrakic, & Przybeck, 1993; Klein, Durbin, Shankman, & Santiago, 2002). Thus, temperament is present early in development (Thomas & Chess, 1977) and is a subset of personality, which emerges over time (Rothbart & Ahadi, 1994; Shiner, 1998).

Is There a Depressive Personality?

Early perspectives on the relation between personality and depression hypothesized that individuals with MDD, as well as their relatives, had a premorbid "depressive personality" (Kraepelin, 1921; Kretschmer, 1925). Akiskal (1983, 1984) identified subtypes of chronic depression that included a "characterological" group, which had a particularly poor prognosis. These subtypes can be subdivided further into (a) subaffective dysthymics, who had an onset before age 25, continuous or intermittent depressive episodes, and a depressive personality type and were responsive to tricyclic antidepressant medications, and (b) character spectrum depressives, who had an even earlier onset; intermittent depressive episodes; and dependent, histrionic, or antisocial personality traits and were unresponsive to medication. Klein and colleagues (Klein, 1990; Klein, Taylor, Dickstein, & Harding, 1988) identified a similar type of early-onset dysthymia who typically became depressed around age 9, had a higher incidence of substance-use disorder as a young adult, was more likely to be diagnosed with borderline or schizotypal personality disorder, and had a less favorable outcome after treatment and a family history of mood disorders.

Some have questioned whether depressive personality and dysthymia are really distinct (Ryder & Bagby, 1999; Widiger, 1989), suggesting, rather, that depressive personality disorder might be a milder form of dysthymia (Ryder, Bagby, & Dion, 2001). Individuals with early-onset dysthymia have a more chronic depressive personality that makes them vulnerable to recurrent episodes (Hurpich, 1998). Others have found, however, that although the constructs do overlap, some individuals meet criteria for one and not the other (e.g., Hirschfeld, 1994; Klein & Shih, 1998; Phillips et al., 1998). Part of the problem in differentiating between depressive personality disorder and dysthymia is related to the somewhat arbitrary categorical diagnostic system used in the *DSM* (Widiger, 1989). Ryder, Bagby, and Schuller (2002) argued that "despite persuasive evidence for the existence of depressive personality traits, support is insufficient for the inclusion of depressive personality disorder as currently defined . . . depressive traits are best conceptualized dimensionally, and as part of an overarching model of personality structure, rather than as a discrete diagnostic entity" (p. 337).

Thus, some evidence exists that a depressive personality exists. Several questions need further research: (a) To what extent is depressive personality distinct from other mood disorders, particularly dysthymia? (b) Is depressive personality a categorical disorder or a dimensional personality trait? (c) If depressive personality is a disorder, should it be an Axis I or Axis II disorder? (d) Are there subtypes or subdimensions of depressive personality? (e) What is the relation between depressive personality and other personality characteristics (e.g., neuroticism, negative cognitive style) and other personality disorders (e.g., dependent, borderline)? (f) What are the developmental origins of depressive personality?

How Are Personality and Depression Related?

Several models have been proposed to explain the relation between personality and depression (Clark, Watson, & Mineka, 1994; Compas, Connor-Smith, & Jaser, 2004; Klein et al., 2002). Simply, these models are consistent with how any two variables might be related: (a) Z can cause both X and Y; (b) X can cause Y; or (c) Y can cause X. Klein et al. (2002) further subdivided these models as follows: (a) common cause—the same etiological process causes both personality and depression; precursor—personality is an earlier manifestation of depression; (b) predisposition—personality increases the risk of depression; pathoplasticity—personality affects the expression or course of depression; (c) state dependence—mood state affects the assessment of personality; complications—episodes of depression alter personality after recovery (p. 116). These models are not mutually exclusive. Some personality traits can predispose individuals to depression while also being affected by the experience of depression itself. For example, high levels of interpersonal sensitivity, that is, hypersensitivity to interpersonal rejection, have been found to be a vulnerability to mood disorders (Boyce & Parker, 1989), particularly atypical depression (Boyce et al., 1993). Then, in turn, depressive symptoms can increase the likelihood of actual rejection by others, thereby heightening individuals' overall interpersonal sensitivity (Coyne, 1976; Hammen, 1991a; Rudolph, 2002). Moreover, both interpersonal sensitivity and depression are partly heritable and may share some common genes (Boyce & Mason, 1996). Thus, a single personality characteristic and depression can be related in all three ways (i.e., common etiology, cause, and consequence).

These various models also might explain the relation between personality and depression at different points in development. For example, cognitive theories of depression (Abramson, Metalsky, & Alloy, 1989; Beck, 1967) hypothesize that a negative cognitive style predisposes individuals to depression. Developmental theorists (Cole & Turner, 1993; Nolen-Hoeksema et al., 1992; Weisz, Southam-Gero, & McCarty, 2001), however, have suggested that negative cognitions emerge over time and their relation with depression increases with development. Indeed, the association between negative cognitions and depressive symptoms has not been found to be as strong in young children as it is in older children and adolescents (Nolen-Hoeksema et al., 1992; Turner & Cole, 1994). Negative attributional style does predict depression in older children (e.g., Abela, 2001; Robinson, Garber, & Hilsman, 1995), and thus it might become a predisposing factor as children develop. On the other hand, depressive symptoms have been shown to predict negative cognitions even in young children (Cole, Martin, Peeke, Seroczynski, & Hoffman, 1998; Nolen-Hoeksema et al., 1992). Thus, earlier in development the complications model may explain the association between depression and negative cognitions, whereas once in place, such negative cognitions may serve as a vulnerability to depression, consistent with the predisposition model. Finally, the common cause model also might explain some of the relation between negative cognitions and depression. For instance, stressful life events and dysfunctional parenting have been found to predict both negative cognitions and depression (e.g., Garber & Flynn, 2001; Nolen-Hoeksema et al., 1992).

Which Personality Characteristics Are Related to Depression?

Although many different dimensions of personality and temperament have been proposed (e.g., Block & Block, 1980; Buss & Plomin, 1984; McCrae & Costa, 1987; Rothbart & Bates, 1998; Thomas & Chess, 1977), they can be categorized into higher-order traits of negative emotionality-neuroticism, positive emotionality-extraversion, constraint-conscientiousness, and agreeableness; lower-order traits, of which these higher-order categories are composed, include sociability, social inhibition, dominance, negative emotionality, aggressiveness, persistence/attention, prosocial disposition, mastery motivation, inhibitory control, and activity level (Shiner, 1998). The personality traits that have been particularly linked with depression are negative and positive emotionality and, to a lesser extent, constraint and attentional control (Clark et al., 1994; Compas et al., 2004; Derryberry & Rothbart, 1988).

Negative emotionality (NE), the propensity to experience negative emotions (e.g., anxiety, fear, sadness, anger), is related to negative affectivity (Clark & Watson, 1991), neuroticism (Eysenck, 1952), the Behavioral Inhibition System (Gray, 1991), stress reactivity (Compas et al., 2004), difficult temperament (Thomas & Chess, 1977), the Emotionality-Activity-Sociability-Impulsivity model (EASI; Buss & Plomin, 1986), behavioral inhibition (Kagan & Snidman, 1991), and harm avoidance (Cloninger, 1987). Although different terms and definitions are used, the conceptual and empirical overlap among these constructs far outweighs their differences. NE reflects a sensitivity to negative stimuli, increased wariness, vigilance, physiological arousal, and emotional distress. Moreover, emotional distress can be divided further into fear and anger, with each having different action tendencies (Buss & Plomin, 1984; Rothbart & Bates, 1998). Whereas fear is associated with anxiety, withdrawal, and inhibition, anger is linked with irritability, frustration, hostility, and aggression. Nevertheless, both forms of distress are related to depression.

Positive emotionality (PE) is associated with positive affectivity (Clark & Watson, 1991), extraversion (Eysenck & Eysenck, 1985), the Behavioral Activation System (Gray, 1991), the EASI model (Buss & Plomin, 1984), activity and approach (Thomas & Chess, 1977), and novelty seeking (Cloninger, 1987). PE is characterized by sensitivity to reward cues, approach, energy, involvement, sociability, and adventurousness. Both NE and PE are consistent with the emergence of the Big 5 as the dominant model of personality structure in children (e.g., Digman & Inouye, 1986; Digman & Shmelyov, 1996), adolescents (e.g., Digman, 1989; Graziano & Ward, 1992), and adults (e.g., Goldberg, 1992; McCrae & Costa, 1987).

Evidence of the Relation Between Personality and Depression

According to the tripartite model (Clark & Watson, 1991; Watson & Clark, 1995), high levels of negative affectivity (NA) are associated with both depression and anxiety, whereas low levels of positive affectivity (PA) are uniquely related to depression, particularly anhedonia. Support for this model has been found in adults (e.g., Brown, Chorpita, & Barlow, 1998; Watson, Clark, & Harkness, 1994) and more recently has been applied successfully to children and adolescents (e.g., Anthony, Lonigan, Hooe, & Phillips, 2002; Joiner & Lonigan, 2000; Phillips, Lonigan, Driscoll, & Hooe, 2002).

Several potential methodological problems, however, could produce spurious correlations between personality and depression. First, self-report questionnaires often are used to assess both personality and depressive symptoms, and overlapping items can inflate the correlation. Second, the actual criteria used to define some personality and mood disorders are identical, making it more likely that they will covary (Farmer, Nelson, & Rosemery, 1990). This is particularly true for the relation between depressive personality disorder and dysthymia. Third, the relation between personality and depression could be inflated as a result of monomethod variance, that is, the tendency for a person to respond to questions about personality and depression in a particular way (i.e., negatively), rather than there being a substantive link between them. Fourth, a related possibility is "state dependence" (Klein et al., 2002, p. 116) such that the mood state distorts individuals' responses to questionnaires so those responses do not reflect how the individuals would answer if they were not in that mood. If so, then responses might be expected to return to baseline after the individual is no longer in a depressive episode.

Individuals report significantly higher levels of neuroticism when they are in an episode of MDD compared to when they are not depressed (Boyce & Mason, 1996; Kendler, Neale, Kessler, Heath, & Eaves, 1993), whereas the levels of extraversion/positive emotionality (E/PE) tend to remain low even after recovery from a MDE (e.g., Hirschfeld, Klerman, Kendler et al., 1993). Some studies, however, have found that the level of neuroticism in remitted depressed patients is still higher compared to nondepressed controls (Hirschfeld & Klerman, 1979; Reich, Noyes, Hirschfeld, Coryell, & O'Gorman, 1987), although others have not found such a difference (Kendler et al., 1993; Liebowitz, Stallone, Dunner, & Fieve, 1979). Taken together, these results indicate that in relation to depression, PE is a relatively stable trait, whereas neuroticism has both a state and trait component (Klein et al., 2002).

Longitudinal studies have shown that neuroticism predicts later negative affect and symptoms of emotional distress (Costa & McCrae, 1980; Levenson, Aldwin, Bosse, & Spiro, 1988), even after controlling for initial symptom levels (Gershuny & Sher, 1998; Jorm et al., 2000). Moreover, neuroticism is a significant risk for the onset, recurrence, and chronicity of MDD (Clark et al., 1994; Hayward, Killen, Kraemer, & Taylor, 1998; Kendler et al., 1993, 2002; Wilhelm, Parker, Dewhurst-Savellis, & Asghari, 1999). In a large adult female twin sample, Kendler et al. (1993) found that neuroticism predicted the onset of MDD over a 1-year period, and using a multifactorial model, Kendler, Gardner, & Prescott (2002) showed that beyond stressful life events, neuroticism was the strongest predictor of the onset of major depression.

Neuroticism is not specific to depression, however, and may be a risk factor for other disorders such as post-traumatic stress disorder following trauma (e.g., Breslau, Davis, & Andreski, 1995; Kulka et al., 1990) and panic attacks (Hayward et al., 1998). Behaviorally inhibited children are at greater risk for the development of multiple phobias and various anxiety disorders in later childhood (Biederman et al., 1993; Hirshfeld et al., 1992) and social phobias in adolescence (Hayward et al., 1998). Thus, neuroticism is a significant predictor of depression, although it might not be a specific vulnerability marker. Rather, neuroticism might be part of a larger causal model in which it interacts with different variables to produce specific outcomes (Garber & Hollon, 1991; Kendler, Gardner, & Prescott (2002).

The relation between neuroticism and depression also may vary by age. For example, among individuals between 31 and 41 years old, Hirschfeld et al. (1989) found that neurotic-like characteristics of decreased emotional strength and increased interpersonal dependency predicted the first onset of depression, but this was not the case for 17- to 30-year-olds. Similarly, Rohde, Lewinsohn, and Seeley (1990) reported that adults with a first episode of MDD had had elevated levels of dependent traits 2–3 years earlier, whereas Rohde, Lewinsohn, and Seeley (1994) found no differences in prior levels of dependency between adolescents who later developed a first MDD and adolescents who were depression-free during a 1-year follow-up period.

In contrast, studies using other measures of neurotic-like traits in children have found evidence of a link with depression. Elevated levels of behavioral inhibition have been observed in laboratory tasks with young offspring of depressed parents (Kochanska, 1991; Rosenbaum et al., 2000). Caspi, Moffitt, Newman, and Silva (1996) reported that children who had been rated as inhibited, socially reticent, and easily upset at age 3 had elevated rates of depressive disorders at age 21. Similarly, physicians' ratings of children's behavioral apathy at ages 6, 7, and 11 have been reported to predict adolescent mood disorders and chronic depression in middle adulthood (van Os, Jones, Lewis, Wadsworth, & Murray, 1997), and a related trait of difficult temperament, characterized by inflexibility, low positive mood, withdrawal, and poor concentration, was found to correlate with depressive symptoms both concurrently and prospectively in adolescents (Davies & Windle, 2001).

The relation between temperament and mood disorders may be moderated by other factors such as gender and parenting behaviors. For example, Gjerde (1995) found that chronic depression during adulthood was predicted by shy and withdrawn behavior in girls and higher levels of undercontrolled behaviors in boys at ages 3 and 4. In a study of families undergoing divorce, Lengua, Wolchik, Sandler, and West (2000) showed that the relation between PE and depression in children was moderated by parental rejection such that low PE predicted higher levels of depressive symptoms among children with high levels of parental rejection, and high levels of impulsivity and depression were significantly associated among children receiving inconsistent parental discipline. Thus, there is some evidence of an association between NE and PE traits during childhood and subsequent depression, although this relation may vary as a function of other factors such as age, gender, context, and how the traits are measured.

Not only do other factors moderate the relation between personality and depression, but personality itself likely moderates the relation between other risk factors (e.g., stress) and depression. Stressful life events clearly are linked with depression (Brown & Harris, 1989; Grant, Compas, Thurm, McMahon, & Gipson, 2004), although important individual differences exist in how people respond to stress. Diathesis-stress models (e.g., Abramson et al., 1989; Beck, 1976; Monroe & Simons, 1991) propose that when exposed to stress, individuals with particular diatheses are more likely to become depressed than are individuals without such vulnerabilities. Various personality characteristics including neuroticism (Eysenck, 1952), negative affectivity (Clark & Watson, 1991), stress reactivity (Compas et al., 2004), attributional style (Abramson et al., 1989), and interpersonal orientation (Beck, Epstein, & Harrison, 1983; Blatt, 1974; Bowlby, 1977) might be the diatheses that affect individuals' interpretations and responses to negative life events when they occur.

For example, interpersonal orientation, also referred to as sociotropy (Beck et al., 1983), interpersonal dependency (Blatt, 1974), or anxious attachment personality style (Bowlby, 1977), has been hypothesized to moderate the relation between negative social events and individuals' responses to those events. Highly interpersonally oriented individuals seek to maintain their self-esteem through their interactions with others. According to the personality-event congruence hypothesis, people who exhibit high levels of this interpersonal orientation are particularly susceptible to becoming depressed following stressful events related to their area of sensitivity, such as the end of a salient interpersonal relationship (Beck et al., 1983; Blatt, 1974; Bowlby, 1977). Supporting this perspective, longitudinal studies with adults (e.g., Hammen et al., 1995; Hammen, Ellicott, Gitlin, & Jamison, 1989; Segal, Shaw, & Vella, 1989) and children (Hammen & Goodman-Brown, 1990; Little & Garber, 2000, 2004, in press) have shown that the interaction between an interpersonal orientation and negative social events significantly predicts increases in depressive symptoms.

Finally, mediation models also are relevant to understanding the relation between personality and depression. Potential mediators of this relation, particularly under condition of stress, have included appraisals, expectations, and coping (Beevers & Meyer, 2002; Compas, Connor-Smith, Saltzman, Thomsen, & Wadsworth, 2001; Lengua, Sandler, West, Wolchik, & Curran, 1999). Compas et al. (2004) suggested that negative affectivity leads to greater emotional arousal, more difficulty modulating emotional reactivity to stress, and a greater likelihood of using avoidance coping. In contrast, high levels of the temperamental characteristic of attentional control can facilitate the use of secondary control coping strategies such as distraction and cognitive restructuring and thereby reduce the likelihood of depression, whereas poor attentional control has been found to be associated with higher levels of depressive symptoms (Thomsen et al., 2002).

EPIDEMIOLOGY

Epidemiological studies of children and adolescents often have yielded different prevalence estimates primarily due to different means of case ascertainment, diagnostic methods, and age groups (Kessler, Avenevoli, & Merikangas, 2001). The incidence and prevalence of depressive disorders varies across developmental periods. Although some have argued that depression in infants exists (e.g., Spitz, 1945; Spitz & Wolf, 1946; Trad, 1987), this is still a matter of dispute. Symptoms considered to be an early form of depression in infants are withdrawal, sad face, apathy, irritability, eating disturbances, abnormal stranger reactions, fussiness, and tantrums (Bowlby, 1980; Spitz & Wolf, 1946; Trad, 1994).

A condition during infancy that has several similarities to depression is failure to thrive (FTT), which is associated with serious undernutrition, psychomotor delay, iron deficiency in the diet, and behavioral and feeding difficulties (Raynor & Rudolf, 1996). The rates of FTT have been reported to be about 1 percent to 5 percent (Iwaniec, 2004). The extent to which infant manifestations of distress share other similarities with childhood and adult mood disorders is not yet known. Do infants with FTT or other depression-like syndromes continue to experience depression later in life? The extent to which FTT has similar correlates with regard to family history, neurobiological dysregulation, or psychosocial stress needs to be studied further.

Depression is also rare in young children. Point prevalence rates of MDD in preschool children have been found to be about 1 percent (Kashani & Carlson, 1987); among prepubertal children (typically aged 6–12 years) rates generally have ranged between 0.4 percent and 2.5 percent (Fleming & Offord, 1990). Since the Fleming and Offord (1990) review, several additional epidemiological studies have reported similar findings. Puura et al. (1997) found prevalence rates of .48 percent for MDD and .06 percent for DD in 8- to 9-year-old children assessed with self-report questionnaires and structured interviews. Cohen et al. (1993) reported a prevalence rate of 2 percent for MDD in children aged 10–13 years based on interviews with parents and children. In a sample of children aged 8–11 years, Polaino-Lorente and Domenech (1993) found prevalence rates of .6 percent for MDD and 3 percent for DD based on information from clinicians, teacher rating scales, and peer nominations, but higher rates (1.8 percent for MDD, 6.4 percent for DD) when diagnoses were based on children's self-report questionnaires. In the Great Smokey Mountain study of children aged 9, 11, and 13 years, Costello et al. (1996) reported 3-month prevalence rates based on interviews with both parents and children to be .03 percent for MDD, .13 percent for DD, and 1.45 percent for D-NOS. Thus, the rates of diagnosed depressive disorders in preadolescents appear to be relatively low, although the rates tend to be higher for children's compared to parents' reports about the children's depression.

In adolescents, the 6-month point prevalence estimates have ranged from 0.4 percent to 9.8 percent (Birmaher et al., 1996; Fleming & Offord, 1990), with an average across 10 studies of 3.6 percent (Lewinsohn & Essau, 2002). Lifetime prevalence rates of MDD in adolescents have ranged from 8.3 percent to 18.5 percent—about 24 percent for females and 11.6 percent for males (Lewinsohn, Hops, Roberts, Seeley, & Andrews, 1993), which is about comparable to the lifetime rates found in adults in the National Comorbidity Survey (NCS; Kessler & Walters, 1998). The NCS was a comprehensive, nationally representative epidemiological study of more than 8,000 persons, ages 15–54, from U.S. households. Among 15- to 18-year-olds, lifetime prevalence of MDD was about 14 percent and an additional 11 percent had a lifetime history of minor depression, with higher rates in females than males. Kessler et al. (2001) reported that risk of the first onset of MDD begins in the early teens and continues to rise through the mid-20s. The authors' onset curves were consistent with findings from other studies of adolescents (e.g., Lewinsohn, Rohde, & Seely, 1998) and cross-national studies of adults (Weissman et al., 1996). The point prevalence for MDD among adults in Western industrialized countries is about 4.9 percent: 2.3 percent to 3.2 percent for men and 4.5 percent to 9.3 percent for women; lifetime prevalence of MDD is about 17 percent: 12.7 percent for men and 21.3 percent for women (Blazer, Kessler, McGonagle, & Swartz, 1994).

The 2:1 sex ratio commonly found in adults (Weissman & Olfson, 1995) has not been seen consistently in preadolescents, where the rate of MDD has been found to be about equal in girls and boys (Angold & Rutter, 1992; Fleming, Offord, & Boyle, 1989) or higher among boys (Anderson, Williams, McGee, & Silva, 1987; Costello et al., 1996; Ryan et al., 1987). Higher rates of prepubertal MDD in boys may be due to the comorbidity with disruptive behavior disorders, particularly attention-deficit/hyperactivity disorder (ADHD), whereas children without this comorbidity tend to have a similar gender representation pre- and postpubertally (Biederman et al., 1995; Costello et al., 1996; Kessler et al., 1992). Interestingly, the prevalence of DD, but not MDD, has been found to be greater in girls than boys among children aged 8–11 years (Polaino-Lorente & Domenech, 1993).

The gender ratio changes after puberty, with the rates particularly increasing among adolescent girls by about age 14 (Hankin et al., 1998; Wade, Cairney, & Pevalin, 2002). Speculations about the causes of the increase in depression in girls during adolescence have included such things as hormonal changes accompanying puberty, genetic regulatory processes, alterations in the frequency of environmental stressors, developmental changes in the availability of either vulnerability or protective factors such as social support, cognitive processes such as learned helplessness and attributional style, and developmental changes in children's experience and expression of emotions (Angold & Rutter, 1992; Cyranowski, Frank, Young, & Shear, 2000; Nolen-Hoeksema & Girgus, 1994).

The clearest evidence of a link between puberty and depression has been reported in a 3-year prospective study of 4,500 boys and girls ages 9, 11, and 13, in which Angold, Costello, and Worthman (1998) found that pubertal status, determined using Tanner staging and hormonal levels, was a better predictor than chronological age of the emergent preponderance of MDD in girls. Whereas boys had a higher rate of MDD at the prepubertal Tanner Stage I, girls' rate of MDD increased and surpassed boys after the puberty Tanner Stage III. Thus, the rates of depressive disorders clearly increase with age, particularly for girls during adolescence. Such epidemiological findings can "capitalize on developmental variations and psychopathologic variations to ask questions about mechanism and processes" (Rutter, 1988, p. 486) such as the following: Why is major depressive disorder less common during childhood? What prevents depression from occurring in childhood, or what happens during adolescence that increases individuals' risk for depression? What accounts for the change in the sex ratio of depression from childhood to adolescence?

Finally, prevalence rates also vary depending on the definition of depression used. Whereas depressive mood occurs most frequently, depressive disorders are less common (Compas et al., 1993). Although by definition, most individuals with depressive diagnoses have dysphoric mood, only a subset of those who experience sadness go on to have a full mood disorder. Point prevalence rates of depressed mood range from 10 percent to 18 percent for preadolescent children (e.g., Kashani & Simonds, 1979) and for adolescents from 10 percent to 20 percent based on parents' report (Achenbach, Howell, Quay, & Conners, 1991) and 20 percent to 40 percent by teens' self-report (e.g., Achenbach, 1991a; Kandel & Davies, 1986), with the rates being generally higher for adolescent girls than boys (e.g., Petersen, Sarigiani, & Kennedy, 1991). The prevalence of irritability is even higher during adolescence (Petersen et al., 1991).

With regard to the syndrome of depression, prevalence rates have ranged from 5 percent (Achenbach, 1991a; Achenbach et al., 1991) to more than 20 percent (Offord et al., 1987), depending on how the syndrome is defined and measured. Surveys of adolescents using self-report depression symptom scales have reported 1-week to 6-month prevalence rates based on established adult cutoff scores for depressive syndrome to be 20 percent to 30 percent (Offord et al., 1987; Reinherz, Giaconia, Hauf, Wasserman, & Silverman, 1999; Wichstrom, 1999). Such self-reported syndrome measures, however, do not differentiate between mild and severe levels of symptoms, type of mood disorder, or other psychiatric syndromes. Overall, the rates of depressed mood are higher than depressive syndrome, which is higher than depressive disorders.

ETIOLOGY

The etiology of depression likely involves a complex interplay of genetic, biological, temperament/personality, cognitive, interpersonal, and environmental factors. No single theory has yet successfully accounted for all major depressive episodes. Rather, it is likely that multiple pathways to depression involve various combinations of several different risk factors (e.g., Akiskal & McKinney, 1975; Brown & Harris, 1978; Monroe & Simons, 1991). Moreover, once an episode of depression occurs, it can affect subsequent risk factors, thereby increasing the likelihood of future episodes (Hammen, 1991a; Lewinsohn, Allen, Seeley, & Gotlib, 1999; Post, 1992).

Genes

Family, twin, and adoption studies have yielded varying results regarding the extent of the genetic contributions to individual differences in depression (Wallace, Schneider, & McGuffin, 2002). Family studies have shown that children of depressed parents are three to four times more likely to experience an episode of depression than are children of normal controls (Beardslee, Versage, & Gladstone, 1998), and the risk of having a depressive episode is higher in relatives of depressed children than in relatives of psychiatric and normal controls (e.g., Harrington et al., 1993). However, family studies confound genetic and shared environmental effects. Familiality of depression also could be caused by psychosocial factors such as maladaptive parenting styles, marital dysfunction, and stress, which also are associated with parental psychopathology (Goodman & Gotlib, 1999).

Twin studies with children have yielded heritability estimates comparable to those found in adults (Sullivan, Neale, & Kendler, 2000). In a study of 41 twin pairs aged 6–16 years, Wierzbicki (1987) reported that monozygotic twins more closely resembled each other in depressive symptoms than did dizygotic twins. Heritability estimates were .32 for child self-report of depression and .93 for parent report of children's symptoms. The Virginia Twin Study of Adolescent Behavioral Development (Eaves et al., 1997) consisted of 1,412 twin pairs aged 8–16 years. Based on child self-report, heritability estimates were small (.15 for girls and .16 for boys), and shared environmental effects were small to moderate (.26 for girls and .14 for boys), whereas when using parent report, heritability estimates were much larger (between .60 for mothers and .65 for fathers) and shared environment effects were negligible. Nonshared environmental factors also played a moderate role in both child (.59 for girls, .70 for boys) and parent report (.35 for mothers, .40 for fathers) of children's depression (Eaves et al., 1997). The higher parent report heritabilities may be partially due to the greater physical similarities between MZ twins. Parents might see MZ twins as more phenotypically similar than DZ twins across constructs, thus elevating heritability estimates based on parent report.

Thaper and McGuffin (1994) also reported large genetic contributions to individual differences in parent-reported depression ($h^2 = .79$) in a sample of 411 twin pairs, aged 8–16 years, and shared environment effects were nonsignificant. When only the 8- to 11-year-old pairs were examined, however, shared environmental effects for parent-reported depression accounted for 77 percent of the variance, and heritability effects were negligible. In adolescents, the heritability estimate for self-reported depression was also high ($h^2 = .70$). Child self-report measures were not available. Finally, in a sample of 395 twin pairs, aged 8–16 years, Eley, Deater-Deckard, Fombonne, Fulker, and Plomin (1998) found similar heritability estimates for both child-reported depression ($h^2 = .48$) and parent report of child depression ($h^2 = .49$). Shared environment effects were greater in adolescents (.28) than children (.08), and heritability estimates were moderate in both groups; $h^2 = .34$ for children and $h^2 = .28$ for adolescents. These results also suggest age differences, but in the opposite direction. In this case, shared environmental effects were stronger in adolescents.

Thus, twin studies indicate that genes account for approximately 30 percent to 50 percent of the variance in child-reported depression. The evidence for environmental effects is mixed. In addition, genetic and environmental influences differ with informant (Eaves et al., 1997; Wierzbicki, 1987) and age (Eley et al., 1998; Thaper & McGuffin, 1994). Early onset (<20 years old) depressions are associated with greater risk for depression in family members (Weissman, Warner, Wickramaratne, & Prusoff, 1988; Weissman et al., 1984, 1986). Alternatively, childhood depression has been associated with greater environmental contributions (Thaper & McGuffin, 1994). It is unclear whether earlier onset depression is due to greater genetic influence or factors within the shared environment of families with a depressed proband (Rutter et al., 1990).

Adoption designs traditionally have been able to directly disentangle shared and nonshared environmental effects. Eley et al. (1998) used an offspring design combined with a sibling design to assess the variance accounted for by genetic and environmental factors in child-reported and parent-reported depression. Neither the sibling nor the parent-offspring correlations showed a significant genetic effect. There was evidence of some shared environmental effects, although these were greater for parent reports, indicating inflation possibly caused by method bias in the relation between mothers' report of their own and their children's symptoms. The results also suggest a substantial role for nonshared environmental effects.

Thus, findings from twin and adoption studies of childhood depression differ. Whereas twin studies suggest a moderate role for genetic influences on individual differences in depression, adoption studies typically have reported negligible genetic effects. Twin studies report nonsignificant effects of shared environment, whereas adoption studies suggest a small but significant shared environment effect. Both designs provide evidence of moderate to large nonshared environmental influences.

Finally, studies of children that have evaluated differences in genetic and environmental effects have reported mixed results as a function of symptom heterogeneity. In two such studies (Eley, 1997; Rende, Plomin, Reiss, & Hetherington; 1993), child report on the Children's Depression Inventory (CDI) was used to establish groups of varying severity. In a sample of 9- to 18-year-olds, Rende et al. (1993) found smaller genetic effects and significant shared environment effects in children with greater severity of symptoms. In contrast, Eley (1997) found in a sample of 8- to 16-year-olds similar heritability estimates for severe groups but less influence of shared environmental factors. Slight differences in age may explain the conflicting results for environmental effects, suggesting that environmental factors may be more important as children get older. In addition, the cutoff points used to identify the groups fell within the mild to moderate range of depressive symptoms (i.e., between 13 and 17 on the CDI).

Neurobiological Vulnerability

Psychobiological studies of depression in children generally have attempted to replicate results of studies with adults (Kaufman, Martin, King, & Charney, 2001). This research has focused on dysregulation in neuroendocrine and neurochemical systems and in disturbances in sleep architecture (Dahl & Ryan, 1996; Emslie, Weinberg, Kennard, & Kowatch, 1994). In addition, functional and anatomical brain differences in depressed and high-risk children are increasingly being investigated (Botteron, 1999; Dawson, Klinger, Panagiotides, Hill, & Spieker, 1992; Field, Fox, Pickens, & Nawrocki, 1995).

Psychoneuroendocrinology

Dysregulation of processes associated with responses to stress are presumed to be linked with abnormalities in the hypothalamic-pituitary-adrenal (HPA) axis (Plotsky, Owens, & Nemeroff, 1998), typically assessed through measures of abnormalities of corticotropic-releasing hormone (CRH) and the dexamethasone suppression test (Ryan & Dahl, 1993). Most studies have not found differences in basal cortisol secretion between depressed and normal children or blunted corticotrophin secretion response to CRH infusion in depressed adolescents, as has been found in adults (Kaufman et al., 2001), although a few have shown elevated cortisol secretion near sleep onset in suicidal and depressed inpatients (Dahl et al., 1991) and differences in evening cortisol secretion between patients with MDD and normal controls (Goodyer et al., 1996).

In contrast to baseline observations, challenging a regulatory system allows observation of its functioning when stressed. Early adversity (e.g., trauma, prenatal stress) is hypothesized to be associated with abnormalities in HPA functioning, which then sensitize the organism to stress in the future (Heim & Nemeroff, 2001). Abnormalities in the HPA axis response to physiological stress have been investigated with the dexamethasone suppression test. Numerous studies have found greater sensitivity in inpatients compared to outpatients (61 percent vs. 29 percent) and in children than in adolescents (58 percent vs. 44 percent), although comparisons with psychiatric controls were stronger in adolescent samples (85 percent) than in child samples (60 percent; Dahl & Ryan, 1996). Developmental changes in the brain and the HPA axis may be responsible for the lack of consistent findings in children as compared to adults (Kaufman et al., 2001). Moreover, currently little evidence exists that HPA axis dysregulation is a stable vulnerability marker. In one of the few longitudinal studies that followed a few depressed children who had elevated cortisol levels, only one of four continued to show elevated levels after recovery (Puig-Antich et al., 1989). Prospective studies of HPA axis functioning in high-risk children are needed to clarify the role that dysregulation in this system may play in onset of depression.

Growth hormone (GH) regulation also has been studied as a possible biological marker of central noradrenergic and serotonergic processes (Birmaher et al., 2000). Growth hormone is normally secreted by the anterior pituitary, functions as a growth-promoting agent throughout the body, and is mostly secreted during sleep in children (Ryan & Dahl, 1993). In response to pharmacologic challenges that artificially stimulate the growth hormone system, depressed children typically show blunted GH secretion. Compared to normal controls, children with MDD have a blunted GH response to stimulation with insulin-induced hypoglycemia, arginine, clonidine, and growth hormone releasing hormone (GHRH; Meyer et al., 1991; Ryan et al., 1994), and prepubertal depressed boys have a blunted GH response to L-dopa and clonidine (Jensen & Garfinkel, 1990). Depressed children show low GH response to GHRH, and the low GH response continues following clinical remission (Dahl et al., 2000). Thus, GH system dysregulation may be a vulnerability marker for depression (Dinan, 1998). Low GH response to GHRH also has been found in children and adolescents with no personal history of depression but with high rates of affective illness in their families (Birmaher et al., 2000). Such high-risk children need to be followed to determine if their blunted GH response predicts future depressive disorders.

Neurotransmitters

Another area of biological dysregulation among depressed patients is in their neurochemistry, with serotonin, norepinephrine, and acetylcholine particularly implicated in the pathophysiology of mood disorders (Thase, Jindal, & Howland, 2002). In comparison to normal controls, depressed children demonstrate hyposecretion of melatonin (Cavallo, Holt, Hejazi, Richards, & Meyer, 1987), a blunted cortisol response, and an increased prolactin response after administration of L-5-hydroxytryptophan, primarily in girls (Ryan et al., 1992). Similar results have been found in never-depressed children with high familial loadings for depression (Birmaher et al., 1997), suggesting a possible serotonergic system marker for depression.

Investigation into the effectiveness of selective seratonin reuptake inhibitors (SSRIs) in reducing depressive symptoms in children also has implicated serotonergic system dysregulation in childhood depression (Emslie et al., 1997). Overall, there is evidence of neurotransmitter involvement in child depression. Moreover, serotonergic system dysregulation may be a risk factor for depression in that it has been found in both high-risk and currently depressed children.

Functional and Anatomical Brain Differences

Abnormal functioning of the prefrontal cortex-limbic-striatal regions in the brain, reduced prefrontal volume, and hippocampal abnormalities have been associated with adult depression (Davidson, Pizzagalli, Nitschke, & Putnam, 2002). Resting frontal brain asymmetry also has been linked with depression in adults and appears to persist into remission (Tomarken & Keener, 1998). Moreover, depressed patients who responded to SSRIs, particularly women, had significantly less relative right-sided activation compared to nonresponders (Bruder et al., 2001). Studies of brain asymmetry in children have found left frontal hypoactivation in infant (Dawson et al., 1992; Field et al., 1995) and adolescent (Tomarken, Dichter, Garber, & Simien, 2004) offspring of depressed mothers compared to offspring of nondepressed mothers. Davidson and colleagues (2002) have proposed that decreased left frontal activation reflects an underactivation of the approach system and reduced positive emotionality. The extent to which this is a marker of vulnerability that predicts depression in children and adolescents is not yet known.

Sleep Architecture Abnormalities

Although depressed children subjectively report sleep disturbance, sleep EEG results are less consistent in children than adults (Ryan & Dahl, 1993). Depressed children show some sleep anomalies, such as prolonged sleep latencies; reduced REM latencies, especially in more severely depressed patients; increased REM density; and decreased sleep efficiency, although findings are inconsistent across studies, and several studies have failed to find differences between depressed and nondepressed children in EEG sleep patterns (Birmaher et al., 1996; Dahl & Ryan, 1996). The absence of consistent patterns of sleep abnormalities in depressed youth has been attributed to the role of maturational changes, suggesting differences in the nature and function of sleep across development (Dahl & Ryan, 1996; Kaufman et al., 2001).

In summary, with the rapid growth of the fields of genetics, neurobiology, and affective neuroscience it will be possible to identify the biological processes that underlie depressive disorders. Depressed children show both neuroendocrine and neurochemical dysregulation. Although basal cortisol levels do not consistently discriminate between depressed and normal children, the HPA axis response to stress does appear to differ between depressed and nondepressed children. Considerable neuroendocrinological evidence exists of dysregulation of the growth hormone system in depressed children; hyposecretion of GH in response to pharmacologic challenge has been demonstrated in high-risk children (Birmaher et al., 1999), suggesting a possible vulnerability marker. Neurochemical dysregulation, particularly in the serotonergic system, has been found in currently depressed and at-risk children (Birmaher et al., 1997), also suggesting a vulnerability for depression. There also is preliminary evidence of functional and anatomical brain differences in depressed children and in offspring of depressed mothers compared to normal controls. Evidence of sleep disturbances in depressed children has been mixed compared to results with adults, possibly due to maturational factors. Thus, the neurobiological literature in children and adolescents is more variable, although not inconsistent with adult findings (Kaufman et al., 2001).

Stress

Stress plays a prominent role in most theories of depression, and there is considerable empirical evidence of a link between stressful life events and depression in children and adolescents (Compas, Grant, & Ey, 1994; Grant et al., 2004). At least three models have been proposed to explain the relation between stress and psychopathology: stress exposure, stress generation, and reciprocal. According to the stress exposure model, individuals who have experienced stressors will be more likely to be depressed than those who have not (Brown & Harris, 1978; Rudolph, Lambert, Clark, & Kurlakowsky, 2001). Cross-sectional studies have shown that minor and major undesirable life events as well as chronic stressors are associated with depressive symptoms in community (e.g., Adams & Adams, 1991; Allgood-Merten, Lewinsohn, & Hops, 1990; Eley & Stevenson, 2000; Petersen et al., 1991) and clinical samples (Goodyer, Kolvin, & Gatzanis, 1986; Williamson, Birmaher, Anderson, Al-Shabbout, & Ryan, 1995) of children and adolescents. Prospective studies showing that stress temporally precedes increases in symptoms have provided support for the stress exposure model (e.g., Aseltine, Gore, & Colton, 1994; Garber, Keiley, & Martin, 2002; Ge, Lorenz, Conger, Elder, & Simons, 1994; Leadbeater, Kuperminc, Blatt, & Hertzog, 1999; Rudolph et al., 2001). Negative life events also have been found to contribute to the onset of depressive disorders in children and adolescents (Garber et al., 2002; Goodyer, Herbert, Tamplin, & Altham, 2000; Hammen, Adrian, & Hiroto, 1988; Lewinsohn et al., 1994; McFarlane, Bellissimo, Norman, & Lange, 1994; Monroe, Rohde, Seeley, & Lewinsohn, 1999). Only two of these studies (Garber et al., 2002; Monroe et al., 1999), however, controlled for lifetime history of MDD to rule out the possibility that earlier depressive disorder contributed to onset.

The stress generation model (Hammen, 1991a) posits that individuals with psychopathology, particularly depression, tend to generate dependent stressors, that is, stressors that occur as a function of their own behavior. Both cross-sectional (e.g., Rudolph & Hammen, 1999; Rudolph et al., 2000; Williamson et al., 1995) and longitudinal studies (e.g., Daley et al., 1997; Davila, Hammen, Burge, Paley, & Daley, 1995; Potthoff, Holahan, & Joiner, 1995) have found support for the stress generation model, particularly with regard to interpersonal relationships. For example, controlling for baseline levels of depression, dependent interpersonal stressors predicted increased levels of depressive symptoms a year later in women aged 17–18 years (Davila et al., 1995). Several studies (e.g., Aseltine, Gore, & Gordon, 2000; Leadbeater et al., 1999; Potthoff et al., 1995), however, have found that externalizing symptoms also predict subsequent stressful life events. Thus, the stressors generated by depressed individuals may be at least partially due to their comorbid behavior problems.

The reciprocal model essentially puts the two prior models together and highlights the vicious cycle that can occur between depression and stress. Symptoms at one time predict stressors at a later time, and similarly, prior stressors are presumed to lead to subsequent symptoms. Studies testing this model have treated both stress and symptoms as predictor and outcome measures across multiple time points. Such analyses allow one to control for earlier levels of stress or symptoms when predicting outcomes and to examine the cross-sectional and longitudinal relations among these variables. Support for the reciprocal model has been found in a few studies of child and adolescent community samples (Carter & Garber, 2005; Cohen, Burt, & Bjork, 1987; Cole, Nolen-Hoeksema, Girgus, & Paul, 2004; Kim, Conger, Elder, & Lorenz, 2003). In other words, depressive symptoms generated more stress, and stress predicted increased symptoms. Kim et al. (2003) tested separate models for stress and internalizing and externalizing symptoms across adolescence and found evidence of a reciprocal model with regard to both types of symptoms and stress. Using path analyses to compare the fit of the three different models, Carter and Garber (2005) showed that peer stress prospectively predicted increases in internalizing and externalizing symptoms, and symptoms predicted increases in peer stress over time as well. Thus, the reciprocal model fit better than either of the alternative models—stress exposure or stress generation.

Thus, there has been considerable progress toward understanding the relation between stress and depression. Several other important and interesting questions concerning the stress-depression link remain. For example, how do negative life events as well as the stress-depression relation vary by age and gender, and what accounts for these differences? Stressful life events have been found to increase for both boys and girls from childhood through adolescence, with increases being greater for girls (Davis, Matthews, & Twamley, 1999; Ge et al., 1994; Larson & Ham, 1993; Rudolph & Hammen, 1999), paralleling increases in rates of depression during this time (Hankin et al., 1998). Moreover, the association between stress and depression appears to grow stronger in adolescence (Ge et al., 1994; Goodyer et al., 1986; Larson & Ham, 1993), particularly in girls (Hankin et al., 1998; Rudolph & Hammen, 1999; Schraedley, Gotlib, & Hayward, 1999). Only a few studies have examined whether gender moderates the relation between stress and depression. Cohen et al. (1987) reported that negative events predicted depressive symptoms in girls who had experienced fewer positive events in the same time interval, and Ge et al. (1994) showed that growth of stressful life events over time predicted growth in depressive symptoms for girls but not boys.

What stressors are particularly likely to be associated with depression? Although no one specific type of stressful event invariably leads to depression in children and adolescents, certain stressors consistently have been found to be associated with depression. Child abuse or maltreatment is an especially potent predictor of depression (Bifulco, Brown, & Adler, 1991; Boudewyn & Liem, 1995; Browne & Finkelhor, 1986), particularly for women (Weiss, Longhurst, & Mazure, 1999; Whiffen & Clark, 1997). Sexual assault during childhood or adulthood increases the risk of depression by 2.4 in women (Burnam et al., 1988). Poverty also is a significant correlate of depression (Grant et al., 2004; McLoyd, 1998). For example, the rates of depression among low-income mothers are about twice as high as in the general population (Bassuk, Buckner, Perloff, & Bassuk, 1998; Brown & Moran, 1997).

To what extent does the relation between stress and depression vary as a function of type of stressors? Stressful life events have been categorized along a number of dimensions, including loss and danger, interpersonal and noninterpersonal, and dependent and independent. Personal disappointments and losses are associated with depression, whereas danger events to self or other contribute to anxiety (Brown, 1993; Eley & Stevenson, 2000; Goodyer, 2001; Surtees, 1997). Interpersonal stressors involve relationships with others (i.e., peer conflict), whereas noninterpersonal events primarily impact only the individual (i.e., failing a test; Rudolph & Hammen, 1999; Rudolph et al., 2000). Interpersonal stress is significantly associated with depression, particularly in girls (Davis et al., 1999; Leadbeater, Blatt, & Quinlan, 1995; Rudolph, 2002; Rudolph et al., 2000); noninterpersonal stress tends to be associated with externalizing behaviors, although in girls noninterpersonal stress predicts both depression and externalizing behaviors (Rudolph et al., 2000).

Dependent events occur largely as a result of the individual's own behavior, whereas independent events are a result of factors unrelated to one's behavior (e.g., Brown & Harris, 1978; Hammen, 1991b; Goodyer, 2001; Rudolph et al., 2000). Depressed individuals experience higher levels of dependent stress than do nondepressed individuals, particularly interpersonal events (Hammen, 1991a; Hankin & Abramson, 1999). Factors that might contribute to the generation of stress include personality (Daley, Hammen, Davila, & Burge, 1998; Nelson, Hammen, Daley, Burge, & Davila, 2001), interpersonal competence (Davila et al., 1995; Herzberg et al., 1998), and comorbid psychopathology (Daley et al., 1997; Rudolph et al., 2000).

By what biological and psychosocial mechanisms does stress increase an individual's vulnerability to depression? Studies that manipulate stress in laboratory animals have shown that antenatal stress impacts the developing physiology of the fetus and later physiological and behavioral outcomes in offspring of stressed rat and primate mothers. Prenatally stressed rat pups show an elevated corticosterone response to novel environments and reduced corticosteroid receptors in the hippocampus, suggesting that prenatal stress may affect the neurobiological development of systems associated with depression, such as the HPA axis (Henry, Kabbaj, Simon, Le Moal, & Maccari, 1994). Such animals also show greater distress and defensive behavior (Fride & Weinstock, 1988; Takahashi, Baker, & Kalin, 1990) and reduced environmental exploration when exposed to aversive or stressful conditions (Fride, Dan, Feldon, Halevy, & Weinstock, 1986; Poltyrev, Keshet, Kay, & Weinstock, 1996). Moreover, prepartum exposure to stress may produce hyperresponsiveness to later stressors. Clarke and Schneider (Clarke & Schneider, 1993; Clarke, Wittwer, Abbott, & Schneider, 1994; Schneider, 1992) showed that prenatally stressed offspring of rhesus monkeys were less likely than nonstressed controls to play and explore the environment and more likely to engage in clinging, which is an indicator of distress in primates. In addition, the prenatally stressed monkeys had significantly higher levels of cortisol and tended to have higher adrenocorticotropic hormone (ACTH) blood levels when anesthetized. Clarke and Schneider suggested that HPA axis functioning is implicated in the hyperresponsiveness to later environmental stressors.

Thus, animal models indicate that stress that occurs as early as conception can influence outcomes that have been associated with depression in humans. In human infants, stress during pregnancy is associated with negative outcomes for offspring (e.g., Lou, Hansen, & Nordenfoft, 1994; Ward, 1991). Although the mechanisms by which stress impacts the developing fetus are still unknown, Glover (1997) hypothesized that fetal neurophysiological development may be sensitive to the intrauterine hormonal environment, and neurophysiological vulnerability (e.g., HPA axis dysregulation) may make these offspring more sensitive to stress and thereby predispose them to depression as they mature.

Another important question is what accounts for individual variability in response to stress. Although stressors often precede mood disorders, not all individuals exposed to stress become depressed. Genetic as well as psychological vulnerability contribute to differences in how people react both physiologically and cognitively to stress. In a longitudinal study of a representative sample of more than 1,000 children followed from ages 3 through 26, Caspi et al. (2003) showed that a functional polymorphism in the promoter region of the serotonin transporter (5-HTT) gene moderated the effect of stressful life events on depression. Depressive symptoms and disorders were significantly more likely after experiencing stressful life events among individuals with one or two copies of the short allele of the 5-HTT promoter polymorphism compared to individuals who were homozygous for the long allele. These findings are consistent with diathesis-stress models of depression in which deviation in the serotonin transporter gene is the diathesis.

Another kind of diathesis that has been hypothesized to moderate the stress-depression link involves a cognitive style that presumably affects the manner in which individuals appraise and react to stressors when they occur. Much of the individual variability is due to differences in appraisals of the meaning of the events with regard to the self and future (Beck, 1967).

Cognitive Vulnerability

Cognitive theories of depression (Abramson et al., 1989; Abramson, Seligman, & Teasdale, 1978; Beck, 1967) assert that depressed individuals have more negative beliefs about themselves, the world, and their future and tend to make global, stable, and internal attributions for negative events. These negative cognitions are expected to be both concurrently associated with depression and to contribute to the onset and exacerbation of depressive symptoms. Cognitive theories of depression are inherently diathesis-stress theories. When confronted with stressful life events, individuals who have such negative cognitive tendencies will appraise the stressors and their consequences negatively and hence are more likely to become depressed than are individuals who do not have such cognitive styles.

Cross-sectional studies with clinic and community samples consistently have shown that compared to nondepressed youth, depressed children report significantly more negative expectations and hopelessness, cognitive distortions, and cognitive errors (for reviews, see Garber & Hilsman, 1992; Kaslow, Adamson, & Collins, 2000; Weisz, Rudolph, Granger, & Sweeney, 1992) and low perceptions of control and competence (e.g., Cole, Martin, & Powers, 1997; Weisz et al., 2001). Meta-analyses have demonstrated moderate to large effect sizes in cross-sectional studies, indicating a strong concurrent association between negative attributional style and higher levels of depressive symptoms in children and adolescents (Gladstone & Kaslow, 1995; Joiner & Wagner, 1995). Evidence of information-processing errors using laboratory tasks with children, however, has been more mixed (Garber & Kaminski, 2000).

Although covariation between negative cognitions and current depression is consistent with there being a cognitive vulnerability, the alternative that cognitions are a concomitant or consequence of a depressive state cannot be ruled out from cross-sectional studies (Barnett & Gotlib, 1988; Haaga, Dyck, & Ernst, 1991). Negative cognitions could be the result of the underlying depressive process and hold no particular causal status. Moreover, the experience of depression itself can contribute to the development of negative cognitions. Nolen-Hoeksema et al. (1992) reported that explanatory style became more pessimistic over time in children with higher levels of depressive symptoms, even after their level of depression declined. They concluded that "a period of depression during childhood can lead to the development of a fixed and more pessimistic explanatory style, which remains with a child after his or her depression has begun to subside" (p. 418).

Some (Barnett & Gotlib, 1988; Wilson, Nathan, O'Leary, & Clark, 1996) have argued that if cognitive style is a stable vulnerability to depression, or type of personality style, then it should be present before, during, and after depressive episodes, although others have questioned this assertion (Just, Abramson, & Alloy, 2001). If negative cognitions are a stable characteristic of depression-vulnerable individuals, then persons whose depression has remitted might be expected to continue to report a more negative cognitive style than never-depressed individuals, although not necessarily at the same level as those who are currently depressed. Although some studies of adults have found support for this, more studies have not shown that negative cognitive styles are present in remitted depressed patients (see Ingram, Miranda, & Segal, 1998; Persons & Miranda, 1992, for reviews). Studies in children also have not found cognitive differences between remitted and nondepressed individuals (Asarnow & Bates, 1988; McCauley, Mitchell, Burke, & Moss, 1988). Although such findings do not support the view that a stable cognitive style exists, Just et al. (2001) noted several limitations of such "remission" studies, including that (a) treatment could have altered formerly depressed patients' cognitions, (b) the formerly depressed group might have been heterogeneous with regard to cognitive style, and (c) cognitive style might need to be activated to be assessed properly. Therefore, it is premature to rule out the possibility that a stable cognitive style exists that makes some individuals particularly vulnerable to depression.

Cognitive vulnerability also has been studied in offspring of depressed parents. If these children are at risk for depression, then they might be more likely to exhibit negative cognitions than children whose parents have not had a mood disorder. Indeed, children of depressed mothers have been found to report significantly lower perceived self-worth and a more depressive attributional style than do children of well mothers (Garber & Robinson, 1997; Goodman, Adamson, Riniti, & Cole, 1994; Jaenicke et al., 1987; Taylor & Ingram, 1999). Thus, children who are at risk for depression but who have not yet experienced depression themselves report a more negative cognitive style that might increase their risk of later depression.

Prospective studies can show the extent to which cognitive vulnerability temporally precedes and predicts increases in depressive symptoms and onset of depressive disorder. Results of longitudinal investigations of the role of cognitions in the prediction of depression in children and adolescents have shown that global self-worth (Allgood-Merton et al., 1990; Hammen, 1988; Vitaro, Pelletier, Gagnon, & Baron, 1995), negative attributions (Dixon & Ahrens, 1992; Hankin, Abramson, & Siler, 2001; Hilsman & Garber, 1995; Lewinsohn, Joiner, & Rohde, 2001; Nolen-Hoeksema et al., 1992; Panak & Garber, 1992; Robinson et al., 1995), inferential style (Abela, 2001), and perceived self-competence in specific domains (Hoffman, Cole, Martin, Tram, & Seroczynski, 2001; Vitaro et al., 1995) predict depressive symptoms (e.g., Allgood-Merton et al., 1990; Vitaro et al., 1995) and diagnoses (Garber et al., 2002; Hammen, 1988), controlling for prior levels of depression and often in interaction with negative life events. These same cognitive constructs, however, also have failed to predict depressive symptoms (Bennett & Bates, 1995; Dubois, Felner, Brand, & George, 1999; Robertson & Simons, 1989) and onset of new episodes (Goodyer et al., 2000; Hammen et al., 1988). Some reasons for these failures have included small samples, not testing cognitions in the context of stress, the possible need to prime negative cognitions with mood or stress inductions, and the use of samples that were receiving treatment (e.g., Robertson & Simons, 1989).

Interpersonal Vulnerability

Interpersonal relationships are particularly important in the development and maintenance of depression (Gotlib & Hammen, 1992; Joiner & Coyne, 1999). Children whose caretakers are consistently accessible and supportive will develop cognitive representations, or working models, of the self and others as positive and trustworthy, whereas those whose caretakers are unresponsive or inconsistent will develop insecure attachments leading to working models of abandonment, self-criticism, and excessive dependency (Bowlby, 1980). These working models likely contribute to the development of cognitive schema about the self and others. Negative working models presumably increase an individual's vulnerability to depression, particularly when exposed to new interpersonal stressors (Cummings & Cicchetti, 1990).

Families of depressed individuals are characterized by problems with attachment, communication, conflict, cohesion, and social support and poor child-rearing practices (for reviews, see Beardslee et al., 1998; Cummings & Davies, 1994; Downey & Coyne, 1990; Kaslow, Deering, & Racusin, 1994; Keitner & Miller, 1990; McCauley & Myers, 1992; Rapee, 1997). Secure attachments help infants explore and cope with the environment, whereas insecure and disorganized attachments lead infants to seek protection by withdrawing from the environment altogether (Bowlby, 1980; Trad, 1994). Securely attached 2-year-old children have been found to be more cooperative, persistent, and enthusiastic; show more positive affect; and function better overall than those with insecure attachments (Matas, Arend, & Sroufe, 1978). In adolescents, depression has been linked with less-secure attachments to parents (Kenny, Moilanen, Lomax, & Brabeck, 1993; Pavlidis & McCauley, 2001). Adolescents undergoing stressful life events are more likely to become depressed if they had insecure attachments compared to securely attached adolescents (e.g., Hammen et al., 1995; Kobak, Sudler, & Gamble, 1991).

Other kinds of dysfunctional family patterns associated with depression in children include chronic criticism, harsh discipline, and serious abuse and neglect (e.g., Kaslow et al., 1994; Rapee, 1997). Maltreatment interferes with the development of emotional competence; leads to avoidant or resistant attachments, especially if the caretaker is the perpetrator of the abuse (Lamb, Gaensbauer, Malkin, & Schultz, 1985); and results in withdrawal behaviors in infants and self-esteem deficits later in childhood (Gaensbauer & Sands, 1979; Trad,

1987). The parent-infant relationship is inevitably worsened from such abuse, which in turn puts the infant in greater danger of being abused again (Trad, 1987).

Interpersonal risk factors have been found to be associated with FTT in infants; these factors include poor parent-child interactions, family dysfunction, and inadequate parental knowledge, all of which also have been linked with depression in children (Boddy & Skuse, 1994; Frank & Drotar, 1994; Raynor & Rudolf, 1996). Temperamental characteristics of the child such as low appetite, inadequate feeding skills, and being shy and undemanding can be maladaptive in feeding situations and thereby contribute to FTT (Wright & Birks, 2000). A noninteractive tendency by these infants can lead to less responsiveness from parents, causing greater withdrawal by the infant and thereby creating a vicious cycle of maladaptive parent-child interactions (Frank & Drotar, 1994; Skuse, 1985). Thus, FTT may be a form of depression in infants.

In older children, two parenting dimensions particularly associated with depression are psychological control/autonomy and acceptance/rejection (e.g., Barber, 1996; Parker, Tupling, & Brown, 1979; Schwarz, Barton-Henry, & Pruzinsky, 1985). In retrospective studies, currently depressed adults recalled their parents to have been critical, rejecting, controlling, and intrusive (Gerlsma, Emmelkamp, & Arrindell, 1990; Parker, 1983). Cross-sectional studies have found that currently depressed children describe their parents as authoritarian, controlling, rejecting, and unavailable (Amanat & Butler, 1984; Stein et al., 2000), and their families as being less cohesive and more conflictual than do nondepressed youth (e.g., Stark, Humphrey, Crook, & Lewis, 1990; Walker, Garber, & Greene, 1993). Mothers of depressed children similarly describe themselves as more rejecting, less communicative, and less affectionate than do mothers of both normal and psychiatric controls (Lefkowitz & Tesiny, 1984; Puig-Antich et al., 1985a). In observational studies, mothers of depressed children have been described as being less rewarding (Cole & Rehm, 1986), more dominant and controlling (Amanat & Butler, 1984; Kobak et al., 1991), and less supportive and positive (Sheeber & Sorenson, 1998) than mothers of nondepressed children. Depressed children also have been observed to have poorer communication and problem-solving skills and are less supportive and assertive than nondepressed children (Kobak & Ferenz-Gillies, 1995; Sheeber & Sorenson, 1998). Dysfunctional family environments, however, are not unique to families with depressed children. For example, Asarnow, Carlson, and Guthrie (1987) found that both depressed and nondepressed inpatient youth reported disrupted family environments.

The relation between interpersonal difficulties and depression is likely to be reciprocal and transactional. Prospective studies have shown that social problems temporally precede depression and that depression contributes to interpersonal difficulties. Several longitudinal studies have found a significant relation between a dysfunctional family environment and subsequent depressive symptoms (e.g., Barber, 1996; Garrison et al., 1997; Ge, Best, Conger, & Simons, 1996; McKeown et al., 1997; Rueter, Scaramella, Wallace, & Conger, 1999; Sheeber, Hops, Alpert, Davis, & Andrews, 1997), although others have reported only cross-sectional analyses despite having longitudinal data available (e.g., Ohannessian, Lerner, Lerner, & von Eye, 1994; Papini & Roggman, 1992), and still others have reported null findings (Burge & Hammen, 1991; Burge et al., 1997). Barber (1996) showed that children's ratings of parents' psychologically controlling behavior predicted their depressive symptoms, controlling for prior levels of depression, although children's prior depressive symptoms also predicted their ratings of their parents' behavior. Other studies that have controlled for prior levels of depressive symptoms also have shown that ratings of family expressiveness predict depression in girls' (Burt, Cohen, & Bjorck, 1988) and adolescents' reports of family adaptability and cohesion (Garrison et al., 1990; McKeown et al., 1997). Perceptions of family support significantly predict increases in depressive symptoms (McFarlane, Bellissimo, & Norman, 1995), and maternal hostile child-rearing attitudes significantly predict increases in children's depressive symptoms (Katainen, Raikkonen, Keskivaara, & Keltikangas-Jarvinen, 1999). Using observational data, Ge et al. (1996) reported that lower levels of parental warmth and higher levels of maternal hostility significantly predicted increases in adolescents' internalizing symptoms. In this same sample, Rueter et al. (1999) found that escalating parent-adolescent conflict predicted increases in adolescent internalizing symptoms, which in turn increased the risk of the onset of internalizing disorders.

Family adversity also contributes to the maintenance or relapse of depressive disorders in youth. Such interpersonal difficulties as low paternal involvement, stressful family environments, and lack of responsiveness to maternal discipline significantly predict persistent depression (Goodyer, Germany, Gowrusankur, & Altham, 1991; Goodyer, Herbert, Tamplin, Secher, & Pearson, 1997; McCauley et al., 1993). In addition, negative attitudes by family members toward depressed children have been found to predict relapse (Asarnow, Goldstein, Tompson, & Guthrie, 1993).

Depressed parents also have been found to have relationship problems with their offspring manifested in greater reported conflict and less coherence in their families, greater hostility toward their children, less involvement and affection with their children, and poorer communication than nondepressed parents (Goodman & Gotlib, 1999; Hammen, 1991b). Observations of depressed mothers interacting with their children reveal that these mothers are more negative and controlling, are less responsive and affectively involved, and use less productive communications (Lovejoy, Graczyk, O'Hare, & Newman, 2000). Depressed mothers spend less time talking to and touching their babies and show more negative affect in their interactions with their infants, who themselves show less positive affect, less activity, and more frequent protests (Field, 1995). Such behaviors by depressed parents can lead to disturbed attachment and an inability by infants to regulate emotions, thereby putting the infant at risk for depression (Gaensbauer, Harmon, Cytryn, & McKnew, 1984). Thus, negative reciprocal interaction patterns also tend to develop between depressed mothers and their children (Hammen, Burge, & Stansbury, 1990).

With regard to peer relationships, self-reported depression significantly correlates with teachers' reports of peer rejection in children (Rudolph, Hammen, & Burge, 1994). Rejection by peers also has been found to predict higher levels of self-reported depressive symptoms among antisocial but not nonantisocial youth (French, Conrad, & Turner, 1995). Panak & Garber (1992) showed that increases in peer-rated aggression predicted increases in self-reported depression through the mediator of increases in peer-reported rejection. Moreover, the relation between peer-rated rejection and self-reported depression was mediated by perceived rejection. Kistner, Balthazor, Risi, and Burton (1999) similarly found that perceived rejection predicted increases in depressive symptoms during middle childhood. Finally, in a longitudinal study of children in sixth grade, Nolan, Flynn, and Garber (2003) found that a composite measure of rejection by peers, family, and teachers significantly predicted depressive symptoms across 3 years. Thus, depression in children is associated with high levels of interpersonal conflict and rejection from various members in their social domain.

COURSE, COMPLICATIONS, AND PROGNOSIS

The reported lengths of depressive episodes tend to vary as a function of the type of sample used. Mean durations for MDD of 32 weeks and 36 weeks have been reported for outpatient children aged 8–13 years (Kovacs, Feinberg, Crouse-Novak, Paulauskas, & Finkelstein, 1984; Kovacs, Feinberg, Crouse-Novak, Paulauskas, Pollock, & Finkelstein, 1984) and inpatient and outpatient adolescents (McCauley et al., 1993; Rao et al., 1995), respectively. These durations are generally similar to those reported in adults (Coryell et al., 1994). Using community samples, Lewinsohn, Clarke, Seeley, and Rohde (1994) found a mean duration of 26 weeks in adolescents; Kessler and Walters (1998) reported a mean of 32.5 weeks for the *longest* lifetime episode; and Rao, Hammen, and Daley (1999) found a median of 8 weeks' duration in a sample of adolescent girls. Finally, in offspring of depressed parents median durations of MDD have been found to be between 12 and 16 weeks (Beardslee, Keller, Lavori, Staley, & Sacks, 1993; Kaminski & Garber, 2002; Warner, Weissman, Fendrich, Wickramaratne, & Moreau, 1992). Kaminski and Garber noted that differences across studies may be due, in part, to the use of the mean versus median episode durations. They recommended that both be reported because the median is less affected by extreme scores and therefore may provide a more accurate representation of episode duration.

The minimum episode length of DD is set at 1 year for children according to the *DSM-IV* (APA, 1994), although this provides little information about the typical length of illness. The mean duration of dysthymia has been found to be 156 weeks and a median length of 203 weeks in clinical samples (Kovacs, Feinberg, Crouse-Novak, Paulauskas, & Finkelstein, 1984), a mean of 130 weeks in a community sample (Lewinsohn, Rohde, Seeley, & Hops, 1991), a median duration of 260 weeks in a high-risk clinical sample (Keller et al., 1988), and a mean of 113.89 weeks and a median of 125 weeks in a community high-risk sample (Kaminski & Garber, 2002).

Minor depression includes a dysphoric mood plus two to four associated symptoms lasting for a minimum of 2 weeks (APA, 1994). The NCS study revealed a mean duration of 21.3 weeks for the longest minor depressive episode (Kessler, Zhao, Blazer, & Swartz, 1997). The duration decreased to 10.3 weeks when only the 15- to 24-year-olds were examined (Kessler & Walters, 1998). In a community high-risk sample (Kaminski & Garber, 2002), the mean length of minor depressive disorders was 28.84 weeks, with a median of 11.0 weeks.

In general, longer depressive episodes are associated with worse functioning over time. Rao et al. (1999) found a link between length of illness and decreased functioning in both romantic relationships and academics among young adult women. Longer depressive episodes also are associated with a shorter time to recurrence (McCauley et al., 1993), and prolonged episodes of dysthymia increase the odds of developing superimposed major depressions (Keller & Shapiro, 1982).

With regard to longer term prognosis, major depression is quite recurrent over the life span and can be chronic (Coryell & Winokur, 1992; Judd et al., 1998). Children with mood disorders have recurrent depressive episodes during adolescence (Costello, Mustillo, Erklani, Keeler, & Angold, 2003; Emslie et al., 1997; Hankin et al., 1998; Kovacs, Feinberg, Crouse-Novak, Paulauskas, & Finkelstein, 1984; Kovacs, Feinberg, Crouse-Novak, Paulauskas, Pollock, & Finkelstein, 1984; Vostanis, Feehan, & Grattan, 1998) and adulthood (Garber, Kriss, Koch, & Lindholm 1988; Harrington, Fudge, Rutter, Pickles, & Hill, 1990; Weissman et al., 1999b), and adolescents have recurrences later in adolescence (Lewinsohn et al., 1994; Rohde, Clarke, Lewinsohn, Seeley, & Kaufman, 2001) and into adulthood (Lewinsohn, Rohde, Klein, & Seeley, 1999; Rao et al., 1995, 1999; Weissman et al., 1999a). Recurrence rates have ranged from 20 percent to 72 percent over 2–10 years (Emslie et al., 1997; Harrington et al., 1990; Kovacs, Feinberg, Crouse-Novak, Paulauskas, & Finkelstein, 1984; Lewinsohn, Rohde, et al., 1999). For example, Kovacs, Feinberg, Crouse-Novak, Paulauskas, and Finkelstein (1984) found that the cumulative probability of a recurrent MDE among children ages 8–13 was .72 over the course of 5 years from the onset of the disorder.

In general, early-onset mood disorders are associated with increased risk of relapse (Gonzales, Lewinsohn, & Clarke, 1985; Keller, Lavori, Lewis, & Klerman, 1983), a more severe course (Hammen, Davila, Brown, Ellicott, & Gitlin, 1992; Kovacs, Feinberg, Crouse-Novak, Paulauskas, and Finkelstein, 1984), and increased familial loading of depression (e.g., Weissman et al., 1988). Recurrent depressive episodes tend to have more negative functional outcomes in school, work, and interpersonal relationships (Lewinsohn, Rohde, Seeley, Klein, & Gotlib, 2003; Rao et al., 1999) and an increased risk of suicide (Kovacs, Goldston, & Gatsonis, 1993; Weissman et al., 1999a). Moreover, the longer depressive episodes last, the more difficult they are to treat (Judd et al., 1998; Thase & Howland, 1994).

Not only are depressed children and adolescents likely to have recurrent depressive episodes as adults, but there also tends to be some specificity in the continuity of mood disorders. Depressed children and adolescents were more likely to have subsequent episodes of depression than were those who had had other psychiatric disorders as children (Harrington et al., 1990) or had had no prior psychiatric history during adolescence (Weissman et al., 1999a). On the other hand, children with prepubertal-onset depressions were more likely than normal controls to develop substance abuse and conduct disorders during the subsequent 10–15 years (Weissman et al., 1999b). Thus, prior depression tends to predict subsequent depressive episodes, although childhood-onset depressions also tend to precede other psychiatric disorders (Pine, Cohen, Gurley, Brook, & Ma, 1998). Moreover, some studies of prepubertally depressed children have not found continuity into adulthood (Harrington et al., 1990; Pine et al., 1998; Weissman et al., 1999b). For example, Harrington et al. (1990) reported that children with prepubertal onset of depression were at significantly *lower* risk of having major depression as adults than were postpubertal patients. Harrington et al. (1990) suggested that this could have been due to artifacts of their methodology such as poor measurement of prepubertal depression or the inaccurate documentation of the onset of puberty. Nevertheless, this interesting result is consistent with the view that prepubertal-onset depressions might differ from adolescent- and adult-onset depressions in several important ways, including phenomenology and outcome.

One other important complication that can affect the course and outcome of depression is the co-occurrence of other psychiatric disorders. Such comorbidity affects risk of recurrence, duration of episodes, suicide attempts, utilization of mental health services, and functional outcomes (Birmaher et al., 1996; Essau, Conradt, & Petermann, 2000; Lewinsohn, Rohde, & Seeley, 1994). Lewinsohn et al. reported that depressed adolescents with another psychiatric diagnosis had poorer global functioning, more academic problems and more suicide attempts and were more likely to have received treatment compared to teens with pure MDD only. Among adolescents receiving cognitive-behavioral group treatment, comorbid substance use problems have been found to be particularly associated with slower recovery from depression (Rohde et al., 2001).

Reviews of studies of comorbidity (Angold, Costello, & Erkanli, 1999; Hammen & Compas, 1994) have shown that depression during childhood and adolescence increased the probability of another disorder by about 20 times. In depressed children, comorbidity has been estimated to range from 53 percent (Angold & Costello, 1993) to between 80 percent and 95 percent (Kovacs, 1996); among depressed adolescents, about 40 percent had one additional disorder and 18 percent had at least two other disorders (Essau et al., 2000). In a meta-analysis of community studies, Angold et al. (1999) reported that a mean odds ratio (i.e., degree of association) of depression with anxiety was 8.2, with ADHD was 5.5, and with conduct/oppositional defiant disorder was 6.6.

Dysthymia has the highest rate of comorbidity; 30 percent of children with MDD had underlying dysthymia and 70 percent of early-onset dysthymia patients had a superimposed major depressive disorder within 2–3 years (Kovacs, Akiskal, Gatsonis, & Parrone, 1994). Children with such so-called double depression have more severe and longer depressive episodes, a higher rate of other comorbid disorders, more suicidality, and worse social impairment than either disorder alone (Goodman et al., 2000). Common comorbid diagnoses with dysthymia are anxiety disorders, conduct disorder, ADHD, and enuresis or encopresis (Kovacs et al., 1994).

Estimates of comorbid disruptive disorders with MDD have ranged from 10 percent to 80 percent (Anderson et al., 1987; Hammen & Compas, 1994). Anxiety disorders are particularly likely to be comorbid with depression, with estimates ranging from 30 percent to 75 percent (Hammen & Compas, 1994; Kovacs, Gatsonis, Paulauskas, & Richards, 1989). Comorbidity of depressive and anxiety disorders is so high that some have challenged the discriminant validity of the two diagnoses (Achenbach, 1991b; Patterson, Greising, Hyland, & Burger, 1997). Others have suggested that anxiety and depression share common causal processes such as negative affectivity (Laurent & Ettelson, 2001; Watson & Clark, 1984), and genes (Kendler et al., 1993; Silberg, Rutter, & Eaves, 2001). Still others have suggested that anxiety precedes depression in children (Avenevoli, Stolar, Li, Dierker, & Merikangas, 2001; Cole, Peeke, Martin, Truglio, & Seroczynski, 1997; Kovacs et al., 1989), although the magnitude of process underlying this relation is unclear.

Studies using dimensional measures also have shown high levels of covariation between depression and other syndromes. Self-report measures of anxiety and depression have correlated between .60 and .80 (Brady & Kendall, 1992), and of aggressive and depressive symptoms between .40 and .73 after controlling for shared method variance in reports of children, parents, and peers (Cole & Carpentieri, 1990; Garber, Quiggle, Panak, & Dodge, 1991). In general, studies using either continuous (e.g., Curran & Bollen, 2001) or categorical (e.g., Rohde, Lewinsohn, & Seeley, 1991; Weissman, Fendrich, Warner, & Wickramaratne, 1992) measures have found that externalizing behaviors typically precede the occurrence of depressive symptoms.

Thus, comorbidity between depression and other internalizing and externalizing problems in children is very common. This raises questions about whether depression in children is a distinct clinical entity that can be differentiated from other forms of psychopathology, and whether the current nomenclature needs to be adjusted to more accurately reflect such covariation among syndromes. Other questions to be explored are (a) to what extent the covariation of depression with other syndromes changes with development, (b) what processes explain such developmental changes, and (c) what mechanisms account for comorbidity between depression and other forms of psychopathology, particularly anxiety and disruptive behavior disorders.

ASSESSMENT AND DIAGNOSIS

Methods of assessing depression in children and adolescents include self-report, others' reports, clinical interviews, projective techniques, physiological and neuroendocrine measures, naturalistic behavioral observations, and laboratory tasks (e.g., Birmaher et al., 1996; Brooks & Kutcher, 2000; Curry & Craighead, 1993; Garber & Kaminski, 2002; Hodges, 1994; Kazdin, 1990; Kendall, Cantwell, & Kazdin, 1989; Myers & Winters, 2002; Reynolds, 1994). A comprehensive review of each of these methods is beyond the scope of this chapter. Rather, we highlight several assessment issues and some of the more widely used methods of measuring depressive symptoms and disorders in children and adolescents.

Several challenges exist in the attempt to accurately assess depression in children. Difficulties may arise in the evaluation process because language, reading, and cognitive abilities are not fully developed in children (Kovacs, 1986, Reynolds, 1994). Also, symptoms that identify problems at one stage of development may not indicate pathology at other stages. Another pitfall is that because assessment of depression in children has evolved as a derivative of assessment of depression in adults, signs of depression unique to children may go undetected. Therefore, accurate assessment must incorporate a global view of child development.

Gathering information from multiple sources including parents, teachers, peers, and the children themselves can provide a more complete picture of the child's psychological state. These various informants, however, have different perspectives and thus often yield different results (Achenbach, McConaughy, & Howell, 1987). Kashani, Holcomb, and Orvaschel (1986) found that parent and teacher ratings of depressive symptoms in preschool children were not correlated, and an evaluation by objective observers showed that teachers were more accurate raters in this school context. Moreover, both teachers and children themselves tend to identify depression more often than do parents (Fleming & Offord, 1990), although depressed parents have been found to overreport their children's depressive symptoms (e.g., Breslau, Davis, & Prabucki, 1988; Youngstrom, Izard, & Ackerman, 1999). In general, ratings of interinformant agreement about child and adolescent depression have tended to be quite low (Kazdin, 1994). Thus, this discrepancy has been related to several factors, including parental psychopathology; actual differences in behaviors across settings; and the difficulty of observing the more subjective symptoms that define depressive disorder such as sadness, hopelessness, worthlessness, and guilt.

Two central concerns regarding the use of more than one informant to assess depression in children are (a) how to determine who is the best source about particular symptoms and (b) how to resolve discrepancies between informants. Many researchers (e.g., Angold et al., 1987; Hammen & Rudolph, 1996; Kazdin & Marciano, 1998; Schwartz, Gladstone, &

Kaslow, 1998) have suggested that individuals may know more about their own internal state such as mood, self-worth, guilt, and hopelessness, whereas others (e.g., parents, teachers) might be better reporters about observable symptoms such as psychomotor problems, changes in eating patterns, and concentration. Studies systematically testing this hypothesis, however, have not yet been conducted. Although some children can report accurately about their symptoms, others lack either the ability or the motivation to do so. In such cases, others, particularly parents, may be the only source of information available. Given that we do not yet know how to identify who will or will not be an accurate informant, the best strategy is to interview both the children and their parent(s) about all depressive symptoms.

How, then, should discrepant information from different informants be combined? Several approaches have been used depending on the interview. For the Schedule for Affective Disorders and Schizophrenia for School-Aged Children (K-SADS; Puig-Antich & Chambers, 1978), the clinical interviewer makes a summary severity rating for each symptom on the basis of all available information. If there are major discrepancies in the child and parent reports, then the clinician interviews parent and child together to clarify their views (Ambrosini, 2000). Another approach has been to use different combination rules: (a) the *or rule* uses the higher of the two ratings; that is, if either person says the symptom is present, then it is. This method tends to overestimate the number of cases; (b) the *consensus rule* counts only those symptoms on which there is agreement, which tends to underestimate cases; and (c) the *best informant rule* uses the child's report for the more subjective symptoms (e.g., sadness, guilt) and the parent's report for more observable symptoms (e.g., psychomotor changes). The validity of each of these approaches is still a matter of debate (McClellan & Werry, 2003).

Thus, despite the general call for using multiple sources when assessing depression in children, there are several reasons for keeping parents' and children's reports separate, including the following: (a) correlations between children's and parents' ratings of depression tend to be relatively small (Achenbach et al., 1987; Herjanic & Reich, 1997); (b) cross-informant stabilities of internalizing symptoms have been found to be smaller than intrainformant stabilities (Hofstra, Van der Ende, & Verhulst, 2000); (c) child- and parent-report measures of children's depression have somewhat different factor structures (Cole, Hoffman, Tram, & Maxwell, 2000); (d) the relation of depression to other constructs such as stressful life events (Compas, Howell, Phares, Williams, & Giunta, 1989; Stanger, McConaughy, & Achenbach, 1992) and perceived control (Weisz et al., 2001) tend to be stronger for children's self-reported depression compared to parents'

reports of children's depression; (f) heritability estimates have been found to be greater for parents' reports of children's depression than children's self-reported depression (Eaves et al., 1997; Thaper & McGuffin; 1994); and (g) parental depression might influence parents' ratings of their children's symptoms (e.g., Breslau et al., 1988; Youngstrom et al., 1999).

Many useful tools are available to assess depression in children and adolescents. Table 12.3 presents information about structured and semistructured interviews that can be used to diagnose mood disorders. Highly structured interviews can obtain a lot of information and are relatively easy to administer. Because the interviewer strictly follows the script, little training is needed. This format does, however, prevent the interviewer from following up on seemingly important responses.

A commonly used, highly structured interview for assessing depression is the Diagnostic Interview for Children and Adolescents (DICA; Herjanic & Reich, 1982), which can be used with children aged 6 or older and covers interpersonal relationships, academic and social functioning, and symptomatology. The DICA has good interrater reliability and moderate validity (Reich, 2000; Shaffer, Fisher, Lucas, Dulcan, & Schwab-Stone, 2000). Compared to less structured clinical interviews, the DICA tends to overdiagnose depression, and it has low parent-child agreement (Reich, 2000). These problems are caused in part by the rigidity of the interview.

In contrast, semistructured interviews have the advantage of having a set agenda but allowing interviewers latitude to pursue what they believe is relevant to the diagnosis. Although this type of interview elicits more information, it does require skilled and experienced clinical interviewers. Moreover, the scoring of the interview is more subjective, which may make it vulnerable to greater variability and possible bias.

The K-SADS is one of the most widely used interviews for diagnosing mood disorders. Developed by Puig-Antich and Chambers (1978), it consists of similar but separate interviews for both the parent and child. The parent is interviewed first to establish onset, duration, and chronicity of the disorder, and both parent and child are given semistructured questions about each symptom. The freedom of the structure necessitates more clinically sophisticated interviewers. The K-SADS has good reliability and validity (Ambrosini, 2000).

The most commonly used clinician-rated measure of just depression symptoms in children and adolescents is the Children's Depression Rating Scale—Revised (CDRS-R; Poznanski, Freeman, & Mokros, 1984; Poznanski, Mokros, Grossman, & Freeman, 1985), which is modeled after the Hamilton Rating Scale for Depression (Hamilton, 1960), used with adults and sometimes adolescents. The CDRS-R

TABLE 12.3 Diagnostic Interviews

Name	Authors	Age	Type of interview	Internal consistency	Test-retest reliability	Interrater reliability	Construct validity	Concurrent validity
ChIPS	Weller et al., 2000	6–18	Structured					Correlates with DICA: .47–.60; concordance with clinicians' diagnoses: κ = .03–.39
DICA	Herjanic & Reich, 2000	6–17	Structured		Ages 6–12: κ = .55–.90 Ages 13–18: κ = .80–.90	κ = .85	Discriminated poorly between psychiatric and pediatric referrals	Concordance with clinicians' diagnoses: κ = .43–.52
DISC	Shaffer et al., 2000	9–17	Structured		Clinical Parent κ = .66 Youth κ = .92 Community Parent κ = .55 Youth κ = .37	κ = .94–1.0	Discriminated well between psychiatric and pediatric referrals	Correlates with CBCL internalizing scale: Parent: .71–.72 Child: .14–.29; Low agreement with K-SADS, and with clinicians' diagnoses: κ = .17
CAPA	Angold & Costello, 2000	9–17	Semi-structured			MDD: κ = .90 Dysthymia: κ = .85	Diagnoses rates of depression similarly or less than are commonly found	
CAS	Hodges et al., 1982	5–17	Semi-structured	α = .80	MDD: κ = .70–.89 Dysthymia: κ = .70–.86	MDD: κ = 1.0 Dysthymia: κ = .71	Discriminated well between inpatients, outpatients, and controls	Correlates well with clinicians' ratings, CDI, CBCL Anx/Dep Subscale: r = .51; good concordance with K-SADS: κ = .52–.75
ISCA	Kovacs, 1985	8–17	Semi-structured		r = .84	r = .96	Differentiated between MDD, Dysthymia, and ADDM	Correlates: CDI: r = .33; CBCL Anx/Dep scale: r = .38
K-SADS	Orvaschel et al., 1982	6–18	Semi-structured	α = .68–.84	KSADS-II: κ = .54 KSADS-III-R: κ = .77 KSADS-P/L: κ = .90 (lifetime: 1.0)	κ = .75	Positive correlation with cognitions associated with depression	Concordance with CAS: κ = .52–.75; CDI: r = .39; Clinicians' diagnoses: κ = .58
CDRS	Poznanski et al., 1984	6–12	Semi-structured		r = .86	r = .80	Problems differentiating depression from anxiety;	r = .87 with clinicians' diagnoses; r = .89 with CDI for females
Dominic-R	Valla et al., 1994	6–11	Pictorial	α = .83	κ = .44–.69 for symptoms	κ = .79–.95		Concordance with clinicians' diagnoses: κ = .80–.88
PICA-III-R	Ernst et al., 1994	6–16	Pictorial	α = .84			Discriminated between depression, psychotic disorder, and ODD/CD: Wilks λ = .67	Positive correlation with clinicians' diagnoses
PRESS	Martini et al., 1990	3–5	Pictorial	α = .89	κ = .86	κ = .84		Correlates: CBCL Anx/Dep scale: r = .55; GRASP: r = .54–.68

Note. α = coefficient alpha; κ = kappa; ADDM = adjustment disorder with depressed mood; CAPA = Child and Adolescent Psychiatric Assessment; CAS = Child Assessment Schedule; CBCL = Child Behavior Checklist; CDI = Child Depression Inventory; CDRS = Children's Depression Rating Scale; ChIPS = Children's Interview for Psychiatric Syndromes; DICA = Diagnostic Interview for Children and Adolescents; DISC = Diagnostic Interview Schedule for Children; GRASP = General Rating of Affective Symptoms in Preschoolers; ISCA = Interview Schedule for Children and Adolescents; K-SADS = Schedule for Affective Disorders and Schizophrenia for School-Age Children; KSADS-II = K-SADS Version 2; KSADS-III-R = K-SADS Version 3; KSADS P/L = K-SADS Present and Lifetime Version; MDD = major depressive disorder; ODD/CD = oppositional defiant disorder/conduct disorder; PICA-III-R = Pictorial Instrument for Children and Adolescents; PRESS = Preschool Symptoms Self-Report.

measures the presence and severity of 17 depressive symptoms. Mothers and children are interviewed separately about the extent of the children's depressive symptoms during the previous 2 weeks. The CDRS-R has good interrater reliability and correlates highly with global ratings of improvement (Emslie et al., 1997).

Another valuable and efficient method for assessing depression is with questionnaires. Self-report measures are the easiest to use and require no interviewer, thereby eliminating any chance for bias or variability in interviewer behavior. Scoring of these measures is standardized and objective. They are more limited, however, in the amount and depth of information obtainable. Self-report depression measures are particularly appropriate for screening but cannot be used to make diagnoses (Craighead, Curry, & Ilardi, 1995; Dierker et al., 2001). They also are less useful for younger children who may lack the linguistic or cognitive ability necessary to read, comprehend, and complete them.

The most widely used self-report measure of depressive symptoms is the Children's Depression Inventory (CDI; Kovacs, 1981). The CDI is a downward extension of the Beck Depression Inventory (Beck, Ward, Mendelson, Mock, & Erbaugh, 1961), which is a self-report measure of depressive symptoms for adults that also can be used with adolescents. The CDI measures cognitive, affective, and behavioral symptoms of depression, and it requires only a third grade reading level. Children rate each of the 27 items for how much they experienced the symptom during the past 2 weeks. The CDI has adequate internal consistency, test-retest reliability, and convergent validity with other self-report measures (e.g., Saylor, Finch, Spirito, & Bennett, 1984; Smucker, Craighead, Craighead, & Green, 1986), differentiates between normal and clinic-referred children (Carey, Faulstich, Gresham, Ruggiero, & Enyart, 1987; Garber, 1984), and correlates moderately with parents' reports of their children's depression (Garber, 1984). One limitation of the CDI is that it has a serious attenuation effect at the second administration (Twenge & Nolen-Hoeksema, 2002), although this probably is not unique to this measure.

Another commonly used self-report depression measure is the Center for Epidemiological Studies Depressive Scale for Children (CES-DC; Radloff, 1977, 1991). Children rate the frequency with which they experienced each of the 20 depressive symptoms over the past week using a 5-point Likert scale. The CES-DC is short and easy to read, has been successfully administered in several large adolescent school samples, and has good psychometrics with youth (Lewinsohn et al., 1991; Roberts, Andrews, Lewinsohn, & Hops, 1990).

Other self-report depression measures used with children and adolescents include the Reynolds Adolescent Depression Scale (Reynolds, 1989), the Depression Self-Rating Scale (Birleson, 1981), the Mood and Feelings Questionnaire (Angold et al., 1987), the Dimensions of Depression Profile for Children and Adolescents (Harter & Nowakowski, 1987), and the Multiscore Depression Inventory for Children (Berndt 1986). The youth self-report version of the Child Behavior Checklist (Achenbach, 1991a) has a subscale that is a combined measure of anxious and depressive symptoms.

Parents, teachers, and peers also have been used to report about children's depressive symptoms. Parent report measures of depressive symptoms include the parent version of the CDI (P-CDI; Cole et al., 2000; Garber, 1984; Kazdin, French, Unis, & Esveldt-Dawson, 1983) and the anxious/depressed subscale of the Child Behavior Checklist (Achenbach et al., 1991). The Child Behavior Checklist—Teacher Report Form (CBCL-TRF; Achenbach & Edelbrock, 1991) is the teacher version of the CBCL that provides a similar profile of the various dimensions of childhood psychopathology. A peer measure of depression is the Peer Nomination Inventory for Depression (Lefkowitz & Tesiny, 1980). Finally, laboratory behavioral measures also can be used to assess depressive symptoms (Garber & Kaminski, 2002); as yet, there are no valid biological tests for diagnosing depression in children (Birmaher, Ryan, Williamson, & Brent, 1996).

IMPACT ON ENVIRONMENT

Depression in children and adolescents is associated with difficulties in many aspects of their environments, including family, school, and peer relationships. Studies that have specifically examined the effects of depressive symptoms or disorders on youths' environments have been relatively rare, and almost all of the available information comes from cross-sectional studies. When longitudinal studies have been conducted, they have focused primarily on environmental factors as predictors of children's depressive symptoms and less on how children's depressive symptoms impact their environment. One exception is a follow-up study of formerly depressed children conducted by Puig-Antich et al. (1985b).

Family

Depression in children and adolescents has been linked to many problems in the family (e.g., Beardslee et al., 1998; Downey & Coyne, 1990; Kaslow et al., 1994). Depressed youth and their parents report higher levels of family stressors with this relation increasing as children get older (Larson & Ham, 1993). Children and adolescents with depressive symptoms report lower levels of cohesion, bonding, and support and have more conflict with their parents (Greenberger, Chen, Tally, & Dong, 2000; Jones, Beach, & Forehand, 2001; McKeown et al., 1997; Sim, 2000; Zimmerman, Ramirez-Valles, Zapert, & Maton, 2003) as well as with their siblings (Puig-Antich et al., 1985a). Children's relationships with their parents were found to improve after their depressive episodes remitted, although there were no changes in parental marital relationships (Puig-Antich et al., 1985b).

Negative parenting also has been concurrently related to depressive symptoms in children and adolescents. Harsh, restrictive parenting or inappropriately peerlike relationships were related to children's higher levels of depressive symptoms (Sagestrano, Paikoff, Holmbeck, & Fendrich, 2003). In addition, parents of depressed children were negatively perceived by their children and had more hostile, critical, and overinvolved parenting styles (McClearly & Sanford, 2002; Messer & Gross, 1995; Rudolph, Hammen, & Burge, 1997).

In two longitudinal studies of the effects of child depression on the child's perception of familial support, neither study found children's depression predicted decreases in family support over time (Sheeber et al., 1997; Stice, Ragan, & Randall, 2004). The failure to find an effect could have been due to stability in family support or the timing of measurement of symptoms and support, given that cross-sectional studies have shown depression to be linked to lower levels of parental support (Sim, 2000; Zimmerman et al., 2000).

Observational studies have been informative about parent-child relationships in families of depressed youth. For example, Sheeber, Hops, Andrews, Alpert, & Davis (1998) found that parents of depressed adolescents responded positively to their adolescent's depressive behaviors such as whining, sadness, anxiety, and self-critical statements, whereas parents of nondepressed adolescents responded less positively to such statements in their children. Moreover, when depressed adolescents displayed depressive behaviors, their mothers were more likely to try to solve their problems or reassure them that things would be okay compared to mothers of nondepressed adolescents. Fathers also were less likely to respond with anger and aggression to depressive behavior in their children. Thus, parents react differently to their adolescents' expressions of depressive symptoms, depending on their frequency and intensity, and parents' responses to their children's depressive symptoms may serve to reinforce and sustain them.

In another sample, parents of depressed children made fewer negative comments in response to their children's depressive statements than did parents of nondepressed children (Slesnick & Waldron, 1997). In this study, depressed children made more depressed statements but did not differ from nondepressed children in their hostile statements and depressive behavior. These observational studies indicate that depressed youth may be differentially reinforced for their expressions of depressive behaviors, and this might be one mechanism by which such behaviors are maintained.

Although there is much evidence suggesting that relationships are impaired in families with depressed youth, several important questions remain. What is the direction of the relation between impaired family functioning and depression? It is most likely that the relations are reciprocal and transactional. What other yet unmeasured variables affect this association? What direct and indirect causal mechanisms influence the relation between the family environment and depression in children and adolescents, and how do these change with development?

School

Depressed youth also have been found to have problems within their school environments. Academic impairment occurs in terms of lower perceived and actual academic competence and lower scores on intelligence tests when depressed (Canals, Domenech-Llaberia, Fernandez-Ballart, & Marti-Hennenberg, 2002; Chen, Rubin, & Li, 1995; Forsterling & Binser, 2002; Greenberger et al., 2000; Ialongo, Edelsohn, & Kellam, 2001; Kistner, David, & White, 2003; Strauss, Forehand, Frame, & Smith, 1984; though also see Hamilton, Asarnow, & Thompson, 1997; Marmorstein & Iacono, 2001). Evidence of an association between depressive symptoms and impaired cognitive functioning has been reported (Ward, Friedlander, & Silverman, 1987), although others have found no difference in actual performance but differences in self-evaluation of performance (Kendall, Stark, & Adam, 1990). Once recovered from an episode, formerly depressed children do not have significantly worse school functioning than normal children (Puig-Antich et al., 1985b). Moreover, impaired academic functioning and intelligence likely are not uniquely related to depression as compared to other psychiatric diagnoses. For example, in a sample of referred youth, no significant differences were found between depressed and nondepressed psychiatric controls with regard to academic performance (McCauley et al., 1993).

Gender differences also have been reported with regard to the relation between depression and school functioning. For boys, both anxious and depressive symptoms alone were found to be associated with significant impairment in multiple domains of social and cognitive functioning, whereas for girls little evidence of associated impairment was found for either anxious or depressive symptoms alone (Ialongo, Edelsohn, Werthamer-Larsson, Crockett, & Kellam, 1996).

Depressed youth experience impairment in other areas of school. They are less likely to hold positions of high status within the school (Chen et al., 1995), are more likely to have classroom behavior problems (Jaffee et al., 2002), and are more likely to report school stressors (Marmorstein & Iacono, 2001). Moreover, depressed youth are at significantly greater risk of dropping out of school (Kandel & Davies, 1986). In particular, adolescents with recurrent depressive episodes have been found to drop out of school at significantly higher rates than depressed adolescents with only one episode or no depression (Rao et al., 1995).

Results of longitudinal studies examining the link between depression and academic performance have been mixed. Cole, Martin, Powers, and Truglio (1996) found that academic competence measured in the beginning of the school year did not predict change in depression 6 months later, after controlling for initial depression. Further, depression at Wave 1 did not predict academic competence at Wave 2 after controlling for Wave 1 competence. Cole et al. argued that this latter finding did not support the view that children's level of academic competence deteriorates because of depression.

In contrast, in a longitudinal study examining whether early-onset depression predicts changes in school functioning, Ialongo et al. (2001) showed that, controlling for academic achievement in first grade, higher levels of self-reported depressive symptoms in first grade significantly predicted higher levels of negative outcomes throughout elementary school. High levels of depressive symptoms in first grade were associated with significantly increased odds of a grade retention and a lower grade point average at age 12 for boys and increased odds of being referred for and receiving special education services for girls. Ialongo et al. cautioned that these findings did not necessarily indicate a causal relation between depressed mood in first grade and later academic outcomes. Rather, the relation between depressive symptoms and academic performance could be bidirectional such that children who struggle in school may experience emotional distress, and emotional distress may interfere with learning. It also is possible that some third variable such as heredity or an inadequate caregiving environment could explain both the school failures and the depressive symptoms. Nevertheless, the longitudinal relation between depression and academic problems needs to be studied further.

Peer Interactions

Depressed children also have significant peer difficulties and social skills deficits (e.g., Altmann & Gotlib, 1988). In laboratory studies, children with depressive symptoms were rated by their peers more negatively than were children without symptoms (Peterson, Mullins, & Ridley-Johnson, 1985), unless the depression was explained by stressful life events (Little & Garber, 1995).

Depressed children are rated by themselves and their peers as having lower levels of peer acceptance and higher levels of peer rejection (Chen et al., 1995; Jaffee et al., 2002; Kiesner, 2002; Kiesner, Poulin, & Nicotra, 2003; Kistner et al., 2003; Rudolph & Clark, 2001); lower rates of positive peer nominations (Ialongo et al., 1996; Puig-Antich et al., 1993); and more peer nominations for behavioral characteristics such as aggressive, shy, and withdrawn (Puig-Antich et al., 1993; Strauss et al., 1984) than nondepressed children. Some evidence exists, however, that depressed youth underestimate their popularity compared to their peers' ratings of their popularity (Brendgen, Vitaro, Turgeon, & Poulin, 2002), suggesting a possible negative reporting bias. Adolescents with MDD also have been found to be more likely to report being teased compared to normal controls (Puig-Antich et al., 1993). Moreover, Puig-Antich et al. (1985b) found that children whose depression had remitted continued to have significantly poorer peer relationships compared to normal controls.

In addition to problems within their peer networks, depressed adolescents tend to have more deviant friends and more disturbances in their friendships (Fergusson, Wanner, Vitaro, Horwood, & Swain-Campbell, 2003; Marmorstein & Iacono, 2001; Rao et al., 1995). These friendship problems, however, do not appear to be related to either demographic or family characteristics (Fergusson et al., 2003). Depressed children similarly have been found to have fewer friends and to spend less time with friends than normal controls, although depressed children did not differ significantly from children with nondepressed psychiatric problems regarding friendships (Puig-Antich et al., 1985a).

In contrast to studies of clinical samples of children and adolescents with diagnoses of depressive disorders, some studies of community samples have failed to find a significant relation between self-reported depressive symptoms and peer ratings of social preference (Hecht, Inderbitzen, & Bukowski, 1998; Prinstein & Aikins, 2004), or between adolescents' level of self-reported depressive symptoms and number of friends (Hogue & Steinberg, 1995). With regard to gender, one longitudinal study found that higher levels of peer rejection, negative attributional style, and overvaluing peer relationships significantly predicted increases in depressive symptoms in girls but not boys (Prinstein & Aikins, 2004). Thus, the association between depression and peer relationships may be moderated by the number and severity of the depressive symptoms as well as gender.

Depressed children also have more negative beliefs regarding their social interactions. They view their own peer status more negatively and rate themselves as less popular than children without depressive symptoms (Rudolph & Clark, 2001; Strauss et al., 1984). They also view their peers more negatively and rate themselves as having less social competence (Greenberger et al., 2000; Hamilton et al., 1997; Rudolph & Clark, 2001) and may be more likely to respond to peer provocations with hostile or passive social strategies compared to children with lower levels of depressive symptoms (Rudolph et al., 1994).

Evidence from longitudinal studies has been mixed, with some studies finding that depression predicts decreases in peer support over time (e.g., Stice et al., 2004) and others failing to find a relation between depressive symptoms and friend support (Sim, 2000; Zimmerman et al., 2000). In a short-term longitudinal study of children in grades 3 and 6, Cole et al. (1996) found that in sixth graders, social competence measured in the beginning of the school year predicted depression 6 months later, after controlling for initial levels of depression. In contrast, depression did not predict change in either social or academic competence over the same period. Cole et al. concluded that their findings were consistent with a social competence deficit model of child depression (Cole, 1991) such that social skills deficits put children at risk for subsequent depression. On the other hand, the results were not consistent with an academic competence deficit model or a model in which depression diminished social or academic competence; that is, the study did not support the perspective that children's levels of social or academic competence deteriorate because of depression, at least over a 6-month interval. It is still possible, however, that performance may be diminished on a particular academic test or in a specific social situation as a result of depression, or if the depression occurs over a more sustained period.

Laboratory studies have shown that children and adolescents with depressive symptoms behave differently than those without. Female children who interacted with high-symptom partners rated them as being more negative during the task. Independent raters provided additional support for this hypothesis by rating more dysphoric participants as less happy and less positive during the task (Baker, Milich, & Manolis, 1996). Adolescent partners of depressed adolescents tend to rate their partners as less popular and less able to make friends. Partners also reported that they liked their depressed partner less than did those interacting with nondepressed partners (Connolly, Gellar, Marton, & Kutcher, 1992; Rudolph et al., 1994).

Viewed as a whole, the social environments of depressed children tend to be more impaired than those of nondepressed children. The interpersonal environment clearly is an important and sometimes stressful context in which children develop schema about themselves and others, which then can serve as a vulnerability to depression. In addition, children's own reactions to these environments can exacerbate and perpetuate negative social exchanges, which furthers the interpersonal vicious cycle, thereby resulting in more rejection and depression (Coyne, 1976). Thus, a transactional model of mutual influence probably best characterizes the association between depressed individuals and their social environment. Future studies should aim to identify those characteristics of depressed children, their social context, and the transactions between them that produce and maintain depressive symptoms and disorders across development.

IMPLICATIONS FOR FUTURE PERSONALITY DEVELOPMENT

Research has shown that having an episode of depression early in development increases the risk of later personality disorders. Less is known about the specific processes by which personality is changed by prior depressive symptoms or episodes. Roberts and Gamble (2001) studied personality features of self-esteem and dysfunctional attitudes in a group of formerly depressed adolescents and found that those with more severe past depressive episodes had lower self-esteem even after controlling for their current symptoms. This is one of the few studies to examine the prospective relation between depression and subsequent personality features.

MDD in children and adolescents appears to be a risk factor for the development of future personality disorders (Kasen, Cohen, Skodol, Johnson, & Brook, 1999; Kasen, Cohen, Skodol, Johnson, Smailes, & Brook, 1999). However, given that studies generally have not measured symptoms of personality disorders before the onset of depressive symptoms, it is not clear whether these personality disorder symptoms existed before or only concurrently with the depressive episode. Nevertheless, an episode of MDD in adolescence appears to be a marker of risk of future personality disorders.

MDD in childhood increases the odds of personality disorders in adolescence. Bernstein, Cohen, Skodol, Bezirganian, and Brook (1996) found that mother-reported depressive symptoms predicted increased rates of Cluster A (paranoid, schizoid, and schizotypal) and Cluster B (antisocial, borderline, histrionic, and narcissistic) personality disorders 10 years later. However, the increased risk associated with earlier depressive symptoms appears to be mediated through comorbid symptoms. When conduct problems, anxiety and fear, and developmental immaturity were included with depression as predictors, depression no longer significantly increased risk. After splitting the sample by gender, depressive symptoms uniquely predicted Cluster A disorders for boys but not girls.

Are Cluster A disorders more common in boys? Bernstein et al. (1996) hypothesized that early depressive symptoms may represent earlier manifestations of personality disorders, although they did not explain why that should be the case specifically for boys. The mean age of participants at their third assessment was 16, which is nearly 2 years before common guidelines recommend diagnosing personality disorders. Moreover, symptoms in childhood were assessed solely by mothers' report, whereas personality symptoms were measured with both parent and youth report. This study also used a symptom criterion of moderate instead of severe to allow for enough cases to test the effects of MDD; perhaps the results would have been different had the standard diagnostic severity level been used. This study likely provided a conservative estimate of the prediction of depressive symptoms to personality disorders in that mothers may not have been the best reporters of children's internal mood states, and personality disorders might have been measured before they were likely to have stabilized (APA, 2000; Hammen & Rudolph, 1996; Kazdin & Marciano, 1998; Schwartz et al., 1998).

MDD in adolescence increases the risk for personality disorders in young adulthood as well. Kasen, Cohen, Skodol, Johnson, Smailes, & Brook (1999) measured depression and personality disorders in early adolescence and young adulthood and found that personality disorders were more prevalent in those who had been diagnosed with MDD during adolescence even after controlling for demographic and family environment variables. Specifically, adolescents with MDD had significantly higher odds of being diagnosed with dependent, antisocial, passive-aggressive, and histrionic personality disorders in young adulthood, in order of descending prevalence. Disruptive and anxiety disorders also increased the odds of a personality disorder, although not as much or with as many types of personality disorders as did MDD. Those adolescents with both MDD and symptoms of personality disorders had the greatest risk for later personality disorders.

Lewinsohn, Rohde, Seeley, and Klein (1997) also found that adolescents with MDD had a greater risk for personality disorder symptoms at age 24. Compared to teens without psychiatric disorders, those with MDD were at greater risk for total number of personality disorders including borderline, dependent, paranoid, schizoid, and schizotypal. Only paranoid and schizoid personality disorders, however, remained significant after controlling for demographic variables and current depressive symptoms. Lewinsohn et al. (1997) also found that adolescents with more depressive symptoms had longer MDD episodes; more recurrent depression; and greater episode severity, mental health service use, and numbers of suicide attempts.

Dysthymia in adolescence also puts young adults at risk for personality disorders. Approximately one third of young adults who had had dysthymia during adolescence met criteria for at least one personality disorder (Rey, Morris-Yates, Singh, Andrews, & Stewart, 1995). In contrast to other studies showing that MDD increased the risk of later personality disorders more than other Axis I disorders, however, Rey et al. showed that disruptive disorders placed adolescents at greater risk for personality disorders than did emotional disorders, including dysthymia.

In a clinical sample of males, antisocial personality disorder during young adulthood was uniquely predicted by depression earlier in adolescence (Loeber, Burke, & Lahey, 2002). MDD and dysthymia, substance use, oppositional defiant disorder, and ADHD all had significant univariate associations with antisocial personality disorder. When all these predictors were entered simultaneously, only depression and marijuana use significantly predicted antisocial personality disorder. Depression in adolescence more than doubled the odds of antisocial personality disorder in adult males.

Adult personality disorders also are elevated in those who were depressed during their youth. In a study using medical records to retrospectively diagnose childhood disorders in hospitalized inpatients and questionnaires to measure adult disorders, Ramklint, von Knorring, von Knorring, and Ekselius (2003) found that 57 percent of participants with a depression history met criteria for some personality disorder in adulthood. Controlling for age, gender, and other comorbidity, formerly depressed individuals were at a greater risk for developing schizoid, schizotypal, borderline, avoidant, and dependent personality disorders as adults. Schizoid was the most frequently occurring personality disorder, with the odds being 10 times greater and the odds for other disorders ranging from 3 to 5 (Ramklint et al., 2003). The higher rates in this study compared to others might be due to the longer follow-up period, use of questionnaires to assess adult personality disorders, and the inclusion of a more impaired inpatient sample.

Finally, in a sample of 160 adult inpatients, Charney, Nelson, and Quinlan (1981) found that individuals diagnosed with *DSM-III* traits of borderline, histrionic, and hostile had an earlier onset of depressive symptoms and a less favorable treatment outcome than non-personality-disordered, nonmelancholic depressive patients. The early age of onset of depressive symptoms and poor treatment prognosis may have reflected the presence of a depressive personality disorder in these patients. Charney et al. concluded that "these findings suggest that personality traits and disorder are not independent ... and that the trait differences among depressive subtypes may reflect different frequencies of personality disorder" (p. 1604).

These studies are notable in that most used clinical diagnoses of both depressive disorders and personality disorders and examined the contribution of other disorders besides depression to future personality disorders. However, the majority of these studies followed their participants only into young adulthood, making it difficult to know if earlier MDD would predict personality disorder in later adulthood. The only study to follow participants past their 20s was retrospective and found slightly higher rates of personality disorders than others (Ramklint et al., 2003).

The *DSM-IV-TR* (APA, 2000) states that symptoms associated with personality disorders need to be present in adolescence or young adulthood and must represent a long-term pattern of functioning. Some of the studies described previously did require participants to have symptoms over multiple assessment periods (e.g., Kasen, Cohen, Skodol, Johnson, & Brook, 1999; Kasen, Cohen, Skodol, Johnson, Smailes, & Brook, 1999), and others were unclear about the time frame used. Another limitation of most of these studies is that they did not measure current symptoms of depression and other Axis I disorders; a notable exception is the Lewinsohn et al. (1997) study. The *DSM-IV-TR* requires that personality disorders not be better accounted for by other Axis I disorders, so it is important that these disorders be measured as well. Moreover, some personality disorders share symptoms with MDD. For example, dependent personality disorder is characterized by low self-worth and reassurance seeking from others, features typical of depression as well. Therefore, studies examining the link between personality and depressive disorders should eliminate symptom overlap to obtain a more conservative estimate of the association.

Given the increasing empirical evidence that MDD predicts later personality disorders, future research should focus on understanding mechanisms and identifying mediators and moderators of this risk. Why are certain clusters of personality disorders more closely related to depressive disorders than others? What are the implications of this relation for treatment?

TREATMENT IMPLICATIONS

Several reviews of treatment of depression in children and adolescents are available (e.g., Curry, 2001; Kaslow & Thomson, 1998; Reinecke, Ryan, & DuBois, 1998). We highlight here some of the main findings from this literature. Despite the success of certain treatments of adult MDD, we cannot assume that these treatments are appropriate and effective with children and adolescents given the biological, developmental, cognitive, and experiential differences between children and adults. Should we start with a top-down approach, whereby we make adult interventions age appropriate, or use a bottom-up approach and start from what we know about children from a developmental perspective? For example, at what age is cognitive therapy appropriate for children, and how should it be modified to make it compatible with children's level of cognitive development? On the other hand, interventions that are not typically used with adults (e.g., family therapy, parent training) may be particularly beneficial when dealing with young children as well as adolescents.

Cognitive-Behavioral Therapy

The majority of the psychotherapy trials for depression in children and adolescents have evaluated the efficacy of various forms of cognitive-behavioral therapy (CBT), and a few have used interpersonal therapy and family therapy (Kaslow & Thomson, 1998). CBT aims to help individuals identify and modify negative thought patterns, realistically evaluate the accuracy of their beliefs, and develop problem-solving and coping skills (Beck, Rush, Shaw, & Emory, 1979). Specific techniques include (1) mood monitoring; (2) cognitive restructuring; (3) behavioral activation, pleasant activity scheduling, and goal setting; (4) relaxation and stress management; (5) social skills and conflict resolution training; (6) assertiveness training; and (7) problem-solving skills (Beck et al., 1979). Although the number of youth depression treatment studies is still relatively small, and different investigators have used various combinations of these CBT techniques, preliminary evidence suggests that CBT packages have beneficial effects on youth depression symptoms (Curry, 2001). In two meta-analyses of treatment of adolescent depression, mean effects of CBT at posttreatment were estimated to be fairly large—1.02 (Lewinsohn & Clarke, 1999) and 1.27 (Reinecke et al., 1998). The recently completed multisite trial (Treatment for Adolescents with Depression Study Team, 2004) is an exception, however. To date, there have been 14 randomized studies of some form of CBT with depressed youth: four in clinically referred samples, four in diagnosed community samples, and six in symptomatic but not diagnosed community samples (see Table 12.4).

Clinic Samples

Wood, Harrington, and Moore (1996) found that by the end of treatment, significantly more patients in the CBT group

TABLE 12.4 Studies of Psychotherapy with Depressed Youth

Clinical Outpatient Samples

Study	Treatment types	# of sessions	Ages	N	Depression criteria	Posttreatment	Follow-up
Wood et al., 1996	CBT vs. relaxation training	5–8 sessions	9–17	53	*DSM-III-R* MDD or RDC minor depression	CBT > relaxation 54% vs. 26% remitted	CBT = relaxation CBT + boosters > CBT only
Vostanis, Feehan, Grattan, & Bickerton, 1996b	CBT vs. NFI (attention placebo)	average 6 sessions	8–17	57	*DSM-III-R* MDD, dysthymia, or minor depression	CBT = NFI 87% vs. 75% did not meet depression criteria	CBT = NFI 71% vs. 75% did not meet depression criteria
Brent et al., 1997	CBT vs. SBFT (family) vs. NST (supportive)	12–16 sessions	13–18	107	*DSM-III-R* MDD	CBT > SBFT = NST 60% > 38% = 39% remitted	CBT = SBFT = NST 6% = 23% = 26% had current MDD
TADS, 2004	CBT vs. fluoxetine vs. placebo vs. CBT + fluoxetine	12 sessions	12–17	439	*DSM-III-R* MDD	CBT + fluoxetine (71%) > fluoxetine (61%) > CBT (43%) = placebo (35%) responded	
Diamond, Reis, Diamond, Siqueland, & Isaacs, 2002	ABFT vs. WLC	12 sessions	13–18	32	*DSM-III-R* MDD	ABFT > WLC 81% > 47% no longer met depression criteria 62% > 19% (BDI < 9)	

Note. ABFT: attachment-based family therapy; BDI = Beck Depression Inventory; CBT = cognitive-behavioral therapy; *DSM-III-R* = *Diagnostic and Statistical Manual of Mental Disorders,* third edition, revised; MDD = major depressive disorder; NFI = nonfocused intervention; NST = nondirective supportive therapy; RDC = Research Diagnostic Criteria; SBFT = systemic behavior family therapy; TADS = Treatment of Adolescent Depression Study; WLC = wait list control.

Diagnosed Community Samples

Lewinsohn, Clarke, Hops, & Andrews, 1990	CWD, CWD + P, WLC	14 group sessions over 7 weeks	14–18	59	*DSM-III* MDD or RDC minor or intermittent depression	CBT = CBT-P > WLC 43% = 48% > 5% no longer met criteria for depression	CBT = CBT+P > WLC at 1-, 6-, 12-, 24- month follow-ups
Clarke, Lewinsohn, Rohde, Hops, & Seeley, 1999	CWD, CWD + P, WLC	16 group sessions	14–18	123	*DSM-III-R* MDD or dysthymia	CBT = CBT-P > WLC 65% = 69% > 48% no longer met criteria for depression	Boosters did not reduce recurrence, but increased recovery
Clarke et al., 2002	CBT vs. usual care	16 group sessions	13–18	88	*DSM-III-R* MDD or dysthymia	CBT = usual care 57.9% = 53.2% recovered	CBT = usual care 89.5% = 92.3% cumulative recovery
Rossello & Bernal, 1999	CBT vs. IPT vs. WLC	12 sessions	13–18	71	*DSM-III-R* MDD or dysthymia	CBT = IPT > WLC 66% = 77% better than WLC	CBT = IPT
Mufson, Weissman, Moreau, & Garfinkel, 1999	IPT vs. clin. mon.	12 sessions	12–18	48	*DSM-III-R* MDD	IPT > clin. mon. 75% > 46% recovered 87% > 58% no longer met criteria for depression 4.5% < 23% worse	
Mufson et al., 2004	IPT vs. usual treatment	12 sessions/ 16 weeks	12–18	63	*DSM-IV* depressive disorder HAM-D ≥ 10 C-GAS ≤ 65	IPT > usual care 50% > 34% HAM-D recovery 74% > 52% BDI < 9	

Note. BDI = Beck Depression Inventory; CBT = cognitive-behavioral therapy; CBT-P = CBT no parents; CBT+P = CBT with parents; C-GAS = Child Global Assessment Scale; Clin. Mon. = clinical monitoring; CWD = coping with depression; CWD + P = coping with depression plus parent group; *DSM-III-R* = *Diagnostic and Statistical Manual of Mental Disorders,* 3rd edition, revised; *DSM-IV* = *Diagnostic and Statistical Manual,* 4th edition; HAM-D = Hamilton Depression Rating Scale; IPT = interpersonal psychotherapy; MDD = major depressive disorder; RDC = Research Diagnostic Criteria; WLC = wait list control.

(continued)

TABLE 12.4 (Continued)

Symptomatic Community Samples

Study	Treatment types	# of sessions	Ages	N	Depression criteria	Posttreatment	Follow-up
Butler, Meizitis, & Friedman, 1980	RP, CR, attention, control	10	Grades 5 & 6	56	CDI	RP = CR > AP = control	
Reynolds & Coats, 1986	CBT, relaxation training, WLC	10	High School Students	30	BDI ≥ 12; RADS ≥ 72	CBT = relaxation > WLC on reducing depressive symptoms	CBT = relaxation > WLC on reducing depressive symptoms (5-week follow-up)
Stark, Reynolds, & Kaslow, 1987	SC, BPS, WLC	12	9–12 yrs	29		SC = BPS > WLC	SC = BPS > WLC (8-week follow-up)
Liddle & Spence, 1990	CBT, attention, NT control	8	7–12 yrs	31	CDI > 40	CBT = attention = control	
Kahn, Kehle, Jenson, & Clark, 1990	CBT, relaxation, self-modeling, NT control		Grades 6–8	68	Self-report depression	CBT = relaxation = SM > control	
Weisz, Thurber, Sweeney, Profitt, & LeGagnoux, 1997	CBT, NT control	8	Mean = 9 yrs	48	CDI, CDRS	CBT > control	CBT > control (9-month follow-up)

Note. AP = attention placebo; BDI = Beck Depression Inventory; BPS = behavior problem solving; CBT = cognitive-behavioral therapy; CDI = Children's Depression Inventory; CDRS = Children's Depression Rating Scale; CR = cognitive restructuring; NT control = no treatment control; RADS = Reynolds Adolescent Depression Scale; RP = role-play; SC = self-control therapy; SM = self-modeling; WLC = wait list control.

had remitted compared to the relaxation training group. At the 6-month follow-up, however, the differences between the groups were reduced, although adding monthly booster CBT sessions after acute treatment for about 6 months resulted in a lower relapse rate (20 percent) compared to acute treatment alone (50 percent; Kroll, Harrington, Jayson, Fraser, & Gowers, 1996). Using a similar CBT treatment package, Vostanis, Feehan, Grattan, and Bickerton (1996a) found the proportion of patients who no longer met depression criteria was not significantly different for those treated with CBT versus a nonfocused intervention (NFI) either at the end of treatment or at the 9-month follow-up (Vostanis, Feehan, Grattan, & Bickerton, 1996b). At the 2-year follow-up, Vostanis, Feehan, and Grattan (1998) found that 52 percent of the overall sample had depressive diagnoses and another 39 percent had reported significant depressive symptoms during the previous year, although these rates did not differ as a function of treatment type.

Brent et al. (1997) found that significantly fewer patients who received CBT (17 percent) continued to have MDD at posttreatment compared to those who received nondirective supportive therapy (NST; 42 percent). Remission, defined as the absence of MDD and at least three consecutive BDI scores <9, was significantly more common for teens treated with CBT than for those in either the NST or systematic behavior family therapy (SBFT) conditions. At the 2-year follow-up, differences between treatment groups on the presence of current MDD were not significant, although they were in the direction of better outcome for CBT participants (Birmaher et al., 2000).

Finally, the recently completed Treatment of Adolescent Depression Study (TADS, 2004) found that the combination of medications (fluoxetine) with CBT was superior to fluoxetine alone, which was, in turn, superior to CBT alone or pill-placebo. Response was defined as ratings of much improved or very much improved on the Clinical Global Impressions (CGI; Guy, 1976). Patients in all four treatment conditions showed a reduction in suicidal ideation, with the greatest change occurring in combined treatment. The authors concluded that there was evidence of a small protective effect of CBT on suicidal ideation.

Thus, clinical trials with diagnosed outpatients have shown mixed results for CBT. Whereas the earlier studies (Vostanis et al., 1996a, 1996b; Wood et al., 1996) had small samples and fewer treatment sessions, the trials by Brent et al. (1997) and TADS (2004) had large samples and thus more power, and also lengthier treatment. The results were quite favorable for CBT in the Brent et al. study, whereas CBT alone did not do as well in TADS. Several possible reasons have been suggested for the poorer showing for CBT in TADS; for example, the TADS patients were more functionally impaired and had more chronic depression (Bridges & Brent, 2004), the CBT was overly structured and less focused in TADS, or the CBT was implemented and supervised by clinicians who were less experienced and possibly less competent with this treatment modality (Bridges & Brent, 2004; Hollon, Garber, & Shelton, 2005). Hollon et al. suggested ways to address these concerns, but this awaits further exploration of the TADS data both within and across sites.

Community Samples

Studies of community samples of youth have recruited primarily from schools or advertisements. Lewinsohn et al. (1990) tested a group Coping with Depression (CWD) course for adolescents, a CWD plus a weekly parent group, and a wait list control (WLC). The CWD course aimed to increase social skills, pleasant events and activities, and problem-solving and conflict resolution skills and reduce anxious and depressive cognitions. At posttreatment, the adolescent-only group and the adolescent-plus-parent group did not differ from each other, and both were significantly better than the WLC; these treatment gains persisted at 1-, 6-, 12-, and 24-month follow-ups. Clarke, Rohde, Lewinsohn, Hops, and Seeley (1999) replicated these results, again finding that the two CWD groups did not differ significantly from each other but both had a significantly better outcome than WLC in terms of the percentage of patients who no longer met diagnostic criteria for MDD or dysthymia at posttreatment. In addition, rerandomization to a one- or two-session booster condition did not reduce the rate of depression recurrence for those who had remitted by posttreatment, but for patients who were not yet improved by the end of the acute treatment phase, booster sessions did accelerate their rate of recovery. Using a similar program with a sample of depressed adolescent offspring of depressed parents, Clarke et al. (2002) found no significant differences between the group CBT versus the treatment-as-usual condition on rate of depressive disorders, depressive symptoms, or functional outcomes at the end of treatment or over the follow-up period. These results by Clarke et al. (2002) are consistent with those reported by Brent et al. (1998), who also found that among teens whose mothers had high levels of depressive symptoms, CBT was not more effective than either family or supportive therapy.

Finally, in a sample of Puerto Rican depressed youth referred by school personnel, Rossello and Bernal (1999) compared individual CBT to interpersonal psychotherapy (IPT) and WLC. At posttreatment, CBT and IPT were not significantly different from each other, but both had achieved clinically significant improvement (cf. Jacobson & Truax, 1991) on the CDI compared to the WLC group. At the 3-month follow-up, CDI scores continued to decrease for the CBT group, though they were not significantly different from the IPT group. Although this study had several limitations (e.g., small sample, substantial attrition, attendance problems, no intent-to-treat analyses conducted, self-report measures only), it was one of the first studies to compare CBT and IPT and to use a sample of depressed Latino adolescents.

Several community studies of children with elevated levels of self-reported depressive symptoms have compared basic CBT (Kahn, Kehle, Jenson, & Clark, 1990; Reynolds & Coats, 1986) or components of CBT including cognitive restructuring (Butler, Meizitis, & Friedman, 1980), social competence training (Liddle & Spence, 1990), self-control training or behavioral problem solving (Stark, Reynolds, & Kaslow, 1987), or primary and secondary control coping (Weisz, Thurber, Sweeney, Proffitt, & LeGagnoux, 1997) to other active treatments (e.g., relaxation training, role-playing, self-modeling) as well as to attention placebo, wait list, and no treatment control groups. In general, these studies have shown that any active intervention is superior to no treatment both immediately posttreatment and at follow-ups ranging from 5 weeks to 9 months. The various CBT interventions, however, did not perform significantly better than the other active interventions. This could have been true for several reasons. First, CBT just might not be any more effective than other interventions for depression in children. Any intervention might work to reduce depressive symptoms, at least in the short term. Second, many of the programs studied were relatively brief and were presented in a group format. It is possible that more extensive and individualized CBT would have a stronger effect. Third, although these authors called their interventions cognitive-behavioral, most of these studies included only components of CBT rather than the comprehensive treatment package. Studies are needed that contrast the full CBT approach with its different components to determine what features are most likely to produce change.

Finally, several individual and family variables have been examined in relation to differential outcome among depressed children and adolescents treated with CBT. Predictors of poor outcome (e.g., lack of recovery, relapse, recurrence) have included older age of onset and lower initial level of functioning (Jayson, Wood, Kroll, Fraser, & Harrington, 1998); comorbid conditions including substance use disorders, attention deficit hyperactivity, disruptive disorders, and substance use disorders (Rohde et al., 2001); greater cognitive distortions; hopelessness; greater severity; prior dysthymia; maternal depression; and family discord (Birmaher et al., 2000; Brent et al., 1998; Clarke, Hops, Lewinsohn, Andrew, & Williams, 1992). An important implication is that for children and adolescents with these predictors, CBT might not be sufficient to address their depression and its associated features. Adjunct or alternative therapeutic approaches may be needed to treat their comorbid condition(s), or family or marital therapies might help to address the parental psychopathology and family conflict. Whether CBT is still necessary and effective in conjunction with some of these other treatments is not yet known. Moreover, although one might think that those with greater negative cognitive distortions would be the most likely to benefit from CBT, these youth might have the most ingrained and least malleable beliefs.

With regard to predicting more positive outcomes, comorbid anxiety has been found to increase the likelihood of improvement in adolescents receiving CBT (Brent et al., 1998; Rohde et al., 2001). It could be that teaching youth to examine their negative cognitions associated with depression also helps them deal with their anxious thoughts. Decreases in anxiety then may serve to reduce the likelihood of future depressive thoughts and symptoms, given that anxiety has been found to precede depression (e.g., Bittner et al., 2004; Pine et al., 1998; Silberg et al., 2001).

Interpersonal Therapies

IPT for depression (Klerman, Weissman, Rounsville, & Chevron, 1984) assumes that depression is related to one (or more) of these interpersonal problems: role transition, grief, interpersonal deficits, and interpersonal disputes. Studies with depressed adults have found that IPT tends to do better than minimal contact control, usual care, or placebo but not better than tricyclic antidepressant medications, medications plus IPT, or cognitive therapy (DiMascio et al., 1979; Elkin et al., 1989; Frank et al., 1990; Schulberg et al., 1996).

Mufson, Weissman, Moreau, and Garfinkel (1999) adapted IPT for use with adolescents (IPT-A) and tested its efficacy in a largely Hispanic and female sample of clinic-referred depressed adolescents randomly assigned to either weekly IPT-A or biweekly to monthly 30-minute sessions of clinical monitoring. IPT-A is a time-limited, focused psychotherapy that addresses common adolescent developmental issues that may contribute to depression, including separation from parents, authority and autonomy issues, development of dyadic interpersonal relationships, peer pressure, loss, and issues related to single-parent families. Rates of recovery (defined by a Hamilton Depression Rating Scale <6 or a BDI <9) favored IPT-A over clinical monitoring. At termination, a lower proportion of those in IPT-A still met criteria for major depression, and a greater number were rated as significantly improved on the Clinical Global Improvement (CGI) Scale.

In a second clinical trial, Mufson et al. (2004) again tested the effectiveness of IPT-A compared with treatment as usual (TAU) in school-based mental health clinics. Adolescents treated with IPT-A compared with TAU showed significantly greater symptom reduction on the Hamilton Depression Rating Scale (HAM-D), improvement in overall functioning on the Children's Global Assessment Scale (CGAS), better overall social functioning on the Social Adjustment Scale—Self-Report, and greater decrease in clinical severity on the CGI scale. These studies, along with the study by Rosello and Bernal (1999), discussed earlier, support the efficacy of IPT for adolescent depression.

Diamond et al. (2002) compared attachment-based family therapy (ABFT) with a wait list control (WLC) in an adolescent sample that was 69 percent African American, poor, and inner-city. ABFT focuses on strengthening family bonds; reducing conflict; improving trust, empathy, affect regulation, and communication; and promoting competence. Those in the WLC group received 15 minutes of weekly telephone monitoring of their clinical condition and a face-to-face assessment at week 6. At posttreatment, significantly more of those treated with ABFT no longer met criteria for depression and had a BDI <9 compared to WLC. One limitation of the study, however, was that the length of treatments was different (ABFT: 12 weeks vs. WLC: 6 weeks). Nevertheless, at the 6-week assessment, significantly more of those in ABFT showed a BDI <9 (56 percent vs. 19 percent). Thus, ABFT may have promise as a treatment for adolescent major depression in a poor African American sample. Further clinical trials need to be conducted comparing various family approaches in the treatment of adolescent depression given the differences in the results of the studies by Diamond et al., which focused on attachment issues, and Brent et al. (1997), which emphasized problem solving and communication.

Medications

Safety

The use of SSRIs with children and adolescents recently has come under increasing scrutiny. In a report dated December 10, 2003, the British Medicines and Healthcare Products Regulatory Agency (MHRA) recommended termination of use of all antidepressants except fluoxetine for depressed individuals under the age of 18. The primary concern stated by the MHRA was that a serious side effect of SSRIs is increased suicidality. Brent (2004; Brent & Birmaher, 2004) has argued, however, that the MHRA overstated the risks and underestimated the possible benefits of antidepressants for the treatment of pediatric depression. Brent reported that although the absolute numbers of cases of suicidality, defined as ideation, self-harm, and actual suicide attempts, were slightly higher in adolescents treated with SSRIs compared to placebo, none of these differences were statistically significant. Moreover, Brent showed that the suicide rate in adolescents actually has

TABLE 12.5 Pharmacotherapy for the Treatment of Depression in Adolescents

Study	Agent(s)	Study length (weeks)	Sample size	Results
Emslie et al., 1997	Fluoxetine (20 mg)	8	64	Fluoxetine > placebo 50% > 33%
Emslie et al., 2002	Fluoxetine (20 mg)	8	219	Fluoxetine = 52% improved vs. placebo = 37%
Keller et al., 2001	Paroxetine(up to 40 mg) Imipramine (up to 300 mg)	8	275	Overall response rates were paroxetine = 66% imipramine = 52% placebo = 48% No differences on the HAM-D
GlaxoSmithKline	Paroxetine	10		Paroxetine = placebo
Wagner et al., 2001	Citalopram (mean = 23 mg)	8	174	Citalopram > placebo 36% vs. 24% Remission (≤28 on CDRS-R)
Wagner et al., 2003	Sertraline (mean = 131 mg)	10	376	Sertraline > placebo 69% vs. 59% Response rate (decrease of ≥40% on CDRS-R)
Rynn et al., 2002	Nefazadone	8	195	Nefazadone = placebo (CDRS-R) Nefazadone > placebo (HAM-D)
Ryan, 2003	Tricyclic antidepressants		500	Tricyclics = placebo
TADS, 2004	Fluoxetine	12	439	Fluoxetine + CBT > fluoxetine > CBT = placebo

Note. CBT = cognitive-behavioral therapy; CDRS-R = Children's Depression Rating Scale—Revised; HAM-D = Hamilton Depression Rating Scale; TADS = Treatment of Adolescent Depression Study.

been decreasing in the last decade and asserted that this is likely due to better detection of depression and suicidality and the dissemination of validated treatments. In particular, increases in the number of prescriptions for SSRIs for adolescents have been found to be associated with a decrease in adolescent suicide (Olfson, Shaffer, Marcus, & Greenberg, 2003).

According to the FDA, the risk of suicidality in children and adolescents receiving SSRIs is real, although small. Therefore, the agency recommended stronger warning labels; close monitoring of patients treated with antidepressants for suicidality, hostility, agitation, and mania; and that clear information be provided to parents and youth about the benefits and risks of these drugs and their possible side effects. The recent TADS (2004) study supported the idea that suicidality in depressed adolescents may be best treated by a combination of cognitive therapy and medication. "Ideally, the FDA, families, and clinicians will find the right balance between the risk of suicidality and another, greater risk: the risk that lies in doing nothing" (Brent, 2004, p. 1600).

Efficacy

Before the introduction of SSRIs, the tricyclic antidepressants (TCAs) were the primary medication used to treat depression in adults and children. Common side effects of TCAs (e.g., imipramine) include dizziness, dry mouth, headache, nausea, and tachycardia. In a review of studies that included more than 500 children and adolescents, Ryan (2003) concluded that double-blind placebo-controlled trials of tricyclic antidepressants in the treatment of pediatric depression have not found TCAs to be superior to placebo. Evidence of the efficacy of SSRIs has been found in several double-blind placebo-controlled trials with several different SSRIs (see Table 12.5). Three studies (Emslie et al., 1997, 2002; TADS, 2004) have now shown that fluoxetine is significantly better than placebo in reducing depression in youth. On the basis of the positive findings of the study by Emslie et al. (2002), fluoxetine received FDA approval for the treatment of major depression in children and adolescents. In a multisite study of adolescent outpatients with MDD, patients were randomly assigned to paroxetine, imipramine, or placebo (Keller et al., 2001). The paroxetine group was much or very much clinically improved compared to the imipramine and placebo groups, although the groups did not differ significantly on the measure of depressive symptoms (HAM-D). The pharmaceutical company, GlaxoSmithKline, conducted a different multicenter, double-blind placebo-controlled trial of paroxetine with both children and adolescents with MDD and found no statistically significant difference in the response rates between the paroxetine and placebo groups. Two other SSRIs have been tested in pediatric patients with MDD in double-blind placebo-controlled trials. Wagner et al. (2001) randomly assigned children aged 7–17 years to either citalopram or placebo and found significantly greater improvement in depressive symptoms from baseline to endpoint for the citalopram compared to the placebo group. The efficacy and safety of sertraline was assessed in depressed children aged 6–17 years randomized to sertraline or placebo (Wagner et al., 2003). The sertraline group showed significantly greater improvement in depression (i.e., CDRS-R change scores from baseline to endpoint) than the placebo group.

Using nefazadone, which is in another antidepressant class, Rynn et al. (2002) randomized depressed adolescents to nefazadone or placebo and found greater improvement with nefazadone compared to placebo. Other antidepressants such as venlafaxine, mirtazapine, and bupropion have not yet been shown to be effective in depressed youth. In addition, due to the need for careful dietary restrictions, monoamine oxidase inhibitors do not seem a viable alternative for pediatric patients.

Thus, based on double-blind placebo-controlled trials, despite the continuing controversy about increased suicidality, only the SSRIs, specifically fluoxetine, have demonstrated efficacy and tolerability for the pharmacotherapeutic treatment of major depression in children and adolescents. An important limitation of several of these studies was that common comorbid disorders were excluded from the clinical trial. Indeed, the presence of comorbid ADHD has been found to significantly reduce response rates in all of the treatment groups (Birmaher, McCafferty, Bellew, & Beebe, 2001; Keller et al., 2001).

Future intervention studies are needed to examine the optimal duration of treatment with medications as well as psychotherapy, and to explore the short- and long-term effects of combining the two. TADS (2004) showed a clear advantage for the combined medication and CBT group. The extent to which CBT is effective in preventing relapse in children and adolescents as it has been in adults (Hollon et al., in press) also should be explored. Studies are needed that allow greater flexibility in both the pharmacotherapy (e.g., augmentation with other medications) and the manner in which CBT is delivered. The best order in which to provide different treatments is not known. Far more research needs to be done testing the efficacy of medications and therapy with younger children. Behavioral approaches with a parenting component might be especially appropriate for children.

Finally, what predicts treatment response, relapse, and recurrence in pediatric depressed patients treated with pharmacotherapy, psychotherapy, or both? Some factors that may be related to outcome include age of onset of depression, severity and duration, comorbid disorders, personality, family history of major depression, and current parental major depression. In particular, how do personality traits and disorders affect treatment response, and what are the implications of this for the development of new interventions?

REFERENCES

Abela, J. R. Z. (2001). The hopelessness theory of depression: A test of the diathesis-stress and causal mediation components in third and seventh grade children. *Journal of Abnormal Child Psychology, 29,* 241–254.

Abramson, L. Y., Metalsky, G. I., & Alloy, L. B. (1989). Hopelessness depression: A theory-based subtype of depression. *Psychological Review, 96,* 358–372.

Abramson, L. Y., Seligman, M. E. P., & Teasdale, J. (1978). Learned helplessness in humans: Critique and reformulation. *Journal of Abnormal Psychology, 87,* 49–74.

Achenbach, T. M. (1991a). *Integrative guide for the child behavior checklist 4-18, youth self-report, and teacher report form profiles.* Burlington: University of Vermont, Department of Psychiatry.

Achenbach, T. M. (1991b). "Comorbidity" in child and adolescent psychiatry: Categorical and quantitative perspectives. *Journal of Child and Adolescent Psychopharmacology, 1,* 271–278.

Achenbach, T. M., & Edelbrock, C. (1991). *Manual for the teachers' report form and 1991 profile.* Burlington: University of Vermont.

Achenbach, T. M., Howell, C. T., Quay, H. C., & Conners, C. K. (1991). National survey of problems and competencies among four- to sixteen-year-olds: Parents' reports for normative and clinical samples. *Monographs of the Society for Research in Child Development, 56*(225), v–120.

Achenbach, T. M., McConaughy, S. H., & Howell, C. T. (1987). Child/adolescent behavioral and emotional problems: Implications of cross informant correlations for situational specificity. *Psychological Bulletin, 101,* 213–232.

Adams, M., & Adams, J. (1991). Life events, depression, and perceived problem solving alternatives in adolescents. *Journal of Child Psychology and Psychiatry and Allied Disciplines, 32,* 811–820.

Akiskal, H. S. (1983). Dysthymic disorder: Psychopathology of proposed chronic depressive subtypes. *American Journal of Psychiatry, 140,* 11–20.

Akiskal, H. S. (1984). Characterologic manifestations of affective disorders: Toward a new conceptualization. *Integrative Psychiatry, 2,* 83–88.

Akiskal, H. S., & McKinney, W. T. (1975). Overview of recent research in depression: Integration of ten conceptual models into a comprehensive clinical framework. *Archives of General Psychiatry, 32,* 285–305.

Allgood-Merton, B., Lewinsohn, P., & Hops, H. (1990). Sex differences and adolescent depression. *Journal of Abnormal Psychology, 99,* 55–63.

Altmann, E. O., & Gotlib, I. H. (1988). The social behavior of depressed children: An observational study. *Journal of Abnormal Child Psychology, 16,* 29–44.

Amanat, E., & Butler, C. (1984). Oppressive behaviors in the families of depressed children. *Family Therapy, 11,* 65–75.

Ambrosini, P. J. (2000). A review of pharmacotherapy of major depression in children and adolescents. *Psychiatric Services, 51,* 627–633.

American Psychiatric Association. (1994). *Diagnostic and statistical manual of mental disorders* (4th ed.). Washington, DC: Author.

American Psychiatric Association. (2000). *Diagnostic and statistical manual of mental disorders* (4th ed., text rev.). Washington, DC: Author.

Anderson, J. C., Williams, S., McGee, R., & Silva, P. (1987). *DSM-III* disorders in preadolescent children. *Archives of General Psychiatry, 44,* 69–76.

Angold, A., & Costello, E. J. (1993). Depressive comorbidity in children and adolescents: Empirical, theoretical, and methodological issues. *American Journal of Psychiatry, 150,* 1779–1791.

Angold, A., & Costello, E. J. (2000). The Child and Adolescent Psychiatric Assessment (CAPA). *Journal of the American Academy of Child and Adolescent Psychiatry, 39,* 39–48.

Angold, A., Costello, E. J., & Erkanli, A. (1999). Comorbidity. *Journal of Child Psychology and Psychiatry, 40,* 57–87.

Angold, A., Costello, E. J., & Worthman, C. M. (1998). Puberty and depression: The roles of age, pubertal status and pubertal timing. *Psychological Medicine, 28,* 51–61.

Angold, A., & Rutter, M. (1992). Effects of age and pubertal status on depression in a large clinical sample. *Development and Psychopathology, 4,* 5–28.

Angold, A., Weissman, M. M., John, K., Merikangas, K. R., Prusoff, B. A., Wickramaratne, P., et al. (1987). Parent and child reports of depressive symptoms in children at low and high risk of depression. *Journal of Child Psychology and Psychiatry, 28,* 901–915.

Anthony, J. L., Lonigan, C. J., Hooe, E. S., & Phillips, B. M. (2002). An affect-based, hierarchical model of temperament and its relations with internalizing symptomatology. *Journal of Clinical Child and Adolescent Psychology, 31,* 480–490.

Asarnow, J. R., & Bates, S. (1988). Depression in child psychiatric inpatients: Cognitive and attributional patterns. *Journal of Abnormal Child Psychology, 16,* 601–615.

Asarnow, J. R., Carlson, G. A., & Guthrie, D. (1987). Coping strategies, self-perceptions, hopelessness, and perceived family environments in depressed and suicidal children. *Journal of Consulting and Clinical Psychology, 55,* 361–366.

Asarnow, J. R., Goldstein, M. J., Tompson, M., & Guthrie, D. (1993). One-year outcomes of depressive disorders in child psychiatric in-patients: Evaluation of the prognostic power of a brief measure of expressed emotion. *Journal of Child Psychology and Psychiatry, 34,* 129–137.

Aseltine, R., Gore, S., & Colton, M. E. (1994). Depression and the social developmental context of adolescence. *Journal of Personality and Social Psychology, 67,* 252–263.

Aseltine, R. H., Gore, S., & Gordon, J. (2000). Life stress, anger and anxiety, and delinquency: An empirical test of general strain theory. *Journal of Health and Social Behavior, 41,* 256–275.

Avenevoli, S., Stolar, M., Li, J., Dierker, L., & Merikangas, K. (2001). Comorbidity of depression in children and adolescents: Models and evidence from a prospective high risk family study. *Biological Psychiatry, 49,* 1071–1081.

Baker, M., Milich, R., & Manolis, M. B. (1996). Peer interactions of dysphoric adolescents. *Journal of Abnormal Child Psychology, 24,* 241–255.

Barber, B. K. (1996). Parental psychological control: Revisiting a neglected construct. *Child Development, 67,* 3296–3319.

Barnett, P. A., & Gotlib, I. H. (1988). Psychosocial functioning and depression: Distinguishing among antecedents, concomitants, and consequences. *Psychological Bulletin, 104,* 97–126.

Bassuk, E. L., Buckner, J. C., Perloff, J. N., & Bassuk, S. S. (1998). Prevalence of mental health and substance use disorders among homeless and low-income housed mothers. *American Journal of Psychiatry, 155*(11), 1561–1564.

Beardslee, W. R., Keller, M. B., Lavori, P. W., Staley, J. E., & Sacks, N. (1993). The impact of parental affective disorder on depression in offspring: A longitudinal follow up in a nonreferred sample. *Journal of the American Academy of Child and Adolescent Psychiatry, 32,* 723–730.

Beardslee, W. R., Versage, E. M., & Gladstone, T. R. G. (1998). Children of affectively ill parents: A review of the past 10 years. *Journal of the American Academy of Child and Adolescent Psychiatry, 37,* 1134–1141.

Beck, A. T. (1967). *Depression: Clinical, experiential, and theoretical aspects.* New York: Harper & Row.

Beck, A. T. (1976). *Cognitive therapy and the emotional disorders.* Oxford, England: International Universities Press.

Beck, A. T., Epstein, N., & Harrison, R. (1983). Cognitions, attitudes and personality dimensions in depression. *British Journal of Cognitive Psychotherapy, 1,* 1–16.

Beck, A. T., Rush, A. J., Shaw, B. F., & Emery, G. (1979). *Cognitive therapy of depression.* New York: Guilford Press.

Beck, A. T., Ward, C. H., Mendelson, M., Mock, J., & Erbaugh, J. (1961). An inventory for measuring depression. *Archive of General Psychiatry, 4,* 561–571.

Beevers, C. G., & Meyer, B. (2002). Lack of positive experiences and positive expectancies mediate the relationship between BAS responsiveness and depression. *Cognition and Emotion, 16,* 549–564.

Bennett, D. S., & Bates, J. E. (1995). Prospective models of depressive symptoms in early adolescence: Attributional style, stress, and support. *Journal of Early Adolescence, 15,* 299–315.

Berndt, D. (1986). *Multi-score depression inventory manual.* Los Angeles: Western Psychological Services.

Bernstein, D. P., Cohen, P., Skodol, A., Bezirganian, S., & Brook, J. S. (1996). Childhood antecedents of adolescent personality disorders. *American Journal of Psychiatry, 153,* 907–913.

Biederman, J., Milberger, S., Faraone, S. V., Kiely, K., Guite, J., Mick, E., et al. (1995). Impact of adversity on functioning and comorbidity in children with attention-deficit hyperactivity disorder. *Journal of the American Academy of Child and Adolescent Psychiatry, 34,* 1495–1503.

Biederman, J., Rosenbaum, J. F., Murphy, E. A., Faraone, S. V., Chaloff, J., Hirshfeld, D. R., et al. (1993). A 3-year follow-up of children with and without behavioral inhibition. *Journal of the American Academy of Child and Adolescent Psychiatry, 32,* 814–821.

Bifulco, A., Brown, G. W., & Adler, Z. (1991). Early sexual abuse and clinical depression in adult life. *British Journal of Psychiatry, 159,* 115–122.

Birleson, P. (1981). The validity of depressive disorder in childhood and the development of a self rating scale: A research report. *Journal of Child Psychology and Psychiatry, 22,* 73–88.

Birmaher, B., Brent, D. A., Kolko, D., Baugher, M., Bridge, J., Iyengar, S., et al. (2000). Clinical outcome after short-term psychotherapy for adolescents with major depressive disorder. *Archives of General Psychiatry, 57,* 29–36.

Birmaher, B., Dahl, R. E., Perel, J., Williamson, D. E., Nelson, B., Stull, S., et al. (1996). Corticotropin releasing hormone challenge in prepubertal major depression. *Biological Psychiatry, 39,* 267–277.

Birmaher, B., Dahl, R. E., Williamson, D. E., Perel, J. M., Brent, D. A., Axelson, D. A., et al. (1999). *Growth hormone secretion in children and adolescents at high risk for major depressive disorder.* Paper presented at the Child and Adolescent Depression Consortium, Western Psychiatric Institute and Clinic, Pittsburgh, PA.

Birmaher, B., Kaufman, J., Brent, D. A., Dahl, R. E., Perel, J. M., Al-Shabbout, M., et al. (1997). Neuroendocrine response to 5-hydroxy-l-tryptophan in prepubertal children at high risk of major depressive disorder. *Archives of General Psychiatry, 54,* 1113–1119.

Birmaher, B., McCafferty, J. P., Bellew, K. M., & Beebe, K. L. (2001). *Disruptive disorders as predictors of response in adolescents with depression.* Poster presented at the 48th annual meeting of the American Academy of Child and Adolescent Psychiatry, Honolulu, HI.

Birmaher, B., Ryan, N. D., Williamson, D. E., Brent, D. A., & Kaufman, J. (1996). Childhood and adolescent depression: A review of the past 10 years. Part II. *Journal of the American Academy of Child and Adolescent Psychiatry, 35,* 1575–1583.

Birmaher, B., Ryan, N. D., Williamson, D. E., Brent, D. A., Kaufman, J., Dahl, R. E., et al. (1996). Childhood and adolescent depression: A review of the past ten years. Part I. *Journal of the American Academy of Child and Adolescent Psychiatry, 35,* 1427–1439.

Bittner, A., Goodwin, R. D., Wittchen, H. U., Beesdo, K., Hofler, M., & Lieb, R. (2004). What characteristics of primary anxiety disorders predict subsequent major depression? *Journal of Clinical Psychiatry, 65,* 618–626.

Blatt, S. J. (1974). Levels of object representation in anaclitic and introjective depression. *Psychoanalytic Study of the Child, 29,* 107–157.

Blazer, D. G., Kessler, R. C., McGonagle, K. A., & Swartz, M. S. (1994). The prevalence and distribution of major depression in a national community sample: The National Comorbidity Survey. *American Journal of Psychiatry, 151,* 979–986.

Block, J. H., & Block, J. (1980). The role of ego-control and ego resiliency in the organization of behavior. In W. A. Collins (Ed.), *The Minnesota symposium on child psychology,* Vol. 13 (pp. 39–101). Hillsdale, NJ: Erlbaum.

Boddy, J. M., & Skuse, D. H. (1994). Annotation: The process of parenting in failure to thrive. *Journal of Child Psychology and Psychiatry, 35,* 401–424.

Botteron, K. (1999). *The role of the medial prefrontal cortex in early onset depression: Current results from an epidemiologic twin study.* Paper presentation at the Child and Adolescent Depression Consortium, Western Psychiatric Institute and Clinic, Pittsburgh, PA.

Boudewyn, A. C., & Liem, J. H. (1995). Childhood sexual abuse as a precursor to depression and self-destructive behavior in adulthood. *Journal of Traumatic Stress, 8,* 445–459.

Bowlby, J. (1977). The making and breaking of affectional bonds: I. Aetiology and psychopathology in the light of attachment theory. *British Journal of* Psychiatry, *130,* 201–210.

Bowlby, J. (1980). *Attachment and loss. Vol. 3: Loss, sadness, and depression.* New York: Basic Books.

Boyce, P., Hickie, I., Parker, G., Mitchell, P., Wilhelm, K., & Brodaty, H. (1993). Specificity of interpersonal sensitivity to non-melancholic depression. *Journal of Affective Disorders, 27,* 101–105.

Boyce, P., & Mason, C. (1996). An overview of depression-prone personality traits and the role of interpersonal sensitivity. *Australian and New Zealand Journal of Psychiatry, 30,* 90–103.

Boyce, P., & Parker, G. (1989). Development of a scale to measure interpersonal sensitivity. *Australian and New Zealand Journal of Psychiatry, 23,* 341–351.

Brady, E. U., & Kendall, P. C. (1992). Comorbidity of anxiety and depression in children and adolescents. *Psychological Bulletin, 111,* 244–255.

Brendgen, M., Vitaro, F., Turgeon, L., & Poulin, L. (2002). Assessing aggressive and depressed children's social relations with classmates and friends: A matter of perspective. *Journal of Abnormal Child Psychology, 30,* 609–624.

Brent, D. A. (2004). Treating depression in children: Antidepressants and pediatric depression—the risk of doing nothing. *New England Journal of Medicine, 351,* 1598–1601.

Brent, D. A., & Birmaher, B. (2004). British warnings on SSRIs questioned. *Journal of the American Academy of Child and Adolescent Psychiatry, 43,* 379–380.

Brent, D. A., Holder, D., Kolko, D., Birmaher, B., Baugher, M., Roth, C., et al. (1997). A clinical psychotherapy trial for adolescent depression comparing cognitive, family, and supportive treatments. *Archives of General Psychiatry, 54,* 877–885.

Brent, D. A., Kolko, D., Birmaher, B., Baugher, M., Bridge, J., Roth C., et al. (1998). Predictors of treatment efficacy in a clinical trial of three psychosocial treatments for adolescent depression. *Journal of the American Academy of Child and Adolescent Psychiatry, 37,* 906–914.

Breslau, N., Davis, G. C., & Andreski, P. (1995). Risk factors for PTSD related traumatic events: A prospective analysis. *American Journal of Psychiatry, 152,* 529–535.

Breslau, N., Davis, G. C., & Prabucki, K. (1988). Depressed mothers as informants in family history research: Are they accurate? *Psychiatry Research, 24,* 345–359.

Bridges, J. A., & Brent, D. A. (2004). Adolescents with depression. Letter to the editor. *Journal of the American Medical Association, 292,* 2578.

Brooks, S. J., & Kutcher, S. (2001). Diagnosis and measurement of adolescent depression: A review of commonly utilized instruments. *Journal of Child and Adolescent Psychopharmacology, 11,* 341–376.

Brown, G. W. (1993). Life events and affective disorder: Replications and limitations. *Psychosomatic Medicine, 55,* 248–259.

Brown, G. W., & Harris, T. O. (1978). *Social origins of depression: A study of psychiatric disorder in women.* London: Tavistock.

Brown, G. W., & Harris, T. O. (1989). Depression. In T. O. Harris & G. W. Brown (Eds.), *Life events and illness* (pp. 49–93). New York: Guilford Press.

Brown, G. W., & Moran, P. M. (1997). Single mothers, poverty, and depression. *Psychological Medicine, 27,* 21–33.

Brown, T. A., Chorpita, B. F., & Barlow, D. H. (1998). Structural relationships among dimensions of the *DSM-IV* anxiety and mood disorders and dimensions of negative affect, positive affect, and autonomic arousal. *Journal of Abnormal Psychology, 107,* 179–192.

Browne, A., & Finkelhor, D. (1986). Impact of child sexual abuse: A review of the research. *Psychological Bulletin, 99,* 66–77.

Bruder, G. E., Stewart, J. W., Tenke, C. E., McGrath, P. J., Leite, P., Bhattacharya, N., et al. (2001). Electroencephalographic and perceptual asymmetry differences between responders and nonresponders to an SSRI antidepressant. *Biological Psychiatry, 49,* 416–425.

Burge, D., & Hammen, C. (1991). Maternal communication: Predictors of outcome at follow-up in a sample of children at high and low risk for depression. *Journal of Abnormal Psychology, 100,* 174–180.

Burge, D., Hammen, C., Davila, J., Daley, S., Paley, B., Lindberg, N., et al. (1997). The relationship between attachment cognitions and psychological adjustment in late adolescent women. *Development and Psychopathology, 9,* 151–168.

Burnam, M. A., Stein, J. A., Golding, J. M., Siegel, J. M., Sorenson, S. B., Forsythe, A. B., et al. (1988). Sexual assault and mental disorders in a community population. *Journal of Consulting and Clinical Psychology, 56,* 843–850.

Burt, C. E., Cohen, L. H., & Bjorck, J. P. (1988). Perceived family environment as a moderator of young adolescents' life stress adjustment. *American Journal of Community Psychology, 16,* 101–122.

Buss, A. H., & Plomin, R. (1984). *Temperament: Early developing personality traits.* Hillsdale, NJ: Erlbaum.

Buss, A. H., & Plomin, R. (1986). The EAS approach to temperament. In R. Plomin & J. Dunn (Eds.), *The study of temperament: Changes, continuities, and challenges* (pp. 67–79). Hillsdale, NJ: Erlbaum.

Butler, L. F., Meizitis, S., & Friedman, R. J. (1980). The effect of two school-based intervention programs on depressive symptoms in preadolescent children. *American Education Research Journal, 17,* 111–119.

Canals, J., Domenech-Llaberia, E., Fernandez-Ballart, J., & Marti-Hennenberg, C. (2002). Predictors of depression at 18: A 7-year follow-up study in a Spanish nonclinical population. *European Child and Adolescent Psychiatry, 11,* 226–233.

Carey, M. P., Faulstich, M. E., Gresham, F. M., Ruggiero, L., & Enyart, P. (1987). Children's Depression Inventory: Construct and discriminant validity across clinical and nonreferred (control) populations. *Journal of Consulting and Clinical Psychology, 55,* 755–761.

Carter, J. S., & Garber, J. (2005). *Reciprocal relations between peer stress and internalizing and externalizing symptoms during adolescence.* Manuscript under review.

Caspi, A., Henry, B., McGee, R. O., Moffitt, T. E., & Silva, P. A. (1995). Temperamental origins of child and adolescent behavior problems: From age three to age fifteen. *Child Development, 66,* 55–68.

Caspi, A., Moffitt, T. E., Newman, D. L., & Silva, P. A. (1996). Behavioral observations at age 3 years predict adult psychiatric disorders: Longitudinal evidence from a birth cohort. *Archives of General Psychiatry, 53,* 1033–1039.

Caspi, A., Sugden, K., Moffitt, T. E., Taylor, A., Craig, I. W., Harrington, H., et al. (2003). Influence of life stress on depression: Moderation by a polymorphism in the 5-HTT gene. *Science, 301,* 386–389.

Cavallo, A., Holt, K. G., Hejazi, M. S., Richards, G. E., & Meyer, W. J. (1987). Melatonin circadian rhythm in childhood depression. *Journal of the American Academy of Child and Adolescent Psychiatry, 26,* 395–399.

Charney, D. S., Nelson, J. C., & Quinlan, D. M. (1981). Personality traits and disorder in depression. *American Journal of Psychiatry, 138,* 1601–1604.

Chen, X., Rubin, K. H., & Li, B. (1995). Depressed mood in Chinese children: Relations with school performance and family environment. *Journal of Consulting and Clinical Psychology, 63,* 938–947.

Clark, L. A., & Watson, D. (1991). Tripartite model of anxiety and depression: Psychometric evidence and taxonomic implications. *Journal of Abnormal Psychology, 100,* 316–336.

Clark, L. A., Watson, D., & Mineka, S. (1994). Temperament, personality, and the mood and anxiety disorders. *Journal of Abnormal Psychology, 103,* 103–116.

Clarke, A. S., & Schneider, M. L. (1993). Prenatal stress has long-term effects on behavioral responses to stress in juvenile rhesus monkeys. *Developmental Psychobiology, 26,* 293–304.

Clarke, A. S., Wittwer, D. J., Abbott, D. H., & Schneider, M. L. (1994). Long-term effects of prenatal stress on HPA axis activity in juvenile rhesus monkeys. *Developmental Psychobiology, 27,* 257–269.

Clarke, G. N., Hawkins, W., Murphy, M., Sheeber, L. B., Lewinsohn, P. M., & Seeley, J. R. (1995). Targeted prevention of unipolar depressive disorder in an at-risk sample of high school adolescents: A randomized trial of group cognitive intervention. *Journal of the American Academy of Child and Adolescent Psychiatry, 34,* 312–321.

Clarke, G. N., Hops, H., Lewinsohn, P. M., & Andrew, J. (1992). Cognitive-behavioral group treatment of adolescent depression: Prediction of outcome. *Behavior Therapy, 23,* 341–354.

Clarke, G. N., Hornbrook, M., Lynch, F., Polen, M. Gale, J., O'Connor, E., et al. (2002). Group cognitive-behavioral treatment for depressed adolescent offspring of depressed parents in a health maintenance organization. *Journal of the American Academy of Child and Adolescent Psychiatry, 41,* 305–313.

Clarke, G. N., Lewinsohn, P.M., Rohde, P., Hops, H., & Seeley, J. R. (1999). Cognitive-behavioral group treatment of adolescent depression: Efficacy of acute group treatment and booster sessions. *Journal of the American Academy of Child and Adolescent Psychiatry, 38,* 272–279.

Clarke, G. N., Rohde, P., Lewinsohn, P. M., Hops, H., & Seeley, J. R. (1999). Cognitive behavioral treatment of adolescent depression: Efficacy of acute group treatment and booster sessions. *Journal of the American Academy of Child and Adolescent Psychiatry, 38,* 272–279.

Cloninger, C. R. (1987). A systematic method for clinical description and classification of personality variants: A proposal. *Archives of General Psychiatry, 44,* 573–588.

Cloninger, C. R., Svrakic, D. M., Przybeck, T. R. (1993). A psychobiological model of temperament and character. *Archives of General Psychiatry 50,* 975–990.

Cohen, L. H., Burt, C. E., & Bjork, J. P. (1987). Life stress and adjustment: Effects of life events experienced by young adolescents and their parents. *Developmental Psychology, 23,* 583–592.

Cohen, P., Cohen, J., Kasen, S., Velez, C. N., Hartmark, C., Johnson, J., et al. (1993). An epidemiological study of disorders in late childhood and adolescence: I. Age- and gender-specific prevalence. *Journal of Child Psychology and Psychiatry, 34,* 851–867.

Cole, D. A. (1991). Preliminary support for a competency-based model of depression in children. *Journal of Abnormal Psychology, 100,* 181–190.

Cole, D. A. (2001). Relation of social and academic competence to depressive symptoms in childhood. *Journal of Abnormal Psychology, 99,* 422–429.

Cole, D. A., & Carpentieri, S. (1990). Social status and the comorbidity of child depression and conduct disorder. *Journal of Consulting and Clinical Psychology, 58,* 748–757.

Cole, D. A., Hoffman, K., Tram, J. M., & Maxwell, S. E. (2000). Structural differences in parent and child reports of children's symptoms of depression and anxiety. *Psychological Assessment, 12,* 174–185.

Cole, D. A., Martin, J. M., Peeke, L. A., Seroczynski, A. D., & Hoffman, K. (1998). Are negative cognitive errors predictive or reflective of depressive symptoms in children: A longitudinal study. *Journal of Abnormal Psychology, 107,* 481–496.

Cole, D. A., Martin, J. M., & Powers, B. (1997). A competency-based model of child depression: A longitudinal study of peer, parent, teacher, and self-evaluations. *Journal of Child Psychology, Psychiatry, and Allied Disciplines, 38,* 505–514.

Cole, D. A., Martin, J. M., Powers, B., & Truglio, R. (1996). Modeling causal relations between academic and social competence and depression: A multitrait-multimethod longitudinal study of children. *Journal of Abnormal Psychology, 105,* 258–270.

Cole, D. A., Nolen-Hoeksema, S., Girgus, J., & Paul, G. (2004). *Stress exposure and stress generation in child and adolescent depression: A latent state-trait error approach to longitudinal analyses.* Manuscript submitted for publication.

Cole, D. A., Peeke, L. A., Martin, J. M., Truglio, R., & Seroczynski, A. D. (1997). A longitudinal look at the relation between depression and anxiety in children and adolescents. *Journal of Consulting and Clinical Psychology, 106,* 586–597.

Cole, D. A., & Rehm, L. P. (1986). Family interaction patterns and childhood depression. *Journal of Abnormal Child Psychology, 14,* 297–314.

Cole, D. A., & Turner, J. E. (1993). Models of cognitive mediation and moderation in child depression. *Journal of Abnormal Psychology, 102,* 271–281.

Compas, B. E., Connor-Smith, J., & Jaser, S. S. (2004). Temperament, stress reactivity, and coping: Implications for depression in childhood and adolescence. *Journal of Clinical Child and Adolescent Psychology, 33,* 21–31.

Compas, B. E., Connor-Smith, J. K., Saltzman, H., Thomsen, A. H., & Wadsworth, M. E. (2001). Coping with stress during childhood and adolescence: Problems, progress, and potential in theory and research. *Psychological Bulletin, 127,* 87–127.

Compas, B. E., Ey, S., & Grant, K. E. (1993). Taxonomy, assessment, and diagnosis depression during adolescence. *Psychological Bulletin, 114,* 323–344.

Compas, B. E., Grant, K. E., & Ey, S. (1994). Psychosocial stress and child and adolescent depression: Can we be more specific? In H. F. Johnston & W. M. Reynolds (Ed.), *Handbook of depression in children and adolescents* (pp. 509–523). New York: Plenum Press.

Compas, B. E., Howell, D. C., Phares, V., Williams, R. A., & Guinta, C. T. (1989). Risk factors for emotional/behavioral problems in young adolescents: A prospective analysis of adolescent and parental stress and symptoms. *Journal of Consulting and Clinical Psychology, 57,* 732–740.

Connolly, J., Gellar, S., Marton, P., & Kutcher, S. (1992). Peer responses to social interactions with depressed adolescents. *Journal of Clinical Child Psychology, 21,* 365–370.

Coryell, W., Akiskal, H. S., Leon, A. C., Winokur, G., Maser, J. D., Mueller, T. I., et al. (1994). The time course of nonchronic major depressive disorder: Uniformity across episodes and samples. *Archives of General Psychiatry, 51,* 405–410.

Coryell, W., & Winokur, G. (1992). Course and outcome. In E. S. Paykel (Ed.), *Handbook of Affective Disorders* (pp. 89–108). New York: Guilford Press.

Costa, P. T., & McCrae, R. R. (1980). Influence of extraversion and neuroticism on subjective well being: Happy and unhappy people. *Journal of Personality and Social Psychology, 38,* 668–678.

Costello, E. J., Angold, A., Burns, B. J., Stangl, D. K., Tweed, D. L., Erkanli, A., et al. (1996). The Great Smoky Mountains Study of youth: Goals, design, methods, and the prevalence of *DSM-III-R* disorders. *Archives of General Psychiatry, 53,* 1129–1136.

Costello, E. J., Mustillo, S., Erklani, A., Keeler, G., & Angold, A. (2003). Prevalence and development of psychiatric disorders in childhood and adolescence. *Archives of General Psychiatry, 60,* 837–844.

Coyne, J. C. (1976). Toward an interactional description of depression. *Psychiatry, 39,* 28–40.

Craighead, W. E., Curry, J. F., & Ilardi, S. S. (1995). Relationship of Children's Depression Inventory factors to major depression among adolescents. *Psychological Assessment, 7,* 171–176.

Cummings, E. M., & Cicchetti, D. (1990). Toward a transactional model of relations between attachment and depression. In M. T. Greenberg, D. Cicchetti, & E. M. Cummings (Eds.), *Attachment in the preschool years: Theory, research, and intervention* (pp. 339–372). Chicago: University of Chicago Press.

Cummings, E. M., & Davies, P. T. (1994). Maternal depression and child development. *Journal of Child Psychology and Psychiatry, 35,* 73–112.

Curran, P. J., & Bollen, K. A. (2001). The best of both worlds: Combining autoregressive and latent curve models. Decade of behavior. In A. G. Sayer & L. M. Collins (Eds.), *New methods for the analysis of change* (pp. 107–135). Washington, DC: American Psychological Association.

Curry, J. F. (2001). Specific psychotherapies for childhood and adolescent depression. *Biological Psychiatry, 49,* 1091–1100.

Curry, J. F., & Craighead, W. E. (1993). Depression. In T. H. Ollendick & M. Hersen (Eds.), *Handbook of child and adolescent assessment* (pp. 251–268). Boston: Allyn & Bacon.

Cyranowski, J. M., Frank, E., Young, E., & Shear, K. (2000). Adolescent onset of the gender difference in lifetime rates of major depression. *Archives of General Psychiatry, 57,* 21–27.

Dahl, R. E., Birmaher, B., Williamson, D. E., Dorn, L., Perel, J., Kaufman, J., et al. (2000). Low growth hormone response to growth hormone-releasing hormone in child depression. *Biological Psychiatry, 48,* 981–988.

Dahl, R. E., & Ryan, N. D. (1996). The psychobiology of adolescent depression. In D. Cicchetti & S. L. Toth (Eds.), *Rochester symposium on developmental psychopathology. Vol. 7. Adolescence: Opportunities and challenges* (pp. 197–232). Rochester, NY: Rochester University Press.

Dahl, R. E., Ryan, N. D., Puig-Antich, J., Nguyen, N. A., Al-Shabbout, M., Meyer, V. A., et al. (1991). 24-hour cortisol measures in adolescents with major depression: A controlled study. *Biological Psychiatry, 30,* 25–36.

Daley, S., Hammen, C., Burge, D., Davila, J., Paley, B., Lindberg, N., et al. (1997). Predictors of the generation of episodic stress: A longitudinal study of late adolescent women. *Journal of Abnormal Psychology, 106,* 251–259.

Daley, S., Hammen, C., Davila, J., & Burge, D. (1998). Axis II symptomatology, depression, and life stress during the transition from adolescence to adulthood. *Journal of Consulting and Clinical Psychology. 66,* 595–603.

Davidson, R. J., Pizzagalli, D., Nitschke, J. B., & Putnam, K. (2002). Depression: Perspectives from affective neuroscience. *Annual Review of Psychology, 53,* 545–574.

Davies, P. T., & Windle, M. (2001). Interparental discord and adolescent adjustment trajectories: The potentiating and protective role of intrapersonal attributes. *Child Development, 72,* 1163–1178.

Davila, J., Hammen, C., Burge, D., Paley, B., & Daley, S. (1995). Poor interpersonal problem-solving as a mechanism of stress generation in depression among adolescent women. *Journal of Abnormal Psychology, 104,* 592–600.

Davis, M. C., Matthews, K. A., & Twamley, E. W. (1999). Is life more difficult on Mars or Venus? A meta-analytic review of sex differences in major and minor life events. *Annals of Behavioral Medicine, 21,* 83–97.

Dawson, G., Klinger, L. G., Panagiotides, H., Hill, D., & Spieker, S. (1992). Frontal lobe activity and affective behavior of infants of mothers with depressive symptoms. *Child Development, 63,* 725–737.

Derryberry, D., & Rothbart, M. K. (1988). Arousal, affect, and attention as components of temperament. *Journal of Personality and Social Psychology, 55,* 958–966.

Diamond, G. S., Reis, B. F., Diamond, G. M., Siqueland, L., & Isaacs, L. (2002). Attachment based family therapy for depressed adolescents: A treatment development study. *Journal of the American Academy of Child and Adolescent Psychiatry, 41,* 1190–1196.

Dierker, L. C., Albano, A. M., Clarke, G. N., Heimberg, R. G., Kendall, P. C., Merikangas, K. R., et al. (2001). Screening for anxiety and depression in early adolescence. *Journal of the American Academy of Child and Adolescent Psychiatry, 40,* 929–936.

Digman, J. M. (1989). Five robust trait dimensions: Development, stability, and utility. *Journal of Personality, 57,* 195–214.

Digman, J. M., & Inouye, J. (1986). Further specification of the five robust factors of personality. *Journal of Personality and Social Psychology, 50,* 116–123.

Digman, J. M., & Shmelyov, A. G. (1996). The structure of temperament and personality in Russian children. *Journal of Personality and Social Psychology, 71,* 341–351.

DiMascio, A., Weissman, M. M., Prusoff, B. A., Neu, C., Zwilling, M., & Klerman, G. L. (1979). Differential symptom reduction by drugs and psychotherapy in acute depression. *Archives of General Psychiatry, 36,* 1450–1456.

Dinan, T. G. (1998). Neuroendocrine markers: Role in the development of antidepressants. *CNS Drugs, 10,* 145–157.

Dixon, J. F., & Ahrens, A. H. (1992). Stress and attributional style as predictors of self-reported depression in children. *Cognitive Therapy and Research, 16,* 623–634

Downey, G., & Coyne, J. C. (1990). Children of depressed parents: An integrative review. *Psychological Bulletin, 108,* 50–76.

DuBois, D. L., Felner, R. D., Brand, S., & George, G. R. (1999). Profiles of self-esteem in early adolescence: Identification and investigation of adaptive correlates. *American Journal of Community Psychology, 27,* 899–932.

Eaves, L. J., Silberg, J. L., Meyer, J. M., Maes, H. H., Simonoff, E., Pickles, A., et al. (1997). Genetics and developmental psychopathology: 2. The main effects of genes and environment on behavioral problems in the Virginia Twin Study of Adolescent Behavioral Development. *Journal of Child Psychology and Psychiatry, 38,* 965–980.

Eley, T. C. (1997). Depressive symptoms in children and adolescents: Etiological links between normality and abnormality: A research note. *Journal of Child Psychology and Psychiatry, 38,* 861–865.

Eley, T. C., Deater-Deckard, K., Fombonne, E., Fulker, D. W., & Plomin, R. (1998). An adoption study of depressive symptoms in middle childhood. *Journal of Child Psychology and Psychiatry, 39,* 337–345.

Eley, T. C., & Stevenson, J. (2000). Specific life events and chronic experiences differentially associated with depression and anxiety in young twins. *Journal of Abnormal Child Psychology, 28,* 383–394.

Elkin, I., Shea, M. T., Watkins, J. T., Imber, S. D., Sotsky, S. M., Collins, J. F., et al. (1989). National Institute of Mental Health Treatment of Depression Collaborative Research Program: General effectiveness of treatments. *Archives of General Psychiatry, 46,* 971–982.

Emslie, G. J., Heiligenstein, J. H., Wagner, K. D., Hoog, S. L., Ernest, D. E., Brown, E., et al. (2002). Fluoxetine for acute treatment of depression in children and adolescents: A placebo-controlled, randomized clinical trial. *Journal of the American Academy of Child and Adolescent Psychiatry, 41,* 1205–1215.

Emslie, G. J., Rush, A. J., Weinberg, W. A., Gullion, C. M., Rintelmann, J., & Hughes, C. W. (1997). Recurrence of major depressive disorder in hospitalized children and adolescents. *Journal of the American Academy of Child and Adolescent Psychiatry, 36,* 785–792.

Emslie, G. J., Weinberg, W. A., Kennard, B. D., & Kowatch, R. A. (1994). Neurobiological aspects of depression in children and adolescents. In W. M. Reynolds & H. E. Johnston (Eds.), *Handbook of depression in children and adolescents* (pp. 143–165). New York: Plenum Press.

Ernst, M., Godfrey, K. A., Silva, R. R., Pouget, E. R., & Welkowitz, J. (1994). A new pictorial instrument for child and adolescent psychiatry: A pilot study. *Psychiatry Research, 51,* 87–104.

Essau, C. A., Conradt, J., & Petermann, F. (2000). Frequency, comorbidity, and psychosocial impairment of depressive disorders in adolescents. *Journal of Adolescent Research, 15,* 470–481.

Eysenck, H. J. (1952). The scientific study of personality. (xiii, 320). Oxford, England: Macmillan.Eysenck, H. J., & Eysenck, M. W. (1985). *Personality and individual differences: A natural science approach.* New York: Plenum Press.

Farmer, R., Nelson, G., & Rosemery, O. (1990). Personality disorders and depression: Hypothetical relations, empirical findings, and methodological considerations. *Clinical Psychology Review, 10,* 453–476.

Fergusson, D. M., Wanner, B., Vitaro, F., Horwood, L. J., & Swain-Campbell, N. (2003). Deviant peer affiliations and depression: Confounding or causation? *Journal of Abnormal Child Psychology, 31,* 605–618.

Field, T. (1995). Presidential address: Infants of depressed mothers. *Infant Behavior and Development, 18,* 1–13.

Field, T., Fox, N. A., Pickens, J., & Nawrocki, T. (1995). Relative frontal EEG activation in 3- to 6-month-old infants of "depressed" mothers. *Developmental Psychology, 31,* 358–363.

Fleming, J. E., & Offord, D.R. (1990). Epidemiology of childhood depressive disorders: A critical review. *Journal of the American Academy of Child and Adolescent Psychiatry, 29,* 571–580.

Fleming, J. E., Offord, D. R., & Boyle, M. H. (1989). Prevalence of childhood and adolescent depression in the community: Ontario Child Health Study. *British Journal of Psychiatry, 155,* 647–654.

Flett, G. L., Vrendenburg, K., & Krames, L. (1997). The continuity of depression in clinical and nonclinical samples. *Psychological Bulletin, 121,* 395–416.

Forsterling, F., & Binser, M. J. (2002). Depression, school performance, and the veridicality of perceived grades and causal attributions. *Personality and Social Psychology Bulletin, 28,* 1441–1449.

Frank, D. A., & Drotar, D. (1994). Failure to thrive. In R. M. Reece (Ed.), *Child abuse: Medical diagnosis and management* (pp. 298–324). Philadelphia: Lea & Febiger.

Frank, E., Kupfer, D. J., Perel, J. M., Cornes, C., Jarrett, D. B., Mallinger, A. G., et al. (1990). Three-year outcomes for maintenance therapies in recurrent depression. *Archives of General Psychiatry, 47,* 1093–1099.

French, D.C., Conrad, J., & Turner, T. M. (1995). Adjustment of antisocial and nonantisocial rejected adolescents. *Development and Psychopathology, 7,* 857–874.

Fride, E., Dan, Y., Feldon, J., Halevy, G., & Weinstock, M. (1986). Effects of prenatal stress on vulnerability to stress in prepubertal and adult rats. *Physiology and Behavior, 37,* 681–687.

Fride, E., & Weinstock, M. (1988). Prenatal stress increases anxiety-related behavior and alters cerebral lateralization of dopamine activity. *Life Sciences, 42,* 1059–1065.

Gaensbauer, T. J., Harmon, R. J., Cytryn, L., & McKnew, D. H. (1984). Social and affective development in infants with a manic-depressive parent. *American Journal of Psychiatry, 141,* 223–229.

Gaensbauer, T. J., & Sands, K. (1979). Distorted affective communications in abused/neglected infants and their potential impact on caretakers. *Journal of the American Academy of Child Psychiatry, 18,* 236–250.

Garber, J. (1984). The developmental progression of depression in female children. *New Directions for Child Development, 26,* 29–58.

Garber, J., & Flynn, C. A. (2001). Predictors of depressive cognitions in young adolescents. *Cognitive Therapy and Research, 25,* 353–376.

Garber, J., & Hilsman, R. (1992). Cognitions, stress, and depression in children and adolescents. *Child and Adolescent Psychiatric Clinics of North America, 1,* 129–167.

Garber, J., & Hollon, S. D. (1991). What can specificity designs say about causality in psychopathology research? *Psychological Bulletin, 110,* 129–136.

Garber, J., & Kaminski, K. M. (2000). Laboratory and performance-based measures of depression in children and adolescents. *Journal of Clinical Child Psychology, 29,* 509–525.

Garber, J., Keiley, M. K., & Martin, N. C. (2002). Developmental trajectories of adolescents' depressive symptoms: Predictors of change. *Journal of Consulting and Clinical Psychology, 70,* 79–95.

Garber, J., Kriss, M. R., Koch, M., & Lindholm, L. (1988). Recurrent depression in adolescents: A follow-up study. *Journal of the American Academy of Child and Adolescent Psychiatry, 27,* 49–54.

Garber, J., Quiggle, N. L., Panak, W. F., & Dodge, K. A. (1991). Depression and aggression in children: Comorbidity and social cognitive processes. In D. Cicchetti and S. Toth (Eds.), *The Rochester Symposium on Developmental Psychopathology, Vol. 2: Internalizing and externalizing expressions of dysfunction* (pp. 225–264). Hillsdale, NJ: Erlbaum.

Garber, J., & Robinson, N. S. (1997). Cognitive vulnerability in children at risk for depression. *Cognitions and Emotions, 11,* 619–635.

Garrison, C., Jackson, K., Marsteller, F., McKeown, R., & Addy, C. (1990). A longitudinal study of depressive symptomatology in young adolescents. *Journal of Child and Adolescent Psychiatry, 29,* 581–585.

Ge, X., Best, K. M., Conger, R. D., & Simons, R. L. (1996). Parenting behaviors and the occurrence and co-occurrence of adolescent depressive symptoms and conduct problems. *Developmental Psychology, 32,* 717–731.

Ge, X., Lorenz, F., Conger, R., Edler, C., & Simons, R. L. (1994). Trajectories of stressful life events and depressive symptoms during adolescence. *Developmental Psychology, 30,* 467–483.

Gerlsma, C., Emmelkamp, P. M. G., & Arrindell, W. A. (1990). Anxiety, depression, and perception of early parenting: A meta-analysis. *Clinical Psychology Review, 10,* 251–277.

Gershuny, B. S., & Sher, K. J. (1998). The relation between personality and anxiety: Findings from a 3 year prospective study. *Journal of Abnormal Psychology, 107,* 252–262.

Gjerde, P. F. (1995). Alternative pathways to chronic depressive symptoms in young adults: Gender differences in developmental trajectories. *Child Development, 66,* 1277–1300.

Gladstone, T. R. G., & Kaslow, N. J. (1995). Depression and attributions in children and adolescents: A meta-analytic review. *Journal of Abnormal Child Psychology, 23,* 597–606.

Glover, V. (1997). Maternal stress or anxiety in pregnancy and emotional development of the child. *British Journal of Psychiatry, 171,* 105–106.

Goldberg, L. R. (1992). The development of markers for the Big Five factor structure. *Psychological Assessment, 4,* 26–42.

Goldsmith, H. H. (1986). Heritability of temperament: Cautions and some empirical evidence. In G. A. Kohnstamm (Ed.), *Temperament discussed: Temperament and development in infancy and childhood* (pp. 83–96). Lisse, Netherlands: Swets & Zeitlinger.

Gonzales, L. R., Lewinsohn, P. M., & Clarke, G. N. (1985). Longitudinal follow up of unipolar depressives: An investigation of predictors of relapse. *Journal of Consulting and Clinical Psychology, 53,* 461–469.

Goodman, S. H., Adamson, L. B., Riniti, J., & Cole, S. (1994). Mothers' expressed attitudes: Associations with maternal depression and children's self-esteem and psychopathology. *Journal of the American Academy of Child and Adolescent Psychiatry, 33,* 1265–1274.

Goodman, S. H., & Gotlib, I. H. (1999). Risk for psychopathology in the children of depressed mothers: A developmental model for understanding mechanisms of transmission. *Psychological Review, 106,* 458–490.

Goodman, S. H., Schwab, S. M., Lahey, B. B., Shaffer, D., & Jensen, P. S. (2000). Major depression and dysthymia in children and adolescents: Discriminant validity and differential consequences in a community sample. *Journal of the American Academy of Child and Adolescent Psychiatry, 39,* 761–770.

Goodyer, I. M. (2001). Life events: Their nature and effects. In I. M. Goodyer (Ed.), *The depressed child and adolescent* (2nd ed., pp. 204–232). New York: Cambridge University Press.

Goodyer, I. M., Germany, E., Gowrusankur, J., & Altham, P. M. E. (1991). Social influences on the course of anxious and depressive disorders in school-aged children. *British Journal of Psychiatry, 158,* 676–684.

Goodyer, I. M., Herbert, J., Altham, P. M. E., Pearson, J., Secher, S. M., & Shiers, H. M. (1996). Adrenal secretion during major depression in 8- to 16-year-olds, I. Altered diurnal rhythms in salivary cortisol and dehydrepiandrosterone (DHEA) at presentation. *Psychological Medicine, 26,* 245–256.

Goodyer, I. M., Herbert, J., Tamplin, A., & Altham, P. M. E. (2000). Recent life events, cortisol, dehydroepiandrosterone and the onset of major depression in high-risk adolescents. *British Journal of Psychiatry, 177,* 499–504.

Goodyear, I. M., Herbert, J., Tamplin, A., Secher, S. M., & Pearson, J. (1997). Short-term outcome of major depression: II. Life events, family dysfunction, and friendship difficulties as predictors of persistent disorder. *Journal of the American Academy of Child and Adolescent Psychiatry, 36,* 474–480.

Goodyer, I. M., Kolvin, I., & Gatzanis, S. (1986). Does age or sex influence the association between recent life events and psychiatric disorders in children and adolescents? A controlled enquiry. *Journal of Child Psychology and Psychiatry and Allied Disciplines, 27,* 681–687.

Gotlib, I. H., & Hammen, C. L. (1992). *Psychological aspects of depression: Toward a cognitive-interpersonal integration.* Chichester, England: Wiley.

Grant, K. E., Compas, B. E., Thurm, A. E., McMahon, S. D., & Gipson, P. Y. (2004). Stressors and child and adolescent psychopathology: Measurement issues and prospective effects. *Journal of Clinical Child and Adolescent Psychology, 33,* 412–425.

Gray, J. A. (1987). The neuropsychology of emotion and personality. In S. D. Iversen and S. M. Stahl (Eds.), *Cognitive neurochemistry* (pp. 171–190). London: Oxford University Press.

Gray, J. A. (1991). The neuropsychology of temperament. In A. Angleitner & J. Strelau (Eds.), *Explorations in temperament: International perspectives on theory and measurement* (pp. 105–128). New York: Plenum Press.

Graziano, W. G., & Ward, D. (1992). Probing the Big Five in adolescence: Personality and adjustment during a developmental transition. *Journal of Personality, 60,* 425–439.

Greenberger, E., Chen, C., Tally, S. R., & Dong, Q. (2000). Family, peer, and individual correlates of depressive symptomatology among U.S. and Chinese adolescents. *Journal of Consulting and Clinical Psychology, 68,* 209–219.

Guy, W. (1976). *ECDEU assessment manual for psychopharmacology* (2nd ed.). DHEW publication 76–388. Washington, DC: U.S. Government Printing Office.

Haaga, D., Dyck, M., & Ernst, D. (1991). Empirical status of cognitive theory of depression. *Psychological Bulletin, 110,* 215–236.

Hamilton, E. B., Asarnow, J. R., & Thompson, M. C. (1997). Social, academic, and behavioral competence of depressed children: Relation to diagnostic status and family interaction style. *Journal of Youth and Adolescence, 26,* 77–87.

Hamilton, M. (1960). A rating scale for depression. *Journal of Neurology Neurosurgery and Psychiatry, 23,* 56–62.

Hammen, C. (1988). Self cognitions, stressful events, and the prediction of depression in children of depressed mothers. *Journal of Abnormal Child Psychology, 16,* 347–360.

Hammen, C. (1991a). The generation of stress in the course of unipolar depression. *Journal of Abnormal Psychology, 100,* 555–561.

Hammen, C. (1991b). *Depression runs in families: The social context of risk and resilience in children of depressed mothers.* New York: Springer-Verlag.

Hammen, C., Adrian, C., & Hiroto, D. (1988). A longitudinal test of the attributional vulnerability model in children at risk for depression. *British Journal of Clinical Psychology, 27,* 37–46.

Hammen, C., Burge, D., Daley, S., Davila, J., Paley, B., & Rudolph, K. (1995). Interpersonal attachment cognitions and prediction of symptomatic responses to interpersonal stress. *Journal of Abnormal Psychology, 104,* 436–443.

Hammen, C., Burge, D., & Stansbury, K. (1990). Relationship of mother and child variables to child outcomes in a high risk sample: A causal modeling analysis. *Developmental Psychology, 26,* 24–30.

Hammen, C., & Compas, B. E. (1994). Unmasking unmasked depression in children and adolescents: The problem of comorbidity. *Clinical Psychology Review, 14,* 585–603.

Hammen, C., Davila, J., Brown, G., Ellicott, A., & Gitlin, M. (1992). Psychiatric history and stress: Predictors of severity of unipolar depression. *Journal of Abnormal Psychology, 101,* 45–52.

Hammen, C., Ellicott, A., Gitlin, M., & Jamison, K. R. (1989). Sociotropy/autonomy and vulnerability to specific life events in patients with unipolar depression and bipolar disorders. *Journal of Abnormal Psychology, 98,* 154–160.

Hammen, C., & Goodman-Brown, T. (1990). Self schemas and vulnerability to specific life stress in children at risk for depression. *Cognitive Therapy and Research, 14,* 215–227.

Hammen, C., & Rudolph, K. D. (1996). Childhood depression. In R. A. Barkley & E. J. Mash (Eds.), *Child psychopathology* (pp. 153–195). New York: Guilford Press.

Hankin, B. L., & Abramson, L. Y. (1999). Development of gender differences in depression: Description and possible explanations. *Annals of Medicine, 31,* 372–379.

Hankin, B. L., Abramson, L. Y., Moffitt, T. E., Silva, P. A., McGee, R., & Angell, K. E. (1998). Development of depression from preadolescence to young adulthood: Emerging gender differences in a 10-year longitudinal study. *Journal of Abnormal Psychology, 107,* 128–140.

Hankin, B. L., Abramson, L. Y., & Siler, M. (2001). A prospective test of the hopelessness theory of depression in adolescence. *Cognitive Therapy and Research, 25,* 607–632.

Harrington, R. C., Fudge, H., Rutter, M. L., Bredenkamp, D., Groothues, C., & Pridham, J. (1993). Child and adult depression: A test of continuities with data from a family study. *British Journal of Psychiatry, 162,* 627–633.

Harrington, R., Fudge, H., Rutter, M., Pickles, A., & Hill, J. (1990). Adult outcomes of childhood and adolescent depression. *Archives of General Psychiatry, 47,* 465–473.

Harris, P. L. (1989). *Children and emotion: The development of psychological understanding.* Cambridge, MA: Blackwell.

Harter, S., & Nowakowski, M. (1987). *Manual for the Dimensions of Depression Profile for Children and Adolescents.* Denver: University of Denver Department of Psychology.

Hartup, W. W., & van Lieshout, C. F. M. (1995). Personality development in social context. *Annual Review of Psychology, 46,* 655–687.

Hays, R. D., Wells, K. B., Sherbourne, C. D., Rogers, W., & Spritzer, K. (1995). Functioning and well-being outcomes of patients with depression compared with chronic general medical illness. *Archives of General Psychiatry, 52,* 11–19.

Hayward, C., Killen, J. D., Kraemer, H. C., & Taylor, C. B. (1998). Linking self reported childhood behavioral inhibition to adolescent social phobia. *Journal of the American Academy of Child and Adolescent Psychiatry, 37,* 1308–1316.

Hecht, D. B., Inderbitzen, H. M., & Bukowski, A. L. (1998). The relationship between peer status and depressive symptoms in children and adolescents. *Journal of Abnormal Child Psychology, 26,* 153–160.

Heim, C., & Nemeroff, C. B. (2001). The role of childhood trauma in the neurobiology of mood and anxiety disorders: Preclinical and clinical studies. *Biological Psychiatry, 49,* 1023–1039.

Henry, C., Kabbaj, M., Simon, H., Le Moal, M., & Maccari, S. (1994). Prenatal stress increases the hypothalamo-pituitary-adrenal axis response in young and adult rats. *Journal of Neuroendocrinology, 6,* 341–345.

Herjanic, B., & Reich, W. (1982). Development of a structured psychiatric interview for children: Agreement between child and parent on individual symptoms. *Journal of Abnormal Child Psychology, 10,* 307–324.

Herjanic, B., & Reich, W. (1997). Development of a structured psychiatric interview for children: Agreement between child and parent on individual symptoms. *Journal of Abnormal Child Psychology, 25,* 21–31.

Herzberg, D. S., Hammen, C., Burge, D., Daley, S. E., Davila, J., & Lindberg, N. (1998). Social competence as a predictor of chronic interpersonal stress. *Personal Relationships, 5,* 207–218.

Hilsman, R., & Garber, J. (1995). A test of the cognitive diathesis-stress model of depression in children: Academic stressors, attributional style, perceived competence, and control. *Journal of Personality and Social Psychology, 69,* 370–380.

Hirschfeld, R. M. A. (1994). Major depression, dysthymia and depressive personality disorder. *British Journal of Psychiatry, 165,* 23–30.

Hirschfeld, R. M., & Klerman, G. L. (1979). Personality attributes and affective disorders. *American Journal of Psychiatry, 136,* 67–70.

Hirschfeld, R. M., Klerman, G. L., Lavori, P., Keller, M. B., Griffith, P., & Coryell, W. (1989). Premorbid personality assessments of first onset of major depression. *Archives of General Psychiatry, 46,* 345–350.

Hirshfeld, D. R., Rosenbaum, J. F., Biederman, J., Bolduc, E. A., Faraone, S. V., Snidman, N., et al. (1992). Stable behavioral inhibition and its association with anxiety disorder. *Journal of the American Academy of Child and Adolescent Psychiatry, 31,* 103–111.

Hodges, K. (1994). Evaluation of depression in children and adolescents using diagnostic clinical interviews. In W. M. Reynolds & H. F. Johnston (Eds.), *Handbook of depression in children and adolescents* (pp. 183–208). New York: Plenum Press.

Hodges, K., McKnew, D., Cytryn, L., Stern, L., & Kline, J. (1982). The Child Assessment Schedule (CAS) diagnostic interview: A report on reliability and validity. *Journal of the American Academy of Child Psychiatry, 21,* 468–473.

Hoffman, K. B., Cole, D. A., Martin, J. M., Tram, J., & Serocynski, A. D. (2001). Are the discrepancies between self- and others' appraisals of competence predictive or reflective of depressive symptoms in children and adolescents: A longitudinal study, Part II. *Journal of Abnormal Psychology, 109,* 651–662.

Hofstra, M. B., Van der Ende, J., & Verhulst, F. C. (2000). Continuity and change of psychopathology from childhood into adulthood: A 14 year follow up study. *Journal of the American Academy of Child and Adolescent Psychiatry, 39,* 850–858.

Hogue, A., & Steinberg, L. (1995). Homophily of internalized distress in adolescent peer groups. *Developmental Psychology, 31,* 897–906.

Hollon, S. D., Garber, J., & Shelton, R. C. (2005). Treatment of depression in adolescents with cognitive behavior therapy and medications: A commentary on the TADS project. *Cognitive and Behavioral Practice 12,* 149–155.

Holsen, I., Kraft, P. A. L., & Vitterso, J. (2000). Stability in depressed mood in adolescence: Results from a 6-year longitudinal panel study. *Journal of Youth and Adolescence, 29,* 61–78.

Ialongo, N., Edelsohn, G., & Kellam, S. (2001). A further look at the prognostic power of young children's reports of depressed mood and feelings. *Child Development, 72,* 736–747.

Ialongo, N., Edelsohn, G., Werthamer-Larsson, L., Crockett, L., & Kellam, S. (1996). Social and cognitive impairment in first-grade children with anxious and depressed symptoms. *Journal of Clinical Child Psychology, 25,* 15–24.

Ingram, R. E., Miranda, J., & Segal, Z. V. (1998). *Cognitive vulnerability to depression.* New York: Guilford Press.

Iwaniec, D. (2004). Children who fail to thrive [electronic resource]: A practice guide. Chichester, England: Wiley.

Jacobson, N. S., & Truax, P. A. (1991). Clinical significance: A statistical approach to defining meaningful change in psychotherapy research. *Journal of Consulting and Clinical Psychology, 59,* 12–19.

Jaenicke, C., Hammen, C., Zupan, B., Hiroto, D., Gordon, D., Adrian, C., et al. (1987). Cognitive vulnerability in children at risk for depression. *Journal of Abnormal Child Psychology, 15,* 559–572.

Jaffee, S. R., Moffitt, T. E., Avshalom, C., Fombonne, E., Poulton, R., & Martin, J. (2002). Differences in early childhood risk factors for juvenile-onset and adult-onset depression. *Archives of General Psychiatry, 59,* 215–222.

Jayson, D., Wood, A., Kroll, L., Fraser, J., & Harrington, R. (1998). Which depressed patients respond to cognitive-behavioral treatment? *Journal of the American Academy of Child and Adolescent Psychiatry, 37,* 35–39.

Jensen, J. B., & Garfinkel, B. D. (1990). Growth hormone dysregulation in children with major depressive disorder. *Journal of the American Academy of Child and Adolescent Psychiatry, 29,* 295–301.

Joiner, T. E., & Coyne, J. C. (Eds.). (1999). *The interactional nature of depression: Advances in interpersonal approaches.* Washington, DC: American Psychological Association.

Joiner, T. E., & Lonigan, C. J. (2000). The tripartite model of depression and anxiety in youth psychiatric inpatients: Relation to diagnostic status and future symptoms. *Journal of Clinical Child Psychology, 29,* 372–382.

Joiner, T. E., & Wagner, K. D. (1995). Attribution style and depression in children and adolescents: A meta-analytic review. *Clinical Psychology Review, 5,* 777–798.

Jones, D. J., Beach, S. R. H., & Forehand, R. (2001). Stress generation in intact community families: Depressive symptoms, perceived family relationship stress, and implications for adolescent adjustment. *Journal of Social and Personal Relationships, 18,* 443–462.

Jorm, A. F., Christensen, H., Henderson, A. S., Jacomb, P. A., Korten, A. E., & Rodgers, B. (2000). Predicting anxiety and depression from personality: Is there a synergistic effect of neuroticism and extraversion? *Journal of Abnormal Psychology, 109,* 145–149.

Judd, L. L., Akiskal, H. S., Maser, J. D., Zeller, P. J., Endicott, J., Coryell., W., et al. (1998). A prospective 12-year study of subsyndromal and syndromal depressive symptoms in unipolar major depressive disorders. *Archives of General Psychiatry, 55,* 694–700.

Just, N., Abramson, L. Y., & Alloy, L. B. (2001). Remitted depression studies as tests of the cognitive vulnerability hypothesis of depression onset: A critique and conceptual analysis. *Clinical Psychology Review, 21,* 63–83.

Kagan, J., & Snidman, N. (1991). Temperamental factors in human development. *American Psychologist, 46,* 856–862.

Kahn, J. S., Kehle, T. J., Jenson, W. R., & Clark, E. (1990). Comparison of cognitive-behavioral relaxation, and self-modeling interventions for depression among middle-school students. *School Psychology Review, 19,* 196–211.

Kaminski, K. M., & Garber, J. (2002). Depressive spectrum disorders in adolescents: Episode duration and predictors of time to recovery. *Journal of the American Academy of Child and Adolescent Psychiatry, 41,* 410–418.

Kandel, D. B., & Davies, M. (1986). Adult sequelae of adolescent depressive symptoms. *Archives of General Psychiatry, 43,* 255–262.

Kasen, S., Cohen, P., Skodol, A. E., Johnson, J. G., & Brook, J. S. (1999). Influence of child and adolescent psychiatric disorders on young adolescent personality disorder. *American Journal of Psychiatry, 156,* 1529–1535.

Kasen, S., Cohen, P., Skodol, A. E., Johnson, J. G., Smailes, E., & Brook, J. S. (1999). Childhood depression and adult personality disorder. *Archives of General Psychiatry, 58,* 231–236.

Kashani, J. H., & Carlson, G. A. (1987). Seriously depressed preschoolers. *American Journal of Psychiatry, 144,* 348–350.

Kashani, J. H., Holcomb, W. R., & Orvaschel, H. (1986). Depression and depressive symptoms in preschool children from the general population. *American Journal of Psychiatry, 143,* 1138–1143.

Kashani, J., & Simonds, J. F. (1979). The incidence of depression in children. *American Journal of Psychiatry, 136,* 1203–1205.

Kaslow, N. J., Adamson, L. B., & Collins, M. H. (2000). A developmental psychopathology perspective on the cognitive components of child and adolescent depression. In A. J. Sameroff, M. Lewis, & S. M. Miller (Eds.), *Handbook of developmental psychopathology* (2nd ed., pp. 491–510). New York: Kluwer/Plenum.

Kaslow, N. J., Deering, C. G., & Racusin, G. R. (1994). Depressed children and their families. *Clinical Psychology Review, 14,* 39–59.

Kaslow, N., & Thompson, M. (1998) Applying the criteria for empirically supported treatments to studies of psychosocial interventions for child and adolescent depression. *Journal of Clinical Child Psychology, 27,* 146–155.

Katainen, S., Raikkonen, K., Keskivaara, P., & Keltikangas-Jarvinen, L. (1999). Maternal child-rearing attitudes and role satisfaction and children's temperament as antecedents of adolescent depressive tendencies: Follow-up study of 6- to 15-year-olds. *Journal of Youth and Adolescence, 2,* 139–163.

Kaufman, J., Martin, A., King, R. A., & Charney, D. (2001). Are child-, adolescent-, and adult-onset depression one and the same disorder? *Biological Psychiatry, 49,* 980–1001.

Kazdin, A. E. (1990). Assessment of childhood depression. In A. M. La Greca (Ed.), *Through the eyes of the child: Obtaining self-reports from children and adolescents* (pp. 189–233). Boston: Allyn & Bacon.

Kazdin, A. E. (1994). Informant variability in the assessment of childhood depression. Issues in clinical child psychology. In H. F. Johnston & W. M. Reynolds (Eds.), *Handbook of depression in children and adolescents* (pp. 249–271). New York: Plenum Press.

Kazdin, A. E., French, N. H., Unis, A. S., & Esveldt-Dawson, K. (1983). Assessment of childhood depression: Correspondence of child and parent ratings. *Journal of the American Academy of Child Psychiatry, 12,* 421–436.

Kazdin, A. E., & Marciano, P. L. (1998). Childhood and adolescent depression. In R. A. Barkley & E. J. Mash (Eds.), *Treatment of childhood disorders* (2nd ed., pp. 211–248). New York: Guilford Press.

Kazdin, A. E., & Weisz, J. R. (1998). Identifying and developing empirically supported child and adolescent treatments. *Journal of Consulting and Clinical Psychology, 66,* 19–36.

Keitner, G. I., & Miller, I. W. (1990). Family functioning and major depression: An overview. *American Journal of Psychiatry, 147,* 1128–1137.

Keller, M. B., Beardslee, W. R., Lavori, P. W., Wunder, J., Drs, D. L., & Samuelson, H. (1988). Course of major depression in non referred adolescents: A retrospective study. *Journal of Affective Disorders, 15,* 235–243.

Keller, M. B., Lavori, P. W., Lewis, C. E., & Klerman, G. L. (1983). Predictors of relapse in major depressive disorder. *Journal of the American Medical Association, 250,* 3299–3304.

Keller, M. B., Ryan, N. D., Strober, M., Klein, R. G., Kutcher, S. P., & Birmaher, B. (2001). Efficacy of paroxetine in the treatment of adolescent major depression: A randomized, controlled trial. *Journal of the American Academy of Child and Adolescent Psychiatry, 40,* 762–772.

Keller, M. B., & Shapiro, R. W. (1982). "Double depression": Superimposition of acute depressive episodes on chronic depressive disorders. *American Journal of Psychiatry, 139,* 438–442.

Kendall, P. C., Cantwell, D. P., & Kazdin, A. E. (1989). Depression in children and adolescents: Assessment issues and recommendations. *Cognitive Therapy and Research, 13,* 109–146.

Kendall, P. C., Stark, K. D., & Adam, T. (1990). Cognitive deficit or cognitive distortion of childhood depression. *Journal of Abnormal Child Psychology, 18,* 255–270.

Kendler, K. S., Gardner, C. O., & Prescott, C. A. (2002). Toward a comprehensive developmental model for major depression in women. *American Journal of Psychiatry, 159,* 1133–1145.

Kendler, K. S., Neale, M. C., Kessler, R. C., Heath, A. C., & Eaves, L. J. (1993). A longitudinal twin study of personality and major depression in women. *Archives of General Psychiatry, 50,* 853–862.

Kenny, M. E., Moilanen, D. L., Lomax, R., & Brabeck, M. M. (1993). Contributions of parental attachments to views of self and depressive symptoms among early adolescents. *Journal of Early Adolescence, 13,* 408–430.

Kessler, R. C., Avenevoli, S., & Merikangas, K. R. (2001). Mood disorders in children and adolescents: An epidemiologic perspective. *Biological Psychiatry, 49,* 1002–1014.

Kessler, R. C., Foster, C., Webster, P. S., & House, J. S. (1992). The relationship between age and depressive symptoms in two national surveys. *Psychology and Aging, 7,* 119–126.

Kessler R. C., & Walters, E. E. (1998), Epidemiology of *DSM-III-R* major depression and minor depression among adolescents and young adults in the national comorbidity survey. *Depression and Anxiety, 7,* 3–14.

Kessler, R. C., Zhao, S., Blazer, D. G., & Swartz, M. (1997). Prevalence, correlates, and course of minor depression and major depression in the national comorbidity survey. *Journal of Affective Disorders, 45,* 19–30.

Kiesner, J. (2002). Depressive symptoms in early adolescence: Their relations with classroom problem behavior and peer status. *Journal of Research on Adolescence, 12,* 463–478.

Kiesner, J., Poulin, F., & Nicotra, E. (2003). Peer relations across contexts: Individual network homophily and network inclusion in and after school. *Child Development, 74,* 1328–1343.

Kim, K. J., Conger, R. D., Elder, G. H.., Jr., & Lorenz, F. O. (2003). Reciprocal influences between stressful life events and adolescent internalizing and externalizing problems. *Child Development, 74,* 127–143.

Kistner, J. A., Balthazor, M., Risi, S., & Burton, C. (1999). Predicting dysphoria in adolescence from actual and perceived peer acceptance in childhood. *Journal of Clinical Child Psychology, 28,* 94–104.

Kistner, J. A., David, C. F., & White, B. A. (2003). Ethnic and sex differences in children's depressive symptoms: Mediating effects of perceived and actual competence. *Journal of Clinical Child and Adolescent Psychology, 32,* 341–350.

Klein, D. N. (1990). Depressive personality: Reliability, validity, and relation to dysthymia. *Journal of Abnormal Psychology, 99,* 412–421.

Klein, D. N., Durbin, C. E., Shankman, S. A., & Santiago, N. J. (2002). Depression and personality. C. L. Hammen and I. H. Gotlib (Eds.), *Handbook of depression* (pp. 115–140). New York: Guilford Press.

Klein, D. N., & Shih, J. H. (1998). Depressive personality: Associations with *DSM-III-R* mood and personality disorders and negative and positive affectivity, 30 month stability, and prediction of course of Axis I depressive disorders. *Journal of Abnormal Psychology, 107,* 319–327.

Klein, D. N., Taylor, E. B., Dickstein, S., & Harding, K. (1988). Primary early-onset dysthymia: Comparison with primary nonbipolar nonchronic major depression on demographic, clinical, familial, personality, and socio-environmental characteristics and short-term outcome. *Journal of Abnormal Psychology, 97,* 387–398.

Klerman, G. L., Weissman, M. M., Rounsville, B. J., & Chevron, E. S. (1984). *Interpersonal psychotherapy of depression.* New York: Basic Books.

Kobak, R. R., & Ferenz-Gillies, R. (1995). Emotion regulation and depressive symptoms during adolescence: A functionalist perspective. *Development and Psychopathology, 7,* 183–192.

Kobak, R. R., Sudler, N., & Gamble, W. (1991). Attachment and depressive symptoms during adolescence: A developmental pathways analysis. *Development and Psychopathology, 3,* 461–474.

Kochanska, G. (1991). Patterns of inhibition to the unfamiliar in children of normal and affectively ill mothers. *Child Development, 62,* 250–263.

Kovacs, M. (1981). Rating scales to assess depression in school-aged children. *Acta Paedopsychiatrica, 46,* 305–315.

Kovacs, M. (1985). The Interview Schedule for Children (ISC). *Psychopharmacological Bulletin, 21,* 991–994.

Kovacs, M. (1986). A developmental perspective on methods and measures in the assessment of depressive disorders: The clinical interview. In M. Rutter, C. Izard, & P. Read (Eds.), *Depression in young people: Developmental and clinical perspectives* (pp. 435–468). New York: Guilford Press.

Kovacs, M., Akiskal, H. S., Gatsonis, C., & Parrone, P. L. (1994). Childhood onset dysthymic disorder: Clinical features and prospective naturalistic outcome. *Archives of General Psychiatry, 51,* 365–374.

Kovacs, M., Feinberg, T. L., Crouse-Novak, M. A., Paulauskas, S. L., & Finkelstein, R. (1984). Depressive disorders in childhood. I. A longitudinal prospective study of characteristics and recovery. *Archives of General Psychiatry, 41,* 229–237.

Kovacs, M., Feinberg, T. L., Crouse-Novak, M., Paulauskas, S. L., Pollock, M., & Finkelstein, R. (1984). Depressive disorders in childhood. II. A longitudinal study of the risk for a subsequent major depression. *Archives of General Psychiatry, 41,* 653–659.

Kovacs, M., Obrosky, D. S., & Sherrill, J. (2003). Developmental changes in the phenomenology of depression in girls compared to boys from childhood onward. *Journal of Affective Disorders, 74,* 33–48.

Kraepelin, E. (1921). *Manic depressive insanity and paranoia.* Edinburgh: E. & S. Livingstone.

Kretschmer, E. (1925). *Physique and character.* New York: Harcourt Brace.

Kroll, L., Harrington, R., Jayson, D., Fraser, J., & Gowers, S. (1996). Pilot study of continuation cognitive-behavioral therapy for major depression in adolescent psychiatric patients. *Journal of the American Academy of Child and Adolescent Psychiatry, 35,* 1156–1161.

Kulka, R. A., Schlenger, W. E., Fairbank, J. A., Hough, R. L., Jordan, B. K., Marmar, C. R., et al. (1990). *Trauma and the Vietnam war generation: Report of findings from the National Vietnam Veterans Readjustment Study.* In Brunner/Mazel psychosocial stress series (No. 18). Philadelphia: Brunner/Mazel.

Lamb, M. E., Gaensbauer, T. J., Malkin, C. M., & Schultz, L. A. (1985). The effects of child maltreatment on security of infant-adult attachment. *Infant Behavior and Development, 8,* 35–45.

Larson, R., & Ham, M. (1993). Stress and "storm and stress" in early adolescence: The relationship of negative events with dysphoric affect. *Developmental Psychology, 29,* 130–140.

Laurent, J., & Ettelson, R. (2001). An examination of the tripartite model of anxiety and depression and its application to youth. *Clinical Child and Family Psychology Review, 4,* 209–230.

Leadbeater, B. J., Blatt, S. J., & Quinlan, D. M. (1995). Gender-linked vulnerabilities to depressive symptoms, stress, and problem behaviors in adolescents. *Journal of Research on Adolescence, 5,* 1–29.

Leadbeater, B. J., Kuperminc, G. P., Blatt, S. J., & Hertzog, C. (1999). A multivariate model of gender differences in adolescents' internalizing and externalizing problems. *Developmental Psychology, 35,* 1268–1282.

Lefkowitz, M. M., & Tesiny, E. P. (1980). Assessment of childhood depression. *Journal of Consulting and Clinical Psychology, 48,* 43–50.

Lefkowitz, M. M., & Tesiny, E. P. (1984). Rejection and depression: Prospective and contemporaneous analyses. *Developmental Psychology, 20,* 776–785.

Lengua, L. J., Sandler, I. N., West, S. G., Wolchik, S. A., & Curran, P. J. (1999). Emotionality and self regulation, threat appraisal, and coping in children of divorce. *Development and Psychopathology, 11,* 15–37.

Lengua, L. J., Wolchik, S. A., Sandler, I. N., & West, S. G. (2000). The additive and interactive effects of parenting and temperament in predicting problems of children of divorce. *Journal of Clinical Child Psychology, 29,* 232–244.

Levenson, M. R., Aldwin, C. M., Bosse, R., & Spiro, A. (1988). Emotionality and mental health: Longitudinal findings from the normative aging study. *Journal of Abnormal Psychology, 97,* 94–96.

Lewinsohn, P. M., Allen, N. B., Seeley, J. R., & Gotlib, I. H. (1999). First onset versus recurrence of depression: Differential processes of psychosocial risk. *Journal of Abnormal Psychology, 108,* 483–489.

Lewinsohn, P. M., & Clarke, G. N. (1999). Psychosocial treatments for adolescent depression. *Clinical Psychology Review, 19,* 329–342.

Lewinsohn, P. M., Clarke, G. N., Hops, H., & Andrews, J. (1990). Cognitive-behavioral treatment for depressed adolescents. *Behavior Therapy, 21,* 385–401.

Lewinsohn, P. M., Clarke, G. N., Seeley, J. R., & Rohde, P. (1994). Major depression in community adolescents: Age at onset, episode duration, and time to recurrence. *Journal of the American Academy of Child and Adolescent Psychiatry, 33,* 809–818.

Lewinsohn, P. M., & Essau, C. A. (2002). Depression in adolescents. In C. L. Hammen & I. H. Gotlib (Ed.), *Handbook of depression* (pp. 541–559). New York: Guilford Press.

Lewinsohn, P. M., Hops, H., Roberts, R. E., Seeley, J. R., Andrews, J. A. (1993). Adolescent psychopathology: I. Prevalence and incidence of depression and other DSM-III-R disorders in high school students. *Journal of Abnormal Psychology, 102,* 133–144.

Lewinsohn, P. M., Joiner, T. E., & Rohde, P. (2001). Evaluation of cognitive diathesis-stress models in predicting major depressive disorder in adolescents. *Journal of Abnormal Psychology, 110,* 203–215.

Lewinsohn, P. M., Pettit, J. W., Joiner, T. E., & Seeley, J. R. (2003). The symptomatic expression of major depressive disorder in adolescents and young adults. *Journal of Abnormal Psychology, 112,* 244–252.

Lewinsohn, P. M., Roberts, R. E., Seeley, J. R., Rohde, P., Gotlib, I. H., & Hops, H. (1994). Adolescent psychopathology: II. Psychosocial risk factors for depression. *Journal of Abnormal Psychology, 103,* 302–315.

Lewinsohn, P. M., Rohde, P., Klein, D. N., & Seeley, J. R. (1999). Natural course of adolescent major depressive disorder: I. Continuity into young adulthood. *Journal of the American Academy of Child and Adolescent Psychiatry, 38,* 56–63.

Lewinsohn, P. M., Rohde, P., & Seeley, J. R. (1994). Psychosocial risk factors for future adolescent suicide attempts. *Journal of Consulting and Clinical Psychology, 62,* 297–305.

Lewinsohn, P. M., Rohde, P., & Seely, J. R. (1998). Major depressive disorder in older adolescents: Prevalence, risk factors, and clinical implications. *Clinical Psychology Review, 18,* 765–794.

Lewinsohn, P. M., Rohde, P., Seeley, J. R., & Klein, D. N. (1997). Axis II psychopathology as a function of Axis I disorder in childhood and adolescence. *Journal of the American Academy of Child and Adolescent Psychiatry, 36,* 1752–1759.

Lewinsohn, P. M., Rohde, P., Seeley, J. R., Klein, D. N., & Gotlib, I. H. (2003). Psychosocial functioning of young adults who have experienced and recovered from major depressive disorder during adolescence. *Journal of Abnormal Psychology, 112,* 353–363.

Liddle, B. J., & Spence, S. H. (1990). Cognitive-behavior therapy with depressed primary school children: A cautionary note. *Behavioral Psychotherapy, 18,* 85–102.

Liebowitz, M. R., Stallone, F., Dunner, D. L., & Fieve, R. R. (1979). Personality features of patients with primary affective disorder. *Acta Psychiatrica Scandinavica, 60,* 214–224.

Little, S. A., & Garber, J. (1995). Aggression, depression, and stressful life events predicting peer rejection in children. *Development and Psychopathology, 7,* 845–856.

Little, S. A., & Garber, J. (2000). Interpersonal and achievement orientations and specific hassles predicting depressive and aggressive symptoms in children. *Cognitive Therapy and Research, 24,* 651–671.

Little, S. A., & Garber, J. (2004). Interpersonal and achievement orientations and specific stressors predict depressive and aggressive symptoms. *Journal of Adolescent Research, 19,* 63–84.

Little, S. A., & Garber, J. (in press). The role of social stressors and interpersonal orientation in explaining the longitudinal relation between externalizing and depressive symptoms. *Journal of Abnormal Psychology.*

Loeber, R., Burke, J. D., and Lahey, B. B. (2002). What are adolescent antecedents to antisocial personality disorder? *Criminal Behaviour and Mental Health, 12,* 24–36.

Lou, H. C., Hansen, D., & Nordenfoft, M. (1994). Prenatal stressors of human life affect fetal brain development. *Developmental Medicine and Child Neurology, 36,* 826–832.

Lovejoy, M. C., Graczyk, P. A., O'Hare, E., & Neuman, G. (2000). Maternal depression and parenting: A meta-analytic review. *Clinical Psychology Review, 20,* 561–592.

Marmorstein, N. R., & Iacono, W. G. (2001). An investigation of female adolescent twins with both major depression and conduct disorder. *Journal of the American Academy of Child and Adolescent Psychiatry, 40,* 299–306.

Martini, D. R., Strayhorn, J. M., & Puig-Antich, J. (1990). A symptom self-report measure for pre-school children. *Journal of the American Academy of Child and Adolescent Psychiatry, 29,* 594–600.

Matas, L., Arend, R. A., & Sroufe, L. A. (1978). Continuity of adaptation in the second year: The relationship between quality of attachment and later competence. *Child Development, 49,* 547–556.

McCauley, E., Mitchell, J. R., Burke, P., & Moss, S. (1988). Cognitive attributes of depression in children and adolescents. *Journal of Consulting and Clinical Psychology, 56,* 903–908.

McCauley, E., & Myers, K. (1992). Family interactions of mood-disordered youth. *Child and Adolescent Psychiatric Clinics of North America, 1,* 111–127.

McCauley, E., Myers, K., Mitchell, J., Calderon, R., Schloredt, K., & Treder, R. (1993). Depression in young people: Initial presentation and clinical course. *Journal of the American Academy of Child and Adolescent Psychiatry, 32,* 714–722.

McCleary, L., & Sanford, M. (2002). Parental expressed emotion in depressed adolescents: Prediction of clinical course and relationship to comorbid disorder and social functioning. *Journal of Child Psychology and Psychiatry, 43,* 587–595.

McClellan, J. M., & Werry, J. S. (2003). Evidence-based treatments in child and adolescent psychiatry: An inventory. *Journal of the American Academy of Child and Adolescent Psychiatry, 42,* 1388–1400.

McCrae, R. R., & Costa, P. T. (1987). Validation of the five factor model of personality across instruments and observers. *Journal of Personality and Social Psychology, 52,* 81–90.

McFarlane, A. H., Bellissimo, A., Norman, G. R., & Lange, P. (1994). Adolescent depression in a school-based community sample: Preliminary findings on contributing social factors. *Journal of Youth and Adolescence, 23,* 601–620.

McKeown, R. E., Garrison, C. Z., Jackson, K. L., Cuffe, S. P., Addy, C. L., & Waller, J. L. (1997). Family structure and cohesion, and depressive symptoms in adolescents. *Journal of Research on Adolescence, 7,* 267–281.

McLoyd, V. C. (1998). Socioeconomic disadvantage and child development. *American Psychologist, 53,* 185–204.

Messer, S. C., & Gross, A. M. (1995). Childhood depression and family interaction: A naturalistic observation study. *Journal of Clinical Child Psychology, 24,* 77–88.

Meyer, W. J., Richards, G. E., Cavallo, A., Holt, K. G., Hejazi, M. S., Wigg, C., et al. (1991). Depression and growth hormone. *Journal of the American Academy of Child and Adolescent Psychiatry, 30,* 335.

Monroe, S. M., Rohde, P., Seeley, J. R., & Lewinsohn, P. M. (1999). Life events and depression in adolescence: Relationship loss as a prospective risk factor for first onset of major depressive disorder. *Journal of Abnormal Psychology, 108,* 606–614.

Monroe, S. M., & Simons, A. D. (1991). Diathesis-stress theories in the context of life stress research: Implications for the depressive disorders. *Psychological Bulletin, 110,* 406–425.

Mufson, L., Dorta, K. P., Wickramaratne, P., Nomura, Y., Olfson, M., & Weissman, M. M. (2004). A randomized effectiveness trial of interpersonal psychotherapy for depressed adolescents. *Archives of General Psychiatry, 61,* 577–584.

Mufson, L., Weissman, M. M., Moreau, D., & Garfinkel, R. (1999). Efficacy of interpersonal psychotherapy for depressed adolescents. *Archives of General Psychiatry, 56,* 573–579.

Myers, K., & Winters, N. C. (2002). Ten year review of rating scales. II. Scales for internalizing disorders. *Journal of the American Academy of Child and Adolescent Psychiatry, 41,* 634–659.

Nelson, D., Hammen, C., Daley, S., Burge, D., & Davila, J. (2001). Sociotropic and autonomous personality styles: Contributions to chronic life stress. *Cognitive Therapy and Research, 25,* 61–76.

Nolan, S. A., Flynn, C., & Garber, J. (2003). The relation between rejection and depression in adolescents. *Journal of Personality and Social Psychology, 85,* 745–755.

Nolen-Hoeksema, S., & Girgus, J. S. (1994). The emergence of gender differences in depression during adolescence. *Psychological Bulletin, 115,* 424–443.

Nolen-Hoeksema, S., Girgus, J. S., & Seligman, M. E. P. (1992). Predictors and consequences of childhood depressive symptoms: A 5-year longitudinal study. *Journal of Abnormal Psychology, 101,* 405–422.

Offord, D. R., Boyle, M. H., Szatmari, P., Rae-Grant, N. I., Links, P. S., Cadman, D. T., et al. (1987). Ontario Child Health Study: II. Six-month prevalence of disorder and rates of service utilization. *Archives of General Psychiatry, 44,* 832–836.

Ohannessian, C. M., Lerner, R. M., Lerner, J. V., & von Eye, A. (1994). A longitudinal study of perceived family adjustment and emotional adjustment in early adolescence. *Journal of Early Adolescence, 14,* 371–390.

Olfson, M., Shaffer, D., Marcus, S. C., & Greenberg, T. (2003). Relationship between antidepressant medication treatment and suicide in adolescents. *Archives of General Psychiatry, 60,* 978–982.

Orvaschel, H., Puig-Antich, J., Chambers, W., Tabrizi, M. A., & Johnson, R. (1982). Retrospective assessment of prepubertal major depression with the Kiddie-SADS-E. *Journal of the American Academy of Child Psychiatry, 21,* 392–397.

Panak, W. F., & Garber, J. (1992). Role of aggression, rejection, and attributions in the prediction of depression in children. *Development and Psychopathology, 4,* 145–165.

Papini, D. R., & Roggman, L. A. (1992). Adolescent perceived attachment to parents in relation to competence, depression, and anxiety: A longitudinal study. *Journal of Early Adolescence, 12,* 420–440.

Parker, G. (1983). Parental "affectionless control" as an antecedent to adult depression: A risk factor delineated. *Archives of General Psychiatry, 40,* 956–960.

Parker, G., Tupling, H., & Brown, L. B. (1979). A parental bonding instrument. *British Journal of Medical Psychology, 52,* 1–10.

Patterson, M. L., Greising, L., Hyland, L. T., & Burger, G. K. (1997). Childhood depression, anxiety, and aggression: A reanalysis of Epkins and Meyers (1994). *Journal of Personality Assessment, 69,* 607–613.

Pavlidis, K., & McCauley, E. (2001). Autonomy and relatedness in family interactions with depressed adolescents. *Journal of Abnormal Child Psychology, 29,* 11–21.

Persons, J. B., & Miranda, J. (1992). Cognitive theories of vulnerability to depression: Reconciling negative evidence. *Cognitive Therapy and Research, 16,* 485–502.

Petersen, A. C., Sarigiani, P. A., & Kennedy, R. E. (1991). Adolescent depression: Why more girls? *Journal of Youth and Adolescence, 20,* 247–271.

Peterson, L., Mullins, L. L., & Ridley Johnson, R. (1985). Childhood depression: Peer reactions to depression and life stress. *Journal of Abnormal Child Psychology, 13,* 597–609.

Phillips, B. M., Lonigan, C. J., Driscoll, K., & Hooe, E. S. (2002). Positive and negative affectivity in children: A multitrait multimethod investigation. *Journal of Clinical Child and Adolescent Psychology, 31,* 465–479.

Phillips, K. A., Gunderson, J. G., Triebwasser, J., Kimble, C. R., Faedda, G., Lyoo, I., et al. (1998). Reliability and validity of depressive personality disorder. *American Journal of Psychiatry, 155,* 1044–1048.

Pine, D. S., Cohen, E., Gurley, D., Brook, J., & Ma, Y. (1998). The risk for early-adulthood anxiety and depressive disorders in adolescents with anxiety and depressive disorders. *Archives of General Psychiatry 55,* 56–64.

Plotsky, P. M., Owens, M. J., & Nemeroff, C. B. (1998). Psychoneuroendocrinology of depression. *Psychoneuroendocrinology, 21,* 293–307.

Polaino-Lorente, A., & Domenech, E. (1993). Prevalence of childhood depression: Results of the first study in Spain. *Journal of Child Psychology and Psychiatry, 34,* 1007–1017.

Poltyrev, T., Keshet, G. I., Kay, G., & Weinstock, M. (1996). Role of experimental conditions in determining differences in exploratory behavior of prenatally stressed rats. *Developmental Psychobiology, 29,* 453–462.

Post, R. M. (1992). Transduction of psychosocial stress into the neurobiology of recurrent affective disorder. *American Journal of Psychiatry, 149,* 999–1010.

Potthoff, J. G., Holahan, C. J., & Joiner, T. E. (1995). Reassurance seeking, stress generation, and depressive symptoms: An integrative model. *Journal of Personality and Social Psychology, 68,* 664–670.

Poznanski, E., Mokros, H. B., Grossman, J., & Freeman, L. N. (1985). Diagnostic criteria in childhood depression. *American Journal of Psychiatry, 142,* 1168–1173.

Poznanski, E. O., Freeman, L. N., & Mokros, H. B. (1984). Children's Depression Rating Scale—revised. *Psychopharmacology Bulletin, 21,* 979–989.

Poznanski, E. O., Grossman, J. A., Buchsbaum, Y., Banegas, M., Freeman, L., & Gibbons, R. (1984). Preliminary studies of the reliability and validity of the Children's Depression Rating Scale. *Journal of the American Academy of Child Psychiatry, 23,* 191–197.

Prinstein, M. J., & Aikins, J. W. (2004). Cognitive moderators of the longitudinal association between peer rejection and adolescent depressive symptoms. *Journal of Abnormal Child Psychology, 32,* 147–158.

Puig Antich J., & Chambers, W. (1978). *The schedule for affective disorders and schizophrenia for school-aged children.* New York: New York State Psychiatric Institute.

Puig-Antich, J., Dahl, R. E., Ryan, N. D., Novacenko, H., Goetz, D., Goetz, R., et al. (1989). Cortisol secretion in prepubertal children with major depressive disorder: Episode and recovery. *Archives of General Psychiatry, 46,* 801–809.

Puig-Antich, J., Kaufman, J., Ryan, N. D., Williamson, D. E., Dahl, R. E., Lukens, E., et al. (1993). The psychosocial functioning and family environment of depressed adolescents. *Journal of the American Academy of Child and Adolescent Psychiatry, 32,* 244–253.

Puig-Antich, J., Lukens, E., Davies, M., Goetz, D., Brennan-Quattrock, J., & Todak, G. (1985a). Psychosocial functioning in prepubertal major depressive disorders. I. Interpersonal relationships during the depressive episode. *Archives of General Psychiatry, 42,* 500–507.

Puig-Antich, J., Lukens, E., Davies, M., Goetz, D., Brennan-Quattrock, J., & Todak, G. (1985b). Psychosocial functioning in prepubertal major depressive disorder. II. Interpersonal relationships after sustained recovery from affective episode. *Archives of General Psychiatry, 42,* 511–517.

Puura, K., Tamminen, T., Almqvist, F., Kresanov, K., Kumpulainen, K., Moilanen, I., et al. (1997). Should depression in young school children be diagnosed with different criteria? *European Child and Adolescent Psychiatry, 6,* 12–19.

Rabkin, J. G., Stewart, J. W., Quitkin, F. M., McGrath, P. J., Harrison, W. M., Klein, D. F. (1996). Should atypical depression be included in *DSM-IV? DSM-IV Sourcebook* (Vol. 2, pp. 239–260). Washington, DC: American Psychiatric Press.

Radloff, L. S. (1977). The CES D Scale: A self-report depression scale for research in the general population. *Applied Psychological Measurement, 1,* 385–401.

Radloff, L. S. (1991). The use of the Center for Epidemiologic Studies Depression Scale in adolescents and young adults. *Journal of Youth and Adolescence, 20,* 149–166.

Ramklint, M., von Knorring, A. L., von Knorring, L., & Ekselius, L. (2003). Child and adolescent psychiatric disorders predicting adult personality disorder: A follow-up study. *Nordic Journal of Psychiatry, 57,* 23–28.

Rao, U., Hammen, C., & Daley, S. E. (1999). Continuity of depression during the transition to adulthood: A 5-year longitudinal study of young women. *Journal of the American Academy of Child and Adolescent Psychiatry, 38,* 908–915.

Rao, U., Ryan, N. D., Birmaher, B., Dahl, R. E., Williamson, D. E., Kaufman, J., et al. (1995). Unipolar depression in adolescents: Clinical outcomes in adulthood. *Journal of the American Academy of Child and Adolescent Psychiatry, 34,* 566–578.

Rapee, R. M. (1997). Potential role of childrearing practices in the development of anxiety and depression. *Clinical Psychology Review, 17,* 47–67.

Raynor, P., & Rudolf, M. C. J. (1996). What do we know about children who fail to thrive? *Child: Care, Health and Development, 22,* 241–250.

Reich, J., Noyes, R., Hirschfeld, R., Coryell, W., & O'Gorman, M. (1987). State and personality in depressed and panic patients. *American Journal of Psychiatry, 144,* 181–187.

Reich, W. (2000). Diagnostic Interview for Children and Adolescents (DICA). *Journal of the American Academy of Child and Adolescent Psychiatry, 39,* 59–66.

Reinecke, M. A., Ryan, N. E., & DuBois, L. (1998). Cognitive-behavioral therapy of depression and depressive symptoms during adolescence: A review and meta-analysis. *Journal of the American Academy of Child and Adolescent Psychiatry, 37,* 26–34.

Reinherz, H. Z., Giaconia, R. M., Hauf, A. M. C., Wasserman, M. S., & Silverman, A. B. (1999). Major depression in the transition to adulthood: Risks and impairments. *Journal of Abnormal Psychology, 108,* 500–510.

Rende, R. D., Plomin, R., Reiss, D., & Hetherington, E. M. (1993). Genetic and environmental influences on depressive symptomatology in adolescence: Individual differences and extreme scores. *Journal of Child Psychology and Psychiatry, 34,* 1387–1398.

Rey, J. M., Morris-Yates, A., Singh, M., Andrews, G., & Stewart, G. W. (1995). Continuities between psychiatric disorders in adolescents and personality disorders in young adults. *American Journal of Psychiatry, 152,* 895–900.

Reynolds, W. M. (1989). *Reynolds Child Depression Scale: Professional Manual.* Odessa, FL: Psychological Assessment Resources.

Reynolds, W. M. (1994). Assessment of depression in children and adolescents by self-report questionnaires. In W. M. Reynolds & H. F. Johnston (Eds.), *Handbook of depression in children and adolescents* (pp. 209–234). New York: Plenum Press.

Reynolds, W. M., & Coats, K. I. (1986). A comparison of cognitive-behavioral therapy and relaxation training for the treatment of depression in adolescents. *Journal of Consulting and Clinical Psychology, 54,* 653–660.

Roberts, J. E., & Gamble, S. A. (2001). Current mood state and past depression as predictors of self esteem and dysfunctional attitudes among adolescents. *Personality and Individual Differences, 30,* 1023–1037.

Roberts, R. E., Andrews, J. A., Lewinsohn, P. M., & Hops, H. (1990). Assessment of depression in adolescents using the Center for Epidemiologic Studies Depression Scale. *Psychological Assessment, 2,* 122–128.

Robertson, J. N., & Simons, R. L. (1989). Family factors, self-esteem, and adolescent depression. *Journal of Marriage and Family, 51,* 125–138.

Robinson, N. S., Garber, J., & Hilsman, R. (1995). Cognitions and stress: Direct and moderating effects on depressive versus externalizing symptoms during the junior high school transition. *Journal of Abnormal Psychology, 104,* 453–463.

Rohde, P., Clarke, G. N., Lewinsohn, P. M., Seeley, J. R., & Kaufman, N. K. (2001). Impact of comorbidity on a cognitive-behavioral group treatment for adolescent depression. *Journal of the American Academy of Child and Adolescent Psychiatry, 40,* 795–802.

Rohde, P., Lewinsohn, P. M., & Seeley, J. R. (1990). Are people changed by the experience of having an episode of depression? A further test of the scar hypothesis. *Journal of Abnormal Psychology, 99,* 264–271.

Rohde, P., Lewinsohn, P. M., & Seeley, J. R. (1991). Comorbidity of unipolar depression: II. Comorbidity with other mental disorders in adolescents and adults. *Journal of Abnormal Psychology, 100,* 214–222.

Rohde, P., Lewinsohn, P. M., & Seeley, J. R. (1994). Are adolescents changed by an episode of major depression? *Journal of the American Academy of Child and Adolescent Psychiatry, 33,* 1289–1298.

Rosenbaum, J., Biederman, J., Hirshfeld Becker, D. R., Kagan, J., Snidman, N., Friedman, D., et al. (2000). A controlled study of behavioral inhibition in children of parents with panic disorder and depression. *American Journal of Psychiatry, 157,* 2002–2010.

Rossello, J., & Bernal, G. (1999). The efficacy of cognitive-behavioral and interpersonal treatments for depression in Puerto Rican adolescents. *Journal of Consulting and Clinical Psychology, 67,* 734–745.

Rothbart, M. K., & Ahadi, S. A. (1994). Temperament and the development of personality. *Journal of Abnormal Psychology, 103,* 55–66.

Rothbart, M. K., & Bates, J. E. (1998). Temperament. In W. Damon (Series ed.) & N. Eisenberg (Vol. ed.), *Handbook of child psychology: Vol. 3. Social, emotional, and personality development* (5th ed., pp. 105–176). New York: Wiley.

Rothbart, M. K, Posner, M. I., & Hershey, K. L. (1995). Temperament, attention, and developmental psychopathology. In D. Cicchetti & D. Cohen (Eds.), *Developmental psychopathology: Vol. 1. Theory and methods* (pp. 315–340). New York: Wiley.

Rudolph, K. D. (2002). Gender differences in emotional response to interpersonal stress during adolescence. *Journal of Adolescent Health, 30,* 3–13.

Rudolph, K. D., & Clark, A G. (2001). Conceptions of relationships in children with depressive and aggressive symptoms: Social-cognitive distortion or reality? *Journal of Abnormal Child Psychology, 29,* 41–56.

Rudolph, K., & Hammen, C. (1999). Age and gender as determinants of stress exposure, generation, and reactivity in youngsters: A transactional perspective. *Child Development, 70,* 660–677.

Rudolph, K. D., Hammen, C., & Burge, D. (1994). Interpersonal functioning and depressive symptoms in childhood: Addressing the issues of specificity and comorbidity. *Journal of Abnormal Child Psychology, 22,* 355–371.

Rudolph, K. D., Hammen, C., & Burge, D. (1997). A cognitive-interpersonal approach to depressive symptoms in preadolescent children. *Journal of Abnormal Child Psychology, 25,* 33–45.

Rudolph, K., Hammen, C., Burge, D., Lindberg, N., Herzberg, D., & Daley, S. (2000). Toward an interpersonal life stress model of depression: The developmental context of stress generation. *Development and Psychopathology, 12,* 215–234.

Rudolph, K. D., Lambert, S. F., Clark, A. G., & Kurlakowsky, K. D. (2001). Negotiating the transition to middle school: The role of self-regulatory processes. *Child Development, 72,* 929–946.

Rueter, M. A., Scaramella, L., Wallace, L. E., & Conger, R. D. (1999). First-onset of depressive or anxiety disorders predicted by the longitudinal course of internalizing symptoms and parent-adolescent disagreements. *Archives of General Psychiatry, 56,* 726–732.

Ruscio, J., & Ruscio, A. M. (2000). Informing the continuity controversy: A taxometric analysis of depression. *Journal of Abnormal Psychology, 109,* 473–487.

Rutter, M. (1988). Epidemiological approaches to developmental psychopathology. *Archives of General Psychiatry, 45*(5), 486–495.

Rutter, M., Macdonald, H., Le Couteur, A., Harrington, R., Bolton, P., & Bailey, A. (1990). Genetic factors in child psychiatric disorders—II. Empirical findings. *Journal of Child Psychology and Psychiatry, 31,* 39–83.

Ryan, N. D. (2003). Medication treatment for depression in children and adolescents. *CNS Spectrum, 8,* 283–287.

Ryan, N. D., Birmaher, B., Perel, J. M., Dahl, R. E., Meyer, V., Al-Shabbout, M., et al. (1992). Neuroendocrine response to L-5-hydroxytryptophan challenge in prepubertal major depression. *Archives of General Psychiatry, 49,* 843–851.

Ryan, N., & Dahl, R. (1993). The biology of depression in children and adolescents. In J. J. Mann & D. J. Kupfer (Eds.), *Biology of depressive disorders, Part B: Subtypes of depression and comorbid disorders* (pp. 37–58). New York: Plenum Press.

Ryan, N. D., Dahl, R. E., Birmaher, B., Williamson, D. E., Iyengar, S., Nelson, B., et al. (1994). Stimulatory tests of growth hormone secretion in prepubertal major depression: Depressed versus normal children. *Journal of the American Academy of Child and Adolescent Psychiatry, 33,* 824–833.

Ryan, N. D., Puig-Antich, J., Ambrosini, P., Rabinovich, H., Robinson, D., Nelson, B., et al. (1987). The clinical picture of major depression in children and adolescents. *Archives of General Psychiatry, 44,* 854–861.

Ryder, A. G., & Bagby, R. M. (1999). Diagnostic viability of depressive personality disorder: Theoretical and conceptual issues. *Journal of Personality Disorders, 13,* 135–141.

Ryder, A. G., Bagby, R. M., & Dion, K. L. (2001). Chronic, low-grade depression in a nonclinical sample: Depressive personality or dysthymia? *Journal of Personality Disorders, 15,* 84–93.

Ryder, A. G., Bagby, R. M., & Schuller, D. R. (2002). The overlap of depressive personality disorder and dysthymia: A categorical problem with a dimensional solution. *Harvard Review of Psychiatry, 10,* 337–352.

Rynn, M. A., Findling, R., Emslie, G., Marus, R. N., Fernandes, L. A., & D'Amico, M. F. (2002, May). *Efficacy and safety of nefazodone in adolescents with MDD.* Paper presented at the 155th annual meeting of the American Psychiatric Association, Philadelphia.

Sagestrano, L. M., Paikoff, R. L., Holmbeck, G. N., & Fendrich, M. (2003). A longitudinal examination of familial risk factors for depression among inner-city African American adolescents. *Journal of Family Psychology, 17,* 108–120.

Saylor, C. F., Finch, A. J., Spirito, A., & Bennett, B. (1984). The Children's Depression Inventory: A systematic evaluation of psychometric properties. *Journal of Consulting and Clinical Psychology, 52,* 955–967.

Schneider, M. L. (1992). Prenatal stress exposure alters postnatal behavioral expression under conditions of novelty challenge in rhesus monkey infants. *Developmental Psychobiology, 25,* 529–540.

Schraedley, P. K., Gotlib, I. H., & Hayward, C. (1999). Gender differences in correlates of depressive symptoms in adolescents. *Journal of Adolescent Health, 25,* 98–108.

Schulberg, H. C., Block, M. R., Madonia, M. J., Scott, C. P., Rodriguez, E., & Imber, S. D. (1996). Treating major depression in primary care practice. Eight-month clinical outcomes. *Archives of General Psychiatry, 53,* 913–919.

Schwartz, J. A. J., Gladstone, T. R. G., & Kaslow, N. J. (1998). Depressive disorders. In M. Hersen & T. H. Ollendick (Eds.), *Handbook of child psychopathology* (3rd ed., pp. 269–289). New York: Plenum Press.

Schwarz, J. C., Barton-Henry, M. L., & Pruzinsky, T. (1985). Assessing child-rearing behaviors: A comparison of ratings made by mother, father, child, and siblings on the CRPBI. *Child Development, 56,* 462–479.

Segal, Z. V., Shaw, B. F., & Vella, D. D. (1989). Life stress and depression: A test of the congruency hypothesis for life event content and depressive subtype. *Canadian Journal of Behavioural Science, 21,* 389–400.

Shaffer, D., Fisher, P., Lucas, C. P., Dulcan, M. K., & Schwab-Stone, M. E. (2000). NIMH Diagnostic Interview Schedule for Children Version IV (NIMH DISC-IV): Description, differences from previous versions, and reliability of some common diagnoses. *Journal of the American Academy of Child and Adolescent Psychiatry, 39,* 28–38.

Sheeber, L., Hops, H., Alpert, A., Davis, B., & Andrews, J. (1997). Family support and conflict: Prospective relations to adolescent depression. *Journal of Abnormal Child Psychology, 25,* 333–344.

Sheeber, L., Hops, H., Andrews, J., Alpert, T., & Davis, B. (1998). Interactional processes in families with depressed and nondepressed adolescents: Reinforcement of depressive behavior. *Behaviour Research and Therapy, 36,* 417–427.

Sheeber, L., & Sorenson, E. (1998). Family relationships of depressed adolescents: A multi-method assessment. *Journal of Clinical Child Psychology, 27,* 268–277.

Shiner, R. L. (1998). How shall we speak of children's personalities in middle childhood? A preliminary taxonomy. *Psychological Bulletin, 124,* 308–332.

Silberg, J. L., Rutter, M., & Eaves, L. (2001). Genetic and environmental influences on the temporal association between earlier anxiety and later depression in girls. *Biological Psychiatry, 49,* 1040–1049.

Sim, H. (2000). Relationship of daily hassles and social support to depression and antisocial behavior among early adolescents. *Journal of Youth and Adolescence, 29,* 647–659.

Skuse, D. H. (1985). Non-organic failure to thrive: A reappraisal. *Archives of Disease in Childhood, 60,* 173–178.

Slesnick, N., & Waldron, H. B. (1997). Interpersonal problem-solving interactions of depressed adolescents and their parents. *Journal of Family Psychology, 11,* 234–245.

Smucker, M. R., Craighead, W. E., Craighead, L. W., & Green, B. J. (1986). Normative and reliability data for the Children's Depression Inventory. *Journal of Abnormal Child Psychology, 14,* 25–39.

Spitz, R. A. (1945). Hospitalism: An inquiry into the genesis of psychiatric conditions in early childhood. *Psychoanalytic Study of the Child, 1,* 53–74.

Spitz, R. A., & Wolf, K. M. (1946). Anaclitic depression; an inquiry into the genesis of psychiatric conditions in early childhood, II. *Psychoanalytic Study of the Child, 2,* 313–342.

Stanger, C., McConaughy, S. H., & Achenbach, T. M. (1992). Three year course of behavioral/emotional problems in a national sample of 4 to 16 year olds: II. Predictors of syndromes. *Journal of the American Academy of Child and Adolescent Psychiatry, 31,* 941–950.

Stark, K. D., Humphrey, L. L., Crook, K., & Lewis, K. (1990). Perceived family environments of depressed and anxious children: Child's and maternal figure's perspectives. *Journal of Abnormal Child Psychology, 18,* 527–547.

Stark, K. D., Reynolds, W. M., & Kaslow, N. J. (1987). A comparison of the relative efficacy of self-control therapy and a behavioral problem-solving therapy for depression in children. *Journal of Abnormal Child Psychology, 15,* 91–113.

Stein, D., Williamson, D. E., Birmaher, B., Brent, D. A., Kaufman, J., Dahl, R. E., et al. (2000). Parent-child bonding and family functioning in depressed children and children at high risk for future depression. *Journal of the American Academy of Child and Adolescent Psychiatry, 39,* 1387–1395.

Stice, E., Ragan, J., & Randall, P. (2004). Prospective relations between social support and depression: Differential direction of effects for parent and peer support. *Journal of Abnormal Psychology, 113,* 155–159.

Strauss, C. C., Forehand, R., Frame, C., & Smith, K. (1984). Characteristics of children with extreme scores on the Children's Depression Inventory. *Journal of Clinical Child Psychology, 13,* 227–231.

Sullivan, P. F., Neale, M. C., & Kendler, K. S. (2000). Genetic epidemiology of major depression: Review and meta-analysis. *American Journal of Psychiatry, 157,* 1552–1562.

Surtees, P. G. (1997). Adversity, vulnerability, and depression. *Stress Medicine, 13,* 185–191.

Takahashi, L. K., Baker, E. W., & Kalin, N. H. (1990). Ontogeny of behavioral and hormonal responses to stress in prenatally stressed male rat pups. *Physiology and Behavior, 47,* 357–364.

Taylor, L., & Ingram, R. E. (1999). Cognitive reactivity and depressotypic information processing in children of depressed mothers. *Journal of Abnormal Psychology, 108,* 202–210.

Thaper, A., & McGuffin, P. (1994). A twin study of depressive symptoms in childhood. *British Journal of Psychiatry, 165,* 259–265.

Thase, M. E., & Howland, R. H. (1994). Refractory depression: Relevance of psychosocial factors and therapies. *Psychiatric Annals, 24,* 232–240.

Thase, M. E., Jindal, R., & Howland, R. H. (2002). Biological aspects of depression. In I. H. Gotlib & C. L. Hammen (Eds.), *Handbook of depression* (pp. 192–218). New York: Guilford Press.

Thomas, A., & Chess, S. (1977). *Temperament and development.* Oxford, England: Brunner/Mazel.

Thomsen, A. H., Compas, B. E., Colletti, R. B., Stanger, C., Boyer, M. C., & Konik, B. S. (2002). Parent reports of coping and stress responses in children with recurrent abdominal pain. *Journal of Pediatric Psychology, 27,* 215–226.

Tomarken, A. J., Dichter, G. S., Garber, J., & Simien, C. (2004). Relative left frontal hypo-activation in adolescents at risk for depression. *Biological Psychology, 67,* 77–102.

Tomarken, A. J., & Keener, A. D. (1998). Frontal brain asymmetry and depression: A self-regulatory perspective. *Cognition and Emotion, 12,* 387–420.

Trad, P. V. (1987). *Infant and childhood depression: Developmental factors.* New York: Wiley.

Trad, P. V. (1994). Depression in infants. In W. M. Reynolds and H. F. Johnston (Eds.), *Handbook of depression in children and adolescents* (pp. 401–426). New York: Plenum Press.

Treatment for Adolescents with Depression Study (TADS) Team. (2004). Fluoxetine, cognitive-behavioral therapy, and their combination for adolescents with depression: Treatment for Adolescents with Depression Study (TADS) randomized controlled trial. *Journal of the American Medical Association, 292,* 807–820.

Turner, J. E., & Cole, D. A. (1994). Developmental differences in cognitive diatheses for child depression. *Journal of Abnormal Child Psychology, 22,* 15–31.

Twenge, J. M., & Nolen-Hoeksema, S. K. (2002). Age, gender, race, socioeconomic status, and birth cohort differences on the Children's Depression Inventory: A meta-analysis. *Journal of Abnormal Psychology, 111,* 1–11.

Valla, J., Bergeron, L., Berube, H., Gaudet, N., & St. Georges, M. (1994). A structured pictorial questionnaire to assess *DSM-III-R*-based diagnoses in children (6–11 years): Development, validity, & reliability. *Journal of Abnormal Child Psychology, 22,* 403–423.

van Os, J., Jones, P., Lewis, G., Wadsworth, M., & Murray, R. (1997). Developmental precursors of affective illness in a general population birth cohort. *Archives of General Psychiatry, 54,* 625–631.

Vitaro, F., Pelletier, D., Gagnon, C., & Baron, P. (1995). Correlates of depressive symptoms in early adolescence. *Journal of Emotional and Behavioral Disorders, 3,* 241–251.

Vostanis, P., Feehan, C., & Grattan, E. (1998). Two-year outcome of children treated for depression. *European Child and Adolescent Psychiatry, 7,* 12–18.

Vostanis, P., Feehan, C., Grattan, E., & Bickerton, W. (1996a). Treatment for children and adolescents with depression: Lessons from a controlled trial. *Clinical Child Psychology and Psychiatry, 1,* 199–212.

Vostanis, P., Feehan, C., Grattan, E., & Bickerton, W. (1996b). A randomised controlled out-patient trial of cognitive-behavioural treatment for children and adolescents with depression: 9-month follow-up. *Journal of Affective Disorders, 40,* 105–116.

Wade, T. J., Cairney, J., & Pevalin, D. J. (2002). Emergence of gender differences in depression during adolescence: National panel results from three countries. *Journal of the American Academy of Child and Adolescent Psychiatry, 41,* 190–198.

Wagner, K. D., Ambrosini, P., Rynn, M., Wohlberg, C., Yang, R., & Greenbaum, M. S. (2003). Efficacy of sertraline in the treatment of children and adolescents with major depressive disorder: Two randomized controlled trials. *Journal of the American Medical Association, 290,* 1033–1041.

Wagner, K. D., Robb, A. S., Findling, R., Jin, J., Gutierroz, M. M., & Heydorn, W. E., (2001). Citalopram is effective in the treatment of major depressive disorder in children and adolescents: Results of a placebo-controlled trial. Poster presented at the 40th annual meeting of the American College of Neuropsychopharmacology, Waikoloa, HI.

Walker, L. S., Garber, J., & Greene, J. (1993). Psychosocial correlates of recurrent childhood pain: A comparison of pediatric patients with recurrent abdominal pain, organic illness, and psychiatric disorders. *Journal of Abnormal Psychology, 102,* 248–258.

Wallace, J., Schneider, T., & McGuffin, P. (2002). Genetics of depression. In I. H. Gotlib & C. L. Hammen (Eds.), *Handbook of depression* (pp. 169–191). New York: Guilford Press.

Ward, A. J. (1991). Prenatal stress and childhood psychopathology. *Child Psychiatry and Human Development, 22,* 97–110.

Ward, L. G., Friedlander, M. L., & Silverman, W. K. (1987). Children's depressive symptoms, negative self statements, and causal attributions for success and failure. *Cognitive Therapy and Research, 11,* 215–227.

Warner, V., Weissman, M. M., Fendrich, M., Wickramaratne, P., & Moreau, D. (1992). The course of major depression in the offspring of depressed parents: Incidence, recurrence, and recovery. *Archives of General Psychiatry, 49,* 795–801.

Watson, D., Clark, L. A. (1984). Negative affectivity: The disposition to experience a versive emotional states. *Psychological Bulletin, 96,* 465–490.

Watson, D., & Clark, L. A. (1995). Depression and the melancholic temperament. *European Journal of Personality, 9,* 351–366.

Watson, D., Clark, L. A., & Harkness, A. R. (1994). Structures of personality and their relevance to psychopathology. *Journal of Abnormal Psychology, 103,* 18–31.

Weiner, B. (1985). An attributional theory of achievement motivation and emotion. *Psychological Review, 92,* 548–573.

Weiss, B., & Garber, J. (2003). Developmental differences in the phenomenology of depression. *Development and Psychopathology, 15,* 403–430.

Weiss, E. L., Longhurst, J. G., & Mazure, C. M. (1999). Childhood sexual abuse as a risk factor for depression in women: Psychosocial and neurobiological correlates. *American Journal of Psychiatry, 156,* 816–828.

Weissman, M. M., Bland, R., Canino, G., Faravelli, C., Greenwald, S., Hwu, H. G., et al. (1996). Cross-national epidemiology of major depression and bipolar disorder. *Journal of the American Medical Association, 276,* 293–299.

Weissman, M. M., Fendrich, M., Warner, V., & Wickramaratne, P. (1992). Incidence of psychiatric disorder in offspring at high and low risk for depression. *Journal of the American Academy of Child and Adolescent Psychiatry, 31,* 640–648.

Weissman, M. M., Merikangas, K. R., Wickramaratne, P., Kidd, K. K., Prusoff, B. A., Leckman, J. F., et al. (1986). Understanding the clinical heterogeneity of major depression using family data. *Archives of General Psychiatry, 43,* 430–434.

Weissman, M. M., & Olfson, M. (1995). Depression in women: Implications for health care research. *Science, 269,* 799–801.

Weissman, M. M., Prusoff, B. A., Gammon, G. D., Merikangas, K. R., Leckman, J. F., & Kidd, K. K. (1984). Psychopathology in the children (ages 6–18) of depressed and normal parents. *Journal of the American Academy of Child Psychiatry, 23,* 78–84.

Weissman, M. M., Warner, V., Wickramaratne, P., & Prusoff, B. A. (1988). Early-onset major depression in parents and their children. *Journal of Affective Disorders, 15,* 269–277.

Weissman, M. M., Wolk, S., Goldstein, R. B, Moreau, D., Adams, P., Greenwald, S., et al. (1999a). Depressed adolescents grown up. *Journal of the American Medical Association, 281,* 1707–1713.

Weissman, M. M., Wolk, S., Goldstein, R. B, Moreau, D., Adams, P., Greenwald, S., et al. (1999b). Children with prepubertal-onset major depressive disorder and anxiety grown up. *Archives of General Psychiatry, 56,* 794–801.

Weisz, J. R., Rudolph, K. D., Granger, D. A., & Sweeney, L. (1992). Cognition, competence, and coping in child and adolescent depression: Research findings, developmental concerns, therapeutic implications. *Development and Psychopathology, 4,* 627–653.

Weisz, J. R., Southam-Gerow, M. A., & McCarty, C. A. (2001). Control-related beliefs and depressive symptoms in clinic-referred children and adolescents: Developmental differences and model specificity. *Journal of Abnormal Psychology, 110,* 97–109.

Weisz, J. R., Thurber, C. A., Sweeney, L., Proffitt, V. D., & LeGagnoux, G. L. (1997). Brief treatment of mild-to-moderate child depression using primary and secondary control enhancement training. *Journal of Consulting and Clinical Psychology, 65,* 703–707.

Weller, E. B., Weller, R. A., Fristad, M. A., Rooney, M. T., & Schecter, J. (2000). Children's Interview for Psychiatric Syndromes (ChIPS). *Journal of the American Academy of Child and Adolescent Psychiatry,* 76–84.

Whiffen, V. E., & Clark, S. E. (1997). Does victimization account for sex differences in depressive symptoms? *British Journal of Clinical Psychology, 36,* 185–193.

Wichstrom, L. (1999). The emergence of gender difference in depressed mood during adolescence: The role of intensified gender socialization. *Developmental Psychology, 35,* 232–245.

Widiger, T. A. (1989). The categorical distinction between personality and affective disorders. *Journal of Personality Disorders, 3,* 77–91.

Wierzbicki, M. (1987). Similarity of monozygotic and dizygotic child twins in level and lability of subclinically depressed mood. *American Journal of Orthopsychiatry, 57,* 33–40.

Wilhelm, K., Parker, G., Dewhurst Savellis, J., & Asghari, A. (1999, July). Psychological predictors of single and recurrent major depressive episodes. *Journal of Affective Disorders, 54,* 139–147.

Williamson, D. E., Birmaher, B., Anderson, B. P., Al-Shabbout, M., & Ryan, N. D. (1995). Stressful life events in depressed adolescents: The role of dependent events during the depressive episode. *Journal of the American Academy of Child and Adolescent Psychiatry, 34,* 591–598.

Williamson, D. E., Birmaher, B., Frank, E., Anderson, B. P., Matty, M. K., & Kupfer, D. J. (1998). Nature of life events and difficulties in depressed adolescents. *Journal of the American Academy of Child and Adolescent Psychiatry, 37,* 1049–1057.

Wilson, G. T., Nathan, P. E., O'Leary, K. D., & Clark, L. A. (1996). *Abnormal psychology: Integrating perspectives.* Boston: Allyn & Bacon.

Wood, A., Harrington, R., & Moore, A. (1996). Controlled trial of a brief cognitive-behavioural intervention in adolescent patients with depressive disorders. *Journal of Child Psychology and Psychiatry, 37,* 737–746.

Wright, C., & Birks, E. (2000). Risk factors for failure to thrive: A population-based survey. *Child: Care, Health and Development, 26,* 5–16.

Youngstrom, E., Izard, C., & Ackerman, B. (1999). Dysphoria related bias in maternal ratings of children. *Journal of Consulting and Clinical Psychology, 67,* 905–916.

Zimmerman, M. A., Ramirez-Valles, J., Zapert, K. M., & Maton, K. I. (2000). A longitudinal study of stress-buffering effects for urban African-American male adolescent problem behaviors and mental health. *Journal of Community Psychology, 28,* 17–33.

CHAPTER 13

Bipolar Disorders

ROBERT A. KOWATCH AND MARY A. FRISTAD

DESCRIPTION OF THE DISORDERS AND CLINICAL PICTURE

Bipolar disorders are severe and persistent mood disorders occurring in approximately 1 percent of adults, children, and adolescents (Geller & Luby, 1997a; Goodwin & Jamison, 1990). These disorders are now recognized as equally prevalent in children and adolescents as in adults, with an estimated prevalence of 1 percent (Kashani et al., 1987; Lewinsohn, Klein, & Seeley, 1995). Wozniak and coworkers (1995) reported that out of 262 consecutively referred children to a pediatric psychopharmacology clinic, 16 percent met *DSM-III-R* criteria (American Psychiatric Association [APA], 1987) for mania. Bipolar disorder seriously disrupts the lives of children and adolescents, with studies showing increased rates of suicide attempts as well as completions, poor academic performance, disturbed interpersonal relationships, substance abuse, legal difficulties, and multiple hospitalizations (DelBello & Geller, 2001; Geller, Bolhofner, Craney, Williams, & Gundersen, 2000; Geller et al., 2002).

The diagnosis of bipolar disorder requires a history of at least one of the following mood episodes: (1) a manic episode, (2) a hypomanic episode and a major depressive episode, or (3) an episode of mixed mania and depression. A single manic episode will result in a diagnosis of bipolar disorder Type I by *DSM-IV* criteria (APA, 1994). A child or adolescent who has had one or more episodes of major depression, no episodes of mania, and at least one episode of hypomania is classified in *DSM-IV* as having a bipolar II disorder. A mixed episode is characterized by both manic and depressive symptoms for at least 1 week. A child or adolescent who is experiencing a mixed episode and who has had an episode of mania or major depression in the past is classified as having a bipolar I disorder, the most recent episode mixed.

Bipolar II disorder, during which an episode of hypomania occurs, is more common in children and adolescents than bipolar I disorder. A hypomanic episode is characterized in *DSM-IV* as an abnormally and persistently elevated, expansive, or irritable mood that lasts at least 4 days. In contrast to a bipolar I disorder, the illness caused by bipolar II disorder is not severe enough to cause marked impairment in occupational functioning (school functioning in children and adolescents), to interfere with social activities or relationships with others, or to necessitate hospitalization, and there are no psychotic features.

Cyclothymia is a mood disorder in which there are hypomanic episodes without a history of major depressive episodes. In cyclothymia, the child or adolescent is not without symptoms for more than 2 months at a time. Retrospective studies of adults with cyclothymia have shown that adolescence is the most common age of onset for cyclothymia. A significant proportion of adolescents with cyclothymia also are at risk to progress to bipolar disorder. In a study by Akiskal et al. (1985) of the offspring of adults with bipolar disorder, 7 out of 10 adolescents with cyclothymia progressed to mania or hypomania within 3 years of diagnosis.

PERSONALITY DEVELOPMENT AND PSYCHOPATHOLOGY

There is very limited information regarding the interrelationship between personality characteristics of children with bipolar disorders and their symptom profiles. Clinical common sense tells us that the more time a child spends in an episode, the more time he or she is not developing in a typical fashion across all developmental milestones—physical, social, emotional, and cognitive. Anecdotally, families frequently complain that their child appears socially or cognitively delayed, or both, often in direct relationship to the amount of time he or she has been ill. Next, we review what is known about premorbid functioning, age of onset, temperament, course of illness, and impact of recurrent episodes on personality development.

The prodromal phase of bipolar disorder is frequently disturbed, suggesting that even prior to establishment of illness onset, development has gone awry. Some clinical writers have described common precursors to full-blown bipolar disorder (Papalos & Papalos, 2002). These include difficulties with sleep and affect regulation from infancy onward, preconciousness, separation anxiety, night terrors, severe rages, oppositional behavior, hypersensitivity to sensory stimuli, peer problems, temperature dysregulation, carbohydrate and sugar cravings, bed-wetting, and soiling. These characteristics have been gleaned from retrospective anecdotal parental reports of behaviors. However, not all children who display these traits as infants, toddlers, or preschoolers go on to develop bipolar disorder in childhood. Prospective studies will be critical to an understanding of their diagnostic utility. We do not yet know how often children who eventually develop bipolar disorders have these traits prior to illness onset in comparison to how often typically developing children or those diagnosed with other psychiatric disorders, such as attention-deficit/hyperactivity disorder (ADHD), Asperger's syndrome, or anxiety disorders, display these characteristics.

Presumably, the younger the child who is diagnosed, the more the illness will affect future personality development. Clear evidence of this exists for childhood depression (Kovacs, 1996). To examine the impact of age of onset on outcome for children with bipolar disorders, it is important to first understand the clinical manifestations of bipolar disorders in young children. Recently, two studies have examined preschool manifestations of bipolar disorders. In the first study, Tumuluru and colleagues (Tumuluru, Weller, Fristad, & Weller, 2003) provided detailed clinical descriptions of six preschoolers aged 3–5 years diagnosed with bipolar disorders while hospitalized in a psychiatric inpatient unit. The children all had irritable mood and a strong family history of mood disorders, and had previously come to clinical attention due to symptoms of ADHD. During their hospitalization, they clearly demonstrated symptoms consistent with bipolar disorders (e.g., grandiosity, pressured speech, decreased need for sleep). Notably, five were prescribed lithium while hospitalized (the family of the sixth child refused this clinical recommendation). All five improved on this medication regime. In the second study, Wilens and colleagues (2003) examined patterns of comorbidity and dysfunction in clinically referred preschoolers and school-aged children diagnosed with bipolar disorders. Wilens et al. examined 44 preschoolers, aged 4–6 years, diagnosed with bipolar disorders and compared them to 29 consecutively ascertained youth aged 7–9 years, also diagnosed with bipolar disorders. The investigators reported that both age groups of children were quite similar in their rates of comorbid psychopathology (ADHD, for example, was reported in 95 percent and 93 percent of the two groups, respectively); symptom profiles for both depression and mania; high rates of mixed state presentations; and substantial impairment in school, peer, family, and overall functioning. A striking finding from their study was that even in the preschoolers, illness onset was 2.6 years, on average, before diagnosis. Thus, children diagnosed with bipolar disorders during their preschool years spent little or no time living in a well state. Clearly, this is deleterious for the healthy development of a child's self-concept.

Temperament has not been well studied in pediatric bipolar disorders. Only one known study to date has examined the role of temperament, defined as the biological, heritable, and stable component of personality; and character, defined as the experience-dependent product of personal decision making over a lifetime, in pediatric bipolar disorders (Tillman et al., 2003). In their study, which is part of the Washington University study of 101 children with bipolar disorders, 68 children with ADHD, and 94 community comparison children, the Junior Temperament and Character Inventory (JTCI) was used to measure temperament and character. The investigators found novelty seeking to be significantly higher in children with bipolar disorders as well as in children with ADHD compared to community controls. Likewise, reward dependence, persistence, self-direction, and cooperativeness were lower in children with bipolar disorders and in children with ADHD relative to community controls. The only reported temperamental or character difference between children with bipolar disorders and those with ADHD were lower rates of parent-reported cooperativeness for children with bipolar disorders compared to those with ADHD.

Related to these findings, Geller and colleagues (Geller, Tillman, Craney, & Bolhofner, 2004) recently completed a 4-year prospective outcome study in which they documented the natural history of mania in children with prepubertal and early adolescent bipolar disorder phenotype. In this study, Geller et al. extended their important, earlier 6-month, 1-year, and 2-year follow-up findings. They reported that time to recovery averaged 60 weeks (SD = 45 weeks). Time to relapse after recovery was 40 weeks (SD = 33 weeks). Children were in episode for two thirds of the time during this 4-year follow-up. A little more than half of the impaired time (56 percent, on average) was spent in a manic or hypomanic episode, while just under half of the impaired time was spent in a depressed state. Psychosis at baseline was the single best predictor of time spent with mania or hypomania ($p < .0008$). Relapse was predicted by low maternal warmth. Most of the 32 children (86 percent) whose mothers were characterized as being low in warmth relapsed, compared to half (50 percent) of those children whose mothers were characterized as being high in warmth. When Geller and colleagues compared their findings to recovery rates reported for adults (Tohen et al., 1990), it becomes clear that early age of onset is associated with a far more pernicious course than is adult-onset bipolar disorders.

Bhangoo and colleagues (Bhangoo et al., 2003) examined 34 children aged 6–17 years (average age 11) with episodic bipolar disorders and contrasted their clinical and associated features with those of 53 children matched for age with chronic bipolar disorders. They found that the children with episodic bipolar disorders were more likely to have had psychotic symptoms, a broader array of manic symptoms (only irritability and psychomotor agitation were equally common between groups), a full depressive episode, a history of suicide attempts, and a parental history of bipolar disorders. Children in the chronic group were more likely to have a comorbid diagnosis of conduct disorder but were no more likely than the episodic group to be violent toward others. Though this study provides useful information on two manifestations of bipolar disorders in youth, its intent was not to determine the impact of bipolar disorders on future personality development. That research remains to be done. It is anticipated that personality development will be greatly impacted by the success (or failure) of current treatments in ameliorating symptoms and, ideally, improving the developmental trajectory of children diagnosed at a young age.

In summary, it appears that pediatric bipolar disorder is associated with a significant prodromal state that negatively alters development. Some children with bipolar disorders can be reliably diagnosed in their preschool years. Of these children, some were ill several years before diagnosis, suggesting very little time had been available for typical development. The one published study of temperament suggests that children with bipolar disorders share numerous traits with children diagnosed with ADHD, and all these traits carry additional psychosocial risk. Additionally, though both chronic and recurrent course of illness in children have their unique drawbacks, Geller's longitudinal study suggests that time to recovery is lengthy and recurrence is frequent in children. Compared to adult outcomes, prognosis appears more impaired. Clearly, far more work is needed to develop efficacious treatments that not only halt episodes, but also increase functional capacity beyond the level of symptom reduction and remission.

EPIDEMIOLOGY

In a large and well-designed population study of the incidence of mood disorders in adolescents, Lewinsohn et al. (1995) reported an overall lifetime prevalence of 1 percent for bipolar spectrum disorders that included bipolar I disorder, bipolar II disorder, and cyclothymia. In this study, the largest groups of adolescent participants were what Lewinsohn and colleagues called the "core-positive" group. These adolescents reported a distinct period of elevated, expansive, or irritable mood and best fit the *DSM-IV* criteria of bipolar disorder not otherwise specified (NOS). These participants had an overall prevalence of 5.7 percent and accounted for 84 percent of the bipolar sample. These bipolar NOS subjects also had very high rates of psychosocial impairment and mental health service utilization, as did the bipolar Type I subjects.

Wozniak et al. (1995) reported that of 262 consecutively referred children to a specialty pediatric psychopharmacology clinic, 16 percent met *DSM-III-R* criteria for mania. Issac (1992) reported that 8 out of 12 students in a special education class met *DSM-III-R* criteria for a bipolar disorder. However, in more specialized psychiatric settings such as a pediatric psychopharmacology clinic, the occurrence of pediatric bipolar disorder is expected to be much greater than that found in the general population.

ETIOLOGY

As with most adult and child psychiatric disorders, the precise etiology of pediatric bipolar disorders is unknown. Bipolar disorder is similar to diabetes in that both are biologic disorders that are strongly affected by the environment with strong genetic influences as well. None of the biologic studies to date have provided a definite etiology for bipolar disorders in adults or children, but two areas of research, molecular genetics and neuroimaging, are beginning to offer clues to their underlying neurobiology.

Two molecular genetics studies in children with bipolar disorders by Geller and colleagues have recently been reported. In the first study of a sample of bipolar children, the serotonin transporter linked promoter region (HTTLPR) short and long alleles were studied and the transmission disequilibrium test was negative in the children with bipolar disorder (Geller & Cook, 1999). The second study examined the linkage disequilibrium of catechol-O-methyltransferase (l-COMT) in bipolar children, and transmission and the disequilibrium tests were not significant for preferential transmission of l-COMT in this sample (Geller & Cook, 2000). It is still very early in our knowledge about the molecular genetics of psychiatric disorders, and it is very likely that multiple genes are involved that interact with each other and are expressed differentially during development (Kelsoe et al., 1993). It is unlikely that a single genetic locus will be identified that is involved in the neurobiology of bipolar disorders in children or adolescents.

Magnetic resonance imaging (MRI) is being widely used to study children and adolescents with bipolar disorder because it is not associated with ionizing radiation and has no known biological risks. Methods of MRI can now provide information about the structure of the central nervous system with structural T1/T2 studies, information about brain activity via functional magnetic resonance imaging (fMRI), and information about in vivo neurochemistry via magnetic resonance spectroscopy (MRS). Structural MRI studies of adults with bipolar disorder have revealed a variety of abnormalities including decreased prefrontal cortex volumes (Drevets et al., 1997; Sax et al., 1999), increases in the volume of the amygdala and putamen (Altshuler, Bartzokis, Grieder, Curran, & Mintz, 1998; Strakowski et al., 1999, 2002), atrophy of the V3 vermal area (DelBello, Strakowski, Zimmerman, Hawkins, & Sax, 1999), and larger lateral ventricles (Strakowski et al., 2002). Another common structural MRI finding in adults with bipolar disorder is the presence of white matter hyperintensities whose significance is unknown (Altshuler et al., 1995; Soares & Mann, 1997; Strakowski et al., 1993). Structural MRI studies of children and adolescents with bipolar disorder have also reported a variety of neuroanatomical abnormalities, including an increased incidence of subcortical white matter hyperintensities (Botteron, Vannier, Geller, Todd, & Lee, 1995; Woods, Yurgelun-Todd, Mikulis, & Pillay, 1995), reduced intracranial volume and increased frontal and temporal sulcal size (Friedman et al., 1999), and reductions in thalamic area (Dasari et al., 1999).

Functional MRI does not involve exposure to ionizing radiation and has the advantage of better temporal resolution than older positron-emission tomography (PET) or single photon-emission tomography (SPECT). Functional MRI also has the capability of acquiring many more scans in a single scanning session, which allows for signal averaging with block designs with a subsequent increase in the signal-to-noise ratio. The ability to recognize unique identities and various forms of affect in human faces is an essential component of human social behavior (Ekman & Oster, 1979), and the use of neurobehavioral probes such as human faces with fMRI may help in identifying the neural circuits involved in bipolar disorders (Breiter et al., 1996; Gur, Erwin, & Gur, 1992; Morris et al., 1996). Three fMRI studies examined the processing of facial emotion in patients with mania. The first report was by Yergelun-Todd and colleagues at Mclean Hospital, who studied 14 adult patients with *DSM-IV* bipolar disorder and 10 normal controls. These participants were studied with a 1.5T system using the Ekman fearful and happy faces as visual stimuli (Yurgelun-Todd, Gruber, Kanayama, Baird, & Young, 2000). They reported a significant increase in signal intensity in the left amygdala and a reduction of signal intensity in the right dorsolateral prefrontal cortex in response to recognition of fearful facial expressions. Although all of their normal controls were able to accurately label 100 percent of the fearful faces, only 10 of 14 (71 percent) bipolar patients were able to correctly identify the fearful Ekman faces. Yergelun-Todd et al. interpreted these findings to suggest that there were abnormalities in fronto-limbic circuitry of the bipolar participants as compared to the normal control participants. A limitation of this study is that the majority of these participants were taking mood stabilizers and antipsychotics when imaged.

Lawrence and colleagues (2004) recently reported the results of an fMRI study in which they compared responses to mild and intense facial expressions of fear, happiness, and sadness in euthymic and depressed adult bipolar patients, healthy control participants, and depressed patients with major depressive disorder (MDD). The mean age of these participants was 41 years, and all of the bipolar and unipolar patients were taking psychotropic medications when studied. There were no residual manic symptoms in the bipolar patients, but three bipolar patients reported mild symptoms of depression and two had moderate to severe depressive symptoms. All of the MDD patients were symptomatic when studied. Lawrence et al. reported that the bipolar disorder patients demonstrated increased subcortical (ventral striatal, thalamic, hippocampal) and ventral prefrontal cortical responses particularly to mild and intense fear, mild happy expressions, and mild sad expressions, whereas the healthy control participants demonstrated increased subcortical responses to intense happy expressions and mild fear, and increased dorsal prefrontal cortical responses to intense sad expressions. The patients with MDD showed diminished neural responses to all emotional expressions except mild sadness. They concluded that compared with healthy controls and MDD patients, bipolar patients demonstrated increased subcortical and ventral prefrontal cortical responses to both positive and negative emotional expressions.

Several studies have researched bipolar patients using MRS. Soares, Krishnan, and Keshavan (1996) reviewed the literature concerning MRS in the pathophysiology of adult mood disorders (unipolar and bipolar studies) and summarized the findings from seven ^{1}H studies in the adult literature to date. These MRS ^{1}H studies reported significant choline/Cr abnormalities in the parietal lobes and basal ganglia of adult bipolar patients (Renshaw, Yurgelun-Todd, Tohen, Gruber, & Cohen, 1995).

Several authors have developed models of the functional networks thought to be involved in the mood dysregulation of patients with mood disorders. These include the limbic-cortical model of Mayberg (Mayberg, 1997), the frontotemporal model of Blumberg, Charney, and Krystal (2002), the ventral/dorsal system of Philips et al. (1997), and the anterior limbic network of Strakowski, DelBello, Adler, Cecil, and Sax (2000). Each of these models involves the amygdala, hippocampus, prefrontal and orbitofrontal cortex, and parts of the striatum.

COURSE, COMPLICATIONS, AND PROGNOSIS

The outcome of bipolar disorder in children and adolescents has received little study. McGlashen interviewed 62 adult patients who met *DSM-III* criteria for mania and divided them into two groups, 35 with adolescent-onset mania and 31 with adult-onset mania (McGlashen, 1988). He reported that the adolescent-onset group had more hospitalizations, displayed more psychotic symptoms, and were more frequently misdiagnosed as having schizoaffective disorder than the adult-onset group. Surprisingly, the adolescent-onset group had outcomes superior to those of the adult-onset group in terms of social relationships and their ability to work. In contrast, Geller, Tillman, Craney, and Bolhofner (2004) reported diagnostic stability in 93 prepubescent and early adolescent subjects. At 4-year follow-up, 86 of the patients were assessed and rate of recovery was 87 percent. However, rate of relapse after recovery was 64 percent. In these studies recovery was defined as no mania or hypomania for at least 2 weeks and relapse was defined as having full *DSM-IV* criteria for mania or hypomania and a Childhood Global Assessment Scale score of less than or equal to 60 for at least 2 weeks.

ASSESSMENT AND DIAGNOSIS

Many children and adolescents are labeled bipolar without careful consideration of the diagnostic complexities and subtypes of this disorder. The symptoms of bipolarity in children and adolescents can be difficult to establish because of the variability of symptom expression depending on the context and phase of the illness, the effects of development on symptom expression, and the mood and behavioral effects of the various psychotropic medications that the patient is taking. Children and adolescents with a bipolar disorder often present with a mixed or dysphoric picture characterized by frequent short periods of intense mood liability and irritability rather than classic euphoric mania (Geller et al., 1995; Wozniak et al., 1995). Clinicians who evaluate children with pediatric bipolar disorders often try to fit them into the *DSM-IV* rapid cycling subtype and find that this subtype does not fit bipolar children very well, in that these children often do not have clear episodes of mania. Rather, researchers are reporting that bipolar children cycle far more frequently than four episodes per year. In 81 percent of a well-defined group of patients, continuous, daily cycling from mania or hypomania to euthymia or depression was reported (Botteron et al., 1995; Geller, Zimerman, et al., 2000). Findling et al. (2001) recently reported that in a sample of 90 bipolar I patients with a mean age of 10.8 years that the age of the first manic episode was 6.7 years, with 50 percent of these patients categorized as rapid cycling (Findling et al., 2001). The picture that emerges from several independent research groups is that prepubertal bipolar children typically have multiple daily mood swings and that irritability is much more common than euphoria (Geller, Zimerman, et al., 2000; Wozniak & Biederman, 1997).

Children and adolescents with bipolar disorders often exhibit the following symptoms:

- Elevated or expansive mood: The child will have a mood that is inappropriately giddy, silly, elated, or euphoric. Often this mood will be present without any reason. It may be distinguished from a transient cheerful mood by the intensity and duration of the episode. Often, these patients have no insight about the inappropriate nature of this mood.
- Irritable mood: The child may become markedly belligerent or irritated with intense outbursts of anger. An adolescent may appear extremely oppositional, belligerent, or hostile.
- Grandiosity or inflated self-esteem: This can potentially be confused with brief childhood fantasies of increased capability. Typically, true grandiosity can be seen as assertions of great competency in all areas of life, which usually cannot be altered by contrary external evidence. Occasionally, this may be bizarre and include delusions of "super powers." One should consider transient identification with recent exposure to media involving a favorite superhero when evaluating this symptom.
- Decreased need for sleep: The child may require little to no sleep over the period of the episode without a subjective feeling of fatigue or evidence of tiredness. Substance use should be considered in this differential, particularly for adolescents.
- Increased talkativeness: The child or adolescent has a sustained period of uncharacteristically increased speech. Lack of inhibition to social norms may lead them to blurt out answers during class or repeatedly be disciplined for talk-

ing to peers in class. Speech is typically very rapid and pressured to the point where it may be continuous and seems to jump between loosely related subjects.

- Flight of ideas or racing thoughts: The child or adolescent may report a subjective feeling that their thoughts are moving so rapidly that their speech cannot keep up. Often this is differentiated from rapid speech by the degree of rapidity with which the patient may express loosely related subjects that to the listener may seem completely unrelated.
- Distractibility, short attention span: During the episode, the child or adolescent may report that it is impossible to pay attention to class or other outside events due to the rapidly changing focus of their thoughts. This symptom must be carefully distinguished from the distractibility and inattention of ADHD, which typically is a more fixed and longstanding pattern rather than a brief episodic phenomenon in a manic or hypomanic episode.
- Increase in goal-directed activity: During a milder episode, the child or adolescent may be capable of accomplishing a great deal of work. However, episodes that are more severe manifest as an individual starts numerous ambitious projects that they are later unable to complete.
- Excessive risk-taking activities: The child or adolescent may become involved in forbidden pleasurable activities that have a high risk for adverse consequences. This may manifest as hypersexual behavior, frequent fighting, increased recklessness, use of drugs and alcohol, shopping sprees, or reckless driving.

Children and adolescents with pediatric bipolar disorders frequently have comorbid diagnoses that complicate their presentation and treatment response. These comorbid disorders most often include ADHD, anxiety disorders, oppositional defiant disorder, and conduct disorder (Kovacs & Pollock, 1995; West et al., 1995; Wozniak et al., 1995). The most common comorbid disorder among pediatric bipolar patients is ADHD, with leading research groups finding comorbid rates as high as 98 percent (Wozniak et al., 1995) and 97 percent (Geller et al., 1998). This may be problematic in that symptoms of distractibility, irritability, increased talkativeness, and risk-taking behaviors may be seen in ADHD. However, these features of ADHD typically are not as severe as those in a manic or hypomanic episode and do not occur within discrete episodes. One must also carefully differentiate between mood swings associated with the development of personality disorders or those that occur purely in the context of medication or substance usage. Common comorbid disorders found in patients with pediatric bipolar disorders are listed in Table 13.1.

TABLE 13.1 Estimated Rates of Comorbid Disorders among Children and Adolescents with Bipolar Disorder

Disorder	Prepubertal	Adolescent
ADHD	70–90%	30–60%
Anxiety disorders	30–40%	30–40%
Conduct disorders	30–40%	30–60%
Oppositional defiant disorder	60–90%	20–30%
Substance abuse	10%	40–70%
Learning disabilities	30–40%	30–40%

IMPACT ON ENVIRONMENT

Bipolar disorder affects children in all spheres of their lives. Family relations are strained, educational performance is impacted, and peer interactions are deleteriously altered. Geller & Zimmerman et al. (2000) documented the psychosocial functioning of children in these arenas, comparing 93 children with prepubertal and early adolescent bipolar disorder (PEA-BD) to 81 children with ADHD and 94 community control (CC) children.

Family

Families are impacted by a child's bipolar disorder in a myriad of ways. Fewer PEA-BD children come from intact, biological families, compared to children with ADHD and CC children (55 percent, 62 percent, and 89 percent, respectively). They are less likely to engage in frequent activities with their mothers (76 percent versus 94 percent for children with ADHD and 99 percent for CC children), confide in their mothers (47 percent, 61 percent, 83 percent, respectively) or fathers (23 percent, 39 percent, 53 percent, respectively), have consistent limits set by mothers (83 percent, 94 percent, 99 percent) or fathers (65 percent, 71 percent, 86 percent), or experience warm relationships with their mothers (45 percent, 75 percent, 95 percent) or fathers (29 percent, 45 percent, 82 percent). They were, however, more likely to experience frequent hostility from their mothers (79 percent, 38 percent, 2 percent) and fathers (48 percent, 24 percent, 2 percent); corporal punishment on a regular basis (i.e., one or more times per month) from their mothers (30 percent, 25 percent, 4 percent) and fathers (28 percent, 19 percent, 3 percent), and overall frequent tension from their mothers (68 percent, 13 percent, 0 percent) and fathers (40 percent, 18 percent, 2 percent).

In addition to behavioral disruption, which can wreak havoc with parent-child, parent-parent, child-sibling, and parent-sibling relationships, caregivers experience a wide range of stressors. In a survey completed with the Child and Adolescent Bipolar Foundation, an online support, information, and advocacy group, Hellander, Sisson, and Fristad (2002) reported that the following were considered most difficult for caregivers: care of a high-needs child, need to advocate in schools, worry about the future, exhaustion, physical illnesses, financial strain, isolation, stigma, guilt, and blame.

Participants in our Multi-Family Psychoeducation Group (MFPG) study have articulately described the impact of the illness on family life as follows:

> ... we were a functioning family until you turn in the mix and add Jason[1] into our family; we become dysfunctional ... logic and education help us to a point [parents are both college graduates], but then again we are human beings and it is just really tough living with Jason. It affects our whole relationship. It affects our marriage....
>
> Mother of a 10-year-old boy with bipolar disorder-NOS

Relationships inside and outside the family suffer.

> I also find it very difficult to facilitate relationships within our household between the siblings and ... neighbors or his teacher or other people. I feel like I'm always having to facilitate when his moods are switching very rapidly or he's highly anxious.
>
> Mother of an 11-year-old boy with bipolar disorder-mixed

Siblings are also affected.

> My husband and I sometimes will argue over what to do with Maria, and the older child believes that she's not getting enough attention because Maria's sucking all of it up.
>
> Mother of a 9-year-old girl with bipolar disorder-NOS

School

Geller and colleagues (Geller et al., 2002) also described school-based impairment in their three cohorts. They reported that children with PEA-BD were more likely than children with ADHD or CC children to have behavior problems at school (79 percent, 30 percent, and 4 percent, respectively) and low grades (44 percent, 21 percent, and 1 percent). They were less likely than CC children to be in advanced placement courses (4 percent versus 17 percent). The children with PEA-BD and ADHD both had similar rates of repeating grades (8 percent and 7 percent, respectively), being placed in a remedial class (11 percent, 12 percent), and having a learning disability (14 percent, 26 percent), whereas no CC children had experienced any of these.

Reasons for school-based problems in children with PEA-BD are many. First and foremost, their primary mood symptoms affect their ability to learn. Children with mood fluctuations, decreased interest, fatigue, impaired concentration, psychomotor changes, poor judgment, pressured speech, and racing thoughts are not ideal students. Second, their comorbid symptoms affect cognition. Because rates of ADHD, anxiety disorders, and learning disabilities are common in children with bipolar disorders (Geller & Luby, 1997b), these also contribute to school difficulties in children with bipolar disorders. Third, treatment itself can have a deleterious effect on schoolwork. Medication side effects can include tremor and cognitive dulling. Children who have frequent therapy and doctor appointments miss a lot of school. Fourth, if school staff are not adequately prepared to manage the behavioral disruption that can accompany manic behavior, children may miss additional days of school due to suspension and, at times, expulsion. Finally, peer relations suffer, as discussed in the next section. As social interactions comprise a vital part of any child's school day, peer difficulties can further distract a child's learning.

Peer Interactions

Children who struggle to read interpersonal cues and have off-putting behavior are easily ostracized. Geller's study (Geller, Bolhofner, et al., 2000) reveals that children with PEA-BD, compared to children with ADHD and CC children, are more likely to have few or no friends (56 percent, 25 percent, and 6 percent, respectively) and poor social skills (63 percent, 30 percent, 5 percent). They were not statistically different from children with ADHD but had more problems than CC children in terms of trouble keeping friends (19 percent, 6 percent, and 0 percent, respectively), experiencing frequent teasing (53 percent, 36 percent, 10 percent), and having poor sibling relations (41 percent, 23 percent, 7 percent).

IMPLICATIONS FOR FUTURE PERSONALITY DEVELOPMENT

Clinically, one can surmise that the impact of bipolar disorder on a child's personality development is profound. Figure 13.1 shows a class assignment completed by a participant in our MFPG study, a 12-year-old girl with a long-standing history of bipolar disorder. Each child was asked to draw a mask that represented themselves, then respond to the prompt "Describe how your mask reflects your personality."

> The black eye represents all the mental punches I get from people. The stars circling above my head represent how I'm confused. My searching eyes represent that I'm trying to find the right path, but I'm lost so I can't find it. My broken face represents that I'm a broken person. The hair across my face shows

Figure 13.1 Self-representation of 12-year-old female with bipolar disorder.

that I can be whipped around easily. The tears are of loneliness. The crystals = dreamer/pretender. Claw and hand = outcast.

Several studies have examined euthymic adults diagnosed with bipolar disorders to determine the impact of episode recurrence on global outcome. These studies hint at the future personality development of children with bipolar disorders. The adult literature suggests that recurrent episodes clearly impact well-being and global functioning (MacQueen et al., 2000; Robb, Cooke, Devins, Young, & Joffe, 1997). MacQueen and colleagues studied 64 euthymic adults with bipolar disorders to determine what variables predict prolonged psychosocial impairment in asymptomatic adults (MacQueen et al., 2000). They differentiated quality of life indicators from broader indices of recovery, such as the ability to live independently or obtain stable employment. MacQueen et al. argued that the latter do not highlight the day-to-day challenges faced by individuals struggling with the burden of their illness. The investigators found that the first several episodes of depression accounted for the majority of functional decline in their sample. Their data are consistent with Post's hypothesis (Post & Weiss, 1996) that recurrent episodes lead to permanent alterations within the brain, such that vulnerability to future episodes increases with each additional episode experienced. Further, Robb and colleagues (Robb et al., 1997) documented how bipolar disorders, even while individuals are in a euthymic state, negatively affect quality of life. Euthymic adults diagnosed with bipolar disorders report levels of illness intrusiveness similar to those of adults with multiple sclerosis and more illness intrusiveness than adults diagnosed with end-stage renal disease or rheumatoid arthritis. In summary, episode recurrence, which is common in children who have bipolar disorders, negatively affects development. Even during remission, quality of life remains impaired, suggesting that treatments need to broadly address outcome, not focus exclusively on symptom reduction.

TREATMENT IMPLICATIONS

Appropriate medication management is, no doubt, the *sine qua non* of successful intervention for children with bipolar disorders. However, treatment adherence data suggest that merely prescribing the right medicine is not enough. Studies indicate that one third to two thirds of children in child and adolescent psychiatry outpatient clinics do not keep scheduled appointments (Brasic, Nadrich, & Kleinrock, 2001). Further, meta-analyses suggest treatment adherence is approximately 50 percent for most children with chronic health conditions (Bryon, 1998). Thus, interventions that are designed to teach children and their parents the components of treatment and the importance of medication adherence are needed. Additionally, the plethora of life skill deficits and spheres of impairment described previously suggest that children with bipolar disorders will need skill development in order to become more fully functional after their diagnosis. In designing a family-based intervention, it is important to keep in mind that historically, families have been blamed for their family member's condition while simultaneously they have not gotten useful information, support, or skill building (Hatfield, 1997). This can result in families being skittish or "defensive" about family-based intervention. It is important to convey a sense of support and to acknowledge a family's struggles while intervening at a family level. Finally, a recently published set of clinical guidelines (Kowatch et al., 2005) for the assessment and treatment of bipolar disorders in youth concluded that environmental intervention at a family level is critical to detect early symptoms of relapse and to decrease factors that would trigger relapses.

Three research groups have developed and tested psychosocial interventions for children and adolescents with bipolar disorders (Fristad & Goldberg-Arnold, 2002; Fristad et al., 2003; Goldberg-Arnold & Fristad, 2002; Miklowitz, George, Richards, Simoneau, & Suddath, 2003; Pavuluri et al., 2004). Because the similarities between these three treatment programs are more pronounced than their differences, a description of the second author's (MF) program is provided here. Family psychoeducation, whether delivered in a multifamily psychoeducation group (MFPG) or to individual families, involves teaching the parents and children about mood symptoms and their interventions, providing support (from the therapist and, in the MFPG version, from other parents and children), and improving problem-solving and communication skills in regard to symptom management. The theoretical orientation can be described as a nonblaming, growth-oriented, biopsychosocial model that uses systems and cognitive-behavioral techniques. Conceptually, we believe that education, support, and skill building will lead to a better understanding of the illness, which in turn should lead to better treatment adherence and less family conflict, which should result in a better outcome for the child and family.

In the MFPG program, we are studying treatment efficacy for 165 children aged 8–11 years with any mood disorder, although three quarters of our sample has a bipolar spectrum diagnosis. The MFPG is delivered in eight 90-minute sessions. Sessions begin and end with parents and children together, with the middle (largest) portion of each session conducted separately for parents and for children. There is one therapist for the parents and two for the children, in that significant attention must be paid to behavior management during these sessions. Children receive in vivo social skills training during recreational activities after the formal lesson of the day is completed. Parents and children receive projects to do between sessions to solidify the day's learning. The eight-session content for parents and children is as follows:

Parents

1. Welcome to the group, review of mood symptoms and disorders
2. Review medications—general classes of medications, how to work with prescribing physicians and how to manage side effects
3. Review systems of care—school team and treatment team—learn the "players" in the system and how to develop comprehensive care teams
4. Review how mood symptoms contribute to a negative family cycle; questions and answers on the first four sessions
5. Learn and practice problem-solving skills in regard to symptom management
6. Learn and practice effective communication in regard to symptom management
7. Learn specific symptom-management techniques
8. Final review of all material; graduate

Children

1. Welcome to the group, review of mood symptoms and disorders
2. Review medications, their target symptoms, and side effects (and how to manage those)
3. Learn about and build a "tool kit" to manage emotions
4. Learn and practice the connection between thoughts, feelings, and actions
5. Learn and practice problem solving
6. Learn and practice effective nonverbal communication
7. Learn and practice effective verbal communication
8. Final review of all material (game-show format); graduate

Although data collection is ongoing, anecdotal endorsement for the intervention is strong. We ask our participants at their final session to share their words of wisdom for the next set of families who will participate in MFPG. We close with several of the children's comments:

> This place is really great. You get to learn a lot and have fun doing it. Don't forget the gym because it's very fun, but class is even funner.
>
> Nobody's judging people by who they are or where they're from. We help each other work out our problems.

Pharmacological Treatment

The clinical use of mood stabilizers and atypical antipsychotic agents in children and adolescents with bipolar disorders has increased significantly over the past few years, despite the few controlled trials in this population. Many of the same psychotropic medications used to treat adults with bipolar disorders are also used for children and adolescents. To date, there have been only two double-blind placebo-controlled studies of the treatment for acute mania in children and adolescents with bipolar disorder (DelBello, Schwiers, Rosenberg, & Strakowski, 2002; Geller et al., 1998) and one uncontrolled maintenance treatment study (Strober, Morrell, Lampert, & Burroughs, 1990).

Lithium is the most studied medication for children and adolescents with bipolar disorder and is the only medication approved by the Food and Drug Administration (FDA) for the treatment of acute mania and bipolar disorder in adolescents or children (ages 12–18 years). Approximately 40 percent to 50 percent of children and adolescents with mania or hypomania will respond to lithium monotherapy (Findling et al., 2003; Kowatch et al., 2000; Youngerman & Canino, 1978). In general, lithium should be titrated to a dose of 30 mg/kg/day in two to three divided doses, which typically results in a therapeutic serum level of 0.8–1.2 mEq/L. Common side effects of lithium in children and adolescents include hypothyroidism, nausea, polyuria, polydipsia, tremor, acne, and weight gain. Lithium levels and thyroid function tests should be monitored as in adults.

Surprisingly, despite their wide use, there are no published placebo-controlled studies of antiepileptic medications for the treatment of pediatric bipolar disorder. Open-label studies of divalproex in manic adolescents have reported response rates ranging from 53 percent to 82 percent (Kowatch et al., 2000; Papatheodorou, Kutcher, Katic, & Szala, 1995; Wagner et al., 2002; West et al., 1994). Several case reports and series have also described the successful use of carbamazepine as monotherapy and adjunctive treatment in children and adolescents with bipolar disorder (Evans, Clay, & Gualtieri, 1987; Puente, 1975). Kowatch and colleagues are currently completing a National Institutes of Mental Health (NIMH)-sponsored clinical trial of the efficacy of lithium and valproate in children and adolescents with bipolar disorder Type I. This trial will provide much-needed data about the efficacy and safety of these two widely used mood stabilizers.

Carbamazepine is used widely for seizure management but less commonly than divalproex in children and adolescents with bipolar disorder. This anticonvulsant must be titrated slowly and requires frequent monitoring of blood levels because of CYP450 drug interactions. Its most common side effects are sedation, rash, nausea, and hyponatremia. Aplastic anemia and severe dermatologic reactions such as Stevens-Johnson syndrome occur uncommonly. Because of these common and rare side effects, carbamazepine is less commonly used in children and adolescents with bipolar disorder (O'Donovan, Kusumakar, Graves, & Bird, 2002). Oxcarbazepine, an analogue of carbamazepine, is a promising agent for acute mania in adults (Hummel et al., 2001; Nassir Ghaemi, Ko, & Katzow, 2002) but no studies in children and adolescents are available.

Several new antiepileptic agents have been developed for the treatment of epilepsy that may have mood-stabilizing properties. Data are presently limited regarding the efficacy and tolerability of these agents for the treatment of pediatric bipolar disorder. However, they may be useful as adjuncts for the treatment of manic and hypomanic episodes. There have been several case reports of lamotrigine as an adjunctive treatment for children and adolescents with bipolar disorder (Kusumakar & Yatham, 1997). However, its use for pediatric bipolar disorder has been limited due to the risk of potentially lethal cutaneous reactions, such as Stevens-Johnson syndrome and toxic epidermal necrolysis. The risk of a serious rash is approximately 2–3 times greater in children and adolescents less than 16 years old compared with adults, but a recent, more conservative dosing schedule appears to have substantially reduced the rate of serious rashes (Messenheimer, 2002; Messenheimer & Guberman, 2000).

Double-blind, placebo-controlled studies of gabapentin have demonstrated that gabapentin is no more effective than placebo for the treatment of acute mania in adults (McElroy & Keck, 2000). However, gabapentin may be effective for the treatment of anxiety disorders in adults (Pande et al., 1999, 2000) and is generally well tolerated in children and adolescents. Therefore, gabapentin may be particularly useful for treating children and adolescents with bipolar disorder who are also diagnosed with a comorbid anxiety disorder. Preliminary data from open studies suggest that topiramate (Yatham et al., 2002) may be effective as an adjunctive treatment for pediatric bipolar disorder (DelBello, Kowatch, Warner, & Strakowski, 2002), although more recent double-blind, placebo-controlled studies in adults with mania suggest that as monotherapy, it is no more effective than a placebo. Word-finding difficulties have been reported in up to one third of adult patients treated with topiramate (Crawford, 1998). Topiramate is associated with anorexia and weight loss (McElroy et al., 2000) and, therefore, may be useful as an adjunctive treatment for children and adolescents with bipolar disorder who have gained weight as a result of treatment with other psychotropic medications.

The atypical antipsychotics are very powerful psychotropic agents that have recently been found to be efficacious in the treatment of adults with schizophrenia and acute bipolar mania (Glick, Murray, Vasudevan, Marder, & Hu, 2001; Kapur & Remington, 2001). These atypical agents not only have antipsychotic activity but also may possess thymoleptic properties with favorable effects on the depressive and manic symptoms of patients with bipolar disorders (Keck, McElroy, & Arnold, 2001). To date, there have been three large controlled studies of olanzapine (Berk, Ichim, & Brook, 1999; Tohen et al., 2000; Tohen et al., 1999), two controlled trials of risperidone (Sachs, Grossman, Ghaemi, Okamoto, & Bowden, 2002; Segal, Berk, & Brook, 1998), and one controlled trial of ziprasidone (Keck, Reeves, & Harrigan, 2001) in the treatment of adults with acute mania.

Several recent case series and open-label reports suggest that atypical antipsychotics clozapine (Kowatch et al., 1995), risperidone (Frazier et al., 1999), olanzapine (Chang & Ketter, 2000; Soutullo, Sorter, Foster et al., 1999), and quetiapine (DelBello, Schwiers, et al., 2002) are effective in the treatment of pediatric mania. However, significant weight gain may be associated with olanzapine and risperidone (Ratzoni et al., 2002). Ziprasidone (Weiden, 2001) can cause QTc prolongation and safety data in children and adolescents are limited. Therefore, ziprasidone should be used with caution in children and adolescents with bipolar disorder, and EKGs should be monitored at baselines and when significant dosage increases are made. In the only double-blind placebo-controlled study of an atypical antipsychotic for the treatment of bipolar adolescents, quetiapine in combination with divalproex ($n = 15$) resulted in a greater reduction of manic symptoms than divalproex monotherapy ($N = 15$), suggesting that the combination of a mood stabilizer and atypical antipsychotic is more effective than a mood stabilizer alone for the treatment of adolescent mania. In this study, quetiapine was titrated to a dose of 450 mg/day in 7 days and was well tolerated (DelBello, Schwiers, et al., 2002).

If a child or adolescent has euphoric mania without psychotic symptoms, then many times a trial of lithium is helpful. Adult patients with dysphoric mania appear to respond better to divalproex than to lithium (Swann, Bowden, Calabrese, Dilsaver, & Morris, 2002). But if psychotic symptoms are present as part of the child or adolescent's mania, then treatment with an atypical antipsychotic agent is indicated. If a patient does not respond to monotherapy with either a traditional mood stabilizer like lithium or valproate, or an atypical antipsychotic, then a combination of a traditional mood stabilizer and any atypical antipsychotic may be effective.

Most children with bipolar disorders will have comorbid ADHD. Mood stabilization with mood stabilizers or atypical antipsychotics is a necessary prerequisite to initiating stimulant medications (Biederman et al., 1999). A recent randomized controlled trial of 40 bipolar children and adolescents with ADHD demonstrated that low-dose Dexedrine can be used safely and effectively for treatment of comorbid ADHD symptoms after the child's bipolar disorder symptoms are stabilized with divalproex (Scheffer, Kowatch, Carmody, & Rush, 2005). Sustained-release psychostimulants may be more effective at reducing rebound symptoms in bipolar children and adolescents. A typical dose of such stimulants for a child with bipolar disorder and ADHD would be 36 mg/day of Concerta or 10–20 mg/day of Adderall XR.

Many agents used to treat children and adolescents with bipolar disorder are associated with weight gain. A series of general medical, metabolic problems may occur as a result of increases in weight. These include Type II (non-insulin-dependent) diabetes mellitus and changes in lipid levels and transaminase elevation (Clark & Burge, 2003; Lebovitz, 2003). Children who experience significant weight gain should be monitored closely for these possibilities and should be referred for exercise and nutritional counseling. Recently the American Diabetes Association in collaboration with the American Psychiatric Association published a monitoring protocol for all patients before initiating treatment with atypical antipsychotics (American Diabetes Association, 2004). This protocol includes inquiring about a personal and family history of obesity, diabetes, dyslipidemia, hypertension, or cardiovascular disease; measuring weight and height—so that body mass index can be calculated; measuring waist circumference (at the level of the umbilicus); monitoring blood pressure; and taking a fasting plasma glucose and a fasting lipid profile. This group recommended that the patient's weight be reassessed at 4, 8, and 12 weeks after initiating or changing therapy with an atypical antipsychotic and quarterly thereafter at the time of routine visits. A patient who gains more than 5 percent of his or her initial weight at any time during therapy should be switched to an alternative agent.

SUMMARY

Pediatric bipolar disorders are prevalent disorders that are often brought to clinical attention because of the severe mood swings and disruptive behaviors that the affected children and adolescents often have. Early recognition is key to providing effective therapy for these sick and often complicated patients. We know that bipolar disorder presents differently in children and adolescents than in adults, and the high morbidity and mortality of bipolar disorders make it important to recognize and diagnose this disorder as early as possible. It is hoped that earlier recognition and treatment of these disorders will lead to improved outcomes for these patients.

NOTE

1. Pseudonyms used to protect family members' confidentiality.

REFERENCES

Akiskal, H. S. (1995). Developmental pathways to bipolarity: Are juvenile-onset depressions pre-bipolar? *Journal of the American Academy of Child and Adolescent Psychiatry, 34,* 754–763.

Altshuler, L. L., Bartzokis, G., Grieder, T., Curran, J., & Mintz, J. (1998). Amygdala enlargement in bipolar disorder and hippocampal reduction in schizophrenia: An MRI study demonstrating neuroanatomic specificity [letter]. *Archives of General Psychiatry, 55,* 663–664.

Altshuler, L. L., Curran, J. G., Hauser, P., Mintz, J., Denicoff, K., & Post, R. (1995). T2 hyperintensities in bipolar disorder: Magnetic resonance imaging comparison and literature meta-analysis. *American Journal of Psychiatry, 152,* 1139–1144.

American Diabetes Association. (2004). Consensus development conference on antipsychotic drugs and obesity and diabetes. *Diabetes Care, 27,* 596–601.

American Psychiatric Association. (1987). *Diagnostic and statistical manual of mental disorders* (3rd ed., rev.). Washington, DC: Author.

American Psychiatric Association. (1994). *Diagnostic and statistical manual of mental disorders* (4th ed.). Washington, DC: Author.

Berk, M., Ichim, L., & Brook, S. (1999). Olanzapine compared to lithium in mania: A double-blind randomized controlled trial. *International Clinical Psychopharmacology, 14,* 339–343.

Bhangoo, R. K., Dell, M. L., Towbin, K., Myers, F. S., Lowe, C. H., Pine, D. S., et al. (2003). Clinical correlates of episodicity in juvenile mania. *Journal of Child and Adolescent Psychopharmacology, 13,* 507–514.

Biederman, J., Mick, E., Prince, J., Bostic, J. Q., Wilens, T. E., Spencer, T., et al. (1999). Systematic chart review of the pharmacologic treatment of comorbid attention deficit hyperactivity disorder in youth with bipolar disorder. *Journal of Child and Adolescent Psychopharmacology, 9,* 247–256.

Blumberg, H. P., Charney, D. S., & Krystal, J. H. (2002). Fronto-temporal neural systems in bipolar disorder. *Seminars in Clinical Neuropsychiatry, 7,* 243–254.

Botteron, K. N., Vannier, M. W., Geller, B., Todd, R. D., & Lee, B. C. (1995). Preliminary study of magnetic resonance imaging characteristics in 8- to 16-year-olds with mania. *Journal of the American Academy of Child and Adolescent Psychiatry, 34,* 742–749.

Brasic, J., Nadrich, R., & Kleinrock, S. (2001). Do families comply with child and adolescent psychopharmacology? *Child and Adolescent Psychopharmacology Update,* 6–10.

Breiter, H. C., Etcoff, N. L., Whalen, P. J., Kennedy, W. A., Rauch, S. L., Buckner, R. L., et al. (1996). Response and habituation of the human amygdala during visual processing of facial expression. *Neuron, 17,* 875–887.

Bryon, M. (1998). Adherence to treatment in medical conditions. In L. Myers & K. Midence (Eds.), *Adherence to treatment in children* (pp. 163–189). Amsterdam: Harwood Academic.

Chang, K., & Ketter, T. (2000). Mood stabilizer augmentation with olanzapine in acutely manic children. *Journal of Child and Adolescent Psychopharmacology, 10,* 45–49.

Clark, C., & Burge, M. R. (2003). Diabetes mellitus associated with atypical anti-psychotic medications. *Diabetes Technology and Therapy, 5,* 669–683.

Crawford, P. (1998). An audit of topiramate use in a general neurology clinic. *Seizure, 7,* 207–211.

Dasari, M., Friedman, L., Jesberger, J., Stuve, T. A., Findling, R. L., Swales, T. P., et al. (1999). A magnetic resonance imaging study of thalamic area in adolescent patients with either schizophrenia or bipolar disorder as compared to healthy controls. *Psychiatry Research, 91,* 155–162.

DelBello, M. P., & Geller, B. (2001). Review of studies of child and adolescent offspring of bipolar parents. *Bipolar Disorders, 3,* 325–334.

DelBello, M., Kowatch, R., Warner, J., & Strakowski, S. (2002). Topiramate treatment for pediatric bipolar disorder: A retrospective chart review. *Journal of Child and Adolescent Psychopharmacology, 12,* 323–330.

DelBello, M., Schwiers, M., Rosenberg, H., & Strakowski, S. (2002). Quetiapine as adjunctive treatment for adolescent mania associated with bipolar disorder. *Journal of the American Academy of Child and Adolescent Psychiatry, 41,* 1216–1223.

DelBello, M. P., Strakowski, S. M., Zimmerman, M. E., Hawkins, J. M., & Sax, K. W. (1999). MRI analysis of the cerebellum in bipolar disorder: A pilot study. *Neuropsychopharmacology, 21,* 63–68.

Drevets, W. C., Price, J. L., Simpson, J. R., Jr., Todd, R. D., Reich, T., Vannier, M., et al. (1997). Subgenual prefrontal cortex abnormalities in mood disorders. *Nature, 386,* 824–827.

Ekman, P., & Oster, H. (1979). Facial expressions of emotion. *Annual Review of Psychology, 30,* 527–554.

Evans, R. W., Clay, T. H., & Gualtieri, C. T. (1987). Carbamazepine in pediatric psychiatry. *Journal of the American Academy of Child and Adolescent Psychiatry, 26,* 2–8.

Findling, R. L., Gracious, B. L., McNamara, N. K., Youngstrom, E. A., Demeter, C. A., Branicky, L. A., et al. (2001). Rapid, continuous cycling and psychiatric co-morbidity in pediatric bipolar I disorder. *Bipolar Disorders, 3,* 202–210.

Findling, R. L., McNamara, N. K., Gracious, B. L., Youngstrom, E. A., Stansbrey, R. J., Reed, M. D., et al. (2003). Combination lithium and divalproex sodium in pediatric bipolarity. *Journal of the American Academy of Child and Adolescent Psychiatry, 42,* 895–901.

Frazier, J., Meyer, M., Biederman, J., Wozniak, J., Wilens, T., Spencer, T., et al. (1999). Risperidone treatment for juvenile bipolar disorder: A retrospective chart review. *Journal of the American Academy of Child and Adolescent Psychiatry, 38,* 960–965.

Friedman, L., Findling, R. L., Kenny, J. T., Swales, T. P., Stuve, T. A., Jesberger, J. A., et al. (1999). An MRI study of adolescent patients with either schizophrenia or bipolar disorder as compared to healthy control subjects [published erratum appears in *Biological Psychiatry, 46*(4), following 584]. *Biological Psychiatry, 46,* 78–88.

Fristad, M. A., & Goldberg-Arnold, J. S. (2002). Working with families of children with early-onset bipolar disorder. In B. Geller & M. DelBello (Eds.), *Child and early adolescent bipolar disorder: Theory, assessment, and treatment.* New York: Guilford Press.

Fristad, M. A., Goldberg-Arnold, J. S., Gavazzi, S. M., Mackinaw-Koons, B., Shaver, A. E., Cerel, J., et al. (2003). Multi-family psychoeducation groups in the treatment of children with mood disorders. *Journal of Marital and Family Therapy, 29,* 491–504.

Geller, B., Bolhofner, K., Craney, J., Williams, M., Del, B. M., & Gundersen, K. (2000a). Psychosocial functioning in a prepubertal and early adolescent bipolar disorder phenotype. *Journal of the American Academy of Child and Adolescent Psychiatry, 39,* 1543–1548.

Geller, B., & Cook, E. H., Jr. (1999). Serotonin transporter gene (HTTLPR) is not in linkage disequilibrium with prepubertal and early adolescent bipolarity. *Biological Psychiatry, 45,* 1230–1233.

Geller, B., & Cook, E. H., Jr. (2000). Ultradian rapid cycling in prepubertal and early adolescent bipolarity is not in transmission disequilibrium with val/met COMT alleles. *Biological Psychiatry, 47,* 605–609.

Geller, B., Cooper, T. B., Sun, K., Zimerman, M. A., Frazier, J., Williams, M., et al. (1998). Double-blind and placebo-controlled study of lithium for adolescent bipolar disorders with secondary substance dependency. *Journal of the American Academy of Child and Adolescent Psychiatry, 37,* 171–178.

Geller, B., Craney, J. L., Bolhofner, K., Nickelsburg, M. J., Williams, M., & Zimerman, B. (2002). Two-year prospective follow-up of children with a prepubertal and early adolescent bipolar disorder phenotype. *American Journal of Psychiatry, 159,* 927–933.

Geller, B., & Luby, J. (1997a). Child and adolescent bipolar disorder: A review of the past 10 years. *Journal of the American Academy of Child and Adolescent Psychiatry, 36,* 1168–1176.

Geller, B., & Luby, J. (1997b). Child and adolescent bipolar disorder: A review of the past 10 years [see comments] [published erratum appears in *Journal of the American Academy of Child and Adolescent Psychiatry, 36*(11), 1642]. *Journal of the American Academy of Child and Adolescent Psychiatry, 36,* 1168–1176.

Geller, B., Sun, K., Zimerman, B., Luby, J., Frazier, J., & Williams, M. (1995). Complex and rapid-cycling in bipolar children and adolescents: A preliminary study. *Journal of Affective Disorders, 34,* 259–268.

Geller, B., Tillman, R., Craney, J. L., & Bolhofner, K. (2004). Four-year prospective outcome and natural history of mania in children with a prepubertal and early adolescent bipolar disorder phenotype. *Archives of General Psychiatry, 61,* 459–467.

Geller, B., Zimerman, B., Williams, M., Bolhofner, K., Craney, J., Delbello, M., & Soutullo, C. (2000). Diagnostic characteristics of 93 cases of a prepubertal and early adolescent bipolar disorder phenotype by gender, puberty and comorbid attention deficit hyperactivity disorder. *Journal of Child and Adolescent Psychopharmacology, 10,* 157–164.

Glick, I., Murray, S., Vasudevan, P., Marder, S., & Hu, R. (2001). Treatment with atypical antipsychotics: New indications and new populations. *Journal of Psychiatric Research, 35,* 187–191.

Goldberg-Arnold, J. S., & Fristad, M. A. (2002). Psychotherapy with children diagnosed with early-onset bipolar disorder. In B. Geller & M. DelBello (Eds.), *Child and early adolescent bipolar disorder: Theory, assessment, and treatment.* New York: Guilford Press.

Goodwin, F. K., & Jamison, K. R. (1990). *Manic-depressive illness.* New York: Oxford University Press.

Gur, R. C., Erwin, R. J., & Gur, R. E. (1992). Neurobehavioral probes for physiologic neuroimaging studies. *Archives of General Psychiatry, 49,* 409–414.

Hatfield, A. (1997). Families of adults with severe mental illness: New directions in research. *American Journal of Orthopsychiatry, 67,* 254–260.

Hellander, M., Sisson, D. P., & Fristad, M. A. (2002). Internet support for parents of children with early-onset bipolar disorder. In B. Geller & M. DelBello (Eds.), *Child and early adolescent bipolar disorder: Theory, assessment, and treatment.* New York: Guilford Press.

Hummel, B., Stampfer, R., Grunze, H., Schlosser, S., Amann, B., Frye, M., et al. (2001). Acute antimanic efficacy and safety of oxcarbazepine in and open trial with on-off-on design. *Bipolar Disorders, 3*(Suppl. 1), 43.

Isaac, G. (1992). Misdiagnosed bipolar disorder in adolescents in a special educational school and treatment program. *Journal of Clinical Psychiatry, 53,* 133–136.

Kapur, S., & Remington, G. (2001). Atypical antipsychotics: New directions and new challenges in the treatment of schizophrenia. *Annual Review of Medicine, 52,* 503–517.

Kashani, J. H., Beck, N. C., Hoeper, E. W., Fallahi, C., Corcoran, C. M., McAllister, J. A., et al. (1987). Psychiatric disorders in a community sample of adolescents. *American Journal of Psychiatry, 144,* 584–589.

Keck, P. J., McElroy, S., & Arnold, L. (2001). Bipolar disorder. *Medical Clinics of North America, 85,* 645–661, ix.

Keck, P. J., Reeves, K., & Harrigan, E. (2001). Ziprasidone in the short-term treatment of patients with schizoaffective disorder: Results from two double-blind, placebo-controlled, multicenter studies. *Journal of Clinical Psychopharmacology, 21,* 27–35.

Kelsoe, J. R., Kristbjanarson, H., Bergesch, P., Shilling, P., Hirsch, S., Mirow, A., et al. (1993). A genetic linkage study of bipolar disorder and 13 markers on chromosome 11 including the d2 dopamine receptor. *Neuropsychopharmacology, 9,* 293–301.

Kovacs, M. (1996). Presentation and course of major depressive disorder during childhood and later years of the life span. *Journal of the American Academy of Child and Adolescent Psychiatry, 35,* 705–715.

Kovacs, M., & Pollock, M. (1995). Bipolar disorder and comorbid conduct disorder in childhood and adolescence. *Journal of the American Academy of Child and Adolescent Psychiatry, 34,* 715–723.

Kowatch, R. A., Fristad, M. A., Birmaher, B., Wagner, K. D., Findling, R. L., & Hellander, M. (2005). Treatment guidelines for children and adolescents with bipolar disorder. *Journal of the American Academy of Child and Adolescent Psychiatry, 44,* 213–235.

Kowatch, R. A., Suppes, T., Carmody, T. J., Bucci, J. P., Hume, J. H., Kromelis, M., et al. (2000). Effect size of lithium, divalproex sodium and carbamazepine in children and adolescents with bipolar disorder. *Journal of the American Academy of Child and Adolescent Psychiatry, 39,* 713–720.

Kowatch, R. A., Suppes, T., Gilfillan, S. K., Fuentes, R. M., Bruce, D., Grannemann, M. S., et al. (1995). Clozapine treatment of children and adolescents with bipolar disorder and schizophrenia: A clinical case series. *Journal of the American Academy of Child and Adolescent Psychopharmacology, 5,* 241–253.

Kusumakar, V., & Yatham, L. N. (1997). An open study of lamotrigine in refractory bipolar depression. *Psychiatric Research, 72,* 145–148.

Lawrence, N. S., Williams, A.M., Surguladze, S., Giampietro, V., Brammer, M. J., Andrew, C., et al. (2004). Subcortical and ventral prefrontal cortical neural responses to facial expressions distinguish patients with bipolar disorder and major depression. *Biological Psychiatry, 55,* 578–587.

Lebovitz, H. E. (2003). Metabolic consequences of atypical antipsychotic drugs. *Psychiatry Quarterly, 74,* 277–290.

Lewinsohn, P.M., Klein, D. N., & Seeley, J. R. (1995). Bipolar disorders in a community sample of older adolescents: Prevalence, phenomenology, comorbidity, and course. *Journal of the American Academy of Child and Adolescent Psychiatry, 34,* 454–463.

MacQueen, G., Young, L., Robb, J., Marriott, M., Cooke, R., & Joffe, R. (2000). Effect of number of episodes on wellbeing and functioning of patients with bipolar disorder. *Acta Psychiatrica Scandinavia, 101,* 374–381.

Mayberg, H. S. (1997). Limbic-cortical dysregulation: A proposed model of depression. *Journal of Neuropsychiatry and Clinical Neuroscience, 9,* 471–481.

McElroy, S. L., & Keck, P. E., Jr. (2000). Pharmacologic agents for the treatment of acute bipolar mania. *Biological Psychiatry, 48,* 539–557.

McElroy, S. L., Suppes, T., Keck, P. E., Frye, M. A., Denicoff, K. D., Altshuler, L. L., et al. (2000). Open-label adjunctive topiramate in the treatment of bipolar disorders. *Biological Psychiatry, 47,* 1025–1033.

McGlashen, T. H. (1988). Adolescent versus adult onset of mania. *American Journal of Psychiatry, 145,* 221–223.

Messenheimer, J. (2002). Efficacy and safety of lamotrigine in pediatric patients. *Journal of Child Neurology, 17*(Suppl. 2), 2S34–32S42.

Messenheimer, J. A., & Guberman, A. H. (2000). Rash with lamotrigine: Dosing guidelines. *Epilepsia, 41,* 488.

Miklowitz, D. J., George, E. L., Richards, J. A., Simoneau, T. L., & Suddath, R. L. (2003). A randomized study of family-focused psychoeducation and pharmacotherapy in the outpatient management of bipolar disorder. *Archives of General Psychiatry, 60,* 904–912.

Morris, J. S., Frith, C. D., Perrett, D. I., Rowland, D., Young, A. W., Calder, A. J., et al. (1996). A differential neural response in the human amygdala to fearful and happy facial expressions. *Nature, 383,* 812–815.

Nassir Ghaemi, S., Ko, J. Y., & Katzow, J. J. (2002). Oxcarbazepine treatment of refractory bipolar disorder: A retrospective chart review. *Bipolar Disorders, 4,* 70–74.

O'Donovan, C., Kusumakar, V., Graves, G. R., & Bird, D.C. (2002). Menstrual abnormalities and polycystic ovary syndrome in women taking valproate for bipolar mood disorder. *Journal of Clinical Psychiatry, 63,* 322–330.

Pande, A. C., Davidson, J. R., Jefferson, J. W., Janney, C. A., Katzelnick, D. J., Weisler, R. H., et al. (1999). Treatment of social phobia with gabapentin: A placebo-controlled study. *Journal of Clinical Psychopharmacology, 19,* 341–348.

Pande, A. C., Pollack, M. H., Crockatt, J., Greiner, M., Chouinard, G., Lydiard, R. B., et al. (2000). Placebo-controlled study of gabapentin treatment of panic disorder. *Journal of Clinical Psychopharmacology, 20,* 467–471.

Papalos, D., & Papalos, J. (2002). *The bipolar child* (2nd ed.). New York: Broadway Books.

Papatheodorou, G., Kutcher, S. P., Katic, M., & Szalai, J. P. (1995). The efficacy and safety of divalproex sodium in the treatment of acute mania in adolescents and young adults: An open clinical trial. *Journal of Clinical Psychopharmacology, 15,* 110–116.

Pavuluri, M. N., Graczyk, P. A., Henry, D. B., Carbray, J. A., Heidenreich, J., & Miklowitz, D. J. (2004). Child- and family-focused cognitive-behavioral therapy for pediatric bipolar disorder: Development and preliminary results. *Journal of the American Academy of Child and Adolescent Psychiatry, 43,* 528–537.

Phillips, M. L., Young, A. W., Senior, C., Brammer, M., Andrew, C., Calder, A. J., et al. (1997). A specific neural substrate for perceiving facial expressions of disgust. *Nature, 389,* 495–498.

Post, R. M., & Weiss, S. R. (1996). A speculative model of affective illness cyclicity based on patterns of drug tolerance observed in amygdala-kindled seizures. *Molecular Neurobiology, 13,* 33-60.

Puente, R. M. (1975). The use of carbamazepine in the treatment of behavioural disorders in children. In W. Birkmayer (Ed.), *Epileptic seizures—behaviour—pain* (pp. 243–252). Baltimore: University Park Press.

Ratzoni, G., Gothelf, D., Brand-Gothelf, A., Reidman, J., Kikinzon, L., Gal, G., et al. (2002). Weight gain associated with olanzapine and risperidone in adolescent patients: A comparative prospective study. *Journal of the American Academy of Child and Adolescent Psychiatry, 41,* 337–343.

Renshaw, P. F., Yurgelun-Todd, D. A., Tohen, M., Gruber, S., & Cohen, B. M. (1995). Temporal lobe proton magnetic resonance spectroscopy of patients with first-episode psychosis. *American Journal of Psychiatry, 152,* 444–446.

Robb, J., Cooke, R., Devins, G., Young, L., & Joffe, R. (1997). Quality of life and lifestyle disruption in euthymic bipolar disorder. *Journal of Psychiatry Research, 31,* 509–517.

Sachs, G. S., Grossman, F., Ghaemi, S. N., Okamoto, A., & Bowden, C. L. (2002). Combination of a mood stabilizer with risperidone or haloperidol for treatment of acute mania: A double-blind, placebo-controlled comparison of efficacy and safety. *American Journal of Psychiatry, 159,* 1146–1154.

Sax, K. W., Strakowski, S. M., Zimmerman, M. E., DelBello, M. P., Keck, P. E., Jr., & Hawkins, J. M. (1999). Frontosubcortical neuroanatomy and the continuous performance test in mania. *American Journal of Psychiatry, 156,* 139–141.

Scheffer, R., Kowatch, R., Carmody, T., & Rush, A. (2005). A randomized placebo-controlled trial of adderall for symptoms of comorbid ADHD in pediatric bipolar disorder following mood stabilization with divalproex sodium. *American Journal of Psychiatry, 162,* 58-64..

Segal, J., Berk, M., & Brook, S. (1998). Risperidone compared with both lithium and haloperidol in mania: A double-blind randomized controlled trial. *Clinical Neuropharmacology, 21,* 176–180.

Soares, J. C., Krishnan, K. R., & Keshavan, M. S. (1996). Nuclear magnetic resonance spectroscopy: New insights into the pathophysiology of mood disorders. *Depression, 4,* 14–30.

Soares, J. C., & Mann, J. J. (1997). The anatomy of mood disorders—review of structural neuroimaging studies. *Biological Psychiatry, 41,* 86–106.

Soutullo, C., Sorter, M., Foster, K., McElroy, S., & Keck, P. (1999). Olanzapine in the treatment of adolescent acute mania: A report of seven cases. *Journal of Affective Disorders, 53,* 279–283.

Strakowski, S., DelBello, M., Adler, C., Cecil, D., & Sax, K. (2000). Neuroimaging in bipolar disorder. *Bipolar Disorders, 2*(3, Pt. 1), 148–164.

Strakowski, S. M., DelBello, M. P., Sax, K. W., Zimmerman, M. E., Shear, P. K., Hawkins, J. M., et al. (1999). Brain magnetic resonance imaging of structural abnormalities in bipolar disorder. *Archives of General Psychiatry, 56,* 254–260.

Strakowski, S. M., DelBello, M. P., Zimmerman, M. E., Getz, G. E., Mills, N. P., Ret, J., et al. (2002). Ventricular and periventricular structural volumes in first- versus multiple-episode bipolar disorder. *American Journal of Psychiatry, 159,* 1841–1847.

Strakowski, S. M., Woods, B. T., Tohen, M., Wilson, D. R., Douglass, A. W., & Stoll, A. L. (1993). MRI subcortical signal hyperintensities in mania at first hospitalization. *Biological Psychiatry, 33,* 204–206.

Strober, M., Morrell, W., Lampert, C., & Burroughs, J. (1990). Relapse following discontinuation of lithium maintenance therapy in adolescents with bipolar I illness: A naturalistic study. *American Journal of Psychiatry, 147,* 457–461.

Swann, A. C., Bowden, C. L., Calabrese, J. R., Dilsaver, S. C., & Morris, D. D. (2002). Pattern of response to divalproex, lithium, or placebo in four naturalistic subtypes of mania. *Neuropsychopharmacology, 26,* 530–536.

Tillman, R., Geller, B., Craney, J. L., Bolhofner, K., Williams, M., Zimerman, B., et al. (2003). Temperament and character factors in a prepubertal and early adolescent bipolar disorder phenotype compared to attention deficit hyperactive and normal controls. *Journal of Child and Adolescent Psychopharmacology, 13,* 531–543.

Tohen, M., Jacobs, T. G., Grundy, S. L., McElroy, S. L., Banov, M. C., Janicak, P. G., et al. (2000). Efficacy of olanzapine in acute bipolar mania: A double-blind, placebo-controlled study. *Archives of General Psychiatry, 57,* 841–849.

Tohen, M., Sanger, T., McElroy, S., Tollefson, G., Chengappa, K., Daniel, D., et al. (1999). Olanzapine versus placebo in the treatment of acute mania. Olanzapine HGEH study group. *American Journal of Psychiatry, 156,* 702–709.

Tohen, M., Waternaux, C., Tsuang, M., & Hunt, A. (1990). Four-year follow-up of twenty-four first-episode manic patients. *Journal of Affective Disorders, 19,* 79–86.

Tumuluru, R. V., Weller, E. B., Fristad, M. A., & Weller, R. A. (2003). Mania in six preschool children. *Journal of Child and Adolescent Psychopharmacology, 13,* 489–494.

Wagner, K. D., Weller, E., Biederman, J., Carlson, G. A., Frazier, J., Wozniak, J., et al. (2002). An open-label trial of divalproex in children and adolescents with bipolar disorder. *Journal of the American Academy of Child and Adolescent Psychiatry, 41,* 1224–1230.

Weiden, P. (2001). Ziprasidone: A new atypical antipsychotic. *Journal of Psychiatric Practice,* 145–153.

West, S. A., Keck, P. E. J., McElroy, S. L., Strakowski, S. M., Minnery, K. L., McConville, B. J., et al. (1994). Open trial of valproate in the treatment of adolescent mania. *Journal of Child and Adolescent Psychopharmacology, 4,* 263–267.

West, S. A., McElroy, S. L., Strakowski, S. M., Keck, P. E., Jr., & McConville, B. J. (1995). Attention deficit hyperactivity disorder in adolescent mania. *American Journal of Psychiatry, 152,* 271–273.

Wilens, T. E., Biederman, J., Forkner, P., Ditterline, J., Morris, M., Moore, H., et al. (2003). Patterns of comorbidity and dysfunction in clinically referred preschool and school-age children with bipolar disorder. *Journal of Child and Adolescent Psychopharmacology, 13,* 495–505.

Woods, B. T., Yurgelun-Todd, D., Mikulis, D., & Pillay, S. S. (1995). Age-related MRI abnormalities in bipolar illness: A clinical study. *Biological Psychiatry, 38,* 846–847.

Wozniak, J., & Biederman, J. (1997). Childhood mania: Insights into diagnostic and treatment issues. *Journal of the Association for Academic Minority Physicians, 8,* 78–84.

Wozniak, J., Biederman, J., Kiely, K., Ablon, J. S., Faraone, S. V., Mundy, E., et al. (1995). Mania-like symptoms suggestive of childhood-onset bipolar disorder in clinically referred children. *Journal of the American Academy of Child and Adolescent Psychiatry, 34,* 867–876.

Yatham, L. N., Kusumakar, V., Calabrese, J. R., Rao, R., Scarrow, G., & Kroeker, G. (2002). Third generation anticonvulsants in bipolar disorder: A review of efficacy and summary of clinical recommendations. *Journal of Clinical Psychiatry, 63,* 275–283.

Youngerman, J., & Canino, I. A. (1978). Lithium carbonate use in children and adolescents. A survey of the literature. *Archives of General Psychiatry, 35,* 216–224.

Yurgelun-Todd, D., Gruber, S., Kanayama, W., Baird, A., & Young, A. (2000). FMRI during affect discrimination in bipolar affective disorder. *Bipolar Disorders, 2,* 237–248.

CHAPTER 14

Mental Retardation

JAMES M. BEBKO AND JONATHAN A. WEISS

DESCRIPTION OF THE DISORDER AND CLINICAL PICTURE

Mental retardation has been characterized by a number of different terms over the past five decades: *intellectual disability, intellectual handicap,* and *general learning disorder* are some examples (Leonard & Wen, 2002). In this chapter we will use the term mental retardation (MR) throughout, as that is the current entry that appears in the *Diagnostic and Statistical Manual of Mental Disorders* (*DSM-IV*; American Psychiatric Association [APA], 1994).

There is often a tendency for what is meant as a descriptive term to become prescriptive, the labels themselves often coming to be used as if they tell us all or much of what we need to know about the target group. Mental retardation is one of these terms. However, MR is more accurately viewed as a heterogeneous group of conditions that all result in cognitive and functional limitation (Murphy, Boyle, Schendel, Decoufle, & Yeargin-Allsopp, 1998). As will be discussed, MR has hundreds of causes, and it follows that, as a group, individuals with MR show tremendous variability in their cognitive, emotional, and social development (Ratey et al., 2000).

In the *DSM-IV* MR is defined by significantly below average general intellectual functioning (operationalized as 2 standard deviations below the average IQ score of 100; Criterion A) that is accompanied by significant limitations in adaptive functioning (Criterion B), and that occurs before the age of 18 years (Criterion C). Other diagnostic systems (e.g., *ICD-10* [World Health Organization, 1992]; American Association on Mental Retardation [AAMR; Luckasson et al., 2002]) also reflect the three aforementioned criteria. MR is often subclassified into four categories by the severity of intellectual impairment: mild (IQ scores between approximately 55 and 70), moderate (IQ scores between 40 and 55), severe (IQ scores between 25 and 40), and profound (IQ scores <25; APA, 1994).

Psychopathology in Mental Retardation

In many texts on childhood psychopathology, MR has been listed as one of the psychopathologies, along with behavioral disorders, emotional disorders, and so forth. However, more recent views identify MR as a typical manifestation of development, simply representing those individuals clustered toward the lower end of the distribution of intellectual and adaptive skills. The term psychopathology is more properly used to describe the presence of mental illness, psychiatric symptoms, or mental or emotional disorders in an individual, whether with MR or without. Historically it was also common to err by attributing psychopathology found in individuals with MR to their intellectual disability, known as diagnostic overshadowing (Dykens & Hodapp, 2001). In more recent years the focus on dual diagnosis has become more prominent, with professionals viewing psychiatric disorder as a separate construct in individuals with MR (O'Brien, 2002).

Individuals with MR tend to exhibit the same kinds of psychopathology as individuals without MR, including psychoses, mood, personality, adjustment, and behavior disorders (Bebko et al., 1998). The clinical-medical approach and the psychometric-empirical approach have both been used to determine psychopathology in MR, and each is fraught with its own set of complications (Wallander, Dekker, & Koot, 2003). The clinical-medical approach, seen in taxonomies such as the *DSM-IV* and *ICD-10,* set clinical symptoms that must be present or not in order to determine a formal discrete diagnosis. The psychometric-empirical system uses statistically derived rating scales typically completed by an informant other than the individual with MR. These scales typically rate behaviors that have been linked to mental illness, such as anxious or aggressive behavior, in terms of their presence, their intensity, or both. This system often results in a more continuous indicator of degree of psychopathology than the clinical-medical approach.

A review of studies of personality disorders in MR led Alexander and Cooray (2003) to suggest that the ability to diagnose personality disorder in mental retardation is not a clear science. They suggested that difficulties are caused by inadequacies in personality conceptualization and instrumentation for individuals with MR; insufficient diagnostic criteria; and communication, sensory, and behavioral disorders associated with intellectual disability that overlap with or confound symptoms of personality disorder. For example, self-injurious behaviors, impulsivity, and emotional lability are often seen in individuals with MR and are also noted as features of borderline personality disorder. Therefore, the prevalence rates cited in research on dual diagnosis in MR must be interpreted with caution.

A number of causal variables are related to the higher rate of psychopathology in individuals with MR. Early common approaches to understanding the psychopathology-MR association have been unidimensional in nature, citing organic dysfunction such as brain damage (Chess, 1977), products of genetic syndromes (O'Brien, 2002), or environmental stressors and family adjustment (Nihira, Meyers, & Mink, 1980). Transactional models have been proposed to attempt to better explain the rise in psychopathology by outlining the dynamic interaction between risk factors intrinsic in individuals with MR and those external to them (i.e., factors in the environment; Bebko et al., 1998). In fact, Dykens and Hodapp (2001) suggested a number of correlated risk factors that lie upon the biopsychosocial spectrum. Many of these risk factors are linked to personality development in individuals with mental retardation, which is discussed in the following sections.

Given the tremendous heterogeneity in the etiology of MR itself, it is fitting that no one pattern of particular psychopathology appears to be associated with overall intellectual disability. At the same time, particular genetic etiological syndromes do show patterns of psychopathology or personality, known as the behavioral phenotype, at least when measured psychometrically (Dykens, 2001; Tonge & Einfeld, 2003).

PERSONALITY DEVELOPMENT AND PSYCHOPATHOLOGY

To understand personality development in individuals with MR, we need to first come to an understanding of what is meant by *personality*. Most authors agree that personality is made up of relatively enduring patterns of cognition, affect, and behavior (McCrae, 2001; Roberts & Caspi, 2001; see Lewis, 2001, for an exception). Others agree with this basic definition, but they either add that motivation should be an integral component of the personality system (Judge & Ilies, 2002; MacDonald, 1995) or they place special emphasis on the importance of interactions with other people (Lewis, 2001; Zayas, Shoda, & Ayduk, 2002). It appears, therefore, that recent conceptualizations of personality encompass a panoply of many psychological domains, including cognition, emotion, behavior, and motivation.

The Sociocognitive View and the Developmental Approach to Personality in Mental Retardation

The sociocognitive theory of personality attempts to understand the affective and cognitive interactions that give rise to consistencies in behavior (Cervone & Shoda, 1999). Many factors moderate personality continuity and change throughout the life span, and these can be most aptly summarized as an ongoing person- (and gene-) environmental transaction (Roberts & Caspi, 2001). By taking a developmental perspective and focusing on the effect that life experiences have on the personality traits exhibited by people with MR, and on how these personality traits in turn influence future experiences, we are able to form a more complete conceptualization of the individual with MR, as Zigler and Hodapp (1986) termed it, seeing "the whole person." The life histories of children with MR may not be equivalent to the experiences of children without MR, and the development of personality-motivational traits can be affected accordingly.

The Traditional Domains of Personality

In the non-MR literature, the most commonly examined traits are known as the Big Five: extraversion, openness, neuroticism, conscientiousness, and agreeableness (Costa & McCrae, 1992). As Judge and Ilies (2002) suggested: "If a consensual structure of traits is ever to emerge, the five factor model is probably it" (p. 798). Despite this apparent support, there is still considerable debate over the validity of openness, conscientiousness, and agreeableness as separate constructs (Eysenck, 1992). However, extraversion and neuroticism are consistently present in most models of personality. Compared to individuals low in neuroticism, highly neurotic individuals are seen as being poorly adjusted in terms of stress, anxiety, and depression and are highly emotional. In general, highly extraverted individuals are defined as being very sociable, positive, and outgoing, whereas highly introverted individuals are seen as less sociable and more focused internally.

Despite the vast literature examining traditional personality constructs in non-MR populations, only a handful of studies over four decades have explicitly looked at factor traits in individuals with MR. Of the studies that do exist, most are limited to extraversion and neuroticism. There exist a greater number of studies that look at particular affective domains, such as anxiety and depression. However, nearly all appear to be in terms of psychiatric disturbances and dual diagnosis (e.g., Esbensen, Rojahn, Aman, & Ruedrich, 2003), and few look at these aspects in terms of traditional personality factors.

Some have suggested that this dearth of literature is due to measurement difficulties (Zigler, Bennett-Gates, Hodapp, & Henrich, 2002) or to the research emphasis placed on the cognitive differences between MR and non-MR populations (Zigler, 2001). As Dykens (2001) aptly notes, the study of typical personality development in people with genetic MR is even more lacking than in familial MR, due to the focus placed on the increased prevalence of psychopathology or maladaptive behavior in this population. It is clear that traditional models of personality have not been readily applied to MR populations. In addition, most of the research that had been conducted before the 1980s used institutionalized individuals, making generalization to individuals living in the present community-care paradigm tenuous.

Alternative Personality Domains

For more than four decades, Zigler and his colleagues have been suggesting alternative personality constructs to explain performance and behavior in individuals with MR (see Switzky, 2001; Zigler & Bennett-Gates, 1999, for a comprehensive review). The authors take a developmental approach, largely focus on familial MR, and suggest that their personality constructs are a result of four causal life experience factors highly relevant in the past (especially within the zeitgeist of institutionalization) and still bearing weight in the present. The first such experiential factor is that the lives of individuals with MR are often marked by repeated failure to succeed in the academic, social, or work milieu. Second, those with MR may have experienced social deprivation, such as from a lack of continuity of care or an impoverished family or institutional environment. Third, along with this social deprivation, they may have experienced consistent disapproval from socialization agents (i.e., their caregivers, siblings, and peers). And finally, they are intellectually impaired and have inefficient learning strategies.

Zigler and his colleagues suggest that two social-related and three task-related personality traits are highly relevant to individuals with MR and are influenced by these experiences. They recently published a questionnaire with psychometric properties supporting the validity of the constructs, at least with individuals with mild familial MR (the EZ-Yale Personality Questionnaire [EZPQ]; Zigler et al., 2002). These constructs share considerable overlap with other conceptualizations of personality and motivational functioning, and these commonalities will be discussed next. As well, Dykens (1999) has suggested a number of intriguing behavioral phenotypes that could also be characterized by these personality traits, and when applicable, these will be included.

Social-Related Personality Domains

Positive Reaction Tendency

One of the first traits suggested is the tendency for an individual to be highly motivated to maintain social interaction with supportive adults, deemed positive reaction. An extreme positive reaction tendency is thought to be brought about by social deprivation (Balla, Butterfield, & Zigler, 1974; Gayton & Bassett, 1972; Harter & Zigler, 1968). In its extreme, this desire manifests as poor social skills, social disinhibition, extreme extraversion, and a dependent or anxious personality (Dykens, 1999). In terms of clustering to any one behavioral phenotype, Dykens (1999) suggested that positive reaction tendencies are prevalent in individuals with Williams syndrome, in that these individuals are often described as being socially disinhibited, anxious, outgoing, and interpersonally oriented (Pober & Dykens, 1996; Tonge & Einfeld, 2003).

Negative Reaction Tendency

Negative reaction tendency is the tendency to be shy of strangers and to be wary, fearful, or mistrustful in social interactions (Harter & Zigler, 1968; Zigler, Balla, & Butterfield, 1968). In the extreme, behaviors might be seen as avoidant, socially inhibited or phobic, or autistic-like (Dykens, 1999) and are thought to be brought about by social deprivation, aversive encounters with strangers, and negative social and family histories. Negative reactions, such as problems with social relationships, an initial wariness of strangers, and withdrawal, are commonly found in individuals with fragile X syndrome (Dykens, 1999; Dykens, Hodapp, & Leckman, 1994). When compared to children without MR, children with fragile X syndrome show significantly greater degrees of socially avoidant behavior (Tonge & Einfeld, 2003).

Positive and negative reaction tendencies are not thought to be mutually exclusive, nor are they thought to lie on one continuum. In fact, the psychometric analysis of the EZPQ found no significant correlation between positive and negative reaction scale scores (Zigler et al., 2002). Thus, an individual might be found to exhibit both positive and negative reaction tendencies and an extreme ambivalence to others.

Task-Related Personality Domains

Zigler et al. (2002) outlined three interrelated, task-focused personality domains, and each is discussed individually here. All three, expectancy of success, outerdirectedness, and effectance motivation, focus on coping with tasks, and all are significantly intercorrelated (all $p < .01$) on the EZPQ, with the strongest correlation between expectancy of success and effectance motivation ($r = .52$).

Expectancy of Success

Expectancy of success (ES) is the tendency to expect to succeed (or fail) when presented with a novel task, and it is believed to be determined by the degree to which one experiences success at tasks (Hoffman & Weiner, 1978; MacMillan & Keogh, 1971). An extreme expectation of failure can result in learned helplessness, a failure-avoiding orientation, affective disturbances (e.g., depression), behavioral disruption, and low self-esteem and self-competence (Dykens, 1999). Though an extremely low ES is possible in any individual experiencing high incidences of failure, individuals with Prader-Willi syndrome have been identified as particularly prone, due to their continued lifelong failure in attempting to control their obsession over food (i.e., hyperphagia; Dykens, 1999; see also Curfs, Hoondert, van Lieshout, & Fryns, 1995).

Switzky (2001) highlights the influence of social learning and locus of control on the formation of ES in his summation of the literature on success striving versus failure avoiding. According to Weiner (cited in Switzky, 2001), locus of control includes the degree of attribution about (a) whether an outcome is due to an internal or external cause (e.g., success or failure based on effort or luck), (b) whether that cause is permanent or impermanent, and (c) the amount of perceived control over the cause (e.g., a lot of control over effort vs. none, based on luck). Individuals who expect to fail have failure-avoiding tendencies, are failure prone, and attribute failure to an internal permanent cause (e.g., lack of ability) and success to an external impermanent cause (e.g., luck). Conversely, individuals who are success seeking expect to succeed more and have internal attributions regarding success (Switzky, 2001).

Considerable evidence suggests that experiences of consistent failure and a low probability of control orient a person to a more negative expectancy outlook (Weisz, 1999). Individuals with MR may have lower beliefs of control over task mastery compared to non-MR peers and, combined with experiences of failure, may be particularly prone to learned helplessness and low ES (MacMillan & Keogh, 1971). A recent comparison of students aged 10–12 with MR, with learning disabilities, and with no disabilities found that children with MR were significantly more externally oriented on measures of locus of control for academic achievement (Wehmeyer & Palmer, 1997). Weisz (1999) further suggested that, along with the increased failure experienced by individuals with MR, helplessness is reinforced by non-MR individuals who lower their performance expectations and attribute failure by the individual with MR to the disability rather than to a lack of effort.

Outerdirectedness

Outerdirectedness (OD) is the tendency to look to others for solutions to difficult problems and is a factor negatively related to both expectancy of success and achievement (Bybee & Zigler, 1999). It is characterized by an overreliance on external cues and a distrust of inner-derived solutions. In its extreme, OD can lead to a general dependence on others for regulation and direction, impulsive problem solving and attention deficits, and low self-worth (Dykens, 1999). Dykens (1999) suggested that children with Smith-Magenis syndrome are particularly prone to be outerdirected and socially demanding, particularly in comparison to children with Prader-Willi syndrome and to children with unknown MR (Dykens & Smith, 1998).

There are a number of known mediators in the development of OD, explored in depth in Bybee and Zigler (1999). Most commonly observed in children with and without MR is the effect of repeated failure, which lowers perceived self-competence and increases a person's desire to look to others for solutions. Outerdirectedness appears to decline with increases in mental age and as a task becomes easier to master. As problem-solving strategies become more inner directed, and as we are able to master tasks more independently, we tend to look to others less for assistance.

The environment is also an important factor in determining OD. Studies of differences between the family environments of children with organic and familial MR suggest that with more disparity between the competencies of the individual with MR and those of their siblings and parents (as is the case of families of organically based MR), the greater the experience of inadequacy and OD. In this case, the environmental expectations may be too great for the individual with MR. Conversely, in infantilizing and autonomy-removing environments, children with MR can also be conditioned to become outerdirected. Caregivers may inadvertently positively reinforce dependence on others by lowering their expectations of independence for individuals with MR and not allowing for unaided attempts at mastery or for choice.

Effectance Motivation

Effectance motivation (EM) is the pleasure an individual feels from attempting and mastering challenging problems (White, 1959). It has been positively related to an individual's ES and creativity and negatively related to OD and to the reaction tendencies (Zigler et al., 2002). Not surprisingly, the consequences of extremely low effectance motivation are similar to those of low ES (Dykens, 1999).

White (1959) proposed that EM stems from an intrinsic need to feel competent in interactions with the world (e.g., play, curiosity, mastery, or exploration) and is reinforced by internal reward as opposed to external reinforcement. Because EM is thought to provide the internal motivation for an individual to have an effect on the environment and master its challenges, it appears synonymous with task-related intrinsic motivation (explored in depth in Switzky, 2001).

Harter (1978) extended EM theory by applying a developmental perspective. In her cyclical model, (a) socialization agents (i.e., peers, parents) model, reinforce, and approve of early attempts at mastery, which in turn (b) cause children to internalize a system of self-reward and standards. This internalization allows children to recognize when they have met the standards of mastery without the need for external cues, and then to reward themselves, which in turn decreases the need for external reinforcement. Consequently, children (c) gain intrinsic pleasure from attempts and mastery that facilitate a perception of competence and internal control of outcomes, which (d) increases their motivation for future mastery. Conversely, children who have life histories of failure become extrinsically oriented due to a lack of reinforcement, resulting in a case where "the poor get poorer" (Haywood, 1992). The lack of positive feedback from socialization agents results in a decrease in exploration and ensuing mastery, a lack of an internalized self-reward system, and a dependence on the external environment to dictate success and pleasure in cases of mastery.

Summary of Zigler Constructs

Within moderation, the aforementioned traits are adaptive qualities. Positive reactions to supportive adults, and negative reactions to strangers, are certainly helpful for more vulnerable individuals. A moderate ES and EM and an ability to look to others for help (OD) are also helpful across development. An extreme ES, however, predisposes to the experience of failure in that too high an expectancy may be set. Likewise, an extreme intrinsic motivation and low level of OD would result in a lack of reliance on others, which could be detrimental. It is only with negative life experiences that these traits are amplified to extremes, which may be the case for many individuals with MR who experience repeated failure and aversive and deficient social experiences, particularly when compared to peers. Such experiences and traits are also critical in forming another important aspect of personality—the self-concept.

Self-Concept

The specific construct of self-concept is a part of the general construct of personality in that it is a relatively enduring cognitive and affective pattern of how we view ourselves. We may distinguish self-concept and personality by defining self-concept as the subjective *self*-perception of our traits, along with the affective evaluations of those traits. Self-concept also includes the beliefs, feelings, and intentions that a person holds in regard to the self (Sherrill, 1993). Despite its extensive research history in the non-MR population, empirical research on the self-concept in MR continues to be lacking, often attributed to difficulties in measurement (Glick, 1999; Switzky, 2001).

Relevant Domains

Self-concept is a multidimensional construct, and many facets (or domains) of the self exist. Though we may see ourselves in general terms (e.g., general self-worth), we also possess distinct self-perceptions within relevant domains of functioning (e.g., academic self-concept vs. physical self-concept). For individuals with MR, self-concept is seen as a cause and consequence of experience, and its development appears to follow a similar sequence of progressive multi-dimensional growth as in individuals without MR, although its progression is largely governed by developmental level (Glick, 1999). It has been suggested that individuals with MR show more undifferentiated self-concepts than age-matched peers without delays (Dykens, Rosner, & Butterbaugh, 1998) and with self-domains more consistent with their mental age (Evans, 1998; Fine & Caldwell, 1967; Loveland, 1987; Mans, Cicchetti, & Sroufe, 1978). Similar to typically developing younger children, children aged 9–12 years with MR (with IQs ranging from 55 to 85) fail to differentiate between their physical and academic selves and do not demonstrate the awareness of an independent sense of general self-worth (Silon & Harter, 1985). By adolescence, a more realistic self-concept appears to develop (Widaman, MacMillan, Hemsley, Little, & Balow, 1992), fitting with the developmentalist approach (Evans, 1998).

Of the many *selves* we might have, Bybee, Ennis, and Zigler (1990) examined general self-worth as well as the physical, cognitive, and social domains in institutionalized and noninstitutionalized adolescents with MR (M age = 15.6 years, M mental age = 9.3 years) using the Perceived Competence Scale for Children (Harter, 1982). Though no differences between institutionalized and noninstitutionalized groups emerged, results suggested that the social and physical domains were self-rated as lower than the cognitive and general self-worth domains. Scores were slightly lower than those reported for non-MR children by Harter (1982), although all were within 1 standard deviation. In their qualitative interviews of salient domains of self-concept in adults with mild to severe MR, Zetlin and Turner (1988) corroborated the findings that the physical and social competence domains are important, reporting that perceived abilities to conform socially, to participate in activities, and to have competent interpersonal skills appeared to matter most in how respondents evaluated themselves.

EPIDEMIOLOGY

Theoretically, based on the statistical properties of the IQ score and normal distribution, it is thought that approximately 3 percent of the population has MR (i.e., 2.28 percent of the population has an IQ score below 70). Actual prevalence rates of overall MR vary from .2 percent to 8.5 percent, with variation attributed to differences in classification schemes and methodologies, and to difficulties primarily with estimating rates for individuals with mild MR (Leonard & Wen, 2002; Roeleveld, Zielhuis, & Gabreels, 1997). Overall, a conservative estimate appears to be that at least 1.2 percent of individuals have some degree of MR (Murphy et al., 1998). Of the population of individuals with MR, approximately 80–85 percent are in the mild range of impairment, 10 percent to 15 percent are in the moderate range, 3 percent to 4 percent are in the severe range, and 1 percent to 2 percent are in the profound range (Leonard & Wen, 2002).

Rates of psychopathology in the MR population vary considerably with sample size and whether studies use the clinical-medical or psychometric approach, with larger-size studies reporting smaller rates of disturbance (Bebko et al., 1998; Dykens & Hodapp, 2001) and psychometric measures yielding higher rates than clinical judgments (Wallander et al., 2003). Rates range from 4 percent to 64 percent in community-based samples of persons with MR (Gillberg, Persson, Grufman, & Themner, 1986; Wallander et al., 2003) but have been found to be as high as 87 percent in children referred for psychiatric evaluation (Philips & Williams, 1975). Commonly cited statistics indicate that approximately 25 percent of individuals with MR also have some form of psychopathology (Dykens & Hodapp, 2001). Studies that use a typically developing comparison group commonly find a three- to sevenfold higher risk of psychopathology for individuals with MR (Koller, Stephen, Richardson, Katz, & McLaren, 1982; Linna et al., 1999; Wallander et al., 2003).

Rates of major depression can range from 1 percent to 11 percent in individuals with MR (Dykens & Hodapp, 2001), with conservative estimates suggesting that it, as well as bipolar disorder, is diagnosed twice as frequently as in the general population (Cooper, 1997; O'Brien, 2002). Although research is lacking, rates of anxiety disorder may range from 2 percent to 25 percent (Matson, Smiroldo, Hamilton, & Baglio, 1997; Ramirez & Kratochwill, 1997). Prevalence rates of schizophrenia most often vary between 1 percent and 8.3 percent, with one study by Gillberg and colleagues (1986) reporting 24 percent (Dykens & Hodapp, 2001). Rates of attention-deficit/hyperactivity disorder (ADHD) in MR are also at least twice as high as in the general population of children without MR, with studies reporting rates of between 7 percent and 15 percent (Dykens & Hodapp, 2001).

ETIOLOGY

Individuals with MR are often grouped into one of two broad etiological groups (i.e., the two-group approach). Most personality research has been applied to the first group, comprised of individuals with unknown causes of MR, deemed familial retardation. Historically, less research has been conducted with the second, organic causation group.

Individuals with familial MR are more likely to be in the mild range of intellectual impairment, have family members who have learning difficulties or lower intelligence themselves, and come from lower socioeconomic status groups (Zigler & Hodapp, 1986). There is considerable debate over the actual causes of familial MR. Commonly cited is the polygenic model of intellectual inheritance that assumes that, as a human trait, intelligence is continuously distributed so that some individuals will find themselves at the lower end of the Gaussian curve (Hodapp & Dykens, 1996). Others explain the development of familial MR as a complex interaction between various biological, environmental, and psychological risk factors (Baumeister & Baumeister, 1995). In terms of searching for a single pattern of personality to typify individuals with familial MR, Zigler (2001) notes: "The great heterogeneity in personality that one can grossly observe in any group of retarded individuals makes it unlikely that a particular set of personality traits is an invariable feature of low intelligence" (p. 13).

The second group of individuals is made up of those with known organic causes of MR. In terms of personality development, individuals with organic etiologies are receiving increasing attention. Biogenetics allows researchers to differentiate organic MR into distinct etiological groups, and behavioral phenotypes are now being linked to certain genetic disorders (Dykens, 1999, 2001). Therefore, in contrast to individuals with familial MR, the exploration of personality development in organic MR requires that we take into account between-group differences as well as within-group variability.

In a recent epidemiological review, Leonard and Wen (2002) noted that between 54 percent and 72 percent of individuals with MR have a known specific prenatal, perinatal, or postnatal cause (for a more comprehensive review of these factors, see Baumeister & Baumeister, 1995; Dykens, 1999, 2001; Luckasson et al., 2002; Ratey et al., 2000). Individuals with organic MR are usually more severely impaired than individuals with no known cause. Individuals with organic cause can account for as much as 77 percent of cases in the moderate-to-profound range of MR, whereas only 39 percent of cases in the mild range (Zigler & Hodapp, 1986).

Prenatal genetic factors are the most commonly cited cause of organic MR, accounting for approximately 30 percent to 40 percent of known MR and 7 percent to 15 percent of all MR (Murphy et al., 1998). It is thought that there are between 500 and 1,000 genetic causes, many of which are extremely rare (Flint & Wilkie, 1996; Hodapp & Dykens, 1996). Perinatal factors, such as birth injuries, anoxia, and fetal malnutrition, may account for up to 18 percent of cases of known MR (Ratey et al., 2000). Postnatal factors, such as environmental contaminants, head trauma, infections, and environmental deprivation, are thought to account for approximately 3 percent to 15 percent of cases (Murphy et al., 1998).

COURSE, COMPLICATIONS, AND PROGNOSIS

The formation of personality development throughout the life span is variable and dependent on experience (and for some, behavioral phenotype). In terms of overall functioning and diagnosis, MR is seen as a lifelong disability for most individuals. The level and cause of impairment, however, are two factors that have been shown to predict later level of functioning.

Jacobson and Mulick (1996) summarized the typical course of development for individuals with MR based on their level of impairment. Children with mild MR show relatively normal linguistic and social development within the preschool and school-aged years. They often demonstrate a substantial degree of play skills, expressive language, social interaction, and basic understanding of numbers. Usually by adolescence, however, with the increased complexity of the academic and social milieu, significant difficulties emerge. It is common for adults with mild MR to have reading and number skills between the first- and sixth-grade levels, and low overall academic and vocational achievement. Many individuals with mild MR will remain unnoticed once out of the school system, in that they will be able to meet necessary adult norms.

Moderate MR is often diagnosed earlier in life than mild MR, with preschool-aged children showing earlier delays of fundamental milestones, especially in language development and play. During the middle school period, academic and adaptive skill acquisition is delayed, and most children with moderate MR will fail to develop functional number and reading skills. By adulthood, a fair degree of communication, daily living skill, and simple vocational skill may be acquired. Most individuals with moderate MR will function in their communities with support and guidance and will live semi-independently as adults in specialized group homes or with family.

The deficits seen in individuals with severe MR are noticed from infancy, in that there are substantial delays in acquiring basic motor and linguistic milestones. Organic neurological dysfunction is also invariably present, and they are at increased risk of epilepsy compared to children with milder forms of MR. School-aged children may use simple one- to three-word utterances, with low intelligibility, and often have better receptive than expressive language skills. Adults may acquire self-care skills such as feeding, dressing, and toileting, although some assistance in completing these tasks is often needed. Independent living is not a possibility due to the substantial impairments in adaptive behavior, and close supervision is often required.

Individuals with profound MR are often noticed from birth and early infancy due to physical malformations, medical issues, early sensory impairment, and a lack of responsiveness. Many individuals have complicated medical problems that can result in death in childhood or adolescence. Expressive and receptive language, social skills, and self-help skills are all markedly impaired, and continuous supervision is needed.

Along with functional level, the type of impairment also contributes information regarding the course of MR throughout the life span. In general, those with organic MR have a poorer prognosis in terms of independent living and intellectual functioning than individuals with familial MR. Within the heterogeneous organic MR group, however, the course of development may vary by etiology. For example, individuals with particular genetic disorders may show a slowing of intellectual and functional (i.e., adaptive skill) development at different ages (Hodapp & Dykens, 1996). Boys with fragile X syndrome have stable IQ scores until around puberty, at which point cognitive development becomes considerably more delayed (Dykens et al., 1994). Similar decreases occur in individuals with Down syndrome, although much earlier in childhood (Hodapp & Zigler, 1990). As well, the presence of multiple handicaps (e.g., deafness) may complicate already impaired learning skills caused by an organic dysfunction.

ASSESSMENT AND DIAGNOSIS

Diagnosis of MR is primarily based on an individual's performance on norm-referenced tests, as opposed to on a common etiology or deviant behavior. The classic assessment of MR requires at minimum a measure of intellectual functioning and adaptive behavior. More comprehensive multimodal assessments that consider emotional, physiological, and environmental variables (Luckasson et al., 2002), as well as the assessment of psychopathology have also been suggested (Hodapp & Dykens, 1996).

Intellectual Functioning

The interpretation of test results based on an IQ test that is administered in a standardized fashion requires that clinicians bear in mind possible cultural, situational, health, and sensory factors that can interfere with performance (Jacobson & Mulick, 1996). One problem found in all intelligence tests is an insufficient testing floor; that is, inadequate standardized data at the lowest ends of the measure or subtests that are inappropriate for individuals with very limited skills, that makes the accurate measurement of intellectual functioning in individuals with profound and severe MR difficult or impossible. When administering an IQ test it is important to consider how well an instrument can discriminate among individuals at the lower range of functioning. As mentioned, an IQ score at or below 70 (2 standard deviations below the mean) is necessary for a diagnosis of MR.

Adaptive Behavior

A low IQ score is not sufficient to diagnose MR, especially when dealing with the large majority of individuals with MR in the mild range of impairment. Considerable debate remains over how adaptive behavior should be defined (Jacobson & Mulick, 1996). Broadly defined, it refers to the collection of functional skills sufficient for meeting the standards of personal independence and social responsibility expected by one's age, immediate environment, and community. The content areas within adaptive behavior may differ slightly among scales; however, all appear to possess the dimensions of social, communicative, academic, physical, and community-vocational competence (Jacobson & Mulick, 1996). Some of the more frequently used scales include the Vineland Adaptive Behavior Scales (Sparrow, Balla, & Cicchetti, 1984), the AAMR Adaptive Behavior Scale (Lambert, Nihira, & Leland, 1993), the Scales of Independent Behavior—Revised (Bruininks, Woodcock, Weatherman, & Hill, 1996), and the Inventory for Client and Agency Planning (Bruininks, Hill, Weatherman, & Woodcock, 1986).

IMPACT ON ENVIRONMENT

Family

Relationships do not emerge in isolation—social behavior first appears in the context of the family. Many authors have argued that early parent-child interactions lay the foundation for relationships throughout life (e.g., Erwin, 1993; Grusec & Lytton, 1988). In this view, the quality of the relationship between parent and child is strongly associated with the development of later social skills, and with subsequent success in the peer culture.

Having a child with MR can place enormous amounts of stress on the family as a system as well as on individual family members (Hauser-Cram et al., 2001). Earlier research examining stress related to raising a child with MR has found that both mothers (Chetwynd, 1985; Crnic, Friedrich, & Greenberg, 1983) and fathers (Bristol, Gallagher, & Schopler, 1988; Cummings, 1976) experience significantly higher levels of stress than parents of typically developing children.

Mothers are most often the primary caregivers of their children and have been the primary focus of studies of parental stress related to children with disabilities. Mothers' stress has been linked with their locus of control over professional care of their child with a disability and the effectiveness of their social support networks (Krauss, 1993). Research on fathers is much less extensive (Lamb & Billings, 1997), although it is becoming more prominent (Ricci & Hodapp, 2003). Several studies have found that mothers and fathers of children with MR report similar levels of stress, although they suggest that some of the factors that influence stress may be different (Dyson, 1997; Roach, Orsmond, & Barratt, 1999). Mothers, compared to fathers, have also reported more stress related to deficiencies in parenting competence and the spousal relationship (Beckman, 1991). Krauss (1993) found that fathers' stress was related to their children's temperament, the father-child relationship, and the quality of the family environment.

Within the parent-child foundation view, it would follow, then, that children with MR who experience atypical parent-child relations may also experience some difficulty in establishing and maintaining effective peer interactions. Children with MR have been hypothesized to be at higher risk for atypical parent-child relations due to a variety of factors, including difficult temperament qualities (e.g., Chess, 1970; Dosen, 1990), passivity, and more interactional directiveness by parents (Buckhalt, Rutherland, & Goldberg, 1978), perhaps in response to child characteristics. Though these variables do not affect all parent-child dyads, nonetheless they represent potential risk factors.

School

Once children have reached the age of 5 or 6 years, they have typically entered a school setting. School represents a new and highly significant environment, in that most children spend approximately a third or more of their waking hours at school, away from the family. For the child with no additional developmental or socioemotional challenges, adaptation to a school ecosystem represents a significant change from the home environment. Among the differences between the two is that in the school setting, external, often comparative measures of learning are being used. A second is that, on the social side, peer interaction becomes nearly continuous, resulting in an evolution of the child's style of interaction and comfort level with peers. For children with MR, the school environment represents the same challenges as for other children. However, children who bring less extensive cognitive, behavioral, or social skills to the school setting are at correspondingly greater risk for difficulty or failure, since these skill areas are among those most required for success at school.

As a result of those risk factors, one of the most central controversies for children with MR in the school system has to do with placement decisions. Debates about the pros and cons of integration, mainstreaming, segregated classrooms, special schools, and other options have been ongoing for decades. (They are beyond the scope of the present chapter, but there are many detailed discussions of these options and their differences; for examples, see Hardman, Drew, & Egan, 2002; Winzer, 1999.) The debates are often quite heated, not only among the education community, but also among advocacy groups and parent groups and in the political and research arenas. Winzer (1999) noted that the research literature and the media often contribute to an inaccurate general perception that inclusion of special needs children in the regular classroom is currently a universally accepted movement and philosophy in special education. However, this is far from accurate. Many parents, professionals, and their advocacy groups support the maintenance of a full continuum of special education services to respond to the wide range of skill levels present in special needs children, with the regular education classroom being but one option. Even where the philosophical principle of full inclusion is accepted, the reality is that there are many potential barriers to implementation. These include concerns with the real social (vs. physical) integration of the child, possibly inadequate teacher preparation, concerns about whether the special needs child will receive adequate instruction and attention, and similar concerns about the nondisabled children if teaching resources are directed more toward the special needs child (Winzer, 1999; Wong, Pearson, Ip, & Lo, 1999).

Data on the psychosocial outcomes of inclusion versus the wider range of placements is very limited due to variations of methodologies used across studies, and variation in the details of the placements themselves. However, a rationale supporting integration for children with MR and other disabilities is the assumed impact of integration in the socioemotional domain; that is, there are increased opportunities to interact with children with more developed social skills and increased opportunities for relationships with nondisabled peers (Ford & Davern, 1989; Winzer, 1999). Students with mild cognitive impairments placed in mainstreamed schools have been reported to experience less depression and less loneliness and participate in more age-appropriate leisure skills than similar students placed in special schools (Heiman, 2000, 2001). However, simply being physically integrated does not guarantee social integration; children with MR are at risk for social isolation from their peers due to less well developed socialization skills. As a result, proponents of a wider range of placement opportunities caution that forced integration for all individuals may be more stressful than beneficial, and that connectedness with a community may be more easily achieved within a community of others with MR, particularly for those with significant disabilities (Cummins & Lau, 2003).

There appears to be no single solution to the issue of classroom placement for all individuals with mental retardation, which is not unexpected given the range of expression of characteristics and adaptive levels described earlier. Rather, variability in success of outcome is a function of a complex interplay among a variety of variables. From the parents' perspective, success in outcomes has been linked to individual child characteristics, parent and family characteristics and values, and the perceived role of the school by the family (Palmer, Borthwick-Duffy, Widaman, & Best, 1998). In addition to these variables, the match between the child's needs and the degree to which those needs can be met by the nature of the placement is critical.

One important component of how well the child's needs are able to be met is related to teacher preparedness. Teacher preparedness is a common theme in almost all reviews of the success of an integrated school placement, whether involving partial or full integration. Winzer (1999) summarized a number of studies that concluded that teachers do not feel well prepared to support students with special needs comfortably, and this is particularly true if children with other or concurrent disabilities are involved (Scheuermann, Webber, Boutot, & Goodwin, 2003). Nearly all teachers working with special needs children identify a need for additional resources in order to appropriately serve children with disabilities (Minke, Bear, Deemer, & Griffin, 1996). However, a number of studies have demonstrated that relatively brief training courses can be highly effective at imparting accurate knowledge and changing attitudes about disabilities, as well as giving school personnel greater confidence and ease in interacting with people with disabilities (e.g., Campbell, Gilmore, & Cuskelly, 2003). Greater familiarity with the children's needs would enable teachers and administrators to adapt curricula with greater confidence and structure potential social interactions among students to increase the possibility of beneficial outcomes for the students with disabilities.

Clearly, however, meeting the needs of children with MR in the school setting is a complex challenge. The ongoing debates on how best to meet the challenge are, in part, a symptom of the lack of clear data on outcomes. However, if there is a mismatch between the needs of the child and the ability of the school placement to meet those needs, it increases the risk of failure for the child, which in turn affects the child's self-esteem and sense of mastery of the environment, which can contribute to later socioemotional difficulties.

Peer Interactions

Given the central role that friendships are hypothesized to play in terms of life satisfaction, self-concept, and social adjustment, it is important to examine the nature and formation of friendship in individuals with MR. Children with MR have been identified repeatedly as having significant difficulties in establishing peer relations (Guralnick, Connor, & Hammond, 1995; Guralnick, Connor, Hammond, Gottman, & Kinnish, 1995; Guralnick & Groom, 1985, 1987a, 1987b) as well as having poor social status (Asher & Taylor, 1981; Brewer & Smith, 1989; Gottlieb & Leyser, 1981; Rothisberg, Hill, & D'Amato, 1994) and unsatisfying friendships (Taylor, Asher, & Williams, 1987). Children who fail to develop social skills, and who become isolated from their peers, are at risk for future adjustment problems (Guralnick, 1986). Furthermore, children who are less able to interact effectively with other children will have less opportunity to learn typical and effective models of social conduct, and to develop appropriate social and cognitive skills. A clear link between lack of peer friendships and maladjustment in childhood and adulthood in non-MR populations has been identified (Erwin, 1993; Hartup, 1983), thus emphasizing the importance of examining friendship formation.

Guralnick and colleagues conducted a series of studies to observe peer interactions in children with MR in integrated preschool settings (Guralnick & Groom, 1985, 1987a, 1987b; Guralnick & Weinhouse, 1984). They found that solitary and parallel play were the dominant forms of social participation, and a majority of the children failed to engage in sustained social interactions. Like unpopular children without disabilities, children with MR were unable to turn simple two-unit initiation/response sequences into more elaborate social exchanges. These features remained stable throughout the entire school year. Others (e.g., Asch, 1989) have also reported that simply placing children with MR and typical children together had little effect on the quality or quantity of their interactions. Jenkins, Odom, and Speltz (1989) found that preschoolers with mild to moderate MR actually spent more time playing alone in an integrated classroom than when in a classroom composed of peers with MR. Only when a play program encouraging social interaction was implemented did the children with MR engage in a higher proportion of interactive play, regardless of the classroom setting.

Bebko and colleagues (1998) concluded that taken together, these research findings indicate that children with MR have social deficits in dyadic as well as group play interactions with non-MR children, and that these deficits are beyond that which would be expected based on developmental level alone. We speculate as a result that many children with MR either do not have, or do not use, the skills required for sustaining social interaction, particularly with non-MR peers. This interactional style may have an impact on, among other things, the ability to develop friendships.

There is evidence to suggest that friendships serve similar functions for children with and without disabilities (Gold, 1985; Guralnick & Groom, 1988). Guralnick and Groom (1988) examined the behaviorally defined friendship patterns of 4-year-old children with MR in a mainstream play group consisting of 3- and 4-year-old children without MR. The authors were specifically interested in whether children with MR would be able to establish unilateral and reciprocal friendships with typical peers. A unilateral friendship occurred if a child with MR directed 33 percent of his or her interactions to a specific companion. A reciprocal relationship was defined when a child with MR directed 33 percent of his or her interactions to a specific companion, who in turn directed 33 percent of his or her interactions to the target child. Children with MR showed a clear preference for the chronological age-matched children in establishing both unilateral and reciprocal friendships. Results also indicated that although the children with MR were able to establish the same number of unilateral friendships as the two typical groups of children, few children with MR met the reciprocal friendship criterion. Thus, according to these measures, the friendships of children with MR were rarely reciprocated.

More qualitative explorations of friendships between children with and without MR have indicated that children with MR are capable of establishing friendships with peers without MR, although it is unclear whether these friendships can be established without the active facilitation of caregivers (Bebko et al., 1998). Gold (1985) found that the children in her study, ranging in age from 6 to 12 years, had developed a variety of friendships, including close peer friendships. These close friendships possessed a quality of "mutuality" (p. 17), suggesting that both children appeared to acknowledge and seek the friendship and found it mutually beneficial. Other qualities of the friendships included humor, affection, understanding, and concern. Efforts on the part of significant adults such as teachers and parents to facilitate friendships were an important component of the process of developing friendships between children with MR and typical peers (Gold, 1985; Gottlieb & Leyser, 1981). This finding is supported by others such as Strully and Strully (1993) and Hamre-Nietupski (1993).

To date, it appears that reciprocal friendships are not readily established by children with MR without the direct intervention of others. For example, in unstructured settings, it is often older typical children who elicit positive social behavior from children with MR. This trend continues into adulthood (Barber & Hupp, 1993). Many adolescents and adults with MR, while being physically integrated into the mainstream, are still largely socially segregated (Hughes et al., 1999). They often have smaller social support networks composed of more service providers and family, and fewer peers, than the networks of non-MR individuals (Rosen & Burchard, 1990). In an investigation of the quality of life of adults with MR, Schalock, Harper, and Carver (1981) found that, along with importance of functional skills (which we can link to ability), respondents reported a consistent desire for more friends. Because of limited social competence and cognitive skills, individuals with MR are often excluded from many common peer situations, and consequently may have less opportunity to learn the social skills needed for effective interactions, resulting in isolation and an inability to function successfully in the social environment (Anderson, Grossman, & Finch, 1983).

With sufficient effort, close relationships that provide many of the benefits associated with friendship can be established and maintained. Without external help, however, the outcome is less optimistic. When left alone among peers, children with MR spend the majority of their time playing alone or not at all; their social interactions are infrequent and brief. Consistent with the extant literature on the importance of friendships, the failure to make friends will likely have profound consequences on other life experiences, and on personality formation.

IMPLICATIONS FOR FUTURE PERSONALITY DEVELOPMENT

In general, the literature suggests a number of powerful, interrelated influences on the development of personality, including (a) experiences of failure related to a lack of ability, (b) poor social networks and perceived social isolation, and (c) negative social comparisons. These contributions are evident in the formation and evaluation of the self-concept.

The effect that repeated failure has on self-concept should be evident, in that it has adverse effects on many task-related personality factors (e.g., self-efficacy, effectance motivation, expectancy of success; reviewed in the previous section on personality development). There is also a negative correlation of self-concept with IQ in individuals with MR (Weiss, Diamond, Demark, & Lovald, 2003), perhaps because the higher functioning an individual is, the greater the ability to reflect upon his or her experiences and to distinguish the real self from the ideal self (Zigler & Hodapp, 1986).

Along with the influence of disability and the experience of failure, social factors play into one's view of the self. The impact of social isolation is clear: A recent study of non-MR elementary school children found that perceived loneliness, and not peer rejection, accounted for a child's negative sense of self-worth and perceived competence (Qualter & Munn, 2002). This is particularly problematic for children with MR, given the deficits in social interaction and friendship formation highlighted in the previous section.

Social comparison theory suggests that in the absence of objective standards of comparison, people will use others in their environment as the basis for evaluating their self-concepts (Festinger, 1954). If people compare themselves with others who are less capable, called a downward comparison, they create a lower reference point by which to evaluate their own situation. Conversely, if they compare themselves to others who are more capable, they make an upward comparison. It was originally thought that downward comparisons served a self-enhancing role and protected against negative self-concept by boosting self-esteem and reducing anxiety

(Wills, 1981), and that upward comparisons produced more negative emotion and lower self-evaluations. More recent work by Buunk, Collins, Taylor, and Van Yperen (1990) suggests that both types of comparisons are capable of generating positive or negative affective evaluations and depend on one's identification with the peer group, prior self-esteem, and perceived level of control. An upward comparison can be positive if the individual identifies with the person that they interpret to be in a better situation. Likewise, a downward comparison could be negative if an individual likens themselves to the individuals that they see as less capable. In general, negative social comparisons are avoided when individuals have high self-esteem and feel in control of their situation.

Very little work has been done in tailoring social comparison theory to individuals with MR, perhaps due to the difficulty in determining to whom children with MR compare themselves (Widaman et al., 1992). In their study of the self-concepts of students with MR in mainstreamed and self-contained classrooms, Silon and Harter (1985) found no difference between groups and concluded that mainstreamed students compared themselves to other mainstreamed students with MR, whereas self-contained students compared themselves to other self-contained students with MR. However, some studies have found that children with MR in mainstreamed classrooms compare themselves to their classmates in general and have lower self-concepts than when they are in self-contained classrooms, presumably making upward comparisons (Battle, 1979; Schurr, Towne, & Joyner, 1972), whereas other studies report positive effects in mainstreamed settings (Calhoun & Elliott, 1977; Madden & Slavin, 1983). Moreover, Coleman (1983) found that the segregated classroom was a more homogeneous social comparison group in regard to ability and that it increased self-concept.

It may be that the most appropriate model of social comparison for populations with MR is one where both upward and downward comparisons occur, which can lead to either positive or negative evaluations, depending on the degree of group belonging (Allen & Gilbert, 1995) and the individual's resilience (Champion & Power, 1995). Group belonging is an individual's perception of social acceptance and identification with the peer group. Resilience includes other mediating factors, such as a person's self-esteem and role complexity.

As shown in Table 14.1, if individuals with MR regard non-MR individuals as their peer group, they would likely engage in upward comparisons (e.g., "They are more competent than I am"). Typically, their self-perceptions would then be more negative in that they would feel less competent. However, if individuals with MR feel a sense of group belonging with that comparison group and have a more complex sense of self and evaluate their worth from alternative

TABLE 14.1 Social Comparison Theory for Individuals with MR

Self-perception	Upward (Non-MR comparison group; more skilled)	Downward (less-skilled group)
Positive	Group belonging and role resilience	Group belonging and role resilience
Negative	I am less competent.	I am more competent, but I do not belong (alienation).

roles, the result might be more positive self-perceptions (e.g., "They are more competent in some areas, but I am good in others, and I am accepted and belong with them"). If individuals with MR compare themselves to other individuals with MR, they might make downward comparisons (e.g., "I am more competent than they are"). Though we might expect that they would, therefore, have a more positive sense of self, a negative self-perception can develop instead, caused by a denigration of their peers with MR and denying membership in that group, increasing alienation (Dagnan & Sandhu, 1999). Alternatively, an individual with MR would be less likely to experience alienation and a negative self-perception if a sense of group belonging is fostered (e.g., "I am more competent in some areas, but they are good, too, and I am accepted and belong with them").

TREATMENT IMPLICATIONS

By outlining relevant personality domains and understanding how they might be influenced within a developmental approach, we are presented with an opportunity to improve functioning by targeting these influencing variables. For example, many interventions aimed at social skills training have been used with children with MR. These interventions have typically involved some combination of direct instruction, modeling, role play, social reinforcement, and practice (Bellack & Hersen, 1979). The work of Strain and colleagues (Strain & Kerr, 1981; Strain, Odom, & McConnell, 1984) has indicated that positive social interactions of children with MR can be increased using both adult- and peer-mediated interventions. These interventions primarily rely on using social and tangible reinforcement as a means of increasing social interaction. Specific behaviors that have been targeted include social play, sharing, appropriate displays of affection, and giving assistance. Although children showed significant improvement during treatment, the acquired skills frequently are not maintained and do not generalize beyond the treatment environment.

In a review of intervention strategies aimed at overcoming the rejection and isolation of cognitively impaired children, Gottlieb and Leyser (1981) described a strategy known as sociometric grouping. This technique involved rearranging the classroom based on the results of sociometric testing so that low-status children were in closer proximity to high-status children. The authors reported that despite the initial increase in peer status, such changes are often not maintained at follow-up. Furthermore, although children's sociometric status may change, their behavior may not. Clearly this would continue to affect their success at forming positive social relationships. Efforts at changing behavior through role-playing have not been found to be successful, although reinforcement, coaching, and modeling have shown some success. Another, more comprehensive program, Special Olympics, holds promise in addressing many of the psychosocial factors that place individuals with MR at high risk. In a study of self-concept and actual competency of Special Olympians with MR, Weiss and colleagues (2003) found significant relations among three self-concept domains (general self-worth, perceived physical competence, and perceived social competence) and various indicators of involvement in the sport organization. Self-concept was measured by an age-appropriate version of Harter's (1982) Perceived Competence Scale for Children and was assessed in interview format with participants. The study used a randomly selected sample with a wide range of ages (9–43 years), etiologies (e.g., unknown, Down, autism, etc.), and ability levels (IQs ranging from 40 to 90).

After statistically controlling for age and IQ, the researchers found that the number of competitions participants experienced was a significant predictor of athletes' sense of general self-worth, accounting for 11 percent of unique variance. The number of years that participants were involved with Special Olympics and the number of sports they played were found to predict their self-perceptions of physical competence, accounting for 26 percent of unique variance. Finally, the number of medals and ribbons participants obtained was found to be a significant predictor of their self-perceptions of social acceptance. Of interest, the number of competitions experienced emerged as a significant predictor for four out of the five adaptive behavior domains used to represent actual competency.

The Weiss and colleagues study (2003) examined the relations among the facet of personality known as self-concept and involvement in Special Olympics and did not directly examine its possible link with traditional personality traits (e.g., extraversion) or task-related and social-related traits (e.g., positive reaction tendency, effectance motivation). However, the concrete indicators of success, effort, and positive experience in Special Olympics (i.e., medals, number of competitions, sports) have been linked with self-concept. These indicators may also be closely associated with social- and task-related traits, given that experiences with success and with relationships have been hypothesized to be central in the formation of personality. Table 14.2 presents a list of interventions suggested in the literature to be effective in addressing social-related and task-related personality styles as well as overall self-concept. Aspects of Special Olympics that incorporate these issues are also indicated.

Social-Related Factors

In targeting social-related personality traits, Bennett-Gates and Zigler (1999) suggested that interventions should meet the social needs of individuals with MR by ensuring an adequate level of appropriate adult and peer interaction. As summarized earlier, individuals with MR often have smaller-than-average social networks, made up more often of service providers and family members than peers (Robertson et al., 2002; Rosen & Burchard, 1990). In fact, many parents of individuals with MR acknowledge that they are their child's best friend, a situation that is uncommon in non-MR families. As such, it is critical that we develop programs that increase the frequency and size of socially accepting peer networks in order to decrease the sense of isolation and loneliness experienced by individuals with MR. There is reason to suspect that Special Olympics programming can address many of Bennett-Gates and Zigler's (1999) recommendations and those in Table 14.2. In Special Olympics, athletes' training occurs on a weekly basis, often year-round, increasing and maintaining the frequency of nonstaff and nonfamily social interaction. These training experiences with MR peers (e.g., other athletes) and non-MR peers (e.g., coaches) can be coupled with various competitions and social events, which are highly socially accepting and foster a sense of group belonging. In their own research, Weiss and colleagues (2003) found that the number of medals and ribbons that peers and coaches gave an athlete was a significant predictor of social self-concept. It is probable that medals and ribbons, which are given to athletes for participation and winning, are tangible representations of social acceptance. As well, the number of competitions participants experience has recently been linked to parents' feelings of child-related stress (Weiss, Diamond, & Sullivan, 2004). Involvement in Special Olympics has also been positively related to a participant's degree of actual social competence (Dykens & Cohen, 1996; Weiss et al., 2003).

Task-Related Factors

There are a number of ways to improve an individual's ES, OD, and EM. Given the detrimental impact that repeated failure has on individuals with MR, programs that can maximize opportunities for success and foster intrinsic motivation are

TABLE 14.2 Treatment Implications for Personality Factors

Recommendation	Special Olympics
Social-related	
• Provide frequent positive social contact (Bennett-Gates & Zigler, 1999)	• Training occurs on weekly basis, year-round
• Provide a socially accepting and supportive environment (Bennett-Gates & Zigler, 1999)	• Small- to large-scale competitions, many peers and adults. Training and social events, and interaction with individuals with and without MR in an accepting way
• Enhance parent-child relationship (Bennett-Gates & Zigler, 1999)	• Parents watch children participate, and feel pride and decreases in stress
Task-related	
• Increase internal locus of control (Hoffman & Weiner, 1978; Zoeller, Mahoney, & Weiner, 1983)	• Focus is on effort
• Focus on task mastery, not comparison with peers (Nicholls, Cheung, Lauer, & Patashnick, 1989; Roberts & Treasure, 1992; Tassi, Schneider, & Richard, 2001)	• Task mastery the only focus in training
• Maximize opportunities for success (Bennett-Gates & Zigler, 1999; Gibbons & Bushakra, 1989; Ollendick, Balla, & Zigler, 1971; Songster, 1984) • Give tasks that are not too easy or too difficult to accomplish, along with small increases in difficulty (Harter, 1978; Vygotsky, 1978) • Gradual increases in performance demands	• In competition, children matched on age, sex, ability, maximizing success • In training, mastery of short-term attainable goals
• Move from tangible to intangible reinforcement (Harter, 1978)	• Tangible: medals and ribbons • Intangible: hugs, cheers, approval, recognition, pride
• Model and reinforce self-reward system (Harter, 1978)	• Pride in accomplishment is modeled and reinforced
• Increase autonomy and agency (choice, Schunk, 1985) • Active agents in setting their own goals and self-standards (Harris, Kasari, & Sigman, 1996)	• Individual's choice in type of sport and role within sport
Self-concept	
• Increase role complexity (Champion & Power, 1995)	• I am an athlete (e.g., a runner, a bowler, a swimmer)
• Resilience in social comparisons: group belonging (Allen & Gilbert, 1995)	• Peer group is MR athletes and non-MR coaches—upward and downward comparisons in light of group belonging
• Improve task-related and social-related factors	• Competition, medals, and sports have been linked to different self-concept components and may be mediated by task-related and social-related factors

critical. Programming such as exists in the Special Olympics model may shift an individual's motivational orientation.

Positive experiences can alter a person's ES, and studies have shown that the failure-avoiding orientation can be shifted to a more success-oriented one depending on the opportunity for success provided in a task (Ollendick, Balla, & Zigler, 1971) and with attribution training (Hoffman & Weiner, 1978; Zoeller, Mahoney, & Weiner, 1983). In working with adults with moderate MR, Hoffman and Weiner (1978) were able to improve task performance by increasing individuals' internal locus of control, ascribing success and failure in task mastery to internal effort (or the lack thereof). Likewise, in Special Olympics, the responsibility for success and failure is ascribed to an athlete's effort and not to external factors such as the coach or luck, and there is concrete feedback in terms of outcome. The importance of effort is seen within the Special Olympics motto: "Let me win, but if I cannot win, let me be brave in the attempt."

As well, it has been recommended that self-efficacy be reinforced in children with MR by teaching that they can be competent and successful in tasks (Bennett-Gates & Zigler, 1999). Children who function at a lower level than their peers and are focused on external evaluations and approval fixate on their failure in relation to others and have low self-efficacy. By directing attention to the mastered task and away from self-evaluations based on comparisons with peers, children with MR are oriented toward their successes and feel more efficacious (Nicholls, Cheung, Lauer, & Patashnick, 1989; Roberts & Treasure, 1992; Tassi, Schneider, & Richard, 2001). Sport training in Special Olympics is highly focused on task mastery, and self-evaluation is based on task performance, as opposed to performance in relation to others. In fact, even during competitions where athletes compete against others, all individuals are matched on age, sex, and ability level to maximize the possibility of success. Finally, ribbons for effort are given to all participating athletes, not only to those who win. Our own research has found that the length of time an athlete spends in Special Olympics, and the number of sports participated in, are significant predictors of perceived physical competence (Weiss et al., 2003).

Along with reinforcing task orientation, it is important that goals be optimally challenging and maximize opportunity for success (Gibbons & Bushakra, 1989; Ollendick et al., 1971; Songster, 1984). For instance, task difficulty should be within a zone of proximal development (Vygotsky, 1978), being within a person's ability to compete but challenging enough for success to truly be an accomplishment. Self-competence cannot be fostered when tasks are too easy or too difficult (Bennett-Gates & Zigler, 1999; Harter, 1978), and challenging tasks should be broken down into smaller short-term attainable goals, each with its own sense of mastery. In Special Olympics training, a new component in a sport, such as running between the lines in a race, is divided into smaller components and mastered sequentially. As well, pride in accomplishing each subgoal is reinforced and modeled by coaches, parents, and peers, thus helping to internalize a self-reward system (i.e., Harter, 1978). Finally, goals must be embedded with a sense of autonomy, and individuals with MR need to be given choice in their goal setting (Schunk, 1985). For example, Harris, Kasari, and Sigman (1996) found that children with Down syndrome whose parents allowed them to take the lead in interactions were more likely to engage in future attempts at mastery. In Special Olympics, the choice of sports, and activities within sports, is largely left up to the athlete, facilitating a sense of ownership over the goals that are mastered.

Self-Concept Factors

Along with addressing social-related and task-related personality functioning, direct interventions related to the evaluation of the self-concept are possible within the framework of social comparison theory (see Table 14.2; Allen & Gilbert, 1995; Champion & Power, 1995; Dagnan & Sandhu, 1999). Namely, positive evaluations of the self can be promoted by increasing an individual's role complexity and sense of group belonging. If an individual's negative self-concept is a result of being defined as incompetent, then developing other facets of the self that are relevant and competent may be influential. For example, the student who feels incompetent in school can feel competent as an athlete. By participating in programs such as Special Olympics, individuals with MR are given an opportunity to redefine themselves as competent athletes. In addition to developing greater role complexity, an increased social network and sense of group belonging are critical variables in promoting positive self-evaluations.

CONCLUSION

The development of personality in individuals with MR is largely contingent on the same influential variables that are instrumental in shaping personality in individuals without MR. The process is sociocognitive, with environmental variables such as experiences of success and failure, socialization agents, and home environment interacting with internal person variables such as genetic contributions and social and intellectual ability. Few in-depth studies of traditional traits exist on individuals with MR, and relevant personality domains centering on social and task-related functioning, and self-concept, are more prominent. Chronic negative life experiences predispose individuals with MR to having poor expectancies of success, maladaptive social reactions, low effectance motivation, and negative self-concepts. There is tremendous individual variability in the presentation of negative traits, and it is important that researchers find active ingredients in intervention programs capable of effecting change. Social skills intervention programs, such as those outlined here, and physical activity programs, such as Special Olympics, offer alternatives for potentially improving personality functioning by facilitating positive experiences of task mastery and social acceptance. However, intervention research into the prevention of psychopathology in people with MR is extremely limited to date, yet it is critical for our understanding of the psychological health of dually diagnosed individuals.

REFERENCES

Alexander, R., & Cooray, S. (2003). Diagnosis of personality disorders in learning disability. *British Journal of Psychiatry, 182* (Suppl. 44), S28–S31.

Allen, S., & Gilbert, P. (1995). A social comparison scale: Psychometric properties and relationship to psychopathology. *Personality and Individual Differences, 19,* 293–299.

American Psychiatric Association. (1994). *Diagnostic and statistical manual of mental disorders* (4th ed.). Washington, DC: Author.

Anderson, S. C., Grossman, L. M., & Finch, H. A. (1983). Effects of a recreation program on the social interaction of mentally retarded adults. *Journal of Leisure Research, 15,* 100–107.

Asch, A. (1989). Has the law made a difference? In D. Kerzner & A. Gartner (Eds.), *Beyond separate education: Quality education for all* (pp. 181–206). Baltimore: Brookes.

Asher, S. R., & Taylor, A. R. (1981). Social outcomes of mainstreaming: Sociometric assessment and beyond. *Exceptional Children Quarterly, 1,* 13–28.

Balla, D. A., Butterfield, E. C., & Zigler, E. (1974). Effects of institutionalization on retarded children: A longitudinal cross-institutional investigation. *American Journal of Mental Deficiency, 78,* 530–549.

Barber, D., & Hupp, S. C. (1993). A comparison of friendship patterns of individuals with developmental disabilities. *Education and Training in Mental Retardation, 28,* 13–22.

Battle, J. (1979). Self-esteem of students in regular and special classes. *Psychological Reports, 44,* 212–214.

Baumeister, A. A., & Baumeister, A. A. (1995). Mental retardation. In M. Hersen & R. T. Ammerman (Eds.), *Advanced abnormal child psychology* (pp. 283–304). Hillsdale, NJ: Erlbaum.

Bebko, J. M., Wainwright, J. A., Brian, J. A., Coolbear, J., Landry, R., & Vallance, D. D. (1998). Social competence and peer relations in children with mental retardation: Models of the development of peer relations. *Journal on Developmental Disabilities, 6,* 1–31.

Beckman, P. J. (1991). Comparison of mothers' and fathers' perceptions of the effect of young children with and without disabilities. *American Journal on Mental Retardation, 95,* 585–595.

Bellack, A. S., & Hersen, M. (1979). *Research and practice in social skills training.* New York: Plenum.

Bennett-Gates, D., & Zigler, E. (1999). Effectance motivation and the performance of individuals with mental retardation. In E. Zigler & D. Bennett-Gates (Eds.), *Personality development in individuals with mental retardation* (pp. 145–164). New York: Cambridge University Press.

Brewer, N., & Smith, J. M. (1989). Social acceptance of mentally retarded children in regular schools in relation to years mainstreamed. *Psychological Reports, 64,* 375–380.

Bristol, M. M., Gallagher, J. J., & Schopler, E. (1988). Mothers and fathers of young developmentally disabled and nondisabled boys: Adaptation and spousal support. *Developmental Psychology, 24,* 441–451.

Bruininks, R. H., Hill, B. K., Weatherman, R. F., & Woodcock, R. W. (1986). *Inventory for Client and Agency Planning.* Allen, TX: DLM Teaching Resources.

Bruininks, R. H., Woodcock, R. W., Weatherman, R. F., & Hill, B. K. (1996). *Scales of Independent Behavior—Revised: Comprehensive manual.* Itasca, IL: Riverside.

Buckhalt, J., Rutherland, R. B., & Goldberg, K. E. (1978). Verbal and nonverbal interaction of mothers with their Down's Syndrome and non-retarded infants. *American Journal on Mental Deficiency, 82,* 337–343.

Buunk, B. P., Collins, R. L., Taylor, S. E., & Van Yperen, N. W. (1990). The affective consequences of social comparison: Either direction has its ups and downs. *Journal of Personality and Social Psychology, 59,* 1238–1249.

Bybee, J., Ennis, P., & Zigler, E. (1990). Effects of institutionalization and the self-concept and outerdirectedness of adolescents with mental retardation. *Exceptionality, 1,* 215–226.

Bybee, J., & Zigler, E. (1999). Outerdirectedness in individuals with and without mental retardation: A review. In E. Zigler & D. Bennett-Gates (Eds.), *Personality development in individuals with mental retardation* (pp. 165–205). New York: Cambridge University Press.

Calhoun, G., & Elliott, R. N. (1977). Self-concept and academic achievement of educable retarded and emotionally disturbed pupils. *Exceptional Children, 43,* 379–380.

Campbell, J., Gilmore, L., & Cuskelly, M. (2003). Changing student teachers' attitudes towards disability and inclusion. *Journal of Intellectual and Developmental Disability, 28,* 369–379.

Cervone, D., & Shoda, Y. (1999). Beyond traits in the study of personality coherence. *Current Directions in Psychological Science, 8,* 27–32.

Champion, L. A., & Power, M. J. (1995). Social and cognitive approaches to depression: Towards a new synthesis. *British Journal of Clinical Psychology, 34,* 485–503.

Chess, S. (1970). Emotional problems in mentally retarded children. In F. J. Menolascino (Ed.), *Psychiatric approaches to mental retardation* (pp. 55–67). New York: Basic Books.

Chess, S. (1977). Evolution of behavior disorder in a group of mentally retarded children. *Journal of the American Academy of Child Psychiatry, 16,* 5–18.

Chetwynd, J. (1985). Factors contributing to stress on mothers caring for an intellectually handicapped child. *British Journal of Social Work, 15,* 295–304.

Coleman, J. M. (1983). Self-concept and the mildly handicapped: The role of social comparisons. *Journal of Special Education, 17,* 37–45.

Cooper, S. A. (1997). Epidemiology of psychiatric disorders in elderly compared with younger adults with learning disabilities. *British Journal of Psychiatry, 170,* 375–380.

Costa, P. T., & McCrae, R. R. (1992). Four ways five factors are basic. *Personality and Individual Differences, 13,* 653–665.

Crnic, K., Friedrich, W., & Greenberg, M. (1983). Adaptation of families with mentally retarded children: A model of stress, coping, and family ecology. *American Journal on Mental Retardation, 88,* 125–138.

Cummings, S. T. (1976). The impact of the child's deficiency on the father: A study of fathers of mentally retarded and chronically ill children. *American Journal of Orthopsychiatry, 46,* 246–255.

Cummins, R. A., & Lau, A. L. (2003). Community integration or community exposure? A review and discussion in relation to people with an intellectual disability. *Journal of Applied Research in Intellectual Disabilities, 16,* 145–157.

Curfs, L. M. G., Hoondert, V., van Lieshout, C. F. M., & Fryns, J. P. (1995). Personality profiles of youngsters with Prader-Willi syndrome and youngsters attending regular schools. *Journal of Intellectual Disability Research, 39,* 241–248.

Dagnan, D., & Sandhu, S. (1999). Social comparison, self-esteem, and depression in people with intellectual disability. *Journal of Intellectual Disability Research, 43,* 372–379.

Dosen, A. (1990). Depression in mentally retarded children. In A. Dosen & F. J. Menolascino (Eds.), *Depression in mentally retarded children and adults* (pp. 113–128). Leiden, Netherlands: Logan.

Dykens, E. M. (1999). Personality-motivation: New ties to psychopathology, etiology, and intervention. In E. Zigler & D. Bennett-Gates (Eds.), *Personality development in individuals with mental retardation* (pp. 249–270). New York: Cambridge University Press.

Dykens, E. M. (2001). Personality and psychopathology: New insights from genetic syndromes. In H. N. Switzky (Ed.), *Personality and motivation differences in persons with mental retardation* (pp. 283–317). Mahwah, NJ: Erlbaum.

Dykens, E. M., & Cohen, D. J. (1996). Effects of Special Olympics International on social competence in persons with mental retardation. *Journal of the American Academy of Child and Adolescent Psychiatry, 35,* 223–229.

Dykens, E. M., & Hodapp, R. M. (2001). Research in mental retardation: Toward an etiologic approach. *Journal of Child Psychology and Psychiatry, 42,* 49–71.

Dykens, E. M., Hodapp, R. M., & Leckman, J. F. (1994). *Behavior and development in Fragile X syndrome.* Thousand Oaks, CA: Sage.

Dykens, E. M., Rosner, B. A., & Butterbaugh, G. (1998). Exercise and sports in children and adolescents with developmental disabilities: Positive physical and psychosocial effects. *Child and Adolescent Psychiatric Clinics of North American, 7,* 757–771.

Dykens, E. M., & Smith, A. C. M. (1998). Distinctiveness and correlates of maladaptive behavior in children and adolescents with Smith-Magenis syndrome. *Journal of Intellectual Disability Research, 42,* 481–489.

Dyson, L. L. (1997). Fathers and mothers of school-age children with developmental disabilities: Parental stress, family functioning, and social support. *American Journal on Mental Retardation, 102,* 267–279.

Erwin, P. (1993). *Friendships and peer relations in children.* New York: Wiley.

Esbensen, A. J., Rojahn, J., Aman, M. G., & Ruedrich, S. (2003). Reliability and validity of an assessment instrument for anxiety, depression, and mood among individuals with mental retardation. *Journal of Autism and Developmental Disorders, 33,* 617–629.

Evans, D. W. (1998). Development of the self-concept in children with mental retardation: Organismic and contextual factors. In J. A. Burack, R. M. Hodapp, & E. Zigler (Eds.), *Handbook of mental retardation and development* (pp. 462–480). Cambridge, England: Cambridge University Press.

Eysenck, H. J. (1992). Four ways five factors are not basic. *Personality and Individual Differences, 13,* 667–673.

Festinger, L. (1954). A theory of social comparison processes. *Human Relations, 7,* 117–140.

Fine, M. J., & Caldwell, T. E. (1967). Self-evaluation of school-related behavior of educable mentally retarded children: A preliminary report. *Exceptional Children, 33,* 324.

Flint, J., & Wilkie, A. O. M. (1996). The genetics of mental retardation. *British Medical Bulletin, 52,* 453–464.

Ford, A., & Davern, L. (1989). Moving forward with school integration: Strategies for involving students with severe handicaps in the life of the school. In R. Gaylord-Ross (Ed.), *Intervention strategies for students with severe handicaps* (pp. 11–32). Baltimore: Brookes.

Gayton, W. F., & Bassett, J. E. (1972). The effect of positive and negative reaction tendencies on receptive language development in mentally retarded children. *American Journal of Mental Deficiency, 76,* 499–508.

Gibbons, S. L., & Bushakra, F. B. (1989). Effects of Special Olympics participation on the perceived competence and social acceptance of mentally retarded children. *Adapted Physical Activity Quarterly, 6,* 40–51.

Gillberg, C., Persson, E., Grufman, M., & Themner, U. (1986). Psychiatric disorders in mildly and severely retarded urban children and adolescents: Epidemiological aspects. *British Journal of Psychiatry, 149,* 68–74.

Glick, M. (1999). Developmental and experiential variables in the self-images of people with mild mental retardation. In E. Zigler & D. Bennett-Gates (Eds.), *Personality development in individuals with mental retardation* (pp. 47–69). New York: Cambridge University Press.

Gold, D. (1985). Children's friendships. *Journal of Insurability, 13,* 4–21.

Gottlieb, J., & Leyser, Y. (1981). Friendship between mentally retarded and nonretarded children. In S. Asher & J. Gottman (Eds.), *The development of children's friendships* (pp. 150–181). Cambridge, England: Cambridge University Press.

Grusec, J. E., & Lytton, H. (1988). *Social development: History, theory, and research.* New York: Springer-Verlag.

Guralnick, M. J. (1986). The peer relations of young handicapped and nonhandicapped children. In P. S. Strain, M. J. Guralnick, & H. M. Walker (Eds.), *Children's social behavior: Development, assessment, and modification* (pp. 93–140). New York: Academic Press.

Guralnick, M. J., Connor, R. T, & Hammond, M. (1995). Parent perspectives of peer relationships and friendships in integrated and specialized programs. *American Journal on Mental Retardation, 99,* 457–476.

Guralnick, M. J., Connor, R. T., Hammond, M., Gottman, J. M., & Kinnish, K. (1995). Immediate effects of mainstreamed settings on the integration of preschool children. *American Journal on Mental Retardation, 100,* 359–377.

Guralnick, M. J., & Groom, J. M. (1985). Correlates of peer-related social competence of developmentally delayed preschool children. *American Journal of Mental Deficiency, 90,* 140–150.

Guralnick, M. J., & Groom, J. M. (1987a). Dyadic peer interactions of mildly delayed and nonhandicapped preschool children. *American Journal of Mental Deficiency, 92,* 178–193.

Guralnick, M. J., & Groom, J. M. (1987b). The peer relations of mildly delayed and nonhandicapped preschool children in mainstreamed playgroups. *Child Development, 58,* 1556–1572.

Guralnick, M. J., & Groom, J. M. (1988). Friendships of preschool children in mainstreamed playgroups. *Developmental Psychology, 24,* 595–604.

Guralnick, M. J., & Weinhouse, E. M. (1984). Peer-related social interactions of developmentally delayed young children: Development and characteristics. *Developmental Psychology, 20,* 815–827.

Hamre-Nietupski, S. (1993). How much time should be spent on skill instructions and friendship development? Preferences of parents of students with moderate and severe/profound disabilities. *Education and Training in Mental Retardation, 28,* 220–231.

Hardman, M. L., Drew, C. J., & Egan, M. W. (2002). *Human exceptionality: Society, school and family.* Boston: Allyn & Bacon.

Harris, S., Kasari, C., & Sigman, M. D. (1996). Joint attention and language gains in children with Down syndrome. *American Journal on Mental Retardation, 100,* 608–619.

Harter, S. (1978). Effectance motivation reconsidered: Toward a developmental model. *Human Development, 21,* 34–64.

Harter, S. (1982). The perceived competence scale for children. *Child Development, 53,* 87–97.

Harter, S., & Zigler, E. (1968). Effectiveness of adults and peer reinforcement on the performance on institutionalized and noninstitutionalized retardates. *Journal of Abnormal Psychology, 73,* 144–149.

Hartup, W. W. (1983). Peer relations. In R H. Mussen (Series ed.) and E. M. Hetherington (Vol. Ed.), *Handbook of child psychology: Vol. 4. Socialization, personality, and social development* (pp. 103–196). New York: Wiley.

Hauser-Cram, P., Warfield, M. E., Shonkoff, J. P., Krauss, M. W., Sayer, A., & Upsher, C. C. (2001). Children with disabilities: A longitudinal study of child development and parent well-being. *Monographs of the Society for Research in Child Development, 66,* 1–131.

Haywood, H. C. (1992). The strange and wonderful symbiosis of motivation and cognition. *International Journal of Cognitive Education and Mediated Learning, 2,* 186–197.

Heiman, T. (2000). Quality and quantity of friendship: Students' and teachers' perceptions. *School Psychology International. 21,* 265–280.

Heiman, T. (2001). Depressive mood in students with mild intellectual disability: Students' reports and teachers' evaluations. *Journal of Intellectual Disability Research, 45,* 526–534.

Hodapp, R. M., & Dykens, E. M. (1996). Mental retardation. In E. J. Mash & R. A. Barkley (Eds.), *Child psychopathology* (pp. 362–389). New York: Guilford Press.

Hodapp, R. M., & Zigler, E. (1990). Applying the developmental perspective to individuals with Down syndrome. In D. Cicchetti & M. Beeghly (Eds.), *Children with Down syndrome: A developmental approach* (pp. 299–331). New York: Wiley.

Hoffman, J., & Weiner, B. (1978). Effects of attributions for success and failure on the performance of retarded adults. *American Journal of Mental Deficiency, 82,* 449–452.

Hughes, C., Rodi, M. S., Lorden, S. W., Pitkin, S. E., Derer, K. R., Hwang, B., et al. (1999). Social interactions of high school students with mental retardation and their general education peers. *American Journal on Mental Retardation, 104,* 533–544.

Jacobson, J. W., & Mulick, J. A. (1996). Definition of mental retardation. In J. W. Jacobson & J. A. Mulick (Eds.), *Manual of diagnosis and professional practice in mental retardation* (pp. 13–53). Washington, DC: American Psychological Association.

Jenkins, J. R., Odom, S. L., & Speltz, M. L. (1989). Effects of social integration on preschool children with handicaps. *Exceptional Children, 55,* 420–428.

Judge, T. A., & Ilies, R. (2002). Relationship of personality to performance motivation: A meta-analytic review. *Journal of Applied Psychology, 87,* 797–807.

Koller, H., Stephen, M. S., Richardson, S. A., Katz, M., & McLaren, J. (1982). Behavior disturbance in childhood and the early adult years in populations who were and were not mentally retarded. *Journal of Preventive Psychiatry, 1,* 453–468.

Krauss, M. W. (1993). Child-related and parenting stress. Similarities and differences between mothers and fathers of children with disabilities. *American Journal on Mental Retardation, 97,* 393–404.

Lamb, M. E., & Billings, L. A. (1997). Fathers of children with special needs. In M. E. Lamb (Ed.), *The role of the father in child development.* New York: Wiley.

Lambert, N., Nihira, K., & Leland, H. (1993). *AAMR Adaptive Behavior Scale: School* (2nd ed.). Austin, TX: Pro-Ed.

Leonard, H., & Wen, X. (2002). The epidemiology of mental retardation: Challenges and opportunities in the new millennium. *Mental Retardation and Developmental Disabilities Research Reviews, 8,* 117–134.

Lewis, M. (2001). Issues in the study of personality development. *Psychological Inquiry, 21,* 67–83.

Linna, S., Moilanen, I., Ebeling, H., Piha, J., Kumpulainen, K., Tamminen, T., et al. (1999). Psychiatric symptoms in children with intellectual disability. *European Child and Adolescent Psychiatry, 8,* 77–82.

Loveland, K. A. (1987). Behavior of young children with Down syndrome before the mirror: Finding things reflected. *Child Development, 58,* 928–936.

Luckasson, R., Borthwick-Duffy, S., Buntinx, W. H. E., Coulter, D. L., Craig, E. M., Reeve, A., et al. (2002). *Mental retardation: Definition, classification, and systems of supports* (10th ed.). Washington, DC: American Association on Mental Retardation.

MacDonald, K. (1995). Evolution, the five-factor model, and levels of personality. *Journal of Personality, 63,* 525–567.

MacMillan, D., & Keogh, B. (1971). Normal and retarded children's expectancy for failure. *Developmental Psychology, 9,* 477–494.

Madden, N. A., & Slavin, R. E. (1983). Mainstreaming students with mild handicaps: Academic and social outcomes. *Review of Educational Research, 53,* 519–569.

Mans, L., Cicchetti, D., & Sroufe, L. A. (1978). Mirror reactions of Down's syndrome infants and toddlers: Cognitive underpinnings of self-recognition. *Child Development, 49,* 1247–1250.

Matson, J. L., Smiroldo, B. B., Hamilton, M., & Baglio, C. S. (1997). Do anxiety disorders exist in persons with severe and profound mental retardation? *Research in Developmental Disabilities, 18,* 39–44.

McCrae, R. R. (2001). Traits through time. *Psychological Inquiry, 21,* 85–87.

Minke, K. M., Bear, G. G., Deemer, S. A., & Griffin, S. M. (1996). Teachers' experiences with inclusive classrooms: Implications for special education reform. *Journal of Special Education, 30,* 152–186.

Murphy, C. C., Boyle, C., Schendel, D., Decouflé, P., & Yeargin-Allsopp, M. (1998). Epidemiology of mental retardation in children. *Mental Retardation and Developmental Disabilities Reviews, 4,* 6–13.

Nicholls, J., Cheung, P., Lauer, J., & Patashnick, M. (1989). Individual differences in academic motivation: Perceived ability, goals, beliefs, and values. *Learning and Individual Differences, 1,* 63–84.

Nihira, K., Meyers, C. E., & Mink, I. T. (1980). Home environment, family adjustment, and the development of mentally retarded children. *Applied Research in Mental Retardation, 1,* 5–24.

O'Brien, G. (2002). Dual diagnosis in offenders with intellectual disability: Setting research priorities: A review of research findings concerning psychiatric disorder (excluding personality disorder) among offenders with intellectual disability. *Journal of Intellectual Disability Research, 46*(Suppl. 1), 21–30.

Ollendick, T., Balla, D., & Zigler, E. (1971). Expectancy of success and the probability learning of retarded children. *Journal of Abnormal Psychology, 77,* 275–281.

Palmer, D. S., Borthwick-Duffy, S. A., Widaman, K., & Best, S. J. (1998). Influences on parent perceptions of inclusive practices for their children with mental retardation. *American Journal on Mental Retardation, 103,* 272–287.

Philips, I., & Williams, N. (1975). Psychopathology of mental retardation: A study of 100 mentally retarded children. I: Psychopathology. *American Journal of Psychiatry, 132,* 1265–1271.

Pober, B. R., & Dykens, E. M. (1996). Williams syndrome: An overview of medical, cognitive, and behavioral features. *Child and Adolescent Psychiatric Clinics of North America, 5,* 929–943.

Qualter, P., & Munn, P. (2002). The separateness of social and emotional loneliness in childhood. *Journal of Child Psychology and Psychiatry and Allied Disciplines, 43,* 233–244.

Ramirez, S. Z., & Kratochwill, T. R. (1997). Self-reported fears in children with and without mental retardation. *Mental Retardation, 35,* 83–92.

Ratey, J. J., Dymek, M. P., Fein, D., Joy, S., Green, L. A., & Waterhouse, L. (2000). Neurodevelopmental disorders. In B. S. Fogel, R. B. Schiffer, & S. M. Rao (Eds.), *Synopsis of neuropsychiatry* (pp. 245–271). Philadelphia: Lippincott, Williams & Wilkins.

Ricci, L. A., & Hodapp, R. M. (2003). Fathers of children with Down's syndrome versus other types of intellectual disability: Perceptions, stress and involvement. *Journal of Intellectual Disability Research, 47,* 273–284.

Roach, M. A., Orsmond, G. I., & Barratt, M. (1999). Mothers and fathers of children with Down syndrome: Parental stress and involvement in child care. *American Journal on Mental Retardation, 104,* 422–436.

Roberts, B. R., & Caspi, A. (2001). Personality development and the person-situation debate: It's déjà vu all over again. *Psychological Inquiry, 12,* 104–109.

Roberts, G. C., & Treasure, D. C. (1992). Children in sport. *Sport Science Review, 1,* 46–64.

Robertson, J., Emerson, E., Gregory, N., Hatton, C., Kessissoglou, S., Hallam, A., et al. (2002). Social networks of people with mental retardation in residential settings. *Mental Retardation, 39,* 201–214.

Roeleveld, N., Zielhuis, G. A., & Gabreels, F. (1997). The prevalence of mental retardation: A critical review of recent literature. *Developmental Medicine and Child Neurology, 39,* 125–132.

Rosen, J. W., & Burchard, S. N. (1990). Community activities and social support networks: A social comparison of adults with and adults without mental retardation. *Education and Training in Mental Retardation, 25,* 193–204.

Rothisberg, B. A., Hill, R., & D'Amato, R. C. (1994). Social acceptance by their peers of children with mental retardation. *Psychological Reports, 74,* 239–242.

Schalock, R. L., Harper, R. S., & Carver, G. (1981). Independent living placement: Five years later. *American Journal on Mental Deficiency, 86,* 170–177.

Scheuermann, B., Webber, J., Boutot, E. A., & Goodwin, M. (2003). Problems with personnel preparation in autism spectrum disorders. *Focus on Autism and Other Developmental Disabilities, 18,* 197–206.

Schunk, D. H. (1985). Participation in goal setting: Effects on self-efficacy and skills of learning disabled children. *Journal of Special Education, 19,* 307–317.

Schurr, K. T., Towne, R. C., & Joiner, L. M. (1972). Trends in self-concepts of ability over 2 years of special education class placement. *Journal of Special Education, 6,* 161–166.

Sherrill, C. (1993). Women with disabilities. In G. L. Cohen (Ed.), *Women in sport: Issues and controversies* (pp. 238–248). Thousand Oaks, CA: Sage.

Silon, E. L., & Harter, S. (1985). Assessment of perceived competence, motivational orientation, and anxiety in segregated and mainstreamed educable mentally retarded children. *Journal of Educational Psychology, 77,* 217–230.

Songster, T. (1984). The Special Olympics Sport program: An international sport program for mentally retarded athletes. In C. Sherrill (Ed.), *Sport and disabled athletes* (pp. 73–79). Champaign, IL: Human Kinetics.

Sparrow, S. S., Balla, D. A., & Cicchetti, D. V. (1984). *Vineland Adaptive Behavior Scale.* Circle Pines, MN: American Guidance Service.

Strain, P. S., & Kerr, M. M. (1981). *Mainstreaming of children in schools.* New York: Academic Press.

Strain, P. S., Odom, S. L., & McConnell, S. (1984). Promoting social reciprocity of exceptional children: Identification, target behavior, and intervention. *Remedial and Special Education, 5,* 21–28.

Strully, J. L., & Strully, C. (1993). That which binds us: Friendship as a safe harbor in a storm. In A. N. Amado (Ed.), *Friendships and community connections between people with and without developmental disabilities* (pp. 213–225). Baltimore: Brookes.

Switzky, H. N. (2001). Personality and motivational self-system processes in persons with mental retardation: Old memories and new perspectives. In H. N. Switzky (Ed.), *Personality and motivation differences in persons with mental retardation* (pp. 57–146). Mahwah, NJ: Erlbaum.

Tassi, F., Schneider, B. H., & Richard, J. F. (2001). Competitive behavior at school in relation to social competence and incompetence in middle childhood. *Revue Internationale de Psychologie Sociale, 14,* 165–184.

Taylor, A. R., Asher, S. R., & Williams, G. A. (1987). The social adaptations of mainstreamed mildly retarded children. *Child Development, 58,* 1321–1334.

Tonge, B. J., & Einfeld, S. L. (2003). Psychopathology and intellectual disability: The Australian child to adult longitudinal study. In L. M. Glidden (Ed.), *International Review of Research in Mental Retardation, 26,* 61–91.

Vygotsky, L. S. (1978). *Mind in society: The development of higher psychological processes.* Cambridge, MA: Harvard University Press.

Wallander, J. L., Dekker, M. C., & Koot, H. M. (2003). Psychopathology in children and adolescents with intellectual disability: Measurement, prevalence, course, and risk. In L. M. Glidden (Ed.), *International review of research in mental retardation* (Vol. 26, 93–134). San Diego: Academic Press.

Wehmeyer, M. L., & Palmer, S. B. (1997). Perceptions of control of students with and without cognitive disabilities. *Psychological Reports, 81,* 195–206.

Weiss, J., Diamond, T., Demark, J., & Lovald, B. (2003). Involvement in Special Olympics and its relations to self-concept and actual competency in participants with developmental disabilities. *Research in Developmental Disabilities, 24,* 281–305.

Weiss, J., Diamond, T., & Sullivan, A. (2004, June). *Involvement in Special Olympics and its relations to maternal and paternal stress.* Poster presented at the 128th Annual Meeting of the American Association on Mental Retardation, Philadelphia.

Weisz, J. R. (1999). Cognitive performance and learned helplessness in mentally retarded persons. In E. Zigler & D. Bennett-Gates (Eds.), *Personality development in individuals with mental retardation* (pp. 17–46). New York: Cambridge University Press.

White, R. H. (1959). Motivation reconsidered: The concept of competence. *Psychological Review, 66,* 297–333.

Widaman, K. F., MacMillan, D. L., Hemsley, R. E., Little, T. D., & Balow, I. H. (1992). Differences in adolescents' self-concept as a function of academic level, ethnicity, and gender. *American Journal on Mental Retardation, 96,* 387–404.

Wills, T. A. (1981). Downward comparison principles. *Psychological Bulletin, 90,* 245–271.

Winzer, M. (1999). *Children with exceptionalities in Canadian classrooms.* Toronto, Canada: Prentice Hall.

Wong, D., Pearson, V., Ip, F., & Lo, E. (1999). A slippery road to equality: Hong Kong's experience of unplanned integrated education. *Disability and Society, 14,* 771–777.

World Health Organization. (1992). *International statistical classification of diseases and related health problems* (10th ed.). Geneva: Author.

Zayas, V., Shoda, Y., & Ayduk, O. N. (2002). Personality in context: An interpersonal systems perspective. *Journal of Personality, 70,* 851–900.

Zetlin, A. G., & Turner, J. L. (1988). Salient domains in the self-conception of adults with mental retardation. *Mental Retardation, 26,* 219–222.

Zigler, E. (2001). Looking back 40 years and still seeing the person with mental retardation as a whole person. In H. N. Switzky (Ed.), *Personality and motivation differences in persons with mental retardation* (pp. 3–55). Mahwah, NJ: Erlbaum.

Zigler, E., Balla, D., & Butterfield, E. C. (1968). A longitudinal investigation of the relationship between preinstitutional social deprivation and social motivation in institutionalized retardates. *Journal of Personality and Social Psychology, 10,* 437–445.

Zigler, E., & Bennett-Gates, D. (Eds.) (1999). *Personality development in individuals with mental retardation.* New York: Cambridge University Press.

Zigler, E., Bennett-Gates, D., Hodapp, R., & Henrich, C. C. (2002). Assessing personality traits of individuals with mental retardation. *American Journal on Mental Retardation, 107,* 181–193.

Zigler, E., & Hodapp, R. M. (1986). *Understanding mental retardation.* New York: Cambridge University Press.

Zoeller, C., Mahoney, G. J., & Weiner, B. (1983). Effects of attribution training on the assembly task performance of mentally retarded adults. *American Journal of Mental Deficiency, 88,* 109–112.

CHAPTER 15

Pervasive Developmental Disorders

BRYNA SIEGEL AND MICHELLE FICCAGLIA

DESCRIPTION OF THE DISORDERS AND CLINICAL PICTURE

The pervasive developmental disorders (PDDs) are a constellation of neuropsychiatric symptoms constituting a neurodevelopmental syndrome characterized by a triad of social impairments (American Psychiatric Association, 1994). This triad of social impairments includes (1) atypical social interactions, (2) atypical communication, and (3) atypical responses to social and perceptual stimuli in the environment. The PDDs encompass several specific diagnostic categories in *DSM-IV.* The main category is autistic disorder (AD). Other manifestations of the syndrome that typically encompass subsets of the symptoms seen in AD include pervasive developmental disorder not otherwise specified (PDD-NOS) and Asperger's disorder, more commonly referred to as Asperger's syndrome (AS). Other variants include Rett syndrome, now understood to have a specific and separate genetic etiology; atypical autism; and the very low incidence childhood disintegrative disorder (<0.2/10,000; Volkmar, 1992). In the last 10 years since the publication of *DSM-IV,* the PDDs have often been referred to as the autistic spectrum disorders (ASDs), and in this chapter we will use those two terms interchangeably as well. This change in terminology has resulted from increased understanding of a broader autistic phenotype and serves to reduce confusion in reference to the PDDs versus PDD-NOS, and to reduce the inaccurate impression that PDD was simply descriptive of pervasive delays—likely to be more appropriately characterized as mental retardation.

The diagnostic criteria for AD, PDD-NOS, and AS revolve around a common set of 12 symptoms, four representing atypical social interactions, four representing atypical communication, and four representing atypical responses to social and perceptual stimuli. The criteria for AS are identical to those for AD, omitting any requirement for atypical communication and requiring onset of single words by age 2 years and phrases or sentences by age 3. AS also requires an IQ above 70 in both verbal and nonverbal domains. Within each of the three categories of PDD symptoms, individual criteria are organized in roughly the order in which they developmentally can be expected to emerge. Signs should be globally rated with respect to overall mental age so as not to confound autistic symptoms with mental retardation, a common co-morbid condition.

The 12 diagnostic criteria for ASDs can be reviewed with respect to how each is associated with altered perception or processing of specific types of social or environmental stimuli. No single criterion for ASDs is remarkably prevalent (or sensitive) *and* also highly unique (specific). Instead, diagnosis requires that two social (A), one communicative (B), and one social-perceptual (C) criteria, and six criteria overall be considered positive to meet criteria for AD. PDD-NOS is typically construed to represent a less full manifestation of AD. If fewer than six criteria but at least two from A and one from B are met, PDD-NOS is diagnosed. PDD-NOS is also diagnosed if more than six criteria are positive but no social-perceptual (C) criteria are met. AS is diagnosed when at least two social criteria and one social-perceptual criterion are met (i.e., as for PDD-NOS). However, unlike with PDD-NOS, language development is considered essentially typical in semantics, morphology, and syntax. Tone of voice (prosody) may be flat or lilting, which may reflect lack of capacity to tie subtle affective information to verbal communication. Individuals with AS typically proceed from a more to a less severe course, with the characteristic neurodevelopmental difference between AD/PDD-NOS and AS manifest by the preschool or early school years. (This is clinically important in that many false positive diagnoses of AS get made when diagnosticians fail to account for very early social developmental patterns being consistent with an ASD.) Because the very earliest symptoms of AS can be consistent with those of PDD-NOS, the differential diagnosis of AS can be very hard to establish before age 3 or 4. High-functioning autism is a designation reserved for those individuals meeting criteria for autism and with verbal and nonverbal IQ in the non–mentally retarded range.

Social Interactive Criteria for PDDs

The earliest signs of ASDs relate to failures in the development of the paralinguistic signaling system and are characterized by the well-known hallmarks of poor eye contact, failure to develop a protodeclarative point, and lack of facial affect that demonstrates reciprocal engagement or shared attention. Children meeting this criterion experience major disability in the primary set of prelinguistic mechanisms for organizing social stimuli as well as foundational skills for spoken language. Spoken language development is facilitated by the child or adult being able to guide attention to a shared perspective. Without such prerequisite paralinguistic capacity, emerging language will almost certainly be atypical. This developmental failure is almost always fundamental to the failure to share enjoyment or attention seeking, which later becomes an even more specific manifestation of the failed development of joint attention. Some children with autism initially develop an instrumental form of joint attending to get a specific need met, but they may fail to generalize the capacity to more purely social situations in which a child typically seeks to share his pleasure in an activity with a caregiver. Later, the lack of mutuality becomes expressed as a lack of peer relations wherein the child, lacking affiliative drive, tends to neither imitate nor join other children because there is no shared frame of reference for the potential relationship. Finally, atypical social interactive qualities manifest as a lack of sympathy, empathy, or any other acknowledgment of reciprocal experience. At this stage, lack of affective response in attunement to social situations is apparent, usually in the form of diminished affective variability, lack of multidimensionality of affect (only happy and sad, not guilty or apprehensive, pleased or proud).

Atypical Communication

The second dimension of the autistic triad of social impairments consists of those involving language comprehension and social use. First noticed and most pervasive is a failure to make compensatory use of gestural communication in the absence of spoken capacity. Much like a typically developed adult who relies on gesture in a foreign language environment, infants and toddlers should engage in comparable practice, using gesture, gaze directing, and pointing to decode and clarify spoken language they do not fully comprehend. Lack of paralinguistic capacity increases the difficulty and limits the compensatory strategies available to the language-emerging child with ASD. Another aspect of language failure associated with ASD is the presence of echolalic or stereotyped utterances with little or no communicative value. Many young children with delayed language development characterized by adequate auditory memory but poor parsing or processing of language, or both, may echo as a functional conversational repair strategy. Children with ASDs often do so without communicative intent (such as repeating whole or fragmented portions of videos or songs in a manner tied to neither action nor communication). Related to this is a lack of use of language for conversational purposes, especially purely social purposes, in that neither affiliative drive, shared frame of reference, nor complete comprehension of what is being said may be intact. Finally, also included as atypical communication is the child with ASD's incapacity to engage in representational or abstract play comparable to that of other children with the same developmental level of communicative competence. Children with ASD typically will not play in a way that represents an attempt to represent their social experiences via their own actions. This not only shows another dimension of the child's failure to see the self as others do—or to be like others—but also represents failure of a mechanism whereby typically developing children can use play to consolidate language meaning through reenactment and rehearsal via playacting.

Atypical Responses to Sensory-Perceptual Stimuli

The third dimension of the triad of social impairments in ASDs encompasses abnormal ways in which individuals with ASDs relate to experiences in their nonsocial world. First is a preoccupation with restricted and narrow interests as well as preoccupation with (sensory) parts of objects. These symptoms can be understood to emerge from a confluence of lack of interest in learning via imitation and the range of atypical social symptoms. In addition, individuals with ASDs often have hyper- or hypoacute sensory thresholds that may drive them to avoid or repetitively seek out stimuli with certain characteristics. Given high levels of comorbid mental retardation, exploratory drive is also often reduced, and this is synergistic with the aforementioned influences. Related to this, adherence to nonfunctional routines and rituals can also be seen as a confluence of other signs of autism: functional routines may well serve language-limited individuals who cannot use language to question or regulate what is happening to them. However, when atypical social symptoms are added to this, the routines that arise may become detached from the socialization pressures that usually shape procedural preferences. Though not specific to the ASDs, many individuals display motor stereotypies that appear to serve as an extension of the difficulties with regulation of sensory thresholds, with increased stereotypies typically in evidence as sensory and social stimulation increase above tolerable limits, or, conversely, sometimes as arousal reducing.

Overall, it is clinically important to qualitatively evaluate the individual for the presence of each of the symptoms of ASDs in relation to others in that it (1) improves validity of diagnosis, and (2) leads to accurate differential diagnosis of the symptom as it might instead present in a related disorder such as a psychotic disorder, a language disorder, or mental retardation.

PERSONALITY DEVELOPMENT AND PSYCHOPATHOLOGY

Developmental Neuropathology

ASDs are a distinctive developmental disability in that the development of its symptoms is preceded by a period of seemingly normal development. Longitudinal and retrospective video studies indicate that the earliest symptoms of autism become distinctive at around the first birthday and increase in both number and intensity following the first birthday and through preschool (DeMyer, 1979; Werner, Dawson, Osterling, & Dinno, 2000). However, it is rare for children to be diagnosed this early. Autism and PDD-NOS are typically diagnosed between 2 and 4 years of age. Typically, parents present to pediatricians with concerns about language development. Soon after, they may express concerns about problems with social skills. The repetitive interests and behaviors associated with ASD diagnoses become more noticeable after the child's second birthday and are not typically reported as primary parental concerns. Children with AS are usually not identified until after 4 years of age (Ozonoff, Dawson, & McPartland, 2002). These children often present with generalized parental and school concerns about social development such as overactivity, social difficulties, and dislike of change (Gilchrist et al., 2001).

First Developmental Concerns

Although language and sometimes social development concerns are often parents' presenting complaints, even earlier social-communication deficits typically precede these concerns. Early red flags include a lack of following gaze, lack of protodeclarative pointing, and lack of interest in animate toys (Siegel, 2004). Key developmental concerns that differentiate young children with ASDs from children with other developmental delays are detailed in the following section.

Deficits in Joint Attention and Pragmatics

In preverbal children with autism the clearest deficits in language development involve difficulties in engaging in joint attention. Joint attention is the ability to knowingly share the focus of attention, to follow another's attentional lead, and to lead another person's attentional focus (Rogers, 1999). In addition, joint attention involves the ability to understand and use common and natural gestures such as pointing to objects and showing objects to others (Mundy, Sigman, & Kasari, 1990). Joint attention skills are a foundation of social-cognitive process, which allows the child to communicate with his or her parents, and are believed to facilitate future language and cognitive development. Specific differences in joint attention skills of children eventually diagnosed with ASDs are evident in retrospective analyses of family video recordings as early as 12 months of age. Osterling and Dawson (1994) found that at their first birthday, children who were later diagnosed with autism oriented to their name less often than typically developing children, showed an object to another person less often than typically developing children, and looked into the face of anther person less often than typically developing children. In addition, none of the children eventually diagnosed with autism pointed. These deficits in nonverbal joint attention have been shown to persist over time in comparison to language-matched mentally retarded children (Mundy et al., 1990). Further, variations in joint attention skills between individuals with ASDs have been correlated to language outcomes.

In verbal children with ASDs, the joint attention difficulties associated with the disorder are evident as impairments in the pragmatics of language. These deficits include difficulties using gestures, eye gaze, prosody, organization of narrative, repairs in breakdowns, and conversational skills when interacting with others (Rogers, 1999).

Deficits in the Development and Nature of Play

The qualitative nature of the play exhibited by children with autism is markedly different from the play of their peers. For instance, children with autism are often described as engaging in repetitive sensory-motor play. Instead of actively exploring their environment, these children are content to repeatedly explore a single object in a monotonous or stereotyped fashion. Further, the play activities of children with ASDs tend to lack the spontaneity, flexibility, and symbolic pretence that are considered to be hallmarks of play. Additionally, the social nature of play is also affected in children with ASDs. Because children with autism have deficits in social understanding, they often find it difficult to participate in social games and imaginary play activities with peers. When children with ASDs do participate in social play, their interactions are often marked by less proximity to peers, fewer responses to social overtures, and more solitary activities.

EPIDEMIOLOGY

The epidemiology of ASDs has become a controversial topic in need of further research. In the last 10 years, there has been a steady rise in the number of cases from a number of sources (see Fombonne, 2003, for the most recent, authoritative review of these issues). At the time that *DSM-III* (American Psychiatric Association, 1980) as well as *DSM-III-R* (American Psychiatric Association, 1989) were published, 4–5 cases per 10,000 were the commonly accepted incidence rates, based on epidemiological samples collected in the 1960s (e.g., Lotter, 1966), even though case finding in this early study was based on a simple rating scale. Additional prevalence studies made between 1966 and 1989 continued to use a variety of nonstandardized criteria for case finding, so it is difficult to compare rates from such studies with subsequent work using *DSM-III, DSM-III-R,* and *DSM-IV* criteria.

Reasons for Rise in Prevalence

It is known that between *DSM-III* and *DSM-III-R* the pervasive developmental disorders were redefined in a way that resulted in about a third more cases in the norming sample meeting *DSM-III-R* criteria compared to the clinically assigned so-called gold standard diagnosis (Spitzer & Siegel, 1990). The revision of the diagnostic criteria was not instantly reflected in clinical practice, but five years later, with the issuance of *DSM-IV* (American Psychiatric Association, 1994), it was clear that many more individuals were being diagnosed as having a PDD. In addition, *DSM-IV* added the diagnosis of Asperger's disorder (AS).

Around that time, it became increasingly common to refer to the PDDs as the ASDs. The understanding of the PDDs as autistic spectrum disorders corresponded to two phenomena. First, the symptoms of autism were increasingly understood to be ubiquitous, meaning that none were completely unique to the ASDs, but rather, to varying extents, that the signs of ASDs were shared with related neurodevelopmental conditions, including language disorders (e.g., echolalia), mental retardation syndromes (e.g., motor stereotypies), and some neuropsychiatric conditions such as obsessive-compulsive disorder (e.g., nonfunctional routines and rituals).

Second, beginning in the mid-1980s with the inception of the Human Genome Project, there was a resurgence of interest in the genetics of autism for the first time since the 1970s when Folstein and Rutter (1988) described risk-recurrence in monozygotic (MZ) and dizygotic (DZ) twins with autism and convincingly supported a genetic etiology for autism. As a result of work in the behavioral genetics of autism and the field of neuropsychiatric genetics in general, it became clear that autism as a syndrome with a range of symptoms as well as a range of phenotypic expression was likely polygenetic. A critical step for research in autism genetics was the development of sensitive clinical technology (such as the Autism Diagnostic Interview—Revised [ADI-R]; Lord, Rutter, & LeCouteur, 1994; and the Autism Diagnostic Observation Schedule [ADOS]; Lord et al., 2000) for measurement of even the mildest forms of symptomatology. With recognition of a mild autistic phenotype, plus the addition of AS, a number of individuals who clearly would not have been diagnosable under *DSM-III* or *DSM-III-R* began to be counted.

The *DSM* directs diagnosticians to diagnose based on significant functional impairment as the result of symptoms—but this has proven to be a very soft threshold. Therefore it is increasingly common in studies of multiplex families to characterize mildly phenotypic parents (though they are married, reproducing, fully educated, and gainfully employed) also as autistic.

Another factor that is posited to play a role in reported autism incidence is early diagnosis. In 1988, Lovaas reported marked success in treating the youngest children with autism. Although the importance of earliness in intervention for neurodevelopmental disorders was well understood before this time, no explicit models for early treatment were widely available or accepted. Special education budgets have risen roughly as have the rates of diagnosis of autism, with autism receiving increasingly larger proportions of special education budgets (Gutner, 2004). With many children receiving upward of $60,000 per year in educational treatments for autism, the diagnosis has become the gateway to the most intensive level of special education services. It has been speculated that high levels of special educational access, therefore, may partly drive increasing rates of autism diagnosis. In addition, educational authorities tend to have fewer diagnostic or descriptive categories to demarcate qualification for special education services, and so some children may be diagnosed and qualified for services as educationally autistic without consideration of the full *DSM* criteria. To be considered educationally autistic, a child must exhibit a "developmental disability significantly affecting verbal and nonverbal communication and social interaction, generally evident before age 3, that adversely affects a child's educational performance" (e.g., California Department of Education).

Current Epidemiology

In 2003, Fombonne updated an original 1999 report of epidemiological surveys of ASDs. He included 32 English-language surveys made between 1966 and 2001 in 13 countries. Each survey found widely varying rates, depending on diagnostic criteria used and methodology for data collection (including screening procedures and confirmatory diagnosis). Over time, however, rates of reported autism have definitely grown. The reported ratio of males to females continues to be consistently reported—between 3:1 and 5:1 (males:females). Overall, the average incidence rates for all PDDs at present now appear to be closer to 30/10,000—or about 6 times higher than in the earliest reported survey (Lotter, 1966). AS alone is alternately rated as much more or much less prevalent than all PDDs together, but the average prevalence is most lower than for other PDDs—about 2.5/10,000—or only about 1/12th the rate of autism plus PDD-NOS. No consistent patterns or higher rates of autism have been found according to ethnicity or social class (Fombonne, 2003). Overall, epidemiological studies of autism make it clear why autism has received so much more attention in recent years. However, it is important to note that none of the epidemiological work to date can serve as confirmation for any etiological hypotheses that may bear on increasing incidence.

ETIOLOGY

Behavioral Genetics

As already noted, the earliest support for autism as a highly genetic neurodevelopmental disorder came from twin studies made in the 1970s (see Folstein & Rutter, 1988). Over time, their estimates and those of others for concordance in MZ twins has ranged from the high 90th percentile to around 60 percent with DZ twin recurrence between 3 percent and 7 percent (similar to or slightly higher than for siblings). Although sibling risk recurrence is considered low at about 3 percent to 5 percent, it is 50- to 100-fold higher than for the general population—also reinforcing our understanding of how highly genetic this disorder is. The most recent work on twins has been done by Bailey, Hatten, Mesibov, Ament, and Skinner (1995), and on families by Bolton et al. (1994). These studies have been subject to further quantitative analyses by Pickles et al. (1995), who concluded that twin and family data, plus dropoff in recurrence among second-degree relatives, suggest that the autism spectrum represents three or four different genes occurring in different subsets and with different phenotypic expressions, including the broader phenotype most often described in parents of probands.

Prenatal Suboptimality

Genetic explanations as to the etiology of autism, however, do not account for why about 70 percent of those with autism have mental retardation, whereas relatives (e.g., parents) with the broader phenotype (and thus assumed to have largely the same genotype) do not have mental retardation, other than to suggest that affected individuals have a larger dose of the gene. Alternatively, the presence of mental retardation in so many of those with autism may be understood to be caused by interaction between autism genetics and other factors. At one time researchers sought to causally correlate pre- and perinatal events to aspects of autism (e.g., Knobloch & Pasamanick, 1975; Siegel, Anders, Ciaranello, Bienenstock, & Kraemer, 1984). Currently, the working hypothesis about suboptimality is inverse—that abnormal fetuses are more likely to accrue suboptimal pre- and perinatal events as in other forms of mental retardation (Simonoff, McGuffin, & Gottesman, 1994).

Other factors that may influence gene degree of expression or the probability of concomitant genetic abnormalities have received relatively little systematic study. Included in these factors are maternal age, which has always been associated with increased rate of birth defects, and assisted conceptions (e.g., in vitro fertilization) that essentially override processes of natural selection (von During et al., 1995). Also poorly understood and characterized are the approximately 10 percent of cases of autism with a second comorbid disorder of known or suspect genetic etiology (Simonoff et al., 1994). Worthy of note here is that of eight studies that have reported comorbidity of autism and fragile X syndrome, the average comorbidity is 0.3 percent—though it was once thought to be much more common in ASDs (Fombonne, 2003).

Environmental Risks

Additional factors have been suspected as triggers for gene expression and severity. These include various specific and nonspecific environmental risks. One type of study has investigated whether there are environmental clusters in autism incidence (e.g., Bertrand et al., 2001), but such work has not resulted in identification of any specific common environmental risks. Most controversial has been the hypothesized impact of either the measles, mumps, and rubella (MMR) vaccination or thimerisol, a preservative in the MMR vaccine and other childhood vaccines. This question has now been very thoroughly studied, and position papers by organizations central to the issue (e.g., American Academy of Pediatrics,

World Health Organization) have all reaffirmed the safety of thimerisol and childhood vaccine regimes based on meta-analyses of numerous nationwide epidemiological studies. The most current of these is the 2004 Institute of Medicine report.

Neuroanatomical Findings

The autistic spectrum is a heterogeneous array of symptoms and symptom severities. Not surprisingly, neuroanatomical research that may explain the implications of any genetic differences have been hard to demonstrate consistently. A wide range of methodologies have been used to study neuropathological processes in autism including autopsy, EEG (electroencephalography); magnetic resonance imaging (MRI); functional MRI; and, most recently, magnetoencephalography. Subject age, gender, degree of mental retardation, and symptoms and severity all factor into reported patterns of findings. There is no single pathophysiological model for ASDs, though there seems to be support for the idea that neuropathological processes begin in utero, with subsequent mediation of effects by various processes influencing early brain plasticity.

Some fairly consistent and repeated findings provide direction for future research in the pathophysiology of autism. Macrocephaly has frequently been reported, though head size at birth is more often normal (Miles, Hadden, Takahashi, & Hillman, 2000). Increased brain volume, particularly at earlier ages, and increased white matter have been reported (Filapek, 1999). Autopsy studies have revealed a number of structural abnormalities—though again, these findings are neither consistent nor linked clearly to function. These include subcortical forebrain abnormalities of the limbic system, anomalies of the cerebellum, abnormalities in brain stem nuclei, reduced numbers of Purkinje cells in the cerebellum, and abnormalities in the amygdala and in the fusiform gyrus (see Newschaffer, Fallin, & Lee, 2002).

A long history of serologic work in autism dates back to studies started in the 1960s on serotonin, a neurotransmitter thought to be active in neuronal differentiation. Studies of serotonin synaptogenesis have not yielded consistent findings, however, nor has work on autoantibodies, neuropeptides, or neurotrophins (also see Newschaffer et al., 2002).

Another long-standing finding is an increased rate of epilepsy (averaging 17 percent; Fombonne, 2003) associated with ASDs, although no specific type(s) of seizure activity has been linked (Deykin & MacMahon, 1979).

Work on perceptual and cognitive processes using various neuroimaging methods have begun to show a pattern of maturational and processing speed differences that include atypicalities in laterality, auditory processing, sensory processing, affect, and facial recognition. Children with autism are often reported to have inconsistent cerebral dominance (e.g., Escalante, Minshew, & Sweeney, 2003); problems in regional specialization, as in facial recognition (e.g., Carver & Dawson, 2002); difficulties in interhemispheric circuitry (Boddaert & Zilbovicius, 2002); and overall differences in size of specific brain structures (Hardan, Minshew, & Keshavan, 2000).

COURSE, COMPLICATIONS, AND PROGNOSIS

Age of Onset

Determining the age of onset for ASDs is made difficult by the necessity to rely on parent report, which can be affected by parental experience, knowledge, denial, and variability within the disorder. Although the literature indicates that the age of onset is spread fairly evenly across the first 30–36 months of life, considerable evidence exists that the population breaks into two separate groups: those with early-onset autism and those with so-called regressive autism.

Individuals designated as having early-onset autism have social and communication symptoms that are identifiable by experts in retrospective analysis as early as 8–10 months of age (Werner et al., 2000). Those designated as having regressive or late-onset autism represent 20 percent to 49 percent of children diagnosed with ASDs. Parents of these children report that their child's earliest development is typical. However, between 12 and 24 months of age parents describe a period where established first words as well as social and play skills plateau, diminish, or are lost. Parental reports of late-onset autism have been substantiated by retrospective video analysis that indicates that the first symptoms of the disorder were not detectable by experts until after the first birthday (Werner et al., 2000). Although verbal and nonverbal (e.g., eye contact) communication losses are the most commonly reported areas of regression, other losses have been reported, including decreases in social, play, and imitation skills (Davidovitch, Glick, Holtzman, Tirosh, & Safir, 2000).

The presence of regressive autism in the population has led to substantial debate about environmental risk factors (including thimerisol in immunizations). Research has failed to find a consistent link between developmental regression and medical history (e.g., fever, exposure to thimerisol) or social factors (e.g., divorce, move to a new home). However, regressive autism has been linked to developmental outcomes. For instance, loss of speech has been associated with lower functioning in a variety of domains, including a greater severity of mental retardation, greater social deficits, and poorer language development (Rogers & DiLalla, 1990).

Developmental Course

Some of the earliest concerns associated with ASDs include poor language development, increasing repetitive behaviors, lack of appropriate toy play, atypical social behavior, and difficulties with eating and toilet training (Rogers, 1999). As children with ASDs get older they often exhibit impairments in a large number of domains, including executive function, cognitive functioning, communication and language use, social-emotional functioning, social engagement, imitation, emotional responsiveness, play, motor functioning, and sensory functioning. Unlike children with mental retardation, children with autism tend to show an uneven developmental profile with relatively lower scores in social and language development in comparison to cognitive, adaptive, and motor skills (Bailey et al., 2000).

What Influences Outcome?

Reviews of model programs have noted that several factors are likely to influence outcomes (e.g., Dawson & Osterling, 1996; National Research Council, 2001; Rogers, 1998). The most frequently noted factors to influence outcome include the age of treatment initiation and treatment intensity. Additionally, research indicates that the child's characteristics before treatment have a significant predictive value in determining outcomes. For instance, children with behavioral problems and higher levels of cognitive impairment tend to do worse. In contrast, children who develop early joint attention, symbolic play, and receptive language tend to do better over time.

Some intervention models, notably those adhering to the Young Autism Project/discrete trial training (YAP/DTT) methods (Lovaas, 1987), claim that if children with autism are treated with the right methodology, they will recover from autism. Perhaps the most frequently quoted statistic in this realm is that of the initial and follow-up Lovaas studies (Lovaas, 1987; Lovaas & Smith, 1989). These studies claimed that 47 percent of the participants in the YAP program recovered normal functioning and were indistinguishable from their peers. General consensus in the field views these claims with a high degree of skepticism, especially given that Lovaas's findings have never been fully replicated after 15 years of attempts. Other researchers, however, do claim to fully integrate a subsample of children into regular education classrooms. These findings range from 14 percent to 54 percent of the children participating in model treatment programs.

Although it is certain that these students had very good outcomes, many of these students continued to require ancillary support in the classroom. There is currently no research definitively predicting with whom the most substantial improvements are likely to occur, though factors such as milder and fewer initial symptoms, fewer behavioral challenges, and higher initial cognitive levels—along with early and intensive treatment—have all been indicated to be important (National Research Council, 2001).

ASSESSMENT AND DIAGNOSIS

Screening

The first step in the identification of autism is surveillance, and the second is screening (Filapek et al., 1999). Surveillance for autism is improving and may be responsible for increased rates of identification. As primary care providers (PCPs) as well as early child care workers become more aware of the signs of autism, they are more likely to understand ASDs as a problem worthy of timely identification. Unfortunately, informal community-based surveillance can be associated with case finding based on tangential, anecdotal descriptions of ASDs (as commonly presented in the media), possibly contributing to the rate of false positive referrals. However, PCP training in awareness of developmental disorders seems to be increasing along with overall earlier identification. Once a potential case of autism is identified (most are parental self-referral to the child's PCP), the first level of screening is to determine whether the child in fact has any developmental differences and whether these are consistent with autism. This is typically done with a paper-and-pencil, parent-report screener such as the Pervasive Developmental Disorders Screening Test-II (PDDST-II; Siegel, 2004), which delineates between clinically referred autism and a developmentally high-risk sample; or a more population-based measure such as the Checklist for Autism in Toddlers (CHAT; Baird et al., 2000; Baron-Cohen et al., 1996), which delineates between ASDs and the general population but tends to thereby overidentify other severely delayed children as having ASDs. The goal of Level 1 screening is to get the child started in the diagnostic process. Screening via parent report, however, is subject to validity threats from child-rearing knowledge and experience and parent over- or underconcern. On the other hand, the parent witnesses low-frequency behaviors that may be of diagnostic importance and knows the child's responses in different settings. This is in contrast to the clinician, who usually sees a child only briefly and in an unfamiliar setting that may greatly attenuate sociability and communication and increase atypical responses to the environment.

The second level of screening takes place after the child has been referred for developmental assessment that may have initially included referral to Early Start, audiology, or a speech and language pathologist. Such clinicians, who serve both those with ASDs and those with non-ASD developmental disorders, may question whether the referred child likely has an ASD and if so, whether the child should be made eligible for autism-specific treatments. Because proceeding with autism-specific assessment will raise parental concern as well as add to the cost of diagnosis by requiring additional clinicians and measures, Level 2 screening is useful to determine the probability that the child has autism rather than another developmental disorder. The only instrument specifically designed for Level 2 screening is the PDDST-II Stage 2 (Siegel, 2004), which delineates among ASDs and other neurodevelopmental disorders.

Diagnosis

Best practice in diagnostic assessment for ASDs stipulates that the assessment be multitrait, multimethod, and interdisciplinary (California Department of Developmental Services, 2002). For an assessment to be multitrait, it must systematically collect information on each of the 12 diagnostic signs of ASDs enumerated in *DSM-IV*. It is important to document that the presence of each is qualitatively consistent with an ASD. The most reliable way to do this is to use an autism-specific inventory, such as the interviewer-mediated semi-structured interview, the ADI-R. However, the ADI-R is seldom practical in clinical settings in that it can take up to 2.5 hours to administer, depending on the age of the child being assessed, the experience of the clinician, and the communication skills of the respondent. Nonetheless, it is the closest thing to a gold standard measure of autism symptoms and a model for any multitrait interview that systematically evaluates for each autism-specific symptom.

It is important that the clinician be trained in differential diagnosis. For example, a trait such as failure to develop peer relationships must be carefully considered given that children with most other childhood neuropsychiatric disorders are also impaired in developing friendships, but they may result from a range of non-autism-specific signs such as shyness, anxiety, depression, overactivity, intrusiveness, or aggressivity.

Diagnostic assessment for autism should use multiple methods to increase validity. Methods to consider can encompass parent history taking; review of records; and direct observation of the child using structured, semistructured, and clinical methods focused on eliciting symptoms of autism. Parent reporting is subject to error based on previous parenting experience, the presence of older typically or atypically developing children in the home, parental anxiety, parental knowledge of child development, or the perception that a diagnosis of autism will lead to desired services. Clinician observation may be skewed because of attenuated range of behavior on display in the assessment setting; no opportunity to observe low-frequency but diagnostically important patterns of behaviors (such as odd routines or rituals); or clinician inexperience, particularly with frequently comorbid conditions such as mental retardation and language disorders.

Finally, the ideal is for assessment to be interdisciplinary, meaning that clinicians from different perspectives should discuss and integrate their diagnostic findings (and assessment plans). Appropriate clinicians include child psychiatrists, clinical and developmental psychologists, general and developmental-behavioral pediatricians, speech and language pathologists, occupational therapists, and educators. The primary advantage of the interdisciplinary team is that differential diagnosis is more likely to be comprehensively considered, and the diagnostic assessment should move directly from assignment of a diagnosis to treatment plans and execution.

Treatment Planning in the Context of Diagnostic Assessment

The final phase of the diagnostic assessment process is treatment planning. Recommendations for treatment should proceed directly from information gathered about which of the individual diagnostic criteria for autism are met, how impairing the presence of each symptom is, and the child's developmental level of function in each area of diagnostic concern. The clinician(s), working together with the family, should identify community resources that fit the child's learning needs and fit well within the family's ecology. This most often means utilizing or emphasizing components of different treatment approaches for autism as well as accessing treating professionals from a variety of disciplines.

IMPACT ON ENVIRONMENT

Family

The Meaning for Parents of a Child with Autism

The literature on parenting a child with an ASD indicates that caring for these children can tax even the most resilient parents. There is a negative impact on all parent-child interactions as a result of the social symptoms associated with ASDs. Children with ASDs do not engage in parent-child reciprocity in the same way as other children do. Although they can be affectionate and responsive, exchanges are typically routinized, on their own terms, and instrumental. In addition, children with ASDs rarely adjust their behavior in response to either positive or negative emotions from their parents.

Several studies indicate that parents of children with ASDs are at increased risk for stress as compared to parents of children with other disabilities such as Down syndrome (Donovan, 1988; Rodrigue, Morgan, & Geffken, 1990; Wolf, Noh, Fisman, & Speechley, 1989). Considerable debate surrounds what it is about ASDs that results in elevated parental stress levels. A cross-national study indicated a characteristic profile of stress among parents of children with autism (Koegel et al., 1992). In this study, major differences from normative data occurred on scales that measured stress associated with issues of dependency and management, cognitive impairment, limits on family opportunity, and life span care. Similarly, the core features of autism such as verbal expressive difficulties and cognitive inconsistency were rated as particularly stressful by parents in another study (Bebko, Konstantareas, & Springer, 1987). Both the severity of these individual factors as well as the overall severity of a child's autism contribute to the degree of stress that parents experience. In addition, Konstantareas and Homatidis (1989) found that self-injurious and hyperirritable behaviors were most likely to predict elevated stress in parents.

Stress can also arise from interactions with the many professionals whom parents of children with ASDs must encounter, especially when the service system puts demands on parents that they may not feel capable of meeting. Recently, a review of model programs by the National Research Council, a committee on educational interventions for children with autism, indicated that a key factor in the success of the children in these programs was parent involvement. Additionally, in community-based settings, parents are often asked to manage and implement much of their child's therapy, requiring that they learn specialized skills to meet their child's needs. Parents are also expected to act as advocates for their child in interactions with service systems. Unfortunately, very little training is available for parents to help them meet these demands.

Mothers who care for children with autism have also been found to exhibit significantly greater depressive symptoms when compared to mothers of typically developing children (Wolf et al., 1989). Further, many parents blame themselves for either the onset of autism or their child's repeated failures to develop normally (Rodrigue et al., 1990). Perhaps coinciding with the increased risks of stress, depression, and self-blame, mothers of children with ASDs are also less likely than mothers of either typically developing children or children with Down syndrome to believe that they have the skills to be a good parent.

Social support is commonly considered a buffer to the types of stress described previously. Unfortunately, the literature indicates that many parents of children with autism find little help from either informal or formal sources of support. Parents of children with ASDs are at increased risk for withdrawal from their social networks because of their child's bizarre and disruptive behavior (Sanders & Morgan, 1997). Parents also find that they have difficulty maintaining social relationships in that friends, family members, and strangers react to the child's diagnosis or odd behavior in ways that are perceived as withdrawal (Easterbrooks, 1988), judgmental (Schall, 2000), or both.

Relatives are often seen as particularly unsupportive when a child is diagnosed with a disability. Randall and Parker (1999) found that 30 percent of parents with a child with autism believed that their relatives blamed them for their child's autism. Another 30 percent felt that their relatives believed they had not gotten their child sufficient help. Although Dyson (1987) found that although parents of children with disabilities did not differ from parents of typically developing children on a measure of total social support, they did perceive that they received less support from their own parents and other relatives. Further research indicates that, at least among parents of older children, mothers of children with autism report less marital satisfaction than mothers of typically developing children or mothers of children with Down syndrome (Rodrigue et al., 1990). Compounding this, more than half of parents felt that professionals either did not listen to them or did not attach importance to what they said (Randall & Parker, 1999).

The Meaning for Siblings of a Child with Autism

The impact of having a sibling with autism has received relatively little attention in the literature. A few studies have shown benefits, such as a higher self-concept, when siblings of children with autism are compared to siblings of typically developing children (e.g., Mates, 1990). Others have indicated that sibling relationships, regardless of whether one has a disability, look relatively similar to one another (McHale, Sloan, & Simeonsson, 1986). However, the preponderance of evidence indicates that siblings of children with autism are at greater risk for psychological maladjustment than their peers.

In comparison to siblings of children with mental retardation or typically developing children, siblings of children with autism have been found to be somewhat more negative about the sibling relationship and were more likely to report feeling lonely (Bagenholm & Gillberg, 1991). Siblings of boys with autism have also been shown to be at greater risk for depression (Gold, 1993). Interestingly, some research indicates that the correlates of depression are different depending on the gender of the affected sibling. Female siblings of boys with autism were more likely to be depressed (1) the longer it had been since their sibling was diagnosed with autism, (2) the older the autistic sibling, (3) when the typically developing sibling was younger, (4) when the sibling's mother found her caregiving responsibilities to be a problem, and (5) when the mother worked full-time (Gold, 1993). In contrast, brothers of boys with autism were more likely to be depressed (1) when they felt there were no good things about having an autistic brother, (2) when their mother had no one available to provide a caregiving break, and (3) when their mother had not participated in a support group (Gold, 1993). In addition, Hastings (2003) found that siblings of children with autism were rated by their mothers as having more peer problems, more overall adjustment problems, and lower levels of prosocial behaviors.

Other research has looked at the relation of parent stress and sibling relationships. When marital stress is greater, siblings report less satisfaction with the sibling relationship and less prosocial behavior directed toward the sibling with autism (Rivers & Stoneman, 2003). Importantly, several studies have indicated that the risks to siblings of children with autism can be mediated by social support (e.g., Gold, 1993; Rivers & Stoneman, 2003).

School

Autism, including the broader spectrum, is one of 10 disability categories that school districts are federally mandated to serve. This federal mandate, the Individuals with Disabilities Education Act (IDEA, 2004), sets forth two broad tenets for educating children with disabilities. These are to (1) provide an individualized free and appropriate education from birth to age 22, and (2) provide this service in the least restrictive or most natural environment possible. The manner in which these services are provided to each child are negotiated yearly by a team composed of the child's parents and educational professionals. Out of this team a document, an individual education plan (IEP), is produced that delineates the child's needs, educational services, and goals for the next year. The district must provide these services regardless of the cost.

It is important to note that IDEA does not use the *DSM-IV* definition of autism to determine whether children qualify for services. Rather, IDEA requires only that (1) the child have a developmental disability that significantly affects verbal and nonverbal communication and social interaction, (2) the disability is evident before age 3 years, and (3) the disability adversely affects the child's educational performance.

Services for children with ASDs are organized in different ways depending on the state and school district in which the child is being served as well as the age of the child. Around the country, services for children from birth to age 3 years are provided by either education, health, or social service agencies (National Research Council, 2001). After age 3, states provide services under the direction of their department of education. The youngest children often receive home-based services. However, the greatest majority of children are served in special education classrooms housed in public schools. In some cases. children who cannot receive an appropriate education in the classes their school district offers are served in nonpublic schools (private schools that states certify to provide school district–funded services to children with disabilities).

Peer Interactions

By definition of the disorder, children with ASDs have markedly impaired peer interactions, as they do with most social relationships. Peer interactions in children with ASDs are characterized by low rates of both initiation and response (National Research Council, 2001). This is especially true in the areas of establishing joint attention and sharing experiences with peers (Mundy & Sigman, 1989). Unlike children with other psychiatric diagnoses, the lack of friendships that characterizes children with ASDs does not stem from peer rejection (e.g., hyperactive children who are too impulsive for their peers or oppositional-defiant children who taunt their peers). Rather, peers seem to lack the same level of importance as learning models and sources of social affiliation for children with ASDs that they have for other children.

Like all characteristics associated with ASDs, the social interaction deficits displayed in children with ASD show a spectrum of severity. Wing and Gould (1979) proposed three subgroupings of children with ASDs that reflect this variation. The first group, the aloof children, are indifferent in all situations but especially when with peers. The second group, the passive children, make few social initiations but respond positively to the initiations of adults and peers. The final group, the active but odd children, actively pursue social interaction and respond to others' initiations. However, the way these children carry out social interactions are unusual. Specifically, their initiations and responses are affected by their use of odd language, obsessional topics, and lack of understanding of others.

Without intervention, it is unlikely that children with ASDs will develop age-appropriate social skills. They can, however, be taught to interact more appropriately with peers through interventions that explicitly teach social skills.

IMPLICATIONS FOR FUTURE PERSONALITY DEVELOPMENT

The Spectrum of Outcomes

Although there is evidence that children with ASDs can shift diagnoses within the spectrum and change in severity of developmental disability, children diagnosed with ASDs generally continue to exhibit the impairments associated with the disorder into adulthood. Approximately 75 percent of individuals with autism function in the mentally retarded range throughout life, with those who also experience seizures or other specific organic brain dysfunction being the most impaired (Freeman, 1997). The least impaired 25 percent have normal intelligence, are able to live and work independently, and in rare cases may marry and have children (Freeman, 1997). The next 25 percent are those with relatively normal motor development who develop communication by age 5 but will need continued supervision in living situations and can often function in supported employment (Freeman, 1997). The remainder need to live in shelters or supervised settings (which may include parental homes), are unlikely to have gainful employment, and may have persisting behavioral problems. However, even the highest functioning, most mildly affected individuals often have difficulty maintaining employment and performing household management tasks (Ritvo, Ritvo, Freeman, & Mason-Brothers, 1994).

High-Functioning Adults

The long-term outcomes of high-functioning adults who have no comorbid mental retardation are particularly interesting. Research indicates that the differences in social functioning characterizing the disorder in childhood are maintained into adulthood. Although the highest functioning adults with normal IQ and diagnoses of high-functioning autism (HFA) or AS may develop friendships, these relationships are less close, less empathetic, less supportive, and less important to the individual when compared with normal controls (Baron-Cohen & Wheelwright, 2003). Adults with HFA or AS are less likely to enjoy social interaction for its own sake (Baron-Cohen & Wheelwright, 2003).

Several studies on adults with HFA and AS make little distinction between the two diagnoses. By definition a key difference in samples of individuals with HFA and those with AS is the presence of language delays in those with HFA. These initial language development differences seem to persist in that individuals with AS continue to show relative strengths on the verbal subtests of standardized tests of intelligence (Gilchrist et al., 2001). Additionally, in structured 1:1 interviews, individuals with AS tend to have better conversational speech (Gilchrist et al., 2001). However, additional research indicates that adults with HFA do not differ from adults with AS in (1) total ADI-R scores or ADI-R domain scores; (2) social, emotional, and psychiatric symptoms; (3) current symptomatology; (4) motor clumsiness; or (5) neuropsychological profiles (Howlin, 2003).

TREATMENT IMPLICATIONS

Current Views on Treatment

With few exceptions, research-based services for children with autism have been based on the philosophy that children with ASDs need very individualized services provided by trained individuals familiar with autism-specific learning differences (Strain, McGee, & Kohler, 2001). Intensity of intervention is the driving force behind all empirically validated intervention models. The theory behind this push for highly intense interventions is that children with ASDs, unlike their typically developing peers, are unable to learn from their environments (Handleman & Harris, 2001; McGee, Morrier, & Daly, 2001). Therefore, it is argued, to match the environmental richness absorbed by typically developing children, children with autism must be provided with intensive intervention that essentially mimics the intensity of learning opportunities experienced by their typically developing peers. Although most experts agree that intensity is required in interventions for children with autism (especially the very young), there is considerable disagreement about how to achieve this intensity.

Much of the debate surrounding treatment for children with autism is a direct result of the paucity of well-designed intervention studies. The literature, to this time, lacks not only comparative research between models, but also indicators of responder characteristics or longitudinal outcome studies for individual models. Certainly, a recognized need exists for this research to be done. However, in the absence of clear efficacy research, treatment decisions are made based on the clinical judgments of school district personnel and community-based psychologists, psychiatrists, and neurologists. This section is designed to provide guidance on how these decisions should be made.

TABLE 15.1 Comprehensive Treatment Models and the Autistic Learning Disabilities Model

Area of autistic learning disability	DTT	TEACCH	Floor-time	Inclusion
Hypothesized Benefits				
Social interaction–based disabilities				
Lack of modeling or imitation	Yes			Yes
Lack of peer affiliation				Yes
Lack of social reference	Yes		Yes	Yes
Lack of response to social reward	Yes	Yes	Yes	Yes
Communication-based disabilities				
Problems comprehending natural gesture and emotional expression	Yes		Yes	
Problems in using natural gestures and facial expressions			Yes	
Preference for visual over auditory modalities	Yes	Yes		
Disabilities based in processing of environmental stimuli				
Stimulus overselectivity/perseveration on parts of objects	Yes	Yes		
Preference for routines/ritual over novelty	Yes	Yes		
Sensory modulation difficulties	Yes	Yes	Yes	

Note. DTT = discrete trial training; TEACCH = Treatment and Education of Autistic and Related Communication Handicapped Children; Floor-time = floor-time play therapy.

Because ASDs involve impairments in multiple areas of development, intervention cannot be narrowly focused. There is no evidence that addressing one aspect of autism will result in improvements across areas of disability. For this reason, many researchers have begun to advocate a highly individualized approach to intervention based on each child's specific profile of autism symptomatology. One such model (Siegel, 1999, 2003) encourages a reconceptualization of ASDs into three broad categories of autistic learning disabilities (ALD). The ALD model is designed to highlight how individual differences in experiences and learning are altered by the presence of each symptom of autism. As can be seen in Table 15.1, these categories, essentially mapping onto the *DSM* description of autism, include (1) social interaction–based disabilities (e.g., inability to reference socially, lack of response to social reward), (2) communication-based disabilities (e.g., difficulties using and comprehending gesture and facial affect), and (3) difficulties processing environmental stimuli (e.g., stimulus overselectivity, low response to novelty). Using this model, features of interventions are selected to target the individual profile of symptoms a particular child exhibits at a specific point in time. As the child's symptoms change as a result of maturation and intervention, the intervention model would be redesigned.

Therapy Models

In this section we will discuss the most prominent intervention models that clinicians drawn on when designing eclectic services for children with ASDs. Instead of targeting individual symptoms of autism, these models are more comprehensive in their attempt to remediate many (but not all) symptoms. Included in this review are the four models most often encountered by parents in the community and considered by some to represent an effective standard of treatment for ASDs. These models include Discrete Trial Training, Division TEACCH, Floor-Time, and Inclusion.

Many therapeutic approaches have been used successfully to provide intensive intervention for children with autism. By and large these approaches can be grouped into two categories: behavioral and developmental. The oldest group of interventions relies on the principles and theories of applied behavior analysis (ABA). The interventions embracing this model focus primarily on skill acquisition and give very little attention to the developmental sequence of learning. More recently, a newer group of interventions have begun to emphasize developmentally sequenced learning. Developmentally sequenced teaching may involve direct instruction and incorporate ABA principles, or may be more child-centered in orientation. The latter also use developmental models while emphasizing a child-centered approach in which the adult follows the child's interest in order to build meaningful interaction through play.

Current thought in the field recognizes the benefits of each intervention model. There has generally been a move away from using one treatment approach in isolation from others. Looking forward, the trend seems to be moving toward eclectic treatment planning guided by a kind of developmental behaviorism. Although ABA methodologies are good for teaching foundational skills such as learning readiness, attention, and imitation, more developmentally oriented treatments facilitate the development of spontaneous language, play, and social skills. The current best practice, therefore, advocates an eclectic model constructed to represent developmentally appropriate intervention. However, because very few community-based interventions provide a truly eclectic approach to intervention, each model is described separately in the following discussion. The ALD model discussed previously provides clinicians with an heuristic to develop and assess individual treatment plans. Table 15.1 provides an overview of how these comprehensive treatment models map onto the specific learning disabilities described in the ALD model.

Discrete Trial Training

Ivar Lovaas pioneered the discrete trial training (DTT) method of working with children with autism in the early 1970s. In his Young Autism Project (YAP) conducted at the University of California at Los Angeles (UCLA), Lovaas examined the impact of a high-intensity (35–40 hours per week, 365 days a year), highly structured one-to-one intervention using the principles of operant learning and discrimination learning with very young children with autism (Smith, McEachin, & Lovaas, 1993).

Today, many different types of programs use the principles of behavior modification and discrete trial training without implementing a full-scale YAP program. Additionally, several newer model programs have developed that base their approach on Lovaas's early research. Some of these programs include the May Center for Early Childhood Education (Anderson, Campbell, & O'Malley-Cannon, 1993), the Douglas Developmental Disabilities Center (Harris, Handleman, Kristoff, Bass, & Gordan, 1990), and the Princeton Child Development Institute (McClanahan & Krantz, 1994). Each of these programs provides 20–30 hours of service to a full age range of children with ASDs, emphasizing a gradual progression of intervention settings from highly segregated 1:1 work in the home to eventual integration into preschool settings.

In community-based settings, practitioners and researchers refer to programs combining elements of YAP using a variety of names, including the Lovaas Method, the Early Intervention Project (EIP), the Young Autism Project (YAP), DTT, and sometimes the general heading of ABA. Many children are treated with DTT interventions in home-based programs that require parents, other family members, community volunteers, students, and paid practitioners to implement the full program. Most empirically validated programs are still highly intensive, requiring 20–40 hours per week of 1:1 structured intervention. However, in community-based settings (Early Start, special education classes), many programs provide 20–25 hours, which is considered to represent sufficient intensity for young children with autism (National Research Council, 2001).

DTT interventions are well designed for developing cause-and-effect understanding, attention, compliance, instructional control, and imitation skills. These interventions are less effective at teaching play, imagination, spontaneous language, and initiation skills. Some researchers have suggested that the strongest responders to this treatment may be children with higher pretreatment cognitive and language abilities (Smith, Groen, & Wynn, 2000).

The TEACCH Method

The Treatment and Education of Autistic and Related Communication Handicapped Children (TEACCH) method was developed at the University of North Carolina in Chapel Hill in the early 1970s by Eric Schopler for nonverbal children with autism (Marcus, Schopler, & Lord, 2001). Like DTT interventions, the TEACCH curriculum uses the principles of ABA. However, TEACCH emphasizes the use of known rules and consequences to impose structure and encourage attention. To some degree, TEACCH also emphasizes developmental theories of autism treatment in that it compiles an individualized assessment of each client's abilities, strengths, and emerging skills to plan curricula. The Chapel Hill TEACCH demonstration program integrates individualized classroom methods, services delivered by outside community organizations, and support services for the family (Ozonoff & Cathcart, 1998). The classroom portion of the TEACCH program emphasizes careful classroom design and scheduling as well as the use of predictable, systematic teaching methods. Parents are seen as partners in the intervention process, and thus the TEACCH program attempts to validate parent perspectives and values their contributions. Parent involvement in every aspect of the intervention is considered essential (Ozonoff & Cathcart, 1998).

The goals of TEACCH programs are adult independence and community integration to the greatest extent possible (Mesibov & Shea, 1996). TEACCH proponents believe that children with autism need special instruction in individualized settings that minimize their deficits and present information in ways they understand (Mesibov & Shea, 1996). The TEACCH curriculum, therefore, emphasizes making modifications to the environment and using visually augmentative teaching strategies to build on existing skills (e.g., strong visual memories, a preference for routine) rather than teaching selected skills that are not in the child's repertoire. For instance, TEACCH classrooms emphasize the use of visual supports such as picture schedules and other cues to signal the beginning and end of activities, steps in individual tasks, and sequence activities in a typical day. Areas of the classroom are clearly demarcated to indicate the purpose of and appropriate activities for each area.

In community-based settings outside North Carolina, families are likely to find only the classroom-based portion of this model. The TEACCH model is used in community classrooms serving moderately to severely affected children with ASDs from preschool through adulthood. It is particularly effective for children who show a preference for visual stimuli, have significant receptive language and auditory processing delays, and naturally rely on visual and procedural memory and predictability of routine.

Floor-Time Play Therapy

Floor-time play therapy is a relatively recent relationship-based individualized therapy developed by Stanley Greenspan at George Washington University. According to Greenspan, the main difference between this intervention model and the behavioral interventions advocated by ABA and TEACCH proponents is that the floor-time model focuses on relationships and affect, developmental level, individual differences, and comprehensiveness (Greenspan & Wieder, 1998). Greenspan and Wieder (1998) describe floor-time as a comprehensive relationship-based approach tailored to the child's and family's individual differences as well as the child's developmental level.

The theoretical rationale underlying floor-time is that the symptoms of autism (e.g., failure to engage in joint attention, failure to use or understand gestures) are often secondary to underlying biologically based processing difficulties (Greenspan & Wieder, 1998). Floor-time interventionists work individually with children to help them learn to work around these processing deficits to explore and learn from things of interest to them. Intervention takes place in 1:1 sessions in which an adult follows a child's interests to initiate communication and interaction. Once the child and adult are involved in an interaction, the goal of intervention is to increase the number of social initiatives and contingent responses, referred to as circles of communication. By carefully building these circles of communication, floor-time is designed to lead to reductions in sensory sensitivities, revealing the child's capacity for more typical social reciprocity.

The floor-time curriculum is generally available in community-based settings for children under 5 years of age. It appears most successful at increasing shared attention and regulation; affective reciprocity and communication through gestures; complex presymbolic, shared social communication and problem solving; symbolic and creative use of ideas; and logical and abstract use of ideas and thinking. A recent variation on the principles of the floor-time model is called relationship-development intervention and relies on the same underpinnings but is manualized in a way to make it more accessible to parents and nonspecialist service providers (Gutstein & Sheely, 2002). Among evidence-based practice standards, floor-time and its derivatives are the least studied empirically and the most theory-based among treatment approaches.

Inclusion

Inclusion is an educational method wherein a pupil with special educational needs is fully or partly included with nondisabled peers in school. The purpose is to provide models of appropriate behavior and segregate the child from unfavorable models. Proponents of inclusion as a civil rights issue note that for some, segregated services have not resulted in adequate gains, and so any gains children achieve while in the mainstream justify such placement. This position is now supported by law. Inclusion research is mired by the fact that inclusion implies a placement, not a curriculum—and an effective curriculum is likely the more powerful factor in any educational outcomes. Typically developing children are thought to benefit from inclusion of children with disabilities because they learn about diversity among individuals, develop positive attitudes toward people with disabilities, and learn altruistic skills (Diamond, Hestenes, & O'Connor, 1994).

Inclusion interventions that purposely employ peers as intervention agents for children with ASDs subscribe to the philosophy that the social deficits associated with the disability are its most handicapping feature. Theoretically, teaching in the natural environment allows the use of typically occurring events, activities, and consequences as a context in which to teach specific skills. Peers are used in these interventions because children with autism do not easily transfer the social skills they learn with adults to naturalistic peer interactions (Rogers, 2000). In addition, they more easily generalize skills between trained peer interventionists and untrained peers (Rogers, 2000). However, a limitation to this approach is that many children with autism have significantly impaired imitation skills and significantly diminished interest in peers.

Several model programs, including the Colorado Model (Strain, 1987) and Walden (McGee et al., 2001), employ typically developing peers in structured interactions with children with autism to facilitate social skills development. These programs have successfully used behavioral methodologies to teach social skills to children with ASDs across a wide range of ages and functioning levels. In the majority of model programs, typically developing peers are taught specific strategies for initiating and maintaining interaction with the autistic child (Rogers, 2000). Interventions have been implemented successfully using a variety of structures, including individual play interactions, classroom-based interventions, play groups, and peer tutoring (Rogers, 2002).

Although model programs of inclusion for children with ASDs use a behavioral orientation and strong supports from expert special staff, such factors often are not available in community-based programs, where the child's primary support in an inclusive setting most often is a paraprofessional aide. Inclusive services span various levels of integration, often with only one or two children with disabilities included within a much larger group of typically developing peers (Harris, 1995; Odom & Speltz, 1983). Children in these settings typically receive a variety of ancillary support services including speech therapy, occupational therapy, respite services, and in-class 1:1 paraprofessional support. The supports may either facilitate participation in the core curriculum or support an adapted curriculum that is significantly different from the one experienced by classmates. There is little to no empirical evidence that most children with autism can benefit from simply being with their typically developing peers, so it is considered better practice to include children with typically developing peers when the child with ASD can meaningfully access the core curriculum.

REFERENCES

American Psychiatric Association. (1980). *The diagnostic and statistic manual of mental disorders* (3rd ed.). Washington, DC: Author.

American Psychiatric Association. (1989). *The diagnostic and statistic manual of mental disorders* (3rd ed., rev.). Washington, DC: Author.

American Psychiatric Association. (1994). *The diagnostic and statistic manual of mental disorders* (4th ed.). Washington, DC: Author.

Anderson, S. R., Campbell, S., & O'Malley-Cannon (1993). The May Center for Early Childhood Education. In S. L. Harris & J. L. Handleman (Eds.), *Preschool education programs for children with autism*. Austin, TX: Pro-Ed.

Bagenholm, A., & Gillberg, C. (1991). Psychosocial effects on siblings of children with autism and mental retardation: A population-based study. *Journal of Mental Deficiency Research, 35,* 291–307.

Bailey D., Jr., Hatten, D. D., Mesibov, G., Ament, N., & Skinner, M. (1995). Early development temperament, and functional impairment in autism and fragile X syndrome. *Journal of Autism and Developmental Disorders, 30,* 49–59.

Baird, G., Charman, T., Cox, A., Baron-Cohen, S., Swettenham, J., Wheelwright, S., et al. (2000). A screening instrument for autism at 18 months of age: A 6-year follow-up study. *Journal of the American Academy of Child and Adolescent Psychiatry, 39,* 694–702.

Baron-Cohen, S., Cox, A., Baird, G., Swettenham, J., Nightingale, N., Morgan, K., et al. (1996). Psychological markers in the detection of autism in infancy in a large population. *British Journal of Psychiatry, 168,* 158–163.

Baron-Cohen, S., & Wheelwright, S. (2003). The Friendship Questionnaire: An investigation of adults with Asperger syndrome or high-functioning autism, and normal sex differences. *Journal of Autism and Developmental Disorders, 33,* 509–517.

Bebko, K. M., Konstantareas, M. M., & Springer, J., (1987). Parent and professional evaluations of family stress associated with characteristics of autism. *Journal of Autism and Developmental Disorders, 17,* 565–576.

Bertrand, J., Mars, A., Boyle, C., Bove, F., Yeargin-Allsopp, M., & Decoufle, P. (2001). Prevalence of autism in a United States population: The Brick Township, New Jersey, investigation. *Pediatrics, 108,* 1155–1161.

Boddaert, N., & Zilbovicius, M. (2002). Functional neuro-imaging and childhood autism. *Pediatric Radiology, 32,* 1–7.

Bolton, P., Macdonald, H., Pickles A., Rios, P., Goode, S., Crawson, M., et al. (1994). A case-control family history study of autism. *Journal of Child Psychology and Psychiatry, 35,* 877–900.

California Department of Developmental Services. (2002). Autistic spectrum disorders: Best practice guidelines for screening, diagnosis, and assessment. Accessed at www.ddhealthinfo.org

Carver, L. J., & Dawson, G. (2002). Development and neural bases of facial recognition in autism. *Molecular Psychiatry, 7,* S18–S20.

Davidovitch, M., Glick, L., Holtzman, G., Tirosh, E., & Safir, M. P. (2000). Developmental regression in autism: Maternal perception. *Journal of Autism and Developmental Disorders, 30,* 113–119.

Dawson, G., & Osterling, J. (1996). Early intervention in autism. In M. J. Guralnick (Ed.), *The effectiveness of early intervention* (pp. 307–326). Baltimore: Paul Brookes.

DeMyer, M. K. (1979). *Parents and children in autism.* New York: Wiley.

Deykin, E. Y., & MacMahon, B. (1979). Incidence of seizures among children with autistic symptoms. *American Journal of Psychiatry, 136,* 1310–1312.

Diamond, K. E., Hestenes, L. L., & O'Connor, C. (1994). *Integrating children with disabilities into preschool* Educational Research Information Clearinghouse Document Reproduction Service No. ED 440497.

Donovan, A. M. (1988). Family stress and ways of coping with adolescents who have mental handicaps: Maternal perceptions. *American Journal on Mental Retardation, 92,* 502–509.

Dyson, L. (1987). *Parent stress, family functioning, and social support in families of young handicapped children.* Educational Research Information Clearinghouse Document Reproduction Service No. ED 202502.

Easterbrooks, M. A. (1988). Effects of infant risk status on the transition to parenthood. In G. Y. Michaels & W. A. Goldberg (Eds.), *The transition to parenthood: Current theory and research.* New York: Cambridge University Press.

Escalante, P. R., Minshew, N. J., & Sweeney, J. A. (2003). Abnormal brain lateralization in high-functioning autism. *Journal of Autism and Developmental Disorders, 33,* 539–543.

Filapek, P. (1999). Neuroimaging in the developmental disorders: The state of the science. *Journal of Child Psychiatry and Psychology, 40,* 113–128.

Filapek, P. A., Accardo, P. J., Ashwal, S., Barenek, G. T., Cook, E. H., Dawson, G., et al. (1999). Practice parameter: Screening and diagnosis of autism. *Neurology, 55,* 468–479.

Folstein, S., & Rutter, M. (1988). Autism: Familial aggregation and genetic implications. *Journal of Autism and Developmental Disorders, 18,* 3–30.

Fombonne, E. (1999). The epidemiology of autism: A review. *Psychological Medicine, 29,* 769–786.

Fombonne, E. (2003). Epidemiological surveys of autism and other pervasive developmental disorders: An update. *Journal of Autism and Developmental Disorders, 33,* 365–382.

Freeman, B. J. (1997). Guidelines for evaluating intervention programs for children with autism. *Journal of Autism and Developmental Disorders, 27,* 641–651.

Gilchrist, A., Cox, A., Rutter, M., Green, J., Burton, D., & Le Couteur, A. (2001). Development and current functioning in adolescents with Asperger syndrome: A comparative study. *Journal of Child Psychology and Psychiatry, 42,* 227–240.

Gold, N. (1993). Depression and social adjustment in siblings of boys with autism. *Journal of Autism and Developmental Disorders, 23,* 147–163.

Greenspan, S. I., & Wieder, S. (1998). *The child with special needs: Encouraging intellectual and emotional growth.* Reading, MA: Perseus Books.

Gutner, T. (2004, May 31). Special needs, crushing costs. *Newsweek,* 94–97.

Gutstein, S., & Sheely, R. K. (2002). *Relationship development intervention with young children.* New York: Jessica Kingsley.

Handleman, J. S., & Harris, S. L. (2001). Preschool programs for children with autism. In J. S. Handleman & S. L. Harris (Eds.), *Preschool programs for children with autism.* Austin, TX: Pro-Ed.

Hardan, A. Y., Minshew, N. J., & Keshavan, M. S. (2000). Corpus callosum size in autism. *Neurology, 55,* 1033–1036.

Harris, S. L. (1995). Educational strategies in autism. In E. Schopler & G. B. Meisibov (Eds.), *Learning and cognition in autism* (pp. 293–310). New York: Plenum Press.

Harris, S. L., Handleman, J. S., Kristoff, B., Bass, L., & Gordon, R. (1990). Changes in language development in autistic and peer children in segregated and integrated preschool settings. *Journal of Autism and Developmental Disorders, 20,* 23–31.

Hastings, R. P. (2003). Behavioral adjustment of siblings of children with autism engaged in applied behavior analysis early intervention programs: The moderating role of social support. *Journal of Autism and Developmental Disorders, 33,* 141–150.

Howlin, P. (2003). Outcome in high-functioning adults with autism with and without early language delays: Implications for differentiation between autism and Asperger syndrome. *Journal of Autism and Developmental Disorders, 33,* 3–13.

Institute of Medicine. (2004).*Vaccines and autism.* http://www.fda.gov/cber/vaccine/thimerosal.htm#iomsafe.

Knobloch, H., & Pasamanick, B. (1975). Some etiologic and prognostic factors in early infantile autism and psychosis. *Pediatrics, 55,* 182–191.

Koegel, R. L., Schreibman, L., Loos, L. M., Dirlich-Wilhelm, H., Dunlap, G., Robbins, F. R., et al. (1992). Consistent stress profiles in mothers of children with autism. *Journal of Autism and Developmental Disorders, 22,* 205–216.

Konstantareas, M. M., & Homatidis, S. (1989). Assessing child symptom severity and stress in parents of autistic children. *Journal of Child Psychology and Psychiatry, 30,* 459–470.

Lord, C., Risi, S., Lambrecht, L., Cook, E. H., Leventhal, B. L., DiLavore, P. C., et al. (2000). The autism diagnostic observation schedule-generic: A standard measure of social and communicative deficits associated with the spectrum of autism. *Journal of Autism and Developmental Disorders, 30,* 205–223.

Lord, C., Rutter, M., & LeCouteur, A. L. (1994). Autism Diagnostic Interview Revised: A revised version of a diagnostic interview for caregivers of individuals with possible pervasive developmental disorders. *Journal of Autism and Developmental Disorders, 24,* 659–685.

Lotter, V. (1966). Epidemiology of autistic conditions in young children. I: Prevalence. *Social Psychiatry, 1,* 124–137.

Lovaas, O. I. (1987). Behavioral treatment and normal educational and intellectual functioning in young autistic children. *Journal of Consulting and Clinical Psychology, 55,* 3–9.

Lovaas, O. I., & Smith, T. (1989). A comprehensive behavioral theory of autistic children: Paradigm for research and practice. *Journal of Behavior Therapy and Experimental Psychiatry, 20,* 17–29.

Marcus, L., Schopler, E., & Lord, C. (2001). TEACCH services for preschool children. In J. S. Handleman & S. L. Harris (Eds.), *Preschool programs for children with autism* (pp. 215–232). Austin, TX: Pro-Ed.

Mates, T. E. (1990). Siblings of autistic children: Their adjustment and performance at home and at school. *Journal of Autism and Developmental Disorders, 20,* 545–553.

McClanahan, L., & Krantz, P. (1994). The Princeton Child Development Institute. In S. L. Harris & J. L. Handleman (Eds.), *Preschool education programs for children with autism*. Austin, TX: Pro-Ed.

McGee, G. G., & Morrier, D. (2001). The Walden early childhood programs. In J. S. Handleman & S. L. Harris (Eds.), *Preschool programs for children with autism* (pp. 157–190). Austin, TX: Pro-Ed.

McHale, S. M., Sloan, J., & Simeonsson, R. J. (1986). Sibling relationships of children with autistic, mentally retarded, and nonhandicapped brothers and sisters. *Journal of Autism and Developmental Disorders, 16*, 399–413.

Mesibov, G. B., & Shea, V. (1996). Full inclusion and student with autism. *Journal of Autism and Developmental Disorders, 26*, 337–346.

Miles, J. H., Hadden, L. L., Takahashi, T. N., & Hillman, R. E. (2000). Head circumference is an independent clinical finding associated with autism. *American Journal of Medical Genetics 95*, 339–350.

Mundy, P., & Sigman, M. (1989). Theoretical implications of joint attention deficits in autism. *Developmental Psychopathology, 1*, 173–183.

Mundy, P., Sigman, M., & Kasari, C. (1990). A longitudinal study of joint attention and language development in autistic children. *Journal of Autism and Developmental Disorders, 20*, 115–128.

National Research Council. (2001). *Educating children with autism*. Washington, DC: National Academy Press.

Newschaffer, C., Fallin, D., & Lee, N. L. (2002). Heritable and nonheritable risk factors for autistic spectrum disorders. *Epidemiology Review, 24*, 137–153.

Odom, S. L., & Speltz, M. L. (1983). Program variation in preschools for handicapped and nonhandicapped children: Mainstreamed vs. integrated special education. *Analysis and Intervention in Developmental Disabilities, 3*, 89–103.

Osterling, J., & Dawson, G. (1994). Early recognition of children with autism: A study of first birthday home videotapes. *Journal of Autism and Developmental Disorders, 24*, 247–257.

Ozonoff, S., & Cathcart, K., (1998). Effectiveness of a home program intervention for young children with autism. *Journal of Autism and Developmental Disorders, 28*, 25–32.

Ozonoff, S., Dawson, G., & McPartland, J. (2002). *A parent's guide to Asperger syndrome and high functioning autism*. New York: Guilford Press.

Pickles, A., Bolton, P., Macdonald, H., Bailey, A., LeCouteur, A., Jordan, H., et al. (1995). Latent class analysis of recurrence risks for complex phenotypes with selection and measurement error: A twin and family history study of autism. *American Journal of Human Genetics, 57*, 717–726.

Randall, P., & Parker, J. (1999) *Supporting the families of children with autism*. West Sussex, England: Wiley.

Ritvo, E. R., Ritvo, R., Freeman, B. J., & Mason-Brothers, A. (1994). Clinical characteristics of mild autism in adults. *Comprehensive Psychiatry, 35*, 149–156.

Rivers, J. W., & Stoneman, Z. (2003). Sibling relationships when a child has autism: Marital stress and support coping. *Journal of Autism and Developmental Disorders, 33*, 383–394.

Rodrigue, J. R., Morgan, S. B., & Geffken, G. (1990). Families of autistic children: Psychological functioning of mothers. *Journal of Clinical Child Psychology, 19*, 371–379.

Rogers, S. J. (1998). Empirically supported comprehensive treatments for young children with autism. *Journal of Clinical Child Psychology, 27*, 168–179.

Rogers, S. J. (1999). Intervention for young children with autism: From research to practice. *Infants and Young Children, 12*, 1–16.

Rogers, S. J. (2000). Interventions that facilitate socialization in children with autism. *Journal of Autism and Developmental Disorders, 30*, 399–409.

Rogers, S. J., & DiLalla, D. L. (1990). Age of symptom onset in young children with pervasive developmental disorders. *Journal of the American Academy of Child and Adolescent Psychiatry, 29*, 863–872.

Sanders, J. L., & Morgan, S. B., (1997). Family stress and adjustment as perceived by parents of children with autism or down syndrome: Implications for intervention. *Child and Family Behavior Therapy, 19*, 15–32.

Schall, C. (2000). Family perspectives on raising a child with autism. *Journal of Child and Family Studies, 9*, 409–423.

Siegel, B. (1999). Autistic learning disabilities and individualizing treatment for autistic spectrum disorders. *Infants and Young Children, 12*, 27–36.

Siegel, B. (2003). *Helping children with autism learn: Treatment approaches for parents and professionals*. New York: Oxford University Press.

Siegel, B. (2004). *The Pervasive Developmental Disorder Screening Test—II*. San Antonio, TX: Psychological Corp..

Siegel, B., Anders, T., Ciaranello, R. D., Bienenstock, B., & Kraemer, H. C. (1984). Empirical subclassification of the autistic syndrome. *Journal of Autism and Developmental Disorders, 16*, 475–491.

Simonoff, E., McGuffin, P., & Gottesman, I. (1994). Genetic influences in normal and abnormal development. In M. Rutter, E. A. Taylor, & L. Hersov (Eds.), *Child and adolescent psychiatry: Modern approaches* (pp. 129–154). Oxford: Blackwell.

Smith, T., Groen, A., & Wynn, J. (2002). Randomized trial of intensive early intervention for children with pervasive developmental disorder. *American Journal of Mental Retardation, 105*, 269–285.

Smith, T., McEachin, J. J., & Lovaas, O. I. (1993). Comments on replication and evaluation of outcome. *American Journal of Mental Retardation, 97*, 385–391.

Spitzer, R. L., & Siegel, B. (1990). The *DSM-III-R* field trials for pervasive developmental disorders. *Journal of the American Academy of Child and Adolescent Psychiatry, 26*, 855–862.

Strain, P. (1987). Comprehensive evaluation of intervention for young autistic children. *Topics in Early Childhood Special Education, 7*, 97–110.

Strain, P., McGee, G. G., & Kohler, F. W. (2001). Inclusion of children with autism in early intervention environments: An examination of rationale, myths, and procedures. In M. J. Guralnick (Ed.), *Early childhood inclusion: Focus on change* (pp. 337–363). Baltimore: Brooks.

Volkmar, F. (1992). Childhood disintegrative disorder: Issues for DSM-IV. *Journal of Autism and Developmental Disorders, 22,* 625–642.

von During, V., Maltau, J. M., Forsdahl, F., Abyholm, T., Kolvik, R., Ertzeid, G., et al. (1995). Pregnancy, birth and newborn after in vitro fertilization in Norway, 1988–1991. *Tidsskr Nor Lægeforen, 115,* 2054–2060.

Werner, E., Dawson, G, Osterling, J., & Dinno, N. (2000). Brief report: Recognition of autism spectrum disorders before one year of age: A retrospective study based on home video tapes. *Journal of Autism and Developmental Disorders, 30,* 157–162.

Wing, L., & Gould, J. (1979). Severe impairments of social interaction and associated abnormalities in children: Epidemiology and classification. *Journal of Autism and Developmental Disorders, 9,* 11–29.

Wolf, L. C., Noh, S., Fisman, S. N., & Speechley, M. (1989). Brief report: Psychological effects of parenting stress on parents of autistic children. *Journal of Autism and Developmental Disorders, 19,* 157–166.

CHAPTER 16

Learning Disabilities

JAMES W. LOOMIS

DESCRIPTION OF THE PROBLEM AND CLINICAL PICTURE

Learning disabilities have been recognized in children since the end of the nineteenth century (Anderson & Meier-Hedde, 2001). Previously known by a series of diagnostic terms including word blindness, minimal brain dysfunction, and developmental lag (Silver & Hagin, 2002), a learning disability (LD) is characterized by a difficulty with academic learning not attributable to low intellectual ability, neurological injury or disorder, or psychiatric illness.

The generally accepted definition of LD comprises five components:

1. The individual has difficulty learning to read, write, perform mathematical operations, reason, or process visuospatial stimuli.
2. These difficulties are related to dysfunction in underlying psychological processes (e.g., auditory processing, memory, phonetic encoding, visual-motor coordination).
3. The primary cause of the learning difficulties is subtle neurological dysfunction, in part genetically determined, and related to anomalies in early neurological development.
4. The learning difficulties reflect a persistent deficit in skills and not a developmental lag that resolves in time.
5. The learning challenges are not caused by, but may be exacerbated by, emotional problems (e.g., depression, anxiety disorders), a lack of environmental support (e.g., poor nutrition, lack of enrichment in the learning environment or limited family support), or inappropriate instructional techniques.

Though at this time consensus exists with regard to the definition of LDs, operationalizing this construct has been extremely difficult. Neuropsychological evaluation can identify the processing difficulties associated with LDs, but the definition requires that there be a significant discrepancy between actual and expected learning achievement. Generally, one assesses this discrepancy by looking at differences between achievement and intellectual ability (i.e., IQ). However, this presents psychometric difficulties in that IQ and achievement are correlated with each other, thus confounding the measurement of differences (Silver & Hagin, 2002). Furthermore, the statistical nature of finding achievement-ability discrepancies makes it easier to identify older students and those with high IQ and more difficult to identify younger students and children with lower IQ (Pennington, 1991). Because of these difficulties, most researchers and professional organizations have moved away from discrepancy criteria. However, school systems, which are charged with identifying children with LDs so they can be eligible for special education services, continue to rely on the discrepancy formulas and so are left with the incumbent problems (Mercer, Jordan, Allsop, & Mercer, 1996).

Individuals with LDs can be separated into four groups according to the type of basic learning challenge. The majority of students with LDs present with reading difficulties or dyslexia (80 percent of all students with LDs, by some estimates; Lerner, 1985). Smaller numbers of students fall into groups marked by challenges in mathematics or writing skills. A fourth category of LD is children with nonverbal learning disabilities (NLD; Pennington, 1991; Rourke, 1989, 1995). These students have difficulty with visual and spatial processing, visual-motor integration, and higher order reasoning and problem solving. A significant amount of overlap exists among these categories, and there are a number of students whose profile of learning challenges makes it difficult to fit them into any of the four categories. Some investigators present support for the existence of an LD related to executive functioning (Denckla, 1994; Welsh, 2002), although research in this area is still developing.

Over the last 35 years, neuropsychological research has attempted to identify subtypes of LDs according to the type of underlying neuropsychological challenge (Rourke, 1985). From this perspective, students with reading disabilities are separated into groups—those with challenges in phonological processing and those with visual motor challenges. Similarly, mathematics LDs have been categorized according to difficulties with procedural operations, semantic memory, or visuospatial skills (Geary, 2004). Researchers have been attempting to establish the validity of subtypes so that they can better differentiate key processing challenges for each group and design more effective interventions. Although some question whether LDs fall into discrete, categorical clusters, subtype analyses have found key differences among groups (Torgesen, 1991).

Along with LDs, many emotional, behavioral, and social challenges can develop secondary to the LD. These include challenges with self-esteem, social competency, anxiety and depression, conduct disorders, and substance abuse (Beitchman & Young, 1997; Osman, 2000). There is disagreement in the literature with regard to the extent of these risks. Our knowledge in this area has been limited by the predominance of studies using simple comparisons between aggregated groups of participants identified as learning disabled and control groups without a diagnosis of LD. This type of study overlooks the diversity among individuals with LDs and makes it difficult to identify factors that impact on outcomes related to LDs. Individuals with LDs vary according to (a) type and severity of neurological, neuropsychological, and academic dysfunction; (b) temperamental predisposition to depression, anxiety, anger, and attentional challenges; (c) level of social motivation and relatedness; (d) age of diagnosis and interventions provided; and (e) environmental context variables, including history of early childcare (e.g., nutrition, educational enrichment), socioeconomic status, and cultural background. These factors are thought to be mediators of the relationship between LDs and outcomes, but empirical examination of these relationships has been limited (Rourke & Fuerst, 1991; Thompson & Kronenberger, 1990).

PERSONALITY DEVELOPMENT AND PSYCHOPATHOLOGY

Relatively little attention has focused on personality development in the LD literature. Most of this work has looked at the psychosocial challenges associated with LDs as they emerge throughout the life span (Osman, 2000; Williams & McGee, 1996). A few studies have used objective personality assessment with LD samples (Waldo, McIntosh, & Koller, 1999). The psychoanalytic and self-psychology literature provides the most detailed discussion of how LDs impact on personality, although this approach has been limited to theory based on case studies of patients in psychoanalytic treatment (Palombo, 2001; Rothstein & Glenn, 1999).

LDs can be seen to affect personality development in three ways: (1) through the emotional experience of not being able to master the learning challenges created by the LD; (2) through the impact that academic difficulties have on key social relationships with parents, teachers, and peers; and (3) through the direct impact of the processing difficulties of the LD on the student's ability to understand the environment and adaptively interact with it.

Emotional Impact

Having an LD can exact a high emotional price on an individual. Although these children (with average or above-average intelligence) may have no problems with understanding games or managing the demands of home routines, in school they are confronted with tasks (reading, writing, mathematics) that are extremely difficult, if not impossible, for them to complete. While they struggle, they see their peers managing the same tasks without great difficulty. This scenario can create confusion, frustration, and stress in the young student (Osman, 2000; Price, 1993). It can lead to tendencies toward self-blame and anger (Shessel & Reiff, 1999). It can interfere with the normal development of self-esteem by undermining the child's sense of self-efficacy (Elbaum & Vaughn, 2003; Klassen, 2002). The child is confronted with impossible challenges, along with clearly unattainable expectations from teachers and parents, potentially leading to learned helplessness, denial in the form of unrealistic self-assessment of abilities, or task-avoidant tendencies (e.g., withdrawal, passivity, disruptive behaviors; Dev, 1998; Shapiro & Rich, 1999). The child may respond by developing narcissistic and grandiose compensatory trends or a negative sense of self (Rothstein & Glenn, 1999). In the terms of self-psychology theory, this situation can disrupt the development of a cohesive sense of self in that it undermines the confident and predictable performance of daily tasks and presents incompatible experiences of being smart yet unskilled (Palombo, 2001).

While attempting to cope with these challenges, the child can come to rely on maladaptive defenses such as denial and avoidance, and ultimately this can lead to character pathology (Rothstein & Glenn, 1999) or internalizing forms of psychopathology, specifically depression and anxiety disorders (Howard & Tryon, 2002). Alternately, with poor sublimation of aggression and if the level of anger is high and there is a greater reliance on disruptive behavior as a coping response, the child is susceptible to externalizing disorders such as conduct disorder and problems with juvenile delinquency (Brier, 1989).

Impact Mediated by the Social Environment

Looking beyond the intrapsychic experience of having an LD, further impacts are mediated by the social environment. Early parent-child bonding can be disrupted by the child's poor language development or other processing challenges. This can impede the child's attainment of object constancy, the process of separation and individuation, and the early development of object relations (Rothstein & Glenn, 1999). At the time of the emergence of school difficulties, parents can struggle with accepting the diagnosis. This situation can lead to chronic conflict or emotional disengagement by the parents and can further compromise the child-parent bond (Culbertson & Silovsky, 1996).

Peer relations can also be impacted in that children who are low achievers are generally less liked by peers, have fewer friendships, and are more frequently rejected (Gresham & MacMillan, 1997; Wallander & Hubert, 1987). Further, in many school systems a stigma can be associated with identification as a special education student. The LD can place the child in a low status and an undesirable position in the peer culture (Vaughn & Hogan, 1990).

In addition, LDs may have a negative impact on relations with teachers. Teachers generally rate students with LDs as less persistent and having poorer task engagement, and feel greater frustration with them because they demand more time and support (Keogh, 2003). Some studies have found that teachers are less responsive to children with LDs and ignore their questions more frequently (Bryan, 1974).

Thus, on top of the emotional challenges, the social environment can be less supportive and less responsive to children with LDs. This can undermine the development of both a positive self-concept and object relations marked by consistent affection and respect (Rothstein & Glenn, 1999). The child may be left with an internalized experience of the world as rejecting, disapproving, and even antagonistic. This sense may lead to further reliance on maladaptive defense mechanisms such as avoidance, denial, and negative attention-seeking behaviors.

Direct Impact of the Processing Challenges

Many researchers also point to the direct impact that the LD has on the student's ability to manage the demands of social and adaptive functioning. The same neuropsychological dysfunction that impedes learning to read, write, and perform mathematics can also undermine social communication skills, social problem solving, skills of daily living, and other non-academic functions. During the earliest years, the social processing difficulties can interfere with the attainment of object constancy and separation and individuation (Rothstein & Glenn, 1999). Establishing friendships may be difficult because the child cannot effectively manage nonverbal communication, conversational turn taking, or social conventions. In adolescence, students with LDs can be particularly vulnerable to the influence of antisocial peers who draw them into negative behaviors. The student with an LD may not be able to discern the manipulation or deception of the antisocial peers and so is easily led into making poor judgments and engaging in destructive behaviors (Pearl & Bryan, 1990).

This is especially true with NLDs, in which individuals have difficulty reading facial expressions, engaging in conversation, and understanding the perspectives of others. These individuals present limited emotional depth in that their verbalizations present as superficial, with many tangential associations and a lack of emotional context. Individuals with NLDs present limited affect, restricted object relations, and high levels of passivity and depression that are seen to arise directly from the LD-related processing challenges (Rourke, 1995; Rourke & Fuerst, 1991).

With all this in mind, it is easy to see how LDs are a risk factor for psychopathology. However, there is considerable disagreement in the literature regarding the level of this risk. A number of studies have found elevated frequencies of psychopathology among individuals with LDs, including depression, anxiety disorders, conduct disorders, and substance-abuse disorders (Beitchman, Wilson, Douglas, Young, & Adlaf, 2001; Bennet, Brown, Boyle, Racine, & Offord, 2003; Brier, 1989; Osman, 2000). At the same time, others have found a weak relationship between LDs and psychopathology and low percentages of individuals with LDs presenting significant mental health challenges (Heath & Ross, 2000; Rourke, 1988). These conflicting results can be attributed in part to differences in measures (clinical interviews vs. self-report instruments vs. behavioral ratings), the bidirectional causal impact between LDs and psychopathology, and difficulties with accurate self-report by individuals with LDs (Moss, Prosser, Ibbotson, & Goldberg, 1996). In any case, groups of individuals with LDs are at each end of the continuum of psychopathology, but further study is needed to determine the distribution across its span.

EPIDEMIOLOGY

The incidence of identified LDs in U.S. schools is in the range of 4 percent to 6 percent of all students (Silver & Hagin, 2002). Most investigators believe that there are high levels of underidentification of students with LDs and estimate a true incidence of LDs closer to 25 percent of all students (Silver & Hagin, 2002).

Reading disorders are seen to account for the greatest percentage of LDs, with some estimating that 80 percent of all LDs are reading related (Lerner, 1985). The Connecticut Longitudinal Study found 17.5 percent of all students presented with dyslexia (Shaywitz, Pugh, Fletcher, & Shaywitz, 2000). In contrast, estimates of mathematics LDs fall between 5 percent and 8 percent of all children (Geary, 2004) and between 8 percent and 15 percent for LDs related to writing (Silver & Hagin, 2002). A significant amount of overlap also exists among these categories, with some estimating that half of all children with mathematics LDs also have reading LDs (Geary, 2004).

The frequency of reported LDs appears to be rising. The U.S. Department of Education reports a 28 percent increase from 1992 to 2001 in children identified with LDs (U.S. Department of Education, 2003). This may reflect improved diagnostic techniques and increased advocacy for services by parents rather than a true increase in the incidence of LDs.

There are significant comorbidities between LDs and ADHD. Though empirical studies support the distinction between the two disorders, it is estimated that 15 percent to 25 percent of individuals with reading LDs have ADHD and that between 25 percent and 50 percent of children with ADHD present with reading LDs (Beitchman & Young, 1997; Silver & Hagin, 2002).

Gender differences are present in the frequencies of children and adolescents referred for LDs, with boys outnumbering girls at a ratio of from 2:1 to 5:1. However, population-based research samples reveal an equal number of boys and girls presenting with LDs (Silver & Hagin, 2002). This difference can be attributed to several factors. First, initiation of referrals may be related in part to problematical behaviors, and so boys, who generally demonstrate more disruptive and challenging behavior, may be more likely to be referred. Second, as Pennington (1991) pointed out, boys generally have higher average IQ scores and lower average achievement scores than girls. This would increase the likelihood of an IQ-achievement discrepancy on statistical grounds alone.

In the United States, the incidence of identified LDs is associated with socioeconomic status. Studies generally find higher frequencies of LDs among children coming from low-income families, with estimates as high as 50 percent of children from the lowest income categories presenting LDs (Silver & Hagin, 2002). There are also some modest differences between races and ethnicities. When compared to all students receiving LD services, Native American and Hispanic children are identified with greater frequency and African American and Asian children are identified with lesser frequency (U.S. Department of Education, 2003).

The frequency of reading LDs varies across different languages, with Japan and China showing the lowest frequency (1 percent) and English-speaking countries evidencing among the highest frequencies (20 percent; Grigorenko, 2001). The incidence of reading difficulties is thought to be related to the level of unique phonological and orthographic processing demands associated with different languages.

ETIOLOGY

Researchers have emphasized etiological factors associated with LDs on three levels: (1) the neuropsychological deficits that undermine learning; (2) the neurological indicators of brain dysfunction associated with LDs; and (3) the familial and genetic factors that are related to LDs. Most of this research has focused on reading LDs.

Neuropsychological Factors

Research has identified four neuropsychological functions essential to successful reading: phonological processing (e.g., phonemic awareness, phonetic segmentation, phoneme-grapheme matching), visual-spatial processing (identifying letters and words), speed/automaticity of processing written symbols, and basic language processing (Grigorenko, 2001; Silver & Hagin, 2002). Studies of dyslexic individuals have found that dysfunction of phonetic processing is central in the majority of cases (Shaywitz et al., 2000).

Math and writing LDs have received much less attention in the literature. A review by Geary (2004) identifies three key processes involved in mathematics: procedural processing (e.g., counting, following multiple steps in computations), semantic memory (retrieving key facts from long-term memory), and visuospatial processing (spatially representing numerical relationships, geometric concepts, and functions). Others separate the neuropsychological challenges of mathematics LDs into verbally based difficulties comprehending numbers and mathematics symbols, problems retrieving number facts from memory, and impediments to executing calculations, and nonverbally based challenges with visual-spatial processing and nonverbal reasoning and concept formation (Rourke & Conway, 1997).

Writing skills are typically categorized at the levels of handwriting, mechanics (spelling, grammar, syntax), and content and organization of ideas (Silver & Hagin, 2002). These are related to a wide range of neuropsychological functions and so potentially comprise a diverse group of students.

Handwriting is based on visual-motor and visual memory skills. Writing mechanics (e.g., spelling, syntax, grammar) involve the processing of language and the retention and recall of rules (verbal and nonverbal) in long-term memory. Skills related to the content and organization of writing generally use higher level reasoning and analysis skills.

Generally, NLDs are seen to be related to challenges to tactile and visual-motor processes affecting attention, memory, and reasoning in these areas, accompanied by relative strengths related to verbal processing. The model uses this pattern of strengths and weaknesses to explain difficulties with higher order reasoning, social skills, and adaptive functioning (Rourke, 1989).

Neurological Factors

Studies of neurological functioning have examined differences in the brain morphology and physiology of individuals with LDs in areas of the brain associated with language processing (e.g., planum temporale, sylvian fissure), executive functioning (e.g., prefrontal cortex), short- and long-term memory (e.g., hippocampus, amygdala), and visuospatial processing (e.g., posterior right hemisphere; Grigorenko, 2001; Pennington, 1991; Semrud-Clikeman & Hynd, 1994). In explaining LDs, findings point to complex relationships among brain centers rather than one key area or lesion (Grigorenko, 2001). Most of these studies examined individuals with reading difficulties. Focusing on the areas of the brain related to language processing, differences between dyslexics and normal readers have been found in brain structure and morphology, electrophysiological activity (EEG), and neuronal activity (e.g., functional MRI; Grigorenko, 2001).

Familial and Genetic Factors

Research findings also support the genetic transmission of LDs. Here again, this research has focused on children with reading LDs. Familial studies show a 35 percent to 40 percent incidence of LDs in first-degree relatives (Beitchmen & Young, 1997) compared to 5 percent in the population at large. Studies have found that 40 percent of boys and 18 percent of girls with an affected parent have dyslexia (Grigorenko, 2001). Twin studies also support genetic factors, with samples of monozygotic twins showing a concordance of 85 percent to 100 percent compared to a concordance of 35 percent to 50 percent in dizygotic twins (Grigorenko, 2001).

In summary, research into LDs (primarily dyslexia) has found multiple etiological factors and complex relationships among contributing components at each level of analysis. At the most basic level, both genetic and environmental factors appear to play a role. Further, it is not a simple, single gene transmission, but rather a process involving multiple chromosomal sites (Grigorenko, 2001). Similarly, at a neurological level, multiple brain centers are involved and outcomes result from complex functions involving multiple sites. At the level of learning and adjustment outcomes, cognitive, emotional, social, and family factors are involved, and we are just at the beginning stage of understanding causal relationships among them.

COURSE, COMPLICATIONS, AND PROGNOSIS

Typically, LDs are not recognized until the child is in the early years of elementary school. Although investigators have attempted to identify early indicators of LDs during the preschool years, predictive factors have been elusive. Some children demonstrate early language problems that are associated with later LDs, but this relationship has not been strong enough to reliably identify LDs before kindergarten or first grade (Satz & Fletcher, 1988; Silver & Hagin, 2002).

Even timely identification in early elementary school is inconsistent. Depending on the teacher's approach and familiarity with LDs, the availability of appropriate assessment resources, and school policies on identifying children for special education services, LDs may go undetected for years. Children with high intellectual abilities can often compensate for the LD-related processing difficulties and master early learning objectives, masking the effects of the LD. Alternately, children with LDs and lower ability levels are often mistaken for children with generally low learning abilities and so fail to qualify as well. In cases of children from families where English is a second language, assessment may attribute learning problems to competency with English rather than to the underlying LD (Silver & Hagin, 2002).

Children with LDs face persistent challenges throughout the school years (Shaywitz et al., 2000). Appropriate interventions can mitigate the extent of the academic deficits, but reading, math, or writing problems are present throughout the life span. Students with LDs follow a number of developmental courses. Children with mild learning challenges, early identification, appropriate instructional adaptations, talents in nonacademic areas, and good family support generally do well with minimal or no psychosocial sequelae. Although these children recognize that they have low academic abilities relative to peers, their global self-concept remains positive (Gans, Kenny, & Ghany, 2003). Their postsecondary academic achievement and vocational attainments are generally seen to be somewhat limited by the basic learning challenges (Klein & Mannuzza, 2000; Spreen, 1988). Still, there are many documented cases of individuals with LDs succeeding in professional schools and even a number of accomplished historical figures thought to have had an LD (e.g., Albert Einstein, Thomas Edison, Winston Churchill).

In contrast, three groups of students with LDs appear at greater risk for more negative outcomes. First, there are children with severe LDs who confront processing difficulties that directly undermine their overall development. This includes severe reading LDs where the individual cannot understand written language to the point that it restricts their functional independence (Reiff & Gerber, 1994). Additionally, LDs that have an impact on social processing interfere with social development, establishing age-appropriate friendships, and experiencing a social support network (Gresham & MacMillan, 1997; Wallander & Hubert, 1987).

A second at-risk group is individuals with LDs whose early temperament and limited affective resilience restrict their ability to take on the emotional and social challenges accompanying an LD (Keogh, 2003; Rothstein & Glenn, 1999). This includes children with poor self-regulation, a less established sense of self, limited social motivation and relatedness, dysphoric trends, or a tendency to respond to frustration with anger or aggression.

The third group at risk for negative outcomes consists of children with environmental and family challenges (Silver & Hagin, 2002). Children growing up with exposure to environmental toxins or psychological trauma, limited parental support, or impoverished early learning environments may have fewer internal learning resources to use to compensate and adapt to LDs. Furthermore, an environment where the school cannot appropriately diagnose and intervene with the LD leaves the child at further risk of being overwhelmed by the learning challenges.

The course of development for these at-risk students is far more difficult, with increased likelihood of low grades, retention, social rejection, behavioral problems, and psychosocial challenges. As adolescents, these individuals are at greater risk for a range of adjustment problems including psychiatric disorders, social isolation, dropping out of school, problems with the law, and substance abuse.

Outcome studies of adults with LDs have yielded conflicting results. These studies have consistently found that the learning challenges persist and that this is related to the severity of the LD in childhood (Kavale, 1988; Spreen, 1988). There also appears to be a significant impact on participation in postsecondary education and occupational attainment. The extent of the impact on vocational achievement and on psychosocial adjustment is not clear, however, in that some studies have found relatively positive outcomes (e.g., Bruck, 1985) and others greater challenges (Satz, Buka, Lipsitt, & Seidman, 1988). In general, outcomes are correlated with IQ, socioeconomic status of family of origin, degree of neurological dysfunction, and extent of services and interventions received (Beitchman & Young, 1997; Kavale, 1988; Silver & Hagin, 2002; Spreen, 1988).

ASSESSMENT AND DIAGNOSIS

Diagnosis of LDs is made through two separate systems, the psychiatrically based *Diagnostic and Statistical Manual of Mental Disorders,* fourth edition (*DSM-IV;* American Psychiatric Association, 1994) and the educationally based federal guidelines for determining eligibility for special education services (IDEA; U.S. Department of Education, 2003). The two diagnoses serve different functions. The psychiatric *DSM-IV* diagnosis guides treatment and establishes eligibility for third-party payment for clinical services. The educational guidelines are used to identify the student as eligible for special education services and to grant certain rights to the parents in advocating for the educational needs of the child.

The *DSM-IV* separates LDs into four diagnostic categories: reading disorder, mathematics disorder, disorder of written expression, and learning disorder not otherwise specified. Diagnostic criteria are based on achievement in the area "as measured by individually administered standardized tests . . . [falling] substantially below that expected for the child's chronological age, measured intelligence, and age-appropriate education" and that the "disturbance . . . significantly interferes with academic achievement or activities of daily living . . ." (American Psychiatric Association, 1994, p. 48). A discrepancy of 2 standard deviations between ability and IQ meets the criterion. (Learning disorder not otherwise specified is a category for disorders of learning that do not meet the criteria for the three other diagnoses.)

The federal guidelines establish 12 categories of special needs, with LDs falling into the category of specific learning disability. The actual criteria are set by each separate state, with most states utilizing a discrepancy between IQ and achievement of between 1 and 2 standard deviations. Other regulations and criteria are also established and followed by each school district.

School-based assessment of LDs includes a psychological evaluation (to determine IQ), an educational evaluation of achievement, and often a speech and language evaluation to further understand language processing skills or an occupational therapy evaluation to further explore visual-motor integration. Schools will also often provide some assessment of emotional functioning (self-concept, anxiety, behavior) and family adaptation. School professionals present the results at an official team meeting (including school administration, teaching staff, pupil personnel specialists, and the parents), and this team determines the educational diagnosis.

Outside of school, clinical assessment should include a comprehensive psychological or neuropsychological evaluation to evaluate the profile of cognitive functioning (intelligence, achievement, and processing deficits), social and emotional functioning, and family dynamics. This includes a range of cognitive tests, behavior rating scales, projective tests, a diagnostic interview/play session, and parent interview to review the child's history. In many settings, the psychologist/neuropsychologist only administers the tests and a psychiatrist or clinical social worker conducts the rest of the evaluation procedures. A neurological evaluation may also be necessary to assess health and neurological status and to rule out other neurological disorders (e.g., seizure disorder). When assessing a child with an LD, it is important to go beyond the cognitive measures needed to make the diagnosis and to fully evaluate the child's emotional condition, social functioning, family dynamics, and neurological status.

IMPACT ON ENVIRONMENT

Family

Having a child with an LD increases stress on a family in a number of ways. This varies depending on the severity of the cognitive challenges; the extent of emotional, social, and behavioral problems; and the level of support from the school. In extreme cases the presence of the LD makes difficult demands on parents and siblings, taxing family coping resources and exacting an emotional cost on the entire family system (Dyson, 1996; Knight, 1999).

The primary impact of the LD on the family is seen through the parents' emotional response to the diagnosis. Parents are challenged to accept the diagnosis, grieve for the child's learning abilities that are experienced as lost, and adjust their expectations for academic (and other) achievements (Knight, 1999). For many parents, this may engender an overly supportive response that may protect the child from some of the difficulties of living with an LD, but may also undermine the child's development of coping skills and ability to become independent (Rothstein & Glenn, 1999). Alternately, parents may struggle with accepting the diagnosis and either emotionally disengage from the child or insist on maintaining unrealistic expectations for him or her (Lerner, 1985).

Beyond the emotional response to the diagnosis, parents are confronted with increased demands for caregiving. This includes helping with the child's learning and homework, communicating and advocating with the school team, and learning about LDs so as to best meet the child's needs. Parenting demands will especially increase with children who present behavioral or emotional demands, because the family must provide extra support in the form of encouragement, nurturance, or behavioral programs in the home. Helping the child complete homework can become a particularly onerous duty for parents, as the child struggles with the frustration of the LD. Demands on parents often extend beyond the usual 20-year period of child rearing. The young adult with an LD may require functional, emotional, and financial support from the family beyond the age of 30 (Bassett, Polloway, & Patton, 1994).

A further source of stress for many families is the development of the relationship with the school team. Parents must learn the challenging skills of advocating for the child, knowing when to push and when to compromise and how to demand resources for their child in the face of budgetary or procedural resistance. For families with rigid boundaries, creating a trusting, functional relationship with the school can be daunting.

The presence of an LD also affects siblings. Siblings usually know something is wrong but do not understand what it is (Culbertson & Silovsky, 1996). They frequently report feeling confused because they are not given any information about the LD or how it affects the brother or sister. Siblings can also feel neglected by the increased attention and time parents give the child with the LD. They can resent the increased responsibilities placed on them and the disruption of family plans caused by the needs of the child with an LD. The LD can evoke a range of difficult emotions in the siblings including shame, anger, and guilt. In peer situations, they may feel the need to defend or protect their brother or sister with an LD in the face of teasing or provocation. Comparisons among siblings can interfere with the parents' normal praise giving in that parents do not want to compliment the achievements of a sibling in front of the child who struggles with the LD. These factors can distort the normal, healthy occurrence of sibling rivalry, intensifying it to destructive levels.

It should also be noted that for families struggling with dysfunction or other challenges, the presence of the LD can exacerbate these problems. For example, marital discord can become extreme, with parents disagreeing about the existence of an LD or how best to parent the child. Families struggling with facilitating the transition of their children to adulthood may avoid providing the supports needed by the adolescent child with LD to become independent. In extreme cases, the LD and its symptoms can serve a function for the family. For example, focus on the LD can distract from marital issues that threaten the family's ability to stay together, or the family may use the LD to express displaced anger to school personnel.

School

Students with LDs provide a challenge for schools that can be daunting to teaching and administrative staff. Such students require a thorough assessment and a carefully designed, individualized program that includes adjustments to the instruction in the mainstream classroom and a coordinated approach with the teaching provided in the resource room. They place demands on school resources, requiring more staff, space, and equipment and materials. Team members must work to provide individualized services and assessments, communicate and coordinate the program, and learn new techniques. It can be particularly challenging for the mainstream teacher to integrate the special needs of the child with an LD into the classroom program.

Many schools embrace these challenges and provide excellent programs that enhance the academic skills and psychosocial development of children and adolescents with LDs. These schools see the positive impact of children with LDs on the school as a means to promote the appreciation of diversity, challenge teachers to provide excellent instruction, and create pride among staff when successes occur. Other schools struggle with coordinating these special requirements. For many schools, stretching limited resources or consistently applying a particular model of education outweighs the needs of the individual child, and so key services are not provided.

Peer Interactions

As noted in previous sections, LDs have a negative impact on peer interactions for many children. Research using nomination techniques and rating scales has consistently found that students with an LD are less accepted and more rejected by peers (Gresham & MacMillan, 1997). They are seen to be less attractive as friends to observers blind to the presence of an LD (Wallander & Hubert, 1987). This does not apply to all children with an LD, however, in that a significant number of students with LDs are as liked and as socially active as typical students. In one meta-analysis, it was estimated that between 16 percent and 22 percent of students with LDs were as accepted as children without LDs (Swanson & Malone, 1992).

The social challenges of children with LDs can be attributed to two factors—the child's social skills and the social culture of the classroom. The presence of poor social skills is reflected in studies that have found that students with LDs demonstrate more negative social behaviors and fewer positive social behaviors (Wallander & Hubert, 1987). This is a problem particularly for children with associated behavior disorders marked by aggression (Gresham & MacMillan, 1997).

The presence of an LD can also put the child in a lower status position in the classroom. A number of studies showed no difference in the social status of children with LDs and children who exhibited low academic achievement (Nowicki, 2003). In general, children who do more poorly with academic achievement are less liked and more rejected by peers within the classroom culture (Vaughn & Hogan, 1990). In this regard, students with resource room placement may have a more positive social experience because they have a supportive peer group outside the classroom.

IMPLICATIONS FOR FUTURE PERSONALITY DEVELOPMENT

A growing body of work is addressing personality development in adults with LDs. This includes surveys of adults with LDs, interview studies, and use of the Minnesota Multiphasic Personality Inventory (Hall, Spruill, & Webster, 2002; Shessel & Reiff, 1999; Waldo, McIntosh, & Koller, 1999). As with the other areas of inquiry, although there is agreement that LDs influence a number of key personality dimensions, there are conflicting results with regard to the extent of the impact.

The presence of an LD can affect the process of adult emotional development (Bassett, Polloway, & Patton, 1994). The developmental process may be generally delayed so that key developmental objectives of adulthood (e.g., independence from family of origin, developing an intimate relationship) may not occur until later than generally expected. There may also be acute difficulties related to a range of important steps of adult development. Dependency on others (emotional and instrumental) may interfere with achieving independence from parents. Challenges with social functioning may undermine efforts to establish an intimate partnership or marital relationship. A conflicted self-concept, vocational struggles, and social challenges may interfere with the establishment of a positive adult sense of identity (Price, 1993; Waldo, McIntosh, & Koller, 1999).

The area receiving the most attention with regard to adult personality is self-concept. Adults with LDs are seen to struggle with a sense of themselves as different and incompetent in some fundamental way. The experience of chronic academic frustration associated with an LD leaves many adults "feeling stupid," with all the expected negative connotations (Price, 1993; Shessel & Reiff, 1999).

Consistent with the fact that LDs are an invisible disability (i.e., not readily apparent to other people upon first meeting them), some investigators report significant manifestations of the imposter phenomenon whereby individuals feel that they are deceiving others who think they are smart and competent and do not know the truth of the cognitive challenges related to the LD (Shessel & Reiff, 1999). This type of challenge can lead some to experience identity confusion, whereby they work to present what they think others find desirable rather than who they really are. Self-psychology views this in terms of difficulties developing a cohesive sense of self and a lack of coherence in the self-narrative (Palombo, 2001).

Closely related to difficulties with self-concept, adults with LDs also confront significant difficulties with their experiences of the social world. In dealing with the challenges of negotiating the social and vocational environments without being able to read, write, or understand numerical computations, they may increasingly depend on others (Price, 1993). Many adults with LDs require the help of family members, friends, teachers, coworkers, or supervisors to meet the daily demands of independence. Further, the chronic childhood experience of frustration in the face of academic, social, and functional demands can lead to greater emotional dependency on others as a coping response. Psychoanalytic studies conceptualize this in terms of the development of object relations and find that an LD can influence the internalized representations of self and others, leading to self-representations marked by dependency on others or the need for the support of others to feel complete (Rothstein & Glenn, 1999).

Complicating this picture, adults with LDs often feel chronically rejected in a world that does not understand them, accept them, or respond to their emotional needs. This can influence the development of trust and lead to socially avoidant tendencies or antisocial conduct. Many report feeling like a loner and regularly experience loneliness (Shessel & Reiff, 1999). Experiencing elevated dependency along with socially avoidant tendencies can leave the individual quite conflicted and lead them to oscillate between dependent and alienating behaviors.

Another area receiving attention is degree of work motivation. There is evidence suggesting that LDs disrupt the development of typical patterns of motivation to take on challenges in school, at work, or in other components of one's life. This body of research has found that adults with LDs experience an overly external locus of control, attribute failure to internal factors and success to external factors, and present lower levels of need for achievement or intrinsic motivation (Dev, 1998; Shapiro & Rich, 1999). These findings are attributed to the chronic experience of frustration associated with growing up with an LD.

This range of challenges fosters high levels of stress, anxiety, and dysphoric affect (Price, 1993; Shessel & Reiff, 1999; Waldo, McIntosh, & Koller, 1999). Some adults with LDs present difficulties with anger, self-blame, sadness, chronic frustration, and anxiety (Price, 1993; Shessel & Reiff, 1999). Psychoanalytic studies have found that LDs affect the presence of particular defense mechanisms and the development of character pathology (Rothstein & Glenn, 1999). For example, an individual with poor organizational skills secondary to an LD can present obsessive and compulsive traits in the service of maintaining order in his life. Alternately, a person may use the LD to manage key conflicts associated with achievement by focusing on his damaged sense of self, thus avoiding new challenges. In extreme cases, a constellation of defenses can be built around the LD, creating a personality disorder. Some psychoanalytic investigators have posited that the primitive defenses and difficulties with integration presented by borderline personality disorders are associated with the processing difficulties of an LD (Rothstein & Glenn, 1999).

This suggestion is consistent with findings of higher frequencies among adults with LDs of externalizing psychopathology such as conduct disorders or internalizing disorders such as depression or anxiety disorders (Price, 1993). However, findings in this area are inconsistent, leading to the conclusion that in some cases adults with LDs are at risk for these behavioral outcomes, and that further study of risk and resilience factors is needed.

The impact on personality of an LD can be even greater for individuals with LDs that are not recognized until adulthood (Hoffschmidt & Weinstein, 2003). This group struggles with the issues noted previously but also frequently confronts attributions of laziness, incompetence, or other negative appraisals from others. The development of a cohesive identity can be challenged by the confusing experience of competence in some areas and deficits in others. Confusion can lead to self-blame or to compensatory efforts to work harder in order to achieve. In this context, it is easy to see why early assessment of LDs is important.

Though the literature has focused on the challenges and negative impacts of LDs on personality, Shessel and Reiff (1999) also found some positive effects. Their study participants reported during interviews that the LD had helped to make them more creative, more sensitive to others, and more motivated to help others. This effect is often overlooked and requires further study. Similarly, Hall, Spruill, and Webster (2002) found higher levels of resiliency and need for achievement in a sample of college students with LDs, compared to peers without LDs.

TREATMENT IMPLICATIONS

Appropriate treatment for LDs includes modified academic programming, social skills training, and psychotherapy.

Academic Programming

Children with LDs require an individualized educational program tailored to fit the pattern of learning strengths and weaknesses that they present. Most children with LDs can be effectively taught in the mainstream, with some individualized services provided in a resource room. Children with more severe LDs may require a program with time equally split between the resource room and the mainstream classroom or even full-time assignment to a special education classroom. Only the most extreme cases with associated behavioral challenges require out-of-district placement in day or residential facilities. Federal guidelines require that the child be educated in the least restrictive setting, and social and academic advantages are associated with greater inclusion in the mainstream (Silver & Hagin, 2002). It is essential, however, to meet the child's educational needs in whatever setting is appropriate.

Modifications to the program of a child with an LD include changing general instructional techniques. Directions and task information may be given through both visual and auditory channels, time limits for tasks or tests may be eliminated, learning objectives and tasks may be broken into smaller components, and cognitive strategies may be taught (Swanson, 1999). Additional teaching geared to the individual student may be provided, along with study aids such as outlines, summaries, and charts.

Special educators also use specific programs or interventions to address learning disabilities. Approaches to reading include building phonemic awareness, teaching phonics skills, building sight word recognition, and addressing reading comprehension through repeated reading or analytic skills (drawing inferences, using story maps, and separating main ideas and supporting details; Bender, 1999; Torgesen et al., 2001). Mathematics programs include multisensory approaches to number recognition, strategies to use with word problems, and ways to master basic computation and the learning of math facts (Bryant & Dix, 1999). Spelling programs use visual imagery, teacher imitation of student errors, and mnemonics to develop memory skills (Johnson & Bender, 1999). Higher order writing skills are developed through teaching the student about the writing process (organizing thoughts, drafting, editing), understanding the audience and purpose of the written work, and using graphic organizers to design structures for the writing (Johnson & Bender, 1999).

Children with LDs receive individual (and group) services from a number of other specialists as well. Speech and language therapists work with the student on oral articulation, building expressive and receptive communication skills, general language processing, and pragmatic skills (the social use of language). Occupational therapists address fine-motor coordination and visual-motor integration skills. School psychologists, social workers, and counselors provide a range of interventions to support self-esteem, coping, and academic motivation. Many children with LDs receive extra teaching and support from private tutors.

Appropriate interventions for LDs do not eliminate or cure the processing difficulties but allow the student to continue to develop academic skills and to be ready for the demands of the curriculum of the higher grades. Without the appropriate support, students fall further behind and are unable to continue to meet the demands of the age-appropriate curriculum. Transitional planning is very important for children with LDs. They encounter a unique set of challenges as they make their way from high school to postsecondary education, employment, and independent living. It is essential that the school team assess functional, social, and vocational needs starting in middle school to ensure that the student is well prepared for life after high school.

Social Skills Training

In many cases challenges with social skills accompany LDs (this is especially important for students with NLD). These challenges include difficulties with processing social information (e.g., reading facial expressions, processing auditory language), which is associated with the neuropsychological deficits underlying the LD, as well as managing the social rejection and exclusion that can accompany the academic challenges. Research has found that a range of social skills training interventions, usually carried out in a group format, are effective at teaching social skills but that it is difficult to promote generalization of the skills to social situations and to ensure maintenance following the completion of the intervention (Bryan & Lee, 1990; Vaughn, McIntosh, & Hogan, 2002; Wallander & Hubert, 1987). For this reason, children with LDs also require opportunities to practice social skills in structured situations with cueing and staff support. Social skills programs address behavioral skills (eye contact, greetings, initiating contact in a group), perspective taking and understanding the viewpoints of others, learning about social conventions and unwritten rules, and social problem solving (Bryan & Lee, 1990; Vaughn et al., 2002). As with academic interventions, the most effective social skills programs are geared to the individual deficits of the child (Vaughn et al., 2002).

Social skills programs are usually offered in school by psychologists, social workers, speech therapists, or special education teachers. In some cases they are also offered by community-based clinicians. Most groups are offered on a time-limited basis, consisting of 10–20 sessions (Vaughn et al., 2002).

Psychotherapy

Individuals with LDs can benefit from a range of psychotherapeutic interventions. Behavior therapy, working with parents or the school, may be necessary to manage difficult behaviors, facilitate motivation, or teach more adaptive coping responses. Cognitive behavioral techniques can be used to help deal with stress or to improve self-esteem. Group therapy is used to teach social skills (see preceding section) or to build self-esteem. Groups can be particularly effective because they help the child with an LD see that she is not the only one, provide supportive and constructive peer feedback, and can lead to the development of friendships. Family therapy is also an important modality of treatment for students with LDs. This work can help families to best support and parent the child, address family systemic dysfunction that is affecting the child, or help resolve conflicts between the school and family systems (Fine & Carlson, 1992).

Individual psychotherapy or counseling is probably the most frequently used intervention. This work typically addresses understanding and integrating the LD and its impact, developing self-esteem, building social relations, and facilitating adaptive coping with the challenges of an LD. Although psychotherapy with children is not fundamentally different from treatment with other diagnostic groups of children, there are key considerations for the therapist to embrace. First, it is very important for the therapist to assess any difficulties with communication or language processing and to understand how they will affect the therapeutic process. Adaptations (e.g., simplifying what the therapist says, avoiding abstract and figurative language, repeating key information) may be necessary to successful intervention. Second, therapists should be sensitive to the potential shame dynamic surrounding the LD, leading to avoidance and a high degree of defensiveness and impeding attempts to examine its impact in therapy. Finally, therapists should consider how the LD is integrated with the therapy. It is important not to focus only on the LD and attribute all problems to its existence. Conversely, therapists need to avoid underemphasizing the emotional impact the LD has on a child or adolescent.

Psychoanalytic investigators have raised the issue of whether some individuals with LDs are not able to benefit from more psychodynamic types of treatment (Rothstein & Glenn, 1999). More recent work has found children and adolescents with LDs generally able to engage in psychodynamic forms of therapy. However, individuals with NLD are found to be poor candidates for this type of treatment because they struggle with understanding emotion and integrating memories, thoughts, and feelings toward personality change.

REFERENCES

American Psychiatric Association. (1994). *Diagnostic and statistical manual of mental disorders* (4th ed.). Washington, DC: Author.

Anderson, P. L., & Meier-Hedde, R. (2001). Early case reports of dyslexia in the United States and Europe. *Journal of Learning Disabilities, 34,* 9–21.

Bassett, D. S., Polloway, E. A., & Patton, J. R. (1994). Learning disabilities: Perspectives on adult development. In P. J. Gerber & H. B. Reiff (Eds.), *Learning disabilities in adulthood: Persisting problems and evolving issues* (pp. 10–19). Boston: Andover Medical.

Beitchman, J. H., Wilson, B., Douglas, L., Young, A., & Adlaf, E. (2001). Substance use disorders in young adults with and without LD: Predictive and concurrent relationships. *Journal of Learning Disabilities, 34,* 317–332.

Beitchman, J. H., & Young, A. R. (1997). Learning disorders with a special emphasis on reading disorders: A review of the past 10 years. *Journal of the American Academy of Child and Adolescent Psychiatry, 36,* 1020–1032.

Bender, W. N. (1999). Innovative approaches to reading. In W. N. Bender (Ed.), *Professional issues in learning disabilities: Practical strategies and relevant research findings.* Austin, TX: Pro-Ed.

Bennett, K. J., Brown, K. S., Boyle, M., Racine, Y., & Offord, D. (2003). Does low reading achievement at school entry cause conduct problems? *Social Science and Medicine, 56,* 2443–2448.

Brier, N. (1989). The relationship between learning disability and delinquency: A review and reappraisal. *Journal of Learning Disabilities, 22,* 546–553.

Bruck, M. (1985). The adult functioning of children with specific learning disabilities. In L. Siegel (Ed.), *Advances in applied developmental psychology* (pp. 91–129). New York: Ablex.

Bryan, T. (1974). An observational analysis of classroom behaviors of children with learning disabilities. *Journal of Learning Disabilities, 7,* 26–34.

Bryan, T., & Lee, J. (1990). Social skills training with learning disabled children and adolescents: The state of the art. In T. E. Scruggs & B. Y. L. Wong (Eds.), *Intervention research in learning disabilities.* New York: Springer-Verlag.

Bryant, D. P., & Dix, J. (1999). Mathematics interventions for students with learning disabilities. In W. N. Bender (Ed.), *Professional issues in learning disabilities: Practical strategies and relevant research findings* (pp. 219–259). Austin, TX: Pro-Ed.

Culbertson, J. L., & Silovsky, J. F. (1996). Learning disabilities and attention deficit hyperactivity disorders: Their impact on children's significant others. In F. W. Kaslow (Ed.), *Handbook of relational diagnosis and dysfunctional family patterns* (pp. 186–209). New York: Wiley.

Denckla, M. B. (1994). Measurement of executive function. In G. R. Lyon (Ed.), *Frames of reference for the assessment of learning disabilities* (pp. 117–142). Baltimore: Paul H. Brookes.

Dev, P. C. (1998). Intrinsic motivation and the student with learning disabilities. *Journal of Research and Development in Education, 31,* 98–108.

Dyson, L. L. (1996). The experiences of families of children with learning disabilities: Parental stress, family functioning, and sibling self-concept. *Journal of Learning Disabilities, 29,* 280–286.

Elbaum, B., & Vaughn, S. (2003). For which students with learning disabilities are self-concept interventions effective? *Journal of Learning Disabilities, 36,* 101–108.

Fine, M. J., and Carlson, C. (Eds.). (1992). *The handbook of family-school intervention: A systems perspective.* Boston: Allyn & Bacon.

Gans, A. M., Kenny, M. C., & Ghany, D. L. (2003). Comparing the self-concept of students with and without learning disabilities. *Journal of Learning Disabilities, 36,* 287–295.

Geary, D. C. (2004). Mathematics and learning disabilities. *Journal of Learning Disabilities, 37,* 4–15.

Gresham, F. M., & MacMillan, D. L. (1997). Social competence and affective characteristics of students with mild disabilities. *Review of Educational Research, 67,* 377–415.

Grigorenko, E. L. (2001). Developmental dyslexia: An update on genes, brains, and environments. *Journal of Child Psychology and Psychiatry, 42,* 91–125.

Hall, C. W., Spruill, K. L., & Webster, R. E. (2002). Motivational and attitudinal factors in college students with and without learning disabilities. *Learning Disability Quarterly, 25,* 79–86.

Heath, N. L., & Ross, S. (2000). Prevalence and expression of depressive symptomatology in students with and without learning disabilities. *Learning Disability Quarterly, 23,* 24–36.

Hoffschmidt, S. J., & Weinstein, C. S. (2003). The influence of silent learning disorders on the lives of women. *Women and Therapy, 26,* 81–94.

Howard, K. A., & Tryon, G. S. (2002). Depressive symptoms in and type of classroom placement for adolescents with LD. *Journal of Learning Disabilities, 35,* 185–190.

Johnson, S. E., & Bender, W. N. (1999). Language arts instructional approaches. In W. N. Bender (Ed.), *Professional issues in learning disabilities: Practical strategies and relevant research findings.* Austin, TX: Pro-Ed.

Kavale, K. A. (1988). The long-term consequences of learning disabilities. In M. C. Wang & M. C. Reynolds (Eds.), *Handbook of special education: Research and practice. Vol. 2: Mildly handicapped conditions* (pp. 303–344). Elmsford, NY: Pergamon Press.

Keogh, B. K. (2003). *Temperament in the classroom: Understanding individual differences.* Baltimore: Paul H. Brookes.

Klassen, R. (2002). A question of calibration: A review of the self-efficacy beliefs of students with learning disabilities. *Learning Disability Quarterly, 25,* 88–102.

Klein, R. G., & Mannuzza, S. (2000). Children with uncomplicated disorders grown up: A prospective follow-up into adulthood. In L. L. Greenhill (Ed.), *Learning disabilities: Implications for psychiatric treatment* (pp. 1–31). Washington, DC: American Psychiatric Press.

Knight, D. (1999). Families of students with learning disabilities. In W. N. Bender (Ed.), *Professional issues in learning disabilities: Practical strategies and relevant research findings* (pp. 263–306). Austin, TX: Pro-Ed.

Lerner, J. W. (1985). *Learning disabilities: Theories, diagnosis, and teaching strategies.* Boston: Houghton Mifflin.

Mercer, C. D., Jordan, L., Allsop, D. H., & Mercer, A. R. (1996). Learning disabilities definitions and criteria used by state education departments. *Learning Disability Quarterly, 19,* 217–232.

Moss, S., Prosser, H., Ibbotson, B., & Goldberg, D. (1996). Respondent and informant accounts of psychiatric symptoms in a sample of patients with learning disabilities. *Journal of Intellectual Disability Research, 40,* 457–465.

Nowicki, E. A. (2003). A meta-analysis of the social competence of children with learning disabilities compared to classmates of low and average to high achievement. *Learning Disability Quarterly, 26,* 171–188.

Osman, B. B. (2000). Learning disabilities and the risk of psychiatric disorders in children and adolescents. In L. L. Greenhill (Ed.), *Learning disabilities: Implications for psychiatric treatment* (pp. 33–57). Washington, DC: American Psychiatric Press.

Palombo, J. (2001). *Learning disorders and disorders of the self: In children and adolescents.* New York: Norton.

Pearl, R., & Bryan, T. (1990). Learning disabled adolescents' vulnerability to victimization and delinquency. In L. Swanson & B. Keogh (Eds.), *Learning disabilities: Theoretical and research issues* (pp. 139–154). Hillsdale, NJ: Erlbaum.

Pennington, B. F. (1991). *Diagnosing learning disorders: A neuropsychological framework.* New York: Guilford Press.

Price, L. (1993). Psychosocial characteristics and issues of adults with learning disabilities. In L. C. Brinckerhoff, S. F. Shaw, & J. M. McGuire (Eds.), *Promoting postsecondary education for students with learning disabilities: A handbook for practitioners* (pp. 137–167). Austin, TX: Pro-Ed.

Reiff, H. B., & Gerber, P. J. (1994). Social/emotional and daily living issues for adults with learning disabilities. In P. J. Gerber & H. B. Reiff (Eds.), *Learning disabilities in adulthood: Persisting problems and evolving issues* (pp. 72–81). Boston: Andover Medical.

Rothstein, A. A., & Glenn, J. (1999). *Learning disabilities and psychic conflict: A psychoanalytic casebook.* Madison, CT: International Universities Press.

Rourke, B. P. (Ed.). (1985). *Neuropsychology of learning disabilities: Essentials of subtype analysis.* New York: Guilford Press.

Rourke, B. P. (1988). Socioemotional disturbances of learning disabled children. *Journal of Consulting and Clinical Psychology, 56,* 801–810.

Rourke, B. P. (1989). *Nonverbal learning disabilities: The syndrome and the model.* New York: Guilford Press.

Rourke, B. P. (Ed.). (1995) *Syndrome of nonverbal learning disabilities.* New York: Guilford Press.

Rourke, B. P., & Conway, J. A. (1997). Disabilities of arithmetic and mathematical reasoning: Perspectives from neurology and neuropsychology. *Journal of Learning Disabilities, 30,* 34–46.

Rourke, B. P., & Fuerst, D. R. (1991). *Learning disabilities and psychosocial functioning: A neuropsychological perspective.* New York: Guilford Press.

Satz, P., Buka, S., Lipsitt, L., and Seidman, L. (1998). The long-term prognosis of learning disabled children: A review of studies 1954–1993. In B. K. Shapiro, P. J. Accardo, & A. J. Capute (Eds.), *Specific reading disability: A view of the spectrum* (pp. 223–250). Timonium, MD: York Press.

Satz, P., & Fletcher, J. M. (1988). Early identification of learning disabled children: An old problem revisited. *Journal of Consulting and Clinical Psychology, 56,* 824–829.

Semrod-Clikeman, M., & Hynd, G. W. (1994). Brain-behavior relationships in dyslexia. In N. C. Jordan & J. Goldsmith-Phillips (Eds.), *Learning disabilities: New directions for assessment and intervention* (pp. 43–65). Boston: Allyn & Bacon.

Shapiro, J., & Rich, R. (1999). *Facing learning disabilities in the adult years.* New York: Oxford University Press.

Shaywitz, B. A., Pugh, K. R., Fletcher, J. M., & Shaywitz, S. E. (2000). What cognitive and neurobiological studies have taught us about dyslexia. In L. L. Greenhill (Ed.), *Learning disabilities: Implications for psychiatric treatment* (pp. 59–95). Washington, DC: American Psychiatric Press.

Shessel, I., & Reiff, H. B. (1999). Experiences of adults with learning disabilities: Positive and negative impacts and outcomes. *Learning Disability Quarterly, 22,* 305–316.

Silver, A. A., & Hagin, R. A (2002). *Disorders of learning in childhood; second edition.* New York: Wiley.

Spreen, O. (1988). Prognosis of learning disability. *Journal of Consulting and Clinical Psychology, 56,* 836–842.

Swanson, H. L. (1999). *Interventions for students with learning disabilities: A meta-analysis of treatment outcomes.* New York: Guilford Press.

Swanson, H. L., & Malone, S. (1992). Social skills and learning disabilities: A meta-analysis of the literature. *School Psychology Review, 21,* 427–443.

Thompson, R. J., & Kronenberger, W. (1990). Behavior problems in children with learning problems. In L. Swanson & B. Keogh, *Learning disabilities: Theoretical and research issues* (pp. 156–174). Hillsdale, NJ: Erlbaum.

Torgesen, J. K. (1991). Subtypes as prototypes: Extended studies of rationally defined extreme groups. In L. V. Feagans, E. J. Short, & L. J. Meltzer (Eds.), *Subtypes of learning disabilities: Theoretical perspectives and research* (pp. 229–246). Hillsdale, NJ: Erlbaum.

Torgesen, J. K., Alexander, A. W., Wagner, R. K., Rashotte, C. A, Voeller, K. K. S., & Conway, T. (2001). Intensive remedial instruction for children with severe reading disabilities: Immediate and long-term outcomes from two instructional approaches. *Journal of Learning Disabilities, 34,* 33–58.

U.S. Department of Education. (2003). *Twenty-fourth Annual Report to Congress on the implementation of the Individuals with Disabilities Education Act.* Washington, DC: U.S. Government Printing Office.

Vaughn, S., & Hogan, A. (1990). Social competence and learning disabilities: A prospective study. In L. Swanson & B. Keogh (Eds.), *Learning disabilities: Theoretical and research issues* (pp. 175–191). Hillsdale, NJ: Erlbaum.

Vaughn, S., McIntosh, R., & Hogan, A. (2002). Why social skills training doesn't work: An alternative model. In D. L. Molfese & V. J. Molfese (Eds.), *Developmental variations in learning: Applications to social, executive function, language, and reading skills* (pp. 279–303). Mahwah, NJ: Erlbaum.

Waldo, S. L., McIntosh, D. E., & Koller, J. R. (1999). Personality profiles of adults with verbal and nonverbal learning disabilities. *Journal of Psychoeducational Assessment, 17,* 196–206.

Wallander, J. L. & Hubert, N. C. (1987). Peer social dysfunction in children with developmental disabilities: Empirical basis and a conceptual model. *Clinical Psychology Review, 7,* 205–221.

Welsh, M. C. (2002). Developmental and clinical variations in executive functions. In D. L. Molfese & V. J. Molfese (Eds.), *Developmental variations in learning: Applications to social, executive function, language, and reading skills* (pp. 139–185). Mahwah, NJ: Erlbaum.

Williams, S., & McGee, R. (1996). Reading in childhood and mental health in early adulthood. In J. H. Beitchman, N. J. Cohen, M. M. Konstantareas, & R. Tannock (Eds.), *Language, learning, and behavior disorders: Developmental, biological, and clinical perspectives* (pp. 530–554). New York: Cambridge University Press.

CHAPTER 17

Oppositional Defiant Disorder

ROSS W. GREENE

DESCRIPTION OF THE DISORDER AND CLINICAL PICTURE

Oppositional defiant disorder (ODD) refers to a recurrent childhood pattern of developmentally inappropriate levels of negativistic, defiant, disobedient, and hostile behavior toward authority figures (American Psychiatric Association, 1994). Specific behaviors associated with ODD include temper outbursts; persistent stubbornness; resistance to directions; unwillingness to compromise, give in, or negotiate with adults or peers; deliberate or persistent testing of limits; and verbal (and minor physical) aggression. These behaviors are almost always present in the home and with individuals the child knows well, and they often occur simultaneously with low self-esteem, mood lability, low frustration tolerance, and swearing.

Perhaps due to its relatively recent introduction into the diagnostic nomenclature, ODD has received limited research attention. It has seldom been considered separately from conduct disorder (CD; e.g., Hinshaw, 1994; Kuhne, Schachar, & Tannock, 1997; Lahey & Loeber, 1994), probably because ODD has merely been viewed as an early variant of CD (as noted by Schachar & Wachsmuth, 1990). Data have, in fact, shown that a majority of children diagnosed with CD exhibit the behaviors associated with ODD concurrently or at an earlier age (e.g., Frick et al., 1991; Hinshaw, Lahey, & Hart, 1993; Lahey, Loeber, Quay, Frick, & Grimm, 1992; Loeber, Green, Lahey, Christ, & Frick, 1992). Thus, to the degree that the behaviors associated with ODD often precede more serious forms of psychopathology—including not only CD but also adult antisocial behavior (see Langbehn, Cadoret, Yates, Troughton, & Stewart, 1998)—the manifestation of these behaviors represents an important window of opportunity for prevention efforts (Greene et al., 2004; Loeber, 1990; Lynam, 1996). However, approximately two thirds of children diagnosed with ODD do *not* subsequently develop CD (e.g., Biederman, Faraone, Mick, et al., 1996; Hinshaw et al., 1993; Hinshaw, 1994; Lahey & Loeber, 1994), leading some researchers to question the practice of combining ODD and CD into a single generic category often called conduct problems (Kuhne et al., 1997) and underscoring the need for a significantly greater study of ODD occurring outside the context of CD. Researchers have found ODD to be a significant predictor of family dysfunction and social impairment in clinically referred psychiatric populations of children and adolescents, even when controlling for CD and other psychiatric disorders (Greene, Biederman, et al., 2002).

PERSONALITY DEVELOPMENT AND PSYCHOPATHOLOGY

Because ODD has been poorly studied outside the context of CD, little is known about the longitudinal course of the disorder or its impact on personality development. What has become clear is that ODD typically occurs in combination with other disorders (Greene et al., 2002) and that noncomorbid ODD is fairly rare. For example, the overlap between ODD and attention-deficit/hyperactivity disorder (ADHD) is very well established (e.g., Abikoff & Klein, 1992; Biederman, Faraone, Milberger, et al., 1996; Hinshaw et al., 1993; Lahey & Loeber, 1994; Loeber, 1990; Loeber & Keenan, 1994; Speltz, McClellan, DeKlyen, & Jones, 1999). Current data show that approximately 65 percent of children diagnosed with ADHD have comorbid ODD, and that more than 80 percent of children diagnosed with ODD have comorbid ADHD (Greene, Biederman, et al., 2002).

The overlap between ODD and mood and anxiety disorders is also increasingly documented. Researchers have shown extremely high rates of ODD in children diagnosed with depression and bipolar disorder (Angold & Costello, 1993; Biederman, Faraone, Mick, et al., 1996; Geller & Luby, 1997; Wozniak & Biederman, 1996; Wozniak et al., 1995). In one recent study, 80 percent of children diagnosed with severe major depression and 85 percent of children diagnosed with bipolar disorder were also diagnosed with ODD (Greene et al., 2002). Indeed, youth with ODD and comorbid mood disorders may be at particular risk for the development of conduct disorder (Greene et al., 2002). Meaningful rates of anxiety disorders have also been found in youth with ODD: in one study, more than 60 percent of youth diagnosed with ODD had a comorbid anxiety disorder, and 45 percent of youth diagnosed with an anxiety disorder had comorbid ODD (Greene et al., 2002). The overlap between ODD and obsessiveness may be particularly compelling (e.g., Budman et al., 2000; Garland & Weiss, 1996).

An association is also demonstrated between ODD and language impairment. Recent data indicate that more than 20 percent of youth diagnosed with ODD have a comorbid language processing disorder, and that 55 percent of youth with language processing disorders are also diagnosed with ODD (Greene, Biederman, et al., 2002). Other recent studies have produced similar findings (Beitchman, Brownlie, & Wilson, 1996; Cantwell & Baker, 1991; Davis, Sanger, & Morris-Friehe, 1991; Gilmour, Hill, Place, & Skuse, 2004; Rogers-Adkinson & Griffin, 1999; Stevens & Bliss, 1995; Westby, 1999).

An emerging literature documents significant overlap between ODD and disorders on the autism spectrum, including Asperger's disorder and nonverbal learning disability. In one study, more than half of clinically referred youth meeting criteria for an autism spectrum disorder met criteria for ODD (Greene et al., 2002). Other research also suggests a clear overlap between ODD and social impairment. For example, in one study the rate of ODD among socially impaired youth with ADHD was more than 80 percent.

EPIDEMIOLOGY

Prevalence rates for ODD range from 2 percent to 16 percent (American Psychiatric Association, 1994). This wide spread is testimony to the historical lack of precision in studying and categorizing ODD, including use of disparate diagnostic guidelines and procedures. For example, little is known about whether there are important differences between children exhibiting mild ODD (e.g., tantrums, crying, screaming) and severe ODD (e.g., physical violence, verbal aggression). Research has shown that stubbornness is likely to emerge as a problem at around age 3 years, followed by defiance and temper outbursts at around age 5 years, arguing, irritability, blaming and annoying others, and anger between ages 6 and 8 years, and swearing at around age 9 years.

ETIOLOGY

Disparate conceptual models have been applied to ODD as well (McMahon & Wells, 1998), including the highly influential coercion, or social interactional, model (e.g., Patterson & Gullion, 1968; Patterson, Reid, & Dishion, 1992; see Taylor & Biglan, 1998). This model has focused on patterns of parental discipline that contribute to the development of coercive parent-child exchanges. As described by Chamberlain and Patterson (1995), four subtypes of parent inadequate discipline have been identified as contributing to the development of coercive parent-child interchanges. These subtypes include *inconsistent discipline* (parents who respond indiscriminately to a child's positive and negative behaviors, evidence poor or inconsistent follow-through with commands, give in when a child argues, and unpredictably change expectations and consequences for rule violations); *irritable explosive discipline* (parents who issue high rates of direct commands; frequently use high-intensity, high-amplitude strategies such as hitting, yelling, and threatening; frequently make humiliating or negative statements about the child; and increase the likelihood that the child will respond with aggressive or defiant behavior); *low supervision and involvement* (parents who are unaware of their child's activities outside of their direct supervision, do not know with whom the child is associating, are unaware of their child's adjustment at school, rarely engage in joint activities with their child, and are unwilling or unable to provide supervision even when aware of the child's association with antisocial peers); and *inflexible rigid discipline* (parents who rely on a single or limited range of discipline strategies for all types of transgressions, fail to take contextual or extenuating factors into account, consistently fail to provide rationales or to use other induction techniques in the context of discipline confrontations, and fail to adjust the intensity of the discipline reaction to the severity of the child's infraction).

However, given compelling data underscoring the reciprocal nature of interactions between parents and their difficult offspring (e.g., Anderson, Lytton, & Romney, 1986; Dumas & LaFreniere, 1993; Dumas, LaFreniere, & Serketich, 1995), the social interactional model has evolved from placing almost exclusive (some might argue unidirectional) emphasis on inept parenting practices as the major determinant of childhood conduct problems (e.g., Patterson, DeBaryshe, & Ramsey, 1989) to an acknowledgment that child characteristics may also contribute to the development of maladaptive parent-child interactions (e.g., Dishion, French, & Patterson, 1995; Patterson et al., 1992). It has been argued that, in its focus on inept parenting practices, research on noncompliance in children has historically overemphasized *adult* characteristics. To achieve a more complete, transactional understanding of ODD, significantly greater attention must be paid to *child* characteristics, and it has been argued that specific attention must be paid to emotion regulation, frustration tolerance, adaptation, and problem-solving skills (Greene & Ablon, 2005, Greene & Doyle, 1999). Developmental psychologists have long underscored these skills as related to a child's capacity to adapt to environmental changes or demands and internalize standards of conduct (e.g., Crockenberg & Litman, 1990; Harter, 1983; Kochanska, 1993, 1995; Kopp, 1982, 1989; Rothbart & Derryberry, 1981). The skill of compliance—defined as the capacity to defer or delay one's own goals in response to the imposed goals or standards of an authority figure—can be considered one of many developmental expressions of a young child's evolving capacities in these domains (e.g., Maccoby, 1980; Perry & Perry, 1983; Stifter, Spinrad, & Braungart-Rieker, 1999). The capacity for compliance is thought to develop in a sequence that includes, in infancy, managing the discomfort that can accompany hunger, cold, fatigue, and pain; modulating arousal while remaining engaged with the environment; and communicating with caregivers to signal that assistance is needed (e.g., Gottman, 1986; Kopp, 1989). With the development of language, more sophisticated mechanisms for self-regulation and affective modulation develop, as children learn to use language to label and communicate their thoughts and feelings, develop cognitive schemas related to cause and effect, and generate and internalize strategies aimed at facilitating advantageous interactions with the environment (e.g., Kopp, 1989; Mischel, 1983).

Researchers have underscored the frustration and emotional arousal that often accompany externally imposed demands for compliance (e.g., Amsel, 1990; Hoffman, 1975; Kochanska, 1993; Kopp, 1989; Stifter et al., 1999). When compliance is viewed both as a complex skill and as a critical milestone on the trajectory of emerging self-regulation and affective modulation, then *non*compliance (i.e., oppositional behavior) can be conceptualized as one of many potential by-products of what might best be described as a "compromised trajectory," or learning disability, in these domains (Greene & Ablon, 2005).

It has been argued that many of the psychiatric disorders that are comorbid with ODD (see earlier discussion) may set the stage for compromised skills in the domains of emotion regulation, problem solving, frustration tolerance, and adaptation. For example, compromised executive skills are commonly found in youth with ADHD. A variety of cognitive skills have been characterized as executive, including *working memory,* defined as an individual's capacity to hold events in his or her mind while bringing to bear hindsight and forethought for the purpose of acting on the events (see Fuster, 1989, 1995; Pennington, 1994); *self-regulation,* defined as an individual's capacity to regulate arousal in the service of goal-directed action (see Barkley, 1997); *shifting cognitive set,* which refers to the efficiency and flexibility by which an individual shifts from the rules and expectations of one situation to the rules and expectations of another (see Hayes, Gifford, & Ruckstuhl, 1996); and *problem solving,* which refers to an individual's capacity to organize a coherent plan of action in response to a problem or frustration (see Borkowski & Burke, 1996).

Deficits in executive skills have the potential to compromise a child's capacity to respond to adult directives in an adaptive (compliant) manner (Greene & Ablon, 2005). For example, a child compromised in the domain of working memory might experience significant difficulty efficiently reflecting upon both the previous consequences of noncompliance (hindsight) and the anticipated consequences of potential actions (forethought). A child compromised in the capacity to regulate arousal might respond to the frustration that occurs in the context of imposed demands for compliance with a high level of emotional reactivity (e.g., screaming, crying, swearing) rather than an appropriate level of reflection (hindsight) and reason. In a child compromised in the skill of shifting cognitive set, one might reasonably expect that the capacity to comply rapidly with adult directives might also be compromised (directives typically require the recipient to shift from the mind-set that immediately preceded the directive to the mind-set being imposed by the environment).

As noted previously, significant overlap exists between ODD and language processing disorders. Cognitive skills such as labeling, categorizing, and communicating feelings and needs, and identifying and selecting corresponding behavioral strategies, are strongly mediated by language (e.g., Bretherton, Fritz, Zahn-Waxler, & Ridgeway, 1986). Language permits children to process verbal feedback about the appropriateness of the behavioral strategies they select, thereby facilitating thinking about and reflecting on previous and future actions (e.g., Kopp, 1989). Those children compromised in the capacity to label emotions (such as frustration or anger) may have difficulty identifying and internalizing an adaptive repertoire of behavior strategies for responding to such emotions. Children limited in the capacity to communicate their emotions and needs may have difficulty participating in give-and-take interactions in a flexible, adaptive manner. Those who have difficulty reflecting on previous and future actions may fail to expand response repertoires, may exhibit delays in problem-solving skills, and may consequently respond to various situations in a manner reflective of a very narrow range of response options (Greene & Ablon, 2005).

Developmental psychologists have long focused on emotion-regulation skills, which are typically lacking in children diagnosed with mood and anxiety disorders. Emotion-regulation skills develop in early infancy and increase in complexity and sophistication as a child matures. Children who fail to develop such skills at an expected or advantageous pace may be over- or underreactive to a wide range of affectively charged situations (e.g., Stifter et al., 1999). Children whose tendency is to overreact to affectively charged situations may find the physiological and emotional arousal associated with such situations difficult to regulate, may become cognitively debilitated in the midst of such arousal (a phenomenon referred to as "cognitive incapacitation" by Zillman [1988]). Consequently, these children may respond to such situations with more affect (e.g., screaming, swearing) than reason (rational problem solving) and a reduced capacity to inhibit aggression (Greene & Ablon, 2005). The "affective storms" (prolonged and aggressive temper outbursts) seen in children with bipolar disorder (described by Wozniak & Biederman, 1996) may be considered an example of such overreactivity. These outbursts—which may include threatening or attacking others—seem to be associated with a pervasive irritable mood (Wozniak & Biederman, 1996). The rage attacks seen in children with Tourette's disorder—explosive anger, irritability, temper outbursts, and aggression—appear to resemble this pattern as well (e.g., Budman, Bruun, Park, & Olson, 1998). Thus, there is a strong suggestion that compromised emotion-regulation skills—in the form of depressed mood, irritability, mood instability, anxiety, or obsessiveness—have the potential to compromise a child's capacity to respond to adult requests in an adaptive (compliant) fashion.

Regarding social skills, Kendall (1993) has distinguished between cognitive *distortions* and cognitive *deficiencies,* with the former referring to dysfunctional thinking processes and the latter to an insufficient amount of cognitive activity in situations in which greater forethought prior to action is needed. Both factors are worthy of consideration as to how they relate to child characteristics that may contribute to the development of ODD.

The notion that cognitive distortions may be implicated in aggression is supported by the work of Dodge and colleagues (e.g., Dodge, 1980; Dodge & Coie, 1987; Dodge, Price, Bachorowski, & Newman, 1990), who have shown that children whose aggression is classified as reactive tend to misinterpret peers' behavior as being hostile and tend to react to ambiguous provocation with aggression, whereas children whose aggression is classified as proactive show fewer signs of distorted social information processing. By what mechanism might the development of the cognitive distortions that typify reactive aggression occur? As noted earlier, the cognitive skills mediating affective modulation and self-regulation evolve in a developmental sequence beginning at birth and, under optimal circumstances, become increasingly broad and more sophisticated over time. Patterns of social responding are said to become increasingly automatic and rigid over time, whether adaptive or maladaptive, and early experience is thought to exert significant influence on the development of these automatic social responses. Indeed, mental representations of past social interactions and their outcomes are thought to govern the manner by which a child will respond to social stimuli in the immediate, ongoing stream of a social interaction. Emotional arousal may also play a significant role in the development and process of social cognition, in that it influences a child's interpretation of a social interaction and the accessibility and selection of response options. The importance of self-regulation and affective modulation skills to this process is clear. Compromised skills in these domains are thought to impose limitations that contribute to incomplete, inaccurate, biased encoding and interpretations of social information; to confine the breadth, accessibility, and enactment of a child's response repertoire; and to set the stage for maladaptive automatic patterns of responding to specific social stimuli (e.g., Akhtar & Bradley, 1991; Dodge, 1993).

Cognitive deficiencies have also been implicated in ODD and aggression, particularly in the domain of problem-solving skills. Researchers have shown that aggressive children tend to have difficulties generating alternative solutions, making decisions about which solutions are most appropriate, and enacting solutions (e.g., Dodge, Pettit, McClaskey, & Brown, 1986; Kendall, Ronan, & Epps, 1991; Richard & Dodge, 1982). Indeed, recent research has shown boys with ADHD with comorbid ODD/CD to evidence greater impairment in problem-solving skills as compared to boys with ADHD alone (Matthys, Cuperus, & Van Egeland, 1999). Other conditions that co-occur with ODD may also set the stage for impaired problem- solving. For example, children with nonverbal learning disability often exhibit deficits in problem-solving skills (see Little, 1993; Rourke, 1989; Rourke & Fuerst, 1995; Semrud-Clikeman & Hynd, 1990), presumably due to rigid, literal, concrete processing and a tendency to focus on details rather than on the "big picture."

Naturally, children's emotional regulation, frustration tolerance, adaptation, and problem-solving skills do not develop independently of the manner by which important adults teach and model these skills (Kochanska, 1993). Nor do children's capacities for complying with adult directives develop independently of the manner by which caregivers impose expectations for compliance and respond to deviations from these expectations. Indeed, adult-child transactions are thought to exert influence on a child's evolving cognitive skills quite early in development and may be especially crucial at the point at which oppositional behavior emerges (Greene, Ablon, & Goring, 2002). As noted earlier, it is at this point in development where two important forces—a child's capacity for compliance and adults' expectations for compliance—are thought to intersect. The method by which caregivers interpret and respond to deviations from expectations for compliance can serve to increase or decrease frustration and arousal in children and adults (e.g., Kochanska & Askan, 1995; Kopp, 1989) and to alter or fuel emerging response biases.

Given the lack of longitudinal study of ODD without CD, little is known about the long-term course of the disorder beyond that it is often a precursor to CD and that it is highly represented in juvenile detention and inpatient psychiatric settings. Some have hypothesized that relatively large numbers of children develop some of the behaviors associated with ODD, with some of these children exhibiting enough of these behaviors to meet criteria for ODD (Lahey & Loeber, 1994). It is further hypothesized that, with increasing age, some children with ODD will cease to exhibit these behaviors, whereas others will continue to exhibit ODD for a long time. As the children who persistently display high numbers of ODD behaviors grow older, some of them add enough CD behaviors to their repertoires to meet diagnostic criteria for that disorder (Lahey & Loeber, 1994). Little is known, however, about the factors that may predispose some ODD youth to the development of CD. Interestingly, socioeconomic status has often not emerged as a significant predisposing factor (Lahey & Loeber, 1994).

COURSE, COMPLICATIONS, AND PROGNOSIS

Although the course of CD has been studied—for example, the distinction between and differential prognosis of early- and late-starter pathways—the course of ODD has received limited attention. As noted earlier, it is clear that the noncompliance and temper outbursts of ODD can precede the stealing, substance abuse, and fighting of CD in about one third of youth with ODD; however, the precise factors mediating this progression are less clear.

Also unclear are prognostic indicators. It has been argued that hyperactivity worsens the prognosis of children with ODD (Abikoff & Klein, 1992). Others have hypothesized that parental perceptions of the child (e.g., Johnston, 1996), parental psychopathology or marital problems (e.g., Amato & Keith, 1991), and parenting stress (e.g., Abidin & Brunner, 1995) may set the stage for poorer prognosis, although it is not clear whether these factors should be considered causes, effects, or both.

Certain comorbidities may worsen prognosis in children with ODD. As noted previously, some evidence suggests that ODD that occurs in combination with mood disorders may heighten the likelihood of CD (Greene et al., 2002). Whether other comorbidities (see earlier discussion) have lesser or greater implications for prognosis is unknown. Nor is it known whether the presence of multiple comorbidities (as opposed to just one) might worsen prognosis.

ASSESSMENT AND DIAGNOSIS

Assessment can be defined as the identification and understanding of, and factors contributing to, compatibility and incompatibility between a given individual and given aspects of his or her environment. This definition of assessment has its roots in transactional or reciprocal models of development (Bell, 1968; Belsky, 1984; Chess & Thomas, 1984; Cicchetti & Lynch, 1993, 1995; Gottlieb, 1992; Sameroff, 1975, 1995), which posit that a child's outcome is a function of the degree of fit or compatibility between child and adult characteristics. A higher degree of adult-child compatibility is thought to contribute to optimal outcomes (in both child and adult), whereas a lesser degree of compatibility is thought to contribute to less advantageous outcomes. From a transactional perspective, oppositional behavior would be viewed as only *one of many possible manifestations of adult-child incompatibility,* in which the characteristics of one interaction partner (e.g., the child) are poorly matched to the characteristics of the second interaction partner (e.g., the parent or teacher), thereby contributing to disadvantageous behavior in both partners, which, over time, contributes to more durable patterns of incompatibility (Greene, Ablon, & Goring, 2002). Such a conceptualization has important implications for the assessment (and later in this chapter for intervention) of ODD because assessments must examine the transactional processes (incompatibilities between child and adult characteristics) that contribute to the development of oppositional behavior.

Along these lines, a variety of assessment components are considered to be useful. First and foremost, a *situational analysis* provides indispensable information about the child, the adult, and the environmental characteristics contributing to oppositional transactions and the adult-child incompatibility that gives rise to such transactions. In other words, with whom (mother, father, peer, soccer coach) is the child interacting when oppositional episodes occur, and how are the combined characteristics of interaction partners related to incompatibility? What cognitive tasks precipitate oppositional episodes, and how is this understood in terms of incompatibility? Where do oppositional episodes occur, and how is this understood in terms of incompatibility?

The following assessment components may apply to *both* the child and his or her adult interaction partners: *developmental history* (e.g., early temperament, trauma history, attachment history, family history), *school history* (e.g., the degree to which the child's oppositional behaviors are cross-situational), and *treatment history* (i.e., previously implemented medical and nonmedical interventions and their effectiveness). Given the prior discussion regarding factors contributing to the development of oppositional behavior, an assessment (formal, informal, or both) is also considered to be invaluable (in both child and adult interaction partners) in the following domains: *general cognitive skills* (provides a backdrop for the general level of expectations and a basis for judging relative strengths and limitations), *executive functions* and *language processing skills; social skills,* and *problem-solving skills.*

IMPACT ON ENVIRONMENT

Family

The behaviors associated with ODD have been shown to have potent and adverse effects on parent-child interactions (Anastopoulos, Guevremont, Shelton, & DuPaul, 1992; Barkley, Anastopoulos, Guevremont, & Fletcher, 1992; Greene, Biederman, et al., 2002; Stormschak, Speltz, DeKlyen, & Greenberg, 1997), and recent findings demonstrate that this is true irrespective of whether ODD occurs in the presence of CD (Greene, Biederman, et al., 2002). ODD is one of the most common problems in referrals to outpatient mental health clinics. Indeed, behaviors associated with ODD have been shown to substantially account for difficult interactions between children with ADHD and their adult caretakers (Anastopoulos et al., 1992; Barkley et al., 1992). In a study mentioned earlier, ODD was found to be the only significant predictor of family conflict when entered into regression analyses that included predictors such as CD, ADHD, major depression, bipolar disorder, and socioeconomic status (Greene, Biederman, et al., 2002). In the same study, ODD was also a significant predictor of problems with siblings.

School

Although poorly studied, ODD impacts interactions between children and their adult caretakers at school. For example, in one study students with ADHD who evidenced a high level of oppositional/aggressive behavior were rated as significantly more stressful to teach than their counterparts with ADHD who did not evidence these associated features (Greene, Beszterczey, Katzenstein, Park, & Goring, 2002). In regression analyses, ODD is a significant predictor of school problems (along with CD, ADHD, and major depression) (Greene, Biederman, et al., 2002).

Peer Interactions

Children with ODD also encounter significant difficulties in peer interactions. Studies have found these children to be rated by their peers as poorly liked and mean, with no differences emerging between ODD youth with and without CD. As noted earlier, the work of Dodge and colleagues has established the significant overlap between deficits in social information processing and oppositional behavior (Dodge et al., 1986). Indeed, children with the combination of ADHD and severe social impairment have been shown to have extremely high rates of oppositional behavior (Greene, Biederman, Faraone, Sienna, & Garcia-Jetton, 1997). And ODD is a significant predictor of problems with peers, along with CD and socioeconomic status (Greene, Biederman, et al., 2002).

IMPLICATIONS FOR FUTURE PERSONALITY DEVELOPMENT

This area necessitates significant speculation, for the impact of ODD on future personality development has not been studied. Because ODD is almost always comorbid, much presumably hinges on the degree to which comorbid conditions (irritability, hyperactivity/impulsivity, language processing delays, social impairments) are identified and addressed. In children whose ODD persists, one would anticipate significant disturbance in relationships with individuals (adults, peers, and siblings) most affected by their oppositionality, noncompliance, and temper outbursts. These children are at significant risk for being overpunished across multiple settings, and they often find this excessive use of punishment to be both incomprehensible and unfair. Thus, these children may be at risk for losing faith in adults' abilities to both understand their difficulties and respond effectively. They may also be at risk for developing cognitive distortions (e.g., "It's not fair," "I always get blamed," "It's always my fault") that may persist into adulthood. These children may eventually feel that adults cannot be trusted or may come to have automatic, distorted reactions to authority figures. If the oppositionality is pervasive—in other words, if the child is alienating interaction partners in multiple settings—over time, one might anticipate that hopelessness, depression, and alienation would result. Currently, there are few data to support these hypotheses.

TREATMENT IMPLICATIONS

Diverse psychosocial treatment approaches have been applied to children's ODD-related behaviors. Intervention options are most potent when they are well matched to the needs of those persons for whom intervention is being designed. In other words, *"What* treatment, by *whom,* is most effective for *this* individual with *that* specific problem, and under *which* set of circumstances?" (Kiesler, 1966).

Models known alternatively as parent training (PT) and behavioral family therapy, while differing slightly in their relative emphases on specific aspects of social learning theory, have focused primarily on altering patterns of parental discipline that contribute to the development of oppositional behavior and problematic parent-child exchanges (McMahon & Wells, 1998). Skills typically taught to parents in such models include positive attending, use of appropriate commands, contingent attention and reinforcement, and use of a time-out procedure (see McMahon & Wells, 1998). In general, research has documented the efficacy of these procedures (see Brestan & Eyberg, 1998, for a comprehensive review), and several intervention programs emanating from these models have been identified as either "well-established" (the *Living with Children* program [Patterson & Gullion, 1968] and videotape modeling parent training [Webster-Stratton, 1984, 1990, 1994]) or as "probably efficacious" (including parent-child interaction therapy [e.g., Eyberg, Boggs, & Algina, 1995]).

However, this same body of research has also documented various limitations of PT. First, a substantial number of parents who receive PT do not fully comply with implementation or drop out of treatment altogether (e.g., Prinz & Miller, 1994), suggesting that this form of intervention may not, in fact, be well matched to the needs and characteristics of many of those responsible for implementation (Greene & Ablon, 2005; Greene, Ablon, & Goring, 2002). Most studies examining the efficacy of PT have presented data only for those who remained in treatment rather than those who began treatment. Among those who remain in treatment, PT has been shown to produce statistically significant changes in oppositional behavior, but very few studies have reported clinically significant changes (Kazdin, 1997). Indeed, 30 percent to 40 percent of those children remaining in treatment continue to evidence behavior problems in the clinical range at follow-up (e.g., Kazdin, 1993; Webster-Stratton, 1990). Data have shown that a significant percentage of children—perhaps higher than 50 percent—are not functioning within the normal range when such treatment is completed (Dishion & Patterson, 1992). Finally, the vast majority of studies examining the efficacy of PT have not included clinically referred youth (Kazdin, 1997; Patterson & Chamberlain, 1994), and have typically failed to examine long-term treatment effects (Kazdin, 1993, 1997), although noteworthy exceptions to the latter issue exist (e.g., Ialongo et al., 1993). In view of these limitations, it is reasonable to conclude the following about PT: (a) a meaningful percentage of children and parents do not derive substantial benefit from PT; and therefore (b) alternative treatments that more adequately address the needs of these children and parents must be developed and studied (Greene & Ablon, 2005).

Alternative models of intervention have placed relatively greater emphasis on *cognitive* factors underlying ODD rather than on behavior per se (see Coie & Dodge, 1998; Crick & Dodge, 1996; Kendall, 1985, 1991; Kendall & MacDonald, 1993). Such models emanate from research highlighting the frustration and emotional arousal that often accompany externally imposed demands for compliance (e.g., Amsel, 1990; Hoffman, 1975; Kochanska, 1993; Kopp, 1989; Stifter et al., 1999). As described previously, a variety of factors may compromise a child's skills in these domains, and these alternative models of intervention have focused on addressing the cognitive deficiencies and distortions of oppositional or aggressive children. Several such intervention models have been identified as "probably efficacious," including problem-solving training (e.g., Kazdin, Esveldt-Dawson, French, & Unis, 1987; Kazdin, Siegel, & Bass, 1992), anger-management programs (e.g., Feindler, 1990, 1991, 1995; Lochman, 1992; Lochman, Burch, Curry, & Lampron, 1984; Lochman, Lampron, Gemmer, & Harris, 1987), and multisystemic therapy (e.g., Henggeler, Melton, & Smith, 1992).

It can be argued that, in its exclusive focus on addressing the cognitive distortions and deficiencies of oppositional children, the cognitive model of intervention is no more focused on improving adult-child compatibility than models aimed at altering patterns of parental discipline. As noted earlier, conceptualizing oppositional behavior as the by-product of *incompatibility* between characteristics of youth compromised in the domains of emotion regulation, frustration tolerance, problem solving, and adaptability and characteristics of their adult caretakers (Greene & Ablon, 2005; Greene & Doyle, 1999) has important implications for the process and goals of treatment (reiterated from previous discussion). First, interventions aimed at reducing children's oppositional behavior must take into account the transactional processes (incompatibilities between child and adult characteristics) giving rise to such behavior. Second, effective treatment requires the active involvement of child *and* adult. Third, the primary goal of treatment is to address and resolve issues related to adult-child incompatibility.

These intervention components have been incorporated into a cognitive-behavioral model of intervention known as the collaborative problem solving (CPS) approach (Greene, 2001; Greene & Ablon, 2005; Greene, Ablon, & Goring, 2002). The specific goals of the CPS approach are to help adults (1) understand the specific adult and child characteristics contributing to the development of a child's oppositional behavior; (2) become cognizant of three basic options for handling unmet expectations, including (a) imposition of adult will; (b) collaborative problem solving, and (c) removing the expectation; (3) recognize the impact of each of these three approaches on parent-child interactions; and (4) become proficient, along with their children, at collaborative problem solving as a means of resolving disagreements and defusing potentially conflictual situations so as to reduce oppositional episodes and improve parent-child compatibility.

The first goal highlights the need for a comprehensive assessment and understanding of the specific factors (reviewed earlier) underlying each child's oppositional behavior. In the CPS model, adults learn to conceptualize oppositional behavior as the by-product of a learning disability in the domains of emotion regulation, frustration tolerance, problem solving, flexibility, or any combination of these. Such a conceptualization helps adults respond to oppositional behavior in a less personalized, less reactive, and more empathic manner and is crucial to helping adults understand the necessity for a specialized approach to intervention emphasizing remediation of these cognitive issues. The role of *adult* characteristics as a contributing factor to a given child's oppositional behavior is typically not a major emphasis early in treatment (thereby facilitating adult participation in treatment) but increases in importance as treatment progresses. Indeed, the second goal speaks to the need to help adults understand that the manner by which they pursue unmet expectations with the child is a major factor influencing the frequency and intensity of oppositional outbursts. Adults are taught that imposing adult will (in the parlance of CPS, this approach to unmet expectations is referred to as Plan A) is the most common precipitant of oppositional outbursts; that removing the expectation (known as Plan C) is effective at reducing tension between child and adult and decreasing explosive outbursts, but is not effective at helping adults pursue unmet expectations; and that collaborative problem solving (Plan B) is an effective way to pursue expectations without increasing the likelihood of oppositional outbursts while simultaneously training and practicing emotion regulation, frustration tolerance, problem solving, and adaptability skills.

Adults are viewed as the facilitators of collaborative problem solving. In fact, adults are often told that their role is to serve as the child's so-called surrogate frontal lobe so as to (a) reduce the likelihood of oppositional outbursts in the moment and (b) train lacking thinking skills over the longer term. Adults are trained to proactively focus on antecedent events that precipitate oppositional outbursts rather than reactively focus on consequences. In other words, adults are strongly encouraged to adopt a crisis prevention mentality instead of a crisis management mentality. As part of this mentality, adults are also helped to focus on situational factors that may be associated with oppositional outbursts and are taught that the majority of such outbursts are, in fact, quite predictable.

The CPS approach is thought to differ from other anger-management and problem-solving training programs in its emphasis on helping adults and children develop the skills to resolve issues of disagreement collaboratively. It has been argued that the equivocal effects of many interventions aimed at training cognitive skills in children have likely been due, at least in part, to the manner in which such interventions were delivered (e.g., Greene & Barkley, 1996; Hinshaw, 1992). For example, in a majority of studies cognitive skills have been trained outside the settings where skills were actually to be performed. It has been suggested that training cognitive skills proximally to the setting(s) where behavior is to be performed might greatly enhance the maintenance and generalization of trained skills (e.g., Greene & Ablon, 2001; Greene & Doyle, 1999) and would be more congruent with a transactional perspective. As has been observed in children with ADHD, the more distant in time and space a treatment is from the situations in which trained skills are to be performed, the less beneficial the treatment is likely to be (e.g., Bloomquist, August, Cohen, Doyle, & Everhart, 1997; Greene & Barkley, 1996; Ingersoll & Goldstein, 1993); presumably, the same notion applies to children with ODD. Training cognitive skills proximally to where such skills are to be performed requires, by necessity, considerably greater involvement from and training of interaction partners (e.g., parents, teachers, classmates) present in the environments where oppositional behavior is most likely to occur (Greene, 1998).

Although CPS is a manualized treatment program, session content is not circumscribed. Rather, therapists choose to focus on any combination of five treatment modules based on their assessment of the needs of each child and family. This feature of the CPS approach is thought to enhance the ecological validity of the model. The modules represent important components of CPS (as described previously) as follows: (1) educating adults about characteristics (of child, adult, and environment) that may contribute to the incompatibilities giving rise to noncompliant behavior, (2) use of the Plans framework, (3) medication education (helping adults understand that some factors may be more effectively treated pharmacologically), (4) family communication (identifying and altering communication patterns that may fuel oppositional outbursts, and (5) cognitive skills training (remediating additional cognitive issues that are not specifically being addressed with Plan B). Empirical evaluation of CPS has provided evidence of its effectiveness (Greene, 2001; Greene et al., 2004.

Finally, given its promise in the treatment of ADHD and mood disorders, pharmacotherapy is an increasingly common consideration in the treatment of ODD. It has been asserted that the target of medical intervention should not be oppositional behavior or aggression per se, but rather the underlying or co-occurring disorder, with the intent of reducing oppositional and aggressive behavior as associated symptoms (Connor & Steingard, 1996). A variety of pharmacologic agents have been shown to be effective in children and adolescents evidencing oppositional and aggressive behavior. Methylphenidate has been shown to reduce oppositional behavior in children with ADHD (e.g., Gadow, Nolan, Sverd, Sprafkin, & Paolicelli, 1990; Hinshaw, Heller, & McHale, 1992; Hinshaw, Henker, Whalen, Erhardt, & Dunnington, 1989; Murphy, Pelham, & Lang, 1992; Schachar, Tannock, Cunningham, & Corkum, 1997), presumably because of its efficacy at improving cognitive flexibility (e.g., Tannock, Schachar, & Logan, 1995), reducing hyperactivity and poor impulse control, and improving a child's capacity to reflect on and evaluate potential responses. Antihypertensive medications, such as clonidine and guanfacine, have also shown some promise in the treatment of aggression in children (e.g., Connor & Steingard, 1996; Kemph, DeVane, Levin, Jarecke, & Miller, 1993), and in reducing the hyperactivity and impulsiveness that may fuel such aggression. Mood-stabilizing and antipsychotic medications may be appropriate for those children whose episodic outbursts are of an affective, explosive type (Green & Kowalik, 1997; Wozniak & Biederman, 1996; see Campbell, Gonzalez, & Silva, 1992). When used to treat the irritability, anxiety, and obsessiveness sometimes seen in aggressive children, antidepressants are also a promising form of pharmacologic treatment (e.g., Connor & Steingard, 1996; Garland & Weiss, 1996).

REFERENCES

Abidin, R. R., & Brunner, J. R. (1995). Development of a Parenting Alliance Inventory. *Journal of Clinical Child Psychology, 24,* 31–40.

Abikoff, H., & Klein, R. G. (1992). Attention-deficit hyperactivity disorder and conduct disorder: Comorbidity and implications for treatment. *Journal of Consulting and Clinical Psychology, 60,* 881–892.

Akhtar, N., & Bradley, E. J. (1991). Social information processing deficits of aggressive children: Present findings and implications for social skills training. *Clinical Psychology Review, 11,* 621–644.

Amato, P. R., & Keith, B. (1991). Parental divorce and the well-being of children: A meta-analysis. *Psychological Bulletin, 110,* 26–46.

American Psychiatric Association. (1994). *Diagnostic and statistical manual of mental disorders* (4th ed.). Washington, DC: Author.

Amsel, A. (1990). Arousal, suppression, and persistence: Frustration theory, attention, and its disorders. *Cognition and Emotion, 4,* 239–268.

Anastopoulos, A. D., Guevremont, D. C., Shelton, T. L., & DuPaul, G. J. (1992). Parenting stress among families of children with attention deficit hyperactivity disorder. *Journal of Abnormal Child Psychology, 20,* 503–520.

Anderson, K. E., Lytton, H., & Romney, D. M. (1986). Mothers' interactions with normal and conduct-disordered boys: Who affects whom? *Developmental Psychology, 22,* 604–609.

Angold, A., & Costello, E. J. (1993). Depressive comorbidity in children and adolescents: Empirical, theoretical, and methodological issues. *American Journal of Psychiatry, 150,* 1779–1791.

Barkley, R. A. (1997). Behavioral inhibition, sustained attention, and executive functions: Constructing a unifying theory of ADHD. *Psychological Bulletin, 121,* 65–94.

Barkley, R. A., Anastopoulos, A. D., Guevremont, D. G., & Fletcher, K. F. (1992). Adolescents with attention-deficit hyperactivity disorder: Mother-adolescent interactions, family beliefs and conflicts, and maternal psychopathology. *Journal of Abnormal Child Psychology, 20,* 263–288.

Beitchman, J. H., Brownlie, E. B., & Wilson, B. (1996). Linguistic impairment and psychiatric disorders: Pathways to overcome. In J. H. Beitchman, N. J. Cohen, M. M. Konstantareas, & R. Tannock (Eds.), *Language, learning, and behavior disorders: Developmental, biological, and clinical perspectives.* New York: Cambridge University Press.

Bell, R. (1968). A reinterpretation of the direction of effects in socialization. *Psychological Review, 75,* 81–95.

Belsky, J. (1984). The determinants of parenting: A process model. *Child Development, 55,* 83–96.

Biederman, J., Faraone, S. V., Mick, E., Wozniak, J., Chen, L., Ouellette, C., et al. (1996). Attention-deficit hyperactivity disorder and juvenile mania: An overlooked comorbidity? *Journal of the American Academy of Child and Adolescent Psychiatry, 35,* 997–1008.

Biederman, J., Faraone, S. V., Milberger, S., Garcia, J., Chen, L., Mick, E., et al. (1996). Is childhood oppositional defiant disorder a precursor to adolescent conduct disorder? Findings from a four-year follow-up study of children with ADHD. *Journal of the American Academy of Child and Adolescent Psychiatry, 35,* 1193–1204.

Bloomquist, M. L., August, G. J., Cohen, C., Doyle, A., & Everhart, K. (1997). Social problem solving in hyperactive-aggressive children: How and what they think in conditions of controlled processing. *Journal of Clinical Child Psychology, 26,* 172–180.

Borkowski, J. G., & Burke, J. E. (1996). Theories, models, and measurements of executive functioning: An information processing perspective. In G. R. Lyon & N. A. Krasnegor (Eds.), *Attention, memory, and executive function* (pp. 235–262). Baltimore: Brookes.

Brestan, E. V., & Eyberg, S. M. (1998). Effective psychosocial treatment of conduct-disordered children and adolescents: 29 years, 82 studies, and 5,272 kids. *Journal of Clinical Child Psychology, 27,* 180–189.

Bretherton, I., Fritz, J., Zahn-Waxler, C., & Ridgeway, D. (1986). Learning to talk about emotions: A functionalist perspective. *Child Development, 57,* 529–548.

Budman, C. L., Bruun, R. D., Park, K. S., Lesser, M., & Olson, M. (2000). Explosive outbursts in children with Tourette's disorder. *Journal of the American Academy of Child and Adolescent Psychiatry, 39,* 1270–1276.

Budman, C. L., Bruun, R. D., Park., K. S., & Olson, M. E. (1998). Rage attacks in children and adolescents with Tourette's disorder: A pilot study. *Journal of Clinical Psychiatry, 59,* 576–580.

Campbell, M., Gonzalez, N. M., & Silva, R. R. (1992). The pharmacologic treatment of conduct disorders and rage outbursts. *Psychiatric Clinics of North America, 15,* 69–85.

Cantwell, D. P., & Baker, L. (1991). *Psychiatric and developmental disorders in children with communication disorders.* Washington, DC: American Psychiatric Press.

Chamberlain, P., & Patterson, G. R. (1995). Discipline and child compliance in parenting. In M. H. Bornstein (Ed.), *Handbook of parenting: Vol. 4. Applied and practical parenting.* Mahwah, NJ: Erlbaum.

Chess, S., & Thomas, A. (1984). *Origins and evolution of behavior disorders: From infancy to early adult life.* New York: Brunner/Mazel.

Cicchetti, D., & Lynch, M. (1993). Toward an ecological/transactional model of community violence and child maltreatment. *Psychiatry, 56,* 96–118.

Cicchetti, D., & Lynch, M. (1995). Failures in the expectable environment and their impact on individual development: The case of child maltreatment. In D. Cicchetti & D. J. Cohen (Eds.), *Developmental psychopathology: Vol. 2. Risk, disorder, and adaptation* (pp. 32–71). New York: Wiley.

Coie, J. D, & Dodge, K. A. (1998). Aggression and antisocial behavior. In W. Damon & N. Eisenberg (Eds.), *Handbook of child psychology. Vol. 3. Social, emotional, and personality development* (5th ed.), pp. 779–862. New York: Wiley.

Connor, D. F., & Steingard, R. J. (1996). A clinical approach to the pharmacotherapy of aggression in children and adolescents. *Annals of the New York Academy of Sciences* (pp. 290–307).

Crick, N. R., & Dodge, K. A. (1996). Social information-processing mechanisms on reactive and proactive aggression. *Child Development, 67,* 993–1002.

Crockenberg, S., & Litman, C. (1990). Autonomy as competence in two-year olds: Maternal correlates of child defiance, compliance, and self-assertion. *Developmental Psychology, 26,* 961–971.

Davis, A. D., Sanger, D. D., & Morris-Friehe, M. (1991). Language skills of delinquent and nondelinquent adolescent males *Journal of Communication Disorders, 24,* 251–266.

Dishion, T. J., French, D. C., & Patterson, G. R. (1995). The development and ecology of antisocial behavior. In D. Cicchetti & D. J. Cohen (Eds.), *Developmental psychopathology: Vol. 2. Risk, disorder, and adaptation* (pp. 421–471). New York: Wiley.

Dishion, T. J., & Patterson, G. R. (1992). Age affects in parent training outcomes. *Behavior Therapy, 23,* 719–729.

Dodge, K. A. (1980). Social cognition and children's aggressive behavior. *Child Development, 51,* 162–170.

Dodge, K. A. (1993). The future of research on the treatment of conduct disorder. *Development and Psychopathology, 5,* 311–319.

Dodge, K. A., & Coie, J. D. (1987). Social information processing factors in reactive and proactive aggression in children's peer groups. *Journal of Personality and Social Psychology, 53,* 1146–1158.

Dodge, K. A., Pettit, G. S., McClaskey, C., & Brown, M. (1986). Social competence in children. *Monographs of the Society for Research in Child Development, 58,* 213–251.

Dodge, K. A., Price, J. N., Bachorowski, J., & Newman, J. P. (1990). Hostile attributional biases in severely aggressive adolescents. *Journal of Abnormal Psychology, 99,* 385–392.

Dumas, J. E., & LaFreniere, P. J. (1993). Mother-child relationships as sources of support or stress: A comparison of competent, average, aggressive, and anxious dyads. *Child Development, 64,* 1732–1754.

Dumas, J. E., LaFreniere, P. J., & Serketich, W. J. (1995). "Balance of power": A transactional analysis of control in mother-child dyads involving socially competent, aggressive, and anxious children. *Journal of Abnormal Psychology, 104,* 104–113.

Eyberg, S. M., Boggs, S. R., & Algina, J. (1995). Parent-child interaction therapy: A psychosocial model for the treatment of young children with conduct problem behavior and their families. *Psychopharmacology Bulletin, 31,* 83–91.

Feindler, E. L. (1990). Adolescent anger control: Review and critique. In M. Hersen, R. M. Eisler, & P. M. Miller (Eds.), *Progress in behavior modification* (pp. 11–59). Newbury Park, CA: Sage.

Feindler, E. L. (1991). Cognitive strategies in anger control interventions for children and adolescents. In P. C. Kendall (Ed.),

Child and adolescent therapy: Cognitive-behavioral procedures (pp. 66–97). New York: Guilford Press.

Feindler, E. L. (1995). An ideal treatment package for children and adolescents with anger disorders. In H. Kassinove (Ed.), *Anger disorders: Definition, diagnosis, and treatment* (pp. 173–195). Washington, DC: Taylor & Francis.

Frick, P. J., Kamphaus, R. W., Lahey, B. B., Loeber, R., Christ, M. A. G., Hart, E. L., et al. (1991). Academic underachievement and the disruptive behavior disorders. *Journal of Consulting and Clinical Psychology, 59,* 289–294.

Fuster, J. M. (1989). *The prefrontal cortex.* New York: Raven Press.

Fuster, J. M. (1995). Memory and planning: Two temporal perspectives of frontal lobe function. In H. H. Jasper, S. Riggio, & P. S. Goldman-Rakic (Eds.), *Epilepsy and the functional autonomy of the frontal lobe* (pp. 9–18). New York: Raven Press.

Gadow, K. D., Nolan, E. E., Sverd, J., Sprafkin, J., & Paolicelli, L. (1990). Methylphenidate in aggressive-hyperactive boys: I. Effects on peer aggression in public school settings. *Journal of the American Academy of Child and Adolescent Psychiatry, 39,* 710–718.

Garland, E. J., & Weiss, M. (1996). Case study: Obsessive difficult temperament and its response to serotonergic medication. *Journal of the American Academy of Child and Adolescent Psychiatry, 35,* 916–920.

Geller, B., & Luby, J. (1997). Child and adolescent bipolar disorder: Review of the past 10 years. *Journal of the American Academy of Child and Adolescent Psychiatry, 36,* 1–9.

Gilmour, J., Hill, B., Place, M., & Skuse, D. H. (2004). Social communication deficits in conduct disorder: A clinical and community survey. *Journal of Child Psychology and Psychiatry, 45,* 967–978.

Gottlieb, G. (1992). *Individual development and evolution: The genesis of novel behavior.* New York: Oxford University Press.

Gottman, J. (1986). The world of coordinated play: Same and cross-sex friendship in children. In J. M. Gottman & J. G. Parker (Eds.), *Conversations of friends: Speculations on affective development* (pp. 139–191). Cambridge, England: Cambridge University Press.

Green, W. H., & Kowalik, S. C. (1997). Violence in child and adolescent psychiatry. *Psychiatric Annals, 27,* 745–751.

Greene, R. W. (1998). *The explosive child: Understanding and parenting easily frustrated, "chronically inflexible" children.* New York: HarperCollins.

Greene, R. W. (2001). *The explosive child: Understanding and parenting easily frustrated, "chronically inflexible" children* (2nd ed.). New York: HarperCollins.

Greene, R. W., & Ablon, J. S. (2001). What does the MTA study tell us about effective psychosocial treatment for ADHD? *Journal of Clinical Child Psychology, 30,* 114–121.

Greene, R. W., & Ablon, J. S. (2005). *Treating Explosive Kids: The Collaborative Problem Solving Approach.* New York: Guilford Press.

Greene, R. W., Ablon, J. S. & Goring, J. C. (2002). A transactional model of oppositional behavior: Underpinnings of the Collaborative Problem Solving Approach. *Journal of Psychosomatic Research, 55,* 67–75.

Greene, R. W., Ablon, J. S., Monuteaux, M., Goring, J., Henin, A., Raezer, L., et al. (2004). Effectiveness of Collaborative Problem Solving in affectively dysregulated youth with oppositional defiant disorder: Initial findings. *Journal of Consulting and Clinical Psychology, 72,* 1157–1164.

Greene, R. W. & Barkley, R. A. (1996). Attention-deficit/hyperactivity disorder: Diagnostic, developmental, and conceptual issues. In M. Breen & C. Fiedler (Eds.), *Behavioral approach to assessment of youth with emotional/behavioral disorders: A handbook for school-based practitioners* (pp. 413–449). Austin, TX: Pro-Ed.

Greene, R. W., Beszterczey, S. K., Katzenstein T., Park, K., & Goring, J.C. (2002). Are students with ADHD more stressful to teach? Predictors of teacher stress in an elementary-age sample. *Journal of Emotional and Behavioral Disorders, 10,* 79–89.

Greene, R. W., Biederman, J., Faraone, S. V., Sienna, M., & Garcia-Jetton, J. (1997). Adolescent outcome of boys with attention-deficit/hyperactivity disorder and social disability: Results from a 4-year longitudinal follow-up study. *Journal of Consulting and Clinical Psychology, 65,* 758–767.

Greene, R. W., Biederman, J., Zerwas, S., Monuteaux, M., Goring, J. C., & Faraone, S. V. (2002). Psychiatric comorbidity, family dysfunction, and social impairment in referred youth with oppositional defiant disorder. *American Journal of Psychiatry.*

Greene, R. W., & Doyle, A. E. (1999). Toward a transactional conceptualization of oppositional defiant disorder: Implications for assessment and treatment. *Clinical and Family Psychology Review, 2,* 129–147.

Harter, S. (1983). Developmental perspectives on the self-system. In P. H. Mussen (Ed.), *Handbook of child psychology* (Vol. 4). New York: Wiley.

Hayes, S. C., Gifford, E. V., & Ruckstuhl, L. E. (1996). Relational frame theory and executive function: A behavioral analysis. In G. R. Lyon & N. A. Krasnegor (Eds.), *Attention, memory, and executive function* (pp. 279–306). Baltimore: Brookes.

Henggeler, S. W., Melton, G. B., & Smith, L. A. (1992). Family preservation using Multisystemic Therapy: An effective alternative to incarcerating serious juvenile offenders. *Journal of Consulting and Clinical Psychology, 60,* 953–961.

Hinshaw, S. P. (1992). Intervention for social competence and social skill. *Child and Adolescent Psychiatric Clinics of North America, 1,* 539–552.

Hinshaw, S. P. (1994). Conduct disorder in childhood: Conceptualization, diagnosis, comorbidity, and risk status for antisocial functioning in adulthood. In D. C. Fowles, P. Sutker, & S. H. Goodman (Eds.), *Experimental personality and psychopathology research 1994* (pp. 3–44). New York: Springer.

Hinshaw, S. P., Heller, T., & McHale, J. P. (1992). Covert antisocial behavior in boys with attention-deficit hyperactivity disorder: External validation and effects of methylphenidate. *Journal of Consulting and Clinical Psychology, 60,* 274–281.

Hinshaw, S. P., Henker, B., Whalen, C. K., Erhardt, D., & Dunnington, R. E. (1989). Aggressive, prosocial, and nonsocial behavior in hyperactive boys: Dose effects of methylphenidate in naturalistic settings. *Journal of Consulting and Clinical Psychology, 57,* 636–643.

Hinshaw, S. P., Lahey, B. B., & Hart, E. L. (1993). Issues of taxonomy and comorbidity in the development of conduct disorder. *Development and Psychopathology, 5,* 31–49.

Hoffman, M. L. (1975). Moral internalization, parental power, and the nature of parent-child interaction. *Developmental Psychology, 11,* 228–239.

Ialongo, N. S., Horn, W. F., Pascoe, J. M., Greenberg, G., Packard, T., Lopez, M., et al. (1993). The effects of a multimodal intervention with attention-deficit hyperactivity disorder children: A 9-month follow-up. *Journal of the American Academy of Child and Adolescent Psychiatry, 32,* 182–189.

Ingersoll, B., & Goldstein, S. (1993). *Attention-deficit disorder and learning disabilities.* New York: Doubleday.

Johnston, C. (1996). Addressing parent cognitions in interventions of families of disruptive children. In K. S. Dobson & K. D. Craig (Eds.), *Advances in cognitive-behavioral therapy* (pp. 193–209). Thousand Oaks, CA: Sage.

Kazdin, A. E. (1993). Treatment of conduct disorder: Progress and directions in psychotherapy research. *Development and Psychopathology, 5,* 277–310.

Kazdin, A. E. (1997). Parent management training: Evidence, outcomes, and issues. *Journal of the American Academy of Child and Adolescent Psychiatry, 36,* 1349–1356.

Kazdin, A. E., Esveldt-Dawson, K., French, N. H., & Unis, A. S. (1987). Problem-solving skills training and relationship therapy in the treatment of antisocial child behavior. *Journal of Consulting and Clinical Psychology, 55,* 76–85.

Kazdin, A. E., Siegel, T. C., & Bass, D. (1992). Cognitive problem-solving skills training and parent management training in the treatment of antisocial behavior in children. *Journal of Consulting and Clinical Psychology, 60,* 733–747.

Kemph, J. P., DeVane, C. L., Levin, G. M., Jarecke, R., & Miller, R. L. (1993). Treatment of aggressive children with clonidine: Results of an open pilot study. *Journal of the American Academy of Child and Adolescent Psychiatry, 32,* 577–581.

Kendall, P. C. (1985). Toward a cognitive-behavioral model of child psychopathology and a critique of related interventions. *Journal of Abnormal Child Psychology, 13,* 357–372.

Kendall, P. C. (1991). Guiding theory for therapy with children and adolescents. In P. C. Kendall (Ed.), *Child and adolescent therapy: Cognitive-behavioral procedures* (pp. 3–22). New York: Guilford Press.

Kendall, P. C. (1993). Cognitive-behavioral therapies with youth: Guiding theory, current status, and emerging developments. *Journal of Consulting and Clinical Psychology, 61,* 235–247.

Kendall, P. C., & MacDonald, J. P. (1993). Cognition in the psychopathology of youth and implications for treatment. In K. S. Dobson & P. C. Kendall (Eds.), *Psychopathology and cognition* (pp. 387–427). San Diego: Academic Press.

Kendall, P. C., Ronan, K. R., & Epps, J. (1991). Aggression in children/adolescents: Cognitive-behavioral treatment perspective. In D. J. Pepler & K. H. Rubin (Eds.), *The development and treatment of childhood aggression* (pp. 241–360). Hillsdale, NJ: Erlbaum.

Kiesler, D. J. (1966). Some myths of psychotherapy research and the search for a paradigm. *Psychological Bulletin, 65,* 110–136.

Kochanska, G. (1993). Toward a synthesis of parental socialization and child temperament in early development of conscience. *Child Development, 64,* 325–347.

Kochanska, G. (1995). Children's temperament, mothers' discipline, and security of attachment: Multiple pathways to emerging internalization. *Child Development, 66,* 597–615.

Kochanska, G., & Askan, N. (1995). Mother-child mutually positive affect, the quality of child compliance to requests and prohibitions, and maternal control as correlates of early internalization. *Child Development, 66,* 236–254.

Kopp, C. B. (1982). Antecedents of self-regulation: A developmental perspective. *Developmental Psychology, 18,* 199–214.

Kopp, C. B. (1989). Regulation of distress and negative emotions: A developmental view. *Developmental Psychology, 25,* 343–354.

Kuhne, M., Schachar, R., & Tannock, R. (1997). Impact of comorbid oppositional or conduct problems on attention-deficit hyperactivity disorder. *Journal of the American Academy of Child and Adolescent Psychiatry, 36,* 1715–1725.

Lahey, B. B., & Loeber, R. (1994). Framework for a developmental model of oppositional defiant disorder and conduct disorder. In D. K. Routh (Ed.), *Disruptive behavior disorders in childhood.* New York: Plenum Press.

Lahey, B. B., Loeber, R., Quay, H. C., Frick, P. J., & Grimm, S. (1992). Oppositional defiant and conduct disorders: Issues to be resolved for the *DSM-IV. Journal of the American Academy of Child and Adolescent Psychiatry, 31,* 539–546.

Langbehn, D. R., Cadoret, R. J., Yates, W. R., Troughton, E. P., & Stewart, M. A. (1998). Distinct contributions of conduct and oppositional defiant symptoms to adult antisocial behavior. *Archives of General Psychiatry, 55,* 821–829.

Little, S. S. (1993). Nonverbal learning disabilities and socioemotional functioning: A review of recent literature. *Journal of Learning Disabilities, 26,* 653–665.

Lochman, J. E. (1992). Cognitive-behavioral interventions with aggressive boys. *Child Psychiatry and Human Development, 16,* 45–56.

Lochman, J. E., Burch, P. R., Curry, J. F., & Lampron, L. B. (1984). Treatment and generalization effects of cognitive-behavioral and goal-setting interventions with aggressive boys. *Journal of Consulting and Clinical Psychology, 52,* 915–916.

Lochman, J. E., Lampron, L. B., Gemmer, T. C., & Harris, S. R. (1987). Anger coping intervention with aggressive children: A guide to implementation in school settings. In P. A. Keller & S. R. Heyman (Eds.), *Innovations in clinical practice: A source book* (Vol. 6, pp. 339–356). Sarasota, FL: Professional Resource Exchange.

Loeber, R. (1990). Development and risk factors of juvenile antisocial behavior and delinquency. *Clinical Psychology Review, 10,* 1–41.

Loeber, R., Green, S. M., Lahey, B. B., Christ, M. A. G., & Frick, P. J. (1992). Developmental sequences in the age of onset of disruptive child behaviors. *Journal of Child and Family Studies, 1,* 21–41.

Loeber, R., & Keenan, K. (1994). Interaction between conduct disorder and its comorbid conditions: Effects of age and gender. *Clinical Psychology Review, 14,* 497–523.

Lynam, D. R. (1996). Early identification of chronic offenders: Who is the fledgling psychopath? *Psychological Bulletin, 120,* 209–234.

Maccoby, E. E. (1980). *Social development.* New York: Harcourt Brace Jovanovich.

Matthys, W, Cuperus, J. M., & Van Egeland, H. (1999). Deficient social problem-solving in boys with ODD/CD, with ADHD, and with both disorders. *Journal of the American Academy of Child and Adolescent Psychiatry, 38,* 311–321.

McMahon, R. J., & Wells, K. C. (1998). Conduct problems. In E. J. Mash & R. A. Barkley (Eds.), *Treatment of childhood disorders* (2nd ed.), pp. 111–210. New York: Guilford Press.

Mischel, W. (1983). Delay of gratification as process and as person variable in development. In D. Magnusson and V. P. Allen (Eds.), *Interactions in Human Development* (pp. 149–165). New York: Academic Press.

Murphy, D. A., Pelham, W. E., & Lang, A. R. (1992). Aggression in boys with attention deficit-hyperactivity disorder: Methylphenidate effects on naturalistically observed aggression, response to provocation, and social information processing. *Journal of Abnormal Child Psychology, 20,* 451–466.

Patterson, G. R., & Chamberlain, P. (1994). A functional analysis of resistance during parent training therapy. *Clinical Psychology: Science and Practice, 1,* 53–70.

Patterson, G. R., DeBaryshe, B. D., & Ramsey, E. (1989). A developmental perspective on antisocial behavior. *American Psychologist, 44,* 329–335.

Patterson, G. R., & Gullion, M. E. (1968). *Living with children: New methods for parents and teachers.* Champaign, IL: Research Press.

Patterson, G. R., Reid, J. B., & Dishion, T. J. (1992). *Antisocial boys.* Patterson, OR: Castalia.

Pennington, B. F. (1994). The working memory function of the prefrontal cortices: Implications for developmental and individual differences in cognition. In M. M. Haith, J. Benson, R. Roberts, & B. F. Pennington (Eds.), *The development of future oriented processes* (pp. 243–289). Chicago: University of Chicago Press.

Perry, D. G., & Perry, L. C. (1983). Social learning, causal attribution, and moral internalization. In J. Bisanz, G. L. Bisanz, & R. Kail (Eds.), C. J. Brainerd (Series Ed.), *Learning in children: Progress in cognitive development research* (pp. 105–136). New York: Springer-Verlag.

Prinz, R. J., & Miller, G. E. (1994). Family-based treatment for childhood antisocial behavior: Experimental influences on dropout and engagement. *Journal of Consulting and Clinical Psychology, 62,* 645–650.

Richard, B., & Dodge, K. A. (1982). Social maladjustment and problem solving in school-aged children. *Journal of Consulting and Clinical Psychology, 50,* 226–233.

Rogers-Adkinson, D., & Griffin, P. (1999). *Communication disorders and children with psychiatric and behavioral disorders.* San Diego: Singular.

Rothbart, M. K., & Derryberry, D. (1981). Development of individual differences in temperament. In M. E. Lamb & A. L. Brown (Eds.), *Advances in developmental psychology* (Vol. 1, pp. 37–86). Hillsdale, NJ: Erlbaum.

Rourke, B. P. (1989). *Nonverbal learning disabilities: The syndrome and the model.* New York: Guilford Press.

Rourke, B. P., & Fuerst, D. R. (1995). Cognitive processing, academic achievement, and psychosocial functioning: A neurodevelopmental perspective. In D. Cicchetti & D. J. Cohen (Eds.), *Developmental psychopathology: Vol. 1. Theory and methods* (pp. 391–423). New York: Wiley.

Sameroff, A. (1975). Early influences on development: Fact or fancy? *Merrill-Palmer Quarterly, 21,* 263–294.

Sameroff, A. (1995). General systems theory and developmental psychopathology. In D. Cicchetti & D. J. Cohen (Eds.), *Developmental psychopathology: Vol. 1. Theory and methods* (pp. 659–695). New York: Wiley.

Schachar, R. J., Tannock, R., Cunningham, C., & Corkum, P. V. (1997). Behavioral, situational, and temporal effects of treatment of ADHD with methylphenidate. *Journal of the American Academy of Child and Adolescent Psychiatry, 36,* 754–764.

Schachar, R. J., & Wachsmuth, R. (1990). Oppositional disorder in children: A validation study comparing conduct disorder, oppositional disorder, and normal control children. *Journal of Child Psychology and Psychiatry, 31,* 1089–1102.

Semrud-Clikeman, M., & Hynd, G. W. (1990). Right-hemisphere dysfunction in nonverbal learning disabilities: Social, academic, and adaptive functioning in adults and children. *Psychological Bulletin, 107,* 196–209.

Speltz, M. L., McClellan, J., DeKlyen, M., & Jones, K. (1999). Preschool boys with oppositional defiant disorder: Clinical presentation and diagnostic change. *Journal of the American Academy of Child and Adolescent Psychiatry, 38,* 838–845.

Stevens, L. J., & Bliss, L. S. (1995). Conflict resolution abilities of children with specific language impairment and children with normal language. *Journal of Speech and Hearing Research, 38,* 599–611.

Stifter, C. A., Spinrad, T. L., & Braungart-Rieker, J. M. (1999). Toward a developmental model of child compliance: The role of emotion regulation in infancy. *Child Development, 70,* 21–32.

Stormschak, E., Speltz, M., DeKlyen, M., & Greenberg, M. (1997). Family interactions during clinical intake: A comparison of families of normal or disruptive boys. *Journal of Abnormal Child Psychology, 25,* 345–357.

Tannock, R., Schachar, R., & Logan, G. (1995). Methylphenidate and cognitive flexibility: Dissociated does effects in hyperactive children. *Journal of Abnormal Child Psychology, 23,* 235–266.

Taylor, T. K., & Biglan, A. (1998). Behavioral family interventions for improving child rearing: A review of the literature for clinicians and policy makers. *Clinical Child and Family Psychology Review, 1,* 41–60.

Webster-Stratton, C. (1984). Randomized trial of two parent-training programs for families with conduct-disordered children. *Journal of Consulting and Clinical Psychology, 52,* 666–678.

Webster-Stratton, C. (1990). Enhancing the effectiveness of self-administered videotape parent training for families with conduct-problem children. *Journal of Abnormal Child Psychology, 18,* 479–492.

Webster-Stratton, C. (1994). Advancing videotape parent training: A comparison study. *Journal of Consulting and Clinical Psychology, 62,* 583–593.

Westby, C. (1999). Assessment of pragmatic competence in children with psychiatric disorders. In D. Rogers-Adkinson & P. Griffith (Eds.), *Communication disorders and children with psychiatric and behavioral disorders* (pp. 177–258). San Diego: Singular.

Wozniak, J., & Biederman, J. (1996). A pharmacological approach to the quagmire of comorbidity in juvenile mania. *Journal of Child and Adolescent Psychiatry, 35,* 826–828.

Wozniak, J., Biederman, J., Kiely, K., Ablon, S., Faraone, S. V., Mundy, E., et al. (1995). Mania-like symptoms suggestion of childhood-onset bipolar disorder in clinically referred children. *Journal of the American Academy of Child and Adolescent Psychiatry, 34,* 867–876.

Zillman, D. (1988). Cognition-excitation interdependencies in aggressive behavior. *Aggressive Behavior, 14,* 51–64.

CHAPTER 18

Conduct Disorder

EVA R. KIMONIS AND PAUL J. FRICK

DESCRIPTION OF THE DISORDER AND CLINICAL PICTURE

One of the most common reasons for referral of children and adolescents to mental health clinics (Frick & Silverthorn, 2001) and residential treatment centers (Lyman & Campbell, 1996) is conduct problems. An explanation for this high rate of referral is the significant disruption that youth with conduct disorder (CD) cause their families (Frick, 1998), schools (Gottfredson & Gottfredson, 2001), and society in general. The costs to society include the high monetary costs associated with juvenile crime, the direct harm to victims of juvenile crime, and the reduction in the quality of life for those individuals who live in high-crime neighborhoods (Loeber & Farrington, 2000; Zigler, Taussig, & Black, 1992). These outcomes are especially problematic when conduct problems remain stable and affect the child's adjustment across the life span (Frick & Loney, 1999). For example, a single youth who steadily engages in delinquent offenses for 4 years of his youth and for a further 10 years as an adult can cost society up to $2.3 million (Cohen, 1998).

The most widely used classification system for the diagnosis of CD is the *Diagnostic and Statistical Manual of Mental Disorders*, fourth edition, text revision (*DSM-IV-TR*; American Psychiatric Association, 2000). The *DSM-IV-TR* defines CD as a repetitive and persistent pattern of behavior that violates the rights of others or major age-appropriate societal norms or rules. The *DSM-IV-TR* distinguishes two subtypes of CD based on the age of symptom onset. Youth are classified with the childhood-onset subtype if they show severe antisocial behavior before age 10. In contrast, youth with the adolescent-onset subtype show severe conduct problems that emerge after age 10, usually coinciding with the onset of puberty.

Besides being one class of symptoms used to diagnose CD, aggressive behavior has also been used to distinguish between subtypes of CD in some classification systems (Frick & Ellis, 1999). The distinction between aggressive and non-aggressive subtypes of CD is important in that children with aggression show a more stable pattern of conduct problems that is particularly resistant to treatment (Huesmann, Eron, Lefkowitz, & Walder, 1984; Kazdin, 1987). There have even been attempts to distinguish between different types of aggression in children with CD. These distinctions, although not included in the *DSM-IV-TR*, focus on the form (i.e., overt and relational aggression) and the function (i.e., reactive and proactive aggression) of aggressive behavior (see Dodge & Pettit, 2003; Little, Jones, Henrich, & Hawley, 2003; Poulin & Boivin, 2000, for reviews).

Overt aggression, which is more common in boys, includes physical and verbal aggression such as hitting, pushing, kicking, and threatening (Coie & Dodge, 1998), whereas relational aggression, which is more common in girls, harms others by damaging their social relationships, friendships, or inclusion and acceptance in a peer group, including gossiping about others and spreading rumors (Crick, Casas, & Mosher, 1997; Crick & Grotpeter, 1995; Crick et al., 1999). The second distinction focuses on the motivation and function of the aggressive behavior. Specifically, reactive aggression is retaliatory and often is a result of real or perceived provocation. In contrast, proactive aggression is usually planned and instrumental, such as to obtain goods or services, to obtain dominance over others, or to enhance one's social status.

Although there is some research comparing the correlates of overt and relational aggression (see Crick, 1996; Crick et al., 1997; Prinstein, Boergers, & Vernberg, 2001), much of the research on aggression subtypes in youth has focused on the reactive and proactive distinction. This research has found that the two forms of aggression often co-occur in children, with correlations of about $r = .70$ found in samples of school-aged children (Brown, Atkins, Osborne, & Milnamow, 1996). Despite this high degree of association, many studies have documented different correlates to the two forms of aggression. For example, reactive aggression has been associated with higher risk for social isolation and social rejection by peers (Dodge & Pettit, 2003; Price & Dodge, 1989) and a temperamental propensity for angry reactivity and emotional dysregulation (Hubbard et al., 2002; Shields & Cicchetti, 1998). Reactively aggressive children also show a number of deficits in their social information processing, such as having difficulty employing effective problem-solving skills in social situations and showing a hostile attributional bias to ambiguous provocation situations (Crick & Dodge, 1996; Dodge, Lochman, Harnish, Bates, & Pettit, 1997). Proactively aggressive children, on the other hand, associate more positive outcomes with their aggressive behavior, and they report significantly fewer symptoms related to anxiety than reactive aggressive children (Dodge et al., 1997; Price & Dodge, 1989; Schwartz et al., 1998).

An important feature of CD is that youth with this disorder often have a number of other problems in adjustment, besides their conduct problems. Specifically, attention-deficit/hyperactivity disorder (ADHD), learning disabilities (LD), and internalizing disorders are common in youth with CD (i.e., Frick, 1998; Lilienfeld & Waldman, 1990; Lynam, 1996). Researchers have found that the rate of a comorbid ADHD diagnosis ranges from 36 percent in community samples (Waschbush, 2002) to as high as 90 percent in some clinic-referred samples of children with severe conduct problems (Abikoff & Klein, 1992). Further, this comorbidity appears to be particularly strong for children with the childhood-onset subtype of CD (Moffitt, 2003). Importantly, youth with comorbid ADHD and CD tend to show a greater frequency and variety of chronic delinquent and aggressive acts in adolescence (Loeber, Brinthaupt, & Green, 1990; Moffitt, 1993) and more violent offending in adulthood (Klinteberg, Andersson, Magnusson, & Stattin, 1993). Some researchers suggest that the combination of ADHD and CD may actually designate a distinct disorder that is qualitatively different from either disorder alone (Lynam, 1996).

Youth with CD also frequently show comorbid learning disabilities (Cantwell & Baker, 1992). However, some controversy exists about whether the learning problems are more related to ADHD than to the conduct problems themselves (Frick, Lahey, Christ, Loeber, & Green, 1991; Maughan, Pickles, Hagell, Rutter, & Yule, 1996). However, this explanation seems to largely apply to children in the childhood-onset group, with some children with learning disabilities developing conduct problems in adolescence without an early history of ADHD or other behavior problems (Hinshaw, 1992).

Internalizing disorders, such as depression and anxiety, are also highly comorbid with CD. It is estimated that between 15 percent and 31 percent of children with CD have comorbid depression, whereas between 22 percent and 33 percent of children with CD have a comorbid anxiety disorder in community samples and between 60 percent and 75 percent have a comorbid anxiety disorder in clinic-referred samples (Russo & Beidel, 1994; Zoccolillo, 1993). Further, children with comorbid CD and depression are found to be at heightened risk for suicidal ideation (Capaldi, 1992). Also, for many children with CD, the presence of anxiety and depression seems to be largely a result of the interpersonal conflicts (e.g., with peers, teachers, and police) and other stressors (e.g., family dysfunction, school failure) that often are experienced by children with severe conduct problems (Capaldi, 1992; Frick, Lilienfeld, Ellis, Loney, & Silverthorn, 1999).

PERSONALITY DEVELOPMENT AND PSYCHOPATHOLOGY

CD seems to be related to several distinct personality profiles, and these profiles differ across subgroups of children with CD. For example, children with the adolescent-onset pattern of CD often do not show distinct temperamental or personality features before adolescence but score higher on measures of rebelliousness and authority conflict when they enter adolescence (Moffitt & Caspi, 2001; Moffitt, Caspi, Dickson, Silva, & Stanton, 1996). This pattern of personality development has led some to suggest that children in the adolescent-onset pathway of CD show an exaggeration of the normative developmental process of identity formation that takes place in adolescence. In this model of adolescent-onset CD, the child's engagement in antisocial and delinquent behaviors is a misguided attempt to obtain a subjective sense of maturity and adult status in a way that is maladaptive but that is encouraged by an antisocial peer group (Moffitt, 1993, 2003).

In contrast, children in the childhood-onset group show a number of distinct temperamental features early in life that seem to place them at risk for developing antisocial and aggressive behavior patterns (Frick & Morris, 2004; Moffitt & Caspi, 2001). At least two distinct temperamental styles seem to be found in this group. Some children within the childhood-onset group show problems regulating their emotion (Frick & Morris, 2004)—that is, some children with childhood-onset CD show a tendency to react with strong angry and hostile emotions. Such angry reactivity can make the child more likely to act aggressively within the context of these strong emotions without thinking of the potential consequences of these acts (Hubbard et al., 2002; Kruh, Frick, & Clements, 2005; Loney, Frick, Clements, Ellis, & Kerlin, 2003; Shields & Cicchetti, 1998). Such intense emotional arousal can also influence a child's ability to interpret and use social cues (Dodge & Pettit, 2003). In addition, children who are susceptible to strong negative affect can have difficulties internalizing parental norms because their intense emotional arousal to discipline encounters prevents them from effectively processing the parental message (Hoffman, 1994; Kochanska, 1993, 1997), or such a temperament can lead to coercive cycles between the child and parent in which the child learns to act in an aggressive and antisocial manner (Patterson, 1986; Patterson, Reid, & Dishion, 1992).

Problems in emotional regulation seem to best explain conduct problems and aggression that are displayed in the context of high emotional arousal. Although many children show conduct problems that involve the overt and angry confrontation of others (e.g., defiance, argumentativeness, fighting, assault), there are also covert conduct problems that do not involve the direct confrontation of others (e.g., lying, stealing, vandalism) and are not associated with high levels of negative affect (Frick et al., 1992; Frick & Ellis, 1999). Evidence exists that this group of children shows a different temperamental style that has been labeled low fearfulness (Rothbart & Bates, 1998) or low behavioral inhibition (Kagan & Snidman, 1991). This temperament can place a child at risk for problems in the normal development of guilt, empathy, and other aspects of conscience, leading to a particularly severe form of antisocial and aggressive behavior (Frick & Morris, 2004).

Consistent with this contention, research has documented a subgroup of children with CD in school-based samples (Frick, Bodin, & Barry, 2000), outpatient mental health clinics (Christian, Frick, Hill, Tyler & Frazer, 1997; Frick, O'Brien, Wootton, & McBurnett, 1994), and juvenile forensic facilities (Caputo, Frick, & Brodsky, 1999; Silverthorn, Frick, & Reynolds, 2001) who show callous and unemotional personality traits (CU; e.g., absence of guilt, failure to show empathy). Consistent with the hypothesized link to a fearless temperament, this group also shows a preference for novel, exciting, and dangerous activities (Frick, Cornell, Bodin, et al., 2003; Frick et al., 1999); is less reactive to threatening and emotionally distressing stimuli (Blair, 1999; Frick, Cornell, Bodin et al., 2003; Loney et al., 2003); and shows a decreased sensitivity to punishment cues in laboratory and social settings (Barry et al., 2000; Fisher & Blair, 1998; Frick, Cornell, Bodin et al., 2003; Pardini, Lochman, & Frick, 2003).

EPIDEMIOLOGY

In community samples of youth, the prevalence of CD ranges from 2 percent to 4 percent (Loeber, Burke, Lahey, Winters, & Zera, 2000). However, prevalence rates of conduct problems can be influenced by a number of factors, such as the exact criteria used to define the disorder (Anderson, Williams, McGee, & Silva, 1987; Offord et al., 1987) and the method used to assess these criteria (Costello et al., 1988). For example, Costello et al. (1988) reported that prevalence estimates for CD were somewhat higher using child reports than when relying on parent reports.

Prevalence estimates of CD also vary significantly across ethnic groups, age groups, and gender. For example, some researchers have found higher rates of conduct problems in African American youth compared with Caucasian youth (Fabrega, Ulrich, & Mezzich, 1993; Lahey et al., 1995). However, these racial differences in prevalence may be a function of adverse contextual factors that may be disproportionately experienced by ethnic minority youth, including neighborhood poverty, crime rates, and violence (Lahey, Miller, Gordon, & Riley, 1999; Peeples & Loeber, 1994). There also appear to be distinct development trends in the prevalence of CD. In a sample of 1,517 youth in a large urban area, Loeber and colleagues (2000) reported prevalence rates of 5.6, 5.4, and 8.3 for boys aged 7, 11, and 13 with CD, respectively, demonstrating an increase in the rates of CD in adolescence. Prevalence rates for CD also differ significantly across sex. Specifically, in childhood, the ratio of boys to girls with severe conduct problems ranges from 2:1 to 4:1 (Cohen et al., 1993; Loeber et al., 2000; Offord et al., 1987; Shaffer, Fisher, Dulcan, & Davies, 1996). However, this strong male predominance is not consistent across development. Before age 5, prevalence rates for boys and girls are roughly equivalent (Keenan & Shaw, 1997). Also, the developmental period of adolescence is marked by a drastic increase in the number of girls engaging in antisocial behavior, whereas this increase for boys is much less dramatic, leading to a much smaller male predominance of CD in adolescence (see Silverthorn & Frick, 1999, for a review).

ETIOLOGY

Research has consistently suggested that CD is associated with a large number of risk factors (Dodge & Pettit, 2003; Frick, 1998; Loeber & Farrington, 2000; Raine, 2002), suggesting that a focus on any single risk factor is inadequate for explaining its development. Instead, causal theories must integrate a large number of dispositional risk factors (i.e., biological abnormalities, maladaptive personality traits), and contextual risk factors (i.e., inadequate parenting, poor quality schools, peer rejection) when explaining the etiology of CD. The most common method for integrating the influence of multiple risk factors is with a cumulative risk perspective that emphasizes the number of risk factors present rather than the type of risk factors. For example, Loeber and Farrington

(2000) illustrated that the risk for CD increases linearly from the presence of no risk factors to the presence of six or more risk factors. Another perspective for integrating the effects of multiple risk factors is through an interactionist perspective. In this case a given risk factor (i.e., impulsivity) may constitute a moderate risk for conduct problems alone but conveys substantial risk when combined with other risk factors (i.e., inadequate socializing experiences, poverty; Lynam et al., 2000).

A third method for understanding how multiple risk factors may lead to CD is to recognize that multiple pathways may be involved in the development of conduct problems, each with a somewhat distinctive causal process involved (Frick, 1998; Moffitt, 1993; Patterson et al., 1992; Richters, 1997). As noted previously, the adolescent-onset subtype of CD has been viewed as an exaggeration of the normal process of adolescent rebellion (Moffitt, 1993; 2003). In contrast, the childhood-onset subtype of CD is associated with multiple dispositional risk factors (e.g., poor emotional regulation, low intelligence) and contextual risk factors (i.e., family dysfunction, poverty) that lead to a more severe and chronic pattern of antisocial behavior (Moffitt, 1993, 2003). As also noted previously, this childhood-onset group can be further divided into two groups, those with and without CU traits, and different causal processes may be operating across these groups as well.

The fearless temperament that children with CU display may interfere with their development of guilt (Kagan, 1998; Kochanska, 1993) and empathy (Blair, 1995; Blair, Colledge, Murray, & Mitchell, 2001; Blair, Jones, Clark, & Smith, 1997) and thus make the child more difficult to socialize (Frick & Morris, 2004). Consistent with these theories, children with CD and CU traits appear less responsive to typical parental socialization practices than other children with conduct problems (Oxford, Cavell, & Hughes, 2003; Wootton, Frick, Shelton, & Silverthorn, 1997), are less distressed by the negative effects of their behavior on others (Blair et al., 1997; Frick et al., 1999; Pardini et al., 2003), are more impaired in their moral reasoning and empathic concern toward others (Blair, 1999; Fisher & Blair, 1998; Pardini et al., 2003), are less able to recognize expressions of sadness in the faces and vocalizations of other children (Blair et al., 2001; Stevens, Charman, & Blair, 2001), and are less reactive to threatening and emotionally distressing stimuli (Blair, 1999; Frick, Cornell, Bodin, et al., 2003; Kimonis, Frick, Fazekas, & Loney, 2004; Loney et al., 2003).

On the other hand, children with CD who show problems in emotion regulation are less aggressive than children high on CU traits and tend to show a more reactive type of aggression (Frick, Cornell, Barry, Bodin, & Dane, 2003) that is typically in response to real or perceived provocation by others (Frick, Cornell, Bodin, et al., 2003). They exhibit high rates of emotional distress (Frick et al., 1999; Frick, Cornell, Bodin, et al., 2003), are highly reactive to the distress of others in social situations (Pardini et al., 2003), and are highly reactive to negative emotional stimuli (Loney et al., 2003). This is consistent with the theory that the problems in emotional dysregulation interfere with the child's appropriate socialization by parents and peers, leading to problems in multiple settings (Frick & Morris, 2004). For example, emotional dysregulation can cause the child to commit impulsive and unplanned antisocial acts that the child is remorseful for afterward, despite his or her inability to control future acts (Frick & Morris, 2004; Pardini et al., 2003).

In addition, a child who shows intense, unregulated displays of negative emotion is more likely to be rejected by his or her classmates (Rubin, Bukowski, & Parker, 1998), and this peer rejection can place the child at risk for school truancy and for associating with other antisocial and aggressive peers (Keenan, Loeber, Zhang, Stouthamer-Loeber, & Van Kammen, 1995). Compared with youth with CU traits, this type of CD is also more strongly associated with dysfunctional parenting practices (Oxford et al., 2003; Wootton et al., 1997) and a history of physical abuse (Dodge, Bates, & Pettit, 1990; Strassberg, Dodge, Pettit, & Bates, 1994), as well as verbal intelligence deficits (Loney, Frick, Ellis, & McCoy, 1998).

In both groups of children with childhood-onset CD, temperamental vulnerabilities appear to place a child at risk for acting in an aggressive and antisocial manner. This would be consistent with twin studies showing rather substantial genetic contributions to the development of CD (Eaves et al., 2000; Eley, Lichenstein, & Stevenson, 1999). These studies have not, however, generally compared the genetic underpinnings of the different pathways to CD. One exception is a large twin study of 6,330 seven-year-old twins (3,165 twin pairs) in which children who scored in the top 10 percent on the level of conduct problems were divided into those with ($n = 359$) and without ($n = 333$) significant levels of CU traits (Viding, Blair, Moffitt, & Plomin, 2003). When the two groups were compared, the group heritability (i.e., percentage of variance in conduct problems that could be accounted for by genetic factors) for children with conduct problems but low on CU traits was .30, whereas the group heritability for children with conduct problems high on CU traits was more than double this estimate (.81).

COURSE, COMPLICATIONS, AND PROGNOSIS

There is substantial stability in conduct problems across the life span. In a review of 12 prospective longitudinal studies of the stability of conduct problems over short periods (from 8 months to 5 years), Frick and Loney (1999) found that the correlations between initial and follow-up assessments generally ranged from .42 to .64. Further, in studies that estimated the degree of stability for diagnoses of CD, about 50 percent of the children diagnosed with CD at an initial assessment were rediagnosed with CD at a follow-up assessment. Frick and Loney (1999) also reviewed the results of nine prospective longitudinal studies investigating the stability of conduct problems over longer periods (i.e., >6 years). These studies still documented fairly substantial, albeit somewhat lower, stability in conduct problems. Specifically, the correlation coefficients for the long-term follow-up studies generally ranged from .20 to .40.

The severity of CD is a consistent predictor of poor outcome. Specifically, the frequency and intensity of the youth's behavior, the variety of symptoms exhibited, and the presence of symptoms in more than one setting have all been related to a more severe and persistent type of CD (Loeber, 1982). For example, Mitchell and Rosa (1981) found that boys who were rated by both parents and teachers to steal or lie were 2 to 6 times more likely to show chronic criminal behavior as adults than boys rated as such by only one informant. In addition to the severity of conduct problems, other predictors of stability include a comorbid diagnosis of ADHD, low intelligence (especially low verbal intelligence), a family history of antisocial behavior, family dysfunction (e.g., poor parental supervision, harsh discipline, parental conflict, low maternal affection), and low socioeconomic status (Frick & Loney, 1999).

Besides being important for understanding differences in etiology, the distinction between childhood-onset and adolescent-onset CD is also important for identifying differences in the life courses of children with CD (Frick & Loney, 1999). Childhood-onset CD is typically preceded by milder oppositional behaviors earlier in development (i.e., between the ages of 3 and 8), which gradually progress into increasingly more severe types of conduct problems over the course of childhood (Loeber, Green, Lahey, Christ, & Frick, 1992). However, there are three important aspects to this developmental trajectory. First, although most children who show the more severe conduct problems of CD begin with the less severe ODD symptoms, a large number of children with ODD never progress to more severe conduct problems (Lahey & Loeber, 1994). Second, most children who progress to CD don't change the types of behaviors they display but rather add the more severe conduct problem behaviors to their existing behavioral repertoire (Lahey & Loeber, 1994). Third, this ODD to CD progression appears to be characteristic of only the childhood-onset pattern of CD and not the adolescent-onset pathway (Hinshaw, Lahey, & Hart, 1993; Moffitt, 1993).

Specifically, youth who show adolescent-onset CD do not typically show the less severe ODD behaviors earlier in development, but instead show a range of both ODD and CD behaviors coinciding with the onset of puberty.

The outcome and severity of behavior for these two subtypes also differ in that youth with childhood-onset CD are more likely to show aggression in childhood and adolescence and are more likely to continue their antisocial and criminal behavior through adolescence and into adulthood (Frick & Loney, 1999). For example, in a prospective study of the adult outcomes of a birth cohort in New Zealand, Moffitt, Caspi, Harrington, and Milne (2002) reported that the adolescent-onset group was 50 percent to 60 percent less likely to be convicted of an offense as an adult, and their offenses tended to be less serious (e.g., minor theft, public drunkenness) and less violent (e.g., property offenses) than children whose chronic conduct problems started before adolescence.

Unfortunately, there has been less research comparing youth with CD and CU traits to youth with CD only. The few studies that are available, however, suggest that the presence of CU traits may account for a significant amount of the stability in the childhood-onset group. That is, the presence of CU traits predicts later delinquency, aggression, the number of violent offenses, and a shorter length of time to violent reoffending in institutionalized antisocial adolescents (Brandt, Kennedy, Patrick, & Curtin, 1997; Forth, Hart, & Hare, 1990; Toupin, Mercier, Dery, Cote, & Hodgins, 1995). Also, in one of the only studies to test the predictive utility of CU traits in a nonreferred sample of children, youth with CU traits showed the highest rate of conduct problems, self-reported delinquency, and police contacts across a 4-year study period (Frick, Stickle, Dandreaux, Farrell, & Kimonis, in press). In contrast, the rate of self-reported delinquency and the rate of police contact in children with conduct problems but without CU traits was not higher than that found in children without conduct problems.

ASSESSMENT AND DIAGNOSIS

As noted previously, one of the most widely used systems of classifying psychological disorders, the *DSM-IV-TR* (American Psychiatric Association, 2000) defines CD as a repetitive and persistent pattern of behavior that violates the rights of others or violates major age-appropriate societal norms or rules. The disorder is operationalized by four main types of behaviors: aggressive conduct that threatens physical harm to other people or animals, nonaggressive conduct that causes property loss or damage, deceitfulness and theft, and serious violations of rules. It is important to note that the *DSM-IV-TR* definition of CD, like most of the definitions of mental disorders included in this classification system, is strictly a behavioral definition. It does not specify causal factors in its definition.

Such a definition has been criticized by some because it fails to account for the social and transactional influences on the development of CD and seems to view it as a stable dysfunction that is within the individual. This is problematic because family, neighborhood, culture, and other important contexts are strong influences on the development of psychopathology in children, and it may be more appropriate to view the context, and the individual's interaction with his or her context, as dysfunctional (Jensen & Hoagwood, 1997). Furthermore, the *DSM* definition defines only two subtypes of CD, the childhood-onset and adolescent-onset subtypes, and this may not adequately capture the heterogeneity in causal pathways that can lead to severe antisocial and aggressive behavior (Frick & Ellis, 1999). For example, it does not consider the presence or absence of CU traits as a potentially important marker for two distinct pathways within the childhood-onset subtype (Frick & Morris, 2004).

Therefore, to adequately assess a child with CD one must go beyond simply documenting the presence of *DSM-IV-TR* criteria. McMahon and Frick (in press) focus on four findings from research on CD that (a) have clear implications for the prevention and treatment of CD and (b) can help to guide comprehensive assessments of children with CD. First, research has indicated that CD encompasses a broad range of antisocial and aggressive behaviors that vary widely in their form and severity. As a result, the first goal of the assessment is to carefully and thoroughly assess the number, types, and severity of the conduct problems and the level of impairment that the behavioral problems are causing for the child or adolescent (e.g., school suspensions, police contacts, peer rejection). To obtain an accurate representation of the referred child's conduct problems, it is important to use multiple methods of assessment that provide information on the child's behavior across different settings (e.g., home and school). Several methods have proven especially helpful in this respect. These include interviews with the parents, child, and other relevant parties (e.g., teachers); behavior rating scales; and behavioral observations in the clinic, home, or school settings, or a combination of these (see Frick, 1998; Kamphaus & Frick, 2002; McMahon & Frick, in press, for specific examples).

Second, children with CD often have a number of significant problems in adjustment, in addition to their conduct problem behaviors, that contribute to the level of impairment experienced by the child. The large number of co-occurring conditions suggests that an assessment must be comprehensive and cover a large number of areas of adjustment and not just focus on the symptoms of CD. Many behavior-rating scales provide information on a number of important areas of adjustment and thus have utility as screening instruments. Like interviews, these rating scales often include forms for parents, teachers, and the child to complete, providing information from multiple informants that can be collected in a time-efficient manner (Frick & Kamphaus, 2001; Kamphaus & Frick, 2002). Further, most scales provide good norm-referenced scores to compare how a child is rated to a reference group. However, to assess many of the comorbid conditions, more detailed information on the history of symptoms and on the level of impairment they cause for the child may be important. This typically requires a clinical or structured interview, or both (Kamphaus & Frick, 2002; Loney & Frick, 2003).

Third, research has also suggested that a large number of risk factors can act in additive, interactive, or transactional manners to contribute to the development of CD. Again, this indicates the need for a comprehensive assessment of the child with CD to assess these many factors that could have important treatment implications (Frick, 1998, 2001). For example, several cognitive deficits have been associated with CD. As reviewed previously, because deficits in intelligence have been associated with CD, a standard intellectual evaluation should be included as part of most assessment batteries for children with conduct problems. Another critical class of risk factors for CD involves various aspects of family functioning. Parenting practices have been assessed through clinical interviews, behavioral observation of parent-child interactions, and parent and child report on behavior rating scales. Also, children with CD frequently have problems with peer interactions (e.g., peer rejection, association with a deviant peer group). Information from behavioral interviews, behavior rating scales, behavioral observations, or any combination of these can assess for problems in the child's social relationships. Finally, the child's broader social ecology is often crucial for understanding the development of CD in many cases. Therefore, it is important to assess such variables as the economic situation of the family, the level of social and community support provided to the child and his or her family, and other aspects of a child's social climate (e.g., neighborhood, quality of school, degree of exposure to violence).

Fourth, research suggests that the specific risk factors that may be involved in the development of CD and how they place a child at risk for acting in an antisocial and aggressive manner may differ across subgroups of children with CD. Stated another way, there are multiple developmental pathways leading to CD. As a result, it is critical to assess important features that distinguish among children in these pathways. One of the most critical pieces of information in guiding assessment and perhaps ultimately intervention is the age at which various serious conduct problems began, in that this provides some indication as to whether the child may be on the childhood-onset or adolescent-onset pathway. An important advantage that many structured interviews have over behavior-rating scales (and behavioral observations) is that they provide a structured method for assessing when a child first began showing serious conduct problems, thereby providing an important source of information on the developmental trajectory of the child's conduct problem behavior. If the child's history of conduct problems is consistent with the childhood-onset pathway, then additional assessment to examine the extent to which CU traits may also be present is important. The Antisocial Process Screening Device (Frick & Hare, 2001), which is a behavior-rating scale completed by parents and teachers, can be used to assess these traits (Christian et al., 1997; Frick et al., 2000).

IMPACT ON ENVIRONMENT

Family

As mentioned in the introduction, youth with CD can cause significant disruption to their families (Frick, 1998). Importantly, the development of conduct problems can be explained from a social interactive perspective, involving reciprocal exchanges between the child and his or her environment (Thornberry & Krohn, 1987). According to this model, a child with a certain biological predisposition may elicit given responses from his or her parents. For example, a child with a difficult temperament may cause his or her parents to become angry easily and respond to the child's misbehavior with harsh discipline (Dodge & Pettit, 2003). This elicited response by the parents then feeds back to the child to affect his or her behavior. Over time this reciprocal process significantly reduces the effectiveness of parental socialization attempts.

Substantial evidence shows that this social interactive process contributes to the development of conduct problems. Anderson, Lytton, and Romney (1986) found that boys with conduct problems and a problematic temperament were more likely than other boys to elicit punitive discipline practices from adults. These punitive parenting strategies predicted future conduct problems. Also, in their early study of 500 delinquents and 500 nondelinquents, Glueck and Glueck (1950) found that effective parenting strategies were undermined by delinquent children, resulting in erratic, threatening, and harsh discipline; low supervision; and weak parent-child attachment. Importantly, these ineffective parenting strategies further increased the risk for later delinquency (Sampson & Laub, 1994). Both studies demonstrate how the child's dispositions evoke responses from others in the child's life and further increase his or her risk for future conduct problems.

School

Ineffective reciprocal exchanges that begin in early childhood between the child and his or her parents can extend to later in childhood when the child begins school (Gottfredson & Gottfredson, 2001). Within the school setting, these negative reciprocal exchanges that begin with the parent are likely to be repeated with teachers, further reducing socialization attempts with the child outside of the home. Further, the behavior of youth with CD often leads to disruptions in the classroom that prevent all students from experiencing an educational setting conducive to learning (Frick, 1998; Zigler et al., 1992). It can become extremely difficult and costly to schools to set up appropriate programs for these youth that meet their educational needs and minimize the disruptions caused to other students in the school (Knoff, 2000). In addition, it is costly for schools to establish additional security procedures to protect the welfare and safety of all students (Gottfredson & Gottfredson, 2001) and to repair schools that have experienced vandalism from youth with CD (Zigler et al., 1992).

Peer Interactions

Youth with CD who typically begin negative reciprocal exchanges with the parent in early childhood and continue these exchanges with teachers at school age are also likely to show such exchanges with peers. Specifically, this child may behave in unacceptable ways with conventional peers, leading him or her to be rejected by them, further causing the child to be socially isolated or to affiliate with other deviant peers (Dodge & Pettit, 2003). For example, a child who shows early aggression or a tendency to perceive innocuous experiences as hostile will likely aggress toward peers, placing him or her at risk for early rejection by conventional peers and depriving him or her of important peer experiences that foster the development of social and cognitive skills (Dodge et al., 1990; Price & Dodge, 1989). In support of this contention, research has found that peer rejection in childhood is related to later maladjustment and antisocial behavior in adolescence (Kupersmidt, Coie, & Dodge, 1990; Parker & Asher, 1987).

Peer rejection in childhood may also make a child more likely to affiliate with deviant peers in adolescence (Coie, Terry, Zakriski, & Lochman, 1995; Dishion, Patterson, Stoolmiller, & Skinner, 1991). Importantly, youth are significantly more likely to engage in antisocial behavior within a peer context (Fergusson, Swain, & Horwood, 2002; Keenan et al., 1995), and association with deviant peers is a strong predictor of later delinquency (Patterson, Capaldi, & Bank, 1991). Although youth within both childhood-onset and adolescent-onset forms of CD seem to associate with deviant peers, the causal mechanisms for this affiliation may differ between the two subgroups (Moffitt, 1993; Moffitt et al., 1996; Moffitt & Caspi, 2001). Children with early-onset CD likely show antisocial and aggressive behaviors prior to affiliation with deviant peers that may be the result of dispositional or contextual risk factors, or both. These early antisocial behaviors may cause the child to seek out nonconventional peers because of rejection by conventional peers or lack of parental supervision (Vitaro, Brendgen, Pagani, Tremblay, & McDuff, 1999). However, affiliation with deviant peers by youth with adolescent-onset CD may provide a more direct causal influence on the development of conduct problems (Moffitt & Caspi, 2001). That is, the association with the deviant group for the adolescent-onset group may be a critical factor in their extreme rebelliousness, rejection of authority, and rejection of societal norms.

IMPLICATIONS FOR FUTURE PERSONALITY DEVELOPMENT

By definition, children with CD show a behavioral disturbance that impacts their psychological, social, or educational functioning in some significant way (Frick, 1998). Whether this behavioral disturbance results from problems in identity formation (adolescent-onset CD), problems in conscience development and response to distress in others (childhood-onset CD with CU traits), or problems regulating emotion (childhood-onset CD without CU traits), it is likely that the problems in development leading to CD and the conduct problems themselves can have an impact on the individual's subsequent personality functioning. To illustrate this impact on adult adjustment, Robins (1966) found that 43 percent of boys and 12 percent of girls who had been referred to a mental health clinic for CD symptoms were later imprisoned at least once as adults. This longitudinal study suggests that the rate of antisocial outcomes is not as high for girls with CD. However, this study did reveal that girls with CD are at heightened risk for other adjustment problems as adults, including somatization, emotional disorders, suicide attempts, and severe impairments in occupational and social adjustment (see also Robins, Tipp, & Pryzbeck, 1991; Silverthorn & Frick, 1999; Zoccolillo, 1993).

Two potential personality outcomes of CD are antisocial personality disorder (APD) and psychopathy. These two personality dimensions are often used interchangeably, but evidence is accumulating that there are important differences between the two constructs. APD simply refers to a pattern of impulsive, irresponsible, aggressive, and antisocial behavior (American Psychiatric Association, 2000). In contrast, psychopathy refers to a constellation of affective traits (e.g., poverty of emotions, lack of empathy and guilt), interpersonal traits (e.g., callous use of others for one's own gain), and self-referential traits (e.g., inflated sense of one's own importance) that may or may not be associated with impulsive and antisocial behavior (Cleckley, 1982; Hare, 1999). Importantly, studies of adult prisoners suggest that, whereas the vast majority of inmates meet the behavioral criteria for APD, only a minority show the interpersonal and affective features associated with the construct of psychopathy (Hare, Hart, & Harpur, 1991; Hare, 1999). This minority of criminals with psychopathy, however, shows a more severe and violent pattern of antisocial behavior, both within the institution and after release (Gendreau, Goggin, & Smith, 2002; Hemphill, Hare, & Wong, 1998; Walters, 2003). In addition, incarcerated adults with and without psychopathic features show a number of distinct cognitive (Newman & Lorenz, 2003), affective (Hare, 1998; Patrick, 2001), and neurological (Kiehl et al., 2001) correlates that could implicate different causal processes involved in the development of antisocial behavior for the two groups of individuals.

Therefore, the presence of psychopathic traits seems to designate an important subgroup of individuals with APD. There is research to suggest that children with CD are at risk for showing APD. In fact, the *DSM-IV-TR* criteria for APD specify that persons with APD must have shown symptoms of CD at least since age 15 (American Psychiatric Association, 2000). This link between APD and CD has been empirically demonstrated in both retrospective (Robins et al., 1991) and prospective (Robins, 1966) studies. However, little research has focused on the risk between CD and adult psychopathy (Edens, Skeem, Cruise, & Cauffman, 2001). The few exceptions are retrospective studies showing that adults with psychopathic traits often have a long history of antisocial behavior beginning in childhood (Hare, McPherson, & Forth, 1988; Marshall & Cooke, 1999). It is possible that the subgroup of CD children who have CU traits may be more specifically at risk for psychopathy as adults, given that they share many characteristics with adults who show psychopathy (see Frick & Marsee, in press; Frick & Morris, 2004, for reviews). Further, these traits are fairly stable across the transition from childhood to adolescence (Frick, Kimonis, Dandreaux & Farrell, 2003). However, prospective studies have not specifically tested whether and at what level these children may be at increased risk for meeting criteria for psychopathy as adults.

TREATMENT IMPLICATIONS

Four primary treatment approaches have been documented to be effective for reducing conduct problems in youth in controlled treatment trials (see Brestan & Eyberg, 1998; Frick, 1998; Kazdin, 1995). First, contingency management programs are based on the assumption that most children with CD experience inadequate socialization that plays a major role in the child's inability to modulate his or her behavior (i.e., delay gratification, conform to parental and societal expectations; Patterson, 1986). This inadequate socialization may result from exposure to an inconsistent and noncontingent environment within their family or a temperamental vulnerability that causes the child to be more susceptible to a noncontingent environment, such as being overfocused on the potential positive consequences of their behavior (i.e., obtaining a stereo) while ignoring the potential negative consequences (i.e., being arrested for stealing) (Barry et al., 2000; Pardini et al., 2003).

A structured behavior management system is designed to overcome these deficiencies in socialization by (a) establishing clear behavioral goals that gradually shape more prosocial behavior in the child, (b) developing a system of monitoring whether the child is reaching these goals, (c) having a system of reinforcing appropriate steps toward reaching these goals, and (d) providing consequences for inappropriate behavior. Research shows that contingency management programs are effective in bringing about behavioral changes in children with conduct problems within the home (Ross, 1981), at school (Abramowitz & O'Leary, 1991), and in residential treatment centers (Lyman & Campbell, 1996). Importantly, these programs must be tailored to the individual child, from the selection of appropriate goals to the types of reinforcers and punishments used to motivate the child.

Second, parent management training (PMT) teaches parents how to develop and implement structured contingency management programs within the home. In addition, PMT programs focus on improving the quality of parent-child interactions (i.e., getting parents more involved in their child's activities, improving parent-child communication, increasing parental warmth and responsiveness), changing the antecedents to the child's behavior to enhance the likelihood that positive prosocial behaviors will be displayed (i.e., how to time and present requests), improving parents' ability to monitor and supervise their children, and using more effective discipline strategies. The effectiveness of PMT is the most consistently documented of any technique to treat conduct problems (Kazdin, 1995). However, two major limitations of PMT are the large number of parents who never complete the program and the low effectiveness for the most dysfunctional families (Kazdin, 1995; Miller & Prinz, 1990).

Third, cognitive-behavioral interventions are designed to target the child's deficits in social cognition and social problem solving. These approaches usually include some method for reducing the child's tendency to respond impulsively or with anger. With this skills-building approach, the child learns a series of problem-solving steps (i.e., how to recognize problems, how to consider alternative responses and their outcomes, how to select the most adaptive response) to deal more effectively with problems that they encounter. The therapist plays an active role by modeling the skills being taught, role-playing social situations with the child, prompting the use of the skills being taught, and delivering feedback and praise for appropriate use of the skills. Because of the iatrogenic effects of group interventions with antisocial youth (Arnold & Hughes, 1999; Dishion, McCord, & Poulin, 1999), it is important for groups to be small, with very structured group interactions. A major limitation of cognitive-behavioral approaches is the difficulty in getting children to use the skills learned in the program outside of the therapeutic setting (Kendall, Reber, McLeer, Epps, & Ronan, 1990) and to maintain the skills over extended periods after the intervention has ended (Lochman, 1992). To enhance generalization, most programs include the practice of skills in a variety of settings. Some programs are designed to be implemented outside of the typical mental health delivery setting, such as in schools (Bierman & Greenberg, 1996). In these programs, the skills are taught in the same environment in which they will be used. Most importantly, all of the programs involve people in the child's natural environment (e.g., parents, teachers, peers) to encourage the use of these skills outside of the therapeutic context.

Fourth, stimulant medication has proven to be effective in reducing conduct problems given that ADHD is highly comorbid with CD (Abikoff & Klein, 1992) and the impulsivity associated with ADHD may directly lead to some of the aggressive and other poorly regulated behaviors of children with conduct problems (Frick & Morris, 2004). Several controlled medication trials have demonstrated the effectiveness of stimulants for reducing conduct problems in children with both ADHD and CD (Hinshaw, 1991; Hinshaw, Heller, & McHale, 1992; Pelham et al., 1993). For example, within a very structured classroom setting, Ritalin significantly decreased the rate of disruptive classroom behaviors, including verbal and physical aggression, teasing, destruction of property, and cheating (Hinshaw et al., 1992). Further, medication was somewhat more effective than an intensive contingency management system in reducing the level of these conduct problems. These results were replicated in a large treatment trial of 579 children diagnosed with ADHD (Swanson, Kramer, & Hinshaw, 2001). Importantly, this study also determined that the combination of stimulant medication and psychosocial treatments, such as PMT and contingency management systems, resulted in somewhat greater reductions in conduct problems than either type of intervention alone.

Although each of these four interventions has proven to be effective in reducing conduct problems, they all have a number of substantial limitations (Kazdin, 1995). First, a significant proportion of children with CD do not show a significant response to these interventions, and, for those who do respond, their behavior problems are often not reduced to a normative level. Second, children under the age of 8 with less severe behavioral disturbances typically show the greatest degree of improvement. Although this finding highlights the need to focus on the prevention of CD in young children who are beginning to show problematic behaviors, it also suggests a strong need for better interventions for older children and adolescents with more severe conduct problems. Third, with some notable exceptions (McNeil, Eyberg, Eisenstadt, Newcomb, & Funderburk, 1991), the generalizability of treatment effects tends to be poor across settings, such that they may be effective in changing a child's behavior in one setting (i.e., mental health clinics) but ineffective in others (i.e., schools). Fourth, and also with some notable exceptions (Long, Forehand, Wierson, & Morgan, 1994), it is difficult to maintain improvements in the child's behavior over time, again especially for older children with severe conduct problems (Lochman, 1992) and for children from very dysfunctional family environments (Kazdin, 1995).

Given these rather substantial limitations, innovative approaches to intervention are being developed that integrate research on developmental models of conduct problems with empirically supported treatments (Frick, 1998, 2001). These novel approaches are comprehensive and thus recognize the multidetermined nature of conduct problems. In addition, they are individualized and thus recognize the different developmental pathways through which children may develop CD. Using this approach, the existing research on these developmental pathways helps in determining which processes may be involved in the development of CD for a particular child, and it guides decisions on the most important targets for the intervention. This approach requires a clear case conceptualization specifying the developmental processes that may have led to the child's behavior problems, and this conceptualization guides the design of a focused and integrated approach to treatment (Frick & McCoy, 2001). Finally, this approach requires the collaboration of multiple professionals and community agencies working together to provide a comprehensive and integrated intervention.

Multisystemic therapy (MST; Henggeler, Schoenwald, Borduin, Rowland, & Cunningham, 1998) involves many of the features of this developmental approach to treatment. It has been tested in controlled treatment outcome studies and found to be effective in reducing severe antisocial and aggressive behavior in children and adolescents (Henggeler, Melton, & Smith, 1992; Henggeler et al., 1998). MST expands on systemic family therapy, which views problems in children's adjustment as being embedded within the larger family context, by including other contexts, such as the child's school, peer group, and neighborhood. Also, MST involves a comprehensive and individualized approach to intervention based on an initial assessment and case conceptualization. This conceptualization attempts to explain how the child's problem behaviors are related to factors in his or her familial, peer, and cultural environments and then targets these factors in an individualized treatment plan based on the specific needs of the child and his or her family.

One of the important contributions of MST to the treatment outcome literature is its demonstration that individualized interventions can be rigorously evaluated through controlled treatment outcome studies. The initial findings on the effectiveness of MST suggest that it is one of the more successful interventions for reducing severe antisocial and aggressive behavior among older youth (Henggeler et al., 1992). For example, in a controlled treatment outcome study of MST at a university-based outpatient clinic, 88 adolescent repeat juvenile offenders underwent MST (Henggeler & Borduin, 1990). To illustrate the individualized nature of the treatment, the length of treatment with MST ranged from 5 to 54 hours (mean of 23 hours). In addition to this variation in intensity, the way in which these hours were utilized varied depending on the needs of the clients. Eighty-three percent of the MST group participated in family therapy, 60 percent participated in some form of school intervention (e.g., facilitation of parent-teacher communication, academic remediation, or help in classroom behavior management), 57 percent received some form of peer intervention, and 28 percent received individual therapy that typically involved some form of cognitive-behavioral skills building intervention. Additionally, in 26 percent of the cases, the adolescent's parents became involved in marital therapy. The outcomes of the group of offenders receiving MST were compared to a control group of 68 offenders who received traditional outpatient services, typically involving individual psychotherapy (Borduin et al., 1995). At a 4-year follow-up, only 26 percent of the youth who underwent MST were rearrested, compared to 71 percent of the control adolescents.

SUMMARY

In summary, the large body of research on CD indicates two important points that guide the assessment and treatment of this disruptive behavior disorder. First, CD often results from multiple interacting risk factors. Second, this constellation of interacting factors may be very different for various subgroups of children with conduct problems. To illustrate these two critical points, research has identified three primary causal pathways to severe conduct problems. In the adolescent-onset pathway, the emergence of serious antisocial behaviors coincides with the onset of puberty and is caused by an exaggeration of the normal developmental process of adolescent rebellion. In contrast, the childhood-onset subgroup begins to show oppositional behaviors early in life, and this behavior worsens into more severe conduct problems over the course of development. The childhood-onset pathway has been tied to distinct premorbid personality features, which lead to problems that transcend a single developmental stage and can be further divided into two distinct subgroups. The two primary premorbid personality traits that have been tied to these subgroups of CD are (a) a callous and unemotional interpersonal style (CU) seeming to indicate a deficit in conscience development, and (b) an impulsive and emotionally dysregulated personality pattern.

Further research is needed to provide a better understanding of the developmental mechanisms leading to conduct problems for children in each of these groups. Also, other pathways may be uncovered that better explain the development of conduct problems for children who do not fit into these subtypes. However, this model of CD illustrates the importance of considering the many different causal processes that can lead to CD. Further, it has important implications for assessment, prevention, and treatment for youth with CD. It suggests that treatments must be comprehensive and individualized in order to target the unique constellation of interacting factors responsible for the development, exacerbation, and maintenance of conduct problems for an individual child. Several treatment models that consider these multiple pathways are being developed and tested, with some initial promising results. Such research provides great optimism that techniques for successfully reducing antisocial and aggressive behavior are possible in the near future.

REFERENCES

Abikoff, H., & Klein, R. G. (1992). Attention-deficit hyperactivity and conduct disorder: Comorbidity and implications for treatment. *Journal of Consulting and Clinical Psychology, 60*, 881–892.

Abramowitz, A. J., & O'Leary, S. G. (1991). Behavioral interventions for the classroom: Implications for students with ADHD. *School Psychology Review, 20*, 220–234.

American Psychiatric Association. (2000). *Diagnostic and statistical manual of mental disorders* (4th ed., text rev.). Washington, DC: Author.

Anderson, J. C., Williams, S., McGee, R., & Silva, P. A. (1987). DSM-III disorders in preadolescent children. *Archives of General Psychiatry, 44*, 69–76.

Anderson, K. E., Lytton, H., & Romney, D. M. (1986). Mothers' interactions with normal and conduct-disordered boys: Who affects whom? *Developmental Psychology, 22*, 604–609.

Arnold, M. E., & Hughes, J. N. (1999). First do no harm: Adverse effects of grouping deviant youth for skills training. *Journal of School Psychology, 37*, 99–115.

Barry, C. T., Frick, P. J., Grooms, T., McCoy, M. G., Ellis, M. L., & Loney, B. R. (2000). The importance of callous-unemotional traits for extending the concept of psychopathy to children. *Journal of Abnormal Psychology, 109*, 335–340.

Bierman, K. L., & Greenberg, M. T. (1996). Social skills training in the FAST Track program. In R. D. Peters & R. J. McMahon (Eds.), *Preventing childhood disorders, substance abuse, and delinquency* (pp. 65–89). Thousand Oaks, CA: Sage.

Blair, R. J. R. (1995). A cognitive developmental approach to morality: Investigating the psychopath. *Cognition, 57*, 1–29.

Blair, R. J. R. (1999). Responsiveness to distress cues in the child with psychopathic tendencies. *Personality and Individual Differences, 27*, 135–145.

Blair, R. J. R., Colledge, E., Murray, L., & Mitchell, D. G. V. (2001). A selective impairment in the processing of sad and fearful expressions in children with psychopathic tendencies. *Journal of Abnormal Child Psychology, 29*, 491–498.

Blair, R. J. R., Jones, L., Clark, F., & Smith, M. (1997). The psychopathic individual: A lack of responsiveness to distress cues? *Psychophysiology, 34*, 192–198.

Borduin, C. M., Mann, B. J., Cone, L. T., Henggeler, S. W., Fucci, B. R., Blaske, D. M., et al. (1995). Multisystemic treatment of serious juvenile offenders: Long-term prevention of criminality and violence. *Journal of Consulting and Clinical Psychology, 63*, 569–578.

Brandt, J. R., Kennedy, W. A., Patrick, C. J., & Curtin, J. J. (1997). Assessment of psychopathy in a population of incarcerated adolescent offenders. *Psychological Assessment, 9*, 429–435.

Brestan, E. V., & Eyberg, S. M. (1998). Effective psychosocial treatments for conduct disordered children and adolescents. *Journal of Clinical Child Psychology, 27*, 180–189.

Brown, K., Atkins, M. S., Osborne, M. L., & Milnamow, M. (1996). A revised teacher rating scale for reactive and proactive aggression. *Journal of Abnormal Child Psychology, 24*, 473–480.

Cantwell, D. P., & Baker, L. (1992). Attention deficit disorder with and without hyperactivity: A review and comparison of matched groups. *Journal of the American Academy of Child and Adolescent Psychiatry, 31,* 432–438.

Capaldi, D. M. (1992). The co-occurrence of conduct problems and depressive symptoms in early adolescent boys, II: A 2-year follow-up at grade 8. *Development and Psychopathology, 4,* 125–144.

Caputo, A. A., Frick, P. J., & Brodsky, S. L. (1999). Family violence and juvenile sex offending: Potential mediating roles of psychopathic traits and negative attitudes toward women. *Criminal Justice and Behavior, 26,* 338–356.

Christian, R. E., Frick, P. J., Hill, N. L., Tyler, L., & Frazer, D. R. (1997). Psychopathy and conduct problems in children: II. Implications for subtyping children with conduct problems. *Journal of the American Academy of Child and Adolescent Psychiatry, 36,* 233–241.

Cleckley, H. (1982). *The mask of sanity.* St. Louis, MO: Mosby.

Cohen, M. A. (1998). The monetary value of saving a high-risk youth. *Journal of Quantitative Criminology, 14,* 5–33.

Cohen, P., Cohen, J., Kasen, S., Velez, C. N., Hartmark, C., Johnson, J., et al. (1993). An epidemiological study of disorders in late childhood and adolescence, I: Age and gender-specific prevalence. *Journal of Child Psychology and Psychiatry, 34,* 851–867.

Coie, J. D., & Dodge, K. A. (1998). Aggression and antisocial behavior. In W. Damon & N. Eisenberg (Eds.), *Handbook of child psychology: Social, emotional, and personality development* (pp. 779–862). Toronto: Wiley.

Coie, J. D., Terry, R., Zakriski, A., & Lochman, J. E. (1995). Early adolescent social influences on delinquent behavior. In J. McCord (Ed.), *Coercion and punishment in long-term perspective* (pp. 229–244). New York: Cambridge University Press.

Costello, E. J., Costello, A. J., Edelbrock, C., Burns, B. J., Dulcan, M. K., Brent, D., et al. (1988). Psychiatric disorders in pediatric primary care. *Archives of General Psychiatry, 45,* 1107–1116.

Crick, N. R. (1996). The role of overt aggression, relational aggression, and prosocial behavior in the prediction of children's future social adjustment. *Child Development, 67,* 2317–2327.

Crick, N. R., Casas, J. F., & Mosher, M. (1997). Relational and overt aggression in preschool. *Developmental Psychology, 33,* 579–588.

Crick, N. R., & Dodge, K. A. (1996). Social information-processing mechanisms in reactive and proactive aggression. *Child Development, 67,* 993–1002.

Crick, N. R., & Grotpeter, J. K. (1995). Relational aggression, gender, and social-psychological adjustment. *Child Development, 66,* 710–722.

Crick, N. R., Werner, N. E., Casas, J. F., O'Brien, K. M., Nelson, D. A., Grotpeter, J. K., et al. (1999). Childhood aggression and gender: A new look at an old problem. In D. Bernstein (Ed.), *The 45th Nebraska symposium on motivation: Gender and motivation* (pp. 75–141). Lincoln: Nebraska University Press.

Dishion, T. J., McCord, J., & Poulin, F. (1999). When interventions harm: Peer groups and problem behavior. *American Psychologist, 54,* 755–764.

Dishion, T. J., Patterson, G. R., Stoolmiller, M., & Skinner, M. L. (1991). Family, school, and behavioral antecedents to early adolescent involvement with antisocial peers. *Developmental Psychology, 27,* 172–180.

Dodge, K. A., Bates, J. E., & Pettit, G. S. (1990). Mechanisms in the cycle of violence. *Science, 250,* 1678–1683.

Dodge, K. A., Lochman, J. E., Harnish, J. D., Bates, J. E., & Pettit, G. S. (1997). Reactive and proactive aggression in school children and psychiatrically impaired chronically assaultive youth. *Journal of Abnormal Psychology, 106,* 37–51.

Dodge, K. A., & Pettit, G. S. (2003). A biopsychosocial model of the development of chronic conduct problems in adolescence. *Developmental Psychology, 39,* 349–371.

Eaves, L., Rutter, M., Silberg, J. L., Shillady, L., Maes, H., & Pickles, A. (2000). Genetic and environmental causes of covariation in interview assessments of disruptive behavior in child and adolescent twins. *Behavior Genetics, 30,* 321–334.

Edens, J., Skeem, J., Cruise, K., & Cauffman, E. (2001). The assessment of juvenile psychopathy and its association with violence: A critical review. *Behavioral Sciences and the Law, 19,* 53–80.

Eley, T. C., Lichenstein, P., & Stevenson, J. (1999). Sex differences in the etiology of aggressive and nonaggressive antisocial behavior: Results from two twin studies. *Child Development, 70,* 155–168.

Fabrega, J. H., Ulrich, R., & Mezzich, J. E. (1993). Do Caucasian and Black adolescents differ at psychiatric intake? *Journal of the American Academy of Child and Adolescent Psychiatry, 32,* 407–413.

Fergusson, D. M., Swain, N. R., & Horwood, L. J. (2002). Deviant peer affiliations, crime and substance use: A fixed effects regression analysis. *Journal of Abnormal Child Psychology, 30,* 419–430.

Fisher, L., & Blair, R. J. R. (1998). Cognitive impairment and its relationship to psychopathic tendencies in children with emotional and behavioral difficulties. *Journal of Abnormal Child Psychology, 26,* 511–519.

Forth, A. E., Hart, S. D., & Hare, R. D. (1990). Assessment of psychopathy in male young offenders. *Psychological Assessment, 2,* 342–344.

Frick, P. J. (1998). *Conduct disorders and severe antisocial behavior.* New York: Plenum Press.

Frick, P. J. (2001). Effective interventions for children and adolescents with conduct disorder. *Canadian Journal of Psychiatry, 46,* 26–37.

Frick, P. J., Bodin, S. D., & Barry, C. T. (2000). Psychopathic traits and conduct problems in community and clinic-referred samples of children: Further development of the Psychopathy Screening Device. *Psychological Assessment, 12,* 382–393.

Frick, P. J., Cornell, A. H., Barry, C. T., Bodin, S. D., & Dane, H. E. (2003). Callous-unemotional traits and conduct problems in the prediction of conduct problem severity, aggression, and self-report of delinquency. *Journal of Abnormal Child Psychology, 31,* 457–470.

Frick, P. J., Cornell, A. H., Bodin, S. D., Dane, H. A., Barry, C. T., & Loney, B. R. (2003). Callous-unemotional traits and developmental pathways to severe conduct problems. *Developmental Psychology, 39,* 246–260.

Frick, P. J., & Ellis, M. (1999). Callous-unemotional traits and subtypes of conduct disorder. *Clinical Child and Family Psychology Review, 2,* 149–168.

Frick, P. J., & Hare, R. D. (2001). *The Antisocial Process Screening Device (APSD).* Toronto: Multi-Health Systems.

Frick, P. J., & Kamphaus, R. W. (2001). Behavior rating scales in the assessment of children's behavioral and emotional problems. In C. E. Walker & M. C. Roberts (Eds.), *Handbook of clinical child Psychology* (3rd ed., pp. 190–204). New York: Wiley.

Frick, P. J., Kimonis, E. R., Dandreaux, D. M., & Farrell, J. M. (2003). The four-year stability of psychopathic traits in non-referred youth. *Behavioral Sciences and the Law, 21,* 713–736.

Frick, P. J., Lahey, B., Christ, M. A. G., Loeber, R., & Green, S. (1991). History of childhood behavior problems in biological parents of boys with attention-deficit hyperactivity disorder and conduct disorder. *Journal of Clinical Child Psychology, 20,* 445–451.

Frick, P. J., Lahey, B. B., Loeber, R., Stouthamer-Loeber, M., Christ, M. A. G., & Hanson, K. (1992).Familial risk factors to conduct disorder and oppositional defiant disorder: Parental psychopathology and maternal parenting. *Journal of Consulting and Clinical Psychology, 60,* 49–55.

Frick, P. J., Lilienfeld, S. O., Ellis, M. L, Loney, B. R., & Silverthorn, P. (1999). The association between anxiety and psychopathy dimensions in children. *Journal of Abnormal Child Psychology, 27,* 381–390.

Frick, P., & Loney, B. R. (1999). Outcomes of children and adolescents with conduct disorder and oppositional defiant disorder. In H. C. Quay & A. Hogan (Eds.), *Handbook of disruptive behavior disorders* (pp. 507–524). New York: Plenum Press.

Frick, P. J., & Marsee, M. A. (in press). Psychopathy and developmental pathways to antisocial behavior in youth. In C. J. Patrick (Ed.), *Handbook of psychopathy.* New York: Guilford Press.

Frick, P. J., & McCoy, M. G. (2001). Conduct disorder. In H. Orvaschel, J. Faust, & M. Hersen (Eds.), *Handbook of conceptualization and treatment of child psychopathology* (pp. 57–76). Oxford: Elsevier Science.

Frick, P. J., & Morris, A. S. (2004). Temperament and developmental pathways to conduct problems. *Journal of Clinical Child and Adolescent Psychology, 33,* 54–68.

Frick, P. J., O'Brien, B. S., Wootton, J. M., & McBurnett, K. (1994). Psychopathy and conduct problems in children. *Journal of Abnormal Psychology, 103,* 700–707.

Frick, P. J., & Silverthorn, P. (2001). Psychopathology in children. In P. B. Sutker & H. E. Adams (Eds.), *Comprehensive handbook of psychopathology* (3rd ed., pp. 881–920). New York: Kluwer.

Frick, P. J., Stickle, T. R., Dandreaux, D. M., Farrell, J. M., & Kimonis, E. R. (in press). Callous-unemotional traits in predicting the severity and stability of conduct problems and delinquency. *Journal of Abnormal Child Psychology.*

Gendreau, P., Goggin, C., & Smith, P. (2002). Is the PCL-R really the "unparalleled" measure of offender risk? A lesson in knowledge cumulation. *Criminal Justice and Behavior, 29,* 397–426.

Glueck, S., & Glueck, E. (1950). *Unraveling juvenile delinquency.* Cambridge, MA: Harvard University Press.

Gottfredson, G. D., & Gottfredson, D.C. (2001). What schools do to prevent problem behavior and promote safe environments. *Journal of Educational and Psychological Consultation, 12,* 313–344.

Hare, R. D. (1998). Psychopathy, affect, and behavior. In D. J. Cooke, A. E. Forth, & R. D. Hare (Eds.), *Psychopathy: Theory, research, and implications for society* (pp. 105–138). Dordrecht, The Netherlands: Kluwer.

Hare, R. D. (1999). *Without conscience: The disturbing world of the psychopaths among us.* New York: Guilford Press.

Hare, R. D., Hart, S. D., & Harpur, T. J. (1991). Psychopathy and the *DSM-IV* criteria for antisocial personality disorder. *Journal of Abnormal Psychology, 100,* 391–398.

Hare, R. D., McPherson, L. E., & Forth, A. E. (1988). Male psychopaths and their criminal careers. *Journal of Consulting and Clinical Psychology, 56,* 710–714.

Hemphill, J. F., Hare, R. D., & Wong, S. (1998). Psychopathy and recidivism: A review. *Legal and Criminological Psychology, 3,* 139–170.

Henggeler, S. W., & Borduin, C. M. (1990). *Family therapy and beyond: A multisystemic approach to treating the behavior problems of children and adolescents.* Pacific Grove, CA: Brooks/Cole.

Henggeler, S. W., Melton, G. B., & Smith, L. A. (1992). Family preservation using multisystemic therapy: An effective alternative to incarcerating juvenile offenders. *Journal of Consulting and Clinical Psychology, 60,* 953–961.

Henggeler, S. W., Schoenwald, S. K., Borduin, C. M., Rowland, M. D., & Cunningham, P. B. (1998). *Multisystemic treatment of antisocial behavior in children and adolescents.* New York: Guilford Press.

Hinshaw, S. P. (1991). Stimulant medication and the treatment of aggression in children with attention deficits. *Journal of Clinical Child Psychology, 20,* 301–312.

Hinshaw, S. P. (1992). Externalizing behavior problems and academic underachievement in childhood and adolescence: Causal relationships and underlying mechanisms. *Psychological Bulletin, 111,* 127–155.

Hinshaw, S. P., Heller, T., & McHale, J. P. (1992). Covert antisocial behavior in boys with attention-deficit hyperactivity disorder: External validation and effects of methylphenidate. *Journal of Consulting and Clinical Psychology, 60,* 274–281.

Hinshaw, S. P., Lahey, B. B., & Hart, E. L. (1993). Issues of taxonomy and co-morbidity in the development of conduct disorder. *Development and Psychopathology, 5,* 31–50.

Hoffman, M. L. (1994). Discipline and internalization. *Developmental Psychology, 30,* 26–28.

Hubbard, J. A., Smithmyer, C. M., Ramsden, S. R., Parker, E. H., Flanagan, K. D., Dearing, K. F., et al. (2002). Observational, physiological, and self-report measures of children's anger: Relations to reactive versus proactive aggression. *Child Development, 73,* 1101–1118.

Huesmann, L. R., Eron, L. D., Lefkowitz, M. M., & Walder, L. O. (1984). Stability of aggression over time and generations. *Developmental Psychology, 20,* 1120–1134.

Jensen, P. S., & Hoagwood, K. (1997). The book of names: *DSM-IV* in context. *Development and Psychopathology, 9,* 231–249.

Kagan, J. (1998). Biology and the child. In N. Eisenberg (Ed.), *Handbook of child psychology: Vol. 3. Social, emotional, and personality development* (pp. 177–235). New York: Wiley.

Kagan, J., & Snidman, N. (1991). Temperamental factors in human development. *American Psychologist, 46,* 856–862.

Kamphaus, R. W., & Frick, P. J. (2002). *Clinical assessment of child and adolescent personality and behavior* (2nd ed.). Boston: Allyn & Bacon.

Kazdin, A. E. (1987). Treatment of antisocial behavior in children: Current status and future directions. *Psychological Bulletin, 102,* 187–203.

Kazdin, A. E. (1995). *Conduct disorders in childhood and adolescence* (2nd ed.). Thousand Oaks, CA: Sage.

Keenan, K., Loeber, R., Zhang, Q., Stouthamer-Loeber, M., & Van Kammen, W. B. (1995). The influence of deviant peers on the development of boys' disruptive and delinquent behavior: A temporal analysis. *Development and Psychopathology, 7,* 715–726.

Keenan, K., & Shaw, D. S. (1997). Developmental and social influences on young girls' behavioral and emotional problems. *Psychological Bulletin, 121,* 95–113.

Kendall, P. C., Reber, M., McLeer, S., Epps, J., & Ronan, K. R. (1990). Cognitive-behavioral treatment of conduct disordered children. *Cognitive Therapy and Research, 14,* 279–297.

Kiehl, K. A., Smith, A. M., Hare, R. D., Mendrek, A., Forster, B. B., Brink, J., et al. (2001). Limbic abnormalities in affective processing by criminal psychopaths as revealed by functional magnetic resonance imaging. *Biological Psychology, 50,* 677–684.

Kimonis, E. R., Frick, P. J., Fazekas, H., & Loney, B. R. (2004). *Psychopathy, aggression, and the processing of emotional stimuli in non-referred children.* Manuscript submitted for publication.

Klinteberg, B. A., Andersson, T., Magnusson, D., & Stattin, H. (1993). Hyperactive behavior in childhood as related to subsequent alcohol problems and violent offending: A longitudinal study of male subjects. *Personality and Individual Differences, 15,* 381–388.

Knoff, H. M. (2000). Organizational development and strategic planning for the millennium: A blueprint toward effective school discipline, safety, and crisis prevention. *Psychology in the Schools, 37,* 17–32.

Kochanska, G. (1993). Toward a synthesis of parental socialization and child temperament in early development of conscience. *Child Development, 64,* 325–347.

Kochanska, G. (1997). Multiple pathways to conscience for children with different temperaments: From toddlerhood to age 5. *Developmental Psychology, 33,* 228–240.

Kruh, I. P., Frick, P. J., & Clements, C. B. (2005). Historical and personality correlates to the violence patterns of juveniles tried as adults. *Criminal Justice and Behavior, 32,* 69–96.

Kupersmidt, J. B., Coie, J. D., & Dodge, K. A. (1990). The role of peer relationships in the development of disorder. In S. R. Asher & J. D. Coie (Eds.), *Peer rejection in childhood* (pp. 274–308). New York: Cambridge University Press.

Lahey, B. B., & Loeber, R. (1994). Framework for a developmental model of oppositional defiant disorder and conduct disorder. In D. K. Routh (Ed.), *Disruptive behavior disorders in childhood* (pp. 139–180). New York: Plenum Press.

Lahey, B. B., Loeber, R., Hart, E. L., Frick, P. J., Applegate, B., Zhang, Q., et al. (1995). Four-year longitudinal study of conduct disorders: Patterns and predictors of persistence. *Journal of Abnormal Psychology, 104,* 93–93.

Lahey, B. B., Miller, T. L., Gordon, R. A., & Riley, A. (1999). Developmental epidemiology of the disruptive behavior disorders. In H. Quay & A. Hogan (Eds.), *Handbook of the disruptive behavior disorders* (pp. 23–48). New York: Plenum Press.

Lilienfeld, S. O., & Waldman, I. D. (1990). The relation between childhood attention-deficit hyperactivity disorder and adult antisocial behavior reexamined: The problem of heterogeneity. *Clinical Psychology Review, 10,* 699–725.

Little, T. D., Jones, S. M., Henrich, C. C., & Hawley, P. H. (2003). Disentangling the "whys" from the "whats" of aggressive behavior. *International Journal of Behavioral Development, 27,* 122–133.

Lochman, J. E. (1992). Cognitive-behavior intervention with aggressive boys: Three-year follow-up and preventive effects. *Journal of Consulting and Clinical Psychology, 60,* 426–432.

Loeber, R. (1982). The stability of antisocial and delinquent child behavior: A review. *Child Development, 53,* 1431–1446.

Loeber, R., Brinthaupt, V. P., & Green, S. M. (1990). Attention deficits, impulsivity, and hyperactivity with or without conduct problems: Relationships to delinquency and unique contextual factors. In R. J. McMahon & R. D. Peters (Eds.), *Behavior dis-*

orders of adolescence: Research, intervention, and policy in clinical and school settings (pp. 39–61). New York: Plenum Press.

Loeber, R., Burke, J. D., Lahey, B. B., Winters, A., & Zera, M. (2000). Oppositional defiant and conduct disorder: A review of the past 10 years, part I. *Journal of the American Academy of Child and Adolescent Psychiatry, 39,* 1468–1482.

Loeber, R., & Farrington, D. P. (2000). Young children who commit crime: Epidemiology, developmental origins, risk factors, early interventions, and policy implications. *Development and Psychopathology, 12,* 737–762.

Loeber, R., Green, S. M., Lahey, B. B., Christ, M. A. G., & Frick, P. J. (1992). Developmental sequences in the age of onset of disruptive child behaviors. *Journal of Child and Family Studies, 1,* 21–41.

Loney, B. R. & Frick, P. J. (2003). Structured diagnostic interviewing. In C. R. Reynolds & R. W. Kamphaus (Eds.), *Handbook of educational assessment of children* (2nd ed., pp. 235–247). New York: Guilford Press.

Loney, B. R., Frick, P. J., Clements, C. B., Ellis, M. L., & Kerlin, K. (2003). Callous-unemotional traits, impulsivity, and emotional processing in antisocial adolescents. *Journal of Clinical Child and Adolescent Psychology, 32,* 139–152.

Loney, B. R., Frick, P. J., Ellis, M., & McCoy, M. G. (1998). Intelligence, psychopathy, and antisocial behavior. *Journal of Psychopathology and Behavioral Assessment, 20,* 231–247.

Long, P., Forehand, R., Wierson, M., & Morgan, A. (1994). Does parent training with young noncompliant children have long-term effects? *Behaviour Research and Therapy, 32,* 101–107.

Lyman, R. D., & Campbell, N. R. (1996). *Treating children and adolescents in residential and inpatient settings.* Thousand Oaks, CA: Sage.

Lynam, D. R. (1996). The early identification of chronic offenders: Who is the fledgling psychopath? *Psychological Bulletin, 120,* 209–234.

Lynam, D. R., Caspi, A., Moffitt, T. E., Wikstrom, P. O., Loeber, R., & Novak, S. P. (2000). The interaction between impulsivity and neighborhood context on offending: The effects of impulsivity are stronger in poorer neighborhoods. *Journal of Abnormal Psychology, 109,* 563–574.

Marshall, L., & Cooke, D. J. (1999). The childhood experiences of psychopaths: A retrospective study of familial and societal factors. *Journal of Personality Disorders, 13,* 211–225.

Maughan, B., Pickles, A., Hagell, A., Rutter, M., & Yule, W. (1996). Reading problems and antisocial behaviour: Developmental trends in comorbidity. *Journal of Child Psychology and Psychiatry and Allied Disciplines, 37,* 408–415.

McMahon, R. J., & Frick, P. J. (in press). Evidence-based assessment of conduct problems in children and adolescents. *Journal Clinical Child and Adolescent Psychology.*

McNeil, C. B., Eyberg, S., Eisenstadt, T. H., Newcomb, K., & Funderburk, B. W. (1991). Parent-child interaction therapy with behavior problem children: Generalization of treatment effects to the school setting. *Journal of Clinical Child Psychology, 20,* 140–151.

Miller, G. E., & Prinz, R. J. (1990). Enhancement of social learning family interventions for childhood conduct disorder. *Psychological Bulletin, 108,* 291–307.

Mitchell, S., & Rosa, P. (1981). Boyhood behavior problems as precursors of criminality: A fifteen year follow-up study. *Journal of Child Psychology and Psychiatry, 22,* 19–33.

Moffitt, T. E. (1993). Adolescence-limited and life-course persistent antisocial behavior: A developmental taxonomy. *Psychological Review, 100,* 674–701.

Moffitt, T. E. (2003). Life-course persistent and adolescence-limited antisocial behavior: A 10-year research review and research agenda. In B. B. Lahey, T. E. Moffitt, & A. Caspi (Eds.), *Causes of conduct disorder and juvenile delinquency* (pp. 49–75). New York: Guilford Press.

Moffitt, T. E., & Caspi, A. (2001). Childhood predictors differentiate life-course persistent and adolescence-limited antisocial pathways among males and females. *Development and Psychopathology,* 355–375.

Moffitt, T. E., Caspi, A., Dickson, N., Silva, P., & Stanton, W. (1996). Childhood-onset versus adolescent-onset antisocial conduct problems in males: Natural history from ages 3 to 18 years. *Development and Psychopathology, 8,* 399–424.

Moffitt, T. E., Caspi, A., Harrington, H., & Milne, B. J. (2002). Males on the life-course-persistent and adolescence-limited antisocial pathways: Follow-up at age 26 years. *Development and Psychopathology, 14,* 179–207.

Newman, J. P., & Lorenz, A. R. (2003). Response modulation and emotion processing: Implications for psychopathy and other dysregulatory psychopathology. In R. J. Davidson, K. Scherer, & H. H. Goldsmith (Eds.), *Handbook of affective sciences* (pp. 1043–1067). London: Oxford University Press.

Offord, D. R., Boyle, M. H., Szatmari, P., Rae-Grant, N. I., Links, P. S., Cadman, D. T., et al. (1987). Ontario Child Health Study: II. Six-month prevalence of disorder and rates of service utilization. *Archives of General Psychiatry, 44,* 832–836.

Oxford, M., Cavell, T. A., & Hughes, J. N. (2003). Callous-unemotional traits moderate the relation between ineffective parenting and child externalizing problems: A partial replication and extension. *Journal of Clinical Child and Adolescent Psychology, 32,* 577–585.

Pardini, D. A., Lochman, J. E., & Frick, P. J. (2003). Callous/unemotional traits and social cognitive processes in adjudicated youth. *Journal of the American Academy of Child and Adolescent Psychiatry, 42,* 364–371.

Parker, J. G., & Asher, S. R. (1987). Peer relations and later social adjustment. *Psychological Bulletin, 102,* 357–389.

Patrick, C. J. (2001). Emotional processes in psychopathy. In A. Raine & J. Sanmartin (Eds.), *Violence and psychopathy* (pp. 57–77). New York: Kluwer.

Patterson, G. R. (1986). Performance models for antisocial boys. *American Psychologist, 41,* 432–444.

Patterson, G. R., Capaldi, D. M., & Bank, L. (1991). An early starter model for predicting delinquency. In D. J. Pepler & K. H. Rubin (Eds.), *The development and treatment of childhood aggression* (pp. 139–168). Hillsdale, NJ: Erlbaum.

Patterson, G. R., Reid, J. B., & Dishion, T. J. (1992). *Antisocial boys.* Eugene, OR: Castilia.

Peeples, F., & Loeber, R. (1994). Do individual factors and neighborhood context explain ethnic differences in juvenile delinquency? *Journal of Quantitative Criminology, 10,* 141–158.

Pelham, W. E., Carlson, C., Sams, S. E., Vallan, G., Dixon, M. J., & Hoza, B. (1993). Separate and combined effects of methylphenidate and behavior modification on boys with attention deficit-hyperactivity disorder in the classroom. *Journal of Consulting and Clinical Psychology, 61,* 506–515.

Poulin, F., & Boivin, M. (2000). Reactive and proactive aggression: Evidence of a two-factor model. *Psychological Assessment, 12,* 115–122.

Price, J. M., & Dodge, K. A. (1989). Reactive and proactive aggression in childhood: Relations to peer status and social context dimensions. *Journal of Abnormal Child Psychology, 17,* 455–471.

Prinstein, M. J., Boergers, J., & Vernberg, E. M. (2001). Overt and relational aggression in adolescents: Social-psychological adjustment of aggressors and victims. *Journal of Clinical Child Psychology, 30,* 479–491.

Raine, A. (2002). Biosocial studies of antisocial and violent behavior in children and adults: A review. *Journal of Abnormal Child Psychology, 30,* 311–326.

Richters, J. E. (1997). The Hubble hypothesis and the developmentalist's dilemma. *Development and Psychopathology, 9,* 193–230.

Robins, L. N. (1966). *Deviant children grown up.* Baltimore, MD: Williams and Wilkins.

Robins, L. N., Tipp, J., & Pryzbeck, T. (1991). Antisocial personality. In L. N. Robins & D. A. Regier (Eds.), *Psychiatric disorders in America* (pp. 224–271). New York: Free Press.

Ross, A. O. (1981). *Child behavior therapy: Principles, procedures, and empirical basis.* New York: Wiley.

Rothbart, M. K., & Bates, J. E. (1998). Temperament. In W. Damon (Ed.), *Handbook of child psychology: Vol. 3. Social, emotional, and personality development* (pp. 105–176). New York: Wiley.

Rubin, K. H., Bukowski, W., & Parker, J. G. (1998). Peer interactions, relationships, and groups. In W. Damon (Ed.), *Handbook of child psychology: Vol. 3. Social, emotional, and personality development* (pp. 619–700). New York: Wiley.

Russo, M. F., & Beidel, D. C. (1994). Comorbidity of childhood anxiety and externalizing disorders: Prevalence, associated characteristics, and validation issues. *Clinical Psychology Review, 14,* 199–221.

Sampson, R. J., & Laub, J. H. (1994). Urban poverty and the family context of delinquency: A new look at structure and process in a classic study. *Child Development, 65,* 523–540.

Schwartz, D., Dodge, K. A., Coie, J. D., Hubbard, J. A., Cillessen, A. H. N., Lemerise, E. A., et al. (1998). Social-cognitive and behavioral correlates of aggression and victimization in boys' play groups. *Journal of Abnormal Child Psychology, 26,* 431–440.

Shaffer, D., Fisher, P., Dulcan, M., & Davies, M. (1996). The NIMH Diagnostic Interview Schedule for Children Version 2.3 (DISC-2.3): Description, acceptability, prevalence rates, and performance in the MECA study. *Journal of the American Academy of Child and Adolescent Psychiatry, 35,* 865–877.

Shields, A., & Cicchetti, D. (1998). Reactive aggression among maltreated children: The contributions of attention and emotion dysregulation. *Journal of Clinical Child Psychology, 27,* 381–395.

Silverthorn, P., & Frick, P. J. (1999). Developmental pathways to antisocial behavior: The delayed-onset pathway in girls. *Development and Psychopathology, 11,* 101–126.

Silverthorn, P., Frick, P. J., & Reynolds, R. (2001). Timing of onset and correlates of severe conduct problems in adjudicated girls and boys. *Journal of Psychopathology and Behavioral Assessment, 23,* 171–181.

Stevens, D., Charman, T., & Blair, R. J. R. (2001). Recognition of emotion in facial expressions and vocal tones in children with psychopathic tendencies. *Journal of Genetic Psychology, 16,* 201–211.

Strassberg, Z., Dodge, K. A., Pettit, G. S., & Bates, J. E. (1994). Spanking in the home and children's subsequent aggression toward kindergarten peers. *Development and Psychopathology, 6,* 445–461.

Swanson, J. M., Kraemer, H. C., & Hinshaw, S. P. (2001). Clinical relevance of the primary findings of the MTA: Success rates based on severity of ADHD and ODD symptoms at the end of treatment. *Journal of the American Academy of Child and Adolescent Psychiatry, 40,* 168–179.

Thornberry, T. P., & Krohn, M. D. (1987). The development of delinquency: An interactional perspective. In S. O White (Ed.), *Handbook of youth and justice* (pp. 289–305). Dordrecht, The Netherlands: Kluwer.

Toupin, J., Mercier, H., Dery, M., Cote, G., & Hodgins, S. (1995). Validity of the PCL-R for adolescents. *Issues in Criminological and Legal Psychology, 24,* 143–145.

Viding, E., Blair, R. J. R., Moffitt, T. E., & Plomin, R. (2003). *Psychopathic syndrome indexes strong genetic risk for antisocial behaviour in 7-year-olds.* Paper presented at the conference "Developmental and Neuroscience Perspectives on Psychopathy," sponsored by the Department of Psychology, University of Wisconsin–Madison, Madison, WI.

Vitaro, F., Brendgen, M., Pagani, L., Tremblay, R. E., & McDuff, P. (1999). Disruptive behavior, peer association, and conduct disorder: Testing the developmental links through early intervention. *Development and Psychopathology, 11,* 287–304.

Walters, G. D. (2003). Predicting criminal justice outcomes with the Psychopathy Checklist and Lifestyle Criminality Screening Form: A meta-analytic comparison. *Behavioral Sciences and the Law, 21,* 89–102.

Waschbusch, D. A. (2002). A meta-analytic examination of comorbid hyperactive-impulsive-attention problems and conduct problems. *Psychological Bulletin, 128,* 118–150.

Wootton, J. M., Frick, P. J., Shelton, K. K., & Silverthorn, P. (1997). Ineffective parenting and childhood conduct problems: The moderating role of callous-unemotional traits. *Journal of Consulting and Clinical Psychology, 65,* 301–308.

Zigler, E., Taussig, C., & Black, K. (1992). Early childhood intervention: A promising preventative for juvenile delinquency. *American Psychologist, 47,* 997–1006.

Zoccolillo, M. (1993). Gender and the development of conduct disorder. *Development and Psychopathology, 5,* 65–78.

CHAPTER 19

Attention-Deficit/Hyperactivity Disorder

JACK STEVENS AND JEANNE WARD-ESTES

DESCRIPTION OF THE DISORDER AND CLINICAL PICTURE

Symptoms of attention-deficit/hyperactivity disorder (ADHD) fall into two domains: inattention and hyperactivity/impulsivity. For a diagnosis of ADHD, combined type, the *DSM-IV* (APA, 1994) stipulates that at least six of nine symptoms of inattention and at least six of nine symptoms of hyperactivity/impulsivity be present for a minimum of 6 months. ADHD, predominantly inattentive type, and ADHD, predominantly hyperactive-impulsive type, require that at least six symptoms be present in one domain but not the other for a minimum of 6 months. In addition, all three ADHD subtypes require that symptoms cause interpersonal or academic/occupational impairment in at least two settings with an age of onset prior to 7 years.

Although all three subtypes fall under the rubric of ADHD, the predominantly inattentive type may be considered distinct from the other two subtypes. Children in all three subtypes often benefit from psychostimulant medication; however, their clinical correlates differ. Children with predominantly inattentive type are at heightened risk for academic underachievement and internalizing disorders, whereas children with the other two subtypes are at heightened risk for other disruptive behavior disorders, namely oppositional defiant disorder (ODD) and conduct disorder (CD).

Problems with inattention manifest themselves in different ways for children with ADHD. These children often have great difficulty sustaining their attention on relevant stimuli over time, as opposed to filtering out irrelevant stimuli. They make careless mistakes on their homework, appear disorganized, and exhibit difficulties following multistep instructions.

Problems with hyperactivity are apparent for most but not all children with ADHD. Examples of hyperactivity include excessive talking and excessive movement of the hands and feet. Due to the overt nature of motor overactivity as well as the developmental inappropriateness of certain inattention symptoms for preschoolers (e.g., careless mistakes in homework, difficulty organizing oneself), the symptoms of hyperactivity are often the first recognized signs of ADHD in children.

Despite the name of the disorder, some experts consider impulsivity to be the central trait of ADHD, with inattention and hyperactivity being secondary (Barkley, 1997; Quay, 1997). Only 3 of the 18 ADHD symptoms reflect impulsivity (i.e., often having difficulty waiting one's turn, often interrupting, often blurting out answers). Nevertheless, deficits in inhibitory control are perhaps the most consistently reported findings in studies using diverse experimental tasks.

Symptom variability is a key feature for the disorder. At times, children with ADHD look much like normally developing children, whereas at other times their behavior stands out. The context of given situations often influences whether ADHD behaviors will be displayed. Children with ADHD perform worse under more familiar and monotonous circumstances (e.g., completing school assignments and chores; Breen & Altepeter, 1990), and they may perform better under more novel and stimulating circumstances (e.g., playing video games). This variation in performance across situations is an important caveat in studying the personality of individuals with the disorder, in that the term *personality* connotes a high level of cross-situational consistency.

Comorbidity is also a key feature of ADHD. Though a small portion of children with ADHD have no co-occurring diagnosis, most children meet criteria for at least one other disorder. To begin with, Green, Wong, Atkins, Taylor, and Feinleib (1999) reviewed several dozen studies on diagnostic patterns for children with ADHD and concluded that they met criteria for ODD or CD. However, difficulties in attributing causes for noncompliance may explain some of the covariation among these disorders. It may be a challenge to determine if a child's failure to adhere to an instruction is due to attentional or processing problems (as in ADHD) or willful defiance (as in ODD).

Approximately one in four children with ADHD meet criteria for anxiety, depression, or both (Biederman, Newcorn,

& Sprich, 1991). Again, difficulty in determining the root of attention problems may explain this greater-than-chance co-occurrence, because such behaviors are nonspecific symptoms of numerous childhood psychiatric disorders. Alternatively, academic and interpersonal difficulties associated with ADHD may lead to secondary feelings of worry and low self-esteem that characterize internalizing disorders.

Finally, a small portion of children with ADHD meet criteria for a specific disability in reading or mathematics. The temporal order of these comorbid conditions can be challenging to identify. Symptoms of ADHD can interfere with the acquisition of basic academic skills. Alternatively, children who fail to master reading and mathematics may become frustrated or disheartened by their academic problems and switch their attention away from these endeavors.

Parents, teachers, and physicians sometimes dismiss ADHD symptoms because nearly all normally developing children are expected to periodically exhibit certain degrees of inattention and motor activity. In contrast, other problem behaviors (e.g., hallucinations, sexually acting out) are somewhat rare for children and may be taken seriously as signs of psychopathology. The frequency and severity of inattention, hyperactivity, and impulsivity as well as the impairment caused by these symptoms are what distinguish ADHD from non-ADHD groups. Children with ADHD have frequent academic problems (e.g., low grades across subjects) and social problems (e.g., difficulties making friends).

PERSONALITY DEVELOPMENT AND PSYCHOPATHOLOGY

Knowledge of the premorbid personality features of children with ADHD is limited for two major reasons. First, methodological challenges have undoubtedly dissuaded researchers from this line of inquiry. Because it is not uncommon for a large percentage of infants and preschoolers to demonstrate hyperactivity and inattention to varying degrees, it is very difficult to predict which particular children will ultimately meet criteria for ADHD someday. Therefore, to achieve an adequate sample of elementary school children with ADHD, investigators face the daunting task of following longitudinally several hundred infants and preschoolers for at least a few years.

Second, premorbid personality characteristics and temperament have not been considered the primary etiological factors for ADHD. Instead, biological and genetic factors have received greater attention in the origins of the disorder. Even the few psychosocial studies of ADHD in preschoolers have focused not on personality per se but rather on more specific behaviors that reflect certain personality characteristics.

DuPaul, McGoey, Eckert, and VanBrakle (2001) found that both parents and teachers of preschoolers with ADHD rated these children as more withdrawn and less cooperative and interactive relative to normally developing children. These behaviors suggest that these children are prone to low levels of extraversion. In addition, DeWolfe, Byrne, and Bawden (2000) found that parents of preschool-age children with ADHD reported that their children were more defiant, less adaptable, and more demanding compared to children in the control group, indicating that children with ADHD are prone to low levels of agreeableness. Furthermore, behavioral disinhibition has been found in preschool children with ADHD (Sonuga-Barke, Dalen, Daley, & Remington, 2002), suggesting that low amounts of conscientiousness may be early personality features of this population.

Despite the aforementioned methodological and etiological challenges, a few researchers have explored the predictive utility of temperament measures on the manifestation of subsequent ADHD behaviors. Caspi, Henry, McGee, Moffitt, and Silva (1995) examined the relationship between preschool temperament measures and later parent and teacher ratings of ADHD symptoms. They found that emotional dysregulation, reflecting "emotional lability, restlessness, short attention span, and negativism" (p. 59) at ages 3 and 5 predicted hyperactivity and inattention at ages 9 and 11. It must be stressed, however, that these temperament characteristics explained only 4 percent to 12 percent of the variation in later ADHD behaviors. Other investigators (Bussing et al., 2003; McIntosh & Cole-Love, 1996) have also identified a relationship between ADHD symptoms and earlier elevated activity levels and attention problems (e.g., poor task orientation, high distractibility). Furthermore, severe infant sleep problems, which reflect other aspects of temperament (e.g., difficulty to soothe), have also been linked to ADHD behaviors during the elementary school years (Thunstrom, 2002).

However, these investigators may have underemphasized the importance of the interaction between young children's constitutional makeup and their environments in predicting later ADHD behaviors. Carlson, Jacobvitz, and Sroufe (1995) investigated the role of both children's temperament and maternal characteristics in predicting hyperactivity at ages 6–8. They found that although children's distractibility level predicted later hyperactivity, intrusive and overstimulating parenting during the first few years of life was also a powerful predictor of subsequent hyperactivity. Morrell and Murray (2003) also explored the role of early parenting in the development of ADHD and found a trend suggesting an interaction between delayed reaching on the A-not-B task and coercive parenting during infancy and subsequent hyperactivity at ages 5 and 8. In summary, various investigators have suggested that ineffective parenting in combination with certain temperament features (e.g., distractibility) may lead to ADHD.

Other environmental factors besides parenting may interact with temperament to produce ADHD behaviors. Sonuga-Barke, Daley, and Thompson (2002) reported that mothers with high levels of ADHD symptoms themselves had preschool children with ADHD who benefited less from a parent training intervention. This finding suggested that maternal ADHD may interact with early-onset ADHD symptoms in children to produce greater symptomatology later in life, possibly because mothers with high levels of ADHD symptoms are at risk for exhibiting the maladaptive parenting behaviors previously described.

In addition, Biederman et al. (1995) found more psychopathology and lower socioeconomic status in mothers of children with ADHD versus normally developing children. Unfortunately, this study did not differentiate between children with only ADHD and those with ADHD and conduct problems. This distinction is vital, given that conduct problems and oppositional behavior have been repeatedly linked to environmental risk factors. When Shaw, Owens, Giovannelli, and Winslow (2001) later examined risk factors in children with only ADHD, they found that parents of these children did not have more psychopathology or rejecting parenting styles relative to parents of normally developing children. However, parents of children with both ADHD and conduct problems had more environmental risk factors than any other groups of parents, including parents of children with only conduct problems. Similarly, Schachar and Tannock (1995) found that children with only CD or CD plus ADHD had more socioeconomic adversity than did children with only ADHD or children in the control group. Therefore, environment may play a subsequent role in later functioning, particularly for those children with comorbid ADHD and ODD or CD.

EPIDEMIOLOGY

Epidemiological studies of ADHD have suggested that the disorder has become more prevalent over the past 15 years. Multiple teams of investigators (e.g., Robison, Skaer, Sclar, & Galin, 2002; Swanson, Lerner, & Williams, 1995) have reported that rates of ADHD have increased two- to threefold since 1990. Greater recognition of the disorder (e.g., wider use of screening measures) and better treatment options (e.g., longer-acting stimulant medications) may explain this increase in prevalence rates.

However, much less consistency exists in the literature regarding precisely what these prevalence rates actually are. Although the American Psychiatric Association (1994) has indicated that 3 percent to 5 percent of elementary school children have the disorder, previous reviews of the epidemiology of ADHD have suggested somewhat higher rates of 4 percent to 12 percent (e.g., Brown et al., 2001). Methodological factors help explain the wide estimates in prevalence rates for the disorder. Studies that have relied on rating scale data have reported consistently higher rates of ADHD (11 percent to 24 percent) than studies requiring a psychiatric diagnosis (5 percent to 9 percent; Swanson et al., 1998).

Nolan, Gadow, and Sprafkin (2001) found that almost 16 percent of children ages 3–18 had clinically significant levels of ADHD based on teacher questionnaire data alone. However, these researchers acknowledged that teachers might have mistaken other psychiatric symptoms for ADHD, leading to spuriously high levels of the disorder. Stevens, Quittner, and Abikoff (1998) found support for this contention by demonstrating that children with solely oppositional behavior are often erroneously rated by teachers as having substantial ADHD symptomatology. In essence, ADHD may be overdetected by rating scales caused by difficulties in differentiating ADHD from other common childhood behavioral and learning problems.

Other factors may explain discrepancies between studies using rating scale versus interview data. To begin with, rating scales do not require that symptoms be present before age 7, whereas this age-of-onset criterion is a feature of a psychiatric diagnosis. Cuffe et al. (2001) reported that this age-of-onset criterion eliminated many children with ADHD symptoms from being formally diagnosed with the disorder. In addition, rating scales do not require that symptoms cause significant impairment, whereas psychiatric diagnoses do. This factor has prompted leading epidemiologists such as Roberts, Attkisson, and Rosenblatt (1998) to call for giving impairment greater attention in estimating the frequency of ADHD in the general population.

ETIOLOGY

In her review of the genetic research on ADHD, Tannock (1998) noted that investigators analyzing differences in the concordance rates between monozygotic twins and dizygotic twins have suggested that approximately 80 percent of the variation in ADHD behaviors appears to be caused by genetic factors. This heritability estimate makes ADHD one of the most genetically linked of psychiatric disorders. Kuntsi and Stevenson (2000) reviewed adoption studies and concluded that greater similarity exists between children with ADHD and their biological versus adoptive parents, again implicating a strong genetic basis for the disorder. Though no gene, sets of genes, or chromosomes have been definitely associated with the disorder, specific genes linked to the transport and postsynaptic activities of dopamine have been frequently implicated (Attention-Deficit/Hyperactivity Disorder Molecular Genetics Network, 2002).

In addition to genetic research, neuroimaging studies have played a large role in highlighting the potential etiology of ADHD. Although magnetic resonance imaging (MRI) and positron-emission tomography (PET) scans are generally not used for diagnosis in individual children, these brain imaging techniques have allowed scientists during the past 15 years to describe more fully the biological basis for groups of affected individuals. Despite the apparent objectivity of these techniques, discrepancies in results exist across studies. Because these technologies are expensive to use and appear intimidating for children and their families, many studies are hampered by small sample sizes, which in turn may influence the reliability of the findings.

Nevertheless, some fairly consistent findings have emerged. The prefrontal and striatal areas of the brain have been repeatedly linked to ADHD (Frank & Pavlakis, 2001; Hale, Hariri, & McCracken, 2000). Given that these portions of the brain play a major role in self-control, planning, and organization, it is not surprising that reduced activity in these portions of the brain are associated with the symptoms of ADHD. Deficits in self-control manifest themselves as impulsivity, which many consider to be the cardinal feature of the disorder (Barkley, 1997; Quay, 1997). Not only do children with ADHD exhibit problems with inhibitory control on different neuropsychological tasks, but also impulsivity may be more severe in this population than in other clinical populations, such as ODD and CD (Halperin et al., 1995).

Besides genetic and neuropsychological influences, three other etiological factors have recently received great attention. First, prenatal maternal substance use has been linked to ADHD. Mick, Biederman, Faraone, Sayer, and Kleinman (2002) studied the prenatal effects of nicotine and alcohol use in children subsequently diagnosed with ADHD. Relative to children without the disorder, those with ADHD were more than two times as likely to have nicotine and alcohol exposure in utero, even after accounting for confounding variables such as maternal psychopathology.

Second, many experts have suggested that sleep difficulties are causal factors in a substantial portion of ADHD cases. For example, Chervin et al. (2002) reported elevated rates of diurnal sleepiness and snoring, a sign of sleep-related disorders such as obstructive sleep apnea, in children displaying ADHD symptoms. In fact, Chervin, Dillon, Bassetti, Ganoczy, and Pituch (1997) speculated that as much as one quarter of children with ADHD could have their symptomatology dramatically decreased if sleep problems were effectively treated. Moreover, multiple authors have noted that removing the tonsils and adenoids preceded significant improvements in attention (Ali, Pitson, & Stradling, 1996; Goldstein, Post, Rosenfeld, & Campbell, 2000), which further suggests a link between sleep problems and this disorder.

Third, Christakis, Zimmerman, DiGiuseppe, and McCarty (2004) recently examined the relationship between TV viewing and ADHD symptoms. They found a positive symptomatic relationship between TV viewing at ages 1 and 3 and inattention at age 7. Although these researchers controlled for multiple confounds, one uncontrolled variable was parental ADHD symptomatology. Therefore, it cannot be determined whether this environmental etiological factor is linked to ADHD above and beyond genetic influences for the disorder.

COURSE, COMPLICATIONS, AND PROGNOSIS

In his seminal review of the developmental trajectory of ADHD symptoms, Willoughby (2003) distinguished between two types of studies: developmental course studies, which highlight the consistency of ADHD symptoms over time, and developmental outcome studies, which highlight the long-term functional outcomes for children with the disorder. Developmental course studies (e.g., Biederman, Mick, & Faraone, 2000) are fairly uniform in noting that parent-report symptoms of hyperactivity and impulsivity remit more quickly as children with ADHD age relative to symptoms of inattention. However, although these more overt symptoms of ADHD may become less noticeable over time, other related but more subtle symptoms may emerge, such as low levels of alertness (Whalen, Jamner, Henker, Delfino, & Lozano, 2002) and feelings of restlessness. Furthermore, the symptoms of hyperactivity and impulsivity do not disappear entirely, in that adolescents with ADHD have exhibited more fidgeting and disinhibition during structured academic activities than do normally developing adolescents (Fischer, Barkley, Edelbrock, & Smallish, 1990).

Researchers have studied not only the maintenance of specific clusters of ADHD symptoms but also the persistence of the diagnosis as a whole from childhood to adolescence. Approximately half of children with ADHD continue to meet the criteria for the disorder once they reach the early teenage years (Steinhausen, Drechsler, Foldenyi, Imhof, & Brandeis, 2003). The reason for this discontinuity for half of children with ADHD is not entirely clear. Perhaps a certain portion of children with ADHD outgrow or compensate for the disorder by the time they reach adolescence. Alternatively, the diagnostic criteria for the disorder, particularly the hyperactive-impulsive subtype, appear most developmentally appropriate for elementary school–age children. Many of the ADHD hyperactive-impulsive symptoms (e.g., the child often cannot sit still, often runs about or climbs excessively, often cannot engage in leisure activities quietly) are unlikely to be displayed by an adolescent considered to be overly active. A final plausible explanation is that young adults with ADHD may underreport their symptoms relative to the perspectives of their parents (Barkley, Fischer, Smallish, & Fletcher, 2002), indicating that longitudinal studies that rely solely on data from probands may overestimate rates of discontinuity.

In terms of developmental outcome studies, adolescents who exhibited ADHD during childhood have substantial difficulties relative to normally developing adolescents. Just like children with ADHD, adolescents with ADHD have elevated levels of CD, depression, and anxiety (Faraone, Biederman, & Monuteaux, 2002). Poor academic performance and social maladjustment were more common in those adolescents with versus without an earlier history of ADHD (Howell, Huessy, & Hassuk, 1985). Thus, comorbidity and impairments associated with ADHD appear consistent over time.

In her literature review of adult outcomes for children with ADHD, Hechtman (1999) identified three key groups. Group 1 consisted of 30 percent of children with ADHD who had no major impairment during the adult years. Group 2 consisted of 50 percent to 60 percent of children with ADHD who had substantial difficulties during the adult years, such as frequent job changing and emotional problems. Group 3 consisted of 10 percent to 15 percent of children with ADHD who exhibited either severe depression or antisocial personality features during the adult years. Although predicting which children with ADHD will fall into Groups 2 and 3 is not fully possible, Hechtman (1999) concluded that low intelligence, comorbidity (especially CD), low socioeconomic status, and parental psychopathology were all important predictors of future impairment. Greater initial severity of ADHD symptoms also predicts the persistence of the disorder into adolescence (Steinhausen et al., 2003).

ASSESSMENT AND DIAGNOSIS

Interviews, ratings scales, psychological tests, and clinical observation are among the four most common assessment methods for determining if diagnosis criteria for ADHD are met. Each of these methods will be discussed in turn.

Diagnostic interviews are frequently administered to parents, rather than children, in cases of suspected ADHD because children are often poor informants of these symptoms. Children with ADHD may fail to comprehend specific items and often underreport symptoms and impairment related to the disorder. Structured interviews, such as the Diagnostic Interview Schedule for Children (Shaffer, Fisher, Lucas, Dulcan, & Schwab-Stone, 2000), have been shown in numerous research projects to have excellent psychometric features. Their structured nature has been shown to increase their reliability over unstructured interviews. Despite their advantages, structured interviews have two noteworthy limitations: their extensive administration time and their lack of well-established norms (Reitman, Hummel, Franz, & Gross, 1998). The first limitation in particular may be a key reason that they are not used more frequently in routine practice settings.

Parents and teachers frequently complete standardized rating scales for ADHD evaluations. Examples of such questionnaires include the Conners' Rating Scale—Revised (Conners, 1997) and the Vanderbilt Assessment Scales (Wolraich et al., 2003). Their short administration time and often excellent normative bases for children of different ages and genders often make them an invaluable technique for determining whether children's symptoms are developmentally inconsistent. Though there are advantages and disadvantages to particular questionnaires, the Conners' Rating Scales—Revised appear to have the most normative and best psychometric data relative to other measures (see Collett, Ohan, & Myers, 2003, for a more complete discussion.)

Three limitations of these questionnaires should be noted. First, children are not considered to be valid providers of rating scale data. Even adolescents, who are presumed to have more insight into their difficulties and better item comprehension compared to elementary school–age children, are often poor informants on self-report questionnaires (Smith, Pelham, Gnagy, Molina, & Evans, 2000).

Second, rater biases (e.g., presence of adult depression) may produce inaccuracies in these data. For example, Stevens et al. (1998) demonstrated that teachers observing a videotaped child displaying only oppositional behavior often erroneously rated the child as having substantial hyperactivity and inattentiveness, even though those problem behaviors were not present. In this case, the authors speculated that oppositional behaviors (e.g., arguing, temper tantrums, making fun of others) are particularly aversive to teachers and may cause a negative halo effect in which teachers have unreasonably harsh perceptions of children with ODD.

Third, although parent and teacher questionnaires appear to be an ideal way of establishing the pervasiveness of symptoms, often only one of the two informants reports clinically significant levels of ADHD symptoms. This requires the diagnostician to consider various explanations for these inconsistent results (e.g., different situational requirements, different developmental expectations for the child, biases leading to underreporting or overreporting by one informant). Though a widely acceptable algorithm for handling inconsistent questionnaire data does not exist, Mannuzza, Klein, and Moulton (2002) stressed that teachers may be more valid informants of ADHD symptoms. They found that children with significant ADHD according to teachers but not parents had similar problems as adults in comparison to children with significant ADHD according to both informants. However, children with significant ADHD according to parents but not teachers had more benign adult outcomes.

Due to the subjectivity of interview and rating scale data, it is not surprising that extensive research has been conducted on neuropsychological tests, which in theory could be more objective measures of inattention, hyperactivity, and impulsivity. Barkley (1998) reviewed the literature on a wide variety of neuropsychological tests (e.g., Trails, Wisconsin Card Sort) and found that nearly all of them had poor sensitivity and specificity for making an ADHD diagnosis. Even when used in combination, these tasks tend to have poor diagnostic utility (Doyle, Biederman, Seidman, Weber, & Faraone, 2000). However, Barkley (1998) concluded that the test with the most, albeit limited, utility for ADHD evaluation was the continuous performance test. For example, Nichols and Waschbusch (2004) concluded that this test is often sensitive to medication effects.

Despite the apparent objectivity of the continuous performance test, two limitations should be highlighted. First, performance on this test is often not indicative of behavior in more familiar, real-world settings (Barkley, 1991). Second, the continuous performance test may have poor discriminant validity. For instance, McGee, Clark, and Symons (2000) found that the Conners' Continuous Performance Test often produced false positives for children with reading problems but not ADHD, presumably because this particular test requires efficient processing of alphanumeric stimuli, a weakness for children with learning disabilities. Versions of the continuous performance test that do not use alphanumeric stimuli could theoretically be less prone to false positives. In summary, greater attention to both developing and selecting psychological tests is warranted for purposes of diagnosing ADHD.

Finally, clinical observation has often played a role in diagnosing this disorder. Although there are cases in which children with ADHD are "bouncing off the walls" in the offices of physicians or psychologists, frequently these children behave normally due to the novelty of the situation and the one-on-one attention. Therefore, clinicians are often urged to give greater weight to teachers and parents, who observe children in everyday settings, than to their own clinical observations. However, clinical observations may be valid for purposes of assessing ADHD symptoms under limited circumstances, such as observing off-task behaviors during the administration of psychological tests (Wilcutt, Hartung, Lahey, Loney, & Pelham, 1999).

IMPACT ON ENVIRONMENT

Family

The impact of ADHD symptoms has been studied most extensively on parental (particularly maternal) well-being. Podolski and Nigg (2001) found that mothers of children with ADHD report more parenting stress compared to mothers of normally developing children. These researchers also found a similar but nonsignificant trend for fathers of children with ADHD relative to fathers of control group children. Harrison and Sofronoff (2002) similarly reported that more severe ADHD behaviors were associated with greater maternal stress even after controlling for confounding variables such as the child's gender and age.

However, these studies are cross-sectional and corelational in nature, thereby precluding the identification of the temporal ordering and possible causation of an ADHD-parenting stress association (McCleary, 2002). Moreover, maternal cognitions appear to play a mediating role in this relationship. Parents of children with ADHD often see these problem behaviors as less controllable and more enduring than do parents of children without ADHD (Johnston & Freeman, 1997). In fact, Harrison and Sofronoff (2002) found that maternal perceptions of the controllability of a child's behavior predicted maternal stress above and beyond the severity of ADHD behaviors. Recent research has shown that stimulant medication, the most empirically supported intervention for ADHD, often leads mothers to view these problem behaviors as more controllable (Johnston et al., 2000), which may in turn reduce parental stress levels.

Aside from parenting stress, other forms of psychological difficulties have been evaluated in families of children with ADHD. First, parents of these children report more depression than do parents of normally developing children (Nigg & Hinshaw, 1998). Again, this finding is cross-sectional in nature, so causation must not be inferred. Nevertheless, maternal depression is an important determinant of ADHD ratings, in that Chi and Hinshaw (2002) reported that maternal depressive symptoms lead to more severe maternal ratings of a child's level of ADHD symptomatology when compared with teacher ratings.

Second, Pelham and Lang (1999) described a series of laboratory studies in which brief parental exposure to a confederate child displaying disruptive versus normal behavior leads to somewhat more alcohol use. This finding held true for parents of children without ADHD as well as parents of children with ADHD. These series of laboratory studies were important, because they suggest some directionality for the association between children's ADHD behaviors and parental alcohol abuse. However, these studies do not eliminate the possibility that parental alcohol problems, either genetically or through the prenatal or postnatal environment, lead to ADHD behaviors.

Third, Johnston and Mash (2001) summarized the literature on marital difficulties in families of children with ADHD. They found inconsistent evidence across studies regarding whether ADHD and marital conflict were related, although they noted that investigators who did report an association always reported a positive one (i.e., ADHD being related to greater marital problems). Fourth, Kendall (1999) used qualitative, uncontrolled data to suggest that siblings of children with ADHD often feel victimized by ADHD probands. However, a closer examination of their responses indicates that the co-occurring ODD behaviors may be producing the negative sibling interactions, as opposed to ADHD per se.

In summary, a rather bleak picture of the impact of ADHD behaviors on parents has been painted. However, three caveats are in order. First, the association between ADHD behaviors and parental psychological difficulties was only modest. Second, a prospective follow-up study of these families (Hechtman, 1996) indicated that family functioning improves as children with ADHD age and particularly when they leave home, suggesting that these family problems are not permanent. Third, Fletcher, Fischer, Barkley, and Smallish (1996) have shown that problematic interactions between adolescents with ADHD and their mothers occur in only a subgroup of adolescents with ADHD.

School

Given the aforementioned academic and behavioral difficulties of individuals with ADHD, the impact of this disorder on the school environment is not surprising. Many children with ADHD repeat grades, require at least part-time special education or tutoring services, and are at heightened risk for suspension and expulsion (Faraone et al., 1993). All of these functional outcomes require extra teacher time and patience as well as additional resources for school districts. In fact, children with ADHD often do not self-report academic problems (Gresham, MacMillan, Bocian, Ward, & Forness, 1998), making remediation very challenging for a group of individuals who often appear unaware of their school difficulties.

The impact of ADHD symptoms on academic functioning is not attributed solely to comorbid conditions. Attention problems may even mediate the association between other forms of psychopathology and academic difficulties (Barriga et al., 2002). In their sample of boys, Faraone et al. (1993) further noted that although comorbidity often predicted educational problems above and beyond only ADHD symptoms, those children with ADHD but without comorbid disorders still had lower IQ scores and school difficulties than did normally developing boys. In his sample of girls, Hinshaw (2002) noted academic deficits in children with ADHD that were not attributed to comorbidity.

Peers

Multiple ADHD behaviors (e.g., distractibility, overly talkativeness, and intrusiveness) could hamper successful peer relations. In terms of boys with ADHD, various researchers have documented that they are at heightened risk for maladaptive peer relations. Hodgens, Cole, and Boldizar (2000) used sociometric ratings of males ages 8–11 and found that relative to boys with ADHD, boys with both the inattentive and combined types of ADHD were less liked by peers. Peers regarded boys with the inattentive type as shy and withdrawn, while boys with the combined type were perceived as aggressive. Girls with ADHD often have substantial peer problems as well. Blachman and Hinshaw (2002) found that throughout the course of their 5-week summer camp, elementary school–age girls with ADHD often had no friend nominations from their peers. In addition to sociometric ratings, observational data suggest that children with ADHD struggle with peer interactions. For example, Hoza, Waschbusch, Pelham, Molina, and Milich (2000) found that children with ADHD were observed to have less social effectiveness, which encompassed behaviors such as friendliness and responsiveness, with a confederate peer.

In summary, family relationships, academic performance, and peer interactions are three domains in which children with ADHD struggle. Given that achieving success in these three areas is regarded as an important developmental challenge for all children, one must conclude that ADHD is associated with substantial, albeit varied, levels of impairment.

IMPLICATIONS FOR FUTURE PERSONALITY DEVELOPMENT

Several cross-sectional studies have documented associations between adult ADHD symptoms and the Big Five personality traits—extraversion, neuroticism, conscientiousness, agreeableness, and openness to experience. In terms of extraversion, Braaten and Rosen (1997) compared adults with high versus low amounts of ADHD symptoms on the Eysenck Personality Questionnaire and found that those in the former group had greater amounts of this personality trait. White (1999) speculated that certain core features of ADHD—sensation seeking and disinhibition—might explain why many individuals with ADHD have larger amounts of extraversion.

However, multiple studies on ADHD and extraversion have failed to find a significant relationship. Ranseen, Campbell, and Baer (1998) found no differences in extraversion between adults with ADHD and clinical controls. Moreover, Nigg and colleagues (2002) utilized six different samples of individuals with ADHD symptoms across the country and found no consistent association between extraversion and ADHD.

The heterogeneity of adults with ADHD may explain these inconsistent findings. Certain adults with ADHD may be prone to extraversion, whereas other adults with ADHD may be considered shy. Canu and Carlson (2003) recently shed some light on this variation across adults with ADHD. They compared the heterosexual skills and experiences of adults with the combined versus inattentive type of ADHD. They found that those in the former group had greater early-onset dating experiences, whereas those in the latter group were more passive and less experienced. In summary, evidence supporting a relationship between ADHD and extraversion appears inconsistent and may reflect the importance of specifying the subtypes of ADHD under examination.

In terms of neuroticism, greater levels of this personality trait have been found in adults with ADHD relative to clinical controls (Ranseen et al., 1998) and normal controls (Braaten & Rosen, 2000). Nigg et al. (2002) reported a mild association between ADHD inattentive symptoms and neuroticism but no relationship between ADHD hyperactive-impulsive symptoms and neuroticism. This finding is consistent with the literature on comorbid internalizing disorders in individuals with ADHD. Those with the inattentive type are at heightened risk for anxiety disorders relative to those with the hyperactive-impulsive and combined subtypes. As with extraversion, neuroticism appears to be a personality trait of only a subgroup of adults with ADHD.

In terms of conscientiousness, Ranseen et al. (1998) reported that adults with ADHD had lower levels of this personality trait relative to clinical controls. Nigg et al. (2002) also found a robust relationship between ADHD inattentive symptoms and decreased amounts of conscientiousness. This finding is not surprising given the negative outcomes of adults with ADHD, including lower amounts of education and occupational prestige (Mannuzza, Klein, Bessler, Malloy, & Hynes, 1997), more alcohol and marijuana abuse and dependence (Murphy, Barkley, & Bush, 2002), and high levels of antisocial personality features (Mannuzza, Klein, Bessler, Malloy, & LaPadula, 1998) relative to normal controls. These outcomes for adults with ADHD all reflect challenges in adhering to societal expectations and delaying gratification, both basic features of conscientious individuals.

Finally, less research has been conducted on the relationship between ADHD symptoms and agreeableness and openness to experience (White, 1999). In terms of agreeableness, hyperactive-impulsive symptoms (Nigg et al., 2002) but not inattentive symptoms (Nigg et al., 2002) or ADHD symptoms as a whole (Ranseen et al. (1998), have been linked to lower levels of this personality trait. Because hyperactive-impulsive symptoms are associated with oppositional and conduct problems, one might expect less altruism and concern for others in this ADHD subgroup. In terms of openness to experience, multiple investigators have reported no relationship between ADHD and this personality trait (Nigg et al., 2002; Ranseen et al., 1998), despite anecdotal reports of higher levels of creativity in selected individuals with ADHD.

The impact of ADHD symptoms has been examined not only on adult personality features but also on adult personality disorders. Using the Millon Clinical Multiaxial Inventory—II, May and Bos (2000) reported on the various personality disorders for four ADHD subgroups. For those adults with just ADHD and no comorbid diagnoses, only one personality pattern was found: mild histrionic features. But adults with both ADHD and ODD had more numerous personality problems, including histrionic, narcissistic, and sadistic features. Moreover, those adults with ADHD, ODD, and internalizing symptoms had the most disturbed personality pattern of all, which included histrionic, narcissistic, sadistic, avoidant, and antisocial tendencies. The fact that histrionic features were found in all ADHD subgroups is not unexpected, given that individuals with histrionic features often seek out stimulating and lively activities. However, the trend of individuals with ADHD who have greater comorbidity to have more problematic personality features does not appear to be an artifact of an overexaggerating style, in that only individuals with valid protocols were included in this study.

The presence of CD symptomatology in individuals with ADHD appears to play a large role in influencing what specific personality features these adults will exhibit. Flory,

Milich, Lynam, Leukefeld, and Clayton (2003) reported that individuals with both ADHD and CD were at greatest risk for marijuana and other illicit drug dependence, whereas those with solely ADHD were at much lower risk. Jensen, Martin, and Cantwell (1997) reviewed the literature on comorbidity in individuals with ADHD and concluded that adult antisocial personality disorder was more likely in children with ADHD and conduct problems than ADHD alone.

TREATMENT IMPLICATIONS

Psychostimulant medication has been the most widely studied and implemented intervention for ADHD. The short-acting formulation of methylphenidate (Ritalin) alone has been studied in over 60 clinical trials with nearly 3,000 children (Schachter, Pham, King, Langford, & Moher, 2001). Given that children with ADHD often have underactive prefrontal areas of the brain and that these medications have been shown to increase blood flow to that anatomical region (Kim, Lee, Cho, & Lee, 2001), the efficacy of stimulant medications should not be surprising.

Approximately three in four children with ADHD show significant short-term reductions in core symptoms on these medications (Greenhill et al., 2001). These success rates may even be higher if children who do not respond to one particular stimulant are tried on a different stimulant. Moreover, stimulant treatment has a frequent secondary benefit of reducing childhood aggression (Connor, Glatt, Lopez, Jackson, & Melloni, 2002). Though treatment response is largely idiosyncratic for specific children, a generally positive dose-outcome relationship has been demonstrated (Greenhill et al., 2001). Longer-acting formulations of stimulant medication, which often require only one time per day dosing as opposed to multiple doses per day for short-acting formulations, have been available for the past few years and appear effective in reducing ADHD symptoms (e.g., Wilens et al., 2003).

Despite all the advantages of stimulant medication, certain caveats must be stressed. First, a substantial minority of patients experience side effects, most notably decreased appetite, insomnia, dizziness, fatigue, and stomachaches (Schachter et al., 2001). Second, research on these medications has been conducted almost entirely on elementary school–age Caucasian males (Biederman, Spencer, & Wilens, 2004). Though more research needs to be conducted on females, members of minority groups, and preschoolers and adolescents with ADHD, differential responsiveness across sociodemographic groups has not been reported. Third, parents, particularly African Americans, frequently have low expectations for these medications despite their success rates (dosReis et al., 2003).

These parents also have many misconceptions about medications, such as their relationship to later substance abuse (Bussing et al., 2003), although current research does not support this belief (Barkley, Fischer, Smallish, & Fletcher, 2003). Fourth, and perhaps most disconcerting, is the dearth of knowledge on the long-term functional outcomes of children prescribed these medicines. As Vitiello (2001) poignantly stated, "It is not known whether the beneficial effects of stimulants extend beyond acute symptomatic relief and affect important outcome variables, such as later psychopathology, educational achievement, antisocial behavior, and social or occupational status. Data from naturalistic follow-up of clinical samples are limited by lack of appropriate controls and self selection biases" (p. 25).

Due to these limitations, other classes of medications have been examined for children with ADHD. Though the newer selective seratonin reuptake inhibitor (SSRI) antidepressant medications have not been useful for reducing ADHD symptoms, the older tricyclic antidepressants have reduced ADHD symptoms in multiple studies (e.g., Popper, 1997). However, due to their lethality in overdose and their potentially serious cardiac side effects, this class of medication is generally considered only for those children who first have been nonresponsive to stimulants. Caballero and Nahata (2003) reviewed the literature on atomoxetine (Strattera), a newly available nonstimulant pharmacological agent for ADHD. This medication reduces ADHD symptoms and has side effects similar to those of stimulants. Parents who are resistant to the idea of their children taking stimulant medication may find atomoxetine a more acceptable treatment option. However, further independent research on this medication is needed, particularly studies that compare newer stimulants and atomoxetine head-to-head.

One nonpharmacological intervention for ADHD has solid scientific support: behavior therapy. Barkley (2002) provided an overview of this treatment alternative. He noted that this psychosocial intervention involves the therapist instructing parents, teachers, or both on specific behavior-modification strategies, including effective commands, differential attention, token economies, time-out, and consequences at home for school misbehavior. It should be noted that cognitive therapy, an alternative psychological intervention, has been found to be much less useful for ADHD, particularly when it involves no explicit behavioral components. For example, DuPaul and Eckert (1997) noted that contingency management, based almost entirely on behavior modification principles, reduced ADHD symptoms more than a blend of cognitive and behavioral strategies in school settings.

Given that stimulants and behavior therapy both have empirical support for reducing ADHD symptoms, the combination of these interventions has been frequently tried. The best known study of the examination of these interventions both in combination and in isolation relative to routine clinical care is the Multimodal Treatment Study of more than 500 children with the combined type of ADHD (Multimodal Treatment Study for ADHD Cooperative Group, 1999). These researchers found that medication was superior to behavior therapy in reducing core ADHD symptoms and that the combination of interventions was no more successful in reducing ADHD symptoms than medication alone. However, these researchers also found that for non-ADHD domains (e.g., oppositional behavior, parent-child interactions), combination treatment was superior to either intervention alone.

Over the last several years, researchers have begun to study treatment options for adults with ADHD. Faraone, Spencer, Aleardi, Pagano, and Biederman (2004) conducted a meta-analysis of methylphenidate studies for adults and concluded that stimulant treatments are just as efficacious for adults as they are for children. This is welcome news for the large portion of affected individuals whose symptoms and impairment do not substantially diminish by adulthood.

REFERENCES

Ali, N. J., Pitson, D., & Stradling, J. R. (1996). Sleep disordered breathing: Effects of adenotonsillectomy on behaviour and psychological functioning. *European Journal of Pediatrics, 155,* 56–62.

American Psychiatric Association. (1994). *Diagnostic and statistical manual of mental disorders* (4th ed.). Washington, DC: Author.

Attention-Deficit/Hyperactivity Disorder Molecular Genetics Network. (2002). Report from the Third International Meeting of the Attention-Deficit/Hyperactivity Disorder Molecular Genetics Network. *American Journal of Medical Genetics, 114,* 272–276.

Barkley, R. A. (1991). The ecological validity of laboratory and analogue assessment methods of ADHD symptoms. *Journal of Abnormal Child Psychology, 19,* 149–178.

Barkley, R. A. (1997). Behavioral inhibition, sustained attention, and executive functions: constructing a unifying theory of ADHD. *Psychological Bulletin, 121,* 65–94.

Barkley, R. A. (1998). Attention-deficit hyperactivity disorder. *Scientific American, 279,* 66–71.

Barkley, R. A. (2002). Psychosocial treatments for attention-deficit/hyperactivity disorder in children. *Journal of Clinical Psychiatry, 63*(Suppl. 12), 36–43.

Barkley, R. A., Fischer, M., Smallish, L., & Fletcher, K. (2002). The persistence of attention-deficit/hyperactivity disorder into young adulthood as a function of reporting source and definition of disorder. *Journal of Abnormal Psychology, 111,* 279–289.

Barkley, R. A., Fischer, M., Smallish, L., & Fletcher, K. (2003). Does the treatment of attention-deficit/hyperactivity disorder with stimulants contribute to drug use/abuse? A 13-year prospective study. *Pediatrics, 111,* 97–109.

Barriga, A. Q., Doran, J. W., Newell, S. R., Morrison, E. M., Barbetti, V., & Robbins, B. D. (2002). Relationships between problem behaviors and academic achievement in adolescents: The unique role of attention problems. *Journal of Emotional and Behavioral Disorders, 10,* 233–240.

Biederman, J., Mick, E., & Faraone, S. V. (2000). Age-dependent decline of symptoms of attention deficit hyperactivity disorder: Impact of remission definition and symptom type. *American Journal of Psychiatry, 157,* 816–818.

Biederman, J., Milberger, S., Faraone, S. V., Kiely, K., Guite, J., Mick, E., et al. (1995). Family-environment risk factors for attention-deficit hyperactivity disorder. A test of Rutter's indicators of adversity. *Archives of General Psychiatry, 52,* 464–470.

Biederman, J., Newcorn, J., & Sprich, S. (1991). Comorbidity of attention deficit hyperactivity disorder with conduct, depressive, anxiety, and other disorders. *American Journal of Psychiatry, 148,* 564–577.

Biederman, J., Spencer, T., & Wilens, T. (2004). Evidence-based pharmacotherapy for attention-deficit hyperactivity disorder. *International Journal of Neuropsychopharmacology, 7,* 77–97.

Blachman, D. R., & Hinshaw, S. P. (2002). Patterns of friendship among girls with and without attention-deficit/hyperactivity disorder. *Journal of Abnormal Child Psychology, 30,* 625–640.

Braaten, E. B., & Rosen, L. A. (1997). Emotional responses in adults with symptoms of attention deficit hyperactivity disorder. *Personality and Individual Differences, 22,* 355–361.

Braaten, E. B., & Rosen, L. A. (2000). Self-regulation of affect in attention deficit-hyperactivity disorder (ADHD) and non-ADHD boys: Differences in empathic responding. *Journal of Consulting and Clinical Psychology, 68,* 313–321.

Breen, M. J., & Altepeter, T. S. (1990). Situational variability in boys and girls identified as ADHD. *Journal of Clinical Psychology, 46,* 486–490.

Brown, R. T., Freeman, W. S., Perrin, J. M., Stein, M. T., Amler, R. W., Feldman, H. M., et al. (2001). Prevalence and assessment of attention-deficit/hyperactivity disorder in primary care settings. *Pediatrics, 107,* E43.

Bussing, R., Gary, F. A., Mason, D. M., Leon, C. E., Sinha, K., & Garvan, C. W. (2003). Child temperament, ADHD, and caregiver strain: Exploring relationships in an epidemiological sample. *Journal of the American Academy of Child and Adolescent Psychiatry, 42,* 184–192.

Caballero, J., & Nahata, M. C. (2003). Atomoxetine hydrochloride for the treatment of attention-deficit/hyperactivity disorder. *Clinical Therapeutics, 25,* 3065–3083.

Canu, W. H., & Carlson, C. L. (2003). Differences in heterosocial behavior and outcomes of ADHD-symptomatic subtypes in a college sample. *Journal of Attention Disorders, 6*, 123–133.

Carlson, E. A., Jacobvitz, D., & Sroufe, L. A. (1995). A developmental investigation of inattentiveness and hyperactivity. *Child Development, 66*, 37–54.

Caspi, A., Henry, B., McGee, R. O., Moffitt, T. E., & Silva, P. A. (1995). Temperamental origins of child and adolescent behavior problems: From age three to age fifteen. *Child Development, 66*, 55–68.

Chervin, R. D., Archbold, K. H., Dillon, J. E., Pituch, K. J., Panahi, P., Dahl, R. E., et al. (2002). Associations between symptoms of inattention, hyperactivity, restless legs, and periodic leg movements. *Sleep, 25*, 213–218.

Chervin, R. D., Dillon, J. E., Bassetti, C., Ganoczy, D. A., & Pituch, K. J. (1997). Symptoms of sleep disorders, inattention, and hyperactivity in children. *Sleep, 20*, 1185–1192.

Chi, T. C., & Hinshaw, S. P. (2002). Mother-child relationships of children with ADHD: The role of maternal depressive symptoms and depression-related distortions. *Journal of Abnormal Child Psychology, 30*, 387–400.

Christakis, D. A., Zimmerman, F. J., DiGiuseppe, D. L., & McCarty, C. A. (2004). Early television exposure and subsequent attentional problems in children. *Pediatrics, 113*, 708–713.

Collett, B. R., Ohan, J. L., & Myers, K. M. (2003). Ten-year review of rating scales. V: Scales assessing attention-deficit/hyperactivity disorder. *Journal of the American Academy of Child and Adolescent Psychiatry, 42*, 1015–1037.

Conners, C. K. (1997). *Conners' Rating Scales—Revised Technical Manual*. North Tonawanda, NY: Multi-Health Systems.

Connor, D. F., Glatt, S. J., Lopez, I. D., Jackson, D., & Melloni, R. H., Jr. (2002). Psychopharmacology and aggression. I: A meta-analysis of stimulant effects on overt/covert aggression-related behaviors in ADHD. *Journal of the American Academy of Child and Adolescent Psychiatry, 41*, 253–261.

Cuffe, S. P., McKeown, R. E., Jackson, K. L., Addy, C. L., Abramson, R., & Garrison, C. Z. (2001). Prevalence of attention-deficit/hyperactivity disorder in a community sample of older adolescents. *Journal of the American Academy of Child and Adolescent Psychiatry, 40*, 1037–1044.

DeWolfe, N., Byrne, J., & Bawden, H. (2000). ADHD in preschool children: Parent-rated psychosocial correlates. *Developmental Medicine and Child Neurology, 42*, 825.

dosReis, S., Zito, J. M., Safer, D. J., Soeken, K. L., Mitchell, J. W., Jr., & Ellwood, L. C. (2003). Parental perceptions and satisfaction with stimulant medication for attention-deficit/ hyperactivity disorder. *Journal of Developmental and Behavioral Pediatrics, 24*, 155–162.

Doyle, A. E., Biederman, J., Seidman, L. J., Weber, W., & Faraone, S. V. (2000). Diagnostic efficiency of neuropsychological test scores for discriminating boys with and without attention deficit-hyperactivity disorder. *Journal of Consulting and Clinical Psychology, 68*, 477–488.

DuPaul, G., McGoey, K., Eckert, T., & VanBrakle, J. (2001). Preschool children with attention-deficit/hyperactivity disorder: Impairments in behavioral, social, and school functioning. *Journal of the American Academy of Child and Adolescent Psychiatry, 40*, 508.

DuPaul, G. J., & Eckert, T. L. (1997). The effects of school-based interventions for attention deficit/hyperactivity disorder: A meta-analysis. *School Psychology Review, 26*, 5–27.

Faraone, S., Biederman, J., & Monuteaux, M. C. (2002). Further evidence for the diagnostic continuity between child and adolescent ADHD. *Journal of Attention Disorders, 6*, 5–13.

Faraone, S. V., Biederman, J., Lehman, B. K., Spencer, T., Norman, D., Seidman, L. J., et al. (1993). Intellectual performance and school failure in children with attention deficit hyperactivity disorder and in their siblings. *Journal of Abnormal Psychology, 102*, 616–623.

Faraone, S. V., Spencer, T., Aleardi, M., Pagano, C., & Biederman, J. (2004). Meta-analysis of the efficacy of methylphenidate for treating adult attention-deficit/hyperactivity disorder. *Journal of Clinical Psychopharmacology, 24*, 24–29.

Fischer, M., Barkley, R. A., Edelbrock, C. S., & Smallish, L. (1990). The adolescent outcome of hyperactive children diagnosed by research criteria: II. Academic, attentional, and neuropsychological status. *Journal of Consulting and Clinical Psychology, 58*, 580–588.

Fletcher, K. E., Fischer, M., Barkley, R. A., & Smallish, L. (1996). A sequential analysis of the mother-adolescent interactions of ADHD, ADHD/ODD, and normal teenagers during neutral and conflict discussions. *Journal of Abnormal Child Psychology, 24*, 271–297.

Flory, K., Milich, R., Lynam, D. R., Leukefeld, C., & Clayton, R. (2003). Relation between childhood disruptive behavior disorders and substance use and dependence symptoms in young adulthood: Individuals with symptoms of attention-deficit/hyperactivity disorder and conduct disorder are uniquely at risk. *Psychology of Addictive Behaviors, 17*, 151–158.

Frank, Y., & Pavlakis, S. G. (2001). Brain imaging in neurobehavioral disorders. *Pediatric Neurology, 25*, 278–287.

Goldstein, N. A., Post, J. C., Rosenfeld, R. M., & Campbell, T. F. (2000). Impact of tonsillectomy and adenoidectomy on child behavior. *Archives of Otolaryngology—Head and Neck Surgery, 126*, 494–498.

Green, M., Wong, M., Atkins, D., Taylor, J., & Feinleib, M. (1999). *Diagnosis of attention deficit hyperactivity disorder* (Technical Review 3). Rockville, MD: Agency for Healthcare Policy and Research.

Greenhill, L. L., Swanson, J. M., Vitiello, B., Davies, M., Clevenger, W., Wu, M., et al. (2001). Impairment and deportment responses to different methylphenidate doses in children with ADHD: The

MTA titration trial. *Journal of the American Academy of Child and Adolescent Psychiatry, 40,* 180–187.

Gresham, F. M., MacMillan, D. L., Bocian, K. M., Ward, S. L., & Forness, S. R. (1998). Comorbidity of hyperactivity-impulsivity-inattention and conduct problems: Risk factors in social, affective, and academic domains. *Journal of Abnormal Child Psychology, 26,* 393–406.

Hale, T. S., Hariri, A. R., & McCracken, J. T. (2000). Attention-deficit/hyperactivity disorder: Perspectives from neuroimaging. *Mental Retardation and Developmental Disabilities Research Reviews, 6,* 214–219.

Halperin, J. M., Newcorn, J. H., Matier, K., Bedi, G., Hall, S., & Sharma, V. (1995). Impulsivity and the initiation of fights in children with disruptive behavior disorders. *Journal of Child Psychology and Psychiatry and Allied Disciplines, 36,* 1199–1211.

Harrison, C., & Sofronoff, K. (2002). ADHD and parental psychological distress: Role of demographics, child behavioral characteristics, and parental cognitions. *Journal of the American Academy of Child and Adolescent Psychiatry, 41,* 703–711.

Hechtman, L. (1996). Families of children with attention deficit hyperactivity disorder: A review. *Canadian Journal of Psychiatry, 41,* 350–360.

Hechtman, L. (1999). Predictors of long-term outcome in children with attention-deficit/hyperactivity disorder. *Pediatric Clinics of North America, 46,* 1039–1052.

Hinshaw, S. P. (2002). Preadolescent girls with attention-deficit/hyperactivity disorder: I. Background characteristics, comorbidity, cognitive and social functioning, and parenting practices. *Journal of Consulting and Clinical Psychology, 70,* 1086–1098.

Hodgens, J. B., Cole, J., & Boldizar, J. (2000). Peer-based differences among boys with ADHD. *Journal of Clinical Child Psychology, 29,* 443–452.

Howell, D. C., Huessy, H. R., & Hassuk, B. (1985). Fifteen-year follow-up of a behavioral history of attention deficit disorder. *Pediatrics, 76,* 185–190.

Hoza, B., Waschbusch, D. A., Pelham, W. E., Molina, B. S., & Milich, R. (2000). Attention-deficit/hyperactivity disordered and control boys' responses to social success and failure. *Child Development, 71,* 432–446.

Jensen, P. S., Martin, D., & Cantwell, D. P. (1997). Comorbidity in ADHD: Implications for research, practice, and *DSM-V. Journal of the American Academy of Child and Adolescent Psychiatry, 36,* 1065–1079.

Johnston, C., Fine, S., Weiss, M., Weiss, J., Weiss, G., & Freeman, W. S. (2000). Effects of stimulant medication treatment on mothers' and children's attributions for the behavior of children with attention deficit hyperactivity disorder. *Journal of Abnormal Child Psychology, 28,* 371–382.

Johnston, C., & Freeman, W. (1997). Attributions for child behavior in parents of children without behavior disorders and children with attention deficit-hyperactivity disorder. *Journal of Consulting and Clinical Psychology, 65,* 636–645.

Johnston, C., & Mash, E. J. (2001). Families of children with attention-deficit/hyperactivity disorder: Review and recommendations for future research. *Clinical Child and Family Psychology Review, 4,* 183–207.

Kendall, J. (1999). Sibling accounts of attention deficit hyperactivity disorder (ADHD). *Family Process, 38,* 117–136.

Kim, B. N., Lee, J. S., Cho, S. C., & Lee, D. S. (2001). Methylphenidate increased regional cerebral blood flow in subjects with attention deficit/hyperactivity disorder. *Yonsei Medical Journal, 42,* 19–29.

Kuntsi, J., & Stevenson, J. (2000). Hyperactivity in children: A focus on genetic research and psychological theories. *Clinical Child and Family Psychology Review, 3,* 1–23.

Mannuzza, S., Klein, R. G., Bessler, A., Malloy, P., & Hynes, M. E. (1997). Educational and occupational outcome of hyperactive boys grown up. *Journal of the American Academy of Child and Adolescent Psychiatry, 36,* 1222–1227.

Mannuzza, S., Klein, R. G., Bessler, A., Malloy, P., & LaPadula, M. (1998). Adult psychiatric status of hyperactive boys grown up. *American Journal of Psychiatry, 155,* 493–498.

Mannuzza, S., Klein, R. G., & Moulton, J. L., III. (2002). Young adult outcome of children with "situational" hyperactivity: A prospective, controlled follow-up study. *Journal of Abnormal Child Psychology, 30,* 191–198.

May, B., & Bos, J. (2000). Personality characteristics of ADHD adults assessed with the Millon Clinical Multiaxial Inventory—II: Evidence of four distinct subtypes. *Journal of Personality Assessment, 75,* 237–248.

McCleary, L. (2002). Parenting adolescents with attention deficit hyperactivity disorder: Analysis of the literature for social work practice. *Health and Social Work, 27,* 285–292.

McGee, R. A., Clark, S. E., & Symons, D. K. (2000). Does the Conners' Continuous Performance Test aid in ADHD diagnosis? *Journal of Abnormal Child Psychology, 28,* 415–424.

McIntosh, D. E., & Cole-Love, A. S. (1996). Profile comparisons between ADHD and non-ADHD children on the Temperament Assessment Battery for Children. *Journal of Psychoeducational Assessment, 14,* 362–372.

Mick, E., Biederman, J., Faraone, S. V., Sayer, J., & Kleinman, S. (2002). Case-control study of attention-deficit hyperactivity disorder and maternal smoking, alcohol use, and drug use during pregnancy. *Journal of the American Academy of Child and Adolescent Psychiatry, 41,* 378–385.

Morrell, J., & Murray, L. (2003). Parenting and the development of conduct disorder and hyperactive symptoms in childhood: A prospective longitudinal study from 2 months to 8 years. *Journal of Child Psychology and Psychiatry and Allied Disciplines, 44,* 489–508.

Multimodal Treatment Study for ADHD Cooperative Group. (1999). A 14-month randomized clinical trial of treatment strategies for attention-deficit/hyperactivity disorder. *Archives of General Psychiatry, 56,* 1073–1086.

Murphy, K. R., Barkley, R. A., & Bush, T. (2002). Young adults with attention deficit hyperactivity disorder: Subtype differences in comorbidity, educational, and clinical history. *Journal of Nervous and Mental Disease, 190,* 147–157.

Nichols, S. L., & Waschbusch, D. A. (2004). A review of the validity of laboratory cognitive tasks used to assess symptoms of ADHD. *Child Psychiatry and Human Development, 34,* 297–315.

Nigg, J. T., & Hinshaw, S. P. (1998). Parent personality traits and psychopathology associated with antisocial behaviors in childhood attention-deficit hyperactivity disorder. *Journal of Child Psychology and Psychiatry and Allied Disciplines, 39,* 145–159.

Nigg, J. T., John, O. P., Blaskey, L. G., Huang-Pollock, C. L., Willcutt, E. G., Hinshaw, S. P., et al. (2002). Big Five dimensions and ADHD symptoms: Links between personality traits and clinical symptoms. *Journal of Personality and Social Psychology, 83,* 451–469.

Nolan, E. E., Gadow, K. D., & Sprafkin, J. (2001). Teacher reports of *DSM-IV* ADHD, ODD, and CD symptoms in schoolchildren. *Journal of the American Academy of Child and Adolescent Psychiatry, 40,* 241–249.

Pelham, W. E., Jr., & Lang, A. R. (1999). Can your children drive you to drink? Stress and parenting in adults interacting with children with ADHD. *Alcohol Research and Health: Journal of the National Institute on Alcohol Abuse and Alcoholism, 23,* 292–298.

Podolski, C. L., & Nigg, J. T. (2001). Parent stress and coping in relation to child ADHD severity and associated child disruptive behavior problems. *Journal of Clinical Child Psychology, 30,* 503–513.

Popper, C. W. (1997). Antidepressants in the treatment of attention-deficit/hyperactivity disorder. *Journal of Clinical Psychiatry, 58,* 14–29.

Quay, H. C. (1997). Inhibition and attention deficit hyperactivity disorder. *Journal of Abnormal Child Psychology, 25,* 7–13.

Ranseen, J. D., Campbell, D. A., & Baer, R. A. (1998). NEO PI-R profiles of adults with attention deficit disorder. *Assessment, 5,* 19–24.

Reitman, D., Hummel, R., Franz, D. Z., & Gross, A. M. (1998). A review of methods and instruments for assessing externalizing disorders: Theoretical and practical considerations in rendering a diagnosis. *Clinical Psychology Review, 18,* 555–584.

Roberts, R. E., Attkisson, C. C., & Rosenblatt, A. (1998). Prevalence of psychopathology among children and adolescents. *American Journal of Psychiatry, 155,* 715–725.

Robison, L. M., Skaer, T. L., Sclar, D. A., & Galin, R. S. (2002). Is attention deficit hyperactivity disorder increasing among girls in the US? Trends in diagnosis and the prescribing of stimulants. *CNS Drugs, 16,* 129–137.

Schachar, R., & Tannock, R. (1995). Test of four hypotheses for the comorbidity of attention-deficit/hyperactivity disorder and conduct disorder. *Journal of the American Academy of Child and Adolescent Psychiatry, 34,* 639–648.

Schachter, H. M., Pham, B., King, J., Langford, S., & Moher, D. (2001). How efficacious and safe is short-acting methylphenidate for the treatment of attention-deficit disorder in children and adolescents? A meta-analysis. *Canadian Medical Association Journal, 165,* 1475–1488.

Shaffer, D., Fisher, P., Lucas, C., Dulcan, M., & Schwab-Stone, M. (2000). NIMH Diagnostic Interview Schedule for Children, version IV (NIMH DISC-IV): Description, differences from previous versions, and reliability of some common diagnoses. *Journal of the American Academy of Child and Adolescent Psychiatry, 39,* 28–38.

Shaw, D. S., Owens, E. B., Giovannelli, J., & Winslow, E. B. (2001). Infant and toddler pathways leading to early externalizing disorders. *Journal of the American Academy of Child and Adolescent Psychiatry, 40,* 36–43.

Smith, B. H., Pelham, W. E., Jr., Gnagy, E., Molina, B., & Evans, S. (2000). The reliability, validity, and unique contributions of self-report by adolescents receiving treatment for attention-deficit/hyperactivity disorder. *Journal of Consulting and Clinical Psychology, 68,* 489–499.

Sonuga-Barke, E. J., Dalen, L., Daley, D., & Remington, B. (2002). Are planning, working memory, and inhibition associated with individual differences in preschool ADHD symptoms? *Developmental Neuropsychology, 21,* 255–272.

Sonuga-Barke, E. J., Daley, D., & Thompson, M. (2002). Does maternal ADHD reduce the effectiveness of parent training for preschool children's ADHD? *Journal of the American Academy of Child and Adolescent Psychiatry, 41,* 696–702.

Steinhausen, H. C., Drechsler, R., Foldenyi, M., Imhof, K., & Brandeis, D. (2003). Clinical course of attention-deficit/hyperactivity disorder from childhood toward early adolescence. *Journal of the American Academy of Child and Adolescent Psychiatry, 42,* 1085–1092.

Stevens, J., Quittner, A. L., & Abikoff, H. (1998). Factors influencing elementary school teachers' ratings of ADHD and ODD behaviors. *Journal of Clinical Child Psychology, 27,* 406–414.

Swanson, J. M., Lerner, M., & Williams, L. (1995). More frequent diagnosis of attention deficit-hyperactivity disorder. *New England Journal of Medicine, 333,* 944.

Swanson, J. M., Sergeant, J. A., Taylor, E., Sonuga-Barke, E. J., Jensen, P. S., & Cantwell, D. P. (1998). Attention-deficit hyperactivity disorder and hyperkinetic disorder. *Lancet, 351,* 429–433.

Tannock, R. (1998). Attention deficit hyperactivity disorder: Advances in cognitive, neurobiological, and genetic research. *Journal of Child Psychology and Psychiatry and Allied Disciplines, 39,* 65–99.

Thunstrom, M. (2002). Severe sleep problems in infancy associated with subsequent development of attention-deficit/hyperactivity disorder at 5.5 years of age. *Acta Paediatrica, 91,* 584–592.

Vitiello, B. (2001). Long-term effects of stimulant medications on the brain: Possible relevance to the treatment of attention deficit hyperactivity disorder. *Journal of Child and Adolescent Psychopharmacology, 11,* 25–34.

Whalen, C. K., Jamner, L. D., Henker, B., Delfino, R. J., & Lozano, J. M. (2002). The ADHD spectrum and everyday life: Experience sampling of adolescent moods, activities, smoking, and drinking. *Child Development, 73,* 209–227.

White, J. D. (1999). Personality, temperament, and ADHD: A review of the literature. *Personality and Individual Differences, 27,* 589–598.

Wilens, T., Pelham, W., Stein, M., Conners, C. K., Abikoff, H., Atkins, M., et al. (2003). ADHD treatment with once-daily OROS methylphenidate: Interim 12-month results from a long-term open-label study. *Journal of the American Academy of Child and Adolescent Psychiatry, 42,* 424–433.

Willcutt, E. G., Hartung, C. M., Lahey, B. B., Loney, J., & Pelham, W. E. (1999). Utility of behavior ratings by examiners during assessments of preschool children with attention-deficit/hyperactivity disorder. *Journal of Abnormal Child Psychology, 27,* 463–472.

Willoughby, M. T. (2003). Developmental course of ADHD symptomatology during the transition from childhood to adolescence: A review with recommendations. *Journal of Child Psychology and Psychiatry and Allied Disciplines, 44,* 88–106.

Wolraich, M. L., Lambert, E. W., Baumgaertel, A., Garcia-Tornel, S., Feurer, I. D., Bickman, L., et al. (2003). Teachers' screening for attention deficit/hyperactivity disorder: Comparing multinational samples on teacher ratings of ADHD. *Journal of Abnormal Child Psychology, 31,* 445–455.

CHAPTER 20

Eating Disorders

ERIC STICE, STEPHEN WONDERLICH, AND EMILY WADE

DESCRIPTION OF THE DISORDERS AND CLINICAL PICTURE

Eating disorders consist of a variety of psychiatric disturbances involving marked abnormalities in eating behaviors, maladaptive efforts to control shape and weight, and disturbances in self-perception regarding body shape. Three eating disorder syndromes are currently recognized in the literature: anorexia nervosa, bulimia nervosa, and binge eating disorder.

The diagnostic criteria for anorexia nervosa include (a) extreme emaciation (less than 85 percent of expected weight for height and age); (b) intense fear of gaining weight or becoming fat despite a low body weight; (c) disturbed perception of weight and shape, an undue influence of weight or shape on self-evaluation, or a denial of the seriousness of the low body weight; and (d) amenorrhea in postmenarcheal females (American Psychiatric Association, 1994). Current diagnostic nomenclature recognizes a restricting type of anorexia nervosa, in which the person does not regularly engage in binge eating or purging (self-induced vomiting or laxative/diuretic use), and a binge eating/purging type of anorexia nervosa, in which the person does engage in these behaviors. This distinction is based on the observation that individuals with the binge/purge type of anorexia nervosa have elevated personal and family histories of obesity and higher rates of impulsive behaviors, including stealing, drug abuse, self-harm, and mood lability, than individuals with the restricting type of anorexia nervosa (Garner, 1993). Several common clinical features are associated with anorexia nervosa, including a relentless pursuit of thinness and overvaluation of body shape, which usually results in extreme dietary restriction and high levels of physical activity (Fairburn & Harrison, 2003). Consequent to this state of semistarvation, individuals experience mood disturbances, preoccupation with food, and ritualistic and stereotyped eating (Wilson, Becker, & Heffernan, 2003). According to the clinical literature (Slade, 1982), anorexia nervosa is also commonly associated with a need for control and dysfunctional relationships with family members, although it is currently unclear whether this is a cause or a consequence of this eating disorder. Because of the extreme pursuit of thinness that characterizes individuals suffering from anorexia nervosa, the eating disorder is often perceived as a personal accomplishment rather than a psychiatric disorder in need of treatment. Accordingly, individuals with anorexia nervosa are often brought to treatment by concerned family members or friends and are typically very resistant to treatment, which invariably involves weight restoration.

The diagnostic criteria for bulimia nervosa includes (a) recurrent episodes (at least 2 days per week for the previous 3 months) of uncontrollable consumption of large amounts of food, (b) recurrent use (at least twice weekly for the previous 3 months) of compensatory behavior to prevent consequent weight gain (e.g., vomiting, laxative abuse, diuretic abuse, fasting, or excessive exercise), and (c) undue influence of weight and shape on self-evaluation (American Psychiatric Association, 1994). If these symptoms occur exclusively during a period in which the individual satisfies diagnostic criteria for anorexia nervosa, this latter diagnosis is given precedence. During binge episodes, individuals with bulimia nervosa (and binge eating disorder) typically consume between 1,000 and 2,000 kcals, which usually involve foods with high fat and high sugar content (Walsh, 1993; Yanovski et al., 1992). Bulimia nervosa is typically associated with marked feelings of guilt and shame regarding eating behaviors, which are often kept secret from friends and family (Wilson et al., 2003). Indeed, it is common for these individuals to seek treatment because they fear they can no longer keep their eating disorder secret (e.g., upon moving in with a romantic partner). One benefit of this shame is that it makes it easier to engage individuals with bulimia nervosa in treatment than is the case for their counterparts with anorexia nervosa (Fairburn & Harrison, 2003). Similar to individuals with anorexia nervosa, those with bulimia nervosa exhibit rigid rules regarding eating and an overvaluation of thinness.

Binge eating disorder involves (a) repeated episodes (at least twice weekly for the previous 6 months) of uncontrollable binge eating characterized by certain features (e.g., rapid eating, eating until uncomfortably full, eating large amounts of food when not physically hungry, eating alone because of embarrassment, and feeling guilty or depressed after overeating), (b) marked distress regarding binge eating, and (c) the absence of compensatory behaviors (American Psychiatric Association, 1994). If these symptoms occur exclusively during a period in which the individual satisfies diagnostic criteria for anorexia nervosa, this latter diagnosis is given precedence. If the symptoms of binge eating disorder occur exclusively during a period in which the individual satisfies diagnostic criteria for bulimia nervosa, this latter diagnosis is given precedence. Binge eating disorder is typically associated with elevated rates of obesity, as well as the medical complications that accompany obesity. These individuals often present with marked shame about their eating behaviors and evidence elevated rates of depression.

In addition to the three widely recognized eating disorders noted previously, the *Diagnostic and Statistical Manual of Mental Disorders,* fourth edition *(DSM-IV),* also allows for the diagnosis of eating disorders not otherwise specified, or EDNOS (American Psychiatric Association, 1994). This category includes subdiagnostic levels of anorexia nervosa, bulimia nervosa, and binge eating disorder (Fairburn & Harrison, 2003). For example, an individual who uses compensatory behaviors only an average of one time per week (versus two times per week) but met all the other diagnostic criteria for bulimia nervosa would likely warrant a diagnosis of EDNOS. The EDNOS category also includes partial syndrome eating disorders. For instance, an individual who does not evidence uncontrollable binge eating but nonetheless engages in weekly compensatory behaviors would probably warrant a diagnosis of EDNOS. Finally, the EDNOS category includes other atypical eating disorders, such as rumination or pica exhibited during adolescence. EDNOS is particularly important during childhood and adolescence because nearly half of individuals in this developmental period who seek treatment for eating pathology do not meet full diagnostic criteria for anorexia nervosa, bulimia nervosa, or binge eating disorder (Fisher, Schneider, Burns, Symons, & Mandel, 2001; Herzog, Hopkins, & Burns, 1993; Williamson, Gleaves, & Savin, 1992).

It is important to note that the current diagnostic system for eating disorders does not require that the eating disorder symptoms cause clinically significant distress or impairment in social, occupational, or other important areas of functioning, as is the case for other psychiatric disorders such as major depression. It is our impression that the addition of these criteria would be useful, particularly because this would provide a way of differentiating clinically meaningful eating pathology that should warrant a diagnosis from less clinically meaningful forms of eating disturbances that should not warrant a psychiatric diagnosis.

Although obesity is characterized by a disturbance in eating wherein caloric intake exceeds caloric expenditure (Rosenbaum, Leibel, & Hirsch, 1997), it is not considered a psychiatric disorder because obesity appears to be largely a product of behavior (excess caloric intake relative to physical activity). Accordingly, obesity is not included in this chapter. Nonetheless, it is noteworthy that depressive symptoms do increase the risk for future onset of obesity (Goodman & Whitaker, 2002; Stice, Presnell, Shaw, & Rohde, 2005), which suggests that psychopathology may play a role in the etiology of this public health problem.

PERSONALITY DEVELOPMENT AND PSYCHOPATHOLOGY

The relations of personality traits to eating disorders have been poorly understood in the theoretical, empirical, and clinical literature. In addition to the continued debates about the nature and assessment of personality (e.g., traits vs. categories, state effects, stability of personality self-report vs. interview), significant uncertainties remain regarding simple cause-and-effect issues in the eating disorder–personality relation. Some of this complexity has been described in recent discussions of possible eating disorder–personality conceptual models (Grilo, 2002; Lilenfeld, Wonderlich, Riso, Crosby, & Mitchell, 2004; Wonderlich & Mitchell, 1997). Although there are minor variations, the predominant models of the eating disorder–personality relation include the following: predispositional, complication, and common cause. These models are depicted in Figure 20.1, which was developed by Lilenfeld et al. (2004).

Predispositional Model

The predispositional model essentially posits that personality traits precede the onset of the eating disorder and serve as a significant risk for its onset. Such a model was implied in Bruch's (1973) early writings regarding characteristics of the anorexic child as fundamentally compliant, perfectionistic, and dependent. Similarly, Strober (1991) posits that personality traits such as low novelty seeking and high harm avoidance (Cloninger, Svrakic, & Przybeck, 1993) may increase the risk of developing anorexia nervosa during adolescence. Rigorous empirical tests of the predispositional model require prospective designs that can clearly delineate the temporal precedence of personality traits in relation to eating disorder

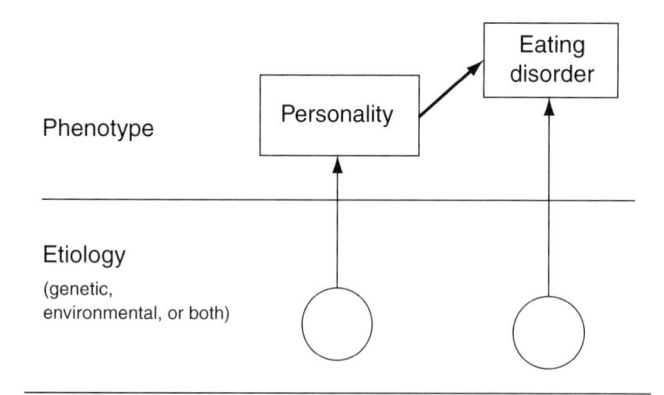

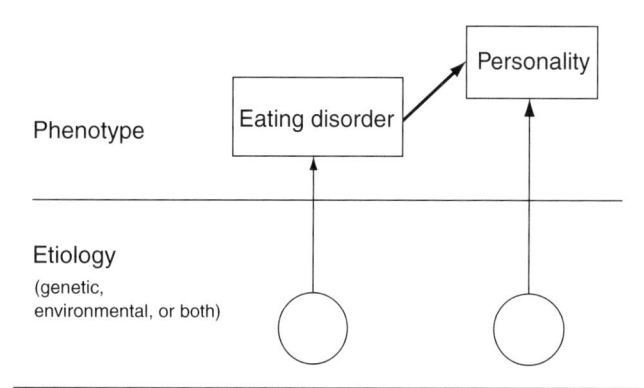

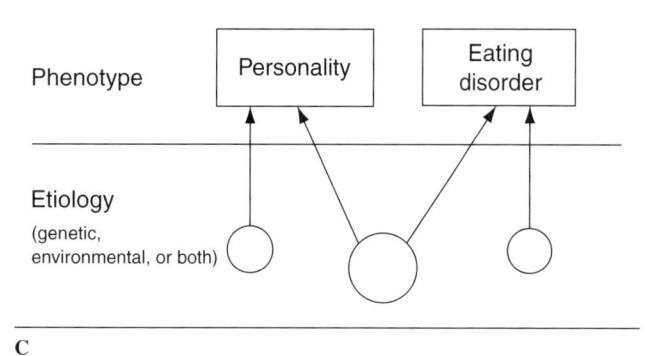

Figure 20.1 A, Predispositional model. B, Complication model. C, Common cause: Third variable model.

onset. Such prospective longitudinal studies of anorexia nervosa are nonexistent, and similar studies of bulimia nervosa or clear bulimic symptomatology are rare. Consequently, most prospective longitudinal studies that examined personality in eating disorders have focused on disordered eating, eating pathology, or some other nondiagnostic measure as the outcome variable. Several early studies failed to find any personality predictors of disordered eating (e.g., Attie & Brooks-Gunn, 1989; Patton, Johnson-Sabine, Wood, Mann, & Wakeling, 1990). More recent studies, using various research designs, have found conflicting evidence for the predictive effects of various personality traits. For example, the personality trait of perfectionism has been associated with the onset of bulimic behavior (e.g., Killen et al., 1994), but this has not been a consistent finding (e.g., Killen et al., 1996). One retrospective case-control study (Fairburn, Cooper, Doll, & Welch, 1999) identified perfectionism as a premorbid risk factor for eating-disordered individuals, particularly anorexic individuals. However, this study was limited by its retrospective measurement strategy for personality. Other research has focused on perfectionism in multifactorial models (e.g., Vohs, Bardone, Joiner, Abramson, & Heatherton, 1999), which has provided some evidence to suggest that perfectionism predicts increases in eating disorder behavior, but only if the individual also displays low self-esteem and high levels of body dissatisfaction; these studies have failed to find any significant main effects for perfectionism. Recent reviews have concluded that perfectionism may be considered a risk factor for bulimic pathology (Stice, 2002) and a specific, retrospective correlate of medium potency for anorexia nervosa and a correlate of all eating disorder diagnoses (Jacobi, Hayword, de Zwaan, Kraemer, & Agras, 2004).

Another trait that has received attention in terms of its risk factor status is the general construct of negative emotionality, and its related constructs of negative affectivity and neuroticism. There has been evidence that high levels of negative affect serve as a risk factor for increases in eating disorder symptoms (Wertheim, Koerner, & Paxton, 2001; Wichstrom, 2000) and bulimic symptoms (Stice & Agras, 1998). However, several studies have also failed to support this finding (Keel, Fulkerson, & Leon, 1997; Leon, Fulkerson, Perry, Keel, & Klump, 1999). Stice (2001) concluded that negative affectivity appears to be a more potent risk factor for binge eating or bulimic symptomatology than for other facets of eating disorder behavior. Two recent studies have provided some evidence to suggest that the related personality trait of neuroticism is a significant risk factor for the onset of actual eating disorder diagnoses (Cervera et al., 2003; Ghaderi & Scott, 2000). Consistent with these findings, recent literature reviews have concluded that negative emotionality or neuroticism may be considered a risk factor for eating pathology (Stice, 2002) or a variable risk factor of unclear potency (Jacobi et al., 2004).

Finally, the personality trait of impulsivity has been posited to have causal significance for the onset of eating disorder behavior. However, several empirical studies have not provided strong support for this idea (see Stice, 2002, for a review). One recent study suggests that the measurement approach for impulsivity, particularly with adolescents, may significantly impact such empirical studies. Wonderlich, Connolly, and Stice (2004) failed to find evidence that impulsivity or disinhibition scales prospectively predicted the onset of eating disorder behavior when measured with traditional personality scales. However, in the same series of studies, impulsivity-related constructs such as substance use and delinquency were significant predictors of eating disorder onset. This raises the important issue of how to assess personality in adolescents, which has been recognized as a very complicated methodological issue for some time (Shiner, 1998).

Complication Model

This model of the personality–eating disorder relation implies that personality traits frequently observed in eating-disordered individuals are not risk factors for eating disorders but in fact are complications or consequences of the starvation, binge-purge, and dietary chaos that characterize the eating disorders. By implication, this line of thinking does not consider the personality traits frequently seen in eating disorders to be actual traits, but instead reflects on disorder-related changes that mimic traits. For example, studies of imposed starvation with healthy participants suggest that starvation is associated with increases in obsessionality and rigidity, which in turn persist as a result of the starved state (Keys, Brozek, Henschel, Mickelsen, & Taylor, 1950). Although prospective, longitudinal designs would be the ideal approach for testing complication models, our scientific knowledge of such phenomena is generally based on designs that either compare recovered individuals to currently ill individuals, in order to identify traits associated with the state of the illness, or compare recovered individuals to never ill individuals, in order to identify personality features that represent long-term scarring complications of the illness.

Several traits have been identified as particularly likely to be complications of eating disorders. In particular, obsessionality, neuroticism, extroversion, emotional lability, and disinhibition all appear to be significantly influenced by the presence of eating disorder behavior (Grilo, 2002; Kennedy, McVey, & Katz, 1990; Pollice, Kaye, Greeno, & Weltzin, 1997; Stonehill & Crisp, 1977). It is important to point out, however, that studies with recovered designs cannot clearly determine whether such traits are indeed complications of the disorder, or if they may have been predisposing traits that continue to persist after recovery.

Common Cause Model

The common cause model is based on the notion that personality traits and the eating disorders are independent entities that frequently co-occur because they share underlying causal factors. Such a model distinguishes itself from the predispositional model because it does not imply that personality increases the risk of eating disorders but implies instead that personality and eating disorders both arise from some third variable. Typically, the third variables most often posited to increase the risk of both conditions are familial in nature, and consequently family study designs have been used to test the common cause model. For example, in studying the relationship between anorexia nervosa and obsessive-compulsive personality disorder (OCPD), a four-cell design would be optimal. The cells would include the following: anorexic probands with OCPD, anorexic probands without OCPD, non–eating disorder probands with OCPD, and non–eating disorder probands without OCPD. If, as the common cause model implies, the familial factor increases the risk of both conditions, elevated rates of both anorexic pathology and OCPD should be found among the relatives of any proband who has either, or both, of the conditions. Some research, using approximations of this design, has found evidence for a common cause for the restricting type of anorexia nervosa and OCPD disorder (Lilenfeld et al., 1998).

Multivariate twin study designs have also examined similar questions regarding common causation of personality traits and eating disorders. One study suggests that the covariation between high-order personality traits, such as negative emotionality, and disordered eating attitudes and behavior (e.g., weight preoccupation) are mediated through shared genes (Klump, McGue, & Iacono, 2002). On the other hand, another recent study, using the same basic methodology, found that the covariation between neuroticism and disordered eating was primarily influenced by nonshared environmental factors rather than shared genetic factors (Wadeet et al., 2000).

EPIDEMIOLOGY

Large community-recruited studies with adolescents that used diagnostic interviews suggest that the lifetime prevalence of anorexia nervosa is between 0.5 percent and 1.0 percent for females and between 0.0 percent and 0.3 percent for males, the lifetime prevalence for bulimia nervosa is between 1.5 percent and 4.0 percent for females and between 0.1 percent and 0.5 percent for males, and the lifetime prevalence for binge eating disorder is between 0.0 percent and 0.5 percent for females and is 0.0 percent for males (Johnson, Cohen, Kasen, & Brook, 2002; Lewinsohn, Hops, Roberts, Seeley, & Andrews, 1993; Newman et al., 1996). Community-recruited samples indicate that for adolescent females, the rates of subthreshold or partial syndrome anorexia nervosa range between 1.1 percent and 3.0 percent, the rates of subthreshold or partial syndrome bulimia nervosa range between

2.0 percent and 5.4 percent, and the rate of subthreshold binge eating disorder is 1.6 percent (Lewinsohn, Streigel-Moore, & Seeley, 2000; Stice, Presnell, & Bearman, 2004). It is noteworthy that these data imply that anorexic and bulimic pathology are more common than binge eating disorder during adolescence—a trend that appears to reverse itself during adulthood (Wilson et al., 2003).

A study that used a combination of retrospective and prospective data suggested that the incidence of new cases of anorexia nervosa and bulimia nervosa ranges between 1.3 percent and 2.8 percent during adolescence and that the risk for onset of these disorders peaks between 16 and 17 years of age (Lewinsohn et al., 2000). This same period of peak risk for onset of threshold and subthreshold anorexia nervosa and bulimia nervosa emerged from a fully prospective study that followed adolescent girls from the ages of 12 through 19 years (Stice, Presnell, & Bearman, 2004). Likewise, a fully prospective study that followed a large cohort of adolescent girls from 13 to 19 years of age indicated that the peak period of risk for onset of bulimic symptoms was between 16 and 18 years of age (Stice, Killen, Hayward, & Taylor, 1998). Another noteworthy feature of these prospective studies is that they consistently imply that anorexia nervosa, bulimia nervosa, and binge eating disorder are relatively rare throughout childhood and the preadolescent developmental period. Thus, eating disorders are somewhat distinct from other psychiatric disorders in that there is a relatively narrow developmental period during which most of the cases of anorexia nervosa and bulimia nervosa will emerge.

ETIOLOGY

Although there are numerous theories regarding the etiologic processes that promote the development of anorexia nervosa, very few prospective studies have investigated factors that predict subsequent onset of anorexic pathology or increases in anorexic symptoms and no prospective tests of multivariate etiologic models. Prospective studies are essential to determining whether a putative risk factor is a precursor, concomitant, or consequence of eating pathology. Theorists have suggested a wide variety of risk factors for anorexia nervosa, including norepinephrine abnormalities, serotonergic abnormalities, childhood sexual abuse, low self-esteem, perfectionism, need for control, disturbed family dynamics, internalization of the thin-ideal, dietary restraint, and mood disturbances (Fairburn & Harrison, 2003; Kaye, Klump, Frank, & Strober, 2000; Wilson et al., 2003).

The only prospective study that tested predictors of subsequent onset of threshold or subthreshold anorexia nervosa found that girls with the lowest relative weight and those with extremely low scores on a dietary restraint scale at baseline were at increased risk for future onset of anorexic pathology over a 5-year period (Stice, Presnell, & Bearman, 2004). In contrast to expectancies, early puberty, perceived pressure to be thin, thin-ideal internalization, body dissatisfaction, depressive symptoms, and deficits in parental and peer support did not predict onset of anorexic pathology. However, these null findings should be interpreted with care because of the low base rate of this outcome. Unfortunately, we were unable to locate any additional studies that focused on predicting onset of anorexic pathology or increases in anorexia nervosa symptoms; all of the other studies that focused on this eating disorder collapsed across anorexic and bulimic pathology (e.g., McKnight Investigators, 2003; Patton et al., 1990; Santonastaso, Friederici, & Favaro, 1999). Thus, surprisingly little is currently known about the risk factors for anorexic pathology or how they work together to promote this pernicious eating disturbance.

Greater strides have been made regarding our understanding of the risk factors for bulimic pathology. According to the sociocultural model, an internalization of the socially sanctioned thin-ideal for females combines with direct pressures for female thinness (e.g., weight-related teasing) to promote body dissatisfaction, which in turn is thought to increase the risk for the initiation of dieting and for negative affect and consequent bulimic pathology (Cattarin & Thompson, 1994; Garner, Olmsted, & Polivy, 1983; Polivy & Herman, 1985; Stice et al., 1998). This body dissatisfaction is thought to lead females to engage in dietary restraint in an effort to conform to this thin-ideal, which paradoxically increases the likelihood of the initiation of binge eating. Dieting also entails a shift from a reliance on physiological cues to cognitive control over eating behaviors, which leaves the individual vulnerable to overeating when these cognitive processes are disrupted. Body dissatisfaction is also theorized to contribute to negative affect, which increases the risk that these individuals will turn to binge eating to provide comfort and distraction from these negative emotional states.

Consistent with this general etiologic model, thin-ideal internalization, perceived pressure to be thin, body dissatisfaction, dietary restraint, and negative affect have been consistently found to increase the risk for future onset of bulimic symptoms and bulimic pathology (Field, Camargo, Taylor, Berkey, & Colditz, 1999; Killen et al., 1994, 1996; Stice et al., 1998; Stice, Presnell, & Bearman, 2004). Experiments have confirmed that a reduction in thin-ideal internalization, body dissatisfaction, and negative affect have produced the expected decreases in bulimic symptoms but have failed to provide support for dietary restraint (see Stice, 2002, for a review). A number of other risk factors have received support in a few prospective studies, such as deficits in social support, substance abuse, and elevated body mass, but these effects have not been consistently replicated (Stice, 2002). Interestingly, several hypothesized risk factors for bulimic pathology have not received support in prospective studies, including early menarche and temperamental impulsivity (Stice, 2002).

To date there has been relatively little theory regarding the etiologic processes that promote binge eating disorder, but those that have been proposed have conceptually overlapped with etiologic theories that have been put forth for bulimic pathology (Vogeltanz-Holm et al., 2000). Prospective studies have provided evidence that initial elevations in body mass, body dissatisfaction, dietary restraint, negative affect, and emotional eating increase the risk for future onset of binge eating (Stice, Presnell, & Spangler, 2002; Stice et al., 1998; Vogeltanz-Holm et al., 2000).

It is probable that genetic factors contribute to the development of eating disorders, but twin studies have produced conflicting results, with heritability estimates ranging from 0.0 percent to 70 percent for anorexia nervosa and from 0.0 percent to 83 percent for bulimia nervosa (Bulik, Sullivan, & Kendler, 1998; Fairburn, Cowen, & Harrison, 1999; Kaye et al., 2000). Other genetic findings are likewise conflicting. For example, one study found that the concordance rate for monozygotic twins was greater than for dizygotic twins (Treasure & Holland, 1989), but another observed findings in the opposite direction (Walters & Kendler, 1995). Similarly, studies that have tried to identify specific receptor genes that are associated with eating disorders have produced highly inconsistent results that have not been replicated (e.g., Hinney et al., 1998, 1999). The large range in parameter estimates suggests fundamental problems with sampling error resulting from small samples, the reliability of diagnostic procedures, or statistical models used to estimate genetic effects. It therefore appears somewhat premature to draw conclusions regarding the genetic heritability of eating disorders at this time.

Several important gaps in the literature should be kept in mind when interpreting etiologic findings. First, we were unable to locate a single prospective study that tested whether any biological variable, including structural or functional abnormalities in the brain or neurotransmitter abnormalities, predicted onset of any eating disorder. Without such studies it is impossible to determine whether any biological abnormalities are a cause or consequence of eating pathology. Second, very few studies have predicted onset of anorexic pathology, bulimic pathology, or binge eating disorder or have focused on comparing and differentiating the risk factors for these three classes of eating disorders. Without these types of studies, it is impossible to differentiate the distinct etiologic processes that give rise to the various types of eating disorders.

COURSE, COMPLICATIONS, AND PROGNOSIS

Anorexia nervosa shows a highly variable course, with some individuals recovering after a single episode, other individuals showing a chronic course that is marked by fluctuating patterns of weight restoration and relapse, and other individuals progressing to other eating disorders (Wilson et al., 2003). This eating disorder also results in severe medical complications, including permanent organ damage, cerebral atrophy, and osteoporosis, which necessitate close medical monitoring during periods of low body weight. Anorexia nervosa is also associated with the highest rates of suicidal ideation and mortality of any psychiatric condition (Herzog et al., 2000; Newman et al., 1996). Because there have been very few randomized clinical trials for anorexia nervosa, primarily because of the low base rate and the medical danger of using control groups, relatively little is known about effective treatments for this eating disorder. However, a consensus is emerging that family therapy is the best treatment option at this time for adolescent girls, although there are promising findings for certain pharmacologic interventions (Kaye et al., 2000).

Community-recruited samples suggest that bulimia nervosa typically shows a chronic course that is characterized by periods of recovery and relapse, but that subthreshold bulimic pathology shows less chronicity (Fairburn, Cooper, Doll, Norman, & O'Connor, 2000; Stice, Burton, & Shaw, 2004). Bulimia nervosa typically results in marked subjective distress and functional impairment (Lewinsohn et al., 2000). In severe cases, bulimia nervosa can result in serious medical complications that can require hospitalization (e.g., esophageal tears) or even cause death (e.g., electrolyte imbalances that result in cardiac arrest). Community-recruited samples indicate that bulimia nervosa is also associated with an increased risk for suicide attempt and elevated rates of comorbid affective disorders, anxiety disorders, and substance abuse (Johnson, Cohen, Kasen, & Brook, 2002; Lewinsohn et al., 1993; Newman et al., 1996). Threshold and subthreshold bulimia nervosa increase the risk for future onset of depression, suicide attempts, anxiety disorders, substance abuse, obesity, and health problems (Johnson et al., 2002; Stice, Cameron, Killen, Hayward, & Taylor, 1999; Stice, Hayward, Cameron, Killen, & Taylor, 2000; Striegel-Moore, Seeley, & Lewinsohn, 2003). The treatment prognosis for bulimia nervosa is fair, in that lasting symptom remission typically occurs for only 30 percent to 40 percent of patients who are provided with the treatment of choice (Agras, Walsh, Fairburn, Wilson, & Kraemer, 2000; Fairburn et al., 1995).

Community-recruited natural history studies suggest that binge eating disorder shows a high auto-remission rate over time, with fewer than 20 percent of cases meeting diagnostic criteria over long follow-up periods (Fairburn et al., 2000; Wilson et al., 2003), although the majority appear to meet criteria for EDNOS. Another noteworthy finding is that a large portion of individuals with binge eating disorder show onset of obesity (Fairburn et al., 2000). Binge eating disorder is associated with elevated major depression and slight elevations in Axis I and Axis II psychiatric disorders as well as obesity and the consequent elevated morbidity and mortality associated with this health problem (Striegel-Moore, Wilfley, Pike, Dohm, & Fairburn, 2000; Telch & Stice, 1998). The prognosis for the treatment of binge eating disorder is good, with psychotherapeutic interventions showing abstinence rates of approximately 60 percent at 1-year follow-up (Wilson et al., 2003). There is also considerable evidence that low-calorie behavioral weight loss interventions are effective treatments for binge eating disorder (Goodrick, Poston, Kimball, Reeves, & Foreyt, 1998; Reeves et al., 2001).

ASSESSMENT AND DIAGNOSIS

A variety of self-report questionnaires and structured diagnostic interviews have been developed to assess eating pathology (Anderson & Paulosky, 2004). We provide a brief overview of the evidence for the reliability and validity of the most widely researched assessment strategies.

The Eating Attitudes Test (EAT; Garner et al., 1979) is a 40-item questionnaire designed to assess the symptoms of anorexia nervosa, but various adaptations of this scale exist, including a 26-item short form, a form for children in grades 3–6, and a form for children in grades 6–8 (Anderson & Paulosky, 2004). There is considerable evidence that the EAT possesses internally consistency, test-retest reliability, and discriminate validity with adolescents and adults; however, this scale cannot discriminate anorexia nervosa from bulimia nervosa or diagnose eating disorders (Anderson & Paulosky, 2004; Garfinkel & Newman, 2001).

The Eating Disorder Inventory (EDI; Garner, Olmsted, & Polivy, 1983) is a multi-item scale that assesses the symptoms and features of anorexia nervosa and bulimia nervosa. The current version (EDI-2; Garner, 1991) includes 11 scales such as the bulimia, body dissatisfaction, drive for thinness, perfectionism, and impulse regulation subscales. Research suggests that the EDI possesses adequate internal consistency and test-retest reliability and good discriminate and predictive validity with adolescents and adults, but that this scale cannot be used to diagnose eating disorders (Anderson & Paulosky, 2004; Garner, 1991).

The Bulimia Test—Revised (BULIT-R; Thelen, Farmer, Wonderlich, & Smith, 1991), and its predecessor, the BULIT, were designed to assess the symptoms of bulimia nervosa. Research has found that the BULIT-R possesses good internal consistency, test-retest reliability, discriminate validity, and predictive validity with adolescents and adults (Anderson & Paulosky, 2004; Thelen et al., 1991). However, this scale cannot be used to diagnose eating disorders.

The Eating Disorder Examination-Questionnaire (EDE-Q; Fairburn & Beglin, 1994) is a questionnaire version of the Eating Disorder Examination interview (EDE; Fairburn & Cooper, 1993), a validated measure of eating pathology. This scale assesses the diagnostic symptoms of anorexia nervosa and bulimia nervosa and contains subscales assessing features that are commonly associated with these eating disorders, such as dietary restraint and eating concern. Research has found that this scale possesses good internal consistency and test-retest reliability with adolescents and adults (Black & Wilson, 1996; Fairburn & Beglin, 1994; Luce & Crowther, 1999; Stice, 2001). Although this scale does assess the symptoms of anorexia nervosa and bulimia nervosa, there are currently no data concerning the agreement between diagnoses made with this scale and those made with validated structured interviews.

The Questionnaire for Eating Disorder Diagnoses (QEDD; Mintz, O'Halloran, Mulholland, & Schneider, 1997) is a questionnaire assessing the diagnostic criteria for anorexia nervosa, bulimia nervosa, and binge eating disorder. Research has found that this scale shows good test-retest reliability and criterion validity (Mintz et al., 1997).

The Eating Disorder Diagnostic Scale (Stice, Telch, & Rizvi, 2000) is a brief self-report scale assessing the *DSM-IV* diagnostic criteria for anorexia nervosa, bulimia nervosa, and binge eating disorder. Research has found that the continuous symptom composite shows good internal consistency, test-retest reliability, and predictive validity, and that the eating disorder diagnoses made with this scale also possess good test-retest reliability and show good criterion validity with interview-based diagnoses (mean $\kappa = .81$; Stice, Fisher, & Martinez, 2004; Stice, Telch, & Rizvi, 2000).

There are structured psychiatric interviews for arriving at *DSM-IV* (American Psychiatric Association, 1994) diagnoses of anorexia nervosa, bulimia nervosa, and binge eating disorder (e.g., the Eating Disorder Examination [EDE; Fairburn

& Cooper, 1993] and the Structured Clinical Interview for *DSM-IV* Axis I [SCID; Spitzer, Williams, Gibbon, & First, 1990]).

The EDE (Fairburn & Cooper, 1993) is a semistructured psychiatric interview assessing the diagnostic criteria for anorexia nervosa and bulimia nervosa. This interview also contains subscales assessing features that are commonly associated with these eating disorders, such as dietary restraint and eating concern. Research has found that the continuous scales from this interview possess good internal consistency, test-retest reliability, and discriminate validity, and that the diagnoses show good interrater reliability and test-retest reliability (Fairburn & Cooper, 1993; Rizvi, Peterson, Crow, & Agras, 2000; Stice, Burton, & Shaw, 2004; Williamson, Anderson, Jackman, & Jackson, 1995).

The SCID (Spitzer et al., 1990) is a semistructured interview that assesses current and lifetime psychiatric status for major Axis I psychiatric disorders using criteria in accordance with the *DSM*. The reliability and validity of the SCID have been well documented, with interrater reliability agreement (*k*) ranging from .70 to 1.00 (Segal, Hersen, & Van Hasselt, 1994; Williams et al., 1992). For instance, one study found that the interrater agreement for SCID diagnoses for anorexia nervosa and bulimia nervosa in a patient sample to be .72 and .86, respectively (Williams et al., 1992). However, we were unable to locate information concerning the test-retest reliability for specific eating disorder diagnosis with the SCID.

IMPACT ON ENVIRONMENT

As noted, clinically significant impairment in social or occupational functioning is not required to meet full diagnostic criteria for anorexia nervosa, bulimia nervosa, or binge eating disorder. However, young people with eating disorders often exhibit marked disturbances in their family, social, and school environments, which can persist even after successful treatment (Striegel-Moore et al., 2003) and well into adulthood (Gortmaker, Must, Perrin, & Sobol, 1993; Johnson et al., 2002). The relationship between family dynamics and the development of adolescent eating disorders has received significant attention in eating disorder literature by both clinicians and researchers, though relatively few studies have examined the impact of eating disorders on adolescents' social and academic functioning. We briefly discuss the growing body of research in the area of adolescent eating disorder impact on environment.

Family

Disturbances in family functioning have consistently been associated with anorexia and bulimia in adolescents (Davis, Shuster, Blackmore, & Fox, 2004; Humphrey, 1994). For example, parents of anorexic offspring are often characterized by overprotection, rigidity, and an excessive focus on thinness (Humphrey, 1994). Anorexics may be eager to meet parental demands and maintain harmony within their families, which can allow their psychopathology to persist, undetected, and result in heightened resistance to treatment (Inbody & Jones, 1985). By contrast, research suggests that families with bulimic offspring may exhibit more family chaos, hostility, stress, and isolation (Humphrey, 1989; Villejo, Humphrey, & Kirschenbaum, 1997). In a study of 20 bulimic adolescent girls, Okon, Greene, and Smith (2003) found that perceived family conflicts increased the occurrence and severity of bulimic symptoms, though longitudinal prospective studies of larger cohorts have not corroborated these findings. Murray, Waller, and Legg (2000) suggested that shame may be a mediating link between family functioning and bulimic pathology. A study of adolescents with binge eating disorder (Hodges, Cochrane, & Brewerton, 1998) found that young people with the disorder reported higher levels of control and conflict in family relationships than did anorexics, bulimics, and controls.

Continued research emphasis on the impact of eating disorders on family functioning may prove useful in identifying risk and protective factors in family environments, understanding the intergenerational persistence of eating disorders in families, preventing unhealthy modeling behaviors among adolescents with eating disorders and their siblings, and improving long-term treatment outcomes for this population.

School

Some studies have suggested that individuals with eating disorders may exhibit higher intelligence than persons without eating disorders (Blanz, Betzner, Lay, Rose, & Schmidt, 1997), though this has not been a consistent finding (Ranseen & Humphries, 1992). Adolescents with anorexia nervosa are often able to sustain academic excellence despite severe malnourishment (Fairburn & Harrison, 2003). Perfectionism, need for control, and strong desire to please may enhance anorexics' academic performance even as their physical and mental health deteriorate (Beumont, 2002; Vitousek, Watson, & Wilson, 1998). Indeed, anorexics who earn good grades and teacher approval through extreme self-discipline may be especially resistant to treatment, which may be viewed as undermining their success (Vitousek et al., 1998). However, decreased energy, impaired concentration, and other medical problems resulting from the anorexic's semistarved condition can hinder academic achievement and prompt teachers, family, and friends to intervene (Lena, Chidambaram, Panarella, & Sambasivan, 2001; Pomeroy, 2004).

Less is known about the effects of bulimia and binge eating disorder on adolescent functioning in school environments. However, because bulimia and binge eating disorder often occur comorbidly with depression, substance use, anxiety, and suicidality, it might reasonably be suggested that adolescents with bulimia and binge eating disorder suffer impairment in school-related activities similar to those of adolescents with associated disorders alone (Ameringen, Mancini, & Farvolden, 2003; Dolgan, 1990; Hallfors et al., 2002). Similarly, some evidence suggests that adolescents with binge eating disorder who are overweight or obese may be at greater risk for poor performance in school than their slimmer peers. Low self-confidence, diminished energy level, and discrimination from teachers and peers have been found to present significant obstacles to achievement among overweight adolescents (Gortmaker, Must, Perrin, & Sobol, 1993; Morrill, Leach, Shreeve, & Radebaugh, 1991; Puhl, & Brownell, 2001). More research is needed to determine whether adolescents with eating disorders encounter distinct difficulties in their school environments that differ from those experienced by young people with other disorders. Such research might usefully inform the creation of effective school-based prevention programs for eating disorders.

Peer Interactions

Peer views of weight and eating seem to strongly influence adolescents' body image concerns. One study found that the importance that peers placed on weight and eating was more strongly related to the development of excessive weight concerns in elementary and middle school adolescent girls than both body mass index and attempts to look like girls or women in magazines and on television (Taylor et al., 1998). Some evidence suggests that individuals with anorexia may exhibit diminished capacity to feel empathy for others (Kucharska-Pietura, Nikolaou, Masiak, & Treasure, 2004) along with higher levels of social anxiety (Hinrichsen, Wright, & Meyer, 2003), and obsessiveness (Fairburn & Harrison, 2003; Sutandar-Pinnock, Blake Woodside, Carter, Olmsted, & Kaplan, 2003) than nonanorexic controls. These factors are thought to contribute to disturbances in anorexics' peer relationships, including excessive competitiveness and social isolation, but their exact role remains unclear (Butow, Beumont, & Touyz, 1993). Troop, Allan, Treasure, and Katzman (2003) suggested that submissive behaviors and social comparison related to adolescents' perceived low social rank may be implicated in the development of both anorexia and bulimia. Hypothetically, because bulimics often hide their disturbed eating behaviors from peers, they may experience less impairment in their social relationships than anorexics, whose restrictive eating habits and low body weight appear more obvious. However, extreme body dissatisfaction; neuroticism; and feelings of guilt, shame, and envy associated with bulimia would seem to disrupt healthy social functioning (Cervera et al., 2003).

The impact of binge eating disorder on peer relationships is clearer, given the recent increase in attention to the social consequences of child and adolescent obesity, a condition associated with binge eating (Fairburn et al., 2000; Williamson & Martin, 1999). Studies have found that children and adolescents often attribute negative characteristics that are unrelated to weight or appearance to overweight individuals, and that overweight adolescents are often the victims of weight-related stigmatization among their peers (Brylinsky, 1994; Hill & Silver, 1995). In addition, overweight adolescents report being victims of teasing, social exclusion, and physical aggression more often than healthy weight control groups, and they may be less likely to engage in romantic relationships (Neumark-Sztainer, Falkner, & Story, 1999; Pearce, Boergers, & Prinstein, 2002). Janssen, Craig, Boyce, and Pickett (2004) suggested that overweight adolescents are more likely to be both victims and perpetrators of bullying and aggressive behaviors than their healthy weight peers. These troubling findings highlight the importance of further investigation into peer relationships and eating disorder development, as well as the creation of prevention and treatment programs sensitive to adolescents' family, school, and peer environments.

IMPLICATIONS FOR FUTURE PERSONALITY DEVELOPMENT

In the last several decades, there has been an increasing awareness that the emergence of psychopathology during adolescence may have a significant effect on a young person's efforts to develop a coherent strategy to cope with both internal and external demands of daily life (i.e., personality). The issue of how an eating disorder may impact emerging personality traits during adolescence, and later in adulthood, refers to the complication model of the eating disorder–personality relationship, which was reviewed earlier (see Figure 20.1C). By comparing recovered eating-disordered patients to ill patients, the personality traits that are accentuated in the short term by the state effects of the eating disorder are revealed. As noted, traits such as obsessiveness, neuroticism, emotional lability, and behavioral disinhibition all are elevated during an episode of the disorder but are substantially reduced following recovery (Grilo, 2002; Kennedy et al., 1990; Pollice et al., 1997; Stonehill & Crisp, 1977). On the other hand, by comparing recovered patients and never eating-disordered comparison individuals, the traits that *may* represent long-term personality scars of the disorder may be elucidated. Unfortunately this research design cannot definitively differentiate such potential long-term complications from potential predispositional traits. Nonetheless, traits such as ineffectiveness, harm avoidance, heightened stress reactivity, and perfectionistic doubting of actions have all been found to be elevated in recovered patients compared to never-ill controls and have not yet been identified as predispostional risk factors in prospective studies, leaving open the possibility that these traits might represent long-term consequences of the disorder on personality (Casper, 1990; Lilenfeld et al., 1998). Thus, it is possible that such traits, which generally reflect anxiousness, interpersonal submissiveness, and perfectionistic doubt, are features of personality that are the result of the experience of an eating disorder.

Another important concept that is relevant to the long-term effects of an eating disorder on personality is the reciprocal, pathoplastic influence that each condition (i.e., personality, eating disorder) has on the other over time. Increasingly, it is clear that certain personality traits influence the course of an eating disorder. For example, Steinhausen (2002), in a comprehensive review of the longitudinal studies in anorexia nervosa, concluded that obsessionality predicts a negative course in anorexia nervosa, whereas hysterical personality traits predict a more favorable course. Similarly, recent studies suggest that certain personality traits influence the phenomenon of diagnostic crossover from anorexia nervosa to bulimia nervosa and conversely from bulimia nervosa to anorexia nervosa. In a large multisite international study, Tozzi et al. (2005) found that low levels of the personality trait of self-directedness predicted crossover from AN to BN and that low levels of novelty seeking, along with low levels of self-directedness, predicted a diagnostic crossover from bulimia nervosa to anorexia nervosa. Given that such crossover is a relatively common phenomenon (25 percent to 30 percent), such personality traits may be important and help elucidate patterns of chronicity and symptomatic change, frequently seen in the eating disorders. Thus, eating disorders and personality traits may ultimately influence each other in a manner that affects symptom formation, course, and diagnostic stability of the eating disorder.

TREATMENT IMPLICATIONS

Treatment of the eating disorders has varied dramatically, depending on which eating disorder diagnosis is being considered. For example, there have been a large number of randomized controlled trials of psychotherapy and pharmacotherapy in bulimia nervosa, and to a lesser extent binge eating disorder, but the research literature on the treatment of anorexia nervosa has been quite limited. Furthermore, psychotherapeutic approaches for bulimia nervosa and binge eating disorder have relied heavily on individual- or group-based models, whereas the treatment for anorexia nervosa has recently moved in the direction of family therapy approaches. Finally, there is substantial support for several moderately efficacious treatments for bulimia nervosa, but such support of treatments for anorexia nervosa is lacking. Next, we will provide a brief overview of the treatment literature for each of the major eating disorders, but the reader is referred to several recent reviews for a more comprehensive overview (e.g., Peterson & Mitchell, 2001; Steinglass & Walsh, 2004; Wonderlich, de Zwann, Mitchell, Peterson, & Crow, 2003).

Anorexia Nervosa

The psychotherapeutic treatment of anorexia nervosa has developed in two rather distinct trends. First, in the psychotherapeutic treatment of adolescent anorexia nervosa there were early efforts at individually oriented therapies that focused on various psychodynamic themes or the concept that anorexia nervosa was a result of a phobic avoidance of adolescence (Bruch, 1973; Crisp, 1980). In contrast to individually oriented therapies, family system approaches to the treatment of anorexia nervosa were also being developed (e.g., Minuchin, Rosman, & Baker, 1978). Although these early approaches were not rigorously tested in randomized controlled trials, a specific form of family therapy called the Maudsley approach has been manualized and studied empirically. This approach focuses on several themes, including empowering families to find solutions to the problem of feeding their child, in-session family meals, and an emphasis on separating the illness from the child (Lock, 2004). This approach has been shown to be most beneficial for anorexic individuals under the age of 19 who display a relatively short duration of the illness (Dare, Eisler, Russell, & Szmukler, 1990; Russell, Szmukler, Dare, & Eisler, 1987).

The second trend in anorexia nervosa treatment has been the use of individual therapy for adult patients. Interestingly, studies of the Maudsley approach have suggested that in contrast to adolescent individuals, adult anorexic individuals tend to benefit more from individually oriented forms of psychotherapy than from family therapy. For example, individual supportive psychotherapy was found to be equivalent or superior to family therapy in the treatment of adult anorexic subjects at 5-year follow-up (Eisler, Dare, Russell, Szmukler, le Grange, & Dodge, 1997). Other studies using individually oriented approaches with both behavioral and psychodynamic strategies have produced modest support for the notion that there may be symptomatic improvement in adult anorexia nervosa when treated with individually oriented therapies (Channon, De Silva, Hemsley, & Perkins, 1989; Treasure et al., 1995).

In addition to psychotherapy studies, a variety of pharmacotherapeutic agents have also been tried in the treatment of anorexia nervosa, but due to the limited understanding of the biological basis of this disorder, the trials have not been adequately grounded on a theoretical basis and generally have proven to be relatively unproductive (Steinglass & Walsh, 2004). Early trials with tricylic antidepressants proved to be ineffective in the treatment of anorexia nervosa, and more recent research has focused on the selective serotonin reuptake inhibitors (SSRIs). However, the single, randomized, placebo-controlled trial of fluoxetine used in the acute phase of anorexia nervosa treatment has failed to provide substantial support for this agent (Attia, Harman, Walsh, & Flater, 1998). Somewhat more promising was a randomized controlled trial studying the maintenance effects of fluoxetine after anorexic participants had been weight stabilized on an inpatient basis. This study, by Kaye and colleagues (2001), found both a statistically and a clinically significant impact of fluoxetine compared to placebo on weight maintenance at 1-year follow-up. However, the dose of fluoxetine was not controlled, nor were additional forms of treatment, thus limiting the strength of inference from this particular study. Furthermore, another naturalistic study with historical control participants failed to support the efficacy of fluoxetine in relapse prevention with anorexic patients, thus leaving the utility of fluoxetine as a maintenance treatment unclear (Strober, Freeman, DeAntonio, Lampert, & Diamond, 1997). Although many other pharmacotherapeutic agents have been tried in the treatment of anorexia nervosa, positive findings have been extremely limited. There is some interest in newer antipsychotics, which have a lower side effect profile and may be helpful in the treatment of anorexia nervosa. For example, olanzapine has shown some promise, but the field awaits further empirical information regarding this drug.

Unfortunately, the consensus in the field is that treatments for anorexia nervosa have very limited efficacy in the reduction of anorexic symptoms and behaviors, and there is currently no empirically supported treatment for anorexia nervosa that has been shown to be even modestly efficacious in randomized controlled trials. Clearly, a strong need exists for large-scale, multicenter treatment trials for anorexia nervosa to begin to identify effective strategies for the treatment of the very complicated and serious disorder.

Bulimia Nervosa

Both psychotherapeutic and pharmacotherapeutic treatments for bulimia nervosa have received considerable empirical support. Cognitive behavior therapy is the most well studied and currently efficacious psychotherapeutic treatment strategy for bulimia nervosa. This treatment focuses on decreasing restrictive dieting, addressing dysfunctional thoughts about shape and weight, interrupting binge-purge behaviors, and ultimately enhancing self-esteem. More than 20 controlled trials have been conducted using individual or group cognitive-behavior therapy (CBT) for bulimia nervosa, with a general consensus that CBT has been shown to be superior to minimal or waiting list controls as well as other interventions including behavior therapy, psychodynamic therapy, supportive psychotherapy, and pharmacotherapy (Wonderlich, Mitchell, Swan-Kremeier, Peterson, & Crow, 2004). Importantly, however, 50 percent to 70 percent of bulimic individuals remain symptomatic at the end of short-term interventions, suggesting that new treatment strategies are needed to enhance outcome for a broader range of patients. Nonetheless, CBT continues to be the treatment of choice for bulimia nervosa (Peterson & Mitchell, 2001), largely due to its relatively rapid action and wealth of evidence suggesting reasonable efficacy.

Several other psychotherapeutic treatments have also shown promise for the treatment of bulimia nervosa. Interpersonal therapy, which targets relationship issues and avoids body shape and weight issues, has been shown to be roughly equivalent to CBT, particularly one or more years following the end of treatment (Agras, Walsh, Fairburn, Wilson, & Kraemer, 2000). Additionally, dialectical behavior therapy has been modified and applied to bulimia nervosa with reasonable outcomes (e.g., Safer, Telch, & Agras, 2001), but more research is needed to assess the efficacy of this personality-based treatment for bulimia nervosa.

Pharmacotherapeutic trials with bulimia nervosa have been more promising than medication studies with anorexia nervosa. General antidepressant therapies including tricyclic antidepressants, monoamine oxidase inhibitors, and SSRIs have all been shown to be fairly effective in reducing bulimic symptoms, without evidence of superiority of one drug over another (de Zwaan, Roerig, & Mitchell, 2004). It is important to note, however, that drug trials frequently report substantial percentage reductions in binge frequency (i.e., 31 percent to 91 percent), but remission rates are significantly lower (i.e.,

4 percent to 34 percent; Steinglass & Walsh, 2004). Also, there is a fairly substantial placebo response in some studies for both binge eating change percentage (i.e., +7 percent to −50 percent) and abstinence percentage (i.e., 0 percent to 16 percent; de Zwaan et al., 2004), which should be considered when evaluating drug therapy efficacy. Treating bulimic individuals with simple drug therapy has also been associated with high drop-out and relapse rates, suggesting that these treatments are best used in combination with psychotherapy, in spite of the fact that adding drug therapy to CBT provides uncertain benefit beyond psychotherapy alone (e.g., Mitchell et al., 1990; Walsh et al., 1997).

Binge Eating Disorder

As in bulimia nervosa, several psychotherapeutic strategies have been used in the treatment of binge eating disorder. The most studied is CBT (e.g., Agras, Telch, Arnow, Eldridge, & Marnell, 1997; Wilfley et al., 2002), although interpersonal therapy (e.g., Wilfley et al., 2002) and dialectical behavior therapy (Telch, Agras, & Linehan, 2001) have also been investigated. All three of these psychotherapeutic approaches for treating binge eating disorder have been quite efficacious in terms of reducing binge eating and promoting abstinence in approximately 50 percent of binge eating disorder patients at 12-month follow-up; significantly greater than wait-list control conditions (e.g., 0 percent to 13 percent abstinent at end of treatment; Telch et al., 2001; Telch, Agras, Rossiter, Wilfley, & Kenardy, 1990). The major limitation of these studies, however, is that binge eating disorder patients, who tend to be obese, do not lose substantial amounts of weight over long-term follow-up, even after reducing binge eating behaviors. However, individuals who attain abstinence from binge eating are most likely to avoid further weight gain in longitudinal studies (Agras et al., 1995).

Binge eating disorder patients have also been treated with simple dieting strategies that do not target many of the cognitive variables associated with binge eating disorder. Dieting strategies have been slightly more effective in weight loss in binge eating disorder than psychotherapeutic strategies (Goodrick et al., 1998; Wonderlich et al., 2003), but more importantly such dieting approaches have also demonstrated a significant reduction in binge eating frequency (Goodrick et al., 1998; Raymond, de Zwaan, Mitchell, Ackard, & Thuras, 2002). This is particularly noteworthy given predictions that dietary restriction in binge eating individuals would promote binge eating rather than reduce it (Polivy & Herman, 1985). Low-calorie diets have likewise been found to produce reductions in bulimic symptoms (Presnell & Stice, 2003). The fact that these experimental findings are incompatible suggests that there may be fundamental problems with the restraint model of eating disorders. It should be noted that the reduction of binge eating through dieting also raises interesting questions about the nature of binge eating disorder, along with its mechanisms of risk and action.

As with other eating disorders, numerous drug therapies have been tested in the treatment of binge eating disorder. Encouraging evidence suggests that SSRIs significantly reduce binge eating behavior and body mass index in binge eating disorder when compared to placebo (de Zwaan et al., 2004). Long-term efficacy of these treatments, however, remains unclear. Newer agents, such as topiramate, have shown promise in open-label studies and in one recent randomized controlled trial (McElroy et al., 2003). In this study, individuals treated with topiramate showed significantly greater reductions than controls in binge frequencies, symptom severity, and also body mass index. Finally, two studies have now examined whether drugs in combination with CBT are more efficacious than CBT alone or drugs alone (Devlin, 2002; Grilo, Masheb, Heninger, & Wilson, 2002). Both of these studies converge to suggest that the addition of drugs adds little to CBT in the treatment of binge eating disorder, and furthermore that drug treatment alone is not significantly more effective than placebo.

REFERENCES

Agras, W. S., Telch, C. F., Arnow, B., Eldredge, K., Detzer, M. J., Henderson, J., et al. (1995). Does interpersonal therapy help patients with binge eating disorder who fail to respond to cognitive-behavioral therapy? *Journal of Consulting and Clinical Psychology, 63,* 356–360.

Agras, W. S., Telch, C. F., Arnow, B., Eldredge, K., & Marnell, M. (1997). One-year follow-up of cognitive-behavioral therapy for obese individuals with binge eating disorder. *Journal of Consulting and Clinical Psychology, 65,* 343–347.

Agras, W. S., Walsh, B. T., Fairburn, C. G., Wilson, G. T., & Kraemer, H. C. (2000). A multicenter comparison of cognitive-behavioral therapy and interpersonal therapy for bulimia nervosa. *Archives of General Psychiatry, 57,* 459–466.

American Psychiatric Association. (1994). *Diagnostic and statistical manual of mental disorders* (4th ed.). Washington, DC: Author.

Ameringen, M. V., Mancini, C., & Farvolden, P. (2003). The impact of anxiety disorders on educational achievement. *Journal of Anxiety Disorders, 17,* 561–571.

Anderson, D. A., & Paulosky, C. A. (2004). Psychological assessment of eating disorders and related features. In J. K. Thompson (Ed.), *Handbook of eating disorders and obesity* (pp. 112–129). Hoboken, NJ: Wiley.

Attia, E., Harman, C., Walsh, T., & Flater, S. (1998). Does fluoxetine augment the inpatient treatment of anorexia nervosa? *American Journal of Psychiatry, 155,* 548–551.

Attie, I., & Brooks-Gunn, J. (1989). Development of eating problems in adolescent girls: A longitudinal study. *Developmental Psychology, 25,* 70–79.

Beumont, P. J. V. (2002). Clinical presentation of anorexia nervosa and bulimia nervosa. In C. G. Fairburn & K. D. Brownell (Eds.), *Eating disorders and obesity: A comprehensive handbook* (2nd ed., pp. 859–867). New York: Guilford Press.

Black, C. M., & Wilson, G. (1996). Assessment of eating disorders: Interview versus questionnaire. *International Journal of Eating Disorders, 20,* 43–50.

Blanz, B. J., Betzner, U., Lay, B., Rose, F., & Schmidt, M. H. (1997). The intellectual functioning of adolescents with anorexia nervosa and bulimia nervosa. *European Child and Adolescent Psychiatry, 6,* 129–135.

Bruch, H. (1973). *Eating disorders: Obesity, anorexia, and the person within.* New York: Basic Books.

Brylinski, J. A. (1994). The identification of body build stereotypes in young children. *Journal of Research in Personality, 28,* 170–181.

Bulik, C. M., Sullivan, P. F., & Kendler, K. S. (1998). Heritability of binge-eating and broadly defined bulimia nervosa. *Biological Psychiatry, 44,* 1210–1218.

Butow, P., Beumont, P., & Touyz, S. (1993). Cognitive processes in dieting disorders. *International Journal of Eating Disorders, 14,* 319–329.

Casper, R. C. (1990). Personality features of women with good outcome from restricting anorexia. *Psychosomatic Medicine, 52,* 156–170.

Cattarin, J. A., & Thompson, J. K. (1994). A 3-year longitudinal study of body image, eating disturbance, and general psychological functioning in adolescent females. *Eating Disorders, 2,* 114–125.

Cervera, S., Lahortiga, F., Martinez-Gonzalez, M. A., Gual, P., de Irala-Estevez, J., & Alonso, Y. (2003). Neuroticism and low self-esteem as risk factors for incident eating disorders in a prospective cohort study. *International Journal of Eating Disorders, 33,* 271–280.

Channon, S., de Silva, P., Hemsley, D., & Perkins, R. (1989). A controlled trial of cognitive behavioral and behavioral treatment of anorexia nervosa. *Behavior Research and Therapy, 27,* 529–535.

Cloninger, C. R., Svrakic, D. M., & Przybeck, T. (1993). A psychobiological model of temperament and character. *Archives of General Psychiatry, 50,* 975–990.

Crisp, A. H. (1980). *Anorexia nervosa: Let me be.* London: Academic Press.

Dare, C., Eisler, I., Russell, G. F. M., & Szmukler, G. I. (1990). Family therapy for anorexia nervosa: Implications from the results of a controlled trial of family and individual therapy. *Journal of Marital and Family Therapy, 16,* 39–57.

Davis, C., Shuster, B., Blackmore, E., & Fox, J. (2004). Looking good: Family focus on appearance and the risk for eating disorders. *International Journal of Eating Disorders, 35,* 136–144.

Devlin, M. (2002, April). *Psychotherapy and medication for binge eating disorder.* Paper presented at the International Conference on Eating Disorders, Boston.

de Zwaan, M., Roerig, J. L., & Mitchell, J. E. (2004). Pharmacological treatment of anorexia nervosa, bulimia nervosa, and binge eating disorder. In J. K. Thompson (Ed.), *Handbook of eating disorders and obesity* (pp. 186–217). Hoboken, NJ: Wiley.

Dolgan, J. I. (1990). Depression in children. *Pediatric Annals,* 45–50.

Eisler, I., Dare, C., Russell, G. F. M., Szmukler, G. I., le Grange, D., & Dodge, E. (1997). Family and individual therapy in anorexia nervosa: A five-year follow-up. *Archives of General Psychiatry, 54,* 1025–1030.

Fairburn, C. G., & Beglin, S. J. (1994). Assessment of eating disorders: Interview or self-report questionnaire? *International Journal of Eating Disorders, 16,* 363–370.

Fairburn, C. G., & Cooper, Z. (1993). The Eating Disorder Examination (12th ed.). In C. Fairburn & G. Wilson (Eds.), *Binge eating: Nature, assessment, and treatment* (pp. 317–360). New York: Guilford Press.

Fairburn, C. G., Cooper, Z., Doll, H. A., Norman, P. A., & O'Connor, M. E. (2000). The natural course of bulimia nervosa and binge eating disorder in young women. *Archives of General Psychiatry, 57,* 659–665.

Fairburn, C. G., Cooper, Z., Doll, H. A., & Welch, S. L. (1999). Risk factors for anorexia nervosa: Three integrated cases—control comparisons. *Archives of General Psychiatry, 56,* 468–467.

Fairburn, C. G., Cowen, P. J., & Harrison, P. J. (1999). Twin studies and the etiology of eating disorders. *International Journal of Eating Disorders, 26,* 349–358.

Fairburn, C. G., & Harrison, P. J. (2003). Eating disorders. *Lancet, 361,* 407–416.

Fairburn, C. G., Norman, P. A., Welch, S. L., O'Connor, M. E., Doll, H. A., & Peveler, R. C. (1995). A prospective study of outcome in bulimia nervosa and the long-term effects of three psychological treatments. *Archives of General Psychiatry, 52,* 304–312.

Field, A. E., Camargo, C. A., Taylor, C. B., Berkey, C. S., & Colditz, G. A. (1999). Relation of peer and media influences to the development of purging behaviors among preadolescent and adolescent girls. *Archives of Pediatric Adolescent Medicine, 153,* 1184–1189.

Fisher, M., Schneider, M., Burns, J., Symons, H., & Mandel, F. S. (2001). Differences between adolescents and young adults at presentation to an eating disorder program. *Journal of Adolescent Health, 28,* 222–227.

Garfinkel, P. E., & Newman, A. (2001). The Eating Attitudes Test: Twenty-five years later. *Eating and Weight Disorders, 6,* 1–24.

Garner, D. M. (1991). *Eating Disorder Inventory—2 manual.* Odessa, FL: Psychological Assessment Resources.

Garner, D. M. (1993). Binge eating in anorexia nervosa. In C. G. Fairburn & G. T. Wilson (Eds.), *Binge eating: Nature, assessment, and treatment* (pp. 50–76). New York: Guilford Press.

Garner, D. M., & Garfinkel, P. (1979). The Eating Attitudes Test: An index of the symptoms of anorexia nervosa. *Psychological Medicine, 9,* 273–279.

Garner, D. M., Olmsted, M. P., & Polivy, J. (1983). Development and validation of a multidimensional eating disorder inventory for anorexia nervosa and bulimia. *International Journal of Eating Disorders, 2,* 15–34.

Ghaderi, A., & Scott, B. (2000). The Big Five and eating disorders: A prospective study in the general population. *European Journal of Personality, 14,* 311–323.

Goodman, E., & Whitaker, R. C. (2002). A prospective study of the role of depression in the development and persistence of adolescent obesity. *Pediatrics, 109,* 497–504.

Goodrick, G. K., Poston, W. S., Kimball, K. T., Reeves, R. S., & Foreyt, J. P. (1998). Nondieting versus dieting treatments for overweight binge-eating women. *Journal of Consulting and Clinical Psychology, 66,* 363–368.

Gortmaker, S. L., Must, A., Perrin, J., & Sobol, A. (1993). Social and economic consequences of overweight in adolescence and young adulthood. *New England Journal of Medicine, 329,* 1008–1012.

Grilo, C. M. (2002). Recent research of relationships among eating disorders and personality disorders. *Current Psychiatry Reports, 4,* 18–24.

Grilo, C. M., Masheb, R. M., Heninger, G., & Wilson, G. T. (2002, April). *Psychotherapy and medication for binge eating disorder.* Paper presented at the International Conference on Eating Disorders, Boston.

Hallfors, D., Vevea, J. L., Iritani, B., Cho, H., Khatapoush, S., & Saxe, L. (2002). Truancy, grade point average, and sexual activity: A meta-analysis of risk indicators for youth substance use. *Journal of School Health, 72,* 205–211.

Herzog, D. B., Greenwood, D. N., Dorer, D. J., Flores, A. T., Ekeblad, E. R., Richards, A., et al. (2000). Mortality in eating disorders: A descriptive study. *International Journal of Eating Disorders, 28,* 20–26.

Herzog, D. B., Hopkins, J., & Burns, C. D. (1993). A follow-up study of 33 subdiagnostic eating disordered women. *International Journal of Eating Disorders, 14,* 261–267.

Hill, A. J., & Silver, E. K. (1995). Fat, friendless and unhealthy: 9-year-old children's perception of body shape stereotypes. *International Journal of Obesity, 19,* 423–430.

Hinney, A., Bornscheuer, A., Depenbusch, M., Mierke, B., Tolle, A., Middeke, K., et al. (1998). No evidence for involvement of the leptin gene in anorexia nervosa, bulimia nervosa, underweight or early onset extreme obesity: Identification of two novel mutations in the coding sequence and a novel polymorphism in the leptin gene linked upstream region. *Molecular Psychiatry, 3,* 539–543.

Hinney, A., Schmidt, A., Nottebom, K., Heibult, O., Becker, I., Ziegler, A., et al. (1999). Several mutations in the melanocortin-4 receptor gene including a nonsense and a frameshift mutation associated with dominantly inherited obesity in humans. *Journal of Clinical Endocrinology and Metabolism, 84,* 1483–1486.

Hinrichsen, H., Wright, F., & Meyer, C. (2003). Social anxiety and coping strategies in the eating disorders. *Eating Behavior, 4,* 117–126.

Hodges, E. L., Cochrane, C. E., & Brewerton, T. D. (1998). Family characteristics of binge-eating disorder patients. *International Journal of Eating Disorders, 23,* 145–151.

Humphrey, L. L. (1989). Observed family interactions among subtypes of eating disorders using structural analysis of social behavior. *Journal of Clinical Psychology, 57,* 206–214.

Humphrey, L. L. (1994). Family relationships. In K. A. Halmi (Ed.), *Psychobiology and treatment of anorexia nervosa and bulimia nervosa* (pp. 263–282). Washington, DC: American Psychiatric Press.

Inbody, D. R., & Jones, J. (1985). Group therapy with anorexic and bulimic patients: Implications for therapeutic intervention. *American Journal of Psychotherapy, 39,* 411–421.

Jacobi, C., Hayward, C., de Zwaan, M., Kraemer, H. C., & Agras, S. (2004). Coming to terms with risk factors for eating disorders: Application of risk terminology and suggestions for a general taxonomy. *Psychological Bulletin, 130,* 19–65.

Janssen, I., Craig, W. M., Boyce, W. F., & Pickett, W. (2004). Associations between overweight and obesity with bullying behaviors in school-aged children. *Pediatrics, 5,* 1187–1194.

Johnson, J. G., Cohen, P., Kasen, S., & Brook, J. S. (2002). Eating disorders during adolescence and the risk for physical and mental disorders during early adulthood. *Archives of General Psychiatry, 59,* 545–552.

Kaye, W., Nagata, T., Weltzin, T., Hsu, L. K., Sokol, M. S., McConaha, C., et al. (2001). Double-blind placebo-controlled administration of fluoxetine in restricting and restricting-purging-type anorexia nervosa. *Biology of Psychiatry, 49,* 644–652.

Kaye, W. H., Klump, K. L., Frank, G. K., & Strober, M. (2000). Anorexia and bulimia nervosa. *Annual Review of Medicine, 51,* 299–313.

Keel, P. K., Fulkerson, J. A., & Leon, G. R. (1997). Disordered eating precursors in pre- and early adolescent girls and boys. *Journal of Youth and Adolescence, 26,* 203–216.

Kennedy, S. H., McVey, G., & Katz, R. (1990). Personality disorders in anorexia nervosa and bulimia nervosa. *Journal of Psychiatric Research, 24,* 259–269.

Keys, A., Brozek, J., Henschel, A., Mickelsen, O., & Taylor, H. L. (1950). *The biology of human starvation.* Minneapolis: University of Minnesota Press.

Killen, J. D., Taylor, C. B., Hayward, C., Haydel, K. F., Wilson, D. M., Hammer, L., et al. (1996). Weight concerns influence the development of eating disorders: A 4-year prospective study. *Journal of Consulting and Clinical Psychology, 64,* 936–940.

Killen, J. D., Taylor, C. B., Hayward, C., Wilson, D., Haydel, K., Hammer, L., et al. (1994). Pursuit of thinness and onset of eating disorder symptoms in a community sample of adolescent girls: A three-year prospective analysis. *International Journal of Eating Disorders, 16,* 227–238.

Klump, K. L., McGue, M., & Iacono, W. G. (2002). Genetic relationships between personality and eating attitudes and behaviors. *Journal of Abnormal Psychology, 111,* 380–389.

Kucharska-Pietura, K., Nikolaou, V., Masiak, M., & Treasure, J. (2004). The recognition of emotion in the faces and voice of anorexia nervosa. *International Journal of Eating Disorders, 12,* 377–384.

Lena, S. M., Chidambaram, U., Panarella, C., & Sambasivan, K. (2001). Cognitive factors in anorexia nervosa: A case history. *International Journal of Eating Disorders, 30,* 354–358.

Leon, G. R., Fulkerson, J. A., Perry, C. L., Keel, P. K., & Klump, K. L. (1999). Three to four year prospective evaluation of personality and behavioral risk factors for later disordered eating in adolescent girls and boys. *Journal of Youth and Adolescence, 28,* 181–192.

Lewinsohn, P. M., Hops, H., Roberts, R. E., Seeley, J. R., & Andrews, J. A. (1993). Adolescent psychopathology: I. Prevalence and incidence of depression and other *DSM-II-R* disorders in high school students. *Journal of Abnormal Psychology, 102,* 133–144.

Lewinsohn, P. M., Striegel-Moore, R. H., & Seeley, J. R. (2000). Epidemiology and natural course of eating disorders in young women from adolescence to young adulthood. *Journal of the American Academy of Child and Adolescent Psychiatry, 39,* 1284–1292.

Lilenfeld, L. R., Kaye, W. H., Greeno, C. G., Merikangas, K. R., Plotniciv, K., Pollice, C., et al. (1998). A controlled family study of anorexia nervosa and bulimia nervosa: Psychiatric disorders in first-degree relatives and effects of proband comorbidity. *Archives of General Psychiatry, 55,* 603–610.

Lilenfeld, L. R. R., Wonderlich, S., Riso, L. P., Crosby, R., & Mitchell, J. E. (2004). *Eating disorders and personality: A methodological and empirical review.* Manuscript submitted for publication.

Lock, J. (2004). Family approaches for anorexia nervosa and bulimia nervosa. In K. Thompson (Ed.), *Handbook of eating disorders and obesity* (pp. 218–231). Hoboken, NJ: Wiley.

Luce, K. H., & Crowther, J. H. (1999). The reliability of the eating disorder examination—self-report questionnaire version (EDE-Q). *International Journal of Eating Disorders, 25,* 349–351.

McElroy, S., Arnold, L., Shapira, N., Keck, P. E., Rosenthal, N. R., Karim, M. R., et al. (2003). Topiramate in the treatment of binge eating disorder associated with obesity: A randomized placebo-controlled trial. *American Journal of Psychiatry, 160,* 255–261.

McKnight Investigators. (2003). Risk factors for the onset of eating disorders in adolescent girls: Results of the McKnight Longitudinal Risk Factor Study. *American Journal of Psychiatry, 160,* 248–254.

Mintz, L. B., O'Halloran, M. S., Mulholland, A.M., & Schneider, P. A. (1997). Questionnaire for eating disorder diagnoses: Reliability and validity of operationalizing *DSM-IV* criteria into a self-report format. *Journal of Counseling Psychology, 44,* 63–79.

Minuchin, S., Rosman, B., & Baker, I. (1978). *Psychosomatic families: Anorexia nervosa in context.* Cambridge, MA: Harvard University Press.

Mitchell, J. E., Pyle, R. L., Eckert, E. D., Hatsukami, D., Pomeroy, C., & Zimmerman, R. (1990). A comparison study of antidepressants and structured group therapy in the treatment of bulimia nervosa. *Archives of General Psychiatry, 47,* 149–157.

Morrill, C., Leach, J., Shreeve, W., & Radebaugh, M. (1991). Teenage obesity: An academic issue. *International Journal of Adolescence and Youth, 2,* 245–250.

Murray, C., Waller, G., & Legg, C. 2000. Family dysfunction and bulimic psychopathology: The mediating role of shame. *International Journal of Eating Disorders, 28,* 84–89.

Neumark-Sztainer, D., & Haines, J. (2004). Psychosocial and behavioral consequences of obesity. In K. Thompson (Ed.), *Handbook of eating disorders and obesity* (pp. 349–371). Hoboken, NJ: Wiley.

Newman, D. L., Moffitt, T. E., Caspi, A., Magdol, L., Silva, P. A., & Stanton, W. R. (1996). Psychiatric disorder in a birth cohort of young adults: Prevalence, comorbidity, clinical significance, and new case incidence from ages 11 to 21. *Journal of Consulting and Clinical Psychology, 64,* 552–562.

Okon, D. M., Greene, A. L., & Smith, J. E. (2003). Family interactions predict intraindividual symptom variation for adolescents with bulimia. *International Journal of Eating Disorders, 34,* 450–458.

Patton, G. C., Johnson-Sabine, E., Wood, K., Mann, A. H., & Wakeling, A. (1990). Abnormal eating attitudes in London schoolgirls—a prospective epidemiological study: Outcome at twelve month follow-up. *Psychological Medicine, 20,* 383–394.

Pearce, M. J., Boergers, J., & Prinstein, M. J. (2002). Adolescent obesity, overt and relational peer victimization, and romantic relationships. *Obesity Research, 10,* 386–393.

Peterson, C. B., & Mitchell, J. E. (2001). Cognitive behavioral therapy for eating disorders. In J. E. Mitchell (Ed.), *The outpatient treatment for eating disorders: A guide for therapists, dietitians, and physicians* (pp. 145–167). Minneapolis: University of Minnesota Press.

Polivy, J., & Herman, C. P. (1985). Dieting and binge eating: A causal analysis. *American Psychologist, 40,* 193–204.

Pollice, C., Kaye, W. H., Greeno, C. G., & Weltzin, T. E. (1997). Relationship of depression, anxiety and obsessionality to states of illness in anorexia nervosa. *International Journal of Eating Disorders, 21,* 367–376.

Pomeroy, C. (2004). Assessment of medical status and physical factors. In K. Thompson (Ed.), *Handbook of eating disorders and obesity* (pp. 81–111). Hoboken, NJ: Wiley.

Presnell, K., & Stice, E. (2003). An experimental test of the effect of weight-loss dieting on bulimic pathology: Tipping the scales in a different direction. *Journal of Abnormal Psychology, 112,* 166–170.

Puhl, R., & Brownell, K. D. (2001). Bias, discrimination and obesity. *Obesity Research, 9,* 788–805.

Ranseen, J. D., & Humphries, L. L. (1992). The intellectual functioning of eating disorder patients. *Journal of the American Academy of Child and Adolescent Psychiatry, 31,* 844–846.

Raymond, N. C., de Zwaan, M., Mitchell, J. E., Ackard, D., & Thuras, P. (2002). Effect of a very low calorie diet on the diagnostic category of individuals with binge eating disorder. *International Journal of Eating Disorders, 31,* 49–56.

Reeves, R. S., McPherson, R. S., Nichaman, M. Z., Harrist, R. B., Foreyt, J. P., & Goodrick, G. K. (2001). Nutrient intake of obese female binge eaters. *Journal of the American Dietetic Association, 101,* 209–215.

Rizvi, S. L., Peterson, C. B., Crow, S. J., & Agras, W. S. (2000). Test-retest reliability of the eating disorder examination. *International Journal of Eating Disorders, 28,* 311–316.

Rosenbaum, M., Leibel, R., & Hirsch, J. (1997). Obesity. *New England Journal of Medicine, 337,* 396–407.

Russell, G. F. M., Szmukler, G. I., Dare, C., & Eisler, I. (1987). An evaluation of family therapy in anorexia nervosa and bulimia nervosa. *Archives of General Psychiatry, 44,* 1047–1056.

Safer, D. L., Telch, C. F., & Agras, W. S. (2001). Dialectical behavior therapy for bulimia nervosa. *American Journal of Psychiatry, 4,* 632–634.

Santonastaso, P., Friederici, S., & Favaro, A. (1999). Full and partial syndromes in eating disorders: A 1-year prospective study of risk factors among female students. *Psychopathology, 32,* 50–56.

Segal, D. L., Hersen, M., & Van Hasselt, V. B. (1994). Reliability of the structured clinical interview for *DSM-III-R:* An evaluative review. *Comprehensive Psychiatry, 35,* 316–327.

Shiner, R. L. (1998). How shall we speak of children's personalities in middle childhood? A preliminary taxonomy. *Psychological Bulletin, 124,* 308–332.

Slade, P. (1982). Towards a functional analysis of anorexia nervosa and bulimia nervosa. *British Journal of Clinical Psychology, 14,* 167–179.

Spitzer, R. L., Williams, J. B., Gibbon, M., & First, M. B. (1990). *Structured Clinical Interview for DSM-III-R (SCID).* Washington, DC: American Psychiatric Press.

Steinglass, J. E., & Walsh, B. T. (2004). Psychopharmacology of anorexia nervosa, bulimia nervosa, and binge eating disorder. In T. D. Brewerton (Ed.), *Clinical handbook of eating disorders: An integrated approach.* New York: Marcel Dekker.

Steinhausen, H. C. (2002). The outcome of anorexia nervosa in the twentieth century. *American Journal of Psychiatry, 159,* 1284–1293.

Stice, E. (2001). A prospective test of the dual pathway model of bulimic pathology: Mediating effects of dieting and negative affect. *Journal of Abnormal Psychology, 110,* 124–135.

Stice, E. (2002). Risk and maintenance factors for eating pathology: A meta-analytic review. *Psychological Bulletin, 128,* 825–848.

Stice, E., & Agras, W. S. (1998). Predicting onset and cessation of bulimic behaviors during adolescence: A longitudinal grouping analysis. *Behavior Therapy, 29,* 257–276.

Stice, E., Burton, E. M., & Shaw, H. (2004). Prospective relations between bulimic pathology, depression, and substance abuse: Unpacking comorbidity in adolescent girls. *Journal of Consulting and Clinical Psychology, 72,* 62–71.

Stice, E., Cameron, R., Killen, J. D., Hayward, C., & Taylor, C. B. (1999). Naturalistic weight reduction efforts prospectively predict growth in relative weight and onset of obesity among female adolescents. *Journal of Consulting and Clinical Psychology, 67,* 967–974.

Stice, E., Fisher, M., & Martinez, E. (2004). Eating disorder diagnostic scale: Additional evidence of reliability and validity. *Psychological Assessment, 16,* 60–71.

Stice, E., Hayward, C., Cameron, R., Killen, J. D., & Taylor, C. B. (2000). Body image and eating related factors predict onset of depression in female adolescents: A longitudinal study. *Journal of Abnormal Psychology, 109,* 438–444.

Stice, E., Killen, J. D., Hayward, C., & Taylor, C. B. (1998). Age of onset for binge eating and purging during adolescence: A four-year survival analysis. *Journal of Abnormal Psychology, 107,* 671–675.

Stice, E., Presnell, K., & Bearman, S. K. (2004). *Risk factors for onset of threshold and subthreshold bulimia nervosa: A 4-year prospective study of adolescent girls.* Unpublished manuscript, University of Texas at Austin.

Stice, E., Presnell, K., Shaw, H., & Rohde, P. (2005). Psychological and behavioral risk factors for obesity onset in adolescent girls: A prospective study. *Journal of Consulting and Clinical Psychology, 73,* 62–71.

Stice, E., Presnell, K., & Spangler, D. (2002). Risk factors for binge eating onset: A prospective investigation. *Health Psychology, 21,* 131–138.

Stice, E., Telch, C. F., & Rizvi, S. L. (2000). A psychometric evaluation of the Eating Disorder Diagnostic Screen: A brief self-report measure for anorexia, bulimia, and binge eating disorder. *Psychological Assessment, 12,* 123–131.

Stonehill, E., & Crisp, A. H. (1977). Psychoneurotic characteristics of patients with anorexia nervosa before and after treatment and at follow-up 4–7 years later. *Journal of Psychosomatic Research, 21,* 187–193.

Striegel-Moore, R. H., Seeley, J. R., & Lewinsohn, P. M. (2003). Psychosocial adjustment in young adulthood of women who experience an eating disorder during adolescence. *American Academy of Child and Adolescent Psychiatry, 42,* 587–593.

Striegel-Moore, R. H., Wilfley, D. E., Pike, K. M., Dohm, F. A., & Fairburn, C. G. (2000). Recurrent binge eating in black American women. *Archives of Family Medicine, 9,* 83–87.

Strober, M. (1991). Disorders of the self in anorexia nervosa: An organismic developmental paradigm. In C. Johnson (Ed.), *Psychodynamic treatment for eating disorders* (pp. 354–373). New York: Guilford Press.

Strober, M., Freeman, R., DeAntonio, M., Lampert, C., & Diamond, J. (1997). Does adjunctive fluoxetine influence the post-hospital course of anorexia nervosa? A 24-month prospective, longitudinal follow-up and comparison with historical controls. *Psychopharmacology Bulletin, 33,* 425–431.

Sutandar-Pinnock, K., Blake Woodside, D., Carter, J. C., Olmsted, M. P., & Kaplan, A. S. (2003). Perfectionism in anorexia nervosa: A 6–24-month follow-up study. *International Journal of Eating Disorders, 33,* 225–229.

Taylor, C. B., Sharpe, T., Shisslak, C., Bryson, S., Estes, L. S., Gray, N., et al. (1998). Factors associated with weight concerns in adolescent girls. *International Journal of Eating Disorders, 24,* 31–42.

Telch, C. F., Agras, W. S., & Linehan, M. M. (2001). Dialectical behavior therapy for binge eating disorder. *Journal of Consulting and Clinical Psychology, 69,* 1061–1065.

Telch, C. F., Agras, W. S., Rossiter, E. M., Wilfley, D., & Kenardy, J. (1990). Group cognitive-behavioral treatment for the nonpurging bulimic: An initial evaluation. *Journal of Consulting and Clinical Psychology, 58,* 629–635.

Telch, C., & Stice, E. (1998). Psychiatric comorbidity in a nonclinical sample of women with binge eating disorder. *Journal of Consulting and Clinical Psychology, 66,* 768–776.

Thelen, M., Farmer, J., Wonderlich, S., & Smith, M. (1991). A revision of the Bulimia Test: The BULIT-R. *Psychological Assessment, 3,* 119–124.

Tozzi, F., Thornton, L. M., Klump, K. L., Bulik, C. M., Fichter, M. M., Halmi, K. A., et al. (2005). Symptom fluctuation in eating disorders: Correlates of diagnostic crossover. *American Journal of Psychiatry, 162,* 732–740.

Treasure, J., & Holland, A. (1989). Genetic vulnerability to eating disorders: Evidence from twin and family studies. In H. Remschmidt & M. H. Schmidt (Eds.), *Child and youth psychiatry: European perspectives* (pp. 59–68). New York: Hogrefe & Huber.

Treasure, J., Todd, G., Brolly, M., Tiller, J., Nehmed, A., & Denman, F. (1995). A pilot study of a randomized trial of cognitive-behavioral analytical therapy vs. educational behavioral therapy for adult anorexia nervosa. *Behavioral Research and Therapy, 33,* 363–367.

Troop, N. A., Allan, S., Treasure, J. L., & Katzman, M. (2003). Social comparison and submissive behaviour in eating disorder patients. *Psychology and Psychotherapy, 76,* 237–249.

Villejo, R., Humphrey, L. L., Kirschenbaum, D. S. (1997) Affect and self-regulation in binge eaters: Effects of activating family images. *International Journal of Eating Disorders, 21,* 237–250.

Vitousek, K., Watson, S., & Wilson, G. T. (1998). Enhancing motivation for change in treatment-resistant eating disorders. *Clinical Psychology Review, 18,* 391–420.

Vogeltanz-Holm, N. D., Wonderlich, S. A., Lewis, B. A., Wilsnack, S. C., Harris, T. R., Wilsnack, R. W., et al. (2000). Longitudinal predictors of binge eating, intense dieting, and weight concerns in a national sample of women. *Behavior Therapy, 31,* 221–235.

Vohs, K. D., Bardone, A. M., Joiner, T. E., Abramson, L. Y., & Heatherton, T. F. (1999). Perfectionism, perceived weight status, and self-esteem interact to predict bulimic symptoms: A model of bulimic symptom development. *Journal of Abnormal Psychology, 108,* 695–700.

Wade, T., Martin, N. G., Tiggeman, M., Abraham, S., Treloar, S. A., & Heath, A. C. (2000). Genetic and environmental risk factors shared between disordered eating, psychological, and family variables. *Personality and Individual Differences, 28,* 729–740.

Walsh, B. T. (1993). Binge eating in bulimia nervosa. In C. G. Fairburn & G. T. Wilson (Eds.), *Binge eating: Nature, assessment, and treatment* (pp. 37–49). New York: Guilford Press.

Walsh, B. T., Wilson, G. T., Loeb, K. L., Devlin, M. J., Pike, K. M., Roose, S. P., et al. (1997). Medication and psychotherapy in the treatment of bulimia nervosa. *American Journal of Psychiatry, 154,* 523–531.

Walters, E. E., & Kendler, K. S. (1995). Anorexia nervosa and anorexia-like syndromes in a population-based female twin sample. *American Journal of Psychiatry, 152,* 64–71.

Wertheim, E. H., Koerner, J., & Paxton, S. (2001). Longitudinal predictors of restrictive eating and bulimic tendencies in three different age groups of adolescent girls. *Journal of Youth and Adolescence, 30,* 69–81.

Wichstrom, L. (2000). Psychological and behavioral factors unpredictive of disordered eating: A prospective study of the general adolescent population in Norway. *International Journal of Eating Disorders, 28,* 33–42.

Wilfley, D. E., Welch, R. R., Stein, R. I., Spurrell, E. B., Cohen, L. R., Saelens, B. E., et al. (2002). A randomized comparison of group cognitive-behavioral therapy and group interpersonal psychotherapy for the treatment of overweight individuals with binge-eating disorder. *Archives of General Psychiatry, 59,* 713–721.

Williams, J. B., Gibbon, M., First, M. B., Spitzer, R. L., Davies, M., Borus, J., et al. (1992). The Structured Clinical Interview for *DSM-III-R* (SCID) II: Multisite test-retest reliability. *Archives of General Psychiatry, 49,* 630–363.

Williamson, D. A., Anderson, D. A., Jackman, L. P., & Jackson, S. R. (1995). Assessment of eating disordered thoughts, feelings, and behaviors. In D. B. Allison (Ed.), *Handbook of assessment methods for eating behaviors and weight-related problems: Measures, theory, and research* (pp. 347–386). Thousand Oaks, CA: Sage.

Williamson, D. A., Gleaves, D. H., & Savin, S. S. (1992). Empirical classification of eating disorder not otherwise specified: Support for *DSM-IV* changes. *Journal of Psychopathology and Behavioral Assessment, 14,* 201–216.

Williamson, D. A., & Martin, C. K. (1999). Binge eating disorder: A review of the literature after publication of *DSM-IV. Eating and Weight Disorders, 4,* 103–114.

Wilson, G. T., Becker, C. B., & Heffernan, K. (2003). Eating disorders. In E. J. Mash & R. A. Barkley (Eds.), *Child psychopathology* (2nd ed., pp. 687–715). New York: Guilford Press.

Wonderlich, S. A., & Mitchell, J. E. (1997). Eating disorders and comorbidity: Empirical, conceptual, and clinical implications. *Psychopharmacology Bulletin, 33,* 381–390.

Wonderlich, S. A., de Zwaan, M., Mitchell, J. E., Peterson, C., & Crow, S. (2003). Psychological and dietary treatments of binge eating disorder: Conceptual implications. *International Journal of Eating Disorders, 34,* 558–573.

Wonderlich, S. A., Mitchell, J. E., Swan-Kremeier, L., Peterson, C., & Crow, S. (2004). An overview of cognitive-behavioral approaches to eating disorders. In T. D. Brewerton (Ed.), *Clinical handbook of eating disorders: An integrated approach.* New York: Marcel Dekker.

Wonderlich, S., Connolly, K. M., & Stice, E. (2004). Impulsivity as a risk factor for eating disorder behavior: Assessment implications with adolescents. *International Journal of Eating Disorders, 36*(2), 172–182.

Yanovski, S. Z., Leet, M., Yanovski, J. A., Flood, M., Gold, P. W., Kissileff, H. R., et al. (1992). Food selection and intake of obese women with binge eating disorder. *American Journal of Clinical Nutrition, 56,* 975–980.

CHAPTER 21

Substance Use Disorders

ERIC F. WAGNER AND ASHLEY M. AUSTIN

DESCRIPTION OF THE DISORDERS AND CLINICAL PICTURE

Most teenagers, by the time they reach their senior year of high school, will have tried alcohol, and fully half will have tried at least one illicit drug. Results from the Monitoring the Future Study, conducted annually by researchers at the Survey Research Center in the Institute for Social Research at the University of Michigan, indicate that 77 percent of 12th graders have used alcohol in their lifetime, 58 percent have been drunk, and 51 percent have tried an illicit substance (Johnston, O'Malley, Bachman, & Schulenberg, 2004). When asked about past-year substance use behaviors, 70 percent reported drinking one or more times, 48 percent reported having been drunk one or more times, and 39 percent reported using an illicit drug one or more times. Finally, when asked about past-month substance use behaviors, 47 percent reported drinking one or more times, 31 percent reported having been drunk one or more times, and 24 percent reported using an illicit drug one or more times. As might be expected, substance use is much less prevalent among 8th graders and somewhat less prevalent among 10th graders compared with 12th graders. Still, sizable numbers of younger adolescents drink and use drugs; for example, 20 percent of 8th graders and 35 percent of 10th graders drank one or more times in the past month. The point here is that substance use among adolescents is not uncommon, and depending on the recall period and age may be the rule rather than the exception.

When does adolescent substance use, a statistically normative behavior, become a disorder? To date, even experts in the field have not completely agreed on what are the sufficient and necessary criteria for determining whether a teenager is exhibiting a substance use problem (Hays & Ellickson, 1996). One approach has been to rely on the diagnostic criteria for substance abuse and substance dependence developed and used with adults. According to the *Diagnostic and Statistical Manual of Mental Disorders,* fourth edition (*DSM-IV;* American Psychiatric Association, 1994), a diagnosis of substance abuse requires at least one of the following four symptoms: (1) recurrent substance use resulting in a failure to fulfill major role obligations at work, school, or home; (2) recurrent substance use in situations in which it is physically hazardous; (3) recurrent substance-related legal problems; and (4) continued substance use despite having persistent or recurrent social or interpersonal problems caused or exacerbated by the effects of the substance. A diagnosis of substance dependence requires three or more of the following seven symptoms within a 12-month period: (1) tolerance to the effects of a substance, as defined by either (a) a need for markedly increased amounts of the substance to achieve intoxication or desired effect or (b) markedly diminished effect with continued use of the same amount of the substance; (2) withdrawal, as defined by either (a) withdrawal syndrome in the absence of substance consumption or (b) using the substance to relieve or avoid withdrawal symptoms; (3) using larger amounts of the substance or using the substance for a longer period than intended; (4) a persistent desire or unsuccessful efforts to cut down or control substance use; (5) a great deal of time spent in activities necessary to obtain the substance, use the substance, or recover from its effects; (6) important social, occupational; or recreational activities given up or reduced because of substance use; and (7) continued substance use despite knowledge of having a persistent or recurrent physical or psychological problem likely to have been caused or exacerbated by using the substance.

Although considerable debate remains as to the fundamental appropriateness of the *DSM-IV* criteria for detecting substance use problems among youth (e.g., see Bailey, Martin, Lynch, & Pollack, 2000; Chung et al., 2000; Martin & Winters, 1999; Wagner, Lloyd, & Gil, 2002), these criteria are actively being used in many clinical and research settings. This is potentially very problematic, in that there are several limitations to applying the *DSM-IV* substance use disorders (SUDs) diagnostic criteria to adolescents. In their concise review of the issues associated with using the *DSM-IV* alcohol use disorders with teenagers, Martin and Winters (1999) noted seven specific concerns, as well as several general concerns. These general concerns, which apply as well to the diagnosis of drug use problems as they do to the diagnosis of alcohol use problems, include the following: a lack of knowledge about the overall validity of the diagnostic criteria for adolescents, the fact that several *DSM-IV* symptoms are atypical for adolescents with substance use problems (e.g., withdrawal, substance-related medical problems), the fact that some symptoms have low specificity in distinguishing adolescents with and without substance use problems (e.g., tolerance to the effects of alcohol), and the fact that some symptoms tend to occur only in particular subgroups of teenagers (e.g., hazardous use and legal problems appear primarily among older conduct-disordered males).

A second approach has been to define substance use problems in terms of the frequency and quantity of substance use behavior. As noted earlier, most adolescents will have tried alcohol or other drugs at some point in their lives by the time they reach their senior year in high school. Most of these adolescents will not develop substance use problems, though it should be noted that even infrequent and light alcohol or other drug use may increase the risk for negative events such as car crashes, unwanted or unprotected sexual encounters, and violent interpersonal exchanges. Adolescents who use substances often and in large quantities are the most likely to suffer negative consequences from their use and the most likely to develop substance use problems. In fact, most experts in the field would agree that teenagers who use alcohol, marijuana, or other drugs on a daily basis for a month are abusing these substances, if not dependent on them. Though statistically rare (the Monitoring the Future Study estimates the lifetime prevalence of monthlong daily marijuana use at 6.0 percent and monthlong daily alcohol use at 3.2 percent among 12th graders), such extreme substance use involvement most certainly represents compulsive consumption, which by most accounts is a cardinal sign of substance use problems.

There are at least three problems with relying exclusively on extremes in frequency and quantity of substance use behavior for detecting substance use problems among teenagers. The first has to do with securing accurate measures of such behavior. Alcohol and other drug use is socially proscribed behavior for teenagers, and as a result adolescents may be motivated to underreport or deny involvement with substances. Collateral reporters (e.g., parents, siblings, friends) are an alternative, but these informants have limited opportunities to observe an adolescent's behavior and may have biases of their own that affect the accuracy of their reports. Biochemical detection methods are an alternative to self- or informant reports. Although such measures can provide information about whether an individual has used within a given window of time (the length of this window varies by substance), they provide only the roughest gauge of the quantity of use and reveal almost nothing about the frequency of use. The second problem has to do with just how frequent and just how heavy substance use has to be before it becomes a problem. If the cutoff for abuse is set too low, false positive rates will be raised; this erroneous labeling of a nonproblem adolescent as substance abusing can have profound and potentially long-lived negative consequences for the teenager. If the cutoff for abuse is set too high, false negative rates will be raised; adolescents who can and should be helped will not get the help they deserve. The third problem is that substance abuse determinations relying on frequency or quantity of use disregard whether an adolescent has experienced negative consequences from their use. As the *DSM-IV* criteria illustrate, a prominent component of a substance use disorder diagnosis is the experience of negative social, occupational, medical, psychological, or legal consequences from the use of substances. For some teenagers, such negative consequences begin to appear only when substances are used chronically and in large quantities; for other teenagers, negative consequences emerge after relatively limited use. Of course, the more an adolescent uses, the greater his or her risk for negative substance-related events, but it is important to recognize that there is individual variation among adolescents in how frequently and in what quantities substances need to be used before a clinically significant substance use problem will emerge.

A third approach has been to define substance use problems not by substance use per se but rather by the experience of problems directly linked to the use of substances. This is the only approach with which experts in the field demonstrate reasonable consensus (Hays & Ellickson, 1996). The *DSM-IV* criteria more or less take this approach, though these signs and symptoms are very general in nature and adult-oriented in their wording and behavioral indicators. Recently developed diagnostic instruments for adolescent substance use problems (e.g., Brown, Myers, Lippke, et al., 1998; Dennis, Funk, Godley, Godley, & Waldron, 2004; Tarter & Hegedus, 1991; Winters, Latimer, & Stinchfield, 1999) ask about developmentally congruent types of substance-related experiences using very specific behavioral indicators worded in language teenagers can understand. Examples of the types of items from these instruments include questions about whether an adolescent's substance use caused problems such as breaking curfews, making excuses to parents, or skipping school. Experiences such as these are common among adolescents with substance use problems, and when they are chronic and many in number they are sine qua non with a diagnosis of alcohol or drug abuse.

So what does an adolescent with substance use problems really look like? We would like to suggest that an adolescent with substance use problems will (1) meet one or more of 10 of the 11 symptoms associated with *DSM-IV*-defined substance abuse and dependence (i.e., we agree with Chung et al.'s [2000] recommendation to drop the tolerance symptom given its low specificity in distinguishing adolescents with and without substance-use problems); (2) be using substances more frequently and in larger amounts than is typical of other teenagers of the same age and gender; and (3) have experienced identifiable and indisputable negative consequences from their use of alcohol or other drugs.

PERSONALITY DEVELOPMENT AND PSYCHOPATHOLOGY

A reasonably large empirical literature exists examining possible linkages between personality development and adolescent substance use involvement. Studies vary as to whether they focus on substance use or substance use problems, as well as whether they focus on younger adolescents or older adolescents. Given age-graded changes in substance use involvement, studies with younger adolescents are more likely to examine substance use–related outcomes (e.g., onset of alcohol use, frequency of marijuana use), whereas studies with older adolescents are more likely to examine substance use problems (e.g., negative consequences related to alcohol or other drug use). Despite such variation in study designs and aims, there is remarkable consistency in findings concerning the role of personality in the etiology of substance use problems.

Chassin and DeLucia (1996) noted that the literature has confirmed that a constellation of personality traits indicating low levels of self-regulation has been found to predict adolescent substance use and substance use problems. Personality characteristics such as low self-regulation, aggressiveness, sensation seeking, and impulsivity all have been shown to be strongly associated with alcohol and drug use during the teenage years. Other personality characteristics found to reliably predict adolescent substance involvement include highly tolerant attitudes toward deviant behavior, low value of and expectation for academic success, and low self-esteem. In addition, the personality factors of negative emotional states (e.g., depression), high emotional intensity, and low threshold for emotional response have been hypothesized to predict adolescent drinking and drug use, although findings regarding the significance of these putative associations have been equivocal.

Nearly every researcher who has examined the impact of personality development on adolescent substance use involvement has stressed that intrapersonal vulnerabilities to substance use are substantially mediated by social and environmental contexts (for a developmental perspective on this process, see Maggs and Schulenberg, 2001). Bates and Labouvie (1995) have referred to this phenomenon as "personality-environment constellations" and note that "it is clear that high levels of personality needs for disinhibition and impulsivity increase risk for substance use initiation and intensity . . . yet these characteristics may foster the emergence of such behavioral outcomes primarily, or only, when coupled with certain environmental contexts" (p. 23). Similar perspectives have been presented by Tarter (Tarter, Moss, & Vanyukov, 1995; Tarter & Vanyukov, 1994) and Zucker (1994), who suggested that the effect of temperament (the developmental precursor to personality) on adolescent tobacco and alcohol use is indirect, mediated through self-control ability and its consequences in areas such as academic involvement, life stress, and peer affiliations. These investigators acknowledge the importance of social factors for shaping the impact of self-regulation problems but also argue that self-regulation problems can lead adolescents to select or elicit social environmental contexts that compound the likelihood of substance use and substance use problems. This latter point is the essence of primary socialization theory (Clayton, Colon, Donohew, & Skinner, 1999), which posits that an individual's personality traits do not directly relate to drug use; rather, they indirectly influence drug use because they affect interactions between the individual and primary socialization sources.

Chassin and colleagues have done some of the best empirical work examining the impact of personality variables on substance use problems in community and high-risk adolescent samples. A recent study by Chassin, Curran, and Hussong (1998) offered support for the role of self-regulation problems, as evidenced by externalizing behaviors, in predicting heavy substance use among teenagers. Externalizing behavior not only was associated with concurrent heavy alcohol use among adolescents, but also prospectively predicted individual differences in change in heavy alcohol use over time. This study also found no support for negative emotional states, as reflected by internalizing symptoms, in predicting future heavy alcohol use by adolescents. These authors interpreted their findings as suggesting that negative affect is unlikely to be a precursor to heavy substance use for most adolescents. Instead, internalizing symptoms, when concurrent with adolescent substance use problems, may be a consequence rather than an antecedent of alcohol and other drug involvement. In another study, Chassin and Colder (1997) further investigated the potential interactions between poor self-regulation and affectivity in predicting adolescent substance use problems. In this study, low levels of positive affectivity were associated with alcohol use and alcohol-related impairment for impulsive adolescents but not for nonimpulsive adolescents. This finding suggests that affectivity can play a role in predicting adolescent substance use and substance use problems, but only among adolescents temperamentally predisposed toward the development of substance-related problems (i.e., demonstrating poor self-regulation). Based on similar results from a study with young adults, Carle, Chassin, Krull, and Loukas (2000) speculated that impulsive individuals may be more motivated to use substances to manage affect because such individuals derive greater stress-response-dampening benefits from the use of substances. The extent to which this proposition is true has yet to be adequately tested.

Wills and colleagues have done some of the best empirical work examining the personality predictors of alcohol and drug use among community samples of middle school–aged children (e.g., see Cleary et al., 2001; Cleary, Wills, & Windle, 1998; DuHamel & Wills, 1995; Wills, Sandy, & Yaeger, 2000). This group of researchers has proposed that personality, as indexed by measures of temperament, is likely to have indirect effects on early-onset substance use. Temperament is thought to be related to substance use given its association with self-control, and temperament dimensions associated with poor self-control include physical activity level, the tendency to be physically active and to have difficulty sitting still, and the tendency to become easily and intensely upset. Temperament dimensions associated with good self-control include the ability to focus attention on a task and ignore distracting stimuli, and the tendency to easily and frequently experience positive mood. Wills and colleagues also include concepts from epigenetic models into their account of the association between personality and substance use, noting that the nature and degree of relations between self-control and substance use may change as adolescents develop progressively more complex cognitive and social skills in response to maturational and environmental demands. Specifically, they argue that poor self-control can lead to substance use problems because poor self-control is associated with experiencing more negative life events and affiliating with substance-using peers, each of which has been consistently linked to substance use. From this perspective, substance use arises from what Moffitt (1993) has termed "a chain of failures" based on a child's temperament profile, social relationships, and self-control abilities. Findings from this research group have been consistent with this model (e.g., see Cleary et al., 1998, 2001; DuHamel & Wills, 1995; Wills et al., 2000), demonstrating that personality factors, and specifically temperament variables, are most accurately conceptualized as vulnerability promoting or vulnerability reducing. The effects of temperament on adolescent substance use are mediated, moderated, or both by variables including self-control, maladaptive coping, novelty seeking, affiliation with substance-using peers, and parental support.

Most studies that have examined associations between self-regulation variables and adolescent substance use have been performed with primarily non-Hispanic White individuals from the United States. However, studies of Colombian, African American, Taiwanese, and Russian teenagers have supported the cross-cultural validity of these associations (Arencibia-Mireles, Brook, Brook, Richter, & Whiteman, 2001; Brody Gerrard, Gibbons, Murry, & Wills, 2003; Chen, Duo, Soong, & Yang, 2002; Eisemann, Hagglof, Koposov, & Ruchkin, 2002). In addition, several studies have identified other personality variables that may influence the relation between poor self-regulation and adolescent substance use and substance use problems. These variables include the following: (a) gender-role attributes and ideology, with traditional attitudes positively related to alcohol use among males and negatively related to alcohol use among females (Cooper & Huselid, 1992); (b) socioeconomic status, with affluent youth more likely to report using substances in order to manage negative affect than less-privileged youth (Becker & Luthar, 2002); (c) cognitive prototypes (i.e., perceptions) of abstainers and substance users (Brody et al., 2003), with more favorable perceptions of users associated with a greater likelihood of use; and (d) risk perceptions, with adolescents who perceive less risk in engaging in substance use more likely to use substances (Burns, Fisher, Hampson, Severson, & Slovic, 2001).

In sum, current thinking regarding possible linkages between personality development and adolescent substance use problems is that problems in self-regulation are the primary personality-related predictors of substance use and substance use problems. This association is indirect and substantially mediated by certain social and environmental contexts (e.g., low academic involvement, high life stress, affiliation with substance-involved peers). At least to some degree, these social and environmental contexts appear be selected or elicited, or both, by adolescents with self-regulation problems.

EPIDEMIOLOGY

Substance use among adolescents in the United States is a serious public health issue. Results from the 2002 Monitoring the Future (MTF) study, a nationwide study exploring drug and alcohol use trends among youth in grades 8, 10, and 12, indicate that nearly 4 out of 5 (78 percent) have consumed alcohol, with a significant proportion having been drunk at least once (Johnston, O'Malley, & Bachman, 2003). Furthermore, findings indicate that more than half (53 percent) of high school students in the United States have tried drugs other than alcohol or cigarettes (Johnston et al., 2003). In addition, high rates of past-month substance use were found among adolescents in the 2002 National Survey on Drug Use and Health (NSDUH; Office of Applied Studies, 2003). Among youth ages 12–20, 28.8 percent reported drinking alcohol in the past 30 days, with 19.3 percent of these youth classified as binge drinkers and 6.2 percent classified as heavy drinkers. Finally, past-month use of any illicit substance was 11.8 percent for youth ages 12–17.

Gender differences exist in drug and alcohol use patterns among adolescents. Data from the MTF study indicate that males have higher rates of past-month drinking than females (37 percent vs. 28.4 percent) and higher rates of past-30-day illicit drug use than females (28.4 percent vs. 22.6 percent). Similar results were obtained in the NSDUH study, with 12.3 percent of males using any illicit substance in the past month compared to 10.9 percent of females. Rates of cigarette smoking among male and female adolescents are roughly equal, with males reporting slightly higher rates in the MTF study (29.7 percent and 28.7 percent) and females reporting slightly higher rates in the NSDUH study (13.6 percent vs. 12.3 percent).

In addition to gender differences, important substance use differences exist across racial and ethnic groups. Native American youth consistently have the highest rates of licit and illicit substance use (Jenson, 1997). Findings from NSDUH (2002) indicate that when compared with rates of all youth ages 12–17, rates of past-month illicit substance use were significantly greater among Native American youth (20.9 percent vs. 11.6 percent). Among the three largest racial and ethnic groups in the United States, African American, Hispanic, and non-Hispanic White (NHW), NHW youth have the highest rates of substance use while African American youth have the lowest rates of substance use across most studies (Johnston et al., 2003; Office of Applied Studies, 2003). Findings indicate that among adolescents, rates of past-month use of alcohol, marijuana, and any illicit substance were highest among NHWs and lowest among African Americans (Johnston et al., 2003; Office of Applied Studies, 2003). These findings are consistent with results from MTF (2003), where rates of substance use were higher for NHW than for African American youth across all substances (Johnston et al., 2003). Rates of substance use among Hispanic youth tend to fall in between rates reported by NHW and African American youth for most but not all substances (Johnston et al., 2003; Office of Applied Studies, 2002). MTF results indicated that Hispanic youth had the highest rates of lifetime crack use (6.1 percent vs. 3.8 percent for NHW and 0.9 percent for Blacks), lifetime cocaine use (6.1 percent vs. 5.5 percent for NHW and 1.0 percent for Blacks), and lifetime Ecstasy use (13.1 percent vs. 12.4 percent for NHW and 3.1 percent for Blacks; Johnston et al., 2003).

Although youth who use drugs or alcohol may not develop substance abuse or dependence, research findings indicate that a disconcerting proportion of adolescents do meet criteria for a substance use disorder. According to NSDUH (2002) data, 8.9 percent of 12- to 17-year-olds met criteria for substance abuse or substance dependence, with the lowest rates among 12- to 13-year-olds (1.8 percent) and highest rates among 16- to 17-year-olds (17.1 percent). Rates of substance use and dependence were similar among male and female adolescents (9.3 percent vs. 8.6 percent). In an interview-based study of randomly selected Oregon high school students, Lewinsohn, Hops, Roberts, Seeley, and Andrews (1993) found that 4 percent developed a *DSM-III-R*-defined substance use problem during the course of a single year. In a survey-based study of Minnesota high school students, Harrison, Fulkerson, and Beebe (1998) found that 13.8 percent of 9th graders and 22.7 percent of 12th graders met *DSM-IV* criteria for substance use problems at some point during the previous year. Regarding racial and ethnic variation in the prevalence of SUDs, Turner and Gil (2002) studied 1,803 multiethnic young adults ages 19–21 from Miami-Dade County, Florida. Though rates of SUDs were alarming across all subgroups of adolescents, when compared with African Americans, NHWs had statistically significantly greater lifetime prevalence rates for all SUDs examined, alcohol abuse (22.2 percent vs. 6.7 percent), alcohol dependence (15.8 percent vs. 4.0 percent), marijuana abuse (18.4 percent vs. 6.7 percent), marijuana dependence (14.2 percent vs. 7.1 percent), and other drug abuse or dependence (14.3 percent vs. 2.4 percent). Similarly, when comparing lifetime prevalence rates of SUDs among U.S.-born and foreign-born non-Cuban Hispanics, U.S.-born youth had statistically significantly greater prevalence rates than foreign-born youth for several SUDs including marijuana abuse (15.3 percent vs. 7.1 percent), marijuana dependence (17.3 percent vs. 9.4 percent), and other drug abuse or dependence (12.3 percent vs. 7.8 percent).

In sum, the research indicates that a majority of adolescents in the United States use alcohol and other substances, with notable differences across subgroups of adolescents. Moreover, although the findings suggest that most adolescents do not evidence substance use problems, a substantial proportion of youth do develop subsequent SUDs, including substance abuse and dependence. Again, important racial and ethnic differences are associated with prevalence of SUDs. The factors associated with differences in the risk for substance use and the development of substance use problems among adolescents will be discussed in the following section.

ETIOLOGY

No universal consensus exists regarding a causal model of adolescent substance abuse; rather, current research indicates that a myriad of biological, psychosocial, and environmental factors are associated with the development of substance use problems during adolescence (Hawkins, Catalano & Miller, 1992; Kaminer, 2001; Kirby & Fraser, 1997; Newcomb, 1992). Factors that both precede and are correlated with substance use problems are labeled risk factors (Hawkins et al., 1992). Research points to the cumulative effect of risk factors, that is, the more risk factors a youth is exposed to or the longer a youth is exposed to a risk factor, the greater the likelihood that a youth will develop substance use problems (Kirby & Fraser, 1997). Further evidence suggests that certain factors may mitigate the impact of risk factors. Accordingly, these factors are labeled protective factors. It is through an exploration of the influence of various risk and protective factors that the current etiological framework for adolescent substance problems can be understood. Different ethnic subgroups of adolescents appear to be differentially exposed to and influenced by risk factors (Gil, Vega, & Turner, 2002; Wallace & Muroff, 2002). As such, we will discuss risk factor research with particular attention to subgroup differences.

Risk Factors

In the presiding risk factor framework, risk factor domains have been classified into two primary categories: (1) individual factors (e.g., personal characteristics and interpersonal relationships) and (2) contextual factors (e.g., societal, environmental, and cultural factors; Hawkins et al., 1992).

Individual Factors

Developmental and Peer Factors. Children exposed to aggression during early childhood are more likely to develop conduct disorder, which is considered a risk factor for substance abuse (Baumrind & Moselle, 1985). Likewise, childhood trouble adjusting successfully to peer relationships and the school environment put youth at risk for peer and teacher discrimination, factors that increase the risk for developing an adolescent alcohol problem (Kaminer, 1994). Peer rejection, poor academic performance, and dropping out of school are all associated with an increased risk for developing substance use problems (Clayton, 1992; Jenson, 1997; Kaminer, 1994). In addition to the impact of peer rejection, other peer influences serve as significant risk factors. Specifically, empirical research has consistently demonstrated that association with friends who use alcohol and other drugs is among the strongest predictors of adolescent substance use problems (Barnes & Welte, 1986; Elliott, Huizinga, & Ageton, 1985; Kandel, 1985; Vega, Zimmerman, Warheit, Apospori, & Gil, 1998).

Family Factors. Teens raised with lax supervision, excessively severe or inconsistent disciplinary practices, or lack of involvement with parents are at greater risk for behavioral problems, including substance use and delinquency (Baumrind, 1991). Moreover, poor parent-child bonding characterized by a lack of closeness between parent and child and low involvement by parents is associated with an increased likelihood of adolescent substance use (Hawkins et al., 1992). In addition, family problems including broken homes, abuse or neglect within the family, and family conflict have been associated with an increased risk of delinquency and adolescent substance abuse (Clayton, 1992; Hawkins et al., 1992; Kaminer, 1994). Finally, drug or alcohol abuse within the family increases a youth's risk for developing substance use problems in a number of ways, including the increased availability of substances in the home, adults modeling drug and alcohol use, tolerant attitudes regarding children's use of substances, and poor parenting practices by the adults under the influence of drugs or alcohol (Clayton, 1992; Hawkins et al., 1992).

Physiological/Biological Factors. Adoption studies reveal consistent evidence for genetic transmission of alcohol use problems among sons of alcoholics (Hawkins et al., 1992). Additionally, research indicates that genetic factors may decrease the likelihood of alcohol use among Asians, many of whom do not have the enzyme associated with decomposing alcohol in the body (Hawkins et al., 1992). Finally, temperamental factors including sensation seeking, low harm avoidance, and low impulse control have been associated with an increased risk of developing substance use problems (Hawkins et al., 1992).

Contextual Factors

Laws, Norms, and Availability of Drugs and Alcohol. Community laws and norms that promote the use and availability of alcohol and drugs lead to an increased risk of teen substance abuse as well as drug- or alcohol-related motor vehicle accidents among teens (Jenson, 1997). Additionally, increased availability of alcohol and other drugs to adolescents is a significant risk factor for substance use among adolescents (Herrenkohl et al., 2000).

Extreme Economic Deprivation and Neighborhood Disorganization. Enmeshment in a culture of poverty or delinquency, or both, as well as living in a neighborhood that is densely populated, high in crime, and highly disorganized have been suggested to contribute to an adolescent's risk for problem behavior (Hawkins et al., 1992; Jenson, 1997). A distinct relationship between poverty and adolescent substance use is unclear. Results from one study indicated that extreme poverty was associated with alcoholism among adults who had antisocial behavior as children (Robins & Ratcliff, 1979). However, other findings point to the existence of a negative relationship between economic status and teen alcohol use (Bachman, Lloyd, & O'Malley, 1981; Zucker & Hatford, 1983). Finally, although neighborhood disorganization has been associated with juvenile offending and serious violence (Sampson & Lauritsen, 1994) there is little empirical research demonstrating the direct influence of neighborhood disorganization on adolescent substance use (Hawkins et al., 1992).

Cultural Factors. Cultural factors such as acculturation, nativity, and perceived discrimination have been found to influence the progression from no substance use to problematic use among adolescents (Vega & Gil, 1998). Findings from epidemiological studies indicate that acculturation and acculturation stress are positively associated with onset and severity of substance use (Vega & Gil, 1998, 1999). Furthermore, among Hispanic/Latino adolescents, nativity is related to adolescent substance use, with U.S.-born adolescents significantly more likely than foreign-born adolescents to use licit and illicit substances (Vega & Gil, 1998, 1999). Finally, research suggests that perceived discrimination may significantly impact psychological adaptation among ethnic minority youth (Aries & Moorehead, 1989; Keefe & Padilla, 1987; Semons, 1991), although the relationship between perceived discrimination and adolescent substance use is unclear.

Protective Factors

Kirby and Fraser (1997) defined protective factors as the "internal and external forces that help children resist or ameliorate risk" (p. 16). Although research on protective factors is recent and far from comprehensive, it is known that many youth do not develop emotional or behavioral problems, including substance use problems, despite exposure to a variety of the risk factors discussed previously (Jenson, 1997). Within the risk and protection model, protective factors are conceptualized as moderators; it is suggested that protective factors temper the negative effects of being exposed to risk factors (Jessor, Van Den Bros, Vanderryn, Costa, & Turbin, 1997). According to Jessor et al. (1997), factors that appear to protect against youth drug and alcohol abuse include parental relationships, religiosity, law abidance, self-efficacy, and bonding to society. Jenson (1997) identifies a positive family milieu, support from the community, and social bonds to positive adults and prosocial peers as important social and environmental protective factors, while capable problem-solving skills, high intelligence, and high levels of self-efficacy are identified as the relevant individual protective factors. Recent research suggests that cultural variables may moderate the risk for substance use. Specifically, preliminary studies suggest that national origin, level of acculturation, familism, and acculturation stress moderate risk of substance use among Hispanic/Latino adolescents (Vega & Gil, 1998). Thus, protective factors appear to play a significant role in impeding the development of substance use and other behavioral problems, yet a better understanding of the specific protective factors, and the interactions between risk and protective factors, is necessary.

Racial and Ethnic Differences

Emerging research suggests that adolescent exposure and vulnerability to risk factors may vary substantially across racial and ethnic groups (Amey & Albrecht, 1998; Gil et al., 2002; Vega, Zimmerman, Warheit, Apospori, & Gil, 1998; Wallace & Muroff, 2002). Findings from Wallace and Muroff (2002) indicated that African Americans and NHWs were differentially exposed to more than half of the 55 risk factors examined. African American students were more likely to be exposed to contextual risk factors and academic risk factors, whereas NHW youth had greater exposure to individual risk factors. Furthermore, findings indicated that the relationship between exposure to risk factors and substance use was stronger for NHW students than for African American students. Of 165 tests for ethnic differences in vulnerability to risk factors, nearly one third were statistically significant. Similarly, Gil et al. (2002) found that African American youth differed from their NHW counterparts in the number of risk factors they experienced as well as their vulnerability to the effects of cumulative risk factors. African American adolescents were found to demonstrate a greater number of risk factors than NHW adolescents; however, first use of alcohol and marijuana occurred later for the African American youth than the NHW youth. This finding suggests that African American youth are less vulnerable to the cumulative effect of risk factors than their NHW counterparts. Finally, research suggests that certain cultural factors differentially impact risk for substance use among U.S.-born and foreign-born Hispanic adolescents. Specifically, acculturation level, acculturation stress, and ethnic identity were found to differentially influence substance use among foreign-born and U.S.-born Hispanic adolescents (Vega, Gil, & Wagner, 1998).

In sum, although the majority of adolescents in the United States try alcohol and drugs by age 18, the transition to substance abuse or dependence varies according to exposure to a myriad of individual and contextual risk factors. The presence of protective factors appears to moderate the impact of risk factors and inhibit the development of substance use problems in adolescents. In addition, recent research findings suggest that (a) exposure to risk factors differs substantially across racial and ethnic groups of adolescents, and (b) vulnerability to specific risk factors as well as the cumulative effect of risk factors may vary across racial and ethnic groups. As such, the presiding risk and protective factor framework may be more accurate in predicting substance use among NHW adolescents than among their ethnic minority counterparts. A better understanding of the influence of specific risk and protective factors on the development of substance use problems is necessary to facilitate the development of effective interventions for adolescents with diverse psychosocial, developmental, and cultural needs.

COURSE, COMPLICATIONS, AND PROGNOSIS

The course and outcome of adolescent substance use varies widely across adolescents who use alcohol and other drugs. The literature indicates that a sequential pattern of substance involvement exists among adolescents whereby the use of licit substances (alcohol and cigarettes) precedes the use of marijuana, and marijuana precedes the use of other illicit substances (Kandel, Yamaguchi, & Chen, 1992). Although a clear sequential course of substance involvement has been identified among adolescents, many substance-using youth stop during early stages of use and do not progress to higher levels of use (Kandel et al., 1992). In that there is wide variation in course and outcome of substance use among adolescents, researchers have worked at identifying the factors associated with distinct trajectories of substance use among adolescents.

Several studies have examined the factors associated with substance use among subgroups of adolescent substance users (e.g., nonusers, users, and problem users). Donovan and Jessor (1978, 1983) examined the psychosocial correlates of adolescent alcohol use problems and found higher levels of adolescent deviant behavior, as well as family and peer modeling and approval of substance use, among problem users than among nonproblem users. Similarly, Baumrind (1991) found that adolescents with substance dependence had more externalizing symptoms and dysfunction related to parental support and control than those adolescents who did not demonstrate problematic alcohol use or did not use alcohol at all. An important limitation of these studies is that causal linkages are difficult to determine in that potential differences associated with the consequences of differing levels of substance consumption were not taken into account.

More recent studies examining differential prediction of problem and nonproblem use among adolescents have controlled for consumption level (Bailey & Rachal, 1993; Stice, Kirz, & Borbely, 2002). Findings from Bailey and Rachal (1993) indicated that peer approval of drinking was positively associated with both alcohol consumption and alcohol problems, whereas parental approval of drinking was positively associated with alcohol consumption but not alcohol problems. In addition, higher levels of problem use were found for males than for females in this study. In a study aimed at differentiating the predictors of adolescent substance use and adolescent problematic substance use, Stice et al. (2002) found that externalizing symptoms and peer substance use were positively associated with both consumption and problem use when controlling for level of consumption. In contrast, parental substance use and level of behavioral undercontrol (e.g., impulsivity, sensation seeking, irresponsibility) were directly associated with consumption but only indirectly associated with problem use. When level of consumption was controlled, these factors no longer predicted problematic use. Thus, although the transition from experimental substance use to problematic use varies greatly among teenagers, it appears that several psychosocial factors, including peer and family substance use and externalizing behavior problems, may be associated with more problematic substance use.

Research further indicates considerable differences in outcomes associated with adolescents who are treated for substance use problems. Among adolescents who receive treatment for drug and alcohol use problems, one half will relapse to substance use within 90 days posttreatment and two thirds will relapse within the first 6 months following treatment (Brown, Mott, & Myers, 1990; Brown, Vik, & Creamer, 1989). Although relapse rates are similar for both adolescents and adults with substance use problems, research from several longitudinal studies suggests that the factors associated with relapse are distinct for adolescents (Brown, 1993; Brown et al., 1990; Latimer, Newcomb, Winters, & Stinchfield, 2000; Latimer, Winters, Stinchfield, & Traver,

2000). Brown (1993) and Brown et al. (1990) conducted longitudinal research examining the factors associated with posttreatment status among adolescents treated for substance use problems. Findings indicated that at 6 months posttreatment one third of adolescents had abstained, 43 percent had returned to problematic levels of drug and alcohol use, and almost one fourth demonstrated minimal alcohol or drug use involvement. The factors associated with relapse among these youth included posttreatment exposure to alcohol and drug use in the social environment as well as a lack of involvement in self-help groups.

In a more recent study examining the predictors of posttreatment substance use among adolescents who participated in a 12-step-based treatment program, Latimer, Newcomb, et al. (2000) found that greater involvement in aftercare services predicted decreased substance use problem severity at 6 months posttreatment. In addition, psychosocial risk status, which included measures of parent and sibling substance abuse, deviant attitudes, deviant behavior, and impulsivity, was positively associated with rates of substance use problem severity 6 months following treatment. Latimer, Winters, et al. (2000) also explored the impact of demographic, individual, and interpersonal factors on substance use outcomes at 6 and 12 months posttreatment. Results indicated that sibling substance use at pretreatment and lack of participation in aftercare services posttreatment predicted both alcohol and drug use at 6 months posttreatment. Predictors of alcohol use and marijuana use at 12 months posttreatment were distinct. Gender, pretreatment substance use, treatment length, alcohol use at 6 months posttreatment, and peer substance use at 6 months posttreatment predicted alcohol use 12 months following treatment. In contrast, pretreatment peer substance use, marijuana use at 6 months posttreatment, psychological dependence at 6 months posttreatment, and peer substance use at 6 months posttreatment predicted marijuana use at 12 months posttreatment.

Thus, research consistently indicates that (a) a majority of adolescents return to substance use by 6–12 months posttreatment and (b) one of the strongest predictors of posttreatment substance use is exposure to peers or family members (or both) who use substances. In addition, findings point to the potential influence of posttreatment involvement in self-help groups and aftercare services on positive long-term outcomes among adolescents.

Psychiatric comorbidity has emerged as one of the most compelling factors associated with substance use outcomes among adolescents with substance use problems. It is estimated that between 22 percent and 82 percent of youth with substance use problems have at least one additional psychiatric diagnosis (Office of Applied Studies, 2003). The psychiatric disorders that most commonly co-occur in treated populations of adolescents with substance use problems are conduct disorder (32 percent to 59 percent) and mood disorders (35 percent to 61 percent) (Wise, Cuffe, & Fischer, 2001). Anxiety disorders, attention-deficit/hyperactivity disorder, and disruptive behavior disorders are also highly associated with substance use problems in adolescents (Lewinsohn et al., 1993; Wise et al., 2001). Recent research consistently indicates that psychiatric comorbidity significantly impacts treatment response and outcomes among adolescents with substance use problems. In particular, a number of studies indicate that externalizing disorders are associated with poor treatment response, retention, and outcomes among adolescents with substance use problems (Galaif, Hser, Grella, & Joshi, 2001; Kaminer, Tarter, Bukstein, & Kabene, 1992; Rounds-Bryant & Staab, 2001; Wise et al., 2001). A study of dually diagnosed adolescents in an inpatient hospital found that a diagnosis of conduct disorder was positively correlated with treatment dropout (Kaminer et al., 1992). Congruent with results from Kaminer et al. (1992), a larger study ($N = 710$), the Drug Abuse Treatment Outcome Studies for Adolescents (DATOS-A), found that a diagnosis of conduct disorder predicted premature departure from both outpatient and residential treatment programs (Galaif et al., 2001). Additionally, the presence of conduct disorder was associated with regular posttreatment marijuana use in a study of 1,094 African American, White, and Hispanic youth in outpatient, residential, and inpatient substance abuse treatment programs (Rounds-Bryant & Staab, 2001). Finally, in a study of 91 adolescents in residential treatment for substance use problems, Wise et al. (2001) found that adolescents diagnosed with disruptive disorders were less successful in treatment.

Research on the role of internalizing disorders such as mood disorders, adjustment disorders, and anxiety disorders on substance abuse treatment–related outcomes has yielded equivocal results. Several studies revealed that internalizing disorders, as well as the combination of internalizing and externalizing disorders, may negatively impact treatment response among adolescents with substance use problems. Fiegelman (1987) found that the presence of moderate to severe depressive symptoms at intake was associated with high rates of dropout from day treatment services. Additionally, among adolescents receiving inpatient substance abuse treatment, depression and anxiety were associated with poorer treatment response (Dobkin, Chabot, Maliantovitch, & Craig, 1998). Moreover, a comparison of adolescent substance abusers with no comorbidity, comorbid externalizing disorders, and comorbid internalizing and externalizing disorders indicated that the youth with no comorbidity had the best substance use outcomes at both 6 and 12 months posttreatment (Rowe,

Liddle, Greenbaum, & Henderson, 2004). Finally, a study by Jainchill, Hawke, and Yagelka (2000) examined the impact of the level of disturbance on treatment outcomes and found that more psychiatric disturbance (i.e., total number of *DSM-III-R* diagnoses) was negatively associated with declines in alcohol use.

In sum, research reveals that although the majority of youth who try alcohol and other drugs do not develop subsequent substance use problems, a subgroup of adolescents go on to develop a myriad of substance use problems, including substance abuse or dependence. Though the transition from substance use to the development of substance use problems appears to vary considerably across adolescents, family and peer influences have been associated with both the transition from nonproblematic substance use to problematic substance use among adolescents, as well as a return to posttreatment substance use among treated adolescent substance abusers. In addition, psychiatric comorbidity, particularly the presence of co-occurring externalizing disorders, has been consistently linked to poor treatment response and outcome among substance-abusing adolescents. Finally, although treatment outcomes vary among subgroups of adolescents, it should be recognized that approximately one third of adolescents treated for substance use problems demonstrate successful treatment outcomes at 6–12 months posttreatment.

ASSESSMENT AND DIAGNOSIS

As noted earlier in this chapter, the *DSM-IV* criteria for SUDs are actively being used in many clinical and research settings. Consequently, many of the assessment and diagnostic approaches used with substance-abusing teens are based on the *DSM-IV*. This state of affairs is quite unfortunate because of the limitations of the *DSM-IV* SUDS criteria when applied to adolescents. Compared to adults with substance use problems, adolescent substance abusers demonstrate a briefer history of involvement with alcohol and other drugs, engage in more episodic use, experience fewer consequences of protracted use, use a greater number and different types of substances, are undergoing faster and more developmental changes, show more interindividual variation in developmental status, are more likely to be diagnosed with co-occurring problems, and have a greater chance of outgrowing substance use problems even without treatment. These differences have obvious implications for how to assess and diagnose substance use problems in a developmentally appropriate manner. In addition, current *DSM*-based methods of estimating adolescent alcohol and other drug problems result in high percentages of diagnostic orphans, that is, adolescents who demonstrate some of the signs and symptoms of SUDs but do not fully meet diagnostic criteria (Pollock & Martin, 1999). In sum, this suggests that relying solely on the *DSM-IV* for diagnosing adolescent substance use problems among teens would be a mistake.

Most experts agree that adolescent substance use problems are best conceptualized as developmental, biological, psychological, and social phenomena. Failure to consider the role of any of these dimensions may result in inaccuracies in assessing and diagnosing adolescent substance use problems. Furthermore, assessment also should include information from a variety of sources, including teenager self-reports (gained through self-monitoring, clinical interview, structured reporting forms, or a combination of these), significant others' reports (e.g., parents, teachers), psychometric testing, direct observation of the adolescent's behavior, and biological measures; a reliance on multiple sources will help ensure the accuracy of the data that are obtained. Given the foregoing, the ideal adolescent substance abuse evaluation will include data collection in the following areas: (1) the substance use behavior itself, (2) the type and severity of psychiatric morbidity that may be present and whether it preceded or developed after the substance use disorder, (3) cognitive processes, with specific attention to neuropsychological functioning, (4) family organization and interaction patterns, and (5) social skills. A comprehensive assessment of adolescent substance use problems also should include data addressing: (1) school or vocational adjustment, (2) recreation and leisure activities, (3) temperament and personality characteristics, (4) peer affiliations, (5) legal status, and (6) physical health status and concerns.

A valid, standardized, and clinically relevant assessment is essential for effective intervention with adolescent substance abusers (Winters et al., 1999). The advantages of standardized assessments include the following: (1) they provide a benchmark against which clinical decisions can be compared and validated, (2) they are less prone to clinician biases and inconsistencies than more traditional assessment methods, and (3) they provide a common language from which improved communication in the field can develop. Until recently, clinicians traditionally relied on clinical judgment or locally developed procedures to diagnose adolescent substance use problems. Thankfully, this has begun to change as standardized and clinically valid instruments such as the Personal Experiences Inventory (Winters et al., 1999), the Drug Use Screening Inventory (Tarter & Hegedus, 1991), the Customary Drinking and Drug Use Record (Brown, Myers, Lippke, et al., 1998), the Teen-Addiction Severity Index (Kaminer, Wagner, Plummer, & Seifer, 1993), and the Global Appraisal of Individual Needs (GAIN; Dennis et al., 2004) have been introduced. Developmental appropriateness is critical to the effectiveness of these instruments. By developmental appropriateness, we mean that items are interpretable by both younger and older adolescents. This requires consideration of factors such as reading level, level of concrete versus abstract reasoning, and world experience. This also means that data-collection methods are relevant to the contexts and lifestyles of adolescents. Some obvious examples include asking about boyfriends or girlfriends rather than spouses; asking about school and workplace rather than careers; and asking about drinking in cars, homes, parks, and locations other than pubs, bars, lounges, and restaurants.

The actual assessment process should begin with a brief open-ended interview with an adolescent and their parents about the presenting problem, especially in regard to its chronicity, severity, and origins. Rather than focusing on the frequency, type, or quantity of substance use, the focus should be on problems that the teenager has experienced because of substance use. It is usually best to openly acknowledge any contradictions in adolescents' and their parents' accounts of the presenting without siding with the adolescent or the parents. A teenager or parent may request a meeting alone with the clinician; such meetings may be helpful but should take place only after issues related to confidentiality are discussed. After the assessment data have been collected and analyzed, providing feedback about the assessment results is crucial for ensuring compliance with treatment recommendations. Miller and Rollnick's (2002) motivational interviewing is a particularly useful approach to feedback, which in the case of adolescent substance use problems has the following characteristics: avoid trying to prove things to teenagers and their families; describe each result, along with the information necessary to understand what it means; avoid a scare tactic tone; solicit and reflect adolescents' and their families' reactions to the assessment information; remain open to feedback from adolescents and their families; and be prepared to deal with strong emotional reactions. The feedback session should conclude with a summary of what has transpired, including the risks and problems that have emerged from assessment findings; teenagers' and their families' own reactions to the feedback, with an emphasis on statements reflecting an interest in making positive changes and a willingness to do so; an invitation for the adolescents and families to add to or correct the summary; and assurance that successful treatments are available.

IMPACT ON ENVIRONMENT

Research has consistently identified negative health risks associated with substance use. For example, driving a motor vehicle while intoxicated increases the risk for accidents, injuries, and death; heavy alcohol use during pregnancy increases the risk of health and developmental problems for the fetus; and cigarette smoking has been associated with increased health problems including cancer, respiratory disease, and cardiovascular functioning (National Institute of Alcohol Abuse and Alcoholism, 1997; U.S. Department of Health and Human Services, 1988, 1994). Moreover, substance use problems among adolescents have been associated with increased risk for suicide, HIV infection, and drug overdose. Though it is expected that serious socioenvironmental consequences are also associated with adolescent substance use, empirical research on the topic is comparatively sparse (Chassin, Pitts, & DeLucia, 1999). Rather, the majority of research has examined the socioenvironmental antecedents of adolescent substance use and abuse rather than their socioenvironmental consequences (Newcomb & Bentler, 1988). It is likely that the causal relationship between adolescent substance use problems and socioenvironmental factors is reciprocal, whereby social and environmental factors such as family problems, poor academic performance, and socialization with deviant peers increase the risk for substance use and abuse among adolescents, which in turn exacerbates family, school, and peer problems.

Family

Adolescent substance use and substance use problems have been linked to poor family functioning, including increases in parent-child conflict and a lack of parental support (Baumrind, 1991; Foxcroft & Lowe, 1991), as well as to negative peer relationships (e.g., associations with substance-using and delinquent peers; Barnes & Welte, 1986; Brown et al., 1989; Elliott, Huizinga, & Ageton, 1985; Jainchill et al., 2000; Latimer, Winters, et al., 2000). The majority of research in this area has examined the impact of negative family and peer influences on the development of substance use behaviors of adolescents; however, preliminary research suggests that adolescent substance use may also exacerbate problematic relationships with family and peers. In a study examining the consequences of adolescent substance use, Chassin et al. (1999) found that illicit substance use among adolescents was associated with lower levels of adolescent autonomy, which in turn is related to problematic parent-child relationships. This finding is consistent with that of Newcomb and Bentler (1988), who found that polysubstance use during adolescence was associated with poor social relationships and a lack of social support. Thus, though research suggests a linkage between adolescent substance use and peer and family problems, it is likely a relationship of mutual causality, with adolescent substance use problems exacerbating already existing problems with family and peers.

School

The relationship between adolescent substance use and academic functioning including school dropout also has begun to be examined. Emerging research suggests that adolescent substance use may significantly contribute to poor academic performance and subsequent school dropout. Several studies have found that adolescents with substance use problems demonstrate lower levels of academic achievement than their counterparts without substance use problems (Braggio, Pishkin, Gameros, & Brooks, 1993; Moss, Kirisci, Gordon, & Tarter, 1994). Other studies reveal that adolescents with drug and alcohol problems demonstrate slightly diminished cognitive and intellectual functioning compared to youth without substance use problems (Moss et al., 1994; Tarter, Mezzich, Hsieh, & Parks, 1995). In some studies, adolescent illicit drug use has been associated with an increased risk of dropping out of school (Garnier, Stein, & Jacobs, 1997; Krohn, Thornberry, Collins-Hall, & Lizotte, 1995); in other studies, cigarette use, but not other types of substance use, has been predictive of high school dropout (Ellickson, Bui, Bell, & McGuian, 1998; Mensch & Kandel, 1988; Newcomb, Abbot et al., 2002; Weng, Newcomb, & Bentler, 1988). Overall, research findings point to the potentially devastating effects of licit and illicit substance use on academic functioning among adolescents and suggest a relationship of mutual causality, with adolescent substance use problems exacerbating already existing academic problems.

Peer Interactions

Baumrind and Moselle (1985) suggested that adolescent substance use promotes a false sense of reality, thereby interfering with the development of necessary coping skills. As such, substance-abusing adolescents may have impaired psychological and emotional functioning that impedes the development of autonomy and age-appropriate interpersonal relationships. An alternative theory proposed by Newcomb and Bentler (1988) suggests that adolescent substance abuse prematurely pushes teenagers into social roles for which they are not emotionally or cognitively prepared. In both cases, it is proposed that substance use during adolescence interferes with developmental processes, which contributes to problematic interpersonal functioning. Although the empirical support for these theories is limited, studies have begun to suggest that substance use during adolescence may negatively affect developmental and psychosocial outcomes, including interpersonal relations (Chassin, Pitts, & DeLucia, 1999).

In sum, although emerging data point to the negative impact of adolescent substance use on interpersonal and academic functioning, findings must be interpreted with caution for two primary reasons. First, as discussed in the etiology section of this chapter, interpersonal and academic problems have been identified as risk factors for the development of substance use problems among adolescents. As such, poor relationships with family members and peers, and poor academic functioning, may be both precursors to and consequences of adolescent substance use problems. Second, it is important to recognize that third-variable explanations may account for apparent connections between socioenvironmental variables and substance use problems (Brook, Cohen, & Brook, 1998). For example, poor interpersonal relationships, academic failure, and substance use problems all may result from a preexisting problem such as a psychiatric disorder or juvenile delinquency. Despite these caveats, it is clear that adolescent substance use problems are associated with problematic family and peer relationships, as well as academic failure and high school dropout.

IMPLICATIONS FOR FUTURE PERSONALITY DEVELOPMENT

The vast majority of studies examining putative relations between personality variables and adolescent substance use problems have focused on substance use problems as an outcome rather than as a predictor (Chassin, DeLucia, & Pitts, 1999). Thus, little is currently known about the implications for future personality development of adolescent substance use and abuse. This is very unfortunate, in that there are multiple mechanisms by which adolescent alcohol and drug use might exert negative effects on personality and psychosocial adjustment (Chassin et al., 1999). These mechanisms include (a) the direct pharmacological effects of substances, such as their performance-impairing effects and psychosocial consequences through a simple addictive model; (b) the indirect psychosocial effects of substances, such as their potential negative impact on adolescent emerging developmental competency; and (c) the secondary effects of poor developmental competency, such as occupational, social, and psychological problems.

In one of the few investigations examining the implications of adolescent substance use problems for future personality development, Chassin et al. (1999) compared children with at least one biological alcoholic parent with a demographically matched group of community controls. These researchers found that adolescent levels of drug use and alcohol use were associated with lowered levels of young adult autonomy, positive activity involvement, and competence. Illegal drug use in adolescence, in particular, had a significant and unique negative impact on later young adult outcomes. In a longitudinal study of community-dwelling adolescents, Brown, Kahler, Lewinsohn, Rohde, and Seeley (2001) found that adolescents with alcohol use problems had significantly higher rates of future alcohol and substance use disorders, depression, and antisocial personality disorder symptoms as young adults than adolescents without alcohol use problems. Females and males did not differ significantly in the course of their alcohol disorder or in the extent to which alcohol use problems predicted other disorders, suggesting that the same developmental pathways are operating for both genders. In a general-population retrospective study, Compton et al. (2002) examined the plausibility of adolescent substance use playing a causal role in the development of adulthood antisocial behavior. These researchers found that being drunk by age 18 or having a drug use–related symptom before age 18 significantly increased the risk for adult antisocial behavior, even after controlling for childhood conduct problems and substance use–related disorders. These results were supported for both females and males, again suggesting a gender-invariant developmental pathway.

Adolescent substance use appears to be especially related to poor adult outcomes among adolescents diagnosed with early-onset and life-course-persistent conduct problems (Caspi, Harrington, Moffitt, & Milne, 2002). Followed to age 26 years, childhood-onset delinquents were significantly more likely than adolescence-limited delinquents to have psychopathic personality traits; mental health problems; substance dependence; multiple offspring; financial problems; work problems; and drug-related and violent crime, including violence against women and children. In a longitudinal study of adolescents who received treatment for substance use problems, Brown, Myers, and Stewart (1998) reported similar findings. These researchers found that those teens who had an onset of conduct disorder behavior at age 10 or earlier, greater diversity of conduct disorder behavior occurring independent of substance involvement, and greater recent use of drugs were significantly more likely to meet criteria for an antisocial personality disorder diagnosis in late adolescence or early adulthood than teens without these characteristics. Recent behavior genetic research supports these findings, and suggests that a heritable developmental pathway to adult substance abuse is characterized by unsocialized behavior and psychopathology in childhood (Carlson, Elkins, Iacono, McGue, & Taylor, 1999). Carlson et al.'s work suggests that the genetic transmission of general disposition toward behavioral disinhibition, rather than the transmission of substance abuse per se, leads to heightened risk for life-course-persistent substance use and conduct problems.

In sum, the implications of adolescent substance use problems for future personality development is an underresearched topic. Nonetheless, recent studies have been consistent in finding that early-onset substance use problems, and especially illicit drug use problems, raise the risk for negative adult outcomes, including alcohol and substance use disorders and antisocial personality disorder. This linkage appears to be especially strong among substance-abusing adolescents with concurrent conduct problems, who are much more likely to demonstrate poor adult functioning than substance-abusing adolescents without conduct problems. Finally, these developmental pathways appear to operate similarly for females and males.

TREATMENT IMPLICATIONS

Multiple intervention approaches have been developed to address alcohol and other drug problems among adolescents. Knowledge about which of these many approaches is most effective for which individuals, and under which conditions, remains limited. Demand for clinical services has been overwhelming and has outpaced demand for empirical research evaluating the effectiveness of treatment approaches. Though a growing number of investigators are conducting controlled clinical trials of various adolescent substance abuse interventions (Wagner, Brown, Monti, Myers, & Waldron, 1999; Wagner & Waldron, 2001), most available substance abuse interventions have not been rigorously evaluated. As Williams, Chang, and the Addiction Centre Adolescent Research Group (2000) pointed out, "There is evidence that treatment is superior to no treatment, but insufficient evidence to compare the effectiveness of treatment types. The exception to this is that outpatient family therapy appears superior to other forms of outpatient therapy" (p. 159). This is well said, though it is important to note that family therapy has relatively high rates of attrition with adolescents. Moreover, studies of the efficacy of family therapy have compared interventions that differ not only on family versus individual involvement, but also on the conceptual underpinnings of the interventions being compared (e.g., systemic vs. cognitive-behavioral). Nonetheless, we do know that the treatment of substance use problems can succeed with adolescents, adolescent treatment outcomes are comparable to those found with adults, and improvement varies across domains of functioning (e.g., school, emotional distress, family relations; Wagner & Tarolla, 2002).

Until very recently, treatment approaches for adolescent substance abuse have mirrored those used for adult substance abuse (Wagner, 2003; Wagner & Kassel, 1995). Though this was a good place to start, clinicians and researchers have begun to question the developmental congruence of adult-derived methods and techniques. It is well recognized that the behavioral manifestations of, the motives underlying, and the factors associated with adolescent substance use problems are markedly different from those associated with adult substance use problems. This suggests that treatment approaches with adolescents, in order to be optimally successful, need to take these developmental differences into account. Compared to adult substance abusers, adolescent substance abusers (a) have a briefer history of substance involvement; (b) are more likely to demonstrate episodic consumption and less likely to demonstrate chronic, daily use; (c) are less likely to suffer from the progressive nature of the disorder, medical complications, and other consequences of protracted use; (d) tend to use a greater number of different types of substances, resulting in more complicated withdrawal and dependency patterns; (e) are undergoing rapid developmental changes, which may mimic or exacerbate drug or alcohol effects; (f) are more likely to present with co-occurring problems, such as depressive symptoms, family disruption, academic problems, problem behaviors, deviance, low levels of conventionality, and peer drug use; (g) may be more likely to outgrow patterns of substance use or abuse by early adulthood, without formal intervention or treatment; and (h) may be less amenable to confrontation-of-denial treatment approaches because of developmental issues associated with independence seeking and achieving autonomy.

It is also important to recognize that adolescents with substance use problems are a diverse group. There are vast individual differences on factors such as the anticipated effects and consequences of substance use, the context and motivations in which use occurs, and the risk factors that contribute to or accompany adolescent substance use and abuse (Wagner & Kassel, 1995). These differences could explain why some substance-abusing teenagers respond to treatment and others do not. Individual difference variables likely to affect treatment response have been labeled amenability to treatment or matching factors (Wagner, 2003). Personality differences are among the most compelling candidates for study as amenability to treatment variables. However, personality variables, as well as other possible moderators of treatment (e.g., gender, acculturation, motivation for change), have received scant attention in the adolescent substance abuse treatment literature. This is exactly the reason that knowledge about which treatment approaches are most effective for which individuals under which conditions remains limited.

At present, several evidence-based, developmentally sensitive approaches are emerging for addressing alcohol, nicotine, and other drug use problems among adolescents (Wagner & Waldron, 2001). Examples of such approaches include family systems approaches (Liddle & Hogue, 2001; Waldron, 1997), brief motivational interventions (Barnett, Monti, & Wood, 2001), guided personal change programs (Brown, 2001; Gil, Tubman, & Wagner, 2001), cognitive-behavioral skills-building treatments (Bry & Attaway, 2001; Donohue & Azrin, 2001; Myers, 2001; Wagner, Myers, & Brown, 1994), and assertive aftercare programs (Harrington, Godley, Godley, & Dennis, 2001). In addition, attention devoted to community-based treatment models has been increasing (e.g., treatment provided in neighborhood clinics, schools, and the home), which have been argued to have greater ecological validity and impact, and fewer barriers to treatment access, than more traditional treatment models (Wagner, Swensen, & Henggeler, 2000; Wagner, Tubman, & Gil, 2004). Examples of empirically derived, community-based treatment models include those described by Brown (2001), Bry and Attaway (2001), Gil et al. (2001), and Wagner, Kortlander, and Leon-Morris (2001).

Group therapy and 12-step programs are commonly used with adolescents, but recent reports suggest that these interventions should be pursued only after careful consideration. Though there is little doubt that group therapy can be successful for some teenagers with substance use problems, it may have iatrogenic effects for other teenagers. Based on developmental and intervention findings, Dishion, McCord, and Poulin (1999) have argued that adolescent peer networks formed on the basis of deviance (e.g., referral to group therapy) may provide a context where problem behaviors are reinforced and exacerbated. This argument is not without controversy, and several researchers are now attempting to replicate and expand the work of Dishion and colleagues (see Macgowan & Wagner, in press). In regard to 12-step programs with teenagers, Kassel and Jackson (2001) critically evaluated the existing literature and concluded that some adolescents respond positively to Alcoholics Anonymous and its derivatives, primarily because of expanded social support for nonuse. This may be especially true for teens who have been involved in intensive substance abuse treatment and use 12-step programs as aftercare support (Brown, 1993; Winters et al., 2000). Other teenagers do not respond positively to 12-step approaches, perhaps because these programs are not sufficiently flexible or sophisticated to accommodate the developmental and diagnostic issues associated with substance use problems among adolescents. At present, more research is needed to understand the strengths and weaknesses of group therapy and 12-step approaches when implemented with adolescents with substance use problems.

In sum, treating adolescent substance use problems results in better short- and long-term outcomes than not treating adolescent substance use problems. However, we currently know very little about what parameters are critical to the success of treatments targeting adolescent alcohol and drug problems. Although treatment factors certainly account for some of the variance in treatment outcomes, intraindividual variables and interindividual differences likely moderate response to treatment in ways yet to be determined. Personality factors are compelling candidates as moderators of treatment response, but so little has been done in the area that nothing definitive can be said about to what degree or in what ways these factors may alter the impact of treatment with substance-abusing teenagers.

REFERENCES

American Psychiatric Association. (1994). *Diagnostic and statistical manual of mental disorders* (4th ed.). Washington, DC: Author.

Amey, C. H., & Albrecht, S. L. (1998). Race and ethnic differences in adolescent drug use: The impact of family structure and the quantity and quality of parental interaction. *Journal of Drug Issues, 28,* 283–298.

Arencibia-Mireles, O., Brook, D. W., Brook, J. S., Richter, L., & Whiteman, M. (2001). Risk factors for adolescent marijuana use across cultures and across time. *Journal of Genetic Psychology, 162,* 357–374.

Armstrong, T. D., & Costello, E. J. (2002). Community studies on adolescent substance use, abuse, or dependence, and psychiatric comorbidity. *Journal of Consulting and Clinical Psychology, 70,* 1224–1239.

Bachman, J. G., Lloyd, D. J., & O'Malley, P.M. (1981). Smoking, drinking, and drug use among American high school students: Correlates and trends, 1975–1979. *American Journal of Public Health, 71,* 59–69.

Bailey, S. L., Martin, C. S., Lynch, K. G., & Pollock, N. K. (2000). Reliability and concurrent validity of *DSM-IV* subclinical symptom ratings for alcohol use disorders among adolescents. *Alcoholism: Clinical and Experimental Research, 24,* 1795–1802.

Bailey, S. L., & Rachal, J. V. (1993). Dimensions of adolescent problem drinking. *Journal of Studies on Alcohol, 54,* 555–565.

Barnes, G. M., & Welte, J. W. (1986). Patterns and predictors of alcohol use among 7–12th grade students in New York State. *Journal of Studies on Alcohol, 47,* 53–62.

Barnett, N. P., Monti, P. M., & Wood, M. D. (2001). Motivational interviewing for alcohol-involved adolescents in the emergency room. In E. F. Wagner & H. B. Waldron (Eds.), *Innovations in adolescent substance abuse intervention.* Oxford, England: Elsevier.

Bates, M. E., & Labouvie, E. W. (1995). Personality-environment constellations and alcohol use: A process-oriented study of intraindividual change during adolescence. *Psychology of Addictive Behaviors, 9,* 23–35.

Baumrind, D. (1991). The influence of parenting style on adolescent competence and substance use. *Journal of Early Adolescence, 11,* 56–95.

Baumrind, D., & Moselle, K. (1985). A developmental perspective on adolescent drug use. *Advances in Alcohol and Substance Abuse, 5,* 41–67.

Becker, B. E., & Luthar, S. S. (2002). Privileged but pressured? A study of affluent youth. *Child Development, 73,* 1593–1610.

Braggio, J. T., Pishkin, V., Gameros, T. A., & Brooks, D. L. (1993). Academic achievement in substance abusing and conduct disordered adolescents. *Journal of Clinical Psychology, 49,* 282–291.

Brody, G. H., Gerrard, M., Gibbons, F. X., Murry, V. M., & Wills, T. A. (2003). Family communication and religiosity related to substance use and sexual behavior in early adolescence: A test for pathways through self-control and prototype perceptions. *Psychology of Addictive Behaviors, 17,* 312–323.

Brook, J., Cohen, P., & Brook, D. (1998). Longitudinal study of co-occurring psychiatric disorders and substance use. *Journal of the American Academy of Child and Adolescent Psychiatry, 37,* 322–330.

Brown, R. A., Kahler, C. W., Lewinsohn, P. M., Rohde, P., & Seeley, J. R. (2001). Natural course of alcohol use disorders from adolescence to young adulthood. *Journal of the American Academy of Child and Adolescent Psychiatry, 40,* 83–90.

Brown, S. A. (1993). Recovery patterns in adolescent substance abuse. In J. S. Baer, G. A. Marlatt, & R. J. McMahon (Eds.), *Addictive behaviors across the lifespan* (pp. 160–183). London: Sage.

Brown, S. A. (2001). Facilitating change for adolescent alcohol problems: A multiple options approach. In E. F. Wagner & H. B. Waldron (Eds.), *Innovations in adolescent substance abuse intervention.* Oxford, England: Elsevier.

Brown, S. A., Mott, M. A., & Myers, M. G. (1990). Adolescent alcohol and drug treatment outcome. In R. R. Watson (Ed.), *Drug and alcohol abuse prevention, drug and alcohol abuse reviews* (pp. 373–403). Clifton, NJ: Humana.

Brown, S. A., Myers, M. G., Lippke, L., Tapert, S. F., Steward, D. G., & Vik, P. W. (1998). Psychometric evaluation of the customary drinking and drug use record (CDDR): A measure of adolescent alcohol and drug involvement. *Journal of Studies on Alcohol, 59,* 427–438.

Brown, S. A., Myers, M. G., & Stewart, D. G. (1998). Progression from conduct disorder to antisocial personality disorder following treatment for adolescent substance abuse. *American Journal of Psychiatry, 155,* 479–485.

Brown, S. A., Vik, P. W., & Creamer, V. A. (1989). Characteristics of relapse following adolescent substance abuse treatment. *Addictive Behaviors, 14,* 291–300.

Bry, B. H., & Attaway, N. M. (2001). Community-based intervention. In E. F. Wagner & H. B. Waldron (Eds.), *Innovations in adolescent substance abuse intervention.* Oxford, England: Elsevier.

Burns, W. J., Fisher, K. J., Hampson, S. E., Severson, H. H., & Slovic, P. (2001). Risk perception, personality factors and alcohol use among adolescents. *Personality and Individual Differences, 30,* 167–181.

Carle, A. C., Chassin, L., Krull, J. L., & Loukas, A. (2000). The relation of personality to alcohol abuse/dependence in a high-risk sample. *Journal of Personality, 68,* 1153–1175.

Carlson, S. R., Elkins, I. J., Iacono, W. G., McGue, M., & Taylor, J. (1999). Behavioral disinhibition and the development of substance-use disorders: Findings from the Minnesota Twin Family Study. *Development and Psychopathology, 11,* 869–900.

Caspi, A., Harrington, H., Moffitt, T. E., & Milne, B. J. (2002). Males on the life-course-persistent and adolescence-limited antisocial pathways: Follow-up at age 26 years. *Development and Psychopathology, 14,* 179–207.

Chassin, L., & Colder, C. R. (1997). Affectivity and impulsivity: Temperament risk for adolescent alcohol involvement. *Psychology of Addictive Behaviors, 11,* 83–97.

Chassin, L., Curran, P. J., & Hussong, A. M. (1998). Pathways of risk for accelerated heavy alcohol use among adolescent children of alcoholic parents. *Journal of Abnormal Child Psychology, 26,* 1–12.

Chassin, L., & DeLucia, C. (1996). Drinking during adolescence. *Life-Stage Issues, 20,* 175–180.

Chassin, L., Pitts, S. C., & DeLucia, C. (1999). The relation of adolescent substance use to young adult autonomy, positive activity involvement, and perceived competence. *Development and Psychopathology, 11,* 915–932.

Chen, W. J., Duo, P., Soong, W., & Yang, H. (2002). Substance use among adolescents in Taiwan: Associated personality traits, incompetence, and behavioral/emotional problems. *Drug and Alcohol Dependence, 67,* 27–39.

Chung, T., Colby, S. M., Barnett, N. P., Rohsenow, D. J., Spirito, A., & Monti, P. M. (2000). Screening adolescents for problem drinking: Performance of brief screens against *DSM-IV* alcohol diagnoses. *Journal of Studies on Alcohol, 61,* 579–587.

Clayton, R. R. (1992). Transitions in drug use: Risk and protective factors. In M. Glantz & R. Pickens (Eds.), *Vulnerability to drug abuse* (pp. 15–51). Washington, DC: American Psychological Association.

Clayton, R. R., Colon, S., Donohew, L., & Skinner, W. F. (1999). Peer networks and sensation seeking: Some implications for primary socialization theory. *Substance Use and Misuse, 34,* 1013–1023.

Cleary, S., Filer, M., Mariani, J., Shinar, O., Spera, K., & Wills, T. A. (2001). Temperament related to early-onset substance use: Test of a developmental model. *Prevention Science, 2,* 145–163.

Cleary, S. D., Wills, T. A., & Windle, M. (1998). Temperament and novelty seeking in adolescent substance use: Convergence of dimensions of temperament with constructs from Cloninger's Theory. *Journal of Personality and Social Psychology, 74,* 387–406.

Cooper, M. L., & Huselid, R. F. (1992). Gender roles as mediators of sex differences in adolescent alcohol use and abuse. *Journal of Health and Social Behavior, 33,* 348–362.

Compton, W. M., Cottler, L. B., Cunningham-Williams, R. M., Ridenour, T. A., Robins, L. N., & Spitznagel, E. L. (2002). Test of the plausibility of adolescent substance use playing a causal role in developing adulthood antisocial behavior. *Journal of Abnormal Psychology, 111,* 144–155.

Dennis, M. L., Funk, R., Godley, S. H., Godley, M. D., & Waldron, H. (2004). Cross-validation of the alcohol and cannabis use measures in the Global Appraisal of Individual Needs (GAIN) and Timeline Followback (TLFB; Form 90) among adolescents in substance abuse treatment. *Addiction, 99*(Suppl. 2), 120–128.

Dobkin, P. L., Chabot, L., Maliantovitch, K., & Craig, W. (1998). Predictors of outcome in drug abuse treatment of adolescent inpatients. *Psychological Reports, 83,* 175–186.

Donohue, B., & Azrin, N. (2001). Family behavior therapy. In E. F. Wagner & H. B. Waldron (Eds.), *Innovations in adolescent substance abuse intervention.* Oxford, England: Elsevier.

Donovan, J. E., & Jessor, R. (1978). Adolescent problem drinking: Psychosocial correlates in a national sample study. *Journal of Studies on Alcohol, 39,* 1506–1524.

Donovan, J. E., & Jessor, R. (1983). Problem drinking and the dimension of involvement with drugs: A Guttman scattergram analysis of adolescent drug use. *American Journal of Public Health, 73,* 543–552.

DuHamel, K., & Wills, T. A. (1995). Activity and mood temperament as predictors of adolescent substance use: Test of a self-regulation mediational model. *Journal of Personality and Social Psychology, 68,* 901–916.

Eisemann, M., Hagglof, B., Koposov, R. A., & Ruchkin, V. V. (2002). Alcohol use in delinquent adolescents from northern Russia: The role of personality, parental rearing and family history of alcohol abuse. *Personality and Individual Differences, 32,* 1139–1148.

Ellickson, P. L., Bui, K., Bell, R. M., & McGuigan, K. (1998). Does early drug use increase the risk of dropping out of high school? *Journal of Drug Issues, 28,* 357–380.

Elliot, D. S., Huizinga, D., & Ageton, S. S. (1985). *Multiple problem youth: Delinquency substance use and mental health problems.* New York: Springer-Verlag.

Fiegelman, W. (1987). Day-care treatment for multiple drug abusing adolescents: Social factors linked with completing treatment. *Journal of Psychoactive Drugs, 19,* 335–344.

Foxcroft, D. R., & Lowe, G. (1991). Adolescent drinking behaviour and family socialization factors: A meta-analysis. *Journal of Adolescence, 14,* 255–273.

Galaif, E. R., Hser, Y. I., Grella, C. E., & Joshi, V. (2001). Prospective risk factors and treatment outcomes among adolescents in DATOS-A. *Journal of Adolescent Research, 16,* 661–678.

Garnier, H. E., Stein, J. A., & Jacobs, J. K. (1997). The process of dropping out of high school: A 19 year perspective. *American Educational Research Journal, 34,* 395–419.

Gil, A. G., Tubman, J. G., & Wagner, E. F. (2001). Substance abuse interventions with Latino adolescents: A cultural framework. In E. F. Wagner & H. B. Waldron (Eds.), *Innovations in adolescent substance abuse intervention.* Oxford, England: Elsevier.

Gil, A. G., Vega, W. A., & Turner, R. J. (2002). Early and mid-adolescence risk factors for later substance abuse by African-Americans and European Americans. *Public Health Reports, 117*(Suppl. 1), 15–29.

Godley, S. H., Godley, M. D., & Dennis, M. L. (2001). The assertive aftercare protocol for adolescent substance abusers. In E. F. Wagner & H. B. Waldron (Eds.), *Innovations in adolescent substance abuse intervention.* Oxford, England: Elsevier.

Harrison, P. A., Fulkerson, J. A., & Beebe, T. J. (1998). DSM-IV substance use disorder criteria for adolescents: A critical examination based on a statewide school survey. *American Journal of Psychiatry, 155,* 486–492.

Hawkins, J. D., Catalano, R. F., & Miller, J. Y. (1992). Risk and protective factors for alcohol and other drug problems in adolescence and early adulthood: Implications for substance abuse prevention. *Psychological Bulletin, 112,* 64–105.

Hays, R. D., & Ellickson, P. L. (1996). What is adolescent alcohol misuse in the United States according to the experts? *Alcohol and Alcoholism, 31,* 297–303.

Herrenkohl, T. I., Maguine, E., Hill, K. G., Hawkins, D. J., Abbott, R. D., & Catalano, R. F. (2000). Developmental risk factors for youth violence. *Journal of Adolescent Health, 26,* 176–186.

Jainchill, N., Hawke, J., & Yagelka, J. (2000). Adolescents in therapeutic communities: One-year posttreatment outcomes. *Journal of Psychoactive Drugs, 32,* 81–94.

Jenson, J. M. (1997). Risk and protective factors for alcohol and other drug use in childhood and adolescence. In M. W. Fraser (Ed.), *Risk and resilience in childhood: An ecological perspective* (pp. 117–139). Washington, DC: National Association of Social Workers.

Jessor, R., Van Den Bros, J., Vanderryn, J., Costa, F. M., & Turbin, M. S. (1997). Protective factors in adolescent problem behavior: Moderator effects and developmental change. In G. A. Marlatt & G. R. VandenBos (Eds.), *Addictive behaviors: Readings on etiology, prevention, and treatment* (pp. 239–264). Washington, DC: American Psychological Association.

Johnston, L. D., O'Malley, P. M., & Bachman, J. G. (2003). *Monitoring the future: National results on adolescent drug use.* Retrieved March 6, 2003, from http://www.monitoringthefuture.org

Johnston, L. D., O'Malley, P.M., Bachman, J. G., & Schulenberg, J. E. (2004). *Monitoring the Future national survey results on drug use, 1975–2003. Volume I: Secondary school students* (NIH Publication No. 04–5507). Bethesda, MD: National Institute on Drug Abuse.

Kaminer, Y. (1994). *Adolescent substance abuse: A comprehensive guide to theory and practice.* New York: Plenum Press.

Kaminer, Y. (2001). Adolescent substance abuse treatment: Where do we go from here? *Psychiatric Services, 52,* 147–149.

Kaminer, Y., Tarter, R. E., Bukstein, O. G., & Kabene, M. (1992). Comparison between treatment completers and noncompleters among dually diagnosed substance-abusing adolescents. *Journal of the American Academy of Child and Adolescent Psychiatry, 31,* 1046–1049.

Kaminer, Y., Wagner, E., Plummer, B., & Seifer, R. (1993). Validation of the Teen Addiction Severity Index (T-ASI): Preliminary findings. *American Journal on Addictions, 2,* 250–254.

Kandel, D. B. (1985). On processes of peer influences in adolescent drug use: A developmental perspective. *Advances in Alcohol and Substance Abuse, 4,* 139–163.

Kandel, D. B., Yamaguchi, K., & Chen, K. (1992). Stages of progression in drug involvement from adolescence to adulthood: Further evidence for the gateway theory. *Journal of Studies on Alcohol, 53,* 447–457.

Kassel, J. D., & Jackson, S. I. (2001). 12-Step based interventions for adolescents. In E. F. Wagner, & H. B. Waldron (Eds.), *Innovations in adolescent substance abuse intervention.* Oxford, England: Elsevier.

Keefe, S. E., & Padilla, A. M. (1987). *Chicano ethnicity.* Albuquerque: University of New Mexico Press.

Kirby, L. D., & Fraser, M. W. (1997). Risk and resilience in childhood. In M. W. Fraser (Ed.), *Risk and resilience in childhood: An ecological perspective* (pp. 10–31). Washington, DC: National Association of Social Workers.

Krohn, M. D., Thornberry, T. P., Collins-Hall, L., & Lizotte, A. J. (1995). School dropout, delinquent behavior and drug use: An examination of the causes and consequences of dropping out of school. In H. B. Kaplan (Ed.), *Drugs, crime, and other deviant adaptations: Longitudinal studies* (pp. 163–183). New York: Plenum Press.

Latimer, W. W., Newcomb, M., Winters, K. C., & Stinchfield, R. D. (2000). Adolescent substance abuse treatment outcome: The role of substance abuse problem severity, psychosocial, and treatment factors. *Journal of Consulting and Clinical Psychology, 68,* 684–696.

Latimer, W. W., Winters, K. C., Stinchfield, R., & Traver, R. E. (2000). Demographic, individual, and interpersonal predictors of adolescent alcohol and marijuana use following treatment. *Psychology of Addictive Behaviors, 14,* 162–173.

Lewinsohn, P.M., Hops, H., Roberts, R. E., Seeley, J. R., & Andrews, J. A. (1993). Adolescent psychopathology I: Prevalence and incidence of depression and other *DSM-III-R* disorders in high school students. *Journal of Abnormal Psychology, 102,* 133–144.

Liddle, H. A., & Hogue, A. (2001). Multidimensional family therapy for adolescent substance abuse. In E. F. Wagner & H. B. Waldron (Eds.), *Innovations in adolescent substance abuse intervention.* Oxford, England: Elsevier.

Macgowan, M. J., & Wagner, E. F. (in press). Iatrogenic effects of group treatment on adolescents with substance use problems: A review of the literature and a presentation of a model. *Journal of Evidence Based Social Work.*

Maggs, J. L., & Schulenberg, J. (2001). Moving targets: Modeling developmental trajectories of adolescent alcohol misuse, individual and peer risk factors, and intervention effects. *Applied Developmental Science, 5,* 237–253.

Martin, C. S., & Winters, K. C. (1999). Diagnosis and assessment of alcohol use disorders among adolescents. *Alcohol Health and Research World, 22,* 95–105.

Mensch, B. S., & Kandel, D. B. (1988). Dropping out of high school and drug involvement. *Sociology of Education, 61,* 95–113.

Miller, W. R., & Rollnick, S. (Eds.). (2002). *Motivational interviewing: Preparing people for change* (2nd ed.). New York: Guilford Press.

Moffitt, T. E. (1993). The neuropsychology of conduct disorder. *Development and Psychopathology, 5,* 135–151.

Moss, H. B., Kirisci, L., Gordon, H. W., & Tarter, R. E. (1994). A neuropsychologic profile of adolescent alcoholics. *Alcoholism: Clinical and Experimental Research, 18,* 159–163.

Myers, M. G. (2001). Cigarette smoking treatment for substance abusing adolescents. In E. F. Wagner & H. B. Waldron (Eds.), *Innovations in adolescent substance abuse intervention.* Oxford, England: Elsevier.

National Institute of Alcohol Abuse and Alcoholism. (1997). *Alcohol and health: The 9th Special Report to Congress* (NIH Publication No. 97–4017). Rockville, MD.

Newcomb, M. D. (1992). Understanding the multidimensional nature of drug use and abuse: The role of consumption, risk factors, and protective factors. In M. Glantz & R. Pickens (Eds.), *Vulnerability to drug abuse* (pp. 255–297). Washington, DC: American Psychological Association.

Newcomb, M. D., Abbot, R. D., Catalano, R. F., Hawkins, J. D., Battin-Pearson, S., & Hill, K. (2002). Mediational and deviance theories of late high school failure: Process roles of structural strains, academic competence, and general versus specific problem behaviors. *Journal of Counseling Psychology, 49,* 172–186.

Newcomb, M. D., & Bentler, P. M. (1988). *Consequences of adolescent drug use.* Beverly Hills, CA: Sage.

Office of Applied Studies. (2003). *National survey on drug use and health (NSDUH).* Retrieved on March 28, 2003, from http://www.samsha.org

Pollock, N. K., & Martin, C. S. (1999). Diagnostic orphans: Adolescents with alcohol symptoms who do not qualify for *DSM-IV* abuse or dependence diagnoses. *American Journal of Psychiatry, 156,* 897–901.

Robins, L. N., & Ratcliff, K. S. (1979). Continuation of antisocial behavior into adulthood. *International Journal of Mental Health, 7,* 96–116.

Rounds-Bryant, J. L., & Staab, J. (2001). Patient characteristics and treatment outcomes for African-American, Hispanic, and White adolescents in DATOS-A. *Journal of Adolescent Research, 16,* 624–641.

Rowe, C. L., Liddle, H. A., Greenbaum, P. E., & Henderson, C. E. (2004). Impact of psychiatric comorbidity on treatment of adolescent drug abusers. *Journal of Substance Abuse Treatment, 26,* 129–140.

Sampson, R., & Lauritsen, J. (1994). Violent victimization and offending: Individual-, situational-, and community-level risk factors. In A. J. Reiss & J. A. Roth (Eds.), *Understanding and preventing violence: Vol. 3. Social influences* (pp. 1–115). Washington, DC: National Academy Press.

Semons, M. (1991). Ethnicity in the urban high school: A naturalistic study of student experiences. *Urban Review, 23,* 137–158.

Stice, E., Kirz, J., & Borbely, C. (2002). Disentangling adolescent substance use and problem use within a clinical sample. *Journal of Adolescent Research, 17,* 122–142.

Tarter, R., & Hegedus, A. M. (1991). The Drug Use Screening Inventory: Its applications in the evaluation and treatment of alcohol and other drug abuse. *Alcohol Health and Research World, 15,* 65–75.

Tarter, R. E., Mezzich, A. C., Hsieh, Y., & Parks, S. M. (1995). Cognitive capacity in female adolescent substance abusers. *Drug and Alcohol Dependence, 39,* 15–21.

Tarter, R. E., Moss, H. B., & Vanyukov, M. M. (1995). Behavioral genetics and the etiology of alcoholism. In H. Begleiter & B. Kissin (Eds.), *The genetics of alcoholism. Alcohol and alcoholism* (pp. 294–326). London: Oxford University Press.

Tarter, R. E., & Vanyukov, M. (1994). Alcoholism as a developmental disorder. *Journal of Consulting and Clinical Psychology, 62,* 1096–1107.

Turner, R. J., & Gil, A. G. (2002). Psychiatric and substance use disorders in South Florida: Racial/ethnic and gender contrasts in a young adult cohort. *Archives of General Psychiatry, 59,* 43–50.

U.S. Department of Health and Human Services. (1988). *The health consequences of smoking: Nicotine addiction: A report of the Surgeon General.* Washington, DC: U.S. Government Printing Office.

U.S. Department of Health and Human Services. (1994). *Preventing tobacco use among young people: Report of the Surgeon General.* Washington, DC: U.S. Government Printing Office.

Vega, W. A., & Gil, A. G. (1998). *Drug use and ethnicity in early adolescence.* New York: Plenum Press.

Vega, W. A., & Gil, A. G. (1999). A model for explaining drug use behavior among Hispanic adolescents. *Drugs and Society, 14,* 57–73.

Vega, W. A., Gil, A. G., & Wagner, E. (1998). Cultural adjustment and Hispanic adolescent drug use. In H. B. Kaplan, A. E. Gottfried, A. W. Gottfried (Series Eds.), W. A. Vega, & A. G. Gil (Vol. Eds.), *Longitudinal research in the social and behavioral sciences: Vol. 2. Drug use and ethnicity in early adolescence* (pp. 125–148). New York: Plenum Press.

Vega, W. A., Zimmerman, R. S., Warheit, G. J., Apospori, E., & Gil, A. G. (1998). Risk factors for early adolescent drug use in four ethnic and racial groups. In P. Balls-Organista, K. M. Chun, & G. Marin (Eds.), *Readings in ethnic psychology* (pp. 178–187). New York: Routledge.

Wagner, E. F. (2003). Conceptualizing alcohol treatment research for Hispanic/Latino adolescents. *Alcoholism: Clinical and Experimental Research, 27,* 1349–1352.

Wagner, E. F., Brown, S. A., Monti, P. M., Myers, M. G., & Waldron, H. B. (1999). Innovations in adolescent substance abuse intervention. *Alcoholism: Clinical and Experimental Research, 23,* 236–249.

Wagner, E. F., & Kassel, J. D. (1995). Substance use and abuse. In R. T. Ammerman & M. Hersen (Eds.), *Handbook of child behavior therapy in the psychiatric setting* (pp. 367–388). New York: Wiley.

Wagner, E. F., Kortlander, S. E., & Leon Morris, S. (2001). The Teen Intervention Project: A school-based intervention for adolescents with substance abuse problems. In E. F. Wagner & H. B. Waldron (Eds.), *Innovations in adolescent substance abuse intervention* (pp. 189–203). Oxford, England: Elsevier.

Wagner, E. F., Lloyd, D., & Gil, A. G. (2002). Racial/ethnic and gender differences in the incidence and onset age of *DSM-IV* alcohol use disorder symptoms among adolescents. *Journal of Studies on Alcohol, 63,* 609–619.

Wagner, E. F., Myers, M. G., & Brown, S. A. (1994). Adolescent substance abuse: Assessment and treatment strategies. In L. VandeCreek (Ed.), *Innovations in clinical practice: A source book.* Sarasota, FL: Professional Resource Press.

Wagner, E. F., Swensen, C. C., & Henggeler, S. W. (2000). Practical and methodological challenges in validating community-based interventions. *Children's Services: Social Policy, Research, and Practice, 3,* 211–231.

Wagner, E. F., & Tarolla, S. (2002). Course and outcome. In C. A. Essau (Ed.), *Substance abuse and dependence in adolescence* (pp. 119–142). London: Brunner Routledge.

Wagner, E. F., Tubman, J. G., & Gil, A. G. (2004). Implementing school-based substance abuse interventions: Methodological dilemmas and recommended solutions. *Addiction, 99,* 106–119.

Wagner, E. F., & Waldron, H. B. (Eds.). (2001). *Innovations in adolescent substance abuse intervention.* Oxford, England: Elsevier.

Waldron, H. B. (1997). Adolescent substance abuse and family therapy outcome: A review of randomized trials. In T. H. Ollendick & R. J. Prinz (Eds.), *Advances in clinical child psychology* (Vol. 19, pp. 199–234). New York: Plenum Press.

Wallace, J. M., & Muroff, J. R. (2002). Preventing substance abuse among African-American children and youth: Race differences in risk factor exposure and vulnerability. *Journal of Primary Prevention, 22,* 235–261.

Weng, L. J., Newcomb, M. D., & Bentler, P. M. (1988). Factors influencing noncompletion of high school: A comparison of methodologies. *Educational Research Quarterly, 12,* 8–22.

White, N. R. (1992). Early problem behavior and later drug problems. *Journal of Research in Crime and Delinquency, 29,* 412–429.

Williams, R. J., Chang, S. Y., & Addiction Centre Adolescent Research Group. (2000). A comprehensive and comparative review of adolescent substance abuse treatment outcome. *Clinical Psychology: Science and Practice, 7,* 138–166.

Wills, T. A., Sandy, J. M., & Yaeger, A. (2000). Temperament and adolescent substance use: An epigenetic approach to risk and protection. *Journal of Personality, 68,* 1127–1151.

Winters, K. C., Stinchfield, R. D., Opland, E., Weller, C., & Latimer, W. W. (2000). The effectiveness of the Minnesota Model approach in the treatment of adolescent drug abusers. *Addiction, 95,* 601–612.

Winters, K. C., Latimer, W. W., & Stinchfield, R. D. (1999). Assessing adolescent drug use with the Personal Experience Inventory. In M. E. Maruish (Ed.), *The use of psychological testing for treatment planning and outcomes assessment* (2nd ed., pp. 599–630). Mahwah, NJ: Erlbaum.

Wise, B. K., Cuffe, S. P., & Fischer, T. (2001). Dual diagnosis and successful participation of adolescents in substance abuse treatment. *Journal of Substance Abuse Treatment, 21,* 161–165.

Zucker, R. A. (1994). Pathways to alcohol problems. A developmental account of the evidence for contextual contributions to risk. In R. A. Zucker, J. Howard, & G. M. Boyd (Eds.), *The development of alcohol problems* (pp. 255–289). Rockville, MD: National Institute on Alcohol Abuse and Alcoholism.

Zucker, R. A., & Harford, T. C. (1983). National study of the demography of adolescent drinking practices in 1980. *Journal of Studies on Alcohol, 44,* 974–985.

CHAPTER 22

Child Physical Abuse and Neglect

DAVID DILILLO, ANDREA R. PERRY, AND MICHELLE FORTIER

DESCRIPTION OF THE PROBLEM AND CLINICAL PICTURE

Although poor and inhumane treatment of children is not a new phenomenon (Doerner & Lab, 1998; Wolfe, 1999), child physical abuse and neglect were not identified as serious social problems until the 1960s, with the publication of Kempe and colleagues' description of battered-child syndrome (Kempe, Silverman, Steele, Droegemueller, & Silver, 1962). In this influential study, Kempe and colleagues described the clinical manifestation of this syndrome in terms of the deleterious physical consequences maltreated children experienced, ranging from undetected outcomes to those that cause significant physical impairments. Rather than exploring the potential psychological sequelae of maltreated children, Kempe focused on detailing the psychiatric profiles of abusive parents. They concluded that, although not all maltreating parents possess severe psychiatric disturbances, "in most cases some defect in character structure is probably present; often parents may be repeating the type of child care practiced on them in their childhood" (p. 112). Since Kempe and colleagues' original characterization of physical abuse, professionals have grappled with exactly how to define child maltreatment. As many have pointed out, child maltreatment is a complex and heterogeneous problem (e.g., Cicchetti, 1990; Wolfe & McGee, 1991; Zuravin, 1991) that is difficult to define (Wolfe, 1987, 1999). In a summary of definitional considerations, Zuravin (1991) suggested that operational definitions of abuse and neglect should differentiate among subcategories of maltreating behavior and should consider issues such as severity and chronicity. Before we discuss the respective definitions of child physical abuse and neglect, we will briefly review the legal aspects of these definitions.

Legal Aspects

In 1974 the federal government established a minimal set of child protection laws (the federal Child Abuse Prevention and Treatment Act [CAPTA]) and required each state to adhere to CAPTA guidelines (National Clearinghouse on Child Abuse and Neglect [NCCAN], 2003b, 2004b). These seminal laws were most recently amended and refined in 2003 by the Keeping Children and Families Safe Act, which conceptualizes child maltreatment minimally as (1) "Any recent act or failure to act on the part of a parent or caretaker which results in death, serious physical or emotional harm, sexual abuse, or exploitation" or (2) "An act or failure to act which presents an imminent risk or serious harm" (NCCAN, 2004b, p. 1). With the exception of these federally mandated criteria, child abuse and neglect laws vary from state to state, including the degree to which they include exemptions (e.g., cultural or religious practices, corporal punishment) and whether they encompass specific or broad definitional categories (NCCAN, 2003a).

Definition of Child Physical Abuse

Aside from these basic federal requirements, a single conceptual framework has yet to emerge for child physical abuse. Establishing an operational definition of child physical abuse is difficult for several reasons. First, there is wide variation in how people view corporal punishment (e.g., spanking, slapping), ranging from the belief that any physical behavior directed at a child is completely unacceptable (e.g., Straus, 2000) to the view that physical punishment is an effective and appropriate method of discipline. This lack of agreement makes it difficult to distinguish between physical acts against a child that represent an extreme disciplinary method and those that qualify as abuse (Hansen, Sedlar, & Warner-Rogers, 1999; Kolko, 2002). In addition, although physical injury may indicate the presence of abuse, it is important also to consider the many factors surrounding abusive behavior, including the prevalence, time frame, severity, age of onset, and chronicity of abuse (Hecht & Hansen, 2001; Widom, 2000; Wolfe, 1987; Zuravin, 1991) as well as the impact of cultural and community values on parents' socialization practices (Wolfe, 1987).

Despite difficulties in formulating a unified definition of child physical abuse, several concepts have converged in the literature to provide some conceptual consistency. For example, because of the direct, explicit, and invasive nature of physical abuse, this form of maltreatment has been conceptualized as an act (or acts) of commission in which a caregiver intentionally inflicts physical pain or injury upon a child (see Hansen et al., 1999; Warner-Rogers, Hansen, & Hecht, 1999; Zuravin, 1991). Consistent with this notion, NCCAN (2004b) defined child physical abuse as "physical injury (ranging from minor bruises to severe fractures or death) as a result of punching, beating, kicking, biting, shaking, throwing, stabbing, choking, hitting (with a hand, stick, strap, or other object), burning, or otherwise harming a child" (p. 2). Within this definitional framework, NCCAN maintains that, regardless of the caregiver's intent, injurious behavior imposed upon a child invariably constitutes abuse. In the Third National Incidence Study of Child Abuse and Neglect (NIS-3), a thorough, federally mandated examination of the incidence, characteristics, and consequences of child abuse in the United States, child maltreatment was defined by two standards: the Harm Standard and the Endangerment Standard (Sedlak & Broadhurst, 1996). According to the former standard, children were classified as abused, neglected, or both if maltreatment resulted in "demonstrable harm" (p. 4). The latter standard expanded this by including children who had been abused, neglected, or both but had not yet suffered from observable or known consequences.

Definition of Neglect

In contrast to the acts of commission that comprise physical abuse, neglect is said to reflect caregiver acts of omission, or deficiencies in providing for the child in a manner that promotes healthy growth and development (see NCCAN, 2001; Warner-Rogers et al., 1999; Zuravin, 1991). More specifically, NCCAN (2004b) defines neglect as a "failure to provide for a child's basic needs" in one or more of the following areas: physical, medical, educational, and emotional (p. 1). These categories have also been extended to include additional subtypes such as mental health neglect (Erickson & Egeland, 2002), supervisory neglect (National Research Council, 1993), and abandonment (Barnett, Miller-Perrin, & Perrin, 1997). Thus, neglectful behaviors include acts such as failure to provide children with proper nutrition, safe and sanitary shelter, and adequate clothing; failure to protect children from harm; failure to be attentive to a child's physical and psychological or emotional needs; and failure to seek appropriate medical, mental health, or educational services for a child (Barnett et al., 1997; Erickson & Egeland, 2002). Finally, it is important to note that neglect may vary across cultures, religions, and communities (NCCAN, 2004b). For instance, NCCAN (2003a) stated that the most prevalent exemption in state statutes is withholding medical care from an ill child because of religious affiliation. In 2003, states including Arizona, Connecticut, and Washington exempted the religious health-related practices of the Christian Science community.

Despite what may initially seem like rather clear-cut definitional criteria, several factors make it difficult to operationalize neglect. One such factor involves the inevitability of placing a subjective description on what so-called adequate parenting or caregiver behavior involves (NCCAN, 2001). Wolfe (1999) delineated this notion by suggesting that parent-child relationships cannot be understood in terms of dichotomous labels. Rather, Wolfe described a continuum of parenting behaviors, including *child-centered behaviors* (e.g., open communication) that encourage healthy growth and development; *borderline methods* that approximate inappropriate parenting behaviors (e.g., rigidity, coerciveness); and lastly, *inappropriate, abusive, or neglectful methods* that reflect readily harmful parent-child interactions. In examining the neglect literature, Straus and Kantor (2003) posited two conceptual concerns that emerged in their review. First, they questioned whether neglectful caregiver behavior must be intentional or whether confounding causes such as poverty and lack of knowledge should be considered as mitigating factors (also discussed by Erickson & Egeland, 2002, and NCCAN, 2001). These authors also considered whether caregivers who do not shield children from potentially deleterious events, such as domestic violence, should be considered neglectful. Regardless of the aforementioned factors, many professionals have suggested that definitions of neglect should not be contingent upon the presence of short-term sequelae because, in many cases, the effects of neglect do not emerge in the immediate aftermath of maltreatment (e.g., Erickson & Egeland, 2002).

Features of Child Physical Abuse and Neglect

Because child physical abuse and neglect involve interactions between a child or adolescent victim and an adult perpetrator, these phenomena are not represented as a unique classification within the *Diagnostic and Statistical Manual of Mental Disorders,* fourth edition, text revision (*DSM-IV-TR;* American Psychiatric Association, 2000). Child maltreatment can, however, manifest in a range of symptoms that span various *DSM-IV* diagnostic criteria. Although there is no telltale symptom pattern indicative of abuse or neglect, examining the range of potential physical, emotional, and behavioral correlates helps to elucidate a typical clinical picture of child maltreatment. In general, physically abused and neglected children may experience a variety of impairments, including intellectual or academic difficulties, diminished peer relationships, and disturbed attachment with caregivers. Studies specifically examining child physical abuse have revealed linkages to affective dysregulation (e.g., depression; Johnson et al., 2002), cognitive impairment (e.g., language-delays; Eigsti & Cicchetti, 2004), and externalizing behaviors (e.g., heightened oppositionality and aggression; Trickett & Kuczynski, 1986). Further, physically abused children may demonstrate fear around adult figures and resist reunification with parents (e.g., after school; NCCAN, 2003c). Research on neglect has documented associations with various internalizing psychological factors (e.g., self-esteem, disrupted attachment; Egeland, 1991) as well as cognitive deficits, particularly when coupled with a child's failure to thrive (Mackner, Starr, & Black, 1997). In addition to these correlates, neglected children may present as physically unclean or unkempt, be repeatedly truant or absent from day care or school, and steal essential items from others (NCCAN, 2003c).

PERSONALITY DEVELOPMENT AND PSYCHOPATHOLOGY

Predisposing Personality Characteristics

As noted, child physical abuse and neglect are inherently interactive phenomena. Most efforts to understand the origins of abuse and neglect have focused on one side of this equation by examining parental risk factors for abusive behavior. It is also possible, however, that certain personality features of children may place them at risk of being abused or neglected. Child temperament and disruptive behavior patterns are two such factors. Although children bear no responsibility for being maltreated, both of these constructs have been examined as factors that may increase their vulnerability to abuse or neglect.

Temperament is believed to encompass the biological rudiments of adult personality (Kagan, 1994). It has been suggested that children who are temperamentally difficult—that is, those who are irritable, cry frequently, are hard to soothe, and display negative emotionality—may elicit physically harsh or neglectful behaviors from caregivers. Presumably, this is because the added stress and demands of caring for temperamentally challenging children can overwhelm parental coping and lead to the use of harsh or neglectful parenting.

This notion is based on early writings highlighting the bidirectional nature of parent-child socialization (e.g., Bell, 1968), as well as the notion that child temperament impacts interactions between caregiver and child (Thomas, Chess, & Birch, 1968). In considering the literature on this topic, Erickson and Egeland (2002) are skeptical of this connection, noting that early writings addressing child irritability and fussiness (e.g., Gil, 1970; Parke & Collmer, 1975; Thomas & Chess, 1977) were limited by retrospective designs and potentially biased parental reports of temperament. They further point out that parental responsiveness to children has been shown to overcome challenging temperamental characteristics (Brachfield, Goldberg, & Sloman, 1980; Sameroff & Chandler, 1975). Hence, based on current evidence, it cannot be concluded that temperamental factors significantly increase the risk of abuse.

Early comparisons of maltreated and nonmaltreated children revealed that youths who had been abused were more likely to exhibit aggressive and defiant behaviors during interactions with parents (Bousha & Twentyman, 1984; Trickett & Kucznyski, 1986). However, these investigations did not reveal whether such behaviors had actually provoked parental abuse or were simply the result of maltreatment. In addressing this issue, other studies have used experimental designs to explore how parents respond to children displaying different degrees of aversive behaviors (Anderson, Lytton, & Romney, 1986), as well as how parents interact with child confederates instructed to behave aggressively toward peers (Brunk & Henggeler, 1984). In both cases, child misbehavior has been found to elicit more coercive parental responses. In a similar vein of research, it has been noted that children with oppositional defiant disorder are more likely to be abused than are children with internalizing disorders or those with other types of externalizing disorders (Ford et al., 1999). Thus, there appears to be some credence to the possibility that disruptive behavior increases a child's risk for experiencing physical abuse.

Personality Factors Associated with Resilience

Although difficult temperament and disruptive behavior have been examined as risk factors for abuse, other personality features may serve to protect against the negative consequences of maltreatment. Moran and Eckenrode (1992) explored whether locus of control and self-esteem buffered against depression in maltreated adolescent females and a comparison group of nonmaltreated peers. An internal locus of control for positive events and higher self-esteem both interacted with maltreatment status in predicting depression, suggesting that they serve a protective function. Further, those who experienced maltreatment during childhood were less likely than those whose abuse started during adolescence to have these protective personality characteristics. Heller, Larrieu, D'Imperio, and Boris (1999) also identified internal locus of control, in addition to external attributions of blame, ego control, and resilience, as personality features that guarded against the negative impact of maltreatment. In examining some of these same attributes longitudinally, Cicchetti and Rogosch (1997) found that the personality characteristics of positive self-esteem, ego resilience, and ego overcontrol were predictive of resilience over a 3-year period. These findings were in contrast to resilience in nonmaltreated children, which was associated more with relationship factors (e.g., emotional availability of mothers) rather than personality characteristics.

The Role of Attachment

Regardless of a child's premorbid characteristics, an important challenge for researchers is to determine whether abuse and neglect impinge upon the course of normal development in ways that disrupt emerging personality organization. An attachment perspective is one theoretical framework that has often been used to understand these processes. The experience of maltreatment has frequently been linked to a range of attachment-related difficulties, including insecure bonding with caregivers, problems with emotional regulation, and negativistic views of self and others. The following is a brief discussion of these issues and their relation to early personality development among maltreated children.

The concept of attachment derives from Bowlby's (1969) theory and refers to the quality of parent-child bonding, which is believed to have a strong influence on how children learn to regulate their emotional responses and behaviors. Classic studies by Ainsworth, using the Strange Situation paradigm, led to the identification and classification of several primary attachment patterns, including secure, anxious ambivalent, avoidant, and disorganized types (Ainsworth, Blehar, Waters, & Wall, 1978; Main & Solomon, 1986). Insecurely attached children (the latter three classifications) are deprived of comforting caregivers who consistently respond in a sensitive manner to their physical and psychological needs. Because the family environments of abused and neglected children are similarly harsh and unresponsive, an attachment framework has been applied to understand the developmental experiences of maltreated children. Studies confirm that physically abused children experience attachment difficulties (Finzi, Cohen, Sapir, & Weizman, 2000). More specifically, physically abused youth have been found to display avoidant attachment styles, while neglect has often been linked to the development of anxious or ambivalent patterns of attachment (Crittenden, 1985; Finzi, Ram, Har-Even, Shnit, & Weizman, 2001). The absence of a secure base of attachment results in maltreated children lagging behind peers in their cognitive and social development (Sroufe, Carlson, Levy, & Egeland, 1999), which may set the stage for later psychopathology and personality difficulties.

An important component of Bowlby's (1969) theory is the notion that infants and children develop mental representations of self and others (known as internal working models), that are derived from the quality of parent-child relationships. Thus, children whose parents are sensitive and responsive to their needs will acquire positive models of self and others. For maltreated children, however, who lack attachment security, internal representations of self and others appear to be negativistic and include perceptions of maternal figures as untrustworthy (Toth, Cicchetti, Macfie, & Emde, 1997). Neglected children, in particular, may have difficulty viewing themselves in positive terms (Toth et al., 1997). Of relevance to personality adjustment is the possibility that negative representational models may endure and be generalized to encounters with other individuals, thereby impacting lifelong interpersonal adjustment (Howes & Segal, 1993; Lynch & Cicchetti, 1992; Toth & Cicchetti, 1996).

A third attachment-related concern is that of emotional regulation, or the ability to effectively manage and control the expression of intense emotional experiences, particularly those that are negative (Cicchetti, Ganiban, & Barnett, 1991). Emotions serve a valuable function as an internal barometer of the external world, allowing for interpretation of external events in positive or negative terms and providing the impetus for adaptive responding. In the case of child maltreatment, the development of emotional regulation may often be disrupted. Abuse and neglect create a harsh and unpredictable world for children, one inhabited by caregivers who fail to provide the guidance and learning experiences needed to make sense of intense emotions. In fact, rather than eliciting comforting responses, negative emotional expressions by children, such as crying, may be met with invalidating or disapproving responses from abusive parents. This is concerning because parental socialization of emotional regulation in children has been shown to mediate between maltreatment experiences and children's management of their emotional expressions (Shipman & Zeman, 2001).

Research with psychiatric patients has linked poor attachment with the long-term development of personality difficulties (Nakash-Eisikovits, Dutra, & Westen, 2002). The same may be true for maltreated children, whose pervasive attachment difficulties may set a course for maladaptive personality formation. Indeed, in one of the few studies to specifically examine early personality characteristics of maltreated children, Rogosch and Cicchetti (2004) applied the Five Factor Model (FFM) to compare abused and nonabused 6-year-olds on several personality dimensions, including extraversion, agreeableness, conscientiousness, neuroticism, and openness to experience. Results showed that, with the exception of extraversion, maltreated children differed from their nonmaltreated peers on all dimensions assessed, in directions that were indicative of poorer adaptation. Abused children were also more likely to be represented in maladaptive personality clusters, while those who had been both physically abused and neglected showed particularly problematic personality profiles. Finally, these researchers found that personality organization was relatively stable between the ages of 6 and 9 years among abused children, suggesting that these maladaptive personality profiles may endure across time.

EPIDEMIOLOGY

As previously discussed, operationally defining child physical abuse and neglect is problematic due to a number of thorny conceptual issues. Despite these challenges, official estimate reports have provided valuable information with which to measure the magnitude of victimization. Although these reports use nationally representative samples, data from several of these wide-scale studies will be presented. Then, a brief overview of demographic variables associated with abuse will be discussed.

National Incidence Studies

Data for the latest National Incidence Study of Child Abuse and Neglect (NIS-3) were collected during 1993 and 1994. Findings from this study, published by Sedlak and Broadhurst (1996), revealed alarming rates of child maltreatment. For example, when utilizing the harm standard (i.e., children who were harmed by abuse or neglect), 381,700 children were physically abused, 338,900 children were physically neglected, and 212,800 were emotionally neglected during the data-collection period. Under the endangerment standard (i.e., children who were abused or neglected but not yet harmed), 614,100 were deemed at risk for harm from physical abuse, 1,335,100 from physical neglect, and 585,100 from emotional neglect (Sedlak & Broadhurst, 1996). Similarly, data from the National Child Abuse and Neglect Data System (NCANDS, 2004a), a database reflecting cases reported to Child Protective Services, revealed that the national victimization rate was 12.3 per every 1,000 children (18.6 percent physically abused; 60.5 percent neglected; NCCAN, 2004a). Finally, according to the *Injury Fact Book,* an estimated 1,100 children died from some form of child abuse or neglect during 2001–2002 (Centers for Disease Control and Prevention, 2001).

Child Age and Gender

In addition to basic prevalence findings, several demographic variables such as child age and gender have been examined in relation to physical abuse and neglect. Official estimate reports have yielded mixed findings regarding associations between age and child physical abuse. Some authors have reported that the risk of abuse peaks between the ages of 3 and 12 years, with children outside of that range experiencing relatively less risk (Wolfner & Gelles, 1993). Others have reported little association between child age and child physical abuse (Connelly & Straus, 1992), or negative associations between minor (but not severe) physical abuse and age (Straus, Hamby, Finkelhor, Moore, & Runyan, 1998). Despite these inconsistencies, it appears clear that young children are more likely to be severely injured as a result of child physical abuse (Lung & Daro, 1996). With regard to neglect, incidence appears to peak around age 6 years and decline thereafter (Sedlak & Broadhurst, 1996). The most serious cases of neglect involving injury or death tend to occur to younger children (Wang & Daro, 1998).

Findings regarding child gender are similarly inconsistent, with some sources showing no gender differences and others reporting differences only in certain circumstances. For example, the second National Family Violence Survey found that boys were more likely to experience child physical abuse, regardless of severity (Wolfner & Gelles, 1993). On the other hand, data from the National Center for Child Abuse and Neglect (DHHS, 1994) revealed that boys 12 and under were more likely to be abused, but that girls 13 and older were at greater risk. Additionally, NIS-3 (Sedlak & Broadhurst, 1996) data documented a greater percentage of boys who experienced emotional neglect than girls. On the whole, there is little evidence that gender is a risk factor for neglect (Claussen & Crittenden, 1991; DHHS, 1994).

ETIOLOGY

Although child abuse has received extensive attention since Kempe and colleagues' (1962) identification of battered child syndrome, the development of a comprehensive etiological framework of child physical abuse and neglect is challenging because of the complex and multidetermined nature of these phenomena. The National Research Council Panel on Research on Child Abuse and Neglect (1993) defined several barriers to formulating an integrative etiological model, including the complexity and deviance of maltreating behavior, the shifting definitions of abuse and neglect, the interactive pathways of maltreatment, and the low overall prevalence of abusive behavior. In addition, Azar (1991) suggested that early attempts to understand child maltreatment were focused on creating and implementing treatments rather than defining the etiology. Consequently, the development of etiological models has been a relatively slow process (Azar, 1991) that resulted in a lag between theory, research, and practice (Runyan et al., 1998). The earliest etiological conceptualizations of child physical abuse and neglect paralleled Kempe and colleagues' medical and psychiatric description of child physical abuse and posited that maltreating parents were inherently pathological (e.g., Wolfe, 1999). By the 1970s, however, researchers and practitioners began to acknowledge the impact of multiple factors contributing to child maltreatment, rather than focusing solely on parental deficits (Wolfe, 1999).

Recently, several researchers have proposed multifaceted explanatory frameworks to account for the complexity of child physical abuse and neglect. Although these models vary in many respects, an assumption common across each framework is that child maltreatment reflects a multisystemic and dynamic interplay of various factors (e.g., distal and proximal, transient and long-standing) at multiple levels (e.g., interpersonal, developmental, familial, and sociocultural; e.g., Belsky, 1993; Hansen et al., 1999; Kolko, 2002; Wekerle & Wolfe, 1996). Provided here is a brief overview of some of the most prominent etiological theories of child physical abuse and neglect, including (in alphabetical order) Belsky's (1980, 1993) ecological model, Cicchetti and Rizley's (1981) transactional model, Milner's (1993) social information processing model, and Wolfe's (1987, 1999) transitional model.

Belsky's (1980, 1993) Ecological Model

In response to increasing disparity among professionals about the etiology of child physical abuse and neglect as well as mounting empirical evidence revealing the complexity of these phenomena, Belsky (1980) proposed an integrative ecological framework of child maltreatment. This pioneering model describes four interrelated, mutually embedded categories that contribute to child maltreatment: (1) *ontogenic development,* (2) *the microsystem,* (3) *the exosystem,* and (4) *the macrosystem.* Within this framework, not only do child and parent biological and psychological characteristics impact the development of child maltreatment, but numerous sociocultural and environmental factors are also interwoven within these multiple ecologies. Specifically, ontogenic development reflects premorbid interpersonal and historical factors (e.g., personal history of childhood victimization) that impact parenting behavior. The second layer, the microsystem, is defined as the "immediate context" (i.e., the family) in which the child experiences abuse or neglect, including the bidirectional influence of parent and child characteristics and other relationships (such as marriage) that may directly or indirectly impact parent-child interactions (Belsky, 1980, p. 321). In contrast, the exo- and macrosystemic levels reflect social or cultural forces that contribute to and maintain abuse or neglect. Specifically, the exosystem encompasses the effects of broader societal systems (e.g., employment) on parent and child functioning, and the macrosystem mirrors temporally driven, sociocultural ideologies (e.g., cultural views of corporal punishment), or a "larger cultural fabric," that inevitably shape functioning at all other levels (Belsky, 1980, p. 328). In his 1993 article describing the developmental-ecological etiology of child maltreatment, Belsky concluded that within these mutually embedded, multifaceted categories that may foster child maltreatment, "maltreatment seems to arise when stressors outweigh supports and risks are greater than protective factors" (p. 427).

Cicchetti and Rizley's Transactional Model; Cicchetti and Lynch's Ecological/Transactional Model

Whereas Belsky's (1980, 1993) ecological model describes the various interrelated ecologies in which child maltreatment occurs, Cicchetti and Rizley's (1981) transactional model highlights the multiple transactions that occur among categories of factors, labeled potentiating (or debilitating) and compensatory, which can be either transient or enduring in nature (see also Cicchetti, 1989; Cicchetti & Lynch, 1993; and Cicchetti & Toth, 2000). As outlined in these writings, the constellations that emerge are enduring potentiating factors (*vulnerability*), transient potentiating factors (*challengers*), enduring compensatory factors (*protective*), and transient compensatory factors (*buffers*). For example, a family may experience chronic unemployment, the stress of which serves as a potentiating factor, increasing the chances of child maltreatment. However, if a parent then finds a new and satisfying job, the risk likely becomes more benign, and the potential for abuse may be reduced. As such, increased stressors (particularly if they are chronic) coupled with decreased compensatory resources heighten the potential for abuse and neglect. Conversely, when significant compensatory factors (either protective or buffers) are present and overshadow potentiating circumstances, abuse and neglect potential may be drastically diminished.

Building on their original transactional model, Cicchetti and Lynch (1993) describe a more integrative ecological/transactional model of child maltreatment. This framework, used to describe outcomes and processes rather than etiology, is based heavily on Belsky's (1980) ecological model and Cicchetti and Rizley's (1981) transactional model (Cicchetti & Lynch, 1993). These authors suggest that children and parents function across multiple ecological dimensions, with short- and long-term potentiating and compensatory factors nested within each of these ecologies. At any given time, the various ecological domains may interact catalytically, just as risk and protective factors may either ignite or buffer maltreatment at the various levels. Cicchetti and Toth (2000) maintain that, through examining compensatory resources in children and their environment, an ecological/transactional framework can aid in understanding children who exhibit resilient outcomes in spite of being maltreated.

Milner's (1993, 2000) Social Information Processing Model

In contrast to the aforementioned models, which deal largely with factors predictive of abusive parent-child interactions, Milner's social information processing model (1993, 2000) focuses more on the cognitive processes associated with abusive behaviors. A core concept in this model is that all parents have *global* and *specific* cognitions, or "preexisting (preprocessing) cognitive schema," related to how they perceive and interact with children (Milner, 1993, p. 277; 2000). Milner (1993, 2000) proposes a four-stage etiological model, with the first three stages reflecting cognitive processes of the parent and the final stage including the actions and cognitions of the parent. The first stage, *perceptions,* refers to distorted and maladaptive beliefs that abusive individuals often hold about children (e.g., "My child should always mind"). In Stage 2, *interpretations, evaluations, and expectations,* parents who are abusive tend to view even routine child misbehavior as malignant, thus heightening caregiver cognitive distortions and reinforcing negative beliefs about the child. As caregivers transition into the third stage, *information integration and response selection,* they will attend primarily to child behaviors that confirm their negative yet distorted cognitions. Thus, parents become blinded to discrepant information (e.g., positive behaviors in the child), and because they notice only negative child characteristics, the potential for the inhibition of aggression decreases. Milner (1993, 2000) notes that, at this stage, it is important to consider the response options that are accessible to the parent, which may be adversely impacted by significant skill deficits. In the fourth stage, *response implementation and monitoring,* abusive parents, for a variety of reasons (e.g., increased distress, diminished affect), are highly ineffective and inflexible in how they respond to their child, thus potentially leading to deleterious consequences and a more perpetual abuse cycle. Finally, Milner (1993, 2000) suggests that at each stage, adults' distortions and biases increase in the face of heightened distress.

Wolfe's (1987, 1999) Transitional Model

Whereas Milner's (1993) social information processing model highlights the specific cognitive patterns of maltreating caregivers, Wolfe's transitional model of child physical abuse describes the specific processes by which maltreating behavior develops and progresses within the family system (Wolfe, 1987, 1999). This model is based on two underlying assumptions: (1) the belief that maltreating behaviors typically develop in a graduated, stepwise manner, with relatively benign parent-child interactions becoming increasingly maladaptive; and (2) the notion that three specific adult psychological characteristics (anger, arousal, and coping reactions) are integral in determining whether abuse will occur (Wolfe, 1987, 1999). Wolfe (1987, 1999) describes three stages through which an increase in negative familial interactions progressively leads to the magnification of maladaptive and abusive parent-child interactions; notably, at each stage, various destabilizing and compensatory factors exist that may either intensify or buffer against maltreatment. The first stage, *reduced tolerance for stress and disinhibition of aggression,* reflects the ways in which parents learn (or fail to learn) how to cope with increasingly stressful situations and either allow or disallow aggression, particularly within the context of the parent-child interaction. In Stage 2, *poor management of acute crises and provocation,* Wolfe suggests that the parent has developed an ineffective coping repertoire and consequently feels a mounting loss of control. As a result, the parent may attempt to discipline a child more harshly or act impulsively, which in turn serves to undermine inhibitions against acts of maltreatment. In the final stage, called *chronic patterns of anger and abuse,* abusive or neglectful caregivers become increasingly exasperated and overwhelmed by unremitting strain, particularly in the context of the parent-child dyad. At this point, caregivers engage in progressively more punitive behavior with children and likely enter an enduring and ever-escalating cycle of distress, arousal, and maltreating behavior.

COURSE, COMPLICATIONS, AND PROGNOSIS

Theoretical Considerations: A Developmental Framework

Some victims of child physical abuse and neglect appear to be asymptomatic and report few maltreatment-related difficulties (e.g., Barnett et al., 1997; Stevenson, 1999). In many cases, however, child maltreatment adversely impacts normal ontogenic processes across the life span and can trigger diverse developmental trajectories for maltreated individuals (see reviews by Cicchetti & Toth, 2000; Wolfe, 1999). Two concepts from the developmental psychopathology literature help shed light on the complex pathways of child maltreatment: *multifinality,* or the notion that similar starting points can lead to a myriad of outcomes (Cicchetti, 1989; Wolfe, 1999), and *equifinality,* the notion that diverse starting points can lead to similar consequences (Cicchetti, 1989). For example, demonstrating the principle of multifinality, it is possible for a child who is neglected to exhibit deleterious maltreatment-related outcomes, such as impaired academic performance and increased withdrawal from peers, whereas another child may emerge unscathed despite exposure to a similar form of neglect. Equifinality may be demonstrated by a physically abused child and a nonabused child who both experience similar difficulties, such as heightened aggression toward peers and depressive symptomatology, despite discrepant abuse histories.

In light of these diverse pathways, the course and prognosis of child maltreatment cannot be understood by an examination of the maltreated individual at a single point in time or in one area of functioning but rather must be conceptualized within a developmental framework. In the course of development, children are presented with various tasks that they attempt to resolve or master (e.g., Cicchetti & Toth, 2000) and that "upon emergence, remain critical to the child's continual adaptation" (Cicchetti, 1989, p. 385). Significant life stressors, such as child maltreatment, can impede the successful resolution and integration of these developmental tasks (Cicchetti & Toth, 2000). Consequently, maltreated children experience impairments in critical areas of development or at "stage-salient" tasks (Cicchetti & Toth, 2000, p. 95; Wolfe, 1999), including attachment, moral and social judgments, autonomy, self-control, and peer relationships (Cicchetti, 1989, 1990; Wolfe, 1999). In some cases, the manifestations of maltreatment may go unrecognized until impaired development is evidenced. For example, when the maltreated child enters school and is faced with academic challenges and peer socialization, he or she may begin to evidence abuse-related problems such as aggression, isolation, and poor academic performance. As Wolfe (1999) stated, "The developmental disruptions and impairments that accompany child abuse and neglect set in motion a series of events that increase the likelihood of adaptational failure and future behavioral and emotional problems" (p. 51).

Longitudinal Findings

With this developmental framework in mind, researchers have conducted longitudinal studies that focus on the short- and long-term developmental effects associated with victimization. Several important findings have emerged from these studies, which include the Longitudinal Studies of Child Abuse and Neglect (LONGSCAN; Runyan et al., 1998), the Lehigh Longitudinal Study (LLS; Herrenkohl, Herrenkohl, Egolf, & Wu, 1991), the Mother-Child Project (M-CP; Egeland, 1991), and Silverman and colleagues' community-based longitudinal study (Silverman, Reinherz, & Giaconia, 1996).

In early childhood, maltreated youth have been shown to experience cold and rejecting interactions with their caregivers (Herrenkohl, Herrenkohl, Toedter, & Yanushefski, 1984) and to present with significant impairments, such as attachment disturbances and anger/noncompliance (physically abused children), as well as frustration and diminished self-esteem (neglected children; Egeland, 1991). Deleterious effects also are apparent during the preschool years, with maltreated children born to adolescent mothers exhibiting significantly more internalizing and externalizing difficulties than nonmaltreated children (Black et al., 2002). Specifically, physically abused children have been shown to exhibit hyperactivity, negativistic outlooks, and lower self-esteem (Egeland, 1991). As maltreated children enter preschool, they continue to show significantly more adverse behavioral and emotional outcomes than do nonmaltreated children (Johnson et al., 2002). For example, unpopularity and self-destructiveness are among the features that characterize physically abused children, and poor academic performance and isolation are associated with neglected individuals (Egeland, 1991).

Unfortunately, the effects of child maltreatment often persist into adolescence. Silverman et al. (1996) compared long-term sequelae in maltreated individuals when they were 15 and 21 years old. They found that, although physically abused females tended to be more negatively impacted than physically abused males, abuse in childhood was linked to impairments in functioning for both. Specifically, for abused males, they found more suicidal ideation at age 15 than for the control group; at age 21, maltreated men had higher rates of depression, antisocial behavior, post-traumatic stress symptoms, and drug abuse than did their nonabused counterparts. At age 15, females with a physical abuse history demonstrated more withdrawal, somatization, aggression, depression, anxiety, attentional deficits, and suicidal ideation than the nonabused control group; at 21, the physically abused women, compared to the nonabused control group, were more likely to exhibit depression, post-traumatic stress symptoms, antisocial behavior, suicidal ideation, and externalizing behavior.

Moderating and Mediating Factors

Although these research findings have illuminated the diverse developmental trajectories among child abuse victims, no single or definitive picture remains of the maltreated individual or of the specific course or prognosis associated with abuse. Whereas abuse sets the stage for subsequent maladjustment, the presence of moderating and mediating factors can significantly impact the course and prognosis of abuse victims. Regarding moderators, Malinosky-Rummell and Hansen (1993) identified four interrelated categories of moderating variables that, depending on their presence or absence, may impact the course of development in various ways. The factors include maltreatment characteristics (e.g., co-occurrence of multiple forms of maltreatment), individual factors (e.g., developmental level of the child or adolescent), family factors (e.g., level of familial distress, presence of domestic violence), and environmental factors (e.g., presence of support systems, socioeconomic status). Although many of these factors exacerbate the impact of maltreatment, others seem to serve a buffering role by explaining resilient outcomes in maltreated children. Herrenkohl et al. (1991) reported that positive parent-child interactions; maternal support, affection, and involvement; parent modeling of resilient outcomes; and higher intelligence scores in children may help protect the child from harmful abuse-related outcomes and contribute to child competency. In reference to mediators, researchers have found that low parental support in childhood mediates the link between child maltreatment and increased depression and diminished self-esteem in adult women (Wind & Silvern, 1994). Finally, treatment or intervention can serve as a buffer against the deleterious outcomes associated with child maltreatment (Stevenson, 1999). Specific forms of treatment will be discussed in a later section.

ASSESSMENT AND DIAGNOSIS

Areas of Assessment

Because physical abuse and neglect arise from a variety of circumstances and produce a range of potential symptoms, each child and family will portray a unique clinical picture (Kolko, 2002). Assessments must therefore include antecedent conditions as well as specific child and parent factors. Antecedent risk factors include parental skill deficits, anger management difficulties, substance abuse, unrealistic expectations of child behavior, inability to cope with stress, and the nature of the parent-child relationship. Child-related factors that increase the risk of maltreatment also serve as areas for assessment (e.g., behavior problems, temperament). However, an assessment of overall child functioning, particularly outcomes related to child physical abuse and neglect, is necessary to determine the needs of the child. These include, but are not limited to, medical/health status, social and developmental functioning, behavior problems, academic needs, and emotional difficulties. Assessment should also focus on the larger context of maltreatment, including overall family functioning, social support, and environmental resources as well as the strengths of the family, including resources and compensatory skills. To provide an accurate conceptualization of the problem, assessment should also include the nature and extent of dysfunction as well as the frequency, severity, chronicity, and context of the abuse and neglect incidents (Hansen & MacMillan, 1990). Specific targets for incidents of neglect may also include the quality of stimulation afforded the child, hygiene, safety, medical health, and quality of affection demonstrated (Hansen & MacMillan, 1990).

Assessment Techniques

Though it is not possible to provide an extensive review of assessment measures here (see Feindler, Rathus, & Silver, 2002, for such a review), we will present a brief description of some of the more popular and well-validated measurement approaches, including interviewing, self-report, observational, and self-monitoring techniques. Clinical interviewing is crucial in ascertaining the antecedents and consequences of abuse as well as the context of incidents of maltreatment. The Parent Interview and Assessment Guide (Wolfe, 1988; Wolfe & McEachran, 1997) is a useful tool that addresses the identification of parent responses to child behavior problems and demands. In addition, Ammerman, Hersen, and Van Hasselt (1988) developed the Child Abuse and Neglect Interview Schedule (CANIS), a semistructured interview that assesses the presence of behaviors of abuse and neglect as well as factors that relate to child maltreatment. With regard to the assessment of neglect, the Childhood Level of Living Scale (CLLS; Hally, Polansky, & Polansky, 1980, as cited in Hansen & MacMillan, 1990) is a measure of parenting skill deficits that may be useful in minimizing error associated with the detection of neglect (Hansen & MacMillan, 1990).

Self-report is another assessment technique that can be used to identify parent and child risk factors that relate to maltreatment as well as provide targets for intervention and monitoring treatment progress. A useful measure to assess the risk of maltreatment is the Child Abuse Potential Inventory (CAP Inventory; Milner, 1986), which provides an abuse potential scale as well as three validity scales. Parental psychological functioning is another important area of assessment. The Minnesota Multiphasic Personality Inventory—2 (MMPI-2; Butcher, Dahlstrom, Graham, Tellegen, & Kaemmer, 1989) and the Symptom-Checklist-90-Revised (SCL-90-R; Derogatis, 1983) are commonly used self-report measures of psychological psychopathology and distress. Measures of parental anger (Parental Anger Inventory; DeRoma & Hansen, 1994;

MacMillan, Olson, & Hansen, 1988), parenting-related stress (Parenting Stress Index; Abidin, 1986), marital violence (Revised Conflict Tactics Scales; Straus, Hamby, Boney-McCoy, & Sugarman, 1996), and child behaviors (Child Behavior Checklist; Achenbach, 1991) are also important areas to assess, in that they constitute risk factors for child maltreatment. Further, to assess neglect from the child's perspective, Kaufman Kantor, Straus, Mebert, and Brown (2001) developed the Multidimensional Neglect Scale—Child Report (MNS-CR) that includes the emotional, cognitive, supervisory, and physical components of neglect.

Due to the inherent potential for bias and distortions related to self-report measures, observations are an important technique to incorporate into the assessment of child abuse and neglect. Observations can provide information regarding the quality of the parent-child relationship, evidence of parenting skills and knowledge, and examples of child behavior problems. Such techniques may involve live or videotaped observations of unstructured parent-child interactions in the home or clinic settings, such as the Child's Game procedure (Forehand & McMahon, 1981). In this task, the child directs play activity, after which the parent instructs the child to clean up the toys. Coding systems may then be used to quantify the parent-child relationship. Examples of coding systems include the Behavioral Coding System (Forehand & McMahon, 1981) and the more complex Dyadic Parent-Child Interaction Coding System (DPICS; Eyberg & Robinson, 1981), which assesses both positive and negative behaviors of the child and parent. Observations may also involve the use of adult actors to assess the ability of the parent to apply behavior management techniques in commonly encountered problem situations, such as through the Home Simulation Assessment (HSA; MacMillan, Olson, & Hansen, 1991).

Self-monitoring techniques may also be useful to assess the occurrence of specific behaviors (e.g., child behavior problems) and allow parents to record the antecedents and consequences of such behaviors in order to provide a more thorough functional analysis of abuse and neglect incidents. Self-monitoring has been shown to be particularly useful in assessing parent responses to situations that cause arousal, such as anger, by providing a description of triggers and responses to the arousal (Hansen, Warner-Rogers, & Hecht, 1998).

Finally, assessment should include information gathered from sources outside of the family. In the case of neglect, for example, a child's teacher may be best able to provide information regarding the child's hygiene or attire (Hansen et al., 1998). Further, professionals from a variety of settings, including health care providers and social services, may have had contact with maltreating families. Information from such professionals may be useful in both initial assessment as well as monitoring treatment progress (Warner-Rogers et al., 1999).

IMPACT ON ENVIRONMENT

The consequences of child abuse and neglect can be far-reaching. In addition to the developmental consequences noted previously, various domains of functioning may be impacted by physical abuse and neglect. These include families, school functioning, and peer interactions.

Family

It is important to remember that child abuse and neglect emanate from family environments that are characterized by a range of other problems (Hecht & Hansen, 2001). Economic impoverishment, other forms of interpersonal violence, parental psychopathology and substance abuse, and negative parent-child interactions are common in families in which abuse and neglect occur (Appel & Holden, 1998; Erickson & Egeland, 2002; Fantuzzo, 1990; Kelleher, Chaffin, Hollenberg, & Fischer, 1994; Whipple & Webster-Stratton, 1991). Much has been written about the general constellation of risk factors associated with maltreatment (Belsky, 1980, 1993). Most authors agree that these contextual factors interact in complex, mutually influential ways, such that they each can feed into or be exacerbated by the occurrence of abuse or neglect (Belsky, 1980; Cicchetti & Rizley, 1981; Hecht & Hansen, 2001).

Aside from the role of maltreatment within generally troubled family environments, the disclosure of abuse or neglect to child protective authorities may itself trigger multiple changes within the family. Local child protective service (CPS) agencies are often notified about abuse by physicians, psychologists, social workers, teachers, and other professionals who are bound by law to hotline suspected maltreatment. Once reports are received, CPS conducts an investigation to determine whether the alleged maltreatment in fact occurred. If maltreatment is verified, some (yet not all) families receive remediating services (DePanfilis & Zuravin, 2001). These services may include parent training, anger management, substance abuse treatment, or other interventions aimed at ameliorating the conditions leading to maltreatment. During this period, children may be removed from the home and placed in foster care to protect them from the risk of continuing abuse. Ongoing risk assessments determine whether family reunification will be possible. Nationally, most children in foster care are eventually either reunited with their families of origin (40 percent) or are adopted by other caregivers (16 percent; Chipungu & Bent-Goodley, 2004). Regardless of outcome, however, it is clear that abuse and neglect, particularly that which comes to the attention of authorities, has a profound impact on family functioning, including the possibility of altering family structure.

School

Early school performance can set the stage for later success or failure in both higher education and employment pursuits (Sylva, 1994). It is easy to envision how child maltreatment could disrupt school performance through various means such as inducing developmental, cognitive, and language delays; low IQ; depression; and diminished self-efficacy. As Shonk and Cicchetti (2001) outlined, empirical studies of these issues can be grouped into those examining direct associations between maltreatment and subsequent academic functioning, and those exploring possible mediating factors in that relationship. Regarding the former, studies have consistently shown that maltreated children experience more school-adjustment problems than do nonmaltreated children. For example, physical abuse has been linked to outcomes including lower test scores and grades, absenteeism, and lower retention in comparison to other schoolchildren and children from disadvantaged (but not abusive) households (Leiter & Johnsen, 1994). More recent work exploring mechanisms that may explain this association has revealed some important mediational factors. For example, Eckenrode, Rowe, Laird, and Brathwaite (1995) found that links between maltreatment and school performance were mediated by family moves and school transfers. Shonk and Cicchetti (2001) reported that level of academic engagement partially mediated linkages between maltreatment and academic maladjustment.

Several factors point to child neglect, in particular, as a source of impaired school performance. Neglectful households may be lacking in various activities that promote cognitive development, including deficits in parent-child verbal interaction, less reading to children, and overall lower parental involvement in children's academic pursuits (e.g., help with homework). Indeed, comparisons of abused and neglected children indicate that neglect may be more harmful than other forms of abuse to a wider range of school-related outcomes (Eckenrode, Laird, & Doris, 1993; Erickson, Egeland, & Pianta, 1989). Moreover, neglect alone may be just as detrimental to grade performance as combined neglect and physical abuse (Kendall-Tackett & Eckenrode, 1996). Problems adapting to the broader school environment have also been linked to neglect. For example, Erickson and colleagues (1989) found that youths who had been neglected were seen by teachers as anxious; inattentive; unable to understand their work; lacking in initiative; and heavily dependent on teachers for help, approval, and encouragement.

Peer Interactions

Early physical abuse has negative implications for subsequent peer interactions as well. This statement is supported by findings that children who are physically maltreated tend to be unpopular and rejected by peers and have a lower social standing among classmates (Bolger, Patterson, & Kupersmidt, 1998; Haskett & Kistner, 1991; Salzinger, Feldman, Hammer, & Rosario, 1993). Some of the best documentation of these difficulties comes from a 5-year longitudinal study of children with verified cases of physical abuse (Dodge, Pettit, & Bates, 1994). Reports from multiple informants showed abused youth to be less well liked by other children and more socially withdrawn than their nonabused peers. To make matters worse, these social problems tended to increase over time (Dodge et al., 1994). Physical abuse has also been linked to subsequent bullying of peers, a relationship that was mediated by difficulties in emotional regulation (Shields & Cicchetti, 2001). In a study of close friendships, direct observation of play and conversation with best friends has shown that the relationships of maltreated children are less positive and involved more conflict and disagreement and less overall intimacy than do the friendships of nonabused children (Parker & Herrera, 1996).

Aggression toward others may account for some of the peer problems observed in maltreated children. A consistent finding in the literature is that abused children display more verbal and physical aggression toward peers than do nonmaltreated youth (e.g., Herrenkohl, Egolf, & Herrenkohl, 1997; Shields & Cicchetti, 1998; Weiss, Dodge, Bates, & Pettit, 1992). Maltreatment history has also been linked to the increased use of verbal and physical violence in adolescent dating relationships, part of what the authors described as a "maladaptive interpersonal trajectory of maltreated children" (Wolfe, Wekerle, Reitzel-Jaffe, & Lefebvre, 1998, p. 61). In a recent study, Bolger and Patterson (2001) found that this heightened physical aggression plays an important contributory role in the rejection that maltreated youth experience by mediating associations between maltreatment and subsequent peer relations. This was especially true for children whose abuse was chronic.

Like physical abuse, neglect has been linked to poor social interactions. Preschool children who have been neglected may show increased apprehension when interacting with peers, avoidance in social situations, and greater social isolation in comparison to nonmaltreated children (Camras & Rappaport, 1993; Erickson et al., 1989). These trends toward withdrawal and avoidance in social interactions appear to remain into the school-age years (Erickson et al., 1989; Kaufman & Cicchetti, 1989).

IMPLICATIONS FOR FUTURE PERSONALITY DEVELOPMENT

Child maltreatment has been linked to a range of subsequent (primarily pathological) personality characteristics. The majority of data making this connection come from retrospective investigations showing that psychiatric patients report unusually high rates of child maltreatment (e.g., Arbel & Stravynski, 1991; Norden et al., 1995). A history of physical abuse, for example, has been found to predict overall personality symptomatology in psychiatric patients (Carter, Joyce, Mulder, & Luty, 2001), while physical abuse and emotional and physical neglect have been linked retrospectively to increased neuroticism in abstinent substance-dependent patients (Roy, 2002). One exception to this general pattern of findings is a study by Gibb, Wheeler, Alloy, and Abrahamson (2001), who failed to find a unique association between child physical abuse and personality dysfunction. However, in addition to the usual limitations of retrospective self-reporting, this study was conducted with college freshmen and assessed only the frequency (not the severity) of abusive acts.

A few investigations have used prospective designs to examine connections between child maltreatment and later personality characteristics. One such study used New York State CPS records of verified abuse and found that those individuals with a history of abuse or neglect were four times more likely to experience personality disorders during early adulthood (Johnson, Cohen, Brown, Smailes, & Bernstein, 1999). Although physical abuse was predictive of a range of personality problems, including antisocial, borderline, dependent, depressive, passive-aggressive, and schizoid symptoms, associations with antisocial and depressive symptoms were especially robust. Documented neglect was most strongly related to antisocial, avoidant, borderline, narcissistic, and passive-aggressive personality disorder symptoms. In a second study using the same longitudinal sample, these authors examined associations between particular subtypes of neglect and the development of personality pathology (Johnson, Smailes, Cohen, Brown, & Bernstein, 2000). Emotional, physical, and supervisory neglect were all related to an increased risk of personality disorders as well as elevations in overall personality symptomatology. Each of these neglect subtypes was also associated with different types of personality disorder symptoms. The authors speculated that attachment processes and levels of social support may play a role in these relationships.

Borderline personality disorder (BPD) has been commonly studied as a correlate of child maltreatment (Golier et al., 2003). This connection seems logical given that the long-term problems associated with abuse are also common to the presentation of BPD (e.g., lack of trust, dissociation, emotional instability; Trull, 2001). Indeed, several investigations have found that patients with BPD have high rates of child maltreatment, including both physical and sexual abuse (e.g., Herman, Perry, & van der Kolk, 1989). Of course, a large proportion of individuals with BPD do not have a history of child abuse, which points to the conclusion that BPD results from multiple etiological factors. In exploring multiple etiological correlates of BPD, Trull (2001) tested a multivariate structural model that included a combined physical and sexual abuse variable as well as parental psychopathology and personality traits of disinhibition and negative affectivity. Results showed that abuse history maintained unique associations with BPD, even when controlling for the other etiological factors. This study is unique in its attempt to simultaneously consider multiple domains that may contribute to BPD. Unfortunately, with few exceptions (e.g., Weaver & Clum, 1993) studies have not attempted to isolate or disentangle the impact of individual forms of abuse on later BPD. It will be important for future work to separate the potential impact of physical abuse from co-occurring sexual abuse, which has itself been linked to BPD.

A second area of personality functioning that has been studied extensively in relation to physical abuse is antisocial behavior patterns. This association could be expected given the previously noted aggressiveness and behavior problems in childhood victims of abuse (e.g., Weiss et al., 1992). Widom and colleagues (e.g., Widom, 1989; Widom & Maxfield, 1996) followed more than 900 abused and neglected children, and a matched cohort of nonmaltreated youth, from childhood through early adulthood. These authors found that women with histories of physical abuse or neglect were more likely than others to be arrested for a violent act (7 percent vs. 4 percent). Interestingly, differences were much smaller between abused and nonabused males, who tended to have higher arrest rates overall (26 percent vs. 22 percent). These criminal characteristics may be part of a larger antisocial personality pattern common among adults who experienced abuse and neglect. Using the same prospective sample, Luntz and Widom (1994) compared the personality styles of young adults with and without abuse histories. These researchers identified clear linkages between childhood abuse and lifetime antisocial symptomatology as well as a diagnosis of antisocial personality disorder. Differences in antisocial personality diagnoses between abused and nonabused participants were greater for men than for women. Other investigations using retrospective designs have also confirmed links between early physical abuse and long-term antisocial personality tendencies (e.g., Bernstein, Stein, & Handelsman, 1998; Lysaker, Wickett, Lancaster, & Davis, 2004; Shearer, Peters, Quaytman, & Ogden, 1990).

A major question facing researchers is whether child maltreatment plays a truly causal role in the development of more prevalent personality problems, such as antisocial personality disorder. On one side of this issue are consistent findings of elevated personality symptoms among adult abuse survivors, which suggest at least the possibility of a causal link. On the other hand, the correlational designs of most of these studies do not permit conclusions about causality. It is possible, therefore, that certain personality features of maltreatment victims, such as antisocial tendencies, result more from genetic factors than from the environmental impact of abuse. According to this notion, an antisocial genotype may be transmitted from maltreating parents to their children and subsequently be expressed phenotypically through antisocial behavior patterns. This possibility is supported by findings that personality traits are largely heritable (Eysenck, 1991; Livesley, Jang, Jackson, & Vernon, 1995; Plomin, DeFries, McClearn, & McGuffin, 2001) and that antisocial tendencies, specifically, have at least a moderate heritable component (Rhea & Waldman, 2002). Some illuminating data addressing the genetic versus environmental contributions to antisocial behaviors of maltreated children come from a recent longitudinal study that followed a large sample of twin pairs from the United Kingdom (Jaffe, Caspi, Moffitt, & Taylor, 2004). By controlling for parental antisocial behaviors and a variety of other factors in the twin sample, these researchers found clear evidence of an environmental impact of maltreatment on later antisocial tendencies. Although their conclusions were limited to childhood antisocial acts, to the extent that there is continuity from childhood conduct problems to adult antisocial behaviors, these findings point toward a causal role for physical abuse in the development of antisocial traits (Jaffe et al., 2004).

TREATMENT IMPLICATIONS

The short- and long-term sequelae of child abuse support the need for intervention, through both preventive measures as well as immediate and follow-up interventions. Historically, treatment of child physical abuse focused primarily on interventions directed at parents, although current methods acknowledge the importance of targeting the broader systemic contexts in which child physical abuse occurs (Barnett et al., 1997). Interventions for child physical abuse include individual (both parent and child) therapy, parent training, family treatment, and multisystemic approaches. With regard to child neglect, interventions primarily focus on parents, parent behaviors, or both and may involve multiple providers working with a single family over a long period. The assessment of child physical abuse and neglect, as well as evaluation of risk, can aid in determining the type of structural interventions (e.g., separation, supervision) that may be called for as well as the type of clinical intervention that may be necessary for any given family (Saunders, Berliner, & Hanson, 2004). A brief overview of some of the major treatment approaches for child physical abuse and neglect will follow.

Child-Focused Interventions

In general, child-focused treatments are designed to assist children in coping with the emotional and behavioral symptoms stemming from child physical abuse and neglect. The majority of interventions for children involve day treatment programs, individual therapy, and play sessions (Barnett et al., 1997). Though there is empirical support for the effectiveness of child-focused interventions for maltreated children (e.g., Oates & Bross, 1995; Wolfe & Wekerle, 1993), most studies in this area involve preschool or young children and do not differentiate between types of abuse. Thus, continued research is necessary to determine the effectiveness of child-focused interventions. Nonetheless, the National Crime Victims Research and Treatment Center has prepared a guide to the treatment of child physical and sexual abuse that includes empirically supported interventions: *Child Physical and Sexual Abuse: Guidelines for Treatment* (revised report, April 26, 2004; Saunders et al., 2004).

One child-focused approach noted in *Guidelines* is individual cognitive-behavioral therapy (CBT), which is designed to help children alter cognitions related to abuse or violence, teach coping skills to reduce the emotional symptoms related to abuse, and increase social competence (Bonner, 2004). An example of a CBT approach is the protocol by Kolko and Swenson (2002), which has received empirical support and consists of child components addressing views of family violence, coping strategies, and interpersonal skills and involves the use of role-playing, feedback, and homework exercises. In addition, this treatment has a parent-focused component that involves identifying cognitions related to violence, cognitive and anger control coping strategies, and child behavior management principles (e.g., positive attention, reinforcement, time-out). Fantuzzo and colleagues' Resilient Peer Training Intervention (RPT; Fantuzzo, Weiss, & Coolahan, 1998) is a classroom-based intervention designed for preschool-aged maltreated children. RPT uses peers, teachers, and parent volunteers to increase social competency and has been shown to be effective with socially isolated, low-income preschool children who have been victims of maltreatment (Fantuzzo, Coolahan, & Weiss, 1997).

Parent Training Interventions

Child physical abuse frequently occurs in the context of increasingly negative parent-child interactions (Chaffin et al., 2004). More specifically, parents who are physically abusive often view their children as defiant and unresponsive to discipline techniques not involving violence (Chaffin et al., 2004). As a result, physically abusive parents may believe that the only way to manage their children's behaviors is through physical tactics. Parent training interventions have recently been used with maltreating caregivers in an effort to interrupt this coercive pattern. In general, these interventions target conduct-disordered children and involve teaching parents skills to increase child compliance, decrease disruptive behaviors, and increase positive parent-child interactions (Brestan & Payne, 2004).

One model of parent training used with physically abusive parents is Parent Child Interaction Therapy (PCIT; Hembree-Kigin & McNeil, 1995), which was recently categorized as an empirically supported treatment (Chambless & Ollendick, 2000). When applied to physical abuse, PCIT is designed to change the dysfunctional parent-child relationship by disrupting the escalating degrees of violence that characterize these interactions. This involves improving the quality of the parent-child relationship and teaching nonviolent behavior-management strategies (Chaffin et al., 2004). PCIT has been shown to be effective in reducing child behavior problems and increasing positive parent-child interactions (Borrego, Urquiza, Rasmussen, & Zebell, 1999), as well as reducing the incidence of future child abuse reports (Chaffin et al., 2004). Further, PCIT has been demonstrated to be effective across a variety of populations (e.g., Hembree-Kigin & McNeil, 1995), and treatment effects have been shown to demonstrate some generalization across time (Eyberg et al., 2001) and settings (McNeil, Eyberg, Eisenstadt, Newcomb, & Funderburk, 1991) and to untreated siblings (Brestan, Eyberg, Boggs, & Algina, 1997). Other parent training interventions that have been used with physically abusive families include Patterson and Gullion's (1968) *Living with Children,* Forehand's (1981) Social Learning Parent Training (as detailed in Forehand & McMahon, 1981), and Barkley's (1997) *Defiant Children.*

Family-Focused Interventions

An ecological model of child physical abuse views abuse as the product not only of the immediate family context, but also of the relationship of the family with the surrounding environmental influences (e.g., Belsky, 1993). Thus, family-focused interventions are multifaceted and target the parent-child relationship and various child (e.g., emotional disruption), parent (e.g., anger management), and family (e.g., boundaries) issues (Ralston & Sosnowski, 2004). Overall, family-focused interventions for child physical abuse have received less empirical evaluation than other treatment approaches (see Wolfe & Wekerle, 1993), although at least one study has indicated that family therapy is comparable to parent training in demonstrating reductions in perceived stress and severity of overall problems (Brunk, Henggeler, & Whelan, 1987).

The Parent-Child Education Program (Wolfe, 1991) is a family-focused intervention designed to reduce parental use of power assertion as discipline and to establish positive parent-child interactions to prevent the use of verbal and physical abuse. Stemming from attachment and social learning theories and using principles of cognitive and behavioral learning, this treatment focuses on effective child-rearing practices, problem solving to increase child compliance, skills training to strengthen the parent-child relationship, reducing child noncompliance, and helping parents cope with stress (Wolfe, 2004). An additional family intervention is Physical Abuse–Informed Family Therapy (Kolko, 1996), which enlists the participation of all family members to enhance cooperation and motivation through developing an understanding of coercive behavior, teaching communication skills, and problem solving. This approach has been shown to be superior to traditional community services in improving child outcomes following abuse and reducing violence (Kolko, 1996). Finally, intensive family preservation programs provide interventions such as crisis intervention therapy and behavior modification (Haapala & Kinney, 1988) and are aimed at preventing the out-of-home placement of abused and neglected children (Barnett et al., 1997). Research has suggested that such interventions can be successful in preventing children from being placed out-of-home (e.g., Bath & Haapala, 1993).

Multisystemic and Societal Approaches

Multisystemic and societal approaches adopt the perspective that behaviors are maintained by any number of factors within the multiple systems surrounding the behavior (e.g., family, school, peer, society) and that such factors have reciprocal influence (Bronfenbrenner, 1979). Hence, these interventions target variables within and between the systems that serve to maintain abuse and neglect, thereby serving to reduce the overall stress level of abusive parents such that therapeutic concerns may be addressed (Barnett et al., 1997). One such intervention is multisystemic therapy (MST; Henggeler, Schoenwald, Borduin, Rowland, & Cunningham, 1998) for maltreated children and their families. Originally intended to address youth antisocial behavior, MST has recently been applied to abusive and neglectful families and, in one randomized trial, was found to be more effective than parent training in improving parent-child interactions related to maltreatment (Brunk et al., 1987). Other approaches that may be classified as multisystemic include home visitation programs, such as Project SafeCare (Gershater-Molko, Lutzker, & Wesch, 2003), which targets families at risk for abuse or neglect and has demonstrated efficacy in promoting positive parent-child interactions and improving home safety and child health care. Prenatal and early childhood home nurse visitation programs have also been shown to improve the quality of infant caregiving, reduce rates of dysfunctional care (including reducing rates of maltreatment and medical encounters related to injury), and improve women's own health care (e.g., Eckenrode et al., 2001; Korfmacher, Kitzman, & Olds, 1998; Olds et al., 1998). Further, home visitation programs provide both support and education for parents (Roberts, Wasik, Casto, & Ramey, 1991, as cited in Barnett et al., 1997) and are recommended in the prevention of child physical abuse (Barnett et al., 1997).

REFERENCES

Abidin, R. R. (1986). *Parenting Stress Index* (2nd ed.). Charlottesville, VA: Pediatric Psychology Press.

Achenbach, T. M. (1991). *Manual for the Child Behavior Checklist/4–18 and 1991 profile*. Burlington: University of Vermont.

Ainsworth, M. S., Blehar, M. C., Waters, E., & Wall, S. (1978). *Patterns of attachment: A psychological study of the strange situation*. Oxford, England: Erlbaum.

American Psychiatric Association. (2000). *Diagnostic and statistical manual of mental disorders* (4th ed., text rev.). Washington, DC: Author.

Ammerman, R. T., Hersen, M., & Van Hasselt, V. B. (1988). *The Child Abuse and Neglect Interview Schedule (CANIS)*. Pittsburgh: Unpublished instrument, Western Pennsylvania School for Blind Children.

Anderson, K. E., Lytton, H., & Romney, D. M. (1986). Mothers' interactions with normal and conduct-disordered boys: Who affects whom? *Developmental Psychology, 22,* 604–609.

Appel, A. E., & Holden, G. W. (1998). The co-occurrence of spouse and physical child abuse: A review and appraisal. *Journal of Family Psychology, 12,* 578–599.

Arbel, N., & Stravynski, A. (1991). A retrospective study of separation in the development of adult avoidant personality disorder. *Acta Psychiatrica Scandinavica, 83,* 174–178.

Azar, S. T. (1991). Models of child abuse: A metatheoretical analysis. *Criminal Justice and Behavior, 18,* 30–46.

Barkley, R. A. (1997). *Defiant children: A clinician's manual for assessment and parent training*. New York: Guilford Press.

Barnett, O. W., Miller-Perrin, C. L., & Perrin, R. D. (1997). *Family violence across the lifespan: An introduction*. Thousand Oaks, CA: Sage.

Bath, H. I., & Haapala, D. A. (1993). Intensive family preservation services with abused and neglected children: An examination of group differences. *Child Abuse & Neglect, 17,* 213–225.

Bell, R. (1968). A reinterpretation of the direction of effects in studies of socialization. *Psychological Review, 75,* 81–95.

Belsky, J. (1980). Child maltreatment: An ecological integration. *American Psychologist, 35,* 320–335.

Belsky, J. (1993). Etiology of child maltreatment: A developmental-ecological analysis. *Psychological Bulletin, 114,* 413–434.

Bernstein, D. P., Stein, J. A., & Handelsman, L. (1998). Predicting personality pathology among adult patients with substance use disorders: Effects of childhood maltreatment. *Addictive Behaviors, 23,* 855–868.

Black, M. M., Papas, M. A., Hussey, J. M., Dubowitz, H., Kotch, J. B., & Starr, R. H., Jr. (2002). Behavior problems among preschool children born to adolescent mothers: Effects of maternal depression and perceptions of partner relationships. *Journal of Clinical Child and Adolescent Psychology, 31,* 16–26.

Bolger, K. E., & Patterson, C. J. (2001). Developmental pathways from child maltreatment to peer rejection. *Child Development, 72,* 549–568.

Bolger, K. E., Patterson, C. J., & Kupersmidt, J. B. (1998). Peer relationships and self-esteem among children who have been maltreated. *Child Development, 69,* 1171–1197.

Bonner, B. (2004). Cognitive-behavioral and dynamic play therapy for children with sexual behavior problems and their caregivers. In B. E. Saunders, L. Berliner, & R. F. Hanson (Eds.), *Child physical and sexual abuse: Guidelines for treatment* (revised report: April 26, 2004). Charleston, SC: National Crime Victims Research and Treatment Center.

Borrego, J., Urquiza, A., Rasmussen, R., & Zebell, N. (1999). Parent-child interaction therapy with a family at high risk for physical abuse. *Child Maltreatment, 4,* 331–342.

Bousha, D. M., & Twentyman, C. T. (1984). Mother-child interactional style in abuse, neglect, and control groups: Naturalistic observations in the home. *Journal of Abnormal Psychology, 93,* 106–114.

Bowlby, J. (1969). *Attachment and loss: Vol. 1. Attachment*. New York: Basic Books.

Brachfield, S., Goldberg, S., & Sloman, J. (1980). Parent-infant interaction in free play at 8 and 12 months: Effects of prematurity and immaturity. *Infant Behavior in Development, 3,* 289–305.

Brestan, E., & Payne, H. (2004). Behavioral parent training interventions for conduct-disordered children. In B. E. Saunders, L. Berliner, & R. F. Hanson (Eds.), *Child physical and sexual abuse: Guidelines for treatment* (revised report: April 26, 2004). Charleston, SC: National Crime Victims Research and Treatment Center.

Brestan, E. V., Eyberg, S. M., Boggs, S. R., & Algina, J. (1997). Parent-child interaction therapy: Parents' perceptions of untreated siblings. *Child and Family Behavior Therapy, 19,* 13–28.

Bronfenbrenner, U. (1979). Contexts of child rearing: Problems and prospects. *American Psychologist, 34,* 844–850.

Brunk, M., Henggeler, S. W., & Whelan, J. P. (1987). A comparison of multisystemic therapy and parent training in the brief treatment of child abuse and neglect. *Journal of Consulting and Clinical Psychology, 55,* 311–318.

Brunk, M. A., & Henggeler, S. W. (1984). Child influences on adult controls: An experimental investigation. *Developmental Psychology, 20,* 1074–1081.

Butcher, J. N., Dahlstrom, W. G., Graham, J. R., Tellegen, A., & Kaemmer, B. (1989). *Minnesota Multiphasic Personality Inventory—2 (MMPI-2): Manual for administration and scoring.* Minneapolis: University of Minnesota Press.

Camras, L. A., & Rappaport, S. (1993). Conflict behaviors of maltreated and nonmaltreated children. *Child Abuse & Neglect, 17,* 455–464.

Carter, J. D., Joyce, P. R., Mulder, R. T., & Luty, S. E. (2001). The contribution of temperament, childhood neglect, and abuse to the development of personality dysfunction: A comparison of three models. *Journal of Personality Disorders, 15,* 123–135.

Centers for Disease Control and Prevention. (2001). *Injury fact book 2001–2002.* Washington, DC: U.S. Department of Health and Human Services.

Chaffin, M., Silovsky, J. F., Funderburk, B., Valle, L. A., Brestan, E. V., Balachova, T., et al. (2004). Parent-child interaction therapy with physically abusive parents: Efficacy for reducing future abuse reports. *Journal of Consulting and Clinical Psychology, 72,* 500–510.

Chambless, D. L., & Ollendick, T. H. (2000). Empirically supported psychological interventions: Controversies and evidence. *Annual Review of Psychology, 52,* 685–716.

Chipungu, S. S., & Bent-Goodley, T. B. (2004). Meeting the challenges of contemporary foster care. *Future of Children, 14,* 75–93.

Cicchetti, D. (1989). How research on child maltreatment has informed the study of child development: Perspectives from developmental psychopathology. In D. Cicchetti & V. Carlson (Eds.), *Child maltreatment: Theory and research on the causes and consequences of child abuse and neglect* (pp. 377–431). New York: Cambridge University Press.

Cicchetti, D. (1990). The organization and coherence of socioemotional, cognitive, and representational development: Illustrations through a developmental psychopathology perspective on Down syndrome and child maltreatment. In R. A. Thompson (Ed.), *36th Annual Nebraska Symposium on Motivation: Socioemotional development* (pp. 259–366). Lincoln: University of Nebraska Press.

Cicchetti, D., Ganiban, J., & Barnett, D. (1991). Contributions from the study of high-risk populations to understanding the development of emotion regulation. In J. Garber & K. A. Dodge (Eds.), *Development of emotion regulation and dysregulation.* New York: Cambridge University Press.

Cicchetti, D., & Lynch, M. (1993). Toward an ecological/transactional model of community violence and child maltreatment: Consequences for children's development. *Psychiatry, 56,* 96–118.

Cicchetti, D., & Rizley, R. (1981). Developmental perspectives on the etiology, intergenerational transmission, and sequelae of child maltreatment. *New Directions for Child Development, 11,* 31–55.

Cicchetti, D., & Rogosch, F. A. (1997). The role of self-organization in the promotion of resilience in maltreated children. *Development and Psychopathology, 9,* 797–815.

Cicchetti, D., & Toth, S. L. (2000). Developmental processes in maltreated children. In D. J. Hansen (Ed.), *46th Annual Nebraska Symposium on Motivation: Motivation and child maltreatment* (pp. 85–160). Lincoln: University of Nebraska Press.

Claussen, A. H., & Crittenden, P. M. (1991). Physical and psychological maltreatment: Relations among types of maltreatment. *Child Abuse & Neglect, 15,* 5–18.

Connelly, C. D., & Straus, M. A. (1992). Mother's age and risk for physical abuse. *Child Abuse & Neglect, 16,* 709–718.

Crittenden, P. M. (1985). Maltreated infants: Vulnerability and resilience. *Journal of Child Psychology and Psychiatry, 26,* 85–96.

DePanfilis, D., & Zuravin, S. J. (2001). Assessing risk to determine the need for services. *Children and Youth Services Review, 23,* 3–20.

Department of Health and Human Services. (1994). *Child maltreatment 1992: Reports from the states to the National Center on Child Abuse and Neglect.* Washington, DC: Government Printing Office.

Derogatis, L. R. (1983). *SCL-90-R: Administration, scoring, and procedures manual—II.* Towson, MD: Clinical Psychometric Research.

DeRoma, V. M., & Hansen, D. J. (1994, November). *Development of the Parental Anger Inventory.* Paper presented at the Association for the Advancement of Behavior Therapy, San Diego, CA.

Dodge, K. A., Pettit, G. S., & Bates, J. E. (1994). Effects of physical maltreatment on the development of peer relations. *Development and Psychopathology, 6,* 43–55.

Doerner, W. G., & Lab, S. P. (1998). *Victimology* (2nd ed.). Cincinnati, OH: Anderson.

Eckenrode, J., Laird, M., & Doris, J. (1993). School performance and disciplinary problems among abused and neglected children. *Developmental Psychology, 29,* 53–62.

Eckenrode, J., Rowe, E., Laird, M., & Brathwaite, J. (1995). Mobility as a mediator of the effects of child maltreatment on academic performance. *Child Development, 66,* 1130–1142.

Eckenrode, J., Zielinski, D., Smith, E., Marcynyszyn, L. A., Henderson, C. R., Kitzman, H., et al. (2001). Child maltreatment and the early onset of problem behaviors: Can a program of nurse home visitation break the link? *Development and Psychopathology, 13,* 873–890.

Egeland, B. (1991). A longitudinal study of high-risk families: Issues and findings. In R. H. Starr, Jr., & D. A. Wolfe (Eds.), *The effects of child abuse and neglect: Issues and research* (pp. 33–56). New York: Guilford Press.

Eigsti, I.-M., & Cicchetti, D. (2004). The impact of child maltreatment on expressive syntax at 60 months. *Developmental Science, 7,* 88–102.

Erickson, M. F., & Egeland, B. (2002). Child neglect. In J. E. B. Myers, L. Berliner, J. Briere, C. T. Hendrix, C. Jenny, & T. A. Reid (Eds.), *The APSAC handbook on child maltreatment* (2nd ed., pp. 3–20). Thousand Oaks, CA: Sage.

Erickson, M. F., Egeland, B., & Pianta, R. C. (1989). The effects of maltreatment on the development of young children. In D. Cicchetti & V. Carlson (Eds.), *Child maltreatment: Theory and research on the causes and consequences of child abuse and neglect.* New York: Cambridge University Press.

Eyberg, S. M., Funderburk, B. W., Hembree-Kigin, T. L., McNeil, C. B., Querido, J. G., & Hood, K. K. (2001). Parent-child interaction therapy with behavior problem children: One and two year maintenance of treatment effects in the family. *Child and Family Behavior Therapy, 23,* 1–20.

Eyberg, S. M., & Robinson, E. A. (1981). *Dyadic Parent-Child Interaction Coding System: A manual* (Manuscript No. 2582). San Rafael, CA: Social and Behavioral Sciences Documents, Select Press.

Eysenck, H. J. (1991). Dimensions of personality: 16, 5, or 3?—Criteria for a taxonomic paradigm. *Personality and Individual Differences, 12,* 773–790.

Fantuzzo, J., Coolahan, K. C., & Weiss, A. D. (1997). Resiliency partnership-directed intervention: Enhancing the social competencies of preschool victims of physical abuse by developing peer resources and community strengths. In D. Cicchetti & S. L. Toth (Eds.), *Developmental perspectives on trauma: Theory, research, and intervention* (pp. 463–489). Rochester, NY: University of Rochester Press.

Fantuzzo, J., Weiss, A., & Coolahan, K. (1998). Community-based partnership-directed research: Actualizing community strengths to treat victims of physical abuse and neglect. In R. J. Lutzker (Ed.), *Child abuse: A handbook of theory, research, and treatment* (pp. 213–238). New York: Pergamon Press.

Fantuzzo, J. W. (1990). Behavioral treatment of the victims of child abuse and neglect. *Behavior Modification, 14,* 316–339.

Feindler, E. L., Rathus, J. H., & Silver, L. B. (2002). *Assessment of family violence: A handbook for researchers and practitioners.* Washington, DC: American Psychological Association.

Finzi, R., Cohen, O., Sapir, Y., & Weizman, A. (2000). Attachment styles in maltreated children: A comparative study. *Child Psychiatry and Human Development, 31,* 113–128.

Finzi, R., Ram, A., Har-Even, D., Shnit, D., & Weizman, A. (2001). Attachment styles and aggression in physically abused and neglected children. *Journal of Youth and Adolescence, 30,* 769–786.

Ford, J. D., Racusin, R., Daviss, W. B., Ellis, C. G., W. B., Thomas, J., Rogers, K., et al. (1999). Trauma exposure among children with oppositional defiant disorder and attention deficit- hyperactivity disorder. *Journal of Consulting and Clinical Psychology, 67,* 786–789.

Forehand, R., & McMahon, R. (1981). *Helping the noncompliant child: A clinician's guide to parent training.* New York: Guilford Press.

Gershater-Molko, R. M., Lutzker, J. R., & Wesch, D. (2003). Project SafeCare: Improving health, safety, and parenting skills in families reported for, and at-risk for child maltreatment. *Journal of Family Violence, 18,* 377–386.

Gibb, B. E., Wheeler, R., Alloy, L. B., & Abramson, L. Y. (2001). Emotional, physical, and sexual maltreatment in childhood versus adolescence and personality dysfunction in young adulthood. *Journal of Personality Disorders, 15,* 505–511.

Gil, D. G. (1970). *Violence against children: Physical abuse in the United States.* Cambridge, MA: Harvard University Press.

Golier, J. A., Yehuda, R., Bierer, L. M., Mitropoulou, V., New, A. S., Schmeidler, J., et al. (2003). The relationship of borderline personality disorder to posttraumatic stress disorder and traumatic events. *American Journal of Psychiatry, 160,* 2018–2024.

Haapala, D. A., & Kinney, J. M. (1988). Avoiding out-of-home placement of high-risk status offenders through the use of intensive family preservation services. *Criminal Justice and Behavior, 15,* 334–348.

Hally, C., Polansky, N. F., & Polansky, N. A. (1980). *Child neglect: Mobilizing services* (DHHS Publication No. OHDS 80–30257). Washington, DC: U.S. Government Printing Office.

Hansen, D. J., & MacMillan, V. M. (1990). Behavioral assessment of child-abusive and neglectful families: Recent developments and current issues. *Behavior Modification, 14,* 255–278.

Hansen, D. J., Sedlar, G., & Warner-Rogers, J. E. (1999). Child physical abuse. In R. T. Ammerman & M. Hersen (Eds.), *Assessment of family violence: A clinical and legal sourcebook* (pp. 127–156). New York: Wiley.

Hansen, D. J., Warner-Rogers, J. E., & Hecht, D. B. (1998). Implementing and evaluating an individualized behavioral intervention program for maltreating families: Clinical and research issues. In J. R. Lutzker (Ed.), *Handbook of child abuse research and treatment* (pp. 133–158). New York: Plenum Press.

Haskett, M. E., & Kistner, J. A. (1991). Social interactions and peer perceptions of young physically abused children. *Child Development, 62,* 979–990.

Hecht, D. B., & Hansen, D. J. (2001). The environment of child maltreatment: Contextual factors and the development of psychopathology. *Aggression and Violent Behavior, 6,* 433–457.

Heller, S. S., Larrieu, J. A., D'Imperio, R., & Boris, N. W. (1999). Research on resilience to child maltreatment: Empirical considerations. *Child Abuse & Neglect, 23,* 321–338.

Hembree-Kigin, T. L., & McNeil, C. B. (1995). *Parent-child interaction therapy.* New York: Plenum Press.

Henggeler, S. W., Schoenwald, S. K., Borduin, C. M., Rowland, M. D., & Cunningham, P. B. (1998). *Multisystemic treatment of antisocial behavior in children and adolescents.* New York: Guilford Press.

Herman, J. L., Perry, C., & van der Kolk, B. (1989). Childhood trauma in borderline personality disorder. *American Journal of Psychiatry, 146,* 490–495.

Herrenkohl, R. C., Egolf, B. P., & Herrenkohl, E. C. (1997). Preschool antecedents of adolescent assaultive behavior: A longitudinal study. *American Journal of Orthopsychiatry, 67,* 422–432.

Herrenkohl, R. C., Herrenkohl, E. C., Egolf, B. P., & Wu, P. (1991). The developmental consequences of child abuse: The Lehigh longitudinal study. In R. H. Starr, Jr., & D. A. Wolfe (Eds.), *The effects of child abuse and neglect: Issues and research* (pp. 57–81). New York: Guilford Press.

Herrenkohl, E. C., Herrenkohl, R. C., Toedter, L., & Yanushefski, A. M. (1984). Parent-child interactions in abusive and nonabusive families. *Journal of the American Academy of Child Psychiatry, 23,* 641–648.

Howes, C., & Segal, J. (1993). Children's relationships with alternative caregivers: The special case of maltreated children removed from their homes. *Journal of Applied Developmental Psychology, 14,* 71–81.

Jaffee, S. R., Caspi, A., Moffitt, T. E., & Taylor, A. (2004). Physical maltreatment victim to antisocial child: Evidence of an environmentally mediated process. *Journal of Abnormal Psychology, 113,* 44–55.

Jang, K. L., Livesley, W. J., Vernon, P. A., & Jackson, D. N. (1996). Heritability of personality disorder traits: A twin study. *Acta Psychiatrica Scandinavica, 94,* 438–444.

Johnson, J., Cohen, P., Brown, J., Smailes, E. M., & Bernstein, D. P. (1999). Childhood maltreatment increases risk for personality disorders during early adulthood. *Archives of General Psychiatry, 56,* 600–606.

Johnson, J., Smailes, E. M., Phil, M., Cohen, P., Brown, J., & Bernstein, D. P. (2000). Associations between four types of childhood neglect and personality disorder symptoms during adolescence and early adulthood: Findings of a community-based longitudinal study. *Journal of Personality Disorders, 14,* 171–187.

Johnson, R. M., Kotch, J. B., Catellier, D. J., Winsor, J. R., Dufort, V., Hunter, W., et al. (2002). Adverse behavioral and emotional outcomes from child abuse and witnessed violence. *Child Maltreatment, 7,* 179–186.

Kagan, J. (1994). *Galen's prophecy.* New York: Basic Books.

Kaufman, J., & Cicchetti, D. (1989). Effects of maltreatment on school-age children's socioemotional development: Assessments in a day-camp setting. *Developmental Psychology, 25,* 516–524.

Kaufman Kantor, G., Straus, M. A., Mebert, C., & Brown, W. (2001). *Measuring neglect through child-report: The Multidimensional Neglect Scale, form C6.* Durham: Family Research Laboratory, University of New Hampshire.

Kelleher, K., Chaffin, M., Hollenberg, J., & Fischer, E. (1994). Alcohol and drug disorders among physically abusive and neglectful parents in a community-based sample. *American Journal of Public Health, 84,* 1586–1590.

Kempe, C. H., Silverman, F. N., Steele, B. F., Droegemueller, W., & Silver, H. K. (1962). The battered-child syndrome. *Journal of the American Medical Association, 181,* 105–112.

Kendall-Tackett, K. A., & Eckenrode, J. (1996). The effects of neglect on academic achievement and disciplinary problems: A developmental perspective. *Child Abuse & Neglect, 20,* 161–169.

Kolko, D. J. (1996). Individual cognitive behavioral therapy and family therapy for physically abused children and their offending parents: A comparison of clinical outcomes. *Child Maltreatment, 1,* 322–342.

Kolko, D. J. (2002). Child physical abuse. In J. E. B. Myers, L. Berliner, J. Briere, C. T. Hendrix, C. Jenny, & T. A. Reid (Eds.), *The APSAC handbook on child maltreatment* (2nd ed., pp. 21–54). Thousand Oaks, CA: Sage.

Kolko, D. J., & Swenson, C. C. (2002). *Assessing and treating physically abused children and their families: A cognitive-behavioral approach.* Thousand Oaks, CA: Sage.

Korfmacher, J., Kitzman, H., & Olds, D. L. (1998). Intervention processes as predictors of outcomes in a preventive home-visitation program. *Journal of Community Psychology, special issue: Home visitation II, 26,* 49–64.

Leiter, J., & Johnsen, M. C. (1994). Child maltreatment and school performance. *American Journal of Education, 102,* 154–189.

Livesley, W. J., Jang, K. L., Jackson, D. N., & Vernon, P. A. (1995). Genetic and environmental contributions to dimensions of personality disorder. *American Journal of Psychiatry, 152,* 479–480.

Lung, C., & Daro, D. (1996). *Current trends in child abuse reporting and fatalities: The results of the 1995 annual fifty state survey.* Chicago: National Committee to Prevent Child Abuse.

Luntz, B. K., & Widom, C. S. (1994). Antisocial personality disorder in abused and neglected children grown up. *American Journal of Psychiatry, 151,* 670–674.

Lynch, M., & Cicchetti, D. (1992). Maltreated children's reports of relatedness to their teachers. In R. C. Pianta (Ed.), *Beyond the parent: The role of other adults in children's lives.* San Francisco: Jossey-Bass.

Lysaker, P. H., Wickett, A. M., Lancaster, R. S., & Davis, L. W. (2004). Neurocognitive deficits and history of childhood abuse in schizophrenia spectrum disorders: Associations with cluster B personality traits. *Schizophrenia Research, 68,* 87–94.

Mackner, L. M., Starr, R. H., & Black, M. M. (1997). The cumulative effect of neglect and failure to thrive on cognitive functioning. *Child Abuse & Neglect, 21,* 691–700.

MacMillan, V. M., Olson, R. L., & Hansen, D. J. (1988, November). *The Development of an Anger Inventory for Use with Maltreating Parents.* Paper presented at the Association for the Advancement of Behavior Therapy, New York.

MacMillan, V. M., Olson, R. L., & Hansen, D. J. (1991). Low and high deviance analogue assessment of parent-training with physically abusive parents. *Journal of Family Violence, 6,* 279–301.

Main, M., & Solomon, J. (1986). Discovery of an insecure-disorganized/disoriented attachment pattern. In T. B. Brazelton & M. W. Yogman (Eds.), *Affective development in infancy.* Westport, CT: Ablex.

Malinosky-Rummell, R., & Hansen, D. J. (1993). Long-term consequences of childhood physical abuse. *Psychological Bulletin, 114,* 68–79.

McNeil, C. B., Eyberg, S. M., Eisenstadt, T. H., Newcomb, K., & Funderburk, B. (1991). Parent-child interaction therapy with behavior problem children: Generalization of treatment effects to the school setting. *Journal of Child Clinical Psychology, 20,* 140–151.

Milner, J. S. (1986). *The Child Abuse Potential Inventory: Manual* (2nd ed.). Webster, NC: Psytec.

Milner, J. S. (1993). Social information processing and physical child abuse. *Clinical Psychology Review, 13,* 275–294.

Milner, J. S. (2000). Social information processing and child physical abuse: Theory and research. In D. J. Hansen (Ed.), *46th Annual Nebraska Symposium on Motivation: Motivation and child maltreatment* (pp. 39–84). Lincoln: University of Nebraska Press.

Moran, P. B., & Eckenrode, J. (1992). Protective personality characteristics among adolescent victims of maltreatment. *Child Abuse & Neglect, 16,* 743–754.

Nakash-Eisikovits, O., Dutra, L., & Westen, D. (2002). Relationship between attachment patterns and personality pathology in adolescents. *Journal of the American Academy of Child and Adolescent Psychiatry, 41,* 1111–1123.

National Clearinghouse on Child Abuse and Neglect. (2001). *Acts of omission: An overview of child neglect.* Washington, DC: U.S. Department of Health and Human Services.

National Clearinghouse on Child Abuse and Neglect. (2003a). *2003 child abuse and neglect state statute series statutes-at-a-glance: Definitions of child abuse and neglect.* Washington, DC: U.S. Department of Health and Human Services.

National Clearinghouse on Child Abuse and Neglect. (2003b). *About the federal child abuse prevention and treatment act.* Washington, DC: U.S. Department of Health and Human Services.

National Clearinghouse on Child Abuse and Neglect. (2003c). *Recognizing child abuse and neglect: Signs and symptoms.* Washington, DC: U.S. Department of Health and Human Services.

National Clearinghouse on Child Abuse and Neglect. (2004a). *Child maltreatment 2002.* Washington, DC: U.S. Department of Health and Human Services.

National Clearinghouse on Child Abuse and Neglect. (2004b). *What is child abuse and neglect?* Washington, DC: U.S. Department of Health and Human Services.

National Research Council. (1993). *Understanding child abuse and neglect.* Washington, DC: National Academy Press.

Norden, K. A., Klein, D. N., Donaldson, S. K., Pepper, C. M., & Klein, L. M. (1995). Reports of the early home environment in *DSM-III-R* personality disorders. *Journal of Personality Disorders, 9,* 213–223.

Oates, R. K., & Bross, D.C. (1995). What have we learned about treating child physical abuse? A literature review of the last decade. *Child Abuse & Neglect, 19,* 463–473.

Olds, D. L., Henderson, C. R., Kitzman, H., Eckenrode, J., Cole, R., & Tatelbaum, R. (1998). The promise of home visitation: Results of two randomized trials. *Journal of Community Psychology, 26,* 5–21.

Parke, R. D., & Collmer, C. W. (1975). Child abuse: An interdisciplinary analysis. In F. D. Horowitz (Ed.), *Review of child development research.* Chicago: University of Chicago Press.

Parker, J. G., & Herrera, C. (1996). Interpersonal processes in friendship: A comparison of abused and nonabused children's experiences. *Developmental Psychology, 32,* 1025–1038.

Patterson, G. R., & Gullion, M. E. (1968). *Living with children: New methods for parents and teachers.* Champaign, IL: Research Press.

Plomin, R., Defries, J. C., McClearn, G. E., & McGuffin, P. (2000). *Behavioral genetics* (4th ed.). Gordonsville, VA: Worth.

Ralston, M. E., & Sosnowski, P. B. (2004). Family focused, child centered treatment interventions in child maltreatment. In B. E. Saunders, L. Berliner, & R. F. Hanson (Eds.), *Child Physical and Sexual Abuse: Guidelines for Treatment* (revised report: April 26, 2004). Charleston, SC: National Crime Victims Research and Treatment Center.

Roberts, R. N., Wasik, B. H., Casto, G., & Ramey, C. T. (1991). Family support in the home: Programs, policy, and social change. *American Psychologist, 46,* 131–137.

Rogosch, F. A., & Cicchetti, D. (2004). Child maltreatment and emergent personality organization: Perspectives from the five-factor model. *Journal of Abnormal Child Psychology, 32,* 123–145.

Roy, A. (2002). Childhood trauma and neuroticism as an adult: Possible implication for the development of the common psychiatric disorders and suicidal behaviour. *Psychological Medicine, 32,* 1471–1474.

Runyan, D. K., Curtis, P. A., Hunter, W. M., Black, M. M., Kotch, J. B., Bangdiwala, S., et al. (1998). LONGSCAN: A consortium for longitudinal studies of maltreatment and the life course of children. *Aggression and Violent Behavior, 3,* 275–285.

Salzinger, S., Feldman, R. S., Hammer, M., & Rosario, M. (1993). The effects of physical abuse on children's social relationships. *Child Development, 64,* 169–187.

Sameroff, A. J., & Chandler, M. J. (1975). Reproductive risk and the continuum of caretaking casualty. In F. D. Horowitz (Ed.), *Review of child development research.* Chicago: University of Chicago Press.

Saunders, B. E., Berliner, L., & Hanson, R. F. E. (2004). *Child physical and sexual abuse: Guidelines for treatment* (revised report: April 26, 2004). Charleston, SC: National Crime Victims Research and Treatment Center.

Sedlak, A. J., & Broadhurst, D. D. (1996). *Executive summary of the third national incidence study of child abuse and neglect.* Washington, DC: U.S. Department of Health and Human Services.

Shearer, S. L., Peters, C. P., Quaytman, M. S., & Ogden, R. L. (1990). Frequency and correlates of childhood sexual and physical abuse histories in adult female borderline inpatients. *American Journal of Psychiatry, 147,* 214–216.

Shields, A., & Cicchetti, D. (1998). Reactive aggression among maltreated children: The contributions of attention and emotion dysregulation. *Journal of Clinical Child Psychology, 27,* 381–395.

Shields, A., & Cicchetti, D. (2001). Parental maltreatment and emotion dysregulation as risk factors for bullying and victimization in middle childhood. *Journal of Clinical Child Psychology, 30,* 349–363.

Shipman, K. L., & Zeman, J. (2001). Socialization of children' emotion regulation in mother-child dyads: A developmental psychopathology perspective. *Development and Psychopathology, 13,* 317–336.

Shonk, S. M., & Cicchetti, D. (2001). Maltreatment, competency deficits, and risk for academic and behavioral maladjustment. *Developmental Psychology, 37,* 3–17.

Silverman, A. B., Reinherz, H. Z., & Giaconia, R. M. (1996). The long-term sequelae of child and adolescent abuse: A longitudinal community study. *Child Abuse & Neglect, 20,* 709–723.

Sroufe, L. A., Carlson, E., Levy, A., & Egeland, B. (1999). Implications of attachment theory for developmental psychopathology. *Development and Psychopathology, 11,* 1–13.

Stevenson, J. (1999). The treatment of the long-term sequelae of child abuse. *Journal of Child Psychology and Psychiatry and Allied Disciplines, 40,* 89–111.

Straus, M. A. (2000). Corporal punishment and primary prevention of physical abuse. *Child Abuse & Neglect, 24,* 1109–1114.

Straus, M. A., Hamby, S. L., Boney-McCoy, S., & Sugarman, D. B. (1996). The Revised Conflict Tactic Scales (CTS2): Development and preliminary psychometric data. *Journal of Family Issues, 17,* 283–316.

Straus, M. A., Hamby, S. L., Finkelhor, D., Moore, D. W., & Runyan, D. (1998). Identification of child maltreatment with the parent-child Conflict Tactics Scales: Development and psychometric data for a national sample of American parents. *Child Abuse & Neglect, 22,* 249–270.

Straus, M. A., & Kantor, G. K. (2003). *Definition and measurement of neglect: Some general principles and their application to self-report measures.* Unpublished manuscript, University of New Hampshire.

Sylva, K. (1994). School influences on children's development. *Journal of Child Psychology and Psychiatry and Allied Disciplines, 35,* 135–170.

Thomas, A., & Chess, S. (1977). *Temperament and development.* New York: Bruner-Mazel.

Thomas, A., Chess, S., & Birch, H. G. (1968). *Temperament and behavior disorders in children.* Oxford: New York University Press.

Toth, S. L., & Cicchetti, D. (1996). Patterns of relatedness, depressive symptomatology, and perceived competence in maltreated children. *Journal of Consulting and Clinical Psychology, 64,* 32–41.

Toth, S. L., Cicchetti, D., Macfie, J., & Emde, R. N. (1997). Representations of self and other in the narratives of neglected, physically abused, and sexually abused preschoolers. *Development and Psychopathology, 9,* 781–796.

Trickett, P. K., & Kuczynski, L. (1986). Children's misbehaviors and parental discipline strategies in abusive and nonabusive families. *Developmental Psychology, 22,* 115–123.

Trull, T. J. (2001). Structural relations between borderline personality disorder features and putative etiological correlates. *Journal of Abnormal Psychology, 110,* 471–481.

Wang, C. T., & Daro, D. (1998). *Current trends in child abuse reporting and fatalities: The results of the 1997 annual fifty state survey.* Chicago: Prevent Child Abuse America.

Warner-Rogers, J. E., Hansen, D. J., & Hecht, D. B. (1999). Child physical abuse and neglect. In V. B. Van Hasselt & M. Hersen (Eds.), *Handbook of psychological approaches with violent offenders: Contemporary strategies and issues.* New York: Kluwer Academic/Plenum Press.

Weaver, T. L., & Clum, G. A. (1993). Early family environments and traumatic experiences associated with borderline personality disorder. *Journal of Consulting and Clinical Psychology, 61,* 1068–1075.

Weiss, B., Dodge, K. A., Bates, J. E., & Pettit, G. S. (1992). Some consequences of early harsh discipline: Child aggression and a maladaptive social information processing style. *Child Development, 63,* 1321–1335.

Wekerle, C., & Wolfe, D. A. (1996). Child maltreatment. In E. J. Mash & R. A. Barkley (Eds.), *Child psychopathology* (pp. 492–537). New York: Guilford Press.

Whipple, E. E., & Webster-Stratton, C. (1991). The role of parental stress in physically abusive families. *Child Abuse & Neglect, 15,* 279–291.

Widom, C. S. (1989). Child abuse, neglect and adult behavior: Research design and findings on criminality, violence, and child abuse. *American Journal of Orthopsychiatry, 58,* 260–270.

Widom, C. S. (2000). Understanding the consequences of childhood victimization. In R. M. Reece (Ed.), *Treatment of child abuse: Common ground for mental health, medical, and legal practitioners* (pp. 339–361). Baltimore: Johns Hopkins University Press.

Widom, C. S., & Maxfield, M. G. (1996). A prospective examination of risk for violence among abused and neglected children. In C. Ferris & T. Grisso (Eds.), *Understanding aggressive behavior in children* (pp. 224–237). New York: New York Academy of Sciences.

Wind, T. W., & Silvern, L. (1994). Parenting and family stress as mediators of the long-term effects of child abuse. *Child Abuse and Neglect, 18,* 439–453.

Wolfe, D. A. (1987). *Child abuse: Implications for child development and psychopathology.* Newbury Park, CA: Sage.

Wolfe, D. A. (1988). Child abuse and neglect. In E. J. Mash & L. G. Terdal (Eds.), *Behavioral assessment of childhood disorders* (2nd ed., pp. 627–669). New York: Guilford Press.

Wolfe, D. A. (1991). *Preventing physical and emotional abuse of children.* New York: Guilford Press.

Wolfe, D. A. (1999). *Child abuse: Implications for child development and psychopathology* (2nd ed.). Thousand Oaks, CA: Sage.

Wolfe, D. A. (2004). Parent-child education program for physically abusive parents. In B. E. Saunders, L. Berliner, & R. F. Hanson (Eds.), *Child physical and sexual abuse: Guidelines for treatment* (revised report: April 26, 2004). Charleston, SC: National Crime Victims Research and Treatment Center.

Wolfe, D. A., & McEachran, A. (1997). Child physical abuse and neglect. In E. J. Mash & L. G. Terdal (Eds.), *Assessment of childhood disorders* (3rd ed., pp. 523–568). New York: Guilford Press.

Wolfe, D. A., & McGee, R. (1991). Assessment of emotional status among maltreated children. In R. H. Starr, Jr., & D. A. Wolfe (Eds.), *The effects of child abuse and neglect: Issues and research* (pp. 257–277). New York: Guilford Press.

Wolfe, D. A., & Wekerle, C. (1993). Treatment strategies for child physical abuse and neglect: A critical progress report. *Clinical Psychology Review, 13,* 473–500.

Wolfe, D. A., Wekerle, C., Reitzel-Jaffe, D., & Lefebvre, L. (1998). Factors associated with abusive relationships among maltreated and nonmaltreated youth. *Development and Psychopathology, 10,* 61–85.

Wolfner, G. D., & Gelles, R. J. (1993). A profile of violence toward children: A national study. *Child Abuse & Neglect, 17,* 197–212.

Zuravin, S. J. (1991). Research definitions of child physical abuse and neglect: Current problems. In R. H. Starr, Jr., & D. A. Wolfe (Eds.), *The effects of child abuse and neglect: Issues and research* (pp. 100–128). New York: Guilford Press.

CHAPTER 23

Child Sexual Abuse

ANTHONY P. MANNARINO AND JUDITH A. COHEN

DESCRIPTION OF THE PROBLEM AND CLINICAL PICTURE

Definitional Issues

Child sexual abuse (CSA) is not a clinical disorder or psychiatric diagnosis. It is an event or series of events to which a child or adolescent is subjected. There is also a wide range of emotional and behavioral responses to CSA that will be discussed. Although the legal definition of CSA varies from state to state, in all states CSA is a criminal act. When it is perpetrated by a member of the child's immediate family (e.g., father, sibling), CSA is typically referred to as incest. Extrafamilial CSA occurs when the perpetrator is someone outside of the family such as a neighbor, an older child or teenager, a member of the clergy, or a teacher. Most reports suggest that CSA is perpetrated by a stranger less than 10 percent of the time (Berliner & Elliott, 2002).

There is no commonly accepted definition as to what actually constitutes CSA. Certainly rape is a clear-cut example. However, at the other end of the spectrum, many people would suggest that noncontact events such as exposing a child to pornographic materials or forcing a child to see an adult's genitalia would also constitute CSA. A common definition used in research studies is that CSA is sexual exploitation involving physical contact between a child and another person. Exploitation implies an inequality of power between the child and the abuser on the basis of age, physical size, the nature of the emotional relationship, or a combination of these (Cohen & Mannarino, 1996, 1998a). Physical contact may involve oral, anal, genital, or breast contact. Thus, many different types of inappropriate sexual contact could fall under this broad definition.

Mandated Reporting

Mandated reporting refers to the requirement that professionals are required to report child abuse, including CSA, to their local child protective service (CPS) organization or appropriate state agency, or both. All 50 states have mandated reporting laws, and mental health professionals in all jurisdictions are subject to these laws. Unfortunately, the mandated reporting laws vary from state to state with respect to how child abuse is defined and the minimal criteria that need to be reached in order for a mandated report to be made (Kalichman, 1993). In most states, suspicion of abuse or reason to believe that abuse has occurred is the threshold for a mandated report. However, in some states a mandated report would be required only if a child directly discloses abuse to a professional, whereas in other states information obtained from other sources, including the alleged abuser, would trigger a mandated report (Mannarino & Cohen, in press).

It is also worth noting that in most states, CSA would fall under the jurisdiction of the CPS system only if it is perpetrated by someone in a caretaking role with the child (i.e., parent, adolescent sibling, sitter) or someone living in the immediate family. Otherwise, CSA would likely fall outside of the purview of CPS, would not trigger a mandated report, and would not be investigated by the state. In such instances, CSA would still be a criminal act. Given the differences from state to state in how CSA is defined and mandated reporting requirements, mental health professionals must become familiar with the CPS and criminal statutes in their individual states in order to practice in a legally and ethically sound manner. Additionally, lack of knowledge of pertinent state laws and regulations would handicap a professional trying to assist a family whose child has been victimized by sexual abuse, particularly when the family is confronted with the often confusing issues that arise when dealing with CPS or the criminal justice system.

Clinical Picture

Child sexual abuse is best conceptualized as a stressful life event. Children's responses to CSA encompass a wide range of behavioral and emotional reactions. Some children may display no detectable negative effects (Kendall-Tackett, Williams,

& Finkelhor, 1993), and it has been estimated that approximately 30 percent of sexually abused children may be asymptomatic at the time of their disclosure (Finkelhor, 1990). In contrast, the majority of sexually abused children display a variety of significant emotional and behavioral difficulties, including depressive symptoms, anxiety, and sexualized behavioral problems (Kendall-Tackett et al., 1993; Mannarino, Cohen, & Gregor, 1989). No particular set of problems or symptoms uniquely characterize sexually abused children, however, and there is absolutely no evidence for a child sexual abuse syndrome.

Despite the wide diversity of responses to CSA and the lack of a unitary syndrome, most professionals consider CSA to be a traumatic event that places the child at risk for the development of post-traumatic stress disorder (PTSD). In fact, some studies have found that as many as 50 percent of sexually abused children suffer from PTSD or experience some PTSD symptoms (McLeer, Deblinger, Atkins, Foa, & Ralphe, 1988; McLeer, Deblinger, Henry, & Orvaschel, 1992).

Although the rate for partial or full PTSD in sexually abused children is quite high, it is very possible that the disorder is underdiagnosed in this population. Current diagnostic criteria for PTSD were not developed based on child or adolescent field trials. Accordingly, they may not be sensitive to developmental factors, particularly the lack of well-developed expressive language skills in young children. Also, children may respond to trauma in unique ways that fall outside the parameters of current diagnostic criteria (Saywitz, Mannarino, Berliner, & Cohen, 2000). In this regard, Scheeringa and his colleagues (Scheeringa, Peebles, Cook, & Zeanah, 2001; Scheeringa, Zeanah, Myers, & Putnam, 2003) have examined alternative PTSD criteria that may better capture how very young children express this disorder. It is also true that children who suffer from PTSD often experience other comorbid disorders, including depression, other anxiety disorders, and attention-deficit/hyperactivity disorder (ADHD).

Because CSA is a criminal act, determining whether a child or teenager has been victimized has serious implications for both the alleged victim and the perpetrator. In this regard, some forensic experts or investigative interviewers have suggested that it is common for sexually abused children to exhibit certain types of symptoms or a specific cluster of symptoms and that the presence of such symptoms would be evidence that CSA has occurred (i.e., pathognomonic of CSA). Unfortunately, this kind of reasoning is faulty. The clinical symptomatology (i.e., PTSD, depression, sexualized behavior problems) that sexually abused children present could be consistent with other life stressors. Moreover, the presence or absence of any particular set of clinical symptoms in no way indicates that CSA has or has not occurred. Particularly with asymptomatic sexually abused children who are either resilient or have received significant familial support, or both, it would be highly inappropriate to suggest that they have not been victimized simply because they are functioning well. Accordingly, in forensic contexts, clinical presentation or psychiatric symptomatology should not be used as evidence to demonstrate the presence or absence of CSA.

PERSONALITY DEVELOPMENT AND PSYCHOPATHOLOGY

Premorbid Personality Features

In the area of child physical abuse, some studies have indicated that children with specific personality qualities or behavioral features may be at higher risk for victimization. For example, children who are oppositional, aggressive, hyperactive, or a combination of these may inherently present difficult challenges for parents and may be at higher risk for physical abuse (Ford et al., 1999; Herrenkohl, Herrenkohl, & Egolf, 1983). In contrast, interviews with sexual abuse offenders have suggested that they may be more likely to assault a quiet, shy, or vulnerable child (Conte, Wolfe, & Smith, 1989). Such children may appear needy and may more easily become the prey of the calculating offender, whose so-called grooming strategies are aimed to achieve access to and cooperation from a potential victim.

Although some studies have demonstrated that specific personality features or behaviors in the child may increase the risk for physical or sexual abuse, the research in this area has largely been equivocal and has not typically involved prospective methodology that would permit a better understanding of antecedents and consequences. There is also the concern that focusing on the child's personality or behaviors could result in victim blame when physical or sexual abuse has occurred. A more fruitful approach would be to examine the impact of abuse on personality development and how the abusive experience alters the normal developmental trajectory.

Self-Esteem and Self-Efficacy

Self-Esteem

The development of positive self-esteem and a strong sense of personal self-efficacy is seen by most developmentalists as essential to solid personality formation. With respect to self-esteem, the research data have been mixed as to whether sexually abused children experience difficulties in this area. In an early study, Mannarino et al. (1989) found that sexually abused girls did not exhibit lower self-esteem than either clinical or normal controls. In fact, at the 6-month follow-up assessment, the sexually abused group actually exhibited higher self-esteem than either the clinical or the normal control group (Mannarino, Cohen, Smith, & Moore-Motily, 1991). In a later study by this research group (Mannarino & Cohen, 1996a, 1996b), sexually abused girls displayed significantly more self-esteem problems than normal controls at an initial assessment and at the 12-month follow-up but not at the 6-month follow-up. Other studies have not found self-esteem problems in cohorts of sexually abused children (Einbender & Friedrich, 1989; Gomes-Schwartz, Horowitz, & Sauzier, 1985).

There may be a number of explanations as to why most studies have not demonstrated self-esteem deficits in sexually abused children. Because self-esteem has typically been based on self-report, it is possible that sexually abused children use denial when completing these instruments, perhaps as a self-protective mechanism. This argument assumes that sexually abused children do indeed have self-esteem problems but are not able to acknowledge them, at least in the context of a research study. A more plausible explanation is that sexually abused children are able to develop adequate self-esteem despite their sexual victimization experience. In this regard, it is possible that disclosing their sexual abuse history helps these children to feel good about themselves, particularly since they often receive positive feedback and praise from parents or the authorities for their disclosure. From a clinical perspective, we have frequently observed that sexually abused children feel very proud that their disclosure may have prevented other children from being victimized.

Self-Efficacy

The belief that an individual can have a significant impact on his or her life or environment is often referred to as personal self-efficacy or a sense of self-competence. In this regard, clinicians in the sexual abuse field frequently report that sexually abused children typically experience powerlessness or helplessness because they were not able to stop or prevent their victimization. This is not surprising given that by definition, CSA assumes an inequity in power between the perpetrator and the victim based on size, age, or the nature of the emotional relationship. From a theoretical perspective, Finkelhor (1987) has posited powerlessness as one of four factors in his traumagenic dynamics model of the impact of child sexual abuse.

Locus of control measures have commonly been used to evaluate whether children believe that their personal outcomes are the result of external factors outside their control or internal factors (i.e., personal self-efficacy). In one study, Mannarino and Cohen (1996a) found that sexually abused children did not differ from normal controls in locus of control at the initial research assessment. However, at the 6- and 12-month follow-up assessments (Mannarino & Cohen, 1996b) the normal controls became increasingly more internal in their locus of control, whereas the sexually abused group did not change. Mannarino and Cohen (1996b) speculated that the sexually abused group may not have exhibited the normal developmental pattern toward a more internalized locus of control because of their perceptions that they were not able to have an impact on specific outcomes in their lives such as family breakups, out-of-home placements, or legal outcomes related to their sexual abuse disclosure. It is also noteworthy that these researchers found in their sexually abused group that an external locus of control was significantly predictive of depressive symptoms at the 6-month follow-up and significantly predictive of depressive symptoms, anxiety, self-esteem problems, and externalized behavior problems at the 12-month follow-up. Thus, sexually abused children appear to be at risk for not moving along the normal developmental trajectory of a more internal locus of control, and this specific developmental deviation significantly increases the likelihood of emotional and behavioral difficulties.

Perceived credibility has also been studied in sexually abused children. This concept refers to the idea that other people believe what the sexually abused child has to say, not only about the sexual abuse experience but about things in general. If the sexually abused child has a solid foundation of perceived credibility, this would enhance overall personal self-efficacy. Unfortunately, research has demonstrated that sexually abused children have lower perceived credibility than normal controls and that this factor is strongly related to self-reported symptomatology, particularly at follow-up assessments (Mannarino & Cohen, 1996a, 1996b; Mannarino, Cohen, & Berman, 1994). Thus, over time, lower perceived credibility has an increasingly negative impact and increases the probability of psychiatric symptoms. The findings from these studies on perceived credibility can be added to the results from investigations examining locus of control and together demonstrate that sexually abused children develop an impaired sense of personal self-efficacy and that this deficit is highly related to the formation of clinical problems in this population.

Personal Responsibility and Shame

Personal Responsibility

Developing an appropriate sense of responsibility for one's personal behavior is an important aspect of development.

With respect to sexually abused children, clinical observations suggest that they often inappropriately take responsibility for their victimization, that is, they engage in self-blame. Self-blame may be directly reinforced by some perpetrators who blame their victims for the abuse or by society for stigmatizing children who disclose what happened to them. Studies of sexually abused children and adolescents (Feiring, Taska, & Chen, 2002; Morrow, 1991) have demonstrated a clear relationship between self-blame for the abusive experience (i.e., internal attributions) and the development of self-esteem problems, depressive symptoms, and PTSD symptoms.

Other research has examined general attributional style independent of the sexual abuse experience. These studies (Feiring, Taska, & Lewis, 1998; Mannarino et al., 1994; Mannarino & Cohen, 1996a) have consistently shown that a self-blaming general attributional style or increased personal attributions for negative events is common among sexually abused children and that this variable is correlated with self-esteem problems, depressive symptoms, and other signs of psychological distress in this population.

Shame

Responsibility and shame are different concepts when evaluating the impact of the sexual abuse experience. Although children may feel that the victimization was not their fault, they may still feel a sense of shame for what occurred. From a clinical perspective, we often see sexually abused children who describe feeling contaminated or damaged by the victimization. In the research arena, Feiring and her colleagues have begun to closely examine the role of shame in the development of psychological symptoms in sexually abused children. Their research has demonstrated that shame is significantly related to PTSD symptoms, depression, and self-esteem problems in this population and that shame specifically mediates not only the relationship between abuse severity and symptom formation but also the relationship between internal attributions for the abuse and symptom development (Feiring et al., 1998, 2002).

Findings from these interrelated areas of research suggest that personal responsibility and shame are important concepts to consider with respect to the personality development of sexually abused children. These youngsters are clearly vulnerable to blaming themselves for their victimization, for experiencing significant shame associated with the abuse, and for developing a general sense that they are responsible for other negative events that occur in their lives. These factors greatly increase the risk that sexually abused children will veer from a normal developmental trajectory and manifest clinically significant psychological difficulties.

Interpersonal Trust

Finkelhor (1987) identified betrayal as one of the significant effects of child sexual abuse in his traumagenic dynamics model of the impact of sexual victimization. This is not surprising given that most children are sexually abused by someone they know and trust. From a clinical perspective, we often see sexually abused children who are slow to trust others and, accordingly, sometimes find it difficult to develop a therapeutic alliance. These clinical observations have been confirmed in research studies. Using the Children's Attributions and Perceptions Scale (CAPS), which was developed to assess abuse-related attributions and perceptions, Mannarino and his colleagues have consistently found that sexually abused children have lower interpersonal trust than normal controls soon after the disclosure and at 6- and 12-month follow-ups (Mannarino et al., 1994; Mannarino & Cohen, 1996a, 1996b). These same investigators have noted, however, that lower interpersonal trust in victimized children is correlated with depressive symptoms, trait anxiety, and self-esteem problems soon after the disclosure but not necessarily at subsequent assessments.

The information reviewed in this section clearly demonstrates that sexually abused children manifest a number of significant problems in their personality development that are related to their victimization experience. Self-esteem deficits, reduced feelings of self-efficacy, self-blame for negative life events, increased shame, and lower interpersonal trust characterize many sexually abused children and increase their risk for PTSD, depressive symptoms, and other clinical difficulties. It is worth stating yet again that these children appear to have been thrown off the course of their normal developmental trajectory in ways that have serious implications for their overall personality development and general psychological well-being.

EPIDEMIOLOGY

The incidence and prevalence of CSA are difficult to estimate. Many sexually abused children do not disclose their victimization experience for a long time, and in some instances, not until adulthood. In fact, some sexually abused children never disclose that they were victimized. Additionally, as discussed earlier, the definition of CSA varies from state to state such that state-by-state statistics will vary accordingly. Finally, there is no national reporting system for crimes perpetrated against children, thus increasing the likelihood that statistics from individual states may prove to be unreliable (Cohen & Mannarino, 1999).

The best data about the prevalence of child sexual abuse have come from national surveys of adults in community-based samples. In one methodologically rigorous study, Finkelhor, Hotaling, Lewis, and Smith (1990) reported that 27 percent of women and 16 percent of men indicated that they had experienced contact sexual abuse before the age of 18. Fairly similar findings were also reported by Elliott and Briere (1995). What is striking about these statistics is the pervasiveness of CSA. Few other medical or psychiatric disorders have such extraordinarily high prevalence rates in American society.

Child sexual abuse occurs across all racial, ethnic, religious, and socioeconomic strata in the United States. Some disagreement exists as to whether children in the lower socioeconomic levels of society are at greater risk for CSA. Some (e.g., Strauss, Gelles, & Steinmetz, 1980) have suggested that it is more common among poorer families. However, this may be an artifact of abuse reporting in that poorer families are more likely to be involved with the CPS system or government-funded health clinics where there might be an increased probability that the authorities will be notified when there is suspicion of abuse (Cohen & Mannarino, 1999). In one widely cited review of the research literature (Finkelhor & Barron, 1986), no relationship between CSA and socioeconomic status was reported.

Gender is a risk factor for CSA in that girls are more likely to be abused than boys. The relationship between CSA and age is unclear in that very young children are less likely to disclose that they have been victimized. Thus, it is quite possible that many more young children have been sexually abused than existing data suggest in the absence of any specific disclosure. In the Finkelhor and Barron (1986) review, a poor parent-child relationship, having a stepfather, having mothers who worked outside of the home, having mothers who were distant emotionally or frequently ill, and having a mother or father who did not reside with the child for an interval of time increased the risk of CSA. Finkelhor (1984) has also reported that family size, crowded living conditions, and alcohol abuse in either parent are not associated with CSA.

ETIOLOGY

As previously noted, child sexual abuse is not a clinical problem or disorder, but rather it is a traumatic event to which a child or adolescent is subjected. Accordingly, any discussion about etiology will differ in many ways from what might be said about the causes of true clinical disorders such as depression or ADHD. So why are children sexually abused? The simple answer is because an older child, adolescent, or adult has a sexual behavior problem or engages in sexually inappropriate behaviors and directs these problematic behaviors toward young victims. Despite that victims are sometimes stigmatized within our society, children are never to blame for their victimization experience, and the cause of CSA does not lie within child victims. There has been some suggestion that perpetrators may choose victims who are shy and vulnerable and therefore less likely to disclose (Conte et al., 1989), but this finding reflects the psychological dynamics of some perpetrators and should not be viewed in any way as implying that the victim is responsible for CSA. As epidemiological data have consistently demonstrated, CSA cuts across race, ethnicity, socioeconomic class, religion, age, and gender (Cohen & Mannarino, 1999). Additionally, clinical observations indicate that sexually abused children do not have a specific personality profile, nor do they exhibit an identifiable clinical syndrome. Given the high prevalence of CSA, sadly, any child or adolescent may potentially be a victim.

Given that perpetrators are responsible for CSA, any discussion as to the causes of this specific type of trauma should focus on why some older children, adolescents, and adults victimize children. In this regard, it would appear that a multitude of pathways exist for individuals to develop deviant sexual behaviors, including biological, psychological, social, familial, and personality determinants. Unfortunately, such a discussion is beyond the scope of this chapter. (For an excellent discussion with respect to adults, adolescents, and children who sexually abuse children, please see Chaffin, Letourneau, & Silovsky, 2002.)

With regard to CSA victims, a more appropriate discussion about etiology pertains to what factors contribute to the scope and severity of the impact of the victimization. In an earlier section of this chapter, we reviewed a number of cognitive, interpersonal, and personality features that increase the risk of significant emotional and behavioral problems in this population. These include self-esteem deficits, reduced feelings of self-efficacy, self-blame for negative life events, increased shame, and lower interpersonal trust. These factors stem from the dynamics of the abusive experience in which victims typically have been betrayed by someone they know, felt powerless to control what occurred, may have blamed themselves for the abuse, and have a sense of being contaminated or damaged by the victimization. Thus, the essential nature of the sexually abusive experience increases the likelihood that these factors will develop, and these factors in turn often mediate symptom formation in this group.

Other factors may worsen the impact of child sexual victimization. These include variables related to legal proceedings. For example, it has been demonstrated that delays in court proceedings can result in child victims continuing to experience significant psychological distress and depression (Runyan, Everson, Edelsohn, Hunter, & Coulter, 1988). Also, there have been concerns about children having to testify in court, particularly in criminal trials. In this regard, studies have indicated that testifying in front of the defendant in a criminal proceeding as well as being subjected to a harsh cross-examination are associated with ongoing psychological distress (Goodman et al., 1992; Whitcomb et al., 1991).

Family factors have also been examined with respect to how they affect the overall impact of the sexual victimization experience. In terms of overall family functioning, one longitudinal study demonstrated that family dysfunction, and in particular, inadequate maternal problem-solving abilities, correlated significantly with behavior problems in the abused child at an 18-month follow-up (Oates, O'Toole, Lynch, Stern, & Cooney, 1994). In a rather odd finding, Mannarino and Cohen (1996c) reported that family adaptability was positively associated with general behavior problems and internalizing symptoms in preadolescent sexually abused girls. These authors speculated that if the family of a CSA victim has to make an excessive number of changes in response to significant stresses (e.g., relocation, reduced income, family member out of the home), this process may be perceived negatively by the abused child and increase the likelihood of emotional and behavioral difficulties. Accordingly, adaptability may ordinarily be a sign of resilience in a family, but not if the family is subjected to frequent, major changes and stresses that challenge its capacity to function as a coherent system.

When nonoffending parents learn that their child has been sexually abused, this knowledge can have a devastating impact on their own psychological well-being. Fear that their child has been damaged permanently by the victimization, guilt over their perceived failure to protect their child, and worries about legal proceedings are just some of the emotional issues that parents manifest after disclosure. Moreover, parental distress appears to be associated with increased psychological difficulties in the victimized child. In one investigation of incestuous families, Hanson, Saunders, and Lipovsky (1992) indeed found that maternal distress was significantly associated with the victim's self-reported fears.

Mannarino and Cohen (1996c) developed the Parent Emotional Reaction Questionnaire (PERQ) to measure the emotional reactions of nonoffending parents to their child being sexually abused. The PERQ assesses fear, sadness, guilt, anger, embarrassment, shame, and emotional preoccupation with the abuse. In the original study involving the PERQ, Mannarino and Cohen (1996c) reported that as the parents' emotional reaction to the abuse intensified, there were corresponding increases in sexualized behavior problems as well as internalizing and externalizing behavior problems. A more striking finding by this research group indicated that for young sexually abused children involved in a treatment outcome study, the parents' significant emotional distress regarding their child's sexual abuse was highly predictive of emotional and behavioral difficulties in the victim at the end of treatment, independent of treatment group (Cohen & Mannarino, 1996b).

Although parental distress may exacerbate the impact of the victimization experience on the child victim, this conclusion is in no way meant to suggest that the nonoffending parent is to blame or is the cause of the child's ongoing symptoms. However, one implication of this finding is that if parents can resolve their own abuse-related distress, this positive change will be correlated with a reduction in symptomatology in the abused child. Hence, reducing parental emotional distress through their participation in the child's treatment or the parents' involvement in their own treatment will likely benefit the child victim as well.

Another family factor that has been examined is parental support for the abused child and its impact on symptom development. Parental support includes both believing that their child was abused and providing ongoing emotional support. One previous study (Leifer, Shapiro, & Kassem, 1993) indicated that low maternal support was correlated with sexualized play or sexually inappropriate behaviors in sexually abused children. In a widely cited study, lack of maternal support significantly increased the risk of foster placement and was significantly related to higher levels of emotional and behavioral difficulties (Everson, Hunter, Runyan, Edelsohn, & Coulter, 1989). Thus, low parental support has been found to correlate with negative outcomes in sexually abused children. On the other end of the continuum, Cohen and Mannarino (1998b) reported that at 1 year after the end of treatment, higher levels of parental support were significantly predictive of symptom reduction in young sexually abused children.

In summary, CSA is the result of children being subjected to sexually inappropriate behaviors by older children, adolescents, or adults. However, a multitude of factors can worsen the impact of the victimization experience. These factors include child-related variables (e.g., lower interpersonal trust, reduced self-efficacy, personal attributions for negative events, shame), certain kinds of involvement in legal proceedings (e.g., harsh cross-examination in criminal court), and family factors (e.g., parental distress; low parental support).

COURSE, COMPLICATIONS, AND PROGNOSIS

Because CSA is not a clinical disorder, it is not possible to describe a typical clinical or developmental course for children who have been victimized. Some sexual abuse victims who are asymptomatic after disclosure may never experience any significant clinical difficulties (Mannarino, 2000). However, there is limited follow-up data or longitudinal research with this subset of victims and therefore a rather small body of knowledge as to their developmental trajectory. In a review of nearly 50 studies, Kendall-Tackett et al. (1993) concluded that the majority of asymptomatic sexually abused children remain symptom free. However, they also reported that a significant minority develop problems over time. In a 5-year follow-up of sexually abused children, Tebbutt, Swanston, Oates, and O'Toole (1997) found that 41 percent who had been asymptomatic at intake developed depressive symptoms while 30 percent developed self-esteem problems.

Accordingly, it appears that some sexually abused children who are asymptomatic soon after disclosure or abuse discovery develop clinical difficulties over time. However, little is known as to what accounts for this deterioration. It is possible that these children develop unique vulnerabilities because of their victimization experience that are not initially detected but that may place them at higher risk for subsequent clinical difficulties. Alternatively, the presence of other stressors (e.g., legal proceedings, placement, forced contact with perpetrator) that occur over time may predict subsequent clinical problems. More extensive research is obviously needed to better explain why most asymptomatic sexually abused children remain symptom free while some deviate from a normal developmental path.

For symptomatic sexually abused children, the existing evidence is conflicting regarding their clinical and developmental course. Mannarino et al. (1991) reported that sexually abused girls displayed significantly fewer internalizing and total behavior problems over the course of 6- and 12-month follow-up assessments. Nonetheless, at both time points, their sexually abused group exhibited significantly more clinical difficulties than normal controls. In a subsequent study with a different sexual abuse cohort (Mannarino & Cohen, 1996b), this research group again reported that at both 6- and 12-month follow-up assessments these children continued to display significantly more depressive symptoms, anxiety, self-esteem difficulties, sexual behavior problems, and internalizing and externalizing difficulties than normal controls. Moreover, in the earlier of these two studies (Mannarino et al., 1991), at the 12-month follow-up, sexually abused girls who had been subjected to intercourse exhibited significantly more depressive symptoms, anxiety, self-esteem problems, and externalizing difficulties as well as reduced involvement in social activities compared with sexually abused girls who had experienced fondling only. The latter findings suggest that there may be a "sleeper effect" related to type of sexual abuse that becomes evident over time.

In a previously cited review, Kendall-Tackett et al. (1993) concluded that sexually abused children generally have reduced symptomatology over time. However, it should be noted that this review included very few studies with available follow-up data. Thus, this conclusion does not necessarily have strong support. Additionally, in the Tebbutt et al. (1997) study, there were no significant changes in depressive symptoms, self-esteem difficulties, or behavior problems over 5 years. In fact, 43 percent of their sexually abused sample were sad or depressed or had self-esteem problems and 46 percent manifested behavioral difficulties at follow-up. Equally as important, although some of these sexually abused children improved in their functioning over time, nearly the same percentage deteriorated.

Overall, the clinical course for sexually abused children remains very unclear. Many improve over time but some have a worsening of symptoms. Also, sexually abused children who are initially asymptomatic will likely continue to do well, but a smaller percentage will develop clinical problems, perhaps due to previously undetected vulnerabilities or subsequent stressors. In previous sections, we have discussed how a variety of factors such as abuse-related attributions and perceptions, personal self-efficacy, responsibility and shame, and parental support may affect symptom formation in this population. We know far less about the impact of these factors on the clinical and developmental course of sexually abused children over many years. Unfortunately, longitudinal data on sexually abused children has generally been limited to 1 or 2 years. More studies involving longer term follow-up, similar to the 5-year follow-up by Tebbutt et al. (1997), are sorely needed to provide greater understanding as to the developmental course of the different subsets of sexually abused children and the factors that may mediate both positive and negative outcomes.

It must be noted that an undetermined proportion of sexually abused children never disclose their sexual abuse history, at least not during childhood. Accordingly, these children do not come to the attention of the local authorities and are not involved in legal proceedings. Obviously these children do not participate in research studies that examine clinical symptomatology or clinical course in victimized children. Thus, even less is known about this group of sexually abused children in terms of developmental trajectory. They may be symptom free and not display any negative effects from their victimization experience. On the other hand, they may exhibit clinically significant difficulties but because their abuse was never disclosed or discovered, the true source of their problems cannot be determined. Some of these children may ultimately disclose their sexual abuse during adulthood. Unfortunately, a history of sexual abuse during childhood is well documented to be a significant risk factor for many types of adult psychopathology (Neumann, Houskamp, Pollock, & Briere, 1996).

ASSESSMENT AND DIAGNOSIS

Forensic Assessment

As was discussed earlier in the chapter, CSA is a criminal act. Accordingly, the first order of business is determining whether a child has been victimized. Although legal processes may vary from state to state, a number of agencies are typically involved in investigating whether a child has been abused, including the local CPS system, the police, and sometimes the local district attorney's office. To assist in the investigative process, local agencies frequently use the services of mental health professionals, who conduct forensic interviews or assessments with the alleged victim and sometimes the alleged perpetrator to help determine the likelihood of abuse. Forensic evaluators then share their findings with the local authorities and often testify as expert witnesses in civil or criminal proceedings.

It is important to note that a forensic evaluator's role in sexual abuse cases should be clearly defined, with clear-cut boundaries. The forensic evaluator's role is essentially limited to assisting the local authorities in determining the likelihood that abuse has occurred. Forensic evaluators need to clarify with victims and their families that the information provided during the assessment is not confidential in that it will be shared with a third party (e.g., CPS, police). Moreover, forensic evaluators are discouraged from accepting therapeutic roles with sexual abuse victims and their families because of the inherent conflict of interest involved in these roles. Unfortunately, greater elaboration of the role of forensic evaluator and the specific nature of forensic assessments in sexual abuse cases is beyond the scope of this chapter. (The reader is referred to Mannarino and Cohen, 2001, for a comprehensive discussion of the professional role conflicts involved in sexual abuse cases and strategies to avoid them.) Also, excellent references are available regarding appropriate investigative interviewing techniques with alleged child sexual abuse victims (Mannarino & Cohen, 2003; Saywitz, Goodman, & Lyon, 2002).

Clinical Assessment

Sexually abused children are frequently referred for clinical assessment after a forensic evaluator or the local authorities (e.g., CPS, police) have determined that there is a significant likelihood that abuse has occurred. Of course, in some instances, forensic investigations do not result in definitive findings. Nonetheless, children in these situations may be referred for clinical assessment as well. The primary purpose of the clinical assessment with sexually abused children is to evaluate the impact of the victimization experience, determine a working clinical diagnosis, and develop an appropriate treatment plan.

At the time of the clinical assessment, abuse-related information is typically gathered via interviews with the child and family. Relevant information includes the identity of the perpetrator, the child's emotional relationship with the perpetrator, the number of abusive episodes, the duration of the abuse, whether the abuse involved penetration or fondling only, and whether the perpetrator used force or coercion. Additionally, it is helpful to gather information about how the perpetrator elicited the child's cooperation in the absence of force or coercion, the disclosure process, the presence or absence of legal proceedings, and the impact of the abuse on the family. All of this information is valuable in helping to elucidate the impact of the victimization on the child.

Abuse-Specific Measures

To more completely capture the full impact of the abusive experience, it is strongly recommended that abuse-specific measures be used. Fortunately, a number of abuse-specific or abuse-related instruments have been developed over the past decade that enhance the clinician's ability to evaluate sexually abused children in a more focused manner. For example, the Trauma Symptom Checklist for Children was designed by Briere (1996) to assess trauma symptoms in children, including sexual concerns. Also, Friedrich's Child Sexual Behavior Inventory (1997) is an excellent parent-report instrument with strong psychometric properties to assess the presence of sexual behavior problems.

Other abuse-specific measures examine shame in sexually abused children (Feiring et al., 1998, 2002) as well as abuse-related attributions and perceptions such as feeling different from other children, self-blame for negative events, lower interpersonal trust, and lower perceived credibility (Mannarino et al., 1994). Additionally, Mannarino and Cohen (1996c) developed the previously mentioned PERQ to assess the nonoffending parent(s)' level of distress in response to the child's sexual abuse disclosure and the Parental Support Questionnaire to examine the nonoffending parent(s)' perception of who is to blame for the abuse and the parents' emotional support for the victim. All of these measures can provide essential information to determine the specific impact of the abusive experience on both the child and the family.

Diagnosis

Sexually abused children may suffer from a variety of clinical disorders, including post-traumatic stress disorder (PTSD), other anxiety disorders, and depression. Because PTSD is commonly diagnosed in this population, measures that specifically evaluate the presence of this disorder can be extremely useful. In this regard, semistructured interviews with a PTSD section such as the Schedule for Affective Disorders and Schizophrenia (Kaufman, Birmaher, & Brent, 1997) are often used in research studies but typically take too long to administer to be practical for clinicians in community settings. Self-report measures of PTSD such as the Child PTSD Symptom Scale (Foa, Johnson, Feeny, & Treadwell, 2001) can be administered in a more efficient manner. One of the advantages of Foa et al.'s (2001) measure over previous self-report PTSD instruments is that it assesses impairment in functioning in addition to evaluating the presence of reexperiencing, avoidance, and hyperarousal symptoms. Standardized measures for depression such as the Children's Depression Inventory (Kovacs, 1985) and general anxiety such as the Multidimensional Anxiety Scale for Children (March, Parker, Sullivan, Stallings, & Conners, 1997) are valuable in determining the presence of other comorbid clinical disorders.

It is worth mentioning that the PTSD symptoms manifested by sexually abused children sometimes overlap with the clinical symptoms exhibited by children diagnosed with ADHD (e.g., difficulties with concentration). In this regard, it is possible that these children are suffering from both disorders or in some instances, children with PTSD only have been incorrectly diagnosed with ADHD. A comprehensive developmental history will enable the clinician to determine whether the attentional problems predated the sexual abuse experience and are truly reflective of ADHD or that these symptoms presented only after the abuse, in which case they are most likely part of the hyperarousal cluster of PTSD.

IMPACT ON ENVIRONMENT

Family

The impact of CSA on the family is largely dependent on whether the abuse is intra- or extrafamilial. If it is intrafamilial, the effect on the family is likely to be dramatic. The nonoffending parent(s) typically are shocked when they learn that their child has been victimized and experience a great deal of emotional distress (Mannarino & Cohen, 1996c). In contrast to earlier beliefs that the nonoffending parent is collusive with the perpetrator and is aware that the abuse has been occurring, research has demonstrated that the nonoffending parent is often the individual who reports the victimization to the authorities as soon as it has been disclosed or discovered (Mannarino & Cohen, 1986).

In cases of intrafamilial CSA, the authorities (CPS or police) typically mandate that the alleged perpetrator (e.g., parent, stepparent, older sibling) leave the home. The sexually abused child may feel relieved that the perpetrator is gone but also responsible for breaking up the family. Feelings of responsibility may be exacerbated if other family members express anger that the victim disrupted the family by disclosing the abuse. If the perpetrator is a parent or stepparent (usually father or stepfather), the mother may feel betrayed. However, many mothers feel caught in the middle. On the one hand, they may want to believe and support their abused child, but on the other hand, they may still care deeply for their spouse and have some disbelief that the abuse actually occurred. Denial by the mother is not surprising given that most adult perpetrators of CSA do not exhibit significant psychiatric symptoms (Chaffin et al., 2002), do not fit the classic stereotype of a child molester, and may well have a decent job and otherwise be upstanding individuals in their community. It is worth noting that lack of maternal support not only is related to increased symptomatology in the abused child but also increases the likelihood that the child will be taken into protective custody by the local CPS (Hunter, Coulter, Runyan, & Everson, 1990).

When the perpetrator is an older sibling, family members face difficult emotional challenges. Clinically we have observed that parents may minimize the abuse or its impact in order to have the older sibling reunited with the family as soon as possible. In some instances, they may permit the older sibling to visit at the home even if the victim remains scared or is not yet ready for a visit. We have also observed clinically that many victims truly miss their older sibling. Although they are relieved that the abuse has stopped, they are also saddened by the older sibling's departure from the family.

Because CSA is a criminal act, families are also confronted in many cases with legal proceedings, regardless of whether the CSA is intra- or extrafamilial. A great deal of research has been devoted to the impact of legal proceedings on the victimized child (Goodman et al., 1992; Whitcomb et al., 1991). However, far less has been written about their impact on other family members. It has been our experience clinically that many parents are very distressed while awaiting criminal or juvenile court proceedings. In particular, they are very concerned about the impact of testifying on their abused child. Also, there is the added burden of anger and a sense that justice has not been served if the perpetrator is acquitted or given a minimal sentence. Fortunately, many jurisdictions now have victims' advocacy agencies that offer assistance to the sexually abused child and other family members to help them to better understand and become more adequately prepared to deal with the legal processes they must face.

School

Data are relatively scarce regarding the impact of CSA on the victimized child's school experience. Although research has clearly demonstrated that sexually abused children manifest significantly more internalizing and externalizing problems, based on parental report, than nonabused children (Mannarino et al., 1989, 1991), it is not known to what degree these difficulties are exhibited at school. In one study relevant to this issue, Boney-McCoy and Finkelhor (1995) conducted a telephone survey with a national sample of children and adolescents ages 10–16 to ascertain their exposure to violence. They reported that victims of sexual assault were significantly more likely to experience difficulties with a teacher at school than non–sexual assault victims. Clinically we have observed that children with PTSD symptoms secondary to their sexual abuse experience may display difficulties with attention in the classroom or may have reexperiencing symptoms at school that can negatively affect their academic performance.

Some sexual abuse victims may be rejected at school because of their allegations, particularly if the alleged perpetrator is a teacher or popular member of the community and there is disbelief that the abuse really occurred. This rejection can be severe and devastating for the abused child and may necessitate a change in schools. This is unfortunate and can exacerbate a sense of stigmatization and self-blame in the victim.

Peer Interactions

Research has demonstrated that sexually abused children are less socially competent than normal controls (Mannarino et al., 1989) and that these deficits continue to be displayed at a 6-month follow-up assessment (Mannarino et al., 1991). On a more encouraging note, this same cohort of sexually abused children were no different from normal controls in their social competence at the 12-month follow-up. However, at this 12-month follow-up (Mannarino et al., 1991), sexually abused girls who had been subjected to intercourse were significantly less involved in school-related social activities than those subjected to fondling only. Thus, although most sexually abused children may become more socially competent over time, those who have experienced the most severe forms of victimization may continue to display significant difficulties in this domain.

IMPLICATIONS FOR FUTURE PERSONALITY DEVELOPMENT

As one would expect, the relationship between a history of CSA and adult personality development is complicated and most likely influenced by many factors. There are currently no longitudinal studies that follow victimized children throughout the course of their development and into their adult years. A longitudinal design would offer the most rigorous examination of the long-term impact of CSA. Instead, existing studies are retrospective in nature. Additionally, some studies have focused on community samples whereas others have included only a clinical population. Accordingly, findings have varied considerably, with some adult survivors coping well and evidencing few difficulties whereas others exhibit substantial psychopathology.

Nevertheless, reviews of the literature have clearly demonstrated that CSA is a significant risk factor for a variety of emotional and behavioral problems during adulthood (Beitchman et al., 1992; Browne & Finkelhor, 1986; Finkelhor et al., 1990). These problems include general anxiety (Gold, Lucenko, Elhai, Swingle, & Sellers, 1999; Murphy et al., 1988), general trauma symptoms and PTSD (Briere & Elliott, 2003; Peleikis, Mykletun, & Dahl, 2004; Saunders, Villeponteaux, Lipovsky, Kilpatrick, & Veronen, 1992), depression (Briere & Runtz, 1993; Browne & Finkelhor, 1986), and increased likelihood of suicide attempts (Briere & Runtz, 1987; Saunders et al., 1992) and other types of self-harming behaviors (Romans, Martin, Anderson, Herbison, & Mullen, 1995). We also know that among adult female survivors of CSA, there is an increased likelihood of relationship dissatisfaction, poorer communication, and lower trust with partners (DiLillo & Long, 1999). (For a more exhaustive review of the relationship between CSA and adult psychopathology, please see the comprehensive discussion by Berliner and Elliott, 2002.)

A history of CSA also appears to have an impact on a survivor's parenting. In this regard, Alexander, Teti, and Anderson (2000) reported that women with a CSA history and current unsatisfactory intimate relationships were significantly more likely to demonstrate emotional overdependence on their children than CSA survivors with satisfactory intimate relationships or nonabused women. Additionally, in a good review article of the relationship between CSA history and parenting characteristics in women, DiLillo and Damashek (2003) concluded that survivors may have a more difficult time establishing generational boundaries, may be more permissive with their children, and may be at increased risk for using harsh physical discipline.

Despite the well-documented link between CSA and adult psychopathology and possibly between CSA and parenting characteristics, little understanding exists as to what factors mediate these relationships. As discussed earlier, there is a considerable body of knowledge regarding what factors mediate the connection between CSA and childhood difficulties (e.g., impaired trust, cognitive distortions, low parental support). Nonetheless, we do not know whether these same factors mediate outcome among adult survivors. From Finkelhor's traumagenic dynamics model, which focuses on the powerlessness, betrayal, stigmatization, and traumatic sexualization associated with CSA (Finkelhor, 1987), one could hypothesize that significant ongoing difficulties in any of these domains would place the adult survivor at a higher risk for the development of psychological difficulties.

In one study with adult females that focused on possible mediating factors, Barker-Collo (2001) reported that survivors who blamed themselves during childhood for their victimization were at higher risk for trauma symptoms and suicide attempts during adulthood. Interestingly, attributions made during adulthood added little power in predicting adjustment and suicidality. Thus, self-blame during childhood for the victimization experience may well have long-term negative implications for adult adjustment.

Many questions are unanswered about the relationship between CSA and adult functioning. Of course, we know nothing about those adults with a history of CSA who have never disclosed their victimization. This population has never been studied. It is quite possible, though, that studies of a variety of adult disorders (e.g., depression and anxiety) may include survivors of CSA who deny this history or even possibly do not have a memory of their previous victimization (Williams, 1994). Additionally, we know little about what happens to the approximately 30 percent of sexually abused children who are asymptomatic during childhood (Mannarino, 2000). Whether they remain symptom free or develop significant emotional or behavioral problems during late adolescence and adulthood is clearly an area that merits investigation. Finally, there is a tremendous gap in knowledge between our understanding of the impact of sexual abuse on children and adolescents and its long-term impact on adult survivors, the latter based on retrospective analyses. In particular, disclosure of CSA and treatment during childhood, a supportive family environment, and other factors may well ameliorate the long-term negative effects of sexual victimization. Longitudinal studies would go a long way in advancing our understanding of these important issues.

TREATMENT IMPLICATIONS

Although sexual abuse can have a significantly negative effect on children's adjustment and development, recent treatment advances offer considerable hope to these children and their families. In this regard, the most widely studied treatment for sexually abused children has been trauma-focused cognitive-behavioral therapy (TF-CBT; Cohen, Mannarino, & Deblinger, 2002). This treatment has a number of components, including psychoeducation, interventions for affective dysregulation, stress inoculation skills building, exposure-based interventions, cognitive reprocessing, and behavior management. Parents are integrally involved in TF-CBT and receive as much intervention as the children. It is a short-term treatment model, with the number of sessions typically ranging from 12 to 16.

Research evidence has now accumulated that strongly supports the efficacy of TF-CBT with sexually abused children and their nonoffending parents. Deblinger, Lippmann, and Steer (1996; Deblinger, Steer, & Lippmann, 1999) found that children who received TF-CBT (with or without the parents in treatment) made significantly greater improvements in PTSD symptoms, whereas children whose parents received TF-CBT (with or without the children in treatment) made significantly greater gains in child-reported depression and parent-rated behavior problems. These gains were maintained over the course of a 2-year follow-up. Deblinger, Stauffer, and Steer (2001) studied a variant of TF-CBT (group format) with young sexually abused children and found greater gains with this model in the areas of maternal distress related to the abuse and children's development of body safety skills compared with supportive group counseling.

Cohen and Mannarino (1996a, 1997, 1998a) have generated similar results in their treatment studies of sexually abused children. With preschool children, they reported (Cohen & Mannarino, 1996a, 1997) that those who received TF-CBT made significantly greater improvements in PTSD symptoms, sexualized behaviors, and internalizing and externalizing problems than those children who received nondirective supportive therapy (NST) and that these gains were maintained at the 1-year follow-up. With sexually abused children ages 8–15, Cohen and Mannarino (1998a) reported that TF-CBT was more effective than NST in reducing depressive symptoms and enhancing social competence. At a 1-year follow-up, treatment completers who received TF-CBT demonstrated significantly greater gains in PTSD and dissociative symptoms than treatment completers who received NST (Cohen, Mannarino, & Knudsen, in press).

The Cohen and Deblinger teams have recently collaborated to complete the largest treatment study to date of sexually abused children. In a multisite investigation of 229 sexually abused children ages 8–14, they found that TF-CBT was superior to child-centered therapy (a variant of their previous NST) in reducing PTSD and depressive symptoms, behavior problems, shame, and abuse-related attributions in the children and depression and abuse-specific distress in the nonoffending parents (Cohen, Deblinger, Mannarino, & Steer, 2004). Moreover, parents who participated in TF-CBT became significantly more supportive of their victimized child and developed better parenting practices than those who participated in child-centered therapy. This study is noteworthy not only because of the impressiveness of the reported findings, but also because the majority of the children had experienced other traumas in their lives in addition to sexual abuse. Thus, the Cohen et al. (2004) results suggest that TF-CBT is successful in treating children who are multiply traumatized and that improvements occur over a number of domains.

Other studies of trauma-focused treatments with sexually abused children have reported somewhat mixed results. King et al. (2000) found that children assigned to individual or family cognitive behavioral therapy made significantly greater gains than those in a wait list condition. However, in two other studies, sexually abused children receiving trauma-focused treatment did not improve to a greater extent with respect to fear and anxiety symptoms (Berliner & Saunders, 1996) or PTSD symptoms (Celano, Hazzard, Webb, & McCall, 1996) compared with those participating in more nonspecific treatments. However, in the latter study (Celano et al., 1996), parents who received cognitive behavioral therapy developed greater support for their child and demonstrated less self-blame.

Unfortunately, other treatments for sexually abused children have not been rigorously studied. Trowell et al. (2002) reported that sexually abused children who received individual psychoanalytic psychotherapy experienced a significantly greater reduction in PTSD symptoms than those who participated in group psychoeducation. However, the two treatments studied differed in terms of length of treatment and whether they were delivered in a group or individual format. Thus, treatment differences may have been the result of these factors and not the actual type of treatment. Additionally, Downing, Jenkins, and Fisher (1988) reported that sexually abused children who received reinforcement therapy made significantly greater gains in the areas of sleep, enuresis, and sexualized behavior problems than those who participated in psychodynamic treatment.

Psychodynamic therapy and other treatments for sexually abused children with some initial empirical support require more extensive investigation in order to demonstrate whether they are truly effective models of intervention for this population. In this regard, researchers should be encouraged to study treatments other than TF-CBT so that a variety of effective treatments may potentially be available for victimized children. At present, TF-CBT is clearly the treatment for sexually abused children with the greatest empirical support. Moreover, research has demonstrated that inclusion of parents in TF-CBT is vital in achieving the best outcomes (Cohen & Mannarino, 1996a, 1998a; Deblinger et al., 1996). Additional study of TF-CBT would be helpful to determine which of its treatment components are most essential and the optimal length of treatment. It should be encouraging for sexually abused children and their families that effective treatment is available and that treatment during childhood will, it is hoped, reduce the likelihood of the long-term emotional and behavioral difficulties often found in adult survivors of child sexual abuse.

REFERENCES

Alexander, P.C., Teti, L., & Anderson, C. L. (2000). Childhood sexual abuse history and role reversal in parenting. *Child Abuse & Neglect, 24,* 829–838.

Barker-Collo, S. L. (2001). Adult reports of child and adult attributions of blame for childhood sexual abuse: Predicting adult adjustment and suicidal behaviors in females. *Child Abuse & Neglect, 25,* 1329–1341.

Beitchman, J. H., Zucker, K. J., Hood, J. E., daCosat, G. A., Akman, D., & Cassavia, E. (1992). A review of the long-term effects of child sexual abuse. *Child Abuse & Neglect, 16,* 101–118.

Berliner, L., & Elliott, D. M. (2002). Sexual abuse of children. In J. E. B. Myers, L. Berliner, J. Briere, C. T. Hendrix, C. Jenny, & T. A. Reid (Eds.), *The APSAC handbook on child maltreatment* (pp. 55–78). Thousand Oaks, CA: Sage.

Berliner, L., & Saunders, B. E. (1996). Treating fear and anxiety in sexually abused children: Results of a controlled 2-year follow-up study. *Child Maltreatment, 1,* 294–309.

Boney-McCoy, S., & Finkelhor, D. (1995). Psychosocial sequelae of violent victimization in a national youth sample. *Journal of Consulting and Clinical Psychology, 63,* 726–736.

Briere, J. (1996). *Trauma Symptom Checklist for Children (TSCC).* Odessa, FL: Psychological Assessment Resources.

Briere, J., & Elliott, D. M. (2003). Prevalence and psychological sequelae of self-reported childhood physical and sexual abuse in a general population sample of men and women. *Child Abuse & Neglect, 27,* 1205–1222.

Briere, J., & Runtz, M. (1987). Post-sexual abuse trauma: Data and implications for clinical practice. *Journal of Interpersonal Violence, 2,* 367–379.

Briere, J., & Runtz, M. (1993). Child sexual abuse: Long-term sequelae and implications for assessments. *Journal of Interpersonal Violence, 8,* 312–330.

Browne, A., & Finkelhor, D. (1986). Impact of child sexual abuse: A review of the research. *Psychological Bulletin, 18,* 66–77.

Celano, M., Hazzard, A., Webb, C., & McCall, C. (1996). Treatment of traumagenic beliefs among sexually abused girls and their mothers: An evaluation study. *Journal of Abnormal Child Psychology, 24,* 1–7.

Chaffin, M., Letourneau, E., & Silovsky, J. F. (2002). Adults, adolescents and children who sexually abuse children: A developmental perspective. In J. E. B. Myers, L. Berliner, J. Briere, C. T. Hendrix, C. Jenny, & T. A. Reid (Eds.), *The APSAC handbook on child maltreatment* (2nd ed., pp. 205–232). Thousand Oaks, CA: Sage.

Cohen, J. A., Deblinger, E., Mannarino, A. P., & Steer, R. (2004). A multisite, randomized controlled trial for sexually abused children with PTSD symptoms. *Journal of the American Academy of Child and Adolescent Psychiatry, 43,* 393–402.

Cohen, J. A., & Mannarino, A. P. (1996a). A treatment outcome study for sexually abused preschool children: Initial findings. *Journal of the American Academy of Child and Adolescent Psychiatry, 35,* 42–50.

Cohen, J. A., & Mannarino, A. P. (1996b). Factors that mediate treatment outcome of sexually abused preschool children. *Journal of the American Academy of Child and Adolescent Psychiatry, 35,* 1402–1410.

Cohen, J. A., & Mannarino, A. P. (1997). A treatment outcome study of sexually abused preschool children: Outcome during one year follow-up. *Journal of the American Academy of Child and Adolescent Psychiatry, 36,* 1228–1235.

Cohen, J. A., & Mannarino, A. P. (1998a). Interventions for sexually abused children: Initial treatment findings. *Child Maltreatment, 3,* 17–26.

Cohen, J. A., & Mannarino, A. P. (1998b). Factors that mediate treatment outcome of sexually abused preschool children: Six and twelve month follow-up. *Journal of the American Academy of Child and Adolescent Psychiatry, 37,* 44–51.

Cohen, J. A., & Mannarino, A. P. (1999). Sexual abuse. In R. T. Ammerman, M. Hersen, & C. G. Last (Eds.), *Prescriptive treatments for children and adolescents* (2nd ed., pp. 308–328). Needham Heights, MA: Allyn & Bacon.

Cohen, J. A., Mannarino, A. P., & Deblinger, E. (2002). *Child and parent trauma-focused cognitive behavioral therapy treatment manual.* Pittsburgh, PA: Allegheny General Hospital.

Cohen, J. A., Mannarino, A. P., & Knudsen, K. (in press). Treating sexually abused children: One year follow-up of a randomized controlled trial. *Child Abuse & Neglect.*

Conte, J. R., Wolfe, S., & Smith, T. (1989). What sexual offenders tell us about prevention strategies. *Child Abuse & Neglect, 13,* 293–302.

Deblinger, E., Lippmann, J., & Steer, R. (1996). Sexually abused children suffering posttraumatic stress symptoms: Initial treatment outcome findings. *Child Maltreatment, 1,* 310–321.

Deblinger, E., Stauffer, L. B., & Steer, R. A. (2001). Comparative efficacies of supportive and cognitive behavioral group therapies for young children who have been sexually abused and their nonoffending mothers. *Child Maltreatment, 6,* 332–343.

Deblinger, E., Steer, R., & Lippman, J. (1999). Two-year follow-up study of cognitive behavioral therapy for sexually abused children suffering posttraumatic stress symptoms. *Child Abuse and Neglect, 23,* 1371–1378.

DiLillo, D., & Damashek, A. (2003). Parenting characteristics of women reporting a history of childhood sexual abuse. *Child Maltreatment, 8,* 319–333.

DiLillo, D., & Long, P. J. (1999). Perceptions of couple functioning among female survivors of child sexual abuse. *Journal of Child Sexual Abuse, 7,* 59–76.

Downing, J., Jenkins, S. J., & Fisher, G. L. (1988). A comparison of psychodynamic and reinforcement treatment with sexually abused children. *Elementary School Guidance Counseling, 22,* 291–298.

Einbender, A. J., & Friedrich, W. N. (1989). Psychological functioning and behavior of sexually abused girls. *Journal of Consulting and Clinical Psychology, 57,* 155–157.

Elliott, D. M., & Briere, J. (1995). Posttraumatic stress associated with delayed recall of sexual abuse: A general population study. *Journal of Traumatic Stress, 8,* 629–647.

Everson, M. D., Hunter, W. M., Runyan, D. K., Edelsohn, G. A., & Coulter, M. L. (1989). Maternal support following disclosure of incest. *American Journal of Orthopsychiatry, 59,* 197–207.

Feiring, C., Taska, L., & Chen, K. (2002). Trying to understand why horrible things happen: Attribution, shame, and symptom development following sexual abuse. *Child Maltreatment, 7,* 26–41.

Feiring, C., Taska, L., & Lewis, M. (1998). The role of shame and attributional style in children's and adolescents' adaptation to sexual abuse. *Child Maltreatment, 3,* 129–142.

Finkelhor, D. (1984). *Child sexual abuse: New theory and research.* New York: Free Press.

Finkelhor, D. (1987). The trauma of child sexual abuse: Two models. *Journal of Interpersonal Violence, 2,* 348–366.

Finkelhor, D. (1990). Early and long-term effects of child sexual abuse: An update. *Professional Psychology: Research and Practice, 21,* 325–330.

Finkelhor, D., & Barron, L. (1986). Risk factors for sexual abuse. *Journal of Interpersonal Violence, 1,* 43–71.

Finkelhor, D., Hotaling, G., Lewis, I. A., & Smith, C. (1990). Sexual abuse in a national survey of adult men and women: Prevalence, characteristics, and risk factors. *Child Abuse & Neglect, 14,* 19–28.

Foa, E. B., Johnson, K. M., Feeny, N. C., & Treadwell, K. R. H. (2001). The Child PTSD Symptom Scale: A preliminary examination of its psychometric properties. *Journal of Clinical Child Psychology, 30,* 376–384.

Ford, J. D., Racusin, R., Daviss, W. B., Ellis, C., Thomas, J., Rogers, K., et al. (1999). Trauma exposure among children with attention deficit hyperactivity disorder and oppositional defiant disorder. *Journal of Consulting and Clinical Psychology, 67,* 786–789.

Friedrich, W. N. (1997). *Child Sexual Behavior Inventory.* Odessa, FL: Psychological Assessment Resources.

Gold, S. N., Lucenko, B. A., Elhai, J. D., Swingle, J. M., & Sellers, A. H. (1999). A comparison of psychological/psychiatric symptomatology of women and men sexually abused as children. *Child Abuse & Neglect, 23,* 683–692.

Gomez-Schwartz, B., Horowitz, J. M., & Sauzier, M. (1985). Severity of emotional distress among sexually abused preschool, school-aged, and adolescent children. *Hospital and Community Psychiatry, 36,* 503–508.

Goodman, G. S., Taub, E. P., Jones, D. P. H., England, P., Port, L. K., Rudy, L., et al. (1992). Emotional effects of criminal court testimony on child sexual assault victims. *Monographs of the Society for Research on Child Development, 57,* 1–163.

Hanson, R. F., Saunders, B. E., & Lipovsky, J. A. (1992). The relationship between self-reported levels of distress in parents and victims of incest families. *Journal of Child Sexual Abuse, 1,* 49–61.

Herrenkohl, R. C., Herrenkohl, E. C., & Egolf, B. P. (1983). Circumstances surrounding the occurrence of child maltreatment. *Journal of Consulting and Clinical Psychology, 51,* 424–431.

Hunter, W. M., Coulter, M. L., Runyan, D. K., & Everson, M. D. (1990). Determinants of placement for sexually abused children. *Child Abuse & Neglect, 14,* 407–418.

Kalichman, S. C. (1993). *Mandated reporting of suspected child abuse: Ethics, law and policy.* Washington, DC: American Psychological Association.

Kaufman, J., Birmaher, B., Brent, D. A., Rao, U., Flynn, C., Moreci, P., et al. (1996). Schedule for Affective Disorders and Schizophrenia for School-Aged Children: Present and Lifetime version (K-SADS-PL): Initial reliability and validity data. *Journal of the American Academy of Child and Adolescent Psychiatry, 36,* 980–988.

Kendall-Tackett, K. A., Williams, L. M., & Finkelhor, D. (1993). Impact of sexual abuse on children: A review and synthesis of recent empirical studies. *Psychological Bulletin, 113,* 164–180.

King, N. J., Tange, B. J., Mullen, P., Myerson, N., Heyne, D., Rollings, S., et al. (2000). Treating sexually abused children with posttraumatic stress symptoms: A randomized clinical trial. *Journal of the American Academy of Child and Adolescent Psychiatry, 39,* 1347–1355.

Kovacs, M. (1985). The Children's Depression Inventory (CDI). *Psychopharmacology Bulletin, 21,* 995–998.

Leifer, M., Shapiro, J. P., & Kassem, L. (1993). The impact of maternal history and behavior upon foster placement and adjustment in sexually abused girls. *Child Abuse & Neglect, 17,* 755–766.

Mannarino, A. P. (2000). Asymptomatic sexually abused children. *Trauma, Violence, and Abuse, 1,* 191–193.

Mannarino, A. P., & Cohen, J. A. (1986). A clinical-demographic study of sexually abused children. *Child Abuse & Neglect, 10,* 17–23.

Mannarino, A. P., & Cohen, J. A. (1996a). Abuse-related attributions and perceptions, general attributions, and locus of control in sexually abused girls. *Journal of Interpersonal Violence, 11,* 162–180.

Mannarino, A. P., & Cohen, J. A. (1996b). A follow-up study of factors that mediate the development of psychological symptomatology in sexually abused girls. *Child Maltreatment, 1,* 246–260.

Mannarino, A. P., & Cohen, J. A. (1996c). Family-related variables and psychological symptom formation in sexually abused girls. *Journal of Child Sexual Abuse, 5,* 105–120.

Mannarino, A. P., & Cohen, J. A. (2001). Treating sexually abused children and their families: Identifying and avoiding professional role conflicts. *Trauma, Violence, and Abuse, 2,* 331–342.

Mannarino, A. P., & Cohen, J. A. (2003). Sexually and physically abused children. In M. Hersen & S. M. Turner (Eds.), *Diagnostic interviewing* (3rd ed., pp. 415–432). New York: Kluwer.

Mannarino, A. P., & Cohen, J. A. (in press). Ethical issues in child abuse practice. In J. Conte (Ed.), *Encyclopedia of trauma and abuse.* Thousand Oaks, CA: Sage.

Mannarino, A. P., Cohen, J. A., & Berman, S. R. (1994). The Children's Attributions and Perceptions Scale: A new measure of sexual abuse-related factors. *Journal of Clinical Child Psychology, 23,* 204–211.

Mannarino, A. P., Cohen, J. A., & Gregor, M. (1989). Emotional and behavioral difficulties in sexually abused girls. *Journal of Interpersonal Violence, 4,* 437–451.

Mannarino, A. P., Cohen, J. A., Smith, J. A., & Moore-Motily, S. (1991). Six- and twelve-month follow-up of sexually abused girls. *Journal of Interpersonal Violence, 6,* 494–511.

March, J. S., Parker, J. D. A., Sullivan, K., Stallings, P., & Conners, C. K. (1997). The multidimensional anxiety scale for children: Factor structure, reliability, and validity. *Journal of the American Academy of Child and Adolescent Psychiatry, 36,* 554–565.

McLeer, S. V., Deblinger, E., Atkins, M. S., Foa, E. B., & Ralphe, D. L. (1988). Posttraumatic stress disorder in sexually abused children: A perspective study. *Journal of the American Academy of Child and Adolescent Psychiatry, 138,* 119–125.

McLeer, S. V., Deblinger, E., Henry, D., & Orvaschel, H. (1992). Sexually abused children at high risk for posttraumatic stress disorder. *Journal of the American Academy of Child & Adolescent Psychiatry, 31,* 875–879.

Morrow, K. B. (1991). Attributions of female adolescent incest victims regarding their molestation. *Child Abuse & Neglect, 15,* 477–483.

Murphy, S. M., Kilpatrick, D. G., Amick-McMullan, A., Veronen, L. J., Paduhovich, L., Best, C. L., et al. (1988). Current psychological functioning of child sexual assault survivors: A community study. *Journal of Interpersonal Violence, 3,* 55–79.

Neumann, D. A., Houskamp, B. M., Pollock, V. E., & Briere, J. (1996). The long-term sequelae of childhood sexual abuse in women: A meta-analytic review. *Child Maltreatment, 1,* 6–16.

Oates, R. K., O'Toole, B. I., Lynch, D. L., Stern, A., & Cooney, G. (1994). Stability and change in outcomes for sexually abused children. *Journal of the American Academy of Child and Adolescent Psychiatry, 33,* 945–953.

Peleikis, D. E., Mykletun, A., & Dahl, A. (2004). The relative influence of childhood sexual abuse and other family background risk factors on adult adversities in female outpatients treated for anxiety disorders and depression. *Child Abuse & Neglect, 28,* 61–76.

Romans, S. E., Martin, J. L., Anderson, J. C., Herbison, P. G., & Mullen, P. E. (1995). Sexual abuse in childhood and deliberate self-harm. *American Journal of Psychiatry, 152,* 1335–1342.

Runyan, D. K., Everson, M. D., Edelsohn, G. A., Hunter, W. M., & Coulter, M. L. (1988). Impact of intervention on sexually abused children. *Journal of Pediatrics, 113,* 647–653.

Saunders, B. E., Villeponteaux, L. A., Lipovsky, J. A., Kilpatrick, D. G., & Veronen, L. J. (1992). Child sexual assault as a risk factor for mental disorders among women: A community survey. *Journal of Interpersonal Violence, 7,* 189–204.

Saywitz, K. J., Goodman, G. S., & Lyon, T. D. (2002). Interviewing children in and out of court: Current research and practice implications. In J. E. B. Myers, L. Berliner, J. Briere, C. T. Hendrix, C. Jenny, & T. A. Reid (Eds.), *The APSAC handbook on child maltreatment* (2nd ed., pp. 349–377). Thousand Oaks, CA: Sage.

Saywitz, K. J., Mannarino, A. P., Berliner, L., & Cohen, J. A. (2000). Treatment for sexually abused children and adolescents. *American Psychologist, 55,* 1040–1049.

Scheeringa, M. S., Peebles, C. D., Cook, C. A., & Zeanah, C. H. (2001). Toward establishing procedural, criterion and discriminant validity for PTSD in early childhood. *Journal of the American Academy of Child and Adolescent Psychiatry, 40,* 52–60.

Scheeringa, M. S., Zeanah, C., Myers, L., & Putnam, F. W. (2003). New findings on alternative criteria for PTSD in preschool children. *Journal of the American Academy of Child and Adolescent Psychiatry, 42,* 561–570.

Strauss, M. A., Gelles, R., & Steinmetz, S. (1980). *Behind closed doors: Violence in the American family.* New York: Doubleday.

Tebbutt, K., Swanston, H., Oates, R. K., & O'Toole, B. I. (1997). Five years after child sexual abuse: Persisting dysfunction and problems of prediction. *Journal of the American Academy of Child and Adolescent Psychiatry, 36,* 330–339.

Trowell, J., Kolvin, I., Weeramanthri, T., Sadowski, H., Berelowitz, M., Glasser, D., et al. (2002). Psychotherapy for sexually abused girls: Psychopathological outcome finding and patterns of change. *British Journal of Psychiatry, 160,* 234–247.

Whitcomb, D., Runyan, D. K., DeVos, E., Hunter, W. M., Gross, T. P., Everson, M. D., et al. (1991). *Child victim as witness research and development program* (Executive Summary, Grant #87-MC-CX-0026). Washington, DC: Office of Juvenile Justice and Delinquency Prevention, Office of Justice Programs, U.S. Department of Justice.

Williams, L. (1994). Recall of childhood trauma: A prospective study of women's memories of child sexual abuse. *Journal of Consulting and Clinical Psychology, 62,* 1167–1176.

CHAPTER 24

Somatization Disorders

BRENDA BURSCH

DESCRIPTION OF THE DISORDERS AND CLINICAL PICTURE

Children and adolescents commonly experience persistent physical symptoms that are not clearly accounted for by identifiable medical illness or tissue pathology (Campo & Fritsch, 1994; Garber, Walker, & Zeman, 1991). The symptoms are sometimes quite severe, and some symptomatic children have great difficulty coping and become disabled. Disabling somatic symptoms can occur in the presence or absence of an identifiable etiology and in the presence or absence of other medical or psychiatric disorders. Those individuals who have unexplained symptoms (not volitionally produced) and who are inexplicably distressed or disabled by symptoms that appear to be in excess of what would be expected from history, physical examination, or laboratory findings are defined by the *DSM-IV* (American Psychiatric Association [APA], 1994) as having a somatoform disorder.

Historically, unexplained chronic somatic symptoms have been considered to be solely the result of stress or a psychiatric problem, leading many to view the symptoms themselves as not real, faked, or exaggerated. Despite the fact that an essential feature of a somatoform disorder is that it is not intentionally produced, some clinicians confuse somatoform disorders with malingering, using language to suggest that the symptoms are volitionally produced for external incentives.

As researchers study the connections between the brain, the digestive system, and the immune system in nonclinical samples, many of these disorders are becoming better understood within a biopsychosocial context. Consequently, a number of symptom clusters that were previously considered fundamentally psychiatric are now called functional disorders, with or without comorbid psychiatric disorders. Research in the area of functional disorders is expanding and deserves mention as it relates to somatization disorders. A functional disorder refers to a disorder or disease where the primary abnormality is an altered physiological function (the way the body works) rather than an identifiable structural cause. Similar to the *DSM-IV*, functional disorder diagnostic criteria are being developed for a number of disorders (e.g., adult and pediatric functional gastrointestinal disorders). Such disorders generally cannot be diagnosed in a traditional way as an inflammatory, infectious, or structural abnormality that can be seen by commonly used examination, X-ray, or laboratory test. As the biological mechanisms causing chronic somatic symptoms are being revealed (e.g., abnormal motility or hypersensitivity in the gastrointestinal tract), there is a heightened interest in better understanding what places someone at higher risk for chronic somatic symptoms and disability, and why some people are disabled by their symptoms and others are not. The main point is that the conceptual understanding of chronic somatic symptoms and somatization disorders is currently evolving, whereas the practice of dichotomizing disorders as biological *or* psychiatric is fading.

Fritz, Fritsch, and Hagino (1997) suggested that somatization disorders can be considered the severe end of a disability continuum that includes functional somatic symptoms in the middle and minor transient symptoms at the other end. Others suggest that disability be assessed and treated similarly regardless of the associated symptoms and presumed etiologies of the symptoms (Bursch, 1999). This would remove the need to determine if the disability is in excess of what would be expected from the disorder. Such attempts at definition clarification reflect research and clinical observations that (1) specific symptom clusters, the presence or absence of a currently defined medical disorders, or level of disability cannot be used in isolation for comprehensive assessment or treatment, and (2) doing so can sometimes hinder appropriate care.

Recently, Sharpe and Mayou (2004) summarized the theoretical and practical limitations of the current use of somatoform disorder criteria and called for reconsideration of this conceptual framework. They cited the main theoretical limitation to be the assumption of psychogenesis when symptoms are not well understood or commensurate with apparent disease severity. They pointed out, as an example, that the symptoms of individuals with cardiovascular disease have only a limited relationship with objectively measured disease severity (Ruo et al., 2003). They listed the following practical limitations: (1) clinician-patient rapport is hindered because patients frequently do not accept the psychogenic implication of the diagnosis (Stone et al., 2002); (2) anxiety and depression may be underdiagnosed when a patient is given a diagnosis of a somatoform disorder; (3) somatoform disorders do not correspond well with the more widely used medical classification of functional somatic syndromes; (4) the accepted criteria for validity or reliability are not met for somatoform disorders; and (5) the diagnosis of a somatoform disorder carries minimal value in guiding treatment recommendations. They recommended that the problems captured by these diagnoses be reassigned to other sections of the *DSM* and the somatoform disorders themselves abolished.

The diagnostic criteria for somatoform disorders were established for adults, and most of the related research is with adult populations. The criteria are applied to children in the absence of child-specific diagnostic criteria. The *DSM-IV* includes diagnostic criteria for seven somatoform disorders: somatization disorder, conversion disorder, pain disorder, hypochondriasis, body dysmorphic disorder (BDD), undifferentiated somatoform disorder, and somatoform disorder not otherwise specified (NOS). The remainder of this section will briefly review the diagnostic criteria for each of the disorders, along with comments about the state of the literature for children and adolescents.

DSM-IV criteria for somatization disorder require several years of physical complaints and associated treatment seeking or disability, with at least four pain symptoms, two gastrointestinal symptoms, one sexual symptom, and one pseudoneurological symptom. Though abdominal pain occurring with other pain (including headache and limb pain) and other somatic symptoms have been shown in pediatric community samples (Aro, Paronen, & Aro, 1987; Zuckerman, Stevenson, & Bailey, 1987), the diagnosis of somatization disorder is relatively rare in children and adolescents, partially due to the requirements for several years of complaints and disability and for one sexual symptom. Consequently, there is little in the literature on this topic for children and adolescents.

The criteria for a conversion disorder require one or more unexplained symptoms or deficits affecting voluntary motor or sensory function that suggest a neurological or other medical condition, and distress or functional impairment. Additionally, this disorder requires that psychological factors be judged to be associated with the symptom or deficit based on the timing of the symptom appearance or exacerbation with conflicts or other stressors. The specified subtypes are with motor symptom or deficit, sensory symptom or deficit, sei-

zures or convulsions, and mixed presentation. In the pediatric literature on this topic, symptoms frequently reported include pseudoseizures, paresis, paresthesia, and gait disturbances (Grattan-Smith, Fairley, & Procopis, 1988; Leslie, 1988; Spierings, Pocls, Sijben, Gabreals, & Renier, 1990; Thomson & Sills, 1988). It is important to note that *La belle indifference,* the lack of concern by the patient for his or her primary symptom, has been reported in as few as 8 percent of pediatric cases (Spierings et al., 1990).

A somatoform pain disorder is diagnosed when a patient's predominant complaint is of unexplained physical pain in one or more body parts that causes distress or impairment and for which "psychological factors are judged to have played a significant role in the onset, severity, exacerbation, or maintenance of the pain" (APA, 1994, p. 461). Subtypes include somatoform pain disorder with psychological factors and with both psychological factors and a general medical condition. It is considered acute if it is present for less than 6 months and chronic if it is present for longer. Children and adolescents frequently report pain (e.g., Fearon, McGrath, & Achat, 1996; Goodman & McGrath, 1991; Perquin, Hazebroek-Kampschreur, Hunfeld, Bohnen, et al., 2000; Perquin, Hazebroek-Kampschreur, Hunfeld, van Suijlekom-Smit, et al., 2000). Although abdominal pain is the most frequent symptom reported among younger children, children and adolescents also report headaches, limb pain, and other body pain. Population-based studies suggest that 15 percent to 20 percent of school-age children and adolescents report at least three episodes of significant pain in the abdominal region within a period of 3 months and that abdominal pain accounts for a substantial portion of all pediatric office visits (Colletti, 1998). The majority of these children (approximately 75 percent) do not have an identifiable disease to account for the pain. Some of them become highly distressed or disabled by their symptoms, and some meet criteria for a somatoform pain disorder due to a preponderance of psychological factors that are thought to be relevant. A growing literature on functional pediatric chronic pain is influencing thinking about somatization in general. It is interesting to note that no psychosocial measures have been found to consistently differentiate children and adolescents with recurrent nonorganic abdominal pain from those with organically based abdominal pain (Pritchard, Ball, Culbert, & Faust, 1988; Walker, Garber, & Greene, 1993; Walker & Greene, 1991). This finding supports a biopsychosocial conceptual framework for abdominal pain rather than the familiar organic/nonorganic dichotomy. Factors that predict disability have been identified and will be discussed elsewhere in this chapter.

Hypochondriasis criteria require 6 months of distress or impairment due to a preoccupation with unexpected fears of having, or the idea that one has, a serious disease based on the misinterpretation of bodily symptoms. Reassurance and thorough medical evaluation do not reduce such fears, but the individual neither is delusional nor meets criteria for BDD or another explanatory anxiety disorder. Additionally, the diagnosis requires that the clinician add the notation "with poor insight" if, for most of the time during the current episode, the person does not recognize that the concern about having a serious illness is excessive or unreasonable. There is very little in the literature about the occurrence of hypochondriasis in children and adolescents. Because children and adolescents typically require their parents to transport them to medical care and also to help them interpret the meaning of bodily sensations, it could be hypothesized that one would be more likely to see hypochondriasis by proxy in pediatric settings.

BDD requires excessive concern or preoccupation with a real or imagined defect in body appearance, not better accounted for by an eating disorder or other psychiatric disorder. One article suggests the presence of this disorder in about 2.3 percent of adolescents in a community sample (Mayville, Katz, Gipson, & Cabral, 1999), with skin concerns being most common.

Undifferentiated somatoform disorder requires 6 months of one or more unexplained physical complaints, and distress or unexpected functional impairment that do not better fit criteria for another somatoform (or other *DSM*) disorder. And somatoform disorder not otherwise specified (NOS) captures other somatoform disorders not meeting criteria for one of the specific disorders. Chronic, distressing, and disabling somatic symptoms that do not meet criteria for one of the other disorders has been systematically identified in the adolescent population, and the related literature crosses a number of symptom cluster domains.

PERSONALITY DEVELOPMENT AND PSYCHOPATHOLOGY

Stuart and Noyes (1999) hypothesized that somatizing behavior is best conceptualized as a behavior that is driven by an anxious and maladaptive attachment style. Research into personality traits of children and adolescents with somatic preoccupation shows some consistency in results. In this section we will review such findings and their implications for the development and maintenance of somatic symptoms and associated disability.

Behaviorally inhibited temperament has been linked to variability in stress reactivity, to a propensity to activate neural circuits that generate distress responses to threatening stimuli, and to the development of anxiety disorders and somatic complaints in childhood (Boyce, Barr, & Zeltzer, 1992; Kagan, Reznick, & Snidman, 1988; Manassis, Bradley, Goldberg, Hood, & Price-Swinson, 1995; Rosenbaum, et al., 1993).

Davison, Faull, and Nicol (1986) studied temperament in a group of 6-year-olds with recurrent abdominal pain and in a control group. They reported that those children with recurrent abdominal pain were temperamentally more difficult than those without pain. They also reported that the girls had more irregular temperamental styles and the boys were more likely to withdraw in new situations. They hypothesized that abdominal pain represents an interaction between a vulnerable temperamental style and environmental stresses.

Campo et al. (2004) examined temperament in 42 pediatric abdominal pain patients and 38 routine care patients without pain (aged 8–15 years) in pediatric primary care. The patients with recurrent abdominal pain, compared to the controls, were significantly more likely to receive a diagnosis of anxiety disorders (79 percent) and depressive disorders (43 percent) and had higher levels of anxiety and depressive symptoms, temperamental harm avoidance, and functional impairment. The authors suggested that functional abdominal pain may be the manifestation of a generalized sensitivity to perceived novel or threatening stimuli. They also noted that harm avoidance has previously been linked with behavioral inhibition, pessimistic worry, fear of uncertainty, tendency to respond to environmental challenge at lower thresholds, vulnerability to anxiety and depressive disorders, and adult functional gastrointestinal symptoms.

As part of a larger study, Olafsdottir, Ellertsen, Berstad, and Fluge (2001) looked at personality profiles of 25 pediatric patients with recurrent abdominal pain (aged 7–15 years) using the Personality Inventory for Children. Of these 25 patients, 16 had high scores on somatic concern, with 8 over the clinical cutoff. Several patients had scores in the clinical range for depression (5), withdrawal (6), and anxiety (7), but the mean scores for the group as a whole were within the normal range for healthy children. Interestingly, 15 patients had scores above (11) or close to (4) the clinical cutoff value on the lie scale. Elevations on the lie scale are most often interpreted as a sign that the parent is denying problem behaviors in the child. However, it is also possibly a sign that the child is relatively passive, is exceedingly well behaved, has high standards, is perfectionistic, or a combination of these. Of note, 10 of the children also reported that they were harassed at school, and 12 frequently missed school due to pain. Ten had moved residence in the last 5 years, and 7 had experienced other severe family stress. Guidetti et al. (1987)

also used the Personality Inventory for Children with 40 children with migraine and in 40 controls (aged 8–14 years). They also found that children with migraines were not globally different from the controls, but they did have significantly higher scores on the somatic concern, depression, and anxiety scales.

Conceptually related are the topics of anxiety sensitivity and catastrophizing. Pain catastrophizing, including rumination, magnification, and helplessness, is one predictor of pain experience and pain-related disability in clinical samples. Catastrophizing has been significantly related to increased lab pain in healthy children and pediatric pain samples as young as 7 years old, and females typically score higher than males on catastrophizing measures (Gil et al., 1993; Keefe et al., 2000; Lester, Lefebvre, & Keefe, 1994; Piira, Taplin, Goodenough, & von Baeyer, 2002; Sullivan et al., 2001; Thastum, Zachariae, & Herlin, 2001; Thastum, Zachariae, Scholer, Bjerring, & Herlin, 1997). Anxiety sensitivity refers to the tendency to interpret anxiety-related bodily sensations (e.g., rapid heartbeat) as dangerous. Anxiety sensitivity in adults has been associated with anxiety disorders (Taylor, 1999) and chronic pain (Asmundson, Norton, & Veloso, 1999). Additionally, parent anxiety sensitivity (AS) and depression have been demonstrated to be strong predictors of child lab pain responses in a sample of healthy children. Watt, Stewart, and Cox (1998) retrospectively studied the relationship between early learning experiences and the development of AS in a nonclinical sample of 551 university students. Interestingly, the learning experiences of high-AS individuals involved increased parental reinforcement of sick-role behavior related to somatic symptoms in general (rather than to only anxiety-specific symptoms). High-AS subjects reported both more somatic symptoms as a child and more special attention from parents when they had symptoms. The authors concluded that AS may arise from learning to catastrophize about the occurrence of bodily symptoms.

Hyman et al. (2002) retrospectively reviewed the charts of 40 patients (aged 13 ± 2 years; range 7–21 years, 18 male) diagnosed with symptom-based criteria for one or more functional gastrointestinal disorders and meeting disability criteria for a somatoform pain disorder. The chief complaints included abdominal pain (30), nausea (5), regurgitation (3), and chest pain (2). Comorbid diagnoses included anxiety disorders (12), depression (5), substance dependence (1), atypical eating disorder (1), pervasive developmental disorders (2), and malingering (1). Almost all had disordered sleep (39). Twenty of the children (50 percent) were described by their parents as highly organized, neat, and perfectionistic in personality. High scholastic, athletic, or artistic achievement, or a combination of these, was present before development of pain-associated disability in 20 patients (50 percent), including many patients with previously unrecognized learning disabilities. More than half of the patients (22) had learning disorders, including subtle receptive or expressive language disorder (15), attention-deficit/hyperactivity disorder (3), pervasive developmental disorders (2), and mild mental retardation (2). Interestingly, parents were aware of the learning disability prior to evaluation in only 13 of these cases, and one case of Asperger's disorder was previously unrecognized. Also identified were unrealistic goals in the perfectionistic, high-achieving children; early childhood pain experiences; passive, dependent coping styles; marital problems in the home; and a parent with chronic illness. All patients had at least two associated factors, and a majority had four or more. Possible triggering events included viral illness in 20, school change in 11, trauma in 2, death of a loved one in 2, and sexual abuse in 2.

With similar findings, Rangel, Garralda, Levin, and Roberts (2000) followed up on 25 adolescents with diagnoses of chronic fatigue syndrome (CFS) and compared them with 15 matched healthy controls. They found that CFS patients were significantly more likely than controls to have personality difficulty, with more frequent personality features than controls that included conscientiousness (fussy, perfectionistic, setting high standards), vulnerability, worthlessness, and emotional lability. They found personality difficulty (high scores) to be significantly correlated with psychological symptoms and decreased social competence.

Wyllie, Glazer, Benbadis, Kotagal, and Wolgamuth (1999) studied 34 pediatric patients who were interviewed by a psychiatrist after diagnosis of pseudoseizures by ictal video electroencephalogram (aged 9–18 years, mean age 14 years; 74 percent female). In addition to conversion disorder, 11 patients (32 percent) had mood disorders, 8 (24 percent) had separation anxiety and school refusal, and 2 (6 percent) had a psychotic disorder. Smaller numbers (1–3 patients) had panic disorder, overanxious disorder, adjustment disorder, oppositional defiant disorder, or impulse control disorder. Eleven patients (32 percent) had a reported history of sexual abuse, and 2 patients (6 percent) had a history of physical abuse. Fifteen (44 percent) had severe family stressors (including parental divorce, marital discord, or death of a close family member). Four patients (12 percent) were deemed to have personality disorders based on *DSM-IV* criteria. Axis II diagnoses included mild mental retardation (2), dependent traits (2), borderline personality disorder (2), mixed personality disorder (1), and histrionic personality disorder (1). Conscientiousness, obsessiveness, or perfectionism were not reported for this patient population.

Shapiro and Rosenfeld (1987) conducted psychological testing with 14 conversion-disordered children who visited a pediatric neurology clinic. Cognitive and academic assessment revealed that 9 of 14 patients had a mild to severe learning disability. The most consistent Wechsler Intelligence Scale for Children—Revised (WISC-R) finding among 10 somatoform-disordered patients was their inability to complete arithmetic calculations compared to their baseline functioning ($p < .05$). Objective personality testing resulted in profiles of patients who often appeared overnormal due to a significant amount of denial of emotional distress. Shapiro and Rosenfeld reported that only one third of their sample had elevated scores on the scales of defensiveness (validity scale K), hypochondriasis (clinical scale 1), and hysteria (clinical scale 3). Rorschach protocols of 14 somatoform-disordered pediatric patients presenting with neurological symptoms revealed significant difficulty in perceptual accuracy in 12 cases. Additionally, the authors noted unusually large numbers of detailed responses, special scores, and false positive results on the schizophrenia index, as well as difficulty responding to emotional stimuli. They found higher levels of pathology in the polysymptomatic patients.

Lambert (1941) was among the first to suggest possible learning disorders among children with chronic pain disorders. In his description of a series of 25 children with recurrent abdominal pain, he reported that despite a relatively high median IQ of approximately 110, many children exhibited difficulties in school. The topic of learning disorders in pediatric chronic pain patients remains understudied despite the high rates of school problems. There is emerging case-based data to suggest that previously undiagnosed pervasive developmental disorders might also be underrecognized in this population (Bursch, Ingman, Vitti, Hyman, & Zeltzer, 2004; Bursch & Zeltzer, 2002; Malloy & Manning-Courtney, 2003). This could account for some pediatric patients, and perhaps even many adult patients, being diagnosed with personality disorders.

EPIDEMIOLOGY

Complaints of recurrent or chronic somatic symptoms in children and adolescents are common. However, epidemiological data for *DSM-IV* somatoform disorders in children are difficult to collect due to diagnostic criteria requirements and are not readily available. Lieb, Pfister, Mastaler, and Wittchen (2000) reported prevalence data from the Early Developmental Stages of Psychopathology study, in which the Munich-Composite International Diagnostic Interview was used to assess 3,021 German respondents aged 14–24 years. They found that specific *DSM-IV* somatoform disorders were relatively rare, with a lifetime rate in this sample of 2.7 percent. When they used an abridged somatization construct, the Somatic Symptom Index, a higher proportion (10.8 percent of the subjects) met criteria for clinically significant somatoform syndromes. Similarly, in a general population survey, Offord et al. (1987) found recurrent distressing somatic symptoms to be present in 11 percent of girls and 4 percent of boys aged 12–16 years. Prepubertal children are most likely to report one symptom, most commonly abdominal pain or headaches (Belmaker, Espinoza, & Pogrund, 1985; Faull & Nicol, 1986; Garber, Zeman, & Walker, 1990). As age increases, so do reports of multiple symptoms, including limb pain, aching muscles, fatigue, and neurological symptoms (Groholt, Stigum, Nordhagen, & Kohler, 2003; Walker & Greene, 1989, 1991). Additionally, somatic complaints and conversion disorders become more common in females than males around the time of puberty (Apley & Naish, 1958; Groholt et al., 2003; Spierings et al., 1990; Steinhausen, von Aster, Pfieffer, & Gobel, 1989; Stickler & Murphy, 1979). Finally, there appears to be a higher rate of somatization among lower socioeconomic groups (Groholt et al., 2003).

Somatization Disorder/Undifferentiated Somatoform Disorder

No studies have been published on the prevalence of somatization disorders in younger children using the current diagnostic criteria. The Lieb et al. (2000) study of older adolescents and young adults (described earlier) found no cases that met full criteria for somatization disorder. However, Garber et al. (1991) evaluated somatic symptoms in a community sample of 540 school-age children and reported that 1.1 percent endorsed the threshold 13 symptoms required for *DSM-III-R* (APA, 1987) diagnosis of somatization disorder. Commonly reported symptoms in the sample included headaches, fatigue, sore muscles, abdominal distress, back pain, and blurred vision. Although the current diagnostic criteria are thought to result in the rare diagnosis of somatization disorder, reports of multiple somatic symptoms are not uncommon, with 15 percent reporting four or more symptoms in the Garber et al. (1991) study.

Conversion Disorder

Similarly, there are no well-designed studies on the prevalence of conversion disorder in children. The Lieb et al. (2000) study of adolescents and young adults found a lifetime conversion disorder prevalence of 0.4 percent and a 12-month prevalence of 0.2 percent. The term pseudoseizure is used to describe paroxysmal nonepileptic events that are thought to be a relatively common conversion disorder symptom. Although there are no population-based studies of the prevalence of pseudoseizure, or even of the broader range of paroxysmal nonepileptic events, some clinical studies do exist. Duchowny, Resnick, Deray, and Alvarez (1988) evaluated 60 children younger than 10 years of age with episodic signs and symptoms of seizures despite repeatedly normal electroencephalograms. The authors used video electroencephalographic (EEG) recording and determined that 9 children (15 percent) had simple partial and atypical absence seizures and 24 (40 percent) had pseudoseizures presenting as rhythmic movements or staring. Bye and Nunan (1992) evaluated 186 children aged 3 weeks to 17 years with prolonged video and EEG monitoring for possible seizure activity. They found that 74 of them were having non-ictal events. Twenty-six of them were developmentally delayed, neurologically impaired, or both. Twenty-four received a specific diagnosis of a non-ictal event, including: spasticity in children with neurological impairment (6), Munchausen syndrome by proxy (5), pseudoseizures (3), breath holding (2), masturbation (2), reflux (2), shudder (1), movement disorder (1), motor tic (1), and pertussis (1). The remaining 51 were described as staring (20), jerks (16), and unusual behavior (15). Grattan-Smith et al. (1988) conducted a retrospective chart review of 52 children (identified from more than 10 years of records) diagnosed with a conversion disorder during admission to a pediatric hospital. They reported that conversion disorder was rare below the age of 8 years and that girls more commonly had this diagnosis (3 to 1). They indicated that 75 percent of the children presented during end-of-year exams or at the beginning of the new school year. Gait disturbance was the primary complaint in 36 children and sensory abnormality, predominantly pain, was present in 40 children. Most children had more than one somatic complaint.

Pain Disorder

The Lieb et al. (2000) study of adolescents and young adults found that the most prevalent somatoform disorder in their sample was pain disorder (lifetime 1.7 percent, 12-month, 1.3 percent). In fact, there is a substantial, and growing, body of literature on the topic of pain problems in childhood and adolescence. The bulk of this research is conceptualized to assess specific pain disorders or pain-associated disability rather than *DSM-IV* somatoform pain disorder. Nevertheless, the overlap is significant and worth reporting here. Headache and recurrent abdominal pain are the most frequently reported painful somatic symptoms, with 10 percent to 30 percent of school-age children and adolescents reporting symptoms as often as weekly (Garber et al., 1991; Larson, 1991; Tamminen et al., 1991). Recurrent abdominal pain (RAP), sometimes meeting criteria for a somatoform pain disorder, is characterized by three or more episodes of abdominal pain that occur over at least 3 months that are severe enough to interfere with activities. Most investigators report that only 5 percent to 10 percent of affected children have an identifiable disease to account for their pain (Apley, 1975; Apley & Naish, 1958). Prevalence rates of RAP vary due to inconsistent use of diagnostic criteria and characteristics of the population being sampled (e.g., age, gender) but range from 9 percent to almost 25 percent (Apley & Naish, 1958; Oster, 1972; Scharff, 1997; Zuckerman et al., 1987). Population-based studies suggest that RAP is experienced by 10 percent to 15 percent of school-age children (Apley, 1975; Apley & Naish, 1958) and about 20 percent of middle school and high school students (Hyams et al., 1996). Hyams, Burke, Davis, Rzepski, and Andrulonis's (1996) study assessed abdominal pain in 507 middle school and high school students. The authors reported that abdominal pain was noted by 75 percent of all students, occurring weekly in 13 percent to 17 percent of the students, and limiting activities in about 21 percent. Irritable bowel syndrome symptoms were reported by 17 percent of the high school students and 8 percent of the middle school students who reported abdominal pain ($n = 381$). Anxiety and depression scores were significantly higher for those with irritable bowel syndrome symptoms. Eight percent of all students had seen a physician for abdominal pain in the previous year. Co-occurrence of RAP with other functional pain, including headache and limb pain, and other types of somatic symptoms has been shown in community samples (Aro et al., 1987; Zuckerman et al., 1987) and in referred samples (Thomsen et al., 2002). The prevalence of headache in children age 7–18 years appears to be about 15 percent, increasing from 8.3 percent for children under 10 years and to approximately 17 percent to 20 percent for those 10 years old or older (Groholt et al., 2003).

Hypochondriasis and Body Dysmorphic Disorder

No epidemiological data are available for hypochondriasis or for BDD in children and adolescents. A series of 188 individuals revealed a mean onset of BDD at age 16.0 years, ± 7.2 years (range = 4–43 years), with 70 percent of cases beginning before age 18 years (Phillips & Diaz, 1997).

ETIOLOGY

It is becoming clearer that somatic symptoms during childhood are the outcome of a dynamic integration of biological processes, psychological factors, and sociocultural context expressed within a particular child's developmental trajectory. Research on the genetics of somatoform disorders is very limited, with little understood about the interplay between genes and other factors in the development of somatoform disorders. Torgersen (1986) conducted a twin study examining somatoform disorders in monozygotic and dizygotic same-sex twins born between 1910 and 1955 in Sweden. Fourteen monozygotic and 21 dizygotic index twins and their cotwins were interviewed. There was a concordance of 29 percent in monozygotic and 10 percent in dizygotic pairs. Torgersen reported that similar childhood experiences seemed to have influenced the concordance rates, suggesting that transmission may be largely environmental. This study also showed a high rate of anxiety disorders, especially generalized anxiety disorders, in the co-twins of somatoform-disordered twins.

Much research has been done examining familial, biological, psychological, and social determinants of pain disorders. Consequently, this body of research might provide the best current model for consideration of somatization in general. Biological processes thought to be relevant for pain disorders (and some other somatic symptoms) include autonomic nervous system reactivity and recovery in response to stress and to symptoms. Psychological processes include attentional biases toward symptom-related stimuli and the ways that children and adolescents cope with environmental stressors and with episodes of symptoms. Social factors include environmental stressors, especially recurrent or chronic stress, and parental responses to children's symptom behavior. Many researchers conceptualize symptom and disability development from a social cognitive theory framework. Within this framework, a significant life event, physical stressor, or developmental challenge has the potential to render a high-risk child somatically vulnerable. An example might be a socially anxious child undergoing significant bullying at school. The child's sense of inefficacy in this situation might result in the appraisal of extreme stress and result in somatic vulnerability. A somatic symptom (such as a functional symptom, flu, or injury) that results in a dependent role and avoidance of the perceived stressor can then strengthen inefficacy beliefs because there is no mastery over the challenge. A progressively declining course can sometimes then occur, with decreasing functioning, increasing distress, and increasing vulnerability to emotional and physical impairment. Well-meaning and concerned family members, as well as health care providers, may sometimes perpetuate the downward spiral of symptoms and disability by fostering the dependent role or by contributing to the child's stress and distress. This framework suggests that children at high risk might have poor coping skills, feel low self-efficacy in specific situations, have preexisting problems with arousal or excessive attentional focus (hypervigilance, obsessiveness or perseverativeness), have a family system with similar attributes, or a combination of these.

Research to date supports this conceptual framework. Developmental risk factors for persistent physical symptoms appear to include prior medical illness, physical injury, and hospitalization; a history of childhood trauma (including physical or sexual abuse); and school problems (Drossman et al., 1990; Lester, Stein, & Bursch, 2003; Livingston, 1993; Pilowsky, Bassett, Begg, & Thomas, 1982; Reilly, Baker, Rhodes, & Salmon, 1999; Reiter, Shakerin, Gambone, & Milburn, 1991; Roelofs, Keijsers, Joogduin, Naring, & Moene, 2002; Walker, Claar, & Garber, 2002; Wyllie et al., 1999). Research on the general topic of perceived coping inefficacy has revealed associated high ratings of subjective distress, autonomic arousal, and plasma catecholamine secretion (Bandura, Reese, & Adams, 1982; Bandura, Taylor, Williams, Mefford, & Barchas, 1985). Exposure to controllable physical stressors has been found to have no adverse physiological effects, but exposure to the same stressors without the ability to control them impairs cellular components of the immune system (Maier, Laudenslager, & Ryan, 1985). In fact, research on children with recurrent abdominal pain has shown that accommodative coping (e.g., distraction, acceptance, positive thinking, cognitive restructuring) is related to less pain (Thomsen et al., 2002; Walker, Smith, Garber, & Van Slyke, 1997). On the other hand, passive coping strategies (e.g., denial, cognitive avoidance, behavioral avoidance, wishful thinking) have been associated with increased levels of pain. The results regarding active coping strategies (e.g., problem solving, emotional expression, emotional modulation, decision making) have been inconsistent (Thomsen et al., 2002; Walker et al., 1997).

Related to the coping appraisal process, Claar, Walker, and Smith (1999) examined self-perceived academic, social, and athletic competence as potential moderators of the relation between symptoms of irritable bowel syndrome and functional disability in adolescents and young adults with a history of RAP. The relationship between symptoms and disability was found to be stronger at lower levels of perceived academic competence. Additionally, the same relationship between symptoms and disability was found for females at lower levels of perceived social competence, and for males at lower levels of perceived athletic competence. In fact, children with RAP experience frequent school absence (Walker, Garber, Van Slyke, & Greene, 1995).

Rates of internalizing disorders in children with RAP, particularly anxiety and depressive disorders and symptoms, have been found to be higher than in well populations, although lower than in children referred for psychiatric problems (Walker, Garber, & Greene, 1993). Campo et al. (2004) recently studied 42 pediatric outpatients with functional abdominal pain and 38 pediatric outpatients obtaining routine care without pain (aged 8–15 years). Pain patients were significantly more likely than those in the control group to meet criteria for a psychiatric disorder and to endorse higher levels of anxiety and depressive symptoms, temperamental harm avoidance, and functional impairment. The diagnostic rates in the pain group included anxiety disorders in 33 patients (79 percent) and depressive disorders in 18 (43 percent). Anxiety disorders (mean age of onset 6.25 years) were most likely to precede RAP (mean age of onset 9.17 years). Overall, studies of depressive symptoms have not found consistent differences between children with RAP and control group children (Hodges, Kliner, Barbero, & Flaney, 1985a; McGrath, Goodman, Firestone, Shipman, & Peters, 1983; Raymer, Weininger, & Hamilton, 1984; Walker & Greene, 1989).

Wyllie et al. (1999) studied 34 patients (25 female) aged 9–18 years (mean age, 14 years) immediately after diagnosis of pseudoseizures by video electroencephalogram. In addition to conversion disorder, they reported that 11 (32 percent) had mood disorders (including major depression, bipolar disorder, or dysthymic disorder), 8 (24 percent) had separation anxiety and school refusal, 3 (9 percent) had PTSD, 3 had other anxiety or behavioral disorders, 2 (6 percent) had brief reactive psychosis, 11 (32 percent) had a history of sexual abuse (especially those with mood disorders: 7 [64 percent] of 11 patients), and 2 (6 percent) had a history of physical abuse. Fifteen patients (44 percent) reportedly had severe family stressors (such as recent parental divorce, parental discord, or death of a close family member), but the symptom did not typically immediately follow a specific psychological stressor. The most common comorbid psychiatric disorders identified in 33 children and adolescents (91 percent female, mean age of 14.9 years, range of 6–17 years) with BDD included major depression (70 percent), obsessive-compulsive disorder (36 percent), and social phobia (30 percent). The onset of social phobia preceded that of BDD by at least 1 year in most cases (80 percent, $n = 8$); however, obsessive-compulsive disorder preceded onset of BDD by at least 1 year in only 40 percent ($n = 4$) of cases, and in major depression in only 17 percent ($n = 4$) of cases (Albertini & Phillips, 1999).

Imbierowicz and Egle (2003) studied psychosocial adversities affecting the childhood of 38 adult fibromyalgia patients compared to those of 71 patients with somatoform pain disorders and to a control group of 44 with medically explained chronic pain. Fibromyalgia patients reported the highest number of childhood adversities, including sexual and physical maltreatment, a poor emotional relationship with both parents, a lack of physical affection, remembering parents' physical quarrels (as well as addiction in the mother), separation, and a poor financial situation before the age of 7 years old. These experiences were found to a similar extent in the somatoform pain patients, but less frequently in the control group.

Research reveals that children with RAP appear to be hyperreactive in sympathetic nervous system arousal to environmental stressors (abnormal perception of gastrointestinal physiological events and a lower threshold for pain), to experience disrupted recovery (parasympathetic) from stressors, and to be hypervigilant to internal and external pain-related cues (Compas & Boyer, 2001; Di Lorenzo et al., 2001; Duarte, Goulart, & Penna, 2000; Thomsen, Compas, Colletti, & Stanger, 2000). The reduced pain threshold is currently thought to be related to biochemical changes in the afferent neurons of the central and enteric nervous systems and influenced by cognitive processes or other sensations.

Research related to the family context reveals that somatizing children have been found to share similar physical symptoms with family members (Garber et al., 1990; Kriechman, 1987; Walker, Garber, & Greene, 1991; Walker & Greene, 1989). Parents of children with RAP endorse high levels of symptoms of depression, anxiety, and somatization (Garber et al., 1990; Hodges et al., 1985a, 1985b). It has been demonstrated that parents can have a direct impact on children's pain experiences and behavior through modeling responses to painful stimuli (Goodman & McGrath, 1999). Some parent behaviors (i.e., reassurance, empathy, apologies, giving control, criticism) are associated with increases in children's distress during painful medical procedures. Other parent behaviors (i.e., nonprocedural talk, commands to use coping strategies, humor) are associated with decreases in child distress (Blount et al., 1989, 1997; Blount, Sturges, & Powers, 1990). One study found that parent behavior accounted for 55 percent of variance in child distress behavior (Frank, Blount, Smith, Manimala, & Martin, 1995). It appears that particular parental behaviors (e.g., discouraging children's coping efforts, providing special attention) are related to long-term distress, difficulties coping with pain, and the likelihood of developing chronic pain (e.g., Walker et al., 1993; Walker & Zeman, 1992). Interestingly, daily stress, including family illness, appears to be more important than major stressors in triggering episodes of abdominal pain (Walker, Smith, Garber, Van Slyke & Claar, 2001). Using the Social Consequences of Pain questionnaire with 151 patients (aged 8–18) with RAP, Walker et al. (2002) assessed four types of social consequences: positive attention, negative attention, activity restriction, and privileges. They found that positive attention and activity restriction predicted greater symptom maintenance and that this effect was moderated by perceived self-worth and academic competence. To the extent that children rated their self-worth and academic competence as low, the impact of social factors on symptom maintenance was stronger. Positive attention for symptoms predicted an increase in symptoms for children with lower self-worth or perceived academic competence and a decrease in symptoms for children with higher self-worth or higher perceived academic competence. Finally, in a study of family and developmental predictors of somatic symptoms in a high-risk community sample, 211 adolescents and their HIV-infected parents were prospectively examined (Lester et al., 2003). The authors found that parental distress over pain predicted adolescent somatic symptoms at baseline and at 2 month follow-up ($p < .001$), that adolescents who experienced their parents as highly rejecting reported more somatic symptoms at follow-up ($p < .001$), and that school problems correlated at baseline with somatic symptoms ($p < .001$) and with parental rejection ($p < .001$).

COURSE, COMPLICATIONS, AND PROGNOSIS

Based on limited research, it appears that some children make full recoveries from somatoform disorders and that some become symptomatic and disabled adults. Variability in the severity of symptoms, nature of treatments completed, comorbid disorders and problems, length of follow-up, or any combination of these may account for differences in outcomes.

The prognosis for conversion disorder appears to be relatively positive. In the retrospective chart review of medically hospitalized children with conversion disorders conducted by Grattan-Smith et al. (1988), 32 of the 52 children identified (in the 10 years of records reviewed) were completely recovered or had improved considerably by the time of discharge. Similarly, Gudmundsson, Prendergast, Foreman, and Cowley (2001) conducted a 6-year symptom survival analysis on patients who had previously been diagnosed with pseudoseizures without epilepsy. A cure was defined as freedom from seizures for 6 months in that no recurrences after this period were noted. Seventeen patients (15 females) were identified. Their mean age at diagnosis was 12 years, 9 months (range, 8 years, 3 months, to 15 years, 9 months). Of the 17 studied, 14 recovered and resumed regular school attendance, and 3 were lost to follow-up before they had recovered. The mean symptom survival time was 1.5 years. Better outcome was associated with younger age at presentation, female sex, having more types of seizures, and not receiving both inpatient and outpatient treatment. In another study of children with a history of pseudoseizures (also predominantly female, mean age 14 years), Wyllie et al. (1999) found that 15 (72 percent) of the 21 patients who could be reached for follow-up reported they achieved freedom from pseudoseizures (follow-up was after 9–55 months; mean, 30 months). For 8 (53 percent) of them, the last pseudoseizure was within 1 month of diagnosis by video EEG. Interestingly, several of the children had started missing school with headaches or abdominal pain but progressed to pseudoseizures when school attendance was enforced. All of these children had been out of school for many weeks by the time pseudoseizures were diagnosed by video EEG.

The course and prognosis for pain disorders appears less promising. Wasserman, Whitington, and Rivara (1988) found that 90 percent of 31 children reported at least one further episode of abdominal pain over a 9-month period. A Finnish population-based study reported that 52 percent of schoolchildren with weekly musculoskeletal pain still had pain at 1-year follow-up (Mikkelsson, Salminen, & Kautiainen, 1997). Oster (1972) found that 74 percent of children who had abdominal pain reported at least one further episode over a 5-year period. Headaches have been reported to change over time (mostly hospital-based childhood migraine studies), with remission in 30 percent to 40 percent and improvement in about 50 percent of cases at 5- to 10-year follow-up (Bille, 1981, 1989; Burke & Peters, 1956; Congdon & Forsythe, 1979; Dooley & Bagnell, 1995; Guidettim & Galli, 1998; Hinrichs & Keith, 1965; Hockaday, 1978; Koch & Melchior, 1969). Long-term studies suggest that abdominal pain (Apley & Hale, 1973; Lewis & Lewis, 1989) and other gastrointestinal complaints (Christensen & Mortensen, 1975) persist into adulthood in some RAP patients, with perhaps only 30 percent to 47 percent experiencing a complete resolution of symptoms. Additionally, the long-term risk for psychiatric disorders, especially depression and anxiety, appears to be significant (Campo et al., 2003; Hotopf, Carr, Mayou, Wadsworth, & Wessely, 1998; Walker, Guite, Duke, Barnard, & Greene, 1998). For example, Walker et al. (1998) studied 76 patients 5 years after an initial RAP diagnosis and compared them to 49 individuals in a control group. They found that patients with a history of RAP reported significantly more episodes of abdominal pain at follow-up than did those in the control group. They also reported significantly higher levels of functional disability, school absence, and clinic visits for abdominal distress. Female patients with RAP were more likely than female control participants to meet criteria for irritable bowel syndrome. And among patients with RAP, higher levels of irritable bowel syndrome symptoms were related to significantly greater functional disability, more clinic visits, more life stress, higher levels of depression, and lower academic and social competence.

ASSESSMENT AND DIAGNOSIS

Psychiatric assessment is geared toward identifying psychiatric symptoms, behavioral reinforcements, or psychosocial stressors that could be exacerbating the symptoms. Common comorbid findings among children who are disabled with somatic symptoms include anxiety disorders, alexithymia, depression, unsuspected learning disorders (even in high-achieving children), developmental or communication disorders, social problems, physical or emotional trauma, family illness, and prominent family distress (Bursch et al., 2004; Bursch & Zeltzer, 2002; Campo, Comer, Jansen-McWilliams, Gardner, & Kelleher, 2002; Campo, Jansen-McWilliams, Comer, & Kelleher, 1999; Egger, Angold, & Costello, 1998; Fritz et al., 1997; Garber et al., 1990; Hodges et al., 1985a, 1985b; Hyman et al., 2002; Lester et al., 2003; Livingston, Witt, & Smith, 1993; Livingston et al., 1995; Schanberg, Keefe, Lefebvre, Kredich, & Gil, 1998; Stuart & Noyes, 1999; Zuckerman et al., 1987).

Assessment recommendations previously published (Campo & Fritz, 2001) include acknowledging patient and family suffering; exploring previous experiences with health care practitioners; investigating fears related to the symptoms; communicating a willingness to suggest further medical assessment if indicated; avoiding excessive tests and procedures; avoiding diagnosis by exclusion; and exploring the symptom timing, context, and characteristics.

Whenever feasible (such as in hospital settings or integrated outpatient clinics), it is ideal to conduct the psychiatric assessment concurrent with the medical evaluation to reinforce team adherence to the biopsychosocial model regardless of the etiology of the symptoms. Before asking psychosocial questions, it can be very helpful to spend a considerable amount of time understanding the specific nature of the child's symptoms from the perspective of both the child and family members, including siblings, who are often the best observers in the family. A discussion of symptoms and previous medical evaluation will result in a determination as to whether further medical evaluation is indicated and will also reassure the patient and family that you believe the symptoms exist.

Table 24.1 presents a list of topics to cover during the assessment. It is important to note that alexithymia might hinder endorsement of emotional descriptors and require an emphasis on somatic symptoms of depression or anxiety. Additionally, for those children who are not attending school, intellectual, academic, or psychological testing may be needed

TABLE 24.1 Clinical Interview: Topics and Areas Targeted for Assessment

Chief complaint and history of present illness
- Onset and course of the current problem (including results of previous evaluations and treatment attempts, including home remedies, and alternative/complementary therapies)
- Locations of symptoms, if relevant
- Symptom intensity at different times and under differing circumstances
- Symptom quality, duration, variability, predictability
- Exacerbating and alleviating factors
- Impact of symptoms on daily life of patient
- Other sensations that accompany the symptoms
- Thoughts and behaviors associated with the symptoms
- Beliefs about what will and will not help symptoms
- Coping responses; ability to tolerate the symptoms
- How the symptoms have impacted the family
- How family members react to symptoms displayed during the interview
- Any unusual behavior, family dynamics, or use of language during the interview
- Review entire body for symptoms, not just the site of the presenting complaint

Past medical history
- Illnesses, hospitalizations, surgeries, injuries, ER visits, allergies
- Birth and early childhood history, developmental milestones
- Family history
- The intensity and types of emotion displayed by the patient and family
- The roles various family members hold and who speaks about which topics
- The child and family history of all somatic and emotional symptoms and diagnoses
- Baseline functioning of the child and of each family member

Social history and current functioning
- School and school absenteeism, including academic difficulties and/or challenges, friends, bullies, teachers, exams, grades, classes, and academic aspirations
- Social history of family, especially significant (positive and negative) life events, including things such as divorce, overt marital tension, sibling problems, changes at school or in living arrangements, and/or traumatic experiences (such as the witnessing or direct experience of physical or sexual assault, a robbery, death, or injury)

Emotional history and current functioning
- Alexithymia; depression; panic (including nonfearful panic); anxiety, worries, or fears related to parents, academic achievement or exams, social situations, or school; obsessive-compulsive traits; post-traumatic stress symptoms; enuresis or encopresis
- Developmental history of the preceding symptoms
- Parents' emotional functioning, marital stress, and coping skills
- Parental behaviors: excessive sympathy and attention for symptoms, external help seeking, strong emotional responses, modeling of symptoms, and support for task avoidance

to identify specific problems that might be difficult to assess through interview alone. If the child is academically behind, has peer problems or weak social problem-solving skills, or has good achievement with a previously unsuspected learning disorder, school can be a significant source of stress. This can be true even if the child does not initially report it as such, especially among perfectionistic children who strongly identify with being a good student, attempt to maintain high grades, or experience pressure to achieve. Due to the time required and the expense of psychological testing, however, such testing might be reserved for children experiencing a progression of disability or who are resistant to treatment recommendations. Testing can sometimes be obtained through the school district if the child is having recognized academic difficulties.

Identification of specific physical and psychiatric symptoms, behavioral reinforcements of disability, and psychosocial stressors allows for logical feedback and targeted interventions that may be more readily acceptable to families than a general description of somatoform disorders. For example, a homebound child with chronic abdominal pain and diarrhea might have irritable bowel syndrome, perfectionistic traits, and a bully at school. His school avoidance might be based on concerns about getting to the bathroom on time, getting all As, and avoiding the bully. It might have been reinforced by his parent, who feared the child had a life-threatening illness.

Motor pseudoseizures can sometimes be brought on with verbal encouragement. Stereotypic motor presentations are often quite different from those of true motor seizures, but they can be difficult to determine from the history or routine EEG data. Symptomatic children can be clinically diagnosed by analyzing confirmed episodes with video EEG (Cohen, Howard, & Bongar, 1992; Duchowny et al., 1988) or by measuring post-ictal elevations in serum prolactin levels (Fisher, Chan, Bare, & Lesser, 1991).

IMPACT ON ENVIRONMENT

In addition to being heavily influenced by the child's environments, somatoform disorders can have significant influences on families, school performance, and peer relationships—that is, the relationship is bidirectional. Recent studies have shown that serious pediatric illness or treatment may also lead to chronic as well as acute symptoms of emotional distress in the parents, which may interfere with their ability to provide support for the children (Young et al., 2003). Though some may not consider a somatoform disorder a serious pediatric disease, many parents perceive it as such, especially before diagnosis. One day of a child missing school because of a somatic complaint also has potential to bring to the parent a degree of stress or anxiety about the health of the child or about the missed day, lost wages, and expenses associated with obtaining medical care. The child may experience similar anxiety or stress, in addition to missed schoolwork and social interaction. This section will focus on what is known about the impact of several functional disorders, including childhood somatoform disorders, on the environment.

Conversion Disorder

Although the impact of a conversion disorder on the family, school, and peer environments can be exceedingly high in the short run, it may be relatively low in the long run compared to other somatoform disorders. School absenteeism and health care utilization are often high during symptom episodes, but, as described earlier in this chapter, the episodes often remit within a month of diagnosis and, for the remainder of identified patients, within 1–2 years (Grattan-Smith, Fairley, & Procopis, 1988; Gudmundsson et al., 2001; Wyllie et al., 1999).

Pain Disorder

Pain and somatoform pain disorders, which are less likely to remit than conversion disorders, have the potential to strongly impact the environment. In fact, when compared to a wide range of chronic illnesses, pediatric chronic pain is associated with the highest rates of school absenteeism (Newacheck & Taylor, 1992). It has been estimated (Stang & Osterhaus, 1993) that almost one million children and adolescents in the United States suffer from migraine headaches, that about 10 percent of them missed at least 1 day of school over a 2-week period due to migraine, and nearly 1 percent missed 4 days. Abu-Arefeh and Russell (1994) reported that children with migraines lose more days of school than children without migraines, even after excluding absences associated with headaches. Further, rates of hospital admission for nonspecific abdominal pain among children aged 5–15 are significantly higher on school days than for holidays or weekends (Williams, Jackson, Lambert, & Johnstone, 1999). Finally, children are most likely to develop significant pain conditions at the beginning of the school year (Antilla, Metsahonkala, & Sillanpaa, 1999). Higher rates of functional disability compared to controls have also been found among children with abdominal pain (Walker & Greene, 1989; Walker et al., 1998), fibromyalgia, and juvenile rheumatoid arthritis (Reid, Lang, & McGrath, 1997). Kashikar-Zuck et al. (2002) studied 18 children with juvenile primary fibromyalgia syndrome and compared them with 18 matched children with nonmalignant chronic back pain (all female, 9–19 years of age). Both groups reported significant disruption in functional abilities and school attendance as a result of chronic pain. Kashikar-Zuck, Vaught, Goldschneider, Graham, and Miller (2001) studied 73 pediatric pain patients with chronic localized musculoskeletal pain or chronic daily headaches. They reported that chronic pain had a significant impact on the children's lives and that depression was strongly associated with functional disability. The musculoskeletal pain group reported significantly higher levels of disability and more difficulty coping than the headache group.

Walker et al. (1998) found that, even after 5 years, patients with a history of RAP reported significantly higher levels of functional disability, school absence, and clinic visits for abdominal distress than controls. They also found that those RAP patients with higher levels of irritable bowel syndrome symptoms had significantly greater functional disability, more clinic visits, more life stress, higher levels of depression, and lower academic and social competence. Not surprisingly, studies of childhood pain in community samples often reflect less environmental impact than studies of clinical samples. For example, Hunfeld et al. (2002) studied a community sample of 77 children with physically unexplained chronic pain (aged 5–11 years). Children had abdominal pain, headaches, limb pain, or a combination of these. The average pain was described as mild (30 mm on a 0- to 100-mm visual analog scale), moderately frequent (present in 34 percent of the three daily pain diary entries), worse as the day progressed, and nondisabling (no significant school absence or problems with functional status). However, pain showed a relatively negative impact on family life, especially maternal reports of restrictions in social life and personal strain. Perquin et al. (2003) followed a community sample of 987 children and adolescents aged 0–18 years for 2 years. They reported that 254 subjects reported chronic benign pain at baseline. Of these, 124 (48 percent) and 77 (30 percent) still experienced chronic pain at 1-year and 2-year follow-up, respectively. However, interestingly, there was a modest decrease in the impact of pain on the child's behavior, social functioning, and use of health care over time.

Body Dysmorphic Disorder

Although not extensively studied, it appears clear from the diagnosis that BDD can have a profound impact on the environment. For example, Albertini and Phillips (1999) studied 33 children and adolescents (91 percent female; mean age of 14.9 years; range of 6–17 years) with BDD. Their findings are consistent with previous BDD case reports. They reported that all individuals spent time engaging in BDD-related behaviors (mean number of behaviors = 4.5; range = 1–9), with 25 percent spending more than 8 hours per day in such activities. The most common behaviors included camouflaging and looking in a mirror. However, many engaged in behaviors that involved others. For example, 73 percent repeatedly questioned others about their appearance, up to 30 times a day. Ninety-four percent experienced social impairment, such as avoidance of friends or dating, due to embarrassment and shame over their appearance. Additionally, 85 percent reported that their BDD obsessions and related behaviors significantly impacted their academic performance. BDD resulted in a relatively high number (39 percent) temporarily missing school and 18 percent dropping out of school (3 percent dropped out temporarily and 15 percent dropped out permanently). Suicidal ideation (67 percent), suicide attempts (21 percent), and physical violence (38 percent) caused by BDD symptoms (e.g., hitting themselves or destroying property due to frustration) were common.

IMPLICATIONS FOR FUTURE PERSONALITY DEVELOPMENT

In adults, somatic preoccupation has been empirically linked with antisocial, passive-dependent, histrionic, narcissistic, avoidant, paranoid, borderline, and obsessive-compulsive personality disorders (Hayward & King, 1990; Hudziak et al., 1996; Rost, Akins, Brown, & Smith, 1992). Such traits have also been identified in some studies of adolescents with somatoform disorders (Wyllie et al., 1999). However, it is unclear if the typical path for children and adolescents with somatoform disorders is reflected in the adult literature. As reviewed earlier in this chapter, most children with conversion disorders and some with chronic somatic symptoms do experience a resolution of symptoms. However, some children have persistent symptoms into childhood, and some appear to be at higher risk for the development of anxiety and depression rather than continued somatic complaints (Campo et al., 2003; Hotopf et al., 1998; Walker et al., 1998). Being female, substance use, and comorbid anxiety disorders appear to be risk factors for the onset of new somatoform conditions and for a stable course over time (Lieb et al., 2002).

Extrapolating from the research in children and adolescents summarized in this chapter, one might also expect a number of other long-term consequences in personality development. Individuals who had a somatoform disorder as a child or adolescent may continue with identified traits such as being harm avoidant, catastrophizing, symptom sensitive, perfectionistic, high achieving, learning impaired, traumatized, socially impaired, dependent, or passive in coping style. In such an individual, difficulties attaining expectations (imposed by others or by oneself) might contribute to preexisting anxiety and somatic symptoms. An injury, illness, or chronic condition might reinforce symptom anxiety and result in subsequent avoidance of the difficult situation, which would prohibit mastery over it. It is easy to see how one might become chronically dependent on the medical system, disability income, or substances in such a disability cycle. Remediation of underlying deficits or problems might become more difficult over time as such individuals become more dependent. And diagnosing adult patients as having personality disorders might, in some cases, preclude assessment of unsuspected learning disorders, developmental disorders, social perception deficits, past trauma, or other issues that might allow for remediation if identified. Some may obtain unhelpful medical procedures that further traumatize and sensitize them. Over time, it would be difficult not to identify such individuals as antisocial, passive-dependent, histrionic, narcissistic, avoidant, paranoid, borderline, or obsessive-compulsive in personality.

Though it has not been researched longitudinally, short-term studies and clinical observations suggest that remediation of underlying deficits, development of self-management skills, aggressive treatment of comorbid disorders and family distress, and a focus on academic intervention (or vocational training) might serve to alter the disability course described previously. For individuals who have received such treatment during childhood or adolescence, one might expect to identify high-achieving, perfectionistic adults, some with episodic or persistent somatic symptoms that are self-managed and that do not lead to disability.

TREATMENT IMPLICATIONS

Families, and treatment teams, often worry about missing a life-threatening problem or a diagnosis that could be easily remedied. This fear is particularly strong when the patient exhibits significant distress about the symptoms. The treatment team must feel that a reasonable evaluation has been completed so they can clearly communicate to the family that no further evaluation is indicated to understand and treat the problem. A rehabilitation approach can improve independent and normal functioning, enhance coping and self-efficacy, and serve to prevent secondary disabilities (Bursch, Walco, & Zeltzer, 1998; Campo & Fritz, 2001; Heruti, Levy, Adunski, & Ohry, 2002). Like traditional physical therapy, functioning (rather than symptoms) should be tracked to determine whether progress is being made. As functioning, coping skills, and self-efficacy improve, symptoms as well as the distress related to the symptoms often remit.

As with any chronic condition that requires treatment adherence, the cornerstone to effective treatment is understandable education about the problem and about the rationale for treatment recommendations. Many patients and families will accept only those explanations that overtly acknowledge the biological processes involved in the disorder. It often does not make sense to families to be told "There is nothing wrong" when the intended message is that there are no structural abnormalities that need repair. For some patients who have had a recent onset of symptoms, patient and family education along with some basic behavioral recommendations focused on reinforcement for normal functioning are enough to reverse the problem. For others, a more comprehensive plan is often needed.

Specific treatment plans target the biological, psychological, and social factors that are exacerbating or maintaining the symptoms and disability. Treatments designed to target underlying sensory signaling mechanisms and specific symptoms can include cognitive-behavioral strategies (e.g., cognitive-behavioral psychotherapy, self-hypnosis training, biofeedback, or meditation), behavioral techniques, family interventions, physical interventions (e.g., massage, yoga, acupuncture, transcutaneous electrical nerve stimulators [TENS], physical therapy, heat and cold therapies, occupational therapy), sleep hygiene, and pharmacological interventions (Fritz et al., 1997; Minuchin, Rosman, & Baker, 1978; Sanders, Shepherd, Cleghorn, & Woolford, 1994; Sanders et al., 1989; Zeltzer & Bursch, 2001). In general, interventions that promote active or accommodative coping are preferred over those that require passive dependence. Most of the currently employed pharmacological strategies are extrapolated from adult trials without evidence of efficacy in children. Classes of medications to consider include tricyclic antidepressants or anticonvulsants for neuropathic pain or irritable bowel syndrome; selective seratonin reuptake inhibitors for symptoms of anxiety or depression (this includes BDD or hypchondriasis when the behavior appears obsessive-compulsive); muscle relaxants for myofascial pain; beta-blockers for anxiety responses to somatic sensations, headaches, or chronic nausea or vomiting; and low-dose antipsychotics (especially those with low potency) for acute anxiety, multiple somatic symptoms with significant distress, chronic nausea, or any combination of these. Benzodiazepines sometimes elicit paradoxical reactions in those children who are hypervigilant to their bodies and concerned about losing control. Blocks, trigger point injections, epidurals, and other invasive assessments and treatments that further stimulate the central nervous system can sometimes exacerbate the problem. Evidence-based treatments should be used whenever available. For example, in adolescent migraine headache, cognitive-behavioral interventions have better evidence for efficacy than triptans, and ibuprofen appears to be more effective than acetaminophen.

School absences are common in this patient population and often represent a significant challenge to patients, parents, and clinicians. Common obstacles to returning to school include worry about work completion or makeup work, concerns about peer relationships, fear of having symptoms at school, an anxiety disorder (social, test, or separation anxiety), a poor relationship with a teacher or school nurse, parental anxiety, or a general life stressor (parental divorce, death in family, etc). Some children will return to school once they are reassured that their symptoms are understood and are not harmful to them. Others return once they have a plan for dealing with their specific obstacles, such as makeup work or a bully. Finally, some children who have completely lost confidence in their ability to attend school will resist even when there is a plan to address the obstacles. If they are required to immediately return to school, chances are that they will have a severe symptom episode in the morning that prevents school attendance. For these children, a gradual return to school is sometimes more effective. A behavior-reinforcement program can be used to track and reward children's progress in attending school and related goals (such as not crying in the morning before school). All parents involved in the child's life should be involved in the program. Children should initially be rewarded for brief periods of school attendance, starting with the least aversive portion of the day (examples include lunch, morning classes, or art class). Later, the rewards should be given for longer periods of attendance. If a child has difficulty separating from one parent, then it can be helpful for the other parent to take the child to school to break this pattern. Some children enjoy verbal praise for school attendance as long as it is not assumed that symptoms are better. Other children will regress if verbally praised. Schools can normally accommodate reentry efforts such as this if there is good communication and a written plan.

REFERENCES

Abu-Arefeh, I., & Russell, G. (1994). Prevalence of headache and migraine in schoolchildren. *British Medical Journal, 309,* 765–769.

Albertini, R. S., & Phillips K. A. (1999). Thirty-three cases of body dysmorphic disorder in children and adolescents. *Journal of the American Academy of Child and Adolescent Psychiatry, 38,* 453–459.

American Psychiatric Association. (1987). *Diagnostic and statistical manual of mental disorders* (3rd ed., rev.). Washington, DC: Author.

American Psychiatric Association. (1994). *Diagnostic and statistical manual of mental disorders* (4th ed.). Washington, DC: Author.

Antilla, P., Metsahonkala, L., & Sillanpaa, M. (1999). School start and occurrence of headache. *Pediatrics, 103,* e80.

Apley, J. (1975). *The child with abdominal pain* (2nd ed.). Oxford: Blackwell.

Apley, J., & Hale, B. (1973). Children with recurrent abdominal pain: How do they grow up? *British Medical Journal, 3,* 7–9.

Apley, J., & Naish. N. (1958). Recurrent abdominal pains: A field survey of 1,000 school children. *Archives of Diseases of Children, 33,* 165–170.

Aro H., Paronen, O., & Aro, S. (1987). Psychosomatic symptoms among 14–16 year old Finnish adolescents. *Social Psychiatry, 22,* 171–176.

Asmundson, G. J., Norton, P. J., & Veloso, F. (1999). Anxiety sensitivity and fear of pain in patients with recurring headaches. *Behaviour Research and Therapy, 37,* 703–713.

Bandura, A., Reese, L., & Adams, N. E. (1982). Microanalysis of action and fear arousal as a function of differential levels of perceived self-efficacy. *Journal of Personality and Social Psychology, 43,* 5–21.

Bandura, A., Taylor, C. B., Williams, S. L., Mefford, I. N., & Barchas, J. D. (1985). Catecholamine secretion as a function of perceived coping self-efficacy. *Journal of Consulting and Clinical Psychology, 53,* 406–414.

Belmaker, E., Espinoza, R., & Pogrund, R. (1985). Use of medical services by adolescents with nonspecific somatic symptoms. *International Journal of Adolescent Medical Health, 1,* 150–156.

Bille, B. (1981). Migraine in children: Prevalence, clinical features, and a 30-year follow-up. In M. D. Ferrari & X. Lataste (Eds.), *Migraines and other headaches.* Carnforth, UK: Parthenon.

Bille, B. (1989). Migraine in childhood and its prognosis. *Cephalalgia, 1,* 71–75.

Blount, R. L., Cohen, L. L., Frank, N. C., Bachanas, P. J., Smith, A. J., Manimala, R. M., et al. (1997). The Child-Adult Medical Procedure Interaction Scale—Revised: An assessment of validity. *Journal of Pediatric Psychology, 22,* 689–705.

Blount, R. L., Corbin, S. M., Sturges, J. W., Wolfe, V. V., Prater, J. M., & James, L. D. (1989). The relationship between adult behavior and child coping and distress during BMA/LP procedures: A sequential analysis. *Behavior Therapy, 20,* 585–601.

Blount, R. L., Sturges, J. W., & Powers, S. W. (1990). Analysis of child and adult behavioral variations by phase of medical procedure. *Behavior Therapy, 21,* 33–48.

Boyce, W., Barr, R., & Zeltzer, L. (1992). Temperament and the psychobiology of childhood stress. *Pediatrics, 90,* 483–486.

Burke, E. C., & Peters, G. A. (1956). Migraine in childhood; a preliminary report. *American Journal of Diseases of Children, 92,* 330–336.

Bursch, B. (1999). Pain-associated disability syndrome and the biopsychosocial model. In P. Hyman (Ed.), *Pediatric functional bowel disorders* (pp. 811–813). New York: Academy of Professional Information Services.

Bursch, B., Ingman, K., Vitti, L., Hyman, P. E., & Zeltzer, L. K. (2004). Chronic pain in individuals with previously undiagnosed autistic spectrum disorders. *Journal of Pain, 5,* 290–295.

Bursch, B., Walco, G., & Zeltzer, L. K. (1998). Clinical assessment and management of chronic pain and pain-associated disability syndrome (PADS). *Journal of Developmental and Behavioral Pediatrics, 19,* 44–52.

Bursch, B., & Zeltzer, L. K. (2002). Autism spectrum disorders presenting as chronic pain syndromes: Case presentations and discussion. *Journal of Developmental and Learning Disorders, 6,* 41–48.

Bye, A. M., & Nunan, J. (1992). Video EEG analysis of non-ictal events in children. *Clinical Experimental Neurology, 29,* 92–98.

Campo, J. V., Bridge, J., Ehmann, M., Altman, S., Lucas, A., Birmaher, B., et al. (2004). Recurrent abdominal pain. *Anxiety and Depression in Primary Care Pediatrics, 113,* 817–824.

Campo, J. V., Comer, D. M., Jansen-McWilliams, L., Gardner, W., & Kelleher, K. J. (2002). Recurrent pain, emotional distress, and health service use in childhood. *Journal of Pediatrics, 141,* 76–83.

Campo, J. V., Dahl, R. E., Williamson, D. E., Birmaher, B., Perel, J. M., & Ryan, N. D. (2003). Gastrointestinal distress to serotonergic challenge: A risk marker for emotional disorder? *Journal of the American Academy of Child and Adolescent Psychiatry, 42,* 1221–1226.

Campo, J. V., & Fritsch, S. L. (1994). Somatization in children and adolescents. *Journal of the American Academy of Child and Adolescent Psychiatry, 33,* 1223–1235.

Campo, J. V., & Fritz, G. (2001). A management model for pediatric somatization. *Psychosomatics, 42,* 467–576.

Campo, J. V., Jansen-McWilliams, L., Comer, D. M., & Kelleher, K. J. (1999). Somatization in pediatric primary care: Association with psychopathology, functional impairment and use of services. *Journal of the American Academy of Child and Adolescent Psychiatry, 38,* 1093–1101.

Christensen, M. F., & Mortensen, O. (1975). Long-term prognosis in children with recurrent abdominal pain. *Archives of Diseases in Children, 50,* 110–115.

Claar, R. L., Walker, L. S, Smith, C. A. (1999). Functional disability in adolescents and young adults with symptoms of irritable bowel syndrome: The role of academic, social, and athletic competence. *Journal of Pediatric Psychology, 24,* 271–280.

Cohen, L. M., Howard, G. F., III, & Bongar, B. (1992). Provocation of pseudoseizures by psychiatric interview during EEG and video monitoring. *International Journal of Psychiatry and Medicine, 22,* 131–140.

Colletti, R. B. (1998). Recurrent abdominal pain. In F. D. Burg, J. R. Ingelfinger, E. R. Wald, & R. A. Polin (Eds.), *Current pediatric therapy* (pp. 671–673). Philadelphia: Saunders.

Compas, B. E., & Boyer, M. C. (2001). Coping and attention: Implications for children's health and pediatric conditions. *Journal of Developmental and Behavioral Pediatrics, 22,* 1–11.

Davison, I. S., Faull, C., & Nico, A. R (1986). Research note: Temperament and behavior in six-year-olds with recurrent abdominal pain: A follow up. *Journal of Child Psychology and Psychiatry, 27,* 539–544.

Di Lorenzo, C., Youssef, N. N., Sigurdsson, L., Scharff, L., Griffiths, J., & Wald, A. (2001). Visceral hyperalgesia in children with functional abdominal pain. *Journal of Pediatrics, 139,* 838–843.

Dooley, J., & Bagnell, A. (1995). The prognosis and treatment of headaches in children—a ten year follow-up. *Canadian Journal of Neurological Science, 22,* 47–49.

Drossman, D. A., Lesserman, J. S., Nachman, G., Zhiming, L. I., Gluck, H., Toomey, T. C., et al. (1990). Sexual and physical abuse in women with functional or organic gastrointestinal disorders. *Annals of Internal Medicine, 113,* 828–833.

Duarte, M., Goulart, E., & Penna, F. (2000). Pressure pain threshold in children with recurrent abdominal pain. *Journal of Pediatric Gastroenterology and Nutrition, 31,* 280–285.

Duchowny, M. S., Resnick, T. J., Deray, M. J., & Alvarez, L. A. (1988). Video EEG diagnosis of repetitive behavior in early childhood and its relationship to seizures. *Pediatric Neurology, 4,* 162–164.

Egger, H. L., Angold, A., & Costello, E. J. (1998). Headaches and psychopathology in children and adolescents. *Journal of the American Academy of Child and Adolescent Psychiatry, 37,* 951–958.

Faull C., & Nicol, A. R.(1986). Abdominal pain in six-year-olds: An epidemiological study in a new town. *Journal of Child Psychology and Psychiatry, 27,* 251–260.

Fearon, I., McGrath, P. J., & Achat, H. (1996). "Booboos": The study of everyday pain among young children. *Pain, 68,* 55–62.

Fisher, R. S., Chan, D. W., Bare, M., & Lesser R. P. (1991). Capillary prolactin measurement for diagnosis of seizures. *Annals of Neurology, 29,* 187–190.

Frank, N. C., Blount, R. L., Smith, A. J., Manimala, M. R., & Martin, J. K. (1995). Parent and staff behavior, previous child medical experience, and maternal anxiety as they relate to child distress and coping. *Journal of Pediatric Psychology, 20,* 277–289.

Fritz, G. K., Fritsch, S., & Hagino, O. (1997). Somatoform disorders in children and adolescents: A review of the past 10 years. *Journal of the American Academy of Child Adolescent Psychiatry, 36,* 1329–1338.

Garber, J., Walker, L. S., & Zeman, J. (1991). Somatization symptoms in a community sample of children and adolescents: Further validation of the children's somatization inventory. *Psychological Assessment, 3,* 588–595.

Garber, J., Zeman, J., & Walker, L. (1990). Recurrent abdominal pain in children: Psychiatric diagnoses and parental psychopathology. *Journal of the American Academy of Child Adolescent Psychiatry, 29,* 648–656.

Gil, K. M., Thompson, R. J., Keith, B. R., Tota-Faucette, M., Noll, S., & Kinney, T. R. (1993). Sickle cell disease pain in children and adolescents: Change in pain frequency and coping strategies over time. *Journal of Pediatric Psychology, 18,* 621–637.

Goodman, J. E., & McGrath, P. J. (1991). The epidemiology of pain in children and adolescents: A review. *Pain, 46,* 247–264.

Goodman, J. E., & McGrath, P. J. (1999, May). *The impact of mothers' behavior on children's pain during a cold pressor task.* Paper presented at the Annual Meeting of the Canadian Psychological Association, Halifax, Nova Scotia.

Grattan-Smith, P., Fairley, M., & Procopis, P. (1988). Clinical features of conversion disorder. *Archives of Diseases of Children., 63,* 408–414.

Groholt, E. K., Stigum, H., Nordhagen, R., & Kohler, L. (2003). Recurrent pain in children, socio-economic factors and accumulation in families. *European Journal of Epidemiology, 18,* 965–975.

Gudmundsson, O., Prendergast, M., Foreman, D., & Cowley, S. (2001). Outcome of pseudoseizures in children and adolescents: A 6-year symptom survival analysis. *Developmental Medicine and Child Neurology, 43,* 547–551.

Guidetti, V., Fornara, R., Ottaviano, S., Petrilli, A., Seri, S., & Cortesi, F. (1987). Personality inventory for children and childhood migraine: A case-controlled study. *Cephalalgia, 7,* 225–230.

Guidetti, V., & Galli, F. (1998). Evolution of headache in childhood and adolescence: An 8-year follow-up. *Cephalalgia, 18,* 449–454.

Hayward, C., & King, R. (1990). Somatization and personality disorder traits in nonclinical volunteers. *Journal of Personality Disorders, 4,* 402–406.

Heruti, R. J., Levy, A., Adunski, A., & Ohry, A.(2002). Conversion motor paralysis disorder: Overview and rehabilitation model. *Spinal Cord, 40,* 327–334.

Hinrichs, W. L., & Keith, H. M. (1965). Migraine in childhood: A follow-up report. *Mayo Clinic Proceedings, 40,* 593–596.

Hockaday, J. M. (1978). Late outcome of childhood onset migraine and factors affecting outcome, with particular reference to early and late EEG findings. In R. Greene (Ed.), *Current concepts in migraine research* (41–48). New York: Raven.

Hodges, K., Kline, J. J, Barbero, G., & Flanery, R. (1985a). Depressive symptoms in children with recurrent abdominal pain and in their families. *Journal of Pediatrics, 107,* 622–626.

Hodges, K., Kline, J. J., Barbero, G., & Woodruff, C. (1985b). Anxiety in children with recurrent abdominal pain and their parents. *Psychosomatics, 26,* 859, 862–866.

Hotopf, M., Carr, S., Mayou, R., Wadsworth, M., & Wessely, S. (1998). Why do children have chronic abdominal pain, and what happens to them when they grow up? Population based cohort study. *British Medical Journal, 316,* 1196–1200.

Hudziak, J. J., Boffeli, T. J., Kreisman, J. J., Battaglia, M. M., Stanger, C., & Guze, S. B. (1996). Clinical study of the relation of borderline personality disorder to Briquet's syndrome (hysteria), somatization disorder, antisocial personality disorder, and substance abuse disorders. *American Journal of Psychiatry, 153,* 1598–1606.

Hunfeld, J. A., Perquin, C. W., Hazebroek-Kampschreur, A. A., Passchier, J., van Suijlekom-Smit, L. W., & van der Wouden, J. C. (2002). Physically unexplained chronic pain and its impact on children and their families: The mother's perception. *Psychology and Psychotherapy, 75,* 251–260.

Hyams, J. S., Burke, G., Davis, P. M., Rzepski, B., & Andrulonis, P. A. (1996). Abdominal pain and irritable bowel syndrome in adolescents: A community-based study. *Journal of Pediatrics, 129,* 220–226.

Hyman, P. E., Bursch, B., Lopez, E., Schwankovsky, L., Cocjin, J., & Zeltzer, L. K. (2002). Visceral pain-associated disability syndrome: A descriptive analysis. *Journal of Pediatric Gastroenterology and Nutrition, 35,* 663–668.

Imbierowicz, K., & Egle, U. T. (2003). Childhood adversities in patients with fibromyalgia and somatoform pain disorder. *European Journal of Pain, 7,* 113–119.

Kagan, J., Reznick, J., & Snidman, N. (1988). Biological bases of childhood shyness. *Science, 40,* 167–171.

Kashikar-Zuck, S., Goldschneider, K. R., Powers, S. W., Vaught, M. H., & Hershey, A. D. (2001). Depression and functional disability in chronic pediatric pain. *Clinical Journal of Pain, 17,* 341–349.

Kashikar-Zuck, S., Vaught, M. H., Goldschneider, K. R., Graham, T. B., & Miller, J. C. (2002). Depression, coping, and functional disability in juvenile primary fibromyalgia syndrome. *Journal of Pain, 3,* 412–419.

Keefe, F. J., Lefebvre, J. C., Egert, J. R., Affleck, G., Sullivan, M. J. L., & Caldwell, D. S. (2000). The relationship of gender to pain, pain behavior, and disability in osteoarthritis patients: The role of catastrophizing. *Pain, 87,* 325–334.

Koch, C., & Melchior, J. C. (1969). Headache in childhood. A five year material from a pediatric university clinic. *Danish Medical Bulletin, 16,* 109–114.

Kriechman, A. M. (1987). Siblings with somatoform disorders in childhood and adolescence. *Journal of the American Academy of Child and Adolescent Psychiatry, 26,* 226–231.

Lambert, J. P. (1941). Psychiatric observations on children with abdominal pain. *American Journal of Psychiatry, 98,* 451–454.

Larson, B. S. (1991). Somatic complaints and their relationship to depressive symptoms in Swedish adolescents. *Journal of Child Psychology and Psychiatry, 32,* 821.

Leslie, S. A. (1988). Diagnosis and treatment of hysterical conversion reactions. *Archives of Diseases in Children, 63,* 506–511.

Lester, N., Lefebvre, J. C., & Keefe, F. J. (1994). Pain in young adults: I. Relationship to gender and family pain history. *Clinical Journal of Pain, 10,* 282–289.

Lester, P., Stein, J. A., & Bursch, B. (2003). Developmental predictors of somatic symptoms in adolescents of parents with HIV: A 12-month follow-up. *Journal of Developmental and Behavioral Pediatrics, 24,* 242–250.

Lewis, C. E., & Lewis, M. A. (1989). Educational outcomes and illness behaviors of participants in a child-initiated care system: A 12-year follow-up study. *Pediatrics, 84,* 845–850.

Lieb, R., Pfister, H., Mastaler, M., & Wittchen, H. U. (2000). Somatoform syndromes and disorders in a representative population sample of adolescents and young adults: Prevalence, comorbidity and impairments. *Acta Psychiatrica Scandanavica, 101,* 194–208.

Lieb, R., Zimmermann, P., Friis, R. H., Hofler, M., Tholen, S., & Wittchen, H. U. (2002). The natural course of *DSM-IV* somatoform disorders and syndromes among adolescents and young adults: A prospective-longitudinal community study. *European Psychiatry, 17,* 321–331.

Livingston, R. (1993). Children of people with somatization disorder. *Journal of the American Academy of Child and Adolescent Psychiatry, 3,* 536–544.

Livingston, R., Witt, A., & Smith, G. R. (1995). Families who somatize. *Journal of Developmental and Behavioral Pediatrics, 16,* 42–46.

Maier, S. F., Laudenslager, M. L., & Ryan, S. M. (1985). Stressor controllability, immune function, and endogenous opiates. In F. R. Brush and J. B. Overmier (Eds.), *Affect, conditioning, and cognition: Essays on the determinants of behavior* (pp. 183–201). Hillsdale, NJ: Erlbaum.

Manassis, K., Bradley, S., Goldberg, S., Hood, J., & Price-Swinson, R. (1995). Behavioural inhibition, attachment and anxiety in children of mothers with anxiety disorders. *Canadian Journal of Psychiatry, 40,* 87–92.

Mayville, S., Katz, R. C., Gipson, M. T., & Cabral, K. (1999). Assessing the prevalence of body dysmorphic disorder in an ethnically diverse group of adolescents. *Journal of Child and Family Studies, 8,* 357–362.

McGrath, P. J., Goodman, J. T., Firestone, P., Shipman, R., & Peters, S. (1983). Recurrent abdominal pain: A psychogenic disorder? *Archives of Diseases in Children, 58,* 888–890.

Mikkelsson, M., Salminen, J. J., Kautiainen, H. (1997). Nonspecific musculoskeletal pain in preadolescents. Prevalence and 1-year persistence. *Pain, 73,* 29–35.

Minuchin, S., Rosman, B., & Baker, L. (1978). *Psychosomatic families.* Boston: Harvard University Press.

Molloy, C. A, & Manning-Courtney, P. (2003). Prevalence of chronic gastrointestinal symptoms in children with autism and autistic spectrum disorders. *Autism, 7,* 165–171.

Newacheck, P. W., & Taylor, W. R. (1992). Childhood chronic illness: Prevalence, severity, and impact. *American Journal of Public Health, 82,* 364–371.

Offord, D. R., Boyle, M. H., Szatmari, P., Rae-Grant, N. I., Links, P. S., Cadman, D. T., et al. (1987). Ontario Child Health Study. II. Six-month prevalence of disorder and rates of service utilization. *Archives of General Psychiatry, 44,* 832–836.

Olafsdottir, E., Ellertsen, B., Berstad, A., & Fluge, G. (2001). Personality profiles and heart rate variability (vagal tone) in children with recurrent abdominal pain. *Acta Paediatrica, 90,* 632–637.

Oster, J. (1972). Recurrent abdominal pain, headache and limb pains in children and adolescents. *Pediatrics, 50,* 429–435.

Perquin, C. W., Hazebroek-Kampschreur, A. A., Hunfeld, J. A., Bohnen, A. M., van Suijlekom-Smit, L. W., Passchier, J., et al. (2000). Pain in children and adolescents: A common experience. *Pain, 87,* 51–58.

Perquin, C. W., Hazebroek-Kampschreur, A. A., Hunfeld, J. A., van Suijlekom-Smit, L. W., Passchier, J., & van der Wouden, J. C. (2000). Chronic pain among children and adolescents: Physician consultation and medication use. *Clinical Journal of Pain, 16,* 229–235.

Perquin, C. W., Hunfeld, J. A., Hazebroek-Kampschreur, A. A., van Suijlekom-Smit, L. W., Passchier, J., Koes, B. W., et al. (2003). The natural course of chronic benign pain in childhood and adolescence: A two-year population-based follow-up study. *European Journal of Pain, 7,* 551–559.

Phillips, K. A., & Diaz, S. F. (1997). Gender differences in body dysmorphic disorder. *Journal of Nervous and Mental Disorders, 185,* 570–577.

Piira, T., Taplin, J. E., Goodenough, B., & von Baeyer, C. L. (2002). Cognitive-behavioral predictors of children's tolerance of laboratory-induced pain: Implications for clinical assessment and future directions. *Behaviour Research and Therapy, 40,* 571–584.

Pilowsky, I., Bassett, D. L., Begg, M. W., & Thomas, P. G. (1982). Childhood hospitalization and chronic intractable pain in adults: A controlled retrospective study. *International Journal of Psychiatry and Medicine, 12,* 75–84.

Pritchard, C. T., Ball, J. D., Culbert, J., & Faust, D. (1988). Using the Personality Inventory for Children to identify children with somatoform disorders: MMPI findings revisited. *Journal of Pediatric Psychology, 13,* 237–245.

Rangel, L., Garralda, E., Levin, M., & Roberts, H. (2000). Personality in adolescents with chronic fatigue syndrome. *European Child and Adolescent Psychiatry, 9,* 39–45.

Raymer, D., Weininger, O., & Hamilton, J. R. (1984). Psychological problems in children with abdominal pain. *Lancet, 1*(8374), 439–440.

Reid, G. J., Lang, B. A., & McGrath, P. J. (1997). Primary juvenile fibromyalgia: Psychological adjustment, family functioning, coping, and functional disability. *Arthritis and Rheumatology, 40,* 752–760.

Reilly, J., Baker, A., Rhodes, J., & Salmon, P. (1999). The association of sexual and physical abuse with somatization: Characteristics of patients presenting with irritable bowel syndrome and non-epileptic attack disorder. *Psychological Medicine, 29,* 399–406.

Reiter, R. C., Shakerin, L. R., Gambone, J. C., & Milburn, A. K. (1991). Correlation between sexual abuse and somatization in women with somatic and nonsomatic chronic pelvic pain. *American Journal of Obstetrics and Gynecology, 165,* 104–109.

Roelofs, K., Keijsers, G. P., Hoogduin, K. A., Naring, G. W., & Moene, F. C. (2002). Childhood abuse in patients with conversion disorder. *American Journal of Psychiatry, 159,* 1908–1913.

Rosenbaum, J. F., Biederman, J., Bolduc-Murphy, E. A., Faraone, S. V., Chaloff, J., Hirshfeld, D. R., et al. (1993). Behavioral inhibition in childhood: A risk factor for anxiety disorders. *Harvard Review of Psychiatry, 1,* 2–16.

Rost, K. M., Akins, R. N., Brown, F. W., & Smith, G. R. (1992). The comorbidity of *DSM-III-R* personality disorders in somatization disorder. *General Hospital Psychiatry, 14,* 322–326.

Ruo, B., Rumsfeld, J. S., Hlatky, M. A., Liu, H., Browner, W. S., & Whooley, M. A. (2003). Depressive symptoms and health-related quality of life: The Heart and Soul Study. *Journal of the American Medical Association, 290*(2), 215–221.

Sanders, M. R., Rebgetz, M., Morrison, M., Bor, W., Gordon, A., Dadds, M., et al. (1989). Cognitive-behavioral treatment of recurrent nonspecific abdominal pain in children: An analysis of generalization, maintenance, and side effects. *Journal of Consulting and Clinical Psychology, 57,* 294–300.

Sanders, M. R, Shepherd, R. W., Cleghorn, G., & Woolford, H. (1994). The treatment of recurrent abdominal pain in children: A controlled comparison of cognitive-behavioral family intervention and standard pediatric care. *Journal of Consulting and Clinical Psychology, 62,* 306–314.

Schanberg, L. E., Keefe, F. J., Lefebvre, J. C., Kredich, D. W., & Gil, K. M. (1998). Social context of pain in children with juvenile primary fibromyalgia syndrome: Parental pain history and family environment. *Clinical Journal of Pain, 14,* 107–115.

Scharff, L. (1997). Recurrent abdominal pain in children: A review of psychological factors and treatment. *Clinical Psychological Review, 17,* 145–166.

Shapiro, E. G., & Rosenfeld, A. A. (1987). *The somatizing child: Diagnosis and treatment of conversion and somatization disorders.* New York: Springer.

Sharpe, M., & Mayou, R. (2004). Somatoform disorders: A help or hindrance to good patient care? *British Journal of Psychiatry, 184,* 465–467.

Spierings, C., Pocls, P. J, Sijben, N., Gabreals, F. J, & Renier, W. O. (1990). Conversion disorders in childhood: A retrospective follow-up study of 84 inpatients. *Developmental Medicine and Child Neurology, 32,* 865–871.

Stang, P. E., & Osterhaus, J. T. 1993. Impact of migraine in the United States: Data from the National Health Interview Survey. *Headache, 33,* 29–35.

Steinhausen, H. C., von Aster, M., Pfeiffer, E., & Gobel, D. (1989). Comparative studies of conversion disorders in childhood and adolescence. *Journal of Child Psychology and Psychiatry, 30,* 615–621.

Stickler, G. B., & Murphy, D. B. (1979). Recurrent abdominal pain. *American Journal of Diseases in Children, 133,* 486–489.

Stone, J., Wojcik, W., Durrance, D., Carson, A., Lewis, S., MacKenzie, L., et al. (2002). What should we say to patients with symptoms unexplained by disease? The "number needed to offend." *British Medical Journal, 325,* 1449–1450.

Stuart, S., & Noyes, R. (1999). Attachment and interpersonal communication in somatization. *Psychosomatics, 40,* 34–43.

Sullivan, M. J., Thorn, B., Haythornthwaite, J. A., Keefe, F., Martin, M., Bradley, L. A., et al. (2001). Theoretical perspectives on the relation between catastrophizing and pain. *Clinical Journal of Pain, 17,* 52–64.

Talley, N. J., Fett, S. L., Zinsmeister, N. R., & Milton, L. J. (1994). Gastrointestinal tract symptoms and self-reported abuse: A population based study. *Gastroenterology, 107,* 1040–1049.

Tamminen, T. M., Bredenberg, P., Escartin, T., Kaukonen, P., Puura, K., Rutanen, M., et al. (1991). Psychosomatic symptoms in preadolescent children. *Psychotherapy Psychosomatics, 56,* 70–77.

Taylor, S. (1999). *Anxiety sensitivity: Theory, research and treatment of the fear of anxiety.* Mahwah, NJ: Erlbaum.

Thastum, M., Zachariae, R., & Herlin, T. (2001). Pain experience and pain coping strategies in children with juvenile idiopathic arthritis. *Journal of Rheumatology, 28,* 1091–1098.

Thastum, M., Zachariae, R., Scholer, M., Bjerring, P., & Herlin, T. (1997). Cold pressor pain: Comparing responses of juvenile arthritis patients and their parents. *Scandinavian Journal of Rheumatology, 26,* 272–279.

Thomsen, A. H., Compas, B. E., Colletti, R. B., Stanger, C., Boyer, M. C., & Konik, B. S. (2002, April). *Coping, temperament, and adjustment in children with recurrent abdominal pain.* Paper presented at the 21st Annual Scientific Sessions of the Society of Behavioral Medicine, Nashville, TN.

Thomsen, A. H., Compas, B. E., Colletti, R. B., Stanger, C., Boyer, M. C., & Konik, B. S. (2002). Parent reports of coping and stress responses in children with recurrent abdominal pain. *Journal of Pediatric Psychology, 27,* 215–226.

Thomson, A. P., & Sills, J. A. (1988). Diagnosis of functional illness presenting with gait disorder. *Archives of Diseases in Children, 63,* 148–153.

Torgersen, S. (1986). Genetics of somatoform disorders. *Archives of General Psychiatry, 43,* 502–505.

Walker, L. S., Claar, R. L., & Garber, J. (2002). Social consequences of children's pain: When do they encourage symptom maintenance? *Journal of Pediatric Psychology, 27,* 689–698.

Walker, L. S., Garber, J., & Greene, J. W. (1991). Somatization symptoms in pediatric abdominal pain patients: Relation to chronicity of abdominal pain and parent somatization. *Journal of Abnormal Child Psychology, 19,* 379–394.

Walker, L. S., Garber, J., & Greene, J. W. (1993). Psychosocial correlates of recurrent childhood pain: A comparison of pediatric patients with recurrent abdominal pain, organic illness, and psychiatric disorders. *Journal of Abnormal Psychology, 102,* 248–258.

Walker, L. S., Garber, J., Van Slyke, D. A., & Greene, J. W. (1995). Long-term health outcomes in patients with recurrent abdominal pain. *Journal of Pediatric Psychology, 20,* 233–245.

Walker, L. S, & Greene, J. W. (1989). Children with recurrent abdominal pain and their parents: More somatic complaints, anxiety, and depression than other patient families? *Journal of Pediatric Psychology, 14,* 231–243.

Walker, L. S., & Greene, J. W. (1991). Negative life events and symptom resolution in pediatric abdominal pain patients. *Journal of Pediatric Psychiatry, 16,* 341–360.

Walker, L. S., Guite, J. W., Duke, M., Barnard, J. A., & Greene, J. W. (1998). Recurrent abdominal pain: A potential precursor of irritable bowel syndrome in adolescents and young adults. *Journal of Pediatrics, 132,* 1010–1015.

Walker, L. S., Smith, C. A., Garber, J., & Van Slyke, D. A. (1997). Development and validation of the Pain Response Inventory for children. *Psychological Assessment, 9,* 392–405.

Walker, L. S., Smith, C. A., Garber, J., Van Slyke, D. A., & Claar, R. (2001). The relation of daily stressors to somatic and emotional symptoms in children with recurrent abdominal pain. *Journal of Consulting and Clinical Psychology, 69,* 85–91.

Walker, L. S., & Zeman, J. L. (1992). Parental response to child illness behavior. *Journal of Pediatric Psychology, 17,* 49–71.

Wasserman, A. L., Whitington, P. F., & Rivara, F. P. (1988). Psychogenic basis for abdominal pain in children and adolescents. *American Academy of Child and Adolescent Psychiatry, 27,* 179–184.

Watt, M. C., Stewart, S. H., & Cox, B. J. (1998). A retrospective study of the learning history origins of anxiety sensitivity. *Behaviour Research and Therapy, 36,* 505–525.

Williams, N., Jackson, D., Lambert, P. C., & Johnstone, M. J. (1999). Incidence of non-specific abdominal pain in children during school term: Population survey based on discharge diagnosis. *British Medical Journal, 318,* 1455.

Wyllie, E., Glazer, J. P., Benbadis, S., Kotagal, P., & Wolgamuth, B. (1999). Psychiatric features of children and adolescents with pseudoseizures. *Archives of Pediatric and Adolescent Medicine, 153,* 244–248.

Young, G. S., Mintzer, L. L., Seacord, D., Castaneda, M., Mesrkhani, V., & Stuber, M. L. (2003). Symptoms of posttraumatic stress disorder in parents of transplant recipients: Incidence, severity, and related factors. *Pediatrics, 111,* e725–731.

Zeltzer, L. K., & Bursch, B. (2001). Psychological management strategies for functional disorders. *Journal of Pediatric Gastroenterology and Nutrition, 32,* S40–S41.

Zuckerman, B., Stevenson, J., & Bailey, V. (1987). Stomachaches and headaches in a community sample of preschool children. *Pediatrics, 79,* 677–682.

PART THREE
TREATMENT APPROACHES

CHAPTER 25

Psychodynamic Treatments

SANDRA W. RUSS

INTRODUCTION

Psychodynamic theory is a rich and comprehensive theory that for many decades has guided the practice of psychodynamic child therapy. With the advent of the move toward empirically supported treatments, psychodynamic therapy is challenged by the need to demonstrate the validity of the approach. Research can test both the effectiveness of the therapy and the validity of the constructs and processes proposed by the theory. Some research has investigated the effectiveness of psychodynamic therapy, and a growing body of studies have supported the validity of major constructs. More research is needed so that the psychodynamic approach can remain viable and be refined. This chapter reviews major principles of psychodynamic practice and constructs of psychodynamic theory. The clinical and research literature is discussed. The role of play in psychodynamic therapy is especially highlighted.

Psychodynamic Approach

The psychodynamic approach focuses on the internal world of the child. A developmental perspective is used to understand underlying cognitive, affective, and interpersonal processes (Shirk & Russell, 1996). The level of development of these processes and the interaction among them largely determines the child's behavior, relationships, and internal state. The therapist applies the psychodynamic framework in order to understand these internal processes and childhood disorders. This psychodynamic understanding determines the specific intervention approach and techniques to be used with a particular child.

Psychoanalysis with children evolved from psychoanalytic theory and treatment of adults. Chused (1988), Tuma and Russ (1993), and Tyson and Tyson (1990) reviewed the history of child psychoanalysis. In essence, the techniques of adult psychoanalysis were applied to children. Hug-Hellmuth (1921, 1924), A. Freud (1927), and Burlingham (1932) adapted psychoanalytic techniques to children. Children's play was especially important in that it was used as a vehicle for communication with the therapist. Also, the therapist actively worked to establish a positive relationship with the child (A. Freud, 1927). Anna Freud made significant contributions to psychoanalytic theory with her work on the ego and mechanisms of defense (1936/1966). Melanie Klein, in a different approach, developed early concepts in object relations theory and interpersonal relations (Tyson & Tyson, 1990). Klein also utilized active interpretation of children's play.

Historically, psychodynamic approaches have evolved from psychoanalytic theory and therapy. As Fonagy and Moran (1990) pointed out, many forms of psychodynamic therapies are based on the psychoanalytic conceptualization of child development. Although similar conceptualizations guide psychoanalytic and psychodynamic approaches, there are a number of differences. First, psychodynamic therapies have less ambitious goals than psychoanalytic therapy (Fonagy & Moran, 1990; Tuma & Russ, 1993). Psychodynamic approaches have immediate goals and tend to be focused on a few underlying issues and processes, whereas psychoanalysis works to achieve major structural changes in personality. Both approaches strive to return the child to normal developmental pathways (A. Freud, 1965; Shirk & Russell, 1996). Second, psychoanalytic therapy is more intense than psychodynamic therapies (Fonagy & Moran, 1990; Tuma & Russ, 1993). Psychoanalytic treatment tends to be carried out five times per week and is long-term, lasting an average of 2 years (Fonagy & Moran, 1990). Psychodynamic therapies are less intensive, usually involve weekly sessions with the child, and may be short-term (6–12 sessions) or long-term. The less frequent and shorter term nature of psychodynamic therapies requires different goals, mechanisms of change, and intervention techniques than psychoanalysis. Tuma (1989) stated that psychoanalysis and psychodynamic approaches differ in degree rather than in the kind of psychotherapy. In psychodynamic approaches, the therapist is more active in pointing out feelings and defenses in order to understand and change behavior. In psychoanalysis, where there is more time, there is more of a focus on understanding the origins of the feelings, especially anxiety (Tuma, 1989).

A third difference is that of flexibility (Russ, 1998). Psychoanalysis involves a very standardized approach over a long time. Psychodynamic approaches are more flexible in terms of the types of intervention techniques used and the integration of other theoretical perspectives and techniques. For example, the therapist might use modeling techniques, role-playing, or family sessions with a particular child, but always within an overall psychodynamic conceptualization of the case.

Interestingly, in a review of the adult research literature, Fisher and Greenberg (1996) concluded that the research does not support a distinction with regard to outcome between psychodynamic and the more intensive psychoanalytic treatment. In fact, evidence suggests that the briefer psychodynamic treatments, which allow for more flexibility in therapist interventions, may be more efficient in helping patients.

MECHANISMS OF CHANGE AND TECHNIQUES

In most forms of psychodynamic therapy, the therapist and child meet individually once a week for a session of 45–50 minutes. The basic understanding between the therapist and the child is that the therapist is there to help the child express feelings and thoughts, understand causes of behavior, and form a relationship with the therapist (Freedheim & Russ, 1992). Goals of treatment are also discussed. Play is a major tool in the therapy. Traditionally, the child has usually structured the hour, chosen the topic to discuss, chosen the toys to play with, and determined the pace of the therapy. But as therapy has become more short-term, therapists are becoming more active and directive within a psychodynamic framework in focusing on specific topics and directing the play (Russ, 2004). Also, for most child therapists, parent guidance and therapy, and education and consultation with the school are essential components to the therapy. Medication, where appropriate, is part of the treatment plan as well. For a review of the practical issues that arise in psychodynamic therapy and for case presentations, see Chethik (1989), Kessler (1966, 1988), and Russ (2004).

What occurs between the therapist and child that results in changes in behavior or internal experiences? How does change occur in psychodynamic psychotherapy? In 1983, Freedheim and Russ identified six major mechanisms of change in individual child psychotherapy. These mechanisms of change were based on those identified in the adult literature by Applebaum (1978) and Garfield (1980). After recent reviews of the literature, we continue to think that these categories of mechanisms of change are most relevant to psychodynamic therapy (Russ, 2004; Russ & Freedheim, 2001). The following emerge as hypothesized mechanisms of change within the child as a result of psychodynamic therapy.

Catharsis and Expression of Feelings

The release of emotion and expression of feelings are thought to be therapeutic by a number of different schools of therapy (Axline, 1947; A. Freud, 1965). Expression of negative feelings in particular is important for many children (Moustakas, 1953). Helping children to feel that they can safely express feelings, through talk or play, is a major task of the therapist. The therapist labels the feeling expressed by the child or puppet, accepts the feeling, and tries to understand the feeling. Words help put the feeling into a context for the child, thus making the feeling less overwhelming.

Corrective Emotional Experience

The therapist accepts the child's feelings and thoughts. Often, the child's learned expectations are not met. The relationship between the therapist and child is especially important for a corrective emotional experience to occur. For example, a child expresses angry thoughts and feelings about his or her mother. The therapist, contrary to the child's expectations, is not angry or punishing. Rather, the therapist is accepting of the feelings and works to understand the reasons for the anger. After a number of these therapeutic events, a corrective emotional experience occurs (Kessler, 1966). The automatic connection between angry thoughts or feelings and anxiety or guilt gradually decreases (or extinguishes). The child then becomes more comfortable with these feelings and thoughts. In children, expression of thoughts and feelings often occurs through play. The therapist works with those expressions and, if possible, connects them to the child's daily life.

Insight and Working Through

The emotional resolution of conflict or trauma is a major mechanism of change in psychodynamic psychotherapy. It is this mechanism that differentiates psychodynamic therapy from other forms of interpersonal therapy. One goal of the therapist is to help the child reexperience major developmental conflicts or situational traumas in therapy. When underlying conflicts are a major issue, then therapy goals are cognitive insight into origins of feelings and conflicts; causes of symptoms; and links between thoughts, feelings, and actions (Sandler, Kennedy, & Tyson, 1980; Shirk & Russell, 1996). Verbal labeling of unconscious impulses, conflicts, and causes of behavior helps lend higher order reasoning skills to understanding problems. Well-timed interpretations by the therapist help to establish these links and to help the child understand the causes of feelings and behavior. In many cases, however, especially with young children, cognitive insight does not occur. Rather, emotional reexperiencing, emotional working through, and mastery of material do occur and result in behavior change and changes in internal feeling states. This is an important mechanism of change and is often overlooked in the literature. Messer and Warren (1995) also stated that the goal of making the unconscious conscious needs to be modified in child therapy with many children. In Erikson's (1963) concept of mastery, the child uses play to gain mastery over traumatic events and everyday conflicts. Resolving conflicts through play is part of normal child development. For normal children who are using play, cognitive insight into underlying issues does not usually occur. But the emotional processing that is occurring in the play helps the child resolve the issues. Therapists who are using play in therapy may be helping the emotional processing occur without cognitive insight in many cases. Freedheim and Russ (1992) described the process of playing out conflict-laden content until the conflict and negative affect are resolved. The psychodynamic therapist helps guide the play, labels the feelings, describes the action, and makes interpretations to facilitate conflict resolution and the working-through process.

Learning Alternative Problem-Solving Techniques and Coping Strategies

The therapist, in a directive approach, helps the child think about alternative ways of viewing a situation and generate problem-solving strategies. Role-playing and modeling of coping strategies are used by the therapist. For example, Singer (1993) gave examples of modeling techniques during therapy. Although this mechanism of change is not often associated with psychodynamic therapy, it is frequently part of an intervention within a psychodynamic conceptualization of a case.

Development of Internal Structure and Processes

Many children have deficits in internal structures and processes that result in serious emotional disorders. Deficits in self/other differentiation and object representations and object relations can result in serious problems with self-esteem regulation, reality testing, attachment, and impulse control. In these children, major deficits exist in underlying cognitive, affective, and interpersonal processes. Structure-building approaches are based on conceptualizations by Mahler (1968) and Kohut (1977). The therapist attempts to be seen as a caring, empathic, stable, and predictable figure.

Development of good object relations is a major goal of therapy with these children. Gilpin (1976) stressed that the role of the therapist is to become an internalized object for the child. The therapist serves as a stable figure who helps the child develop these ego functions as much as possible. The relationship between the therapist and the child is probably the most important aspect of the therapy in helping this process to occur. The expression of empathy by the therapist for the child's experience is an essential technique that enables the child to develop better internal representations of others.

Nonspecific Variables

Nonspecific variables in therapy are increasingly being recognized as important mechanisms of change in their own right. Possible nonspecific variables in child therapy are that the child no longer feels so alone, sees that the problem is being attended to, has expectations of change, or is aware of family involvement (Gaffney, 1986; Miller, 1988).

TREATMENT APPROACHES WITH SPECIFIC POPULATIONS

Three major types of psychodynamic treatment approaches emerge in the child psychotherapy literature (Chethik, 1989; Freedheim & Russ, 1992; Russ, 1998). They are insight-oriented therapy, structure-building approaches, and supportive approaches. Each type of approach emphasizes different mechanisms of change. However, there is rarely a pure type of therapy, and frequently all of the mechanisms of change occur in one case. Catharsis and corrective emotional experience usually occur in all three types of therapy.

Insight-Oriented Therapy

The form of therapy most associated with the psychodynamic approach is insight-oriented therapy, and it is most appropriate for the child with anxiety and internalized conflicts (Tuma & Russ, 1993). This approach is appropriate for children who have age-appropriate ego development; show evidence of internal conflicts; can trust adults; and, for young children, can use play effectively. Insight-oriented therapy is most appropriate for children with internalizing disorders involving anxiety or depression. Children with internalizing disorders often experience internal conflicts, have good development in major areas, and have good attachment and object relations. Goals of therapy are to resolve conflicts. The major mechanism of change is insight and working through. The therapist actively interprets thoughts and feelings in play and in talk about the child's life. As mentioned earlier, often cognitive insight does not occur. Rather, the child reexperiences difficult emotions, processes these feelings, and develops a better understanding of them. Through the use of play and the therapist's reflection and interpretation of thoughts and feelings, the child expresses "forbidden fantasy and feelings, works through and masters developmental problems, and resolves conflicts" (Freedheim & Russ, 1983, p. 982).

Insight and working through can also be helpful for children with good internal resources who have experienced a major trauma. For example, Altschul (1988) described the use of psychoanalytic approaches in helping children to mourn the loss of a parent. Chethik (1989) discussed focal therapy as therapy that deals with focal stress events in the child's life. Chethik listed events such as death in the family, divorce, hospitalization, and illness as examples of specific stressors. Focal therapy focuses on the specific problem and is usually of short duration. It is a psychodynamic approach that uses insight and working through. Chethik viewed this approach as working best with children who have accomplished normal developmental tasks before the occurrence of stressful events.

Structure-Building Approaches

A second major form of psychodynamic therapy is the structure-building approach, which is used with children with deficits in object relations and interpersonal processes (Russ, 1998). For children with impaired object relations, self/other boundary disturbances, and problems distinguishing reality from fantasy, the therapist uses techniques that foster the development of object permanence, self/other differentiation, modulation of affect, and impulse control. The major mechanism of change is the development of these internal processes. The development of object relations is especially important. Mahler (1968) articulated the separation-individuation process and described the development of object constancy and object representations. Blank and Blank (1986) pointed out that object relations plays a major role in the organization of other intrapsychic processes. Children with severely impaired object relations, such as borderline children and children with psychotic and characterological disorders, have early developmental problems in a variety of areas. Also, they tend to have severe dysfunction in the family and often a genetic predisposition.

In a structure-building approach, empathy on the part of the therapist is a much more important intervention than interpretation (Kohut & Wolfe, 1978). Kohut and Wolfe discussed the failure of empathy from the parent that is the major issue in faulty parent-child interaction. Because of the frequency of this occurrence in the interaction between the child and parent, empathy from the therapist around the history of empathic failure becomes an important part of therapy. The empathy from the therapist results in the therapist being internalized and becoming a stable internal figure for the child. Chethik (1989) and Russ (2004) have case presentations of psychotherapy with borderline children. Often, help with problem solving and coping is used with these children as well. Therapy with these children is usually long term (1–2 years).

Supportive Approaches

A third form of psychodynamic therapy with children is supportive psychotherapy, most appropriate for children with externalizing disorders. The broad syndrome of externalizing disorders includes labels of acting out, antisocial disorders, character disorders, oppositional defiant disorders, and conduct disorders (Baum, 1989). Theoretically, psychodynamic theory views these children as having major developmental problems. These children have not yet adequately developed the processes necessary for impulse control and delay of gratification. In addition, these children frequently are egocentric, demonstrate an absence of shame and guilt, and have impaired ability to empathize with others. Kessler (1988) suggested that structured supportive therapy is more helpful to these children than any other kind of psychodynamic therapy. Therapy focuses on the here and now and on problem solving and coping skills. For example, the therapist might role-play with the child how to handle teasing at school or work on anger-management techniques.

THE ROLE OF PRETEND PLAY IN THERAPY

Play has been a part of therapy with children since Melanie Klein and Anna Freud first began using play techniques in child psychotherapy in the 1930s. Kessler (1966, 1988) discussed the major influence of psychoanalytic approaches in the utilization of play in child treatment. Both Klein and Freud stressed the role of play in communication and in the understanding of internal conflicts and fantasies (Gerard, 1952). Currently, play is used in therapy from a variety of theoretical traditions. As of 1992, play in some form was used in child therapy by a majority of clinicians, as reported by Koocher and D'Angelo (1992).

In the child therapy literature, four broad functions of play emerge as important in therapy (Russ, 2004). First, play is a natural form of expression in children. Chethik (1989) refers to the language of play. Children use play to express feelings and thoughts. Chethik stated that play emerges from the child's internal life and reflects the child's internal world. Therefore, children use play to express affect and fantasy and, in therapy, to express troubling and conflict-laden feelings.

Second, the child uses the language of play to communicate with the therapist. By understanding these communications, the therapist develops a therapeutic relationship with the child (Chethik, 1989). The therapist actively labels, accepts, empathizes with, and interprets the play expressions, which in turn helps the child feel understood (Russ, 1995). These play expressions are important in enabling mechanisms of change to occur in therapy. For example, a corrective emotional experience can occur by the therapist accepting and understanding angry feelings expressed in play. Also, for many children, the feeling of empathy from the therapist around the play facilitates change in their internal representations and interpersonal functioning.

A third major function of play is as a vehicle for the occurrence of insight and working through. The emotional resolution of conflict or trauma and negative feelings is a major mechanism of change in psychodynamic child therapy. Children reexperience major developmental or situational trauma in therapy. Many of these conflicts are expressed in play. The play process itself has been thought of as a form of conflict resolution. For example, Waelder (1933) described the play process as one in which the child repeats an unpleasant experience over and over until it becomes manageable. Erikson (1963) presented the concept of mastery, in which the child uses play to gain mastery over traumatic events and everyday conflicts. During this process the therapist labels and interprets the play. The therapist will also tie the observations and interpretations to events in the child's life. Although there is controversy in the psychodynamic literature about how much interpretation to use (A. Freud, 1966; Klein, 1955), there is general agreement that working through and mastery are important mechanisms of change.

A fourth major function of play in therapy is to provide the child opportunities to practice with a variety of ideas, behaviors, interpersonal behaviors, and verbal expressions. Because play is occurring in a safe environment in a pretend world, with a permissive, nonjudgmental adult, the child can try out and rehearse a variety of expressions and behaviors without concern about real-life consequences. In some forms of play therapy, the therapist is quite directive in guiding the child to try new behaviors.

Knell (1993) developed a cognitive behavioral play therapy approach that actively uses modeling techniques and a variety of cognitive behavioral techniques. Many of these techniques can be used within a psychodynamic framework.

Although these functions of play occur in normal play situations, the therapist builds on these normal functions by enhancing the play experience. The therapist creates a safe environment, gives permission for play to occur, actively facilitates play, and labels the thoughts and feelings expressed. For the psychodynamic therapist, interpretation specifically aids conflict resolution.

For most children younger than 10 years of age in psychodynamic therapy, therapy is a mixture of play and talk. How play is used in psychotherapy depends on the child's ability to use play, developmental level, age, and ability to verbalize as well as the overall treatment approach and goals. A number of practical issues arise in using play in therapy, such as issues of how to get the child started in using play, kinds of play materials, how much the therapist should engage in play, how much to interpret, and how much to set limits (see Chetthik, 1989; Russ, 2004; Singer, 1993).

RESEARCH WITH PSYCHODYNAMIC TREATMENTS AND CONSTRUCTS

The major challenge for psychodynamic therapy today is to establish empirical support for its effectiveness. Recently, there has been a strong movement in the field of child psychotherapy to identify empirically supported treatments (Lonigan, Elbert, & Johnson, 1998). Most of the therapy outcome studies have been efficacy studies that are conducted under controlled conditions that involve random assignment, control groups, and single disorders. Effectiveness studies, on the other hand, are clinical utility studies that focus on treatment outcome in real-world environments such as mental health clinics. Empirically supported treatment reviews have focused on efficacy studies (Kazdin, 2000). Reviews of the research literature spell out the criteria they have used to evaluate the treatment. Criteria usually include studies that use random assignment to conditions, have specific child populations, use treatment manuals, and use multiple outcomes with blind raters (Kazdin, 2000). Some controversy exists about how stringent the criteria should be before it is concluded that a treatment has been empirically validated. One approach used by the Task Force on Promotion and Dissemination of Psychological Procedures of the American Psychological Association placed treatments into categories of well-established or probably efficacious treatments (Chambless et al., 1996). The task force focusing on child therapies adopted this approach, with few exceptions (Lonigan et al., 1998). Kazdin (2000) concluded that there are empirically supported treatments for children, but at this time, they are relatively few in number. The list is composed of mainly cognitive-behavioral treatments. Kazdin recommended placing treatments on a continuum from 1 to 5, with 1 being treatments that have not been evaluated and 5 being best treatments (more effective than one or more other well-established treatments). Using this kind of scale would distinguish among those studies that have not yet been investigated, those that have been investigated and are promising, and those that have been investigated but were not effective. For the most part, psychodynamic treatments have not been investigated in well-controlled studies.

Weisz and Weiss (1993) pointed out the low number of psychodynamic therapy outcome studies in the literature. Fonagy and Moran (1990) stated that one reason for the lack of research is that the rather global approach and broad goals of psychodynamic approaches do not lend themselves easily to carefully controlled outcome studies. In the three types of treatment approaches previously discussed (insight, structure-building, and supportive), the goals and mechanisms of change are broad. Because therapy is so individualized and the therapist is making decisions about intervention on a moment-to-moment basis, specific research guidelines based on research findings are few (Russ, 1998). However, specificity in research is essential for the field to progress. Weisz and Weiss (1993) concluded that the studies showing positive results in psychotherapy research tend to be the ones that focus on a specific problem with careful planning of the intervention. Freedheim and Russ (1983) stated that we need to become very specific and investigate which specific interventions impact which cognitive, affective, and personality processes. Shirk and Russell (1996) developed a framework for conceptualizing intervention research that ties specific treatment processes to underlying cognitive, affective, and interpersonal processes within a developmental framework. Psychodynamic conceptualizations such as the effect of conflict or of deficits in object relations should be testable within their framework. They stress the importance of investigation of specific processes and change mechanisms. Single-case designs are also appropriate for psychodynamic approaches (Kazdin, 1993).

There has been some progress in the area of psychodynamic psychotherapy research with children. Fonagy and Moran (1990) applied many of the current guidelines for psychotherapy outcome research to evaluating the effectiveness of child psychoanalysis. Their studies are models for how to investigate the efficacy of psychodynamic approaches. They have carried out different types of studies that are well suited to the psychoanalytic or psychodynamic approach. In one study (Moran & Fonagy, 1987) they used a time series analysis to study the 184 weeks of treatment of a diabetic teenager. Time series analysis investigates whether there is a time-bound relationship between events. A relationship was found between major themes in analysis and diabetic control. Moran and Fonagy concluded that the interpretation of conflicts in the treatment brought about an improvement in diabetic control. The improved control led to temporary increases in anxiety and guilt. The improved diabetic control appeared to increase the likelihood of manifest psychological symptomatology. This pattern fit the psychodynamic understanding of brittle diabetes.

In a second study, an inpatient program for diabetes was evaluated (Fonagy & Moran, 1990). Eleven patients received psychotherapy and medical supervision while the comparison group received medical treatment with no psychotherapy. The analytic treatment was well defined and based on the psychoanalytic understanding of brittle diabetes as being caused by unconscious emotional factors influencing the significance of the disease or its treatment regimen. This leads to disregard for normal diabetic care. The goal of therapy was to make conscious the conflicts and anxieties that were interwoven with the diabetes treatment regimen. The treated group showed significant improvement in diabetic control. None of the untreated group showed improvement. Improvement was maintained at 1-year follow-up. Fonagy and Moran stressed the importance and feasibility of systematic and specific intervention research that investigates changes in psychic structure such as affect regulation and empathy as a result of psychoanalysis.

Shirk and Russell (1996) reviewed a number of research programs and measures relevant to assessing change in psychodynamic psychotherapy. Wallerstein (1988) and Kernberg (1995) have coding systems for dimensions relevant to psychodynamic treatment. The Affect in Play Scale (Russ, 1993) could also be used to measure change in play processes in psychodynamic therapy.

Muratori, Picchi, Bruni, Patarnello, and Romagnoli (2003) evaluated short- and long-term effects of time-limited psychodynamic psychotherapy for children with internalizing disorders. Fifty-eight outpatient children (6–10 years old), who met *DSM-IV* (American Psychiatric Association, 1994) criteria for depressive or anxiety disorder were assigned to therapy or community services. Children were assessed at baseline, 6 months, and 2-year follow-up by the Children's Global Assessment Scale (C-GAS) and Child Behavior Checklist (CBCL). Group assignment was not random. Assignment to the treatment group occurred if there was an opening. If no opening was available, the child was referred to community services. There was no significant difference at baseline between the groups on major variables. Therapy consisted of 11 sessions that followed a protocol—5 parent-child sessions, 5 sessions with the child alone, and a final parent-child session. There appear to be clear guidelines about therapist intervention in each session. The treatment approach focused on pointing out the nature of the core conflictual theme and connecting it to the child's symptoms and the representational world of the parent. In the child sessions, the therapist labeled feelings and connected feelings, mental contents, and symptoms. Play was seen as an important part of the therapy. Therapists were trained in this approach. Therapists' interventions were videotaped and discussed weekly to monitor adherence to the protocol.

The results of this study indicated major improvements in the treatment group on the C-GAS and CBCL. C-GAS improvements were observed at 6 months and CBCL findings were at 2-year follow-up. The changes in the internalizing syndrome on the CBCL at the follow-up only is evidence for the "sleeper effect"—a delayed response to the treatment. Muratori et al. (2003) concluded that changes in the shared representational world brought about by the therapy resulted in changes in parent-child interaction only after a length of time. Also, the treatment group sought mental health services less than the comparison group during the 2-year period. This evaluation was a well-done study that followed many methodological guidelines for adequate research design described by Weisz and Weiss (1993). The sample was relatively homogeneous (anxious and depressed), a treatment protocol was followed, therapists were trained, and therapists were monitored to make sure they adhered to the intervention techniques. In addition, there was a theoretical rationale for why this approach should affect this syndrome. This type of rigorous research needs to occur in the psychodynamic area.

More studies are also needed that investigate specific mechanisms of change in therapy. A good example of this kind of study is one by Wiser and Goldfried (1998). This study was with adults, but it is a good model for the child area because it investigates specific types of interventions on specific processes. The authors investigated the effectiveness of therapeutic interventions on emotional experiencing. Theoretically, the expression of emotion in session has been thought to be important for different mechanisms of change to occur. An important question, then, with adults and children is how to facilitate emotional experiencing in the session. Wiser and Goldfried coded interventions by therapists with outpatient adults who were anxious, depressed, or both in either psychodynamic or cognitive-behavioral therapy. They found that interventions of reflections and acknowledgments, affiliative and noncontrolling interventions, or interventions highlighting nonspecific client content were associated with maintaining high emotional experiencing in both approaches (reflections were nonsignificant in the psychodynamic approach but may have been significant with a larger sample size). Interestingly, no type of intervention was associated with a shift to higher emotional experiencing. Some interventions were related to shifts to low experiencing—those that were lengthy and those that were affiliative but moderately controlling. It is important to know which techniques to use that increase emotional experiencing and that decrease emotional experiencing. Both types of interventions are therapeutic at different times with different populations. The Wiser and Goldfried (1998) study is an excellent example of the type of therapy process research that needs to be carried out with children.

The relationship with the therapist is also important to investigate in psychodynamic therapy. Using meta-analytic procedures, Shirk and Karver (2003) reviewed associations between therapeutic relationship variables and treatment outcomes in child and adolescent therapy. Results found a modest association (.20), which is similar to that of adult studies. This relationship was found across diverse types and modes of child treatment.

Target (2002) reported on results from a retrospective chart study of treated children at the Anna Freud Center who were in psychodynamic or more intensive psychoanalytic treatment. Although this study was retrospective and there was no randomized design or comparison groups, the results are important and provide guidance. Looking first at anxiety or depressive disorders, 72 percent of those treated for at least 6 months showed clinically significant improvement (Target & Fonagy, 1994). Phobic disorders were most likely to remit and depressive disorders least likely. Variables that identified children most likely to improve were higher IQ, younger age, longer treatment, good peer relations, poor overall adjustment of the mother, presence of anxiety in the mother, concurrent treatment of the mother, and absence of maternal antisocial behavior.

In a chart review of disruptive disorders, improvement rates were lower than for the internalizing disorders, with one third terminating prematurely. Of those who stayed in treatment, 69 percent were no longer diagnosable upon termination. Predictors of improvement were the presence of an anxiety disorder, absence of other disorders, younger age, intensive treatment, longer treatment, maternal anxiety disorder, treatment of the mother, and foster care for the child. Target and Fonagy (1996), in discussing this study, concluded that psychodynamic therapy was effective with disorders involving anxiety, even when the anxiety was coupled with disruptive disorders. A different picture emerged with the disruptive (externalizing) disorders. When therapy was effective, it was when intensive treatment was used. Fonagy reported that the oppositional disorders were most likely to improve and conduct disorders the least likely.

We need to think carefully before recommending psychodynamic therapy for externalizing disorders in which anxiety is not a major factor. Cognitive-behavioral approaches have been found to be effective. For example, parent-child interaction therapy is very effective with oppositional defiant disorder (Bodiford-McNeil, Hembree-Kigin, & Eyberg, 1996). If psychodynamic therapy is recommended, two things should be kept in mind and shared with the family: (1) there is no solid empirical support for psychodynamic therapy with externalizing disorders, and (2) the intensive therapy that would be attempted would be costly in resources.

Research studies that do exist in the area support the use of psychodynamic therapy for internalizing disorders where anxiety and conflict are important factors. The play intervention research that exists also supports the use of a psychodynamic conceptualization for reducing anxiety and negative affect.

Play Intervention Studies

As Russ (1995, 2004) has reviewed, play intervention studies have investigated the effect of play on specific types of problems and in specific populations. I labeled these studies play intervention because the focus is highly specific, usually involving only a few sessions with the child. These studies have been focused on reducing anxiety in children in medical settings or dealing with separation anxiety. In two different studies, puppet play reduced anxiety in children facing medical procedures when compared with children in a control group (Cassell, 1965; Johnson & Stockdale, 1975). Rae, Worchel, Upchurch, Sanner, and Daniel (1989) found that children in a therapeutic play group showed significantly more reduction in self-reported hospital-related fears than children in three other groups. This was a well-done study that controlled for time spent with an adult, verbal support, and play activity. The authors concluded that fantasy activity in the play resulted in fear reduction. Milos and Reiss (1982) found that thematic play reduced separation anxiety in preschoolers when compared with children in a control group. Also, the quality of play ratings were significantly negatively related to posttest anxiety. High-quality play was defined as play that showed more separation themes and attempts to resolve conflicts. They concluded that their results supported the underlying assumption of play therapy—that play can reduce anxiety associated with psychological problems. The results are consistent with psychodynamic theory.

A well-designed study by Barnett (1984) also investigated separation anxiety and expanded on the work of Barnett and Storm (1981) in which free play was found to reduce distress in children following a conflict situation. In the 1984 study, a natural stressor, the first day of school, was used. Seventy-four preschool children were observed separating from their mothers and were rated anxious or nonanxious. These two groups were further divided into a play or no-play story-listening condition. For half of the play condition, play was solitary. For the other half, peers were present. The story condition was also split into solitary and peers-present segments. Play was rated by observers and categorized into types of play. Play significantly reduced anxiety in the high-anxious group. Anxiety was measured by the Palmer Sweat Index. There was no effect for low-anxious children. For the high-anxious children, solitary play was best in reducing anxiety. High-anxious children spent more time in fantasy play than did low-anxious children, who showed more functional and manipulative play. High-anxious children also engaged more in fantasy play when no other children were present. Barnett interpreted these results to mean that play was used to cope with a distressing situation. The findings supported her concept that it is not social play that is essential to conflict resolution, but rather imaginative play qualities that the child introduces into playful behavior.

The results of these studies suggest that play helps children deal with fears and reduce anxiety and that something about play itself is important and serves as a vehicle for change. Results of several studies suggest that fantasy and make-believe are involved in the reduction of anxiety. The studies effectively controlled for the variable of an attentive adult. Results also suggest that children who are already good players are more able to use play opportunities to resolve problems.

These research findings are consistent with psychodynamic theoretical and clinical literature that utilizes play to help with internal conflict resolution and mastery of internal issues, as well as with external traumas and stressful life events. As a result of this conflict resolution and problem solving, anxiety is reduced. Psychodynamic approaches also suggest the use of insight, conflict-resolution approaches for children whose fantasy skills are normally developed and who can use play in therapy.

Future research should focus on the mechanisms that account for the finding that play reduces anxiety. Conceptualizations and research from other theoretical frameworks could apply to play therapy. For example, Harris (2000) views play as helping the child construct a situation model that is revisable. Children go back and forth between an imagined world and reality and develop a new cognitive appraisal of the situation. Pennebaker's work is also relevant. Adults who develop a coherent and meaningful narrative of an event through an emotional writing exercise have improved mental and physical health (Pennebaker & Graybeal, 2001). Children may be developing meaningful and coherent narratives in play therapy.

Future research should also investigate techniques in therapy that facilitate play in therapy. Russ, Moore, and Farber (2004) developed play intervention protocols that resulted in increased fantasy and imagination and increased affect in first- and second-grade children. In five 30-minute sessions with a play trainer, the child was instructed to play out various story scripts. In the affect play group, the child was asked to play out stories with different emotions and to express emotion. In the imagination play group, the child was asked to play out stories with a high fantasy content and high organization of the story. The instructions and prompts by the play trainer were standardized. The affect play group had higher scores on all play abilities when compared to a control group on the outcome play measure (Affect in Play Scale). The imagination play group had higher scores on affect play variables. There was a significant affect of group on creativity, coping, and life satisfaction measures. The results suggest that a brief standardized play intervention can improve play skills that may be related to creativity, coping, and life satisfaction. The structured play technique used in this study could be used to increase emotional expression in play in children in psychotherapy. This technique could be especially helpful for affect constricted children or children with posttraumatic stress disorder (PTSD), where the expression of affect in a safe setting can be therapeutic. By having children make up various stories and directing them to express affect, with modeling and reinforcement by the therapist, children could increase affect expression quickly. The play intervention scripts and prompts used in this study could be used by therapists at various points in the therapy.

Research on Psychodynamic Constructs

Research that investigates the constructs and hypotheses of psychodynamic theory also helps establish an empirical base to psychodynamic therapy. Although not directly investigating psychodynamic therapy, empirically supported constructs should guide therapy research in terms of what to focus on and what therapy techniques to emphasize. Westen (1998) had a major review of the research literature and identified a number of psychodynamic constructs and propositions that have been supported. Much of the research has been carried out in cognitive, social, developmental, and personality psychology. Often, psychodynamic terminology is not used or referred to. Concepts are placed in a more contemporary cognitive-affective framework. Westen identified the following constructs and principles of psychodynamic theory that have received significant empirical support: unconscious processes, ambivalence and conflict, importance of childhood origins of personality and social dispositions, mental representations of self and others, and developmental dynamics.

Primary process thinking is another construct that has a large body of research support (Holt, 1977; Suler, 1980). A large number of studies have found a relationship between access to primary process thinking and creativity, as psychoanalytic theory predicts, in adults and children (Russ, 1996; Suler, 1980). Russ (1996) has discussed these relationships within current cognitive-affective conceptualizations.

SHORT-TERM PSYCHODYNAMIC PSYCHOTHERAPY

Short-term psychotherapy (6–12 sessions) is a frequent form of psychodynamic psychotherapy with children (Messer & Warren, 1995). The practical realities of HMOs and of clinical practice in general have led to briefer forms of treatment. Often, the time-limited nature of the therapy is by default, not by plan (Messer & Warren, 1995). The average number of sessions for children in outpatient therapy is 6 or fewer in private and clinical settings (Dulcan & Piercy, 1985).

There is little research or clinical theory about short-term therapy with children (Messer & Warren, 1995). A few research studies have shown that explicit time limits reduced the likelihood of premature termination (Parad & Parad, 1968) and that children in time-limited therapy showed as much improvement as those in long-term therapy (Smyrnios & Kirby, 1993). The time is right for the development of theoretically based short-term interventions for children. Messer and Warren (1995) suggested that the developmental approach utilized by psychodynamic theory provides a useful framework for short-term therapy. One can identify the developmental problems and obstacles involved in a particular case. The authors also stressed the use of play as a vehicle of change and, as Winnicott (1971) has said, of development. They suggested that the active interpretation of the meaning of play can help the child feel understood, which in turn can result in lifelong changes in self-perception and experience.

In other words, the understanding of the metaphors in a child's play could give the child insight, or an experience of empathy, or both. This lasting change could be accomplished in a short time.

As previously discussed, Chethik (1989) developed focal therapy to deal with specific stressful events in the child's life. Basic principles of psychodynamic therapy are applied in this short-term approach, with the basic mechanism of change being insight and working through. Chethik views this approach as working best with children who have accomplished normal developmental tasks before the stressful event occurred.

In general, brief forms of psychodynamic intervention are seen as more appropriate for the child who has accomplished the major developmental milestones. Proskauer (1969) stressed the child's ability to quickly develop a relationship with the therapist, good trusting ability, the existence of a focal dynamic issue, and flexible and adaptive defenses as criteria for short-term intervention. Messer and Warren concluded that children with less severe pathology are more responsive to brief intervention than children with chronic developmental problems. The Muratori et al. (2003) study that found that short-term intervention with anxious and depressed children was effective is consistent with this conclusion. The research and clinical literature suggest that internalizing disorders are most appropriate for brief psychodynamic intervention (Russ, 2004). The therapist is active, at times directive, and uses all mechanisms of change in the therapy. Insight and working through are essential, but modeling, rehearsal, and problem-solving strategies are also part of the therapy. Children with major deficits in object relations and with early developmental problems need longer term structure-building approaches.

Shelby (2000) described the importance of using developmentally appropriate interventions in brief therapy with traumatized children. In working with traumatized children in Sarajevo, Shelby used play and drawing. She described an experiential mastery technique in which children drew pictures of the thing that frightened them. Children were encouraged to verbalize their feelings to the drawing.

Structured play techniques would be especially useful in short-term therapy. The MacArthur Story Stem Battery (MSSB), although designed as an assessment tool, can be used to structure the play situation. Kelsay (2002), in an innovative approach, used the MSSB to structure play therapy. The MSSB is a set of story beginnings (e.g., parents arguing over lost keys) and the child is asked to complete the story. The therapist can choose appropriate story stems tailored to the issues that the child is dealing with. This structured approach could move the therapy to central issues more quickly.

Structured play techniques have also been used with very young children. Gaensbauer and Siegel (1995) described structured play techniques with toddlers who have experienced traumatic events. They conceptualized the mechanisms of change when play is used as being similar to those in older children with PTSD. With these very young children, the therapist actively structures the play to re-create the traumatic event. Gaensbauer and Siegel outlined three purposes of structured play reenactment. First, play enables the child to organize the fragmented experiences into meaningful narratives. Second, the interpretive work by the therapist helps the child understand the personal meanings of the trauma. Third, there is desensitization of the anxiety and fear and other negative emotions associated with the trauma. The authors stressed that the key element that enables the child to use play adaptively, rather than in a repetitive fashion, is the "degree to which affects can be brought to the surface so the child can identify them and integrate them in more adaptive ways" (p. 297).

The play protocol developed by Russ et al. (2004) could be useful in short-term therapy. These play stories could be used to structure the play and help the child gain access to and express emotion. We found that the affect play group did increase their expression and range of emotion in a different play task. The therapist could choose and develop stories that related to the specific issues with which the child is struggling.

FUTURE RESEARCH

Given the results of the research in the area, a research agenda that would be the most fruitful and have the most immediate impact on the field would focus on the following:

1. Internalizing disorders: Well-controlled studies with anxiety disorders, post-traumatic stress disorders, depression, and focused problems involving anxiety and conflict should be carried out with psychodynamic therapy.
2. Short-term therapy approaches: Short-term interventions should be investigated and refined.
3. Mechanisms of change in therapy, especially insight and emotional working through: We need to identify what leads to anxiety reduction and reduction of negative affect.
4. Research on play processes and techniques that facilitate play in therapy.

Demonstration of effectiveness of structure-building approaches with seriously emotionally disturbed children is also necessary. Because the therapy is so long-term and complex with these children, single case designs would be appropriate.

SUMMARY

The psychodynamic approach focuses on the internal world of the child from a developmental perspective. Three different types of psychodynamic treatment emerge in the child psychotherapy literature: insight-oriented therapy; structure-building approaches, and supportive therapy. Each type of treatment emphasizes different mechanisms of change. Major mechanisms of change are catharsis and expression of feelings, corrective emotional experience, insight and working through, learning alternative problem-solving and coping strategies, and developing internal structure and processes. Pretend play is an important part of psychodynamic therapy in all approaches.

The form of therapy most associated with the psychodynamic approach is insight-oriented therapy with an emphasis on insight and working through. An important point is that often, with young children, emotional working through and emotional processing and reexperiencing occurs without cognitive insight. Play is especially helpful with the process of expressing, mastering, and regulating emotions in therapy. Insight-oriented therapy was intended for children with anxiety and conflicts. The few well-controlled psychodynamic psychotherapy outcome studies in the literature support the use of psychodynamic therapy with internalizing disorders—disorders that involve anxiety, conflict, or depression. In addition, well-designed play intervention studies have found that pretend play reduces anxiety in specific stressful situations. These findings in the play area are consistent with psychodynamic theory. A number of psychodynamic constructs and principles have also received empirical support.

It is essential that psychodynamic psychotherapy establish a solid base of empirical support for it to remain a viable form of treatment for children. Research that would be the most fruitful and have the most immediate impact would investigate psychodynamic therapy with internalizing disorders; short-term therapy with internalizing disorders; mechanisms of change, especially insight and emotional processing and working through; and pretend play processes and facilitation techniques. By building an empirical base in this way, the field will learn about the effectiveness of psychodynamic therapy and the development of personality processes in children.

REFERENCES

Altschul, S. (1988). *Childhood bereavement and its aftermath.* New York: International Universities Press.

American Psychiatric Association. (1994). *Diagnostic and statistical manual of mental disorders* (4th ed.). Washington, DC: Author.

Applebaum, S. (1978). Pathways to change in psychoanalytic therapy. *Bulletin of the Menninger Clinic, 42,* 239–251.

Axline, V. M. (1947). *Play therapy.* Boston: Houghton-Mifflin.

Barnett, I. (1984). Research note: Young children's resolution of distress through play. *Journal of Child Psychology and Psychiatry, 25,* 477–483.

Barnett, I., & Storm, B. (1981). Play, pleasure and pain: The reduction of anxiety through play. *Leisure Science, 4,* 161–175.

Baum, C. G. (1989). Conduct disorders. In T. H. Ollendick & M. Hersen (Eds.), *Handbook of child psychopathology* (2nd ed., pp. 171–196). New York: Plenum Press.

Blank, R., & Blank, G. (1986). *Beyond ego psychology: Developmental object relations theory.* New York: Columbia University Press.

Bodiford-McNeil, C., Hembree-Kigin, T. L., & Eyberg, S. (1996). *Short-term play therapy for disruptive children.* King of Prussia, PA: Center for Applied Psychology.

Burlingham, D. (1932). Child analysis and the mother. *Psychoanalytic Quarterly, 4,* 69–92.

Cassell, S. (1965). Effect of brief puppet therapy upon the emotional responses of children undergoing cardiac catheterization. *Journal of Consulting Psychology, 29,* 1–8.

Chambless, D. L., Sanderson, W. C., Shoham, V., Johnson, S. B., Pope, K. S., Chris-Christoph, R., et al. (1996). An update on empirically validated therapy. *Clinical Psychologist, 49,* 5–18.

Chethik, M. (1989). *Techniques of child therapy: Psychodynamic Strategies.* New York: Guilford Press.

Chused, J. (1988). The transference neurosis in child analysis. *Psychoanalytic Study of the Child, 43,* 51–81.

Dulcan, M., & Piercy, P. (1985). A model for teaching and evaluating brief psychotherapy with children and their families. *Professional Psychology: Research and Practice, 16,* 689–700.

Erikson, E. H. (1963). *Childhood and society.* New York: Norton.

Fisher, S., & Greenberg, R. (1996). *Freud scientifically reappraised.* New York: Wiley.

Fonagy, P., & Moran, G. S. (1990). Studies on the efficacy of child psychoanalysis. *Journal of Consulting and Clinical Psychology, 58,* 684–695.

Freedheim, D. K., & Russ, S. W. (1983). Psychotherapy with children. In C. E. Walker & M. E. Roberts (Eds.), *Handbook of clinical child psychology* (pp. 978–994). New York: Wiley.

Freedheim, D. K., & Russ, S. W. (1992). Psychotherapy with children. In C. E. Walker & M. Roberts (Eds.), *Handbook of clinical child psychology* (2nd ed., pp. 765–780). New York: Wiley.

Freud, A. (1927). Four lectures on child analysis. In *The writings of Anna Freud* (Vol. 1, pp. 3–69). New York: International Universities Press.

Freud, A. (1965). Normality and pathology in childhood: Assessments of development. In *The writings of Anna Freud* (Vol. 6). New York: International Universities Press.

Freud, A. (1966). The ego and the mechanisms of defense. In *The writings of Anna Freud* (Vol. 2). New York: International Universities Press. (Original work published 1936)

Gaensbauer, T. J., & Siegel, C. H. (1995). Therapeutic approaches to posttraumatic stress disorder in infants and toddlers. *Infant Mental Health Journal, 16,* 292–305.

Gaffney, B. (1986). Toward integration and independence: A four-year-old boy's use of thirteen months of psychotherapy. *Journal of Child Psychology, 12,* 79–97.

Garfield, W. (1980). *Psychotherapy: An eclectic approach.* New York: Wiley.

Gerard, M. W. (1952). Emotional disorders of childhood. In F. Alexander & H. Ross (Eds.), *Dynamic psychiatry* (pp. 165–210). Chicago: University of Chicago Press.

Gilpin, D. (1976). Psychotherapy of borderline psychotic children. *American Journal of Psychotherapy, 30,* 483–496.

Harris, P. (2000). *The work of the imagination.* Oxford, England: Blackwell.

Holt, R. R. (1977). A method for assessing primary process manifestations and their control in Rorschach responses. In M. Rickers-Ovsiankina (Ed.), *Rorschach psychology* (pp. 375–420). New York: Kreiger.

Hug-Hellmuth, H. (1921). On the technique of child-analysis. *International Journal of Psychoanalysis, 2,* 287–305.

Hug-Hellmuth, H. (1924). *New paths to the understanding of youth.* Leipzig-Wein, Germany: Franz Deuticki.

Johnson, P. A., & Stockdale, D. E. (1975). Effects of puppet therapy on palmar sweating of hospitalized children. *Johns Hopkins Medical Journal, 137,* 1–5.

Kazdin, A. (1993). Evaluation in clinical practice: Clinically sensitive and systematic methods of treatment delivery. *Behavior Therapy, 24,* 11–45.

Kazdin, A. (2000). *Psychotherapy for children and adolescents.* New York: Oxford University Press.

Kelsay, K. (2002, October). *MacArthur Story Stem Battery as a therapeutic tool.* Paper presented at the meeting of the American Academy of Child and Adolescent Psychiatry, San Francisco.

Kernberg, P. (1995, October). *Child psychodynamic psychotherapy: Assessing the process.* Paper presented at the meeting of the American Academy of Child and Adolescent Psychiatry, New Orleans.

Kessler, J. (1966). *Psychopathology of childhood.* Englewood Cliffs, NJ: Prentice Hall.

Kessler, J. (1988). *Psychopathology of childhood* (2nd ed.). Englewood Cliffs, NJ: Prentice Hall.

Klein, M. (1955). The psychoanalytic play technique. *American Journal of Orthopsychiatry, 25,* 223–237.

Knell, S. (1993). *Cognitive-behavioral play therapy.* Northvale, NJ: Aronson.

Kohut, H. (1977). *The restoration of the self.* New York: International Universities Press.

Kohut, H., & Wolfe, E. R. (1978). The disorders of the self and their treatment: An outline. *International Journal of Psychoanalysis, 59,* 413–424.

Koocher, G., & D'Angelo, E. J. (1992). Evolution of practice in child psychotherapy. In D. K. Freedheim (Ed.), *History of psychotherapy* (pp. 457–492). Washington, DC: American Psychological Association.

Lonigan, C., Elbert, J., & Johnson, S. (1998). Empirically supported psychosocial interventions for children: An overview. *Journal of Clinical Child Psychology, 27,* 138–145.

Mahler, M. S. (1968). *On human symbiosis and the vicissitudes of individuation.* New York: International Universities Press.

Messer, S. B., & Warren, C. S. (1995). *Models of brief psychodynamic therapy.* New York: Guilford Press.

Miller, J. (1988). A child losing and finding her objects: An unusual therapeutic intervention in the nursery school. *Bulletin of the Anna Freud Center, 11,* 75–89.

Milos, M., & Reiss, S. (1982). Effects of three play conditions on separation anxiety in young children. *Journal of Consulting and Clinical Psychology, 50,* 389–395.

Moran, G. S., & Fonagy, P. (1987). Psychoanalysis and diabetic control: A single case study. *British Journal of Medical Psychology, 60,* 352–372.

Moustakas, C. (1953). *Children in play therapy.* New York: McGraw-Hill.

Muratori, F., Picchi, L., Bruni, G., Patarnello, M., & Romagnoli, G. (2003). A two-year follow-up of psychodynamic psychotherapy for internalizing disorders in children. *Journal of the American Academy of Child and Adolescent Psychiatry, 42,* 331–339.

Parad, L., & Parad, N. (1968). A study of crisis-oriented planned short-term treatment, Part 1. *Social Casework, 49,* 346–355.

Pennebaker, J. W., & Graybeal, A. (2001). Patterns of natural language use: Disclosure, personality, and social integration. *Current Directions in Psychological Science, 10,* 90–93.

Proskauer, S. (1969). Some technical issues in time-limited psychotherapy with children. *Journal of the American Academy of Child and Adolescent Psychiatry, 8,* 154–169.

Rae, W., Worchel, R., Upchurch, J., Sanner, J., & Daniel, C. (1989). The psychosocial impact of play on hospitalized children. *Journal of Pediatric Psychology, 14,* 617–627.

Russ, S. W. (1993) *Affect and creativity: The role of affect and play in the creative process.* Hillsdale, NJ: Erlbaum.

Russ, S. W. (1995). Play psychotherapy research: State of the science. In T. Ollendick & R. Prinz (Eds.), *Advances in clinical child psychology* (Vol. 17, pp. 365–391). New York: Plenum Press.

Russ, S. W. (1996). Psychoanalytic theory and creativity: Cognition and affect revisited. In J. Masling & R. Borstein (Eds.), *Psychoanalytic perspectives on developmental psychology* (pp. 69–103). Washington, DC: American Psychological Association.

Russ, S. W. (1998). Psychodynamically based therapies. In T. Ollendick & M. Hersen (Eds.), *Handbook of child psychopathology* (3rd ed., pp. 537–556). New York: Plenum Press.

Russ, S. W. (2004). *Play in child development and psychotherapy: Toward empirically supported practice.* Mahwah, NJ: Erlbaum.

Russ, S. W., & Freedheim, D. (2001). Psychotherapy with children. In C. E. Walker & M. Roberts (Eds.), *Handbook of clinical child psychology* (3rd ed., pp. 840–859). New York: Wiley.

Russ, S. W., Moore, M., & Farber, B. (2004). Effects of play intervention on play skills and adaptive functioning. Manuscript submitted for publication.

Sandler, J., Kennedy, H., & Tyson, R. L. (1980). *The technique of child psychoanalysis: Discussion with Anna Freud.* Cambridge, MA: Harvard University Press.

Shelby, J. (2000). Brief therapy with traumatized children: A developmental perspective. In A. Kaderson & C. Schaefer, (Eds.), *Short-term play therapy for children* (pp. 69–104). New York: Guilford Press.

Shirk, S. W., & Karver, M. (2003). Prediction of treatment outcome from relationship variables in child and adolescent therapy: A meta-analytic review. *Journal of Consulting and Clinical Psychology, 71,* 452–464.

Shirk, S. W., & Russell, R. (1996). *Change processes in child psychotherapy: Revitalizing treatment and research.* New York: Guilford Press.

Singer, D. (1993). *Playing for their lives.* New York: Free Press.

Smyrnios, K., & Kirby, R. I. (1993). Long-term comparison of brief versus unlimited psychodynamic treatments with children and their families. *Journal of Counseling and Clinical Psychology, 61,* 1020–1027.

Suler, J. (1980). Primary process thinking and creativity. *Psychological Bulletin, 88,* 144–165.

Target, M. (2002). The problem of outcome in child psychoanalysis: Contributions from the Anna Freud Center. In M. Leuzinger-Bohleber & M. Target (Eds.), *Outcomes of psychoanalytic treatment* (pp. 240–251). New York: Brunner-Routledge.

Target, M., & Fonagy, P. (1994). The efficacy of psycho-analysis for children with emotional disorders. *Journal of the American Academy of Child and Adolescent Psychiatry, 33,* 361–371.

Target, M., & Fonagy, P. (1996). The psychological treatment of child and adolescent psychiatric disorders. In A. Roth & P. Fonagy (Eds.), *What works for whom* (pp. 263–320). New York: Guilford Press.

Tuma, J. M. (1989). Traditional therapies with children. In T. H. Ollendick & M. Hersen (Eds.), *Handbook of child psychopathology* (2nd ed., pp. 419–437). New York: Plenum Press.

Tuma, J. M., & Russ, S. W. (1993). Psychoanalytic psychotherapy with children. In T. Kratochwill & R. Morris (Eds.), *Handbook of psychotherapy with children and adolescents* (pp. 131–161). Boston: Allyn & Bacon.

Tyson, P., & Tyson, R. L. (1990). *Psychoanalytic theories of development: An integration.* New Haven, CT: Yale University Press.

Waelder, R. (1933). Psychoanalytic theory of play. *Psychoanalytic Quarterly, 2,* 208–224.

Wallerstein, R. S. (1988). Assessment of structural change in psychoanalytic therapy and research. *Journal of the American Psychoanalytic Association, 36*(Suppl.), 241–261.

Weisz, J., & Weiss, B. (1993). *Effects of psychotherapy with children and adolescents.* Beverly Hills, CA: Sage.

Westen, D. (1998). The scientific legacy of Sigmund Freud: Toward a psychodynamically informed psychological science. *Psychological Bulletin, 124,* 333–371.

Winnicott, D. W. (1971). *Playing and reality.* London: Tavistock.

Wiser, S., & Goldfried, M. (1998). Therapist interventions and client emotional experiencing in expert psychodynamic-interpersonal and cognitive-behavioral therapies. *Journal of Counseling and Clinical Psychology, 66,* 634–640.

CHAPTER 26

Cognitive-Behavioral Treatments

JOSEPH A. DURLAK

INTRODUCTION

Cognitive-behavioral therapy (CBT) has become a prominent paradigm for psychosocial interventions for children and adolescents. For example, surveys of Ph.D. clinical programs suggest that CBT is by far the most frequently mentioned primary orientation within child and adult training programs (Durlak, Maltby, & Allen, 2004). Several factors account for the popularity of CBT approaches.

Considerable research data have documented the positive impact of CBT treatments for child and adolescent populations. CBT has been applied successfully to a wide range of problems and is, therefore, suitable for many different clinical situations. Managed care pressures tend to favor approaches such as CBT, not only because of the existing empirical evidence, but also because CBT is effective as a short-term intervention and can be delivered by those with master's- or baccalaureate-level training. More recently, CBT techniques have been incorporated effectively into several preventive and health promotion programs and have thus ridden the wave of enthusiasm for these alternative means of serving more children and promoting their development. Finally, as a psychosocial intervention, CBT can be easily integrated with current conceptualizations of psychopathology, creating a natural bridge between theories of psychopathology and intervention.

The purpose of this chapter is to present an overview of current CBT interventions for children and adolescents. First, CBT is defined and its major distinctive features are described. Second, the empirical evidence on the impact of CBT is summarized, and details on several representative programs are provided. Third, several aspects of CBT interventions are discussed, including its focus on cognitive functioning. Fourth, and finally, a few important issues needing attention in future work are presented.

For ease of discussion, unless otherwise noted, the terms *child* and *children* will be used to refer to both child and adolescent populations, and treatment will be used to refer generally to psychosocial interventions that may include prevention and health promotion.

WHAT IS CBT?

Historically, CBT arose as an extension of behavior therapy and retained the central belief that behavior is learned. Therefore, CBT recognizes the importance of environmental stimuli and contingencies in the learning process and uses many of the techniques of behavior therapy (e.g., shaping, prompting, modeling, behavioral rehearsal, reinforcement, and response cost procedures) to establish desirable behavior and reduce or eliminate undesirable behavior. In other words, behavioral procedures are an essential component of CBT.

Moreover, CBT adherents have no argument with ecological theories or the application of a risk and protective factor paradigm to understand maladjustment. It is important to view behavior within its environmental context in order to understand its adaptive goals and its cultural relevance, and it may be prudent to intervene in the child's natural environment (e.g., with parents, teachers, or peers, at home or in school) instead of, or in addition to, working directly with the child. Furthermore, CBT acknowledges that adjustment is multiply determined; it is wise to consider multiple factors that may lessen (protective factors) or increase (risk factors) the likelihood of later problems. In addition to cognitive processes, other previous and concurrent influences on adjustment should be considered, with the usual candidates being parental practices and the family environment, school and neighborhood, and peer group.

Finally, CBT is congruent with the more recent movements toward positive psychology and positive youth development that focus attention on the development of competencies and skills and deemphasize a pathologically oriented view of human development. In fact, CBT always strives to develop both cognitive and behavioral skills.

One obvious characteristic that distinguishes CBT from many other forms of intervention is its central theoretical tenet that cognitive processes play a major role in adjustment. All other things being equal, it is believed that children who develop and use cognitive processes appropriately will be better adjusted than those who do not, whereas maladjustment is often associated with poorly developed or distorted cognitive processes. In other words, either cognitive deficiencies or cognitive distortions may lead to maladjustment. Children may fail to develop the necessary cognitive skills that will help them cope effectively, or they may possess the necessary basic skills but err when they apply them. In some cases, both cognitive deficiencies and cognitive errors may be present. In sum, CBT asserts that cognitive functioning is influential in the development and maintenance of many different types of competencies and coping skills, whereas poor cognitive skills are related to the development and maintenance of a variety of behavioral and social problems and symptoms. Given this orientation, change agents using CBT techniques attempt to modify different cognitive processes to improve strengths and competencies; diminish symptoms and problems; and, often, to accomplish both these goals simultaneously.

Notwithstanding the central importance of cognitive functioning, there are other distinctive features of CBT. For example, Blagys and Hilsenroth (2002) concluded that six main features distinguish CBT from psychodynamic and interpersonal approaches with adults, and these features apply well to work with child and adolescent populations. In addition to a focus on cognitive functioning, Blagys and Hilsenroth (2002) reported that CBT is characterized by five other features: (1) the use of homework and outside-the-session activities; (2) considerable structure and direction by the therapist; (3) the teaching of specific skills; (4) education of the client about what will happen in the intervention and what is known about their current level of functioning; and (5) an emphasis on the client's future experiences (i.e., helping the client anticipate positive outcomes from their efforts). In sum, CBT is an empirically supported, short-term, skill-oriented strategy of behavioral change in which the change agent serves in the role of an educator and uses a structured approach to teach clients how to use various cognitive processes to improve their adjustment.

RESEARCH ON CBT OUTCOMES

An extensive empirical literature confirms the value of CBT for children and adolescents. Table 26.1 presents the standardized mean effects found in eight meta-analyses of outcome studies. The positive mean effects listed in Table 26.1 illustrate the superiority of treated participants over controls obtained in the 277 studies, involving more than 9,000 participants, that were part of these eight reviews. These effects are large in magnitude, averaging 0.71. By comparison, Lipsey and Wilson (1993) reported that the average effect size obtained in 156 meta-analyses of psychosocial interventions was only 0.48.

Focusing on specific findings among the meta-analyses in Table 26.1 adds further evidence for the impact of CBT in several ways. First, reviewers have reported that few studies produce negative mean effects, which would indicate that treated children do worse than untreated controls. It seems that CBT rarely affects children negatively. Second, when follow-up data are available for analysis (Bennett & Gibbons, 2000; Durlak, Furhman, & Lampman, 1991; Reinicke, Ryan, & DuBois, 1998; Robinson, Smith, Miller, & Brownell, 1999), results indicate that the effects of treatment endure over time, although the follow-up periods vary across studies. Third, subgroup analyses indicate that CBT is effective for children or adolescents who have clinically relevant problems such as anxiety and somatic disorders (Grossman & Hughes, 1992) or depression (Grossman & Hughes, 1992; Reinicke, et al., 1998). Durlak et al. (1991) also demonstrated the clinical significance of program effects by comparing the functioning of treated children before and after intervention on normed assessment measures. Whereas children's scores on normed measures suggest they are functioning beyond normal limits before intervention, their behavior falls within normal limits on these same measures after intervention. The clinical significance of CBT treatment effects has also been demonstrated on outcome measures assessing important areas of functioning such as impulsivity and aggression (Robinson et al., 1999) and antisocial behavior (Bennett & Gibbons, 2000).

Another way to assess the practical benefits of CBT treatment is to convert the mean effects obtained in meta-analyses to success rates using the binomial effect size display developed by Rosenthal and Rubin (1982). This involves converting mean effects into percentages that reflect the success rate achieved by treated children and controls in outcome studies. Averaging the mean effects from all the group studies in the meta-analyses listed in Table 26.1 yields an average success rate for treated children of 68 percent versus only 32 percent for controls. Put another way, youth with adjustment problems are more than twice as well off after receiving CBT treatment than children who do not receive any intervention.

Other data support the efficacy of CBT. Results of individual studies and, in a few cases, narrative reviews indicate that CBT is effective in treating children who have been traumatized (Cohen, Mannarino, Berliner, & Deblinger, 2000), have obsessive-compulsive disorders (March, 1995), have anxiety disorders (Kendall, Safford, Flannery-Schroeder, & Webb, 2004), or have symptoms of conduct disorder or op-

TABLE 26.1 Summary of Selected Meta-Analyses of Cognitive Behavioral Therapy Outcomes

Author	Number of studies/ participants in studies	Population	Target problem(s)	Mean effect size
Bennett & Gibbons (2000)	30/678	Ages 5–18	Antisocial behavior	0.23
Baer & Nietzel (1991)	36/1,550	Ages 4–18	Impulsivity	0.77
Durlak, Furhman, & Lampman (1991)	64/2,654	Ages 5–13	Behavioral and social problems	0.56
Dush, Hirt, & Schroeder (1989)	48/1,111	Ages 5–16	Clinically relevant problems	0.47
Grossman & Hughes (1992)	20/712	Ages 9–18	Anxiety, depression, or somatic disorders	0.74[a]
Kibby, Tyc, & Mulhern (1998)	42/1,084	Ages 3–18	Chronic medical conditions	1.12
Reinicke, Ryan, & DuBois (1998)	14/217	Ages 13–18	Depression	1.02
Robinson, Smith, Miller, & Brownell (1999)	23/1,132	Ages 6–18	Impulsivity or aggression	0.74

Note. Results are reported from these meta-analyses using weighted mean effects.
[a] = Results from control group studies.

positional defiant disorder (Durlak, Rubin, & Kahng, 2001; Lochman, Magee, & Pardini, 2003).

There are also demonstrations that CBT is successful with children who present with comorbid conditions (Rapee, 2003), and for members of different racial and ethnic groups (Ginsburg & Drake, 2002; Pina, Silverman, Fuentes, Kurtines, & Weems, 2003; Rosselló & Bernal, 1999). Some limitations exist regarding the problems treated via CBT. CBT has been used least often for children with severe cognitive impairments (e.g., autism spectrum disorders and severe developmental delays), and its efficacy with attention-deficit/hyperactivity disorder (ADHD) has not been demonstrated.

Finally, another approach in evaluating interventions is to apply strict methodological criteria to reach conclusions about the efficacy of a particular treatment for a particular problem. When this is done, CBT is well represented among child treatments that have received empirical support in carefully controlled studies (Kadzin & Weisz, 1998; Ollendick & King, 1998). Divisions 53 (Child and Adolescent Clinical Psychology, www.clinicalchildpsychology.org) and 54 (Society for Pediatric Psychology, www.apa.org/divisions/54) of the American Psychological Association maintain Web sites with updated information on the research support that exists for different types of treatments for children and adolescents, and provide explanations of how conclusions are reached.

Exemplars of Intervention

To provide the reader with some concrete examples of effective interventions, I offer details on a few treatment- and prevention-oriented interventions. In terms of treatment, two independent research teams who have reported impressive results for children with anxiety disorders merit attention. Each team conducted well-controlled randomized clinical trials with children who met diagnostic criteria for an anxiety disorder; several of these children had comorbid conditions (e.g., depression, conduct disorder, oppositional defiant disorder, or ADHD). For example, Kendall (1994) investigated the impact of a 16-session individual treatment regimen using behavioral techniques such as modeling, relaxation training, and reinforcement to teach 9- to 13-year-old children four cognitive skills: (1) how to identify anxious feelings and signs of somatic distress; (2) how to recognize the application of any unrealistic or negative attributions in relation to anxiety-arousing situations; (3) how to modify anxious self-talk and replace it with effective coping self-talk and effective coping behaviors; and, finally, (4) how to evaluate one's performance and reinforce oneself appropriately. A treatment manual, called the Coping Cat Workbook, guided the intervention.

At posttreatment, treated children demonstrated significant gains across a variety of outcome measures completed by parents and children, and, depending on the specific outcome measure, a majority of the treatment group fell within normal limits of functioning on normed instruments. A 3.35-year follow-up study indicated that previous treatment gains were by and large maintained, and a majority of the treated children continued to function within normal limits (Kendall & Southam-Gerow, 1996). Similarly impressive posttreatment and long-term findings were reported in a second randomized trial by Kendall and colleagues (Kendall et al., 2004).

A second research team adapted Kendall's treatment manual for an Australian sample (appropriately called the Coping Koala Workbook) and assigned 7- to 14-year-old anxious children to a 12-session individual regimen of CBT, a control condition, or a family condition involving 12 individual child sessions plus family sessions completed after each child session (Barrett, Dadds, & Rapee, 1996). The intent of the family sessions was twofold: (1) to provide each child with additional support, guidance, and reinforcement from their parents; and (2) to help parents deal with their own anxiety in stressful situations. Parents were trained on how to reward their child's nonanxious behavior, prompt their child for more effective coping behavior, model effective problem solving, and deal with their own anxieties.

Both treatment conditions demonstrated significant improvement compared to controls across a variety of outcome measures and maintained their major gains during a long follow-up period. For example, 6 years after treatment, less than 15 percent of each treatment group met diagnostic criteria for any type of anxiety disorder, with no between-group differences (Barrett, Duffy, Dadds, & Rapee, 2001). The value of involving parents in CBT treatments is discussed further in a later section.

As mentioned earlier, CBT strategies have been used effectively in prevention programs. Two examples are now presented, one focusing on anxiety and one on conduct problems. Several members of the Australian research team described previously have also successfully conducted a school-based intervention to prevent anxiety problems in young children (Dadds, Spence, Holland, Barrett, & Laurens, 1997). These investigators used a multigating screening procedure to identify 7- to 14-year-old schoolchildren who were at risk for later anxiety problems based on their scores on self-report measures, teacher ratings, and parental interviews. Children selected for intervention were then assigned to intervention or control conditions. The intervention involved 10 group sessions using the Coping Koala procedures and three group parental sessions, each essentially using similar procedures from the earlier treatment study (Barrett et al., 1996) to help children deal with their anxiety and guide parents in supporting and reinforcing their children's efforts.

Results confirmed the importance of collecting follow-up data and considering preintervention status when assessing the preventive impact of the intervention. Whereas some differences emerged between the intervention and control groups at posttreatment, stronger effects were evident at 6-month follow-up. Among those children with the highest initial levels of anxiety, 53 percent fewer children in the intervention than in the control group met diagnostic criteria for an anxiety disorder. Among those with the lowest initial levels of anxiety, 70 percent fewer intervention than control group children met criteria for an anxiety disorder. In other words, this well-timed school-based intervention seemed effective for children at both higher and lower risk for subsequent anxiety problems. A 2-year follow-up (Dadds et al., 1999) showed some diminution of effects, but significant differences still favored intervention-group children.

Lochman and his colleague (Lochman & Wells, 2002, 2004) have successfully applied CBT techniques to prevent externalizing problems in young boys. Their interest was in teaching aggressive boys how to deal with anger and other negative emotions, which are frequently difficult for these children. Building on clinical and developmental research and past findings for anger-control treatments, their school-based Coping Power program was spread out over a 15-month period, encompassing two school years, and consisted of 33 group sessions for the boys and 16 parent group sessions. The intervention targeted multiple skills, including awareness of negative feelings and physiological arousal, generation of effective coping self-statements, relaxation or distraction techniques when provoked, realistic goal setting, and interpersonal problem-solving skills. In the parent sessions, parents were taught how to reinforce and extend their child's newly acquired skills at home and in the neighborhood and how to adopt more effective parenting practices as needed. The Coping Power program has successfully achieved several important outcomes, such as reducing aggressive and disruptive behavior and substance use and improving social competence. These effects have been observed immediately following intervention and during a 1-year follow-up period (Lochman & Wells, 2002, 2004).

INTERVENTION ISSUES

It is not possible in this brief chapter to discuss all of the issues relevant to CBT interventions. Instead, this section discusses a few select topics: assessment, the cognitive processes typically targeted for intervention, some common CBT techniques, and the importance of a developmental perspective.

Assessment

There is a dual assessment challenge in CBT treatment. The first involves determining the nature and severity of maladjustment in reference to diagnostic status, symptom levels, or functional impairment. The second involves assessing the child's cognitive skills related to effective coping. The first challenge is easier to overcome than the second. Substantial improvements in child psychopathology research over the past few years have produced a useful, although not perfect, array of assessment techniques suitable for many situations. These include structured diagnostic interviews for parents and children, self-report measures, parent and teacher rating scales, and observational methods (see Mash & Barkley, 2003; Velting, Setzer, & Albano, 2004). Assessing cognitive processes accurately is problematic, however, due to the lack of standardized methods to evaluate these skills. Most current methods for assessing different cognitive processes are either unwieldy for clinical use or have not gained wide acceptance. The development of reliable, valid, and easy-to-use assessments of cognitive functioning is a top priority for the future. Therefore, it is not unusual for cognitive assessments to occur informally during the course of treatment. The clinician begins an intervention only to learn that a child needs more practice and training in some cognitive areas because the expected abilities are not sufficiently developed.

Cognitive Processes

Cognitive processes can be viewed as a collection of thinking and reasoning skills that serve as a basis for understanding the world, oneself, and others as well as evaluating the appropriateness of one's behavior in different situations, and include the ability to solve interpersonal problems and pursue personal goals through activities related to regulating, monitoring, and reinforcing oneself effectively and appropriately. Table 26.2 lists several cognitive processes that in one way or another have been targeted in CBT interventions. Admittedly, liberties are taken in listing these constructs. The developmental and clinical research literatures have not consistently used the same conceptualizations, terminology, or definitions for the same phenomena. Nevertheless, Table 26.2 is designed to capture the flavor of cognitive processes that are believed to be amenable to change and important in developing effective coping skills.

The importance of different cognitive processing is intuitively appealing. For example, it should be helpful for children to attend to important aspects of a situation, avoid distracting stimuli as they perform tasks, and maintain their attention as needed. It is reasonable to believe that children should be aware of their own thoughts, feelings, and behavior; how their actions or responses may affect others; and whether their personal reactions and behaviors are appropriate to the situation. It also seems helpful if children could learn effective methods of solving interpersonal problems and conflicts. An extensive research base indicates that the cognitive processes listed in Table 26.2 are correlated with children's adjustment status, although confirming which processes are causal is more difficult. For instance, children with

TABLE 26.2 Important Cognitive Processes That Are Targets for Intervention in CBT

Attentional processes
    Attention to relevant stimuli
    Avoidance of distracting stimuli
    Maintenance of attention

Self-awareness/understanding
    Awareness of one's thoughts, behaviors, and feelings

Self-regulation/self-control
    Of thoughts, feelings, and behaviors

Attributions
    Regarding self, others, and the environment

Interpersonal problem-solving skills
    Identification of the problem
    Generation of alternative problem solutions
    Consideration of possible consequences of each alternative
    Selection of one alternative
    Execution of problem-solving strategies
    Evaluation of performance

Interpersonal understanding/sensitivity
    Interpretation of others' nonverbal and verbal cues
    Distinguishing others' thoughts, behaviors, feelings, and intentions

Self-efficacy
    Accurate assessment of one's skills, abilities
    Confidence in one's ability to do what is necessary for goal attainment

Self-monitoring/self-evaluation skills
    Monitoring one's performance
    Rewarding oneself

Various coping processes
    Reactions to errors, failure, or criticism
    Dealing with stress, pressure, or challenges
    Ability to relax or self-soothe

Decision-making and goal-setting skills

Self-talk
    Use of language to guide one's behavior, thoughts, and feelings

Note. These areas of cognitive functioning exist along a continuum rather than on an all-or-none basis, are often connected to each other, and can be evaluated in terms of how appropriately or realistically they are applied to different situations.

conduct problems often display difficulties in accurately interpreting others' behaviors, selecting appropriate strategies to solve interpersonal conflicts, and preventing negative emotions from unduly influencing their behaviors. Children with anxiety problems attend too frequently to the negative aspects of situations, are overly self-critical, and tend to be distracted or overwhelmed by negative emotions and negative self-talk (e.g., "I am not doing well," "I am no good"). It should be kept in mind that many of the cognitive processes listed in Table 26.2 are connected; that is, when a child is confronted with a social situation that requires coping, the child's cognitive abilities involving attention, memory, self-evaluation, problem solving, and self-regulation all come into play. Individual children's competencies in these areas will vary, however, allowing the therapist to concentrate on those aspects of cognitive functioning most in need of improvement.

Common Cognitive-Behavioral Therapy Techniques

CBT is not a single set of techniques but an amalgamation of many different related strategies directed at behavioral change. The major techniques of CBT include self-instructional training and self-monitoring, cognitive restructuring, stress inoculation training, training in interpersonal problem-solving skills, and various self-reinforcement strategies. These procedures are often combined and can be used with various behavioral change strategies such as shaping, modeling, and behavioral rehearsal in many different ways. A 1991 review found that eight different therapeutic techniques were used in 42 different ways in 64 studies (Durlak et al., 1991). Several additional techniques have been added to the CBT clinical armamentarium in the ensuing years.

The most common CBT technique is self-instructional training, which involves teaching children how to use internal speech to guide and evaluate their thoughts, behaviors, and feelings. Children learn to talk to themselves before they act and in response to their internal cues of physiological arousal and negative emotional states. Self-talk is important for children with either externalizing or internalizing problems. Children with externalizing problems tend to misperceive neutral or benign social situations as hostile or threatening; easily become angry and defensive; and then respond impulsively to others, sometimes with aggression. The therapist uses self-instructional training in these cases to help children to (1) delay their response, (2) evaluate the situation more appropriately, and then (3) make a more reasoned and appropriate response. Self-instructional training helps children with internalizing difficulties, but for different reasons. For example, anxious children also tend to misinterpret social situations, but the threat they perceive makes them anxious. This, coupled with their usual self-critical stance, often makes them feel unable to perform what is required; they then worry excessively about potential negative evaluations and failure and frequently use avoidance and withdrawal as ineffectual coping responses. In these situations, self-instruction training affords the therapist the opportunity to teach children how to focus more on the positive aspects of situations and their possible resolution, calm down if they become anxious, use positive self-talk to increase self-confidence, and employ more direct coping strategies that will elicit positive reactions from others and lessen concerns of being incompetent.

Cognitive restructuring, another widely used CBT technique, is often applied in conjunction with self-instructional training and involves teaching children how to replace their distorted attributions and expectations with more realistic and positive ones. As a result, both aggressive and anxious children can learn how to make more positive attributions involving others' behaviors and intentions, and to entertain more positive expectations about their ability to cope when feeling threatened or anxious.

Finally, another popular technique is training in interpersonal problem-solving skills. The typical training scenario divides problem solving into five separate cognitive steps. Children learn how to (1) identify the problem, (2) generate different possible solutions, (3) evaluate the potential consequences and success of each solution, (4) initiate the problem-solving approach by selecting an appropriate solution, and (5) evaluate the outcomes of their chosen solution and self-reinforce for a successful solution.

Homework

Although use of the term *homework* may not be wise for children with negative school experiences, CBT therapists do ask their child clients to do out-of-session tasks and activities to further therapeutic progress. These activities may involve self-monitoring of behaviors, thought diaries, practice of skills in new situations, or relaxation procedures. Malouff and Schutte (2004) offer a useful set of practical guidelines to facilitate homework completion. These guidelines include modeling the task first during the session, starting with simple, concrete tasks and working toward more complicated assignments, and asking parents to prompt, remind, and reinforce child adherence. In general, the guidelines emphasize six factors that affect homework compliance: Do clients have the necessary understanding, ability, self-efficacy, motivation, opportunity, and memory to complete the tasks?

Developmental Considerations

Developmental considerations are paramount in CBT because of the evolving nature of cognitive abilities in children and adolescents. At a very basic level, CBT should work only for children who are able to distinguish, evaluate, and understand the connections among thoughts, feelings, and behaviors. This set of related skills is often essential to learning the different coping skills taught in CBT. Yet, our understanding of when different cognitive abilities emerge is sketchy and frequently rests on generalizations related to age. For example, research suggests that by 6–7 years of age, children can recognize their inner speech, 5-year-olds can report some details regarding their thoughts, preschoolers can learn a step-by-step cognitive approach for solving interpersonal problems, 8-year-olds seem able to learn how to use self-talk to guide task-oriented behavior, and so on. These findings, like many others in the clinical and developmental literature, provide information only on the mean performance of children, and usually performance across age groups and within each age level varies considerably.

For example, in one study designed to examine how well children could distinguish thoughts from behaviors, the mean accuracy of children between 7 and 8 years of age and 10 and 11 years of age was beyond chance, suggesting that children in each age group could make such distinctions (Quakley, Coker, Palmer, & Reynolds, 2003). However, the mean score of the older group was only slightly better than that of the younger group; individual scores for the younger group ranged from 60 percent to 100 percent correct while scores for the older group ranged from 85 percent to 100 percent, and a majority of both younger (84 percent) and older (63 percent) children made some errors.

Unfortunately, treatment outcome research has infrequently attended to developmental issues. One review found that only one quarter of CBT interventions considered developmental issues in the design or evaluation of their treatments (Holmbeck et al., 2000). As a result, clinicians must ascertain the level of each child's abilities instead of assuming the presence of such abilities based on age. Moreover, proficiencies within a child usually vary across areas in terms of attention, memory, thinking, language, and self-evaluative processes.

At a practical level, then, it is not surprising that CBT is not a single standardized methodology with a prescribed moment-to-moment sequence of activities, but a more flexible application of different strategies depending on client needs. Many treatment manuals have been prepared for different CBT programs, but most allow the change agent to move according to the child's pace and to modify activities to suit the child's developmental level; they also permit other procedural departures to insure skill mastery. In other words, adaptations to treatment plans are acceptable as long as the central focus remains on the development and application of more effective cognitively based coping skills.

Developmental modifications for younger children might also include reducing session length; making home visits; including parents in sessions; and the use of play, stories, picture books, and drawings ("thought bubbles") to teach skills. In contrast, adolescents may be able to profit from complicated cognitive techniques involving abstract thinking, meta-cognition, and logical analysis (Friedberg & McClure, 2002).

FUTURE PRIORITIES

This final section discusses a few issues whose resolution would greatly enhance future research and practice in CBT. The importance of matching treatment techniques to children's developmental level and creating psychometrically sound and clinically useful assessment procedures for different aspects of cognitive functioning have already been noted, so this section focuses on involvement of parents, identifying moderators and mediators of intervention impact, and training in CBT approaches.

Involvement of Parents

On the one hand, it seems logical to include parents in CBT interventions. It would seem that the more resources directed at helping young people, the better the results of any intervention. On the other hand, inconsistent findings have been obtained for parent involvement; in some studies it has led to better outcomes, but in others it has not (cf. Barrett, 1998; Nauta, Scholing, Emmelkamp, & Minderaa, 2003). These inconsistencies may occur for several reasons, such as the differences across samples, problems, and treatments evaluated. They could also result from the different reasons for incorporating parents.

Parents may be viewed as (a) ancillary to their child's treatment, (b) important because there is a need to change or improve their customary parenting practices, or (c) necessary because of the parents' personal problems. In the first case, parents would typically been seen briefly and asked to merely support and encourage their treated child. In the second case, parents would typically be seen as often as their child, in either separate or concurrent training sessions. Finally, in the last case, parents would receive treatment for their own problems, usually in addition to their child receiving treatment. Each of these scenarios has resulted in positive benefits. For example, in the last case, data indicate that helping parents who have high levels of anxiety does improve the impact of CBT for their anxious children (Cobham, Dadds, & Spence, 1998). Future work needs to clarify what types of parental involvement enhance intervention gains under different clinical circumstances.

Furthermore, consistency in the application of the CBT model suggests the importance of examining any maladaptive parental cognitions that might interfere with effective treatment for their child. It is well known that parental attributions play a major role in determining which families arrive for child mental health services (Morrissey-Kane & Prinz, 1999). Table 26.3 contains a partial listing of some of the maladaptive parental beliefs and attributions that deserve consideration, depending on the role parents are asked to assume. These beliefs include such things as views about the nature, severity, and cause of their child's difficulties as well as the prognosis; how responsible or guilty parents feel for what has happened; their level of confidence in being able to help

TABLE 26.3 Some Potentially Maladaptive Parental Cognitions about Child Problems and Intervention

General beliefs
  That's just the way she is.
  He does that to get back at me.
  I have no influence over her.
  We cannot get him to change.
  When she gets into one of her moods, there's nothing we can do.
  I don't think he'll ever outgrow this.

Beliefs about treatment
  It is up to the therapist to fix my child.
  I really don't expect this to work.
  If this is going to work, then change should come quickly, and there won't be any setbacks or reverses.
  You're missing the true problem; why work with me when my child has the problem?
  The onus for change is on my child and the therapist.
  Treatment won't demand too much of me.

their child; disagreements between parents about any of these issues; and expectations for treatment.

What Moderates and Mediates the Effects of CBT?

Despite the extensive amount of outcome research on CBT, it is not possible to offer firm conclusions regarding what factors moderate or mediate treatment impact. Although at first this might seem surprising, this situation is not very different from other types of psychosocial interventions for children, especially with respect to treatment mediation. In general, a moderator is a variable that identifies conditions that make a treatment more or less effective, whereas a mediator explains why a treatment works or by what mechanism change is achieved.

Age has appeared as one important moderator of CBT outcomes in at least three meta-analyses. Although younger children do benefit from intervention, older children seem to benefit even more (Bennett & Gibbons, 2000; Durlak et al., 1991; Dush, Hirt, & Schroeder, 1989). The differences are more apparent the wider the age range of the children; for example, 11- to 13-year-olds versus 6- to 8-year-olds. Presumably, these findings result from the ability of older as opposed to younger children to make greater use of CBT treatment because of their more sophisticated and developed cognitive abilities. However, such an effect may also occur because change agents have not effectively modified customary CBT strategies to match younger children's developmental level. Moreover, because age serves only as a gross marker of developmental level, the real reasons that older children benefit more from CBT than younger ones remain unclear.

On the one hand, the most obvious and theoretically relevant mediational variable in CBT is cognitive functioning. After all, CBT places major emphasis on the role of cognitive processing in adjustment. On the other hand, confirmation that CBT outcomes are mediated by changes in cognitive functioning has not been obtained. The two primary factors accounting for this appear to be the very limited number of research studies that have explicitly tested for possible treatment mediators, and limitations in measurement. As noted earlier, there is a lack of standardized assessments of cognitive processes. The use of methods of unsubstantiated psychometric quality introduces considerable measurement error that can obscure mediational phenomena if they are present. For example, in a review of 25 CBT group outcome studies with anxious children, Prins and Ollendick (2003) reported that fewer than half (44 percent) collected any measures of cognitive change, 11 different measures were used, and many were subject to possible response bias and measurement error. Prins and Ollendick (2003) stressed the need for researchers to develop cognitive assessment instruments that tap the typical cognitive functions targeted in CBT studies.

Training

The research literatures in both the child and adult areas are remarkably barren on how to train change agents in the successful administration of CBT interventions. In fact, this statement holds for all types of child interventions and treatments. It is now widely recognized that a doctoral degree is not a prerequisite for an effective helper (see Christensen & Jacobson, 1994; Durlak, 1979), but it is not known which training techniques are most successful in developing the necessary competencies in individuals with varying levels of education and experience. The lack of training procedures with documented efficacy and the personnel to administer them are some of the barriers standing in the way of transporting CBT into the hands of more practitioners in real-world settings. In turn, this also prevents us from learning from practitioners how to modify customary CBT approaches to suit different family, community, and individual circumstances.

SUMMARY

CBT has become a popular paradigm for treating children and adolescents, and extensive outcome data indicate its efficacy for a wide range of problems. This chapter has explained the main features of CBT, discussed some of the major research findings on therapeutic outcomes, described some common CBT techniques, and discussed a few other issues such as the importance of a developmental perspective. For CBT to advance in theoretical sophistication and clinical efficacy and become widely used in more real-world clinical settings, it is important that future research and practice emphasize a few central issues. These include developing clinically useful and valid assessments of children's cognitive functioning at different ages, determining the factors that moderate and mediate treatment outcomes, understanding how best to incorporate parents into interventions, and devising methods of training others efficiently and effectively in different CBT approaches. The positive findings to date on the impact of CBT for many child and adolescent problems should encourage work in these needed areas.

REFERENCES

Baer, R. A., & Nietzel, M. T. (1991). Cognitive and behavioral treatment of impulsivity in children: A meta-analytic review of the outcome literature. *Journal of Clinical Child Psychology, 20,* 400–412.

Barrett, P. M. (1998). Evaluation of cognitive-behavioral group treatment for childhood anxiety disorders. *Journal of Clinical Child Psychology, 27,* 459–468.

Barrett, P. M., Dadds, M. R., & Rapee, R. M. (1996). Family treatment of childhood anxiety: A controlled trial. *Journal of Consulting and Clinical Psychology, 64,* 333–342.

Barrett, P. M., Duffy, A. L., Dadds, M. R., & Rapee, R. M. (2001). Cognitive-behavioral treatment of anxiety disorders in children: Long-term (6-year) follow-up. *Journal of Consulting and Clinical Psychology, 69,* 2001, 135–141.

Bennett, D. S., & Gibbons, T. A. (2000). Efficacy of child cognitive-behavioral interventions for antisocial behavior: A meta-analysis. *Child and Family Behavior Therapy, 22,* 1–15.

Blagys, M. D., & Hilsenroth, M. J. (2002). Distinctive activities of cognitive-behavioral therapy. A review of the comparative psychotherapy process literature. *Clinical Psychology Review, 22,* 671–706.

Christensen, A., & Jacobson, N. S. (1994). Who (or what) can do psychotherapy: The status and challenge of nonprofessional therapies. *Psychological Science, 5,* 8–14.

Cobham, V. E., Dadds, M. R., & Spence, S. H. (1998). The role of parental anxiety in the treatment of childhood anxiety. *Journal of Consulting and Clinical Psychology, 66,* 893–905.

Cohen, J. A., Mannarino, A. P., Berliner, L., & Deblinger, E. (2000). Trauma-focused cognitive behavioral therapy for children and adolescents. *Journal of Interpersonal Violence, 15,* 1202–1223.

Dadds, M. R., Holland, D. E., Laurens, K. R., Mullins, M., & Barrett, P. M. (1997). Early intervention and prevention of anxiety disorders in children: Results at two-year follow-up. *Journal of Consulting and Clinical Psychology, 67,* 145–150.

Dadds, M. R., Spence, S. H., Holland, D. E., Barrett, P. M., & Laurens, K. R. (1997). Prevention and early intervention for anxiety disorders: A controlled trial. *Journal of Consulting and Clinical Psychology, 65,* 627–635.

Durlak, J. A. (1979). Comparative effectiveness of paraprofessional and professional helpers. *Psychological Bulletin, 86,* 80–92.

Durlak, J. A., Furhman, T., & Lampman, C. (1991). Effectiveness of cognitive-behavior therapy for maladapting children: A meta-analysis. *Psychological Bulletin, 110,* 204–214.

Durlak, J. A., Maltby, N., & Allen, G. J. (2004). *Outcomes from the 2003 CUDCP Biennial Survey.* Unpublished manuscript, Loyola University Chicago.

Durlak, J. A., Rubin, L. A., & Kahng, R. D. (2001). Cognitive behavior therapy for children and adolescents with externalizing problems. *Journal of Cognitive Psychotherapy, 15,* 183–194.

Dush, D. M., Hirt, M. L., & Schroeder, H. E. (1989). Self-statement modification in the treatment of child behavior disorders: A meta-analysis. *Psychological Bulletin, 106,* 97–106.

Friedberg, R. D., & McClure, J. M. (2002). *Clinical practice of cognitive therapy with children and adolescents: The nuts and bolts.* New York: Guilford Press.

Ginsburg, G. S., & Drake, K. L. (2002). School-based treatment for anxious African-American adolescents: A controlled pilot study. *Journal of the American Academy of Child and Adolescent Psychiatry, 41,* 768–775.

Grossman, P. B., & Hughes, J. N. (1992). Self-control interventions with internalizing disorders: A review and analysis. *School Psychology Review, 21,* 229–245.

Holmbeck, G. N., Colder, C., Shapera, W., Westhoven, V., Kenealy, L., & Updegrove, A. (2000). Working with adolescents: Guides from developmental psychology. In P. C. Kendall (Ed.), *Child and adolescent therapy: Cognitive-behavioral procedures* (2nd ed., pp. 334–385). New York: Guilford Press.

Kazdin, A. E., & Weisz, J. R. (1998). Identifying and developing empirically supported child and adolescent treatments. *Journal of Consulting and Clinical Psychology, 66,* 19–36.

Kendall, P. C. (1994). Treating anxiety disorders in children: Results of a randomized clinical trial. *Journal of Consulting and Clinical Psychology, 62,* 100–110.

Kendall, P. C., & Southam-Gerow, M. (1996). Long-term follow-up of treatment for anxiety disordered youth. *Journal of Consulting and Clinical Psychology, 64,* 724–730.

Kendall, P. C., Safford, S., Flannery-Schroeder, E., & Webb, A. (2004). Child anxiety treatment: Outcomes in adolescence and impact on substance use and depression at 7.4-year follow-up. *Journal of Consulting and Clinical Psychology, 72,* 276–287.

Kibby, M. Y., Tyc, V. L., & Mulhern, R. K. (1998). Effectiveness of psychological intervention for children and adolescents with chronic medical illness: A meta-analysis. *Clinical Psychology Review, 18,* 103–117.

Lipsey, M. W., & Wilson, D. B. (1993). The efficacy of psychological, educational, and behavioral treatment. *American Psychologist, 48,* 1181–1209.

Lochman, J. E., Magee, T. N., & Pardini, D. A. (2003). Cognitive-behavioral interventions for children with conduct problems. In M. A. Reinicke & D. A. Clark (Eds.), *Cognitive therapy across the lifespan* (pp. 441–476). Cambridge, England: Cambridge University Press.

Lochman, J. E., & Wells, K. C. (2002). The Coping Power Program at the middle school transition: Universal and indicated prevention effects. *Psychology of Addictive Behaviors, 16,* S40–S54.

Lochman, J. E., & Wells, K. C. (2004). The Coping Power Program for preadolescent aggressive boys and their parents: Outcome effects at the 1-year follow-up. *Journal of Consulting and Clinical Psychology, 72,* 571–578.

Malouff, J. M., & Schutte, N. S. (2004). Strategies for increasing client completion of treatment assignments. *Behavior Therapist, 27,* 1–4.

March, J. S. (1995). Cognitive-behavioral psychotherapy for children and adolescents with OCD: A review and recommendations for treatment. *Journal of the American Academy of Child and Adolescent Psychiatry, 34,* 7–18.

Mash, E. J., & Barkley, R. A. (Eds.). (2003). *Child psychopathology* (2nd ed.). New York: Guilford Press.

Morrissey-Kane, E., & Prinz, R. J. (1999). Engagement in child and adolescent treatment: The role of parental cognitions and attributions. *Clinical Child and Family Psychology Review, 2,* 183–198.

Nauta, M. H., Scholing, A., Emmelkamp, P. M. G., & Minderaa, R. B. (2003). Cognitive-behavioral therapy for children with anxiety disorders in a clinical setting: No additional effect of a cognitive parent training. *Journal of the American Academy of Child and Adolescent Psychiatry, 42,* 1270–1278.

Ollendick, T. H., & King, N. J. (1998). Empirically supported treatments for children with phobic and anxiety disorders. *Journal of Clinical Child Psychology, 27,* 156–168.

Pina, A. A., Silverman, W. K., Fuentes, R. M., Kurtines, W. M., & Weems, C. F. (2003). Exposure-based cognitive-behavioral treatment for phobic and anxiety disorders: Treatment effects and maintenance for Hispanic/Latino relative to European-American youths. *Journal of the American Academy of Child and Adolescent Psychiatry, 42,* 1179–1187.

Prins, P. J. M., & Ollendick, T. H. (2003). Cognitive change and enhanced coping: Missing mediational links in cognitive behavior therapy with anxiety-disordered children. *Clinical Child and Family Psychology Review, 6,* 87–105.

Quakley, S., Coker, S., Palmer, K., & Reynolds, S. (2003). Can children distinguish between thoughts and behaviors? *Behavioural and Cognitive Psychotherapy, 31,* 159–168.

Rapee, R. M. (2003). The influence of comorbidity on treatment outcome for children and adolescents with anxiety disorders. *Behaviour Research and Therapy, 41,* 105–112.

Reinicke, M. A., Ryan, N. E., & DuBois, D. L. (1998). Cognitive-behavioral therapy of depression and depressive symptoms during adolescence: A review and meta-analysis. *Journal of the American Academy of Child and Adolescent Psychiatry, 37,* 26–34.

Robinson, T. R., Smith, S. W., Miller, M. D., & Brownell, M. T. (1999). Cognitive behavior modification of hyperactivity-impulsivity and aggression: A meta-analysis of school-based studies. *Journal of Educational Psychology, 91,* 195–203.

Rosenthal, R., & Rubin, D. B. (1982). A simple, general purpose display of magnitude of experimental effect. *Journal of Educational Psychology, 74,* 166–169.

Rossello, J., & Bernal, G. (1999). The efficacy of cognitive-behavioral and interpersonal treatments for depression in Puerto Rican adolescents. *Journal of Consulting and Clinical Psychology, 67,* 734–745.

Velting, O. N., Setzer, N. J., & Albano, A. M. (2004). Update on and advances in assessment and cognitive-behavioral treatment of anxiety disorders in children and adolescents. *Professional Psychology: Research and Practice, 35,* 42–54.

CHAPTER 27

Pharmacological Treatments

SANJEEV PATHAK

INTRODUCTION

Psychopharmacology is the mainstay of pediatric psychiatry. Yet until recently, many considered the field of pediatric psychopharmacology to be in its infancy (Vitiello & Jensen, 1997). Although there is a long way to go before the field reaches a stage of desirable maturity, efforts by the National Institute of Mental Health (NIMH) and the Food and Drug Administration (FDA) have increased pharmacological research in pediatric psychiatry. Large multisite clinical trials such as the multimodal treatment of attention-deficit/hyperactivity disorder (ADHD) study and the Treatment for Adolescent with Depression Study have provided useful scientific information that will guide treatment for common psychiatric disorders in times to come (Multimodal Treatment of ADHD [MTA] study, 1999; Treatment for Adolescents with Depression Study Team, 2004). Despite this progress, clinicians use many psychopharmacological interventions that have been investigated exclusively in adults. Moreover, recent studies have reported an increase in the use of psychotropics in pediatric age groups (Rappley et al., 1999; Zito et al., 2000). A multitude of reasons may account for this increase, such as better recognition of psychopathology, increased availability of services, and possible increase in psychopathology (Lewinsohn, Hops, Roberts, Seeley, & Andrews, 1993). However, concerns have been expressed in the professional literature and media about this growth because of the paucity of data regarding the short-term and long-term efficacy, safety, and tolerability of these agents in young patients (Charatan, 2000; Coyle, 2000; Kalb, 2000; Shute et al., 2000; Zito et al., 2000). Psychopharmacological research clearly lags behind clinical care in pediatric age groups. Randomized controlled trials with psychopharmacological interventions for psychiatric problems in children and adolescents are urgently needed. Legislation such as the Best Pharmaceuticals for Children Act has increased pharmaceutical research in child psychiatry (www.fda.gov/opacom/laws/pharmkids/contents.html). This act has encouraged pharmaceutical companies to conduct pediatric studies of on-patent drugs that are used in pediatric populations but are not labeled for such use by extending their market exclusivity.

This chapter discusses the psychopharmacological interventions commonly used with children and adolescents, namely selective serotonin inhibitors, stimulants, antipsychotics, and mood stabilizers, along with the supporting empirical research, beginning with the important developmental issues in clinical pharmacology of psychotropics.

DEVELOPMENTAL ISSUES IN PHARMACOKINETICS AND PHARMACODYNAMICS OF PSYCHOTROPICS

In all fields of medicine, medication selection and dosing are influenced by the clinical pharmacology of the specific drug. In pediatric psychopharmacology, dosing choices are often based on adult data, which is problematic because of pharmacokinetic and pharmacodynamic differences between children and adults.

Pharmacokinetics

Percentage of body fat varies significantly as children and adolescents grow. Body fat increases in the first year of life, then decreases until adolescence, when it increases again. Because psychotropics are highly lipid soluble, their storage is affected by body fat percentage. Thus prepubertal children have relatively less drug storage capability compared to adults. This reduces half-life and requires more frequent dosing. In addition, preschoolers have relatively greater hepatic capacity, which increases metabolism for hepatically metabolized drugs. Thus they may require higher doses per unit body weight than adults. Glomerular filtration rates in children reach adult rates by age 1 year. Because children have higher fluid intake than adults, they also have higher and more rapid renal elimination. Therefore medications such as lithium that are excreted by the kidney without being metabolized may need higher doses than would be expected from weight alone.

Pharmacodynamics

The neurotransmitter systems and the brain develop through childhood, adolescence, and adulthood, resulting in variable pharmacodynamic response at different stages of development. This variation could result in differing drug response and side effects. For instance, the lack of efficacy of noradrenergic tricyclic antidepressants may be due to the relative immaturity of the noradrenergic system in children. Similarly, the dopamine system changes with decreases in receptor density beginning at age 3 years. However, the serotonin system seems to remain unchanged through development. Therefore, selective serotonin reuptake inhibitors may have utility for anxiety disorders across the life span.

SELECTIVE SEROTONIN REUPTAKE INHIBITORS

The selective serotonin reuptake inhibitors (SSRIs), fluoxetine, paroxetine, sertraline, fluvoxamine, citalopram, and escitalopram, are all approved by the FDA for at least one indication in adults (see Table 27.1). Currently, three SSRIs have FDA approval for use in children and adolescents. They are fluvoxamine (for obsessive-compulsive disorder), sertraline (for obsessive-compulsive disorder), and fluoxetine (for obsessive-compulsive disorder and major depressive disorder).

Adult data show that all SSRIs are well absorbed after oral administration, and peak blood levels are obtained within 1 to 8 hours. Fluoxetine, paroxetine, and sertraline each undergo more than 95 percent protein binding, whereas for citalopram and escitalopram the figure is about 50 percent. All SSRIs undergo extensive hepatic metabolism, but only in the case of fluoxetine is there an active metabolite of any significance. Fluoxetine, which is sequestered in the lungs, has a half-life of about 2 or 3 days, and its active metabolite, norfluoxetine, has a much longer half-life of from 7 to 10 days. The other SSRIs have half-lives of from 1 to 1.5 days. Few pharmacokinetic studies have been conducted in children and adolescents. Wilens et al. (2002) evaluated the pharmacokinetic profile of fluoxetine and its major metabolite, norfluoxetine, in 21 children and adolescent patients. Participants were administered 20 mg fluoxetine for 60 days, with sparse blood samples taken throughout the open-label study. The patients contributed 168 plasma concentrations. Pharmacokinetic parameters were estimated using a mixed effects nonlinear model. Mean steady-state fluoxetine and norfluoxetine of 127 ng/mL and 151 ng/mL, respectively, were achieved in children and adolescents after 4 weeks of treatment, with high between-patient variability. Fluoxetine was twofold higher and norfluoxetine was 1.7-fold higher in children relative to adolescents. However, when normalized to body weight, fluoxetine and norfluoxetine were similar for both age groups. Age, body weight, body mass index, and body surface area, modeled independently as continuous variables, significantly improved the population pharmacokinetic model when evaluated as patient factors. The authors concluded that children have twofold higher fluoxetine and norfluoxetine relative to adolescents, a finding that appears to be related to indices of body size.

Findling et al. (1999) enrolled 30 depressed youths who received a single 10-mg dose of paroxetine followed by 5 days of blood and urine collection for pharmacokinetic analyses. The patients subsequently received open treatment for 8 weeks, and weekly blood samples were obtained for plasma concentration measurements. There was tremendous interindividual variability in paroxetine disposition. The mean half-life of paroxetine was 11.1 ± 5.2 (SD) hours. The average clearance was 88.7 ± 66.4 mL/min/kg. The mean area under the plasma drug concentration curve was 0.09 ± 0.10 micro-

TABLE 27.1 Selective Serotonin Reuptake Inhibitors

Agent	Clinical use	FDA pediatric labeling	Dose (mg/day)	Schedule	Potential adverse effects
Fluoxetine		OCD, MDD (7–17 years)	5–60	QD	Suicidality, irritability, insomnia akathisia, GI disturbance, headache, rash, flulike symptoms on rapid discontinuation, CYP inhibition
Paroxetine	Anxiety disorders, MDD, DD, body dysmorphic disorder	N/A	10–30	QD	
Sertraline		>6 years for OCD	25–200	QD	
Fluvoxamine		>8 years for OCD	12.5–200	QD	
Citalopram		N/A	10–40	QD	
Escitalopram		N/A	5–30	QD	

Note. CYP = Cytochrome P450; DD = dysthymic disorder; MDD = major depressive disorder; OCD = obsessive-compulsive disorder; QD = once per day.

gram/mL/hr. Within-subject variability of plasma paroxetine concentrations was generally not significant. Findling and colleagues concluded that paroxetine is more rapidly cleared in youths than adults and may be given once daily in this population.

Labellarte et al. (2004) studied the pharmacokinetics of fluvoxamine in children and adolescents by titrating fluvoxamine to a target dose of 100 mg, twice daily, in children (6–11 years) and 150 mg b.i.d. in adolescents (12–17 years) with obsessive-compulsive disorder or another disorder requiring fluvoxamine treatment. Serum samples were collected over 12 hours after 12 or more consecutive doses of 25, 50, 100, and 150 mg. Sixteen children (seven females, nine males) and 18 adolescents (nine females, nine males) were included in the pharmacokinetic analyses. Children demonstrated higher mean peak plasma concentration, higher mean area under the plasma concentration–time curve, and lower apparent oral clearance compared with adolescents. Compared with male children, female children had higher mean area under the plasma concentration–time curve, higher mean peak plasma concentration, and more reports of adverse events. However, the area under the plasma concentration–time curve was not directly correlated with frequency or severity of adverse events. Pharmacokinetics were nonlinear over the dose range studied. These pharmacokinetic results suggest that children (especially females) have a higher exposure to fluvoxamine than adolescents.

Axelson et al. (2002) assessed the pharmacokinetics of sertraline in adolescents by evaluating steady-state withdrawal kinetics in 10 adolescents taking 50 mg/day and in 6 adolescents taking 100–150 mg/day. The mean steady-state half-life of 50 mg was significantly shorter (15.3 ± 3.5 hours) than the single-dose half-life (26.7 ± 5.2 hours; $t = 6.4$, $p \leq .001$) and the steady-state half-life at 100–150 mg/day (20.4 ± 3.4 hours; $t = 2.9$, $p = .01$). Thus the half-life of 50 mg sertraline becomes significantly shorter from the initial dose to steady-state, and many adolescents may benefit from twice-per-day dosing. The steady-state half-life increases as the dose increases. Taken together, the clinical significance of the interindividual variability in the pharmacokinetic profile is unclear at this time.

Clinical Trials

The first large pediatric trial of SSRIs in obsessive-compulsive disorder (OCD) used fluvoxamine in 120 participants aged 8–17 years (Riddle et al., 2001). This double-blind, placebo-controlled study implemented 10 weeks of core treatment followed by a 1-year extension phase. Average daily dose of fluvoxamine was approximately 150 mg/day, and the dose range was between 50 and 200 mg/day. Significant improvement of OCD symptoms began at week 1 and continued over the course of the study. Improvement was noted on three outcome measures, the Children's Yale-Brown Obsessive-Compulsive Scale (CY-BOCS), the National Institute of Mental Health Obsessive-Compulsive Scale (NIMH-OCS), and the Clinical Global Impressions-Improvement Scale (CGI-I). Fluvoxamine was well tolerated and few patients dropped out due to lack of efficacy (9 percent) or untoward effects (3 percent). These data helped fluvoxamine earn an FDA indication for treatment of OCD in children and adolescents aged 8–17 years.

The next large controlled SSRI trial for OCD was a sertraline study of 187 children and adolescents aged 6–17 years (March et al., 1998). Patients were treated with sertraline during a 4-week titration up to 200 mg/day, followed by 8 weeks at a stable dose. Significant differences between sertraline and placebo emerged at week 3 and persisted for the duration of the study. In intent-to-treat analyses, patients treated with sertraline showed significantly greater improvement than did placebo-treated patients on the CY-BOCS (adjusted mean, -6.8 vs. -3.4), the NIMH-OCS (-2.2 vs. -1.3), and the CGI-I (2.7 vs. 3.3) scales. Significant differences in efficacy between sertraline and placebo emerged at Week 3 and persisted for the duration of the study. These data resulted in an FDA indication for sertraline treatment of OCD in children and adolescents aged 6–17 years. This was followed up by a randomized controlled trial of sertraline, cognitive-behavioral psychotherapy (CBT), and a combination of CBT and sertraline in 112 children and adolescents diagnosed with OCD (Pediatric OCD Treatment Study [POTS] Team, 2004). Intent-to-treat random regression analyses indicated a statistically significant advantage for sertraline alone ($p = .007$) and combined treatment ($p = .001$) compared with placebo. Combined treatment also proved superior to CBT alone ($p = .008$) and to sertraline alone ($p = .006$), which did not differ from each other. The rate of clinical remission for combined treatment was 53.6 percent (95 percent confidence interval [CI], 36 percent to 70 percent); and for sertraline alone was 21.4 percent (95 percent CI, 10 percent to 40 percent).

Rosenberg, Stewart, Fitzgerald, Tawile, and Carroll (1999) used paroxetine in a 12-week open-label trial of paroxetine with 20 patients diagnosed with OCD, aged 8–17 years. They were treated for OCD with daily doses ranging from 10 to 60 mg. Paroxetine appeared effective in this small sample as mean CY-BOCS scores decreased significantly ($z = 3.49$, $p = .0005$), from 30.6 ± 3.5 to 21.6 ± 6.8. The only other psychotropic agent with controlled safety and efficacy data for pediatric OCD is clomipramine (DeVeaugh-Geiss et al., 1992; Flament, Rapoport, & Kilts, 1985; Leonard et al.,

1989), a tricyclic antidepressant with potent serotonin (5-HT) reuptake inhibitor activity in addition to noradrenergic activity. Because of efficacy data and its noteworthy serotonergic properties, clomipramine is included here in discussions of SSRIs. DeVeaugh-Geiss et al. enrolled 60 children aged 10–17 years diagnosed with OCD and demonstrated significant improvements in OCD symptoms as early as 3 weeks into treatment (DeVeaugh-Geiss et al., 1992). Clomipramine resulted in adverse effects such as tachycardia, decreased systolic blood pressure, dry mouth, somnolence, dizziness, fatigue, tremor, and constipation, which are typical of tricyclic antidepressants. Geller et al., in a meta-analysis, demonstrated that clomipramine was statistically superior to SSRIs in reducing OCD symptoms but may not be a first-line treatment due to its side effect profile (Geller et al., 2003). The SSRIs examined in this meta-analysis were more or less comparably effective in this population (Geller et al., 2003).

SSRI trials in major depressive disorder (MDD) have had mixed results, and fluoxetine is the only SSRI approved by the FDA for pediatric depression. In a landmark treatment study of fluoxetine in children and adolescents (aged 7–17 years) with MDD, Emslie et al. (1997) utilized a double-blind, placebo-controlled, 8-week trial design. Ninety-six patients were randomized to 8 weeks of treatment with fluoxetine or placebo. Fifty-six percent of the fluoxetine-treated sample responded to fluoxetine treatment compared to 33 percent of the placebo group ($p < 0.05$). These results were replicated by Emslie et al. (2002) in a multisite study with fluoxetine in pediatric MDD. Using a trial design similar to that of Emslie et al. (1997), 122 children and 97 adolescents with MDD were randomly assigned to placebo or fluoxetine (Emslie et al., 2002). After a 1-week placebo lead-in, fluoxetine-treated patients received fluoxetine 10 mg/day for 1 week, then fluoxetine 20 mg/day for 8 weeks. Fluoxetine was associated with greater mean improvement in Children's Depression Rating Scale—Revised (CDRS-R; Poznanski & Mokros, 1996) score than placebo after 1 week ($<.05$). Significantly more fluoxetine-treated patients (41 percent) met the prospectively defined criteria for remission than did placebo-treated patients (20 percent; $<.01$). This data resulted in FDA approval of fluoxetine for MDD in children and adolescents (aged 7–17 years). Fluoxetine is the only antidepressant that has demonstrated efficacy in more than one placebo-controlled, randomized clinical trial of pediatric depression.

The efficacy of fluoxetine in MDD was again supported by the NIMH-sponsored Treatment for Adolescents with Depression Study (TADS), the largest clinical trial conducted in adolescents with depression (Treatment for Adolescents with Depression Study Team, 2004). TADS randomized 439 patients with MDD between the ages of 12 and 17 years to 12 weeks of fluoxetine alone (10–40 mg/day), CBT alone, CBT with fluoxetine (10–40 mg/day), or placebo. Compared with placebo, the combination of fluoxetine with CBT and fluoxetine alone were statistically significant on the CDRS-R.

Data are emerging on the efficacy of SSRIs in anxiety disorders such as social phobia (SP), separation anxiety disorder (SAD), and generalized anxiety disorder (GAD). However, no SSRI is currently approved by the FDA for treatment of the aforementioned disorders. The Research Unit on Pediatric Psychopharmacology (RUPP) Anxiety Study Group (RUPP, 2001) studied 128 children who were 6–17 years of age; met the criteria for SP, SAD, or GAD; and had received psychological treatment for 3 weeks without improvement. The children were randomly assigned to receive fluvoxamine (at a maximum of 300 mg/day) or placebo for 8 weeks. Patients in the fluvoxamine group had a mean ($\pm$ SD) decrease of 9.7 ± 6.9 points in symptoms of anxiety on the Pediatric Anxiety Rating Scale (range of possible scores 0–25, with higher scores indicating greater anxiety), as compared with a decrease of 3.1 ± 4.8 points among children in the placebo group ($p \leq 0.001$). On the CGI-I scale, 48 of 63 children in the fluvoxamine group (76 percent) responded to the treatment, as indicated by a score of less than 4, as compared with 19 of 65 children in the placebo group (29 percent; RUPP, 2001).

Birmaher et al. (2003) assessed the efficacy of fluoxetine for the acute treatment of pediatric GAD, SAD, SP, or a combination of these by randomizing youths (aged 7–17 years) who had significant functional impairment due to the above diagnoses to fluoxetine (20 mg/day; $n = 37$) or placebo ($n = 37$) for 12 weeks. Using intent-to-treat analysis, 61 percent of patients taking fluoxetine and 35 percent taking placebo showed much to very much improvement. Despite this improvement, a substantial group of patients remained symptomatic. Youths with SP and GAD responded better to fluoxetine than placebo, but only SP moderated the clinical and functional response. Severity of the anxiety at intake and positive family history for anxiety predicted poorer functioning at the end of the study (Birmaher et al., 2003).

In a multicenter, 16-week randomized double-blind, placebo-controlled trial with flexible-dose paroxetine, Wagner et al. (2004) enrolled 322 children (aged 8–11 years) and adolescents (aged 12–17 years) with SAD as their predominant psychiatric illness. Patients were randomized to receive paroxetine (10–50 mg/day) or placebo. At the week 16 end point, the odds of responding (CGI-I score of 1 or 2) were statistically significantly greater for paroxetine (77.6 percent response) than for placebo (38.3 percent response [59/154]; adjusted odds ratio, 7.02; 95 percent confidence interval, 4.07

to 12.11; $p \leq .001$). The proportion of patients who were very much improved (CGI-I score of 1) was 47.8 percent (77/161) for paroxetine compared with 14.9 percent (23/154) for placebo.

Adverse Effects of Selective Serotonin Reuptake Inhibitors

On September 14, 2004, a joint advisory committee for the FDA voted in favor of a black box warning indicating that antidepressants could increase suicidality in pediatric patients. The warning states, "Antidepressants increase the risk of suicidal thinking and behavior (suicidality) in children and adolescents with major depressive disorder (MDD) and other psychiatric disorders. Patients who are started on therapy should be observed closely for clinical worsening, suicidality, or unusual changes in behavior." This warning was based on a pooled analysis of short-term (4–16 weeks) placebo-controlled trials of nine antidepressant drugs (SSRIs and others) in children and adolescents with MDD and other anxiety disorders including OCD. This analysis included a total of 24 trials with approximately 4,400 patients and revealed a greater risk of adverse events representing suicidal thinking or behavior (suicidality) across all antidepressants and almost all trials during the first few months of treatment in those receiving antidepressants. The average risk of such events on the drug was 4 percent, twice the placebo risk of 2 percent. No suicides occurred in these trials. Before the FDA decision to go with the black box warning, in December 2003, Britain's equivalent of the FDA, the Medicines and Healthcare Products Regulatory Agency (MHRA), contraindicated all antidepressants except fluoxetine in the pediatric age group. The FDA, on the other hand, has chosen a black box warning instead, which still allows for off-label prescriptions of SSRIs, as many scientists have argued that other antidepressants should be available for patients who do not benefit from fluoxetine (Brent, 2004). With these recent developments, utilization of SSRIs is difficult for clinicians as well as for patients and their families. Despite the concerns of increased suicidal behavior in some pediatric patients, SSRIs remain an important depression treatment in this population. This is because untreated depression carries serious morbidity and mortality, and psychosocial interventions do not work for all (Carroll, 2004; Treatment for Adolescents with Depression Study Team, 2004).

SSRIs may also produce stomachache, nausea, vomiting, diarrhea, and anorexia (Birmaher et al., 2003; Scharko, 2004). Weight loss may occur but is generally seen only in those who were overweight prior to treatment; exceptions to this rule, however, do occur, especially among the elderly, who may lose substantial amounts even if they were of normal weight before treatment. Uncommonly, patients may gain weight. Sexual dysfunction is seen in almost half of treated adults and may consist of decreased libido, erectile dysfunction, delayed ejaculation, or anorgasmia. This effect has not been well studied in pediatrics. Scharko (2004) did a literature review of SSRI-induced sexual dysfunction in adolescents and found that only one male of 1,346 pediatric patients receiving an SSRI reported sexual dysfunction. This is presumed to result from inadequate reporting and gathering of data. Anxiety, tremor, agitation, and insomnia may occur. Conversely, some patients may experience sedation or an urge to take a nap. A minority of patients may experience an akathisia that may at times be severe and may be associated with an increase in any preexisting agitation or suicidal ideation. Dystonia or parkinsonism may also occur, but these are generally mild in patients with preexisting Parkinson's disease. In bipolar patients, mania may be precipitated. Occasionally, a syndrome of inappropriate antidiuretic hormone secretion may occur with hyponatremia. Rarely, an SSRI may precipitate a systemic vasculitis. Physical symptoms are rare, and usually SSRIs are well tolerated. On the other hand, the psychiatric adverse effects need to be monitored carefully. None of these SSRIs have been associated with major malformations in infants. However, there may be an increased risk of miscarriage with fluoxetine if used in pregnant teenagers (Simon, Cunningham, & Davis, 2002).

Because all SSRIs inhibit cytochrome P450 2D6 (CYP2D6), interactions between SSRIs and other drugs can produce adverse effects. The potency of SSRIs in this regard varies widely: fluoxetine and paroxetine are the most potent; sertraline has only modest effects in this regard. Fluvoxamine, citalopram, and escitalopram have minimal effect. Of the many drugs metabolized by CYP2D6 whose blood levels may be increased with inhibition of CYP2D6, the most important are the tricyclic antidepressants, whose levels may be increased into toxic ranges by fluoxetine or paroxetine. SSRIs, especially fluoxetine and paroxetine, may increase warfarin levels, thus increasing the risk of bleeding. Phenytoin, metoprolol, and tricyclic antidepressant levels may also be increased. Concurrent use of an SSRI with a monoamine oxidase inhibitor (MAOI) is contraindicated because it may result in confusion, myoclonus, agitation, hyperthermia, long-tract signs, and possibly death. Potentially harmful effects of drug interactions can be avoided with astute clinical decisions. If a patient is initially taking an MAOI, at least 2 weeks should elapse after discontinuing the MAOI before starting the SSRI to allow for a regeneration of monoamine oxidase. If the patient was initially taking the SSRI, at least 2 weeks should elapse between discontinuing paroxetine or sertraline and starting the MAOI. In the case of fluoxetine, given its longer half-life, generally 4 weeks should pass before starting the MAOI.

Dosing

Given that there is little pharmacokinetic data on SSRI dosing in children and adolescents, most predictions of pediatric daily dosages have been extrapolated from adult pharmacokinetic data. The starting dose is usually lower than that given to adults. The dose can be increased weekly to reach the final dose, which is equivalent to the adult dose. It is reasonable to wait 4–6 weeks for improvement after a reasonable target dose of SSRIs has been achieved. SSRIs are usually given in the morning. Uncommonly, these agents can cause sedation, and in such a case changing the dose time to before bedtime can help. Most sedation and activation should improve over time at a given dosage. A patient can usually lessen gastrointestinal distress by eating before taking the SSRI. Withdrawal symptoms should also be observed during SSRI discontinuation, particularly with shorter acting SSRIs such as paroxetine.

ATYPICAL (SECOND-GENERATION) ANTIPSYCHOTICS

No currently available second-generation antipsychotic (SGA), a category that includes clozapine (Clozaril®), risperidone (Risperdal®), olanzapine (Zyprexa®), quetiapine (Seroquel®), aripiprazole (Abilify®), and ziprasidone (Geodon®), is approved for use in the pediatric age group (see Table 27.2). However, child and adolescent psychiatrists prescribe antipsychotics frequently, but with more than 30 percent of psychiatric patients receiving them (Kaplan, Simms, & Busner, 1994). Although the FDA labels them primarily as treatments for psychosis and mania in adults (Glick, Murray, Vasudevan, Marder, & Hu, 2001; Kapur & Remington, 2001), antipsychotics are prescribed for youths who suffer from a wide variety of diagnoses including schizophrenia, psychotic depression, schizoaffective disorder, bipolar disorder, conduct disorder, pervasive developmental disorders, and Tourette's syndrome.

Clinical Trials

Several reports have suggested that atypical antipsychotics such as clozapine (Kowatch et al., 1995), risperidone (Frazier et al., 1999), olanzapine (Chang & Ketter, 2000; Khouzam & el-Gabalawi, 2000; Soutullo, Sorter, Foster, McElroy, & Keck, 1999) and quetiapine (DelBello, Schwiers, Rosenberg, & Strakowski, 2002) are effective in the treatment of pediatric bipolar disorder (BPD). In an 8-week open-label prospective study of olanzapine monotherapy (dose range 2.5–20 mg/day). Frazier et al. (2001) treated 23 children and adolescents with BPD and reported that olanzapine treatment was associated with a response rate of 61 percent on the Young Mania Rating Scale (YMRS) and Clinical Global Impression—Severity (CGI-S). The response rate was based on a predefined criterion for improvement of >30 percent decline in YMRS and a CGI-S mania score of <3 at end point. In another retrospective chart review of outpatients ($N = 28$), Frazier et al. (1999) investigated the effectiveness and tolerability of risperidone for the treatment of pediatric mania. These children received a mean daily dose of 1.7 ± 1.3 mg risperidone over an average period of 6.1 ± 8.5 months. Using a CGI Improvement score of = 2 (very much/much improved) to define improvement, 82 percent showed improvement in manic symptoms. Barzman et al. (2004) conducted a retrospective chart review of 30 patients and found a statistically significant improvement in CGAS scores (48 ± 11 to 65 ± 11, signed rank = 191, $p < 0.0001$) and CGI-S scores (4.2 ± 0.8 to 2.8 ± 1.0, signed rank = $-172, p < 0.0001$, effect size = 1.90) from baseline to end point.

TABLE 27.2 Second-Generation Antipsychotics

Agent	Clinical use	FDA pediatric labeling	Dose (mg/day)[1]	Schedule	Potential adverse effects
Clozapine	Bipolar disorder, phychosis, schizophrenia, schizoaffective disorder, conduct disorder	N/A	12.5–900	BID	Agranulocytosis, leucopenia, seizures, hypersalivation for clozapine; weight gain, hyperglycemia, QTc prolongation, tardive dyskinesia, orthostatic hypotension, neuroleptic malignant syndrome for all
Risperidone			10–30	BID/QD	
Olanzapine			2.5–30	QD/BID	
Quetiapine			50–800	BID	
Aripiprazole			5–30	QD/BID	
Ziprasidone			20–160	QD/BID	

Note. BID = two times per day; QD = once per day.
[1] Start with the least possible dose and have weekly increments to reach the target dose for outpatients.

Although these studies are limited by small samples and retrospective and uncontrolled designs, findings suggest that these SGAs may be effective for the treatment of mania. In addition, data are emerging that the addition of an atypical antipsychotic to a mood stabilizer decreases manic symptoms and improves overall response rates. DelBello et al. (2002) conducted a placebo-controlled study examining the efficacy, safety, and tolerability of quetiapine as an adjunct to divalproex for acute mania in adolescents with BPD. In this study, 30 adolescent inpatients, ages 12–18 years, with manic or mixed bipolar I received an initial divalproex dose of 20 mg/kg and were randomized to a double-blind 6-week treatment with quetiapine ($n = 15$) or placebo ($n = 15$), which was titrated to 450 mg/day. The primary efficacy measure was changed from baseline to end point in YMRS score. The divalproex + quetiapine group demonstrated a statistically significant greater reduction in YMRS scores from baseline to end point than the valproate + placebo group. Moreover, YMRS response rate was significantly greater in the divalproex + quetiapine group than in the DVP + placebo group (87 percent versus 53 percent).

Kafantaris, Coletti, Dicker, Padula, and Kane (2001) enrolled acutely manic adolescents with psychotic features who received treatment with lithium and an adjunctive antipsychotic medication. If their psychosis resolved, the antipsychotic medication dose was gradually tapered and discontinued after 4 weeks of therapeutic lithium levels. Patients were continued on maintenance lithium monotherapy for up to 4 weeks. Significant improvement was seen in 64 percent of the sample with psychotic features after 4 weeks of combination treatment. However, 43 percent did not maintain their response after discontinuation of the antipsychotic medication, suggesting that longer than 4 weeks of antipsychotic treatment is required for some adolescents with psychotic mania. These studies suggest that pediatric BPD may benefit from treatment with both a mood stabilizer and an atypical antipsychotic to achieve a full response.

There have been few controlled trials with SGA in schizophrenia. In a 6-week double-blind comparison of clozapine and haloperidol for childhood-onset schizophrenia ($N = 21$, mean age = 14), clozapine was found to be more efficacious than haloperidol for positive and negative symptoms (Kumra et al., 1996). In this study, however, seizures and neutropenia were major concerns with clozapine (Kumra et al., 1996).

A prospective 6-week, open-label study of 10 adolescents with schizophrenia found significant symptom reduction during risperidone therapy (Armenteros, Whitaker, Welikson, Stedge, & Gorman, 1997). At the end of this trial, 6 of 10 youths were rated as being much or very much improved. The mean risperidone dosage at the end of the study was 6.6 mg/day. The most common side effects were sedation and weight gain. Two patients had acute dystonic reactions, and three developed drug-induced parkinsonism. Seven open-label studies ($N > 100$) have suggested that olanzapine may be efficacious for pediatric psychosis (ages 6–18, 2.5–20 mg/day). In a double-blind parallel study of risperidone, olanzapine, and haloperidol for psychosis in adolescents ($N = 50$, age range = 8–19, mean age = 15), risperidone (0.5–3 mg), olanzapine (2.5–12.5 mg), and haloperidol (1–5 mg) produced significant reductions in psychotic symptoms measured on the Brief Psychiatric Rating Scale for Children (Sikich, Hamer, Bashford, Sheitman, & Lieberman, 2004).

Although conduct disorder is neither a psychotic disorder nor a mood disorder, emerging data support the use of SGAs in conduct disorder and aggression in pediatric patients (Aman, DeSmedt, Derivan, Lyons, & Findling, 2002; Findling et al., 2000; Snyder et al., 2002). Snyder et al. evaluated whether risperidone is effective in reducing symptoms of disruptive behaviors (such as aggression, impulsivity, defiance of authority figures, and property destruction) associated with conduct disorder, oppositional defiant disorder, and disruptive behavior disorder not otherwise specified in children with subaverage IQs (Snyder et al., 2002). This study consisted of a 1-week, single-blind, placebo run-in period and was followed by a 6-week, double-blind, placebo-controlled treatment of 110 children (aged 5–12 years, inclusive) with IQs of 36–84 with a disruptive behavior disorder and a score of at least 24 on the conduct problem subscale of the Nisonger Child Behavior Rating Form (NCBRF). Risperidone doses ranged from 0.02 to 0.06 mg/kg/day. The intention-to-treat analysis of risperidone-treated participants showed a significant ($p < .001$) reduction in mean scores (from 33.4 at baseline to 17.6 at end point; 47.3 percent reduction) versus placebo-treated participants (mean baseline of 32.6 to 25.8 at end point; 20.9 percent reduction) on the conduct problem subscale of the NCBRF. Between-group differences in favor of risperidone were seen as early as week one and were significant at all postbaseline visits. The authors concluded that risperidone appears to be an adequately tolerated and effective treatment in children with subaverage IQs and severe disruptive behaviors such as aggression and destructive behavior.

Adverse Effects of Second-Generation Antipsychotics

SGAs have a lower risk of extrapyramidal symptoms (EPS) compared to typical antipsychotic medications such as haloperidol, which is particularly important in children and adolescents (Sikich et al., 2004). In addition, side effect profiles differ among the SGAs. This may be because SGAs have different receptor-blocking affinities for dopamine, histamine, acetylcholine, α−1, and serotonin receptors. Serious adverse effects of SGAs include weight gain, glucose dysregulation, EPS, hyperprolactinemia, QTc prolongation, orthostatic hypotension, and agranulocytosis (Blair, Scahill, State, & Martin, 2005; Boehm, Racoosin, Laughren, & Katz, 2004). Children and adolescents may be more sensitive to some of these side effects because their central nervous systems are still developing. Examples of EPS include acute dystonia (severe muscle stiffness), parkinsonism, akathisia (restlessness), and tardive dyskinesia and are thought to be the consequence of D2 blockade. In general, SGAs are much less likely to cause EPS (including tardive dyskinesia) than conventional antipsychotics because they have lower D2 blockade. However, children may be more sensitive to EPS in that D2 densities are highest in infancy and decrease during childhood. Rates of EPS increase with higher dosages or faster titration schedules of SGAs. Olanzapine appears to be less associated with EPS as a result of its muscarinic receptor blockade properties. The rate of EPS for quetiapine is not significantly different from that for placebo. In general, there is a negligible risk of EPS with clozapine and quetiapine.

Tardive dyskinesia (TD) is involuntary movements of the facial muscles, tongue, trunk, and extremities. Studies suggest that the risk of TD with a specific SGA is related to the dose and duration of treatment as well as the rate of EPS from that agent. Although the risk for TD is much lower than with conventional antipsychotics, each of the SGAs can potentially induce TD. It is difficult to estimate the incidence of TD with the SGAs because some children and adolescents have been treated with conventional antipsychotics in the past. Furthermore, there are limited long-term data regarding the risk of TD in children and adolescents. Clozapine may be useful in the treatment of severe TD. The annual incidence of TD with risperidone and olanzapine treatment has been estimated to be approximately 1 percent and 1.5 percent in the pediatric population, respectively. In contrast, the prevalence of TD in children and adolescents who were treated with typical antipsychotics has been estimated to be relatively high, with a wide range of 0 percent to 51 percent. The American Psychiatric Association Task Force on TD reported that the incidence of TD is 5 percent per year of typical antipsychotic exposure in adults. Children and adolescents may be at greater risk than adults for developing hyperprolactinemia (Saito et al., 2004). Hyperprolactinemia can lead to sexual dysfunction, galactorrhea, amenorrhea, diminished bone density, cardiovascular disease, and breast and endometrial cancer. Elevations in prolactin levels are associated with greater D2 blockade. Risperidone, which has a high affinity for D2 receptors, is the only SGA associated with significant increases in prolactin levels. The increase in prolactin level is dose related in children and adolescents.

Weight gain is one of the greatest concerns with the use of SGAs. This is more concerning in children and adolescents in that their well-documented morbidity and mortality are associated with obesity, especially when it starts early in life (Dietz, 1998). In addition, substantial concern has been raised over diabetes with SGAs (Boehm et al., 2004). Obesity can lead to other health problems including hypertension, hypercholesterolemia, sleep apnea, and cardiovascular disease. Additionally, weight gain may lead to poor self-esteem and medication noncompliance, especially in adolescents who are usually concerned with their appearance. Ziprasidone is the only atypical antipsychotic that has not been associated with weight gain, whereas clozapine and olanzapine have been associated with the most weight gain, followed by risperidone. Aripiprazole leads to less weight gain than the other SGAs except for ziprasidone. The FDA has required a warning of the risk of diabetes on the drug labels for SGAs. Clozapine has been associated with agranulocytosis at a rate of about 1 percent to 2 percent. Adult and pediatric patients appear to have similar risks for agranulocytosis. Patients are at the highest risk for developing agranulocytosis during the first 3–6 months of treatment with clozapine. However, the risk decreases thereafter. White blood cell and granulocyte counts need to be monitored weekly for the first 6 months and then every other week, making clozapine an impractical treatment option for many children and adolescents. Sedation induced by SGAs may be more impairing for children and adolescents because of the negative impact on learning and school performance. Although all of the SGAs frequently cause sedation, some are more likely to do so than others: clozapine > quetiapine > olanzapine > risperidone > ziprasidone = aripiprazole. Sedation is usually temporary and improves with time. Another serious adverse effect can be QTc prolongation, which can cause malignant ventricular arrhythmias like torsades de pointes (Blair et al., 2005; Welch & Chue, 2000). Before starting a child or adolescent with BPD on an atypical antipsychotic that is known to affect the QTc interval, such as ziprazidone, it would be wise for a clinician to get a thorough family cardiac history as well as a baseline electrocardiogram (ECG) and then repeat the ECG whenever a significant dose change is made. The clinician needs to be aware of other risk factors that prolong the QTc, including any medications, obesity, hypoglycemia, athletic training, cardiac diseases, alcoholism, hypothyroidism, and electrolyte disturbances (deficiencies or excesses of calcium, magnesium, or potassium). Few studies have examined SGA-induced QTc prolongation in children and adolescents. Based on studies of adults, the order of likelihood for causing QTc prolongation is ziprasidone = clozapine > quetiapine > risperidone > olanzapine > aripiprazole.

Because children and adolescents appear to be more sensitive to side effects with SGAs, they need close monitoring when they are prescribed these agents. Baseline laboratory tests should include a complete blood count (for clozapine only), electrolytes (for ziprasidone only), liver function tests, a pregnancy test, a prolactin level, fasting glucose and insulin levels, height, and weight (for body mass index). It is recommended that the QTc remain less than 460 ms. A repeat ECG should be performed after steady-state drug concentrations have been reached and before and after concomitant meds are added. For EPS, the clinician should use the Abnormal Involuntary Movement Scale (National Institute of Mental Health, 1985). It is recommended that the clinician perform the Abnormal Involuntary Movement Scale at baseline and every 6 months to monitor for TD. Monitoring of body mass index during the course of treatment is recommended, along with blood pressure and fasting plasma glucose and lipids. The clinician needs to explore a personal and family history of obesity, cardiovascular disease, diabetes, dyslipidemia, and hypertension. Exercise and nutrition counseling should be offered to overweight and obese patients. If a patient gains ≥5 percent of their baseline weight (taking into account weight gain from growth) or develops insulin resistance or hyperlipidemia, the clinician should cross-titrate the patient to another medication with less liability for these adverse effects. Cross-titration in this case would involve lowering and discontinuing one medication while simultaneously starting and titrating a new medication with a lower risk of weight gain.

Dosing

For children and adolescents, the optimal dose may be similar to that for adults. Although children and adolescents have a greater hepatic metabolism for their weight, they also have lower amounts of adipose tissue and a lower degree of protein binding. The starting dose and the rate of titration depend on the clinical setting. A child or adolescent who is admitted to an inpatient unit may need a more rapid titration with close monitoring by medical staff. For psychotic disorders, the optimal dose of SGAs may be higher than for other indications for children and adolescents. Because prepubescent children metabolize rapidly, they seem to need dosing at least twice a day, whereas adolescents can tolerate dosing once a day at bedtime. It may be helpful to give the SGA between 5 p.m. and 7 p.m. to decrease sedation in the following morning.

MOOD STABILIZERS

Lithium, valproate, carbamazepine, and the newer atypical antipsychotics are the commonly used mood stabilizers (see Table 27.3). Ghaemi defines a mood stabilizer as "an agent with efficacy in at least one of the three phases of bipolar disorder (acute mania, acute depression, or prophylaxis), and it should not cause affective switch to the opposite mood state nor should it worsen the acute episode" (Ghaemi, 2001, p. 155).

Clinical Trials

Lithium is the best-studied mood stabilizer in adults and has demonstrated efficacy for mania in adults (McElroy & Keck, 2000). There have been several controlled trials of lithium in children and adolescents with BPD, though many have small sample sizes and methodological limitations (Delong & Nieman, 1983; Gram & Rafaelsen, 1972; Lena, 1979; McKnew et al., 1981). Valproate (divalproex sodium) is another mood-stabilizing agent that is commonly used in pediatric BPD and has established efficacy in adults with BPD (Bowden et al., 1994; Pope, McElroy, Keck, & Hudson, 1991). A number of case reports and open prospective trials of valproate in children and adolescents with BPD suggest its effectiveness (Deltito, Levitan, Damore, Hajal, & Zambenedetti, 1998; Kastner, 1992; Kastner, Plummer, Ruiz, Henning, 1990; Papatheodorou & Kutcher, 1993; Papatheodorou, Kutcher, Katic, & Szalai, 1995; West & McElroy, 1995; West et al., 1994; Whittier, West, Galli, & Raute, 1995). In addition, in an open-label prospective study, Kowatch et al. (2000) compared the relative efficacy of three mood stabilizers, lithium, valproate, and carbamazepine, in the acute phase treatment of 42 bipolar I or II children and adolescents during a mixed or manic episode. Using a ≥50 percent change from baseline to exit in the YMRS scores to define response, the response rates after 6–8 weeks of treatment were carbamazepine, 38 percent; lithium, 38 percent; and sodium divalproex, 53 percent ($\chi^2 = 0.85$, $p = 0.60$). Each of the three mood stabilizers was well tolerated and no serious adverse effects were seen.

Carbamazepine is an anticonvulsant agent that is structurally similar to imipramine. There have been no controlled studies of carbamazepine as a mood stabilizer for the treatment of children and adolescents with BPD. The one comparative study, described previously, compared carbamazepine's relative efficacy to valproate and lithium (Kowatch et al., 2000). Carbamazepine is metabolized by the P450 hepatic system to an active metabolite, carabamazepine-10,11-epoxide. Carbamazepine induces its own metabolism, and this autoinduction is complete 3–5 weeks after the start of a fixed dose.

TABLE 27.3 Mood Stabilizers

Agent	Clinical use	FDA pediatric labeling	Dose	Schedule	Potential adverse effects
Valproate	Bipolar disorder	N/A	15–20 mg/kg/day	BID/QHS	Hepatotoxicity, PCOS, thrombocytopenia, Stevens Johnson syndrome, hyperammonemia, nausea, diarrhea, weight gain, alopecia, nystagmus
Lithium		≥12 years	30 mg/kg/day	TID/BID/QHS	Hypothyroidism, leukocytosis, tremors, diarrhea, nausea, ventricular arrythmias
Carbamazepine		Only approved for epilepsy in pediatrics	200–1,000 mg/day (12–15 years) 200–1,200 mg/day (>15 years)	BID	Aplastic anemia, hyponatremia, Stevens Johnson syndrome, drowsiness, ataxia, nystagmus, blurred vision

Note. BID = two times per day; PCOS = polycystic ovarian syndrome; QHS = once every night; TID = three times per day.

The half-life for initial carbamazepine serum ranges from 25 to 65 hours and then decreases to 9–15 hours after autoinduction of the P450 enzymes.

Adverse Effects of Mood Stabilizers

Common side effects of valproate include nausea, increased appetite, weight gain, sedation, thrombocytopenia, transient hair loss, tremor, and vomiting. Rarely, pancreatitis and liver failure, which are potentially life-threatening adverse effects, can also occur. Baseline studies prior to the initiation of treatment with valproate should include general medical history and physical examination, liver function tests, complete blood count with differential and platelets, and a pregnancy test for sexually active females. A complete blood count with differential, platelet count, and liver functions should be checked every 6 months or when clinically indicated. Adolescent females must employ adequate birth control measures because valproate is associated with an increased rate of neural tube defects. Concern has been expressed in the literature regarding the possible association between divalproex and polycystic ovarian syndrome (PCOS). O'Donovan, Kusumakar, Graves, and Bird (2002) reported that rates of menstrual irregularities and PCOS were higher in women with BPD who were taking divalproex than in those who were not taking divalproex and a comparison group of healthy volunteers. Ernst and Goldberg (2002) recommended that females treated with valproate undergo the following: a body mass index measurement before treatment with valproate and at each follow-up visit, a baseline assessment of menstrual cycle patterns and monitoring for irregularities, and baseline and annual lipid profiles. A female patient treated with valproate who develops hirsutism, alopecia, or acne should be referred to an endocrinologist for a further workup for PCOS. Valproate is metabolized in the liver by the P450 system; some medications that also are metabolized by this system may increase valproate levels, including erythromycin, SSRIs, cimetidine, and salicylates. Valproate may increase levels of phenobarbital, primidone, carbamazepine, phenytoin, tricyclics, and lamotrigene.

Lithium has a narrow therapeutic index, and lithium toxicity can be lethal. Possible side effects include weight gain, nausea, polyuria, polydipsia, tremor, acne, and hypothyroidism. Baseline evaluation before a patient starts lithium should include a basic medical history and physical examination, serum electrolytes, creatinine, blood urea nitrogen, serum calcium levels, thyroid function tests, ECG, complete blood count with differential, and a pregnancy test for sexually active females. Renal function should be tested every 3 months during the first 6 months of treatment with lithium carbonate, and thyroid function should be tested once during the first 6 months of treatment. Thereafter, renal and thyroid functions should be checked every 6 months or when clinically indicated. Chronic treatment with lithium can cause hypoparathyroidism, hypothyroidism, or interstitial nephritis, so serum calcium, thyrotropin-stimulating hormone (TSH), free T4 levels and renal profiles should be checked once a year. Drug interactions with lithium are possible, and patients should be advised not to take any other medications without first consulting with their physician. Medications that may increase serum lithium levels include antibiotics (e.g., ampicillin and tetracycline), nonsteroidal anti-inflammatories (e.g., ibuprofen), antipsychotic agents, propanolol, and SSRIs (e.g., fluoxetine; Ciraulo, Shader, Greenblatt, & Creelman, 1995). Females of childbearing age must use adequate birth control measures because lithium is associated with an increased rate of congenital cardiac abnormality (Cohen, Friedman, Jefferson, Johnson, & Weiner, 1994).

Adverse effects of carbamazepine in children and adolescents include sedation, ataxia, dizziness, blurred vision, nausea, and vomiting. Baseline studies before initiation of treatment with carbamazepine should include a basic medical history and physical examination, complete blood count with differential, liver function tests, and a pregnancy test for sexually active females. Because of its stimulation of the hepatic P450 system, carbamazepine has many clinically significant drug interactions in children and adolescents. Carbamazepine decreases lithium clearance and increases the risk of lithium toxicity. Medications that will increase carbamazepine levels include erythromycin, cimetidine, fluoxetine, verapamil, and valproate. Carbamazepine decreases levels of valproate, olanzapine, and tricyclic antidepressants due to induction of hepatic enzyme activity (Ciraulo et al., 1995).

Dosing

Lithium is readily absorbed from the gastrointestinal system and is excreted by the kidneys without metabolism. Its serum half-life in children and adolescents is estimated to be approximately 18 hours (Vitiello et al., 1988). Weller, Weller, and Fristad (1986) devised guidelines for dosing lithium based on body weight. According to these guidelines, in a 6- to 12-year-old child, a dose of 30 mg/kg/day in three divided doses will produce a lithium level of 0.6–1.2 mEq/L within five days. In children, lithium is usually administered 2–3 times per day. After an adequate serum level is reached, it may be administered once in the morning and once at bedtime in a controlled-release preparation. In adolescents, lithium may be administered once daily, usually at bedtime. Serum lithium levels in the range of 0.8–1.2 mEq/L are necessary for mood stabilization during treatment of a child or adolescent during a manic episode, with trough serum levels measured 12 hours after the last dose.

Valproate has a serum half-life of between 8 and 16 hours in children and adolescents (Cloyd, Fischer, Kriel, & Kraus, 1993). A starting dose of divalproex sodium of 15 mg/kg/day in 2 or 3 divided doses in children and adolescents will produce serum valproate levels in the range of 50–60 mg/mL. Once this low serum level has been obtained, the dose is usually titrated upward depending on the patient's tolerance and response, and it is best to measure trough serum valproate levels 8–12 hours after the last dose. Optimum serum levels among manic adults are between 75 and 110 mg/mL (Bowden et al., 1996). A starting dose of divalproex sodium of 15 mg/kg/day in 2 or 3 divided doses in children and adolescents will produce serum valproate levels in the range of 50–60 mg/mL. Once this low serum level has been obtained, the dose is usually titrated upward depending on the patient's tolerance and response.

For patients who are 6–12 years of age, a reasonable starting dose of carbamazepine is 100 mg twice daily and in patients aged 12 and older, 100 mg three times daily. Serum level of carbamazepine between 8 and 11 mg/mL is necessary for mood control. The maximum daily dose of carbamazepine should not exceed 1,000 mg/day in children aged 6–12 years and 1,200 mg/day in patients age 13 and older.

PSYCHOSTIMULANTS AND ATOMOXETINE

Psychostimulants have a long history of use in pediatric psychiatry and are some of the best-studied medications in pediatrics (see Table 27.4). Bradley (1938) reported the successful use of benzedrine, a psychostimulant, in 30 children in 1938. This has been followed by more than 10 double-blind placebo-controlled clinical trials of psychostimulants, each showing a robust effect size of approximately 1.0, the largest effect size of any psychopharmacological agent (Pliszka, 1998). Psychostimulants are effective in decreasing hyperactivity and impulsivity, improving attention and academic performance, reducing interpersonal conflicts and oppositional behavior, and improving parent-child interactions (MTA, 1999).

Clinical Trials

In the multimodal treatment of ADHD study, 579 children aged 7–10 years were recruited from six sites. All children had ADHD, combined type. There were four treatment arms: medication alone, behavioral therapy alone, combined medication and behavior therapy, and a community control group. For the core symptoms of hyperactivity and impulsivity, the medication and combined therapies worked equally well and better than behavior therapy alone and the community control groups, even though approximately half the community sample was on medication. The superiority of the treatment group may have been the result of the more frequent dosage (three times a day) and a slightly higher total dose of medication (the study group received a mean daily dose of 37.7 mg of methylphenidate compared with a mean daily dose of 22.6

TABLE 27.4 Psychostimulants and Atomoxetine

Agent	Preparations	FDA pediatric labeling	Dose (mg/day)	Duration of action hours	Strength (mg)	Potential adverse effects
Methylphenidate	Concerta	≥6 years for ADHD; approved for narcolepsy in adults	18–72	12	18, 27, 36, 54	Hypertension, appetite suppression, weight loss, growth suppression, headache; extremely rare side effects are seizure and psychosis
	Metadate CD		20–60	10	20, 30	
	Ritalin LA		25–200	8	10, 20, 30, 40	
	Ritalin			4	5, 10, 20	
Adderall (mixed amphetamine salts)	Adderall	≥3 years for ADHD; ≥6 years for narcolepsy	5–40	6 (dose BID)	5, 7.5, 10, 12.5, 15, 20, 30	
	Adderall XR	≥6 years for ADHD	5–30	12	5, 10, 15, 20, 25, 30	
Dextro-amphetamine	Tablets and Spansules (extended release capsules)	≥3 years for ADHD; ≥6 years for narcolepsy	5–40	6; Spansules, 8 hours	5, 10; Spansules, 5, 10, 15	
Atomoxetine		≥6 years	10–100	12	10, 18, 25, 40, 60	Dry mouth, fatigue, hypertension, weight loss, mood swings, hepatoxicity (2 cases reported)

Note. BID = two times per day.

mg in the community control group). This study convincingly demonstrated the efficacy of psychostimulants for ADHD. The MTA cooperative group published another report on the effectiveness of these treatments 24 months after enrollment in the trial (MTA, 2004a). Of 579 children who entered the study, 540 (93 percent) participated in the first follow-up 10 months after the end of treatment (which was given for 14 months). The MTA psychostimulant treatment showed persisting significant superiority over community control and behavior therapy for ADHD and oppositional defiant symptoms at 24 months, although not as great as at 14 months.

Two agents are commonly used as psychostimulants for treatment of ADHD: methylphenidate (MPH) and amphetamine salts. Many preparations currently are available. Methylphenidate has short-acting (approximately 4 hours) and longer acting (8–12 hours) forms. Amphetamines also are available in short- and long-acting compounds. Concerta® is a new formulation of MPH that was released in August 2000; it uses a new osmotic drug delivery technology (OROS) that allows MPH to be taken once daily in the morning and released in a gradual controlled fashion, resulting in 12-hour effectiveness. It employs an osmotically driven trilayer core encased in a semipermeable membrane that releases MPH gradually through a laser-drilled hole on one end. The trilayer core is covered with an overcoat that contains 22 percent of the available MPH in the tablet, producing an initial plasma concentration in approximately 1–2 hours. OROS results in an ascending MPH serum profile that prevents tachyphylaxis. Metadate CD® is a new long-acting MPH formulation produced by Celltech that contains coated beads in 20-mg capsules. Thirty percent of the MPH is immediate release and 70 percent is in an extended-release form. Ritalin LA® is another long-acting preparation; it results in beneficial levels for about 8 hours. Focalin® (dexmethylphenidate hydrochloride), an immediate-release preparation, is the d-*threo*-enantiomer of racemic methylphenidate hydrochloride and was approved by the FDA in November 2001 for use in patients with ADHD. These long-acting preparations are gaining popularity because of ease of dosing. They can be dosed once or twice a day and eliminate the need for dosing at school.

Their use has been supported by randomized controlled trials demonstrating equivalent efficacy to short-acting stimulants. Wolraich et al. (2001) conducted a randomized controlled trial to determine the safety and efficacy of Concerta®, a long-acting (12-hour) methylphenidate preparation using OROS technology. Children with ADHD ($n = 282$), all subtypes, aged 6–12 years, were randomized to placebo ($n = 90$), immediate-release methylphenidate 3 times a day (dosed every 4 hours; $n = 97$), or Concerta® once a day ($n = 95$) in a double-blind 28-day trial. Outcomes in multiple domains were assessed, and data were analyzed using analysis of variance and Kaplan Meier product limit estimates for time to study cessation. Children in the Concerta® and methylphenidate groups showed significantly greater reductions in core ADHD symptoms than did children given placebo. This was true both at the end of Week 1 and at the end of treatment on the basis of mean teacher and parent Iowa Conners ratings (Loney & Milich, 1982). Immediate release methylphenidate and Concerta® did not differ significantly on any direct comparisons. Forty-eight percent of the placebo group discontinued early, compared with 14 percent and 16 percent in the immediate-release methyphenidate and Concerta® groups, respectively.

Biederman, Lopez, Boellner, and Chandler (2002) tested the efficacy and safety of Adderall XR® compared with placebo in the treatment of ADHD in children in a multicenter (47 sites) randomized double-blind, parallel-group placebo-controlled trial. After a 1-week washout of any previous stimulant medication, patients were randomized to receive single-daily morning doses of placebo or Adderall XR® 10 mg, 20 mg, or 30 mg for 3 weeks. The primary efficacy parameter was the Conners Global Index Scale for Teachers (Biederman et al., 2002). Secondary efficacy parameters included the Conners Global Index Scale for Parents, the CGI-I for improvement, and the Parent Global Assessment for improvement. Five hundred eighty-four children were randomized, 563 were included in the intent-to-treat population, and 509 completed the entire study. Intention-to-treat analysis of Conners Global Index Scale for Teachers and Conners Global Index Scale for Parents scores revealed significant improvement in morning, afternoon, and late afternoon behavior for all active treatment groups versus placebo. The authors concluded that Adderall XR® is an efficacious once-daily treatment for children with ADHD. The use of pemoline, another stimulant, has declined because of the life-threatening side effect of hepatic toxicity, and it is therefore usually avoided by clinicians.

Over the years, it was assumed that all stimulants are equally effective and have similar types and frequencies of side effects. Elia and colleagues tested this assumption by conducting a double-blind crossover study of placebo, dextroamphetamine, and methylphenidate in 48 boys with ADHD (Elia, Borcherding, Rapoport, & Keysor, 1991). All 48 patients were given 9 weeks of treatment (3 weeks each of placebo, methylphenidate, and dextroamphetamine). The mean doses for each week of the methylphenidate phase were 0.9 mg/kg, 1.5 mg/kg, and 2.5 mg/kg per dose, whereas for the dextroamphetamine phase they were 0.4 mg/kg, 0.9 mg/kg, and 1.3 mg/kg. These doses are higher than those used in clinical practice. A physician blind to the child's drug status titrated the dose upward each week. Forty percent of the participants could not tolerate an increase to the full dose. A nonresponder was defined as a patient who either did not experience improved behavior or experienced side effects that were too severe even if the behavior had improved. Overall, 79 percent of participants responded to methylphenidate and 88 percent responded to dextroamphetamine. Only 4.2 percent of participants failed to respond to at least one of the two drugs. Sixteen percent of patients who failed to respond to methylphenidate did respond to dextroamphetamine; in contrast, 8.3 percent of patients who did not respond to dextroamphetamine did respond to methylphenidate. Seventy-one percent of the sample responded equally well to both drugs. In a meta-analysis of four studies, Greenhill et al. (1996) found that 35 percent of participants did better on dextroamphetamine, 26 percent improved more on methylphenidate, and the remaining 38 percent did equally well on both psychostimulants. Adderall is a combination of dextroamphetamine (75 percent) and levoamphetamine (25 percent). This amphetamine is a mixed salt of saccharate, sulfate, and aspartate and is believed to have similar efficacy to dextroamphetamine.

Atomoxetine

Atomoxetine is a potent inhibitor of the presynaptic norepinephrine transporter, with minimal affinity for other noradrenergic receptors or for other neurotransmitter transporters or receptors. It is metabolized through the cytochrome P450 2D6 (CYP 2D6) pathway and has a plasma half-life of approximately 4 hours in CYP 2D6 extensive metabolizers and 19 hours in CYP 2D6 poor metabolizers. Several randomized placebo-controlled trials have demonstrated efficacy of atomoxetine in children and adolescents (Kelsey et al., 2004; Kratochvil et al., 2002; Michelson et al., 2001, 2002; Spencer et al., 2002). Michelson and colleagues randomized a total of 297 children and adolescents (aged 8–18 years) with ADHD to placebo or atomoxetine dosed on a weight-adjusted basis at 0.5 mg/kg/day, 1.2 mg/kg/day, or 1.8 mg/kg/day for an 8-week period (Michelson et al., 2001). Approximately 67 percent of patients in this study met criteria for mixed subtype (both inattentive and hyperactive/impulsive symptoms), and the only common psychiatric comorbidity was oppositional defiant disorder (approximately 38 percent of the sample). At baseline, symptom severity was rated as moderate to severe for most children. At end point, atomoxetine 1.2 mg/kg/day and 1.8 mg/kg/day were consistently associated with superior outcomes in ADHD symptoms compared with placebo and were not different from each other. The dose of 0.5 mg/kg/

day was associated with intermediate efficacy between placebo and the two higher doses, suggesting a graded dose response. The authors concluded that atomoxetine is associated with a graded dose response, and 1.2 mg/kg/day seems to an appropriate initial target dose for most patients.

Adverse Effects of Psychostimulants and Atomoxetine

Transient hepatitis and liver failure has been reported following treatment with pemoline, and therefore its use has declined (Jaffe, 1989). On December 17, 2004, the U.S. Food and Drug Administration (FDA) stated that the labeling for atomoxetine was being updated with a bold warning about the potential for severe liver injury following two reports (one teenager and one adult) in patients who had been treated with atomoxetine for several months (both recovered). The label warns that severe liver injury may progress to liver failure, resulting in death or the need for a liver transplant in a small percentage of patients. The label also notes that the number of actual cases of severe liver injury is unknown because of underreporting of postmarketing adverse events. The bold warning indicates that the medication should be discontinued for patients who experience jaundice or exhibit laboratory evidence of liver injury.

Psychostimulants might reduce growth in children treated with them on a long-term basis (Safer, Allen, & Barr, 1972). In addition, a common side effect of stimulant medication is the suppression of appetite, with possible weight loss. Growth might rebound when the psychostimulant is discontinued, a condition that encourages practitioners to try "drug holidays" on weekends and during summers (Safer, Allen, & Barr, 1975). The MTA study corroborated the concerns about growth suppression (MTA, 2004b). The greatest difference was observed in groups assigned to medication only (growth, 4.75 cm, and weight, 1.64 kg) and behavior therapy only (growth: 6.19 cm and 4.53 kg). Thus, the medication versus behavior therapy comparison provides conservative estimates of height suppression (4.75–6.19 cm = −1.44 cm over 14 months = −1.23 cm/year) and weight suppression (1.64–4.53 kg = −2.89 kg over 14 months = −2.48 kg/year) that occurred during the initial 14-month treatment phase of the MTA.

Psychostimulants can exacerbate tics and are usually avoided in children with Tourette's syndrome and tic disorders (Lowe, Cohen, Detlor, Kremenitzer, & Shaywitz, 1982). This finding, however, is not supported by a large clinical trial of methylphenidate in children with ADHD and Tourette's syndrome (Tourette's Syndrome Study Group, 2002). Because a significant percentage of children with tic disorders have comorbid ADHD, and if ADHD results in more social and academic dysfunction than the tics, stimulants can be tried. An alternative may be to use atomoxetine, which may not exacerbate tics. Difficulty sleeping is often noted but can be managed with adjustment of dose, timing of dose, or improvement of sleep hygiene.

Dosing

The use of medication is an important element in the management of ADHD. Because psychostimulants have a long history of safe and effective usage in the treatment of ADHD and are supported by scientific literature, they would be the drugs of first choice in this condition. ADHD deserves treatment with at least two different classes of stimulants before moving to nonpsychostimulant agents. The average dose of methylphenidate is 1.0 mg/kg/day and aderall/dextroamphetamine is 0.5 mg/kg/day, though the medication can be started at a lower dose. As long as side effects are not troublesome, higher dosages may be used to adequately control the ADHD symptoms.

REFERENCES

Aman, M. G., DeSmedt, G., Derivan, A., Lyons, B., & Findling, R. L. (2002). Double-blind, placebo-controlled study of risperidone for the treatment of disruptive behaviors in children with subaverage intelligence. *American Journal of Psychiatry, 159,* 1337–1346.

Armenteros, J. L., Whitaker, A. H., Welikson, M., Stedge, D. J., & Gorman, J. (1997). Risperidone in adolescents with schizophrenia: An open pilot study. *Journal of the American Academy of Child and Adolescent Psychiatry, 36,* 694–700.

Axelson, D., Perel, J., Birmaher, B., Rudolph, G., Nuss, S., Bridge, J., et al. (2002). Sertraline pharmacokinetics and dynamics in adolescents. *Journal of the American Academy of Child and Adolescent Psychiatry, 41,* 1037–1044.

Barzman, D. H., DelBello, M. P., Kowatch, R. A., Gernert, B., Fleck, D. E., Pathak, S., et al. (2004). The effectiveness and tolerability of aripiprazole for pediatric bipolar disorders: A retrospective chart review. *Journal of Child and Adolescent Psychopharmacology, 14,* 593–600.

Biederman, J., Lopez, F. A., Boellner, S. W., & Chandler, M. C. (2002). A randomized, double-blind, placebo-controlled, parallel-group study of SLI381 (Adderall XR) in children with attention-deficit/hyperactivity disorder. *Pediatrics, 110,* 258–266.

Birmaher, B., Axelson, D. A., Monk, K., Kalas, C., Clark, D. B., Ehmann, M., et al. (2003). Fluoxetine for the treatment of childhood anxiety disorders. *Journal of the American Academy of Child and Adolescent Psychiatry, 42,* 415–423.

Blair, J., Scahill, L., State, M., & Martin, A. (2005). Electrocardiographic changes in children and adolescents treated with ziprasidone: A prospective study. *Journal of the American Academy of Child and Adolescent Psychiatry, 44,* 73–79.

Boehm, G., Racoosin, J., Laughren, T., & Katz, R. (2004). Consensus Development Conference on Antipsychotic Drugs and Obesity and Diabetes: Response to consensus statement. *Diabetes Care, 27,* 2088–2089.

Bowden, C. L., Brugger, A. M., Swann, A. C., Calabrese, J. R., Janicak, P. G., Petty, F., et al. (1994). Efficacy of divalproex vs. lithium and placebo in the treatment of mania. The Depakote Mania Study Group. *Journal of the American Medical Association, 271,* 918–924. (Published erratum appears in *Journal of the American Medical Association, 271* [June 15, 1994], 1830.)

Bowden, C. L., Janicak, P. G., Orsulak, P., Swann, A. C., Davis, J. M., Calabrese, J. R., et al. (1996). Relation of serum valproate concentration to response in mania. *American Journal of Psychiatry, 153,* 765–770.

Bradley, C. (1938). The behavior of children receiving benzedrine. *American Journal of Psychiatry, 94,* 577–585.

Brent, D. A. (2004). Antidepressants and pediatric depression—the risk of doing nothing. *New England Journal of Medicine, 351,* 1598–1601.

Carroll, B. J. (2004). Adolescents with depression. *Journal of the American Medical Association, 292,* 2578–2585.

Chang, K., & Ketter, T. (2000). Mood stabilizer augmentation with olanzapine in acutely manic children. *Journal of Child and Adolescent Psychopharmacology, 10,* 45–49.

Charatan, F. (2000). Mrs. Clinton aims to reduce psychoactive drugs in young children. *British Journal of Medicine, 320,* 893.

Ciraulo, D. A., Shader, R. J., Greenblatt, D. J., & Creelman, W. L. (Eds.). (1995). *Drug interactions in psychiatry.* Baltimore: Williams & Wilkins.

Cloyd, J. C., Fischer, J. H., Kriel, R. L., & Kraus, D. M. (1993). Valproic acid pharmacokinetics in children. IV. Effects of age and antiepileptic drugs on protein binding and intrinsic clearance. *Clinical Pharmacological Therapy, 53,* 22–29.

Cohen, L. S., Friedman, J. M., Jefferson, J. W., Johnson, E. M., & Weiner, M. L. (1994). A reevaluation of risk of in utero exposure to lithium [published erratum appears in Journal of the American Medical Association 1994 May 18;271(19):1485] [see comments]. *Journal of the American Medical Association, 271,* 146–150. (Published erratum appears in *Journal of the American Medical Association, 271* [May 18, 1994], 1485 [see comments]).

Coyle, J. T. (2000). Psychotropic drug use in very young children. *Journal of the American Medical Association, 283,* 1059–1060.

DelBello, M., Schwiers, M., Rosenberg, H., & Strakowski, S. (2002). Quetiapine as adjunctive treatment for adolescent mania associated with bipolar disorder. *Journal of the American Academy of Child and Adolescent Psychiatry, 41,* 1216–1223.

Delong, G. R., & Nieman, M. A. (1983). Lithium-induced behavior changes in children with symptoms suggesting manic-depressive illness. *Psychopharmacology Bulletin, 19,* 258–265.

Deltito, J. A., Levitan, J., Damore, J., Hajal, F., & Zambenedetti, M. (1998). Naturalistic experience with the use of divalproex sodium on an in-patient unit for adolescent psychiatric patients. *Acta Psychiatrica Scandinavica, 97,* 236–240.

DeVeaugh-Geiss, J., Moroz, G., Biederman, J., Cantwell, D., Fontaine, R., Greist, J. H., et al. (1992). Clomipramine hydrochloride in childhood and adolescent obsessive-compulsive disorder—a multicenter trial. *Journal of the American Academy of Child and Adolescent Psychiatry, 31,* 45–49.

Dietz, W. H. (1998). Health consequences of obesity in youth: Childhood predictors of adult disease. *Pediatrics, 101,* 518–525.

Elia, J., Borcherding, B. G., Rapoport, J. L., & Keysor, C. S. (1991). Methylphenidate and dextroamphetamine treatments of hyperactivity: Are there true nonresponders? *Psychiatry Research, 36,* 141–155.

Emslie, G. J., Heiligenstein, J. H., Wagner, K. D., Hoog, S. L., Ernest, D. E., Brown, E., et al. (2002). Fluoxetine for acute treatment of depression in children and adolescents: A placebo-controlled, randomized clinical trial. *Journal of the American Academy of Child and Adolescent Psychiatry, 41,* 1205–1215.

Emslie, G. J., Rush, A. J., Weinberg, W. A., Kowatch, R. A., Hughes, C. W., Carmody, T., et al. (1997). A double-blind, randomized, placebo-controlled trial of fluoxetine in children and adolescents with depression. *Archives of General Psychiatry, 54,* 1031–1037.

Ernst, C., & Goldberg, J. (2002). The reproductive safety profile of mood stabilizers, atypical antipsychotics, and broad-spectrum psychotropics. *Journal of Clinical Psychiatry, 63*(Suppl. 4), 42–55.

Findling, R. L., McNamara, N. K., Branicky, L. A., Schluchter, M. D., Lemon, E., & Blumer, J. L. (2000). A double-blind pilot study of risperidone in the treatment of conduct disorder. *Journal of the American Academy of Child and Adolescent Psychiatry, 39,* 509–516.

Findling, R. L., Reed, M. D., Myers, C., O'Riordan, M. A., Fiala, S., Branicky, L., et al. (1999). Paroxetine pharmacokinetics in depressed children and adolescents. *Journal of the American Academy of Child and Adolescent Psychiatry, 38,* 952–959.

Flament, M. F., Rapoport, J. L., & Kilts, C. (1985). A controlled trial of clomipramine in childhood obsessive compulsive disorder. *Psychopharmacology Bulletin, 21,* 150–152.

Frazier, J., Meyer, M., Biederman, J., Wozniak, J., Wilens, T., Spencer, T., et al. (1999). Risperidone treatment for juvenile bipolar disorder: A retrospective chart review. *Journal of the American Academy of Child and Adolescent Psychiatry, 38,* 960–965.

Frazier, J. A., Biederman, J., Jacobs, T. G., Tohen, M. F., Toma, V., Feldman, P. D., et al. (2001). A prospective open-label treatment trial of olanzapine monotherapy in children and adolescents with bipolar disorder. *Journal of Child and Adolescent Psychopharmacology, 11,* 239–250.

Geller, D. A., Biederman, J., Stewart, S. E., Mullin, B., Martin, A., Spencer, T., et al. (2003). Which SSRI? A meta-analysis of pharmacotherapy trials in pediatric obsessive-compulsive disorder. *American Journal of Psychiatry, 160,* 1919–1928.

Ghaemi, S. N. (2001). On defining "mood stabilizer." *Bipolar Disorder, 3,* 154–158.

Glick, I., Murray, S., Vasudevan, P., Marder, S., & Hu, R. (2001). Treatment with atypical antipsychotics: New indications and new populations. *Journal of Psychiatric Research, 35,* 187–191.

Gram, L. F., & Rafaelsen, O. J. (1972). Lithium treatment of psychotic children and adolescents. A controlled clinical trial. *Acta Psychiatrica Scandinavica, 48,* 253–260.

Greenhill, L. L., Abikoff, H. B., Arnold, L. E., Cantwell, D. P., Conners, C. K., Elliott, G., et al. (1996). Medication treatment strategies in the MTA Study: Relevance to clinicians and researchers. *Journal of the American Academy of Child and Adolescent Psychiatry, 35,* 1304–1313.

Jaffe, S. L. (1989). Pemoline and liver function. *Journal of the American Academy of Child and Adolescent Psychiatry, 28,* 457–458.

Kafantaris, V., Coletti, D. J., Dicker, R., Padula, G., & Kane, J. M. (2001). Adjunctive antipsychotic treatment of adolescents with bipolar psychosis. *Journal of the American Academy of Child and Adolescent Psychiatry, 40,* 1448–1456.

Kalb, C. (2000). Drugged-out toddlers. A new study documents an alarming increase in behavior-altering medication for preschoolers. *Newsweek, 135,* 53.

Kaplan, S. L., Simms, R. M., & Busner, J. (1994). Prescribing practices of outpatient child psychiatrists. *Journal of the American Academy of Child and Adolescent Psychiatry, 33,* 35–44.

Kapur, S., & Remington, G. (2001). Atypical antipsychotics: New directions and new challenges in the treatment of schizophrenia. *Annual Review of Medicine, 52,* 503–517.

Kastner, F. (1992). Verapamil and valproic acid treatment of prolonged mania. *Journal of the American Academy of Child and Adolescent Psychiatry, 31,* 271–275.

Kastner, T., Friedman, D. L., Plummer, A. T., Ruiz, M. Q., Henning, D. (1990). Valproic acid for the treatment of children with mental retardation and mood symptomatology. *Pediatrics, 86,* 467–472.

Kelsey, D., Sumner, C., Casat, C., Coury, D., Quintana, H., Saylor, K., et al. (2004). Once-daily atomoxetine treatment for children with attention-deficit/hyperactivity disorder, including an assessment of evening and morning behavior: A double-blind, placebo-controlled trial. *Pediatrics, 114,* e1–8.

Khouzam, H., & el-Gabalawi, F. (2000). Treatment of bipolar I disorder in an adolescent with olanzapine. *Journal of Child and Adolescent Psychopharmacology, 10,* 147–151.

Kowatch, R. A., Suppes, T., Carmody, T. J., Bucci, J. P., Hume, J. H., Kromelis, M., et al. (2000). Effect size of lithium, divalproex sodium and carbamazepine in children and adolescents with bipolar disorder. *Journal of the American Academy of Child and Adolescent Psychiatry, 39,* 713–720.

Kowatch, R. A., Suppes, T., Gilfillan, S. K., Fuentes, R. M., Grannemann, B. D., & Emslie, G. J. (1995). Clozapine treatment of children and adolescents with bipolar disorder and schizophrenia: a clinical case series. *Journal of Child and Adolescent Psychopharmacology, 5,* 241–253.

Kratochvil, C., Heiligenstein, J., Dittmann, R., Spencer, T., Biederman, J., Wernicke, J., et al. (2002). Atomoxetine and methylphenidate treatment in children with ADHD: A prospective, randomized, open-label trial. *Journal of the American Academy of Child and Adolescent Psychiatry, 41,* 776–784.

Kumra, S., Frazier, J. A., Jacobsen, L. K., McKenna, K., Gordon, C. T., Lenane, M. C., et al. (1996). Childhood-onset schizophrenia. A double-blind clozapine-haloperidol comparison. *Archives of General Psychiatry, 53,* 1090–1097.

Labellarte, M., Biederman, J., Emslie, G., Ferguson, J., Khan, A., Ruckle, J., et al. (2004). Multiple-dose pharmacokinetics of fluvoxamine in children and adolescents. *Journal of the American Academy of Child and Adolescent Psychiatry, 43,* 1497–1505.

Lena, B. (1979). Lithium in child and adolescent psychiatry. *Archives of General Psychiatry, 36,* 854–855.

Leonard, H. L., Swedo, S. E., Rapoport, J. L., Koby, E. V., Lenane, M. C., Cheslow, D. L., et al. (1989). Treatment of obsessive-compulsive disorder with clomipramine and desipramine in children and adolescents. A double-blind crossover comparison. *Archives of General Psychiatry, 46,* 1088–1092.

Lewinsohn, P. M., Hops, H., Roberts, R. E., Seeley, J. R., & Andrews, J. A. (1993). Adolescent psychopathology: I. Prevalence and incidence of depression and other *DSM-III-R* disorders in high school students. *Journal of Abnormal Psychology, 102,* 133–144.

Loney, J., & Milich, R. (1982). Hyperactivity, inattention, and aggression in clinical practice. In M. Wolraich & D. K. Routh (Eds.), *Advances in Development and Behavioral Pediatrics,* pp. 113–147. Greenwich, CT: JAI Press.

Lowe, T. L., Cohen, D. J., Detlor, J., Kremenitzer, M. W., & Shaywitz, B. A. (1982). Stimulant medications precipitate Tourette's syndrome. *Journal of the American Medical Association, 247,* 1729–1731.

March, J. S., Biederman, J., Wolkow, R., Safferman, A., Mardekian, J., Cook, E. H., et al. (1998). Sertraline in children and adolescents with obsessive-compulsive disorder: A multicenter randomized controlled trial. *Journal of the American Medical Association, 280,* 1752–1756.

McElroy, S., & Keck, P. J. (2000). Pharmacologic agents for the treatment of acute bipolar mania. *Biological Psychiatry, 48,* 539–557.

McKnew, D. H., Cytryn, L., Buchsbaum, M. S., Hamovit, J., Lamour, M., Rapoport, J. L., et al. (1981). Lithium in children of lithium-responding parents. *Psychiatry Research, 4,* 171–180.

Michelson, D., Allen, A., Busner, J., Casat, C., Dunn, D., Kratochvil, C., et al. (2002). Once-daily atomoxetine treatment for children and adolescents with attention deficit hyperactivity disorder: A randomized, placebo-controlled study. *American Journal of Psychiatry, 159,* 1896–1901.

Michelson, D., Faries, D., Wernicke, J., Kelsey, D., Kendrick, K., Sallee, F., et al. (2001). Atomoxetine in the treatment of children and adolescents with attention-deficit/hyperactivity disorder: A randomized, placebo-controlled, dose-response study. *Pediatrics, 108,* E83.

Multimodal Treatment of ADHD. (1999). A 14-month randomized clinical trial of treatment strategies for attention-deficit/hyperactivity disorder. The MTA Cooperative Group. Multimodal Treatment Study of Children with ADHD. *Archives of General Psychiatry, 56,* 1073–1086.

Multimodal Treatment of ADHD. (2004a). National Institute of Mental Health Multimodal Treatment Study of ADHD follow-up: 24-month outcomes of treatment strategies for attention-deficit/hyperactivity disorder. *Pediatrics, 113,* 754–761.

Multimodal Treatment of ADHD. (2004b). National Institute of Mental Health Multimodal Treatment Study of ADHD follow-up: Changes in effectiveness and growth after the end of treatment. *Pediatrics, 113,* 762–769.

National Institute of Mental Health. (1985). Abnormal Involuntary Movement Scale (AIMS). *Psychopharmacological Bulletin, 21,* 1077–1080.

O'Donovan, C., Kusumakar, V., Graves, G. R., & Bird, D. C. (2002). Menstrual abnormalities and polycystic ovary syndrome in women taking valproate for bipolar mood disorder. *Journal of Clinical Psychiatry, 63,* 322–330.

Papatheodorou, G., & Kutcher, S. P. (1993). Divalproex sodium treatment in late adolescent and young adult acute mania. *Psychopharmacology Bulletin, 29,* 213–219.

Papatheodorou, G., Kutcher, S. P., Katic, M., & Szalai, J.P. (1995). The efficacy and safety of divalproex sodium in the treatment of acute mania in adolescents and young adults: An open clinical trial. *Journal of Clinical Psychopharmacology, 15,* 110–116.

Pediatric OCD Treatment Study (POTS) Team. (2004). Cognitive-behavior therapy, sertraline, and their combination for children and adolescents with obsessive-compulsive disorder: The Pediatric OCD Treatment Study (POTS) Randomized Controlled Trial. *Journal of the American Medical Association, 292,* 1969–1976.

Pliszka, S. R. (1998). The use of psychostimulants in the pediatric patient. *Pediatric Clinics of North America, 45,* 1085–1098.

Pope, H. G., Jr., McElroy, S. L., Keck, P. E., Jr., & Hudson, J. I. (1991). Valproate in the treatment of acute mania. A placebo-controlled study. *Archives of General Psychiatry, 48,* 62–68.

Poznanski, E. O., & Mokros, H. (1996). *Children's Depression Rating Scale—Revised (CDRS-R).* Los Angeles: Western Psychological Services.

Rappley, M. D., Mullan, P. B., Alvarez, F. J., Eneli, I. U., Wang, J., & Gardiner, J. C. (1999). Diagnosis of attention-deficit/hyperactivity disorder and use of psychotropic medication in very young children. *Archives of Pediatric and Adolescent Medicine, 153,* 1039–1045.

Research Unit on Pediatric Psychopharmacology (RUPP). (2001). Fluvoxamine for the treatment of anxiety disorders in children and adolescents. The Research Unit on Pediatric Psychopharmacology Anxiety Study Group. *New England Journal of Medicine, 344,* 1279–1285.

Riddle, M. A., Reeve, E. A., Yaryura-Tobias, J. A., Yang, H. M., Claghorn, J. L., Gaffney, G., et al. (2001). Fluvoxamine for children and adolescents with obsessive-compulsive disorder: A randomized, controlled, multicenter trial. *Journal of the American Academy of Child and Adolescent Psychiatry, 40,* 222–229.

Rosenberg, D. R., Stewart, C. M., Fitzgerald, K. D., Tawile, V., & Carroll, E. (1999). Paroxetine open-label treatment of pediatric outpatients with obsessive-compulsive disorder. *Journal of the American Academy of Child and Adolescent Psychiatry, 38,* 1180–1185.

Safer, D., Allen, R., & Barr, E. (1972). Depression of growth in hyperactive children on stimulant drugs. *New England Journal of Medicine, 287,* 217–220.

Safer, D. J., Allen, R. P., & Barr, E. (1975). Growth rebound after termination of stimulant drugs. *Journal of Pediatrics, 86,* 113–116.

Saito, E., Correll, C. U., Gallelli, K., McMeniman, M., Parikh, U. H., Malhotra, A. K., et al. (2004). A prospective study of hyperprolactinemia in children and adolescents treated with atypical antipsychotic agents. *Journal of Child and Adolescent Psychopharmacology, 14,* 350–358.

Scharko, A. (2004). Selective serotonin reuptake inhibitor-induced sexual dysfunction in adolescents: A review. *Journal of the American Academy of Child and Adolescent Psychiatry, 43,* 1071–1079.

Shute, N., Locy, T., Pasternak, D., Brink, S., Lord, M., MacNeil, J. S., et al. (2000, March 6). The perils of pills. The psychiatric medication of children is dangerously haphazard. *U.S. News and World Report, 128,* 44–50.

Sikich, L., Hamer, R. M., Bashford, R. A., Sheitman, B. B., & Lieberman, J. A. (2004). A pilot study of risperidone, olanzapine, and haloperidol in psychotic youth: A double-blind, randomized, 8-week trial. *Neuropsychopharmacology, 29,* 133–145.

Simon, G. E., Cunningham, M. L., & Davis, R. L. (2002). Outcomes of prenatal antidepressant exposure. *American Journal of Psychiatry, 159,* 2055–2061.

Snyder, R., Turgay, A., Aman, M., Binder, C., Fisman, S., & Carroll, A. (2002). Effects of risperidone on conduct and disruptive behavior disorders in children with subaverage IQs. *Journal of the American Academy of Child and Adolescent Psychiatry, 41,* 1026–1036.

Soutullo, C., Sorter, M., Foster, K., McElroy, S., & Keck, P. (1999). Olanzapine in the treatment of adolescent acute mania: A report of seven cases. *Journal of Affective Disorders, 53,* 279–283.

Spencer, T., Heiligenstein, J., Biederman, J., Faries, D., Kratochvil, C., Conners, C., et al. (2002). Results from 2 proof-of-concept, placebo-controlled studies of atomoxetine in children with attention-deficit/hyperactivity disorder. *Journal of Clinical Psychiatry, 63,* 1140–1147.

Tourette's Syndrome Study Group. (2002). Treatment of ADHD in children with tics: A randomized controlled trial. *Neurology, 58,* 527–536.

Treatment for Adolescents with Depression Study Team. (2004). Fluoxetine, cognitive-behavioral therapy, and their combination for adolescents with depression: Treatment for Adolescents with Depression Study (TADS) Randomized Controlled Trial. *Journal of the American Medical Association, 292,* 807–820.

Vitiello, B., Behar, D., Malone, R., Delaney, M. A., Ryan, P. J., & Simpson, G. M. (1988). Pharmacokinetics of lithium carbonate in children. *Journal of Clinical Psychopharmacology, 8,* 355–359.

Vitiello, B., & Jensen, P. S. (1997). Medication development and testing in children and adolescents. Current problems, future directions. *Archives of General Psychiatry, 54,* 871–876.

Wagner, K., Berard, R., Stein, M., Wetherhold, E., Carpenter, D., Perera, P., et al. (2004). A multicenter, randomized, double-blind, placebo-controlled trial of paroxetine in children and adolescents with social anxiety disorder. *Archives of General Psychiatry, 61,* 1153–1162.

Welch, R., & Chue, P. (2000). Antipsychotic agents and QT changes. *Journal of Psychiatry and Neuroscience, 25,* 154–160.

Weller, E. B., Weller, R. A., & Fristad, M. A. (1986). Lithium dosage guide for prepubertal children: A preliminary report. *Journal of the American Academy of Child Psychiatry, 25,* 92–95.

West, K., & McElroy, S. L. (1995). Oral loading doses in the valproate treatment of adolescents with mixed bipolar disorder. *Journal of Child and Adolescent Psychopharmacology, 5,* 225–231.

West, S. A., Keck, P. E. J., McElroy, S. L., Strakowski, S. M., Minnery, K. L., McConville, B. J., et al. (1994). Open trial of valproate in the treatment of adolescent mania. *Journal of Child and Adolescent Psychopharmacology, 4,* 263–267.

Whittier, M. C., West, S. A., Galli, V. B., & Raute, N. J. (1995). Valproic acid for dysphoric mania in a mentally retarded adolescent. *Journal of Clinical Psychiatry, 56,* 590–591.

Wilens, T., Cohen, L., Biederman, J., Abrams, A., Neft, D., Faird, N., et al. (2002). Fluoxetine pharmacokinetics in pediatric patients. *Journal of Clinical Psychopharmacology, 22,* 568–575.

Wolraich, M. L., Greenhill, L. L., Pelham, W., Swanson, J., Wilens, T., Palumbo, D., et al. (2001). Randomized, controlled trial of oros methylphenidate once a day in children with attention-deficit/hyperactivity disorder. *Pediatrics, 108,* 883–892.

Zito, J. M., Safer, D. J., DosReis, S., Gardner, J. F., Boles, M., & Lynch, F. (2000). Trends in the prescribing of psychotropic medications to preschoolers. *Journal of the American Medical Association, 283,* 1025–1030.

Author Index

Abbott, D. H., 176
Abela, J. R. Z., 168, 178
Abidin, R. R., 289, 376
Abikoff, H. B., 285, 289, 300, 307, 318
Ablon, J. S., 287–289, 291–292
Aboitiz, F., 33
Abramowitz, A. J., 307
Abramson, L. Y., 167, 170, 176–178, 332
Abu-Arefeh, I., 413
Accardo, P. J., 29–30
Achat, H., 404
Achenbach, T. M., 6, 11, 69–70, 89, 124, 142, 171–172, 182–183, 185, 376
Achlien, B., 44
Acierno, R., 40–41, 52
Ackerman, B. P., 77, 153, 182
Adam, T., 186
Adams, H. E., 3–4
Adams, J., 175
Adams, M., 175
Adams, N. E., 409
Adamson, L. B., 177–178
Addiction Centre Adolescent Research Group, 360, 366
Ader, H. J., 151
Adlaf, E., 274
Adler, C., 221
Adler, Z., 176
Adrian, C., 175
Adunski, A., 415
Ageton, S. S., 353, 358
Agras, W. S., 332, 336–337, 340–341
Ahadi, S. A., 150, 166
Ahrens, A. H., 178
Aikins, J. W., 187
Ainsworth, M. S., 87, 370
Akhtar, N., 288
Akins, R. N., 414
Akiskal, H. S., 167, 172, 181, 217
Aksan, N., 64, 75
Albano, A. M., 38, 117, 119, 123–125, 136–137, 140, 442
Albertini, R. S., 410, 414
Aldwin, C. M., 54, 169
Alegria, M., 52
Alexander, R, 233
Algina, J., 291, 380
Algozzine, R., 109
Ali, N. J., 319
Alkon, A., 71
Allan, S., 338
Allen, A., 461
Allen, G. J., 446
Allen, J. P., 101, 103, 105, 107
Allen, L., 6–7, 32
Allen, N. B., 172

Allen, R., 120
Allen, S., 244, 246–247
Allgood-Merton, B., 175, 178
Alloy, L. B., 167, 177, 378
Allsop, D. H., 272
Almeida, D. M., 55
Almqvist, F., 211, 251
Alnaes, R., 143–144
Alpert, A., 179, 186
Al-Shabbout, M., 175
Altepeter, T. S., 316
Altham, P. M. E., 175, 179
Altmann, E. O., 187
Altschul, S., 428
Altshuler, L. L., 220
Alvarez, L. A., 408
Amado, H., 156
Aman, M. G., 235, 454, 461
Amanat, E., 179
Amato, P. R., 53, 289
Amaya-Jackson, L., 149, 159
Ambrosini, P. J., 11, 183
Ament, N., 258
American Academy of Child and Adolescent Psychiatry, 88, 149–150, 153, 155
American Psychiatric Association, 4, 10, 31, 88, 117, 135–136, 148, 153, 155, 165, 217, 227, 233, 254, 257, 277, 285–286, 299, 330–331, 336, 341, 348, 368, 403, 430, 455
American Psychological Association, 6, 429, 440
Ameringen, M. V., 338, 341
Amey, C. H., 354
Ammerman, R. T., 42, 135, 375
Amsel, A., 287, 291
Anastopoulos, A.D., 290
Anders, T. F., 33, 90–91, 258
Anderson, C. L., 397
Anderson, D. A., 336–337
Anderson, J. C., 119, 171, 175, 182, 301
Anderson, K. E., 52, 286, 305, 369
Anderson, P. L., 272
Anderson, S. C., 243
Anderson, S. R., 266
Andreas, D., 74, 87
Andreski, P., 150, 169
Andrews, G., 120
Andrews, J. A., 120, 171, 179, 185–186, 314, 333, 448
Angell, R., 153
Angelosante, A., 128
Angold, A., 6, 10, 14, 53, 93, 119, 122, 140, 171, 181, 182, 184–185, 285, 412
Anthony, J. L., 69, 117, 119, 168
Antilla, P., 413

Aoki, Y., 91
Apley, J., 407–408, 411
Apospori, E., 353–354
Applebaum, S., 426
Arbel, N., 378
Archambault, M. A., 32
Archus, D., 120, 138, 169
Arencibia-Mireles, O., 351
Arend, R. A., 178
Arias, E., 17
Armenteros, J. L., 454, 461
Arnold, L. E., 227
Arnold, M. E., 307
Arnow, B., 341
Aro, H., 404
Aro, S., 404
Arrindell, W. A., 179, 204
Arsenault, L., 82
Asarnow, J. R., 151, 178–179, 186
Asch, A., 242
Aselliine, R. H., 175
Asendorpf, J. B., 69
Asghari, A., 169
Asher, S. R., 242, 305
Askan, N., 289
Asmundson, G. J., 406
Atkins, M. S., 148, 153, 299, 316, 389
Attar, B. K., 52
Attaway, N. M., 361
Attention-Deficit/Hyperactivity Disorder Molecular Genetics Network, 319
Attia, E., 340
Attie, I., 332
Attkisson, C. C., 318
August, G. J., 292, 459
Avenevoli, S., 101–102, 110, 137, 170, 182
Avison, W. R., 53–55, 405
Axelson, D. A., 450
Axline, V. M., 426
Ayduk, O. N., 234
Azar, S. T., 372
Azrin, N. H., 41, 361

Bachanas, P. J., 416
Bachman, J. G., 348, 352, 354, 362, 364
Bachmann, J. P., 97
Bachorowski, J., 288
Backes, W., 33
Baer, R. A., 323, 440
Bagby, R. M., 167
Bagenholm, A., 263
Baglio, C. S., 238
Bagnell, A., 411
Bailey, D., Jr., 258, 260
Bailey, K., 140
Bailey, S. L., 348, 355

Bailey, V., 404
Baird, G., 220, 260
Baker, I., 339
Baker, L., 121, 286, 300, 409, 415
Baker, M., 176, 188
Bakersmans-Krankenburg, M. K., 91
Bakshi, S., 91
Baldwin, A. L., 54
Baldwin, C. A., 54
Ball, J. D., 93, 404
Balla, D. A., 235, 240, 246
Balthazor, M., 180
Bandura, A., 42, 106, 409
Bank, L., 306
Barak, A., 43
Barbarin, O. A., 52
Barber, B. K., 179
Barber, D., 243
Barbero, G., 410
Barbetti, V., 325
Barchas, J. D., 409, 416
Bardone, A. M., 332
Bare, M., 413
Barer, M. L., 48
Barker, L. M., 38, 40
Barker-Collo, S. L., 398
Barkley, R. A., 11, 64, 72, 287, 290, 292, 316, 319–324, 380, 442
Barlow, D. H., 6, 52, 117–119, 124, 168
Barmish, A., 117, 128
Barnard, K., 411
Barnes, G. M., 358
Barnes, H. V., 52
Barnett, D., 66
Barnett, I., 432
Barnett, N. P., 361
Barnett, O. W., 368, 370, 373, 379–381
Barnett, P. A., 177
Barnett, W. S., 52
Barocas, R., 52
Baron, P., 178
Baron, R. M., 75
Baron-Cohen, S., 260, 264
Barr, C. L., 405, 461
Barr, R., 405, 461
Barratt, M., 240
Barrett, P. M., 40, 121, 127, 441, 444
Barriga, A. Q., 322
Barrios, B. A., 123
Barron, L., 392
Barry, C. T., 301–302, 307
Barry, R. J., 32
Barton-Henry, M. L., 179
Bartzokis, G., 220
Bashford, R. A., 454
Bass, L., 266, 291
Bassett, D. L., 319, 409

467

Bassett, D. S., 278–279
Bassett, J. E., 235
Bassetti, C., 319
Bassuk, E. L., 176
Bassuk, S. S., 176
Bates, J. E., 54, 64–65, 67–70, 72, 158, 166, 168, 178, 300–302, 377
Bates, M. E., 350
Bates, S., 178
Bath, H. I., 380
Battle, J., 244
Baum, C. G., 428
Baumeister, A. A., 73, 238
Baumeister, R.F., 73, 238
Baumrind, D., 353, 355, 358–359
Bawden, H., 317
Bayles, K., 70
Beach, S. R. H., 186
Bear, G. G., 242
Beardslee, W. R., 52, 172, 178, 180, 185
Beauregard, M., 73
Bebko, J. M., 233, 238, 242–243
Bebko, K. M., 262
Beck, A. T., 126, 150, 154, 167, 170, 177, 185, 190–192
Beck, J., 72
Becker, B., 101, 351
Becker, C. B., 330
Becker, D. R., 137
Becker, K. B., 55
Beckman, P. J., 241
Beebe, K. L., 196
Beebe, T. J., 352
Beevers, C. G., 170
Begg, M. W., 409
Beglin, S. J., 336
Beidel, D. C., 11, 117, 120, 135–139, 141–143, 300
Beitchman, J. H., 119, 273–275, 277, 286, 397, 399
Bell, K., 105
Bell, M. A., 68
Bell, R. M., 359
Bell, R. Q., 100–101, 289, 369
Bellack, A. S., 244
Bell-Dolan, D. J., 119
Bell-Dolan, D. J., 119
Bell-Dolan, D. J., 177
Bell-Dolan, D. J., 119
Bellissimo, A., 175, 179
Belloiu, A., 43
Belmaker, E., 407
Belsky, J., 50, 66
Bem, D. J., 139
Bemis Vitousek, K., 9
Benbadis, S., 406
Bender, W. N., 281
Bengtson, V. L., 56
Bennett, D. S., 70, 178, 185
Bennett-Gates, D., 235, 245–247
Benoit, D., 87, 90, 92–93, 95
Benson, D. F., 29
Bent-Goodley, T. B., 377
Bentler, P. M., 358–359
Berk, M., 227
Berkes, J. L., 142
Berkey, C. S., 334
Berkman, L. F., 49
Berlin, R., 30
Berliner, L., 148, 159, 379, 388, 397, 399, 439

Bernal, G., 193–194, 440
Bernat, J. A., 4
Berndt, D., 185
Berndt, T. J., 106
Bernstcin, D. P., 153, 188–189, 378–379
Berrueta-Clement, J. R., 52
Berstad, A., 405
Bertrand, J., 258
Bertz, E., 126
Besalel, V., 41
Best, K. M., 179
Best, S. J., 241
Betancourt, H., 107
Betzner, U., 337
Beuhring, T., 58
Beumont, P., 337–338
Bezirganian, S., 188
Bhangoo, R. K., 219
Bickerton, W., 191–192
Biederman, J., 21, 24, 90, 118, 120, 137, 169, 171, 221, 285–286, 288, 290, 316, 318–321, 324, 460–461
Bienenstock, B., 258
Bierer, L. M., 176
Bifulco, A., 176
Biglan, A., 286
Bille, B., 411
Billings, L. A., 240
Binser, M. J., 186
Birch, H. G., 64, 66, 101, 369
Bird, D. C., 226, 457
Bird, H. R., 52
Birleson, P., 185
Birmaher, B., 11, 123, 140, 171, 174–175, 181–182, 185, 192–194, 396, 451–452, 461
Birns, B., 9
Bisserbe, J. C., 140
Bittner, A., 194
Bjerring, P., 406
Bjorck, J. P., 179
Bjork, J. P., 175
Blachman, D. R., 322
Black, C. M., 336
Black, M. M., 369, 374
Blackman, J. A., 52
Blackmore, E., 337
Blagys, M. D., 439
Blair, C., 68
Blair, R. J. R., 301–302
Blair-Greiner, A., 344–345
Blais, M. A., 152
Blake Woodside, D., 338
Bland, R., 215
Blank, G., 428
Blank, R., 428
Blanz, B. J., 337
Blashfield, R., 126
Blatt, S. J., 102–103, 105–106, 170, 175–176
Blazer, D. G., 171
Blehar, M. C., 87, 370
Bliss, L. S., 286
Block, J. H., 168
Block, M. R., 168
Bloomquist, M. L., 292
Blount, R. L., 410, 416
Blum, H. M., 53, 57
Blumberg, H. P., 221
Bocian, K. M., 322
Boddaert, N., 259

Boddy, J. M., 179
Bodiford-McNeil, C., 432
Bodin, S. D., 301–302
Boehm, G., 455
Boellner, S. W., 460–461
Boergers, J., 106, 288, 338
Bogels, S. M., 122, 138
Boggs, K., 10–11
Boggs, S. R., 291, 380
Bohman, M., 17–26
Bohnen, A. M., 404, 419
Boileau, H., 62
Boivin, M., 31, 299
Boldizar, J. P., 108, 322
Bolduc-Murphy, E. A., 120
Bolger, K. E., 377
Bolhofner, K., 217, 218, 221
Bollen, K. A., 182
Bolton, P., 258
Boney-McCoy, S., 376, 397, 399
Bongar, B., 413
Bonner, B. L., 379
Boomsma, D. I., 19, 26
Borbely, C., 355, 365
Borcherding, B. G., 460
Borduin, C. M., 308
Boris, N. W., 86–88, 91, 93–94, 370
Borkevec, T. D., 126
Borkowski, J. G., 287
Borrego, J., 380
Borthwick-Duffy, S. A., 241
Bosse, R., 169
Botteron, K. N., 173, 220–221
Bouchard, T. J., Jr., 20
Boudewyn, A. C., 176
Bourke, M., 40
Bousha, D. M., 369
Boutot, E. A., 242
Bowden, C. L., 227, 456, 458
Bowen, R. C., 119–120
Bower, G. H., 43
Bowlby, J., 105, 170, 178
Boyce, P., 167, 169
Boyce, W. F., 338, 405
Boyce, W. T., 71
Boyer, C. B., 105
Boyer, M. C., 410
Boyer, P., 140
Boylan, A., 74
Boyle, C., 233
Boyle, M. D., 53, 274
Boyle, M. H., 49, 171
Boyum, L. A., 88, 97
Braaten, E. B., 323
Brabeck, M. M., 178
Brachfield, S., 369
Bradley, C., 30, 32, 458
Bradley, E. J., 288
Bradley, S., 405
Brady, E. U., 119–120, 122, 182
Braggio, J. T., 359
Braithwaite, J., 383
Bramsen, I., 151
Brand, S., 178
Brandt, J. R., 303
Brannigan, A., 51
Brasic, J., 225
Braun, C. M., 32
Braungart, J. M., 65, 72–76, 287
Braungart-Rieker, J. M., 75, 76, 287
Bravo, M., 10, 52
Breen, M. J., 316

Breiter, H. C., 220
Brendgen, M., 71, 87, 306
Brent, D. A., 11, 123, 140, 185, 191–195, 396, 452, 461
Breslau, N., 150, 169, 182–183
Brestan, E. V., 7, 291, 307, 380
Bretherton, I., 287
Brewer, N., 242
Brewerton, T. D., 337
Bricker, D., 93
Bridge, J., 192–193
Brier, N., 273–274
Briere, J., 156, 392, 397
Brinthaupt, V. P., 300
Bristol, M. M., 240
Broadhurst, D. D., 368, 371
Broca, P., 29
Brodsky, S. L., 301
Brody, G. H., 9, 54, 77, 351
Bronfenbrenner, U., 49–50, 65, 74, 102, 104, 106–107, 380
Bronson, M. B., 65, 74
Brook, D. W., 351, 359
Brook, J. S., 52, 181, 188–190, 333, 335, 351, 359
Brook, S., 227
Brooks, D. L., 359
Brooks, S. J., 182
Brooks-Gum, J., 53–54, 332
Bross, D. C., 379
Brown, C. R., 32
Brown, E. J., 150, 154
Brown, F. W., 414
Brown, G. W., 170, 172, 175–176, 179, 181
Brown, J., 153, 376, 378
Brown, K. S., 274, 299
Brown, M. M., 288
Brown, R. T., 318
Brown, S. A., 349, 355–356, 358, 360–361
Brown, T. A., 119, 124, 126, 168
Brownell, M. T., 338, 439–440
Brownlie, E. B., 286
Brozek, J., 333
Bruce, J., 72
Bruce, S. E., 108, 122
Bruch, B., 138
Bruch, H., 331, 339
Bruck, M., 277
Bruder, G. E., 174
Bruininks, R. H., 240
Brumback, R. A., 29, 31–33
Bruni, G., 430
Brunk, M., 369
Brunner, J. R., 289
Bruun, R. D., 288
Bry, B. H., 361
Bryan, T., 274
Bryant, D. P., 281
Brylinski, J. A., 338
Bryon, M., 228
Buckhalt, J., 241
Buckner, J. C., 176
Budman, C. L., 288
Buhrmester, D., 105
Bui, K., 359
Buka, S., 277
Bukowski, W. M., 118, 125, 187, 302
Bukstein, O. G., 356
Bulik, C. M., 335

Bullock, B. M., 105
Bums, C. D., 331
Burack, J. A., 102
Burch, P. R., 291
Burchard, S. N., 243, 245
Burge, D., 175–176, 179–180, 182, 186
Burge, M. R., 227
Burke, E. C., 408, 411
Burke, J. D., 189, 301
Burke, J. E., 287
Burke, P., 178
Burlingham, D., 425
Burnam, M. A., 176
Burns, B. J., 331
Burns, C. D., 351
Burroughs, J., 226
Bursch, B., 403, 407, 409, 412, 415
Burt, C. E., 175, 179
Burton, C., 180
Burton, E. M., 335, 337
Burton, R., 29
Bush, T., 323, 501
Bushakra, F. B., 247
Buss, A. H., 3, 64–66, 73, 168
Bussing, R., 70, 317, 324
Butcher, J. N., 9, 375
Butler, C., 179
Butler, G., 124
Butler, I. J., 31
Butler, L. F., 192–193
Butow, P., 338
Butterbaugh, G., 237
Butterfield, E. C., 235
Buunk, B. P., 244
Buur, H., 66
Bybee, J., 103–104, 236, 238
Bye, A. M., 408
Byrne, C., 317

Caballero, J., 324
Cabral, K., 405
Cado, S., 151
Cadoret, R. J., 285
Cairney, J., 47, 49, 55, 57, 171
Calabrese, J. R., 227
Caldwell, T. E., 237
Calhoun, G., 244
Calhoun, K. S., 138
California Department of Developmental Services, 257, 261
Calkins, S. D., 64–69, 71–77
Cam, S., 411
Camargo, C. A., 334
Cameron, R., 335
Campbell, D. A., 319, 323
Campbell, J., 242
Campbell, L. A., 126
Campbell, M., 293
Campbell, N. R., 299, 307
Campbell, S. B., 9, 51–52, 72, 78
Campo, J. V., 403, 405, 410–412, 414–415
Campos, J. J., 65
Canals, J., 186
Canino, G. J., 52
Canino, I. A., 8, 226
Cantwell, D. P., 21, 33, 121, 182, 286, 300, 324
Canu, W. H., 323

Capaldi, D. M., 300, 306
Caputo, A. A., 301
Carbonneau, R., 52
Card, J. A., 67, 321
Carey, G., 119
Carey, M. P., 119, 185
Carle, A. C., 351
Carlson, C. L., 282
Carlson, E. A., 370, 382–383
Carlson, G. A., 162, 170, 179
Carlson, S. R., 317, 323, 360
Carmichael, A., 51
Carmody, T. J., 227
Carpenter, K. M., 47
Carpentieri, S., 182
Carroll, B. J., 452
Carroll, E., 450
Carter, J. C., 165, 175, 338
Carter, J. D., 378
Carver, L. J., 243
Casas, J. F., 299
Casper, R. C., 339
Caspi, A., 64, 70, 72, 119, 136, 139, 166, 169, 177, 234, 300, 303, 306, 317, 360, 379
Cassidy, J. F., 3
Castlebury, F. D., 153
Catalano, R. F., 353
Catanzaro, S., 119
Cathcart, K., 266
Cattarin, J. A., 334
Cauce, A. M., 102
Cauffman, E., 306
Cavallo, A., 174
Cavell, T. A., 302
Ceballo, R., 54
Cecil, D., 221
Cervera, S., 332, 338
Cervone, D., 234
Chabot, L., 356
Chaffin, M., 376, 380, 392, 396
Chamberlain, P., 286, 291
Chambers, W., 10, 183
Chambless, D. L., 6, 380, 430
Chan, D. W., 413
Chance, P., 42
Chandler, M. C., 369, 460
Chang, K., 227
Chang, S. Y., 360
Channon, S., 340
Chansky, T. E., 122, 125
Chapman, J. P., 68
Chapman, L. J., 68
Charatan, F., 448
Charman, T., 302
Charney, D. S., 173, 189–190, 221
Chassin, L., 350–351, 358–359
Chaudry, A., 53
Chavira, D. A., 140
Chazan, R. Z., 69
Chen, C., 186
Chen, K., 391
Chen, W. J., 351, 355
Chen, X., 71, 142, 186–187
Cheney, C. D., 38, 41
Chervin, R. D., 91, 319
Chesney, M. A., 71
Chess, S., 9, 64–66, 101, 136, 166–168, 234, 241, 289, 369
Chethik, M., 426–429, 434
Chetwynd, J., 240
Cheung, P., 246–247

Chevron, E. S., 194
Chidambaram, U., 338
Chipungu, S. S., 377
Chisolm, K., 91
Cho, S. C., 324
Choate, M., 6–7
Chorpita, B. F., 38, 117–119, 124, 168
Christ, M. A. G., 285, 300
Christakis, D. A., 319
Christensen, A., 445
Christensen, M. F., 411
Christian, R. E., 301, 305
Christophersen, E. R., 123–124
Chronis, A., 7
Chu, B., 127
Chue, P., 455
Chun, A., 52
Chung, H., 139
Chung, T., 348, 350
Chused, J., 425
Ciaranello, R. D., 258
Cicchetti, D. V., 66, 77, 93–94, 100–102, 104, 106, 108, 178, 237, 240, 289, 300, 367, 369–374, 376–378
Ciraulo, D. A., 458
Citak, E. C., 33
Claar, R. L., 409–410
Clark, C., 227
Clark, D. O., 56
Clark, F., 302
Clark, L. A., 167–170, 175–177, 182, 187–188, 192–193
Clark, R., 5, 88–89, 91–92
Clark, S. E., 321
Clarke, A. R., 32
Clarke, A. S., 176–177
Clarke, C., 90, 118
Clarke, G. N., 190–191, 193
Claussen, A. H., 371
Clay, T. H., 226
Clayton, P. J., 169
Clayton, R. R., 324, 350, 353
Cleary, S., 351
Cleckley, H., 306
Cleghorn, G., 415
Cleminshaw, H. K., 53
Click, M., 227, 259
Clements, C. B., 300
Cleminshaw, H. K., 53
Cloninger, C. R., 17, 166–168, 331
Cloyd, J. C., 458
Clum, G. A., 378
Coats, K. I., 192–193
Cobham, V. E., 127, 444
Cochrane, C. E., 337
Coffey, C. E., 29, 31
Cohen, B. M., 213, 220
Cohen, C., 292
Cohen, D. J., 245
Cohen, J. A., 9, 95, 148, 155, 159–160, 170, 333, 335, 388–396, 398–399
Cohen, L M., 413
Cohen, L. S., 458, 461
Cohen, M. A., 299, 301
Cohen, M. M., 62, 77
Cohen, O., 370
Cohen, P., 9, 52, 120, 170, 175–176, 179, 181, 188–190, 333, 378
Cohen, R. D., 49

Cohn, S., 9
Coie, J. D., 9, 11, 101, 288, 291, 299, 305
Coker, S., 444
Colder, C. R., 350
Colditz, G. A., 334
Cole, D. A., 167–168, 175, 177–179, 182–183, 185, 187–188
Cole, P. M., 76
Cole, R. E., 52
Cole-Love, A. S., 317
Coleman, J. M., 244
Colledge, E., 302
Collett, B. R., 155, 320
Colletti, R. B., 404, 410, 454
Collins, M. H., 177
Collins, R. L., 244
Collins-Hall, L., 359
Collmer, C. W., 369
Colon, S., 350
Colton, M. E., 175
Compas, B. E., 165, 167–168, 170–171, 175, 181–183, 410
Compton, S. N., 128
Compton, W. M., 360
Cone, J. D., 3
Conger, R. D., 9, 54, 175, 179
Conlin, S., 91
Connelly, C. D., 371
Conner, R.
Conners, C. K., 11, 123, 171, 320–321, 396
Connolly, J., 188
Connolly, K. M., 332
Connor, D. F., 293
Connor, R. T., 242
Connor-Smith, J., 167, 170
Conrad, J., 180
Conradt, J., 181
Constantino, J. N., 21
Conte, J. R., 389, 392
Conway, J. A., 275
Cook, B. L.
Cook, C. A., 90, 389
Cook, E. H., Jr., 219
Cooke, D. J., 306
Cooke, R., 224
Coolahan, K. C., 379–380
Coolbear, J., 90
Cooley, M. R., 135
Cooney, G., 393
Cooper, A. B., 52
Cooper, G., 95
Cooper, M. L., 351
Cooper, S. A., 238
Cooper, T. B., 148
Cooper, Z., 332, 335–337
Coplan, R. J., 68, 77
Copotelli, H., 11
Corcoran, M. E., 53
Corkum, P. V., 293
Corley, R. P., 21
Corrigan, P., 11
Coryell, W., 169, 180
Costa, P. T., Jr., 136, 150–151, 168–169, 234, 354
Costello, A. J., 156
Costello, E., 6, 10, 53
Costello, E. J., 119–120, 122, 148, 171, 181, 184, 285, 412
Cote, G., 303
Coulter, M. L., 150, 393, 396

Courchesne, E., 32
Cox, A., 52–53, 406
Coyne, J. C., 167, 178, 185, 188
Craig, W., 356
Craig, W. M., 338
Craighead, L. W., 185
Craighead, W. E., 182, 185
Cramer, B., 95
Craney, J. L., 217–218, 221
Craske, M. G., 121
Crawford, P., 227
Creamer, V. A., 355
Creelman, W. L., 458
Crichton-Browne, J., 30
Crick, N. R., 291, 299–300
Crisp, A. H., 333, 339
Crittenden, P. M., 370–371
Crnic, K., 240
Crockenberg, S., 87, 287
Crockett, L., 121, 186
Cronk, N. J., 19
Crook, K., 179
Crosbie, J., 40, 42, 135, 331
Cross, S. E., 43
Crouse-Novak, M. A., 180–181
Crow, S. J., 337, 339–340
Crowell, J. A., 93–94
Crowley, T. J., 22
Crowther, J. H., 336
Cruise, K., 306
Cuffe, S. P., 153, 318, 356
Culbert, J., 404
Culbertson, J. L., 274, 278
Cummings, E. M., 78, 87, 178, 201
Cummings, J. L., 31
Cummings, S. T., 241
Cunningham, C., 293
Cunningham, P. B., 308, 381
Cunningham-Williams, R. M.
Cuperus, J. M., 288
Curfs, L. M. G., 236
Curran, J. G., 220
Curran, P. J., 122, 170, 182, 350
Curry, J. F., 53, 182, 185, 190, 291
Curtin, J. J., 303
Cuskelly, M., 242
Cyranowski, J. M., 171
Cytryn, L. Y., 140, 180

Dadds, M., 11
Dadds, M. R., 121, 127, 441, 444
Dagnan, D., 244, 247
Dahl, A., 397
Dahl, R. E., 173–174
Dahlstrom, W. G., 375
Daigneault, S., 32
Dalen, L., 317
Daley, D., 317–318
Daley, S., 175–176, 180
Dalgleish, T., 122
Damashek, A., 397
D'Amato, R. C., 242
Damore, J., 456
Dan, Y., 176
Dana, R., 9
Dandes, S. K., 142
Dandreaux, D. M., 303
Dane, H. E., 302
D'Angelo, E. J., 429
Daniel, C., 232
Dare, C., 339
Daro, D., 371

Dasari, M., 220
Daugherty, T. K., 124
Davern, L., 241
David, C. F., 186
David, D., 43
Davidovitch, M., 259, 301
Davidson, J. R., 68, 72, 139, 152, 158–159
Davidson, R. J., 174
Davies, M., 171, 187
Davies, P. T., 78, 169, 178
Davila, J., 175–176, 181
Davis, A. D., 286
Davis, B., 179, 186
Davis,C., 337
Davis, E. P., 68, 72
Davis, G. C., 150, 169, 182
Davis, J. M., 408, 452
Davis, L. W., 379
Dawson, G., 173–174, 256, 259–260
Dawson, K., 291
DeAntonio, M., 340
Deater-Deckard, K., 172
DeBaryshe, B. D., 105, 286
DeBellis, M. D., 150, 152
Deblinger, E., 148, 153–154, 159, 389, 398–399, 439
Decoufle, P., 233
Dedmon, S., 64–66, 74–75
Deemer, S. A., 242
Deering, C. G., 178
Defries, J. C., 379
DeGangi, G. A., 67, 90
Dekker, M. C., 233
DeKlyen, M., 89, 285, 290
DelBello, M. P., 217, 220–221, 226–227, 454, 461
Delfino, R. J., 319
Delgado, S. V., 461
Delong, G. R., 456
Deltito, J. A., 456
Demark, J., 243
Denckla, M. B., 272
Denney, D., 17
Dennis, M. L., 349, 361
Department of Health and Human Services, 49, 358
Depner, C. E., 52
Deray, M. J., 408
Derivan, A., 454, 461
Derogatis, L. R., 375
DeRoma, V. M., 375
Derryberry, D., 65, 168, 287
Dery, M., 303
de Silva, P., 340
DeSmedt, G., 454, 461
Detlor, J., 461
Detzer, M. J., 341
Dev, P. C., 273, 280
DeVeaugh-Geiss, J., 450–451
Devins, G., 224
Devlin, M., 341
deWet, T., 52
Dewhurst Savellis, J., 169
DeWolfe, N., 317
Deykin, E. Y., 259
de Zwaan, M., 332, 340–341
Diamond, G. M., 191, 194, 243, 245
Diamond, G. S., 191, 194
Diamond, J., 340
Diamond, K. E., 245, 267

DiBartolo, P. M., 136
Dichter, G. S., 174
Dick, D. M., 16, 19–21
Dicker, R., 454
Dickerson, F., 11
Dickson, N., 70, 300
Dickstein, S., 167
Diener, M., 75
Dierker, L. C., 182, 185
Dietz, S. G., 31
Dietz, W. H., 455
Diez-Roux, A. V., 47
DiGiuseppe, D. L., 319
Digman, J. M., 168
DiLalla, D. L., 260
DiLalla, L. F., 64
DiLillo, D., 367, 397
Dillon, J. E., 91, 319
Di Lorenzo, C., 410
Dilsaver, S. C., 227
DiMascio, A., 194
Dinan, T. G., 174
Dinno, N., 256
Dion, K. L., 167
DiPietro, J. A., 67
Dirlich-Wilhelm, H., 269
Dishion, T. J., 40, 105–106, 286, 291, 301, 305, 307, 361
Dix, J., 281
Dixon, J. F., 178
D'Imperio, R., 370
Dobkin, P. L., 356
Dodge, K. A., 11, 43, 54, 69–70, 158–159, 182, 288, 290–291, 299–302, 305, 340, 377
Doerner, W. G., 367
Doherty, M. E., 40–41
Dohm, F. A., 336
Doll, H. A., 332, 335
Domenech, E., 171
Domenech-Llaberia, E., 186
Dong, Q., 186
Donohew, L., 350
Donohue, B., 38, 40–42, 361
Donovan, A. M., 262
Donovan, J. E., 355
Donovan, W. L., 54, 75
Dooley, J., 411
Dooley, M. D., 53
Doris, J., 43, 377
Dosen, A., 241
dosReis, S., 324
Douglas, L., 274
Doussard-Roosevelt, J. A., 67, 76
Dowd, J. J., 56
Down, J. L. H., 30
Downing, J., 399
Doyle, A. E., 24, 291–292, 321
Dozois, D. J. A., 40
Drake, K. L., 440
Drapeau, A., 53
Drechsler, R., 319
Drel, M. J., 148
Drevets, W. C., 220
Drew, C. J., 241
Drewes, M. J., 138
Driscoll, K., 69, 168
Droegemueller, W., 367
Drossman, D. A., 409
Drotar, D., 179
Duarte, M., 410

DuBois, D. L., 178, 190, 439–440
Duchowny, M. S., 408, 413
Dugas, M. J., 118
DuHamel, K., 351
Duke, M., 411
Dulcan, M. K., 10, 156, 183, 301, 320, 433
Dumas, J. E., 286
Dunitz-Scheer, M., 5
Dunn, J., 53
Dunner, D. L., 169
Dunnington, R. E., 293
Duo, P., 351
DuPaul, G. J., 290, 317, 324
Durbin, C. E., 167
Durlak, J. A., 438–440, 443, 445
Dush, D. M., 40, 445
Dutra, L., 370
Dworkin, P. H., 33
Dyck, I., 122, 126
Dyck, M., 177
Dykens, E. M., 233–240, 245
Dykman, R. A., 153
Dyson, L. L., 240, 262, 278

Earls, F., 52
Easterbrooks, M. A., 262
Eaton, W. W., 137
Eaves, L. J., 18–21, 120, 137, 169, 172, 182–183, 302
Eckenrode, J., 43, 52, 369, 377
Eckert, T., 317, 324
Edelbrock, C. S., 6, 69, 156, 185, 319
Edelsohn, G. A., 121, 150, 186, 393
Edens, J., 306
Egeland, B., 52, 121, 368–370, 374, 376–377
Egger, H. L., 412
Egolf, B. P., 158, 374, 377, 389
Ehmann, M., 461
Eiben, L. A., 91
Eigsti, M., 369
Einbender, A. J., 390
Einfeld, S. L., 234, 235, 237
Eisemann, M., 52, 351
Eisen, A. R., 117, 125, 127
Eisenberg, J. G., 45, 52
Eisenberg, N., 71, 76–77, 119
Eisenstadt, T. H., 308, 380
Eisler, I., 339
Ekman, P., 220
Ekselius, L., 143, 189
Elardo, R., 52
Elbert, J., 6, 429
Elder, G. H., Jr., 54, 139, 175
Eley, T. C., 120, 172–173, 175–176, 302
Elhai, J. D., 397
Elia, J., 460
Elkin, I., 194
Elkins, I. J., 360
Ellertsen, B., 405
Ellickson, P. L., 348–349, 359
Ellicott, A., 170, 181
Elliott, D. M., 388, 392, 397
Elliott, D., S., 353, 358
Elliott, R. N., 244
Ellis, M. L., 299–302, 304
Emde, R. N., 87–88, 91, 370
Eme, R., 9

Emery, R. E., 9, 52–53
Emmelkamp, P. M. G., 179, 204, 444
Emmons, C., 106
Emslie, G. J., 33, 173–174, 181, 185, 195, 451
Endicott, J., 31
Engler, L. B., 117, 125
Ennis, P., 238
Enyart, P., 185
Epps, J., 288, 307
Epstein, A. S., 52
Epstein, N., 170
Erbaugh, J., 185
Erickson, M. F., 52, 368–369, 376–378
Erikson, E. H., 429
Erkanli, A., 6, 53, 119, 148, 181
Ernst, C., 457
Ernst, D., 177, 184
Eron, L. D., 299
Erwin, R. J., 220, 240, 242
Esbensen, A. J., 235
Escalante, P. R., 259
Espinoza, R., 407
Essau, C. A., 171, 181
Essex, M. J., 68
Estes, L. S., 316
Esveldt-Dawson, K., 185, 291
Ettelson, R., 182
Ettner, S. L., 55
Evans, D. W., 237–238
Evans, M. A., 48, 141–142
Evans, R. W., 226
Everson, M. D., 150, 393, 396
Ewens, W. J., 25
Ey, S., 165, 175
Eyberg, S. M., 7, 291, 307–308, 376, 380, 432
Eysenck, H. J., 161, 168, 170, 234, 323, 379
Ezpeleta, L., 53

Fabes, R. A., 77
Fabrega, J. H., 301
Fagot, B. I., 51
Fairbank, J. A., 148
Fairbanks, L., 155
Fairburn, C. G., 330–332, 334–338, 340
Fairley, M., 392, 404, 413
Fallon, P., 158
Famularo, R., 159
Fantuzzo, J., 376, 379–380
Faraone, S. V., 24, 32, 120, 285, 290, 319–322
Farchione, T. R., 33
Farmer, J., 336
Farmer, R., 56, 168
Farrell, A. D., 108
Farrell, J. M., 303, 306
Farrington, D. P., 51, 299, 301
Farvolden, P., 338, 341
Fauerbach, J. A., 151–152, 158–159
Faull, C., 405, 407
Faulstich, M. E., 185
Faust, D., 404
Favilla, L., 122
Fazekas, H., 302
Feagans, L., 33
Fearon, I., 404
Feehan, C., 181, 191–192

Feeny, N. C., 156, 396
Feighner, J. P., 31
Feinberg, T. L., 180–181
Feindler, E. L., 291, 375
Feinleib, M., 316
Feiring, C., 150, 154, 391, 395
Feldman, R. S., 158, 377
Feldman, S. S., 93
Feldon, J., 176
Felner, R. D., 178
Fendrich, M., 180, 182, 186
Fenton, T., 159
Ferenz-Gillies, R., 179
Ferguson, H. B., 134
Fergusson, D. M., 139, 187, 306
Fernandez-Ballart, J., 186
Ferraro, K. F., 56
Festinger, L., 243
Fick, A. C., 108
Fiegelman, W., 356
Field, A. E., 334
Field, T., 19, 21, 100, 173–174, 180
Fiese, B. J., 86–87
Fieve, R. R., 169
Filapek, P., 259–260
Filer, M., 106
Finch, A. J., Jr., 119, 151, 185
Finch, H. A., 243
Findling, R. L., 221, 449–450, 454
Fine, M. J., 237, 282
Finkelhor, D., 176, 371, 389–392, 397–399
Finkelstein, R., 180–181
Finzi, R., 370
Firestone, P., 410
Fischer, E., 376
Fischer, J. H., 458
Fischer, M., 319–320, 322, 324
Fischer, T., 356
Fisher, K. J., 351
Fisher, M., 331, 336
Fisher, P., 10, 123, 156, 320
Fisher, R. S., 399, 413
Fisher, S., 426
Fisman, S., 262
Fitzgerald, H., 69
Fitzgerald, K. D., 450
Fitzpatrick, K. M., 108
Flament, M. F., 450
Flannery, D. J., 107
Flannery-Schroeder, E., 118, 120, 125, 127, 439
Fleisig, W., 11
Fleming, J. E., 53, 170–171, 182
Fletcher, J. M., 31, 275–276
Fletcher, K., 320, 322, 324
Fletcher, K. E., 150, 152, 156–157
Fletcher, K. F., 290
Flett, G. L., 165
Flor, D. L., 77
Flory, K., 323
Fluge, G., 405
Flynn, C. A., 168, 180
Foa, E. B., 148, 153–154, 156, 389, 396
Foldenyi, M., 319
Follette, V. M., 154
Follette, W. C., 3, 154
Folstein, S., 257–258
Fombonne, E., 172, 257–259
Fonagy, P., 87, 425, 430–432
Ford, A., 241

Ford, J. D., 156, 369, 389
Ford, T., 6
Forde, D. R., 153
Fordham, K., 136
Forehand, R., 9, 52, 125, 186, 308, 376, 380
Foreyt, J. P., 336
Forness, S. R., 33, 322
Forsterling, F., 186
Forsythe, A. B., 411
Forth, A. E., 303, 306
Foster, K., 227
Foucault, M., 29
Fox, N. A., 65, 67–69, 72, 74, 76–77
Fox, T. L., 121, 127
Foxcroft, D. R., 358
Foy, D., 154
Frame, C. L., 125, 142, 186
Francis, G., 122
Franco, N., 121
Frank, D. A., 179
Frank, E., 194
Frank, G. K., 319, 334
Frank, N. C., 410
Frankel, K. A., 88
Franklin, M. E., 122
Franz, D. Z., 10
Fraser, J., 192–193
Fraser, M. W., 353–354
Frazer, D. R., 301
Frederick, C., 30, 155–156
Freedheim, D. K., 426–428, 430
Freeman, B. J., 264
Freeman, L. N., 26, 33, 183
Freeman, R., 340
Freeman, W. S., 321
French, D.C., 180, 286
French, N. H., 185, 291
Freud, A., 425–426, 428, 431
Freud, S., 30, 34, 100, 154
Frick, P. J., 6, 125, 139, 142, 285, 299–308
Fride, E., 176
Friedberg, R. D., 444
Friederici, S., 334
Friedlander, M. L., 186
Friedman, J. M., 458
Friedman, L., 220
Friedman, R. J., 192–193
Friedrich, W. N., 159–160, 240, 390, 395
Friesen, D., 21
Frieze, I. H., 154
Fristad, M. A., 217–218, 223, 225, 458
Frith, U., 32
Fritsch, S., 403
Fritz, G. K., 287, 403, 412, 415
Frosch, C., 75
Fryns, J. P., 236
Fudge, H., 181
Fuentes, R. M., 440
Fuerst, D. R., 273–274, 288
Fueyo, M., 93
Fulker, D. W., 172
Fulkerson, J. A., 332, 352
Fuller, J. L., 19
Funderburk, B. W., 308, 380
Funk, R., 349
Furer, P., 147
Furmark, T., 137, 143

Furstenberg, F. F., 53
Fuster, J. M., 287

Gabreels, F. J., 238, 404
Gadow, K. D., 293, 318
Gaensbauer, T. J., 178, 180, 434
Gaffney, B., 427
Gagnon, C., 178
Galaburda, A. M., 33
Galaif, E. R., 356
Galin, R. S., 318
Gall, F. J., 29
Galli, V. B., 411, 456
Gamble, S. A., 188
Gamble, W., 178
Gambone, J. C., 409
Gameros, T. A., 359
Ganiban, J., 66, 370
Ganoczy, D. A., 319
Gans, A. M., 276
Garber, J., 165–166, 168–170, 175, 177–182, 185, 187, 193, 403–404, 407–410, 412
Garcia, I. G., 157
Garcia-Coll, C. T., 69, 87, 90
Garcia-Jetton, J., 290
Gardner, J. F., 412
Garfield, W., 426
Garfinkel, B. D., 174, 191
Garfinkel, P. E., 336
Garfinkel, R., 194
Garland, E. J., 10, 286, 293
Garner, D. M., 330, 334, 336
Garnier, H. E., 359
Garralda, E., 406
Garrison, C. Z., 157, 179
Garvey, M. A., 32
Gary, F. A., 70
Gatsonis, C., 181–182
Gayton, W. F., 235
Ge, X. J., 54, 175–176, 179
Geary, D. C., 273, 275
Gelernter, J., 137
Geller, B., 217–223, 226, 285, 451
Gelles, M., 67
Gelles, R., 392, 402
Gelles, R., 371
Gemmer, T. C., 291
Gendreau, P., 306
Gentile, C., 156
George, C., 30, 32, 87
George, E. L., 225
George, G. R., 178
George, P. J., 277
Gerber, P. J., 277
Gerlsma, C., 179
Germain, A., 44
Gershater-Molko, R. M., 381
Gershuny, B. S., 169
Gersten, J. C., 52
Gerull, F. C., 121
Geschwind, N., 33
Ghaemi, S. N., 226–227, 456
Ghany, D. L., 276
Giaconia, R. M., 172, 374
Gibb, B. E., 378
Gibbon, M., 337
Gibbons, F. X., 351
Gibbons, J., 113
Gibbons, S. L., 246–247
Gibbons, T. A., 439–440, 445
Giedd, J., 32
Gil, A. G., 53, 348, 352–355, 361

Gil, D. G., 369
Gil, E., 159
Gil, K. M., 406, 412
Gilbert, P., 244, 246–247
Gilchrist, A., 256, 264
Gilchrist, L., 54
Gill, K. L., 65, 73–75
Gillberg, C., 238, 263
Gilliom, M., 72, 75, 89
Gilpin, D., 427
Gilson, E., 29
Ginsburg, G. S., 128, 440
Giovannelli, J., 51, 64, 69, 89, 318
Gipson, M. T., 405
Gipson, P. Y., 170
Girgus, J. S., 166, 171, 175
Gitlin, M., 170, 181
Gjerde, P. F., 169
Gladstone, T. R., 52, 172, 177, 182
Glascoe, F. P., 93
Glassman, M., 54
Glatt, S. J., 324
Glazer, J. P., 406
Glenn, J., 273–274, 277–278, 280
Glick, L., 237
Glueck, E., 48, 305
Glueck, S., 48, 305
Gnagy, E., 320
Gobel, D., 407
Godley, M. D., 349, 361
Godley, S. H., 349, 361
Goedhart, A. W., 138
Goenjian, A. K., 159
Goggin, C., 306
Gold, D., 242–243
Gold, N., 263
Gold, S. N., 397
Goldberg, D., 269, 274
Goldberg, J., 457
Goldberg, K., 241
Goldberg, S., 369, 405
Goldberg-Arnold, J. S., 225
Goldfried, M., 431
Goldschneider, K. R., 413
Goldsmith, H. H., 64–66, 73, 75, 79, 166
Goldstein, M. J., 180
Goldstein, N. A., 319
Goldstein, S., 292
Golier, J. A., 378
Gonzales, L. R., 181
Gonzalez, N. M., 293
González-Soldevilla, A., 105
Goodenough, B., 406
Goodlin-Jones, B., 90
Goodman, E., 53, 331
Goodman, G. S., 393, 395–396
Goodman, J. T., 404, 410
Goodman, R., 6
Goodman, S. H., 172, 178, 180, 181
Goodman Brown, T., 170
Goodrick, G. K., 336, 341
Goodwin, F. K., 217
Goodwin, J., 242
Goodwin, R. D., 139
Goodyer, I. M., 173, 175–176, 178–179
Gordon, B. L., 29
Gordon, H. W., 359
Gordon, J., 175
Gordon, R. A., 301
Gore, S., 175

Gorman, J., 454
Gorman, J. M., 135
Gorman, L. F., 135
Gorman-Smith, D., 108–109
Gortmaker, S. L., 338
Gotlib, I. H., 54, 172, 176–178, 180–181, 187
Gottesman, I., 16, 103, 258
Gottfredson, G. D., 54, 299, 305
Gottfredson, M., 54, 299, 305
Gottman, J. M., 9, 52, 67, 76, 242, 249, 287
Gough, H. G., 48
Goulart, E., 410
Gould, R. A., 11, 263
Grace, M. C., 148
Graczyk, P. A., 125, 180
Graham, J. R., 375
Graham, T. B., 413
Gram, L. F., 456
Granic, I., 105
Grant, K. E., 165, 170, 175–176
Grattan, E., 181, 191–192
Grattan-Smith, P., 404, 408, 411, 413
Graves, G. R., 226, 457
Gray, D. B., 33
Gray, J. A., 166, 168
Graybeal, A., 433
Graziano, W. G., 168
Green, B. J., 185
Green, B. L., 148
Green, M., 316
Green, S. M., 285, 300, 303
Green, W. H., 293
Greenberg, M., 240, 290, 307
Greenberg, R., 426
Greenberg, T., 195
Greenberger, E., 186, 188
Greenblatt, D. J., 458
Greene, A. L., 337
Greene, J., 179, 404, 407, 409–411, 413
Greene, R. W., 285–293
Greenhill, L. L., 324, 460
Greeno, C. G., 333
Greenough, W. T., 31
Greenwald, E., 151
Greenwald, R., 156
Gregor, M., 389
Gregory, N., 38
Greiner, M., 230
Greising, L., 182
Grella, C. E., 356
Gresham, F. M., 185, 274, 277, 279, 322
Grieder, T., 220
Griffin, P., 286
Griffin, R., 10
Griffin, S. M., 242
Grigorenko, E. L., 275–276
Grills, A. E., 100
Grilo, C. M., 331, 333, 339, 341
Grimm, S., 285
Grisham, J. R., 126
Groen, A., 266
Groom, J. M., 242
Gross, A. M., 3, 10, 186
Gross, J. J., 73
Grossman, F., 227
Grossman, J., 33
Grossman, J. A., 183

Grossman, K. E., 87
Grossman, L. M., 243
Grossman, P. B., 439–440
Grotpeter, J. K., 299
Gruber, S., 220
Grufman, M., 238
Grusec, J. E., 240
Grzywacz, J. G., 55
Gualtieri, C. T., 31, 226
Guberman, A. H., 226
Gudmundsson, O., 411
Guerra, N. G., 52
Guevremont, D. C., 290
Guidetti, V., 405, 411
Guidubaldi, J., 52–53
Guite, J. W., 411
Gundersen, K., 217
Gunderson, J. G., 153
Gunnar, M. R., 67–68, 72, 74, 87
Guo, C., 53
Gur, R. C., 220
Gur, R. E., 220
Guralnick, M. J., 242
Gurley, D., 181
Guthrie, D., 179
Gutner, T., 257
Gutstein, S., 267
Guy, W., 192
Guyer, B., 17
Guyll, M., 43
Guze, S. B., 31

Haaga, D., 177
Haapala, D. A., 380
Haapsalano, J., 54
Hack, S., 125
Hadden, L. L., 259
Hagell, A., 300
Hagglof, B., 52, 351
Hagin, R. A., 272, 274–277, 281, 403
Hagino, O., 403
Haglund, B., 53
Hajal, F., 456
Hale, B., 411
Hale, T. S., 319
Halevy, G., 176
Haley, A., 103
Hall, C. W., 279–280
Hall, J. G., 17
Hallfors, D., 338
Hally, C., 375
Halperin, J. M., 319
Ham, M., 176, 185
Hamer, R. M., 454
Hamilton, D., 6
Hamilton, E. B., 183–186, 188, 191, 194–195
Hamilton, J. R., 410
Hamilton, M., 238
Hammen, C. L., 167, 170, 172, 175–176, 178–182, 186, 189
Hammer, M., 158, 377
Hampson, S. E., 351
Hamre-Nietupski, S., 243
Handleman, J. S., 264, 266
Hanis, S., 246
Hankin, B. L., 171, 176, 178, 181
Hanks, C., 94
Hann, D. M., 108
Hans, S. L., 54
Hansen, C., 121

Hansen, D. J., 177, 367–368, 372, 375–376
Hanson, R. F., 159, 379, 393
Hardan, A. Y., 259
Harding, K., 167
Hardman, M. L., 241
Hare, R. D., 303, 305–306
Har-Even, D., 370
Hariri, A. R., 319
Harkness, A. R., 168
Harman, C., 340
Harmon, R. J., 74, 88, 159, 180
Harper, C. R., 32–33
Harper, D. C., 44, 52, 197
Harper, R. S., 243
Harpur, T. J., 306
Harrigan, E., 227
Harrington, H., 303, 360
Harrington, R., 21, 172, 181, 191, 192–193
Harrington, S., 361
Harris, P., 433
Harris, S., 247
Harris, S. L., 264, 266, 268
Harris, S. R., 291
Harris, T. O., 165, 170, 172, 175–176
Harrison, C., 321
Harrison, P. J., 30, 330–331, 334–335, 337, 352
Harrison, R., 170
Hart, C. H., 72
Hart, E. L., 285
Hart, S. D., 303, 306
Harter, S., 185, 235, 237–238, 244, 246–247, 287
Hartmann, D. P., 123
Hartung, C. M., 321
Hartup, W. W., 166, 242
Haskett, M. E., 377
Hassuk, B., 320
Hastings, P., 71
Hastings, R. P., 263
Hatfield, A., 225
Hatten, D. D., 258
Hauf, A. M. C., 172
Hauser-Cram, P., 104, 240
Hawkins, J. D., 353–354
Hawkins, J. M., 220
Hawkins, R. P., 5
Hawley, P. H., 299
Hay, D. A., 21
Hayes, C., 127
Hayes, S. C., 3, 154, 287
Hays, R. D., 165, 348–349
Hayward, C., 118, 144, 169, 176, 334–335, 414
Hazebroek-Kampschreur, A. A., 404
Hazen, R. A., 119
Hazlett, R. L., 126
Healy, L. J., 40
Heath, A. C., 18–20, 52, 120, 137, 169
Heath, N., 274
Heatherton, T. F., 332
Hecht, D. B., 187, 367–368, 376
Hechtman, L., 320, 322
Heffelfinger, A. K., 88, 90
Heffernan, K., 330
Heflin, A., 154, 159–160
Hegedus, A. M., 349
Heilman, K. M., 32

Heim, C., 173
Heiman, T., 241
Heimberg, R. G., 138
Hejazi, M. S., 174
Hellander, M., 223
Heller, S. S., 52, 91, 370
Heller, T., 293, 307
Hembree-Kigin, T. L., 380, 432
Hemphill, J. F., 306
Hemsley, D., 340
Hemsley, R. E., 238
Henderson, A. S., 120
Henderson, C. R., Jr., 52, 94
Henderson, H. A., 65, 67
Henggeler, S. W., 110, 291, 308, 361, 369, 380–381
Heninger, G., 341
Henker, B., 52, 293, 319
Henrich, C. C., 103, 105, 108, 235, 299
Henriques, J. B., 68
Henry, B., 30, 52, 54, 64, 70, 119, 166, 317
Henry, C., 176
Henry, D., 389
Henry, D. E., 159
Henschel, A., 333
Herberman, R., 44
Herbert, J., 175, 179
Herbert, J. D., 143–144
Herbert, M. R., 32
Herbison, P. G., 397
Hergenhan, B. R., 38
Herjanic, B., 140, 156, 183–184
Herlin, T., 406
Herman, C. P., 334, 341
Herman, J. L., 378
Herrenkohl, E. C., 158, 354, 374–375, 377, 389
Herrenkohl, R. C., 158, 354, 374–375, 377, 389
Herrera, C., 377
Hersen, M., 40–41, 120, 135, 244, 337, 375
Hershey, K. L., 65, 166
Hertzig, M., 64, 66
Hertzog, C., 102, 175
Heruti, R. J., 415
Hervas, A., 21
Herzberg, D. S., 176
Herzog, D. B., 331, 335
Hestenes, L. L., 267
Heston, L. L., 16–17
Hetherington, E. M., 52–53, 173
Hewitt, J. K., 21
Hill, A. J., 338
Hill, B. K., 240, 242, 286
Hill, D., 173, 181
Hill, N. L., 301
Hillman, R. E., 259
Hilsenroth, M. J., 439
Hilsman, R., 168, 177–178
Hinney, A., 335
Hinrichs, W. L., 411
Hinrichsen, H., 338
Hinshaw, S. P., 44, 52, 69, 72, 109–111, 285, 292–293, 300, 303, 307–308, 321–322
Hinshaw-Fuselier, S., 96, 99
Hinshelwood, J., 30
Hiroto, D., 175
Hirsch, J., 345

Hirschfeld, R. M. A., 167, 169
Hirschl, T. A., 54
Hirshfeld, D. R., 120, 169
Hirshfeld Becker, D. R., 137
Hirt, M. L., 440, 445
Hjern, A., 53
Hoagwood, K., 304
Hock, E., 54
Hockaday, J. M., 411
Hodapp, R. M., 103, 233–235, 238–240, 243
Hodgens, J. B., 322
Hodges, K. H., 140, 182, 184, 337, 410, 412
Hodgins, S., 303
Hoehn-Saric, R., 126
Hoffman, K., 95, 168, 178, 183, 236, 246, 287, 291, 301
Hoffmann, H., 30, 32
Hoffschmidt, S. J., 280
Hogan, A., 274, 279, 281
Hogue, A., 187, 361
Holahan, C. J., 175
Holeva, V., 151–152, 158
Holland, D. E., 441
Hollenberg, J., 376
Hollon, S. D., 169, 193, 196
Holmbeck, G. N., 186, 444
Holmes, D. S., 42–43
Holmes, E., 11
Holt, K. G., 174
Holt, R. R., 433
Holtzman, G., 259
Homatidis, S., 262
Honig, A. S., 52
Hood, J. E., 119, 405
Hooe, E. S., 69, 119, 168
Hoondert, V., 236
Hopkins, J., 31, 331
Hops, H., 171, 175, 179–180, 185–186, 191, 193, 333, 352, 448
Horowitz, J. M., 390
Horwood, L. J., 139, 187, 306
Hotopf, M., 411, 414
House, J. S., 48, 51
Houskamp, B. M., 395
Howard, G. F., III, 413
Howard, K. A., 273
Howell, C. T., 142, 171, 182–183
Howell, D. C., 320
Howes, C., 370
Howland, R. H., 174, 181
Howlin, P., 264
Hoza, B., 322
Hser, Y. I., 356
Hu, R., 227
Huang, B., 53
Huang, C. C., 54
Huang-Pollock, C. L., 72
Hubbard, J. A., 300
Hubert, N. C., 274, 277, 279, 281
Hudson, J. I., 456
Hudson, J. L., 120–122, 130, 140, 456
Hudziak, J. J., 414
Huessy, H. R., 320
Huffman, L. C., 67
Hug-Hellmuth, H., 425
Hughes, C. W., 146, 163, 243
Hughes, J. N., 302, 307, 439–440
Huizinga, D., 353, 358
Hummel, B., 226

Hummel, R., 10, 320
Humphrey, L. L., 179, 337
Hunfeld, J. A., 404, 414
Hunter, W. M., 150, 393, 396
Hupp, S. C., 243
Huselid, R. F., 351
Hussong, A. M., 350
Huston, A., 9
Huston, L., 121
Hutz, M. H., 32
Hwang, B., 250
Hwu, H. G., 215
Hyams, J. S., 408
Hyland, L. T., 182
Hymel, S., 142
Hyman, S. E., 406–407, 412
Hynd, G. W., 125, 142, 276, 288
Hynes, M. E., 323

Iacono, W. G., 20, 186–187, 333, 360
Ialongo, N., 121, 186–187
Ialongo, N. S., 121, 186–187, 291
Ibbotson, B., 274
Ichim, L., 227
Ijzendoorn, M. H., 71, 87, 91
Ilardi, S. S., 185
Ilies, R., 234
Imhof, K., 319
Inderbitzen, H. M., 187
Ingman, K., 407
Ingram, J., 121
Ingram, R. E., 177–178
Inouye, J., 168
Institute of Medicine, 259
Ip, F., 241
Ireland, W. W., 30
Isaacs, L., 191
Isabella, R. A., 66
Isen, A. M., 43
Israel, A. C., 3–4
Izard, C. E., 182

Jackman, L. P., 337
Jackson, A. P., 54
Jackson, D., 324, 413
Jackson, S. I., 361
Jackson, S. R., 337
Jacobi, C., 332
Jacobs, J. K., 359
Jacobs, M. R., 9
Jacobson, J. W., 239–240
Jacobson, L., 43
Jacobson, N. S., 193, 445
Jacobvitz, D., 317
Jaenicke, C., 178
Jaffee, S. R., 187
Jahoda, M., 3
Jainchill, N., 358
Jamison, K. R., 170, 217
Jamner, L. D., 319
Jang, K. L., 379
Janoff-Bulman, R., 154
Jansen-McWilliams, L., 412
Janssen, I., 338
Jardine, R., 20
Jarecke, R., 293
Jarvinen, L., 179
Jaser, S. S., 167
Jayson, D., 192–193
Jefferson, J. W., 458
Jenkins, J. M., 53

Jenkins, J. R., 242
Jenkins, S. J., 399
Jennings, K. D., 104
Jensen, P. S., 6, 9–10, 21, 304, 354, 448
Jenson, J. M., 352–354
Jenson, W. R., 103
Jessor, R., 54, 354–355
Jessor, S. L., 54
Jindal, R., 174
Joffe, R., 224
John, O. P., 119
Johnson, D. L., 52
Johnson, E. M., 458
Johnson, J. G., 153, 188–189, 333, 335, 337, 369, 374, 378
Johnson, K. M., 156, 396
Johnson, L., 65
Johnson, M. C., 73–75
Johnson, M. O., 118
Johnson, M. R., 143
Johnson, P. A., 432
Johnson, S., 6, 429
Johnson, S. E., 281
Johnson-Sabine, E., 332
Johnston, C., 289, 321–322
Johnston, M. V., 32
Johsnston, L. D., 348, 352
Joiner, T. E., Jr., 119, 166, 168, 175, 177–178, 332
Jones, B. R., 53
Jones, D. J., 186
Jones, J., 337
Jones, J. G., 153
Jones, K., 285
Jones, K. L., 30
Jones, L., 302
Jones, P., 169
Jones, S., 64
Jones, S. M., 299
Jordan, L., 272
Jorm, A. F., 169
Joshi, V., 356
Jouriles, E. N., 9, 52
Joyce, P. R., 378
Judd, L. L., 165, 180–181
Judge, T. A., 234
Juffer, F., 71
Jung, K. G., 156
Jurkovic, G. J., 103, 108
Just, N., 177–178

Kabbaj, M., 176
Kabene, M., 356
Kadushin, C., 159
Kaemmer, B., 375
Kafantaris, V., 454
Kagan, J., 65, 67, 69, 90, 118, 120, 136–138, 143, 168, 301–302, 369, 405
Kahler, C. W., 360
Kahn, J. S., 192–193
Kahn, R. S., 53
Kahng, R. D., 440
Kaiser, P., 71
Kakiuchi, C., 25
Kalb, C., 448
Kalichman, S. C., 388
Kalin, N. H., 176
Kalis, R., 156
Kamboukos, D., 108
Kaminer, Y., 353, 356

Kaminski, K. M., 180, 182, 185
Kamphaus, R. W., 6, 124, 140, 304
Kanayama, W., 220
Kandel, D. B., 171, 187, 353, 355, 359
Kane, J. M., 454
Kane, M. T., 127
Kanner, L., 31
Kantor, G. K., 368, 376
Kaplan, A. S., 338
Kaplan, G. A., 49
Kaplan, H. I., 148, 154
Kaplan, N., 87
Kaplan, R. F., 32
Kaplow, J. B., 122
Kaprio, J., 19–21
Kapur, S., 227
Karbon, M., 76
Karver, M., 431
Kasari, C., 246–247, 256
Kasen, S., 188–190, 333, 335
Kashani, J. H., 33, 119, 170–171, 182, 217
Kashdan, T. B., 143
Kashikar-Zuck, S., 413
Kaslow, N. J., 177–179, 183, 185, 190, 192–193
Kastner, F., 456
Katainen, S., 179
Katic, M., 226, 256
Katz, L. F., 9, 52
Katz, M., 238
Katz, R. C., 405, 455
Katzelnick, D. J., 290
Katzenstein, T., 290
Katzman, M., 338
Katzow, J. J., 226
Kaufman, J., 11, 123, 140, 156, 173–175, 181, 376, 378, 396
Kautiainen, H., 411
Kavale, K. A., 277
Kavanagh, J. F., 33
Kawachi, I., 49
Kaye, W. H., 333–335, 340
Kazdin, A. E., 7, 101–102, 105, 110, 120, 135, 182, 185, 189, 291, 299, 307–308, 429–430
Keane, S. P., 74
Kearney, C. A., 121, 124
Keck, P. J., 226–227, 456
Keefe, F. J., 406, 412
Keefe, K., 103, 106
Keefe, S. E., 354
Keel, P. K., 332
Keeler, G., 6, 53, 119, 181
Keenan, K., 52, 64, 69–70, 72, 89, 285, 301–302, 306
Keener, A. D., 174
Kehle, T. J., 192–193
Keijsers, G. P., 409
Keil, J. E., 49
Keiley, M. K., 69, 175
Keith, B. R., 53, 289, 411
Keitner, G. I., 178
Kellam, S., 121, 186
Kelleher, K., 376, 412
Keller, M. B., 119, 121–122, 126, 139–140, 143, 169, 180–181, 195–196
Keller, T. E., 54
Kelly, J. B., 53

Kelsay, K., 434
Kelsey, D., 460
Kelsoe, J. R., 219
Keltikangas-Jarvinen, L., 179, 207
Kemmelmeier, M., 52, 60
Kenardy, J., 341
Kendall, P. C., 117–127, 182, 186, 288, 291, 307, 322, 439–440
Kendall-Tackett, K. A., 377, 388–389, 394
Kendell, R. E., 7
Kendler, K. S., 118–120, 137, 169, 172, 182, 335
Kennard, B. D., 173
Kennedy, H., 427
Kennedy, R. E., 171
Kennedy, S. H., 333, 339
Kennedy, W. A., 303
Kenny, D. A., 75
Kenny, M., 150, 154
Kenny, M. C., 276
Kenny, M. E., 178
Keogh, B. K., 274, 277
Kernberg, P., 430
Kerr, M. M., 139
Keshavan, M. S., 220, 259
Keshet, G. I., 176
Keskivaara, P., 179
Kessler, J., 426, 428
Kessler, R. C., 18–19, 51, 120, 137, 169–171, 180
Kestenbaum, R., 74, 87
Ketter, T., 227
Keys, A., 333
Keysor, C. S., 460
Kibby, M. Y., 440
Kiesler, D. J., 291
Kiesner, J., 187
Kilgore, K., 54
Killen, J. D., 118, 169, 332, 334–335
Kilpatrick, D. G., 153, 397
Kilts, C., 450
Kim, B. N., 324
Kim, K. J., 175
Kimonis, E. R., 299, 302–303, 306
King, H., 6
King, J., 324
King, N. J., 6, 100, 121, 127, 159, 399
King, R. A., 173, 414
Kingston, L., 70
Kinney, J. M., 380
Kinney, W. T., 172
Kinnish, K., 242
Kinzie, J. D., 153
Kirby, L. D., 253–254
Kirby, R. I., 433
Kirisci, L., 52, 359
Kirschenbaum, D. S., 337
Kirz, J., 355
Kistner, J. A., 180, 187, 377
Kitzman, H. J., 52, 94, 381
Klaric, S. H., 156
Klassen, R., 273
Klein, D. N., 166–169, 181, 189, 217
Klein, M., 425, 428–429
Klein, R. G., 128, 276, 285, 289, 300, 307, 321, 323
Kleinman, S., 319

Kleinrock, S., 225
Klerman, G. L., 169, 181, 194
Klimes-Dougan, B., 69
Kline, J., 140
Klinger, L. G., 173
Klump, K. L., 332–334
Knauer, D., 97
Knell, S., 429
Knight, D., 278
Knobloch, H., 258
Ko, J. Y., 226
Kobak, R. R., 178–179
Kocgel, R. L., 262
Koch, M. W., 181, 411
Kochanska, G., 169, 287–289, 291, 301–302
Koerner, J., 332
Kogan, E., 40–41
Kohut, H., 427–428
Kolko, D. J., 150, 154, 159, 367, 372, 375, 379–380
Koller, H., 238
Koller, J. R., 273, 279–280
Kolvin, I., 175
Konstantareas, M. M., 262
Koocher, G., 429
Koot, H. M., 69, 233
Koposov, R. A., 351
Kopp, C. O., 66, 73–74, 76, 287, 289, 291
Korn, S., 64, 66
Korotitsch, W., 119
Kortlander, E., 361
Koskenvuo, M., 21
Kotagal, P., 406
Kotler, L., 335
Kovacs, M., 181, 184–185, 218, 222, 396
Kowatch, R. A., 33, 173, 217, 225–227, 456, 461
Kraemer, H. C., 118, 169, 258, 308, 332, 336, 340
Kraepelin, E., 4, 167
Kraft, P. A. L., 166
Krain, A., 117
Kranzler, E., 156
Krasnegor, N., 33
Kratochvil, C. J., 460
Kratochwill, T. R., 238
Kraus, D. M., 458
Krauss, M. W., 104, 240–241
Krauter, K. S., 21
Kredich, D. W., 412
Kremenitzer, M. W., 461
Kretschmer, E., 167
Kriechman, A. M., 410
Kriel, R. L., 458
Krishnan, K. R., 220
Kriss, M. R., 181
Kristoff, B., 266
Krohn, M. D., 305, 359
Kroll, L., 192–193
Kropp, J., 9
Kruh, I. P., 300
Krull, J. L., 351
Krystal, J. H., 221
Kucharska-Pietura, K., 338
Kuczynski, L., 369
Kudler, H., 152
Kuhne, M., 285
Kulka, R. A., 169

Kumpfer, K. L., 110
Kunst, A. E., 49
Kuntsi, J., 318
Kuperminc, G. P., 100–103, 105–108, 175
Kupersmidt, J. B., 305, 377
Kurlakowsky, K. D., 175
Kurnra, S., 454
Kurtines, W. M., 440
Kusumakar, V., 226, 457
Kutcher, S. P., 182, 188, 226, 456
Kvas, E., 5

Lab, S. P., 367
Labellarte, M., 450
Labouvie, E. W., 350
Ladouceur, R., 118
LaFreniere, P. J., 286
La Greca, A. M., 117, 141–142, 151
Lahey, B. B., 6, 9, 52, 125, 142, 189, 285, 289, 300–301, 303, 321
Laird, M., 43, 52, 377
Lally, J. R., 52
Lamb, M. E., 178, 240
Lambert, N., 240
Lambert, P. C., 413
Lambert, R., 32
Lambert, S. F., 175
Lambert, W. W., 139
Lampert, C., 226, 340
Lampman, C., 439–440
Lampron, L. B., 291
Lancaster, R. S., 379
Land, D., 105, 111
Lane, R. D., 31, 72
Lang, A. R., 293, 322
Lang, B. A., 413
Lang, S., 74, 87
Langbehn, D. R., 285
Lange, P., 175
Langner, T. S., 52
LaPadula, M., 323
Lapidus, R. B., 108
Larocque, C., 32
Larrieu, J. A., 86–87, 91, 148, 370
Larson, B. S., 408
Larson, C. L., 72
Larson, N. C., 54
Larson, R., 176, 185
Last, C. G., 9, 117, 121–122, 135, 137
Last, C. L., 120, 135, 137
Latimer, W. W., 349, 355–356, 358
Lau, A. L., 241
Laub, J. H., 305
Laudenslager, M. L., 09
Lauer, J., 246–247
Laugesen, N., 118
Laughren, T., 455
Laurens, K. R., 441
Laurent, J., 119, 182
Lauritsen, J., 354
Lavigne, J. V., 88–89
Lavori, P. W., 180–181
Lawrence, J. W., 151
Lawrence, N. S., 220
Lawrence, P. S., 40
Lay, B., 337
Leach, J. N., 338

Leadbeater, B. J., 102–103, 105–107, 175–176
Leavitt, L. A., 75
LeBlanc, M., 52
Lebovitz, H. E., 227
Leckman, J. F., 235
LeCouteur, A., 257
Lecrubier, Y., 140
Lederer, A. S., 11, 136
Lee, B. C., 220
Lee, D. Y., 43
Lee, J., 281
Lee, J. S., 324
Lee, N. L., 259
Lee, S. S., 44
Leerkes, E., 87
Lefebvre, J. C., 406, 412
Lefebvre, L., 158, 377
Lefkowitz, M. M., 185, 299
LeGagnoux, G. L., 193
Leger, E., 118
Legg, C., 337
Legrand, L., 20
Le Grange, D., 340
Leifer, M., 393
Leino, E. V., 52
Leitenberg, H., 151
Leiter, J., 377
Leland, H., 240
LeMare, L. J., 142
Lemery, K. S., 64, 68
Le Moal, M., 176
Lena, B., 456
Lena, S. M., 338
Lengua, L. J., 68, 119, 169–170
Lentz, C., 54
Leon, G. R., 332
Leonard, H. L., 233–234, 238, 450
Leon Morris, S., 361
Lepine, J. P., 139–140
Lerner, J. V., 179
Lerner, J. W., 272, 275, 278
Lerner, M., 318
Lerner, R. M., 179
Lesser, R. P., 413
Lester, N., 406
Lester, P., 411–412
Letourneau, E., 192–193
Leukefcld, C., 324
Leve, L. D., 51
Leventhal, T., 53
Levesque, J., 73
Levin, G. M., 293
Levin, M., 406
Levitan, J., 176, 456
Levy, A. K., 370, 415
Levy, F., 21
Levy, S. M., 44
Lewinsohn, M., 122
Lewinsohn, P. M., 122, 166, 169, 171–172, 175, 178, 180–182, 185, 189–191, 193, 217, 219, 333–335, 352, 356, 360, 448
Lewis, C. E., 181, 411
Lewis, G., 169
Lewis, I., 391–392
Lewis, K., 179
Lewis, M., 72, 150, 235, 391
Lewis, M. A., 411
Lewis, M. L., 87
Lewis, M. S., 54
Lewis, S., 72

Leyser, Y., 242–244
Li, J., 182, 186
Lichenstein, P., 302
Liddle, H. A., 361
Liddle, P. F., 192–193
Lieb, R., 137, 407–408, 414
Lieberman, A. F., 95
Lieberman, J. A., 454
Liebowitz, M. R., 169
Liem, J. H., 176
Lightel, J., 53
Lilenfeld, L. R., 331, 333, 339
Lilienfeld, S. O., 300
Lindgren, S. D., 52
Lindholm, L., 181
Lindy, J. D., 148
Linehan, C., 341
Link, B. G., 48–49
Linna, S., 238
Lipman, E. L., 49, 53
Lipovsky, J. A., 149, 156, 393, 397
Lippke, L., 349
Lippman, M., 44
Lippmann, J., 154, 159, 398
Lipsey, M. W., 439
Lipsitt, L., 277
Litman, C., 287
Little, S. A., 170, 187
Little, S. S., 288–289
Little, T. D., 299
Little, W. J., 29, 34
Liu, X., 53
Livesley, W. J., 379
Livingston, R., 409, 412
Livingston, S., 30
Lizotte, A. J., 359
Lloyd, D. A., 48, 50, 53, 348
Lloyd, D. J., 354
Lo, E., 241
Lochman, J. E., 291, 300–301, 305, 307–308, 440–441
Loeber, R., 22, 189, 285, 289, 299–303
Lofthouse, N., 69
Lomax, L., 65
Lomax, R., 178
Loney, B. R., 299–304
Loney, J., 321, 460
Long, B.
Long, J. H., 142
Long, P., 308
Long, P. J., 135, 397
Longhurst, J. G., 176
Lonigan, C. J., 6, 69, 119, 151, 168, 429–430
Loomis, J. W., 272
Lopez, F. A., 460
Lopez, I. D., 324
Lord, C., 257, 266
Lorenz, A. R., 306
Lorenz, F. O., 54, 175
Lotter, V., 257–258
Lou, H. C., 177
Loukas, A., 351
Lovaas, O. I., 257, 260, 266
Lovald, B., 243
Lovejoy, M. C., 180
Loveland, K. A., 237
Lowe, G., 358
Lowe, N., 24
Lowe, T. L., 461

Lozano, J. M., 319
Luby, J. L., 88–90, 217, 223, 285
Lucas, C. P., 10, 123, 183, 320
Luce, K. H., 336
Lucenko, B. A., 397
Lucey, J. V., 32
Luckasson, R., 233, 239–240
Lukon, J., 72
Lundin, R., 11
Lung, C., 371
Luntz, B. K., 378
Luthar, S. S., 101, 105, 351
Luty, S. E., 378
Lutzker, J. R., 381
Luu, P., 72
Lydiard, R. B., 143
Lykken, D. T., 20
Lyman, R. D., 299, 307
Lynam, D. R., 285, 300, 302, 324
Lynch, D. L., 393
Lynch, J. W., 49
Lynch, K. G., 348
Lynch, M., 289, 370, 372–373
Lyon, G. R., 33
Lyon, T. D., 395
Lyons, B., 454
Lyons, J., 9
Lyons-Ruth, K., 87, 97
Lysaker, P. H., 379
Lytton, H., 9, 19, 52, 240, 286, 305, 369

Ma, Y., 103–104, 181
Macari, S., 5
Maccari, S., 176
Maccoby, E. E., 9, 287
MacDonald, J. P., 291
MacDonald, K., 234
MacDonald, M., 22
Macfie, J., 370
Macgowan, M. J., 361
Machan, J. T., 122
Mackenbach, J. P., 49
MacKenzie, M. J., 101, 105, 110
Mackner, L. M., 369
MacMahon, B., 259
MacMillan, D. L., 236, 238, 322
MacMillan, H., 33
MacMillan, V. M., 375–376
MacQueen, G., 224
Madden, N. A., 244
Madden, P. A., 52
Maddox, G. L., 56
Madon, S., 43
Maes, H. H., 21
Magee, T. N., 440
Magee, W. J., 137
Maggs, J. L., 350
Mahler, M. S., 427–428
Mahoney, G. J., 246
Maier, S. F., 409
Main, M., 87, 370
Maita, A. K., 76
Maker, A. H., 52
Maliantovitch, K., 356
Malinosky-Rummell, R., 375
Malkin, C. M., 178
Malone, S., 279
Malouff, J. M., 443
Maltby, N., 438
Maluish, A., 44

Manassis, K., 405
Mancini, C., 139, 338
Mandel, F. S., 331
Mangelsdorf, S. C., 66, 72–75, 87
Mangione, P. L., 52
Manimala, M. R., 410
Mann, A. H., 332
Mann, J. J., 220
Mannarino, A. P., 95, 148, 159–160, 388–399, 439
Mannuzza, S., 276, 321, 323
Manolis, M. B., 188
Mans, L., 237
Manson, S., 153
Marakovitz, S., 51
March, J. S., 123, 149, 159, 396, 439, 450
Marchand, J. F., 54
Marciano, P. L., 182, 189
Marcus, L., 266
Marcus, S. C., 195
Marder, S., 227
Mariani, J., 106
Markides, K. S., 56
Marmar, C. R., 48
Marmorstein, N. R., 186–187
Marnell, M., 341
Marsee, M. A., 306
Marshall, L., 306
Marshall, P. J., 67
Marshall, T. R., 65, 68–69
Marteinsdottir, I., 143
Marti-Hennenberg, C., 186
Martin, A., 173, 455
Martin, C. S., 52, 348
Martin, D., 21, 324
Martin, J. A., 9
Martin, J. K., 410
Martin, J. L., 397
Martin, J. M., 168, 177–178, 182, 187
Martin, N. C., 175
Martin, N. G., 20, 338
Martin, P. P., 104
Martinez, E., 336
Martinez, P., 108
Martini, D. R., 184
Marton, P., 188
Marvin, R., 95
Marzolf, D., 72–73
Mash, E. J., 40, 322, 442
Masheb, R. M., 341
Masi, G., 122
Masiak, M., 338
Mason, C., 167, 169
Mason, D. M., 70
Mason-Brothers, A., 364
Masse, L. C., 52
Mastaler, M., 407
Masten, A. S., 101, 105, 110, 142
Maszk, P., 76
Matas, L., 178
Mates, T. E., 262
Matheny, A.P., 67
Mathijssen, J. P., 69
Maton, K. L., 186
Matson, J. L., 238
Matthews, A., 124
Matthews, K. A., 176
Matthews, Z., 157
Matthys, W., 288
Maudsley, H., 30, 339

Maughan, B., 300
Maxfield, M. G., 378, 387
Maxwell, S. E., 183
May, R., 323
Mayberg, H. S., 221
Mayou, R., 403, 411
Mayville, S., 405
Mazure, C. M., 176
McAlpine, D. D., 53
McBurnett, K., 301
McCafferty, J. P., 196
McCarthy, E. D., 52
McCarthy, R., 32
McCarty, C. A., 167, 319
McCarty, J., 9
McCauley, E., 178–180, 186
McClanahan, L., 266
McClaskey, C., 288
McClearly, L., 186, 321
McClearn, G. E., 20, 27, 379
McClellan, J., 89, 183, 285
McCloskey, L. A., 55
McClure, J. M., 444
McCombs, A., 9, 52
McConaughy, S. H., 142, 182–183
McConnell, S., 244
McCord, J., 307, 361
McCoy, M. G., 302, 308
McCracken, A., 51
McCracken, J. T., 32, 319
McCrae, R. R., 136, 168–169, 234
McCrath, C., 413
McDonald, C., 121
McDonough, S. C., 95
McDuff, P., 306
McEachin, J. J., 266
McEachran, A. B., 375
McElroy, S. L., 226–227, 341, 456
McFadyen-Ketchum, S., 68, 70, 72
McFarlane, A. H., 175, 179
McGee, G. G., 264, 267
McGee, R. A., 327
McGee, R. O., 64, 70, 119–120, 166, 171, 264, 267, 273, 301, 317, 367
McGlashen, T. H., 221
McGoey, K., 317
McGonagle, K. A., 137, 171
McGrath, P. J., 404, 410
McGraw, K. L., 135
McGue, M., 20, 333, 360
McGuffin, P., 19, 21, 172–173, 183, 258, 379
McHale, J. L., 75
McHale, J. P., 293, 307
McHale, S. M., 262
McHenry, L. C., Jr., 30
McHugh, K. M., 38
McIntosh, D. E., 279–280, 317
McIntosh, R., 281
McKelvey, J. R., 32
McKeown, R. E., 179
McKinney, W. T., 172
McKnew, D. H., 140, 180, 456
McKnight, C. D., 128
McKnight Investigators, 334
McLaren, J., 238
McLeer, S. V., 148, 153, 159, 307, 389
McLeod, D. R., 126

McLeod, J., 51
McIntosh, D. E., 279–281, 317
McLoyd, V. C., 54, 107, 176
McMahon, R. J., 91, 286, 304, 376, 380
McMahon, S. D., 170
McMullin, J. A., 56
McNeil, C. B., 5, 308, 380
McNichol, K., 71
McPartland, J., 256
McPherson, R. S., 306
McPherson, W. B., 153
McRae, K., 72
McVey, G., 333
Meadows, E. A., 154
Mebert, C., 376
Mefford, I. N., 409
Meier-Hedde, R., 272
Meizitis, S., 192–193
Melchior, J. C., 411
Melloni, R. H., Jr., 324
Melton, G. B., 52, 291, 308
Meltzer, H., 6
Mendelson, M., 185
Mensch, B. S., 359
Mercer, A. R., 272
Mercer, C. D., 272
Mercier, H., 303
Merckelbach, H., 118
Merikangas, K. R., 69, 137, 170, 182
Mesibov, G. B., 258, 266
Messenheimer, J., 226
Messer, S. B., 427, 433–434
Messer, S. C., 186
Mesulam, M. M., 33
Metalsky, G. I., 167
Metsahonkala, L., 413
Metzger, R. L., 124
Meyer, B., 170
Meyer, C., 338
Meyer, E. C., 87
Meyer, T. J., 124
Meyer, W. J., 174, 200
Meyers, C. E., 211, 234
Mezzacappa, E., 76
Mezzich, A. C., 359
Mezzich, J. E., 301
Micheal, S. T., 52
Michel, M. K., 76
Michelson, D., 460
Michienzi, T., 156
Mick, E., 24, 285, 319
Mickelsen, O., 333
Mikkelsson, M., 411
Miklowitz, D. J., 225
Mikulis, D., 220
Milberger, S., 285
Milburn, A. K., 409
Miles, J. H., 259
Milich, R., 188, 322, 324, 460
Milkulich, S. K., 22
Miller, E., 41
Miller, G. E., 291, 307
Miller, I. W., 178
Miller, J. C., 413, 427
Miller, J. Y., 353
Miller, L. S., 108
Miller, M. L., 124
Miller, R. A., 32
Miller, R. L., 293
Miller, S., 72

Miller, T. L., 301
Miller, W. R., 358
Miller-Perrin, C. L., 368
Milnamow, M., 299
Milne, B. J., 303, 306
Milner, J. S., 373, 375
Milos, G., 432
Miltenberger, R. G., 41
Minderaa, R. B., 444
Mineka, S., 118, 167
Mink, I. T., 234
Minke, K. M., 242
Minshew, N. J., 259
Mintz, J., 220
Mintz, L. B., 336
Minuchin, S., 339, 415
Minzer, K., 32
Miranda, J., 177
Mitchell, C., 107
Mitchell, J. E., 331, 339–341
Mitchell, J. R., 178
Mitchell, S., 302–303
Mock, J., 185
Moene, F. C., 409
Moffitt, T. E., 52, 64, 70, 118–119, 166, 300, 302–303, 306, 317, 351, 360, 379
Moher, D., 324
Moilanen, D. L., 178
Mokros, H. B., 33, 183, 451
Molina, B. S., 320–321
Mollina, S., 126
Monroe, S. M., 170, 172, 175
Monti, P. M., 360–361
Monteaux, M. C., 320
Moore, C. W., 101, 105
Moore, D. W., 371
Moore, G. J., 33, 51
Moore, M., 433
Moore, P., 190
Moore-Motily, S., 390
Moradi, A. R., 122
Moran, G. S., 425, 430
Moran, P. B., 369
Moran, P. M., 176
Morgan, A., 308
Morgan, S. B., 262
Morgan, S. P., 53
Morgan, W. P., 30
Morison, P., 142
Morrell, J., 317
Morrell, W., 226
Morrier, D., 264
Morrill, C. M., 338
Morris, A. S., 69
Morris, A. S., 300–302, 304, 307
Morris, D. D., 60, 227, 437
Morris, J. S., 220
Morris, T. L., 5–6, 9, 139, 141
Morris-Friehe, M., 286
Morrissey-Kane, E., 444
Morris-Yates, A., 189
Morrow, K. B., 391
Moselle, K., 353, 359
Mosher, M., 299
Moss, H. B., 350, 359
Moss, S., 178, 274
Mott, M. A., 355
Mottron, L., 32
Moustakas, C., 426
Mowrer, O. A., 152, 154
Moyer, D., 76

Mrakotsky, C., 88–89
Mucci, M., 122
Mufson, L., 191, 194
Mulder, R. T., 378
Mulhern, R. K., 440
Mulholland, A. M., 336
Mulick, J. A., 239–240
Mullen, P. E., 397
Mullins, L. L., 187
Multimodal Treatment of ADHD, 448, 458
Mun, E., 69, 71
Mundy, P., 256, 263
Munn, P., 243
Munster, A. M., 151
Muratori, F., 430–431, 434
Muris, P., 118, 124, 138
Muroff, J. R., 353–354
Murphy, B. C., 76
Murphy, C. C., 233, 238–239
Murphy, C. M., 52
Murphy, D. A., 293
Murphy, D. B., 407
Murphy, K. R., 323
Murphy, S. M., 397
Murray, C., 337
Murray, L., 302, 317
Murray, M. C., 159
Murray, R., 169
Murray, S., 227
Murry, V. M., 351
Must, A., 337
Mustillo, S., 6, 119, 181
Myers, K. M., 155, 178, 182
Myers, L., 88, 389
Myers, M. G., 320, 349, 355, 360–361
Mykletun, A., 397
Mynatt, C. R., 40–41

Nachmias, M., 74–75
Nadder, T. S., 21
Nader, K., 155, 159–160
Nadrich, R., 225
Nagin, D. S., 55
Nahata, M. C., 324
Naish, N., 407–408
Nakash-Eisikovits, O., 370
Narikiyo, T., 9
Naring, G. W., 409
Nassir Ghaemi, S., 226
Nastasi, B. K., 52
Nath, S., 117
Nathan, P. E., 177
National Clearinghouse on Child Abuse and Neglect, 367
National Institute of Alcohol Abuse and Alcoholism, 358
National Institute of Mental Health, 10, 123, 165, 448, 450
National Research Council, 260, 262–263, 266, 268, 371
Nauta, M. H., 127
Nawrocki, T., 173
Neal, A. M., 11, 136
Neale, M. C., 18–19, 120, 137, 169, 172
Neighbors, B. D., 119
Nelson, D. A., 176
Nelson, E., 52
Nelson, G., 168
Nelson, J. C., 189

Nelson-Gray, R. O., 169
Nemeroff, C. B., 173
Neshat-Doost, H. T., 122
Neugebauer, R., 108
Neumann, D. A., 395
Neumark-Sztainer, D., 338
Neupert, S. D., 55
Newacheck, P. W., 413
Newby, K., 51
Newcomb, K., 308, 380
Newcomb, M. D., 353, 355–356, 358–359
Newcorn, J., 21, 316
Newman, A., 336
Newman, D. I., 122
Newman, D. L., 70, 169, 180, 306, 333, 335–336
Newman, J. P., 288
Newschaffer, C., 259
Newton, J. E. O., 153
Nicholls, J., 246–247
Nichols, S. L., 321
Nicol, A. R., 405, 407
Nicotra, E., 187
Nielsen, T. A., 44
Nieman, M. A., 456
Nigg, J. T., 72, 321, 323
Nightingale, J., 151–152, 158
Nihira, K., 234, 240
Nikolaou, V., 338
Nitschke, J. B., 174
Noh, S., 262
Nolan, E. E., 293, 318
Nolan, S. A., 180
Nolen-Hoeksema, S. K., 166–168, 171, 175, 177–178, 185
Norden, K. A., 378
Nordenfoft, M., 177
Nordhagen, R., 407
Norman, G. R., 175, 179
Norman, P. A., 335
Norton, P. J., 406
Nowakowski, M., 185
Nowicki, E. A., 279
Noyes, R., 169, 405, 412
Nunan, J., 408
Nyborg, V. M., 53

Oakman, J., 139
Oates, R. K., 379, 393–394
Oberklaid, F., 64, 70–71, 87
O'Boyle, C., 73
O'Brien, K. M., 233–234, 238, 301
Obrosky, D. S., 166
Ochsner, K. N., 73
Odom, S. L., 242, 244
O'Donovan, C., 226, 457
Office of Applied Studies, 352, 356
Offord, D. R., 47, 49, 53, 119, 170–172, 182, 274, 301, 407
O'Gorman, M., 169
O'Halloran, M. S., 336
Ohan, J. L., 155, 320
Ohannessian, C. M., 179
O'Hare, E., 180
Ohry, A., 415
Okamoto, A., 227
Okon, D. M., 337
Olafsdottir, E., 405
Olds, D. J., 52, 94
O'Leary, K. E., 52
O'Leary, S. G., 177, 307

Olfson, M., 171, 195
Ollendick, T. H., 6, 100–101, 109–110, 121, 127, 137, 246–247, 380, 440, 445
Olsen, S. F., 72
Olson, M., 288
Olson, R. L., 376
Olson, S. L., 54, 70
O'Malley, P. M., 348, 352, 354
O'Malley-Cannon, B., 266, 268
Opler, M. K., 52
Orr, S. P., 157
Orsmond, G. I., 240
Orvaschel, H., 52, 119–120, 182, 184, 389
Osberg, J. S., 56
Osborne, M. L., 299
Osler, W., 29–30
Osman, B. B., 273–274
Osofsky, J. D., 108
Ost, L., 138
Oster, H., 220
Oster, J., 408, 411
Osterhaus, J. T., 413
Osterling, J., 256, 260
O'Toole, B. I., 393–394
Otto, M. S., 139
Owens, E. B., 51, 64, 70, 77, 318
Owens, M. J., 173
Oxford, M., 302

Padilla, A. M., 354
Padula, G., 454
Pagani, L., 306
Page, G. P., 137
Pagni-Kurtz, L., 52
Paikoff, R. L., 186
Paley, B., 175
Palmer, D. S., 236, 241
Palmer, K., 444
Palombo, J., 273, 280
Panagiotides, H., 173
Panak, W. F., 178, 180, 182
Panarella, C., 338
Pande, A. C., 226
Pantin, H., 105
Papalos, D., 218
Papalos, J., 218
Papanicolaou, A. C., 33
Papatheodorou, G., 226, 456
Papini, D. R., 179
Paquette, V., 73
Parad, M., 433
Parad, N., 433
Pardini, D. A., 301–302, 307, 440
Paris, J., 150, 153, 158
Park, C., 54
Park, K. S., 288, 290
Parke, R. D., 369
Parker, G., 169, 179
Parker, J. D. A., 123, 132, 396
Parker, J. G., 123, 125, 302, 305, 377
Parker, K., 87
Parker, Randall, 262
Parks, S. M., 359
Paronen, A., 227
Parrone, P. L., 181
Patashnick, M., 246–247
Pathak, S., 448
Patrick, C. J., 303, 306
Patterson, C. J., 377

Patterson, G. R., 40, 44, 51, 54, 105–106, 286, 291, 301–302, 305–307, 380
Patterson, M. L., 182
Patton, G. C., 332, 334
Patton, J. R., 109, 278–279
Paul, G., 175
Paulauskas, S. L., 180–182
Paulosky, C. A., 336
Paulson, A., 91
Pavlakis, S. G., 319
Pavlidis, K., 178
Pavlov, I. P., 38
Pawl, F. H., 95
Pawl, J. H., 95
Paxton, S., 332
Payne, H., 380
Pearce, M. J., 338
Pearl, R., 274
Pearlin, L. I., 50
Pearson, J., 179
Pederson, S., 110
Pediatric OCD Treatment Study (POTS) Team, 450
Pedlow, K., 70
Pedlow, R., 87
Peebles, C. D., 90, 389
Peeke, L. A., 168, 182
Pelcovitz, D., 153, 157–158
Peleikis, D. E., 397
Pelham, W. E., Jr., 7, 293, 307, 320–322
Pelissolo, A., 139
Pellegrini, D., 142
Pelletier, D., 178
Penick, E. C., 31
Penn, D., 11
Penna, F., 410
Pennebaker., J. W., 433
Pennington, B. F., 272, 275–276, 287, 297
Perkins, R., 340
Perloff, J. N., 176
Perquin, C. W., 404, 414
Perrin, J., 337–338
Perrin, R. D., 368
Perrin, S., 40, 120, 135, 155–157
Perrino, T., 105
Perry, A. R., 367
Perry, C. L., 332
Perry, D. G., 287
Perry, J. C., 52–53, 63, 378
Perry, L. C., 287
Persons, J. B., 177
Petermann, F., 181
Peters, C. P., 379
Peters, G. A., 411
Peters, S., 410
Petersen, A. C., 171
Peterson, C., 44
Peterson, C. B., 337, 339–340
Peterson, D. R., 124
Peterson, J., 52–53
Peterson, L., 187
Peterson, R., 11
Petri, H. L., 42
Pettit, G. S., 54, 69–70, 158, 299–302, 305, 377
Pettit, J. W., 166
Pevalin, D. J., 51, 53, 55, 57, 171
Pfister, H., 407
Pham, B., 324

Phelan, J., 48–49
Phelps, C., 94
Philips, I., 221, 238
Phillips, B. M., 69, 119, 167–168
Phillips, K. A., 211, 408, 410, 414
Piacentini, J. C., 151
Pianta, R. C., 377
Picchi, L., 430
Pickens, J., 173
Pickering, K., 53
Pickett, W., 338
Pickles, A., 181, 258, 300
Pierce, E. W., 51
Pierce, W. D., 38, 41
Piercy, P., 433
Pihl, R. O., 52
Piira, T., 406
Pike, K. M., 336
Pilcher, J. J., 44
Pillay, S. S., 220
Pilowsky, I., 409
Pimentel, S., 122–123, 128
Pina, A. A., 123, 134
Pincus, A. L., 126
Pine, D. S., 76, 181, 194
Pinquart, M., 111
Pipe, B., 139
Pishkin, V., 359
Pitson, D., 319
Pitts, S. C., 358–359
Pituch, K. J., 319
Pizzagalli, D., 174
Place, M., 286
Platt, R., 53
Pliszka, S. R., 458
Plomin, R., 19, 66, 168, 172–173, 302, 379
Plotsky, P. M., 173
Plummer, A. T., 456
Plummer, C. M., 118
Pober, B. R., 235
Pock, P. J., 404
Podolski, C. L., 321
Pogrund, R., 407
Polaino-Lorente, A., 171
Polansky, N. A., 375
Polansky, N. F., 375
Poli, P., 122
Polivy, J., 334, 336, 341
Pollack, M. H., 348
Pollice, C., 333, 339
Pollock, M., 180–181, 222
Pollock, V. E., 395
Polloway, E. A., 278–279
Poltyrev, T., 176
Pomeroy, C., 338
Pope, H. G., Jr., 456
Popper, C. W., 324
Porges, S. W., 67, 76, 90
Portales, A.L., 67
Porter, F. L., 67
Posner, M. I., 64–66, 72, 74, 76, 166
Post, J. C., 319
Post, R. M., 224
Poston, W. S., 336
Potter, L., 93
Potthoff, J. G., 175
Poulin, F., 299, 361
Poulin, L., 187
Powell, B., 95
Powell, K. B., 32

Power, M. J., 244, 246–247
Powers, B., 177, 187
Powers, S. W., 410
Poznanski, E. O., 33, 183–184, 451
Prabucki, K., 182
Preisig, M. A., 69
Prendergast, M., 411
Presnell, K., 331, 334–335, 341
Price, J. M., 299–300, 305
Price, J. N., 288
Price, L., 273, 279–280
Price-Swinson, R., 405
Prins, P. J. M., 445
Prinstein, M. J., 105, 159, 187, 299, 338
Prinz, R. J., 291, 307, 444
Prior, M., 64, 70–71, 87
Pritchard, C. T., 404
Procopis, P., 404, 413
Proskauer, S., 434
Prosser, H., 274
Prusoff, B. A., 173
Pruzinsky, T., 179
Przybeck, T. R., 21, 166, 331
Puente, R. M., 226
Pugh, K. R., 275
Puig-Antich, J., 10, 174, 179, 183, 185–187
Pulkkinen, L., 19–21
Putnam, F. W., 88, 389
Putnam, K. M., 72, 174
Puttler, L. I., 69
Puura, K., 170
Pynoos, R. S., 151–152, 155–157, 159

Qian, Q., 32
Quakley, S., 444
Qualter, P., 243
Quay, H. C., 124, 171, 285, 316, 319
Quaytman, M. S., 379
Quiggle, N. L., 182
Quinlan, D. M., 176, 189
Quittner, A. L., 318

Rabian, B., 11
Rachal, J. V., 355
Racine, Y., 49, 53, 274
Racoosin, J., 455
Racusin, G. R., 178
Radebaugh, M. R., 338
Radloff, L. S., 185
Rae, W., 432
Rafaelsen, O. J., 456
Ragan, J., 186
Raikes, H. A., 105
Raikkonen, K., 179
Ralphe, D. L., 148, 153, 389
Ralston, M. E., 380
Ram, A., 370
Ramey, C. T., 52, 87, 381
Ramirez, S. Z., 238
Ramirez-Valles, J., 186
Ramklint, M., 189–190
Ramsey, E., 105, 286
Randall, J., 119
Randall, P., 186, 262
Rangel, L., 406
Rank, M. R., 53
Ranseen, J. D., 323, 337
Rao, U., 11, 140, 180–181, 187

Rapee, R. M., 120–121, 124, 127, 140, 178, 440–441
Rapoport, J. L., 450, 460
Rappaport, S., 377
Rappley, M. D., 448
Rasmussen, E. R., 21
Rasmussen, R., 380
Ratcliff, K. S., 354
Ratey, J. J., 233, 239
Rathus, J. H., 375
Ratzoni, G., 227
Rauch, S. L., 143
Raute, N. J., 456
Raymer, D., 410
Raymond, N. C., 341
Raynor, P., 170, 179
Reber, M., 307
Reeves, K., 227
Reeves, R. S., 336
Rehm, L. P., 179
Reich, J. H., 123, 126
Reich, W., 11, 137, 140, 157, 169, 183–184
Reid, G. J., 413
Reid, H., 106
Reid, J. B., 40, 51, 301
Reid, J. C., 162
Reiff, H. B., 273, 277, 279–280
Reilly, J., 409
Reinherz, H. Z., 172, 374
Reinicke, M. A., 439–440
Reis, B. F., 191
Reiss, D., 173, 432
Reitman, D., 10, 320
Reitzel-Jaffe, D., 158, 377
Remington, G., 227, 317
Rende, R. D., 173
Renier, W. O., 404
Rennie, T. A. C., 52
Renshaw, P. F., 220
Research Unit on Pediatric Psychopharmacology, 451
Resick, P., 154
Resnick, H. S., 52
Resnick, S., 65, 74
Resnick, T. J., 408
Rey, J. M., 189
Reynolds, A. J., 52
Reynolds, C. A., 182, 185, 192–193
Reynolds, C. R., 6, 123–124, 140–141
Reynolds, R. W., 301
Reynolds, S., 444
Reynolds, W. M., 205, 207
Reznick, J. S., 67, 69, 81, 405
Reznick, S. J., 90, 118, 120
Rhee, S. H., 21
Rhodes, J., 409
Ribera, J., 10
Ricci, L. A., 240
Rich, R., 273, 280
Richard, B., 246–247, 288
Richards, G. E., 83, 174, 182
Richards, J. A., 225
Richardson, S. A., 238
Richmond, B. O., 123, 141
Richter, L., 52, 351
Richters, J. E., 108
Rickels, K., 128
Riddle, M. A., 450
Ridge, B., 70

Ridgeway, D., 287
Ridley Johnson, R., 187
Riese, M. L., 67
Rietschlin, J., 55
Riggs, P. D., 159
Riley, A., 301
Riley, B., 19
Riniti, J., 178
Riordan, K., 65, 74
Risi, S., 180
Riso, L. P., 331
Ritvo, E. R., 31, 264
Ritvo, R., 264
Rivara, F. P., 411
River, L., 11
Rivers, J. W., 263
Rizley, R., 376
Rizvi, S. L., 336–337
Rizzotto, L., 128
Roach, M. A., 240
Robb, A. S., 224
Roberson-Nay, R., 138
Roberts, B. R., 234, 246–247
Roberts, H., 406
Roberts, N., 171
Roberts, R. E., 185, 188, 318, 352, 448
Roberts, R. N., 381
Robertson, J., 178, 251
Robin, J. A., 117
Robins, E., 31, 119
Robins, L. N., 48, 52, 306, 354
Robinson, C. C., 72
Robinson, E. A., 376
Robinson, N. S., 168, 178
Robinson, T. R., 439–440
Robison, L. M., 318
Rodrigue, J. R., 262
Rodriguez, N., 156
Roeleveld, N., 238
Roelofs, K., 409
Roemer, L., 126
Roerig, J. L., 340
Rogers, S. J., 256, 260, 267–268
Rogers, W., 165
Rogers-Adkinson, D., 286
Roggman, L. A., 179
Rogler, L., 8
Rogosch, F. A., 370–371
Rohde, L. A., 32
Rohde, P., 122, 169, 171, 175, 178, 180–182, 189, 191, 193–194, 331, 360
Rojahn, J., 235
Rollnick, S., 358
Romagnoli, G., 430
Roman, T., 32
Romano, R., 122
Romans, S. E., 397
Romeny, D., 9
Romer, D., 105
Romig, C. J., 52
Romney, D. M., 52, 286, 305, 369
Ronan, K. R., 288, 307
Root, M. P., 158
Rosa, P., 303
Rosario, M., 106, 158, 377
Rose, F., 337
Rose, G., 47–48
Rose, R. J., 19–22
Rosemery, O., 168
Rosen, G. D., 33

Rosen, J. W., 243, 245
Rosen, L. A., 323
Rosen, M., 53
Rosenbaum, J. F., 120, 169, 405
Rosenbaum, M., 331
Rosenberg, D. R., 33, 450
Rosenberg, H., 226
Rosenblatt, A., 318
Rosenfeld, A. A., 319, 407
Rosenthal, R., 43, 439
Rosicky, J., 65, 76
Rosman, B., 339, 415
Rosner, B. A., 237
Ross, A. O., 307
Ross, D., 42
Ross, S. A., 42, 283
Rossello, J., 191, 193
Rossiter, E. M., 341
Rost, K. M., 414
Roth, W. T., 153, 157
Rothbart, M. K., 64–70, 72–74, 76, 150, 166–168, 287, 301
Rothbaum, B. O., 154
Rotheram-Borus, M., 106
Rothstein, A. A., 273–274, 277–278, 280
Rounds-Bryant, J. L., 356
Rounsville, B. J., 194
Rourke, B. P., 33, 272–276, 288
Rousseau, C., 53
Rowe, C. L., 356
Rowe, D. C., 107
Rowe, E., 52, 377
Rowland, M. D., 308, 381
Roy, A., 378
Rubin, K. H., 71, 77, 125, 142, 156, 186, 302, 439–440
Rubio-Stipec, M., 10, 52
Ruchkin, V. V., 52, 54, 351
Ruckstuhl, L. E., 287
Rudolf, M. C. J., 170, 179
Rudolph, K. D., 167, 175–177, 180, 182, 186–189
Ruedrich, S., 235
Rueter, M. A., 179
Ruff, H., 65, 73
Ruggiero, L., 185
Rumsey, J. M., 33
Runyan, D. K., 150, 371, 374, 393, 396
Ruo, B., 404
Rush, A. J., 190, 227
Russ, S. W., 425–430, 432–434
Russell, A., 72
Russell, G. F. M., 339–340
Russell, R., 425, 427, 430
Russo, M. F., 300
Rutanen, M., 31
Rutherland, R. B., 241
Rutman, J., 31
Rutter, M. L., 11, 21, 52–53, 100, 151, 171, 173, 181–182, 257–258, 300
Ruzicka, D. L., 91
Ryan, E., 154
Ryan, N. D., 11, 140, 166, 171, 173–175, 185, 190, 195
Ryan, N. E., 439–440
Ryan, S., 121
Ryan, S. M., 409
Ryder, A. G., 167
Rzepski, B., 408

Saavedra, L. M., 123
Sabo, A. N., 153
Sachs, G. S., 227
Sack, A., 105
Sack, W. H., 122, 153
Sacks, N., 180
Sadeh, A., 90
Sadock, B. J., 148, 154
Safer, D. J., 461
Safer, D. L., 340
Safir, M. P., 259
Sagestrano, L. M., 186
Saigh, P. A., 157
Saito, E., 455
Salminen, J. J., 411
Salmon, P., 409
Salonen, J. T., 49
Saltzman, H., 170
Salzinger, S., 158, 377
Sambasivan, K., 338
Sameroff, A. J., 52, 54, 65, 74, 86–87, 91, 100–101, 104–105, 110, 289, 369
Sampson, R., 305, 354
Sanders, J. L., 262
Sanders, M. R., 11, 415
Sanderson, W. C., 126
Sandhu, S., 244, 247
Sandler, I. N., 68, 169–170
Sands, K., 179
Sandy, J. M., 70, 351
Sanford, M., 186
Sanger, D. D., 286
Sanner, J., 432
Sanson, A., 64, 70–71, 87
Santiago, N. J., 166
Santonastaso, P., 334
Sapir, Y., 370
Sarafino, E. P., 38
Sarigiani, P. A., 171
Sas, L., 156
Satz, P., 276–277
Saunders, B. E., 35–36, 159, 393, 397, 399
Saunders, L., 379
Sauzier, M., 390
Sax, K. W., 220–221
Sayer, J., 319
Saylor, C. F., 185
Saywitz, K. J., 389, 395
Scahill, L., 455
Scaramella, L., 179
Schachar, R. J., 285, 318
Schachter, S., 43, 324
Schall, C., 262
Schalock, R. L., 243
Schanberg, L. E., 412
Scharff, L., 408
Scharko, A., 452
Scheer, P., 5
Scheeringa, M. S., 87–88, 90, 148–149, 389
Scheffer, R., 227
Schendel, D., 233
Scheuermann, B., 242
Schiller, M., 65, 70, 74
Schilling, E. M., 70
Schmidt, C. W., 151
Schmidt, L. A., 67–68
Schmidt, M. H., 337
Schmitz, S., 71

Schneider, M. L., 176–177, 246–247, 331
Schneider, P. A., 336
Schneider, R., 74
Schneider, T., 172
Schnicke, M. K., 154
Schniering, C. A., 140
Schnur, J., 43
Schnurr, P. P., 150, 152, 158–159
Schoenwald, S. K., 308, 381
Scholer, M., 406
Scholing, A., 444
Schonberg, M., 72
Schopler, E., 240, 266
Schoppe, S. J., 66
Schraedley, P. K., 176
Schroeder, H. E., 120, 440, 445
Schuckit, M. A., 140
Schuengel, C., 91
Schulberg, H. C., 194
Schulenberg, J. E., 348, 350
Schuller, D. R., 167
Schulte, A., 159
Schultz, A., 159
Schultz, D., 77
Schultz, L. A., 178
Schunk, D. H., 246–247
Schutte, N. S., 443
Schwab-Stone, M. E., 10, 108, 123, 183, 320
Schwartz, C. E., 143
Schwartz, D., 300
Schwartz, J. A. J., 182, 189
Schwartz, S. E., 47
Schweinhart, L., 52
Schwiers, M., 226–227
Sclar, D. A., 318
Scott, B., 332
Scotti, J. R., 5–6, 9
Secher, S. M., 179
Sedlak, A.J., 368, 371
Sedlar, G., 367
Seed, M., 69
Seedat, S., 128
Seeley, J. R., 122, 166, 169, 171–172, 175, 180–182, 189, 191, 193, 217, 333–335, 352, 360, 448
Segal, D. L., 337
Segal, J., 227, 370
Segal, Z. V., 170, 177
Seidman, E., 110
Seidman, L. J., 277, 321
Seifer, R., 52, 54, 65, 74
Seligman, M. E. P., 110, 166, 177
Selikowitz, M., 32
Sellers, A. H., 397
Semrud-Clikeman, M., 276
Serbin, L., 9
Serketich, W. J., 286
Serna, L., 109
Seroczynski, A. D., 168, 178, 182
Sevcik, R. A., 104
Severson, H. H., 351
Shader, R. J., 458
Shafer, M., 105
Shaffer, D., 10, 123, 140, 183–184, 195, 301, 320
Shahar, G., 103
Shakerin, L. R., 409
Shalev, R. S., 33
Shankman, S. A., 166
Shannon, M. P., 151

Shapiro, A. K., 32
Shapiro, E., 32
Shapiro, E. G., 407
Shapiro, J. P., 393
Shapiro, J. R., 72–73, 273, 280
Shapiro, R. W., 180
Shapiro, S. E., 124
Sharpe, M., 403
Shaver, A. E., 111
Shaver, D., 80
Shaw, B. F., 170
Shaw, D. S., 51–53, 64, 69–70, 72, 77, 89, 301
Shaw, H., 331, 335, 337
Shaw, K., 142
Shayka, J. J., 123
Shaywitz, B. A., 275, 461
Shaywitz, S. E., 33, 275–276
Shea, V., 266
Shear, K., 171
Sheeber, L. B., 179, 186
Sheely, R. K., 267
Sheitman, B. B., 454
Shelby, J., 434
Shelton, K. K., 302
Shelton, R. C., 193
Shelton, T. L., 290
Shepherd, R., 415
Sher, K. J., 169
Sherboume, C. D., 165
Sherman, F. G., 33
Sherrill, C., 237
Sherrill, J., 10, 166
Shevell, M., 32
Shields, A., 300, 377
Shih, J. H., 167
Shin, L. M., 143
Shiner, R. L., 64, 72, 166–168, 333
Shipman, K. L., 74, 370
Shipman, R., 410
Shirk, S. W., 425, 427, 430–431
Shmelyov, A. G., 168
Shnit, D., 370
Shoda, Y., 234
Shonk, S. M., 377
Shonkoff, J. P., 104
Shortt, A. L., 121, 127
Shreeve, W. C., 338
Shull, R. L., 40
Shuster, B., 337
Shute, N., 448
Shy, C. M., 48
Sickel, R., 90
Siebelink, B. M., 138
Siegel, B., 256–258, 260–261, 265
Siegel, C. H., 434
Siegel, L., 117
Siegel, T. C., 291
Sienna, M., 290
Sigman, M. D., 246–247, 256, 263
Sigvardsson, S., 17
Sijben, N., 404
Sikich, L., 454
Silbereisen, R. K., 111
Silberg, J. L., 21, 182, 194
Siler, M., 178
Silk, J. S., 117
Sillanpaa, M., 413
Silon, E. L., 237, 244
Silovsky, J. F., 274, 278, 392
Silva, P. A., 52, 64, 70, 119, 136, 166, 169, 171, 300–301, 317

Silver, A. A., 272, 274–277, 281
Silver, E. K., 343
Silver, H. K., 367
Silver, L. B., 375
Silverman, A. B., 172, 374
Silverman, F. N., 367
Silverman, R., 95
Silverman, W. K., 11, 117, 120, 123, 127, 140, 144, 151, 159, 186, 440
Silvern, L., 375
Silverthorn, P., 39, 299–302, 306
Sim, H., 186, 188
Simeon, J., 128
Simeonsson, R. J., 262
Simmons, A., 36
Simon, G. E., 452
Simon, H., 176
Simonds, J. F., 33, 171
Simoneau, T. L., 225
Simonian, S. J., 142
Simonoff, E., 21, 258
Simons, A. D., 170, 172
Simons, R. L., 54, 175, 178–179
Singer, D., 427, 429
Singer, H. S., 32
Singer, J., 43
Singh, M., 189
Siqueland, L., 121, 128, 191
Sisson, D. P., 223
Skaer, T. L., 318
Skeem, J., 306
Skerlec, L. M., 119
Skinner, B. F., 39–42
Skinner, M., 100, 258
Skinner, M. L., 305
Skinner, W. F., 350
Skodol, A. E., 188–190
Skuse, D. H., 179, 286
Slade, P., 330
Slattery, M. J., 69
Slavin, R. E., 244
Slesnick, N., 186
Sloan, J., 262
Slovic, P., 351
Slutske, W. S., 22
Smailes, E. M., 153, 188–190, 378
Smallish, L., 319–320, 322, 324
Smart, D., 64, 70–71
Smider, N. A., 68
Smiroldo, B. B., 238
Smith, A. C. M., 236
Smith, A. J., 410
Smith, A. M., 302
Smith, B., 320
Smith, C., 392
Smith, C. A., 409–410
Smith, C. L., 73–75
Smith, D., 103, 108–109
Smith, E. A., 33
Smith, G. R., 412, 414
Smith, J. A., 390
Smith, J. E., 337
Smith, J. M., 242
Smith, K., 186
Smith, L. A., 291, 308
Smith, M., 76, 302, 336
Smith, M. G., 118
Smith, P., 155, 306
Smith, S. W., 439–440
Smith, T., 260, 266

Smucker, M. R., 185
Smulders, D., 138
Smyrnios, K., 433
Snider, L. A., 33
Snidman, N., 65, 67, 69, 90, 118, 120, 137–138, 168, 301, 405
Snyder, J. J., 54, 454
Soares, J. C., 220
Sobol, A., 337–338
Sofronoff, K., 321
Solomon, J., 370
Somberg, D., 43, 45
Songster, T., 246–247
Sonuga-Barke, E. J., 317–318
Soong, W., 351
Sorenson, E., 179
Sorter, M., 227
Sosnowski, P. B., 380
Southam-Gerow, M. A., 127, 167, 440
Soutullo, C., 227
Spangler, D., 335
Sparrow, S., 34, 93, 240
Speechley, M., 262
Speltz, M. L., 89, 242, 285, 290
Spence, M. A., 121, 127, 193
Spence, S. H., 441, 444
Spencer, T., 324, 460
Spieker, S. J., 54, 173
Spielberger, C. D., 123
Spielman, R. S., 25
Spierings, C., 404, 407
Spinrad, T. L., 76, 287
Spirito, A., 106, 185
Spiro, A., 169
Spitz, R. A., 170
Spitzer, R. L., 31, 257, 337
Spoth, R. L., 43
Spreen, O., 276–277
Sprich, S., 21, 317
Springer, J., 262
Spritzer, K., 165
Spruill, K. L., 279–280
Spurlock, J., 8
Spurzheimer, J. C., 29
Squires, J., 93
Srole, L., 52
Sroufe, A. L., 73
Sroufe, L. A., 9, 87, 100, 102, 121, 178, 237, 317, 370
Staab, J., 356
Stafford, B., 88–89
Staley, J. E., 180
Stallings, M. C., 21
Stallings, P., 123, 396
Stallone, F., 169
Stams, G. J., 71
Stang, P. E., 413
Stanger, C., 183, 410
Stansbury, K., 67–68, 180
Stanton, W. R., 70, 300
Stark, K. D., 179, 186, 192–193
Starr, R., Jr., 369
State, M., 455
Staton, R. D., 33
Stauffer, L. B., 159, 398
Stedge, D. J., 454
Steele, B. F., 367
Steele, H., 87
Steele, M., 87
Steer, R., 154, 159, 398–399
Stein, D., 179

Stein, M. B., 128, 132, 137, 140, 153
Steinberg, A. M., 151, 156
Steinberg, L., 101–102, 110–111, 121, 187
Steiner, H., 157–158
Steingard, R. J., 293
Steinglass, J. E., 339–341
Steinhausen, H. C., 319–320, 339, 407
Steinhauser, K., 56
Stemberger, R. T., 138
Stephen, M. S., 238
Stern, A., 393
Stern, D. N., 91, 95
Stern, L., 140
Stern-Bruschweiler, N., 91
Stevens, D., 302
Stevens, J., 318, 320
Stevens, L. J., 286
Stevens, M. A., 32
Stevenson, J., 175–176, 302, 318, 404
Stevenson-Hinde, J., 136
Stewart, C. M., 450
Stewart, D. G., 360
Stewart, G. W., 120, 189
Stewart, M. A., 285
Stewart, S., 71, 80, 83
Stewart, S. H., 71, 406
Stewart-Brown, S., 52
Stice, E., 186, 188, 331–332, 334–337, 341, 355
Stickle, T. R., 303
Stickler, G. B., 407
Stifter, C. A., 65, 67, 72–76, 287–288, 291
Stigum, H., 407
Still, G. F., 30
Stinchfield, R. D., 349, 355
Stockdale, D. E., 432
Stolar, M., 182
Stone, J., 404
Stone, W. L., 141–142
Stonehill, E., 333, 339
Stoneman, Z., 263
Stoolmiller, M., 17, 305
Storm, B., 432
Stormschak, E., 290
Stouthamer-Loeber, M., 22, 54, 119, 302
Stradling, J. R., 319
Strain, P., 244, 264, 267
Strakowski, S. M., 226
Strassberg, Z., 302
Straus, M. A., 367–368, 371, 376
Strauss, C. C., 9, 122, 124–125, 135, 142, 186–188
Strauss, M. A., 392
Stravynski, A., 378
Striegel-Moore, R. H., 335–337
Strober, M., 226, 331, 334, 340
Strobino, D. M., 17
Strully, C., 243
Strully, J. L., 243
Stuart, S., 405, 412
Stuber, M. L., 156
Sturges, J. W., 410
Suddath, R. L., 225
Sudler, N., 178
Sue, D., 8
Sue, S., 8

Suess, G. J., 87
Sugarman, D. B., 376
Suijlekom-Smit, L. W., 404
Suler, J., 433
Sullivan, K., 123, 396
Sullivan, L., 31
Sullivan, M. J., 406
Sullivan, P. F., 172, 245, 335
Surtees, P. G., 176
Sutandar-Pinnock, K., 338
Swain, N. R., 306
Swain-Campbell, N., 187, 203
Swan-Kremeier, L., 340
Swann, A. C., 227
Swanson, J. M., 279, 281, 308, 318
Swanston, H., 394
Swartz, M. S., 171
Swearingen, L., 77
Swedo, S. E., 32–33
Sweeney, J. A., 192–193, 259
Sweeney, L., 177
Swendsen, J. D., 69
Swenson, C. C., 154, 160, 379
Swingle, J. M., 397
Switzky, H. N., 235–237
Symons, D. K., 321
Symons, H., 331
Szalai, J. P., 226, 456
Szapocznik, J., 105
Szmukler, G. I., 339–340

Taghavi, M. R., 122
Taibleson, C., 123
Takahashi, L. K., 176, 259, 270, 426
Tally, S. R., 186
Tamminen, T., 408
Tamplin, A., 175, 179
Tannock, R., 285, 318
Taplin, J. E., 406
Target, M., 431
Tarolla, S., 360
Tarrier, N., 151–152, 158
Tarter, R. E., 349–350, 356, 359
Taska, L. S., 150, 391
Tassi, F., 246–247
Tatelbaum, R. C., 52
Taussig, C., 299
Tawile, V., 450
Taylor, A., 379
Taylor, C. B., 118, 169, 334–335, 338, 409
Taylor, C. M., 151
Taylor, E. B., 167
Taylor, H. L., 333
Taylor, J., 316, 360
Taylor, L., 178
Taylor, S., 406
Taylor, S. E., 44, 242, 244
Taylor, T. K., 286
Taylor, W. R., 413
Tellegen, A., 375
Teasdale, J., 177
Tebbutt, K., 394
Telch, C. F., 336, 340–341
Terr, L. C., 154–155
Terry, R., 305
Tervo, K., 138
Tesiny, E. P., 179, 185
Teti, L. O., 76, 397
Thakkar-Kolar, R., 154
Thaper, A., 21, 172–173
Thase, M. E., 174, 181

Thastum, M., 406
Thelen, M., 336
Themner, U., 238
Thomas, A., 9, 64–66, 100, 136, 156, 277, 289
Thomas, H., 166–168, 409
Thomas, J., 5–6, 369
Thomas, J. R., 88–89
Thompson, J. K., 334
Thompson, M. C., 186, 318
Thompson, R. A., 78, 105
Thompson, R. J., 273
Thompson, R. L., 121
Thompson, W. R., 19, 22
Thomsen, A. H., 170, 408–409
Thornberry, T. P., 359
Thorpe, C., 55
Thunstrom, M., 317
Thurber, C. A., 192–193
Thurm, A. E., 170
Tillfors, M., 143
Tillman, R., 218, 221
Timbers, D. M., 56
Tipp, J. E., 306
Tirosh, E., 259
Todd, J., 38
Todd, R. D., 16, 19, 21, 220
Toedter, L., 374
Tohen, M. F., 218, 220, 227
Tolan, P. H., 52, 54, 103, 108–109
Tomarken, A. J., 174
Tompson, M., 179
Tonge, B. J., 234, 235
Torgersen, S., 143, 409
Torgesen, J. K., 273, 281
Toth, S. L., 77, 94, 100–102, 104, 106, 108, 370, 372–374
Toupin, J., 303
Touyz, S., 338
Towne, R. C., 244
Tozzi, F., 339
Tracey, S. A., 117, 124
Trad, P. V., 170, 178–179
Tram, J. M., 178, 183
Traver, R. E., 355
Treadwell, K. H., 120
Treadwell, K. R., 117, 156, 396
Treasure, D. C., 246–247
Treasure, J. L., 335, 338, 340
Treatment for Adolescents with Depression Study Team (TADS), 190, 448, 451–452
Treffers, P. D., 138
Tremblay, R. E., 51–52, 54–55, 71, 306
Trickett, P. K., 369
Troop, N. A., 338
Troughton, E. P., 285
Trowell, J., 399
Truax, P., 193
Truglio, R., 182, 187
Trull, T. J., 378
Tryon, G. S., 273
Tschann, J. M., 71, 72, 105
Tubman, J. G., 361
Tucker, D. M., 72
Tuma, J. M., 425, 427
Tuomilehto, J., 49
Tupling, H., 179
Turbin, M. S., 354
Turgeon, L., 187
Turkheimer, E., 103, 107

Turner, J. B., 51
Turner, J. E., 167–168
Turner, R. J., 48, 50, 238, 352–353
Turner, S. M., 120, 135, 137–139, 141–144
Turner, T. M., 180
Twamley, E. W., 176
Twenge, J. M., 185
Twentyman, C. T., 369
Twombly, E., 93
Tyc, V. L., 440
Tyler, L., 301
Tyson, P., 425
Tyson, R. L., 425, 427

Udry, J. R., 57
Uhlemann, M. R., 43
Ulrich, R., 301
Unis, A. S., 185, 291
Upchurch, J., 432
Urquiza, A., 380
U.S. Department of Education, 275, 277

Valla, J., 184
Valliere, J., 91
Van Ameringen, M., 139
VanBrakle, J., 317
Van Den Bros, J., 354
van der Kamp, L. J., 151
van der Kolk, B., 154
van der Ploeg, H. M., 151
Vanderryn, J., 354
van de Ven, M., 118
Van Egeland, H., 288
Van Hasselt, V. B., 40–41, 337, 375
van Ijzendoorn, M., 71, 87, 91
Van Kammen, W. B., 302
van Lieshout, C. F. M., 166, 236
van Oosten, A., 138
van Os, J., 169
Van Slyke, D. A., 409–410
van Suijlekom-Smit, L. W., 404, 419
Van Yperen, N. W., 244
Vanyukov, M., 350
Vasey, M. W., 119
Vasudevan, P., 227
Vaughan, R., 106
Vaughn, B., 66
Vaughn, S., 273–274, 279, 281
Vaught, M. H., 413
Vazsonyi, A. T., 107
Vega, W. A., 353–355
Vella, D. D., 170
Veloso, F., 406
Velting, O. N., 442
Verduin, T. L., 120, 122
Verhulst, F. C., 69, 183
Vernberg, E. M., 159, 299
Vernon, P. A., 379
Veronen, L. J., 397
Versage, E. M., 172
Viding, E., 302
Vielhauer, M. J., 150, 152, 158–159
Vik, P. W., 355
Viken, R. J., 19–21
Villejo, R., 337
Villeponteaux, L. A., 397
Vitaro, F., 52, 71, 178, 187, 306
Vitaro, R., 52

Vitiello, B., 324, 448, 458
Vitousek, K., 9, 337–338
Vitterso, J., 166
Vitti, L., 407
Voeller, K. K. S., 32–33
Vogeltanz-Holm, N. D., 335
Vohs, K. D., 73, 332
Volkmar, F. R., 6, 32, 34, 254
von Aster, M., 407
von Baeyer, C. L., 406
Vondra, J. I., 52, 70, 77
von During, V., 258
Von Eye, A., 179
von Knorring, A. L., 189
von Knorring, L., 189
Vostanis, P., 181, 191–192
Vygotsky, L. S., 246

Waas, G. A., 125
Wachsmuth, R., 285
Wade, T., 333
Wade, T. J., 51–55, 57, 171
Wadsworth, M. E., 169–170, 411
Wagner, A. D., 144
Wagner, E. F., 53, 348, 355, 360–361
Wagner, K. D., 177, 195–196, 226, 451
Wakefield, J., 4
Wakeling, A., 332
Wakschlag, L. S., 54, 89, 93
Walco, G., 415
Walder, L. O., 299
Waldman, I., 21, 300, 379
Waldo, S. L., 273, 279–280
Waldron, H. B., 186, 349, 360–361, 366
Waldron, M., 103
Walker, J. R., 153
Walker, L. S., 179, 403–404, 407, 409–411, 413–414
Walker, T., 52
Walkup, J. T., 128
Wall, S., 87, 370
Wallace, J., 172
Wallace, J. M., 353–354
Wallace, L. E., 179
Wallander, J. L., 233, 238, 274, 277, 279, 281
Waller, G., 337
Wallerstein, J. S., 53
Wallerstein, R. S., 430
Walsh, B. T., 69, 330, 336, 339–341
Walsh-Allis, G., 51
Walters, A. S., 44
Walters, E. E., 171, 180, 306, 335
Wang, C. T., 371
Wang, E. E., 95
Wang, Y., 32
Wanner, B., 187
Ward, A. J., 177
Ward, C. H., 185
Ward, D., 168
Ward, L. G., 86
Ward, M. J., 66
Ward, S. L., 322
Warfield, M. E., 104
Warheit, G. J., 353–354
Warkany, J., 30
Warman, M. J., 117
Warner, J., 226
Warner, V., 173, 180, 182

Warner-Rogers, J. E., 367–368, 376
Warnke, S., 141
Warren, C. S., 427, 433–434
Warren, S. L., 121
Warshaw, M., 126
Waschbusch, D. A., 300, 321–322
Wasik, B. H., 381
Wasserman, A. L., 411
Wasserman, G. A., 108
Wasserman, M. S., 172
Wasserstein, S. B., 151
Waters, E., 87, 370
Watson, D., 118–119, 167–168, 170, 182
Watson, S., 337
Watt, M. C., 406
Wayne, H., 32
Weatherman, R. F., 240
Weaver, T. L., 378
Webb, A., 127, 399, 439
Webber, J., 242
Webster, R. E., 279–280
Webster-Stratton, C., 291
Weems, C. F., 117, 440
Wehmeyer, M. L., 236
Weiden, P., 227
Weikart, D. P., 52
Weiller, E., 140
Weinberg, W. A., 31–33, 173
Weiner, B., 166, 236, 246, 458
Weinhouse, E. M., 242
Weininger, O., 410
Weinstein, C. S., 280
Weinstock, M., 176
Weintraub, S., 33
Weiss, A. D., 379–380
Weiss, B., 166, 377, 430–431
Weiss, J. A., 243, 245
Weiss, S., 69
Weissberg, R. P., 110
Weissman, M. M., 171, 173, 176, 180–182, 191, 194, 286, 293
Weisz, J. R., 103, 167, 177, 183, 192–193, 236, 430–431, 440
Weitoft, G. R., 53
Weizman, A., 370
Wekerle, C., 119, 158, 372, 377, 379–380
Welch, P., 455
Welch, S. L., 332
Welikson, M., 454
Weller, E. B., 184, 218, 458
Weller, R. A., 458
Wells, K. B., 165
Wells, K. C., 286, 291, 441
Welner, A., 11
Welner, Z., 156
Welsh, M. C., 33, 272
Welte, J. W., 253, 258
Weltzin, T. E., 333
Wen, X., 233, 238–239
Weng, L. J., 359
Werner, E. E., 256, 259
Werry, J. S., 6, 117, 183
Werthamer-Larsson, L., 121, 186
Wertheim, E. H., 332
Wesch, D., 381
Wessel, I., 118
Wessely, S., 411
West, D. J., 51, 54
West, S. A., 222, 226, 270, 456
West, S. G., 68, 111, 169–170

Westen, D., 370, 433
Westenberg, P. M., 138
Weston, D. R., 95
Wetzler, S., 126
Wewers, S., 1018
Whalen, C. K., 293, 319
Wheaton, B., 50
Wheeler, R., 378
Wheeler, T., 7
Wheelwright, S., 264
Whelan, J. P., 380
Whiffen, V. E., 176
Whipple, E. E., 376
Whitaker, A. H., 454
Whitaker, R. C., 331
Whitcomb, D., 393, 396
White, B. A., 186
White, J. D., 237, 323
Whiteman, M., 351
Whitington, P. F., 411
Whittier, M. C., 456
Wichstrom, L., 172, 332
Wick, P., 142
Wickett, A. M., 379
Wickramaratne, P., 173, 180, 182
Wicks-Nelson, R., 3–4
Widiger, T. A., 167
Widom, C. S., 54, 158, 367, 378
Wieder, S., 267
Wierson, M., 52, 308
Wierzbicki, M., 38, 172
Wilens, T. E., 218, 324, 449
Wilfley, D. E., 336, 341
Wilhelm, K., 169
Wilkie, A. O. M., 239
Wilkinson, R. G., 53
Willcutt, E. G., 321
Williams, H., 51
Williams, J. A., 193
Williams, J. B., 337
Williams, L., 153, 318, 398
Williams, M., 217
Williams, N., 238, 242, 413
Williams, R. A., 183
Williams, R. J., 360
Williams, R. M., 151–152, 158
Williams, S., 119, 171, 273, 409
Williamson, D. A., 331, 337–338
Williamson, D. E., 175, 185
Willms, D. J., 53
Willoughby, M. T., 319
Wills, T. A., 106, 244, 351
Wilson, B., 67, 76, 274, 286
Wilson, D. B., 439
Wilson, D. R., 177
Wilson, G. T., 330, 334–337, 340–341, 346
Wilson, H., 33
Wilson, R. S., 67
Wind, T. W., 375
Windle, M., 169, 351
Wing, L., 32, 263
Winnicott, D. W., 433
Winokur, G., 180
Winslow, E. B., 51, 64, 70, 318
Winters, A., 301
Winters, K. C., 348–349, 355–356, 358, 361
Winters, N. C., 182
Winzer, M., 241–242
Wise, B. K., 88, 356
Wiser, S., 431

Witt, A., 412
Wittchen, H. U., 137, 407
Wittwer, D. J., 176
Wolchik, S. A., 169–170
Wolf, K. M., 170
Wolf, L. C., 262
Wolfe, D. A., 367–368, 372–375, 377, 379–380
Wolfe, E. R., 428
Wolfe, V. V., 68, 156, 158, 387, 389
Wolfner, G. D., 371
Wolgamuth, B., 406
Wolraich, M. L., 320, 459
Wonderlich, S. A., 330–332, 336, 339–341
Wong, D., 241
Wong, M., 316
Wong, S., 306
Wood, A., 190–193
Wood, K., 332
Wood, M. D., 361
Woodcock, R. W., 240
Woods, B. T., 220
Woods, S. W., 137
Woodside, D. B., 338
Woodward, S. A., 138

Woolford, H., 415
Woolston, J., 6
Wootton, J. M., 301–302
Worchel, R., 432
World Health Organization, 5, 10, 91, 233, 259
Worobey, J., 66
Wozniak, J., 217, 219, 221–222, 285, 288
Wright, C. I., 143
Wright, E. J., 52
Wright, F., 179, 338
Wu, P., 374
Wyllie, E. B., 406, 409–411, 413–414
Wynn, J., 266

Yaeger, A., 351
Yamaguchi, K., 355
Yang, H. M., 351
Yang, L., 32
Yang, R., 9
Yanovski, J. A., 330
Yanovski, S. Z., 330
Yanushefski, A. M., 374
Yarrow, L. J., 104
Yates, W. R., 285

Yatham, L. N., 226
Ye, R., 150
Ye, W. J., 51
Yonkers, K., 126
Young, A., 273–277
Young, B. J., 140, 144
Young, G. S., 413
Young, L., 220, 224
Young, M., 171
Young, S. E., 21–22
Youngstrom, E. A., 77, 182–183
Yule, W., 122, 155, 157, 300
Yurgelun-Todd, D. A., 220

Zachariae, R., 406
Zahn-Waxler, C., 69, 71–72, 287
Zakriski, A., 305
Zambenedetti, M., 456
Zapert, K. M., 186
Zax, M., 54
Zayas, V., 234
Zeanah, C. H., 86–88, 90–95, 389
Zebell, N., 380
Zeitlin, M. F., 51
Zelis, K., 42
Zeltzer, L. K., 405, 407, 412, 415
Zeman, J. L., 370, 403, 407, 410

Zera, M., 301
Zerbe, G. O., 22
Zero to Three National Center for Clinical Infant Programs, 5, 85, 88
Zetlin, A. G., 238
Zhang, F., 302
Zhao, S., 146, 180
Zhou, R., 32
Ziaie, H., 73
Zie, M., 22
Zielhuis, G. A., 238
Zigler, E., 246
Zilbovicius, M., 259
Zill, N., 52–53
Zillman, D., 288
Zimmerman, M. E., 186, 188, 220
Zimmerman, R. S., 353–354
Zinbarg, R., 122
Zipes, J. D., 30
Zito, J. M., 448
Zlotkin, S. H., 95
Zoccolillo, M., 52, 300, 306
Zoeller, C., 246
Zucker, R. A., 69, 350, 354
Zuckerman, B., 404, 408, 412
Zuravin, S. J., 367–368, 376

Subject Index

Abilify. *See* Aripiprazole
Abnormal Involuntary Movement Scale (AIMS), 456
Acetylcholine, 156, 174, 456
Acute stress disorder, 90, 155
Adaptability, 69–70, 136, 179, 291–292, 393
Adderall XR, 227, 459–460
Addiction Centre Research Group, 360
Adoption, 16–17, 19, 26, 107, 120, 172–173, 318, 353
Adrenocortical system, 68, 150, 152, 173–175, 177
Adrenocorticotropic hormone (ACTH), 177
Adult Attachment Interview (AAI), 87
Affect in Play Scale, 430, 433
Affective illnesses, 31, 33, 174, 335
African Americans
    ADHD, 324
    behavioral problems, 53, 77
    CD, 301
    class theoretical studies, 106
    MDD, 194
    SUDs, 351–352, 354–356
Aggression
    imitation, 42
    modeling, 42
    overt, 299
    peer sociometric report, 11
    social conditions contributing to, 52, 55
    suicide, 42
    temperament, 70–72, 77
    violence exposure, 108
Agranulocytosis, 455
Akathisia (restlessness), 32, 117, 122, 319, 449, 452, 455
Alcoholics Anonymous, 361
Alcoholism. *See also* Substance use disorders (SUDs)
    adolescent, 22
    in adoptive parents/adopted children, 17
    case-control association studies, 24–25
    Cloninger's study, 17
    forms of, 17
Amenorrhea, 330, 455
American Association on Mental Retardation (AAMR), 233
    Adaptive Behavior Scale, 240
American Diabetes Association, 227
American Psychiatric Association, 227
    Task Force on TD, 455
American Psychological Association
    Divisions 53 and 54 Web sites, 440
    Task Force on Promotion and Dissemination of Psychological Procedures, 429–430
Amphetamines, 30, 459–460
Ancillary classification system, 5–6
Anger management, 77, 291, 375–376, 380, 428
Anhedonia, 149, 166, 168
Anna Freud Center, 431
Anorexia nervosa. *See* Eating disorders

Anterior attention system, 66, 72
Anterior cingulate cortex (ACC), 72
Anticonvulsant medications, 226, 415, 456
Antidepressants. *See* Tricyclic antidepressants (TCAs)
Antiepileptic medications, 226
Antihypertensive medications, 293
Antipsychotic medications, 32, 227, 293, 453–455
Antisocial behavior, 17, 44, 51–52, 55
Antisocial personality disorder (APD), 306
Antisocial Process Screening Device (APSD), 305
Anxiety disorders
    behavioral abnormalities, 39
    Childhood Anxiety Sensitivity Index (CASI), 11
    early childhood, 90
    PTSD symptoms, 90
    trait, 123, 126, 134, 138, 143, 151, 391
Anxiety disorders. *See also* Generalized anxiety disorder (GAD)
Anxiety Disorders Interview Schedule—Child/Parent (ADIS-C/P), 123
Anxiety Disorders Interview Schedule for Children (ADIS-IV-C), 140
α-1, 455
Appetite
    ADHD, 324
    MDD, 89, 166, 179, 183
    mood stabilizers, 457, 459, 461
Applied behavior analysis (ABA), 265–267
Aripiprazole (Abilify), 453, 455–456
Asperger's syndrome (AS), 32, 34, 254, 257, 286, 406
Asphyxia neonatorum, 29
Asylums, 29
Atomoxetine (Strattera), 324, 459–461
Attachment-based family therapy (ABFT), 191, 194
Attachment disorders, 91, 149
Attachment security, 105, 370
Attachment theory, 95, 105
Attention-deficit/hyperactivity disorder (ADHD), 316–325
    appetite, 324
    assessment/diagnosis of, 88–89, 320–321
    attentional functions of the brain, 32, 396
    Barkley's ADHD Behavior Rating Scale, 11
    comorbidity, 21
    course, complications, prognosis of, 319–320
    description/clinical picture of, 89, 316–317
    environmental impact, 321–322
        family, 321–322
        peer interactions, 322
        school, 322
    epidemiology of, 318
    etiology of, 318–319
    genetic subtype disorders of, 21, 24
    infants, 89

    IQ, 322
    neuroticism, 323
    personality development, 317–318
        future implications for, 323–324
    self-esteem, 317
    treatments for, 324–325
        amphetamines, 30, 32
        multimodal, 325, 448, 458–461
Augmentative communication devices, 104
Autism, 31–32. *See also* Pervasive developmental disorders (PDD)
    Asperger's syndrome, 34
    description of, 31–32
    MR, 31
    ODD, 286
    PDDs, 254, 265
    SAD, 135
    social class influences, 258
Autism Diagnostic Review—Revised (ADI-R), 257, 261, 264
Autistic disorder (AD), 254
Autistic learning disabilities (ALD), 265
Autistic spectrum disorders. *See* Pervasive developmental disorders (PDDs)
Automatic cognition, 42
Autonomic nervous system (ANS), 76, 409
Aversive behaviors, 39, 71, 74, 142, 320, 369
Avoidance behaviors, 39–40, 121, 144, 154, 235, 273, 280, 370
Avoidant personality disorder (APD), 126, 143, 153, 189, 323, 378, 414–415
Awfulizing, 43
Axis disorders
    I, 126, 143, 167, 189–190, 336–337
    II, 88, 143, 167, 336, 406
    III, 88
    V, 88

Barkley's ADHD Behavior Rating Scale, 11
Basal ganglia, 32–33, 220
Beck Depression Inventory (BDI), 191–192, 194
Behavior
    adoption studies, 16–17
    associative learning models, 38–39
    deviant, 4, 8, 42, 54, 101, 240, 350, 355–356
    genetics, 19–21
    intervention, 54
    language development, 92
    maladaptive, 3–4, 9, 41–42, 101, 235
    normal, defining, 4–5
    reinforcement, 40–41
    self-control, lack of, predisposition to, 54
    violent, 108
    withdrawal, 69, 77, 179
Behavioral Assessment System for Children (BASC), 6, 124, 140
Behavioral Coding System (BCS), 376
Behavioral contributions. *See* Cognitive and behavioral contributions

484 Subject Index

Behavioral disinhibition
   ADHD, 317, 319, 323
   attachment disorders, 91
   borderline personality disorder, 378
   eating behavior disorder, 333, 339
   positive reaction tendencies, 235
   SUDs, 350, 360
Behavioral inhibition (BI)
   anxiety disorders, 90
      generalized, 118, 126
      in infants, 90
      social, 136–137, 142–143
   harm avoidance, 405
   MDD, 168–169
   temperament, 69, 77, 301
Behavioral Inhibition System (BIS), 168
Belsky's ecological model, 372
Benzodiazepines, 128, 415
Bertillon Classification, 5
Best Pharmaceuticals for Children Act, 448
Big Five, 136, 168, 234, 371
Binge eating. *See* Eating disorders
Bipolar disorder
   assessment/diagnosis of, 221–222
   classification, 217
   course, complications, prognosis of, 221
   description of, 217
   environmental impact, 222–223
      family, 222–223
      peers, 223
      school, 223
   epidemiology of, 219
   etiology of, 219–221
   gene identification, 25
   inflated self-esteem, 221
   personality development, 217–219
      future implications for, 223–224
      prepubertal and early adolescent, 222–223
   suicide, 217, 219
   symptoms of, 221–222
   treatment of, 224–227
      pharmacological, 226–227
         antiepileptic medications, 226
         antipsychotics, 226–227, 453–456
         lithium, 218, 226–227
Body dysmorphic disorder (BDD), 404, 408, 414
Borderline personality disorder (BPD), 150, 152–153, 234, 280, 378, 406
Bottom-up research, 3, 120, 190
Brain, 29–34
   behavior, 30
   DSM classification, 4
   dyslexia, 33
   early studies of, 29–30
   imaging of, 31, 33
   MDD, etiology, 172, 174–175
   temperament assessment, 67–69, 72, 74, 76–77
Brain stem, 32, 259
Bulimia nervosa. *See* Eating disorders
Bulimia Test—Revised (BULIT-R), 336
Bupropion, 196, 415, 458

Callous and unemotional personality traits (CU), 301–306, 309
Cancer, 44, 153, 358, 455
Carbamazepine, 226, 456–458
Carbamazepine-10, 456
Cardiovascular disease, 227, 404, 455–456
Catechollamine, 150, 152, 409
Catechol-O-methyltransferase (1-COMT), 219
Center for Epidemiological Studies Depressive Scale for Children (CES-DC), 185

Cerebellum, 32, 259
Cerebral cortex, 32
Cerebral palsy, 29–30, 33
Checklist for Autism in Toddlers (CHAT), 260
Child Abuse and Neglect Interview Schedule (CANIS), 375
Child Abuse Potential Inventory (CAP), 375
Child Abuse Prevention and Treatment Act (CAPTA), 367
Child and Adolescent Bipolar Foundation (CABF), 222
Child and Adolescent Psychiatric Assessment (CAPA), 10, 140
Child Behavior Checklist (CBCL), 6, 124, 140, 185, 376, 430–431
Child Behavior Checklist—Teacher Report Form (CBCL-TRF), 185
Child development
   associative learning, 38–39
   cognition, 42–44
   considerations, 8–9
      cultural, 8
      developmental, 8–9
      pragmatic, 7
   diagnostic assessment tools and methods, 9–12
      core components of, 10
         labeling, 11–12
         multiple informants and auxiliary measures, 11
         structured/semistructured interview formats, 10–11
   issues
      children with contexts, 9
      environmental influences, 48, 51–52, 54
      ethical, 7–8
      mental health, 44, 50–52
         disadvantaged environments, 50, 52–53, 57
         gender, 57
         maternal depression, 51, 54
         nocturnal awakenings, 44
      race/ethnicity, 8, 53, 57
      social/economic influence, 52–53
   modeling, 42
   operant conditioning, 39–42
      punishment, 41–42
      reinforcement, 39–41
   social structural factors on, 49
   sociological contributions, 47–58
      distal/proximal risk factors, 48–53, 55–57
         community violence, 52
         family environment, 51–52
         master status, 56
         multiplexity of, 55–57
         social conditions/structures, 51, 55
         social exposure, 50, 54–55
         social vulnerability, 51, 55
      epidemiologic *vs.* sociologic approaches, 47–49
   twin studies, 17–19
Childhood Anxiety Sensitivity Index (CASI), 11
Childhood Level of Living Scale (CLLS), 375
Childhood PTSD Interview—Child Form, 157
Childhood spastic diplegia. *See* Cerebral palsy
Child physical abuse and neglect, 367–381
   adult functioning, 398
   assessments/diagnosis of, 375–376
      areas of, 375
      techniques of, 375–376
   course, complications, prognosis of, 373–375
      longitudinal findings, 374

      moderating/mediating factors, 374–375
      theoretical considerations, 373–374
   description/clinical picture of, 367–369
      definition of physical abuse, 367–368
         of neglect, 368
      features of, 368–369
      legal aspects of, 367
   environmental impact, 376–378
      family, 376–377
      peer interactions, 377–378
      school, 377
   epidemiology of, 371
      child age/gender, 371
      national incidence studies, 371
   etiology, 371–373
      Belsky's ecological model, 372
      Cicchetti and Rizley's models and, 372–373
      Milner's social information processing model, 373
      Wolfe's transitional model, 373
   language development, 377
   MDD, 176
   neuroticism, 378
   parenting behaviors, 368
   personality development of, 369–371
      attachment, role of, 370–371
      future implications for, 378–379
      predisposing personality characteristics, 369
      resilience, personality factors associated with, 369–370
   self-esteem, 369–370, 374–375
   treatments for, 379–381
      interventions, 379–380
         child-focused, 379–380
         family-focused, 380
         parent training, 380
      multisystemic approaches, 380–381
Child Physical and Sexual Abuse: Guidelines for Treatment (National Crime Victims Research and Treatment Center), 379
Child protective services (CPS), 376, 378, 388, 392, 395–396
Child PTSD Symptom Scale (CPSS), 156, 396
Children's Assessment Schedule (CAS), 140
Children's Attributions and Perceptions Scale (CAPS), 391
Children's Depression Inventory (CDI), 173, 184–185, 192–193, 396
Children's Depression Rating Scale—Revised (CDRS-R), 183, 185, 451
Children's Global Assessment Scale (CGAS), 194
Children's Global Assessment Scale (C-GAS), 430–431
Children's Impact of Traumatic Events Scale—Revised (CITES-R), 156
Children's PTSD Inventory (CPTSDI), 157
Children's Yale-Brown Obsessive-Compulsive Scale (CY-BOCS), 450
Child Report of Post-Traumatic Symptoms (CROPS), 156
Child sexual abuse (CSA), 388–399
   assessment of, 395
      clinical, 395
      forensic, 395
   CBT, 95
   course, complications, prognosis of, 393–395
   diagnosis of, 396
   description/clinical picture of, 388–389
      definitional issues of, 388
      mandated reporting of, 388

environmental impact, 396–397
  family, 393, 396–397
  peer interactions, 397
  school, 397
 epidemiology of, 391–392
 etiology of, 392–393
 gender, 392
 incidence/prevalence of, 391–392
 legal implications of, 396–397
 personality development, 389–391
  future implications, 397–398
  personal responsibility, 390–391
  premorbid features of, 389
  self-efficacy, 390
  self-esteem, 389–392, 394
  shame, 391
 PTSD, 389, 391, 396
  ADHD, 396
  psychoanalytic psychotherapy, 399
  school, 397
 sleeper effect of, 394
 suicide, 397–398
 treatments for, 398–399
  clinical course of, 394
  trauma-focused cognitive-behavioral therapy, 398–399
 unreported incidents of, 394
Child Sexual Behavior Inventory (CSBI), 395
Child's Game procedure, 376
Christian Science community, 368
Cicchetti and Lynch's ecological/transactional model, 372–373
Cicchetti and Rizley's transactional model, 372–373
Circle of Security, 95
Citalopram, 195–196, 449, 452
Classical conditioning, 38–39
Classification. See Diagnosis and classification
Class theoretical studies, 106–107
Clinical Global Impressions-Improvement Scale (CGI-I), 450–453, 460
Clomipramine, 450–451
Clonidine, 174, 293
Clozapine (Clozaril), 227, 453–456, 455–456
Clozaril. See Clozapine
Clumsy child syndrome, 33
Cognitive and behavioral contributions, 38–44
 associative learning, 38–39
  higher order conditioning, 38–39
  sensory preconditioning, 39
 cognition, 42–44
 description of, 438–439
 environmental influences, 38
 future priorities, 444–445
  moderating/mediating effects of CBT, 445
  parental involvement, 444–445
  training, 445
 intervention issues, 441–444
  assessment, 441–442
  CBT techniques, 95, 443
   homework and, 443
  cognitive processes, 442–443
   developmental considerations, 443–444
   exemplars of, 440–441
 involuntary cognition, 42
 language development, 42, 73–74, 104, 369, 444
 operant conditioning, 39–42
  punishment, 41–42
  reinforcement, 39–41
 outcomes, research on, 439–441
 social learning, 42

Cognitive-behavioral therapy (CBT), 438–446
 child physical abuse and neglect, 379
 CSA, 398–399
 eating disorders, 340–341
 explained, 438–439
 future priorities in, 444–445
  moderations/mediations of the effects of CBT, 445
  parental involvement, 444–445
  training, 445
 GAD, 127–128
 intervention, 440–441
  issues of, 441–444
   assessment challenge, 441–442
   cognitive processes, 442–443
   common techniques, 443
   developmental considerations, 443–444
   homework, 443
 MDD, 190–194
  clinical samples of, 192–193
  community samples of, 193–194
  studies of, 191–192
 outcomes of, research on, 439–440
 positive impact of, 438
 PTSD, 159–160
 SAD, 144
 SSRIs, 450–451
 trauma-focused, 159, 398–399
Collaborative problem solving (CPS), 292–293
Colorado Child Temperamental Inventory (CCTI), 71
Colorado Model, 267
Community controls (CC), 222–223
Comorbidity, 6–7, 21–22, 122, 139–140, 181–182, 316
Concentration
 eating disorders, 338
 GAD, 117, 122
 MDD, 89, 169, 183
 PTSD, 149, 157–158
Concerta®, 227, 459–560
Concerta^B®, 459
Conditioned stimulus, 39
Conduct disorder (CD), 299–309
 ADHD, 300, 307–308
 assessment/diagnosis of, 88–89, 303–305
 comorbidity, 21–22
 course, complications, prognosis of, 302–303
 description/clinical picture of, 89, 299–300
 emotional disorders, 306
 environmental impact, 305–306
  family, 305
  peer interactions, 301–302, 304–306
  school, 305
 epidemiology of, 301
 etiology of, 301–302
 in infants, 89
 internalizing disorders, 300–301
 personality development, 300–301
  future implications for, 306–307
 suicide, 306
 treatments for, 307–308
Congenital word blindness, 30
Connecticut Longitudinal Study (CLS), 275
Conners' Continuous Performance Test (CPT), 321
Conners' Global Index Scale for Teachers (CGIS-T), 460
Conners' Rating Scale—Revised (CRS-R), 320
Contexts
 care giving, 72, 87
 in child physical abuse, 379

data-collection methods in SUDs, 358
developmental
 children, 8–9
 exosystemic/macrosystemic, 108–109
 proximal, 47, 50, 108
 social exposure, 54
 socioenvironmental factors on, 47–48, 350–351
emotional, 43, 65, 73
environmental, 48, 91–92, 304, 308, 350–351
exposure-based model, 54
forensic, 389
in infant mental health, 85–87, 91–92
 infant-parent/caregiver relationships, 87
 intrinsic characteristics, 86–87
relationship, 91
social-interactional, 74
Continuous Performance Task (CPT), 11
Coping Cat Workbook, 440
Coping Koala, 441
Coping with Depression (CWD), 193
Copralalia, 32
Cortex
 anterior cingulate (ACC), 32
 cerebral, 32
 frontal, 76
 middle cingulate, 32
 orbital frontal, 221
 prefrontal, 72, 174, 220, 276
 right frontal premotor, 32
 right temporal, 32
Corticotropic-releasing hormone (CRH), 173
Cortisol, 68, 150, 152, 173–175, 177
CYP450, 226
CYP2D6, 452, 460
Cystic fibrosis, 23

DC: 0-3, 5, 88–91
Defiant Children (Barkley), 380
Demandingness, 43
Depression. See Major depressive disorder (MDD)
Depression Self-Rating Scale, 185
Depressive disorder not otherwise specified (D-NOS), 165, 171
Der Struwwelpeter (Hoffmann), 30
Developmental dyscalculia, 33
Developmental dysgraphia, 33
Developmental dyspraxia, 33
Developmental Gerstmann syndrome, 33
Developmental pathways, 109
Developmental psychopathology, 100–111
 assessment, 109
 challenges of, 100–102
  ecological-transactional model, 102
  person-environment transactions, 101
  resilience, 101
  risk and protection, 101
 exosystemic/macrosystemic processes in, 102–103, 106–109
  community violence, direct/distal processes of, 108
  immigration and acculturation, 108–109
  gender and ethnicity, moderating role of, 107
  intelligence heritability, social class differences in, 107–108
 future directions, 110–111
 intervention, 109–110
 microsystemic processes in, 102–108
  parent-child relationships, quality of, 105

Developmental psychopathology, microsystemic processes in *(continued)*
  peers, impact of, 105–106
  school climate, role of, 106
 ontogenetic processes in, 102–104
  cognitive universals, 102–104
  language development, 104
Developmental trajectories, 109
Deviant behavior, 4, 8, 42, 54, 101, 240, 350, 355–356
Dexedrine, 227
Dextroamphetamine, 460–461
Diabetes, 227, 430, 455
Diagnosis and classification, 3–12
 of abused and neglected children, 368, 381
 of aggression, 288
 of alcohol use, 352
 ancillary, 5–6
 assessment tools and methods, 9–11
  child diagnostic evaluation, core components of, 10
  interview formats, 10–11
 of attachment in parents, 87
 of behavioral inhibition, 118
 of bipolar disorder, 217
 of cerebral palsy, 30
 current systems, 4–5
 of depressive disorder not otherwise specified (D-NOS), 165
 of DZ/MZ twins, 19
 historical antecedents, 4
  Kraepelin's model, 4
 of infant mental illness, 87–88
 international statistical, 5
 issues and challenges, 7–9
  children with contexts, 9
  cultural considerations, 8
  developmental considerations, 8–9
  ethical issues, 7–8
  pragmatic considerations, 7
 labeling, 11–12
 of MR, 30, 233
 multiple informants and auxiliary measures, 11
 of PTSD, 155
 reliability, validity, clinical utility, 6–7
 of substance use, risk factors, 353
The Diagnostic and Statistical Manual of Mental Disorders (DSM), 4–5, 31, 89
Diagnostic Classification of Mental Health and Developmental Disorders of Infancy and Early Childhood (DC: 0-3), 5, 88–91
Diagnostic Interview for Children and Adolescents (DICA), 10, 156, 182, 184
Diagnostic Interview for Children and Adolescents—Revised (DICA-R), 11, 123, 140
Diagnostic Interview Schedule for Children (DISC-IV), 10, 140, 156, 320
Diagnostic Interview Schedule—PTSD, 157
Differential diagnosis, 9
Dimensions of Depression Profile for Children and Adolescents (DDPC), 185
Dimensions of Temperament Survey (DOTS), 71
Discrete Trial Training (DTT), 265–266
Distal risk factors, 48
Distress
 emotional, 168–169, 187, 302, 306, 393, 396, 407, 413
 family, 412, 415
 GAD and, 117

 maternal, 121, 393, 398
 psychological, 391, 393
 PTSD related, 157
 somatic, 440
Divalproex, 226–227, 454, 456–458
Division TEACCH, 265
Dopamine D_4 receptor (DRD4), 24, 32, 454
Dopamine transporter (DAT), 24, 32
Double-blind placebo controlled trials, 195–196, 226–227, 450–452, 454, 458
Douglas Developmental Disabilities Center, 266
Down syndrome, 30, 240, 247, 262
Drug Use Screening Inventory (DUSI), 357
DSM, 4–5, 89
DSM-II, 117
DSM-III, 5, 122, 148, 189, 221, 257
DSM-III-R
 GAD and OAD labeling of, 117
 mania, 219
 PDDs diagnostic criteria, redefined, 257
 PTSD diagnostic criteria, 148–149
 SAD diagnostic criteria, 137
 somatization disorders diagnostic criteria, 407
 SUDs, 352
DSM-IV
 Asperger's syndrome, 257
 on avoidant personality disorder in adults, 126
 bipolar disorder diagnostic criteria, 217, 219–220
 child physical abuse and neglect, 368
 dysthymic disorder, episode length, 180
 eating disorders
  diagnostic criteria, 336–337
  not otherwise specified, diagnosis of, 331
 GAD, 117
  community prevalence rates of, 119
 infant/children diagnostics, 88–90
 learning disorders diagnostic categories, 277
 mania, 221
 MR, clinical-medical approach to, 233
 PDDs
  diagnostic criteria, redefined, 257
  12 diagnostic signs of, 254, 261
 PTSD
  diagnostic criteria, 148–149, 153, 155–157
  lifetime rates of, 153
  on nightmares, 149
 SAD diagnostic criteria, 135–136
 self-report questionnaires, 123
 somatization disorders, defined, 403–404, 406–408
 SUDs, diagnostic criteria, 348–350, 352, 357
DSM-IV-TR
 CD, 299, 303–304
 child physical abuse and neglect, 368
 GAD, 117, 122
 MDD, 165, 190
 MR, 233
D2 blockade, 455
Duchenne muscular dystrophy, 23
Dutch Temperament Questionnaire, 71
Dyadic Parent-Child Interaction Coding System (DPICS), 376
Dyadic therapy, 95
Dyslexia, 30, 33, 272, 275–276
Dysthymic disorder (DD), 139, 165–167, 171, 180–182, 189, 193, 410
Dystonia, 452, 455

Early Developmental Stages of Psychopathology study (EDSP), 407

Early Intervention Project (EIP), 266
Early Start, 261, 266
Eating Disorder Diagnostic Scale (EDDS), 336
Eating Disorder Examination interview (EDE), 336–337
Eating Disorder Examination-Questionnaire (EDE-Q), 336
Eating disorders, 330–341
 anorexia nervosa, 339–340
 assessment/diagnosis of, 336–337
 binge eating, 341
 bulimia nervosa, 340–341
 CBT, 340–341
 course, complications, prognosis of, 335–336
 description/clinical picture of, 330–331
 environmental impact, 337–338
  family, 337
  peer interactions, 338
  school, 337–338
 epidemiology of, 333–334
 etiology of, 334–335
 impulsivity, 332–333
 neuroticism, 332–333, 338–339
 not otherwise specified, diagnosis of, 331, 336
 obsessive-compulsive personality disorder, 333
 perfectionism, 226, 332, 334, 337
 personality development, 331–333
  future implications, 338–339
  models of, 331–333
 self-esteem, 332, 334, 340
 suicide, 335
 treatments of, 339–341
  anorexia nervosa, 339–340
  binge eating disorder, 341
  bulimia nervosa, 340–341
Echolalia, 32
Ecological model, 49, 101–102, 372–373, 380
Ecological-transactional model, 102–103
Effectance motivation (EM), 236–237, 243, 245, 247
Effortful control (EC), 119
Electrocardiogram (ECG), 455–457
Electroencephalography (EEG), 31, 67–68, 77, 259, 276, 408, 411, 413
11-epoxide, 456
Elimination disorders, 10
Emotion
 regulation of, 65, 73–77
 two-factor theory of emotion, 43
Emotional disorders
 CD, 306
 dysthyemia, 189
 language development, 92
 negative effect syndrome, 6–7
 psychodynamic treatments, 427
 psychopathology, 233
 sociological contributions, 53
Emotionality, Activity, Sociability, Impulsivity Survey (EASI), 168
Emotionality, Activity, Sociability Temperament Survey (EAS), 72
Endoplasmic reticulum stress response (ER), 25
Epilepsy, 29–30, 226, 239, 259, 411, 457
Escitalopram, 449, 452
Ethnicity. *See* Race/ethnicity
European Study of the Epidemiology of Mental Disorders (ESEMeD/MHEDEA), 139
Exosystemic processes, 49, 102–103, 106–109, 111, 372
Expectancy of success (ES), 236–237, 245–246

Externalizing disorders
  child physical abuse and neglect, 369
  heritability of, 21
  infant mental health evaluations, 88–89
  LDs, 273
  psychodynamic therapy, 428, 432
  SUDs, 356–357
  in victimized juvenile delinquents, 157
Extrapyramidal symptoms (EPS), 454–456
Extroversion
  eating disorders, 333
  MDD, 168
  PTSD, 150, 152–153, 158–159
  SAD, 136
Eysenck Personality Questionnaire (EPQ), 323
EZ-Yale Personality Questionnaire (EZPQ), 235–236

Failure to thrive (FTT), 170, 179
Familial contributions
  in alcoholism, 17
  on child development, 48, 51–52, 54
  clustering of OCD and Tourette's syndrome, 33
  in LDs, 33, 276
  in MDD, 172–173, 179, 185–186
  in MR, 235, 237–239
  risk factors within, 51
  in SAD, 137–138
Family anxiety management (FAM), 127–128
FEAR, 127
Feeding disorders, in infants, 90
Finnish Twin Studies, 20
Five Factor Model (FFM or Big Five), 136, 168, 234, 371
Floor-Time, 265, 267
Fluoxetine, 192
  adverse effects of, 458
  for eating disorders, 340
  for MDD, 191–192, 194–196, 449, 451–452
  for OCD, 449
  for SAD, 144
  treatment studies of, 451–452
Fluvoxamine, 128, 449–452
Focalin, 459
Follicle stimulating hormone (FSH), 17
Follow-up Interview Schedule for Adults (FISA), 10
Food and Drug Administration (FDA), 195, 226, 448–452, 455, 457, 459, 461
Fragile X syndrome, 31, 235, 240, 258
Frontal lobe, 32, 76, 292
Functional imaging studies, 32
Functional magnetic resonance imaging (fMRI), 220

Gabapentin, 226
Galactorrhea, 455
Gazing, 73–74, 255–256
Gender differences
  in child development, 57
  in CSA, 392
  in developmental process comparison, 107
  in diagnosis/classification considerations, 9
  in GAD, 119–120
  in internalizing disorders, 107
  in MDD, 186–188
    girls vs. boys, 57
    peer relationships, 187–188
    prepubertal ratios, 171
    school functioning, 186–187
  in social class, 56, 107
  in SUDs, 352

Generalized anxiety disorder (GAD), 117–128
  assessment of, 123
    parent/teacher reports, 124
    self-report questionnaires, 123–124
  concentration, 117, 122
  course, complications, prognosis of, 121–122
    comorbidity, 122
    development/complications of, 121–122
  diagnostics
    criteria for, 122
    differential, 122–123
    interviews, 123
  description/clinical picture of, 117–118
  environmental impact of, 124–126
    family, 124
    peers, 125–126
    school, 125
  epidemiology, 119–120
    community prevalence rates, 119
    gender, differential diagnosis, 119–120
  etiology of, 120
    environmental contributions, 120–121
      attachment, 121
      cumulative vulnerability, 121
      parenting behavior, 120–121
    genetics, 120
  neuroticism, 126
  perfectionism, 117–118, 124–125
  personality development
    future implications of, 126–127
    problems/disorders in adults with Gad, 126–127
  psychopathology, 118–119
    behavioral inhibition, 118
    effortful control, 119
    negative/positive affects, 118–119, 126
    physiological hyperarousal, 118–119
  self-criticism, 118, 124, 442–443
  suicide, 122
  treatment of
    CBT, 127–128
      FEAR acronym, 127
    future directions of, 128
    pharmacological, 128
    fluoxetine, 451
Genetic contributions, 16–25. See also Twins
  behavior genetics, evolving field of, 19–22
    developmental changes, 19–20
    disorders, 21–23
    gene-environment interaction, 20–21
      comorbidity between, 21–22
      subtyping, 21
  detection, traditional methods of, 16–19
    adoption studies, 16–17
    limitations, 17
    family studies, 16
  DNA sequences, 22–23
  identifying specific genes, 22–25
    methods of, 23–25
      association studies and candidate genes, 24
      case-control association studies, 24–25
      family-based association studies, 25
      linkage approaches, 23–24
  MDD, 172–173
Geodon. See Ziprasidone
George Washington University, 267
Global Appraisal of Individual Needs (GAIN), 357
Glucose dysregulation, 455
Growth hormone (GH), 174–175
Guanfacine, 293

Haloperidol, 32, 454
Hamilton Rating Scale for Depression (HAM-D), 185, 194
Harvard/Brown Research Program (HARP), 139–140
Head Start, 47, 52
Heart rate
  PTSD, 157
  RSA suppression, 67
  SAD, 135, 141
  temperament assessment, 67, 75–76
  vagal tone, 67, 75–76
High-functioning autism (HFA), 264
Histrionic personality disorders, 153, 167, 188–189, 323, 406, 414–415
HIV, 358, 411
Home Stimulation Assessment (HSA), 376
HPA axis, 33, 173–177
Human Genome Project, 257
Huntington's disease, 23
Hyperactivity. See Attention-deficit/hyperactivity disorder (ADHD)
Hyperprolactinemia, 455
Hypochondriasis, 404–405, 407–408
Hypoglycemia, 174, 455
Hypomania, 217–218, 221, 226
Hypothalamic-pituitary-adrenal. See HPA axis
Hypothyroidism, 226, 455, 457

Ibuprofen, 415–416, 458
ICD, 5
ICD 10, 5, 10–11, 88, 91, 233
Identity by descent (IBD) marker, 23–24
Imaging studies, 32–33
Immigrants
  acculturation of, 108–109
  language development, 149
Impulsivity
  ADHD, 316–317, 319, 321
  CBT, 439
  CD, 302, 307
  Continuous Performance Task, 11
  developmental psychotherapy, 110
  eating disorders, 332–333, 335
  infant mental health, 88–89
  MDD, 169–170
  MR, 234
  ODD, 290
  psychostimulants, 458
  risperidone, 454
  SUDs, 350, 355–356
  temperament, 66, 71, 77
Inclusion, 265
Individual education plan (IEP)
Individuals with Disabilities Education Act (IDEA), 263, 277
Infans, 29
Infant mental health, 85–96
  assessment, 91–94
    approaches to, 93–94
    content of, 91–92
    Crowell Procedure of, 93–99
    infant-caregiver/parent interactions, 87, 91–92, 94
    process of, 92–94
  development of, 85–86
  diagnostic systems, 88
  disorders, 88–91
    attachment, 91
    in clinical settings, 88
    externalizing, 88–89
    feeding, 90

Infant mental health, disorders (continued)
  internalizing, 89–90
    regulatory, 90
    relationship, 91
    sleep, 90–91
  interrelated contexts of, 86–87
  intervention, 94–95
    Circle of Security, 95
    dyadic therapy, 95
    Nurse Family Partnership, 94
    prevention, 94–95
    therapist-patient relationship, 95
    treatment, 95
  psychopathology of, 87–88
  subjectivity, 86
Infant Temperament Questionnaire (ITQ), 71
Infirmary for Nervous Diseases, 30
Injury Fact Book, 371
Internalizing disorders
  ADHD, 316–317, 323
  anxiety, 90, 121, 124
  behavior characterization, 72
  CD, 300
  child physical abuse neglect, 369
  depressive, 89–90, 179
  diagnostic rates of, 88
  effortful control/negative affects, 119
  gender/ethnicity, 107
  insight-oriented therapy, 427–428
  LDs, 280
  psychodynamic therapy, 430–435
  recurrent abdominal pain, 409
  self-regulation, 77
  substance use treatment-related outcomes, 356
  temperament, 64
Internal working model, 92, 105, 370
International Classification of Diseases, 10
International List of Causes of Causes of Death, 5
International Statistical Classification of Diseases (ICD), 5. See also *ICD 10*
Interpersonal psychotherapy (IPT), 191, 193–194
  for use with adolescents (IPT-A), 194
Interview Schedule for Children and Adolescents (ISCA), 10
Introversion, 136, 139, 143
Inventory for Client and Agency Planning (ICAP), 240
IQ
  ADHD, 322
  Asperger's syndrome, 254
  child physical abuse and neglect, 377
  discrepancy criteria, 272, 275, 277
  genetic effects on, 103, 107
  hereditability, 20
  high-functioning autism, 264
  MR, 233, 238, 239–240
    fragile X syndrome, 240
    self-concept, 243, 245
  psychodynamic treatments, 431
  self-fulfilling prophesy, 43
  social exposure-based model, 54
  somatization disorders, 407
  studies of adult LDs, 277
Irrational beliefs, 43
Isle of Wight Study, 52

John's Hopkins Hospital
  Harriot Lane Home, 31
Junior Temperament and Character Inventory (JTCI), 218

Karolinska Scales of Personality (KSP), 143
Keeping Children and Families Safe Act, 367
Kiddie-SADS. *See* Schedule for Affective Disorders and Schizophrenia for School-Aged Children (K-SADS)
Kraepelin's model of classification, 4
K-SADS. *See* Schedule for Affective Disorders and Schizophrenia for School-Aged Children (K-SADS)

Labeling, 43
Laboratory Temperament Assessment Battery, 66
Lamotrigene, 226, 457
Language
  augmentative communication devices, 104
  behavioral/emotional problems, 92
  body, 34
  child physical abuse and neglect, 377
  cognitive development, 42, 73–74, 104, 369, 444
  copralalia, 32
  diagnostic classification of ethnically diverse children, 8
  immigrants, 149
  LDs, 274–277, 281–282
  MDD, assessment of, 182
  MR, 239
  ODD, 286–287, 290
  PDDs, 254–258, 260–261, 263–267
  of play, 429
  PTSD and ability to describe events, 149, 389
  somatization disorders, 403, 406
Latino adolescents, 107, 109, 193, 354
Lazars, 29
L-dopa, 174
Learned helplessness, 171, 236, 273
Learning, social, 42
Learning disabilities (LDs), 272–282
  assessment/diagnosis of, 277–278
  autistic, 265
  course, complications, prognosis of, 276–277
  description/clinical picture of, 272–273
  developmental, 33
  environmental impact, 278–279
    family, 278–279
    peer interactions, 279
    school, 279
  epidemiology of, 274–275
  etiology of, 275–276
    familial/genetic factors of, 276
    neurological factors of, 276
    neuropsychological factors of, 275–276
  language development, 274–277, 281–282
  nonverbal, 33–34, 272, 281–282
  personality development, 273–274
    emotional impact on, 273
    future implications of, 279–280
    processing challenges, direct impact of, 274
    social environment, impact mediated by, 274
  reading, 33, 272–273, 275, 277
  self-esteem, 273, 281–282
  speech, 34
  treatments of, 280–282
    academic programming, 281
    psychotherapy, 282
    social skills training, 281
Levoamphetamine, 460
L-5-hydroxytryptophan, 174
Limbic system, 69, 72, 259
Lithium, 218, 226–227, 454–458
Little's disease. *See* Cerebral palsy
Liver failure, 457, 461

Living With Children (Patterson, Guillion), 291, 380
Longitudinal studies
  on ADHD, 320
  on anorexia nervosa, 332, 339
  on binge eating disorder, 341
  on CD, 302–303
  on child physical abuse and neglect, 374
  on CSA, 397–398
  on depressive disorders, 166
    academic performance, 187
    child's perception of familial support, 186
    cortisol levels, 174
    dysfunctional families, 179
    environmental factors, 185
    neuroticism, 169
    peer support, 188
    stress generation model, 175
    symptoms, 170, 179, 185
  on PTSD symptoms, 155
  on SAD, 139
  on SUDs, relapse, 355–356
  on temperament, 68–70
Longitudinal Studies of Child Abuse and Neglect (LONGSCAN), 374
Lovaas Method, 266

MacArthur Story Stem Battery (MSSB), 434
Macrosystemic processes, 102–103, 106–109, 372
Magnetic resonance imaging (MRI), 31, 220, 259
Magnetic resonance spectroscopy (MRS), 220
Major depressive disorder (MDD), 165–196
  appetite, 89, 166, 179, 183
  assessment/diagnosis of, 182–185
    discrepancies from multiple informants, 182–183
    interviews, 183–185
    questionnaires, 185
    self-report, 185
    tools for, 183–184
  concentration, 19, 89, 183
  course, complications, prognosis of, 180–182
  depressive symptoms of
    alcohol, effects on, 20
    CBT packages, 190
    Children's Depression Rating Scale-Revised (CDRS-R), 183, 185
    developmental changes in the phenomenology of, 166
  disorders of, described, 165–166
    depressive disorder not otherwise specified, 165, 171
    dysthymic disorder, 165–167, 171, 180–182, 189
  environmental impact of, 185–188
    family, 185–186
    peers, 187–188
    school, 186–187
  epidemiology of, 170–172
  etiology of, 172–180
    adoption studies, 173
    cognitive vulnerability, 177–178
    elevated genetic/environmental differences, 172–173
    interpersonal vulnerability, 178–180
    neurobiological vulnerability, 173–175
      brain differences, functional/anatomical, 174
      neurotransmitters, 174
      psychoneuroendocrinology, 173–174
      sleep abnormalities, 89, 174–175

stress, 175–177
  twin studies, 172–173
  failure to thrive, 170, 179
  in girls vs. boys, 57
  in infants, 89–90
  language and assessment of, 182
  maternal, 49, 51–52, 54–55, 94, 175, 180, 193
  neuroticism, 167–170
  peer rejection, 180, 187
  personality development, 166–170
    future implications of, 188–190
    premorbid depressive personality, 167
    relationship between personality and depression, 167–168
      characteristics of, 168
      evidence of, 168–170
      mediation models, 170
      moderating factors of, 170
  prepubertal, gender ratios, 171
  schizoid, 188–189
  and school failure, 33
  self-criticism, 178, 186
  self-esteem, 170, 179, 188
  sleep disorders, 89
  suicide, 181, 189, 195, 452
  treatments of, 190–196
    CBT, 190–194
      clinic samples, 192–193
      community samples, 193–194
      specific techniques of, 190
      studies of, with depressed youth, 190–191
      symptomatic community samples, 192
    interpersonal therapies, 194
    medications, 194–196
      antidepressants, 194–196, 451–452
      efficacy of, 195–196
      safety of, 194–195
Major depressive episodes (MDEs), 165–166, 169, 181
Maladaptive behavior, 3–4, 9, 41–42, 101, 235
Maltreatment
  antisocial tendencies, 379
  attachment related difficulties, 370
  bipolar disorder, 378
  defining, 367–368
  emotional/behavioral reactions to, 148–149
  etiology of, 372
  fibromyalgia, 410
  home nurse visitation programs, 381
  MDD, 176, 179
  psychiatric symptoms/diagnosis, 100, 368–369
  rates of, 371
  resilience to, 369–370
Mania, 33, 227
  acute, 226–227, 456
  as affective illness, 31–33
  antidepressant risks, 195
  DSM-III-IV criteria for, 221
  dysphoric, 227
  euphoric, 221, 227
  facial emotions, 220
  hypomania, 217–218, 221, 226
  manic-depressive illness, 33
  pharmacological treatments of, 452, 454, 456
May Center for Early Childhood Education, 266
Mediators, 75–77, 90, 180, 445
Medicines and Healthcare Products Regulatory Agency (MHRA), 194–195, 452
Melancholia, 30
Melatonin, 174
Mental age (MA),and MR, 103–104, 236–238, 254

Mental health. *See also* Infant mental health
  defined, 3–4
  DSM, 4
  economic hardship, 52
  ethnic minorities, research, 8
  family environment's influence on, 50–51
  nocturnal awakenings, 44
  stress, 50
Mental retardation (MR), 29–30
  assessment/diagnosis, 240
    adaptive behavior, 240
    intellectual functioning, 240
  autism, 31
  course, complications, prognosis, 239–240
  description/clinical picture of, 233–234
  environmental impact, 240–243
    family, 240–241
    peer interactions, 242–243
    school, 241–242
  epidemiology, 238
  etiology, 238–239
  familial, 234, 235, 237–238
  IQ, 233, 238
    fragile X syndrome, 240
    self-concept, 243, 245
  language development, 239
    augmentative communication devices, 104
  mental age, 103–104, 236–238, 254
  neuroticism, 234–235
  organic, 234, 239
  personality development, 234–238
    alternative domains of, 235
    future implications of, 243–244
    self-concept, 237
    social comparison theory, 243–244, 247
    social-related personality domains of, 235
    sociocognitive theory of, 234
    task-related domains of, 236–237
      effectance motivation, 237
      outer directedness, 236–237
      success expectancy of, 236
      Zigler constructs, 237
    traditional domains of, 234–235
  self-esteem, 236, 242–244
  treatments for, 244–247
    factors of, 245–247
      self-concept, 247
      social-related, 245
      task-related, 245–247
    sociometric grouping, 244–245
    Special Olympics, 245–247
Metadate CD®, 459
Methylphenidate (MPH), 293, 324–325, 458–461
Microsystemic processes, 49, 102–108, 372
Midtown Manhattan Survey of Psychiatric Impairment in Urban Children in New York City, 52
Millon Clinical Multiaxial Inventory—II (MCMI-II), 323
Milner's social information processing model, 373
Minnesota Multiphase Personality Inventory—2 (MMPI-2), 375
Minnesota Multiphasic Personality Inventory (MMPI), 279
Minnesota Twin Family Study, 20
Mirtazapine, 196
Modeling, 42
  of aggression, 42
  biometrical, 19

of child development
  behavioral, 42
  Bronfenbrenner's ecological model, 49–50
  home, school, community contextualization, 50
  social-structure factors, 49
Cicchetti and Lynch's ecological/transactional, 372–373
Cicchetti and Rizley's transactional, 372–373
Colorado, 267
familial, 355
on intervention, 52
parental/adult, 353, 375, 410
peer, 355
of stress linked to mental health, 50
therapist's role in, 426–427
transactional, 188, 234, 372–373
tripartite, 118–119, 168
Walden, 267
Wolfe's transitional, 373
Molecular biology, 31
Mongolian idiot. *See* Down syndrome
Monitoring the Future Study (MTF), 348, 351–352
Monoamine oxidase inhibitors (MAOI), 196, 340, 452–453
Mood and Feelings Questionnaire (MFQ), 185
Mother-Child Project (M-CP), 374
Motivation
  academic, 281–282
  of aggressive behavior, 299
  effectance, 237, 243, 245, 247
  homework, 443
  intrinsic, 237, 245–246
  mastery, 104, 168
  to perform modeled behavior, 42
  to perform undesired behavior, 40, 43–44
  personality, 103, 234–235
  reinforcers, 40, 307
  social, 273, 277
  SUDs, 349, 351, 361
    for change, 361
    denial, 349
    impulsiveness, 351
    interviewing, 358
  temperament, 64, 71–72, 77
  work, 280
Moving to Opportunity, 53
Multidimensional Anxiety Scale for Children (MASC), 123, 396
Multidimensional Neglect Scale—Child Report (MNS-CR), 376
Multi-Family Psychoeducation Group (MFPG), 223, 225–226
Multimodal Treatment Study for ADHD Cooperative Group (MTA), 325, 448, 458–461
Multi-score Depression Inventory for Children (MDI-C), 185
Multisystemic therapy (MST), 308, 381

Narcissistic personality disorders, 153, 188, 273, 323, 378, 414–415
National Center for Child Abuse and Neglect (DHHS), 371
National Center for Clinical Infant Programs, 5
National Child Abuse and Neglect Data System (NCANDS), 371
National Clearinghouse on Child Abuse and Neglect (NCCAN), 367–369, 371
National Comorbidity Survey (NCS), 171

National Crime Victims Research and Treatment Center, 379
National Family Violence Survey, 371
National Incidence Study of Child Abuse and Neglect (NIS-3), 371
National Institute of Mental Health (NIMH), 226, 448
  Abnormal Involuntary Movement Scale of, 456
  Diagnostic Interview Schedule for Children Version IV (DISC-IV), 10, 123, 140, 156, 320
  Obsessive-Compulsive Scale (NIMH-OCS), 450
  Treatment for Adolescents with Depression Study (TADS), 191–193, 195–196, 448, 451
National Longitudinal Survey of Adolescent Health, 57
National Longitudinal Survey of Children and Health, 57
National Research Council Panel on Research on Child Abuse and Neglect, 371–372
National Survey on Drug Use and Health (NSDUH), 352
Nefazadone, 195–196
Negative affect (NA), 118–119, 126
Negative emotionality (NE), 69, 74–75, 168, 332–333, 369
Negative reinforcement, 40
Neurochemical dysregulation, 175
Neurophysiology, 31
Neuropsychiatric contributions, 29–34
  future of, 34
  historical perspective, 29–31
  pediatrics, advances in, 31–34
    ADHA, 32
    affective illness, 33
    autism, 31–32
    OCD, tics, Tourette's syndrome, Sydenham chorea, PANDA, 32–33
    verbal/nonverbal LDs, 33–34
Neuroscience, developmental, 30, 68, 72, 175
Neuroticism
  ADHD, 323
  child physical abuse and neglect, 378
  eating disorders, 332–333, 338
  GAD, 126
  MDD, 167–170
  MR, 234–235
  PTSD, 150–153, 158–159
  SAD, 136, 143
New York Longitudinal Study, 66
Nisonger Child Behavior Rating Form (NCBRF), 454
No Child Left Behind, 47
Nonparametric linkage analysis, 23–24
Nonsteroidal anti-inflammatories, 458
Nonverbal learning disabilities, 33
Norepinephrine, 138, 174, 334, 460
Norfluoxetine, 449
Nurse Family Partnership, 94

Obesity, 227, 330–336, 338, 455–456
Obsessive-compulsive disorder (OCD)
  CBT, 40, 439
  GAD, 119, 123
  neuropsychiatry, 32–33
  PDDs, 257
  pharmacological treatments for, 449–451
  SAD, 140
  somatization disorders, 410
  Tourette's syndrome, 32

Obsessive-compulsive personality disorder (OCPD), 333, 414
Olanzapine (Zyprexa), 227, 340, 454–456, 458
Ontario Child Health Study, 52–53
Ontogenetic development, 102–104, 107, 372
Operant conditioning, 39–41
Oppositional defiant disorder (ODD), 285–293
  assessment/diagnosis of, 88–89, 289–290
  autism, 286
  comorbidity, 21
  course, complications, prognosis of, 289
  description of, 89, 285
  environmental impact, 290
    family, 290
    peer interaction, 290
    school, 290
  epidemiology of, 286
  etiology of, 286–289
  in infants, 89
  language development, 286–287, 290
  personality development, 285–286
    future implications for, 290
  treatments for, 291–293
Optimists, 44
Orthostatic hypotension, 455
Osmotic drug delivery technology (OROS), 459
Outerdirectedness (OD), 236–237, 245
Overanxious disorder (OAD), 117, 127, 139–140, 142, 406. See also Generalized anxiety disorder (GAD)

Pain disorders, 404, 406–410, 413
  somatoform, 404, 406, 408, 410, 413
Palilalia, 32
PANDA (pediatric autoimmune neuropsychiatric disorder associated with streptococcus), 32–33
Panic attacks, 136, 169
Paranoid personality disorder, 188–189, 414–415
Parasympathetic nervous system, 67, 76, 410
Parental Anger Inventory, 375
Parental anxiety management (PAM), 128
Parental Support Questionnaire, 395
Parent Child Education Program, 380
Parent Child Interaction Therapy (PCIT), 380
Parent Emotional Reaction Questionnaire (PERQ), 393, 395
Parent Global Assessment, 460
Parenting Stress Index, 376
Parent Interview and Assessment Guide, 375
Parent management training (PMT), 307–308
Parent Report of Children's Reaction to Stress, 156
Parent Report of Post-Traumatic Symptoms (PROPS), 156
Parkinsonism, 452, 454–455
Paroxetine, 144, 195–196, 449–453
Passive-dependent personality disorders, 406, 414–415
Pediatric OCD Treatment Study (POTS), 450
Peer Generalization Programming, 144
Peer Nomination Inventory for Depression (PNID), 185
Peer pressure
  decision making influence of, 105–106
  genetic influences, 20
  interpersonal therapies, 194
  SUDs and, 353, 358
Peer rejection
  adult interaction in peer-related conflict, 125
  autistic spectrum disorders, 263

CD, 301–302, 304–305
MDD, 180, 187
microsystemic processes, 105
self-worth, 243
social incompetence, 100
SUDs, 353
Peer sociometric report, 11
Penn State Worry Questionnaire—Child (PSWQ-C), 124
Perfectionism
  bulimic behavior, 332, 336
  cognitive theories, irrational beliefs, 43
  eating disorders
    anorexia nervosa, 334, 337
    bulimic behavior, 332, 336
  GAD, 117–118, 124–125
  somatization disorders, 406
Persistence, 69, 77, 104, 168, 218
Personal Experiences Inventory (PEI), 357
Pervasive developmental disorder not otherwise specified (PDD-NOS), 254, 256
Pervasive developmental disorders (PDDs), 254, 268
  assessment/diagnosis of, 260–261
    diagnosis, 261
    screening, 260–261
    treatment planning, diagnostic assessment, 261
  autistic disorder, 254, 265
  course, complications, prognosis of, 259–260
    age of onset, 259–260
    developmental course, 260
    outcome, influences on, 260
  description/clinical picture of, 254–256
    communication, atypical, 255
    diagnostic criteria for, 254
    sensory-perceptual stimuli, atypical responses to, 255–256
    social interactive criteria for, 255
  environmental impact, 261–264
    family, 261–263
      parents of autistic child, 261–262
      siblings of autistic child, 262–263
    peer interactions, 263–264
    school, 263
  epidemiology of, 257–258
    current, 258
    prevalence, reasons for rise in, 257
  etiology of, 258–259
    behavioral genetics, 258
    environmental risks, 258–259
      measles, mumps, rubella, 258–259
    neuroanatomical findings, 259
    prenatal suboptimality, 258
  language, 254–258, 260–261, 263–267
  personality development, 256–257
    concerns of, 256–257
    joint attention/pragmatics deficits, 256
    play, deficits in development nature of, 256–257
  future implications for, 264
    high-functioning adults, 264
  pervasive developmental disorder not otherwise specified, 254, 256
  treatments for, 264–268
    current views on, 264–265
    therapy models, 265–268
      applied behavior analysis, 265–267
      discrete trial training, 266
      floor-time play therapy, 267
      inclusion, 267–268
      TEACCH method, 266–267

Pervasive Developmental Disorders Screening Test—II (PDDST-II), 260–261
Pharmacological treatments, 448–461
  for ADHD, 32
  for affective illnesses, 33
  antipsychotics, second-generation, 453–456
    adverse effects of, 454–456
    clinical trials of, 453–454
    dosing of, 456
  atomoxetine, 460–461
    adverse effects of, 461
  description of, 448
  developmental issues in, 448–449
    pharmacodynamics, 449
    pharmacokinetics, 448–449
  mood stabilizers, 456–458
    adverse effects of, 457–458
    clinical trials of, 456–457
    dosing of, 458
  neuropsycho, 31
  paroxetine, 144
  psycho, 159, 448, 458
  psychostimulants, 458–460
    adverse effects of, 461
    clinical trials of, 458–460
  SSRIs, 449–453
    adverse effects of, 452–453
    clinical trials of, 450–452
    dosing of, 453
  tricyclic antidepressants, 128, 195
Phenobarbitol, 457
Phenytoin, 452, 457
Physical Abuse-Informed Family Therapy, 380
Physiological hyperarousal (PH), 118–119
Plasma concentration, 449–450, 459
Plausible cognition, 42
Polycystic ovarian syndrome (PCOS), 457
Polydipsia, 226, 257
Polyuria, 226, 457
Population health research, 47–48, 56
Positive affect (PA), 118–119
Positive emotionality (PE), 168–170
Positron-emission tomography (PET), 31, 220, 319
Post-traumatic stress disorder (PTSD), 148–160
  anxiety disorders, 44, 90
  assessment of symptoms, 155–157
    clinician-administered scales, 156–157
    psychopathological, 157
    reexperiencing events, 155
    self-administered instruments, 156
  concentration, 149, 157–158
  course, complications, prognosis of, 154–155
  CSA, 389, 391, 396–397
  description/clinical picture of, 148–150
  diagnostic criteria for, 148–149, 155
  environmental impact of, 157–158
    behavioral/emotional impact, 157
    family, 157
    future implications of, 158–159
    peer interactions, 158
    school, 157–158
  epidemiology of, 153
  etiology of, 152–153
    two-factor learning theory, 154
  extroversion, 150, 152–153, 158–159
  increased arousal, 90
  language and ability to describe events, 149, 389
  neuroticism, 150–153, 158–159
  personality development and psychopathology, 150–153
    BPD, 150, 152–153
    hyperarousal, 152

moderating factors of, 150–151
personality disorders, 152–153
PTSD's influence on, 151
reexperiencing, avoiding, 90, 152
trauma, 151–152
sleep disorders, 157
treatment of, 159–160
  structured play technique, 433–434
victimizing, 158
Post-Traumatic Stress Disorder Reaction Index (PTSD-RI), 156
Potent serotonin, (5-HT), 451
Poverty, 8, 48, 50, 52–53, 57
Prader-Willi syndrome, 236
Prefrontal executive dysfunction, 32
Prepubertal and early adolescent bipolar disorder (PEA-BD), 222–223
Primidone, 457
Princeton Child Development Institute, 266
Problem solving
  bipolar disorder, 225
  CBT, 42, 104, 441–443
  CD, 300, 307
  child physical abuse, 380
  CSA, 393
  definition of, 287
  GAD, 118
  LDs, 272, 274, 281
  MDD, 190, 192–194
  MR, 236
  ODD, 287–288, 291–292
  PDDs, 267
  psychodynamic treatments, 427–428, 432, 434–435
  PTSD, 152, 158
  somatization disorders, 409, 412
  SUDs, 354
Process paradigms, 107
Project SafeCare, 381
Prolactin levels, 174, 413, 455–456
Propanolol, 458
Proximal risk factors, 48
Psychoanalysis, 425–426, 430
Psychoanalytic psychotherapy, 399
Psychodynamic treatments, 425–435
  approach of, 425–426
  change and techniques, mechanisms of, 426–427
    catharsis/expression of feelings, 426
    corrective emotional experience, 426
    insight and working through, 426–427
    internal structure/processes, development of, 427
    problem-solving techniques/coping strategies, 427
    variables, nonspecific, 427
  future research of, 434
  pretend play, therapy, 428–429
  short term, 433–434
  treatment approaches, 427–428
    insight-oriented therapy, 427–428
    structure-building, 428
    supportive, 428
  treatments/constructs research, 429–433
    play intervention studies, 432–434
    research on psychodynamic constructs, 433
Psychopathology, 4
Psychostimulant medication, 227, 316, 324, 458–461
PTSD Checklist Parent Report on Child (PCL-PR), 156
Punishment, 41–42

QTc prolongation, 227, 455–456
Questionnaire for Eating Disorder Diagnosis (QEDD), 336
Quetiapine (Seroquel), 227, 454–456

Race/ethnicity, 8, 53. *See also* African Americans
  child development issues, 8, 53, 57
  developmental process comparison, 107
  diagnosis and classification considerations, 8
  internalizing disorders, 107
  language and diagnostic classification of, 8
  mental health research on, 8
  multiplexity of risk factors, 57
  poverty, 8, 53
  SUDs, 351–352, 354–355
    Asians, 353
    Hispanic-Latino adolescents, 354
    non-Hispanic Whites, 352, 354–355
Rapid eye movement (REM), 174
Reactive attachment disorder (RAD), 91
Reactivity
  to anxiety-provoking stimuli, 119
  autonomic nervous system, 409
  emotional, 65–68, 74, 136, 151, 170, 287
  frustration, 74–75
  overreactivity, 288
  physiological, 76, 151, 155
  stress, 68, 168, 170, 339, 405
  temperamental, 65, 69–70, 72, 74, 76–78, 300
Recurrent abdominal pain (RAP), 408–411, 414
Regulatory disorders, 88, 90
Reinforcement, 39–41
Relationship disorders, 5, 91
Research Unit on Pediatric Psychopfarmacolgy Anxiety Study Group (RUPP), 451
Resilient Peer Training (RPT), 379–380
Respiratory sinus arrhythmia (RSA), 67, 76
Restlessness. *See* Akathisia
Rett syndrome, 32, 254
Revised Behavior Problem Checklist (RBPC), 124
Revised Children's Manifest Anxiety Scale (RCMAS), 123, 141
Revised Conflict Tactics Scales, 376
Reynolds Adolescent Depression Scale (RADS), 185
Right hemisphere LDs, 33
Risperdal. *See* Risperidone
Risperidone (Risperdal), 227, 454–456
Ritalin®, 307–308, 324, 459
Ritalin LA®, 459
Rochester Longitudinal Study, 54
Role-playing, 127, 193, 245, 307, 379, 426

Scales of Independent Behavior—Revised (SIB-R), 240
Schedule for Affective Disorders and Schizophrenia for School-Aged Children (K-SADS), 10–11, 183, 396
Schedule for Affective Disorders and Schizophrenia for School-Aged Children—Present and Lifetime Version (K-SADS-PL), 123, 140, 156
Schizoid personality disorder, 153, 188–189, 378
Schizophrenia, 16–17, 43, 227, 238, 454
School failure, 33, 105, 187, 300
Screen for Childhood Anxiety Related Emotional Disorders (SCARED-R), 123
Second-generation antipsychotic (SGA), 453–455

492 Subject Index

Selective serotonin reuptake inhibitors (SSRIs)
    adverse effects of, 452–453, 457–458
    clinical trials on, 450–452
    for eating disorders, 340–341
    FDA approved, 449–450
    for GAD, 127
    for MDD, 174, 194–196
Self-control, 54
Self-criticism
    GAD, 118, 124, 442–443
    MDD, 178, 186
    SAD, 136
    self-loathing, 43
    of students and positive perception of school climate, 106
    vulnerabilities to, 102–103, 107
Self-esteem
    ADHD, 317
    child physical abuse and neglect, 369–370, 374–375
    criticism, 44
    CSA, 389–392, 394
    dysthymic disorder, 166
    eating disorders, 332, 334, 340
    GAD, 126
    hyperarousal symptoms, 152
    inflated, in bipolar disorder, 221
    LDs, 273, 281–282
    MDD, 170, 179, 188
    microsystemic processes, 105
    MR, 236, 242–244
    psychodynamic treatments, 427
    SUDs, 350
    weight gain, and medication noncompliance, 455
Self-fulfilling prophesy, 43–44
Self-loathing, 43
Self-regulation
    CBT, 442
    infant mental health, 92–93
    LDs, 277
    ODD, 287–288
    SUDs, 350–351
    temperament, 65, 72–78
Self-report
    of ADHD, 322
    of anxiety, 69–70, 182
    of CBT, 441–442
    of child physical abuse and neglect, 375–376, 378
    of CSA, 390, 393, 396
    of CU, 303
    of eating pathology assessment, 336
    of GAD, 117–119, 123–124
    of LDs, 274
    of MDD, 69–70, 168, 170–172, 180, 182–183, 185, 187, 193
    of personality stability, 331
    of play intervention, 432
    of PTSD, 155–157, 396
    questioners, 21, 123, 185, 320
    of SAD, 140–142
    twin studies, 21
Self-soothing, 67, 73–74
Separation anxiety, 122–124, 135, 140, 149, 218, 406, 410, 432, 451
Seroquel. *See* Quetiapine
Serotonergic system dysregulation, 174–175
Serotonin transporter (5-HTT), 177
Serotonin transporter linked promoter region (HTTLPR), 219
Sertraline, 133, 195–196, 449–450, 452

Sexual dysfunction, 452, 455
Show That I Can (STIC), 127
Shyness, 68–69, 136, 140, 261
Single-nucleotide polymorphisms (SNPs), 23–24
Single-parent households, 48–49
Single-photon emission computed tomography (SPECT), 31, 220
Situational analysis, 289
Situational traumas, 426, 429
Sleep apnea, 90–91, 319, 455
Sleep disorders
    ADHD, 319317
    apnea, 90–91, 319, 455
    dysthymic disorder, 166
    in infants, 89–91
    MDD, 89, 166
    PTSD, 149–150, 157
    SAD, 141
Smith-Magenis syndrome, 236
Smoking, 48
Social anxiety disorder (SAD), 135–144
    anxiety disorders, 90
    assessment/diagnosis of, 140–141
    behavioral inhibition, 118
    course, complications, prognosis of, 138–140
    description/clinical picture of, 135–136
    DSM classification of, 5
    effective parenting, 141
    environmental impact of, 141–143
        family, 141
        peer interactions, 142–143
        school, 141–142
    epidemiology of, 137
    etiology of, 137–138
        familial aggregation/genetics, 137–138
        observational learning/conditioning, 138
        parenting practices, 138
    personality development and psychopathology, 136–137
    future implications for, 143
    self-criticism, 136
    suicide, 139
    treatment of, 140, 143–144
    fluoxetine, 451
Social Anxiety Scale for Children (SASC-R), 141
Social class
    autism, 258
    ethnicity, 107
    gender, 56, 107
    heritability differences in, 107–108
    ineffective parenting, 54
    preterm infants, 87
    smoking rates, 48
    social status determinants, 48
Social Effectiveness Therapy for Children (SET-C), 144
Social exposure hypothesis, 50
Social Learning Parent Training (Forehand), 380
Social Phobia and Anxiety Inventory for Children (SPAI-C), 141
Social phobia (SP). *See* Social anxiety disorder (SAD)
Social position, determinants of, 48–49
Social vulnerability hypothesis, 51
Social withdrawal, 69–70, 77, 89, 142, 166
Socioeconomic status (SES), 17, 49
Sociometric grouping, 244–245
Somatic Symptom Index (SSI), 407
Somatization disorders (SD), 403, 416
    assessment/diagnosis of, 412–413
    BDD, 404–405, 408, 410, 414–415
    course, complications, prognosis of, 411–412

    description/clinical picture of, 403–405
    DSM-IV diagnostic criteria for, 403–404, 406–408
    disorders
        body dysmorphic, 404, 408, 414
        conversion, 404, 406–408, 410–411, 413–414
        fibromyalgia, 410, 413
        hypochondriasis, 404–405, 407–408
        in language, 403, 406
        migraine headaches, 406, 411, 413, 415
        pain, 404, 406–410, 413–414
        pseudoseizures, 406–408, 410–411, 413
        recurrent abdominal pain, 408–411, 414
        somatization disorder, 407
        undifferentiated somatoform, 404–405, 407
    environmental impact, 413–414
    epidemiology of, 407–408
    etiology of, 408–411
    personality development, 405–407
    future implications, 414–415
    school absences, 416
    suicide, 414
    treatments for, 415–416
Somatoform pain disorder, 404, 406, 408, 410, 413
Special Olympics, 245–247
Spectroscopy (MRS), 31
Speech. *See* Language
State-Trait Anxiety Interview for Children (STAIC), 123
Stevens-Johnson syndrome, 226, 457
Stimulant medications
    for ADHD, 24, 227, 316, 318, 321, 324
    for CD, 307–308
    clinical trials of, 460–461
Strange Situation Procedure, 87, 370
Stress
    generation model, 175
    MDD, 175–177
    mental health, 50
    poverty, 107
Striatum, 32, 221
Structured Clinical Interview for DSM-III-R (SCID), 337
Substance use disorders (SUDs), 348, 362
    assessment/diagnosis of, 357–358
    course, complications, prognosis of, 355–357
    description/clinical picture of, 348–350
    DSM-IV diagnostic criteria for, 348–350
    environmental impact, 358–359
        family, 358–359
        peer interaction, 359
        school, 359
    epidemiology of, 351–353
    etiology of, 353–355
        risk factors, 353–355
        racial/ethnic differences, 354–355
    motivation
        for change, 361
        denial, 349
        impulsiveness, 351
        interviewing, 358
    peer pressure, 353, 358
    personality development, 350–351
        future implications for, 359–360
    self-esteem, 350
    treatments for, 360–362
Suicide
    aggression, influence of modeling, 42
    antidepressant side effects, 195
    bipolar disorder, 217, 219

bulimia nervosa, 335
CD, 306
CSA, 397–398
GAD, 122
MDD, 181, 189, 195
SAD, 139
somatization disorders, 414
SUDs, 358
Survey Research Center (Institute for Social Research), 348
Sydenham chorea, 32–33
Symptom-Checklist-90-Revised (SCL-90-R), 375
Systematic behavior family therapy (SBFT), 191–192

Tanner Stage I, III, 171
Tardive dyskinesia (TD), 455
Task Force on Promotion and Dissemination of Psychological Procedures(American Psychological Association), 429–430
Teacher's Report Form (TRF), 124
Teen-Addiction Severity Index (T-ASI), 357
Temperament, in early development, 64–78
    defined, 64
    effects of, 74–76
    emotional development, 64–68
        adrenocortical functioning, 68
        behavioral assessments of, 66–67
        brain electrical activity, 67–68
        heart rate, 67
        psychobiological assessments of, 67–68
        theories of, 64–66
    psychopathology, development of, 68–72
        externalizing, 70–72
        internalizing, 69–70
        self-regulation of, 76–77
    reactivity/self-regulation, 65
        effort control, 66
    temperament-psychopathology relations, self-regulatory framework for examining, 72–74
Testbusters, 144
Textbook of Psychiatry, 4

Thyrotropin-stimulating hormone (TSH), 457
Tics, 32–33, 461
Topiramate, 226–227, 341
Tourette's syndrome, 32–33, 288, 461
Toxic epidermal necrolysis, 226
Transient hepatitis, 461
Transmission disequilibrium test (TDT), 25
Trauma-focused cognitive-behavioral therapy (TF-CBT), 159, 398–399
Trauma-related disorders, 88
Trauma Symptom Checklist for Children (TSCC), 156, 395
Treatment and Education of Autistic and Related Communication Handicapped Children (TEACCH), 265–266
Treatment as usual (TAU), 194
Treatment for Adolescents with Depression Study (TADS), 191–193, 195–196, 448, 451
Tricyclic antidepressants (TCAs). *See also individual listings*
    for ADHD, 324
    adverse effects of, 449, 451–452, 458
    for eating disorders, 340
    for GAD, 128
    for MDD, 194–196
    for ODD, 293
    for somatization disorders, 415
Tripartite model, 118–119, 168
Twins, 17–19
    Dizygotic (DZ), 17–19
    follicle stimulating hormone (FSH), 17
    genetics
        biometrical modeling, 19
        developmental changes, 19–20
        disorders, 21–22
            comorbidity between, 21–22
            subtyping, 21
        gene-environment interaction, 20–21
        identification studies, using for, 25
        registries, population-based, 19
    studies, 17–18, 20–21
        Finnish Twin Studies, 20
        limitations, 18–19
        Minnesota Twin Family Study, 20

Monozygotic (MZ), 17–19, 25, 31
    zygosity, 19
Two-factor learning theory, 154
Two-factor theory of emotion, 43

Undifferentiated somatoform disorder, 404–405, 407
Universals, cognitive, 102–103
University of California at Los Angeles (UCLA), 266
University of Michigan, 348
University of North Carolina (Chapel Hill), 266

Vagal tone, 67, 75–76
Valproate (divalproex sodium), 226–227, 454, 456–458
Van der Woude syndrome, 25
Venlafaxine, 196
Verapamil, 458
Vineland Adaptive Behavior Scales (VABS), 240
Virginia Twin Study of Adolescent Behavioral Department (VTSABD), 172
Visual-motor disability, 33

Wait list control (WLC), 127, 144, 191–194, 341
Walden Model, 267
Wechsler Intelligence Scale for Children—Revised (WISC-R), 407
Weight
    gain, 90, 166, 226–227, 330, 341, 454–457
    loss, 166, 227, 336, 341, 452, 459, 461
Weinberg syndrome, 32
When Bad Things Happen Scale (WBTH), 156
Williams syndrome, 235
Wolfe's transitional model, 373

Young Autism Project/discrete trial training (YAP/DTT), 260, 266
Young Autism Project (YAP), 266
Young Mania Rating Scale (YMRS), 453–454, 456

Ziprasidone (Geodon), 227, 453, 455–456
Zyprexa. *See* Olanzapine